LEO BAECK INSTITUTE

YEAR BOOK

1991

The turn of history – 1990
One of the last stamps of the German Democratic Republic
issued on the eve of the Jewish New Year shows the
Berlin New Synagogue. The proceeds of the 15 Pf. surcharge
went to the Jewish research foundation Centrum Judaicum

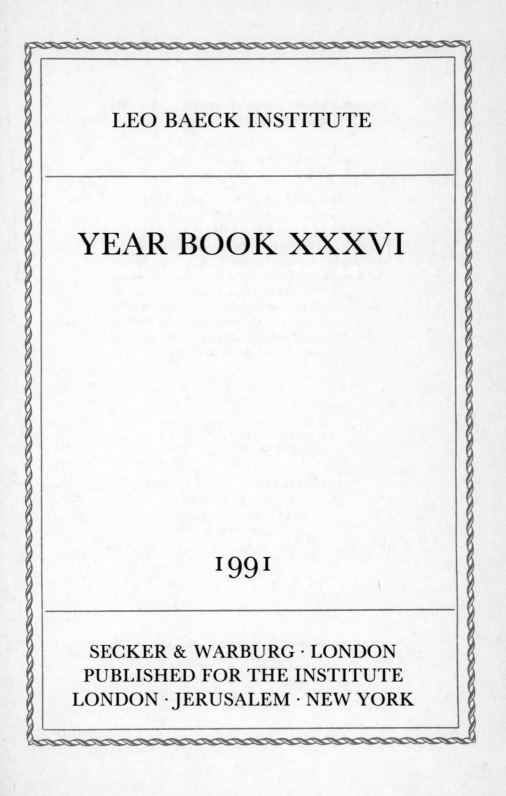

LEO BAECK INSTITUTE

YEAR BOOK XXXVI

1991

SECKER & WARBURG · LONDON
PUBLISHED FOR THE INSTITUTE
LONDON · JERUSALEM · NEW YORK

FOUNDER EDITOR: ROBERT WELTSCH (1956–1978)
EDITOR: ARNOLD PAUCKER

Editorial office: Leo Baeck Institute
4 Devonshire Street, London W1N 2BH

THE LEO BAECK INSTITUTE
was founded in 1955 by the
COUNCIL OF JEWS FROM GERMANY
for the purpose of collecting material on and
sponsoring research into the history of the Jewish
Community in Germany and in other German-
speaking countries from the Emancipation to its
decline and new dispersion. The Institute is
named in honour of the man who was the last
representative figure of German Jewry in Germany during the Nazi period.

LEO BAECK INSTITUTE

JERUSALEM: 33 Bustanai Street
LONDON: 4 Devonshire Street, W.1
NEW YORK: 129 East 73rd Street

THIS PUBLICATION WAS SUPPORTED
BY GRANTS FROM
THE BRITISH ACADEMY
AND THE
MEMORIAL FOUNDATION FOR JEWISH CULTURE

© Leo Baeck Institute 1991
Published by Martin Secker & Warburg Limited
Michelin House, 81 Fulham Road, London SW3 6RB
ISBN 0 436 25550 2
Photoset by Wilmaset, Birkenhead, Wirral
Printed in Great Britain by Richard Clay (The Chaucer Press), Limited,
Bungay, Suffolk

Contents

IV. NAZI DOMINATION

V. GENTILES AND JEWS AFTER 1945

VI. FRANZ ROSENZWEIG

Illustrations

Preface

Year Book XXXVI is introduced by Michael Meyer with an essay on the Jewish and the German historiographical approaches to the history of German Jewry. This is of course related to the problem of whom to define as "Jewish" for the purpose of German-Jewish studies. There is no complete agreement among scholars – many incline to a very elastic interpretation when it comes to certain aspects of the story of Germany's Jews or the "Jewish Question". Meyer's is a plea for a further integration of the two approaches – and the four-volume comprehensive history of German Jewry now commissioned by the Leo Baeck Institute (of which he himself is the general editor) must be viewed as a step towards such a synthesis. Written by scholars from England, Germany, Israel and the United States, it is to be published simultaneously in English, German and Hebrew in 1995, forty years after the founding of the Leo Baeck Institute.

With the opening section of this Year Book we return mainly to the eighteenth century. Steven Lowenstein is right to stress, at the beginning of his study of Berlin Jewry's Orthodox and poor, that the ones who maintained their traditional way of life for much longer, and those who were indigent and less articulate are overlooked by most historians, who tend to give pride of place to those striving for modernity. The kind of instructive social history Lowenstein pursues here is something we need. The world that he depicts was still far removed from 'The World of Moses Mendelssohn' sketched by Eva Engel Holland in an examination of memoirs and letters of the Jewish enlightener. In telling juxtaposition we can see almost contemporaneous and yet vastly differing stages in the evolution of Jewish emancipation.

As Michael Meyer pointedly states in his Introduction, even the most voluminous of post-war "general histories of Modern Germany" fail to mention the *Centralverein deutscher Staatsbürger jüdischen Glaubens*. It is indeed more than strange that the topic of Jewish self-defence and assertion of civil rights is so studiously avoided in these works, when one considers that in Jewish historical research this topic has almost become a sort of sub-discipline in which – it should be emphasised – a number of younger German historians also play their part. This plethora of studies testifying to an ever-growing interest in the *Centralverein* and the Jewish defence in Germany is – *pace* Gershom Sholem – most certainly not unconnected with the fact that Jews in the countries of the West have opted for a continued existence in the pluralistic societies which obtain there. Thus in one of the central sections of this Year Book five further studies deal once again with questions of the emergence of Jewish defence organisations in Wilhelminian Germany and the history of the *Centralverein* until 1933. Jacob Toury in an overview and Jacob Borut in a very detailed study concentrate on the years 1889 to 1895, on the fledgling C.V. and its precursors, with divergent viewpoints on some issues. Evyatar Friesel contrasts the *Centralverein* with the American Jewish Committee; there are both close parallels and considerable variants in these major civil rights organisations, operating in different societies and under differing conditions. This is precisely the type of comparative treatment German-Jewish historiography ought to aim at in the future. Sibylle Morgenthaler and Cyril Levitt, in their studies of the efforts of the *Centralverein* to combat, by legal means, boycott and antisemitic agitation in the Weimar Republic, give, on the whole, a pessimistic picture. There is some consensus that in warding off boycott measures the Jewish defence could register a degree of success, but when it came to the efficacy of legal means to curb the antisemites in other areas, Levitt – much concerned with lessons to be drawn today – comes to entirely negative conclusions, indulging in a harsh critique of the more "optimistic" findings arrived at previously by other scholars. In 1991 self-defence on the part of minority groups is, unhappily, topical as never before.

For almost twenty years now the New York Leo Baeck Institute has conducted regular sessions at the Annual Meetings of the American Historical Association, and the latest, on 'The German Professionals and their Jewish Colleagues', which took place on 29th December 1989 during the 104th Annual Meeting of the AHA in San Francisco is, like many of its forerunners, given a place in this Year Book. In Year Book text sequence we aptly proceed here from the "law" to the "lawyers", as Konrad Jarausch dealt in his opening address with the relationship between the German jurists and their Jewish *confrères*. Perhaps what transpired in the Weimar Republic already foreshadowed the break-up and Nazification of a liberal/illiberal profession, the elimination of its Jewish component and the total suppression of any degree of justice in Germany. The medical profession was, of course, another sizeable sector in which Jews were over-represented when measured in "racialist" terms. Geoffrey Cocks in his contribution ventures into the largely unexplored field of doctor/patient relationships and professional competition against the background of "Aryanisation", the prostitution of medical ethics, and the possible utilisation of the remnants of the Jewish medical potential in the Nazi war effort. Fritz Ringer casts a glance at the representation of Jews in German academia with some hints as to what comparative studies would elicit were we to extend our investigations to other countries. Fritz Stern, once more the commentator at a Leo Baeck Institute session, rounds off the debate with the judicious observation that quantification and tabulation are only one side of the picture. The complex history of German-Jewish life lends itself to a multiplicity of methods.

We supplement this AHA session on German/Jewish relations with two further contributions, by Paul Rose and Shlomo Na'aman. It would seem that any such chapter cannot but include the figure of Richard Wagner, whose role in stimulating German antisemitism continues to exercise the minds of many scholars, Jewish and Gentile alike. Rose traces here the evolving conflict between the composer and the Jewish writer Berthold Auerbach. Na'aman in his essay on the nineteenth-century Social Democratic leader, Wilhelm Hasenclever, certainly shows a degree of careful differentiation in his study of this particular Socialist politician, as also with the more general topic of "antisemitism" within the German labour movement. Ever since Edmund Silberner started the ball rolling almost half a century ago, there has been intense controversy on the factor of antisemitism in German – and European – Socialism. There were – apart from total condemnation of antisemitic rabble-rousers and demonstrations of solidarity with vilified Jews – so many differing shades and variations; from general irreligiosity, commonplace prejudice, anti-philosemitism to indifference, non-concern and on the extreme edge, blatant antisemitism; all these were present in the German working class and amongst its leaders. Tarring Social Democracy itself (and later on the Communists) with the broad brush of anti-Jewishness is too simplistic. This was also brought out forcefully in a seminar, organised jointly by the Steinheim Institute of Duisburg and the London Leo Baeck Institute, on 'Jews and the German Labour Movement' in Mülheim in December 1990. Despite some severe stricture of prominent Socialist leaders and ideologues, there was also – as emerged in heated debates – a great deal of support for the view of the Socialists as none the less trustworthy allies of the Jewish minority. After all it cannot be ignored that the last years of the Weimar Republic had led to a very close collaboration between middle-class activists of the Jewish defence and many functionaries of the Left against Nazism. The Mülheim proceedings are to be published jointly by the two Institutes in the *Schriftenreihe wissenschaftlicher Abhandlungen des Leo Baeck Instituts*.

The other major section of the Year Book has as its theme once again the fate of Germany's Jews after the Nazi takeover; that of the more fortunate who succeeded in fleeing the country and of the many who remained behind until the bitter end. In recent years the behaviour of those who then led the Jewish community has been subjected to much scrutiny and by now we have seen a spate of writings not especially distinguished by scholarly exactitude – rather they are motivated by post-war politicking, tempered with hindsight. That we face here perhaps the most sensitive and convoluted question of modern German-Jewish history cannot be denied, nor that it is all too easy to pinpoint the failings of people confronted with impossible odds and an evil beyond their conception. Francis Nicosia, who here looks at Zionist policies *vis-à-vis* the Nazi regime, has a body of work on this topic to his credit and to the Editor's mind gives an assessment that is cool and balanced. And, of course, there can be no doubt that although the Zionists were by outlook and intellectual training better equipped than most of their co-religionists to face the total collapse of the Jewish position in Germany, they too can be faulted for their shortcomings and miscalculations. But then, they were only one of several Jewish groups which harboured "illusions". Of those closely involved in Zionist politics at that time, the man foremost in castigating, in retrospect, Zionist "illusions" and naivity was Robert Weltsch, the editor of the *Jüdische Rundschau*. He combined in his personality an unusual mixture of honesty, directness and cynicism which enabled him to look back on those years without blinkers. Robert Weltsch was born one hundred years ago on 20th June 1891 in Prague and the anniversary of his birth is remembered with affection in the Year Book he founded.

Christhard Hoffmann and Daniel Schwartz give a vivid account of the abortive attempts to transfer two great centres of Jewish studies in Germany to safety before the extinction of all Jewish scholarly foundations by the Nazi dictatorship. As a story of frustration and failure the two accounts link up conveniently; though one exposes the inner- Jewish religious bickering and altercation from Palestine to Lithuania (Poland), while the other, though revealing the dithering, misgivings and a certain lack of urgency, also shows the genuine concern in the United Kingdom to safeguard a great citadel of Jewish research. Both *Rabbinerseminar* and *Hochschule* were eventually submerged in the welter of destruction; though the traditions of Jewish learning were continued after the war by various bodies, amongst which is the Leo Baeck Institute.

In her analysis of the reception French Jews accorded those fleeing from Hitler Vicki Caron writes on the perpetual conflict and the clash of interests between an established community and an influx of "brethren" from abroad. What the *Ostjuden* experienced in Germany was bound to repeat itself, to some degree at any rate, for the German-Jewish émigrés elsewhere. The author's conclusions are cautious, but she has furnished enough evidence to show that fear and insecurity undoubtedly did dictate attitudes in certain French-Jewish quarters (not solely elitist) which may be reprehensible; but then such stances are definitely not an exclusive feature of Jewish life alone. Wandering minority groups will always produce friction between those who feel safely entrenched and the newcomers seen by them as a threat to their own security and integration.

British official attitudes to crimes committed by the Nazis against the Jews of Germany are investigated by Priscilla Dale Jones. This policy was largely guided by the belief that the refugees – Germans deprived of their citizenship by racialist legislation, some of them political exiles as well – could be expected to return to Germany after its defeat or "liberation", and that therefore they constituted quite a different category of Hitler's victims. Many politicians and civil servants quite obviously indulged in wishful thinking. In fact the vast majority of those admitted to the United Kingdom between 1933 and 1939 elected to remain, fitted in well, and made a considerable contribution to their new country. The story of this group has just been told in a wide-ranging symposium volume of the London Leo Baeck Institute: *Second Chance. Two Centuries of German-speaking Jews in the United Kingdom.*

The ways in which the Jewish press in Nazi Germany, as long as it was suffered to exist, tried to give moral guidance to the community, boost Jewish self-assertion and, by many subterfuges, evade censorship, have been discussed more than once in this Year Book. Most of the authors, younger scholars, have had to arrive at their conclusions by careful analysis of the available documentation. We are, however, fortunate that there are still amongst us some survivors of the time who can act as witnesses. Arno Herzberg, whose recollections we print in this volume, was himself a prominent journalist who played a role in the

Jewish press in those days and who risked many dangers. Thus historians and participants can combine in illuminating the final era of the substantial Jewish press which existed in Germany until its abolition by the Nazis.

The section concludes with Konrad Kwiet's essay on the Jewish men and women inducted into the factories of war-time Berlin and labour gangs elsewhere, to serve the German industrial war machine. This was the prelude to the last phase of German Jewry's enslavement and extermination. That there still remained a spirit of defiance and resistance amongst some of the conscript labour force is probably the only heartening feature of the story. Further documentary evidence, which now comes to light from the hitherto closed archives of the defunct German Democratic Republic, on the long-term Nazi planning of the disposal of Germany's Jewish population – unwelcome perhaps to new schools of historical revisionism – will help to demolish the argumentation of the present-day apologists and the *terribles simplificateurs*.

Immediate post-war history is dealt with in the next section by Robert Knight and Constantin Goschler – and this is not the first time that we have extended our scope beyond 1945. Austria's coming to terms – or rather not coming to terms – with the guilt of its past, posing as an innocent victim of German aggression and therefore not liable to offer restitution to those driven out is a subject which has already sparked some fierce disputes. Bavarian reactions to both German-Jewish returnees and Jewish survivors from the East is a very relevant theme in 1991. This year may well see millions on the march; a westward migration is likely to include an influx of Soviet Jews into Germany; an intriguing pointer to a greatly increased Jewish community in Germany in the next century, with all the attendant problems, bringing a further test for German democracy.

Another two contributions in the wake of the Rosenzweig centenary complete the volume. The anniversary celebrations of the birth of one of the great philosophers of twentieth-century German Jewry have prompted many reassessments. Stefan Meineke's analysis certainly points to more "conservative" stances in Rosenzweig's political thinking than those hitherto highlighted in the pages of this Year Book; while William Hallo provides further documentation and insight into Rosenzweig's works.

In the year 1990 the Leo Baeck Institute suffered many losses from the ranks of its older generation, most of whom had been connected with the Institute from its inception. Five men, because of their important roles in the Institute or their close links with the Year Book, are commemorated here.

Lux Furtmüller, who died in April 1990 in Reading, in his 80th year, was closely associated with the Year Book for over twenty years. He was our Translator-in-Chief, a prince amongst translators who rendered the essays of our

German authors into elegant, idiomatic English (which was not his mother tongue) surpassing himself year by year. Formerly a physicist and also a gifted mathematician, he became, after leaving his native Vienna, a foreign language monitor and B.B.C. editor. A writer and general editor too, he also contributed essays to the Year Book. A man of ability and forceful character, he leaves a great gap.

Nahum N. Glatzer, born in 1903, Professor of Jewish History at Brandeis University and Professor of Religion at the University of Boston until his retirement, and a member of the New York Board of the Leo Baeck Institute, died in Watertown, Mass. in his 87th year. One of the foremost Jewish philosophers, he was the author of numerous works on Jewish history and theology, a.o. *Franz Rosenzweig. His Life and Thought* (1953) and *Hillel the Elder* (1956). His formidable academic career after his emigration to the United States earned him wide recognition; it had been preceded by a scholarly life in Germany as a disciple of Rosenzweig and Buber. He, too, was a contributor to the Year Book, and significantly, one of the first two publications issued by the Leo Baeck Institute bears his name.

Lothar Kahn, Professor of Modern Languages of Central Connecticut State University, born in 1922 in Rehlingen (Saar) died early last year. He was a versatile literary historian, equally at home with German nineteenth-century literature, the writings of the Weimar Republic and German post-war literature, of which he proved himself a shrewd analyst. Between 1967 and 1986 he contributed to this publication an entire series of articles which culminated in a brilliant essay on the image of America in the works of early German-Jewish writers. He has immensely enriched the literary side of the Year Book.

Fred W. Lessing, one of the central personalities of the Leo Baeck Institute, born 1915 in Bamberg, died on 6th May 1990 in his 76th year in New York. An industrialist, and a philanthropist in the truly grand style, he was associated with numerous charities and organisations of which his chairmanship of the Wiener Library in London deserves special mention. It was he above all who helped it to continue in difficult times. But it is as Chairman and Treasurer of the New York Leo Baeck Institute that he is remembered in this Year Book. And if we were to call him only our benefactor that would be an understatement. It behoves us to record that in the whole history of our Institute there has been no one anywhere nearly so generous and so concerned. To him the recording of German-Jewish history and the preservation of its chronicles and documentation became an all-absorbing interest. Moreover, an Institute distributed over three continents needs at times a skilled diplomat and intermediary. He fitted this role to perfection with his great charm and tact; fuelled by an inveterate optimism, he believed that solutions could always be found. His death is an irreplaceable loss and saddens us immensely.

Hans Seidenberg, *Landsgerichtsrat a.D.* and holder of the *Grosses Bundesverdienst-kreuz*, died on 17th February 1990 near Frankfurt, shortly after his 80th birthday. For some twenty years he had been Chairman of the *Freunde und Förderer des Leo Baeck Instituts* in the *Bundesrepublik*, a task he fulfilled with dignity, verve and distinction. Before the war he had been an active Zionist and a functionary of the *Palästina-Amt*. On his return to Germany he also played a strong role in the search for Christian–Jewish understanding. In his person he was a truly gentle man.

———————————————

As we have pointed out in the Preface to Year Book XXXIII, the growth of German-Jewish studies has forced us to become increasingly selective in our Bibliography. For lack of space alone some subjects, such as participation in culture, have had to be relegated to a later volume. There has also been a change of our staff. Barbara Suchy who joined us some time ago has taken over as bibliographer from Irmgard Foerg, who has retired after giving a decade of dedicated service. The Institute owes a great debt to her special skills, and also to her predecessor, Bertha Cohn, who died early this year. The Editor wishes to record his personal gratitude to them and to Annette Pringle, who over the years has provided continuity to the work of all our bibliographers. There will be a further occasion to thank all those who have helped to make the Year Book what it is.

London   *Arnold Paucker*

Jews as Jews versus Jews as Germans
Two Historical Perspectives
Introduction to Year Book XXXVI

BY MICHAEL A. MEYER

The historiography of modern diaspora Jewries is burdened by methodological problems that are the specific consequence both of these Jewries' modernity and their diaspora status. Until modern times Jewish communities, with rare exceptions, constituted religiously and culturally self-contained units whose internal autonomy was established by political contract and which were related to the outside world mostly by economic ties. There were few religious or cultural differences among Jews living in Poland, Germany, or Eastern France. The principal distinction among them was between Ashkenazim (Yiddish-speaking Central and East European Jews) and Sephardim (Jews of Iberian origin). Jews in German lands considered themselves Jewish, not German, and they were similarly regarded by non-Jews. Consequently, general historians of Medieval Central Europe have treated the Jews in terms of ongoing political and economic relationships as well as of outbreaks of hostility. Historians of Medieval Jewry have added to these externals the closed inner circle of communal and religious life.

Beginning in the eighteenth century, however, the lines began to blur. Increasingly, Jews identified themselves with the countries in which they lived and with the culture of Central and Western Europe. German Jews became differentiated from Jews in England and France, and especially from the still self-contained Jewish communities in the East.[1] As they ceased to live wholly within a Jewish cultural orbit, they entered German history as an internal element. It therefore became necessary for historians of the Jews to treat this modern German Jewry within its German and European cultural context, differentiating it and comparing it with Jewish communities elsewhere. And it became necessary for historians of Germany to deal with the Jewish element within, not outside of, German culture. Thus the Enlightenment and its political concomitants established a new location for German Jewry, one that removed the clear distinction between German and Jew even as it created distinctions among the various communities of the Jewish Diaspora. It became difficult to differentiate Jews as Jews from Jews as Germans. What are the consequences of this situation for the historiography of German Jewry?

For Jewish historians it became necessary to note the increasing differences

---

[1] For a description of this process see Jacob Katz, 'From Ghetto to Zionism. Mutual Influences of East and West', in Isadore Twersky (ed.), *Danzig. Between East and West. Aspects of Modern Jewish History*, Cambridge, Mass., 1985, pp. 39–48.

between German Jews and those in other lands: their adoption of the German language, their religious reform, their participation in German culture, their rise to bourgeois status. They were also forced to note that as these processes went forward they were accompanied by a general diminution in Jewish consciousness as Jewish identity shrank to make room for other identifications. They therefore saw it as their task to trace a constricting circle of Jewishness as assimilation spread within German Jewry and – aside from chronicling the course of antisemitism and Jewish defences against it – to concentrate on vicissitudes within the remaining Jewish sphere: the Jewish communities and their various activities, Jewish religious thought and ideologies. Reflecting their own narrower view of the nature of Jewishness, some nineteenth-century historians of the Jewish experience went so far as to single out the religious element as the one permanently differentiating feature. Others kept a broader perspective that included the Jewish community as historical agent, although that community now lacked the coercive authority of its medieval forbear. Beyond these domains lay the most problematic area: the role of individual Jews whose degree of Jewishness now varied along a spectrum from Orthodoxy at the one extreme to merely residual elements remaining beyond apostasy on the other. Later Jewish historiography also sometimes tended to view the Jewish experience in Germany through the lens of the Holocaust. German Jewry seemed the best lesson for Jews elsewhere in the perils of self-delusion.

From the viewpoint of German history, modern Jews have been seen quite differently. When it did not ignore them almost entirely or treated them as mere objects of legislation, nineteenth-century general German historiography regarded most German Jews as recalcitrant for daring to retain elements of Jewish differentiation.[2] More recent writing on German history in general has been interested in analysing the effects of Jewish integration, economically, politically, and culturally, upon German society and the reaction of German society to that integration. Like its Jewish counterpart, it has also focused on the Jews largely from the perspective of the Holocaust. But in this instance that has been less an attempt to explain the Jewish failure to anticipate it than to see the persecution of the Jews within the larger context of Nazism and seek an explanation of why the German people did not sufficiently resist it. German historians down to the present have given little attention to the continuing inner life of the Jews in Germany from the eighteenth century onwards. Those who deal with German Protestantism and Catholicism ignore the Jewish religion and the workings of the Jewish community as if these somehow remained foreign to the German scene.[3] On the other hand, cultural historians do deal with those

---

[2]Michael A. Meyer, 'Heinrich Graetz and Heinrich von Treitschke. A Comparison of their Historical Images of the Modern Jew', *Modern Judaism*, 6 (1986), pp. 1–11.

[3]Gordon Craig, for example, in his *Germany 1866–1945*, New York – Oxford 1978, devotes a great deal of attention to antisemitism and to the Holocaust, but when dealing with religion mentions only Jewish numbers – and that in the uninformed belief that the 567,884 German Jews in the 1890 census were all "orthodox" (p. 181). When Craig expanded upon the subject of religion in modern Germany in a chapter especially devoted to it in his later volume, *The Germans*, New York 1982, he limited his discussion there to Protestantism and Catholicism. The Jews appeared in the same volume segregated and separated in a chapter entitled 'Germans and Jews'.

Jews whose cultural influence has been the broadest. Yet such individuals are often far removed from Judaism, and it seldom seems to matter much, if at all, whether they are converts to Christianity.

In short, historians of the Jews have been mainly interested in German Jews as Jews while modern German historians have been interested in them as Germans.

However, it seems that neither perspective does justice to the phenomenon in its totality. German Jews as Jews and German Jews as Germans may be the two sides of a coin, but obverse and reverse images must adhere to each other. Can the two perspectives be brought together?

The difficulty of that task becomes apparent from a few examples. Moses Mendelssohn, the eighteenth-century philosopher and first prominent modern German Jew, has *prima facie* significance for Jewish as for German history. For the former he represents the first clear articulation of a boundary between a new European/German identity and a Jewish one. Because his internalisation of Enlightenment values could be understood as an extension of purview, with his Jewishness – in religious terms – remaining intact, he became a paradigm for Jewish Orthodoxy. Because he was the first German Jew highly regarded by non-Jews for his cultural achievements he became no less a paradigm for non-traditional Jews. As the perceived fountainhead of Jewish acculturation, Mendelssohn's importance for German history is likewise beyond dispute, since without that acculturation the individual and collective influence of Jews in Germany would have been negligible and the reaction to Jews very different. The change in Jewish political and economic status, though not directly related to Mendelssohn and beginning somewhat later, was the concomitant of that acculturation.

It is in the post-Mendelssohnian period that the perspectives diverge.[4] Here those individuals who assume the greatest importance in the inner life of the Jewish community – who are the most Jewish in their identity and in their spheres of influence – are not the Jews of interest to historians of Germany since they were little noticed by non-Jews. This clearly holds true for religious developments and those individuals associated with them. The establishment in Germany of a modern orthodoxy, a conservative middle path, and a religious liberalism slowed the process of assimilation. Each of them maintained a publicly acknowledged form of Jewish distinctiveness and even destiny. From the viewpoint of Jewish history, their significance is of the first order. Yet almost all overviews of German history ignore them completely, an omission which seems unjustified on two grounds. First, it indicates a failure to recognise that such figures as Samson Raphael Hirsch, Zacharias Frankel, and Abraham Geiger assume an importance for Jewish history that extends beyond the realm of what is often called the "inner history" of German Jewry: their formulations of Jewish identity had consequences for Jewish-Gentile relationships as well.

---

[4] Thus James J. Sheehan, in his *German History 1770–1866*, Oxford 1989, devotes two full paragraphs to Mendelssohn (pp. 178–179), but is silent on the Jewish Enlightenment that followed, although he deals with its Catholic counterpart. His sections on religion in the nineteenth century deal with Protestantism and Catholicism, but not with Judaism.

Second, and more importantly, it implies the questionable assumption that what goes on mainly within German Jewry is not of consequence for German history, somewhat in the way France becomes important for German historians only in terms of its relations with Germany. But if Jews in Germany from the late eighteenth century onwards did indeed become Germans, then surely their inner history is also a part of German history.

Similarly, the development of *Wissenschaft des Judentums*, like the modernisation of Judaism, is a topic almost exclusively discussed from the perspective of Jewish history. Historians of Germany deal with the rise of scientific scholarship generally and with its influence on Christianity. Radicals like David Friedrich Strauss and adherents of the Tübingen School receive attention on account of the challenge they presented to Protestantism in the *Vormärz*. But the parallel effect of the critical study of Jewish sources on Judaism and indirectly on Jewish identity in Germany, that stemmed originally from the circle of Leopold Zunz in the early nineteenth century and widened in succeeding decades, is not noted outside the circle of Jewish historiography.

Although the history of antisemitism in Germany is common to both historiographies, the history of Jewish responses to it is not. The monograph literature on the largest of all Jewish organisations in modern Germany, the *Centralverein deutscher Staatsbürger jüdischen Glaubens*, is considerable, yet the mention of this organisation – to say nothing of its leadership – has remained absent from even the thickest general histories of modern Germany. I could, likewise, find no reference to the *Reichsvertretung der deutschen Juden*, the representative organisation of German Jewry during the 1930s, nor to its remarkable leader, Rabbi Leo Baeck. Antisemitism is judged an important part of German history; its effect on the Jews and their reaction to it is not.

The same, finally, can be said for the history of German Zionism, a subject likewise much studied in recent years but similarly absent from the standard general works on German history. It is of course possible to justify this omission – and those mentioned above – by noting the small percentage of Jews in Germany. In the case of German Zionism, moreover, the movement initially attracted only a very small proportion of this already small number. But for German Jewry Zionism became increasingly important as antisemitism grew stronger, and by the Nazi period it had come to play a very important role. Moreover, by that time Zionism had become a significant consideration for those planning to rid Germany of its Jews.

These phenomena – religious and intellectual developments, communal organisations and strategies, and Jewish ideologies – almost without exception have been left to historians of the Jews; they have been considered a part of Jewish history, but either outside of German history or too insignificant for inclusion in any but specialised studies. If at all aware of them, German historians relegate such matters to the history of Jews acting as Jews within, but not as part of, Germany.

In general, historians of Germany have given the most attention to those Jews furthest removed from Jewishness. Their motives for this preference have been at once deplorable and justifiable. The prevailing conception in German historiography until recent times, that Jews could not be fully German and yet remain Jews in any significant sense, necessarily led to their inclusion only when they had been willing to give up Jewishness entirely, or nearly so. It was not possible for a writer like Heinrich von Treitschke, for example, to regard a fully conscious Jew as a major contributor to German life. More justifiable is concentration on Jewishly peripheral figures simply because in most instances those individuals who achieved the greatest importance for German history were subjectively removed from the inner circle of Jewish life, and often they were converts. Yet there were figures of some importance within the German cultural orbit whose Jewishness – however unorthodox – remained personally and positively signifi-cant. Einstein, Freud, and Kafka would be the most outstanding names, but one could add the philosopher Hermann Cohen, the painter Ludwig Meidner and quite a few others. In such cases, their Jewishness was more than a point of origin and thus deserves more than passing attention.

Still, as noted above, the history of the modern German Jews does describe a curve of decreasing Jewish differentiation, if that differentiation is measured by adherence to indigenously Jewish traditions. But to accept that as the whole picture is to ignore a remarkable phenomenon to which George L. Mosse has repeatedly called our attention: the coming into existence of a new type of differentiation, grounded not in Jewish tradition but in the very experience of acculturation and emancipation itself.[5] Mosse has provided an influential new criterion for historically significant Jewishness that extends beyond community involvement but does not descend to racial considerations. He has argued that acculturating German Jews, beginning in the eighteenth century, developed a lasting attachment to the particular form of *Bildung* that was paradigmatic in the German Enlightenment. They continued to cherish its ideals of toleration, rationalism, and optimism long after most segments of German society had abandoned them. Thus this attachment, which was originally the result of a desire to be like their fellow Germans, came increasingly to distinguish the German Jews from them and form a sort of Jewish identity that was non-Jewish in content but nonetheless marked them as Jews regardless of their closeness or distance from Judaism. The role of *Bildung* in German-Jewish history is clearly of importance both from the side of Jewish history as acculturation and from the side of German history as a significant cultural orientatation, rooted in a segment of the German population, and running counter to powerful trends that culminate in the Nazi period.

It is clear also that Jews who converted to Christianity might carry their anachronistic attachment to Enlightenment values with them into their new faith and thus preserve, at least for a time, the residue of a phenomenon that was the product of a collective response of German Jews to their intellectual environment at the beginning of their integration into it. Jewish history does indeed extend beyond the line of apostasy. However, contrary to still common practice, it would seem difficult on these grounds to designate as significantly Jewish the orientation and accomplishments of any decidedly anti-Enlighten-

[5]See especially his *German Jews Beyond Judaism*, Bloomington – Cincinnati 1983.

ment figure, such as the Jewish-born theoretician of the German-Christian state, Friedrich Julius Stahl. Indeed, by any but racial criteria, Stahl stands outside German-Jewish history.[6]

Yet it is remarkable how little significance most writers, Jewish and non-Jewish, have attached to the fact of apostasy, assuming that conversion does not extinguish racial characteristics. Writing about Jewish actors in 1927, Arnold Zweig described them collectively as Mediterranean types whose organ of thought was the ear and whose organ of speech was their bodies. Whether they identified themselves as Jews or Christians did not matter. On the stage they always remained "Jews".[7] More remarkable, in the collective volume entitled *Juden im deutschen Kulturbereich*, which, though originally prepared in the early 1930s was still being revised until its first public distribution in 1959, the editor Siegmund Kaznelson stated that his criterion for inclusion was descent rather than religious affiliation not only as a counterthrust to antisemitic minimisation of Jewish achievement, but also "not to expose ourselves to the – justified – reproach of not paying attention to clear biological and historical facts".[8] Specifically, Kaznelson's criterion for determining the participation of the "Jewish element"[9] in German culture was one Jewish parent. In an appendix he added the names of individuals often thought to be Jewish but who, in fact, did not meet this minimal racial standard.[10]

A more recent Gentile compiler of short biographies of notable German Jews, Walter Tetzlaff, limited his purview to *Volljuden*, since "half Jews could as well be counted for the other side". But he did include all the baptised without distinction, justifying his decision by what he regarded as the Jews' own definition of themselves as a people rather than a religious denomination.[11] Joseph Walk, in his biographical compilation of twentieth-century German Jews, offered a yet different criterion for including baptised Jews and *Mischlinge*: they were also affected by the Nazis' anti-Jewish measures.[12] Although Tetzlaff's and Walk's criteria may have some justification in biographical dictionaries, they possess only limited validity for a synthetic history, which must also consider the degree to which baptised Jews still consider themselves Jewish and

[6]Yet Franz Schnabel, in his *Deutsche Geschichte im neunzehnten Jahrhundert*, 2nd edn., 4 vols., Freiburg 1948–1951, three times refers to Stahl's Jewish origins (vol. II, pp. 36, 249; vol. IV, p. 539), while not mentioning the religious identity of men who remained Jewish their entire lives, like Ferdinand Lassalle and Berthold Auerbach. His fourth volume, which bears the subtitle *Die religiösen Kräfte* does not discuss the Jewish religion at all. A chapter on Stahl is included in Manfred Treml and Wolf Weigand (eds.), *Geschichte und Kultur der Juden in Bayern. Lebensläufe*, Munich 1988, pp. 117–120.
[7]Arnold Zweig, *Juden auf der deutschen Bühne*, Berlin 1927, pp. 22–23.
[8]Siegmund Kaznelson (ed.), *Juden im deutschen Kulturbereich. Ein Sammelwerk*, Berlin 1959, pp. 1043–1044.
[9]*Ibid.*, p. xii.
[10]Thus Nahida Remy, who was born non-Jewish but then converted to Judaism and wrote on Jewish subjects, is relegated to the appendix. Stahl, however, appears six times in the text.
[11]Walter Tetzlaff, *2000 Kurzbiographien bedeutender deutscher Juden des 20. Jahrhunderts*, Lindhorst 1982, p. i. In this compilation it is half-Jews who are relegated to the appendix, with a notation as to which parent was Jewish.
[12]Joseph Walk, *Kurzbiographien zur Geschichte der Juden 1918–1945*, Munich 1988. Publication of the Leo Baeck Institute, p. vii.

whether their attitudes and accomplishments show any evidence, not only of response to racial antisemitism, but also of identifiable, if residual Jewish influences. Germans treated as Jews by the Nazis, who are no longer such by their own or any other legitimate identity criteria, remain Jews in no sense but that of the oppressor.

Where, then, do the German Jews fit properly into the framework of German historiography? I think at four kinds of junctures. The first are those where Jews have most often been mentioned: when they became the objects of emancipation and the victims of antisemitism. Their acceptance or rejection, as Golo Mann and others have pointed out, clearly reveals much about the state of German society[13] and, as Fritz Stern has noted, also about the German ambivalence to modernity.[14] The Jews' response to changing attitudes, I would add, also reveals something about their self-perceived role in German society. A second kind of juncture occurs with regard to individuals whose contribution to German society or culture is in some way traceable to Jewish influence. Merely to mention the Jewishness of a leading figure in passing, as is commonly done in general works, has little value when a cogent argument, however brief, is not made for its explanatory role – if only to block the reader's flight to a racial explanation. Third, some attention should be given to inner Jewish developments in terms of demographic and identity shifts, the effects of emancipation, the course of acculturation, religious Reform, intellectual and ideological developments, and community activity.[15] Hajo Holborn's history of Germany pioneered in introducing discrete sections on the Jews, but antisemitism remained the focal point of his treatment, inner developments sandwiched between references to outer rejection.[16] The first attempts of which I am aware to do justice in a balanced way to the inner life of the Jews in a brief history of modern Germany have come in the excellent summary sections devoted to them in recent works on the nineteenth century by Thomas Nipperdey[17] and Reinhard Rürup.[18] Yet what remains lacking even in their work is the fourth juncture: the mention of

---

[13]Golo Mann, *Deutsche Geschichte des 19. und 20. Jahrhundert*, Frankfurt a. Main 1958, pp. 466–467.

[14]See especially his *The Politics of Cultural Despair. A Study in the Rise of the Germanic Ideology*, Berkeley 1961.

[15]These categories are absent and the Jews treated only as objects in the widely circulated volume by Hellmut Diwald, *Geschichte der Deutschen*, Frankfurt a. Main 1978.

[16]Hajo Holborn, *A History of Modern Germany 1648–1840*, New York 1964, includes a section entitled 'The Status of the Jews' (pp. 285–288) plus separate treatments of Moses Mendelssohn and of Jewish emancipation. There is virtually nothing on inner Jewish developments after Mendelssohn. His *A History of Modern Germany 1840–1945*, New York 1969, collects Jewish material under 'The Jewish Question' (pp. 277–280), beginning and ending with antisemitism. Later references to Nazi persecution do not include how German Jews dealt with such animosity.

[17]Thomas Nipperdey, *Deutsche Geschichte 1800–1866*, Munich 1983. The section which gathers almost all of Nipperdey's references to German Jewry suggests an external approach in its title, 'Das Problem der Minderheit. Die Juden' (pp. 248–255). However, it includes a full page on inner reorientation.

[18]Reinhard Rürup, *Deutschland im 19. Jahrhundert 1815–1871*, Göttingen 1984. His section on the Jews (pp. 105–109) bears a title similar to Nipperdey's: 'Minderheiten. Die Juden'. Rürup, the best versed in Jewish history among historians of Germany, here not only relates the emancipation of the German Jews to the emancipation of the bourgeoisie, but also draws comparisons between German Jewry and Jews in other lands.

relevant parallel phenomena among the Jews and within Judaism when such matters as historical criticism or religiously motivated political activity are discussed for German Protestantism and Catholicism.[19]

Clearly the expansion of Jewish history is also necessary, although I have not dwelt on it here. The history of the Jews in Germany cannot be fully understood without frequent reference not only to the German political context but also to parallel social phenomena among other minority groups[20] and to religious developments within Christianity. This becomes the more important as Jewish integration proceeds during the nineteenth century and in most instances the Jew as Jew gives way more and more to the Jew as German. The composition of the image is altered as German elements merge with or displace Jewish ones.

Where does that leave the historian whose treatment of the German Jews is not intended exclusively either for the framework of German history or for that of Jewish history? Clearly it involves a consideration of both contexts and the shifting location of German Jewry within each of them.[21] It means trying to determine how Jews in different ways and to various degrees became Germans and what the outcome of that process was for themselves, for Jews elsewhere, and for Germany.[22]

[19]The one volume of which I am aware that contains such integration, at least to a limited degree, is a book already a generation old: Koppel S. Pinson, *Modern Germany. Its History and Civilization*, New York 1954. Thus Pinson, for example, in dealing with intellectual life in the Weimar period, relates the Jewish thinker Martin Buber to a trend among Protestants and Catholics to seek out the mystical foundations of religion and ethics (pp. 456–457, 461).

[20]The Huguenots are one such group. See Stefi Jersch-Wenzel, *Juden und 'Franzosen' in der Wirtschaft des Raumes Berlin/Brandenburg zur Zeit des Merkantilismus*, Berlin 1978.

[21]This is the composite goal set for the Leo Baeck Institute's projected synthetic history of the Jews in German-speaking lands since the seventeenth century. The collaborative four-volume work is scheduled to appear in 1995 in Hebrew, English and German, marking the fortieth anniversary of the Institute.

[22]After this introduction was written, two relevant evaluations of German-Jewish historiography appeared in *LBI Year Book XXXV* (1990): Moshe Zimmermann, 'Jewish History and Jewish Historiography. A Challenge to Contemporary German Historiography', pp. 35–52; and Reinhard Rürup. 'An Appraisal of German-Jewish Historiography', pp. xv–xxiv. In a broadly-based survey Zimmermann differentiates between what he terms "exclusive" and "inclusive" approaches, noting that most German-Jewish historiography remains exclusive, *i.e.* unintegrated into German history. Especially interesting in Rürup's appraisal is his detection of ambivalence on the part of German historians towards stressing differences that marked Jews off within German society. While expanding upon such differences pays tribute to the special role of Jews in German society, it also serves to stress their otherness – a consequence that seems to some undesirable against the background of Nazi antisemitism. Rürup persuasively argues that neglecting the peculiarities of Jewish distribution in the various sectors of German life falsifies reality. From the standpoint of a historian of modern Germany, he also maintains that the approaches of Jewish history and German history are both legitimate and both necessary. Beyond that mutual recognition, of course, lies the task of integrating the two.

Burgeoning Emancipation

Two Silent Minorities: Orthodox Jews and Poor Jews in Berlin 1770–1823

BY STEVEN M. LOWENSTEIN

Berlin Jewry in the last third of the eighteenth century and the first quarter of the nineteenth underwent a very rapid transformation from a rather traditional Jewish community to one with all the characteristics of modern Jewish life. Berlin was one of the pioneering communities in this transformation; the changes there were more rapid than in most other places and the controversies and difficulties more acute than elsewhere.

The transformation of Berlin Jewry has played a large role in most histories of Modern Jewry. It is quite understandable that writers have been mainly interested in the groups that changed the most – the Jewish Enlightenment, the women of the salons, early Reform and the "Taufepidemie" (epidemic of baptisms).* The groups that changed least have had the least attention.

All the evidence seems to show that the changes in Jewish religious and cultural life were most common among the Jewish upper class. This was the group that tended to be most articulate, that first turned to new lifestyles, supported the Enlightenment and was most likely to convert to Christianity. The poor and the less well-to-do seem to have played a lesser role.

For these reasons neither those Berlin Jews who remained Orthodox nor those who were not wealthy have generally held the centre of the stage in discussions of the transformation of Berlin Jewry.

Attention in this essay will focus on these two groups, not only because they have been neglected, but because studying them will help put into perspective the actual shape of the events which took place between 1770 and 1830 in Berlin. First of all, it will enable us to determine with more precision to what extent the equation modernist/wealthy and Orthodox/poor is accurate. Secondly, by looking at traditionalists and their way of life we can see both what the modernists were fighting against and how the traditionalists themselves changed over time. Finally, by looking both at the lifestyles of the Orthodox and the life of the poor, we can get a more accurate picture of the variety of Jewish life during the period of rapid change. After all, what characterises the modern period is not that all Jews are equally modern, but rather that in place of uniformity there is ever increasing diversity in Judaism. Berlin Jewry, like Modern Jewry as a whole, was characterised by a growing chasm between different types of lifestyles.

---

*On this see the most recent studies of Peter Honigmann, 'Jewish Conversions – A Measure of Assimilation? A Discussion of the Berlin Secession Statistics of 1770–1941', in *LBI Year Book XXXIV* (1989), pp. 3–39; and *idem, Die Austritte aus der Jüdischen Gemeinde Berlin 1873–1941*, Frankfurt a. Main – Bern – New York – Paris 1988 – (Ed.).

Steven M. Lowenstein

ORTHODOX JEWRY IN BERLIN

It would seem that Berlin Jewry before the middle of the eighteenth century was no less (and perhaps more) traditional than other German-Jewish communities.[1] The Berlin community, though founded as late as 1671, had all the institutions of a traditional community. Its Chief Rabbi and his assistants formed a rabbinical court; its paid officials included a cantor and assistant cantor with their traditional accompanying bass and "Singer", beadles (*shamoshim*)[2] including those whose job it was to summon community members to the rabbinic court, ritual slaughterers (4 of them in 1764) and butchers for kosher meat. Its charity institutions included a burial society, hospice for the sick (*bikur cholim*), collections for the Land of Israel and for education for the poor (Talmud Torah).

The creation of traditional institutions continued through much of the eighteenth century. In 1729 the community set up a separate fund for the support of poor Jews in Hebron in addition to the special fund already existing for the Land of Israel.[3] A costlier and more influential institution was created in Berlin in 1743–1744 when the *Beth Hamidrash* (Talmud Study House) was founded. The *Beth Hamidrash* had its own facilities in a building adjacent to the synagogue, and chose three rabbis whose job it was to "occupy themselves day and night with the Torah".[4] Private study houses continued to be founded even a generation later by such leaders of the community as Veitel Heine Ephraim and his son Zacharias Veitel Ephraim in their testaments of 1775 and 1779. Even though many leaders of that later generation already supported the Enlightenment, they left foundations for private synagogues and for traditional Talmud study as well. Many of these private synagogues continued to exist well into the nineteenth

---

[1] It is noteworthy that relatively few of the incidents of incipient modernity in early eighteenth-century German Jewry quoted in Azriel Shohet, *Im Hilufei Tekufot. Reshit Hahaskala Beyahadut Germaniya*, Jerusalem 1960, come from Berlin. Evidence from Berlin is far outnumbered by examples from Hamburg-Altona.

[2] In this article two forms of transliteration of Hebrew are used. Where the original source contains a transliteration, I have followed the original even where the results may seem bizarre to those who know modern Hebrew (e.g. *Zanduko*). Elsewhere, I have transliterated using the Ashkenazic pronunciation which is much closer to the original pronunciation of the documents than the usual Sephardic transcription.

[3] Joseph Meisl (ed.), *Protokollbuch der Jüdischen Gemeinde Berlin (1723–1854)* (*Pinkas Kehilat Berlin*), Jerusalem 1962 (hereafter referred to as: *Pinkas*), p.28.

[4] Although this traditional formulation was used to describe the duties of the rabbis of the *Beth Hamidrash*, their actual duties were a good deal more circumscribed. They were to be prepared to teach a daily *Mishna* class for an hour after morning prayers and a daily class in *Shulchan Aruch* (*Orech Chaim*) for an hour before afternoon prayers. The audience was to consist of members of the *Beth Hamidrash* and any other community members who wished to attend.

When Sanwil Neugas was appointed a rabbi of the *Beth Hamidrash* in 1766 his duties included being present all morning to hear the lessons of students from *bar mitzvah* age to age 18. In the afternoon he was to study together with all who wished to come "whether great classes or small classes (*shiura rabba veshiura zuta*)". He was not to leave the building for classes in a private home except with two or more persons and then only after afternoon prayers. He was to supervise the study of the *yeshiva* students (*bachurim*) "day and night" and to teach a class in *Pirke Avot* on Sabbath afternoons. Similar duties were set for Rabbi Loeb Farrnbach in 1770 (Moritz Stern, 'Das Vereinsbuch der Berliner Beth Hamidrasch', *Beiträge zur Geschichte der Jüdischen Gemeinde zu Berlin*, 4 [1931], pp. III, XIV, XV).

century.[5] As late as 1792 a new traditional society *Machasikim Lomde Thora* was created for the support of poor "Talmudisten und andere Gelehrte".[6]

The traditional nature of Berlin Jewry was not only shown by its institutions. There is also evidence of strict religious practice and of continuing traditional ideas until mid-century at least. Regulations on kosher meat issued in 1729 show that only "glatt kosher" meat was permitted in the city, in contrast to more lenient practices in neighbouring small towns.[7]

The traditional self-image of the Jews as a nation in exile waiting for redemption by the Messiah was still taken for granted by many community leaders well into the eighteenth century. This is evident in the language of the communal minute book on numerous occasions, one of them as late as 1802. Even quite routine transactions were dated "until the Messiah comes" or talked about the Jews living "on foreign soil".[8] Besides such examples of traditional language and stereotypically traditional concepts, there are even communal documents from the middle of the eighteenth century which see the coming of the Messiah as a concrete possibility for the near future and include clauses in contracts on how to act in case the Messiah arrives.[9]

The continued use of traditional concepts and phrases does not mean that there were no inroads of modernity. In the early and middle eighteenth century

[5]In 1815 the community sent a list of 12 prayer-houses outside the main synagogue to the government. Of these 10 bear the names of individuals, some of them those of wealthy Jews who left behind foundations for their upkeep. In at least two cases the services were in the homes of persons who had converted (or were soon to convert) to Christianity. (Central Archives for the History of the Jewish People [hereafter referred to as CAHJP] P-17/ 578; K GE 2/10). This compares to 22 private religious services around the year 1774 (*Pinkas*, p. LV).

[6]K GE 2/120 -CAHJP.

[7]*Pinkas*, p. 45, paragraph 61. Those who imported meat from those small towns whose practices were more lenient were to pay a fine of ten Reichstaler (a substantial sum) and their dishes were declared non-kosher. Only meat from towns which forbade meat from animals with growths on the lungs (*sirchos*) could be brought into Berlin.

[8]A record from 1745, for instance, talks about the practice of various large communities "*asher begolus yisroel*" (in the Jewish exile). In 1754 when the community was forced to buy certain goods from the king at a loss, they declared all members of the community to be fully responsible partners "*vecho yihye vecho yikom benenu ad bo goel tsidkenu*" (and so shall it be and so shall it occur until our redeemer comes). The last example of such language occurs as late as 1802. In a document dealing with the attempt to convince the communal elder Liepmann Meyer Wulff not to resign his post, the introduction speaks of Jewish leaders who show God's grace "*miyom bo am behiro al admas nechor*" (since the day when His chosen people have come onto foreign soil). (*Pinkas*, §125, 159, 348).

[9]One such example is shown in a document dated 1762 (in the middle of the Seven Years War) which concerns a loan of 6,300 *Reichstaler* by the community of Halberstadt to the Berlin community. Evidently the community of Berlin felt endangered by war conditions. Therefore article 3 of the contract began "Should our redeemer come with the help of God to bring us up to the Holy Land (*Bevo goel tsidkenu be'ezras hashem yisborach lehalosenu el hooretz hakedosho*) or if another reason should cause our community, heaven forbid to move and scatter its individual members from here" they would first have to repay the loan to the community of Halberstadt. A similar "Messianic" passage is found in the communal record book of Berlin dated 1746. Again a loan is taken out and the principal is to be kept by the institution (only interest is to be paid out) "until our redeemer comes. And if our redemption should come soon (*veim tihyeh geulosenu bizman korov*) or if there be a reason which we cannot write down that the community has to scatter", then the loan has to be repaid. (*Pinkas*, §129, 198, The 1762 example is also quoted by Shohet, *op. cit.*, p. 195.)

This seems to be counter-evidence to Gershom Scholem's claim that the failure of the Sabbatai Zvi movement in the 1660s caused Jews to despair of the coming of the Messiah.

the communal officials tried to deal with signs of cultural modernity with traditional methods, including the use of coercion against innovators. In 1738 when Jeremias Cohen appeared in the synagogue with his beard shaven and wearing a wig, the community ordered that he should be punished. The punishment however was quite mild.[10] In 1747, in a similar case, Abraham Posner (Hirschel) was reported to the government by Veitel Heine Ephraim, the later communal elder, for having shaved his beard. An unconfirmed story claims that the ancestor of Gerson Bleichröder was expelled from Berlin in 1746 for possessing a German book.[11] Evidence of attempts by communal leaders to suppress non-traditional thought are found as late as the 1770s.

Another example of the survival of traditional ideas is the continued use of sumptuary law to limit luxury in dress and celebrations as late as the 1760s and 1770s.[12] Epitaphs of the period also still routinely use traditional and pious language and refer to the traditional piety of the deceased.[13]

By the 1760s and 1770 the Jewish elite of Berlin was beginning to break with some of the habits of tradition. These changes were noticeable both in lifestyle and in support for the Mendelssohnian Enlightenment. Still, the evidence about the modernism of the Berlin Jewish leadership of the generation is highly

[10]Since he had "broken the fence and acted contrary to the law and religion of our Torah and Jewish custom (*poratz geder venohag atzmo neged din vedas torosenu uminhag yisroel*)", he was not to be called to the Torah on the holidays (but could be called on Sabbath and weekdays) and he could not stand in the place of honour next to the Torah reader at all. (*laamod lisgan*) (Pinkas, §80.)

[11]On the Veitel Heine Ephraim–Abraham Posner case see Leiser Landshuth, 'Veitel Heine Ephraim als Anwalt des Judenbarts' [written, 1872], published by Moritz Stern in 1909 as the first of a never-completed series *Beiträge zur Geschichte der Juden in Berlin*. Landshuth claims that Ephraim got involved in the case more out of spite against Posner than out of religious conviction. The story of the expulsion of a Bleichröder for reading a German book is mentioned in Meyer Kayserling, *Moses Mendelssohn. Sein Leben und seine Werke*, Leipzig 1862, and is repeated in Heinz Knobloch's popular, *Herr Moses in Berlin. Ein Menschenfreund in Preussen. Das Leben des Moses Mendelssohn*, Berlin 1982, but not in Alexander Altmann's scholarly biography, *Moses Mendelssohn. A Biographical Study*, London 1973.

[12]A record of 1765 speaks of making a *Kleiderordnung* against luxury which causes much "desecration of God's name". A decision of 1777 during an economic recession strictly limited the number of guests at circumcision feasts and weddings (*Pinkas*, §233, 300). Both these types of action were typical of pre-modern Jewish communities.

[13]Many epitaphs up to the end of the eighteenth century (and even beyond in certain cases) refer to the deceased as learned in Rabbinics ("*hatorani*", "*haraboni*") or as a righteous and proper person ("*ish kosher veyosher*"). Although there are a few noticeable changes between some of the epitaphs of the 1760s and 1770s and those of the early eighteenth century, they are relatively minor compared with what came later.

In the late 1780s we first encounter a number of epitaphs with Hebrew poems in the *Haskalah* (Enlightenment) style.

The clearest examples of Modernity, however are not found until the 1810s. Many epitaphs beginning then are in High German in Hebrew characters rather than in Hebrew and they contain such typically modern and German sentiments as "Hier ruht die irdische Hülle von . . ." (here lie the earthly remains of . . .). Such epitaphs also often contain sentimental language of a type not found in the traditional epitaphs (e.g. "die liebevollste Gattin, zärtlichste Mutter und edelste Wohltäterin" (the most loving spouse, tenderest mother, noblest benefactress).

Even in the nineteenth century, however, there were still some epitaphs with very traditional motifs.

The LBI Archives, New York (LBIA), Jacobson Collection I – 66–70, and elsewhere, contains copies of all epitaphs in the old Jewish cemetery in Berlin copied by Leiser Landshuth covering the period 1671–1827.

ambiguous. On the one hand, virtually the whole Berlin Jewish upper class subscribed to Mendelssohn's Bible translation and to many other Hebrew works printed by the followers of the Enlightenment; they sponsored the first modern Jewish school, the *Jüdische Freischule* (founded 1778); most seem to have given their children a secular education. A number of the wealthiest Berlin Jews of the period built mansions decorated with art work, possessed book or art collections and dressed like non-Jewish Berliners. Leaders like Daniel Itzig (1723–1799) are depicted as clean-shaven and bareheaded, and wearing wigs.[14]

It would seem, however, that most of the elite generation born in the 1720s and 1730s still observed traditional Jewish ritual. Daniel Itzig's mansion had a room that could be converted into a *sukka*. Moses Isaac-Fliess's testament ordered that his non-kosher wine (presumably used in his commerce but not drunk by him) be sold only to non-Jews. It also contained numerous provisions concerning prayers and Talmud study to be undertaken for the benefit of his soul.[15] The will of Veitel Heine Ephraim (1703–1775) provided for the disinheriting of children who did not follow Jewish practice.[16]

It would seem that besides their support for Enlightenment projects, the modernism of this generation was restricted to matters of cultural style. Travellers' reports of the 1770s describe their surprise that Jews in Berlin dressed like non-Jews and regularly attended the theatre, but not until 1780[17] is there mention of widespread violations of the Sabbath and the dietary laws.

However important the Jewish leadership of the 1770s was in supporting and defending[18] Enlightenment projects, not all perceived them as modernists. Henriette Herz spoke of the Jewish elders of the time who had forbidden a theatre performance in a private home as "die reichsten und angesehensten, aber auch

---

[14]On the subscribers to Mendelssohn's Bible translation and other Enlightenment works see Steven Lowenstein, 'The Readership of Mendelssohn's Bible Translation', *Hebrew Union College Annual*, 53 (1982), pp. 179–211.

For a description of the mansions, art collections and libraries of the Berlin Jewish elite see Friedrich Nicolai, *Beschreibung der königlichen Residenzstädte Berlin und Potsdam*, Berlin 1786, pp. 6, 787, 852, 931, 934–935.

The change in dress and hairstyles was not always complete. Quite a few leaders in the community in the 1770s wore fashionable three-cornered hats and wigs, but still had partial or full beards – a practice virtually unknown to non-Jews of the time. This is the way Moses Mendelssohn is depicted. For another such case see the portrait of Ephraim Marcus Ephraim (1716–1776) in *LBI Year Book XXIV* (1979), opposite p. 232.

[15]On Daniel Itzig's *sukka* see Nicolai, *op. cit.*, p. 852. For a German translation of Moses Isaac-Fliess's last will and testament see LBIA, Jacobson Collection, I–97.

[16]Ludwig Geiger, 'Vor Hundert Jahren', *Zeitschrift für die Geschichte der Juden in Deutschland*, 3 (1889), p. 210, states that the testament of Veitel Heine Ephraim allowed his fiduciaries to suspend heirs who left the "Mosaischen Gesetze oder gar die Religion seiner Väter" and to exclude them if they did not improve within two years.

[17]Michael A. Meyer, *The Origin of the Modern Jew. Jewish Identity and European Culture in Germany 1749–1824*, Detroit 1967, p. 40, quotes a letter by the portrait painter Chodowiecki in 1780 which states: "It seems that where you live the Jews are still orthodox; here, with the exception of the lower classes, they are so by no means. They buy and sell on Saturdays, eat all forbidden foods, keep no fast days etc . . ."

[18]For instance, when the Chief Rabbi of Berlin threatened to punish Hartwig Wessely for writing his tract in favour of a radical change in Jewish education (*Divrei Shalom Ve'emet*, 1782), Daniel Itzig's son and son-in-law (Isaac Daniel Itzig and David Friedländer) convinced Itzig to take steps to protect Wessely. Altmann, *Moses Mendelssohn, op. cit.*, pp. 483–485.

orthodoxesten Gemeindemitglieder". Salomon Maimon, who arrived in Berlin during the same decade was expelled from the city by the charity wardens because he planned a commentary on Maimonides's *Guide to the Perplexed* and was thus suspected of heresy.[19] The synagogue leadership remained Orthodox even longer than the overall communal leadership; in the mid-1780s they refused to allow Lazarus Bendavid to lead prayers after his father's death because of his violation of various ritual laws.[20]

The education given to children of the Berlin elite in the middle of the eighteenth century or later was a two-sided and sometimes ambiguous one. Benjamin V. Ephraim (born 1743) was the youngest son of communal elder Veitel Heine Ephraim. The Ephraims were involved both in traditional religious activities and in support for the Enlightenment. Their ambiguous attitude was reflected in Benjamin's education. Benjamin's mother, whom he describes as "eine sehr gottesfürchtige Frau und äusserst orthodox", allowed no German book into the house except Luther's Bible translation. Benjamin was instructed in Talmud and Hebrew but later also received tutoring in German (for three months!) and in French (the same amount of time). Still later his instruction was guided by Lessing and Mendelssohn.[21] The autobiography of Lazarus Bendavid (born 1762) shows a similar combination of traditional and Enlightened influence. Even though Bendavid's parents are described by him as less than totally Orthodox, he received several years of instruction from Polish Talmud tutors.[22]

The ambiguity of the position of the Jewish leadership of the period is one indication of the fact that Orthodox and Enlightenment parties had not yet rigidly

[19]Julius Fürst (ed.), *Henriette Herz. Ihr Leben und ihre Erinnerungen*, Berlin 1850, p. 88; *idem*, *The Autobiography of Solomon Maimon* (J. Clark Murray tr.), London 1954, pp. 97–98.

Salomon Maimon seems to have arrived in Berlin for the first time in the late 1770s. His autobiography is a rich source of information on cultural attitudes in Berlin in the late 1770s and 1780s. On Maimon's second trip to Berlin he again encountered trouble from the "Jewish police-officer L.M.", whose job it was to inquire into the background of newcomers in all hotels in Berlin. L.M. flew into a rage at seeing a copy of *Milloth Higgayon* by Maimonides with notes by Mendelssohn in the possession of Maimon (p. 107). Obviously not all Berlin Jews of the time supported Mendelssohn's efforts.

On the other hand, Maimon was able to find wealthy protectors (the family of D____ P____ [David Präger=David Hirsch?]) who helped get him lodging and Sabbath meals. There were a number of other wealthy families willing to help a Polish Jew searching for Enlightenment in Berlin. Maimon's involvement with a circle of high-living young men seems to have alienated him from Mendelssohn and some of his other influential protectors (pp. 109–119).

[20]Lazarus Bendavid, *Autobiography* (copy with handwritten notes in Leo Baeck Institute, New York), pp. 53–54. The text speaks of Bendavid's violation of four (unnamed) *Ceremonialgesetze*.

[21]Benjamin Veitel Ephraim, *Ueber meine Verhaftung und einige andere Vorfälle meines Lebens*, Berlin 1807, pp. 82–86. Ephraim claims that before the Seven Years War he had already read Montesquieu's *L'Esprit des Loix*, and Hume's *Discours Politique*, studied Euclid with the Jewish mathematician Swa and been urged by Lessing to study English and Latin.

[22]Bendavid, *op. cit.*, pp. 9–22. Bendavid states that when he was three years old his mother taught him how to read German from a book. At the age of about four he was taught both the Hebrew Bible and elementary arithmetic. In his sixth year he was sent "zu einem Polen in eine thalmudische Schule" which he later recalled with horror. After being removed from that school he was sent to another Talmud school at the age of eight; the Polish teacher of that school whom Bendavid recalls fondly taught other subjects as well including Bible, Hebrew grammar and Aristotle's *Logic* with Maimonides's commentary. He also received private tutoring in writing, arithmetic, and bookkeeping and later also had French lessons. He also read widely including the Koran, works by Wolf, Voltaire and Rousseau.

split by the late 1770s. There was still considerable cross-over between Orthodox and Enlightenment activity. Of 77 members of the *Chevra Kadisha* (burial society) in 1778, one of the bulwarks of Orthodoxy in Berlin, at least 14 were also subscribers to Mendelssohn's Bible translation.[23] The boards of officers of the *Beth Hamidrash* between 1770 and 1783 included more subscribers to Mendelssohn (including Moses Mendelssohn himself) than members of the burial society.[24] A generation later, in the 1810s, the degree of overlap between Reformers and Orthodox was much less, and the lines of division were much clearer.[25]

There was some degree of social differentiation between those engaged in "Orthodox" activities and those supporting the Enlightenment in the 1770s, but there were also social differences between various Orthodox activities. Subscribers to Mendelssohn's Bible translation paid almost three times as much tax per person as did members of the burial society. The trustees of the *Beth Hamidrash*, however, paid close to twice as high taxes as those in the burial society.[26]

There is a consensus among scholars that the abandonment of traditional religious practice increased greatly after the death of Mendelssohn in 1786. Although it is difficult to trace the exact stages of the change, it seems likely that this is true. By the early nineteenth century, the non-Orthodox nature of Berlin Jewry seemed established. The communal board which was chosen in 1808 seems to have been the first to have had a majority of members who were not Orthodox.[27]

[23]The following were listed both as subscribers of the Mendelssohn Bible translation and as members of the burial society in 1778:
   Jeremias Bendix, Isaac Esaias Riess, Joseph Hirsch, Moses Isaac Riess, Levin Joel, Liepmann Meyer Wulff, Abraham Marcuse, Hirsch Samuel Speyer, Assur Ephraim Marcus, Joseph Veitel Ephraim, Loeb Bresselau von Bressendorf, Joseph Wolff Rintel, Joel Samuel Nauen, Abraham Nauen. Jacob Borchart was probably also both a subscriber and a member of the burial society. The only ambiguity is that there were two persons in Berlin by that name.
[24]Sixteen of the 45 persons who served on the *Beth Hamidrash* boards or signed its official documents during the period were also subscribers to the Bible translation. Only nine were members of the burial society.
[25]Of the 70 members of the burial society in 1813 only about six were also listed as attendees of the Reform service: Moses Alexander Benda, Pesach Fraustadt, Joseph Levin Meyer, Jacob Joel Sachs, Israel Joel Sachs and Daniel Salomon Levy. Levin Gerson Wolff seems to have been listed as a Reform service attendee and as a signer of an anti-Reform petition.
[26]The average highest tax [i.e. the highest tax listed for that individual in any year up to 1789] paid by subscribers to Mendelssohn's Bible translation was 6 Reichstaler, 3 Groschen, 1 Pfennig (among 86 subscribers who paid any tax to the Jewish community), while the average for members of the *chevra kadisha* in 1778 was only 2 Reichstaler, 4 Groschen, 6 Pfennig (of 68 taxpayers).
   For officers of the *Beth Hamidrash* the average highest tax was 4 Reichstaler, 5 Groschen, 11 Pfennig (44 taxpayers) but this figure is a bit skewed since it includes the richest Jew in Berlin – Daniel Itzig. If he is excluded, the average highest tax is then only 3 Reichstaler, 6 Groschen.
   Officeholders for typically Orthodox charity funds (*Erez Israel*, Hebron and Talmud Torah) after 1770 were even poorer than members of the burial society, with an average tax of only 1 Reichstaler, 11 Groschen, 4 Pfennig (21 taxpayers).
[27]The elders (*Parnassim*) elected in December 1808 were Liepmann Meyer Wulff (Tausk), Samuel Nathan (Bendix) Bernsdorff, David (Präger) Hirsch, Ruben Samuel (Breslau) Gumpertz and David Friedländer. Salomon (Kronke) Friedländer declined his nomination as an elder. All but Hirsch and Wulff were later outspoken adherents of religious Reform. Liepmann Meyer Wulff was already ill at the time of his election and attended virtually no meetings of the communal board. Three of the four alternates to the elders (*Tovim* and *Ikkurim*), Ascher Schönfliess, Liebermann Schlesinger, Juda Herz Beer and Abraham (Bendix) Bendemann were also leaders in the fight for Reform. (CAHJP-Stern Collection P–17/451.)

Despite the decline of Orthodoxy, there was still a substantial Orthodox presence in the city and a distinct Orthodox milieu still existed.[28] A good picture of this milieu is given by the memoirs of Jacob Adam, a youth from the province of Poznań who arrived in Berlin around 1803 to study at the *yeshiva*. The attitude in his hometown towards Berlin was ambiguous. On the one hand, the *yeshiva* in Berlin was well known; on the other hand, it was feared that the boy might be influenced by the atmosphere of the city and lose his piety there. When he arrives in Berlin, Adam finds relatives who no longer observed *kashruth* and who predict that if Adam were to remain in Berlin he too would change.[29]

The Orthodox in Berlin as described by Adam were not all alike. Some were still recognisable on the street. Adam and his travelling companion were unable to find the synagogue until they encountered "einen Juden mit Bart" who could give them directions. Not all the Orthodox in Berlin were so unacculturated. On the way to the city the two travellers had met a coach with a passenger whom Adam described as "a very good looking corpulent man . . . with a powdered wig and three-cornered hat". Only later, when they asked others who the man was, did they realise that he was a Jew. It turned out that this man, Isaac Moses Gerhard, was a leader of Berlin Orthodoxy, head of the Talmud Torah, member of the burial society and a later anti-Reform petitioner.[30] Gerhard, too, expressed his fear that they would become "Epicureans" (heretics) in Berlin. Another Orthodox leader mentioned by Adam was "Lipman Tausk" (Liepmann Meyer Wulff) who was "der reichste und der frömmste unter den Juden in Berlin". From 1799 to 1812 he was also the head of the Jewish community.

The Orthodox institutions included the *yeshiva* which had forty *bachurim* (students), who studied Talmud with the three rabbis of the city. The forty received 2 Taler a month from the Talmud Torah fund. In addition there were ten alternates (*Beisitzer*), who attended the classes but received no funds. There were so many Talmud students at the time that Adam was unable to obtain a regular place in the *yeshiva* but merely became a hanger-on who attended the class ("schier") of one of the rabbis. At the time, he writes, there were still many pious Jews in Berlin who had much respect for Torah learning and were glad to

[28]Berlin Orthodoxy still functioned as a supplier of religious functionaries to the very traditional Jewish communities in small towns near Berlin in the first two decades of the nineteenth century. The memoirs of Aron Hirsch Heymann, *Lebenserinnerungen* (ed. by Heinrich Loewe), Berlin 1909, make several references to such men coming from Berlin to his native town of Strausberg.

Mohalim (ritual circumcisers) came from Berlin (pp. 32, 173). So did the wedding jester Reb Leib Lenzen. A private individual whom Heymann calls Reb Mausche Samter and describes as a *mohel*, a *lambdon* (learned man in Talmud) and a good cantor came to Strausberg from Berlin to dedicate the local synagogue in 1817 (pp. 112, 127–128). (This last case may be somewhat ambiguous. Moshe Samter seems to be identical with Moses David Alexander Benda who is found both on the list of members of the Orthodox burial society and on the list of participants in the Reform service.)

[29]Adam's relative Abel who sees that he will not eat without his hat and that he eats only kosher, advises him to eat in a kosher "*Speisehaus*". He told him "I would have given you, but you won't want to eat non-kosher yet" (Du wirst doch noch kein Treif essen wollen). He also told him "If you plan to remain in Berlin, you won't remain like this long". (Jacob Adam, *Memoirs* [Memoir No. 2/M.E. 317 in LBI Archives, New York], pp. 21–22, 23.)

[30]In the *Memoirs* he is referred to merely as "Bankier Goever", but the *Pinkas*, shows that the head of the Talmud Torah was Eisik Gewer, a banker, who later took the name Isaac Moses Gerhard. (For the name change see LBIA, Jacobson Collection I 82 individual G16/46.)

support those Talmud students who "could flatter well and appear to be pious". Another source of income was as paid members of the *minyan* (quorum of ten) in the many private synagogues in Berlin where daily services took place.[31] Others earned money baking matzos for Passover. Adam eventually gave up his Talmud study and attended the *Jüdische Freischule*.

Although the Orthodox milieu still had its own institutions and its supporters in 1803, it was clearly already in a weakened state. One indication of this is evident from the position of Berlin rabbis. In the mid-eighteenth century, at least some of the rabbis of the city had belonged to or married into leading Berlin families. David Fränkel, Mendelssohn's teacher, who was rabbi of Berlin from 1743 till his death in 1762, was the brother-in-law of Veitel Heine Ephraim, chief elder of the community.[32] These prestigious connections became much less common after 1800. Rabbis now seemed to marry mainly into Orthodox families and not into the most prestigious of communal families. Their ability to ensure the Orthodoxy even of their own families seems to have been impaired. In his memoirs Adam mentions that his relative, who evidently no longer observed the dietary laws, was a close family friend of one of the *yeshiva* rabbis Leiser Zilz.[33] The rabbi's daughter is described as his "beloved" (*Geliebte*) and the two later married.

Another sign of the weakened state of the rabbinate was the fact that no successor was chosen to the Chief Rabbi (*Oberlandesrabbiner*) Hirschel Levin after his death in 1800. His successor Meyer Simcha Weyl (1766–1826) was given only

---

[31]Adam, *Memoirs, op. cit.*, pp. 20–21.

[32]On the ancestry of David Fränkel see Jacob Jacobson, *Jüdische Trauungen in Berlin 1759–1813*, Berlin 1968, pp. 117–118, 9–11. Because of Fränkel's influential relatives in the city, the community had to make special provision for an extra rabbinical judge for cases involving the Chief Rabbi's relatives, in which the rabbi was disqualified to participate. (*Pinkas*, pp. 108–111 [paragraphs 111–113].) Fränkel's nephew, who was assistant rabbi in Dessau also married into a Berlin elite family (the daughter of the very wealthy Abraham Strelitz).

The descendants of Samuel Bendix (Sanwil Dayan), assistant rabbi of Berlin from 1719 to 1742 included a host of wealthy and distinguished Berliners who married into the Abraham Moses, David Friedländer and Ephraim Marcus families. Many were bankers. Among the rabbi's grandchildren and great-grandchildren were several active leaders of the Reform community (e.g. Samuel Bernsdorff and August Heinrich Bendemann); several of the great-grandchildren converted to Christianity.

Another distinguished Berlin family, the Gumperz's, also had rabbis in the family. One of these, Bendit Gumperz, served as rabbi of Breslau from 1744 to 1754. The rabbi's son, Samuel Bendix Gumperz, who left an estate of 400,000 Taler, was a follower of the Enlightenment and the father of the banker Ruben Samuel Gumpertz a leader of the Reform movement in Berlin.

Of the Berlin rabbis who followed David Fränkel only a few had wealthy Berlin relatives and even these (for instance the relatives of Simon Joachim Landsberger) were not nearly as influential as some of the relatives of earlier rabbis. It would seem that by the last years of the eighteenth century it was much more likely for leading Berlin families to wish to have a physician in the family than to wish to be connected with a rabbi.

[33]It would seem that the reference is to Lazarus Horwitz. (Adam, *Memoirs*, p. 22); the identification of Lazarus Horwitz as Leiser Zilz comes from *Pinkas*, p. 510. Horwitz was born in 1747 and died in 1818. Jacob Jacobson, in his *Die Judenbürgerbücher der Stadt Berlin*, Berlin 1962, p. 148, lists Jacob Adam's relative as: Joachim Hirsch Fromm, merchant, Rosenthaler Strasse 54, born in Chodziesen (Grand Duchy of Poznań) in 1776. Originally called Joachim Hirsch Abel. Married on 26th May 1817 to Frommet, daughter of Lazarus Horowitz, member of the Jewish court.

the title of Vice-Chief Rabbi and after Weyl's death, only a caretaker rabbi was appointed.[34]

A list of Jewish institutions in Berlin in 1811 still lists mainly traditional organisations, though such modern ones as the *Jüdische Freischule* and the *Gesellschaft der Freunde* also figure in the list. Even some individuals who are usually thought of as being supporters of Reform were officers of such traditional *chevras* as the "*Zanduko*" (society for paying for circumcising poor children), the *Beth Hamidrash* and *Ohel Jescharim* (rent subsidies for the poor).[35]

When the new pro-Enlightenment administration took over governance of the community in December 1808, it began to put pressure on some of the remaining Orthodox institutions of the city. The new elders took over at a time of great crisis for Berlin Jewry. The city had been occupied by French troops since 1806 and the economy was severely damaged. In the struggle to balance the communal budget, the Orthodox strongholds were among the areas on which the elders decided to save money. A long and sometimes bitter struggle took place between the elders and the heads of the Orthodox Talmud Torah society between 1809 and 1813. The elders tried to cut both the number of Talmud students in the city and the amount of subsidy to the Talmud Torah. David Friedländer, who led the drive to cut the subsidies, seems to have been motivated both by the feeling that it was a waste of money to underwrite Talmud students and by the desire to cut an Orthodox power base.[36]

[34] Monika Richarz, *Jüdisches Leben in Deutschland. Selbstzeugnisse zur Sozialgeschichte 1780–1871*, Stuttgart 1976, Veröffentlichung des Leo Baeck Instituts, p. 234, note 16.

[35] The *Rendant* of the *Zanduko* was Ruben Samuel Gumpertz (see note 32), Samuel Nathan Bernsdorff was an officer of the *Beth Hamidrash*, and Liebermann Schlesinger was head of the *Ohel Jescharim*. Other traditional societies listed were: *Bickur Chaulim* (care for the sick), Talmud Torah (education of children), *Haspakoth Ebionim* (care for the poor), *Gemiluth Chessadim* (burial society), *Machsikim Laumde Thora* (aid for poor Talmud scholars), *Shomer Laboker* (charity for mourners) and *Malbisch Erumim* (clothes for the poor). (CAHJP – K Ge 2/120.)

[36] A customary subsidy of 500 Reichstaler annually had been set aside to support 40 *yeshiva* students (*bachurim*). In February 1809 the elders asked the heads of the Talmud Torah to introduce the thirty students who were still in Berlin to the elders so they could judge if they were worthy. In March 1809 David Friedländer proposed the end of all subsidies to *yeshiva* students from out of town. ("Bei der Überzeugung in welcher alle rechtliche Leute sind, dass der Unterricht der fremden Bachurim aus fremden Städten, völlig unzweckmässig ist, der Unterhalt dieser Bachurim künftighin wegfallen und der Gemeindekasse nichts dazu bei getragen werden soll.") (CAHJP – P 17–451.) By August 1809 the Talmud Torah had agreed to a reduced list of 15 *bachurim* which the elders accepted with some conditions. The amount of the subsidy seems still to have been 250 Reichstaler per half year.

By the end of 1812 the elders were attempting to cut the subsidy of 500 Reichstaler a year by stating that it was for the education of the poor, not necessarily just for those in the Talmud Torah. (In a report to the city government of Berlin in 1812 David Friedländer informed them of the decision to cut the 500 Thaler subsidy to the Talmud Torah. He states that the subsidy had only been instituted because the bonds which had formerly supported the institution no longer brought in income.) They demanded a list of those being supported before they would pay the subsidy. In January 1813 the Talmud Torah wrote that they supported a Talmud Torah school and also gave subsidies to ten poor parents for educating their children. Since discretion was needed they refused to give a list. The elders then refused the subsidy. One tradition-orientated elder protested, but Friedländer stated the money was being denied not to the needy children but to the officers of the Talmud Torah who were acting in an arbitrary manner. After all, he continued, they were in league with the Vice-Chief Rabbi Weyl who was only causing trouble. ("Nicht den armen Kindern welche Unterricht bedürfen soll das Lehrgeld entzogen werden sondern den Herren Vorsteher, welche

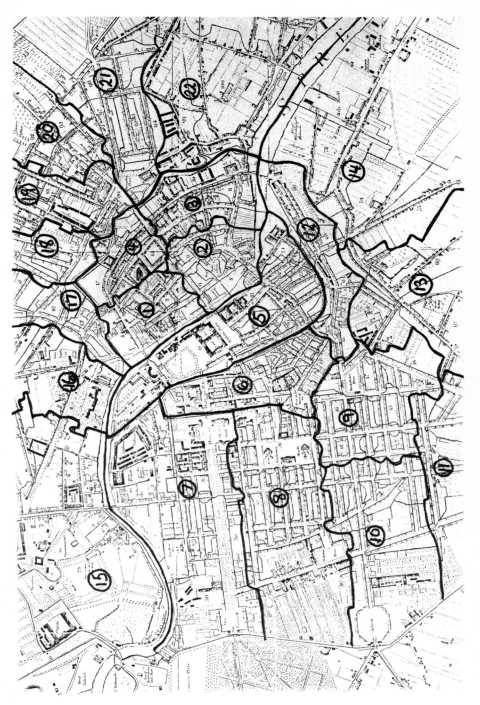

Police districts in Berlin, 1812

Aron Beer
Cantor of Berlin in contemporary dress
(with only the hint of a beard)
1808

Streets and alleys inhabited by poor Berlin Jews
Above: Reetzengasse, 1831, painting by Edvard Gärtner
Below: Nicolaikirchhof and Eiergasse, photo, c. 1880 by F. A. Schwarz

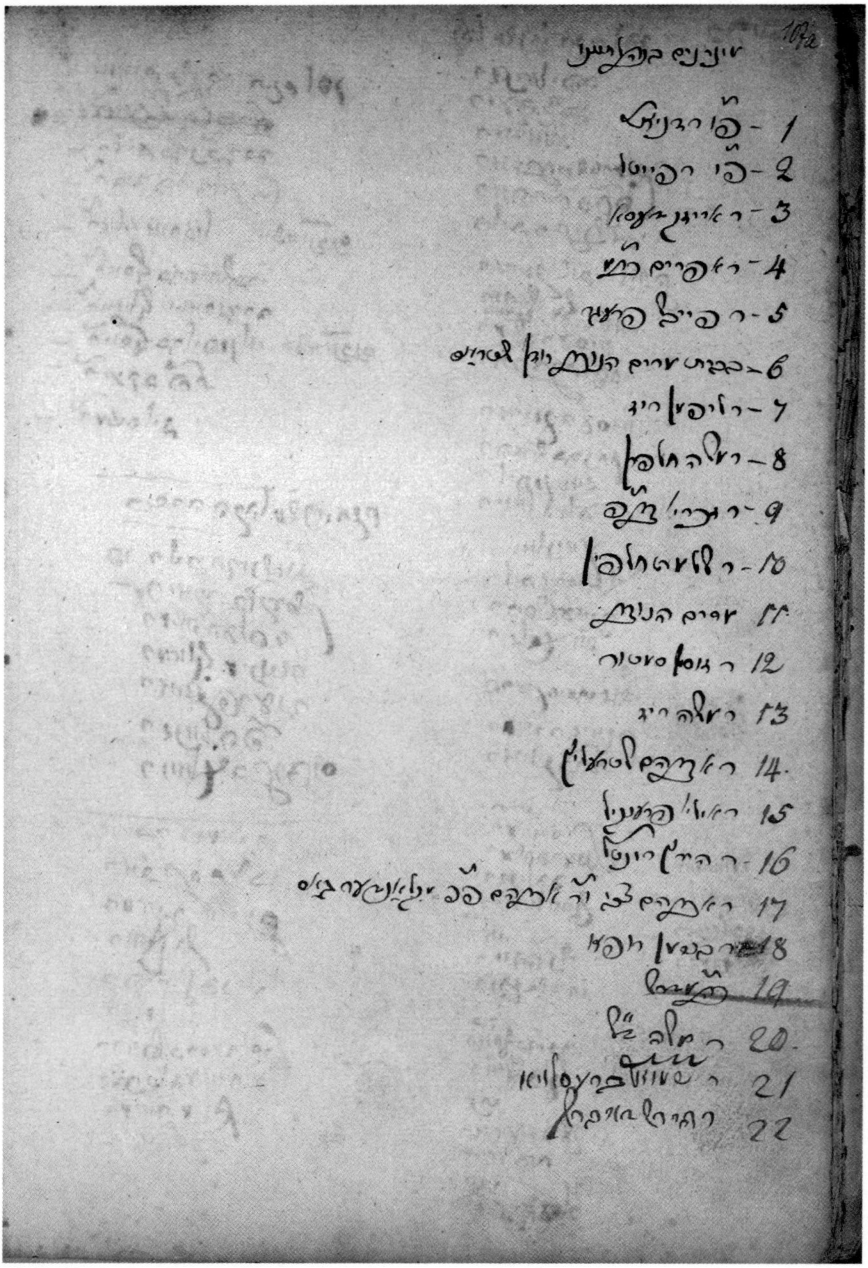

List of private synagogues in Berlin
in the 1770s

From the Archives of the Leo Baeck Institute, New York
(Jacob Jacobson Collection)

Not all Talmud study came to an end in Berlin with the cutting of the Talmud Torah subsidy, but, instead of a real *yeshiva*, by 1812 Berlin had only a number of small and scattered institutions teaching Talmud on the elementary or the advanced level.[37]

Beginning in 1812 a number of Berlin families expressed the desire for a Reform of the synagogue service. Between 1815 and 1823 the Jewish community was split on this matter into a Reform and an Orthodox party. The strength of the Reform party can be gauged by a list dating from 1818 which gives the names of 245 male heads of family (not counting their wives and children who were also listed), 162 unmarried men, 16 widows and 12 unmarried women who supported the *"Neue Gemeinde"*.[38] This would seem to represent fully one third of all married Berlin Jews. The "altgläubige Gemeindeglieder" seemed less well organised and no full list of their supporters survives, though one estimate places it at only one-half as many as the Reformers.

The distinction between Reformers and Orthodox was becoming sharper. Few Reformers belonged to the Orthodox burial society. Relatively few of the known Orthodox[39] had brothers who were Reformers, though a few more had sisters and brothers-in-law among the Reformers. Still, the Reform-Orthodox division did split many families. Among more distant relatives (cousins, uncles, aunts) it was rather common to have members on both sides of the division. In general the family relationships indicate that Orthodoxy was losing ground over the generations. Only seven of the members of the burial society in 1778 had known-Orthodox sons, while at least seventeen had sons or daughters in the Reform

---

nach Willkühr darüber disponieren, und nicht einmahl nur, den Aeltesten, die Nahmen der Empfänger wollen wissen lassen. Es ist unerhört, wie sich gaboim unterstehen können, dergl. Anträge zu machen. *Aber sie sind es auch nicht; da halten sie sich in Gemeinschaft mit dem V. O. L. Rabbiner so einen Kahlmauser der ihnen die Ideen angiebt, und nur Sottisen schreiben: das Handwerk muss ihnen gelegt werden.*") (CAHJP – P17–523.)

The personal conflict between the Orthodox Weyl and the radical Reformer Friedländer also shows itself in other incidents, not all of them directly related to the conflict over the Reform service. Thus Rabbi Weyl wrote to the elders on another occasion that the government was investigating a Jew for tax evasion and had asked for an attestation to his financial situation. He turned to the elders for the information. Friedländer wrote in the margin "Herr Weyl nimmt, sich Dinge heraus, die wir nicht dulden müssen" (Mr. Weyl takes on things we need not tolerate). (CAHJP – P 17–523.)

After much discussion the community granted a semi-annual subsidy of 100 Reichstaler and the Talmud Torah presented a list of 8 names.

[37]In a description of the educational institutions in Berlin in 1812 Friedländer no longer mentions a *yeshiva*, but he does mention several schools which teach Talmud. They include Abraham Marcus Lewusch – 8 students between 8 and 12 years old, teaches only Hebrew and Talmud; Samuel Hirsch Waresch – 8 students between 8 and 14 years old, teaches only Hebrew and Talmud; Liepmann Meyer Wulff Institute – 6 young Talmud students; Talmud Torah school – 16 students aged 6 to 16, learn Hebrew and Talmud, and writing and arithmetic in the evening; Joachim Simon – rabbinical judge – teaches Talmud to students aged 16–18 (no number given); Vice-Chief Rabbi Weyl – 7 Talmud students; in the Ephraim institute in which six students aged 12 to 16 studied secular and Jewish subjects, Rabbi Horwitz taught Talmud. In total 17 institutions were listed – the largest had little or no talmudic study. (Moritz Stern, 'Gutachten und Briefe David Friedländers', *Zeitschrift für die Geschichte der Juden in Deutschland*, 6 [1936], pp. 113–118.)

[38]CAHJP – K GE 2/83.

[39]The Orthodox are here defined as those who either belonged to the burial society in 1813 or who signed the anti-Reform petitions dated 1st March 1816 or 5th May 1817.

community. Even among the children of the Orthodox members of the 1810s, there were two sons and seven married daughters who were Reform and only three known-Orthodox sons. It was much less common for the children of Enlighteners or Reformers still to be Orthodox in the 1810s.[40]

Another indication of the degree of strength of tradition in the 1810s comes from the records of the kosher meat tax. Approximately one half of the persons on the meat tax list paid the tax. The purchase of kosher meat is an indication of traditional religious practice but is not by any means identical with Reform or anti-Reform affiliation. In fact, approximately 36% of Reform families listed had indications that they purchased kosher meat. In general the social patterns of kosher meat taxpayers differed only slightly from those of the Orthodox except that they tended not to be poorer than non-kosher taxpayers.[41]

The Orthodox and the Reformers of the 1810s were different both socially and in their geographical distribution. The Reformers paid almost twice as much average communal taxes as did the Orthodox.[42] The tendency to convert and leave the Jewish community also seems to have been more widespread among the rich than among the poor.

The correlation between wealth and ideological position or conversion is far from complete, however. There were a few wealthy Orthodox Jews and quite a few poor Reformers or apostates. In fact the most common position of poor Berlin Jews seems to have been indifference. Even though members of the burial society, for instance, were poorer than the Reformers of their time, they had incomes near the middle rather than at the bottom of the Jewish social pyramid. Those at the bottom are rarely found on any list of activists.[43]

The only fabulously wealthy Orthodox Jew in Berlin, Liepmann Meyer Wulff, died in 1812. Fewer than 20% of the surviving Orthodox activists paid 80 Taler or more in annual taxation (as compared to about 40% of Reformers).[44]

[40]Of the children and grandchildren of Mendelssohn subscribers who married as Jews in Berlin, 128 (in 36 families) were known to have been associated with the Reform community and only 10 with the Orthodox. (It must be remembered, however, that the total number of Reformers listed in the sample was 246 while only 53 Orthodox were listed.) Although a number of those listed as attending the Reform service had married children also listed, none seems to have had any children listed as Orthodox.

[41]About 20% of Orthodox families were not listed as paying any kosher meat tax, but in most cases this can be traced directly to the fact that they paid no tax on capital either. The amount of capital tax (*Erech*) paid by the kosher meat purchasers was almost identical to those of the non-kosher purchasers. Within each ideological group, however, the kosher meat taxpayers were wealthier than non-kosher taxpayers. Reform kosher meat taxpayers who paid any tax on capital averaged 109 Reichstaler annual communal taxes (N=34), while Reform non-kosher taxpayers paid only 84 (N=48). Among the Orthodox the figures were 52 (N=46) and 5 (N=4) respectively. This is not surprising since the ability to buy enough kosher meat to have it taxed would be higher among the wealthy than among the poor. (CAHJP – P17–466.)

[42]The 108 members of the Reform community listed in the tax list of 1809 averaged 75.5 Reichstaler in annual tax while the 71 Orthodox averaged 40.3 Reichstaler.

[43]Among those who were affiliated with the Reform service 30% paid 25 Taler or less a year in taxes in 1809 (N=95), of the Orthodox (members of the burial society or signatories of anti-Reform petitions) 58% paid 25 Taler or less (N=70). Among those in neither category 65% paid 25 Taler or less (N=417).

[44]Two of the 13 Orthodox activists (members of the burial society or anti-Reform petitioners) who paid over 80 Talers in taxes were also on the list of Reform affiliates.

Poor Reform Jews made up only a minority of the Reformers. Only about thirty percent of Reform families on the tax list paid 25 Taler a year or less (as against almost 60% of Orthodox leaders). There were, however, many single men who attended the Reform service, some of whom were in such dependent occupations as teacher, bookkeeper or commercial employee.

Reformers and Orthodox also had a tendency to live on different streets. Just over 80% of Reformers and over 90% of the Orthodox lived in the four police districts of Central Berlin where the traditional Jewish settlement had been. Well over 90% of all kosher meat purchasers lived in these four police districts as well.[45] Within Central Berlin there was considerable difference in geographical distribution. The Orthodox were concentrated in the area south-east of Königstrasse, where 60% of known Orthodox Jews in the city but only about 1/3 of known Reformers lived.[46] Within specific districts certain streets were more heavily inhabited by traditional Jews than others. This was especially true of some of the less elegant streets of the South-Eastern area like Jüdenstrasse and Stralauerstrasse, as well as some of the narrow alleys near them. Orthodox Jews seem also to have concentrated on the narrow streets near the synagogue, but this is harder to determine since few of the Jews there were taxpayers. The elegant streets overlooking the Spree had only a small percentage of traditional Jews.[47]

Even the wealthy Orthodox tended to live near other Orthodox Jews rather than near other wealthy ones. Poor adherents of Reform seem to have been about equally as likely to live near rich Reformers as near poor Orthodox residents.[48]

The geographical concentration of the Orthodox seems to have had little to do with the prohibition of riding to the synagogue on the Sabbath. In fact most of the streets with a heavy concentration of traditionalists were at least as far from the synagogue as those with many Reformers. All of them were in easy walking

[45]Berlin had 24 police districts in all. Most of the kosher meat purchasers and Orthodox who did live outside the four traditional Jewish districts lived in the 17th district which immediately bordered the traditional section on the North-West. Two-thirds of those who lived outside the four districts and were not kosher meat taxpayers lived outside the 17th district as well. Among those who did not pay the kosher meat tax, over 25% lived outside the traditional four districts.

[46]This represents the percentage in districts 2 and 3. The kosher meat taxpayers were somewhat less concentrated in districts 2 and 3 (c. 48%). This is because those Reform Jews who paid the kosher meat tax were heavily concentrated in district 1 (44% of Reform Jews who paid the meat tax).

[47]On Stralauer and Jüdenstrasse, 26 persons were listed as paying kosher meat tax and 7 as paying none. Overlooking the Spree on the elegant Burg- and Poststrassen, where the mansions of the Itzigs and the Ephraims were located, only 8 of 22 were listed as buying kosher meat. The figures for Orthodox versus Reform were similar: Stralauer/Jüdenstrasse 20 Orthodox, 8 Reform; Burg/ Poststrasse 1 Orthodox, 19 Reform. Some of the main streets of the district like the Spandauerstrasse and Neue Friedrichstrasse were more evenly balanced between traditionalists and non-traditionalists.

[48]Eight of the thirteen Orthodox activists who paid at least 80 Taler in annual taxes lived in the second police district where Orthodox Jews tended to concentrate and only one of these on one of the streets where the wealthy were common (Burgstrasse). Of the 28 Reform members who paid less than 25 Talers, four were wealthy men exempt from taxation. Of the others, 3 lived on the "poor and Orthodox" Stralauerstrasse and 3 on the wealthy Burg or Poststrasse; 3 lived in wealthy districts far to the south-west of the Jewish neighbourhood and 3 lived in district 17 just north-east of the four Jewish districts. A total of 4 of the 24 "poor Reformers" lived in the second police district and four in the similar third district.

distance of the Heidereutergasse Synagogue. In any case, many of the Orthodox attended the dozen or so private synagogues scattered around the Jewish district.[49] The distinction seems to have been more between elegant streets on which the Jewish presence was relatively new, and less elegant ones where Jews had lived since the early eighteenth century. In fact there is a great similarity between the patterns of streets with high Orthodox concentration in 1812 and the centres of Jewish concentration in 1744.[50] Presumably many of the Orthodox Jews on these relatively unfashionable streets lived with none of the luxury so well known from descriptions of the Jewish elite.

In the great crisis of baptisms which struck Berlin Jewry between 1780 and 1830, Orthodox families were not untouched, but they were less affected than were their Reform and Enlightenment opponents. The lesser degree of involvement is found both among the children of the Orthodox in the 1770s and the children of the Orthodox of the 1810s. Only five (7.5%) of sixty-seven identified members of the burial society in 1778 had children who were baptised, as against 26 (28.2%) of ninety-two identified subscribers to Mendelssohn's Bible translation. If grandchildren and great-grandchildren are included the contrast was only a little less great – 34% of the members of the burial society and 56% of the subscribers to Mendelssohn's Bible translation had at least one child, grandchild, or great-grandchild who was baptised. Those members of the burial society who had children who were baptised were far richer than the average member of the society.[51]

Identified Orthodox activists of the 1813–1818 period also had a far lower

---

[49]Lists of the Jewish places of worship in Berlin in 1815 and 1816 are found in CAHJP – K GE 2/10 and P 17–578. The 1815 list includes 13 places, all of them traditional. Besides the synagogue, *Beth Hamidrash* and Jewish hospice it includes synagogues founded by various (mainly wealthy) Berlin Jews: Zacharias Veitel Ephraim, Liepmann Meyer Wulff, David Alexander, Ruben Meyer, Moses Beschütz, Moses Fliess, Jacob Marcuse, Veitel Heine Ephraim, David Hirsch, Hertz Abraham Leffmann. The 1816 list also includes two Reform places of worship: the homes of Israel Jacobson and of Herz Beer.

The memoirs of both Jacob Adam and of Aron Hirsch Heymann speak of the importance of the private *minyanim* in the religious life of Berlin Jewry.
[50]In 1744 the streets with the largest number of Jewish households were Spandauerstrasse (56), Rosenstrasse (56) and Jüdenstrasse (46 plus 12 in the Grosser Judenhof). Neue Friedrichstrasse was not in existence yet. Poststrasse and Burgstrasse where so many of the wealthy and Reform Jews of the early nineteenth century lived had a total of only 7 Jewish households (all on Poststrasse). The narrow alleys near the Nikolaikirche, where many of the poor Jews lived in 1812 had a total of 59 Jewish households in 1744. (Probstgasse, Nikolai Kirchstrasse, Bollengasse, Kronengasse, Siebergasse, Reezengasse). (Jacobson Collection I 37.)
[51]The statistics for grandchildren and great-grandchildren include only those whose parents were married in a Jewish ceremony in Berlin. It is quite likely that the percentages of those with converted grandchildren and great-grandchildren would be even higher if we had information on children who married outside Berlin. If we look at the number of individual descendants who were baptised, the contrast between burial society members and Mendelssohn subscribers becomes even greater. 83 of 379 known descendants of burial society members (22%) and 176 of 396 descendants of Mendelssohn subscribers (43%) were baptised.

The average highest tax for members of the burial society of Berlin in 1778 was only 2 Taler, 4 Groschen, 6 Pfennig; for the five burial society members who had children who converted the average was 6 Taler, 3 Groschen. The board members of the *Beth Hamidrash* (talmudic study society), who were a good deal richer than the burial society members, also had a much higher rate of children who were baptised (20% of the 45 members between 1770 and 1783).

percentage of children who converted than did Reformers. In addition a considerable number of Reform petitioners were themselves later baptised. A similar contrast is found between those who purchased kosher meat and those who did not. Of those who paid the kosher meat tax only 15% had children who were later baptised as compared to 36.8% of those who paid no meat tax.[52] Unlike the earlier period, however, there was little difference in wealth between Orthodox parents of apostates and other Orthodox parents.

The controversy between Orthodox and Reformers between 1814 and 1823 was a very vehement one, which soon involved the intervention of the government. Led in a forceful manner by Gottschalk Helfft, an elderly financial agent, and by Vice-Chief Rabbi Weyl, the Orthodox eventually were able to secure the government decree forbidding all reforms in the liturgy.[53] The large pro-Reform section of the Berlin community was unable to counter the alliance between government and Orthodoxy.

Yet in many ways the victory of the Orthodox was a Pyrrhic one. It is certainly not accurate to say that the laws against Reform had any substantial effect in creating the wave of baptisms which spread through Berlin Jewry during the first third of the nineteenth century.[54] But it is also not accurate to think that the end of Reform did anything to slow down or change the movement away from Judaism. The crisis of Berlin Jewry persisted at least until 1830.[55]

The picture one gets of Berlin Orthodoxy in the 1830s is a rather dreary one. Its main source is the humorous memoir of Aron Hirsch Heymann, a later founder of the separatist Orthodox *Adath Jisroel*. Although one suspects some of

---

[52]8.5% of members of the burial society in 1813 had children who converted as against 21.6% for Reform petitioners in 1812. Another 6.5% of the petitioners were themselves later baptised. Of those who paid kosher meat tax, one was later converted and 12 had apostate children. Of those who were listed as paying no kosher meat tax, 11 were later baptised and 38 had children who were baptised.

[53]For a detailed discussion of the Reform controversy in Berlin see Michael A. Meyer, 'The Religious Reform Controversy in the Berlin Jewish Community, 1814–1823', in *LBI Year Book XXIV* (1979), pp. 139–155.

[54]A number of historians sympathetic to Reform have pointed to conversionist intentions in the anti-Reform policies of Friedrich Wilhelm III of Prussia. The implication is that the existence of the Reform alternative helped prevent some acculturated Jews from converting and that the removal of this alternative would have increased conversions.

[55]According to the *Judenkartei* (card index of baptisms of persons of Jewish ancestry made by the Nazis) of Protestant baptisms in Berlin in the *Evangelisches Zentralarchiv* the number of baptisms by five-year period in the early nineteenth century was as follows:

1800–1804	96
1805–1809	144
1810–1814	179
1815–1819	218
1820–1824	234
1825–1829	381

Although this might suggest a considerable exacerbation of the "Taufepidemie" after the prohibition of Reform at the end of 1823, there is reason to doubt a direct relationship. Most of the adult converts of the 1820s came from outside Berlin. Many converted for career reasons. Outside Berlin the decree against Reform would have had little impact.

his characterisations are overdrawn for effect or to contrast with later improvements he claimed to have made, the general picture does fit with other known facts.

The two beadles who led weekday services in the main synagogue were both elderly old-style pious Jews. The assistant cantor, who was also the chief notary (*ne'eman*) of the community, knew no Hebrew grammar and made money from the sale of synagogue seats. *Oberkantor* Lion had been the cantor of the Beer Reform Temple but in his own humorous phrase, had been "*kashered*". He was accompanied by the traditional bass and singer whose performance Heymann mocks. Few were present at the beginning of Sabbath services since they attended the early services in private synagogues and only came to the main synagogue afterwards. The rabbis Jacob Joseph Oettinger and Elchanan Rosenstein could barely speak German and were not able to give a real sermon. Some of the other synagogue attenders of the time are also depicted with thick Yiddish accents. Many seats in the synagogue were ownerless since their possessers had either converted or died. The ritual bath was dilapidated and the meat market (*Fleischscharren*) in the synagogue courtyard was a distraction.

Even the leaders of the Orthodoxy had to accept the fact that they and their institutions had lost influence. At weddings Rabbi Oettinger didn't do the traditional handkerchief dance with the bride since his policy was always to leave before dinner so as not to insult those whose dinners were not kosher. In 1829 the rabbis had to accept the removal of the charity for the Land of Israel from the list of seven charities with special privileges.[56]

Orthodoxy in the 1830s survived in its old form, but even its supporters like Heymann felt the need for some changes to make it viable for the future. The arrival of Rabbi Michael Sachs in 1844 was the beginning of the updating and

---

[56]The Orthodox rabbis Oettinger and Rosenstein signed the document dated 3rd December 1829 which stated that the "Anstalt Erez Israel" would no longer be one of the seven charities to divide the monies collected at funerals. (The other charities were: Talmud Torah, *Malbish Arumim* (clothes for poor), *Gemilus Chasodim* (burial society), *Hachnasat Kalla* (dowries), *Bikur Cholim* (care of the sick), *Ner Tamid* (Eternal light).) Instead the 1/7th share would now go to the *Armen Anstalt Haspakat Ebionim*. The collections in the synagogue for the Land of Israel would now also become collections for the poor relief institute. The money already collected for Israel as well as any future money expressly donated for that purpose would still go exclusively for the poor in Palestine.

It would seem that the justification for the change was the fact that the money could not be sent to Palestine (perhaps because of the War of Greek Independence against Turkey). However, when similar circumstances had occurred, in the eighteenth century, the community did not resort to "demoting" the charity for the Land of Israel. In 1750 when it was impossible to send the money from the *Erez Israel* fund for a lengthy period, it was decided that the communal treasury would borrow the 351 Reichstaler in the *Erez Israel* fund. As soon as collectors from Palestine would come the loan would be returned. Between 1774 and 1785 the communal records list 16 visits by "*yerushalmim*" to Berlin and the donation of various sums (some large, many small) to these collectors. It seems clear that the reason for the change in 1829 was not merely convenience, but a loss of belief in the value of donations to Palestine and in the Messianic promises of return to the Holy Land. (Jacobson Collection, I, 49, pp. 112a and 113; *Pinkas*, pp. 153–154, 412–413.)

revival of Berlin Orthodoxy. But the days when Orthodoxy represented the bulk of Berlin Jewry were over.

POOR JEWS IN BERLIN

From the foregoing it seems clear that the constituency of Berlin Orthodoxy was less wealthy than the constituency of the Enlightenment or Reform. Nevertheless, this equation is not total. There were poor Reformers and wealthy Orthodox. What is more, many of the very poor had other concerns than the ideological conflicts within the community. For some, the question of subsistence was more vital.

It is well known that Prussian laws which divided Prussian Jewry into various legal categories discriminated in favour of the rich and against the poor. To reach the rank of a *Schutzjude* one was required to pay an annual tax (*Schutzgeld*). The highest ranking – *General Privileg* – which suspended most of the restrictions on Jews, was reserved for the especially wealthy. But even the rank of *Ordinarius* (regularly protected Jew) which included the right to settle one or, if wealthy, two children in the country was limited to the wealthy. The *Extraordinarius*, whose rights were only personal, ranked lower. Below these ranked the merely tolerated who could neither marry nor engage in independent business legally. As is well known, beggars and other Jewish visitors to Berlin were stopped at the gates of the city and limited in their entry.

In 1806 the following estimates were made about the number of Berlin Jewish families in each category:[57]

Ordinarii Priviligirte	249
Generalpriviligirte	61
Widows of *Ordinarii*	65
Extraordinarii	
(husbands or widows)	78
TOTAL	453

This would seem to place the vast majority of Berlin Jewish families in the highest categories. In addition the entire Itzig family had been naturalised in 1791 and was excluded from the list.

The actual facts are, however, not quite so straightforward. First of all there was another category of family in Berlin – the *Publique Bedienten* (public servants) – who were employees of the community and did not need individual residence permits. These included such leaders as the rabbis, cantors and doctors of the Jewish hospice, but also less wealthy and prestigious beadles, ritual slaughterers,

---

[57]This compares to the situation in 1750 when there were 203 ordinarily protected Jews and 63 extraordinary ones. See Selma Stern Täubler, *Der Preussische Staat und die Juden*, Tübingen 1971, III/ 2–1 (Schriftenreihe wissenschaftlicher Abhandlungen des Leo Baeck Instituts 24/2), pp. 236–244.

butchers, gravediggers etc. Between 1759 and 1802, about 7% of all Berlin marriages involved *Publique Bedienten.*

Besides these categories of Jews, all of whom had the legal right to an independent familial existence, there were many Jews who were merely tolerated and lived in the household of a *Schutzjude.* Among these were the very numerous maids and cooks who represented at least 5% of all Berlin Jews in 1812, and the equally large number of unmarried male "commercial servants" (*Handlungs-diener*).[58] About 190 Jewish men and 85 Jewish women over the age of 40 were unmarried. Not all these persons were poor, but quite a few probably were.

Most of the Jewish heads of households with legal permission to live in Berlin were included on the tax lists. The number of those so listed grew with the growth of the Jewish population of Berlin in the early and mid-eighteenth century from 225 in 1733 to 308 in 1745 and 430 in 1764. It then tended to stagnate reaching only 471 in 1780. In 1809 the tax list had about 500 names on it.

Despite the usual description of Berlin Jewry as top-heavy with wealthy families,[59] the tax lists present a picture of a more "normal" distribution. Among the taxpayers the vast majority were assessed for quite moderate amounts. In 1780 for instance, 30 taxpayers were totally exempt from tax, and just over 50% of the rest paid less than one Taler in periodic taxation. This was the approximate cut-off point for the lowest of the three categories of taxpayers in the Berlin community and was the rough equivalent of about 7,200 Reichstaler[60] in wealth. The middle category of 7,200–16,000 Taler included some 25 percent of those on the tax list. The remaining 20% of the taxpayers (95 heads of household or widows) were assessed at over 16,000 Taler. Even within this highest category the very rich stood out. In 1789, for instance, the top ten percent of Berlin Jewish

---

[58]In the family list of all Jews in Berlin in 1812 there are 166 persons listed as *Dienstmägde* and 3 as cooks. (Jacobson Collection I 82.) In the address list of the same year the number of Jewish *Dienstmägde* is 197 and the number of cooks is 28. (CAHJP– P17/508.) In the family list there are 215 male *Handlungsdiener* (commercial employees) and 48 bookkeepers. In the address list there are 110 and 27 respectively.

[59]See for instance Deborah Hertz, *Jewish High Society in Old Regime Berlin*, New Haven 1988, pp. 40–42, who equates the protected families with the wealthy and states: "One historian claimed that there were 600 Jewish families in the city; other scholars estimated that there were 450. Using the first estimate, 600 as the denominator, the 300 to 400 wealthy protected families would constitute almost half the families. Using the smaller estimate, 450, the wealthy protected families would constitute as much as two-thirds of the community . . . By any measure, the Berlin community was therefore top-heavy with rich financiers able to pay the extensive taxes and still prosper."

Raphael Mahler, *A History of Modern Jewry 1780–1815*, London 1971, p. 139, quotes a contemporary description of the Berlin community as consisting of: "50 fabulously wealthy bankers; about 150 well-to-do merchants; 150 rich industrialists and free professionals; and about 100 middlemen-pedlars, 'court Jews', and petty 'house Jews' (Hausjuden), the remaining 150 families lived on charity." Although Mahler stresses the importance of the very poor, he also sees the wealthy as the majority of the community.

[60]The actual assessment (*Erech*) amount which marked the lowest from the middle tax class was 1,800 Reichstaler and 4,000 Reichstaler marked the division between the middle tax group (*benonim*) and the wealthy (*ashirim*). The *Erech*, in most cases, was calculated as one-fourth of a person's total wealth.

taxpayers (47 persons) paid over 53% of all taxes, while the lower half paid only 9%. The ordinary Berlin Jewish taxpayer was quite different from the millionaires at the top of the scale. They were also much more numerous.

The wealth of Jews in Berlin was not only unevenly distributed; it was also very unstable. Periodic crises caused the bankruptcy even of very respected families. On occasion a member of a family of millionaires could end up asking for aid from the Jewish community.[61] Few families remained near the top of the tax lists for three generations.

Probably the most severe economic crises to hit Berlin Jewry took place in the aftermath of the French occupation of Berlin in 1806. Communal records of the time show that most families were unable to pay their tax debts for the year and many were deeply in arrears. In 1809 the community listed only 216 persons as able to pay their full tax assessments (including some who were tax exempt). Reduced payments were listed for 104 families; 41 paid only *Schutzgeld* but no capital levy; and 131 were completely unable to pay any tax.[62]

The strong differential between big Jewish taxpayers and small ones in Berlin and the fact that many families who were wealthy at one time were impoverished or bankrupt at other times should cause us to be cautious in assuming that the strict monetary requirements for residence permits necessarily mean that Berlin Jewry was overwhelmingly rich.

Comparing the level of wealth of Berlin Jews to those of Berlin non-Jews in the eighteenth and early nineteenth century is extremely difficult. Certainly we know that a small number of Jewish firms (many of whose heads later converted) made up a disproportionate percentage of the richest firms in Berlin.[63] Below that level, however, it is hard to state.

Jewish lifestyles and forms of business were so different from the lifestyles of typical Berlin Christian craftsmen or shopkeepers that it would be hasty to conclude that equal amounts of capital meant equal amounts of actual disposable wealth. The section of Berlin in which most Jews lived was inhabited by a wide cross-section of the Berlin population. It would be difficult to characterise it as either a wealthy or a poor neighbourhood. The fact that the infant mortality rate in 1769 was much lower for Jews than for the city as a whole

---

[61] A number of members of the Itzig family became bankrupt in 1797 and later. In the bankruptcy of the converted Jew Ephraim Cohen, Cohen's mother-in-law, Fanny Bernhard née Fliess, was also impoverished. Although her father had left an estate of 750,000 Taler in 1776 and her husband's family (partners of Moses Mendelssohn) were also among Berlin's wealthiest, Fanny Bernhard was so poor that she needed an attestation of poverty so that the Berlin poor commission could pay for the expenses of her suit to recover her share of her father's trust fund. (19th January 1813. CAHJP – P 17 523.)

[62] CAHJP – P 17–466.

[63] A list from Spring 1814 giving the estimated wealth of rich Berliners for a forced loan, contains some 70 names of persons with estimated wealth ranging from 50,000 Taler up to one million. Of these persons at least 46 were Jewish. Twelve of the wealthy Jews on the list eventually converted to Christianity. A list of contributors to forced loans from 1812–1815, with amount, also shows a majority of Jewish names. (Hugo Rachel and Paul Wallich, *Berliner Grosskaufleute und Kapitalisten*, vol. II, Berlin 1967, pp. 294–297.)

might be an indication that Jews were better off economically. But it might also be explainable in terms of different cultural habits or family structures.[64]

We know that the majority of Berlin Jews had less than 7,200 Taler in taxable capital in the eighteenth century. It is quite difficult to assess income levels from such figures. If, by way of a very rough estimate, we calculate an income figure from the prevailing interest rates of the period (5%) we come out with an income figure of some 360 Taler a year – approximately equal to the income of a medium government employee and about 50% higher than the income of a master craftsman. If this very rough calculation is even close to accurate, the income of Jews in the middle of the Jewish tax scale would be about three times that of the average Berliner.[65] The middle of the Jewish tax scale would thus be approximately equal to the top ten percent of Berlin households. In 1780 eighty-seven (almost 20%) of 471 Jews on the tax list paid 9 Groschen taxes and 30 paid nothing. Nine Groschen taxes would mean the equivalent of 167 Taler a year in income,[66] just above the average income of Berlin non-Jews. Quite possibly however, Jewish income levels were more than 5% of capital and consequently, Jewish incomes were even higher.

Whatever the economic position of the small Jewish taxpayers in Berlin might have been, there were many Jews who were poorer than they. The Berlin community, like others of the time, had an extensive charity system. This included not only the famous poorhouse outside the Rosenthaler Tor but also a system of meal tickets for poor non-residents passing through the city. There were also a number of Berlin Jewish residents who needed the support of the

---

[64]Helga Schultz, *Berlin 1650–1800. Sozialgeschichte einer Residenz*, Berlin 1987, p. 182, gives the following statistics for infant and child mortality up to age 12 by church or synagogue (for 1769):

Jerusalemskirche (Friedrichstadt)	74.5%
Dreifaltigkeitskirche (,,)	64.3
Garnisonskirche	58.5
Nikolai und Marienkirche (Alt Berlin)	43.5
Jüdische Gemeinde	34.7
Berlin overall	57.8%

[65]The estimates for general income levels in Berlin are very rough ones calculated by Helga Schultz, *op. cit.*, pp. 150–157. Schultz's estimates, like my own, are based on a great deal of guesswork and fairly sparse documentation. Interestingly, she too calculates the income of merchants on the basis of 5% of their capital. Schultz's figures are for the first half of the eighteenth century, while our figures come from the second half of the century. Because our figures do not take into account inflation, they may somewhat exaggerate the prosperity of the average Jewish taxpayer.

Even though our estimate for average income of Jewish taxpayers far exceeds the estimated income of the average Berliner, it was far lower than Schultz's estimate of the income of Berlin merchants (3,600 Taler). (Perhaps, there is a tendentiousness in Schultz's figures since as an East German she may wish to emphasise the gap between worker's income and the income of the bourgeoisie.) Fewer than two dozen Berlin Jews would have had such a high income in 1780 according to our extrapolations from the Jewish tax tables.

[66]The calculation was made as follows: in 1780 Jews had to pay their tax amounts 42 times a year. 9 Groschen times 42 equals 378 Groschen or 15 Taler, 18 Groschen a year. In the 1790s the annual tax was calculated at 1 7/8% of the "*Erech*". A tax of 15 Taler, 18 Groschen would mean an "*Erech*" of about 835 Taler. The *Erech* was calculated at one fourth of total wealth. Therefore the total wealth would have been about 3340 Taler. If income were 5% of wealth, then it would be about 167 Taler a year.

Jewish charities. In the 1770s some 100 Berlin residents were listed as recipients of poor relief. In the crisis year of 1809, 22 widows and 19 male heads of household with residence permits were receiving charity from the Jewish community.[67] In 1812 the sum of 1,200 Reichstaler was asked for grain for Passover food for the poor.

The situation of the Jews at the bottom of the social scale in Berlin was often quite desperate. Many of the poor were old or infirm and had no family which could support them. Quite a few files of individual cases of the poor asking for attestations of poverty are extant. They show a whole milieu of Berlin Jewish residents unable to support themselves. On the narrow alleys between the Nikolaikirche and Klosterstrasse, the majority of Jewish inhabitants were on charity, unemployed or employed as domestic servants.[68]

The elders of the community were often unhappy about the demands for support by the poor, especially the non-resident poor. They even complained to the government about the burden of the many non-resident beggars, men, women and children. The elders complained that many of them were good-for-nothings (*Taugenichtse*) and that others engaged in illegal trade.

In a few cases Jewish poverty was associated with other types of social pathology. The elders complained to the police that they were asked to put up one Jacob Moses of Strasburg/Uckermark in their hospice for the poor – a man they characterised as a "fremder Landsteicher" (foreign vagabond) with an incurable disease. Another unfortunate case involved an insane woman in the Berlin workhouse who was described as "schwachsinnig und ganz entkräftet". The woman was said to have periods of lucidity and to require the aid of the Jewish community because she could not eat the non-kosher food of the workhouse.

The most desperate case of all came to light in a police investigation in 1814. A Jewish woman gave birth to a child in the Jewish hospital of Berlin. She was a widow and had a four-year-old boy as well. The community paid for her transportation out of the city and gave her a letter of recommendation. Approximately four weeks later, in despair, she drowned her baby and was arrested. Infanticide of this type occurred on occasion among the non-Jewish

---

[67] In a report from David Präger to David Friedländer in June 1809 it states that these are the number of widows or of those who are "*baale batim baale kiyumim mekable Kitzvo*" (householders with residence permits who are recipients of poor relief). (CAHJP – K Ge 2/18.) Of 101 persons listed in the 1770s under the heading "*kitzvo*" (poor relief), fifty-three seem to have been male household heads and 32 were widows. It is not certain that all of these persons received charity in the same year. (LBIA, Jacobson Collection I, 49, pp. 116a–118a.)

[68] On the Kronengasse, Probstgasse, Nikolai Kirchgasse, Nikolai Kirchhof, Nagelgasse, Bollengasse, Siebergasse, Eyergasse and Reetzengasse, 60 Jewish residents were listed. Of these 11 are listed as on charity, 8 as unemployed, 12 as domestics (*Diener, Dienstmagd, Wartefrau*). Other occupations of Jews in these alleys included: old clothes seller (*alte Kleiderhändler* or *Trödler*) (6), teacher (5) and commercial employee (*Handlungsdiener* or *Handlungscommis*) (3). Only three paid any communal taxes, and only 9 were listed on the communal tax lists.

Ismar Freund, *Die Emanzipation der Juden in Preussen*, Berlin 1912, vol. II, p. 396, quotes a Prussian official in 1811 who states that "in the Rätzen-, Kronen-, Lieber[sic], Nagel-Gasse almost every house has an old clothes business (*alter Kleider-Dormino-Handel*)".

poor in Berlin as well. In this case at least the desperation of poverty was equally strong for a Jewish woman.[69]

Life for those at the bottom of the Jewish social scale was so different from life for those at the top that it is hard to imagine them being part of the same community. Despite the attention which has so frequently been given to the small number of elite families in Berlin, they were not really typical of the community as a whole. Neither, for that matter, were the wretchedly poor who have just been described. The largest proportion of Berlin Jews were, in fact, small taxpayers. In 1780 239 families had estimated capital of about 2,400 to 7,200 Taler. These families of relatively modest means probably included over one-third of all Berlin Jewish residents. Another 108 families possessed from about 7,200 to 16,000 Taler. Fewer than 100 families had over 16,000 Taler in capital. The unmarried, the dependent occupations (maid, bookkeeper etc.), and those too poor to be listed certainly were far less than half, and probably less than a quarter of all communal residents.

The occupations of the modest taxpayers seem to have changed somewhat between the eighteenth and nineteenth century. Such categories as *Handelsmann* (dealer), pawnbroker or [old] clothes dealer were fairly common in both periods. In the eighteenth century craft occupations were much more often mentioned – especially printer, *Goldscheider*, baker, grave digger and seal engraver (*Petschierstecher*). In the nineteenth-century lists petty commercial fields like money changer (*Wechsler*), broker (*Courtier* or *Makler*) as well as persons living on savings (*Rentier*) were more common and craftsmen figured less frequently.[70]

Some of the same occupations were common among adults who were not listed on the tax lists at all. In addition, besides the very numerous maids and commercial employees there were over a dozen teachers, many students – some from out of town – a dozen women who supported themselves by sewing or knitting, and such unusual occupations as *Bartzwicker*,[71] *Krankenwärter* (orderly in the Jewish hospital), musician, innkeeper, *Hühneraugenoperateur* (corn-cutter),

---

[69]CAHJP – P17–522 (case of Jacob Moses), P17–523 (case of insane woman in workhouse), P17–524 – case of infanticide.

[70]The most common occupations listed for modest taxpayers (under 1 Taler, 1 Groschen) in Jacob Jacobson's *Jüdische Trauungen* (marriages before 1813) were: *Handelsmann*-15, *Kleiderhandel*-10, *Bäcker*-5, *Drucker/Setzer*-5, *Goldscheider*-5, *Pfandleiher*-5, *Petschierstecher/Wappenstecher*-4, *Wechsler*-4 (total number of modest taxpayers with known occupations–113).

Of those listed as modest taxpayers (under 25 Taler) or too impoverished to pay in 1809 the following were the most common occupations: *Kaufmann*-11; *Rentier*-10, *Handelsmann/handelt*-9, *Alte Kleiderhändler*-8, *Wechsler*-7, *Pfandleiher*-6, *Makler/Courtier*-5, *Lederhändler*-4 (total number of small taxpayers with known occupations – 98).

The differences between the distribution of occupation can be explained in a number of ways. The restrictions on occupation of the eighteenth century as well as the existence of special categories of communal employees encouraged individuals to list themselves in non-commercial categories such as seal engravers, bakers, grave diggers. Because 1809 was a year of crisis, a considerable number of persons in commercial occupations who might otherwise have been relatively prosperous suffered economically and were listed as modest taxpayers or unable to pay.

[71]These were individuals who shaved Jewish men using scissors instead of a razor in order not to violate the biblical command against "destroying the beard". There were two such individuals listed in 1812.

dancing teacher and gardener. Most of these persons were probably not well-off financially.

The typical Berlin Jewish family, often headed by a small merchant, dealer, pawnbroker or old clothes dealer, could make a living in good years and might be in danger of bankruptcy in years of crisis. They would be unlikely to own a house and would probably possess few luxuries. Modest taxpayers were not eligible for the post of elder but could be appointed to lesser posts. In communal elections they had less of a vote than the wealthy whom they outnumbered.[72] In old age or widowhood, a minority of people in these families might have had to depend on communal charity, but most might manage with the help of family members.

It would probably be inaccurate to call these people desperately poor. Certainly they were better off than the vast number of German-Jewish *Betteljuden*, who wandered from town to town and received meals in the homes of their co-religionists. They were also probably better off than most Christian textile workers, small-scale artisans or labourers in Berlin. Still their modest businesses and relatively simple daily lives separated them from the Jewish elite which lived in mansions, collected art and helped to finance the Jewish Enlightenment.

[72]Elections for major communal officials were made by choosing 7 electors by lot. These electors then chose the major officers by majority vote. In 1777 and 1780 the electors consisted of 4 from the rich, 2 from the medium taxpayers and one from the small taxpayers (*Pinkas*, §303 and 314). The community had a long-standing rule not to appoint anyone as a *Parnas* (elder), or a substitute (*tov* or *ikkur*) who did not have an *Erech* of at least 4,000 Taler (= capital of 16,000 Taler) (*Pinkas*, §312). Because of the difficulty of finding enough candidates, a decision of 1780 temporarily lowered the property qualification for *tovim* and *ikkurim* to an *Erech* of 2,500 Reichstaler.

The World of Moses Mendelssohn

BY EVA ENGEL HOLLAND

I

In 1929, now more than sixty years ago, the erudite editors and collaborators of the Jubilee edition of Moses Mendelssohn's *Gesammelte Schriften* were able to give public evidence of their plan to publish what was to be the first historico-critical edition of the writings of the sage who lived from 1729 to 1786.

In keeping with eighteenth-century usage, a not insignificant part of the ideas of the man known to the general public by the early twentieth century either as "the grandfather of the composer", or safely labelled "the friend of Lessing", lay tucked away in letters. And there were many hundreds of these. In an edition originally planned to encompass sixteen volumes, the corpus of letters by and to him was to account for four.

The first of these volumes, 225 letters, written between early 1754 and December 1762 was published in 1932 by the man whose erudition, patience and exemplary editing we wish to recall and honour today: Bruno Strauss (1889–1969). That Strauss was unable to see further volumes of the letters into print is one of the innumerable personal and yet public tragedies that befell as a result of the establishment of Nazi rule in Germany.

Fortunately, Günther Holzboog, the publisher who as philosopher-idealist undertook the continuance of the edition, contributed an article in 1979 on its history to the fourth volume of *Mendelssohn Studien*. In it, he recalled that when approached in 1964, Bruno Strauss no longer felt up to taking part in the edition, and that he wrote:

> "The very mention of the Mendelssohn edition grieves me. You will be aware that I was the editor of the first volume of Mendelssohn's letters and that this was published in 1932. When I was forced to leave Germany in 1939, the manuscript for volume 2 of the letters was ready for the printer. By a most unhappy concatenation of unforeseeable factors, the manuscript, as well as all my Mendelssohn notes, my drafts and correspondence, my books, indeed, all I had ever owned were lost – despite the fact that I had done my utmost to safeguard the just completed typescript of the second volume. The loss cut such a deep wound, that even now, so many decades later, it causes me to lose sleep from time to time."[1]

Holzboog went on to say that all his attempts to locate the lost material, like those attempts of Strauss before him, were in vain.

This meant that all the labour and expertise that had gone into at least seven years of searching for, of studying and annotating extensive, hard to unearth material were forfeited, and that the search had to be begun anew.

It is not over yet. Since 1972, when the Jubilee edition officially began to be under way again under the general editorship of the late Alexander Altmann and

---

[1] *Mendelssohn Studien*, vol. IV, Berlin 1979, pp. 282f.

published by the Frommann publishing house in Stuttgart, a wealth of hitherto "unknown" letters became available; so that by now five volumes of letters are to hand in volumes XI, XII.1, XII.2, XIII and XIX. Of these volumes XII.2 and XIII contain names of correspondents, and groups of highly informative letters, notably on the subject of the Pantheism Dispute, that were left to be discovered by the expertise and diligence of Professor Altmann.

And yet, there is more to come. In the last few months before his death, Alexander Altmann had examined the *res gestae* of some 140 letters that had become known in 1985 as a result of a public inquiry in Western Europe and the USA conducted by myself with the support of the *Herzog August Bibliothek* in Wolfenbüttel. We hope to present these letters, and any that may still surface, in the supplementary volume of an edition that will eventually number not the original sixteen volumes envisaged in 1929 but twenty-two (in thirty-one parts).

II

It is time that we turn to the letters themselves; letters written in the third quarter of the eighteenth century, over a span of thirty years. This was the time of impressive minds like Condillac, Diderot, d'Alembert, Montesquieu, Rousseau and Voltaire, of Boscovich and Euler, of Kant, Hume and Lord Kames: it was the age of the beginning of modern science, of tools like electricity and algebra, of the discovery of the planet Uranus, of hydrogen and oxygen. It was that part of the century which witnessed the onset of a second Golden Age for German literature and *belles lettres* with the writings of men like Lessing, Mendelssohn, Winckelmann, Herder, Goethe, C. P. Moritz, and Schiller.

Reform and revolution were in the air; reinforcing Heine's subsequent contention that any revolution in arms must be preceded by a revolution of mind. In the third quarter of the eighteenth century, this turned out to be as valid for politics as for the judicial system, as true for education as for thinking, in all realms affecting the "destiny of man". The occurring of reform, occasioned by rebellion against the *status quo ante*, is made evident in all its paradoxical complexity by the Prussian philosopher-sovereign, Frederick II, concurrently responsible for the bloodshed, impoverishment, decay caused by three long wars, and also for multiple social and judicial reforms, for stupendous growth of mercantilism, and for the flowering of an *Académie Royale des Sciences et Belles Lettres* that during his reign outshone the *Académie de Paris* and the London Royal Society.

In the face of all the handicaps that beset a Jew in Europe in these decades of the eighteenth century, it is not an idle assertion that Mendelssohn turned out to be, and was regarded as, one of the "Shakers and Movers" of his time. The evidence is to hand in the letters that survive and the words of those who turned to him. Some twelve hundred letters are extant. They derive from about one hundred correspondents. However, figures, meaningless in themselves, have body and substance once we translate them into people, problems, ideas. There was a device used some years ago to accord these letter-writers visibility at a glance.

In 1986, an exhibition was held in the small North German town of Wolfenbüttel, till 1754 the residence of the Dukes of Brunswick, and since 1572 also the seat of a vast ducal library, now called *Herzog August Bibliothek*. Leibniz was librarian there for twenty-six years, and Lessing from 1770 to his death in 1781. At the very entrance to the exhibition we had mounted an eighteenth-century map of Europe. On it, red dots indicated the towns from which non-business letters had gone out to Moses Mendelssohn in Berlin. The letters had come from as far North as London and Copenhagen, as far South as Rome. They had come from the West in Paris and the Hague, to the East from Königsberg and Riga. Others had reached Mendelssohn from towns like – to name a few – Basel, Braunschweig, Breslau, Bückeburg, Dessau, Dresden, Düsseldorf, Genf, Göttingen, Halle, Hamburg, Lausanne, Mannheim, Weimar, Wien, Zürich. More to the point than such geographical directives are the names of the correspondents, and most to the point, the pleas and projects, the thoughts and concerns that had caused the writers to turn to Mendelssohn for advice and comment. For, extraordinarily enough, out of all these dozens of people, philosophers, ministers of state, poets, theologians, noblemen, only three – Fürst Leopold von Anhalt-Dessau, the heir to the throne of the duchy of Braunschweig, and the philosopher Kant – were not the ones who had started the correspondence.

From this chorus of voices, we hear the echoes of topics, incidents, projects and discussions that punctuated the life of the man whom his contemporaries spoke of as the Socrates, the Plato of the eighteenth century, and the quality of whose writings, they maintained, was excelled only by the even greater quality of his character. Yet, for Mendelssohn, it was not an easy life, ever, despite considerable plaudits for intellectual achievements and respect for his professional success as a silk-manufacturer.

III

Only twice in his lifetime, in 1774 and in 1782, did Mendelssohn volunteer information about his life to strangers. The first was a concise, reticent outline, in answer to the inquiry by the librarian Johann Jacob Spiess (1730–1814) for Part 5 of *Brandenburgische Münzbelustigen* (published in Anspach in 1774). This is how Mendelssohn summarises the facts of his life:

"I was born in Dessau in the year 1729. My father was a schoolmaster there and *sofer*. I studied the Talmud with Rabbi Fränkel, then Chief Rabbi of Dessau. Having become famous because of his commentary on the *Jerusalem Talmud*, he was called to Berlin about the year 1743. I followed him there that very same year. In Berlin, Gumpertz who subsequently became doctor of medicine aroused in me a liking for many kinds of knowledge. He also helped me to learn about them. Soon after, I became tutor to the children of a wealthy Jew, later his bookkeeper and eventually, and to this day, manager of his silk-factory. I was married in my thirty-third year and have five living children. By the way, I have never attended a university, never heard a lecture there. This proved to be one of the greatest of my handicaps as I had to acquire all my knowledge through my own effort and diligence. Indeed, I overdid it, and for three years now I have been afflicted by a nervous debility that stops me from following all intellectual pursuits."[2]

The second statement is a summary of his philosophy of life. Strictly speaking, it derives not from a letter but from a very personal, dated, preface: namely Mendelssohn's introduction to Manasseh Ben Israel's *Vindiciae Judaeorum* (1656). The high measure of elation which speaks from Mendelssohn's opening sentences was occasioned by the news of the so-called *Toleranzedikt* of Joseph II in 1781. Till now, Mendelssohn went on to say, tolerance was always taken to apply to members of the three accredited Christian denominations, never to the Heathen, the Jew, the Mohammedan, or the believer in natural religion. And that it had taken a Lessing and his *Nathan der Weise*, a Dohm and his *Über die bürgerliche Verbesserung der Juden*, and a Joseph II to reflect and ponder on how to link the natural rights of mankind and the destiny of man. Mendelssohn continued:

"I am too far removed from even nudging any meeting of cabinet ministers and thus prevented from taking part in this great task. I live in a State which flourishes in the arts and sciences through the active intervention of one of the wisest rulers ever. Moreover this sovereign has established such an atmosphere of freedom of thought that its effects are noticeable even in the least of his subjects. Under his glorious rule, I myself have had cause and opportunity to grow mentally, to think about my destiny and that of my co-religionists in this world. And to the extent of my abilities I have thought about mankind, its fate, and its destiny. However, I have always been at a remove from the Great, have always lived hidden away, have never felt called upon to intervene in the skirmishes of the world. Throughout the years, I have communicated only with a circle of like-minded friends."[3]

[2] *Moses Mendelssohn Jubiläumsausgabe* (henceforth *JubA*), Stuttgart 1970ff., vol. XII, 2, pp. 44f.: "Ich bin im Jahre 1729 zu Dessau geboren. Mein Vater war daselbst Schulmeister und Zehngebotschreiber, oder Sopher. Unter Rabbi Fränkel, der damals in Dessau Oberrabbiner war, studirte ich den Talmud. Nachdem sich dieser gelehrte Rabbi, durch seinen Commentar über den hierosolymitanischen Talmud, bei der jüdischen Nation großen Ruhm erworben, ward er etwa im Jahre 1743 nach Berlin berufen, wohin ich ihm noch in demselben Jahre folgte. Allhier gewann ich durch den Umgang mit dem nachherigen Doctor der Arzneigelartheit, Herrn Aron Gumperz (der vor einigen Jahren zu Hamburg verstorben), Geschmack an den Wissenschaften, dazu ich auch von demselben einige Anleitung erhielt. Ich ward hierauf in dem Hause eines reichen Juden Informator, hernach Buchhalter, und endlich Aufseher über desselben seidene Waaren-Manufactur, welches ich noch auf diese Stunde bin. In meinem drei und dreißigsten Jahr habe ich geheirathet, und seitdem sieben Kinder gezeugt, davon fünfe am Leben. Übrigens bin ich nie auf einer Universität gewesen, habe auch in meinem Leben kein Collegium lesen hören. Dieses war eine der größten Schwierigkeiten, die ich übernommen hatte, indem ich alles durch Anstrengung und eigenen Fleiß erzwingen mußte. In der That trieb ich es zu weit, und habe mir endlich durch Unmäßigkeit im Studiren seit drei Jahren eine Nervenschwäche zugezogen, die mich zu aller gelehrten Beschäftigung schlechterdings unfähig macht."

[3] *JubA*, VIII, p. 4: "Von den Cabineten der Großen, und von allem, was auf dieselbe Einfluß hat, bin ich allzuweit entfernt, um an diesem großen Geschäft auch nur den mindesten Theil nehmen, und mitwürken zu können. Ich lebe in einem Staate, in welchem einer der weisesten Regenten, die je Menschen beherrscht haben, Künste und Wissenschaften blühend, und vernünftige Freyheit zu denken so allgemein gemacht hat, daß sich ihre Wirkung bis auf den geringsten Einwohner seiner Staaten erstrecket. Unter seinem glorreichen Zepter habe ich Gelegenheit und Veranlassung gefunden, mich zu bilden, über meine und meiner Mitbrüder Bestimmung nachzudenken, und über Menschen, Schicksal und Vorsehung, nach Maßgabe meiner Kräfte, Betrachtungen anzustellen. Aber von allen Großen und ihrem Umgange bin ich stets entfernt gewesen. Ich habe jederzeit im Verborgenen gelebt, niemals Antrieb oder Beruf gehabt, mich in die Händel der würksamen Welt einzumischen, und mein ganzer Umgang hat sich von je her blos auf den Zirkel einiger Freund eingeschränkt, die mit mir ähnliche Wege gegangen sind."

Both of these pen-portraits are as remarkable for what they include, as for what they omit! What both extracts stress is Mendelssohn's affirmation of being a Jew, and that a kind of relative obscurity was his by choice. What the 1782 preface omitted to go into were the slights he had suffered at the hands of Frederick II when, in 1771, the King refused to accept the recommendation of members of the Academy that would have made Mendelssohn one of their number. Nor did he mention any of the humiliations that even "le Juif de Berlin", "der berühmte Herr Moses" had had to endure, or the repeated pleas to the King to obtain *Niederlassungsrecht*, or, that when the right of residence was bestowed at last, that it was granted only to him for his life time, and not to be inherited by his family. Then there was the degradation of having to pay poll-tax on entering and leaving the town – as if he were a head of cattle: and this befell the same man of whom the royal physician Johann Georg Zimmermann wrote in the periodical *Deutsches Museum* in 1778: "And here, my learned sirs, we have this philosopher whose fame, intellectuality and innate dignity is rivalled by none." There was the poignancy of having people whom he did not know, nor did they know him, jeering at his children and hurling stones.[4] And above all, the certainty that like him, his gifted sons would have no option in choosing a profession, so that at best they would have to make do like their father, with being a Jack of two trades: merchant by day, philosopher by candlelight.[5] It was not a fate that he cherished, nor one that he found easy to put up with himself. Occasionally, in letters to very close friends, he expressed his longing to be a philosopher: not by the hour but all day. On 11th June 1766 he wrote to Thomas Abbt in the tiny court residence of Bückeburg:

> "Having pondered on the destiny of mankind in general for quite a while, it seemed high time to think of my own in particular. I just don't think that I can put up with Berlin much longer. You once said that in order to do something outstanding, one ought to do something that petty minds might consider foolish. I feel capable of doing something extra foolish . . . I would be willing to give up being a business man and to live in some small township just for my own work . . . But the absolute minimum of requirements that I would expect are 1) the presence

---

[4] *JubA*, XII, 2, p. 200: "Ich ergehe mich zuweilen des Abends mit meiner Frau und meinen Kindern. Papa! fragt die Unschuld, was ruft uns jener Bursche dort nach? warum werfen sie mit Steinen hinter uns her? was haben wir ihnen gethan? – Ja, lieber Papa! spricht ein anderes, sie verfolgen uns immer in den Straßen, und schimpfen: Juden! Juden! Ist denn dieses so ein Schimpf bei den Leuten, ein Jude zu seyn? und was hindert dieses andere Leute? – Ach! ich schlage die Augen unter, und seufze mit mir selber: Menschen! Menschen! wohin habt ihr es endlich kommen lassen?"

[5] *JubA*, XIII, No. 636, p. 185: "In Absicht auf seine künftige Lebensart haben wir noch nichts bestimmt. Ich bin noch immer ungewiß wozu ich ihm rathen soll. Seine Talente und guten Anlagen zu den gründlichen Wissenschaften lassen in diesem Fache etwas Vorzügliches von ihm erwarten. Als Jude aber kann er bloß Arzneykunst treiben, und zu dieser hat er weder Lust noch Genie. Ihn der Handlung zu widmen, ist, wie mich dünkt, noch zu früh. Er mag also vor der Hand alles lernen, wozu er Lust und Trieb empfindet. Zum Kaufmanne wird er dadurch wenigstens nicht verdorben. Er mache es allenfalls, wie sein Vater es hat machen müssen, stümpere sich durch, bald als Gelehrter, bald als Kaufmann; ob er gleich Gefahr läuft, keines von beyden ganz richtig zu werden."

of some, though not many, Jewish families, 2) a letter of protection, at not too great an expense, 3) books, or at the very least, the means to have news of what is going on in the world of scholarship."[6]

Neither the sketch to the librarian, nor the preface of 1782 had made mention that the King's famous insistence "bei mir kann jeder auf seine Fasson selig werden" had saved Mendelssohn from repeated attempts to force him into apostasy. While Mendelssohn had made no public show of the indignities of his life as a Jew in Frederick II's Prussia, Mendelssohn had omitted, too, any mention of contact with the Christian world, any mention of his achievements: first and foremost the truly unbelievable amount of knowledge that he had amassed since he arrived in Berlin, on foot, late in 1743. At that time he knew Hebrew and Western Yiddish, he had read the Talmud, the Torah and Maimonides. None of this learning was likely to help him to survive among the Berliners. The first requirement for that, was the acquisition of German and French. With these languages, and presently with Latin, English, and finally with Greek, books opened up not only whole new worlds, but worlds of whose existence he had never even known.

Information about his youth, i.e. the years between 1743 and the year 1754 (the year from which dates the first of his extant letters) has to be pieced together from contemporary references. These are mostly from Nicolai, Sulzer and Lessing, either in subsequent reports, or in letters exchanged by these poets and scholars in Berlin, and the poet Gleim in Halberstadt, with the critic Bodmer in Zürich, with the orientalist Johan David Michaelis in Göttingen. Thus we know that he was helped by the young Huguenot Louis de Beausobre who took him to classes on Greek and Roman literature and philosophy at the *Joachimsthalsches Gymnasium*. This in turn implies that by 1747/1748 he knew enough Latin to follow lectures held in that language. Presently he gained access to two literary clubs with a cross section of mathematicians, poets, officers, academicians and writers who met for lively discussion of the learned papers they took it in turn to present.

We therefore have to think of this young, stuttering hunchback with the high forehead and expressive eyes as an integral member of several worlds: the Jewish, the Christian, the world of silk manufacture, the world of learning. In access to this last realm, he was fortunate indeed. For instance, the rector of the *Joachimsthalsches Gymnasium*, Johann Philipp Heinius, was a member of the Berlin Royal Academy. Also, Mendelssohn's main Jewish mentor, Gumpertz, was secretary to Maupertuis, permanent president of the Berlin Academy. Thus, it

[6]*JubA*, XII, No. 278, pp. 112 f. (11th June 1766): "Nachdem ich lange Zeit über die Bestimmung des Menschen überhaupt nachgedacht, schien es mir endlich einmal auch Zeit an die Meinige zu denken. Ich glaube nicht, dass ichs noch lange in Berlin machen werde. Sie haben gesagt, um grosse Dinge zu beginnen, müsste man so was thun, das kleinen Geistern wie Thorheit scheinet. Ich finde mich ziemlich zu so was fähig, das einer Thorheit ähnlich siehet . . . Ich bin Willens mich aller Geschäfte zu entschlagen, und an einem kleinen Orte, womöglich, ganz mir selbst zu leben . . . Aber dieser Ort müsste auch folgende Erfordernisse haben. 1) es müssten bereits einige, aber nicht viele jüdische Familien allda wohnen. 2) Ich müsste mit wenig Unkosten herrschaftlichen Schutz bekommen können. 3) Der Ort müsste nicht ganz leer von Litteratur seyn, wenigstens die Bequemlichkeit haben, dass man von den Neuigkeiten in der gelehrten Welt Nachricht bekommen könte."

may be assumed that just as he had been invited to join the Monday Club and the lively intellectuals of the *Gelehrtes Kaffeehaus*, that he also knew a fair number of the members of the Berlin Academy.

By the date of the first extant letter, i.e. by 1754, Mendelssohn had astounded the Berlin circles of his aquaintance by the fact that, though a Jew, he could write in German, in admirable style, and that he was a first rate mathematician. Gleim was to confirm to the poet Uz (12th February 1756), this was "kein erdichteter, sondern ein würcklicher Jude, noch sehr jung, und von einem treflichen Genie, der es, ohne Lehrer, in allen Wißenschaften sehr weit gebracht (hat), der die Algebra zum Zeitvertreib gebraucht, wie wir die Poesie, und doch von Jugend auf, in einer jüdischen Handlung sein Brod verdienet hat". Lessing had been even more explicit. On 16th October 1754 he had told Michaelis that here was a model of a human being, a Jew "welcher ohne Anweisung in Sprachen, in der Mathematik, in der Weltweisheit, in der Poesie eine so große Stärke erlangt hat, daß ihm zu einem zweiten Spinoza nichts fehlt als die Irrthümer".[7]

By the time that Lessing had written this letter to Michaelis, Lessing had not only encouraged Mendelssohn to publish philosophical essays, he had also involved him as his partner in answering a deliberately insulting and trickily worded theme: "All is best", set for the prize essay for the year 1755 of the Berlin Royal Academy.

In other words, already by 1754 Lessing regarded Mendelssohn intellectually, stylistically, as a highly desirable collaborator. How much sophistication Mendelssohn had at his command is borne out by the first of the extant letters. It is addressed to Christian Nicolaus Naumann (1720–1797) and dates from the early months of 1754. Mendelssohn was then twenty-four years of age, Naumann, an inventive if undisciplined writer, was almost ten years his senior. From the context it is clear that Naumann, Lessing's friend of long-standing, had, of all things, asked Mendelssohn to criticise a treatise of his on free-thinkers.

Clearly, Mendelssohn had taken his opponent's measure, and in carrying out the latter's request at length, he adjusted his own logical method wittily and tellingly to the somewhat scatter-brained argumentation of the man from Bauzen. The ability to address any recipient in the man's own language was to become a hallmark of Mendelssohnian letters.

Obviously, Mendelssohn's letters set out from given topics, but their treatment, the choice of metaphors, the style is, unselfconsciously, in sensitive response to the mental calibre and the level of awareness of the recipient. While never withholding his own opinion, nor shortchanging his interlocutor, Men-

---

[7] *Lessings Sämtliche Schriften*, ed. by Karl Lachmann; 3rd edn. by Franz Muncker, Stuttgart–Leipzig 1886–1924 (henceforth *L-M*), vol. XVII, p. 40: Lessing to J. D. Michaelis, 16th October 1754. (See also Mendelssohn to A. Gumpertz, end of June 1754 [*JubA*, XI, No. 3, 16th October 1754].)

a.   "Not a fictitious but a live Jew – very young still – and marvellously intelligent. Without anyone's help he has gone a long way in all kinds of learning; and, for a pastime, is turning to algebra, as we do to poetry.
  And yet, all along he's had to earn his living as a merchant's employee."

b. . . . "who without benefit of instructor has become so knowledgeable in languages, mathematics, in philosophy that – short of that man's fallacies – he looks like becoming a second Spinoza".

delssohn never deliberately discouraged anyone. Moreover, like many other famous bilingual writers (e.g. Joseph Conrad), Mendelssohn had a vast vocabulary and a whole quiverful of verbal nuances and ingenious neologisms at his command. It was Kant who remarked upon this explicitly (16th August 1783):

> "Es sind wehnige so glücklich, vor sich und zugleich in der Stelle anderer dencken und die ihnen allen angemessene Manier im Vortrag treffen zu können. – Es ist nur ein Mendelssohn."[8]

A great many of the letters to and from Mendelssohn are of more than intrinsic interest, both for topics they raise and for incidents and plans that are being discussed. Thus, it is not easy to decide which letters to put before you first. Are we to concentrate on famous correspondents, on exciting contemporary schemes, on concepts in aesthetics and metaphysics, on Mendelssohn's statements about Judaism, on the letters in print, on those still to be published?

Scarcity of time, and the difficulty of doing justice in translation to Mendelssohn's superb style preclude quoting more than snippets of actual letters. Let me therefore attempt a broad panorama of the concept of "destiny of man", a burning topic through the ages, and one to which in the eighteenth century, next to Rousseau in his *Second Discourse* (1755), Mendelssohn added notable highlights.

IV

The most significant among the correspondents with whom there was a sustained exchange, is, first and foremost, Lessing – right up to his death in February 1781. The correspondence began when Lessing left Berlin suddenly in October 1755, thereby interrupting a year of almost daily discussion on points of philosophical and literary interest arising from Leibniz, Wolff, Shaftesbury, and the young men's discontent with the non-existence of objective criticism in Germany, and thus, the necessity for reform.[9] Many of the letters between Lessing, Mendelssohn and Nicolai between October 1755 and Lessing's return to Berlin in May 1758 have been republished early in the twentieth century as *Briefe über das Trauerspiel*.[10] Definitions here hammered out of Aristotelian terms like "tragic", "compassion", "fear", "hero", "terror" precede and are pivotal to

---

[8]"Few men are so fortunate as to think for themselves and others simultaneously; and to choose a style appropriate to all. – Mendelssohn, and only he, is capable of this feat."

[9]*Gotthold Ephraim Lessings Leben, nebst seinem noch übrigen Nachlasse*, Erster Teil, Berlin 1793, pp. 449f. (=LSS); LSS vol. 26, Berlin 1794, pp. 19*f.; Friedrich Nicolai, *Über meine gelehrte Bildung*, Berlin – Stettin 1799, p. 42.

[10]*Lessings Briefwechsel mit Mendelssohn und Nicolai über das Trauerspiel*. Nebst verwandten Schriften Nicolais und Mendelssohns. Hrsg. Robert Petsch, Leipzig 1910.

Lessing's *Laokoön*, his *Hamburgische Dramaturgie*, as well as to Schiller's aesthetic. Between May 1758 and November 1760, Lessing's presence in Berlin obviated letters. Hence, there is no documentation to accompany discussion arising from their own published or anticipated writings, nor observations relating to the review articles in the new venture of the three friends: *Briefe die neueste Litteratur betreffend* (1759–1765).

The remainder of the Lessing/Mendelssohn correspondence was dictated by Lessing's absence from Berlin – always remembering, however, that letter writing was not Lessing's forte anyhow. And clearly while Lessing *was* in Berlin (May 1765–June 1766 and September 1766–April 1767) we are not going to find any written statements of their discussions. But between 1763 and 1777 there are six important Mendelssohn letters that testify to the close link of friendship and intellect between them. After 1777, the letters from Lessing's brother Karl let us follow the exchange of opinion on topics and progress of Lessing's final three summaries of his quest for truth; *Ernst und Falk, Erziehung des Menschengeschlechts, Nathan der Weise*. It is worth stressing, in view of F. H. Jacobi's assertion in 1783, i.e. after Lessing's death, that the intellectual link between Lessing and Lessing's "oldest and worthiest friend"[11] had never snapped, and that to the end, the topics raised were crucial to their respective work in progress. Both men were torn apart publicly for their moral courage in discussing the destiny of man: the letters offer us insight into their inner state of mind. In 1763, Mendelssohn's letter is addressed to the friend who – though currently secretary to a general – has turned to the reading of Spinoza once more. In 1770, in the thick of Mendelssohn's religious confrontation with Lavater, Mendelssohn made a special journey to Wolfenbüttel, apparently to be entrusted with the highly explosive document, the so-called *Fragmente eines Ungenannten*, i.e. the *Apologie, oder Schutzschrift für die vernünftigen Verehrer Gottes* by the Hamburg theologian-philosopher Hermann Samuel Reimarus. The author had wisely decided to leave his attack on the fundamentalist interpretation of the New Testament unpublished during his life-time. On his departure from Hamburg late in 1769 in order to take up his appointment as librarian to the Duke of Braunschweig-Lüneburg, the "hot" manuscript had been given to Lessing by the older Reimarus children. Lessing intended to see the treatise into print, withholding the name of the author and pretending that the material had been discovered in the ducal library.

Apart from Johann and Elise Reimarus, only Mendelssohn seems to have been in Lessing's confidence, and he appears to be the only one to have been asked for his views on the contents of the manuscript and on the advisability of publishing it. Two letters, one to Lessing, one by him, survive to testify to the ensuing discussion. To the best of my belief, neither letter has been taken notice of in the history of the fierce attack on Lessing that resulted from eventual publication. As Mendelssohn knew only too well, any critique of the accepted canon of the church was fraught with danger. The issue for Mendelssohn was one of manner

[11]See Lessing to Ebert on 7th November 1769.

and method. He disagreed with Reimarus's interpretation on grounds of common sense reasoning. Reimarus had seen Christ as the puppet in the hands of a group of political adventurers, cashing in, so to speak, on Messianic prophecies. This struck Mendelssohn as modish and dictated by non-objective partisanship: to his mind, it should be a case of:

> "Den Menschen als Menschen zu betrachten, ihn nach den Sitten, Gewohnheiten und Kenntnissen seiner Zeit und in Vergleichung mit seinen Nebenmenschen zu beurtheilen, dazu muß man weder Vorurtheile haben, noch sich aus Abscheu gegen Vorurtheile zur Unbilligkeit verleiten lassen; dazu muß man das Mass der menschlichen Kräfte kennen, und keine Phantome im Kopfe haben, die uns schwindlich machen. Indessen ist das Manuscript in aller Betrachtung sehr wichtig."[12]

Equally decisively, friend argued with friend when Mendelssohn in Letter 390 (1st February 1774) dealt with an erroneous interpretation of a quotation from Leibniz in Lessing's second report on the 'Treasures of the Ducal Library', namely the article entitled 'Des Andreas Wissowatius Einwürfe wider die Dreieinigkeit' – once again a dangerous discussion, you would think, for a Jew to enter into. Having closely followed Lessing's argumentation, he takes Lessing up on an interpretation tucked away in a footnote, contrasts Lessing's distinction between "*intelligibile, intelligens, intellectus*" with "our Cabbalists' *principium emanaticum, emanens, emanatum*" and wittily clinches his objection to the concept, Trinitarianism, clothing his point of view in an anecdote.

My final two Mendelssohn-to-Lessing letters date from the eve of the last meeting of the two friends, and the first and only meeting of their wives, in December 1777 in Wolfenbüttel. The second of these letters is important for Mendelssohn's suggestion that both men go to Hannover to investigate the Leibniz bequest of notes and papers. The earlier letter (11th November, Letter 456) is a gem for many reasons. It offers a pen-portrait of Lessing, as Mendelssohn had seen him in the past, his burning desire to meet Lessing just now, partly to confirm the mental image of a man at last more at peace with himself, partly to take him to task in this next stage of Lessing's search for religious truth by asserting in the *Ernst und Falk. Gespräche für Freimaurer*: "I am as truly a freemason as I am a Christian." And, just in case the friends might exhaust the tangents of this ever present topic of "Die Wahrheit rühret in mehr als einer Gestalt",[13] Mendelssohn suggested another one: "association of ideas"; "damit wir in der Menge der Dinge, die wir uns zu sagen haben, ein unverrücktes Augenmerk behalten". The two final proofs of friendship are contained in Lessing's last extant letter to Mendelssohn on 19th December 1780 – he died on 15th February 1781 – and the no less moving epitaph that Mendelssohn sent to

---

[12]*JubA*, XII, 1, No. 352, pp. 237f.: "Judging an individual according to the customs, the traditions, and the state of knowledge of his era necessitates the absence of prejudice as much as not being unfair just because prejudice is distasteful. In addition, you need to be aware of the extent of human frailty and not have your head full of delusions that would render you giddy."
[13]*L-M*, IV, p. 277.

Karl Lessing on receiving the news of the death of the man "der meine Seele gebildet hat".[14]

V

We turn now to two minds who – next to Lessing – became his most invigorating partners in the exchange of ideas. The earliest of these was Thomas Abbt whom Mendelssohn "discovered" late in 1760. They met for several months in the summer of 1761, and, among other ventures, planned to translate all the writings of Lord Shaftesbury.[15] From 1761 to Abbt's death in his twenty-eighth year in November 1766, Abbt became Mendelssohn's most notable letter partner. Isaak Iselin, the Basle Town Clerk, author, philosopher and co-founder of the *Patriotische Gesellschaft*, came a close second.

Thomas Abbt, born in 1738, son of a rope-maker in Ulm, was nearly nine years younger than Mendelssohn and Lessing, five years younger than Nicolai. In 1761, then officially a university professor of mathematics, he attracted the attention of Mendelssohn by a little work published by Nicolai, entitled *Vom Tode für das Vaterland*. At Mendelssohn's suggestion, Nicolai invited the young man to become a collaborator for *Literaturbriefe*. Abbt accepted with alacrity.

Their subsequent correspondence consists of at least thirty-one letters by Abbt and some sixty letters by Mendelssohn and Nicolai to him. In addition to these letters in print in the *Jubiläumsausgabe* and in Abbt's *Vermischte Werke* there is a large treasure trove of unpublished material. Also, there is the summary of Mendelssohn's correspondence on "Bestimmung des Menschen" as it appears in *Literaturbrief* 287 in June and July 1764, and then there are the important and extensive "Notes" which Mendelssohn added when their exchange of letters was published in Part III of Abbt's *Vermischte Werke* in 1782. All their letters sport long, lively, witty reflections of their thinking and feeling. The about forty unpublished letters between 1761 and 1766 almost exclusively relate to books reviewed, or to be reviewed for Nicolai's two periodical publications: *Literaturbriefe* and, after 1765, *Allgemeine deutsche Bibliothek*. They are still in the archives of the Prince zu Schaumburg-Lippe. Bruno Strauss knew of them and paraphrased or quoted from them in the notes to the letters in *Jubiläumsausgabe* XI, which covers the letters up to the end of 1762. In that year, Abbt spent some time travelling in Switzerland where he made the acquaintance of men of calibre who also affected the life of Mendelssohn: Iselin, Rousseau, Voltaire, Bonnet, Lavater, Prince Ludwig Eugen of Württemberg.

At the onset of their correspondence, Abbt had raised the topic of the sublime, had analysed Baumgarten's definition of poetry as speech rendered sensual

---

[14]Letter 532 [Berlin, Februar 1781]: "Mit gerührtem Herzen dank' ich der Vorsehung für die Wohlthat, daß sie mich so früh, in der Blüthe meiner Jugend, hat einen Mann kennen lassen, der meine Seele gebildet hat, den ich bey jeder Handlung, die ich vorhatte, bey jeder Zeile, die ich hinschreiben sollte, mir als Freund und Richter vorstellte, und den ich mir zu allen Zeiten noch als Freund und Richter vorstellen werde, so oft ich einen Schritt von Wichtigkeit zu thun habe."
[15]Anthony Ashley Cooper, 3rd Earl of Shaftesbury (1671–1713).

("poema est oratio sensitiva perfecta") and other concepts of the recent new branch of philosophy, i.e. aesthetics – not realising that the treatise, *Über das Erhabene und Naive in den schönen Wissenschaften*, published in 1758 in Nicolai's earliest periodical, was by Mendelssohn himself.[16]

No doubt, the years after the summer of 1761 in Berlin saw the follow-up of these literary discussions and established an outspoken, friendly, mentor-to-very-bright-pupil relationship, and all the fun of being the onlooker in the sprightly Hamann-Mendelssohn altercation and parodying by voicing and rebuffing with superb use of irony their individual reactions to Rousseau's novel, *Julie, ou la Nouvelle Heloïse*, in *Literaturbrief* 192 of the 22nd October 1761. This in turn gave further dimension to the discussion of style, of styles in relation to the content of a piece of writing, as also to the function of the reviewer. The climax of this particular discussion was reached in Mendelssohn's fable about Jupiter's plan for the ideal world (No. 194, April 1762) and in Mendelssohn's superb descriptive comparison of the stylistic ability of Shaftesbury with that of the thinker whom he admired most in this respect, Plato (No. 217, 4th July 1762).

In order to preserve the main thread of this essay – Mendelssohn's steps to arrive at and analyse what he understood by "Bestimmung des Menschen" – we need to skip events important in themselves, Mendelssohn's wedding for instance (June 1762), or the publication veto imposed on the *Literaturbriefe* by the censor for eleven days in April 1762. This *Zensurverbot* had been caused by the spite of a vain author. From the beginning the *Literaturbriefe* with their outspoken, anonymous reviews had raised a rich crop of authors who considered themselves to have been treated unjustly. About this time, the middle of the year 1762, Mendelssohn himself had had to deal with the unjustifiable reaction of an otherwise esteemed thinker, H. S. Reimarus. To Abbt's more impetuous nature, Mendelssohn's reply had seemed "lammsfromm". However, inwardly Mendelssohn felt outraged, to the point of protesting to Abbt that there was no love of truth in contemporary Germany and no room for healthy criticism. Out of this mood, he read in Abbt's letter of November 1762 (No. 233) the rhetorical question "whither the destiny of man?".

This must have given new life to "an idea that I have been fondling for many years", the topic being, as he wrote to Iselin (No. 232, 5th July 1763): *Phädon, oder über die Unsterblichkeit der Seele*. The catalyst that fused Mendelssohn's ideas on immortality of the soul with the concept of aspects "destiny of man" has probably to be sought in Abbt's letter of 11th January 1764 (No. 239). He wrote:

> "Instead of discussing bad authors, let me for once put down what I have been wanting to say a thousand times. You are the only human being with whom I can, and want to, discuss matters of real importance, i.e. those which all learning aspires to. Would you permit me to put my thoughts and doubts before you and let me hear you agree or disagree . . . My point of departure would be that of the 'destiny of man', a matter submerged in many clouds as far as I am concerned . . . If you tell me 'spare me, I don't want to hear or discuss such matters', – it

---

[16] *Bibliothek der schönen Wissenschaften und der freyen Künste*, II, 2 (January 1758), pp. 229–267. See also *JubA*, I, pp. 191–218 and pp. 455–495.

won't put an end to our corresponding. Maybe you have pondered on this matter *ad nauseam* – that you never thought about it, I consider quite impossible."[17]

Mendelssohn was "extraordinarily impatient" to hear which doubts the twenty-five-year-old wanted to put forward. He encouraged Abbt to be outspoken. These two letters and the ones that now followed need to be read, on the one hand, in conjunction with the version of their exchange of beliefs, published as 'Zweifel' and 'Orakel' (*Literaturbrief* 287, June-July 1764), on the other, with those writings of Mendelssohn that owe their final shape to Abbt's initiative, demanding the discussion, as well to the shock of Abbt's untimely death in 1766, the death of Mendelssohn's eleven-month-old daughter, and that of his father, Mendel Heyman: namely *Phädon* (1767) and the treatise on the *Immateriality of the Soul* (*Von der Unkörperlichkeit der Seele*) that was in manuscript by the summer of 1774.

In other words, their discussion did not end with the publication of *Literaturbrief* 287. While Abbt attempts to continue the discussion, Mendelssohn has taken up work on *Phädon* (No. 260, 16th February 1764):

> "Da ich aber, wie Sie längst wissen, ein Werkchen über die Unsterblichkeit der Seele unter der Feder habe, so bin ich willens den zweyten Theil desselben mit Betrachtungen über unsere Bestimmungen zu füllen und will mir also Zeit lassen, gehörig darüber nachzudenken. Fahren Sie fort, liebster Freund mir Einwürfe zu machen, und Zweifel zu erregen."[18]

Since he considers Abbt's doubts to begin to lose weight, Mendelssohn summarised his own belief in the letter of 26th March 1765 (No. 265).[19] It is too long to do it justice by mere summary, and a document that deserves close analysis and also comparison with Lessing's *Erziehung des Menschengeschlechts*, published more than a decade later (No. 267, 14th June 1765; and No. 281, 22nd

---

[17]"Doch, anstatt von schlechten Autoren zu sprechen, lassen Sie mich einmal das hieher setzen was ich tausendmal habe sagen wollen. Sie sind der einzige Mensch, mit dem ich über die wichtigsten Dinge, worauf endlich alles Lernen sich beziehen muß, sprechen kann und mag. Wollen Sie wohl erlauben, daß ich ihnen meine Gedanken und Zweifel darüber vortrage, und Sie dagegen oder mit mir einstimmig höre. Unsere Briefe würden nicht bloß

Jovi Congregatori Nubium sacrae;

ich hoffe, daß wir einige Sachen sicher und gewiß ausmachen werden. Auch dürfen Sie nicht befürchten, daß ich meinen nächsten Brief mit einem

Heus age, responde, nimium est, quod scire laboro.
De Jove quid sentis?

anfangen werde. Mein Punkt, von dem ich ausgehen möchte, ist die Bestimmung des Menschen, über der für mich so viele Wolken liegen, und der Satz, der mir so wahr zu seyn scheinet, daß keine Tugend und kein Laster eine Belohnung nach diesem Leben, wenn auch die Seelen unsterblich seyn, zu fordern haben; weil sich beyde hier selbst belohnen, und kein sicherer Maaßstab für Vergnügen und Mißvergnügen, Glück oder Unglück ist.

Vor allen Dingen wiederhohle ich ihnen feyerlich, daß Sie mir aufrichtig sagen können: ich will von diesen Sachen nichts hören, noch weniger sagen, ohne daß dieses Geständniß unserm Briefwechsel den geringsten Abbruch thun werde. Es kann seyn, daß Sie sich schon bis zum Eckel an diesen Materien satt gedacht haben: denn gar nicht, dies ist unmöglich."

[18]*JubA*, XII, 1, p. 76: "As you know, for quite a while I've been at work on a small book on the Immortality of the Soul. Hence, I intend to leave our mutual reflections for Part II of it, and thus gain time to give more thought to the matter. Therefore, dear friend, do go on raising objections and formulating your doubts."

[19]*JubA*, XII, 1, pp. 86–88.

July 1766).[20] Handsomely, Mendelssohn acknowledged his indebtedness to Abbt in 1766: "It was your questioning that roused me into completing a piece of work begun many years ago" (No. 281).[21] The work he was speaking of was *Phädon*. In his preface to it, Mendelssohn regards it for what it truly is, a memorial to an exceptional friendship.

VI

The friendship with Iselin is documented by a very small number of letters so far: six by Iselin, seven to him. Undoubtedly more evidence can be found in the archive in Basle and in the over two hundred, unfortunately very hard to decipher, letters in the *Nicolai Nachlass* in the *Staatsbibliothek Preussischer Kultur-besitz* (SBPK). Valuable work on Iselin has been done by Ulrich Im Hof. May there be more of it.

Clearly, Mendelssohn knew of Iselin's historico-philosophical publications long before they started to correspond in April 1762. More than a year earlier, Mendelssohn had written to Lessing about Abbt on 11th February 1761 (No. 92): "Er gefällt mir besser als Iselin."

When Iselin approached him, it was to invite Mendelssohn to become a member of the Swiss *Patriotische Gesellschaft*. Similar invitations had gone out to men like Sulzer, Michaelis, Rousseau. However, only at a second remove did Mendelssohn accept. Originally he had felt:

> "Zwar blühet unter der Regierung eines Friderichs die Freyheit zu denken fast in republika-nischer Schönheit; allein Sie wissen, wie wenig Antheil meine Glaubensbrüder an allen Landesfreyheiten zu haben pflegen. Die bürgerliche Unterdrükung zu welcher uns ein zu sehr eingerissenes Vorurtheil verdamt, liegt wie eine todte Last auf den Schwingen des Geistes, und macht sie unfähig, den hohen Flug des Freygebohrnen jemals zu versuchen. Ich besitze Selbsterkentnis genug, um in diesem Stüke meine Schwäche einzusehen, und allzuviel Hochachtung für die Gesellschaft, um ihre dieselbe nicht zu gestehen."[22]

Once Mendelssohn had been persuaded to join the *Patriotische Gesellschaft*, he helped to publicise their aims and their prize competitions in the *Literaturbriefe* and in the *Allgemeine deutsche Bibliothek*. He also wanted to aid their programme and therefore inquired whether the Society would be interested in two of the writings he was engaged on just at that time: a translation of Plato's *Republic* and his own treatise entitled *Phädon*.

Four months later, on the 16th November 1763, Mendelssohn sent the first part of *Phädon* to the *Patriotische Gesellschaft*.[23] His accompanying letter accommo-dates itself to topics of interest to Iselin and, by association of ideas, moves from

---

[20]See also *JubA*, XII, 1, p. 92; and *ibid.*, p. 119.

[21]*JubA*, XII, 1, p. 118.

[22]"Though freedom of thought flourishes in almost republican splendour under the reign of Frederick, you know yourself that my co-religionists have little share in civil freedoms. The civil suppression to which an all too firmly established prejudice has condemned us, renders us incapable of ever attempting to soar as high as those born free. I know myself sufficiently to realise my own weakness in this respect, and I think too highly of your Society not to admit this."

[23]*JubA*, XII, 1, No. 237.

final causality to philosophical history, to history of mankind, the moral good, public good, the query whether society can bring about improvement of moral standards, whether an individual (like the then very famous Swiss "philosophical peasant") could stand up to being always in the public eye. – What part does punishment play in society, and what does the then recent book by Cesare Beccaria, *Dei Delitti e delle Pene* ("Crime and Punishment") contribute? – It would therefore seem that contact with Iselin kindled a real concern in "society and natural law".

Mendelssohn's *Phädon* received two known responses from members of the *Patriotische Gesellschaft*. Iselin's response was rediscovered only last year. He mainly comments on individual words and reproves Mendelssohn for small slips in style. The second, rather more analytical commentary reached Mendelssohn from Lausanne, from Ludwig Eugen, brother of the reigning Duke of Württemberg (and later, briefly, himself Duke of Württemberg). The young Duke's first letter on *Phädon* written on the 27th June 1767,[24] suggests that Mendelssohn's wording[25] with reference to our comprehension of God needs further clarification. Ludwig Eugen here attributed to Mendelssohn himself what in the context applied to Socrates. Of him Mendelssohn had suggested that he gained insight into the Creator and Sustainer of all things "durch das reine Licht der Vernunft auf die lebendigste Art". In the last paragraph of the Duke's, very courtly, weirdly punctuated, second letter (of the 4th August 1767)[26] the point about "the purest light of reason" ("wegen der Stelle von dem reinesten Liechte der Vernunft und ihrer lezten Erklärung") is taken up. It is the Duke's contention that a Christian philosopher, having been brought up, so to speak, to accept the doctrine of Revelation, is at a disadvantage. He cannot define *Offenbarung* with any exactitude – a non-Christian rationalist might. In short, though barricaded behind telescopic jumps within the argument, the Christian Duke accepts a rationalist definition of our ability to comprehend the numinous. – The topic as such is clearly part of the discussion that involved Jew and Christian alike in the eighteenth century. To his Christian contemporaries, it held part of the fascination that emanated from Mendelssohn: that this could lead to a dialogue.

VII

Herein lay the special significance of *Phädon*. Over the years, this work was translated into eleven languages. It brought Mendelssohn European recognition, the soubriquet of "the Socrates of the eighteenth century", and more and more scholars and petitioners who turned to him for advice. Fame, however, made him "visible" and subject to repeated attempts to pressure him into becoming a Christian. The first of the resultant religious discussions that he was forced into (in 1769), caused important statements to be made in letters to minds

[24]*JubA*, XII, 1, No. 294.
[25]*JubA*, III, 1, p. 16.
[26]*JubA*, XII, 1, No. 296.

as diverse as the hereditary prince of Braunschweig-Lüneburg and to Lavater, the Zürich clergyman who tried to convert all around him, Goethe included, into becoming followers of Christ. Friends and interested onlookers alike considered Lavater's clumsy ardour irritating in the extreme. Outwardly, Mendelssohn bore himself with dignity and remained unshakeable in the affirmation of his faith. But his physique collapsed under the strain, and for years there was great concern over his health. He turned his back on modern philosophy, and his sole mental energy seems to have been directed to Jewish concerns. In the letters after 1770, the discussions revolve around interpretation and translation of psalms into German, around utopian plans for Jewish states that various noblemen brought to his attention, around more realistic plans to improve and modernise the education of young Jews, plans to educate Jewish and Christian children in the same school, to set up a model school, to contribute to a primer that was regarded as a model by the minister of education in Prague.

From Hamburg, Lessing had watched the distasteful conduct of Lavater with concern, but without stepping in publicly. A few months later, however, he himself was to embark on an equally explosive appeal for truth in matters concerning belief. We saw how he had turned to Mendelssohn for advice; though being Lessing, he did not act upon it.

VIII

Throughout Mendelssohn's life, men and women appealed to his judgement and sought his help. Two highly unusual instances of this occurred in 1780. One was the case of the Benedictine monk in Erfurt who, in his quest for eternal verities, had come across *Phädon*. The second was that of a young baron, Franz Clemens von Fürstenberg (1755–1827), nephew of the Prince-Bishop of Hildesheim and Paderborn. In 1775 the young man, then twenty years old, had run away from home. In 1780, on horseback, he had made his way as far as Mendelssohn's house. The story became known in Berlin, and it was through *Kriegsrat* Dohm (the Prussian state official about to publish *Über die bürgerliche Verbesserung der Juden*), that the *Fürstbischof* requested information about his nephew's whereabouts.

The incident would be totally forgotten, if it were not for Mendelssohn's, hitherto unpublished, report:

> "He seemed to place special confidence in me and frequented my house so trustingly and confidently. He never passed the time of day, or uttered a word of thanks, and, whether I was at home or not, behaved as if he were one of us. If he did not find me at home, he entered, never saying a word, into whatever room had its door ajar, or he went into my library, took a book, read for about half an hour and then crept away again. My people were so used to him that eventually they paid no attention to him. 'It's the foreign sir, who doesn't talk to anyone', they used to say. He put up near me at the Golden Eagle. Presumably you know how he came by his clothes. On his return from calling on the Minister, he told me secretly that he had the choice of a post in Minden or one here in Berlin, but that he would prefer Minden, in order not to be too far away from home. And that he wanted to petition for the title of *Kriegsrat*, in order to make a better impression on his family."

"I was in the habit of being outspoken with him and not mincing my words. He seemed to like that, though it never affected his decisions. Several times he exclaimed loudly: 'Tolerance, not only in matters of religion but also in secular matters and in politics.' "[27]

How could we possibly find more apt words in conclusion?

[27]"Ich soll Ihnen berichten mein Herr Kriegsrath, was für Partikularien mir von dem Hrn Baron Fürstenberg bekant sind. Ich bedaure, daß meine Geschichte nicht viel weiter reicht, als dasjenige, was Ihnen schon bekant ist. Er schien ein besonderes Zutrauen zu mir zu haben, ging in meinem Hause so vertraulich aus und ein, so zuversichtlich, ohne zu grüßen oder recht zu danken, ich mochte zu Hause oder nicht zu Hause seyn, als wenn er zu uns gehörte. Fand er mich nicht, so ging er, ohne ein Wort zu sprechen, in das nächste Zimmer, das er offen sahe, oder in meine Bücherstube, las etwa eine 1/2 Stunde und schlich sich wieder davon. Meine Leute waren dies schon so gewohnt, daß sie sich am Ende nicht mehr nach ihm umsahen. Es ist der fremde Herr, hieß es, der mit niemanden spricht . . . Ich war gewohnt, ihm bey allen Gelegenheiten herbe Wahrheiten zu sagen, die er gern zu hören schien; aber ohne von seinem Vorhaben in nichts abzugehen. 'Toleranz', schrie er öfters, 'Toleranz, nicht nur in Religionssachen, sondern auch in Welthändeln . . .' " (Archiv von Fürstenberg-Stammheim, No. 23.85).

Jewish Self-Defence

Anti-Anti 1889/1892

BY JACOB TOURY

One of the more recent publications on antisemitism in Germany[1] stresses the "drastically" retarded "tempo of antisemitic agitation" in the decade between the elections of 1881 and 1890, without arousing comment or contradiction. A partial explanation for this optimistic evaluation (and its acceptance today)* may be found in the strict limitation of the cited treatise to *party*-antisemitism, as manifested within the boundaries of the German *Reich* until 1914, thus excluding even the German-speaking parts of the Habsburg Monarchy;[2] moreover, such a stance seems not inconsistent with the position taken by the contemporary Jewish public and its press, which often overlooked, or at least played down, alarming signs of successful antisemitic propaganda – the most glaring being the ascent of Otto Böckel (since 1886), the "Peasants' King" and cock of the walk in various parts of Hesse.[3]

But even in the face of Jewish quietism, the antisemitic mood spread like a cancer, without regard to parties or boundaries, playing havoc with "the deep aversion of German Jews to open resistance, an aversion best exemplified by the policy of the board" of the then largest German community of Berlin, which pointedly refrained from fighting antisemitism and sometimes even restrained others from doing so.[4]

I. INDIVIDUAL FEATS

The first instances of individual endeavours to combat antisemitism[5] developed from rather unexpected quarters: first in Vienna (1882, *Kadimah*) and soon after (1886, *Viadrina*) in Breslau (today: Wroclaw), followed by other German

---

[1]Sanford Ragins, *Jewish Responses to Anti-Semitism in Germany, 1870–1914*, Cincinnati 1980, pp. 36f.

*See also the following essay by Jacob Borut, 'The Rise of Jewish Defence Agitation in Germany, 1890–1895: A Pre-History of the C.V.?', in this volume of the Year Book – (Ed.).

[2]In the following, it will be asserted that developments, at least in Austria proper, ran parallel to those in the *Reich* and although their interconnection was not then regarded as important in Jewish affairs, it must have been stronger than estimated up to now.

[3]There are, as a matter of fact, various commentaries in Jewish papers on the surprising scope of this success, i.a. by Rabbi Isaak Rülf, himself born and brought up in Hesse (*Allgemeine Zeitung des Judenthums*, LIV, Nos. 19, 20 [23rd and 30th May 1890]) and – in partial response to it – by the economist Gustav Tuch of Hamburg, *ibid.*, Nos. 23 and 24 (20th and 27th May 1890); but their tenor is rather in conformity with Ragins's (note 1) characterisation of Jewish "quietism", notwithstanding the fact that Böckel and his followers carried four Hessian seats in the elections to the *Reichstag* in February 1890.

[4]Ismar Schorsch, *Jewish Reactions to German Anti-Semitism, 1870–1914*, New York 1972, pp. 65f.

[5]Apart from Professor Moritz Lazarus's rather pathetic attempts of 1879/1880, on which cf. Schorsch, *op. cit.*, pp. 60ff.

university-towns, Jewish students organised almost spontaneously, in order to stand up for themselves and fight, if need be, with sword, sabre or pistol, against their antisemitic detractors.[6] One of the first to fight a duel with sabres and to disable his antisemitic adversary, was a young theologian from Breslau, the later Rabbi Benno Jacob,[7] who was destined to become one of the spiritual leaders of German Jewry. Another Silesian Jew, cand. med. Königsfeld, in 1889 killed his adversary in a pistol-duel in Würzburg. He was sentenced to two and a half years incarceration in a Bavarian fortress, but was soon pardoned by the Prince Regent and is said to have left Germany.[8] Not all of the duelists were so lucky: somewhat earlier (1888), another medical student, named Blum, had been shot by his adversary, a member of the antisemitic *Verein deutscher Studenten*.[9] More than one year later, Assessor Ziegel fell in a duel with an antisemitic *Referendar*,[10] and another duel between members of the legal profession, although without fatal results, was reported from the vicinity of Ratibor.[11]

Most of these cases concern only Jews from the Eastern parts of Germany and although this fact is rather suggestive of a continuation of Jewish self-awareness in the regions of relative Jewish concentration, in later years examples from other parts of Germany and Austria were occasionally reported,[12] despite the fact that duels as such were deemed a criminal offence. Thus, most of them remained shrouded in silence. In any case, they did not develop into a system of individual – let alone collective – defence-activities. For, apart from their illegality, soon antisemites "on principle" refused to "honour" Jews by consenting to fight; in Jewish circles, too, critical voices were raised[13] against the blind imitation of one of the more glaring feats of *furor teutonicus*. In short, towards the end of the century, duelling as an expression of the Jewish will to combat antisemitism became more or less obsolete.[14]

Another individual form of early activity against antisemitic propaganda, which demanded no less courage than duelling (and more brain!), was public discussion in antisemitic meetings, in order to refute the anti-Jewish allegations of the speakers. At first, the organisers in fact promised (and sometimes the promise was kept) free speech, and occasionally Jews utilised the opportunity to debunk the more hair-raising propaganda clichés of "ritual murder" and other "talmudic immoralities", or of alleged Jewish "influence" on German political

---

[6]On the Vienna *Kadimah* cf. *Festschrift der Kadimah*, Vienna 1933; on the Breslau *Viadrina* see Adolph Asch and Johanna Philippson, 'Self-Defence in the Second Half of the 19th Century. The Emergence of the K.C.', in *LBI Year Book III* (1958), pp. 122–139. It ought to be stressed, however, that duelling never was the foremost aim of Jewish students' organisations.

[7]Asch and Philippson, *loc. cit.*, p. 135 note.

[8]*Allgemeine Zeitung des Judenthums*, LV, No. 11 (15th March 1891), Gemeindebote, p. 2 (and family tradition – J.T.).

[9]*Jüdische Presse*, No. 51 (1888), pp. 201f.

[10]*Israelitisches Gemeindeblatt*, (Köln–) Mülheim (1891), p. 100.

[11]*Ibid.*, p. 171.

[12]E.g. *Jüdische Presse*, 1890, pp. 98, 353, 485.

[13]E.g. *Allgemeine Zeitung des Judenthums* (1890) Gemeindebote, No. 29, p. 3.

[14]Yet, two such occurrences in Austria are still mentioned in 1897. Cf. J. Toury 'Self-improvement and Self-defence in Central Europe (1890–1933)', *Yalkut Moreshet*, 42 (1986), pp. 7–54 (in Hebrew). Sources in note 24.

and economic life. One of the more successful speakers was the already mentioned young Jewish Rabbi of Göttingen, Dr. Benno Jacob, and another was Rabbi David in Düsseldorf.[15] But free discussion in the assemblies of the hate-mongers was never completely assured and could only be enforced with non-Jewish help. "Non-Jewish" in this context meaning: more or less organised cadres of progressive, and most often Social Democratic, leanings.

And, in fact, Social Democrats tended to flock to meetings of certain antisemitic groups, in order to utilise the anti-establishment propaganda promulgated there for their own purposes. Sometimes, propagandists of Jewish origin led the Socialists' onslaught,[16] and one of the most successful was the Socialist editor (of the representative Left-wing *Frankfurter Zeitung*) Dr. Max Quarck. Yet, the antisemites soon learned to take care of the trouble by organising strong-arm squads, who either ensured the quick close of the meeting with three rousing cheers to the Emperor and the singing of the anthem, or they left it to the attending police-officers to disperse the meeting as soon as disorder broke out. Anyhow, the co-operation between Jews and Social Democrats against antisemites remained an episode, which – although tried again *in nuce* during the days of the *Reichsbanner Schwarz-Rot-Gold* and the *Eiserne Front*[17] – never became an established part of the fight against antisemitism.

II. THE FIRST ORGANISED STEPS AGAINST ANTISEMITISM

But there were some other instances of non-Jews joining the anti-antisemitic front, and some of them even seem to have arisen without any Jewish involvement. The first occurrence of the latter kind was initiated by an Austrian Catholic member of the legal profession, *Kaiserlicher Rat* Karl Ritter von Kissling of Linz. Kissling did what he felt to be his duty, without apparent contact with the rather timid Jewish community of the town. In the summer of 1889 he founded a local *Verein zur Abwehr des Antisemitismus* (*Abwehrverein*), that seems to have been the first of its kind anywhere in the world, and soon after he established a fortnightly paper, named *Zeitschrift zur Bekämpfung des Antisemitismus* (Verlag Tagwerker, Linz, octavo). The first issue is said to have appeared on 1st July 1889, but as not even *one* of its thirty or more numbers seem to have survived Nazism and war, only a bibliographical note[18] and two hints in German-Jewish papers testify to its existence.

[15] *Ibid.*, pp. 12, 13.
[16] *Ibid.*, pp. 13, 14.
[17] *Ibid.*, pp. 36ff. On the co-operation between C.V. and *Reichsbanner* and the *Eiserne Front* in the Weimar Republic see in detail Arnold Paucker, *Der Jüdische Abwehrkampf gegen Antisemitismus und Nationalsozialismus in den letzten Jahren der Weimarer Republik*, Hamburg 1968, especially chapter VII, 'Kampf gegen den Nationalsozialismus', pp. 110–128 and notes, pp. 275–281.
[18] *Materialien zur landeskundlichen Bibliographie Oberösterreichs* (ed. by Hans Commenda), Linz 1890, p. 353. This item was brought to my attention by my friend and colleague Professor Moshe Mishkinsky of Tel-Aviv University, who was informed of its existence through the good offices of Dr. H. Hautmann, Linz, and Mr. Ortner of the *Zentralkatalog der wissenschaftlichen Bibliotheken Oberösterreichs*, Linz. Through them we were also obligingly furnished with a photocopy of the booklet mentioned below, note 24.

Kissling and his activities were first mentioned in the *Israelitische Gemeinde-Zeitung* of Prague. An essay, appropriately called 'Der Appell', utilised the opportunity of the non-Jewish defence-activities of Kissling and his helpers in order to exhort Jews and non-Jews alike to step up the fight against antisemitism.[19] The second mention of the activities at Linz occurred in a leading article of a provincial Jewish paper in the Rhineland, the *Israelitisches Gemeindeblatt*, Mülheim (IGB), about eight or nine months later,[20] testifying to the fact that "influential Catholic clerics" had persevered in bringing their anti-anti periodical into its second year. But the article is quick to add that their exertions so far had "not brought forth even the least measure of success".[21]

There seems to be a slight discrepancy between the bibliographic facts and the mention of clerical circles behind the Linz venture; for was not Kissling of Linz a rather well-known legal theoretician with several learned books and periodical publications to his credit?[22] By chance, and with the help of learned colleagues,[23] this discrepancy resolves itself in a manner which adds to our knowledge of the first non-Jewish anti-anti organisation. In a booklet published by Kissling[24] a year or more after the demise of his *Zeitschrift zur Bekämpfung des Antisemitismus*, he once more takes up the fight against an anti-Jewish attack of the Conservative-clerical *Linzer Volksblatt*. This booklet lays bare the background of the group around Kissling in its fight against the anti-Jewish tendencies in Catholic circles. And thus the author introduces himself and his friends.[25]

> ". . . Not only do I stand at the head of the *Verein zur Abwehr des Antisemitismus*, but I am – together with my friend, *Consistorialrat* and Professor (emeritus) of Ecclesiastical Law at the Catholic-Theological faculty of Salzburg, Dr. Joseph Schöpf – the moral initiator of the ever-widening spiritual fight against antisemitism . . ."

It stands to reason that the "clerical circles" mentioned in IGB and the theologian Professor Schöpf, declared by Kissling as his co-initiator and co-fighter, are identical. Both belonged to the – albeit rather small – liberal wing of Austrian Catholicism. It only remains questionable, whether the editor of IGB was really in possession of such internal information, or simply equated Catholicism with clericalism, but it is of little consequence in our context and

---

[19] *Israelitische Gemeinde-Zeitung*, Prague, No. 16 (1889). I am grateful to Dr. Gila Fatran, once a student of mine, who in the course of a seminar discovered the article in question and brought it to my attention.

[20] *Israelitisches Gemeindeblatt*, 1890, p. 177 (leading article). The meaning of "second year" is probably the beginning of a new volume early in 1890.

[21] ". . . doch nicht den mindesten Erfolg aufzuweisen hat . . ." *Ibid.*

[22] For bibliographical particulars, cf. i.a. the printed Catalogue of the British Library, s.v. Kissling. A periodical for lawyers edited by Kissling is also mentioned in *Materialien, op. cit.*, p. 353.

[23] As mentioned above, note 18.

[24] Full title *Offenes Schreiben an den Hochwürdigen Herrn Johann Hauser, Redacteur des "Linzer Volksblattes"*, Linz 1893, Verleger: Dr. Karl von Kissling (18 pp.). Contains: 'Euer Hochwürden' (a prologue addressed to J. Hauser, dated: Xmas 1892), signed K.v.Kissling (pp. 3–10); an 'Anhang' (pp. 11–13), containing a full reprint of the offending article, 'Jüdische Irrwege', ex: *Linzer Volksblatt*, No. 293 (1892) and finally a short treatise: 'Schreiben des Pfarrers S . . . an seinen Mitbruder Sch . . .' (pp. 14–18), culminating in the following question and answer: "Kann ein katholischer Geistlicher mit den Antisemiten Hand in Hand gehen?" – "Nie und nimmer." (p. 18).

[25] *Offenes Schreiben*, p. 3.

does not shed additional light on the first anti-anti organisation and its newssheet. But there is one relevant fact that has to be mentioned: whatever the results of Kissling's and Schöpf's local struggle against clerical antisemitism in Salzburg and in Linz – their society took part in the founding of the central Austrian *Verein zur Bekämpfung des Antisemitismus* and Kissling himself was elected as one of the members of the Vienna board at the first general meeting of the *Verein*[26] on 1st June 1891.

III. FIRST INNER-JEWISH CONTROVERSIES ON DEFENCE-STRATEGY

An additional positive contribution may possibly be ascribed to Kissling's circle at Linz. By its mere existence it seems to have fostered an intermittent discussion in some German-Jewish periodicals on ways and means of combating antisemitism, and one of the foremost papers in this respect was the aforementioned IGB, founded in 1888 by the teacher Carl Brisch in Mülheim (= Cologne). Brisch established good contacts with rabbis and teachers, in i.a. Bohemia, as proven by their contributions to his paper. Through them he seems to have been informed of the activities of the Kissling group.

One of the contributions from Bohemia was a lengthy treatise on 'The Social Question in Judaism' by Rabbi Dr. Adolf Kurrein of Teplitz (Bohemia), which touched – albeit in an oblique way – on a moot point in anti-antisemitic ideology. Kurrein's defence was two-fold: Judaism was social in theory and practice, but it had nothing to do with Socialism, let alone anarchism. The latter point was again stressed in a concluding editorial 'Zur Arbeiterbewegung',[27] which pusillanimously shirked the actual issues of the day. The author expressed his utter satisfaction with his findings that during the latest instances of labour-unrest no Jewish mine-owners, or in general, industrial entrepreneurs, were involved and that among the striking miners, carpenters, builders, brewers no Jewish workmen were to be found. Not even the beneficial influence of labour unions or of the (Jewish) Fathers of Socialism was favourably mentioned; and above all, Wilhelm II's new imperial initiative of not prolonging the anti-Socialist emergency-legislation was not accorded a single word of praise. Was the glib editorial – more bourgeois-Liberal in outlook than the Liberal press itself in the way it glanced over all the positive aspects of Social Democracy again becoming a legal mass-movement – really serving the best German-Jewish interest in its struggle against antisemitism? Had not the Socialists already proved themselves in various mass-meetings, especially in the Rhineland and Westphalia, as potential anti-antisemitic allies? But even so, to Brisch and his IGB belongs the merit of having opened the discussion on the politics of

---

[26] So reported in *Jüdische Presse* (1891), pp. 272f. The spelling is erroneously "Kiesling".
[27] *Israelitisches Gemeindeblatt*, 1890, during the whole first quarter of the year. The concluding leader: pp. 122 f.

"Abwehr", notwithstanding the fact that most of his editorials criticised the defence-politics of other circles. Thus, he found fault also with certain proposals of the ultra-Orthodox *Der Israelit*, which had called for the establishment of non-sectarian societies for the propagation of enlightening literature (*Verein zur Verbreitung aufklärender Schriften*),[28] in order to fight antisemitic lies by a concerted distribution of vast quantities of booklets containing an explanation of the Jewish point of view. The IGB, however, was quick to debunk the proposal: "If we start distributing anti-antisemitic literature, our adversaries will certainly be ready to dump their libellous elaborations in still larger quantities . . . [moreover] it is evident that humorous or satiric pamphlets find far more readers than an earnest and solid treatise." (In this context, the author mentions Kissling's fiasco in Linz.)

What then, if not a literary campaign, has Brisch to propose as a positive step against antisemitism? He, personally, seems to be still hemmed-in by the historic Jewish inheritance of "Shtadlanuth" (= intercession) by personalities of weight and influence and puts his trust in their ability to mobilise "the authorities . . . against the breakers of the peace".[29]

Brisch seems to have been one of the old school, and it took him at least half a year to understand the fact that the majority of his readers did not share his outlook. But before he could adjust to a more modern attitude, a change of generations had taken place, i.a. in the oldest and until then most prestigious German-Jewish paper, the *Allgemeine Zeitung des Judenthums* (AZJ), founded in 1837 by Ludwig Philippson and edited by him until his death in December 1889. Soon after, AZJ was taken over by the vigorous Berlin publisher Rudolf Mosse, who installed as acting-editor the Bohemia-born Gustav Karpeles. He was aided by another young immigrant, Albert Katz, and at first the change of the paper's spirit led to some rather erratic digressions, especially in the field of organisational initiatives. For instance, at the same moment that *Der Israelit* and the IGB had locked horns over the question of the "Society for the Propagation of Enlightened Literature", quite a peculiar, although in fact practicable, concept for an anti-antisemitic organisation was propounded in the pages of AZJ. The anonymous propounder is easily identifiable as the Hamburg-born economist and philanthropist Gustav Tuch.[30] In his endeavour to correct some socio-economic observations in another essay dealing with the growth of antisemitism in Hesse,[31] Tuch gives prominence to his idea of a new anti-anti organisation to be created by non-Jews. He even chooses as title for his deliberations the

---

[28]Quoted here according to a verbatim reprint in *Israelitisches Gemeindeblatt*, No. 24 (1890), p. 177.

[29]*Ibid*. The article praises the valiant fight of Drs. J. S. Bloch and Zucker in the Austrian *Reichsrat*, in counter-distinction to the German-Jewish parliamentarians, who remain silent in the face of antisemitic provocations. With his plea for Jewish intercessors he possibly alludes to Gerson von Bleichröder and Professor Moritz Lazarus, who however did not prevail with Emperor Wilhelm I. The new Emperor Wilhelm II had not yet established his circle of "Kaiserjuden".

[30]Tuch's obituary with biographical notes in *Allgemeine Zeitung des Judenthums* 1909, pp. 76f.

[31]'Entstehung und Bedeutung des Antisemitismus in Hessen', by Rabbi I. Rülf of Memel, *Allgemeine Zeitung des Judenthums*, LIV, Nos. 19, 20 (1890); also as separate booklet, Mainz 1890, 30 pp.

provocative caption 'Philosemitism vs. Antisemitism'.[32] In the operative clause near the end of the second essay Tuch advocates the formation of a *"Philosemiten-Bund* in conjunction with all those who are willing to join us in the fulfilment of the most noble duty, the love of humanity . . . If we succeed in bringing them together, it will mean first and foremost the defeat of antisemitism."

No specific response to Tuch's articles is known, although it seems obvious that the first contacts towards the establishment of the German *Verein zur Abwehr des Antisemitismus* must have taken place just in the period of their publication.[33] In any case, another contribution to the anti-anti deliberations in the pages of AZJ does not soar into the realm of humanitarianism, but sticks to the small vicissitudes of the day-to-day struggle against Jew-baiters. Its author was Arnold Budwig, one of the then leaders of the *Deutsch-Israelitischer Gemeindebund* (DIGB). In his article,[34] Budwig advocates the relentless daily refutation of even the smallest inaccuracy by anti-Jewish speakers and writers; for if each deviation from the truth is not instantly branded as a lie and immediately rectified, the antisemitic propaganda-mechanism tends to grab it as its own, in order to promote it as "an incontestable fact (*unbestrittene Tatsache*) from now to eternity".

These words of Budwig might have sounded far more impressive and convincing, if his organisation had acted on an earlier and somewhat similar proposal from Hesse in the same paper,[35] asking the DIGB to train and dispatch "roving troubleshooters" to antisemitic strong-points, and generally as discussants (*Reiseprediger*) in public meetings. Somewhat later, another proposal from Hesse, addressed to Brisch's IGB, urged the establishment of "societies for legal protection" (*Rechtsschutzvereine*) by and for Jewish businessmen, in order to repulse the antisemitic calumniation of Jewish merchants and their shops.[36] However, Brisch's editorial policy of "wait and see" was upheld for him by an anonymous contributor ("Felix"),[37] who from a legal point of view explained all the difficulties and ambiguities inherent in the Prusso-German judicial and constitutional system, which made it almost impossible to defend Judaism as a collective entity – i.a. because of the Jewish organisations' lack of legal authorisation to act as plenipotentiaries for individuals – obstacles which the *Österreichisch-Israelitische Union* (ÖIU) in Vienna (and later the *Centralverein deutscher Staatsbürger jüdischen Glaubens* [C.V.] in Germany) would experience to their chagrin only too thoroughly .

In all, the above summary of the first public discussion on *Abwehrarbeit* in 1890, sketches a surprisingly clear outline of most of the basic concepts and problems of the later organised defence-activities against antisemitism.

---

[32]'Philosemitismus contra Antisemitismus' ("Hamburg, im Juni"), *Allgemeine Zeitung des Judenthums*, LIV, Nos. 23, 24 (1890). Quotations from p. 324.

[33]On the founding of the *Abwehrverein*, cf. below, note 40.

[34]Leader: 'Tatarennachrichten', signed A.B. (=Arnold Budwig), *Allgemeine Zeitung des Judenthums*, LIV, No. 29 (1890).

[35]*Allgemeine Zeitung des Judenthums*, LIV (1890), Gemeindebote, April 19th, p. 3.

[36]*Israelitisches Gemeindeblatt*, No. 4 (1891). The authorship of a Hessian Jew is mentioned, *ibid.*, p. 50.

[37]*Israelitisches Gemeindeblatt*, Nos. 5–7 (1891).

IV. SOME EARLY PRACTICAL STEPS IN GERMANY

However, one of the most curious occurrences in the development of the first practical steps aimed at combating antisemitism is their sudden emergence at different and far-flung places, seemingly without connection to one another and apparently also without relation to the discussions in the Jewish press.

Thus, the next practical anti-defamatory venture appears, so to speak, out of the blue in the far north, at Danzig. There, as in Linz, the initiator was a non-Jew, the printer and editor A. W. Kafemann. No other person is mentioned by name as belonging to the Danzig "group of men who act, according to the dictate of their conscience, in the best interest of the public weal and with personal sacrifices". Thus they introduced themselves in the foreword to the bound edition of their anti-anti oeuvre, the *Antisemiten-Spiegel* (first instalment: Danzig-Gdańsk, September 1890 – two further instalments 1891, 1892).[38] Only some paltry facts could so far be ascertained on Kafemann and his printshop: besides the *Antisemiten-Spiegel*, bibliographical and other references ascribe to him until 1891 just two items: the 'Kultus- und Gebetsordnung' for the "New Synagogue" at Danzig (1888)[39] and a series of *Anschauungsbilder* for the classroom, entitled, 'The Seasons'. From the first item Kafemann's connection with Jewish circles emerges beyond doubt. Moreover, insofar as he needed Jewish advice for his first instalment of the *Antisemiten-Spiegel*, it appears rather obvious that his primary adviser was none other than the rabbi of the *Neue Synagoge*, Dr. Cosman Werner (later of Munich). Somewhat more problematical is the connection between Kafemann's publication and the German *Verein zur Abwehr des Antisemitismus*, which was still *in statu nascendi*, when the first instalment of the *Antisemiten-Spiegel* made its appearance. But at least *ex post facto* such a connex has been established:[40] One of the *Abwehrverein*'s most active members of latter years, the writer Ludwig Jacobowski, after a private anti-anti venture of his, on which see below, is mentioned in passing as one of the contributors to the *Antisemiten-Spiegel*, probably to the second and third instalments.[41] Moreover, in the same context Kafemann's publication is pertly characterised as "the *Abwehrverein*'s handbook". But it is beyond doubt that the first instalment predates the *Abwehrverein* by at least three months, whereas the later issues definitely benefited from material and spiritual help of the *Abwehrverein*.

At the onset of the year 1891, still another anti-anti paper was published, which predated the *Abwehrverein*, or at least coincided with its foundation. From January 1891 a Berlin weekly entitled *Wahrheit und Gerechtigkeit* was put together

---

[38]The Jewish papers reacted only in October, mostly with short commendatory notices. But in the preface to the bound edition of all three instalments (Danzig 1892, [2]1900), the editor states that the first issue appeared in summer 1890. The date given above (September) is a compromise, and so is the title. The first instalments were hyphenated (*Antisemiten-Spiegel*), but later the title was contracted into one word (*Antisemitenspiegel*).

[39]Samuel Echt, *Die Geschichte der Juden in Danzig*, Leer/Ostfriesland 1972, p. 62; and cf. the bibliography quoted below, note 43, s.v.Kafemann.

[40]A well-documented paper on the *Abwehrverein* has been published by Barbara Suchy, in *LBI Year Books XXVIII, XXX* (1983, 1985), The above reference in vol. *XXVIII*, pp. 205f.

[41]*Ibid.*, p. 215.

by F. P. Huber. On Huber and his weekly even less is known than on Kafemann. Huber declared that he wanted to combat "antisemitism, together with other cancerous growths of present times". From No. 2 on, he printed a series of articles on the Talmud, written "with quite a store of knowledge".[42] But it is not known, who his Jewish helpers were. As far as ascertainable from Huber's additional publications,[43] he seems to have been a teacher, or at least a man of pedagogic interests, his outlook being liberal and anti-clerical in scope. It is not known how long he managed to keep his anti-anti paper alive, but although not a single issue has so far come to light, it seems to have lasted for almost a year. A connection between Huber and the *Abwehrverein* could not be established, but is by no means impossible (as will be proven by his successor Karl Schneidt).

As the emergence and development of the *Abwehrverein* has been exhaustively researched and documented,[44] it remains for us to sketch some of the Jewish reactions to its foundation and to other anti-anti activities mentioned so far. It was again Carl Brisch's *Gemeindeblatt* from Mülheim, which – in a correspondence from Berlin[45] – expressed open scepticism, both with regard to Kafemann's or Huber's publications and to the *Abwehrverein*. The correspondent criticised their limited appeal: as long as the papers reached only a preponderantly Jewish public, as proven by the list of their subscribers, their impact would be nil; and the *Abwehrverein* would immediately lose its appeal to the general public if Jewish membership grew in number and influence. Jews should therefore refrain from joining the *Abwehrverein* (in fact, the Vienna *Abwehrverein* barely avoided a decision to exclude Jewish membership!).

It is remarkable that the *Allgemeine Zeitung des Judenthums*, whose editor, Karpeles, had joyfully greeted[46] the establishment of the *Abwehrverein*, some weeks later printed an unsigned leader, in which – quite similar to the correspondence in IGB – antisemitism was characterised as stultifying, brutal and *unteachable*.[47] "Consequently, neither polemics, nor lamentations, nay, not even scientific proof are of value. It is almost impossible to fight an adversary who does not *want* to be taught and is not choosy in his methods. There remains no way but to pass by him in silence, hoping and trusting that the invincible power of *truth* shall finally overcome even the thick fog of hate-incited antisemitism."

A more favourable and optimistic note was sounded by the Orthodox *Jüdische Presse*, whose editor, Hirsch Hildesheimer, was one of the most dedicated public spokesmen against antisemitism. In his paper, he warmly recommended the *Antisemiten-Spiegel* and especially praised an essay in its second issue, entitled

---

[42]All the information is contained in a short review, *Allgemeine Zeitung des Judenthums*, LV, Gemeindebote, No. 5 (16th January 1891), p. 1.

[43]*Gesamtverzeichnis des deutschen Schrifttums 1700–1910*, vol. 65, Munich 1982, s. v. Huber F. P. (no more); *Dogmenlose Sittenlehre für Schule und Haus*, Berlin 1892; *In letzter Stunde. Offenes Sendschreiben bezüglich des Volksschulgesetzentwurfes* etc., Berlin 1892; *Mein letztes Wort über den Jesuitenorden*, [Berlin?] 1895.

[44]Suchy, as in note 40.

[45]*Israelitisches Gemeindeblatt*, 1891, p. 61.

[46]*Allgemeine Zeitung des Judenthums*, LV, No. 4 (1891), leading article signed G.K. (=Gustav Karpeles).

[47]*Allgemeine Zeitung des Judenthums*, LV (1891), pp. 121f., unsigned leader. Quotation from p. 122.

'The Dark Schemes of the Jew Montefiore', which refuted alleged plans for Jewish "World Domination".[48] But this was only a first trial-balloon of the new antisemitic horror-propaganda, featuring 'The Final Plans of Jewry', as propounded in an alleged speech by a "Grand Rabbin" in Theodor Fritsch's newssheet. Here, the *Abwehrverein* for the first time entered the fracas with its first leaflet destined for mass propaganda,[49] and Hildesheimer's *Jüdische Presse* gave its argumentation due prominence. Not only did the leaflet (and Hildesheimer's report on it) denounce the fictitious character of the speech, but also its source was exactly stated as a "low-brow novel" (published in Berlin, 1868) by Hermann Goedsche, alias John Retcliff, who "reported" a midnight meeting of thirteen Jewish "spirits", *quasi* "Sanhedrin" amidst the tombstones of "the Jewish cemetery of Prague" – a phantasy that later became known the world over as the "Protocols of the Elders of Zion".

Yet, the meritorious leaflet of the *Abwehrverein* and Hildesheimer's jubilant endorsement of its contents remained utterly devoid of public resonance. It is really amazing that such a canard, immediately and ably refuted as a rather primitive phantasy, thrived in the decades to come as a centrepiece of world antisemitism and has not been extirpated up to today, despite scores of trials and hundred of printed denouements. Does this not hint that Hirsch Hildesheimer's favourable comment on the positive influence of the *Abwehrverein* – and all the other organisations of similar character – was over-optimistic, or even misplaced?

V. AN ACTIVIST ORGANISATION?*

Yet, there still remained sufficient numbers of believers in the possibility of active measures of defence against anti-Jewish propaganda tactics. One of the believers was Carl Küchenmeister of Berlin, like Kafemann the owner of a printing shop. Küchenmeister – as might be gleaned from some bibliographical references[50] – seems to have dabbled in psychology and what was later called "public relations". Thus, it is perhaps possible that he was activated by some Jewish friends, for instance, the writer Ludwig Jacobowski, who just in 1891 had published his first really successful novel, *Werther der Jude*, which vacillated "between severe criticism" of his Jewish co-religionists and "defiant reaffirmation of his Judaism".[51] But a Berlin correspondent of AZJ asserted by

[48]*Jüdische Presse*, 1891, p. 93, editor's footnote.
[49]*Jüdische Presse*, 1891, pp. 92f. The price of the leaflets was quoted in a footnote as follows: 100 for 0.50 Mk.; 1000 for 4,50 Mk., obtainable at the offices of the *Abwehrverein*.
*The apparent overlapping of this essay with the contribution by Jacob Borut would seem to present a challenge to the student of history both in general direction and as to individual facts. There are certain discrepancies which invite further investigation, which would in turn advance our knowledge of the subject matter as a whole – (Ed.).
[50]*Gesamtverzeichnis, op. cit.* (note 43), s. v. Küchenmeister Carl.
[51]Schorsch (as in note 4), p. 95. And cf. the literary analysis of Fred. B. Stern, in *Bulletin des Leo Baeck Instituts*, No. 26 (1964), pp. 101ff.

inference that the initiator of the new anti-antisemitic venture was Küchenmeister himself, while Jacobowski seems to have been won over by him as his star orator. In any case, Küchenmeister and Jacobowski proceeded from the fact, established by previous experience,[52] that no free discussion was possible in the meetings convened by antisemites. Therefore, it was now decided to organise anti-antisemitic assemblies, in which – it was hoped – the initiative ought to rest with the forces of law and order. But already the first attempt by Küchenmeister seems to have failed (end of December 1891), probably because it was an entirely private venture, and thus he arrived at his organisational solution:[53] the founding of a *Vereinigung zur Bekämpfung der Rassenhetze*.

This new association introduced itself with an open meeting on 6th January 1892, in which for the first time Jacobowski was scheduled as central speaker. But instead of an orderly discussion, the antisemites were intent on disrupting the procedure and ridiculing the speakers. Finally, bedlam broke out and the assembly was closed by the police. In consequence, the *Vereinigung* decided to give access to its further meetings to holders of valid invitations only. But apparently, this security measure could not be enforced, and anyhow the meetings became less frequent and less turbulent. Among the scheduled speakers were mostly journalists and young writers, of whom at least one – F. Schupp – was not a Jew; but all of them seem to have been systematically heckled by the public.

The first to lose heart was the founder, Küchenmeister, and in April a new chairman was elected in his stead. This was the writer Karl Schneidt,[54] who in January 1892 had founded a new anti-anti weekly newsletter named *Die Schmach des Jahrhunderts*,[55] which took the place of F. P. Huber's defunct *Wahrheit und Gerechtigkeit*. A Jewish source hailed Schneidt's newssheet as the initiation of a new "Kulturkampf", whose praiseworthy aim was the exposure of the anti-semitic "witch-hunt".[56]

Schneidt, like Jacobowski, was very active in publishing refutations of the propaganda slogans, with which the then most notorious antisemite, Hermann Ahlwardt, established his short-lived fame as "Rektor aller Deutschen" (1891/ 1892). Both, Schneidt and Jacobowski had also enrolled as members of the *Abwehrverein*, but whereas Jacobowski became one of its central figures until his untimely demise in 1900, Schneidt and his newssheet started criticising the policies of the *Abwehrverein* and its newly-founded *Mitteilungen*, which were soon

---

[52]Cf. above, text & notes 14, 15.

[53]This chronology is based on a correspondence from Berlin, *Allgemeine Zeitung des Judenthums*, LVI (1892), Gemeindebote, No. 3, p. 2. On the whole development of the "Vereinigung zur Bekämpfung der Rassenhetze" cf. also the small notices, *ibid.*, Nos. 2–7, 12, 18.

[54]Karl Schneidt was born near Saarbrücken in 1854; he lived near Berlin (Strausberg) and was for a time the editor of the Berlin *Tribüne*. Cf. *Gesamtverzeichnis, op. cit.* (note 43), vol. 128. He published quite a large number of novels and plays, also at least one pamphlet against Social Democracy (1892). *Ibid.*, having in his youth adhered to its tenets.

[55]Reported as a pithy saying of (the then Crown Prince) Friedrich III in an audience granted to town-councillor Meir Magnus.

[56]Both expressions in praise of Schneidt and his paper in *Allgemeine Zeitung des Judenthums*, LVI (1892), Gemeindebote, No. 4, p. 1 and No. 18, p. 4.

to overshadow Schneidt's *Schmach des Jahrhunderts*. The altercation was not free
from personal friction between Schneidt and the very active secretary of the
Abwehrverein, Graebner. Moreover, Schneidt started collecting contributions
from his readers, which – as Graebner averred – were often destined for the
coffers of the *Abwehrverein*.[57] But even so, Schneidt barely managed to bring his
paper to the end of the year 1892. Needless to say, under this chairmanship the
Vereinigung zur Bekämpfung der Rassenhetze did not regain its strength and already
during the summer of 1892 it seems to have dwindled away.

When one evaluates these first attempts at fighting antisemitism, it becomes
clear that their social and ideological base was very small, indeed. Liberal
intellectuals or semi-intellectuals of good will and of a certain obstinate
singularity of mind took up an almost quixotic attempt to tilt with the brittle
lance of reason against the flailing windmills of prejudice and hate. They did not
take into account that rabble-rousers like Bernard Foerster, Liebermann von
Sonnenberg, Böckel, Hermann Ahlwardt and their successors mattered only
insofar as they helped prepare the soil for the firm implantation of antisemitism
in party-politics and in the socio-psychological makeup of most political parties,
and especially of all the Conservatives, the Junkers and the higher and highest
echelons of the military and civil hierarchy. And very soon, a first decisive
victory of antisemitism had to be registered in the form of an *Arierparagraph* in the
so-called "Tivoliprogramm" of the Conservative Party (December 1892). From
the programmatic step of the representative National-German Right-wing party
it must have become clear, that the first round in the struggle against
antisemitism had ended with a stinging rebuff to the anti-antisemitic forces,
whoever they might have been.

As immediate follow-up in the anti-anti campaign, the founding of the
Centralverein deutscher Staatsbürger jüdischen Glaubens was achieved. It rang in a
second round of the bout. After the failure of the first non-Jewish or mixed
endeavours, the Jewish character of this stage of the fight undoubtedly became
the most conspicuous aspect of the struggle. But as no other spectacular
innovation arose together with the founding of the C.V., the prognosis for a
successful outcome of the struggle against antisemitism was indeed not too
sanguine.

[57]These facts are gleaned from the one and only issue of the paper that could be located in the *Stadt-
und Universitätsbibliothek Frankfurt a. Main*, namely No. 21, dated 8th November 1892. Another issue
(No. 16) is catalogued at the Wiener Library, but could not be located.

The Rise of Jewish Defence Agitation in Germany, 1890–1895: A Pre-History of the C.V.?

Much of the modern research dealing with German Jewry[1] concerns itself with the central organisation of that Jewry for the Second *Reich* up to the Nazi period – the *Centralverein deutscher Staatsbürger jüdischen Glaubens*, known as the C.V.[2]

Most historians[3] described the founding of the C.V. as a "major change", some even as a "Wendepunkt"[4] in the political and organisational history of German Jewry. The C.V. marked a shift from a passive, sometimes even submissive, political attitude to a self-conscious "Jewish Activism". Before 1893 the Jews avoided taking a public stand against antisemitism.* They preferred to keep silent, believing that it would disappear by itself with the inevitable progress of society. In the meantime, one should not stand up in public as a Jew, because that would only add credence to antisemitic charges that Jews were a separate group that had not integrated into German society.

The C.V. acted in a completely different way. Its leaders were convinced that Jews could and should combat antisemitism publicly, "Im Lichte der Öffentlichkeit",[5] without fear of identifying themselves openly as Jews protecting their own interests.

---

[1] I would like to thank Prof. Michael Graetz, Prof. Moshe Zimmermann and Dr. Henry Wassermann for their help and advice in preparing this article. The kind financial assistance provided by the Leo Baeck Institute in Jerusalem, the Warburg Foundation, the Memorial Foundation in New York, the R. Koebner Chair of German History at the Hebrew University, Jerusalem, and the *Deutscher Akademischer Austauschdienst* helped in meeting the costs involved in the research.

[2] An annotated bibliography of the C.V. is to be found in Arnold Paucker, 'Die Abwehr des Antisemitismus in den Jahren 1893–1933', in Herbert A. Strauss, Norbert Kampe (eds.), *Antisemitismus. Von der Judenfeindschaft zum Holocaust*, Bonn 1984, pp. 164–171; and see *idem*, 'Zur Problematik einer jüdischen Abwehrstrategie in der deutschen Gesellschaft', in *Juden im Wilhelminischen Deutschland 1890–1914*. Ein Sammelband herausgegeben von Werner E. Mosse unter Mitwirkung von Arnold Paucker, Tübingen 1976 (Schriftenreihe wissenschaftlicher Abhandlungen des Leo Baeck Instituts 33), pp. 479–548.

[3] Ismar Schorsch, *Jewish Reactions to German Anti-Semitism 1870–1914*, New York 1972; Jehuda Reinharz, *Fatherland or Promised Land. The Dilemma of the German Jew 1893–1914*, Ann Arbor 1975; Marjorie Lamberti, *Jewish Activism in Imperial Germany. The Struggle for Civil Equality*, New Haven 1978; Sanford Ragins, *Jewish Responses to Anti-Semitism in Germany 1870–1914*, Cincinnati 1980.

[4] Paucker, 'Abwehr', *loc. cit.*, p. 146. Lamberti, *op. cit.*, calls it: "The most important event in the history of German Jewry" between "the Emancipation and the Holocaust", p. 176.

* In conjunction with this contribution see also the preceding essay by Jacob Toury, 'Anti-Anti 1889/1892', in this volume of the Year Book – (Ed.).

[5] This important slogan of the C.V. was emphasised already in its first *Aufrufe*. See *Allgemeine Zeitung des Judenthums*, LVII, No. 21 (26th May 1893), Gemeindebote (Gb.), p. 1; *Aufruf* in Central Archives for the History of the Jewish People (CAHJP) TD/24, esp. p. 6. It was constantly repeated in its publications, and described as the main characteristic of the C.V.'s activity in comparison with

This major change is mainly attributed to the rise of antisemitism, and especially the acceptance of the Tivoli programme by the Conservative Party (December 1892).[6] But the fact remains that Jews had suddenly started acting in a manner that would indeed confirm accusations about their unwillingness to integrate. The C.V., as one historian noted, "was emphasising the value of precisely those attributes that had in 1870 been regarded as obstacles to German Jews becoming Jewish Germans",[7] and Jews organising publicly for defence was one of those obstacles. One might logically expect that Jews in 1893 would not supply more ammunition to their enemies, especially as there existed a Christian organisation against antisemitism – the *Verein zur Abwehr des Antisemitismus*.

According to modern research, the all-important change in Jewish strategy was initiated by a small group of Berlin Jews: the founders of the C.V. It was this group that had re-moulded the political perception of the Jews and caused them to abandon their former passivity.[8]

This article aims to show that active Jewish defence did not begin in Berlin with the founding of the C.V., but several years before, and that new defence efforts took place not only in Berlin, but in different parts of the *Reich*. This is demonstrated by an examination of Jewish local responses to antisemitic politics – a field little studied so far. Thus we hope to help in filling what one historian recently called "a gap in knowledge", partly caused by the concentration on "organisational and ideological responses by Jews at the national level", with little or no attention given to "local responses to concrete antisemitic episodes".[9]

Moreover, we claim that the major change in Jewish public behaviour which took place during those years was not merely a reaction to the continuing growth of antisemitism, but a more complicated process of readjustment to a new kind of politics developing in Germany at that time. Jews chose to defend their interests publicly because this was exactly what other groups were doing by then. Hence, Jews could indeed defend themselves without appearing to be "different" and unwilling to integrate.

Before continuing I would like to explain the choice of the term "defence

---

earlier defence efforts. See also Wilhelm Levinger, 'Abwehr des Antisemitismus', *Jüdisches Lexikon*, Berlin 1927, vol. 1, col. 66, and Ragins, *op. cit.*, p. 87.
[6]On the "Tivoliprogramm" see Paul W. Massing, *Rehearsal for Destruction. A Study of Political Antisemitism in Imperial Germany*, New York 1949, pp. 60–68; Peter Pulzer, *The Rise of Political Anti-Semitism in Germany and Austria*, New York 1964, [2]1988, pp. 119–120; Werner Jochmann, 'Struktur und Funktion des deutschen Antisemitismus 1878–1914', in Strauss, Kampe (eds.), *op. cit.*, pp. 129–130.
[7]Peter Pulzer, 'Why was there a Jewish Question in Imperial Germany?', in *LBI Year Book XXV* (1980), p. 142.
[8]See especially Lamberti, *op. cit.*, chap. 2.
[9]David Peal, 'Jewish Responses to German Antisemitism. The Case of the Böckel Movement, 1887–1894', *Jewish Social Studies*, XLVIII, Nos. 3–4 (Summer–Fall 1986), p. 269. For one study that does deal with that subject see Jacob Toury, 'Self-Improvement and Self-Defence in Central Europe (1890–1933)', *Yalkut Moreshet*, 42 (1986), pp. 7–54 (in Hebrew). Orthodox responses were discussed by Mordechai Breuer, 'The Reaction of German Orthodoxy to Antisemitism', in Shmuel Almog *et al.* (eds.), *Israel and the Nations. Essays presented in Honor of Shmuel Ettinger*, Jerusalem 1987, pp. 185–213 (in Hebrew), and in his *Jüdische Orthodoxie im Deutschen Reich 1871–1918. Sozialgeschichte einer religiösen Minderheit*, Frankfurt a. Main 1987, Veröffentlichung des Leo Baeck Instituts, pp. 301–316.

agitation" for the activities about to be explored. The term most commonly used by German Jews in the 1880s and 1890s to specify that kind of defence is "energische Abwehr" or "energische Vertheidigung". "Agitation" is another term used and its characteristics: "Eine Agitation wird regelmässig durch öffentliche Reden in Versammlungen und durch die Presse, durch Flugblätter, Verteilung von Wahlzetteln u. dgl. betrieben".[10] This term was derived from the time of the French Revolution, designating the kind of activity performed by revolutionary spokesmen. In the second half of the nineteenth century it was used mostly to denote Socialist propaganda. The term "Agitator" retained strong negative connotations even by the beginning of the twentieth century. The terms "Agitation" and "Agitieren", however, had lost their negative meanings by the end of the nineteenth century.[11]

Therefore, "agitation" seems a proper term to describe Jewish defence activities carried by public means such as open rallies or the distribution of leaflets. The term "agitator", which even today retains a negative connotation, was not used for the Jews who performed defence agitation. I chose to call them "defence activists", emphasising their break with former passivity towards antisemitism.

About the time researched: the years 1890–1895 constitute a specific period, or cycle, concerning that type of activity, as can be seen from Tables D and F in Appendixes I and II, respectively. The reasons for this will be discussed later.

I. TRADITIONAL REACTIONS TO ANTISEMITISM

It would be incorrect to claim that there was no active Jewish defence against antisemitism before 1890. Anti-Jewish propaganda did not remain unanswered, and in particular the "great debate" of 1880–1881 produced a significant number of responses against Stoecker and Treitschke, some of them by leading Jewish intellectuals.[12] We can identify several Jews who advocated, and sometimes financially supported, endeavours to combat antisemitism through distribution of defence literature. Some of them were in prominent positions, as, for instance, Moritz Lazarus, a respected Jewish scholar and public leader,[13] and member of the *Repräsentantenversammlung* of the Berlin community.

---

[10]*Meyers Konversations-Lexikon*, vol. I, Leipzig–Wien 1896, col. 203.

[11]See the article 'Agitator', in O. Ladendorf, *Historisches Schlagwörterbuch*, Strassburg – Berlin 1906, p. 2.

[12]See Michael Meyer, 'Great Debate on Antisemitism. Jewish Reaction to New Hostility in Germany 1879–1881', in *LBI Year Book XI* (1966), pp. 137–170. A description of some of the lesser-known writings surrounding that debate is found in Johann de le Roi, 'Neuere Litteratur über die Judenfrage', *Nathanael*, 3 (1887), pp. 65–89. (I thank Alan Levinson for bringing that source to my attention.) Some of the writings were reproduced in Walter Boehlich (ed.), *Der Berliner Antisemitismusstreit*, Frankfurt a. Main 1965.

[13]On Lazarus see Ingrid Belke (ed.), *Moritz Lazarus und Heymann Steinthal. Die Begründer der Völkerpsychologie in ihren Briefen*, vol. I, Tübingen 1971 (Schriftenreihe wissenschaftlicher Abhandlungen des Leo Baeck Instituts 21), pp. XIV–LXXX.

But the efforts of a few activists did not change the general picture, and the rising tide of antisemitism did not meet a resolute Jewish response. The brochures written in 1880–1881 proved to be one-time efforts, and almost all their authors avoided taking further steps against antisemitism. An attempt by the *Deutsch-Israelitischer Gemeindebund* to fight antisemitism by legal action did not arouse interest in Jewish ranks.[14]

This passivity was led by the Jewish elites, that is, community and social leaders, and also the few Jews who had gained prominence in the German political and social arena.[15] Members of these groups were among the main proponents of Jewish assimilation in German society. When they were faced with antisemitism, they declined fighting it as Jews, as that would appear to be an "Absonderung". They also held strong Liberal convictions, including a belief in the inevitability of progress.[16] Antisemitism they considered to be a reactionary, outmoded phenomenon, which would disappear by itself as society progressed. For those reasons, the Jewish leadership preferred to ignore antisemitism rather than fight it.

This was illustrated when Ludwig Philippsohn, editor of the *Allgemeine Zeitung des Judenthums*, tried to create a framework for defence in 1880/1881. He wrote to the leaders of the big communities, then to the leaders of the bigger provincial communities, imploring them to begin talks aimed at establishing such a framework. But his pleas were rejected or ignored.[17]

Early calls for a change in defence methods[18] found no response. The few Jews and Christians who tried to fight back found themselves isolated and lacking support. Franz Delitzsch, a Christian clergyman who tried to discredit antisemitic slanders against Judaism,[19] complained bitterly in his private correspondence about lack of interest in his pamphlets.[20]

This goes to show that the passivity we encounter was not limited to the elites, but shared by the majority of the Jewish population, as is also illustrated by the

---

[14]See Schorsch, *op. cit.*, pp. 39–47.

[15]I cannot discuss here the subject of Jewish elites and their composition, recruiting pattern etc. See Jacob Toury's important article, 'Zur Problematik der jüdischen Führungsschichten im deutschsprachigen Raum 1880–1933', *Tel Aviver Jahrbuch für Deutsche Geschichte*, XVI (1987), pp. 251–281.

[16]On this assumption as a part of the Liberal creed from its inception see Dieter Langewiesche, *Liberalismus in Deutschland*, Frankfurt a. Main 1988, pp. 20–21.

[17]*Allgemeine Zeitung des Judenthums*, XLIV, No. 46 (16th November 1880), p.723; XLV, No. 39 (27th September 1881), p. 637; XLV (11th October 1881), pp. 669–670.

[18]For one interesting, far-sighted call by a provincial teacher see *Der Israelit*, XXI, No. 1 (7th January 1880), p. 6. I did not refer to the anti-antisemitic activities of Jewish students, as they consisted during the 1880s of nothing more than duels against antisemitic students. This is well attested by memories of old *Viadrina* members. See, for example, *K. C. Blätter*, II, No. 1 (1st October 1911), p. 6. See also Benno Jacob's article (in note 100), p. 49, where Jacob – a founder and active member of the *Viadrina*, wrote that prior to 1892, he never attended an antisemitic meeting, and had no clue to what the speaker was going to say, nor any literary materials to counter him.

[19]On Delitzsch see *Neue Deutsche Biographie*, vol. III, Berlin 1957, pp. 581–582.

[20]See his letters to Lazarus, Jewish National and University Library (JNUL) DCM, Ms. Var. 298/94, Delitzsch letters, No. 4 (17th February 1881), No. 11 (5th January 1883).

fate of the *Jüdisches Comité vom 1. Dezember 1880*,[21] a defence organisation founded by Moritz Lazarus and led by a group of Berlin Jewish notables.

The *Comité*, and Lazarus himself, distributed throughout the country a brochure containing two speeches by Lazarus,[22] apparently in order to enlist support for their cause. The answers sent to Lazarus[23] show that none of the recipients had even considered acting personally against antisemitism. An echo of Lazarus's feelings can be found in one of those letters. Sigmund Maybaum, then still in Saaz (Hungary), praised Lazarus for his speeches, but asked for "permission to keep silent" about their contents. Alongside that sentence, a remark was pencilled: "Sehr Bequem!".[24]

In April 1881 the *Comité* organised a big public meeting of Jewish war veterans, as a protest against antisemitic accusations that Jews were avoiding army service.[25] In the meeting, a resolution was put forward, protesting against the accusations, without even mentioning who was behind them. But the organisers met with tough opposition. Two leading members of the Berlin community came to the meeting in order to voice their resentment of the organisation's strategy. They brought speeches declaring that antisemites should be answered only by contempt, not by resolutions. The "self glorification" in the form of the proposed resolution was pointless.

A very heated debate ensued, and the meeting split into two camps, between whom there was, according to one reporter, a "grelle Dissonanz". Then came the vote, and the resolution proposed by the *Comité* was defeated by a large majority. After that failure, the *Comité* withdrew into the background and avoided any public activity.

Although practically all the editors of the Jewish press had supported the calls for a more intensive and public defence effort, they could not arouse the Jewish public (most of whom were not such keen readers of Jewish papers) from its apathy. Jewish public opinion was not prepared for an activist defence. It was the elites, mainly the leaders of the big communities, that were blocking the few defence efforts, with most of the Jewish population complying with their standpoint that antisemitism should not be fought, especially not publicly, by Jews.

---

[21]See Schorsch, *op. cit.*, pp. 59–65; Ragins, *op. cit.*, pp. 33–35. I deal more extensively with this organisation in Chapter 2 of my *A New Spirit among our Brethren in Ashkenaz. German Jewry in the Face of Economical, Social and Political Changes in the Reich at the End of the 19th Century*, unpubl. diss., Hebrew University of Jerusalem 1991.

[22]*Unser Standpunkt*, Berlin 1880. The speeches were reprinted in Moritz Lazarus, *Treu und Frei*, Leipzig 1887, pp. 115–155.

[23]They survived in his archive at the JNUL/DCM. A few were published by Ingrid Belke, 'Liberal Voices on Antisemitism in the 1880s. Letters to Moritz Lazarus, 1880–1883', in *LBI Year Book* XXIII (1978), pp. 61–87.

[24]JNUL/DCM, Ms. Var. 298–94.

[25]On the meeting: *Allgemeine Zeitung des Judenthums*, XLV, No. 15 (12th April 1881), pp. 239–240; *Israelitische Wochenschrift*, XII, No. 14 (6th April 1881), pp. 121–122; *Der Israelit*, XXVII, No. 14 (6th April 1881), pp. 341–343.

II. THE BACKGROUND FOR CHANGE: SOCIO-ECONOMIC AND POLITICAL DEVELOPMENTS

Before examining the profound changes in Jewish defence in the early 1890s, one must understand the developments that took place in German politics during that period, as well as the changes in the socio-economic sphere that were their cause.[26]

In the second half of the nineteenth century, and including up to 1914, Germany had undergone a process of massive industrialisation, unequalled in the West.[27] Its industrial output grew at a tremendous pace. Between 1880 and 1913 coal production in Germany had risen by about 290% (compared with a rise of 80.4% in England); pig-iron production increased by about 390% (13.3% in England); and steel production by no less than 1,335%. Germany's share in overall world production of these goods rose from 14.6% to 25.2%, making it second only to the USA.

Following industrialisation came comprehensive social changes,[28] connected with the process of urbanisation and a revolution in communication possibilities. Inner migration, as people moved from the country to expanding industrial towns, transformed German society from rural-agricultural to urban. The percentage of people living in cities with more than 100,000 inhabitants grew from 7.7 in 1852 to 53.2 in 1910. Corresponding changes occurred in the occupational structure, as the numbers of the employed in industry and crafts overtook the number of those living off agriculture, while the percentage of occupation in commerce and communications leaped between 1843 and 1907 from 1.9 to 13.7.

In 1847, the length of the Prussian railway network stood at 2,754 km. By 1875 it was 16,169 km. The "Verkehrsrevolution" which took place all over Germany was a part of a wide process by which newspapers, periodicals, books and the telegraph – combined with the building of roads and canals – created

---

[26]The following line of reasoning is based mainly on Geoff Eley, *op. cit.* (see note 35), chapter 2; David Blackbourn, *Class, Religion and Local Politics in Wilhelmine Germany. The Centre Party in Württemberg*, New Haven 1980, esp. pp. 8–18; *idem* (note 33), pp. 152–184; Hans-Ulrich Wehler, 'Zur Funktion und Struktur der Nationalen Kampfverbände im Kaiserreich', in Werner Conze, Gottfried Schramm, Klaus Zernack (eds.), *Modernisierung und Nationale Gesellschaft im ausgehenden 18. und im 19. Jahrhundert*, Berlin 1979, pp. 113–124. Discussion of the complex events can only be short and very general.

[27]The literature concerning German economic development during the nineteenth century is vast, and cannot be discussed here. To mention just the works that might be useful for the general reader: Helmut Böhme, *An Introduction to the Social and Economic History of Germany*, Oxford 1978, is an excellent introduction in English. Werner Sombart, *Die deutsche Volkswirtschaft im neunzehnten Jahrhundert*, Berlin ²1909, is still a useful source of information. The major source for data regarding economic development, in spite of some criticism about its processing methods, is Walter G. Hoffmann, unter Mitarbeit von Franz Grumbach und Helmut Hesse, *Das Wachstum der deutschen Wirtschaft seit der Mitte des 19. Jahrhunderts*, Berlin–Heidelberg–New York 1965. Hermann Aubin and Wolfgang Zorn (eds.), *Handbuch der deutschen Wirtschafts- und Sozialgeschichte*, vol. II, Stuttgart 1976, contains excellent articles summarising the knowlege in these fields. Further references concerning the various subjects can be found there.

[28]Again we cannot enter into the huge literature concerning German social history. Helmut Böhme's *Introduction, op. cit.*, and the relevant articles in Aubin and Zorn, *Handbuch, op. cit.*, can provide further references.

new avenues for communication all over the country. One should add, in that connection, the expansion of education and the educational system.[29]

These socio-economic processes combined with the "Staatsgründungen" of 1867 and 1871 to allow for a re-orientation of the political system. The new phenomena of universal suffrage (for men), a central state parliament and the rise of land-wide political parties pushed that re-orientation forward, towards what Hans Rosenberg termed "Der politische Massenmarkt".[30] The people were more educated, had more free time, and better ways to know and understand what was happening throughout the country. Through the universal vote they received some amount of power, and they were beginning to realise that this power could be used to advance their particular interests.

The masses were developing a political consciousness and entering the political game. One indication of that trend was the growing participation in the elections. (1871: 52%; 1878: 63.1%; 1887: 77.2%; 1912: 84.5%). Others were the rise in the number of candidates per constituency (from an aggregate of 2.43 in 1871 to 4.15 in 1893[31]), and in the numbers of "Stichwahlen". (43 in 1871, 178 in 1893.[32]) Public interest in politics became so manifest, that a black market developed for tickets to the *Reichstag* gallery. For one important debate in 1911 people were reportedly willing to pay prices comparable to those for an appearance by Caruso.[33]

The traditional mode of politics, termed "Honoratiorenpolitik",[34] was ill-adapted to a time of growing political participation. It was characterised by a leadership of notables who had little connection with most of the voters. Candidates were selected with little regard to the broad electorate. They usually began to campaign just a few weeks before an election, and, for the most part, came in contact with only small groups of influential voters. Thus in the *Reichstag* elections of 1887 the incumbent of the Marburg seat arrived in the area just three weeks before the election and held only closed meetings with important merchants, teachers and professionals. That kind of electioneering had sufficed for victory in the previous campaign, as the candidate had been chosen by the leading notables of the constituency. By this election, however, times had changed. An unknown candidate, the antisemite Dr. Böckel, had for some

---

[29]On the connection between industrialisation and the expansion of education, with data about Germany, see Peter Lundgreen, *Bildung und Wirtschaftswachtum im Industrialisierungsprozess des 19. Jahrhunderts*, Berlin 1973.

[30]Hans Rosenberg, *Grosse Depression und Bismarckzeit. Wirtschaftsablauf, Gesellschaft und Politik in Mitteleuropa*, Frankfurt a. Main 1967, chaps. 3, 4.

[31]Hans Fenske, *Wahlrecht und Parteisystem. Ein Beitrag zur deutschen Parteiengeschichte*, Frankfurt a. Main 1972, pp. 109–110.

[32]*Ibid.*, p. 116.

[33]David Blackbourn, 'The Politics of Demagogy in Imperial Germany', *Past and Present*, 113 (November 1986), p. 158.

[34]See M. Weber, *Wirtschaft und Gesellschaft*, Tübingen [5]1976, pp. 170ff., 841–842. For a general discussion see James Sheehan, 'Politische Führung im Deutschen Reichstag 1871–1918', in Gerhard A. Ritter (ed.), *Die deutschen Parteien vor 1918*, Cologne 1973, pp. 81–99.

months worked through the area from village to village. Due to his efforts, he carried the votes of the peasants and achieved a stunning victory.[35]

The 1890s were the time when the trends became clearly evident throughout the country, causing "a general rearrangement of political life".[36] Reaching the "little people" became vital, even in areas that were always considered "safe seats" (*Stammsitze*).

A good example is the Fusangel affair.[37] In early 1892 Josef Fusangel, a newspaper editor known for his promotion of popular causes, challenged the Centre Party's official candidate for a by-election in the party's safe *Reichstag* seat of Olpe-Meschede, Westphalia. The party rallied to support its candidate. Major leaders came to speak on his behalf, and clergymen denounced Fusangel from their pulpits. (And were thereupon scolded by some of his adherents.)[38] Editors of the newspapers close to the party, most of whom supported Fusangel, were asked not to publicise opinions that could undermine party unity.[39] Fusangel, however, won the election by a ratio of more than three to one. This was one of several cases in the early 1890s where popular leaders managed to beat official party candidates in safe seats.[40]

The entry of the masses into politics changed the style of election campaigns, and of running politics in general. One had to reach and influence a large public in order to succeed. Politicians began, therefore, to utilise mass propaganda methods. Mass rallies were held in the constituencies, and advertised beforehand to ensure a large audience. Brochures and leaflets, written in popular style, were mass-distributed by post or by hand. Developments in the social and economic realms by the late 1880s and early 1890s proved beneficial to those kinds of propaganda. For example, the assembling of mass rallies was made easier by the great expansion of inner-city transportation after 1890.[41] Distribution of political literature was helped by the combined growth of education, standard of living and spare time, leading to an eight-fold increase in the expenditure per individual on "Bildung und Erholung" between the middle and the end of the century.[42]

---

[35]Pulzer, *op. cit.*, pp. 108–110; Richard Levy, *The Downfall of the Anti-Semitic Political Parties in Imperial Germany*, New Haven 1975, pp. 55–56; Geoff Eley, *Reshaping the German Right. Radical Nationalism and Political Change after Bismarck*, New Haven 1980, p. 23; David Peal, *Anti-Semitism and Rural Transformation in Kurhessen. The Rise and Fall of the Böckel Movement*, unpubl. diss., Columbia University, 1985, pp. 160–162.

[36]Eley, *op. cit.*, p. 11.

[37]On the affair see [Julius Bachem], 'Olpe-Meschede Arnsberg', *Historisch-Politische Blätter für das katholische Deutschland* (HPB), 111 (1893), pp. 564–568. Important bits of information are also contained in P. M. [Paul Majunke?], 'Der Zerfall der Alten Parteien', *ibid.*, pp. 630–640. For an overview see John Zeender, *The German Center Party 1890–1906*, Philadelphia 1976, pp. 31–32.

[38]Ursula Mittmann, *Fraktion und Partei. Ein Vergleich von Zentrum und Sozialdemokratie im Kaiserreich*, Düsseldorf 1976, p. 158, note 89.

[39]*Ibid.*, p. 251, note 270. See also P. M., *loc. cit.*, p. 633.

[40]See the examples in Mittmann, *op. cit.*, p. 159, note 91; P. M., *loc. cit.*, pp. 630–631; and in [Julius Bachem], 'Eine Ära von Schwierigkeiten', HPB, 111 (1893), p. 450.

[41]See Sombart, *op. cit.*, pp. 261–262. For information about Berlin, see Frank B. Tipton, *Regional Variations in the Economic Development of Germany during the Nineteenth Century*, Middletown, Conn. 1976, p. 105. By 1891, public transportation prices there became so low, that workers could use it daily.

[42]Hoffmann, *op. cit.*, p. 134.

Another, connected, development was the growing particularisation of German politics. The new participants in the political game did not want the elites to protect them from above, but began to take their fate in their own hands in working for their needs and demands. A major characteristic of the times was the many new pressure groups, representing a variety of interests. The people forming and supporting those organisations no longer relied on the parties to represent their cause, but applied pressure through these groups on both parties and government in order to advance it.[43] Thus an extra-parliamentary political system came to life, which was, but for some exceptions, built outside the ruling political elite, in many cases against its will.[44] Political activism from below had become a dominant factor.

As for the Jews, the processes described above applied to them even more than to other groups. They participated fully in the urbanisation and modernisation of economy and society, and by 1890 appear as a highly modernised socio-economic group by all the accepted indicators: heavy urban concentration, a high grade of education, a low birth rate, etc.[45]

Mass-propaganda methods, such as mass rallies and the distribution of brochures, began to play an increasing role in inner-Jewish politics, most of all in Berlin. The reign of a well-established, elitist and highly-assimilated community leadership was challenged from below, as an opposition party, called the *Zentralverein für die Interessen der jüdischen Gemeindewähler in Berlin*, came to life. This group, calling for more Judaism and democracy in the community, applied the methods of mass agitation, and managed to get some of its members into the *Repräsentantenversammlung*. The Liberals, in turn, started to apply agitation methods of their own. The process was completed by 1895. The campaign taking place in that year was a heated, intensive mass-propaganda effort by both sides, each holding large meetings in every part of the town, distributing brochures and leaflets to every voter, and using the Jewish press as an advertising aid. The Jewish papers themselves gave intensive coverage to the campaign, making it

[43]Thomas Nipperdey, 'Interessenverbände und Parteien in Deutschland vor dem Ersten Weltkrieg', *Politische Vierteljahresschrift*, 2 (1961), pp. 262–280; Hans-Jürgen Puhle, 'Parlament, Parteien und Interessenverbände 1890–1914', in Michael Stürmer (ed.), *Das kaiserliche Deutschland 1870–1914*, Kronberg 1977, pp. 340–377. Wehler, *loc. cit.*, connects the growth of particularism to the power vacuum created at the top after Bismarck's resignation (and see also Puhle, *loc. cit.*, p. 347).

[44]Again, we cannot discuss here all the literature concerned with that subject. See especially Eley, *op. cit.*, Blackbourn, *op. cit.*, and the articles in Richard J. Evans (ed.), *Society and Politics in Wilhelmine Germany*, New York 1978. And see the various references mentioned in those sources.

[45]See among others: Steven M. Lowenstein, 'The Pace of Modernisation of German Jewry in the Nineteenth Century, in *LBI Year Book XXI* (1976), pp. 41–56; Avraham Barkai, 'Die Sozio-ökonomische Entwicklung der Juden in Rheinland-Westfalen in der Industrialisierung (1850–1910)', *Bulletin des Leo Baeck Instituts*, No. 66 (1983), pp. 53–81; *idem, Jüdische Minderheit und Industrialisierung*, Tübingen 1988 (Schriftenreihe wissenschaftlicher Abhandlungen des Leo Baeck Instituts 46); Arthur Prinz, *Juden im Deutschen Wirtschaftsleben 1850–1914* (Bearbeitet und herausgegeben von Avraham Barkai), Tübingen 1984 (Schriftenreihe wissenschaftlicher Abhandlungen des Leo Baeck Instituts 43).

more open and public.[46] One need only compare this campaign to the sleepy campaigns of the early 1880s (when the press hardly bothered to report even the results), to realise how deep were the changes in Jewish public life.

At least one interest united all Jews: the defence of their rights in the face of growing antisemitism. Moreover, the party that was their traditional ally, the *Freisinnige*, was losing much of its popular support, and its ability – and will – to defend their cause was decreasing. In short, the factors that encouraged broad-based political activism among various segments of the German society, existed – and all the more so – for the Jews.

As specific interests of different groups were increasingly influencing political life, Jews did not have to be afraid of appearing "egotistic" or unassimilating when standing up for their own needs. After all, the super-patriotic Prussian *Junker* were doing exactly that,[47] challenging the government, even the *Kaiser* himself. Some of the Jews took note of the new political winds, and called for applying them to the benefit of their cause.

III. THE RISE OF A NEW JEWISH ACTIVISM

As we have seen, the notables who comprised the Jewish leadership were opposed to a particularistic Jewish activity. But the feelings among other sections of the Jewish population were changing. From 1890 onwards we can observe a growing activist mood.

An increasing number of articles in the Jewish press dealt with the success of politically organised antisemitism, and the need for defence. The writers of such articles attributed the progress of the movement to its utilisation of the above-mentioned new propaganda techniques, which were in tune with the new times. They suggested that if the Jews wanted to defend themselves successfully, they should: a) start acting themselves, instead of remaining passive or relying on friendly non-Jews; b) utilise these new propaganda techniques.

Press articles and contemporary reports conveyed a sense of danger and urgency regarding the spread of antisemitism, combined with outrage that nothing was done against it. "Unser Haus brennt, und man hielt uns einen ästhetischen Vortrag", fumed one writer.[48] That metaphor was used by other writers as well. "Die Wand unseres Wohnhauses ist schon heiss, wollen wir

---

[46]The only modern research I found that mentions the "Zentralverein für die Interessen . . ." is Shmuel Maayan, *The Elections in the Jewish Community of Berlin in the Years 1901–1920*, Givat Haviva 1977 (in Hebrew). A few details about its founding are given on p. 59. About the campaign of 1895 see pp. 60–61, and especially the Berlin Jewish papers of the time: *Allgemeine Zeitung des Judenthums, Jüdische Presse*, and the *Jeschurun (Allgemeine Israelitische Wochenschrift)*. See also my dissertation, *op. cit.*, chap. 3.

[47]Hans-Jürgen Puhle, *Agrarische Interessenpolitik und preussischer Konservatismus im wilhelminischen Reich (1893–1914)*, Bonn – Bad Godesberg 1975.

[48]*Israelitische Wochenschrift*, XXII, No. 8 (19th February 1891), p. 58.

warten bis das Feuer hell-lodernd brennt?"[49] The behaviour of those who claimed that antisemitism should not be fought publicly was symbolised by another metaphor: that of the ostrich, sticking its head in the sand when danger arrives. The expression "Vogelstrausspolitik" was commonly used in articles denouncing the inactivity of Jews against the dangers facing them.

A growing awareness of the new political mode of mass-propaganda is clear in these articles. Whoever objects to propaganda activity, declared one writer, is "one who does not know our modern, public life". He described that life as characterised by the actions of "strong agitational forces" that influence the public, which in turn induces its elected representatives to stand for certain ideas in the parliament. "Der Schwerpunkt liegt in der Bearbeitung des Volkes in Volksversammlungen", he wrote, emphasising the importance of "dem lebendigen, die Massen ergreifenden, begeisternden, entflammenden Wort". He called upon Jewish leaders to visit public meetings. They should address the crowds, and do it in the right manner – powerfully, decisively, with some humour.[50]

The success achieved by the antisemites themselves was the example used by most writers to demonstrate the efficiency of mass-propaganda. "Lernen wir doch von unseren Gegnern", declared one.[51] Antisemitism in Hesse was especially employed for that purpose. The victories of antisemitic candidates in 1890 and 1893 were attributed to their massive publishing activities and door-to-door canvassing.[52] Alarmed writers called for a fightback using similar methods, such as sending "Gegenredner" to the countryside[53] or using "Schlagwörter", which are "much more persuasive" – when dealing with the masses – "than scientific arguments".[54] Others warned against the danger of the flood of antisemitic brochures and leaflets, and especially against the activities of Theodor Fritsch's "factory" in Leipzig.[55] A recurring theme was the call for action, warning that continuing passivity would enable antisemitism to grow to uncontrollable dimensions.

Many writers felt that counter-propaganda would be more effective if carried out, not by Jews but by friendly Christians. "The Jew who stands up for his own belief and group is not as forceful as the Christian."[56] Hence, the founding of the *Verein zur Abwehr des Antisemitismus* (*Abwehrverein*) in 1891 seemed an answer to

---

[49]A local report from Alzey (Rheinhessen), signed R., *Israelitische Wochenschrift*, XXI, No. 16 (17th April 1890), p. 118. I believe that it was written by the local Rabbi David Rothschild, who frequently published in the *Israelitische Wochenschrift*. See about him the obituary in *Israelitische Wochenschrift*, XXIII, No. 6 (5th February 1892), pp. 44–45.

[50]*Israelitische Wochenschrift*, XXV, No. 24 (15th June 1894), p. 187. Signed B. I was unable to identify the writer. (It is not Benno Jacob, who used to sign B. J., and published another article in the same number.)

[51]Probably Hirsch Hildesheimer, *Jüdische Presse*, XXII, No. 14 (2nd April 1891), p. 163.

[52]See, for example, *Allgemeine Zeitung des Judenthums*, LIV, No. 14 (18th April 1890), Gb., p. 3; *Jüdische Presse*, XXI, No. 16 (17th April 1890), p. 196.

[53]*Allgemeine Zeitung des Judenthums*, LIV, No. 14 (18th April 1890), Gb., p. 3, for one of many examples.

[54]*Israelitische Wochenschrift*, XXV, No. 19 (9th March 1894), p. 75.

[55]Karl Wiesenthal, a Jewish author residing in Leipzig, was especially aware of that danger. See *Der Israelit*, XXXI, No. 86 (3rd November 1890), pp. 1150–1151, as well as other reports. See also *Israelitische Wochenschrift*, XXII, No. 11 (12th March 1891), pp. 83–84.

[56]*Israelitische Wochenschrift*, XXII, No. 10 (5th March 1891), p. 75.

many a prayer.[57] (One should note, in this context, that Socialist activists waged a bitter war against antisemitic agitators in several parts of Germany, especially Hesse and Westphalia.[58] The Jews, however, felt uncomfortable with help from "Vaterlandslosen Gesellen", and preferred to ignore it. The Jewish press did not report most of that activity, and in some cases when it did, any mention of the Socialists was omitted.[59])

The *Abwehrverein* leaders did attempt to fight antisemitism through public, agitational methods. They published brochures and leaflets for mass-distribution, organised public meetings, (especially in 1891–1892, when Graebner was their secretary), and some activists visited antisemitic rallies and tried to present their views.[60] There were also other Christians – mainly Liberals – who publicly tried to fight antisemitism in their locality. Usually, it was a one-time effort, and not a prolonged activity.[61] In general, the number of Christians that were prepared to enter into confrontation with the antisemites was not large, and these people suffered grave insults and harassment – including physical attacks on their persons and property – which gradually diminished their ability to continue their activities.[62]

Liberal elements associated with the fight began to call upon the Jews to participate in their own defence. One such call was published by a progressive newspaper in Darmstadt, the *Hessischer Volksfreund*, in November 1890.[63] From 1892 the same line was taken by the organ of the *Abwehrverein* itself, and in no compromising terms.[64] Apparently, the organisation had begun to realise that it was not achieving the results it hoped for, and its *Freisinnige* leaders were tiring of the *Judenschutztruppe* stigma attached to their party. The *Mitteilungen aus dem Verein zur Abwehr des Antisemitismus* declared several times that fighting antisemitism was not only a task for Christians, and "it was *an unquestionable duty* of the Jews to

---

[57]On that organisation see Barbara Suchy, 'The Verein zur Abwehr des Antisemitismus (I). From Its Beginnings to the First World War', in *LBI Year Book XXVIII* (1983), pp. 205–239.

[58]See especially Rosemarie Leuschen-Seppel, *Sozialdemokratie und Antisemitismus im Kaiserreich. Die Auseinandersetzungen der Partei mit den konservativen und völkischen Strömungen des Antisemitismus 1871–1914*, Bonn 1978.

[59]See, for example, the report from Schleswig-Holstein in *Israelitische Wochenschrift*, XXIV, No. 21 (14th May 1893), pp. 161–162; and compare with the *Mitteilungen aus dem Verein zur Abwehr des Antisemitismus* (MVAA), III, No. 20 (14th May 1893), pp. 209–210.

[60]Most active were the architect Hermann Schoeler from Hanover and journalist–author Arthur Weigt from Berlin. The *Mitteilungen aus dem Verein zur Abwehr des Antisemitismus* (MVAA) contain many reports of their activities, especially in 1894.

[61]One exception was Dr. Waltemath in Hamburg, who made a habit of appearing at the antisemitic meetings in his town. See *Die Menorah* (Hamburg), I, No. 2 (6th March 1891), p. 21; No. 25 (14th August 1891), pp. 383–384; No. 29 (11th September 1891), pp. 441–442.

[62]Several examples are found in the MVAA.

[63]The editors must have been aware of the growing power of antisemitism, because the newspaper itself was sold to antisemites a few weeks later. See Adelheid Schaefer, *Hessische Zeitungen*, No. 127 (Darmstadt 1978); and see also Nos. 121, 125, 128. On the call itself see *Der Israelit*, XXXI, No. 91 (21st November 1890), pp. 1633–1634; *Jüdische Presse*, XXII, No. 47 (20th November 1890), p. 552.

[64]See Paucker, 'Die Abwehr des Antisemitismus', *loc. cit.*, p. 147, and in the revised English version, 'The Jewish Defense against Antisemitism in Germany 1893–1933', in Jehuda Reinharz (ed.), *Living with Antisemitism. Modern Jewish Responses*, Hanover–London 1987, p. 110.

come out publicly against antisemitism . . . but instead we often encounter indecisiveness and fearfulness".[65]

Such explicit calls could not be ignored. But even before 1892 many Jews came to realise that it was up to the Jews to defend themselves, and not let Christians do their work. The writer of an article in *Der Israelit*, entitled 'Auf, Israel, zum Streite',[66] declared: "Israel kann und wird seine Sache selbst führen und vertheidigen, es bedarf keines Fremden, der seine Streitigkeiten führt". The article called for the founding of Jewish organisations that would prepare and distribute defence brochures *en masse*, and repeated several times the theme "Sich wehren, bringt Ehren". The feeling of urgency was so strong, that it called upon Jews of all religious viewpoints to unite in that fight – not a common step among *Austrittsorthodoxen*. The editor of *Der Israelit* himself added a note supporting the article, calling upon Jews ready to act to contact the newspaper, and offering free copies of the article to anyone interested.

All over the *Reich* the feeling was growing that Jews must act with the times and defend themselves publicly. And that feeling was manifested, soon enough, in widespread activities.

Activities of defence agitation can be generally classified in two categories: printed defence and verbal defence. The printed defence consists of brochures, leaflets and newspaper articles aimed at refuting slander and attacking the slanderers themselves. Verbal defence consists of participation in antisemitic gatherings and taking the platform in order to refute the main speaker, or the organisation of "anti-anti" public meetings.

Upon examination of the actual activities that took place, a distinction was discerned, as we shall see, between the activities in Berlin and those in the provinces.

IV. VERBAL DEFENCE IN BERLIN

On 5th January, 1892, a new organisation was announced in the press. It was called the *Vereinigung zur Bekämpfung der Rassenhetze* (VBR), and its goal was to fight antisemitism by "mündliche Agitation" in public rallies.[67]

The presidents of the new organisation were Christians. The first was Carl Küchenmeister, a writer and literary critic turned printing-house owner. He was followed by Karl Schneidt, a veteran Socialist (he was jailed for his opinions, and left Germany in 1878 because of the anti-Socialist laws) and newspaper editor. In Berlin he edited literary periodicals and publishing brochures, including some

---

[65]MVAA, III, No. 16 (16th April 1893), pp. 175–176. Emphasis in the original. See also *ibid.*, II, No. 34 (21st August 1892), p. 281; III, No. 1 (1st January 1893), p. 4.

[66]*Der Israelit*, XXXI, No. 45 (9th June 1890), pp. 805–807.

[67]*Berliner Volkszeitung*, XL, No. 3 (5th January 1892), 1. Blatt, 3rd page; *Israelitische Wochenschrift*, XXIII, No. 2 (7th January 1892), p. 14; *Allgemeine Zeitung des Judenthums*, LVI, No. 2 (8th January 1892), Gb., p. 2. Jacob Toury, 'Self-Improvement', *loc. cit.*, p. 14, is the only modern research I found to mention that group.

exposés of the Socialist Party, with which he must have broken by that time.[68] The men who performed the actual propaganda work, by carrying speeches in public meetings, were Jews: the poet Ludwig Jacobowski,[69] the journalist and writer Heinrich Blankenburg, and the writer Edmund Lichtenstein.[70]

All of these activists were young people (the oldest was Schneidt, who was 38 in 1892; Jacobowski was 24 at the time), who were part of the literary world – in fact, of what can be termed "the periphery" of that world,[71] and had no connection with the Jewish or Liberal establishments. They were all born away from Berlin, and – except for Jacobowski – educated outside of it.[72]

Jacobowski and Küchenmeister began fighting antisemitism in 1891, following an attack on the famous Jewish banker Gerson von Bleichröder.[73] They wrote pamphlets[74] and went to antisemitic gatherings.[75] Shortly afterwards Karl Schneidt had began publishing an anti-antisemitic bi-weekly, entitled *Die Schmach des Jahrhunderts*.[76] The next step by Jacobowski and Küchenmeister was founding the *Vereinigung zur Bekämpfung der Rassenhetze*, which launched a sequence of public meetings, beginning on the 18th December 1891[77] (that is, before its official foundation was announced), in which the speakers attacked antisemitism. But they did not take their opponents into account.

Large numbers of antisemites came to their rallies, and they did not show any tendency towards intellectual discourse. They preferred to shout, scream and sometimes sing loudly during speeches. ('Deutschland über Alles' was their favourite.) Jacobowski, who suffered from a speech-defect, was not the right orator for that atmosphere: all his speeches, but one, were disrupted before reaching their end. Other speakers had to shorten their lectures in order to finish. As VBR supporters did not remain idle, fights and brawls broke out, and most of

---

[68]On Küchenmeister see *Deutsches Literatur-Lexikon*, Bd. IX, Bern–Munich 1984. cols. 595–596; Bernhard Fabian (ed.), *Deutsches Biographisches Archiv*, Microfiche, Munich [n.d.], Card 717, frame 403; Carl Leyst, *Neosozialismus*, Zoppot, Leipzig–Berlin 1919, pp. 538–539. (Leyst was a pseudonym of Küchenmeister.) On Schneidt see *Deutsches Literatur-Lexikon*, Bern ²1956, Bd. 3, III cols. 2552–2553, and Fabian (ed.), *op. cit.*, Card 1126, frames 287/288.

[69]Jacobowski's biographer was unaware of his participation in that group: Fred B. Stern, *Ludwig Jacobowski. Persönlichkeit und Werk eines Dichters*, Darmstadt 1966, p. 27.

[70]On Lichtenstein see *Deutsche Literatur-Lexikon*, Bd. IX, Bern–Munich 1984, cols. 1367–1368.

[71]On categories within (modern) German writers see Jürgen Gerhard, Helmut K. Anheier, 'Zur Sozialposition und Netzwerkstruktur von Schriftstellern', *Zeitschrift für Soziologie*, XVI, No. 5 (Oktober 1987), pp. 385–394.

[72]Information about the Jewish members of the VBR was kindly supplied to me by Dr. Renate Heuer of the *Archiv Bibliographia Judaica* in Frankfurt a. Main.

[73]See Fritz Stern, *Gold and Iron. Bismarck, Bleichröder and the Building of the German Empire*, New York – London 1976, pp. 533–540.

[74]Ludwig Jacobowski, *Offene Antwort eines Juden an Herrn Ahlwardt's "Der Eid eines Juden"*, Berlin 1891. It was printed in Küchenmeister's printing-house; Kaberlin [pseudonym for Küchenmeister], *Kritische Proteste eines Germanischen Christen an die Neueste Bleichröder- und Judenhetze*, Berlin 1891.

[75]For Jacobowski see Stern, *op. cit.*, p. 27. For Küchenmeister see *Schmach des Jahrhunderts*, vol. I, No. 2 (1892), p. 62.

[76]It was published in 1892 and ceased publication in 1893, apparently due to financial difficulties. Most of the articles were written by Schneidt himself. The other participants were writers, probably members within the same circle of the VBR activists.

[77]The events during that meeting are recorded in the brochure, *Antwort des Herrn Carl Küchenmeister in der Volksversammlung vom 18. Dezember 1891 . . .*, Berlin 1892.

the meetings reached an unplanned end when the police officer in charge ordered their dismissal.

The society encountered a hostile attitude from the Jewish press and leadership. It was attacked for acting in a manner that would only give the antisemites free publicity.[78] The stormy events that accompanied every meeting only strengthened these criticisms. The view of the Jewish press, which supported, in principle, public agitation against antisemitism, is exemplified by an article that recommended public rallies against antisemitism, but not in Berlin, where the people coming to them already made up their minds and were merely looking for entertainment.[79] A riotous meeting on 9th March was the last one reported by the Jewish press. Afterwards it boycotted the VBR altogether. (Although some meetings were mentioned here and there, these were just in short notices, not reflecting any interest in the organisation). Most Liberal newspapers adopted a similar, negative standpoint towards it, and the organ of the *Abwehrverein* ignored it totally. The one newspaper in Berlin that clearly supported the group was the Liberal-Radical *Berliner Volkszeitung.*[80]

The VBR leaders themselves were obviously embarrassed by the turn of events. After the March meeting Küchenmeister was replaced by Schneidt as president, but the riots in the meetings continued. At this stage Jacobowski apparently left the VBR and joined the *Abwehrverein.*[81]

In the second half of 1892 the society's fortunes changed. By denying entrance to antisemites, it managed to solve the problem of disturbances. In July and August the VBR held three meetings which were the most successful in its short history. Not only were they not suspended by the police, they aroused considerable public attention. This was due to the appearance of a new speaker, Edmund Lichtenstein, who collected material about Hermann Ahlwardt and found evidence of a number of criminal felonies, including the offering of bribes and financial misdeeds.[82] The findings were impressive enough to shake even the *Mitteilungen aus dem Verein zur Abwehr des Antisemitismus* out of its boycott and cause it to mention the group for the first time.[83]

After August 1892 the VBR suddenly vanished. There were no further reports about it in the press, nor any clues that might explain this puzzling disappearance.[84] The only reasonable explanation one can suggest is connected with the cholera epidemic which struck Germany during this period and caused hundreds

---

[78]See, for example, *Allgemeine Zeitung des Judenthums*, LVI, No. 4 (22nd January 1892), p. 38.

[79]*Ibid.*, No. 1 (1st January 1892), p. 1. And see *ibid.*, No. 3 (15th January 1892), Gb., p. 2.

[80]On the paper, see Peter de Mendelssohn, *Zeitungsstadt Berlin. Menschen und Mächte in der Geschichte der deutschen Presse*, Berlin 1982, p. 156.

[81]On his activity in the *Abwehrverein* see Suchy, *loc. cit.*, pp. 214–215.

[82]Lichtenstein's attacks on Ahlwardt are summed up in the brochures *Ahlwardts Ende! Authentische Enthüllungen Eingeweihter*, Berlin 1892; *Ahlwardt im Kampf mit dem Gesetz*, Berlin 1892. Both were published in the Van-Groningen publishing house in the series "Berliner Fanfaren", of which Lichtenstein was the editor.

[83]MVAA, II, No. 33 (14th August 1892), p. 276.

[84]More information could perhaps be found in the Berlin city archives (especially in the police files), but these are located at Potsdam, and I could not get access there at the time this article was prepared.

of deaths, especially in Hamburg.[85] The end of August 1892, the time after the last public meeting of the VBR, was the time when the first signs of panic were found in Berlin's newspapers. A result of that panic was the cancelling of many public events, and this could well be the reason for halting the meetings.

Unlike the case of most organisations, this stoppage might have been fatal for the VBR, because this group lacked any solid organisational structure. It did not manage to agree even upon a common platform.[86] It did not publish a journal,[87] and it seems that its whole operation consisted of organising public meetings. Without that activity it simply disintegrated.

To sum up the VBR's activity, one should note that in contrast to the established Jewish leadership in Berlin, these young people – who were detached from it – chose to fight antisemitism in a public, open way. They had attacked Jewish passivity towards antisemitism, and claimed that this was a major reason for the success of that movement. As Küchenmeister declared in the first meeting:

> "Deshalb wäre es ein Fehler, diesem Treiben [Antisemitismus] immerwährend ruhig zuzusehen ... Die politische Zurückhaltung ist mehr eine Tugend des Privatlebens, im öffentlichen Leben kann sie sehr leicht eine gefährliche Naivität werden. Die Sache liegt also so, dass nur die Zurückhaltung der Juden den Antisemiten so kühn gemacht hat ..."[88]

We should note the distinction made between private and public spheres, and the claim that "Zurückhaltung" does not fit the public, political one. Obviously, the speaker is talking about different politics from "Honoratiorenpolitik". He refers to the new political style, characterised by mass-propaganda. "Billige Schriften und tüchtige Redner", declared another VBR activist, were the means the Jews should apply in their coming battles.[89] The VBR leaders, aware of the new political conditions, believed that mass agitation should be used to fight antisemitism.

The youth of the members was an important element in their self-perception. They felt themselves to be members of a new generation, quite different from the older one in their activities and ideas.[90] In one of their first meetings, they declared that "leider so viele Juden, insbesondere die älteren, ihrem eigensten Interesse gegenüber sich lässig verhalten und ... einen passiven Standpunkt einnehmen".[91] It is interesting that other Jewish supporters of defence agitation in Berlin also had the feeling of being members of a new and different generation.[92]

---

[85]See in detail: Richard Evans, *Death in Hamburg*, Oxford 1977, pp. 275–568.

[86]See Küchenmeister's speech, reported in the *Berliner Volkszeitung*, XL, No. 194 (20th August 1892), 1. Blatt, 3rd page.

[87]The *Schmach des Jahrhunderts* was not an organ of the VBR, and hardly mentions that group. It is quite possible that Schneidt had opposed any suggestion – if such were made – of founding a literary organ for the VBR, that would compete with his own periodical.

[88]Küchenmeister. *Antwort, op. cit.*, p. 4. See also p. 5.

[89]Lichtenstein, *Ahlwardts Ende, op. cit.*, p. 35.

[90]See, for example, *Kritische Proteste, op. cit.*, p. 8; Jacobowski, *Offene Antwort, op. cit.*, pp. 29, 31.

[91]*Berliner Volkszeitung*, XL, No. 6 (8th January 1892), 1. Blatt, 3rd page.

[92]See, for example, Heinrich Meyer-Cohn, 'Vor 25 Jahren – eine Erwiderung', *Allgemeine Zeitung des Judenthums*, LVIII, No. 29 (20th July 1894), pp. 338–340.

Apparently, there were other attempts made by Jews to oppose Berlin's antisemites verbally.[93] But the prevailing opinion, even of those who supported public defence, was that Berlin was not the place for such encounters. Thus we find that two Jewish activists from Berlin travelled to other locations, where they clashed with antisemitic agitators.[94] We should note that these activists, Edmund Friedemann and Heinrich Loewe, shared the characteristics of the VBR activists: youth, birthplace outside of Berlin, an academic-literary background, and lack of connections with the community leadership. (Although both of them, and especially Friedemann, were public figures of some importance.[95]) That leadership did not take part in any effort to combat antisemitism publicly.

V. VERBAL DEFENCE IN THE PROVINCES

Unlike Berlin, where verbal defence encountered wide resistance and was quite rare, in the provinces the attitude towards that sort of defence was favourable, and it was much more widespread.

First, we should explain what we mean when referring to "the Provinces". There was, in the consciousness of contemporary German Jews, a feeling of contrast between the bigger communities (especially Berlin, which symbolised the big metropolitan community), and the smaller ones. This feeling was based on stereotypes attached to the members of such communities. Many a Berlin Jew looked down upon provincial Jews as backward, too conservative, and unsophisticated. The provincial Jews saw the Berliners as arrogant and uprooted, criticising the latter for their aloofness, detachment and neglect of Judaism.[96]

Apart from Berlin, there were three other communities which can be designated as "big" (according to membership figures): Hamburg, Breslau and Frankfurt a. Main.

Concerning the issue of verbal defence, no trace was found of such activity being performed by Jews in these three communities, although antisemitic agitation was carried out openly in their cities.[97] So, when we deal with "the

---

[93]See *Populär-Wissenschaftliche Monatsblätter*, XI, No. 2 (February 1891), p. 43; *Israelitische Wochenschrift*, XXIV, No. 24 (9th June 1893), p. 187. Typically, the Jewish papers of Berlin avoided any publicity of these cases.

[94]*Allgemeine Zeitung des Judenthums*, LVIII, No. 23 (8th June 1894), Gb., p. 2.

[95]For biographical details see Salomon Wininger, *Grosse Jüdische Nationalbiographie*, Czernowitz 1925–1936, vol. II, p. 327 (Friedemann) and vol. V, p. 382 (Loewe).

[96]See *Allgemeine Zeitung des Judenthums*, LIII, No. 40 (3rd October 1889), p. 626, and No. 44 (31st October 1889), pp. 687–689. The *Israelitische Wochenschrift*, published in Magdeburg, is full of attacks on Berlin Jewry. For a typical example see XXIV, No. 27 (30th June 1893), p. 209. Similar relations existed in the German milieu. For an example see the article 'Die "Provinz" gegen Berlin', *Berliner Tageblatt*, XXXVI, No. 228 (6th May 1907), 1st page. On the animosity towards the big cities, as a reaction against modernism and industrialism, see Klaus Bergmann, *Agrarromantik und Großstadtfeindschaft*, Meisenheim a. Glan 1970.

[97]Information about that is found in the Jewish press and the MVAA. (In Frankfurt antisemites began to agitate openly only in 1895.) See the letter sent to the *Abwehrverein* by the Hamburg community leadership (quoted in Suchy, *loc. cit.*, p. 212), claiming that antisemitism did not strike roots in their town (1892), and compare with the large gains made by the party in Hamburg in the elections of 1893.

provinces" in this article, we deal with all communities except the four bigger ones.

In the provinces there were also voices opposing the presence of Jews in antisemitic rallies. But those advocating participation were much more numerous. And, indeed, Jews had began to appear at such gatherings. Their numbers were growing, and their efforts were treated very favourably by the Jewish press, which encouraged others to follow.

The biggest impression on Jewish public opinion was made by the Göttingen rabbi, Benno Jacob.[98] Jacob had the necessary qualities for appearing at antisemitic rallies: a tall, impressive build, a strong voice, a sharp tongue, and also a great knowledge of the subject (useful for such occasions, but not as important as the former qualities). From his student days he bore duelling scars, the *Schmisse*, that were a source of pride and social appreciation. Once he brought a volume of the Talmud to the stand, and asked the antisemitic agitator to show him the exact place from which he was supposedly quoting. When the speaker admitted his inability to do so, due to his unfamiliarity with Hebrew, the "surprised" Jacob expressed his puzzlement at the fact that someone allowed himself to attack a text that he had never read, and never would be able to.

Jacob made his first appearance in his home town, Göttingen, after being officially invited by the antisemitic agitator Liebermann von Sonnenberg.[99] He declared that he came reluctantly to the meeting, and would have preferred to stay at home and study Talmud. But even so, Jacob managed to undermine completely his adversary's credibility. The next day Jacob travelled to another Liebermann rally, and opposed him successfully for the second time. His successes drew enthusiastic responses from the Jewish press,[100] and he continued to appear at antisemitic rallies.

Afterwards the number of Jews willing to fight antisemitism in public increased significantly. I found reports concerning such activities by 48 men from the provinces between 1890 and 1895.[101] Some of the important variables concerning them and their activity have been collected in Appendix I.

Table A of this Appendix shows the professional composition of the activists. The clear dominance of preachers–teachers (both functions were usually fulfilled by the same person) and rabbis immediately strikes the eye. This is not hard to explain, as these men, educated and knowledgeable about Judaism, were obvious choices for the role of providing answers to antisemitic slanders. The

---

[98]On his life see Kurt Wilhelm, 'Benno Jacob, a Militant Rabbi', in *LBI Year Book VII* (1962), pp. 75–94. Jacob published many articles for the *Israelitische Wochenschrift* (under the initials B.J.) which reflect his views about Jewish defence.

[99]This invitation was probably extended after Liebermann von Sonnenberg managed to defend himself successfully against another Jewish speaker at a meeting in Hanover. See *Der Israelit*, XXXIII, No. 97 (8th December 1892), pp. 1856–1858, and *Jüdische Presse*, XXIII, No. 49 (9th December 1892), pp. 396–398, for the most detailed reports.

[100]Jacob published his memories of these meetings in *K.C. Blätter*, II, No. 3 (1st December 1911), pp. 49–53. And see wide reports in the Jewish press and the MVAA between 16th and 22nd December 1892.

[101]A complete list, with references to reports of the activities and biographical sources, is found in Appendix 3 of my dissertation.

Allgemeine Zeitung des Judenthums defined the fight against antisemitism as "Eine neue Aufgabe" of Jewish rabbis and teachers,[102] and that was the prevailing view among proponents of public defence. The self-image of the teachers themselves was consonant with that opinion, as they regarded themselves as spiritual leaders and "Pioniere des Judenthums" in their communities, as well as the representative figures of Judaism towards Christians.[103] As such, it was they who should handle the task of combatting antisemites in public. We should note that in contrast to Berlin, these activists were functionaries and spiritual leaders of their communities.

As regards the other activists, it is interesting that most of them had a high social and economic status. This was made clear not only by their professions (merchants, lawyers, an industrialist, a banker, a university professor), but also by personal information collected about them. Benjamin Hirsch of Halberstadt, for example, was a major leader of his community and its chairman for many years, a highly respected member of the town council and *Handelskammer*, and also one of the leaders of moderate Orthodoxy in Germany.[104] Albert Meyer of Ulm (Württemberg) was a leading politican and a later *Landtag* member.[105] Another activist, from Hamm in Westphalia, was a community chairman.[106] Thus it seems that many Jewish notables and leaders participated actively in the defence effort, and the contrast with Berlin is clear.

At least 14 of the activists had an academic education, and 10 of them held doctoral degrees (a few more earned that title later). If we add professions that required a good education, though not necessarily academic (teachers, journalists, bookkeepers),[107] we come to a total of 35 out of 40 activists whose profession is known. There is only one record of a worker: a *Gerbermeister* in Krojanke, Poznań Province, who offered to demonstrate on Ahlwardt his ability to handle skins.[108]

Another variable that appears to be significant is the age of the activists. (See Appendix I, Table B.) The uncertainty factor here is much higher (compared with the professional analysis), but we cannot ignore the fact that about half the

---

[102]*Allgemeine Zeitung des Judenthums*, LVII, No. 14 (7th April 1893), p. 157.

[103]This statement is based on many articles written by and for teachers in the various Jewish papers. For a good example, see the article, 'Wie kann der israelitische Lehrer dem Antisemitismus und seinen Agitatoren wirksam entgegentreten?', *Blätter für die Israelitische Schule, Beilage der Israelit*, XXXI, No. 99 (18th December 1890) [n.p.]. A study about the self-image and the real social position of Jewish *Kultusbeamte* is still lacking.

[104]See Yoseph Hirsch, 'Le-Toldot Beit Hirsch', *Reshumot*, No. 4 (1947), pp. 38–61 (in Hebrew).

[105]*Pinkas Kehillot Württemberg-Hohenzollern-Baden*, Jerusalem 1985, pp. 26. (and note 110), 36 (in Hebrew).

[106]*Der Israelit*, XXXIV, No. 97 (7th December 1893), pp. 1843–1844. The source gives only the initials H. Z., which do not conform to the initials of any of Hamm community's chairman. (See *Statistisches Jahrbuch des Deutsch-Israelitischen Gemeindebundes 1893*, p. 32; *1895*, p. 35.) Presumably he was M. Herz, a member of an old and respected Jewish family in the town. See Anna Dartmann, *Die soziale wirtschaftliche und kulturelle Entwicklung der jüdischen Gemeinde in Hamm, 1327–1943*, Hamm 1977, p. 61.

[107]On the non-academic "Gebildete" as part of the "Intelligenz" see Theodor Geiger, *Aufgaben und Stellung der Intelligenz in der Gesellschaft*, Stuttgart 1949, pp. 5–12.

[108]MVAA, IV, No. 17 (20th April 1894), p. 133; *Israelitische Wochenschrift*, XXV, No. 18 (4th May 1894), p. 136; *Allgemeine Zeitung des Judenthums*, LVIII, No. 19 (11th May 1894), Gb., p. 4.

activists, whose age was identified, were in their early thirties at the time, and all but two were under 55. (Of the exceptions, one was 57. The other, a most obvious exception, was a rabbi in Sondershausen, who attended an antisemitic meeting a week before his 80th birthday.[109]) This factor is consonant with what we know about verbal activists in Berlin, most of whom were 30 or under.

Another variable characterising activists both in Berlin and the provinces concerns their birthplace. (See Appendix I, Table E). Almost all of them were born outside the area in which they became activists, in fact in a different *Provinz* or *Land* altogether. And a clear majority were born in the East. That does not say much for the provinces, not only because information about most activists is lacking, but mainly because most of them were teachers and rabbis, and it was common for members of these professions to come from other places, and mostly from the East. For Berlin, where none of the activists was a teacher or a rabbi, that variable is much more significant.

Other variables analysed, including the targets of Jewish defence activity (that is, which antisemitic agitators were confronted) or time in office (for rabbis and teachers) produced no coherent or meaningful results.

An interesting point concerning the religious standpoints of rabbis and teachers among the activists (the religious stand of laymen is much harder to establish) is that representatives of the extremist religious views were scarcely to be found. I could identify only one extreme Liberal (Felix Coblenz of Bielefeld) and one possible *Austrittsorthodoxer* (a certain Kahn in Wiesbaden, who might have been the teacher of the local *Austrittsgemeinde*).[110]

Beyond the analysis concerning individual defence activists, we should emphasise that there were cases where Jews came to antisemitic gatherings in groups, ready to respond with force to antisemitic provocations. The Jewish press and the *Mitteilungen aus dem Verein zur Abwehr des Antisemitismus* reported a few of these cases,[111] but it appears that others were not disclosed to their readers, especially if they ended in a brawl. A case in point is the report of a trial following a riot at an antisemitic meeting in Inowrozlaw, where the 15 defendants, "Four of whom were Christians", were acquitted.[112] The only Jewish newspaper to report this case did so only a year and a half after the incident, following the acquittal of the Jews concerned, and did not report the incident itself. In fact, the report mentioned briefly that another trial had taken place several weeks before, in which "mehrere jüdische junge Leute" were accused of participation in a large brawl on the day of the aforementioned meeting. The verdict was not reported, so one can assume that the defendants were found

[109]MVAA, IV, No. 22 (2nd June 1894), p. 172; *Allgemeine Zeitung des Judenthums*, LVIII, No. 25 (22nd June 1894), Gb., p. 2.
[110]For more information about them see my dissertation, *op. cit.*, Appendix 3, Nos. 7 and 22. On the whole subject see *ibid.*, chap. 4.
[111]MVAA, I, No. 5 (22nd November 1891), p. 7 (Lahr, Baden); *Jüdische Presse*, XXIII, No. 16 (23rd April 1892), p. 191 (Bruchsal); *Der Israelit*, XXXV, No. 30 (12th April 1894), p. 548 and MVAA, IV, No. 16 (22nd April 1894), p. 128 (Bonn); *Der Israelit*, XXXV, No. 61 (2nd August 1894), p. 1137 and MVAA, IV, No. 31 (4th August 1894), p. 247 (Duisdorf, near Bonn).
[112]*Allgemeine Zeitung des Judenthums*, LIX, No. 16 (19th April 1895), Gb., p. 2.

guilty. The earlier trial was not reported at all by the Jewish press or the organ of the *Abwehrverein*.

We can deduce that these newspapers and their local "Berichterstatter" declined to report incidents involving group appearances by Jews in antisemitic gatherings. When a single Jew came to such a meeting, he came to debate his case, in accordance with accepted Liberal rules of the game. The presence of many Jews, on the other hand, signalled a readiness for a physical confrontation, an idea less tasteful to Liberals. But the very need for group appearances arose from the fact that antisemites did not abide by Liberal rules. They disturbed and abused, sometimes even physically mishandled, opposing speakers. So some Jewish defence activists assumed that without the presence of a number of supporters, their ability to speak would be greatly inhibited. Thus, when Benjamin Hirsch, a highly respected public figure in Halberstadt, decided to appear at an antisemitic rally, he made sure that all strong and young members of his community would be present.[113] Their presence was not mentioned in Jewish reports of the meeting.

Examination of the geographical dispersion of defence activities (see Appendix I, Table C), shows that they were concentrated on two *foci*. The most important one was Western Germany, from Oldenburg in the North down to Baden and Württemberg. It was especially extensive in the province of Hanover, where one writer had boasted that no antisemitic meeting could be held without the presence of a counter-speaker.[114] Although this claim is clearly exaggerated, it is obvious that verbal defence activities were more abundant in this province than in any other part of the *Reich*.[115] This is probably due to Jacob's influence and successes, but more to the fact that the popular Guelph Party[116] opposed antisemitic agitation in the province, and sometimes its members joined the defence effort. This must have encouraged other defence activists in their operation.

Rhineland and Westphalia were other centres of defence. The operations there were led by the Cologne branch of the *Abwehrverein* – the only local branch of that organisation comprised solely of Jews. That branch will be dealt with later, but we should note that it had organised verbal defence operations in the two provinces, the extent of which remains unknown.[117]

The second focus of defence activities was in the Eastern and mid-Eastern Prussian provinces of Brandenburg, Saxony, Silesia and Poznań. The operations here were much less extensive than in the West, and were based on one-time

[113]Yoseph Hirsch, *loc. cit.*, p. 48.

[114]*Israelitische Wochenschrift*, XXV, No. 22 (1st June 1894), p. 173.

[115]The numbers in Table C refer only to Jewish activities. If we had included the activities of Christians, who included some highly active members of the *Abwehrverein*, and occasionally members of the Guelph Party, they would have been much higher.

[116]On the party see Stewart A. Stehlin, *Bismarck and the Guelph Problem 1866–1890*, The Hague 1973, chap. 5.

[117]See the letter from Feilchenfeld (Cologne) to Lichtenstein (Hagen), 11th August 1893, CAHJP NW/35. The report for 1893, in the same file, shows an expenditure of 1,401 Mark on "Salair an Redner, Gehälter, Botenlöhne".

efforts of individuals. Only one activist here was involved in more than one operation.

Where was verbal defence not conducted? first of all in Bavaria, the second largest Jewish concentration in Germany.[118] It was very poor, or non-existent, in the major centres of antisemitic agitation and parliamentary successes. Four operations in Hesse and two in Hesse-Nassau were a far cry from the scale of antisemitic propaganda there. But extensive anti-antisemitic efforts were performed there by Socialists, and in some years by members of *Abwehrverein*.[119] The same cannot be said for the kingdom of Saxony or Pomerania, where the Socialists hardly tried to combat antisemitism. Still, we recorded only one Jewish verbal defence operation in Pomerania, and none in Saxony. We should also note the lack of activity in East and West Prussia.

A last word should be said about the venue chosen by the activists. As indicated by Table F in Appendix I, most of them chose to appear in antisemitic arenas, which meant going to antisemitic rallies. Some of them chose "defence arenas", that is, public meetings organised by opponents of antisemitism (in most cases by themselves). In those meetings, there were better conditions for the speaker, but they carried the danger of convincing the already convinced. A few activists chose both options (designated as "mixed" in the Table). Only one instance was recorded of appearing in a neutral arena, that is, a meeting of a group not concerned directly with antisemitism, and used by antisemites for agitation. (In this case, a meeting of Silesian *"Gastwirte"*.[120]) As such occasions were fertile ground for antisemitic propaganda aimed at crowds that were not their *a priori* sympathisers, the poor Jewish counter efforts constituted a big gap in defence activity.

VI. PRINTED DEFENCE

Another way of fighting antisemitism was through printed matter, such as leaflets, brochures or articles in German newpapers.[121] For verbal defence the

---

[118]The lack of activity is evident upon examination of two surviving community archives. The Regensburg archive contains a special file on "Emancipation and defence against Antisemitism", holding various documents about defence activities in Bavaria and the whole of Germany. There are no materials from the early 1890s, except for one publication of the *Abwehrverein*, CAHJP, HM/1555. The Nuremberg archive contains the protocols of the community *Vorstand*, CAHJP, HM/2/3621, which record some financial contributions towards defence efforts, all of which were outside Bavaria.

[119]See Peal, *loc. cit.*, pp. 276–278.

[120]*Jüdische Presse*, XVI, No. 10 (5th March 1890), pp. 120–121. I did not include in my survey Orthodox defence activities concerning the *Schechita* (ritual slaughter of animals). These efforts involved many Jewish appearances in neutral arenas, such as animal welfare societies.

[121]Appendix 4 of my dissertation, *op. cit.*, contains a list of 44 people who performed such activities. Included in that list and the subsequent data break-down were only writers of articles, books or brochures aimed at the general public, and not writers of defence articles in the Jewish press or Liberal periodicals with a limited and specific readership, such as the MVAA or *Die Nation*. Modern studies describe some of the brochures that were written in Berlin in early 1893, just before the founding of the C.V. See Schorsch, *op. cit.*, pp. 105–113; Reinharz, *op. cit.*, pp. 39–43; Lamberti, *op. cit.*, p. 9; Ragins, *op. cit.*, pp. 43–44, 47–50. The brochures written by Ludwig Jacobowski are surveyed in Stern, *op. cit.*, chap. 8.

prime requirement was rhetorical prowess. Those engaged in printed defence did not need this skill, nor did they have to suffer the threatening mood of antisemitic meetings, but other qualities were called for: writers of books and pamphlets needed money to cover the printing costs. To have articles printed in the press writing skills and local prestige (or contacts with editors) were imperative. One could also publish *Inseraten* in the papers, but again that demanded financial backing.

This combination of *desiderata* affected the professional composition of activists in printed defence.[122] Whilst verbal defence was composed mostly of teacher-preachers, that profession had only one representative among printed-defence activists. (One other, listed as a teacher in Appendix II, was a school director.) Teachers in Jewish communities did not receive high salaries and their social status was relatively low.[123] The number of rabbis and members of the liberal professions active in printed defence was, on the other hand, significantly higher – in particular, of course, journalists and writers with their established contacts.

There is a partial correlation between the profession of the activist and the means of publication chosen. Rabbis were the large majority (10 out of 15) of those who published in the press – clearly local prestige and recognition as experts in their field were factors in this. Members of the liberal professions, especially journalists and writers, were in the majority among authors of brochures, and here financial means or access to printing houses must have been of overriding importance. Those who wrote or translated books were rabbis, journalists, and one physician, Marcus Hirsch (a son of Samson Raphael Hirsch), who was a prolific writer and published many articles in the Orthodox press. Writing skills and wide knowledge were clearly the dominant factors here, while money was of secondary importance as, apparently, for such well-known and respected personalities some material help towards publication was available.[124]

Examination of the geographical dispersion[125] and religious standpoints of printed-defence activists indicate an involvement of sectors that did not take part in verbal defence. We should note especially the activity in Berlin, in which 12 of the 44 activists resided. The activists in Berlin can be roughly grouped in three categories:

a. Young *literati*, all of whom were born in the Eastern Provinces or Russia.

b. Notables, who had not taken part in Jewish matters before the 1890s, although some of them attempted (or wanted to attempt) to fight antisemitism before.[126]

c. Leaders of the Orthodox *Austrittsgemeinde*.

---

[122]See Appendix II, Table A.

[123]See the complaints in Lion Wolf, *Der Jüdische Lehrer. Sein Leben und Wirken*, Rostock 1881.

[124]Paul Nathan, scion of a rich banking family, seems the only one amongst them who could have afforded the printing himself.

[125]See Appendix II, Table D.

[126]Edmund Friedemann already published a brochure, *Das Judentum und Richard Wagner*, in 1869. Paul Nathan wrote his book, *Der Prozess von Tisza Eszlar. Ein antisemitisches Kulturbild*, Berlin 1892, in 1882, but did not publish it for ten years.

If we compare this with our findings about verbal defence, we see that categories b and c had no representation among verbal-defence activists in Berlin. These categories indicate, in fact, the much higher social standing of their members. Category a, on the other hand, is precisely the one from which members of the VBR came. (And indeed two activists engaged in printed defence were members of the VBR also.) But most of the activists in this category as well had a higher social standing than the VBR members. It is also interesting that in all the categories we again encounter Jews who had no connections with the leadership of the main community.

Another striking dissimilarity between verbal and printed defence is to be seen in the printed-defence efforts in Frankfurt a. Main.[127] In the other big communities no trace was found of any Jewish defence activity. Otherwise, the geographical distribution of printed-defence activity is generally similar to the picture we drew upon examination of verbal defence, with the Western border[128] and the mid-Eastern provinces being the centres of activity. The few brochures and newspaper articles published in Bavaria, Hesse, the North-Eastern provinces[129] and Saxony hardly bear witness to a combatant spirit among the Jews there.

Concerning religious standpoints, we see that printed-defence efforts were joined by holders of extreme viewpoints, whose absence we had noted when considering verbal defence. Leaders of *Austrittsorthodoxie* played an important part in the activities, especially in Berlin and Frankfurt, and among them were no less than three of Samson Raphael Hirsch's sons. No established leaders of extreme Liberalism were among the activists, but some of the brochures were clearly written by extreme Liberals, and contained calls for widespread Reform of the Jewish religion.[130] One brochure – which turned out to be the most influential among them – contained a sharp diatribe against Jewish Orthodoxy, even calling for a complete break with it.[131] The majority of activists, however, held more moderate religious views.

Turning to the other variables characterising printed-defence activists, we find important similarities with verbal defence. Education, especially academic education, is again, obviously, a major factor.[132] In fact, more than half the activists (23) had doctorates. The other important characteristic is again the age group, two thirds of the activists whose age was identified were under 50.[133]

---

[127]All five activities listed under Hessen-Nassau in Table D took place in Frankfurt a. Main.

[128]Again we must note that some activities in this field were carried out by the Cologne branch of the *Abwehrverein*. A number of brochures are mentioned in the report for 1893, CAHJP NW/35. The scope of that activity is unknown to me.

[129]For the listing of West Prussia in Table D see Appendix II, note 3.

[130]Other brochures that were published by Liberal Jews, calling for wide reforms in the face of growing antisemitism, but not for any other means of defence, were not included in this survey. For one of them, see note 160.

[131][Raphael Löwenfeld], *Schutzjuden oder Staatsbürger? Von einem jüdischen Staatsbürger*, Berlin 1893. For a discussion of its contents see Schorsch, *op. cit.*, pp. 105–113; Reinharz, *op. cit.*, pp. 39–42; Lamberti, *op. cit.*, p. 9; Ragins, *op. cit.*, pp. 47–50.

[132]See Appendix II, Table A.

[133]See Appendix II, Table B.

As with verbal defence the large majority were born in places other than their residence, and mostly in the Eastern provinces, or East of the *Reich*. Again, the large percentage of rabbis (especially the Orthodox ones) offers a partial explanation. To them we should also add the group of journalists and writers, also coming mostly from the East.

Other variables, such as the targets of defence activity or time in office (for rabbis) produced no meaningful results.

VII. NON-AGITATIONAL ACTIVITY AGAINST ANTISEMITISM

Besides the activities we termed "agitational" (that is, endeavouring to counter antisemitism by public propaganda measures), there were also efforts to fight antisemitism by other means, such as boycott, spreading personally abusive information, attempting to sabotage the distribution of pamphlets, etc. If verbal- and printed-defence activities were aimed against antisemitic propaganda, these activities were aimed against antisemitic propagandists, trying to damage them, or the physical means of their operation (such as brochures or newspapers). This kind of activity received little public exposure, and this was preferable from the operational point of view. In many cases it was publicised only after – and because – it had failed.

Surviving information of such activities is scant, partial, and abounds with records of blunders and failures. Still, I consider it to be important, as it testifies to a tendency existing among the Jewish population at that time – a tendency towards a sharp, acute combat "with the gloves off" against antisemitism. Due to lack of space, we can only deal with two interesting efforts, which demonstrate the limits of these attempts.

The most comprehensive attempt for direct action against antisemitic bodies was an initiative of the Orthodox newspaper *Der Israelit* to mount a nationwide Jewish boycott of local papers deemed supportive of antisemitism. These papers did not identify themselves publicly as antisemitic, but supported antisemitic standpoints through their articles and reports.[134]

In September 1893 *Der Israelit* sent a letter to various local papers, announcing that it intended to publish fortnightly a list of "Philosemitic Newspapers", in which its readers could advertise without fearing that their money would benefit antisemitism. The recipients of the letter were asked to inform *Der Israelit* if they wished to be included in the list.[135]

The letter evoked sharp and hostile reactions from non-Jewish,[136] as well as

---

[134]The idea for this initiative probably originated in the two-part article, 'Arische Lokalpresse und Semitische Annoncen. Auch ein Wink zur Abwehr', *Der Israelit*, XXXIII, No. 91 (17th November 1892), pp. 1733–1734; 92 (21st November 1892, pp. 1757–1758. Its writer warned of the dangerous role played by such papers, and suggested that Jews should neither read them nor advertise in them.

[135]The letter was printed in MVAA, III, No. 40 (1st October 1893), p. 370.

[136]*Ibid.* The MVAA itself apparently agreed with the criticism.

Jewish sources.[137] *Der Israelit* was deterred and withdrew the initiative, after publishing a bitter reply[138] complaining about the lack of unity within the Jewish camp.

This case shows the limits put on the use of Jewish financial power as a weapon against antisemitism. Public opinion, including that of Liberals and Liberal Jews, was sharply opposed to any such step.[139] Thus, efforts to deter or punish antisemitic businesses by economic means had to be limited to a local or sub-local level, and could not be organised on a wider and more effective scale. Such efforts did take place,[140] but we have no way of knowing how many.

Another attempt to attack and deter antisemites took place in Leipzig, home of Theodor Fritsch, one of the leading agitators of the period.[141] Karl Wiesenthal, a young writer[142] who reported to *Der Israelit* on Fritsch's activities,[143] organised a group aimed at encouraging every Jew slandered by Fritsch to prosecute him before the court.[144]

After one month, however, Wiesenthal completely withdrew. He could not tolerate the heavy pressure to which he was subjected, including fines imposed on him by local courts.[145] After suffering "hateful attacks" and "the worst and most malicious insults", and receiving letters that "bore witness to the incredibly low moral standards of their writers", Wiesenthal published a letter "to clarify the situation",[146] in which he declared that the planned initiative had never materialised.

Karl Wiesenthal and his organisation were the precursors of Eugen Fuchs and the C.V., who also combatted antisemites through legal measures. Their story illustrates the pressures defence activists had to endure, especially in centres of antisemitism, thus providing some explanation for the fact we noted earlier, that defence efforts were scarce in such surroundings. An organisation could better endure the pressures.

Apart from these instances, Jewish papers give evidence to quite a number of anti-antisemitic operations such as collecting and distributing harmful personal information, disturbing the sale of pamphlets and brochures – sometimes by

---

[137]This is clear from the reply of *Der Israelit*. See the next note.

[138]*Der Israelit*, XXXIV, No. 83 (19th October 1893), pp. 1563–1564.

[139]See also the response in the *Allgemeine Zeitung des Judenthums*, LVIII, No. 31 (3rd August 1894), p. 372, to a report on an attempted boycott in Halberstadt.

[140]Evidence of one such effort was unearthed in the archive of a small Hessian village. See Eugen Caspary, 'Jüdische Mitbürger in Oberbrechen 1711–1941', in Helmut Gensicke and Egon Eichhorn (eds.), *Geschichte von Oberbrechen*, Brechen-Oberbrechen 1975, pp. 207–208.

[141]On Fritsch see Pulzer, *op. cit.*, pp. 53–54; Levy, *op. cit.*, pp. 37–39; R. H. Phelps, 'Theodor Fritsch und der Antisemitismus', in *Deutsche Rundschau*, No. 87 (1961), pp. 442–449; Moshe Zimmermann, 'Two Generations in the History of German Antisemitism. The Letters of Theodor Fritsch to Wilhelm Marr', in *LBI Year Book XXIII* (1978), pp. 89–99.

[142]He was born in Leipzig in 1860. This information was also supplied to me by Dr. Renate Heuer.

[143]See note 55.

[144]*Der Israelit*, XXXII, No. 19 (5th March 1891), p. 361. On the immediate background to that initiative see *ibid.*, No. 18 (2nd March 1891), p. 337.

[145]*Israelitische Wochenschrift*, XXIII, No. 5 (29th January 1892), p. 39.

[146]*Der Israelit*, XXXII, No. 30 (13th April 1891), pp. 579–580). The letter was undoubtedly published in local papers in Leipzig as well.

violent means, and even "arranging" for a strong Socialist presence in antisemitic rallies.[147] The Jewish and Liberal press was quite reluctant to print these stories (the antisemitic press, on the other hand, loved them, especially those linking Jews with Socialists, and invented many out of thin air) and did so only when special circumstances arose.

A case in point is that of a Jewish merchant in Thuringia, who was charged with libel by an antisemitic editor after trying to dissuade a local "Gastwirt" from keeping the antisemitic paper on his premises. A judge in Vacha sentenced the merchant to fourteen days in prison, explaining that a fine would not suffice, as it would be paid by the "Gesammtheit der Juden". After a successful appeal to a higher court, the punishment was reduced to a fine of 50 marks.[148]

It took a combination of two factors to have that story publicised: the disparaging decision of the lower legal body, and its revocation by a higher court. Before the first decision was revoked, no Jewish paper printed the story. The same goes for other defence operations which were reported to the public: a special reason was needed before they were published. The reasons were either a big blunder, with the ensuing report as a criticism and warning to others; or a legal process, initiated against Jews, which concluded with acquittal or a relative success. Defence efforts that were publicised because of their achievements were very, very rare, and dealt exclusively with the collection of damaging personal information on antisemitic agitators.[149] It appears that most efforts were not made public when they occurred. About some of them we can learn from local archives, some survive in family memoirs,[150] and others will apparently remain unknown.

It is interesting that many participants in the non-agitational defence efforts were Jewish merchants from villages and small towns, sectors that were hardly represented in defence agitation, either verbal or printed. Defence agitation measures could be applied by only a small part of the Jewish population, those who had a good, and recognised, knowledge of Jewish subjects and considerable rhetorical, writing, or financial capabilities. Clearly, most German Jews did not enjoy all, or even some, of these qualities, and thus could not participate in these efforts. Nevertheless, some evolved their own methods of combat, which were somewhat rougher than the ones used by the big town *bourgeoisie*. Other such activists were students or young *literati*, while others were themselves members of the *bourgeoisie*. We have only scant information about this kind of activity, and cannot measure its scope, but there is no doubt of its wide existence.

---

[147]For more information see my dissertation, *op. cit.*, chap. 4.

[148]*Jüdische Presse*, XXV, No. 2 (11th January 1894), p. 16.

[149]One such case was the information collected by the teacher Lion Wolf on the agitator Schwenhagen. See Lion Wolf, *50 Jahre Lebenserfahrungen eines Jüdischen Lehrers und Schriftstellers*, Leipzig 1919, pp. 260–269.

[150]See the memoirs of Wilhelm Buchheim in Monika Richarz (ed.), *Jüdisches Leben in Deutschland. Selbstzeugnisse zur Sozialgeschichte im Kaiserreich*, Stuttgart 1979 (Veröffentlichung des Leo Baeck Instituts), pp. 166–168.

VIII. A BROAD AWAKENING

So far, we have dealt with defence activities carried out by individuals. The number of these individuals is not very great: we have personally identified 89 activists. In a few places, such as Bonn or Bruchsal, a greater number of Jews were involved in defence operations. But did that activist minority reflect the wider opinion of the Jewish population? We have seen that there was an activistic minority among the Jews in the early 1880s, but it was isolated. Did the events in the early 1890s reflect a major change in Jewish public opinion, or were they also isolated occurrences?*

We mentioned that the Jewish press enthusiastically supported the new defence initiatives. This, however, is no yardstick, as the press supported the defence initiatives of the 1880s as well, but their support did not move the largely indifferent or opposing public opinion.

On the 1890s, however, we have information that clearly indicates a widespread awakening of the Jewish public to the need for actively fighting antisemitism. This awakening proved to be a major change in Jewish attitudes, not only in reactions to antisemitism, but in the whole mode of Jewish relations with surrounding German society. Instead of constant apprehension of appearing to be an unassimilating society, a self-isolated and self-concerned "state within a state", there came the call for Jews to start defending their own interests publicly, to take care of their own needs and concerns, without fear of doing so as Jews.

One clear sign of the attitude towards defence operations is the support given to it by communal leadership in the provinces. We have seen that the spiritual leadership – rabbis and teacher-preachers – formed, alongside local notables, the major portion of defence activists, and some community chairmen personally participated in the activity. Several community and district leaders who did not themselves take part, supported their local activist rabbis with appreciative letters, financial awards, or the publishing of their speeches.[151]

In two parts of Germany, regional defence organisations were formed, which – although founded by local individuals – appealed to, and relied on, a wide affiliation with communities. These were the *Abwehrverein* branch in Cologne, and the *Vereinigung Badischer Israeliten*.

The *Abwehrverein* in Cologne was formed by a group of Jewish notables, who invited the communities of the Rhine province and Westphalia to send their representatives to a big meeting in Cologne. The meeting was held on 21st June 1893, in the presence of delegates from 41 communities, while 24 other communities sent messages of support. At the meeting,[152] the Cologne branch, the only Jewish branch of the *Abwehrverein*, was constituted.[153] The number of

---

*Note the contrary opinion of Toury in his essay in this volume, Section III – (Ed.).

[151]See *Jüdische Presse*, XXIII, No. 25 (1st September 1892), pp. 447–448; and XXIV, No. 22 (1st June 1893), p. 256; *Allgemeine Zeitung des Judenthums*, LIX, No. 7 (15th February 1895), Gb., p. 3.

[152]Invitations, agenda and a report of the meeting are found in CAHJP, NW/35.

[153]For some information about that branch see Suchy, *loc. cit.*, p. 214; and chap. 5 of my dissertation, *op. cit.*

communities involved, and the amount of funds raised,[154] demonstrate a wide support for that group among Jewry in those provinces.

The *Vereinigung Badischer Israeliten* was another defence organisation, founded in early 1893 by a group of prominent Jews in Karlsruhe. Again, these notables appealed to Baden communities for affiliation and support, and elicited a wide response.[155]

Another attempt to organise for defence at a regional level was made in a meeting of community leaders from the Grand Duchy of Hesse.[156] The meeting agreed that an organisation should be formed, which would fight antisemites through open propaganda via the press, public speakers and the distribution of brochures. Apparently, some plans for defence activities were prepared,[157] but there is no indication that they, or the envisioned organisation, ever materialised. Still, what is significant is the evidence that Jewish communal leaders in several provinces and *Länder* actively supported defence against antisemitism by the new, public means. This is an obvious change when compared with former periods.

Support was spreading among the Jewish population, in spite of still existing opposition. At a meeting of the *Mendelssohnverein* in Elberfeld, dedicated to the question of how to fight antisemitism, one speaker (member of the local *Freisinnige* Party leadership) called for a "Todtschweigen" policy, based on a "vornehmes Nichtbeachten". This view, which was dominant in the 1880s, was sharply criticised by the other speakers. The meeting adopted by a large majority a decision to fight antisemitism with every available force.[158] A Liberal group of Frankfurt Jews also organised a special meeting on the subject, where the speakers emphasised the "duty" to combat antisemitism more resolutely than before.[159] Members of the student fraternity *Badenia* in Heidelberg decided in 1892 to try and disseminate similar ideas. They called upon Jews to come and fulfill their "sacred duty" to defend Jewish honour, declaring that so far they had worked in Heidelberg, but now they felt the time had come to "scatter their seeds" in other places. The students obviously felt that there was now a fertile ground for those seeds to fall on.

It is interesting that one speaker at the Frankfurt meeting, Fritz Auerbach,

---

[154]No less than 9,000 Marks were collected in 1893, and that does not include some communities which kept their funds for local activities. See the report for 1893 in CAHJP, NW/35.

[155]See information and membership lists in the *Bericht des Vorstandes der Vereinigung Badischer Israeliten über seine Tätigkeit bis 1. Januar 1895*, Karlsruhe 1895. This is the best source about the organisation's early history. See also Schorsch, *op. cit.*, pp. 115–116, and chap. 5 of my dissertation, *op. cit.*

[156]*Der Israelit*, XXXI, No. 96 (8th December 1890), p. 1737. The meeting took place in Frankfurt, which might indicate that Jewish leaders from the Prussian province of Hesse-Nassau were also present.

[157]See *Der Israelit*, XXXII, No. 31 (16th April 1891), p. 592. There is an undated document, entitled 'Thesen für den zu gründenden Centralverein zur Bekämpfung des Antisemitismus', located in CAHJP, Inv/1412(2). The document, signed by "the delegates from Frankfurt am Main", contains a detailed plan for a national organisation to fight antisemitism, and was obviously prepared for a meeting dedicated to that topic. Possibly, this document was connected with the group of Hessian community leaders we are dealing with.

[158]*Jüdische Presse*, XXIV, No. 49 (7th December 1893), p. 538.

[159]*Allgemeine Zeitung des Judenthums*, LIX, No. 13 (29th March 1895), Gb., p. 3.

had published a few years earlier a brochure on the rise of antisemitism.[160] In this pamphlet, Auerbach had not called for an active defence, but only suggested changes in the Jewish religion, to eliminate everything that still separated Jews from their Christian neighbours. His speech at the meeting shows that he had changed his opinions. We can identify some other individuals, such as Heinrich Loewe and Paul Nathan, who similarly changed their views, from a belief that no action should be taken, to themselves participating in defence activities.[161]

The most clear indication of changes in feelings about the ways of reacting to antisemitism is the response to the plan, initiated by the *Gemeindevorstand* of Berlin at the end of 1892, to meet with the *Kaiser* and ask for his protection. The proposal was leaked to the radical daily *Berliner Volkszeitung*, and was sharply attacked by it in a leading article, entitled 'Reichs-Schutzjuden??'.[162]

The publication caused a storm. The plan was strongly criticised in Jewish and Liberal papers,[163] and even the *Berliner Tageblatt* of Rudolf Mosse, himself a member of the *Repräsentantenversammlung*, initially joined the critics. The Berlin *Vorstand* had to withdraw. The plan was cancelled, and two of its members, the initiators of the plan, resigned. The most powerful body of German Jewry was defeated by the pressures of an activistic public opinion.[164]

All the evidence we put forward clearly demonstrates that during the early 1890s (in fact, as the Berlin affair shows, by the end of 1892), the opinion that antisemitism should be fought by new, public means had become dominant among German Jewry. Only a few were active themselves, but the public view was favourable and supportive of such activities. This represents a major departure from the views which were dominant in the 1880s; a departure that should be attributed to the changes that took place within German politics as a whole.

IX. A PRE-HISTORY OF THE C.V.?

The storm of protest raised by the plan to meet with the *Kaiser* led to the formation of a big and influential Jewish defence organisation: the C.V. This organisation promulgated, from its very beginning, concepts identical with the perceptions of the Jewish activistic defence which we have dealt with: "Selbstvertheidigung, im Lichte der Öffentlichkeit".[165]

---

[160]Fritz Auerbach, *Der Antisemitismus und das freisinnige Judenthum. Ein offenes Wort an die freidenkenden Juden*, Frankfurt a. Main 1893.

[161]For details see my dissertation, *op. cit.*

[162]*Berliner Volkszeitung*, XL, No. 305 (29th December 1892), 2. Blatt, 1st page. The formulations in that article, concerning the difference between acting as "Schutzjuden" and as equal citizens, were used later by Raphael Löwenfeld in his famous brochure (see note 131). As Löwenfeld had connections with the *Berliner Volkszeitung*, I believe that this article was his inspiration (or perhaps inspired by him?).

[163]See the angry reactions in *Israelitische Wochenschrift*, XXIV, No. 1 (1st January 1893), pp. 4–5; No. 2 (7th January 1893), pp. 11–12; No. 3 (14th January 1893), pp. 19–20. See there also quotations from other papers.

[164]For short summaries of the affair see also Reinharz, *op. cit.*, p. 39; Lamberti, *op. cit.*, p. 8.

[165]See the references in note 5.

But, when examining the activities of the C.V. in its first years, one can observe that it did *not* follow the lines of operation carried out by Jewish defence activists. It did not send speakers to antisemitic rallies, nor did it hold public rallies of its own to counter antisemitic slanders. (The public meetings it organised were for Jews, not for the general population, and were not meant to be a forum for fighting antisemitism.) The C.V. did not publish or distribute anti-antisemitic brochures or leaflets,[166] nor did it initiate any press articles on the matter.[167] Thus, the organisation deviated from its own plans, as published in its first public exhortations. Instead, it chose to operate in a different manner: to act as a Jewish interest group, representing the Jewish case before the authorities.[169]

The one way the C.V. used in directly combatting German antisemites was through the law, helping maligned private individuals to bring their slanders before the courts. We encountered one unsuccessful effort to do the same thing in Leipzig. The C.V., as a strong organisation using professional jurists, had more success. But the question remains: as the C.V. did not follow the operational path of Jewish defence activists, can the defence activity be regarded in any way as a "pre-history" of that organisation?

I believe that this question should be answered in the affirmative, though not because of similarities in the actual operational sphere.

Our observations in this article indicate that in the early 1890s large parts of the Jewish population came to realise the need for an activist defence. That was the background for activities performed by individuals, and as some of these individuals were successful, and their actions received wide acknowledgment through the press, the tendency of Jewish public opinion to support further defence actions, carried out in public, continued to increase. A large reservoir for a potential national defence organisation was therefore created.

Through articles in the Jewish press we can identify some members of this reservoir. Dr. Heinrich Meyer-Cohn, son of a rich and respected Berlin family was one. He commenced with a career in community politics, and was appointed member of the most important community body, the *Vorstand*, in 1893. But he chose to give up that appointment,[169] and became instead a member of several defence organisations,[170] including the C.V. Another activist writer and future C.V. member was the journalist, Isidor Kastan.[171] One could also mention Martin Spanier, a teacher and secretary of the Magdeburg community, Dr. Richard Landau of Frankenberg in Saxony, and many others.

There was a widespread feeling that passivity towards antisemitism must

---

[166] Apart from one exception: Walter Pohlmann, *Die Juden und körperliche Arbeit*, Berlin 1894. This was the text of a lecture given at a C.V. meeting: that is, to a Jewish audience.

[167] That changed somewhat when the C.V. began to publish its own organ, *Im deutschen Reich*, in 1895. But that organ was also aimed, first and foremost, at Jewish readers.

[168] I hope to deal with that subject in a separate article about the early history of the C.V. See also chap. 6 in my dissertation.

[169] *Allgemeine Zeitung des Judenthums*, LVII, No. 2 (13th January 1893), Gb., p. 1.

[170] On his part in the *Abwehrverein* see Suchy, *loc. cit.*, pp. 228–229.

[171] See his articles in the *Allgemeine Zeitung des Judenthums*, LVII, No. 2 (13th January 1893), pp. 14–15; No. 13 (31st March 1893), pp. 148–149. For biographical information see Wininger, *Grosse Jüdische Nationalbiographie, op. cit.*, vol. VII, p. 158.

come to an end, that an extensive defence effort must be waged. This feeling had reached a climax by the end of 1892 and the beginning of 1893. A sharp article, published during this period denounced prevailing passivity as "Schmach" and "Thorheit", and ended with an excited appeal for action:

> "Wie lange noch, um Himmelswillen wie lange noch?! Wann endlich wird der Bann gebrochen werden, in den stumpfe Theilnahmslosigkeit und kleinmüthiges Zagen das heutige Geschlecht gezwungen? Auf zur That, zur schleunigen, kräftigen, opferfreudigen, nimmer rastenden That!"[172]

This demand, indeed craving, for something to be done provided the climate in which the C.V., as well as other Jewish organisations dedicated solely to defence, was established. The initiative to found the C.V. was launched as a result of the overwhelming public response towards Raphael Löwenfeld's brochure.[173] The pamphlet, with its call for abandonment of the old "Schutzjuden" ways and for proudly standing for one's rights as a "Staatsbürger", had struck the right note, and the Jewish public responded far and wide. Following that, a group of Jewish personalities gathered around Löwenfeld and reached the decision that a new organisation of German-Jewish "Staatsbürger" could and should be established.[174]

The C.V., after being formed, encountered resistance from Christian Liberal and some Jewish elitist circles[175] (not to mention the Jewish Orthodox). It was opposed, behind the scenes, by the established Jewish Berlin leadership, as its foundation could be, and was, regarded as challenge to that leadership in the wake of the embarrassing failure of its plan to meet with the *Kaiser*.[176] Several years before, the modest ambitions of the *Jüdisches Comité vom 1. Dezember 1880* were hamstrung in the face of lesser opposition. The C.V., on the other hand, succeeded in establishing itself, mobilising a large membership, and gaining a leading position within German Jewry in quite a short time.

This achievement was based on its ability to mobilise the existing "reservoir of potential support for activistic defence" and get it to support its own activities (although they were not "defence agitation" operations as we have defined them). The emergence of the C.V. as a contender for German-Jewish leadership, and its subsequent success, would have been unthinkable, had that reservoir not been formed. Therefore, the rise of Jewish activistic defence should indeed be seen as a "pre-history" of the C.V.

---

[172] *Jüdische Presse*, XXIII, No. 49 (8th December 1892), p. 608.

[173] See the third printing of *Schutzjuden oder Staatsbürger?*, *op. cit.*, in 1893, pp. 17–24.

[174] Paul Rieger, *Ein Vierteljahrhundert im Kampf um das Recht und die Zukunft der deutschen Juden. Ein Rückblick auf die Geschichte des Centralvereins deutscher Staatsbürger jüdischen Glaubens in den Jahren 1893–1918*, Berlin 1918, pp. 18–19; *C. V. Kalender für das Jahr 1929*, Berlin 1929, p. 34.

[175] Rabbi Dr. Singer of Coblenz said that it should be included in "die Kategorie der krankhaften Erscheinungen unseres fin-de-siècle". See *Israelitische Wochenschrift*, XXIV, No. 42 (20th October 1893), pp. 325–326.

[176] See, for example, the speech of Adolf Brüll, in Frankfurt a. Main reprinted in *Populär-Wissenschaftliche Monatsblätter*, XIII, No. 4 (1st April 1893), pp. 73–74. The denial by Löwenfeld of any intentions to challenge the communal leadership (*Schutzjuden*, 3rd printing, p. 17) also indicates that the brochure was seen in that light. The relations between the C.V. and the Berlin community are treated in my dissertation, *op. cit.*, chap. 6.

We must add that support in the provinces was not automatically forthcoming for any national Jewish organisation. Provincial Jews were inclined to be suspicious of Berliners contemplating leading such a group.[177] Another defence organisation from Berlin, the *Verein zur Abwehr Antisemitischer Angriffe*, led by notables who were patronising in their treatment of provincial Jewry, failed to establish itself as a leading national organisation. The C.V. leaders, on the other hand, openly displayed their regard for views and ideas voiced by provincial Jews, and this, it would seem, was a major reason for their success.[178]

Finally, one might ask how can we regard defence operations occurring in late 1893, 1894 and 1895 as a "pre-history" of an organisation founded in early 1893? The answer is that it took the C.V. some time before it became known, and accepted, throughout the country. In 1893 the C.V., still grappling to find its own course of activity, did very little in public. It received more public attention in 1894, thanks especially to its "legal defence bureau" (as indicated both by attention to it in the press, and by appeals for help and advice addressed to it by other Jews). But even when it became known, it was perceived largely as a Berlin group, not necessarily connected with defence in the provinces.[179]

Only by late 1895, when it had organised big meetings which received a wide response from provincial Jewry, and when leaders of other defence organisations joined its ranks and accepted its leadership, can we ascertain that the C.V. was nationally regarded as a leader in defence matters. And I believe that the big reduction in the number of defence operations in 1895 was in large measure a result of the acceptance of that leadership. Therefore, the performance of defence operations up to that time should certainly be considered a "pre-history" of the C.V., since it was still a part of building the atmosphere which enabled it to reach this leadership position.

CONCLUSION

We have surveyed Jewish activities against antisemitism, and identified some of their important characteristics:

1. The centres of activity were Berlin, the Western border, and the Eastern and middle-Eastern Prussian provinces.

2. In Berlin, the communal leadership resented, or at least ignored, these activities, and they were carried out by people who were not connected with it. In the provinces, on the other hand, most activists were associated with the communal leadership and supported by it. Subsequently we saw that some activists in Berlin developed distinct feelings of belonging to a new generation, more in tune with the times than the older, passive one. There was no feeling of such a "generation gap" in the provinces.

---

[177]See, for example, *Israelitische Wochenschrift*, XXIV, No. 10 (3rd March 1893), pp. 74–75; and No. 48 (1st December 1893), p. 379.
[178]See my dissertation, *op. cit.*, chaps. 5 and 6. I hope to deal with that subject separately.
[179]For a clear expression of that perception see the *Bericht* (as in note 155), p. 8, and see also p. 30.

3. The characteristics most distinctive of the activists as a group were: being born outside their place of residence, relative youth and a wide education.

The role of the changes taking place within the surrounding society has been emphasised as the main factor initiating the change in Jewish defence methods. The leading part played here by academics and intellectuals deserves closer attention.[180] Intellectuals are, of course, generally perceived as initiators of cultural, social and political change[181] – and even when not initiators they often sense the changing climate and transmit this to other sectors of a given society.[182] It seems that in a minority group like German Jewry academics were the ones in closer contact with the changing winds[183] and acted as "carrier group".

It is a *sine qua non* that when a break with tradition occurs, younger and educated people lead the change. In Berlin, where the established leadership sharply opposed the attempt for change, we have found another characteristic of verbal defence activists: their marginality to and detachment from formal Jewish life. It is interesting that similar characteristics were found regarding another, much older, Berlin group, which wanted to lead a break with formal traditions in another sphere.[184] These people were more ready to break with dominant norms, and less prone to retreat in the face of opposition by traditional leaders.

An overview of the activities presents one striking fact: the scale of Jewish defence activity was far below that of their adversaries.[185] Most Jewish "defence activists" performed one, and only one, recorded defence activity. Out of 89 activists 22 performed more than one operation, and only 9 (out of the 22) more than two. When we try to look for Jews who were engaged continuously, for more than a year, in defence operations, we find only Benno Jacob of Göttingen and Hirsch Hildesheimer of Berlin. And they had been active only once every several months.

On the other side, dozens of antisemitic agitators operated – writing or speaking publicly – at a steady pace of several times per month, appearing all over the country. (Jewish activists operated only in or near their place of residence.) In almost every big or medium-sized town, some kind of antisemitic organisation was active, spreading by various means the message that "the Jews

---

[180]The percentage of academics in political leadership positions is usually higher than their percentage in the general population. Still, the representation of Jewish academics among defence activists and in the leadership of the C.V. is disproportionately high.

[181]For a general, balanced discussion of that topic see S. N. Eisenstadt, 'Intellectuals and Tradition', in *idem* and S. R. Graubard (eds.), *Intellectuals and Tradition*, New York 1973, pp. 1–19.

[182]Klaus Mehnert, 'The Weather Makers', in Malcolm Macdonald (ed.), *The Intellectuals in Politics*, Austin 1966, pp. 93–94.

[183]The fact that Jewish students were strongly integrated into German society and values is a recurring theme in Monika Richarz, *Der Eintritt der Juden in die akademischen Berufe. Jüdische Studenten und Akademiker in Deutschland 1678–1848*, Tübingen 1974 (Schriftenreihe wissenschaftlicher Abhandlungen des Leo Baeck Instituts 28).

[184]Ismar Schorsch, 'Breakthrough into the Past. The *Verein für Cultur und Wissenschaft der Juden*', in *LBI Year Book XXXIII* (1988), p. 4.

[185]I must emphasise that the following observations are not meant as a criticism, based on hindsight, of German Jewry and its behaviour. Their purpose is solely to shed some light on a subject, not widely discussed, concerning Jewish reactions towards antisemitism.

are our misfortune". Meetings were held, printed material distributed, newspapers printed, all amounting to a constant bombardment of public opinion.

The major antisemitic agitators of the 1890s were professionals. Sales of written material and entry tickets to their meetings were a major source of their income. The masses were their economic, as well as ideological, target. They needed to reach the wider public and get its support. The successful agitators were those who had the talent to gather crowds, to write "best-selling" propaganda pieces. Those who were in possession of such talent suffered no economic retraint, or lack of time, to interfere with their operation.

The Jews had no professional defenders. Those who endeavoured to fight, did so in their own spare time, using their own private means. They did not receive recompense for their efforts, as costly and time-consuming as they might be. And costly they were – from publishing a leaflet to hiring a meeting place. The least expensive activity was attending an antisemitic meeting – requiring only fares and entrance tickets. But there one had often to pay the high emotional price of being subjected to insults and threats. Not many were able to pay such a price.

The only reward Jewish defence activists could and did get was social: public endorsement of their activities. For this the press was the major vehicle. This social compensation was of value for rabbis and teachers, as it could better their standing in the community, enhance their reputation in other communities, and thereby improve their bargaining position *vis-à-vis* community leaders, and thus indirectly lead to economic compensation. This explains why some teachers and rabbis were at pains to publicise their activities in the press. Members of other professions, especially the liberal professions, could also use the "social credit" gained by public recognition of their activities.[186]

Those in need of securing "social credit" through public activity are generally young and from elsewhere. The old-established residents of a town consolidate their place in society and business through existing kinship and social networks.

But even if this socio-economic explanation for the motivations of Jewish defence activists (many of whom were already well established, socially and economically), were true, it would give only part of the picture. There were other, much more comfortable avenues through which one could obtain social credit. An aspiring rabbi could excel in the field of study. An aspiring professional could involve himself in the quickly-developing life of Jewish societies, or – where possible – move into local politics. The network of societies for Jewish history and literature, growing and developing in the very period under discussion, provided one kind of organisation in which many a rabbi, teacher and educated layman could and did acquire social prestige.[187] They did not need the messy business of fighting antisemitism.

---

[186]On the importance of "social credit" for lawyers see Hannes Siegrist, 'Die Rechtsanwälte und das Bürgertum', in Jürgen Kocka (ed.), *Bürgertum im 19. Jahrhundert. Deutschland im europäischen Vergleich*, vol. 2, Munich 1988, p. 116.

[187]See Jacob Borut, 'Vereine für jüdische Geschichte und Literatur. The Popularization of Judaism and the Science of Judaism, 1890–1895', in *Proceedings of the Tenth Congress of Jewish Studies*, Division B, vol. I, Jerusalem 1990, pp. 251–258.

Indeed, the fact that most defence activists operated only once, and that individual defence activities dwindled in 1894 and 1895, as organised groups took the task upon themselves, indicates that the Jewish activists did not operate out of personal motives. Otherwise, they would have continued their engagement. Rather, they performed what they believed to be their duty, and that duty turned out to be a very unpleasant one. Not many could carry on for long, without receiving sufficient compensation for their material and emotional losses. The same is true – even more so – for Christian activists against antisemitism, who did not enjoy the social compensation given to Jews for their efforts.

The solution was the creation of organisations, where the individuals were part of a supporting group, and where large financial resources could be concentrated and distributed to those who could utilise them best. Such organisations were indeed founded in the early 1890s. But – apart from the short-lived Cologne branch of the *Verein zur Abwehr des Antisemitismus* – they chose to concentrate their efforts on other fronts. That is especially true for the C.V., which fought antisemitism through the courts and government institutions, but rarely through public propaganda. As the number of activist defence efforts had dwindled in the middle of the decade, at least partly due to the appearance of the C.V., the public propaganda stage was left open to the antisemites.

It must be emphasised again, that no criticism was intended by these observations. One cannot judge, even today, what chance a prolonged propaganda campaign might have had, especially as parts of the public were, *a priori*, unreceptive to any arguments presented by Jews. It is quite possible that the course taken by the C.V. might have had more success in the long run, had history taken a different course.

The fact remains that Jewish defence, indeed its whole public behaviour and self-perception, changed sharply in the early 1890s, as Jews stopped acting like *Schutzjuden* and began openly to champion their own rights. They did not conceal their Jewish identity, and their own self-recognition, even self-pride, were formulated publicly. These qualities persisted with most German Jews, even when that time came when nothing was left to them of their former position in German society and in the German state.

APPENDIX I

Jewish Verbal Defence Activists in the Provinces

A. *Professions*		B. *Year of Birth*		C. *Province or Land*	
Rabbi	9	Before 1830	1	Prussia (total)	35
Teacher-preacher	19	1831–1840	3		
Merchant	2	1841–1850	2	Silesia	2
Lawyer	3	1851–1860	3	Poznań	2
Journalist-writer	2	1861–1870	7	Pomerania	1
Industrialist	1	Unknown	32	Brandenburg	5
Banker	1			Saxonia (Prov.)	4
Lecturer	1	Total	48	Hessen-Nassau	2
Bookkeeper	1			Hanover	9
Gastwirt	1			Rhine prov.	3
Gerbermeister	1			Westphalia	6
Unknown	8			Schl.-Hostein	1
Total	49*			Baden	4
				Württemberg	2
				Hessen (Duchy)	4
				Oldenburg	1
				Braunschweig	1
				Schwarzbg.-Sonsh.	1
				Bremen	1
				Total	49**

* Elieser David performed two anti-antisemitic operations: one in 1892 whilst a teacher in Hanover, the other in 1894, when he was a rabbi in Düsseldorf. He was therefore counted twice in this table.

** See note *

D. *Year of Activity*		E. *Birthplace of Activist*		F. *Operation Arena*	
1890	1	Silesia	3	Antisemitic	34
1891	6	Poznań	1	Defensive	10
1892	13	Pomerania	1	Mixed	3
1893	21	Saxonia (Prov.)	1	Neutral	1
1894	18	Hessen-Nassau	1		
1895	1	Hanover	1	Total	48
		Rhineland (Saarland)	1		
Total	60***	Württemberg	1		
		Russia	1		
		Unknown	37		
		Total	48		

*** In this table I summed up the total number of defence operations, which is larger than the number of activists, as some of the latter performed more than one defensive operation.

APPENDIX II

Jewish Printed Defence Activists

A. *Professions*		B. *Year of Birth*		C. *Type of Publication*	
Rabbi	17	Before 1830	2	Brochures	24
Journalist-writer	4	1831–1840	5	Books	7
Journalist	3	1841–1850	10	Press Articles	15
Writer	2	1851–1860	5	Press *Inseraten*	4
Lawyer	3	1861–1870	5	Leaflets	3
Teacher-preacher	2	Unknown	17		
Industrialist	1			Total	53*
Merchant	2	Total	44		
Physician	1				
Theatre Director	1				
House-Owner	1				
Gastwirt	1				
Unknown	6				
Total	44				

* 8 of the activists produced 2 publications, and 1 produced 3. 2 produced 1 jointly.

D. *Province of Land*		E. *Birthplace of Activist*		F. *Year of Activity*	
Prussia (total)	34	Silesia	4	1890	3
		Poznań	3	1891	6
Hessen-Nassau	5	West Prussia	2	1892	18
Hanover	4	Pomerania	1	1893	19
Rhine prov.	3	Brandenburg	2	1894	6
Westphalia	1	Berlin	2	1895	1
Saxonia (Prov.)	3	Oldenburg	2		
Silesia	1	Baden	1	Total	53***
Poznań	1	Hessen (Duchy)	1		
Pomerania	1	Saxony-Meiningen	1		
Brandenburg	2				
West Prussia	1	Hungary	3		
Berlin	12	Russia	3		
		Holland	1		
Baden	4	Unknown	18		
Saxony (Kdm.)	1				
Hessen (Duchy)	1	Total	44		
Lübeck	2				
Oldenburg	1				
Bavaria	1				
Total	44**				

** In this table I referred to the places where activists resided, rather than to those where the publications were printed. Of the 53 publications, 4 were not printed in the writer's town of residence. The only significant case is the printing in Berlin of a brochure whose author lived in Danzig. The other cases, e.g. the printing in Berlin of a brochure by the Rabbi of Potsdam, are not significant. In two cases – one in Bavaria and one in Lübeck – I had no information on the author's residence, so used the place of publication, assuming it to be in the same province.

*** See note*.

The Centralverein and the American Jewish Committee: A Comparative Study

BY EVYATAR FRIESEL

From the second half of the nineteenth century, Jews in Western Europe were adapting to the social ways and cultural norms of the general environment – were integrating in general society. At the same time they began to formulate new concepts and to create new organisational structures that expressed Jewish interests and concerns, as seen against the events of the late nineteenth century.*

The Jewish rights' associations were products of that new situation. The prototype of these organisations was the *Alliance Israélite Universelle*, established in Paris, in 1860.[1] Similar societies were formed in diverse countries, such as the *Allianz* in Germany and in Austria, or the Anglo-Jewish Association in England, all in the 1870s. The *Centralverein deutscher Staatsbürger jüdischen Glaubens* (C.V.) was founded in Berlin in 1893, and the American Jewish Committee in New York, in 1906. By the 1930s, Jewish civil-rights organisations were active in almost every country with sizeable Jewish communities.

Basically, the aim of these associations was the implementation of civil and political rights for Jews in countries where such rights were still non-existent, or existed but were not observed. The civil rights associations developed characteristics of their own in each country, reflecting local conditions and necessities. Later they fanned out into new directions. The *Alliance Israélite Universelle* created a well-known educational system: a network of schools spanning most countries of the Mediterranean basin and beyond. Other associations became active in philanthropy. Most participated, in one way or other, in that very important Jewish issue in modern times, Jewish migration.

In the twentieth century, the Jewish rights' associations were much criticised by the Jewish Nationalists and by the Zionists, who considered them as assimilationist oligarchic groups who were not entitled to speak for the broader

*The present article originated from a suggestion of my friend Dr. Arnold Paucker, the editor of the Leo Baeck Institute Year Book. It brought me into a direction of thought and research that I had not considered before, for which I am deeply grateful to him. Research was done in the Blaustein Library of the American Jewish Committee, where I was assisted by the Chief Librarian, Cyma Horowitz. I had also several very helpful conversations with the director of the research department of the AJC, Dr. David Singer. Part of the research and the writing was done in the American Jewish Archives, in Cincinnati, Ohio, assisted by a Rapoport Grant. It was my fourth stay at the Archives, where a large part of my work dealing with the history of American Jewry has been done. Dr. Jacob R. Marcus and Dr. Abraham J. Peck, the directors of the Archives and friends of many years, were again extremely helpful. Sincere thanks are due to the staff of the institutions mentioned for their patience, interest and help.

[1]There are a considerable number of works on different organisations created for the defence of the civil rights of Jews, but so far no general study or comprehensive history has been written. On

Jewish public. The critiques referred to the fact that the Jewish rights'
associations were initiatives of Jewish notables, usually members of the new
Jewish upper-middle class. Workers, people from the lower-middle class,
Orthodox Jews or new immigrants were conspicuously absent from their
councils. Indeed, they had no rank-and-file, but were small groups of self-
appointed spokesmen for Jewish causes.

At the beginning, this was exactly how the founders of the Jewish civil-rights
societies wanted to be and to act. They shunned publicity, or open action with the
participation of the larger Jewish public. They preferred quiet efforts behind the
scenes, and looked suspiciously upon the Jewish "masses", the newcomers, as they
saw them, with foreign accents and outlandish ideas, who had still to work out how
a proper German or American citizen of the Jewish faith should behave. As
always, it was not only a matter of style, but also of principle. If Jews were to appear
before the authorities as a broadly organised and vocal body, would that not cast a
shadow over their standing as good citizens? General society, they felt, was still
doubtful about the Jewish presence in its midst. Too assertive a stance on the part
of the Jews might only fuel the flames of antisemitism, always smouldering
beneath the surface of the still unsolved matter of full Jewish integration in the
different walks of general society. Such feelings were perhaps more clearly formulated among the activists of the *Centralverein* than among those of the American
Jewish Committee, but in practice the broad attitude of both was not dissimilar.

In historical perspective, the Jewish rights' societies appear in a new light,
different from the opinions of both supporters and detractors. Considered under
the conditions of the second half of the nineteenth century, these associations
represented a new and original step in Jewish self-definition. The growing
integration of West European Jews usually brought with it a loosening of Jewish-
orientated ties. Nevertheless, the Jewish rights' activists expressed a high
awareness of the problems facing Jews in different countries and a readiness to
act against persecution or discrimination. In addition, the structure of the
associations was a new phenomenon in Jewish life: country-wide, neutral (in
principle) as regards the diverse religious tendencies in Jewish society, they were
among the first examples of what may be called "secular" Jewish organisations.
It is true that the activists kept stressing their own and their likes' good
citizenship and attachment to their countries. But as we shall see, the internal
dynamics of those organisations worked into a direction that was the opposite of
assimilation. Whoever assimilated, in the social circles of these activists, did not
do so because of his activities in a Jewish civil-rights association.

Among these organisations, the *Centralverein** and the American Jewish Committee represented special cases, because both experienced evolutions which had

the *Alliance Israélite Universelle*, see André Chouraqui, *Cent ans d'histoire: l'Alliance Israélite Universelle et
la renaissance juive contemporaine 1860–1960*, Paris 1965; Michael Graetz, *Les Juifs en France au XIX* Siècle*,
Paris 1989, pp. 380–430.
*For the *Centralverein* and its antecedents see also the two preceding essays by Jacob Toury, 'Anti-Anti
1889/1892', and Jacob Borut, 'The Rise of Jewish Defence Agitation . . .', in this volume of the Year
Book – (Ed.).

much in common, and which led them far beyond their original intentions.[2] Both associations underwent a gradual change in their attitudes *vis-à-vis* the political life in their countries. Their organisational structures expanded. They worked on the formulation of broader Jewish self-definitions.

There were also differences. Both organisations reflected diverse Jewish experiences, in Germany and in the United States. The *Centralverein* was active only in Germany, and concentrated on the fight against antisemitism.* The American Jewish Committee, which was formed in the wake of the Kishinev riots of 1903, focused its attention at the beginning on the situation of the Jews in Russia, later expanded its interests to other countries, and became active also in the United States. Their respective attitudes towards Zionism were not the same, although that point deserves careful analysis: one should remember that they were active in different times.

There were only limited contacts between the *Centralverein* and the Committee, and they started, it seems, not before the late 1920s. In August 1920, Louis Marshall, the AJC's president, wrote to Julius Brodnitz, chairman of the C.V., and observed that "in many respects your organization resembles the American Jewish Committee of which I have the honor of being president. It occurs to me that some kind of cooperation might be feasible between our respective organizations."[3] The worsening political situation in Germany in the early 1930s stimulated collaboration between the two organisations. Contacts continued also after 1933, but they were hampered by the restraints imposed by the new German reality.[4]

---

[2]The *Centralverein* has benefited from a sizeable amount of historical research. For the Imperial era and Wilhelminian Germany in particular see among other works: Ismar Schorsch's *Jewish Reactions to German Anti-Semitism, 1870–1914*, New York–Philadelphia 1972; Jehuda Reinharz's *Fatherland or Promised Land. The Dilemma of the German Jew, 1893–1914*, Ann Arbor, Mich. 1975; Marjorie Lamberti's *Jewish Activism in Imperial Germany. The Struggle for Civil Equality*, New Haven–London 1978. Especially worthwhile is Arnold Paucker's long article, 'Zur Problematik einer jüdischen Abwehrstrategie in der deutschen Gesellschaft', in *Juden im Wilhelminischen Deutschland 1890–1914*. Ein Sammelband herausgegeben von Werner E. Mosse unter Mitwirkung von Arnold Paucker, Tübingen 1976 (Schriftenreihe wissenschaftlicher Abhandlungen des Leo Baeck Instituts 33), pp. 479–548; see also (for Weimar Germany) his *Der jüdische Abwehrkampf gegen Antisemitismus und Nationalsozialismus in den letzten Jahren der Weimarer Republik*, Hamburg 1969; Evyatar Friesel, 'The Political and Ideological Development of the Centralverein before 1914', in *LBI Year Book XXXI* (1986), pp. 121–146. For a comprehensive *Centralverein* bibliography until 1985 see Arnold Paucker, 'Die Abwehr des Antisemitismus in den Jahren 1893–1933', in Herbert A. Strauss, Norbert Kampe (Hrsg.), *Von der Judenfeinschaft zum Holocaust*, Bonn 1985ff., pp. 164–171.

On the American Jewish Committee, see Naomi W. Cohen, *Not Free to Desist. The American Jewish Committee 1906–1966*, Philadelphia 1972. There is plenty of material relating to the AJC in secondary sources.

*The reader should also consult the following two essays on legal aspects of the C.V.'s fight against antisemitism; Sibylle Morgenthaler, 'Countering the Pre-1933 Nazi Boycott against the Jews'; and Cyril Levitt, 'The Persecution of Antisemites by the Courts in the Weimar Republic; Was Justice Served?', in this volume of the Year Book – (Ed.).

[3]10th August 1927 – Blaustein Library (New York), AJC Archives, file 'Germany and Centralverein 1925–1932'.

[4]See Cohen, *Not Free to Desist, op. cit.*, pp. 156–188.

Although aware of the methodological pitfalls of doing so, I suggest that the similarities and differences between the *Centralverein* and the American Jewish Committee should be considered while relativising the time factor. German Jewry was "older" than American Jewry. Consequently there was, usually, a hiatus of two generations or more in any like patterns of development in the *Centralverein* and the Committee. For example, the broadening of the organisation of the *Centralverein* happened from 1905 on; that of the Committee, after 1944. The AJC adopted positions regarding certain issues which, although not unlike those taken by the C.V., went farther. This did not necessarily express a greater inherent dynamism on the part of the American Jewish Committee, but was perhaps a result of the differing periods in which each organisation was active.

The natural development of the *Centralverein* came to an end in 1933 (although it existed for some years more), while the American Jewish Committee continues to be active and evolve up to today. Like most non-Zionist organisations, after the creation of Israel the AJC redefined its attitude towards Jewish statehood and the ideological issues related to it.

POLICY AND ACTIVITIES: PRINCIPLES AND CHANGES

Considering themselves full citizens of their respective countries, the founding fathers of both the *Centralverein* and the American Jewish Committee saw their religious specificity as of similar standing to that of the Protestant and Catholic citizens. The *Centralverein*, as it proclaimed in its first statement in 1893, defined itself as a group of German citizens of the Jewish faith who had come together to work for their civil and social equality, as well as for the cultivation of their German-mindedness (*deutsche Gesinnung*).[5] The 1906 founding charter of the American Jewish Committee mentioned only that the task of the new association was the defence of the civil and religious rights of the Jews. Nevertheless, their sense of full American citizenship and the dedication of its members to the interests and welfare of the United States were obvious and taken for granted.

It was a firm principle of both associations not to take a stand in political matters, since this would have meant mixing religion and politics. This did not mean, however, that German and American Jews did not have recognisable political leanings. In Imperial Germany, most Jews voted for the Left-Liberal (or Progressive) Parties. In the years prior to the outbreak of the First World War, Jews also began to vote for the Social Democrats. Those tendencies continued after 1918, during the Weimar Republic. A majority of the Jews voted then for the *Deutsche Demokratische Partei* (DDP), the successor to the Left-Liberals of

---

[5]See Reinharz, *Fatherland or Promised Land, op. cit.*, pp. 48–49; Friesel, 'The Political and Ideological Development', *loc. cit.*, p. 125.

Imperial Germany. A growing minority supported the *Sozialdemokratische Partei Deutschlands* (SPD).[6]

Jews voted for the Progressives because they were the most committed to the values that were essential for Jewish civil integration in German society: the inviolability of the rights of the individual, political and legal equality of all citizens, constitutional government, separation of Church from State. It was not a political relationship without tensions. Many Jews thought the Progressive Parties inconsequential in German politics. Worse, they were considered lukewarm in their attitude towards the rights of Jews, and apt to enter into electoral coalitions with antisemitic candidates of other parties. In the first decade of the twentieth century there was talk about alternative political options, but nothing came of it.[7]

Probably, nothing could have come of it. Not only because the Jews were too few and too divided amongst themselves to run any realistic electoral chance with a candidate of their own; but because it would have gone counter to their views about being citizens like any other, different only in religion. The fact that the German Catholics were doing exactly that – defining themselves politically along religious lines (the Catholic *Zentrum*), and very successfully – did not count. On the contrary, the Catholics were criticised for it: they practised "confessional politics".[8] Political Catholicism in Germany, observed Ludwig Philippson, the editor of the most important German-Jewish weekly, the *Allgemeine Zeitung des Judenthums*, took away everything the Jews had attained in Germany in the last hundred years.[9]

In the United States, the electoral picture among Jews was different. Republicans and Democrats were equally devoted to the civil and political principles of the American Republic. The situation of the Jews was much easier in the United States than in Germany: not because antisemitism was unknown, but because the Jews were but one "defined" group among many others. There were other groups living in America that were much more the object of discrimination than Jews (although on different basis and kind), such as blacks and Chinese.

In the first part of the century, American Jewry was still largely a community of immigrants. Among the older segment of the community, of German origin (which included the founders of the American Jewish Committee), there was

---

[6]Until 1908, the Progressive or Left-Liberal (as against the National Liberal) Parties were the *Freisinnige Vereinigung* and the *Freisinnige Volkspartei*. After 1910, all Left-Liberals united in the *Fortschrittliche Volkspartei*. On the political tendencies of German Jews, see Jacob Toury, *Die politischen Orientierungen der Juden in Deutschland. Von Jena bis Weimar*, Tübingen 1966 (Schriftenreihe wissenschaftlicher Abhandlungen des Leo Baeck Instituts 15); on the later period (although with an introduction on the pre-1914 years) see Ernest Hamburger and Peter Pulzer, 'Jews as Voters in the Weimar Republic', in *LBI Year Book XXX* (1985), pp. 3–66, especially p. 65.
[7]See Friesel, 'The Political and Ideological Development', *loc. cit.*, pp. 133–135.
[8]Eugen Fuchs, *Um Deutschtum und Judentum, Gesammelte Reden und Aufsätze*, Frankfurt a. Main 1919, pp.85–86, 243. Peter Pulzer, in his article, 'Religious and Judicial Appointments in Germany, 1869–1918', in *LBI Year Book XXVIII* (1983), pp. 183–204, deals extensively with the political situation of the Jews and the Catholics in Imperial Germany, and comments also on the relations between them.
[9]Quoted in Toury, *Die politischen Orientierungen, op. cit.*, pp. 249–250, from the *Allgemeine Zeitung des Judenthums*, XXXIX (1st January 1875), p. 1.

much support for the Republicans. The growing sector of Americanised immigrants of East-European origin, or their children, started the Democrat-orientated electoral pattern that came to characterise American Jewry from the 1930s on. From that time American Jewry became clearly committed to liberal causes, in the United States and elsewhere.[10]

However, the *Centralverein* and the American Jewish Committee recognised that as Jewish organisations they had to steer clear from identifying themselves with one of the parties in the spectrum of the political life in their respective countries. "We are a central organisation which encompasses all Jews 'with no difference regarding their political party tendency'. As Jews, we do not belong to any political party. Political opinion is, like religious opinion, a matter for the individual." Thus Eugen Fuchs of the C.V., in 1898.[11] "We have no political interests which are different from those of our fellow-citizens. We would subject ourselves to just criticism if we organized political clubs of our own. There is no such thing as a Jewish Republican or a Jewish Democrat." Thus Louis Marshall of the AJC, in 1912.[12]

Having said this (and meaning every word of it), they proceeded to develop in a direction that, in essence, was almost opposite.

The same year it was founded, in 1893, the *Centralverein* had established a legal-defence commission (*Rechtsschutzkommission*), headed by Eugen Fuchs, to act through the courts against antisemitic actions and publications. The commission symbolised the pattern of action of the C.V., and it became the most viable of the means at the disposal of the organisation. The results were relatively positive, although it became clear that the courts were not the most effective place to fight antisemitism.[13]

The *Centralverein* took its first step towards politics-connected activities in the German elections of 1898. It did so carefully, keeping itself within the formal framework of its aims: the decision was not to support candidates, but to oppose antisemitic ones. Even so, the C.V.'s move brought a storm of criticism from many of its members, who saw it as a deviation from the C.V.'s principles.[14] They understood well that in the German electoral district system, to fight one (antisemitic) candidate meant to support the opposing one, who in most cases was a Left-Liberal.

Once the C.V. took its first decision, further steps followed almost naturally. At the beginning, the desirable candidate was (discreetly) supported financially. With time, more money was expended.[15] As the next step, the C.V. would appeal

---

[10]On the electoral characteristics of American Jewry, especially in the second half of the century, see Murray Friedman, *The Utopian Dilemma. New Political Directions for American Jews*, Washington 1985.

[11]Fuchs, 'Bestrebungen und Ziele', in *Um Deutschtum und Judentum, op. cit.*, p. 57.

[12]Letter to Benjamin Marcus, 8th March 1912, in Charles Reznikoff (ed.), *Louis Marshall Champion of Liberty. Selected Papers and Addresses*, vol. II, Philadelphia 1957, p. 809.

[13]See Paul Rieger, *Ein Vierteljahrhundert im Kampf um das Recht und die Zukunft der deutschen Juden*, Berlin 1918, pp. 26–32; Schorsch, *Jewish Reactions, op. cit.*, pp. 123–132.

[14]For an explanation of the C.V.'s decision, see Eugen Fuchs, 'Konfessionelle Kandidaturen', in *Um Deutschtum und Judentum, op. cit.*, pp. 66–83; see also Lamberti, *Jewish Activism, op. cit.*, pp. 23–26.

[15]See Schorsch, *Jewish Reactions, op. cit.*, pp. 132–148.

to the Jewish voters, recommending its man. Later it would appeal to voters in general, openly. Gradually the level of the *Centralverein*'s involvement in political activities increased. In the 1920s, the organisation's leadership recognised early enough the dangers embodied in the National Socialists led by Hitler. In the last free elections in Germany the *Centralverein* did its best to fight, by every legal and political means at its disposal, the upsurge of Nazism. By the early 1930s, the *Centralverein* had become as political as possible.[16]

In the United States, only in the 1960s did the American Jewish Committee broaden the realm of issues in American life it took interest in, and adopt positions that were consistently liberal. For the first half century of its existence, the main occupation of the AJC had been matters related to discrimination against Jews and antisemitism, in the United States and elsewhere. Even then, although its constituency in those earlier years had been ideologically much more conservative than its later membership, the argumentation against antisemitism was always based on liberal principles. The same happened also with the *Centralverein*. The reason is obvious: only liberal arguments had any meaning, in the debate against modern antisemitism.

Since the beginning, there had been also a second theme close to the AJC's attention: to keep open the gates of the country for immigrants. Obviously, it was Jewish immigrants that were foremost in the AJC's endeavours. In 1906, Jacob H. Schiff, considered by many as the outstanding American Jewish figure at that time, was thinking in terms of two million new Jewish immigrants in the next five to ten years.[17] As a public attitude, the support for immigration was significant. "Older" Americans were becoming lukewarm, or even hostile (each social group for its own reasons) towards uncontrolled immigration.[18] The leadership of German-Jewish extraction, for its part, was moving in the opposite direction. During the first decades of the century, this was one of the very few issues in American public life in which the German-Jewish notables associated with the Committee ran against the "WASP" establishment.

The Johnson Acts of 1921 and 1924 limited severely the immigration of Jews. Agitating for the approval of more generous immigration laws by Congress remained an important item on the AJC's agenda over the next decades. It was an issue that suited ideally the Committee's style of action: here was a matter where there was a clear fusion of interests that were American and Jewish, and which could be acted upon within the frame of a coalition of many bodies interested in the same goal. The Committee participated in a large public forum, the American Immigration and Citizenship Conference (AICC), in which tens of ethnic and religious associations collaborated. The Conference influenced the

---

[16]See Paucker, *Der jüdische Abwehrkampf, op. cit.*, especially chapt. VII.

[17]Zosa Szajkowski, 'Paul Nathan, Lucien Wolf, Jacob H. Schiff and the Jewish Revolutionary Movements in Eastern Europe (1903–1907)', *Jewish Social Studies*, XXIX (1967), p. 24; see also Cohen, *Not Free to Desist, op. cit.*, pp. 37–53.

[18]On that theme, see Edward G. Hartmann, *The Movement to Americanize the Immigrant*, New York 1948; Cohen, *Not Free to Desist, op. cit.*, pp. 43–53.

approval by Congress of the Law of October 1965, which radically changed American immigration policy.[19]

A broad social-action programme in American life was adopted in the 1960s. In a sense, it was an expansion of the traditional civil rights attitudes of the Committee, which so far had concentrated on action against discrimination, for separation of Church from State, and for better immigration laws. It represented an adaptation of the AJC to the new tenor of public life in the United States and the pressure from the ever-growing rank-and-file of the Committee.

A 1988 statement by the AJC included the protection of human rights in general, with a specific condemnation of apartheid in South Africa. Issues relating to civil rights and civil liberties in the United States were central themes, with emphasis on the separation of Church from State, social policy, family policy, immigration and public education. The American Jewish Committee took a position on the growing debate in American society on abortion, supporting the "pro-choice" camp.[20]

Obviously, however, the Committee remained rooted in Jewish issues, which were its *raison d'être*. Important among these were Israel's security, the fight against antisemitism, and assistance to Russian Jewry. In the 1980s, the defence of Israel had become a foremost item in most statements published by the American Jewish Committee.[21]

At the same time, the American Jewish Committee began to work for the improvement of "the quality of Jewish life in the United States". This was one of the expressions of a new direction and style of work already decided upon by the Committee in 1943,[22] although it took more than two decades to develop this particular theme into a full programme. By 1963, when John Slawson, the forceful Executive Vice-President of the AJC, was stating that ". . . to many leaders of Jewish communities, defense against assimilation now seems more urgent than defense against discrimination",[23] that additional line of action had matured. The establishment of a Department of Jewish Communal Affairs transformed the theme into one of the important fields of activity of the AJC.[24] However, the new topic also involved difficult conceptual problems for the AJC, which will be mentioned again in this paper.

In later years, the AJC defined itself as a "human relations agency", stressing its pioneer role in the United States.[25] In its large array of activities the liberal

---

[19]See Sidney Liskovsky, 'United States Immigration Policy', *American Jewish Yearbook*, 67, (1966), pp.164–175; for former efforts, see American Jewish Committee, *Americanizing our Immigration Laws*, New York 1949; see also Cohen, *Not Free to Desist, op. cit.*, pp. 368–374.

[20]American Jewish Committee, *On the Issues*, December 1988.

[21]*Ibid*; American Jewish Committee: Ira Silverman, *Living in Two Civilizations. Jews in the Political Process*, New York 1989; *AJC, Annual Report 1987*, New York n.d.; *AJC, Annual Report 1988*, New York n.d.

[22]See John Slawson, 'Principles Underlying our Program', *AJC, Annual Report, 1943*, New York 1944, pp. 99f.

[23]John Slawson, 'The Quest for Jewish Identity in America,' *Journal of Jewish Communal Service*, XL, No. 1 (1963), p. 17.

[24]See American Jewish Committee: Bertram H. Gold, *Faith, Patience and Optimism*, New York 1988, p. 10; *AJC, Annual Report 1988*, pp. 44–48.

[25]American Jewish Committee, *On the Issues*.

approach to life in America was consistently maintained, but since the Committee was always shy of formulations of principle, the liberal position was defined as such only long after being adopted. As late as 1984, David M. Gordis, then the Executive Vice-President of the AJC, still preferred to use the concept "active centrism".[26] However, in 1989 the new Executive Vice-President, Ira Silverman, stated that "there must be some specific substance for our lobbying and our resolutions and our articles, a program affirming a liberal approach to public policy". The liberal approach, explained Silverman, was rooted in the Jewish political tradition and "also consistent with our self-interest – our interest in promoting a stable society made up of satisfied individuals and groups, that is tolerant of diversity and provides the kind of fertile ground in which groups like ours may best flourish".[27]

Obviously, the liberal approach in civil and political questions was a reflection of the political views of the membership of the American Jewish Committee, as it has been of the *Centralverein* in its time. However, scholars have commented upon the significant contradiction apparent in these political trends, in Germany as in the United States. The constituency of the C.V. and of the AJC belonged, in their respective countries, to the middle and upper-middle class. In terms of their social and economic interests, it was to be expected that many more Jews would adopt and defend conservative positions in the political life of their countries.[28] We shall deal later with the reasons for this incongruity.

The style of the Committee had also changed dramatically. Commenting about criticisms that had appeared in American television against the American Israel Public Affairs Committee (AIPAC), the pro-Israeli lobby in Congress, the Executive Vice-President of the AJC declared, at the Committee's annual meeting in 1989: "We must not let ourselves be bullied or cowed. We have a right to be heard. Neither we nor others should question our patriotism. Like other Americans, we have multiple loyalties – to country, to people, to religion, to community, to school and so forth."[29]

It should be added that the American Jewish Committee was not the only Jewish organisation in the United States to deal with the questions mentioned on its agenda. The American Jewish Congress, founded in 1916 and re-founded in 1922, had rather similar aims. AIPAC, founded in 1959, was a registered lobby that acted in Congress for the interests of Israel, and was considered highly successful in its task. The Anti-Defamation League (created in 1913 by the Order *B'nai B'rith*) concentrated on the struggle against antisemitism, and operated with a budget and a professional staff significantly larger than those of the American Jewish Committee. The National Jewish Community Relations Advisory Council (NJCRAC), started in 1944 as a co-ordinating agency, was, by the late 1980s, developing activities of its own, in the same fields as the AJC. And

---

[26]See AJC, *New Steps in the American Jewish Experiment*, New York 1984, p. 15.

[27]Silverman, *Living in Two Civilizations, op. cit.*, pp. 6–7.

[28]Regarding Germany, see Paucker, 'Zur Problematik', *loc. cit.*, pp. 494–497, 505; about the United States, see Murray Friedman, *The Utopian Dilemma. New Political Directions for American Jews*, Washington 1985.

[29]Silverman, *Living in Two Civilizations, op. cit.*, p. 5.

the Conference of Presidents of Major American Jewish Organizations, or Presidents' Conference, formed in 1959 (in which the American Jewish Committee participated only as an observer), dealt with matters relating to American policy towards Israel.[30]

It was a situation quite different from what the *Centralverein* had experienced in its time. In spite of the transformations it underwent, the *Centralverein* remained concentrated on the same tasks that had brought about its formation in 1893, namely, the struggle against antisemitism in Germany, in Germany only. In the late 1920s, the growing power of antisemitism and Nazism enhanced the political character of the C.V. and its participation in the efforts against fascism in Germany. Among German Jews, the *Centralverein* was the leading entity in that work.[31] Nobody in Germany disputed the representativeness of the *Centralverein*: as we shall see, in the 1920s it expressed, directly or indirectly, the civil aspirations of the majority of German Jewry.

Is there some conclusion to be drawn from the fact that the *Centralverein* attained in its day a much broader level of representativeness than the American Jewish Committee? Could it be, that had the Committee changed earlier and faster its ideological positions and its organisational structure, the appearance of competing associations would have been avoided? Apparently, not. The conditions of American Jewry were different: more open, non-centralised, prone to reject any body claiming to represent all American Jews. But obviously, the existence of other strong and active Jewish agencies limited in some measure the influence of the American Jewish Committee.

THE BROADENING OF THE ORGANISATIONAL STRUCTURE

From the beginning, the American Jewish Committee had considered ways to broaden (somewhat) its organisation, so as to add to its representativeness. The idea was not to create a large membership of individuals, but to give a (limited) voice to Jewish communities and associations. Several steps to that effect were taken over the next thirty years. In theory, the AJC's membership reached, in the early 1940s, close to four hundred. In practice, half a dozen members of the executive committee established policies and took decisions, as it had been in the beginning. The style of action had remained the same too: discreet, behind the scenes, through contacts with (and occasional pressure on) key congressmen or members of the government.[32]

In its earlier years, no such thoughts about enlarging their association were considered by the *Centralverein*. Its leaders seemed sensitive to the possible

---

[30]Information about these and other organisations, their aims, budgets, staffs and publications is found in the annual reports of the *LCBC Report* (Large City Budgeting Conference).

[31]See Paucker, *Der jüdische Abwehrkampf, op. cit.*, Jehuda Reinharz, 'The Response of the *Centralverein deutscher Staatsbürger jüdischen Glaubens* to Antisemitism during the Weimar Republic', in Shmuel Almog *et al.* (eds.), *Israel and the Nations. Essays Presented in Honor of Shmuel Ettinger* (in Hebrew), Jerusalem 1987, pp. LXXXV-CX.

[32]See Cohen, *Not Free to Desist, op. cit.*, pp. 19–29.

allegations which a broader Jewish organisation might arouse among the ever-present German antisemites. The C.V.'s methods of action were as discreet as those of the AJC. The *Centralverein* worked mainly on the legal level: it was a style in accordance with its principles, and in any case the C.V. had no access to the higher spheres of German political life, such as the Committee enjoyed in the United States.

What brought the *Centralverein* to a radical reconsideration about its organisational structure were stirrings among the broader German-Jewish public about the need to create more effective means of Jewish self-defence. In September 1900, Martin Philippson, a distinguished historian and son of Ludwig Philippson, issued a call for a *Judentag*, an assembly of Jewish delegates.[33] The *Judentag* was suggested as a permanent body of political character, democratically elected and representing all German Jews. Its aim was to act against the growing problem of politically organised antisemitism in Germany.

Philippson was aware that the aims of the body he proposed overlapped those of the *Centralverein*. While recognising that the C.V. had done valuable work, Philippson pointed out that it was too small and represented only a limited sector of German Jewry. The *Judentag* envisaged by him should be broad and representative, with goals far beyond those stated by the *Centralverein*.

Jews from diverse sectors of Jewish life in Germany responded with interest to Philippson's ideas, which indicated that a new mood of Jewish awareness had been developing in the rank-and-file of German Jewry, more incisive than the rather bland and careful line advocated by the *Centralverein*. Indeed, Philippson's initiative represented a problem, seen from the *Centralverein*'s angle: to accept it, or to leave it unchallenged, might have made the *Centralverein* redundant, and brought about, sooner or later, its decline or even demise.

The leadership of the *Centralverein* reacted in three ways, not necessarily clearly defined, not co-ordinated, and spreading over several years: they began to reconsider the Jewish self-definition of their association; they started to plan the broadening of their own organisational structure; and last but not least, they proceeded to neutralise Philippson's initiative. Half knowingly, it seems, they decided to adopt as many of the features of the proposed *Judentag* as feasible – so as to make the *Judentag* superfluous.

Maximilian Horwitz and Eugen Fuchs, the two main leaders of the *Centralverein* in the first years, participated actively in all the deliberations on Philippson's initiative, and were instrumental in the shaping of the result, the creation of the *Verband der Deutschen Juden* in 1904. From the clear-cut self-definition in its title ("German Jews," against the blurred "German Citizens of the Jewish Faith" in the C.V.'s name), to the size of the organisation envisaged, the *Verband* looked impressive indeed. In fact, it was little more than a baroque façade, a castrated version of the far-reaching ideas expressed in the *Judentag* proposal of 1900. Its members were only organisations, not individuals; its tasks were of represen-

[33]See Schorsch, *Jewish Reactions, op. cit.*, pp. 149–162; also, Friesel, 'The Political and Ideological Development', *loc. cit.*, pp. 133–135.

tation, but not political action. The *Verband* said little and did less, which apparently suited well enough the *Centralverein* leaders, who watched over it carefully. Philippson, who recognised quite clearly what had happened, was less happy.[34]

In 1906, the general assembly of the *Centralverein* approved a radical reorganisation plan, with two main components. One, the formation of local chapters in Jewish communities throughout Germany, with as broad individual participation as possible. The other resolution was the transformation of the annual general assembly, at which theoretically all members could participate (in practice, only those living in Berlin, and fitting into a small hall could), to a convention of democratically elected representatives from all the newly formed C.V. branches in the country. Additional steps were taken over the next years, aiming to strengthen the new structure, to improve contact between the centre in Berlin and the branches in the other cities, and to induce the local chapters to activate themselves.[35]

Any worries about the growth of the local branches turned out to be needless. The local associations were a success, and the *Centralverein* developed significantly over the next years. From 17,000 members in 1905, the C.V. reached 34,000 in 1912, and a highpoint of over 72,000 in 1924. The real numerical strength was even greater, since in many cases only the head of the family registered as a member. In addition, the *Centralverein* also had a corporate membership, through Jewish associations affiliated to it. There seems to be no exaggeration in the claim that in the 1920s well over half of all German Jews were directly or indirectly connected with the *Centralverein*.[36]

As for the American Jewish Committee, it decided to transform its organisational structure in 1943–1944, while in the midst of an internal crisis over its decision to leave the American Jewish Conference, because of its pro-Zionist bent. The same meeting that approved the resignation from the Conference, on 24th October 1944, decided also to enlarge the membership of the Committee. Thoughts about broadening the Committee, in order to strengthen its influence, must have been discussed before. But the actual decision was clearly related to the withdrawal from the American Jewish Conference, and the consequent criticism of the AJC inside American Jewry.[37]

In fact, the structural reorganisation of the American Jewish Committee was only one expression of additional changes of attitude. In the words of Jacob Blaustein, the Chairman of the Executive Committee, the Committee decided to

[34]*Ibid.*, p. 135; Marjorie Lamberti, 'The Attempt to Form a Jewish Bloc. Jewish Notables and Politics in Wilhelmian Germany', *Central European History*, 3 (1970), pp. 85–86.

[35]See Friesel, The Political and Ideological Development', *loc. cit.*, pp. 135–140.

[36]See Reinharz, *Fatherland or Promised Land, op. cit.*, pp. 52–56.

[37]See 'Report of the Executive Committee', *AJC, Annual Report for 1943*, New York 1944, pp. 40–41; for the new by-laws, see *ibid.*, pp. 147ff.; for the former by-laws, see *AJC, Annual Report for 1942*, New York, 1943, pp. 136ff.; see also: A Summary of the Changes in the By-Laws of the American Jewish Committee 1906–1943 – Blaustein Library. See also Cohen, *Not Free to Desist, op. cit.*, pp. 260–264; Henry Feingold, *Past as Prologue, The American Jewish Committee*, New York 1987, p. 11.

A late and an early edition of the C.V.'s famous handbook against antisemitic argumentation

Deutsche Juden! wollt ihr ein Hitler - Deutschland?

Wollt ihr eure wirtschaftliche Existenz durch Boykott-Hetzer gefährden lassen?

Wollt ihr eure Kinder in eine haßerfüllte Zukunft hineinwachsen lassen?

Muß man die ehrliebenden und verantwortungsbewußten jüdischen Deutschen erst anfeuern, daß sie sich helfen?

Unser Abwehrkampf erfordert die gleichen ungeheuren Mittel, über die unsere erbitterten Feinde verfügen. Auf jeden Presseangriff, auf jedes Inserat, auf jede Wahlzeitung auf jedes Plakat wollen wir die Antwort geben: auf jedes Flugblatt das Gegenflugblatt, auf jeden Versammlungsvorwurf die Entkräftung! **Mit Pfennigen** ist diese **Arbeit nicht zu tun.** Die Nationalsozialisten opfern erhebliche Teile ihres Einkommens. Wer M, 100 — verdient, gibt mindestens M. 8.— für die Partei.

Dort gibt man Geld um Haß zu säen.
Wir wollen entgiften, aufklären, uns wehren!

Wir betteln nicht um Geld. Wir schildern jedem einsichtigen deutschen Juden die Gefahr objektiv, so wie sie ist und wir erwarten von ihm, daß er sich einreiht in unsere Kampffront, den

die Notgemeinschaft der deutschen Juden

Jeder gebe für den Kampffonds so viel, wie ihm der Schutz seiner Existenz, die Wahrung seiner Ehre und die Zukunft seiner Kinder wert ist. Die deutsche Judenheit wird das Schicksal haben, das sie sich selbst schafft!

Central-Verein
deutscher Staatsbürger jüdischen Glaubens E.V.
Berlin SW 68, Lindenstraße 13

Appeal by the C.V. to the Jews of Germany to contribute financially
to defeat the Nazi Party in the September 1930 elections

By courtesy of the Central Archives for the History of the Jewish People

reach out, "to have the benefit of participation in its program by more like-minded Jews over the land".[38] A step relating to that intention was the launching of *Commentary*, in 1945. And as mentioned before, the new interest in "the quality of Jewish life in America" started at the same time.[39]

The organisational structure of the Committee underwent further modifications over the next years. By the 1980s, the Committee claimed a membership of about 50,000. The AJC's frame was more complex than that of the *Centralverein*, two generations earlier. The highest power of decision belonged to the National Executive Council (with about 850 members), which worked through a smaller Board of Governors (of about 120 members). Day-to-day operations were carried out by an Executive Committee. The Committee was served by a number of commissions, committees, institutes and centres.[40] As far as they were involved in policy-making questions, they did not seem bound by too strict directives from the Executive Committee. As was characteristic also of other American Jewish organisations, the professional staff, and especially the heads of the diverse departments, had a large voice in policy-shaping.[41]

Although the C.V. and the AJC ended by developing structures that had many similarities, the scope of the work of those structures differed greatly. The *Centralverein* remained concentrated on the same tasks that had brought about its formation in 1893, namely, the struggle against antisemitism in Germany. The American Jewish Committee, for its part, expanded in to a wide array of Jewish and non-Jewish fields, and acted, generally, in a much less centralised way.

Furthermore, while the *Centralverein* was an organisation of German Jews, the Committee became open-minded on that issue. From the 1970s, members could be "Jews, their spouses and children [i.e. not necessarily Jewish] who are citizens or resident aliens [i.e. non-Americans] of the United States . . ."[42] Another example of the broader latitude of the Committee's operation was the editorial policy of its publications. The *Centralverein*'s organs, *Im deutschen Reich*, and (from 1922) *C.V.-Zeitung* remained under the strict control of the C.V. and concentrated on Jewish self-defence issues. The two organs of the Committee, *Commentary* and *Present Tense*, as well as the *American Jewish Year Book* (AJYB), were editorially independent. The AJYB became the best source of current information about the situation of Jewish communities throughout the world. *Commentary*, which developed into one of the leading American intellectual monthlies and covered a broad span of general and Jewish subjects, adopted in the 1980s an editorial line labelled "neo-conservative," rather at variance with the liberal position of the Committee.

[38]AJC, 'Annual Report for 1944', *American Jewish Year Book*, 46, (1945), pp. 546–547.
[39]On the relationship between the issues, see John Slawson, 'Principles Underlying our Program', *AJC, Annual Report 1943*, pp. 99ff.
[40]The American Jewish Committee. Bylaws (as amended in 1988), Blaustein Library. *AJC, Annual Report 1988*; *LCBC Report*, No. 10 (1988).
[41]In 1988, the AJC staff counted 318 members, of which 165 professionals.
[42]AJC, by-laws, 1980 – Blaustein Library.

THE SEARCH FOR A BROADER SELF-DEFINITION

It seems difficult to understand the change of policies and the organisational alterations of the *Centralverein* and of the American Jewish Committee without relating them to changes that occurred in the self-definition of both organisations. This was a matter of high complexity, since it touched the foundations of one of the most basic issues in modern Jewish life: the blend of Jewish and "general" ideas and values that characterised the self-definition of the modern Jew.

The questioning started with deceptive simplicity. In the first decade of the century the leaders of the *Centralverein* began to reconsider the definition of aims of their association, and to search for a broader formulation that would go beyond their essentially negative formulation as a self-defence group (*Selbstverteidigungsverein*). As stated by Eugen Fuchs, who in those years can be seen as the most important ideologist of the C.V., it had become clear that a fuller formulation of Jewish aims was essential for the continuing activity of the *Centralverein*. Consequently, the organisation should adopt a positive Jewish conception about itself and explain the Jewish values it stood for (to become a *Gesinnungsverein*). While in 1905 Fuchs had written that the *Centralverein* was "essentially a self-defence organisation, and in its nature more anti-antisemitic than positively Jewish", by 1913 he admitted that he and his colleagues had reconsidered their position. Without knowledge about Judaism and loyalty to Jewish values, he explained now, their defence work remained empty. Consequently, they wanted "to take part in the renaissance of Judaism".[43] As mentioned before, it seems that the growing membership of the reorganised *Centralverein* was one of the impulses in the search for a fuller Jewish self-understanding.

The intention was easier stated than realised. While balancing their Jewishness against their "Germanness", the *Centralverein* activists were restrained by certain ideological barriers which they could not overcome. Scholars have expressed the opinion that the perennial emphasis of the *Centralverein* on its good Germanness (stressed in the very first article of its statutes), or its seemingly unconditional willingness to integrate into German society, or its recurring declarations of loyalty to the German State and *Kaiser*, were the result of self-deception, or of lack of self-confidence.[44] One may wonder if such a critique does not result from reading present experience into the past, or perhaps it reflected preconceptions of ideological (Jewish Nationalist or Zionist) character. To be sure, there was much meekness in many of the *Centralverein*'s leaders' utterances. But ideologically considered, what were their alternatives?

The status of the *Centralverein* members as German citizens (or later, for that matter, of the AJC members as American citizens), was rooted in concepts of the

---

[43]Fuchs, *Um Deutschtum und Judentum, op. cit.*, p. 272; *ibid*, pp. 236–237; for similar opinions from 1918, *ibid*, pp. 327, 328.

[44]See the opinions of Chaim Schatzker and of Abraham Margaliot, in the debate on the *Centralverein* published in *LBI Year Book XXXIII* (1988), pp. 97–106; also, Peter Pulzer, 'Why was there a Jewish Question in Imperial Germany?' in *LBI Year Book XXV* (1980) especially p. 141.

eighteenth-century Enlightenment. Those hated aliens, the Jews, had then been accepted as citizens on the strength of the principle of the equal and inalienable rights of all men; the belief in the basic goodness of human nature and the capability of improvement of man (given the right conditions); and the concept that men live together in the frame of a social contract because this is for their common and mutual benefit.

On such terms, the only matter that made Jews different from the other citizens was, supposedly, their creed. In accordance with Enlightenment values, this was religion reduced to its minimum: to one of the rights of expression of the individual, even if, in the case of Jews, a rather suspicious expression, given past history. And regarding the characteristics of Jewish religion, the legislators of the French Revolution had been clear-minded indeed: nothing that bound together Jews as Jews was acceptable, if they wanted to enjoy full citizenship.

The condition had been well understood by those Jewish groups that began to look for integration into general society. Stimulated as much by need as by conviction, they formulated a Jewish religious position that reflected the concepts of the age: the developing Reform position in Judaism, in the first half of the nineteenth century, was rational, enlightened and explainable according to the concepts of general society. And if, considered from a Jewish point of view, it generated little heat, it at least responded to the needs and creeds of those sectors of Jewish society that were nurturing it.

As it happened, in the meantime the prevailing political ideas in the general environment had changed. While integrating Jewish society in Western Europe was still working on its Reform-inspired Jewish self-definition (which was encountering considerable opposition in traditional-minded Jewish quarters), European civil and political thought had long entered the age of Romantic Nationalism. Religion lost now its mantle of rationality – rationality itself was questioned, as a guiding light for social cohesion. What united men was no longer some social contract: men were forged into a people by organic bonds of historical character deeply rooted in the past. Language, geography, history, and very much religion too, these were the components of the national make-up of a people, according to the new concepts.

How did the Jews fit into the new scheme – if at all? The question was not made simpler by the fact that European political life, by the second half of the nineteenth century, was an uneasy amalgamation of principles inherited from the Enlightenment with ideas accepted from nineteenth-century Nationalism. Most West European countries insisted on the principle of the inalienable rights of the citizen, but in the setting of a National State. The ideological contradictions inherent in such circumstances explain much of the internal political unrest in European countries during the nineteenth century.

Theoretically considered, the Jews – including the generation that had created the *Centralverein* – were in a very complicated situation. They still had not finally worked out their condition in purely Enlightenment terms, and did not know – theoretically – how to cope with the new questions posed by Romantic Nationalism. They were caught by a recurrent phenomenon of modern times: Jewish society absorbed slow and late the new ideologies arising in the general environment. It was quite clear that the most reliable (up to a point) foundation for Jewish integration in the general environment was still the ideas of the Enlightenment, based on the principles about the natural rights of the individual and the rational character of man and society. Indeed, Romantic Nationalism, stressing the irrational ties of society and its organic and historical character, presented for the Jews barriers much more difficult to overcome.

Consequently, the ideological attitudes of integrating German Jewry in the late nineteenth century (the activists of the *Centralverein* included), were hardly the result of self-deception or lack of moral fibre, but reflected an ideological state in which the conditions for the existence of Jews as Jews were increasingly precarious.

Life, however influenced by political theory, has rules of its own, and here was the *Centralverein*, in the first decade of the twentieth century, compounding its ideological problems by trying to broaden its Jewish self-definition. But aside from emotionally charged pledges of loyalty to Jewishness and Germanness,[45] there was little help to be found in the ideological arsenal of integrating German Jewry. Groping for an answer, it was in Zionist thought that, strangely or not, some assistance was found. In 1910, Franz Oppenheimer, a well-known sociologist and an ideologically moderate Zionist, had published an article, 'Stammesbewusstsein und Volksbewusstsein', (roughly, "clan-consciousness and nationality-consciousness").[46] Drawing on concepts in vogue in early-century German sociology, Oppenheimer established hair-splitting distinctions between clan (*Stamm*) and people (*Volk*), community-of-descent (*Abstammungsgemeinschaft*), community-of-likemindedness (*Gesinnungsgemeinschaft*) and community-of-cultural-likemindedness (*Kulturgemeinschaft*). The aim of that rather talmudic exercise was to establish a distinction between Jews and non-Jews in Western Europe, as well as between Jews in Western Europe and Eastern Europe.

Eugen Fuchs adopted some of Oppenheimer's categories: Jews were no people, but a "clan-community" (*Stammesgemeinschaft*). Indeed, there were significant differences between East European and West European Jews, and for the East Europeans, he said, a Jewish state in Palestine may be a feasible solution (the classical position had been that each Jewish community has to work for its rights in its own country).[47] However, one may wonder how much the new concepts solved the *Centralverein*'s ideological dilemma. Its members were still defined as "German citizens (*Staatsbürger*) of the Jewish faith", which meant citizens in the German-political and German-national sense and Jewish in the confessional sense. "We are a *Centralverein* of Jewish Germans", stated Fuchs. It implied some semantic change, but it did not add to much.[48] Although they came to recognise that there were some special ingredients in their Jewishness, the representatives of the C.V. never managed to elaborate the theme properly. In the 1920s, a new concept appeared in the vocabulary of the *Centralverein*: Jews

---

[45]See Fuchs, 'Glaube und Heimat', in *Um Deutschtum und Judentum, op. cit.*, pp. 247–262.
[46]*Die Welt*, 25th March 1910, pp. 257–260.
[47]See, Fuchs, *Um Deutschtum und Judentum, op. cit.*, pp. 240–245.
[48]*Ibid*; for a full explanation of that issue as late as 1913, see the analysis of Eugen Fuchs's position, in Reinharz, *Fatherland and Promised Land, op. cit.*, pp. 77–79.

as a "community bound by a common fate" (*Schicksalsgemeinschaft*).[49] It too was never elaborated.

It is to be doubted that non-Jews ever paid attention to that laborious "*pilpul*" on Jewish self-definition, that they understood it if they did, and that they agreed to it if they understood. Those who did understand were the small ideological opposition the *Centralverein* faced on the Right, the *Verband nationaldeutscher Juden*, led by Max Naumann. Founded in 1920, the *Verband* represented a politically Right-Wing Jewish association, and Naumann, who cultivated a "Prussian" military bearing which included duelling scars (he had been a captain in the Bavarian army in the First World War), castigated the *Centralverein* for what he considered its ideological indecision.[50] For all his aggressiveness and sarcasm, Naumann's position was similar to that of the *Centralverein* back in 1893. The difference lay in his political identification with the German Right. In fact, the *Verband* had few followers. But for the *Centralverein* it represented an irritant, and by recognising and stressing the C.V.'s problems of Jewish self-definition, it may have made further ideological moves on the C.V.'s part more difficult.

Compared to the almost tortuous search of the *Centralverein* for a broader Jewish identity, the American Jewish Committee's evolution, which commenced from the 1940s, was calmer. The reason was that the actual battles around an evolving Jewish self-definition happened not within the AJC, but parallel to it, in the religious group most of the Committee's members were associated with: the Reform movement.

The Reform movement in American Judaism, which had been created in the second half of the nineteenth century by Jews of German origin, was more extreme in its religious position than the parallel religious liberal movement of German Jewry. Nevertheless, its religious and civil premises were not basically different: Jews as good and loyal (American) citizens, Judaism as a religious faith. Zionism, and what it stood for in terms of Jewish self-definition had been fiercely denounced in 1897 and 1898 by the Central Conference of American Rabbis (CCAR) and by the Union of American Hebrew Congregations, respectively the associations of Reform Rabbis and of Reform congregations.[51] But the American Reform movement had been less static in its stance. A

[49]See Ludwig Holländer, *Deutsch-jüdische Probleme der Gegenwart. Eine Auseinandersetzung über die Grundfragen des Central-Vereins deutscher Staatsbürger jüdischen Glaubens*, Berlin 1929, p. 9. The effort to reach a broader Jewish definition is well illustrated in the brochure by Friedrich Brodnitz, Kurt Cohn and Ludwig Tietz, *Der Central-Vereine der Zukunft. Eine Denkschrift zur Hauptversammlung 1928 des Central-Vereins . . .* [1928].

[50]On the position of the *Verband*, see Max Naumann, *Vom nationaldeutschen Juden*, Berlin 1920; *idem, Der nationaldeutsche Jude in der deutschen Umwelt*, Berlin 1921; *idem, Von deutscher Zukunft*, Berlin 1924. On the discussions between the two organisations, see Ludwig Holländer, *Denkschrift über die Bestrebungen des Rechtsanwalts Dr. Max Naumann in Berlin auf Begründung eines Verbandes nationaldeutscher Juden*, Berlin 1921; and Naumann's answer, *Denkschrift über die Treibereien des Syndikus Dr. Ludwig Holländer in Berlin betreffend den Verband nationaldeutscher Juden*, Berlin 1921. On the *Verband*, see the informative, although apologetic work of Klaus J. Herrmann, *Das Dritte Reich und die deutsch-jüdischen Organisationen 1933–1934*, Köln–Berlin–Bonn 1969. For a more critical essay on the *Verband* see Carl J, Rheins, 'The Verband nationaldeutscher Juden 1921–1933', in *LBI Year Book XXV* (1980), pp. 243–268.

[51]See Michael Meyer, *Response to Modernity. A History of the Reform Movement in Judaism*, New York–Oxford 1988, pp. 293–295.

minority of Reform rabbis, a highly prestigious one, had identified with Zionism since the beginnings of the movement. American Jewry was still in the making, masses of East European Jews arriving year after year. Since the early twentieth century, the Reform movement was challenged by the growing conservative movement, whose Jewish self-definition was broader, and which identified itself with Zionism from the start. And last but not least, America was different: American political conditions did not impose upon the citizens the ideological burdens of European-style Nationalism. The boundaries for Jewish self-affirmation were much broader in the American system, then they had ever been in continental Europe.[52]

By the mid-1930s, the Reform movement, whose membership was increasingly of East European stock, was moving towards more positive definitions of Jewishness. How did they cope with the Gordian knot of the ideological obstacles that had defeated their German counterparts? They never cut it, they simply ignored it. The 1937 meeting of the CCAR approved (by a small majority) a resolution recognising that the Jews were a people and that the rebuilding of Palestine was a most worthy goal.[53] However, when the CCAR went a step further and in February 1942 approved a call for the formation of a Jewish army in Palestine, the American Reform movement was precipitated into what has been considered the worst crisis in its existence. A group of rabbis and laymen, opposed to Zionism and holding to the classic positions of Reform, rejected the Jewish army decision and the ideological presumptions underlying it. To act on their opinions, they and others established in June 1942 the American Council for Judaism.[54] In spite of the obvious local differences, there was much ideological similarity between the American Council for Judaism and the *Verband nationaldeutscher Juden* of the 1920s and early 1930s.

While the debate inside the Reform movement was heating up, other groups in American Jewry had convened an American Jewish Conference, to consider ways to help the Jewish community in Palestine. After hesitations and negotiations, the American Jewish Committee agreed to participate. The Committee tried to divert the Conference from following an extreme line of support for Zionist plans, including a call for the establishment of a Jewish commonwealth in Palestine. However, in October 1943 the American Jewish Conference did decide to endorse the maximalist Zionist programme, which caused the Committee to resign.[55] Ideological conviction went, most probably, hand-in-hand with political expediency: the prudent leadership of the American Jewish Committee may have decided to avoid the risks of an internal tempest like the one then raging in the Reform movement.

But the reaction to the AJC's withdrawal was quite tempestuous. Members resigned, affiliated organisations dissociated themselves from the Committee,

---

[52]See Evyatar Friesel, 'American Zionism and American Jewry. An Ideological and Communal Encounter', *American Jewish Archives*, XL (April 1988), pp. 5–23.
[53]See Howard R. Greenstein, *Turning Point. Zionism and Reform Judaism*, Chico, Cal. 1981, chap. I; Meyer, *Response to Modernity, op. cit.*, pp. 388–391.
[54]Greenstein, *Turning Point, op. cit.*, chap. II.
[55]See Cohen, *Not Free to Desist, op. cit.*, pp. 249–260.

and the annual meeting in January 1944 was one of the most agitated in the history of the AJC.[56]

If the AJC leaders were suprised by the vehemence of the negative response to their step, unprepared for it they were not. Obviously, they had been sensing the mood of a new generation of American Jews. At the same time exactly, they decided to widen the structure of the AJC and to transform it into a body open to all interested Jews.

One may well ask what was the possible connection between a political debate with the participants of the American Jewish Conference and the reorganisation of the Committee, which must have been considered long before? But we should remember that something quite similar had happened four decades earlier in the *Centralverein*: pressures from the Jewish rank-and-file had led the C.V. to widen its organisational structure. In this connection, this author has argued that those steps, in the context of the Jewish civil-rights associations, were more than straight means to a new end, i.e, to widen the influence and representativeness of the C.V. or the AJC. They had a further meaning: hemmed in by the constraining characteristics of its ideological self-definition, the *Centralverein* (as later the American Jewish Committee) "expressed" itself through the broadening of its organisational structure.[57]

As in the case of the *Centralverein* in the first decade of the century, the organisational opening of the Committee went together with a new awareness about what was called "the development of an America-centered Jewish life".[58] Here the connections were clear: the growing membership in both organisations, each in its own time, pressured for more comprehensive definitions regarding their Jewishness. In the case of the American Jewish Committee, the issue was complicated by the existence and the influence of Israel. It seems that for the rank-and-file of the AJC, both themes, i.e, a broader Jewish self-definition and a positive attitude towards the Jewish State, were emotionally related. The leadership of the Committee, for its part, found it difficult to formulate these feelings in ideological terms. Worse, they were also motivated by a negative reasoning: As early as 1949, John Slawson, the strong Executive Vice-President of the Committee, had expressed his apprehension that "American Jewish life [may] become centripetal to Israel".[59] In addition, although the issue of the "quality of Jewish life" became a permanent theme in the annual reports of the Committee, it seems that the AJC did not know exactly how to deal with it. "The American Jewish Committee has pioneered in helping American Jews search for a new, meaningful sense of Jewish identity. In this quest we have sometimes

[56]*Ibid.*, p. 259.

[57]Friesel, 'The Political and Ideological Development', *loc. cit.*, pp. 140–144.

[58]John Slawson spoke then about "the adoption of, and adherence to, an appropriate theory of Jewish adjustment to the American scene", *AJC, 37th Annual Report*, (1943), New York 1944, p. 99. Differently, Henry L. Feingold believes that only in 1962 did Slawson start to work towards "a more survivalist direction". See his *Past as Prologue, op. cit.*, p. 10. See John Slawson, 'The Quest for Jewish Identity in America', *Journal of Jewish Communal Service*, vol. XL, No. 1 (1963), pp. 17–25.

[59]John Slawson, 'Major Programs and Policies in 1949', *AJC, 42nd Annual Report*, New York 1949, pp. 124–125. That issue – the ambivalent attitude towards Israel – is more extensively developed in the chapter on Zionism.

failed . . ." said Bertram Gold, in 1987.[60] It seems that the Committee found itself facing the same difficulties that the *Centralverein* had encountered in its time: insufficient ideological room to manoeuvre.

Some of the components of that ideological narrowness became especially clear in the case of the American Jewish Committee. For one there were the already mentioned limitations which the original self-definition of the civil-rights organisations imposed on their Jewish identity. Another component was the inherent impossibility for them to identify explicitly with any given political tendency in general society. And last, their equally inherent inability to adopt a clear position regarding the diverse religious trends, and most of the public issues, in Jewish life.[61]

No solution was found for the last question, which touched the broad spectrum of the problems of Jewish life in contemporary conditions. As it became evident in the case of the AJC, the Committee was reduced, in matters regarding the internal life of the Jewish community, to a consultant or research capacity. With respect to the first issue, here again it was among its Reform "partners" that the American Jewish Committee found some answers. Like the *Centralverein* in its time, it was in the arsenal of Zionist ideology that the American Reform movement came upon concepts and definitions fitting its quest. In the second half of the twentieth century, American Reform Jewry underwent a process of "Zionisation" which was not inspired by the official ideological positions presented by the World Zionist Organisation, but drew inspiration from two other sources. One was from the very existence of a Jewish State. The other was a brand of Zionist ideology that had developed over the years in American Judaism; Americal cultural Zionism, which merged classical Zionist ideas with the principle of the continuation of Jewish life outside Israel also – meaning, in America.[62] A clear expression of the new concepts of the Reform movement was contained in the San Francisco Platform, adopted by the CCAR in 1976, which recognised the Jews as a people and declared their support for Israel.[63]

The American Jewish Committee accepted these new ideas, more or less tacitly, at any rate without much discussion. If an ideological *cul-de-sac* appeared, it was simply ignored. In the 1980s, the term Jewish "peoplehood" – semantically, an American Zionist formulation going back to the 1920s and 1930s – was used in the Committee's publications, with all its many implications: "What does unite most Jews is a sense of peoplehood – the idea that Jews everywhere are bound together by inextricable ties of mutual commitment and extended family obligation deriving from four millennia of Jewish experience and that we share a

[60]See AJC: Gold, *Faith, Patience and Optimism, op. cit.*, p. 10; *idem, The American Jewish Committee and the Dialectic of Change*, New York 1988, p. 10; Henry Feingold, *A Jewish Survival Enigma. The Strange Case of the American Jewish Committee*, New York [1981], p. 16; *idem, Past as Prologue, op. cit.*, pp. 7–8.

[61]The leaders of the AJC were aware of that problem, but gave it their own interpretation. See David M. Gordis, *New Steps in the American Jewish Experiment*, New York 1984, p. 15.

[62]See Evyatar Friesel, 'Ahad-Haamism in American Zionist Thought', in Jacques Kornberg (ed.), *Ahad Haam. At the Crossroads*, Albany, N.Y. 1983, pp. 133–141, 195–198; *idem*, 'American Zionism and American Jewry', *loc. cit.*, pp. 5–23.

[63]See Meyer, *Response to Modernity, op. cit.*, pp. 391–394.

common destiny."[64] The activists of the *Centralverein* in the late 1920s would have balked at using the concept – peoplehood – but part of them would have accepted the contents of the definition. By the late 1980s, representatives of the American Jewish Committee were ready to use the concept "people", to define the Jews.[65]

However, one should perhaps not accord much importance to these semantics. The Committee had never been a laboratory for ideological experiment. Even when dealing with the Israel-American Jewry equation, the AJC mostly kept clear from the thorny ideological issue of Zionism, and addressed itself to political questions relating to Israel the State.

ZIONISM AS PROBLEM AND AS INFLUENCE

Theoretically, Zionist ideas should have played a limited role in the evolution of the *Centralverein* and the American Jewish Committee. Zionism represented the very opposite prognosis of modern Jewish life, a fact the Jewish civil-rights activists were very much aware of. But reality turned out to be very different.

The positions of the C.V. and of the AJC regarding Zionism developed on two levels, ideological and political. As we have seen, in the *Centralverein* both levels intertwined, while in the American Jewish Committee they were kept relatively separate, the brunt of the ideological debate with Zionism being borne not by the AJC, but by the American Reform movement.[66]

Until the beginning of the 1910s the relations in Germany between the *Centralverein* and the *Zionistische Vereinigung für Deutschland* (ZVfD) were good. The earlier leadership of the ZVfD stated its ideological position in terms that have been called "moderate". They valued their status as German citizens and many indicated that the endeavours of the Zionist movement were to alleviate the social and political pressures upon the Jews in Eastern Europe, by creating a "Homeland" for them in Palestine.[67] The C.V. counted quite a number of Zionists among its members. Over the years, the two organisations even seemed to become closer.[68]

[64]See American Jewish Committee, *Peoplehood and Pluralism. Relations between American Jews and Israel*, New York 1988.
[65]See Naomi W. Cohen, 'Share Tefila Congregation v. Cobb. A New Departure in American Jewish Defense?', *Jewish History* (Univ. of Haifa), 3 (1988), pp. 95–108. The AJC participated actively in the process, which reached the Supreme Court of the United States in 1987. Jews were presented in the case as a people, as well as members of a religious group. Whatever doubts about the exact meaning, the term has been used also on other occasions. Speaking before the annual meeting of the AJC in 1989, the Executive Vice President, Ira Silverman, said that the programme of the Committee "starts with securing the needs of our people". American Jewish Committee, *Living in Two Civilizations, op. cit.*
[66]See Reinharz, *Fatherland or Promised Land, op. cit.*, chap. V; Moses Rischin, 'The Early Attitude of the American Jewish Committee to Zionism (1906–1922)', *Publications of the American Jewish Historical Society*, XLIX (1959–1960), pp. 188–201; Naomi W. Cohen, 'The Reaction of Reform Judaism in America to Political Zionism, (1897–1922)', *Publications of The American Jewish Historical Society*, XL (1950–1951), pp.361–394; Friesel, 'American Zionism and American Jewry', *loc. cit.*, pp. 5–23.
[67]See Reinharz, *Fatherland or Promised Land, op. cit.*, pp. 117–121.
[68]The most extensive research on that issue is *ibid.*, see, especially, chapter V.

However, in 1912–1913 there was a breakdown in relations, due to several factors: electoral competition in several larger Jewish communities, the debate on Werner Sombart's ideas about the Jews, the question of influence on German-Jewish youth, etc. But the main reason, it has been said, was the radicalisation of German Zionism. Led by Kurt Blumenfeld, the Poznań conference of the German movement approved resolutions which stressed the commitment of the German Zionists to Palestine, and established that Zionists should "incorporate into their life's program a personal emigration to Palestine. Every Zionist should at least establish personal interests in Palestine."[69]

Nevertheless, it seems that it was not only the German Zionist movement that was undergoing a process of radicalisation. As we have indicated, the *Centralverein* was radicalising too, although along its own, and divergent, ideological lines. If so, it is the confrontation between the C.V. and the Zionists for the influence over German-Jewish youth, going on in 1910–1912, that should be considered a major factor in the new tension that arose between the two organisations: the youth associations were the obvious human reservoir of both.[70] In March 1913, the *Centralverein* convened a special meeting to discuss its attitude towards Zionism. The resolution adopted formulated clearly the ideological gulf separating the two organisations. Its last sentence read: "We must remove ourselves, however, from the Zionist who denies German national feeling, who regards himself as a guest within a foreign host-country, and who affirms only Jewish national feeling."[71] Several weeks later the Zionist organisation answered in kind: it demanded the resignation of German Zionists who belonged to the *Centralverein*.[72]

From now on, relations between the *Centralverein* and the German Zionist movement were consistently chilly. In the 1920s, the C.V. opposed participation in activities related to the economic development of the Jewish National Home in Palestine. However, many of its members (including leading ones), while remaining non-Zionist, were ready to participate in the activities of the *Keren*

---

[69]*Ibid.*, p. 161; the whole topic is developed there, in chapt. IV.

[70]See Marjorie Lamberti, 'From Coexistence to Conflict, Zionism and the Jewish Community in Germany, 1897–1914', in *LBI Year Book XXVII* (1982), pp. 53–86.

[71]The full resolution said: "The *Centralverein deutscher Staatsbürger jüdischen Glaubens* aims, in accordance with paragraph one of its statutes, to unite all German Jews regardless of their religious and political affiliations under its leadership to strengthen them in their struggle to retain their political and social position and to further cultivate them in German *Gesinnung*. From this premise comes the position of the C.V. toward the Zionists. We demand from our members not only the fulfilment of their civic duties, but also German *Gesinnung* and the implementation of this *Gesinnung*, in their daily life.

We do not want to solve the German Jewish question internationally. We want to participate in German culture as Germans and on the soil of the German fatherland. At the same time we want to remain loyal to our Jewish community which has been sanctified by our religion and history. As long as the German Zionist is striving to find a secure home for the dispossessed Jews of the East or to uphold the pride of the Jews in their history and religion, he is welcome as a member [in the C.V.]. We must remove ourselves, however, from the Zionist who denies German National feeling, who regards himself as a guest within a foreign host-country, and who affirms only Jewish national feeling." We have used the translation of Jehuda Reinharz, *Fatherland or Promised Land, op. cit.*, pp. 212–213.

[72]*Ibid.*, p. 217.

Hayesod, the Palestine Foundation Fund, or advocated better relations with the Zionists.[73] Only in the late 1920s, under the worsening political circumstances in Germany, did the C.V. and the Zionists begin to collaborate in the struggle against Right-Wing antisemitism, and even then it was an uneasy alliance.[74]

This was the situation regarding political relations. But, as mentioned above, in the ideological development of the *Centralverein,* the C.V. leaders adopted some concepts that were taken over from Zionist thought. Later, after 1933, the two organisations collaborated in the general representation of German Jews then formed, the *Reichsvertretung der deutschen Juden.* By then, however, any normality of development for Jewish organisations in Germany was no longer possible.

In the United States, the American Jewish Committee for many years maintained an attitude of suspicious neutrality to Zionism in general, and to public matters initiated or supported by the Zionists. To present a basically Zionist issue under the organisational aegis of a broad coalition of Jewish organisations was a recurring and highly successful Zionist tactic. It posed a dilemma the Committee always had trouble coping with: to oppose it meant (almost) to oppose American Jewry. And how could the American Jewish Committee, which supposedly, was speaking for the Jews in the United States, negate "their" undertaking?

For their part, the Zionists, and the Jewish organisations allied with them, were most interested in the participation of the American Jewish Committee: the Committee stood for public influence, social prestige, financial means. Long and sometimes bitter discussions took place with the leadership of the AJC. Compromises were hammered out, agreements reached – or not. In the short range, it was always a nerve-racking effort. But in the long range it was part of that great process of inner evolution which in time transformed American Jewry into a civic body working with a broader basis of Jewish public support than any other Jewry in modern times.

The first time the Committee was drawn (reluctantly) into a Zionist-sponsored initiative was the first American Jewish Congress, in 1916–1920.[75] Shortly after the agreement regarding the Congress, the American Jewish Committee acknowledged (cautiously) the Balfour Declaration of November 1917.[76] However, Louis Marshall, the President of the Committee, was one of the leading figures in the Congress delegation sent to the 1919 Paris Peace Conference to participate in the negotiations regarding Jewish affairs in Eastern Europe. Marshall had accepted the principle that national rights be demanded

---

[73]See Ludwig Foerder, *Die Stellung des Centralvereins zu den innerjüdischen Fragen in den Jahren 1919–1926,* Breslau 1927, pp. 23ff.; see the incisive formulation of Brodnitz, Cohn and Tietz, *Der Central-Verein der Zukunft, op. cit.,* especially on pp. 17–21. All three belonged to the younger generation of C.V. activists. Friedrich Brodnitz was the son of Julius Brodnitz, the chairman of the C.V. The opposing position was strongly formulated by the administrative director of the C.V., Ludwig Holländer, in *Deutsch-jüdische Probleme der Gegenwart, op. cit.,* especially on p. 30.

[74]See Paucker, *Der jüdische Abwehrkampf, op. cit.,* pp. 39–44.

[75]Examples of the difficult route of the American Jewish Committee towards participation in the American Jewish Congress are found in Reznikoff (ed.), *Louis Marshall Champion of Liberty. op. cit.,* pp. 507–548. See also Cohen, *Not Free to Desist, op. cit.,* pp. 90–101.

[76]*Ibid.,* pp. 108–110.

for Jews in the new East European states. This did not stop another leading figure of the American Jewish Committee, Oscar S. Straus, a man of considerable influence in American political circles, from coming to Paris on his own, and (among other matters) working *against* such rights.[77]

Louis Marshall was later the leading American non-Zionist partner in the establishment of the enlarged Jewish Agency, formed in 1929. His interest also attracted other figures from the Committee, especially Felix Warburg. In the 1920s, Marshall attained a *de facto* position of leadership in American Jewry which no other figure had reached, or would, to date, reach again. Although constantly stressing that he was neither a Jewish Nationalist nor a Zionist, Marshall had developed a commitment to Palestine and for the creation of a Jewish National Home there that ran far beyond the interest of his colleagues at the Committee, although he influenced part of them. Nevertheless, it was in their personal capacity that they participated in the Palestine-directed activities, not as representatives of the Committee. Marshall's death, in September 1929, was a severe setback for the newly created Jewish Agency.[78]

Zionist matters again played a significant role in the Committee's activities in the 1940s. As mentioned before, the decision to leave the American Jewish Conference, in 1943, triggered the AJC's resolution to enlarge its organisational structure. But the Committee did not change its basic position regarding Zionism, not then nor later, after 1948. Its statements in the 1940s were (carefully) ambiguous: the Committee was for Jewish immigration, for the development of a Jewish National Home, against British policy in Palestine, but also against a Jewish State – although without saying as much.[79]

After 1948, the Committee declared that the establishment of the State of Israel was "an event of historical significance". But in the next sentence it was added that "citizens of the United States are Americans and citizens of Israel are Israelis . . . and just as our own government speaks only for its citizens, so Israel speaks only for its citizens".[80] The leaders of the AJC must have been surprised to discover that none other than the Israeli Prime Minister, David Ben Gurion, agreed with them. In what should be considered one of the wisest steps in his political career, Ben Gurion, in August 1950, proceeded to sign an agreement with the Committee's President, Jacob Blaustein, in which Ben Gurion recognised the political distinction between Jewish citizens of Israel and of the United States.[81] Ben Gurion had his own reasons for his decision, but for American Jews of the type associated with the American Jewish Committee, the Blaustein–Ben

---

[77]See Naomi W. Cohen, 'An American Jew at the Paris Peace Conference of 1919', in Joseph L. Blau *et al.* (eds.), *Essays on Jewish Life and Thought*, New York 1959, pp. 159–168; Reznikoff (ed.), *Louis Marshall Champion of Liberty*, *op. cit.*, pp. 539–548.

[78]See Cohen, *Not Free to Desist*, *op. cit.*, pp. 149–153.

[79]A statement on Zionism was approved in January 1943 – see Cohen, *Not Free to Desist*, *op. cit.*, pp. 253–256; an additional statement, calling for the "immediate abrogation" of the 1939 White Paper, was approved in 1946 – see *AJC, 40th Annual Report (1946)*, New York 1947, pp. 94–96.

[80]*AJC, 42nd Annual Report (1948)*, *op. cit.*, pp. 8–9.

[81]See *American Jewish Yearbook*, 53 (1952), pp. 551–552, 564–568; Cohen, *Not Free to Desist*, *op. cit.*, pp. 312–313.

Gurion Agreement solved with one stroke the old dual-loyalty dilemma, and opened broad roads for further dealings between both sides.

To reach an understanding with Israel was one thing, to change basic concepts, another. A tone of aggressive defensiveness regarding Israel (and certainly regarding Zionism) could be found in many of the statements of AJC spokesmen from the 1950s, continuing in fact until the early 1980s. As mentioned before, shortly after the establishment of Israel, John Slawson had opposed the possibility that American Jewry might become spiritually dependent on Israel.[82] Slawson never changed his attitude, and although he was a man of strong personal opinions, one may suppose that his position on Israel and Zionism was not out of line with that of the Committee's leadership. In 1956 he declared, regarding the violently anti-Zionist American Council for Judaism, that there was nothing wrong with the principles of the Council, only with its methods.[83] Five years later, in 1961, he said: "There is no obligation for anybody to go to Israel. The State of Israel exists for those Jews who wish to go there or have to go there. Our relationship with the Jews of Israel is based upon religion, culture and history, and upon a certain obligation we have toward one another. The concept of a world Jewish nation, as propagated by the president of the World Zionist Organization, is repugnant to us."[84] More than ten years later one finds the next Executive Vice-President of the Committee, Bertram H. Gold, asking rhetorically: "Are we not encouraging Israelis . . . to take a distorted view . . . [and] perceive American Jewry as a 'service community, a tributary appendage', whose primary, and even sole, function is to serve and support the State of Israel."[85] As recently as 1980, Bertram Gold was reporting, in a (guardedly) hopeful vein, that the members in the AJC chapters had become more interested in local issues, and less in Israel.[86]

Did the tone change, after that? "We may accept a central role for Israel in Jewish life, but we reject totally the principle that because we do not live in Israel we are only peripheral to Jewish life", thus in 1984.[87] "There is no question that American Jews – and the American Jewish Committee – remain not only committed to Israel's security, but fascinated by its symbolism as well", this again Bertram Gold, in 1987.[88] "The American Jewish Committee . . . has been dedicated to Israel's security and its survival as a democracy ever since the Jewish state's founding in 1948[!]. The Committee advocates a strong Israel and

---

[82]Slawson, 'Major Programs and Policies in 1949', *loc. cit.*, pp. 124–125.

[83]'Zionist and Pro-Israel Activities in the United States', address at the meeting of the Executive Board of the AJC, 27th October 1957 – Slawson file, Blaustein Library.

[84]'The American Jewish Committee and What It Does', address, 17th September 1961 – Slawson file, Blaustein Library.

[85]American Jewish Committee, *Who speaks for the Jews?* – address at the annual meeting of the AJC, New York 1972, p. 12.

[86]American Jewish Committee, *New Realities in American Jewish Life* – address at the annual meeting of the AJC, New York 1980.

[87]American Jewish Committee: David M. Gordis, *The American Jewish Committee at Mid-Decade*, November 1984, p. 8. Gordis was then the Executive Vice-President of the AJC.

[88]*Idem, Faith, Patience and Optimism. The American Jewish Committee and the Dialectic of Change*, New York 1988, p. 6. Gold was again Executive Vice-President in 1987.

encourages negotiations that will lead to peace in the Middle East", thus in 1988.[89] In the late 1980s, Israel had become one of the major themes of the American Jewish Committee's endeavours.[90]

Last but not least, in the late 1980s the American Jewish Committee seemed to be getting drawn into a matter which would involve it in questions it had, so far, managed to steer clear of: the issue of religion and state in Israel. To keep it on a civil-rights level, the AJC's activists preferred to call it the quest for "religious pluralism" in Israel.[91] However, everybody involved in the problem was aware that the Committee might be pushed into a type of confrontation it had always preferred to avoid: one that involved religion; that involved ideology; and all this is a country which, at least in principle, was a "foreign" one.

CONCLUSIONS

The German-Jewish *Centralverein* and the American Jewish Committee should be considered as the outstanding organisations of their type, in modern Jewish history. Both attained a level of ideological and organisational development much higher than that of the comparable Jewish associations, the *Alliance Israélite Universelle* included.

The American Jewish Committee may have shown more elasticity in its actions than the *Centralverein* did in its time. But then the Committee has existed longer, and the general background against which it has operated has given it much more latitude than the *Centralverein* enjoyed. Jewish activity has always been easier in the United States than it was in Germany. The fact that many of the developments of the AJC came about after the creation of Israel should not be ignored either. The existence of the Jewish State has been a powerful lever in Jewish organisational life everywhere.

Historically compared, the evolution of the C.V. and the AJC showed most significant similarities, but developments that only sprouted in the *Centralverein*, later blossomed fully in the American Jewish Committee. In three fields the C.V. and the AJC unfolded in like ways: in their orientation regarding the political life

---

[89] *AJC, Annual Report 1988*, p. 17.

[90] Thus, the *1988 Annual Report*, in the chapter 'Safeguarding Israel's Security', p. 17: "The American Jewish Committee – the first American Jewish organization to establish an office in Israel – has been dedicated to Israel's security and its survival as a democracy ever since the Jewish state's founding in 1948. The Committee advocates a strong Israel and encourages negotiations that will lead to peace in the Middle East. It strives to foster constructive and mutually beneficial relations between the United States and Israel, and to deepen the friendship between the two countries. The AJC also seeks to strengthen the ties between Israelis and American Jews, and to further Israel's understanding and appreciation of the American Jewish community."

[91] See Gordis, *New Steps in the American Jewish Experiment, op. cit.*, p. 11; *AJC, Annual Report 1988*, p. 20. And especially, 'American Jewish Committee Statement on American Jewish-Israeli Relations', *AJC, Peoplehood and Pluralism*, pp. 2–4.

in their countries, in their organisational evolution, and in their Jewish self-definition.

In general politics, the orientation of both organisations ended firmly in the Liberal camp. It was an evolution that deserves attention: in principle, the C.V. like the AJC, had been opposed that their associations, because they were "confessional", take position in general political matters; it took time and much soul-searching to change direction. Two related reasons, among possible others, for that transformation stand out: Liberalism represented the best political anchor for Jews as Jews, and the rank-and-file of both organisations pulled in the Liberal direction. This led us to another observation: it was to be expected that the largely middle- to upper-middle-class constituency of both organisations gravitate towards more Conservative attitudes. It did not. In spite of the obvious political differences in and between Germany and the United States, it seems that, whatever its rationalisation, the political behaviour of the Jews in both countries was deeply influenced by what, in the last analysis, seemed to be *Jewish* considerations.

Having started as small groups of self-appointed Jewish activists, both the *Centralverein* and the American Jewish Committee ended by changing themselves into large and democratic organisations. At some point in their work it was felt that their small and non-representative framework encumbered the effectiveness of their action. Similarly, there were large sectors of the Jewish public, in Germany or later in the United States, which became interested in participating in the C.V.'s or the AJC's activities.

The progression of both associations towards a broader Jewish self-definition was of seminal importance. It was a condition for their organisational enlargement and the growing incisiveness of their political attitudes. True, it may appear that both in Germany and in the United States the new political attitudes and the organisational modifications of the C.V. and the AJC were adopted *before* new Jewish self-definitions were outlined. But this happened because the ideological path of both associations was hemmed in between limitations that made any evolutionary progress exceedingly slow and difficult. The historical analysis of both organisations seems to indicate that new stirrings about their Jewishness were very much there, albeit tricky to formulate. Indeed, it is suggested here that these very changes in political attitudes and organisation were an expression of an unformulated (and sometimes unformulatable) Jewish consciousness, which "spoke" through these changes.

The evolution each association underwent came about because historical events forced them to face new issues, in each country according to its own circumstances. The ultimate success of both the C.V. and the AJC lay in the fact that once compelled to confront a new reality in Jewish life, they did so positively: they accepted it and incorporated it into their programme of action, even when it contradicted their ideological foundations, or ran against ideas traditionally held. Instead of losing in strength in doing so, both associations ultimately benefited in terms of power and influence.

It is interesting to note that the executive secretaries of both organisations (the Executive Vice-President in the case of the AJC, the *Syndikus* in the case of the

C.V.), used the concept "movement", when referring to their respective organisations.[92] But the C.V. and the AJC could not be seen as movements; not because they lacked the right numbers – in the 1920s the *Centralverein* was the largest German-Jewish organisation – but because they lacked the right spirit. Deeply embedded in the ideological structure of both organisations there was a corrosive plug: the fact that the ultimate success of their original endeavours would have weakened German or American Jewry, and not strengthened them. Even if later developments had neutralised such a possibility, it had not disappeared. It seemed to express itself in a certain lack of the ideological fervour that would have been characteristic of a movement. The term, then, hardly applied, although it was a meaningful indication of a trend of thought in the leadership of both organisations.

One difference between the *Centralverein* and the American Jewish Committee was that the first was active only in Germany, and concentrated almost entirely on the fight against antisemitism. Conversely, the American Jewish Committee acted in the United States and also world-wide, and covered a broad spectrum of Jewish and general political and civil issues. In the second half of the century the AJC also developed an interesting (although not unproblematic) programme dealing with internal Jewish life. Probably the differences between both organisations were, in that case, more the result of diverse circumstances, than of basic conception. It should be remembered that the fight against discrimination and antisemitism had been the very *raison d'être* for the formation of both the *Centralverein* and the American Jewish Committee. The circumstances of Jewish life in Germany caused the *Centralverein* to remain very close to those first issues. One may suspect that the broad range of activities that has characterised the Committee in the last three decades can encompass the first aim of the AJC but not abolish it, and could flourish because antisemitism in the United States had remained dormant.

It is impossible not to recognise the role – for the researcher, the challenging role – that Zionism fulfilled in the development of both organisations. This is especially true for the American Jewish Committee, whch remained active in the era of Zionism fulfilled and at last adopted a most positive stand regarding Israel.

Zionism represented the very opposite prognosis of modern Jewish life from that which had given birth to the *Centralverein* and to the American Jewish Committee. The activists of both organisations were very much aware of it, and for a long time they maintained an attitude that ran from opposition to reserve. However, from the moment they began considering a broader Jewish self-definition, a quite remarkable change took place: confined in the narrow conceptual boundaries of their original ideological positions, it was in the arsenal

---

[92]See Ludwig Holländer's most interesting article, 'Die demokratische Grundlage des C.V.', *Im deutschen Reich*, January 1912, pp. 1–10; for comments on it, see Friesel, 'The Political and Ideological Development', *loc. cit.*, pp. 143–144. Slawson, 'The American Jewish Committee and What It Does', *loc. cit.*

of Zionist definitions that the leaders of the C.V. looked (with reservations) for some new ideas. The same happened later also to the AJC.

A plausible reason for the growing interest of the American Jewish Committee in Israel and to lesser extent in Zionism is that the organisation was bowing to the will of its membership. This author accepts that assumption, but believes that it does not offer a full explanation for what happened. For one, it does not explain the first timid steps of the *Centralverein* – at least on the ideological level – in the direction of Zionism: in German Jewry of the early twentieth century, no rank-and-file pull towards Zionist ideas has, so far, been recognised. In addition, accepting that the pro-Israeli interests of the Committee's membership did influence the AJC's position, from where were these members themselves influenced?

Therefore, another possibility deserves consideration: that there existed a more general Jewish tendency that affected the political and ideological evolution of the *Centralverein* and of the Committee in their respective countries. A tendency that directed their steps towards the broadening of their organisational structures, their internal progression towards a deeper Jewish self-definition, their adoption of liberal attitudes in civil matters affecting general society. Last but not least, that as part of this process these organisations also came closer to Zionism – and at least in American Jewry, Zionism closer to them. In other words, that there was a convergence of issues, positions and ideas, each one influencing the other, and all together being pulled in a certain direction.

Scholars influenced by the Jerusalem school of Jewish history, stress the balance between centripetal and centrifugal tendencies as a central characteristic of modern Jewish history, indeed, of Jewish history in general. From a broader perspective, the comparison between the *Centralverein* and the American Jewish Committee seems to give an additional example of that process.

One should also remember that there were deep differences between the *Centralverein* and the American Committee: they existed in dissimilar times, they acted in the midst of very unlike general societies. If they developed as they did, in ways that were similar when one might have expected the opposite, it is to be doubted that this was due to the circumstances in their countries: where conditions for Jewish life, in the positive as in the negative sense, remained more or less stable, in each country according to its own pattern. It was Jewish society that changed, moving gradually towards more centripedal attitudes in its self-definition and its patterns of action. Essentially, what both organisations had in common was that they were highly responsive to similar Jewish historical dynamics.

That centripetal process, which influenced almost all expressions of Jewish existence from about the beginnings of the twentieth century, defined itself in different ways in each walk of Jewish life, according to the specific Jewish and general views of each segment of Jewish society. In that broad framework, the original "rights-for-Jews" organisations, and especially the *Centralverein* and the American Jewish Committee went their own, albeit similar, paths.

Countering the Pre-1933 Nazi Boycott against the Jews

BY SIBYLLE MORGENTHALER

I

From the outset those organising the anti-Jewish boycott in Germany saw it as a "legitimate" measure of self-defence against Jewish influence which they perceived as powerful and dangerous. The assumption was that the Jewish population acted as a unified powerful group within society and the individual Jew was regarded *per se* as a member of this group. Seen from this perspective, the Christian businessman's Jewish competitor was not merely to be judged by his actions, but at the same time was to be regarded as a representative of a "power" that had to be warded off.

Yet at the beginning of the Weimar Republic the Jews constituted a minority, which was demographically as well as economically in decline. This was a process accelerated by changes in the economic structure, and by inflation as well as the world economic crisis. At the same time, so-called "normal" economic relationships between the Jewish minority and the non-Jewish community were increasingly established.

None the less there was, of course, still a considerable difference between the employment pattern of Jews and non-Jews. Although the Jews made up less than one per cent of the population, they were strikingly "visible" in certain fields, such as trade, law or medicine, and this favoured antisemitic propaganda. The economic independence, which large numbers of Jews enjoyed, furthered in a certain sense a boycott primarily aimed at the self-employed Jews.

The anti-Jewish boycott before 1933, which reached its peak during the world economic crisis, has not, so far, been comprehensively treated. Essentially, the boycott of that period had its origins in the Nazi Party, which initiated and carried it out; and it could be seen as a precursor of Hitler's *Judenpolitik* after 1933. Despite its significance, the boycott in Weimar Germany has only received scant attention in German-Jewish historiography.

II

The idea of causing damage to the Jews by means of an economic boycott was not an invention of the Nazis. In fact the catchword "Do not buy from Jews", along with leaflets containing slogans such as "Buy your Christmas presents only in Christian shops", dates back at least to the nineteenth century. At that time, these slogans expressed an anti-Jewish reaction to the economic crisis which had begun in 1873, during the years of rapid industrial expansion in Germany.[1] A decision by the *Reichsgericht* of 1906 which, among other things, makes reference to the boycott of Jewish shops, furnishes evidence of such attempts at boycotting Jews.[2]

During the first years of the Weimar Republic, the boycott was merely an insignificant side-effect of antisemitism. The situation changed, however, in the period of inflation with the development of an "economic antisemitism", which was mainly supported by the *Deutschvölkischer Schutz- und Trutz-Bund* (DSTB) as well as certain other Right-wing parties and associations.[3] While it is true that there is little evidence of public appeals to boycott Jews (which the DSTB tried to avoid), it could often be ascertained that secret Nationalist societies existed, whose members vowed to avoid any business with Jews.[4] As the inflation eased, the boycott died down, owing to the re-organisation of the economy and the general shortage of credit and other goods. The reports of the *Centralverein deutscher Staatsbürger jüdischen Glaubens* (C.V.) reveal that, for this latter reason, the boycott of merchants was then designed to become a boycott of customers ("Do not sell to Jews").[5] The fact that Paul Oertmann's juridical paper, *Der politische Boykott* (1925), which, among other problems, dealt with the Communist boycott of *völkisch* groups and *vice versa*, takes into account the boycott of Jews, indicates that the administration of justice even at that time had already begun to occupy itself with the problem.

Only the Nazis practised the boycott of Jews both systematically and rigorously, and to an extent that was unprecedented in the history of antisemitism. The Nazi propaganda against Jews began at the precise moment when competition became fierce during the slow economic upturn in Germany.[6] During the so-called stabilisation period from 1925 until 1929, "the quiet boycott increasingly gained ground".[7] From September 1927, the first signs of an organised boycott by the NSDAP were becoming apparent.[8] The first court decisions on boycott cases* date back to 1926,[9] and they occurred ever increasingly until Hitler seized power. In the summer of 1932, the *C.V.-Zeitung* reports on a collection of judgements containing more than 150 decisions against

---

[1]Henry Wassermann and Eckhart Franz, ' "Kauft nicht bei Juden". Der politische Antisemitismus des späten 19. Jahrhunderts in Deutschland', in *Juden als Darmstädter Bürger*, ed. by Eckhart G. Franz, Darmstadt 1984, p. 129.

[2]Ludwig Foerder, 'Der wirtschaftliche Boykott gegen die Juden', in *Jüdische Wohlfahrtspflege und Sozialpolitik*, vol. III (1932), p. 155.

[3]Uwe Lohalm, *Völkischer Radikalismus. Die Geschichte des Deutschvölkischen Schutz- und Trutz-Bundes 1919–1923*, Hamburg 1970, p. 139.

[4]*C.V.-Zeitung*, V, No. 14 (1st April 1926).

[5]*C.V.-Zeitung*, IV, No. 13 (27th March 1925).

[6]Heinrich Uhlig, *Die Warenhäuser im Dritten Reich*, Köln–Opladen 1956, p. 31.

[7]*C.V.-Zeitung*, V, No. 44 (19th October 1926).

[8]Uhlig, *op. cit.*, p. 35.

[9]*C.V.-Zeitung*, V, No. 18 (30th April 1926).

*On the courts' handling of antisemitism in Weimar Germany see also the following essay by Cyril Levitt, 'The Prosecution of Antisemites by the Courts in the Weimar Republic: Was Justice Served?' – (Ed.).

the economic boycott. And by the end of that year it states: "Another collection of 25 judgements has just been published."[10]

Before investigating the roles and behaviour of those who actively and passively participated in the boycott, it is necessary to give a brief definition of the concepts involved. Oertmann defines the boycott, or "Verruf" (disparagement or slander) as "a social sanction or coercion by means of which the organisers try to cause certain other persons to break off legal or personal relationships with a third party which is the target of the boycott, or at least to ensure by means of rules and bans that these relationships will not be established".[11] According to Rudolf Callmann, there are basically three parties involved: the inciters (those who urge people to boycott), the boycotters (the target group of the incitement) and the boycotted.[12] These three categories will now be investigated closely.

The Nazi Party's most powerful tools for the organisation of the boycott were the newspapers under their control, first and foremost *Der Stürmer*. To a large extent, the boycott campaigns were apparently planned and carried out independently by the press, the district associations and other Party institutions. Since 1929 the NSDAP had tried to encourage the German middle classes, who were the directly affected competitors of the Jews, to form economic associations and action groups. These were also important for the organisation of the boycott. For instance, in the district of Munich/Upper Bavaria a certain Party member, Sturm, founded the *Kampfgemeinschaft gegen Warenhaus und Konsumverein*, which took action against Jewish shops.[13] The organisation could only be joined by "purely German" firms. In the summer of 1932, the action group was formally integrated into the Party organisation of the NSDAP and became the head office for the boycott. The *C.V.-Zeitung* wrote with consternation:

> "The 'Völkischer Beobachter', No. 95 announces on page 3 'special instructions from the chief of the main department IV (economy)'. The instructions convey the remarkable fact that this economic department has its own affiliated 'institution' for the organisation of the boycott movement', led by Party member Sturm of the *Kampfgemeinschaft gegen Warenhaus und Konsumverein*. Hence there is no doubt that the boycott is a planned action, which is controlled by a head office."[14]

The *Deutschnationaler Handlungsgehilfenverband* was the professional organisation of shop assistants with the majority of members. This influential union played an important part in the boycott. It was run by functionaries who were members of Right-wing parties and promoted fascist ideas, and could only be joined by "businessmen of German blood and origin". Jews were not admitted.[15] Another union which officially supported the Nazi Party's *Judenpolitik* was the *Kampfbund des gewerblichen Mittelstandes* under Party member Dr. von Renteln. This group

[10]*C.V.-Zeitung*, XI, No. 28 (8th July 1932).
[11]Paul Oertmann, *Der politische Boykott*, Berlin 1925, p. 7.
[12]Rudolf Callmann, *Zur Boykottfrage. Ein Gutachten*, Berlin 1932, p. 8.
[13]Bundesarchiv: NSD 73 No. 13.
[14]*C.V.-Zeitung*, XI, No. 36 (2nd September 1932).
[15]Christian Zentner and Friedemann Bedürftig (eds.), *Das große Lexikon des Dritten Reiches*, München 1985, p. 124.

admitted "all self-employed businessmen, especially manual workers and retailers of Christian origin".[16] Further inciters were the *Reichsverband zur Bekämpfung der Warenhäuser e.V.* and the *Arbeitsgemeinschaft deutscher Geschäftsleute*. A *Frauenarbeitsgemeinschaft zum Schutze der deutschen Arbeit* was engaged, among other things, in instigating a boycott of Jewish employees.[17]

At the beginning of the Depression, these middle-class unions made little impact. They did not gain popularity until the consequences of the Depression became noticeable and began to threaten the livelihoods of a great proportion of the lower-middle class. In 1932, no fewer than twenty-two professional groups counting more than 4,000 members were founded by the Nazis in the Munich/Upper Bavaria district alone.[18] In his defence brochure, Fritz Marburg writes that the economic incitement directed against Jews, which was supported by various associations, was now practised "in every single corner of Germany".[19] In some cities even *Krankenkassen* (medical insurance companies) boycotted Jewish customers.

The association mentioned above did their best to support the Nazis in their boycott actions. Numerous suggestions with regard to the boycott were communicated to the *Reich* Propaganda Department of the NSDAP or to *Der Stürmer*. For instance, the chairman of the *Wirtschaftsgruppe für Handel, Handwerk und andere Gewerbe*, Julius Starke, sent Streicher an *Aufklärungsschrift* with a 'Guideline to the Jewish Question', asking him to publish it. Starke demanded, among other things, an "auditorium" at the institution in charge of economic control, in order to improve the co-ordination of the boycott:

> ". . . If it becomes known to this institution that the supplier is a Jewish house or that a supplier preferably supplies the cooperative societies, branches and other businesses of that type, then the boycott of that house will be carried out in the entire German *Reich* within 8 days . . ."[20]

The attempts by Nazi Provincial Governments and City Councils to legalise the anti-Jewish boycott even before 1933 give a foretaste of the official boycott actions under Hitler's rule. In October 1932, the Nazi majority in the City Council of Neustadt a.d. Aisch decided that from then on no Jewish businesses could be taken into consideration when the city awarded contracts. As a result of complaints from the C.V., however, the decision was declared illegal and rescinded by the superior authorities.[21] In Thuringia a Nazi provincial government had even proceeded to public boycott actions. Its secretary, Marschler, announced at a conference of retailers in Weimar that the government was going to pass an edict which demanded of all officials not to make any purchases in Jewish shops or "Jewish" department stores. Instead, they were asked to buy from Christian retailers only.[22]

[16]Bundesarchiv: NSD 73 No. 13.
[17]Bundesarchiv: Hauptarchiv der NSDAP, NS 26/2021.
[18]Uhlig, *op. cit.*, p. 66.
[19]Fritz Marburg, *Der Antisemitismus in der deutschen Republik*, Wien 1931, p. 55.
[20]Bundesarchiv: Nachlaß Streicher.
[21]*C.V.-Zeitung*, XI, No. 45 (4th November 1932).
[22]*C.V.-Zeitung*, XI, No. 49 (2nd December 1932).

In addition, NSDAP deputies frequently put forward motions against the Jews. In June 1932, they made an application in the Prussian *Landtag* or diet asking the government to instruct the relevant institutions "to terminate contracts with actors of non-German origin as soon as possible" and "not to conclude such contracts in the future".[23] Another request determined that all contracts between the German broadcasting company and artists of foreign origin were to be terminated immediately.[24]

However, the Nazis were not the only party using this kind of method to woo voters. In Pomerania, one of Hitler's strongholds where the *Deutschnationale Volkspartei* (DNVP) feared to lose votes, parliamentary deputy, Friedrich Everling, tried to woo away voters from the NSDAP by demanding that a new tax, which was designed to aid the middle classes, should be imposed on people who bought from Jews or had business connections with them.[25]

The mottoes "Do not buy from Jews", "Avoid Jewish doctors", "Do not consult Jewish lawyers" or – indirectly – "Germans, buy from Germans only", were spread via leaflets, posters, placards, pamphlets and circulars as well as at meetings. Silly and vulgar as they were, the slogans which recurred *ad nauseam* in the Nazi newspapers were designed to stick in the readers' minds:

> "Kauf nicht beim Jud', das ist nicht recht, der Jud' ist Deutschlands Henkersknecht. Unterstützt den deutschen Gewerbestand, dann bleibt Euer Geld in deutscher Hand."[26]

In December 1928 *Gauleiter* Koch organised a parade with vans carrying posters that asked the population to boycott certain Jewish shops. One picture showed a Jew with a fist over his head and a caption reading "The blow must hit home."[27] This image indicated the physical dimension of the solution to the Jewish Question even at that time. In Görlitz and Plauen the Nazis distributed lists of names of local Jewish firms, doctors and lawyers.[28] In Osnabrück they published a special map in order to show the population the "right" way.[29] In Hirschberg, for instance, a group of Nazis daubed the windows of Jewish shops with swastikas and the slogan "Germans, do not buy from Jews. Hepp Hepp!"[30] In the market in Torgau stormtroopers posted themselves in front of Jewish market stalls in order to keep customers away.[31] The main criterion in the boycott of firms was that of name. As a consequence, an "Aryan" once complained to *Der Stürmer* about being boycotted for his "Jewish" name.[32]

Christmas had always provided an opportunity to incite buyers to boycott. Typically and naturally, the antisemites had no scruples in creating and utilising religious prejudices:

[23]Bundesarchiv: Hauptarchiv der NSDAP, NS 26/504.
[24]Bundesarchiv: Hauptarchiv der NSDAP, NS 26/504.
[25]*C.V.-Zeitung*, XI, No. 19 (6th May 1932).
[26]Cited in *C.V.-Zeitung*, IX, No. 3 (17th January 1930).
[27]*C.V.-Zeitung*, IX, No. 20 (17th May 1929).
[28]*C.V.-Zeitung*, XI, No. 5 (29th January 1932); X, No. 32 (7th August 1931).
[29]*C.V.-Zeitung*, VII, No. 51/52 (21st December 1928); VIII, No. 43 (25th October 1929).
[30]*C.V.-Zeitung*, VII, No. 24 (15th June 1928).
[31]*Israelitisches Familienblatt*, XXIX (2nd July 1931).
[32]Bundesarchiv: Nachlaß Streicher.

"Once again the Jew, who laughs and mocks at our Christian religion, seeks to make great profit from it . . . The Jew is not ashamed to make money out of such a holy Christian feast. For Christmas buy from German Christian traders!"[33]

In 1932, a Christian toy shop was specially opened in Glatz. In Essen's *Nationalzeitung* the children were asked to encourage their parents to boycott: "And you, German boys and girls! Tell your parents that you do not want anything from the Jewish department store, no gifts from the Jewish shop for Christmas."[34] It is of interest to see how strongly the NSDAP, which had a rather restrained attitude towards Christianity, emphasised the religious motivation of antisemitism. The Nazi Party was well aware that this dimension of anti-Jewish attitudes was still very characteristic of the population in rural areas. Such traditional prejudice was certainly stronger than the pseudo-scientific "racial theory" promoted by Gobineau and Günther.

For the purpose of mobilising the middle classes to boycott, the so-called superior economic strength of the department stores served as a more effective argument than the religious one. The department stores as well as the chain stores or cut-price stores were defamed as a "Jewish invention" which should not be allowed to exist. Their "palatial style", low prices and the "musical entertainment" in the cafeterias were described as an imitation of the oriental bazaar, devised by "foreign elements".[35] Certain scandals were created to prevent customers from shopping in department stores. There were claims that the food was bad or poisoned.[36] Through these and other arbitrary accusations the antisemites tried to give the population the notion of reprehensible practices within the Jewish business world.[37]

The Nazi press distorted facts and spread gross lies in order to create dislike and fear. The conjuring up of the "ordinary German businessman's" powerlessness before the "Jewish superiority" was not only designed to cause anger and panic, but also to induce self-pity:

"You are forgetting that nowadays the businessman who runs a small or medium-sized business has to struggle for his existence; that the 'Pfälzer Courier' is complaining about its lot while at the same time destroying the effectiveness of the small advertisements of honourable businessmen by publishing the gigantic advertisements of Jewish department stores."[38]

The *Schlesischer Beobachter* and the *Neue Nationale Zeitung* in Augsburg published a drawing in which Christ on the cross was portrayed next to a huge department store, where an impoverished businessman has hanged himself. Pictures of this kind are usually accompanied by demands for a boycott.[39] *Der Stürmer* and other Nazi newspapers warned against Jews who had "perfidiously" adopted "German names" or, to avoid being boycotted, packed their products in anonymous

---

[33]Cited in *C.V.-Zeitung*, XI, No. 11 (11th March 1932).
[34]*Ibid.*
[35]Peter Dehn, *Die Großbasare und Massenzweiggeschäfte*, Berlin 1899, cited in Uhlig, *op. cit.*, p. 15.
[36]*Heidelberger Beobachter*, 27th October 1931.
[37]*Heidelberger Beobachter*, 21st March 1931.
[38]*Heidelberger Beobachter*, 16th December 1931.
[39]*C.V.-Zeitung*, XI, No. 5 (29th January 1932).

wrapping without company names.[40] From time to time the story was put about that the Jews themselves were instigating boycotts – this as a pretext to justify a return boycott as "self-defence".[41]

With appeals to "German national feeling" the Nazis tried to incite the "German" population to hate foreigners. One standard misrepresentation was the assertion that Jewish shops offered mainly foreign goods.[42] On every occasion it was drummed into the people that they had to behave in a "German" way:

> "German men and women! Buy from Germans and avoid foreigners! Those who buy from Jews buy goods which have the sweat and blood of our German brothers upon them. Only if we support each other like brothers will we win over Juda."[43]

By asserting, albeit wrongly, that most Germans went along with the boycott, the antisemites set out to intimidate those who did not participate in it and tried to get them to believe that they lacked a feeling of solidarity.[44] Those who still dared to ignore the boycott were labelled traitors: "Men and women who buy from Jews and scorn German goods are betraying the German fight for freedom."[45] In a period overshadowed by the Treaty of Versailles, this was a clever and, for many people, a serious reproach. Such Nazi slogans clearly had an impact during this era of so-called national frustration. Thus, even before Hitler seized power the Nazis managed to carry out the threat that they would harry and pillory as "traitors of the people" all those who could not otherwise be intimidated. Especially in small towns and villages, SA and SS men stood, as watchdogs, in front of Jewish shops in order to write down customers' names and to stop them from entering. In Altenburg (Thuringia), for instance, they threatened to publish the names of customers of Jewish shops on posters or in the newspapers.[46]

Naturally, the boycott worked in favour of those whose competitors were thereby eliminated or weakened. Certain Nazi businessmen, doctors or lawyers did not shrink from utilising antisemitic statements as a means of propaganda for their own businesses or practices and therefore openly mentioned the boycott. A painter in Hildesheim was convicted of unfair competition because he had reproached a potential customer for having given his Jewish competitor a job, while remarking that the customer lacked national feeling.[47] In order that boycotters should not be afraid of the courts, the Party granted them protection. The *Kampfgemeinschaft gegen Warenhaus und Konsumverein* offered free legal defence in cases against Jewish suppliers and department stores.[48]

[40]Dennis E. Showalter, *Little Man, What Now? 'Der Stürmer' in the Weimar Republic*, Hamden, Ct. 1982, p. 128.
[41]*Heidelberger Beobachter*, 19th August 1931.
[42]Showalter, *op. cit.*, p. 11.
[43]*Heidelberger Beobachter*, 18th March 1931.
[44]*Heidelberger Beobachter*, 23rd October 1931.
[45]Cited in *C.V.-Zeitung*, XI, No. 2 (8th January 1932).
[46]*C.V.-Zeitung*, X, No. 45 (6th November 1931); XI, No. 34 (19th August 1932).
[47]*C.V.-Zeitung*, IX, No. 31 (1st August 1930).
[48]Bundesarchiv: NSD 73 No. 13.

"Registers of German Businessmen" and "Directories of the Sources of Supply" of "purely Aryan" businesses and those which sympathised with the Party and were advertised in the Nazi press, represented unfair competition as well, as it was not the quality of the products but political criteria that were relevant for the purchase. Shop owners who toed the line were strongly advised to mark their shops by placing swastikas on the doors and shop windows.[49]

Violent assaults on Jews, looting and demolition of Jewish shops, tear-gas bombs thrown in department stores etc., were, from the middle of 1932, part of the everyday practice of the Nazis, even though this was not tolerated by the authorities. The wave of violence surged mainly in East Prussia and Silesia.[50] The outrages continued in spite of the emergency decree of 9th August 1932, which was directed against political terror and primarily referred to the violent clashes between Nazis and Communists.

Thus, the national boycott called openly by the Nazis in April 1933, was organised and tested in a increasingly systematic way well in advance. From the time of the Depression, the *Hetzboykott* had become one of the most popular means of antisemitic harassment with the aim of weakening the Jewish population economically even without anti-Jewish laws, which were of course inconceivable before 1933. Once installed in power, the Nazi regime clearly acted less aggressively at first and for tactical reasons restricted itself with regard to the economic elimination of the Jews. Yet, the NSDAP's boycott activities during the Weimar Republic can still be regarded as symptomatic of what was in store for German Jewry.

III

The reactions to and the result of the boycott actions constitute a criterion for judgement of the nature and extent of antisemitic moods in the populace. Because of the sparsity of source material, it is hard to provide conclusive answers to the questions involved. Their participation in the boycott gave the antisemites an opportunity to put their basic convictions into practice without much effort or use of force. "Staying away" did not even arouse public attention. The fact that – except for the inciters and those who were boycotted, that is, the Nazis and the Jews (here essentially represented by the C.V.) – hardly anybody at that time gave serious attention to the boycott problem, might lead to the conclusion that the boycott met with little public approval. However, the sources only partly support this assumption.

First of all, notice must be taken of the considerable regional differences. As early as the beginning of 1925 the *C.V.-Zeitung* reported that the boycott in the country and in small towns was generally more effective than in the cities.[51] But here again one has to differentiate. In certain towns in North Germany the Jews

[49]Bundesarchiv: Nachlaß Streicher.
[50]*C.V.-Zeitung*, XI, No. 33 (12th August 1932).
[51]*C.V.-Zeitung*, IV, No. 13 (27th March 1925).

were more affected by the boycott, than, for instance, in Baden and the Ruhr.[52] As to the geographic divergencies, the national boycott propaganda gained its first results in Pomerania. East Prussia and Vogtland.[53] In spring 1932 the *C.V.-Zeitung* mentions a "state of emergency" in Pomerania. It emphasised that the Jews in that part of Germany were "seriously threatened" by the economic boycott.[54] In one small town in Pomerania antisemites even tried to starve the Jews systematically.[55]

A comparison of this C.V. survey with the election results at that time reveals interesting parallels, as the extent of participation in the boycott can be determined from the percentage of votes gained by the NSDAP and the *Deutschnationale Volkspartei* (DNVP). What is important is the fact that in Berlin, where 32.1 per cent of the total of German Jews lived at that time, the National parties gained no more than 31.6 per cent of the total of votes. In Hamburg and Leipzig the situation was similar. In most of the other regions with a low percentage of votes for the Nazi Party or the DNVP, the Catholic parties were particularly successful. Frequent boycott actions can also be noted in the strongholds of the *Zentrum* and the *Bayerische Volkspartei* of Upper Bavaria, Franconia, Oppeln and Westphalia.[56] In particular the region around Nuremberg, where *Der Stürmer* was published, was regarded as very "brown". Their editorial office allegedly received numerous letters of complaint about Jewish business methods.[57]

On the other hand, one can conclude from other sources and reports that a large proportion of the population did not follow the exhortations to boycott. The *Israelitisches Familienblatt*, though, registers an "enormous increase" of antisemitic currents in Schleswig-Holstein, which also had its effect on Jewish shops. According to the business people most affected in the small towns, however, only ten per cent of the customers stayed away out of hatred for Jews, while ninety per cent did so because of financial problems caused by the Depression.[58] The Zionist editor Robert Weltsch as well as C.V. functionaries such as Hans and Eva Reichmann could not remember Nazi boycott actions ever having been successful.[59] People continued buying from Jews, if not "out of love", then from the conviction that they offered good quality products.[60] This held true even for

[52]*C.V.-Zeitung*, VII, No. 3 (20th January 1928).

[53]*C.V.-Zeitung*, V, No. 14 (1st April 1926).

[54]*C.V.-Zeitung*, XI, No. 19 (6th May 1932).

[55]Arnold Paucker, *Der jüdische Abwehrkampf gegen Antisemitismus und Nationalsozialismus in den letzten Jahren der Weimarer Republik*, Hamburg 1968, p. 76.

[56]*C.V.-Zeitung*, VII, No. 43 (25th October 1929); VIII, No. 50 (13th December 1929); IX, No. 3 (17th January 1930); IX, No. 6 (7th February 1930); IX, No. 17)9th May 1930); IX, No. 33 (15th March 1931); XI, No. 2 (8th January 1932); XI, No. 14 (1st April 1932); XI, No. 49 (2nd December 1932).

[57]Arnd Müller, *Geschichte der Juden in Nürnberg*, Nürnberg 1968, p. 200.

[58]*Israelitisches Familienblatt*, XXIX (10th April 1931).

[59]Robert Weltsch, *Die deutsche Judenfrage. Ein kritischer Rückblick*, Königstein/TS 1981, p. 53; Eva G. Reichmann, *Flucht in den Haß. Die Ursachen der deutschen Judenkatastrophe*, Frankfurt a. Main 1968, p. 281; Hans Reichmann, 'Der Centralverein deutscher Staatsbürger jüdischen Glaubens', in *Festschrift zum 80. Geburtstag von Rabbiner Dr. Leo Baeck*, London 1953, p. 70.

[60]Weltsch, *op. cit.*, p. 53.

antisemitic fellow travellers. The following report was given by a non-Jewish businessman from Thuringia in 1931:

"On the surface, the Nazi schemes were carried out strictly even in the smallest towns. Though not convinced by Nazi ideas, one had to be at the organisation's disposal. Within, however, one remained the same person, smiled at the hullaballoo and did what one considered right. This includes the boycott of Jewish shops. Although one could not dare, especially in small towns, to act in opposition to the boycott slogans in public, people did so even more thoroughly by way of the backdoor and at night after the shops had ostensibly closed . . ."[61]

Many non-Jewish shop owners were not even aware of the fact that they had been included in the "Register of Christian Businesses". Almost half of those on the list of firms complained about this to the C.V., from which they had received the register. Moreover, there were public protests against it.[62] In Heidelberg, for instance, an initiative of retailers organising themselves against the department stores and cooperative societies offered Jews the opportunity to become members, so as not to be suspected of acting in antisemitic ways.[63]

While the attitude of "the man in the street" decided the success or failure of the boycott against shops, lawyers, doctors etc., the boycott of Jewish employees depended basically on the employer alone. The battle against Jewish employees was fought quietly, but all the more emphatically, and the Nazis abstained, in this respect, from direct boycott propaganda in the press. In the managers' offices and personnel departments of big companies there could often be found someone who was susceptible to antisemitic slogans and who made sure that Jewish personnel was taken into account when it came to dismissal but ignored with regard to applications. Some firms openly apologised for rejecting Jewish applicants by saying that being "Christian firms" they did not employ Jews on principle.[64] Apparently, non-Jewish shops were also boycotted if they employed Jews. Owners of firms felt obliged to dismiss Jewish personnel even when they were satisfied with their work:

"Dear Sir! I am extremely sorry to have to inform you today that I cannot employ your brother in the long term. The permanent increase of radical political influence on a large section of my customers is alarming. I have already suffered damage and expect more trouble in future. In your brother I shall lose an excellent employee . . ."[65]

One cannot rule out that employees of smaller businesses fell in with boycott demands, for fear of harassment, even before Hitler seized power. Or was the alleged fear of the Nazis just a pretence in order to hide antisemitic attitudes?

Quantifications with regard to the extent of the compliance with the boycott, which came to its peak during the Depression, cannot be made for the reasons mentioned above, and evaluations as well as judgements are hard to make. What is certain is the fact that in rural areas and in small towns more people went along with the boycott than in cities and, secondly, that geographical variations existed

---

[61] *Israelitisches Familienblatt*, XXIX (10th April 1931).
[62] Foerder, *op. cit.*, p. 159.
[63] *Heidelberger Beobachter*, 23rd October 1931.
[64] Vereinigte Zentrale für Jüdische Arbeitsnachweise (ed.), *Unser Recht auf Arbeit*, Berlin 1932, p. 8.
[65] *Unser Recht auf Arbeit*, *op. cit.*, p. 9.

(which mainly – though not exclusively – ran parallel to the NSDAP's share of votes in the elections). Moreover, it seems justified to conclude that, compared with the actions against shops and employees, little attention was paid to boycotting Jews in the liberal professions.

Motives for participation in the boycott were very complex and, presumably, opportunism played a part even then. If, on the one hand, the population's fundamental reluctance to follow the boycott could lead to the conclusion that antisemitism was of little importance in Germany, one could on the other hand interpret the lack of interest in taking effective measures against the boycott as an indication of a relevant, even though subliminal, anti-Jewish attitude. Likewise, the sources at hand provide little evidence of an active political resistance to the boycott on the part of most of the Jewish community. The abundant antisemitic propaganda was never met – nor could it have been met – by equivalent counter-actions by the Jewish population – let alone by the non-Jewish population.

The most significant attempt from the non-Jewish side to counteract the boycott systematically was made by the *Verein zur Abwehr des Antisemitismus (Abwehrverein)*, which admittedly also had a considerable number of Jewish members. Their monthly *Abwehrblätter* contained contributions by such respected lawyers as Paul Oertmann, whose treatise *Der politische Boykott*, published as early as 1925, had received much public attention. Here, Oertmann expressly subscribed to Rudolf Wertheimer's term of *Hetzboykott*[66] and emphasised the illegality of boycotting.[67] Under the title 'Swastika-Doctors' the *Abwehrblätter*, for instance, pilloried a Nazi doctor in 1932 who had let a seriously injured boy die after he had heard the boy's Jewish name.[68]

Another organisation which supported the Jews was the *Hansa-Bund*, which was founded in 1909 and, according to the *C.V.-Zeitung*, set up an office for protection against boycotting in May 1932.[69] As a group representing the interests of business, trade and industry, this association, which likewise had Jewish members, opposed agrarian conservatism. The desired unification of the middle-class merchants, however, was not achieved. Their aversion to bankers, who decisively supported the *Hansa-Bund*, as well as antisemitic tendencies, stopped large numbers from joining this organisation. In addition, however, the *Verband der Waren- und Kaufhäuser*, which was treated with hostility by the conservative middle classes and in which Jews also played a part, also joined the *Hansa-Bund*.[70]

What must be pointed out is the fact that neither the political parties nor the trade unions and economic associations – even though they accepted and followed the principles of democracy – took concrete measures of defence against the boycott. Similarly, the *Reich* and *Länder* governments also restricted themselves to restrained comments on the issue. The government itself took hardly any initiatives: the Ministry of the Interior of Hesse came out against the boycott

[66]Rudolf Wertheimer, *Der Hetzboykott. Einige Gedanken zum Boykottproblem*, Wiesbaden 1931, p. 32.
[67]Paul Oertmann, 'Der Hetzboykott', in *Abwehrblätter*, vol. XLII, No. 8/9 (1932), p. 186.
[68]*Abwehrblätter*, vol. XLII, No. 6 (1932), p. 136.
[69]*C.V.-Zeitung*, XI, No. 20 (13th May 1932).
[70]Siegfried Mielke, *Der Hansa-Bund für Gewerbe, Handel und Industrie 1909–1914*, Göttingen 1976, p. 103.

on 30th December 1932. In response to a request by Nazi representative Lenz concerning the question as to why the government could not instruct the police authorities to stop impeding or preventing "propaganda activities carried out in a permissible way, in favour of German businesses and against the purchase of goods from department stores, Jewish shops etc.", the government sent the following circular to the authorities:

"In response to the request of 29th November 1932 from Party representative Lenz and his Party, I have the honour of replying that the agitation against Jewish businessmen, at present practised on a large scale and mainly consisting of leaflets asking the population to avoid shops whose owners are Jewish and to buy only from Christians, has already led to serious disturbances of law and order. In Giessen and Mainz, tear-gas and stink bombs were thrown in several department stores last Sunday, which considerably disturbed the visitors to these stores. In the interest of law and order I have therefore given instructions to put a stop to this agitation most vigorously as it poses a threat to law and order."[71]

The C.V. suspected that the circular had been published in agreement with *Reich* Minister of the Interior Bracht, because a few days later he had sent a message to the regional governments concerning 'Measures Against the Increasingly Occurring Cases of Boycott Against Certain Shops': "The police . . . are authorised and obligated to intervene against this kind of disturbance to law and order."

The democratic press, whether it was dependent on party politics or not, was also somewhat hesitant when it came to fighting the boycott. Exceptions to this were made in instances where the effects were directly felt. The Socialist paper *Freie Presse*, for instance, criticised the boycott in Pforzheim after antisemitic slogans had been daubed on the windows of the editorial office.[72] The *Bürger-Kurier*, too, felt obliged to condemn the demands for a boycott in 1930, after the city Baden-Baden, which depended on tourism, had suffered as a result:

"The resort of Baden-Baden is now experiencing the economic results of Nazi antisemitism. From Baden-Baden it is reported that leaflets have been distributed in the cities to warn the Jewish population against visiting Baden-Baden, after repeated occurrences of Jewish houses being daubed and defaced with swearwords . . . The employers' and employees' associations of Baden-Baden have banded together against the hooliganism which was severely damaging their interests."[73]

Usually, only the C.V. used the argument that the boycott did not only damage the Jews but also the German economy.

How is this passivity, including as it does the inactivity of those who had a certain amount of sympathy for the Jews, to be interpreted? A possible explanation may be that their own worries and struggle for existence during the economic crisis stopped people from involving themselves in the problems of others, and the boycott campaign was conducted on such a crude and vulgar level that otherwise well-meaning people often made the mistake of not taking the Nazis and their antics seriously.

[71]Cited in *C.V.-Zeitung*, XII, No. 3 (19th January 1933).
[72]*Freie Presse*, 6th October 1923.
[73]*Bürgerkurier*, 11th July 1930.

IV

Like everyone else in Germany, the Jews were affected by the economic crisis. The *Vereinigte Zentrale für Jüdische Arbeitsnachweise in Deutschland* asserted that, because of their particular professional and social structure, Jews suffered more serious distress than their non-Jewish fellow citizens.[74] The boycott campaign doubtlessly aggravated the situation, but it is hard to ascertain to what extent. For instance, the different causes for a Jewish firm's bankruptcy can hardly be listed separately and there are only a few individual reports on the direct consequences of the boycott. The C.V. and other observers of the Jewish economic situation, however, increasingly drew attention to the fact that, at this time, the boycott was jeopardising the whole economic existence of the Jews in Germany. In the summer of 1932, the *C.V.-Zeitung* reported that the editorial office was receiving numerous letters concerning boycott actions and violence every day.[75] By the end of the Weimar Republic this type of Nazi agitation had spread into every sector of the economy.

The Jewish business world suffered, particularly in the country and small towns. In some towns Jewish shopkeepers noted a decrease in sales of up to twenty per cent as a result of the boycott. In smaller towns shop-owners were sometimes forced to close down and to change their residence.[76] The boycott made itself felt among Jewish craftsmen, too. A glasscutter from Berlin reported in a survey by the C.V. that it was often insinuated that Jewish master-craftsmen were not sufficiently well-trained.[77] The number of jobs given to Jewish workmen decreased gradually. After demands for a boycott appeared in Nazi newspapers, customers suddenly cancelled their orders and did not collect the goods produced for them.[78] Others refused to have Jewish workmen in their houses. Non-Jewish firms dismissed Jewish apprentices.[79]

Apparently, Jewish employees and workers in particular were strongly affected by the boycott. As early as the summer of 1928 the *C.V.-Zeitung* reported on employment negotiations where the employers enquired about the applicant's religion. "If the answer is 'Jewish', the personnel manager's interest often drops to zero."[80] The boycott became noticeable even on the management level of big corporations. Doctors and lawyers, however, suffered less, although they too were targets. But they were less affected by traditional anti-Jewish polemics than, for instance, businessmen, and since their relations with patients or clients were ones of confidentiality and trust, it was not easy to discredit them. In a pamphlet *Die Juden in der Medizin*, however, the author laments that for the first time in history Jewish doctors were being boycotted by a considerable number of their patients. It was a fact that Christian colleagues had ceased to consult

[74] *Unser Recht auf Arbeit, op. cit.*, p. 4.
[75] *C.V.-Zeitung*, XI, No. 33 (12th August 1932).
[76] *Unser Recht auf Arbeit, op. cit.*, p. 6.
[77] *C.V.-Zeitung*, X, No. 33 (14th August 1931).
[78] *C.V.-Zeitung*, XI, No. 7 (12th February 1932).
[79] Jakob Lestschinsky, *Das wirtschaftliche Schicksal des deutschen Judentums*, Berlin 1933, p. 155.
[80] *C.V.-Zeitung*, VII, No. 26 (29th June 1928).

Jewish authorities or specialists. The consequences of the race-theory were becoming noticeable.[81]

The boycott also had its effects in the realm of press and culture. Editors dismissed Jewish journalists. Some newspapers owned by Jews folded up, as in the case of the *Kasseler Tageblatt*.[82] Jewish artists reported that they were not allowed to sign their work with their Jewish names, as this "would have made a bad impression on the higher level".[83] Anti-Jewish trends could be noted in the theatres particularly.[84]

Jews were not only boycotted economically but socially as well. In many towns, for instance in Nuremberg, it became increasingly difficult for Jews to find a place to live. From Nuremberg it was also reported that young Jewish people were accepted with reluctance in the schools and that in some classes, no one even spoke to them.[85]

V

The most important work in fighting the boycott was done by the *Centralverein*. In its *Anti-Anti*, economic prejudices utilised by the Nazis were disproved. Of necessity, the department stores were an important issue in this debate. It could hardly be denied that the majority of department stores were owned by Jews. In order to counteract the exploitation of this fact for propaganda purposes, one could either dissociate oneself from the department stores – while emphasising that these big stores were harmful competition for Jewish retailers too – or one could justify the department stores as an institution as such. The latter seemed to commend itself last but not least – it must be admitted – because the Tietz Concern (and later other department stores mobilised by them), who felt a threat to their economic basis, were prepared to render financial support to a camouflaged campaign against the NSDAP.[86] The advocates of the department stores, above all the *Schutzgemeinschaft der Großbetriebe des Einzelhandels*, repeatedly rejected the reproach of their alleged superior strength. Compared with the turnover of other branches of the retail trade, the turnover of the department stores was only 3.9 per cent. This figure was published by the *Forschungsstelle für den Handel* and the *Institut für Konjunkturforschung*.[87]

Certainly it had been Jewish businessmen who had introduced the department stores to Germany. The Nazis' claim, however, that the department store was altogether a Jewish invention was false. There was not a single Jew among the founders of the first department stores in France, which were followed by those in

[81]Heinrich Rosin, *Die Juden in der Medizin*, Berlin 1926, p. 25.
[82]Frieda H. Sichel, 'The Rise and Fall of the Kasseler Tageblatt', in *LBI Year Book XIX* (1974), pp. 242–243.
[83]*C.V.-Zeitung*, X, No. 33 (14th August 1931).
[84]Lestschinsky, *op. cit.*, p. 168.
[85]Müller, *op. cit.*, pp. 179 and 208.
[86]Paucker, *op. cit.*, p. 111.
[87]Centralverein (ed.), *Anti-Anti. Tatsachen zur Judenfrage*, Berlin 1928, p. 75a.

Deutsche kauft beim Deutschen

Meidet den Konsum-Verein

MITTEILUNGSBLATT DER KAMPFGEMEINSCHAFT GEGEN WARENHAUS UND KONSUMVEREIN

Folge 1   Kaiserslautern im Juli 1931

Deutsche Hausfrau
in Stadt und Land!

Gerade an Dich wenden wir uns! Für Dich ist dieses Blatt geschrieben! Du sollst es beherzigen, denn durch Deine Hände geht der größte Teil des deutschen Volks-Einkommens.

An Dir liegt es, den deutschen Geschäftsmann vor dem Verderben zu schützen. Der deutsche Kleingewerbetreibende und Handwerker bilden mit den Verbrauchern zusammen die Grundlage eines gesunden Staates. Werden diese vernichtet, wird der Wunsch der Marxisten nach Veredensung des deutschen Einzelhandels erfüllt und die Trust-Psychose gefördert. Die Steuerquellen versiegen und Sozialversicherungen sowie Pensionen kommen in Wegfall.

Was ist nun Deine Aufgabe deutsche Hausfrau?

Den deutschen Geschäftsmann vor dem Untergang zu schützen, indem Du das Warenhaus meidest und Deine Einkäufe beim Deutschen Geschäftsmanne vornimmst, denn das Warenhaus drückt die Preise auf Kosten des Arbeiters und Unternehmers. Der Satz „Die Masse wird es bringen", täuscht den Käufer.

Der deutsche Geschäftsmann ist Dein Volksgenosse!

Ihm stehen die ungeheueren Mittel wie den jüdischen Warenhäusern und Ramschhändlern für marktschreierische Reklame nicht zur Verfügung. Mit Deinem Geld baut der Jude seine großen Paläste. Du verhilfst ihm zu einem Leben in Saus und Braus, während Du selbst darbst.

Der Jude merkt noch nichts von der Not des Volkes, doch Dir wird der Brotkorb immer höher gehängt!

Glaube nicht, daß Du im Warenhaus billiger kaufst!

Die billigeren Preise gehen immer auf Kosten der Qualität. Dagegen kaufst Du gute Ware im deutschen Geschäftshaus billiger wie im Warenhaus.

Auch Du deutsche Bauersfrau

kaufst gedankenlos ins Warenhaus und zum Ramschjuden und unterstützt dadurch die Totengräber Deines Standes.

Call to the German housewife
to boycott Jewish department stores

Boykott!

Nationalsozialisten! Fort mit den Halbheiten!

Boykottiert die Warenhäuser, Konsumvereine und jüdischen oder jüdisch beeinflußten Geschäfte! Laßt nur Juden und Judengenossen in diesen Läden kaufen! Uebt Disziplin!

Wir veröffentlichen hiermit eine Liste der Leipziger Geschäfte, in denen kein Nationalsozialist kauft:

Boykott den jüdischen Geschäften!

Damen= u. Kinderbekleidung:
Hirschfeld, Gebr., Petersstr. 42

Herren= und Knabenkleidung:
Bamberger & Hertz, Goethestr. 1
Fischel, Moritz, Gundorferstr. 13
Heinau, Julius, Wurznerstr. 20
Heller u. Sohn, Gundorferstr. 2
Jackson, Bernhard, Windmühlenstr. 41
Jackson, David, Zeitzerstr. 9
Jacobowitz, Siegmund, Zeitzerstr. 57
Kanner, Ascher, Eisenbahnstr. 5
Kanner, Jacob, Wurznerstr. 15 a
Manes, Gebr., Reichstr. 11
Sprung, Gebr., Gerberstr. 16, Windmühlenstr. 52, Eisenbahnstr. 35, Karl=Heine Str. 71
Wronker, D. u. Co., Karl=Heinestr. 44
Wronker, Julius, Dieskaustr 63

Lederwaren:
Baron, Reginenstr. 2

Schuhwaren:
Bottina, Hainstr., Windmühlenstr., Am Hallischen Tor
Buzbaum, Mittelstraße
Cahane, Schützenstr.
Fried, Windmühlenstr., Reichsstr.
Hasnes, Windmühlenstr.

Schuhwaren:
Königsberg, Königsplatz, Täubchenweg, Diestaustr., Am Hallischen Tor, Markthallenstr.
Ingwer, Täubchenweg
Kormann, Am Hall. Tor, Zweinaundorferstr.
Mercedes, Petersstr.
Nordheimer, Petersstr., Hainstr., Grimmaischestr., Eisenbahnstr.
Salamander, Petersstr.
Schuh=Baer, Gundorferstr., Karl=Heine Str.
Schuh=Bahr, Ranstädtersteinweg, Eisenbahnstr., Merseburgerstr.
Selinger, Gerberstraße
Speyer, Petersstraße
Tack, Conrad, Hainstr. 16/18

Textilwaren:
Hodes, S., Neumarkt
Jacoby, Seidenhaus, Petersstr.
Sonder & Co., Petersstr.
Pergamenter, Gebr., Windmühlenstr., Frankfurterstr Härtelstr.

Wäsche:
Blum, Hugo, Reich=str.

Warenkreditgeschäfte:
Ehmler, H. & Co., Hainstr.
Goldwasser, Hainstr.

Boykott den Warenhäusern und Konsumvereinen!

Kaufhaus des Nordens, Hallisch=str. 122
Kaufhaus Th. Althoff
Kaufhaus Brühl, G. m. b. H.
Kaufhaus Urn, Gebr.
Kaufhaus Held, Gebr., Merseburgerstr.
Epa, Einheitspreis A.=G.
Kaufhaus Fried, Gebr., Windmüh'enstr.
Kaufh. Joske, M. & Co., Karl=Heine Str.
Konsumverein Leipzig=Plagwitz & Umg.
Wohlwert=Handelsgesellschaft m.b.H.
Wächterstraße 8, Wurzner Str. 10, Eisenbahnstraße 39
Woolworth, Petersstraße

Diese Liste ist aus der Zeitschrift der sächsischen jungen Nationalsozialisten, der **"Parole", dem Kampfblatt der sächsischen Jugend** entnommen, die sie regelmäßig veröffentlicht.

(Die Aufzählung erhebt keinen Anspruch auf Vollständigkeit. Nennt weitere jüdische Geschäfte dem Gaupresseamt der sächs. nat. soz. Jugendorganisationen, Leipzig C 1, Weststr. 79 II Aufg. A. Wir brauchen aber nur einwandfreies Material!)

Nationalsozialisten! So kämpft die nat. soz. Leipziger Jugend schon seit langer Zeit. Der "Verband der deutschen Waren= und Kaufhäuser" in Berlin, sowie der "Konsumverein Leipzig=Plagwitz" versuchten die "Parole" durch kostspielige Prozesse tot zu machen, weil sie zum Boykott aufrief. Es hat ihnen nichts genützt! Ihr Angriff scheiterte am Opferwillen der Leipziger Jugend. Nur "herabsetzende Äußerungen" und die "öffentliche" Bekanntgabe derjenigen, die trotzdem in die boykottierten Geschäfte kaufen, wurde uns untersagt. Den Boykott selber aber haben sie uns nicht verbieten können und so rufen wir denn lauter als zuvor:

Boykott den Warenhäusern und Konsumvereinen!

Nationalsozialisten! Unterstützt auch Ihr uns in unserem Kampf! Lest alle die **"Parole", das Kampfblatt der sächsischen Jugend!**

Preis 15 Pfennig!   Überall zu haben!

Nazi boycott appeal

By courtesy of Bundesarchiv, Koblenz

England and the USA. The *Anti-Anti* pointed out that many large German stores such as C&A, Theodor Althoff, Rudolf Herzog, Zeeck, Oberpollinger and others, as well as most non-German corporations (e.g. Woolworth) were owned by non-Jews.[88]

Moreover, it was hoped that the argument that the boycott did harm not only to Jews but also to the national economy would convince the public of its senselessness. In the long run, no economy could sustain the notion that any group could be violently driven out for political or religious reasons. The *C.V.-Zeitung* noted in 1929:

"As far as economic ethics are concerned, the boycott will judge itself, for in its ultimate consequence it must lead to the destruction of the economy. Just as the Nationalist boycotts the Jew, the Catholic could economically paralyse the Protestant, the Southern German the Northern German, the members of one political party the members of another. An economy within the framework of a state would thus be sentenced to death, the state itself would lose its right to exist."[89]

The C.V.'s legal battles demonstrate that in addition to declarations people also defended themselves in a practical way. In October 1931, the regional C.V. of Bavaria, for instance, provided its local groups and confidants with guidelines concerning actions in cases of boycott:[90] They were advised first to inform their regional association and ask them for counsel. Next, they were recommended to "make sure that details of evidence were immediately collected and searched for (procurement of several prints of the demand for a boycott); if, as in the case of posters, this is impossible, production of verbatim copies or photos". With regard to demands for a boycott by way of leaflets and posters, it was pointed out that the incident could be reported to the police and petitions for confiscation could be filed because, according to the Bavarian police regulations of 8th May 1929, such material could only be distributed or put up if the police had given permission. If the appeal was published in the newspapers, the lawyers appointed by the C.V. had to obtain "power of attorney from all or at least a large number of the affected businessmen (or doctors and lawyers etc.)", in order to institute proceedings for refraining from further distribution, which otherwise could be done only by the injured parties themselves. Quick action was a necessity as, otherwise, the courts could put off the charge for lack of urgency. The guidelines contained the advice not to make a report to the police in cases of verbal appeals for a boycott, such as at a public meeting, for experience had shown that the precise wording could not be ascertained. If the persons involved were unable to bear the necessary costs, the regional association was willing to allow them full or partial legal support. However, if the persons involved acted on their own authority, the C.V. refused to bear the costs.

The latter point shows the C.V.'s strong interest in taking legal actions itself or at least in controlling them. The C.V. had a great deal of past experience. Every judgement was scientifically evaluated, duplicated and sent to all jurists who

[88]*Ibid.*, p. 75b.
[89]*C.V.-Zeitung*, VIII, No. 50 (13th December 1929).
[90]Bundesarchiv: Nachlaß Streicher, Circular letter of the C.V. Bavaria of October 1931.

worked with the C.V. This was intended to guarantee unified practice.[91] (Unfortunately, the relevant collection had disappeared. It can be assumed that it was destroyed, along with other documents of the C.V. soon after the Nazis seized power.) The guidelines point to the fact that the C.V. attached great importance to proceeding only in cases which were factually and legally certain.[92]

In order prove in court that the boycott was against the law, the C.V. had legal reports drawn up. The exactitude of argument which was needed to convince the court was noteworthy. There were no unified judgements by the *Reichsgericht* and the administration of justice was fragmented. As the *Reichsgericht* had not yet looked into the boycott problem thoroughly, some judges referred to a decision of 1906 by which a request by the bakers of a town to boycott bakeries which denied their workers better payment and working conditions had been declared permissible. This boycott was compared to a boycott against Jewish traders.[93]

In his treatise of 1925, Oertmann opposed the practice of referring to this testimony of the judges of Leipzig in connection with the national boycott. It might be legal to try and inform the public of an alleged economic dominance of the Jews, but a "witch-hunt" against certain or all Jews because of their Jewishness was prohibited by the new Weimar Constitution (which had not been in force when the ruling of 1906 was made). Those who would fight against religious and racial equality (Article 109) could only do so within the framework of a political programme; not, however, in the name of the entire population. Consequently, antisemitic boycott actions were a type of political boycott.[94] From Article 118 of the Constitution Oertmann concluded that the political boycott in general was not only against the moral code but also directly against the law. Under Article 118 violating freedom of thought in any way (e.g. through an economic boycott) by trying to attack representatives of specific trends of opinion was prohibited. Boycotting human beings merely because of their existence was all the more dangerous and odious. Oertmann's expert opinion had a most positive effect in court proceedings.[95]

In his defence pamphlet, Wertheimer placed much importance on judging the boycott of Jews in a light other than that of an economic or political boycott. Most of all the jurisdiction of the *Reichsgericht* lacked the important bases of relevant objectives. Unlike the antisemitic boycott, the general boycott was not aiming to damage the persons affected economically; for the Jews were unable to stop the boycott by acting according to the wishes of their opponents. From the *völkisch* point of view one could not even voluntarily renounce one's Jewishness through baptism or by leaving the Jewish faith, nor could one change one's "race". A boycott which only intended to harm the opponent was an end in itself and had to be regarded as uneconomic and immoral.[96] After all, a boycott

[91]Bundesarchiv: Nachlaß Streicher, Report of the C.V. around 1931.
[92]*C.V.-Zeitung*, V, No. 14 (1st April 1926).
[93]Cited in Foerder, *loc. cit.*, p. 155.
[94]Oertmann, *Der politische Boykott*, *op. cit.*, p. 59.
[95]Udo Beer, *Die Juden, das Recht und die Republik*, Frankfurt a. Main 1986, p. 261.
[96]Wertheimer, *op. cit.*, pp. 13f.

against Jews was not an economic battle, as on the one hand no form of economic entity along racial or *völkisch* lines existed and on the other hand the inciters in no way claimed to act as economic opponents. For all these reasons, Wertheimer concluded, the only appropriate term for this agitation was *"Hetzboykott"*.[97]

The Nazi Party's programme was not aimed at completely eliminating the Jews just from economic life: the *völkisch* boycott aspired to abolish their constitutionally attested rights (Articles 111, 118, 136, 151), and strove for their ostracism and their exclusion from the civil community. Given this insight, said Hans Lazarus, the lawyer of the C.V., in October 1931 when numerous cases had already come to court, the fight against the boycott would have been very easy. In practice, however, this view caught on increasingly but by slow degrees.[98] The Provincial High Court and Court of Appeal in Bamberg argued against the *Koburger Nationalzeitung* in 1931:

> "The boycott in question is particularly reprehensible because it refuses German citizens the right to exist in the economic sector for no other reason than their affiliation to the Jewish race. Such slander is against the moral code as well as against the spirit of the constitution of the German *Reich*. These proceedings have nothing in common with an objective fight against excesses in the economic sector . . ."[99]

The most effective method of defence against demands for a boycott was the obtaining of an interim injunction from the appropriate courts on penalty of civil action. With its decision of 15th February 1927 – which was welcomed by the C.V. – the *Reichsgericht* gave up its previous point of view according to which a preventive injunction suit could not be instituted if the prohibited action was a penal offence.[100] As the Criminal Code contained no special regulations with regard to the boycott, the fight against it had to be based mainly on the Civil Code. Particularly relevant were claims for compensation under §823 and §826 of the German Civil Code.[101] In additional cases, however, requirements of Criminal Law were also met, namely §240 (coercion), §253 (extortion) as well as §360,11 (public nuisance). Legal action could also be taken against incitement to class hatred (§130) and religious insults (§166). However, legal proceedings were successful only in exceptional cases. The Nazis strictly avoided direct public incitement to violence. Instead, they preferred circumlocutions so as not to commit an offence.[102]

Most frequently the courts granted interim injunctions on grounds of unfair competition. According to several courts the press was capable of practising unfair competition as well, since the support of someone else's competition also met the competition's purpose.[103] In some cases publishers and printers were

[97]*Ibid.*, p. 32.

[98]*C.V.-Zeitung*, X, No. 43 (23rd October 1931).

[99]Cited in *C.V.-Zeitung*, XI, No. 5 (29th January 1932).

[100]Beer, *op. cit.*, p. 261.

[101]Oertmann, *Der politische Boykott, op. cit.*, pp. 76ff., comprised by Beer, *op. cit.*, p. 259.

[102]Paucker, *op. cit.*, p. 78.

[103]*C.V.-Zeitung*, XI, No. 5 (29th January 1932).

fined on grounds of violation of the press law, because they were proved to have knowingly spread lies.[104]

Slander and libel against the individual were punishable offences. Difficulties arose when the requests to boycott certain shops, doctors etc. were expressed through general phrases – "Germans, buy only from Germans!" A large number of courts held the view that the use of these phrases was also a penal offence. According to a decision by the *Reichsgericht* of 13th December 1929, it was not necessary for the name of the insulted person to be mentioned. It was sufficient that the person referred to was recognisable from the context.[105] This also applied to collective slander and libel (§185). As the Jews were excluded from protection against collective slander/libel by a judgement of the *Reichsgericht* of 6th October 1881, an individual Jew was not regarded as a victim if the insults were directed against Jews in general.[106] In such cases it was, therefore, rarely possible to institute criminal proceedings or to obtain an interim injunction.

Also significant were legal opinions which recognised a violation of German national feeling in certain demands for a boycott. In one case the defendants had issued a flier accusing Germans who bought from department stores of "undermining" the German middle class and of contributing to the "subjugation of the German economy". They were convicted by the Provincial Court of Appeal in Braunschweig on grounds of "abuse of national feelings". The Court of Appeal in Jena considered the threat of publishing the names of customers of Jewish firms to be just as illegal:

> "Under the law every individual is free to buy wherever he likes. Whether he buys from department stores or from other shops is entirely his own business. It is impermissible to prevent him from doing this and to try to manipulate him by threats, however covert, of exposure . . ."[107]

Offenders against interim injunctions were usually fined, but the sums were mostly insignificant. Generally they ranged between twenty and 150 Reichsmark for the printers and between 200 and 500 Reichsmark for the authors of the articles or leaflets as well as for the editors of the newspapers.[108] The low fines were sometimes justified by the insolvency of the offenders. In the majority of cases, however, this argument was untenable as the Nazi Party acted as the paymaster.[109] Thus, the penalty became senseless and could even have the opposite effect of motivating the offenders to further action. Nazis who were sentenced were celebrated as martyrs just as the courts had feared.[110]

The fact that the courts sometimes ruled against Jews even in clear-cut cases indicates that certain judges were not willing to punish those behind the *völkisch*

[104]*C.V.-Zeitung*, XI, No. 50 (12th December 1932).

[105]*C.V.-Zeitung*, IX, No. 29 (18th July 1930).

[106]Lohalm, *op. cit.*, p. 238.

[107]Cited in *C.V.-Zeitung*, XI, No. 33 (19th August 1932).

[108]*C.V.-Zeitung*, VIII, No. 43 (25th October 1929); VIII, No. 51 (20th December 1929); IX, No. 13 (28th March 1930); IX, No. 19 (9th May 1930); XI, No. 50 (29th January 1932).

[109]Donald L. Niewyk, 'Jews and the Courts in Weimar Germany', in *Jewish Social Studies*, vol. XXXVII, No. 2 (Spring 1975), p. 105.

[110]*Ibid.*, p. 103.

boycott. Some courts refused to grant interim injunctions. Sometimes they justified their rejection or lenient sentences by asserting that the accused were political extremists who could not be influenced and would not learn their lesson by being convicted.[111] Occasionally young Party members were favoured by extenuating circumstances because they were "instruments of fanatic agitators".[112] Some public prosecutors who were antisemitically inclined simply held that the boycott was a matter for the populace rather than the courts. The Court of Appeal dismissed an injunction suit filed by boycotted firms in Hof and argued that every German enjoyed freedom of speech. Neither the slogan "Do not buy from Jews" not the comparison of German and Jewish shops could be regarded as an insult.[113] On the basis of these arguments the judge accepted the *völkisch* distinction between "German" and "Jewish", which fundamentally implied that he did not regard the German Jews as Germans.

The accused used similar assertions to defend themselves in court and referred to freedom of speech.[114] The demand for a boycott was not motivated by political reasons but merely economic ones since, according to *Gauleiter* Koch in a Königsberg court in May 1929, the Jews were an economic superpower in Germany which had to be combatted. This statement was followed by presenting the case against Jewish department stores.[115] The C.V. lamented that in court the Nazis behaved like "harmless little innocents".[116] A councillor in Glatz, who was a Nazi, denied having incited the population to use violence against Jews. Had his request to boycott been incitement Hitler would not have permitted it. The Party did not use violence and applied legal methods only. While the councillor was fined 300 *Reichsmark* for inciting the use of violence he was found not guilty of slander. By using the expression "traitor to the people" he had not intended to insult the Jews but was referring to the German customers.[117]

Nevertheless, the C.V. reports on boycott trials convey the impression that, on the whole, the courts were taking the protection of the Jews seriously. The majority of cases were settled quickly and with a verdict in favour of the plaintiff.[118] The C.V.'s legal measures of defence against the boycott are said to have been the most successful.[119] "Yet", says Udo Beer, "in the long run the processes of civil law cannot operate successfully unless the poison is taken out of political life, and that did not happen."[120] This implies that with regard to other offences against Jews the courts hesitated to give antisemites an appropriate sentence, if they sentenced them at all. Theo Rasehorn, Ambrose Doskow,

[111]*Ibid.*, p. 103.

[112]*Israelitisches Familienblatt*, XXIX (2nd July 1931).

[113]Callmann, *op. cit.*, p. 7.

[114]*C.V.-Zeitung*, XI, No. 11 (11th March 1932).

[115]*C.V.-Zeitung*, VIII, No. 20 (17th March 1929).

[116]*C.V.-Zeitung*, VIII, No. 20 (17th March 1929).

[117]*Israelitisches Familienblatt*, XXIX (2nd July 1931).

[118]Ambrose Doskow and Sidney Jacoby, 'Anti-Semitism and the Law in Pre-Nazi Germany', in *Contemporary Jewish Record*, vol. III, No. 5 (September-October 1940), pp. 507ff.

[119]Paucker, *op. cit.*, p. 75; Niewyk, *loc. cit.*, p. 108.

[120]Udo Beer, 'The Protection of Jewish Civil Rights in the Weimar Republic. Jewish Self-Defence through Legal Action', in *LBI Year Book XXXIII* (1988), p. 169.

Sidney Jacoby, Ernest Hearst, Elizabeth and Heinrich Hannover as well as Arnold Paucker also came to this conclusion.[121] Donald Niewyk, however, disputes it and holds that court decisions which discriminated against Jews were "isolated occurrences", which were in no way characteristic of the attitude of German courts.[122] From an examination of 321 judgements concerning the boycott, he found that only 32 – approximately 10 per cent – could be regarded as too lenient.[123] His analyses of their geographical aspects deserve attention, as they reveal parallels to the regional differences in the extent of antisemitism and the success of the boycott in Germany. While in East Prussia, Bavaria, Mecklenburg, Anhalt and Bremen a particularly large number of antisemites stood trial, the number of charges in Baden, Württemberg, Hesse and the Rhineland were below the national average.[124] Among the 32 judgements that were too lenient seven were in East Prussia, five in Bavaria and four in Lower Silesia.[125]

It remains difficult, however, to provide a final evaluation of the extent of anti-Jewish attitudes with regard to the courts. At that time, the politically as well as socially explosive proceedings were certainly a challenge to the judges. All in all the boycott trials do not reflect badly on the courts, especially if one takes into account their legally positive phraseology. On the other hand it must not be forgotten that the courts took no measure against the boycott on their own initiative. The same applies to the legislative and executive branches in the *Reich* and the *Länder*, which hardly made any attempt to stop the boycott systematically.

What must be strongly emphasised is that the C.V. persistently defended the only recently obtained full rights of the Jews. Over and over again the C.V. objected to discriminatory judgements and was successful. Thus the Jewish Defence Association motivated many Jews who – out of fear or because of over-confidence – had not stood up in court to assert their rights. The fact that most boycott proceedings were decided in favour of the C.V. can be put down last but not least to the great expertise of the C.V.'s lawyers, men such as the brilliant Ludwig Foerder from Lower Silesia, to give just one excellent example.[126]

VI

In addition to taking political and legal measures, the Jews occasionally reacted to the boycott with a "defence boycott" by which their adversaries were fought

---

[121]Theo Rasehorn, *Justizkritik in der Weimarer Republik. Das Beispiel der Zeitschrift "Die Justiz"*, Frankfurt a. Main 1985, p. 167; Doskow and Jacoby, *loc. cit.*, p. 509; Ernest Hearst, 'When Justice Was Not Done. Judges in the Weimar Republic', in *The Wiener Library Bulletin*, vol. XIV, No. 1 (1960), pp. 10f.; Elisabeth and Heinrich Hannover, *Politische Justiz 1918–1933*, Hamburg 1966, pp. 263ff.; Paucker, *op. cit.*, pp. 77 and 84.

[122]Niewyk, *loc. cit.*, p. 106.

[123]*Ibid.*, p. 101.

[124]*Ibid.*, p. 101.

[125]*Ibid.*, p. 107.

[126]Beer, *Die Juden, das Recht und die Republik*, *op. cit.*, p. 248.

with exactly the same methods they used themselves.[127] The Jewish press, for instance the *Israelitisches Familienblatt* and the *C.V.-Zeitung*, published registers of anti-Jewish resorts and restaurants under the heading "Jews unwanted".[128] According to Oertmann this typical defence boycott was permissible, as it had "just the opposite purpose of the offensive boycott": "Just as it is legal to ward off an illegal attack, it is also morally valid to ward off attacks which violate the moral code."[129] However, this was not a systematic defence boycott (of the kind that after Hitler's seizure of power many Jewish organisations called for in foreign countries against German firms and products). It can be assumed that most Jews avoided those shops and resorts regarded as antisemitic.

On the other hand it is out of the question that out of solidarity business connections were mainly or exclusively maintained with Jewish firms. The Orthodox *Der Israelit* regarded it as a "moral rule" to buy from Jews and to employ Jews.[130] This attitude was criticised by the more assimilated majority. The *C.V.-Zeitung* disapproved of lists of Jewish doctors, lawyers, workmen and shops which served the express purpose of mutual economic support. If there was a chance to take measures other than counter-boycott, then the opportunity should be taken. Moreover, a more general antisemitic attitude could not be regarded as a sufficient reason for calling a boycott.[131] Most Jewish organisations knew that they ought to avoid actions which, as was frequently the case, could serve the Nazis as a pretext. In this connection the *Verband nationaldeutscher Juden* emphatically opposed the *Jüdisches Adressbuch für Grossberlin*.[132] According to Foerder, the most effective means for fighting the *Hetzboykott*, other than by taking legal action, was still the "appeal to moral sense and reason".[133]

The endeavours of Jewish businessmen not to attract too much attention can also be regarded as an economic measure of defence. Apparently, Jewish employers increasingly tended not to employ Jews in order to avoid the reproach of "nepotism". As early as June 1928 the *C.V.-Zeitung* complained about this attitude.[134] *Der Israelit* opined that the employment of young Jewish people should not be seen primarily as a reaction to the antisemitic *Zeitgeist* and as an answer to the anti-Jewish boycott, but, rather, stood for the fulfilment of a Jewish duty in a general sense.[135] In November 1932 the economic committee of the *Preußischer Landesverband jüdischer Gemeinden* organised a public campaign with the slogan "Our Right to Work", to spread the idea of "the Jewish employment exchange and procurement of work". The campaign of the *Vereinigte Zentrale für Jüdische Arbeitsnachweise* in Germany, which aimed at combatting antisemitism in the economic sector, addressed itself to the entire population, to the authorities

[127]*Ibid.*, p. 263.
[128]See e.g., *Israelitisches Familienblatt*, XXX (30th June 1932).
[129]Oertmann, *Der politische Boykott, op. cit.*, pp. 61f.
[130]*Der Israelit*, LXXIII (27th October 1932).
[131]*C.V.-Zeitung*, V, No. 14 (1st April 1926).
[132]*Der nationaldeutsche Jude*, No. 7 (July 1929).
[133]Cited in Foerder, *loc. cit.*, p. 159.
[134]*C.V.-Zeitung*, VII, No. 26 (29th June 1928).
[135]*Der Israelit*, XXIII (10th November 1932).

as well as the economic associations, and appealed especially to Jewish employers.

VII

The anti-Jewish boycott represents a form of antisemitism which, Austria apart, only manifested itself in Germany. There can be no doubt as to its great economic, social, political and psychological significance even before 1933 and that it markedly increased during the Depression, culminating in the brutality of the measures employed in 1932.

The instigators were mainly Nazis, whose boycott campaign also served as a useful exercise for future action. The boycott must not, therefore, be minimised as merely part of the political programme of a minority. What was so fatal was that the Nazi Party made such rapid advances until the July 1932 elections despite these antisemitic practices. And the Nazis operated their *Hetzboykott* increasingly and with an equal degree of both perverse inventiveness and unscrupulousness.

What appears so paradoxical about the increase of boycott actions during the Weimar Republic is that the Jewish population (which decreased continuously from the turn of the century on) economically adapted to the non-Jewish German population; an "assimilatory" process which grew apace after the November Revolution; that their economic influence was on the wane; that they too suffered from the economic crisis and that, therefore, the Nazis' assertion of economic "exploitation" by the Jews was even more groundless. This holds true even for the department stores which were owned by Jews and thus offered the Nazi Party a welcome target for attack. Due to their urbanisation and concentration in certain professions, the Jews attracted more attention; although – except for the growing number of *Ostjuden* – their "different nature", which in view of the traditional lack of "ethnic pluralism" in Germany had always been marked, had gradually lessened.

In tune with the variety of political trends within German Jewry, the defence strategies of the boycotted and their motives were not uniform. Here the C.V. played a decisive and, with regard to the court proceedings, a not unsuccessful role. Apparently it was employees who suffered most from the boycott, those in the liberal professions least of all, although regional differences must be taken into account.

The place to be allotted to the boycott as part of general antisemitism in Germany, which doubtless intensified during the economic crises in accordance with the "scapegoat theory", is problematic. Problems arise not least because it is difficult to assess the reactions of the German population, since this was not yet the time of the opinion polls and as the extent to which people followed the Nazi boycott behests, often enforced through blackmail, is hard to quantify. Here the largely Jewish literature on the subject reaches contradictory conclusions. It would appear significant that Eva Reichmann, who as a C.V. functionary had been familiar with boycott problems, has in retrospect taken up the cudgels on behalf of the non-Jewish Germans. Moreover, the half-hearted participation in the April 1933 boycott for which, now, the new rulers called, rather indicates that people had been even more restrained before. As could be demonstrated, there were considerable differences between rural and urban areas as well; in Berlin, where about a third of the Jewish population and a majority of the *Ostjuden* resided, the situation was pointedly more favourable. On the other hand, the fact that non-Jews – apart from exceptions across the range of the political spectrum (the Nazis and the DNVP on one side or the *Hansa-Bund* and the *Abwehrverein* on the other) – concerned themselves only marginally with the boycott, does not necessarily provide a positive testimonial. A more favourable judgement can probably be passed on the courts, which in the majority of cases increasingly sought to check the boycott within the framework of their authority.* But then Germany, at that time, could still be called a *Rechtsstaat* in which a degree of justice obtained.

---

*On a general dismissive judgement on the Weimar courts see again the essay by Levitt in this volume of the Year Book – (Ed.).

The Prosecution of Antisemites by the Courts in the Weimar Republic: Was Justice Served?

BY CYRIL LEVITT

In 1940 an article appeared in the *Contemporary Jewish Record* which provided "an account of the German experience with legal proceedings against anti-Semitic agitators"[1] during the Weimar Republic. Without issuing a blanket condemnation of the Weimar administration of justice *vis-à-vis* the prosecution of antisemites, the authors nevertheless outlined a number of serious obstacles to the realisation of justice in these cases. It is clear that their view generally reflected the position of the legal experts in the *Centralverein deutscher Staatsbürger jüdischen Glaubens* (C.V.), the major defence organisation of German Jewry during the Weimar Republic. When these matters were raised anew in the sixties as part of the growing general interest in Jewish defence and resistance efforts before the Nazi Juggernaut[2] the same general assessment of the deficiencies of the Weimar administration of justice in relation to anti-Jewish acts was made.[3]

But in the Spring of 1975, Donald L. Niewyk published an article in *Jewish Social Studies* in which he analysed data from 336 court cases gathered from several German sources.[4] On the basis of his statistical analysis he argued that "the record of German courts in prosecuting antisemites and Jews will not support the view that the Weimar years were ones 'when justice was not done' ".[5] He concluded that "given the virulence of racist propaganda against the Jews, the right-wing sympathies of many judges who were holdovers from Imperial Germany, and the brutality of Nazi activities in the last years of the Republic, German courts achieved an uneven but generally positive record of sheltering Jews from their detractors".[6] Furthermore, he suggested that this relatively

---

[1]Ambrose Doskow and Sidney B. Jacoby, 'Anti-Semitism and the Law in Pre-Nazi Germany', in *Contemporary Jewish Record*, vol. III, No. 5 (September–October 1940), p. 498.

[2]See Ernest Hearst, 'When Justice Was Not Done. Judges in the Weimar Republic', in *The Wiener Library Bulletin*, vol. XIV, No. 1 (1960), pp. 10ff; Arnold Paucker, 'Der jüdische Abwehrkampf', in *Entscheidungsjahr 1932. Zur Judenfrage in der Endphase der Weimarer Republik*. Ein Sammelband herausgegeben von Werner E. Mosse unter Mitwirkung von Arnold Paucker, Tübingen 1966 (Schriftenreihe wissenschaftlicher Abhandlungen des Leo Baeck Instituts 13), pp. 405–499; *idem*, *Der jüdische Abwehrkampf gegen Antisemitismus und Nationalsozialismus in den letzten Jahren der Weimarer Republik*, Hamburg 1968, pp. 74–84. On the history of this discussion see Arnold Paucker, 'Jewish Self-Defence', in *Die Juden im Nationalsozialistischen Deutschland/The Jews in Nazi Germany 1933–1943*, herausgegeben von Arnold Paucker mit Sylvia Gilchrist und Barbara Suchy, Tübingen 1986 (Schriftenreihe wissenschaftlicher Abhandlungen des Leo Baeck Instituts 45), pp. 55–65.

[3]See, for example, Paucker, *Der jüdische Abwehrkampf, op. cit.* (book edition quoted), p. 84.

[4]Donald L, Niewyk, 'Jews and the Courts in Weimar Germany', in *Jewish Social Studies*, vol. XXXVII, No. 2 (Spring 1975), pp. 99–113; see also *idem*, *The Jews in Weimar Germany*, Baton Rouge–London 1980, pp. 74–77.

[5]Niewyk, 'Jews and the Courts', *loc. cit.*, p. 111.

[6]Niewyk, 'Jews and the Courts', *loc. cit.*, p. 113.

favourable assessment was generally shared by lawyers working on behalf of the *Centralverein*.[7]

More recently, Udo Beer, in the most comprehensive study to date of the law in relation to Jews and antisemitism in the Weimar Republic, has taken up the thread of Niewyk's earlier writings.[8] After examining the many aspects of Weimar law and administration of justice Beer concludes:

> "Whether the Jews in the Weimar Republic were disadvantaged in legal terms to the extent of being in a state of distress is more than dubious in the light of the present study . . . Those in charge of the C.V. Legal Defence Department, too, declared themselves satisfied by the judicial decisions of the German courts . . .
> In the light of the relevant facts, then, it is plain that at least in the field of legal defence the Jews were far more widely recognised as equal citizens with equal rights than has so far been accepted. Indeed, during the life of the Weimar Republic the collective and individual rights of the Jews were effectively protected and enforced by the State and the Jewish organisations."[9]

Beer acknowledges that there were some Jewish lawyers in the *Centralverein* who took the view that the Jews in the Weimar Republic found themselves in a state of legal distress, but he in no way suggests that they might have represented the dominant view in the organisation. In fact, some may infer from his work, although it is not clearly stated, that Erich Eyck, Ludwig Foerder, Hermann Großmann, Alfred Klee, and others associated with the *Republikanischer Richterbund*, the Liberal-Left League of Republican Judges, were in the minority while Kurt Alexander and Max Hachenburg, and other more conservative Jewish jurists, spoke for the majority of the Legal Defence Department of the C.V.

Furthermore, Beer correctly suggests that the charge of Jewish legal distress had to be understood in terms of the general debate on the crisis of the administration of Weimar justice, although he nowhere analyses the relation between the Jewish debate and the more general discussion. His conclusion that no such crisis existed in spite of the odd, troubling example of misjudgement tacitly supports the view of the Conservative parties in the Weimar *Reichstag* whose spokesmen were willing to admit to single instances of bias and error in court proceedings and practices of state attorneys and judges, yet denied any systemic problem in the administration of law or a lack of trust in it by the population as a whole.[10]

In what follows, the question of the state of Jewish legal distress will be assessed both in relation to the debate on the general crisis of law and administration of justice in the Weimar Republic and in relation to the dominant

---

[7]The three lawyers which he cites in this connection are Kurt Alexander, Hans Reichmann and Erich Eyck. For the quotation from Niewyk, 'Jews and the Courts', *loc. cit.*, p. 106, see p. 164 below.

[8]Udo Beer, *Die Juden, das Recht und die Republik. Verbandswesen und Rechtsschutz 1919–1933*, Rechtshistorische Reihe 50, Frankfurt a. Main–Bern–New York 1986. See also *idem*, 'The Protection of Jewish Civil Rights in the Weimar Republic. Jewish Self-Defence through Legal Action', in *LBI Year Book XXXIII* (1988), pp. 149–176.

[9]Beer, 'The Protection', *loc. cit.*, pp. 175–176. For the German text see Beer, *Die Juden, op. cit.*, pp. 303–305.

[10]The most comprehensive general work on the crisis of law in the Weimar Republic is Robert Kuhn, *Die Vertrauenskrise der Justiz (1926–1928). Der Kampf um die Rechtspflege in der Weimarer Republik*, Köln 1983.

views of the Legal Defence Department of the C.V. The following points will be made: (1) In the prevailing view of those jurists involved in the legal defence work of the *Centralverein* as represented in the *C.V.-Zeitung* and publications of the C.V.'s *Philo Verlag* the administration of justice could not be relied upon to rule fairly and equally where Jewish interests were concerned. (2) Jewish legal distress was directly linked to the question of a general crisis of law in the Weimar Republic. (3) The source of both Jewish and general mistrust of the administration of justice lay in the political allegiances and social provenance of the judiciary, the outmoded legal code which could not be revised due to the political polarisation of the times and the growing influence of *völkisch* and antisemitic ideas upon judges and state attorneys. (4) Many verdicts arrived at by means of a narrow interpretation of the law in cases of Jewish concern were not accepted by Jews as fair decisions by judges concerned with the protection of freedom of expression but rather were seen as part of a double standard, as a front for Conservative and Nationalist judges to play political favourites through the courts. Had the judiciary consistently applied civil libertarian principles in adjudicating its cases then there would have been no crisis of law and the general political culture would have been much healthier. After having addressed these matters we shall return to consider the writings of Niewyk and Beer in greater detail. It will be argued that the views expressed by Niewyk and Beer could be utilised by historical revisionists to detach the Nazi period from German history and thus help pave the way for a new German Nationalism which avoids coming to grips with its past.

THE ADMINISTRATION OF JUSTICE AND THE CRISIS OF LAW

During the years of the Weimar Republic opinion was bitterly divided on the question of the impartiality of the justice system. Spokesmen for the *Sozialdemokratische Partei Deutschlands* (SPD) and the Left-Liberal *Deutsche Demokratische Partei* (DDP) time and again referred to a "crisis of trust" in the administration of law, to a general "crisis of law and the administration of justice" in Germany. Within the legal establishment these charges were forcefully levelled by supporters of the *Republikanischer Richterbund*, who suspected a large number of their fellow judges of monarchical tendencies and of interpreting the law in a way which was not consonant with the intent of the Weimar constitution.[11] Representatives of the Right-Liberal *Deutsche Volkspartei* (DVP), of the Catholic *Zentrum* and the Nationalist *Deutschnationale Volkspartei* (DNVP) generally rejected this charge as a fabrication of the Liberal-Left. The mainstream judges' association (*Deutscher Richterverein*) also rejected the charges and viewed the attempt to "politicise" the dispensation of justice by the *Republikanischer Richterbund* with suspicion.

---

[11]For the positions of the SPD and DDP as well as those of more Conservative parties, see Kuhn, *op. cit.* On the attitude of the *Republikanischer Richterbund* towards their non-republican colleagues, see Birger Schulz, *Der Republikanische Richterbund (1921–1933)*, Rechtshistorische Reihe 21, Frankfurt a. Main–Bern 1982.

There is a rich literature both from the Weimar period itself and from the Federal Republic of Germany concerning the debate about the crisis of law then. Post-war scholarly assessments have generally upheld the position of the Weimar Liberal-Left. An attempt by Neusel[12] to defend the Conservative view has been independently refuted by Jasper,[13] Rasehorn,[14] and Schulz[15]. The claim that Weimar justice was "blind in its right eye", that it treated the politically motivated crimes of the Right more leniently than those of the Left has been confirmed by most post-war legal historians.[16]

There is also a general agreement that the reasons for the problems in the administration of justice were to be found in the circumstances surrounding the formation of the Weimar Republic. Wishing to guarantee an independent judiciary, the framers of the Weimar constitution established the principle of the independence of judges from government control. This was done, however, without taking into consideration that the judges who were thus free from governmental review were, to a very large extent, monarchists with anti-democratic leanings. This act was tantamount to giving large numbers of authoritarian judges a free hand in dispensing justice. As Wolf Rosenbaum suggests: "The meaning of judicial independence, however, turned into its opposite when it was made to work, consciously or unconsciously, against the democratic foundation of the state from an untouchable position."[17]

Conservative jurists argued that under the monarchy sectional interests could not influence the impartial dispensation of justice because judges were loyal to the *Kaiser* (the head of state) and not to the *Reichstag* which represented only the forces of competing interests. With the abdication of the *Kaiser* and the founding of the Republic many judges sought to continue their loyalty to the state without recognising its new democratic form.[18] The Republican jurists argued that in so doing the Conservatives, either consciously or unconsciously, would simply allow their own values to determine the character of their conduct and rulings in

---

[12]Werner Neusel, *Die Spruchtätigkeit der Strafsenate des Reichsgerichts in politischen Strafsachen in der Zeit der Weimarer Republik*, Marburg 1971.

[13]Gotthard Jasper, 'Justiz und Politik in der Weimarer Republik', in *Vierteljahrshefte für Zeitgeschichte*, Heft 2 (1982), pp. 171–172, 192.

[14]Theo Rasehorn, *Justizkritik in der Weimarer Republik. Das Beispiel der Zeitschrift 'Die Justiz'*, Frankfurt a. Main–New York 1985, pp. 157–158.

[15]Schulz, *op. cit.*, pp. 119–120, 124–125.

[16]See Heinrich Hamburger und Elisabeth Hamburger-Drück, *Politische Justiz 1918–1933*, Frankfurt a. Main–Hamburg 1966; Jasper, *loc. cit.*; Klaus Petersen, *Literatur und Justiz in der Weimarer Republik*, Bonn 1988; Rasehorn, *op. cit.*; Schulz, *op. cit.* Jasper has also dealt with the attempt by Hattenhauer and others to shift attention away from the one-sidedness of the criminal courts by arguing that it was the excessive criticism of the League of Republican judges which should be looked upon as the basis for the problem in the administration of justice. See Karl Dietrich Erdmann und Hagen Schulze (Hrsg.), *Weimar. Selbstpreisgabe einer Demokratie. Eine Bilanz heute*, Düsseldorf 1980, p. 170; Hans Hattenhauer, *Geschichte des Beamtentums*, Köln 1980, p. 336; Friedrich-Christian Schröder, *Der Schutz von Staat und Verfassung im Strafrecht*, München 1970, p. 115; Jasper, *loc. cit.*, pp. 169–170.

[17]Wolf Rosenbaum, *Naturrecht und positives Recht*, Neuwied–Darmstadt 1972, p. 71; cf. Hans Hattenhauer, *Die geistesgeschichtlichen Grundlagen des deutschen Rechts*, Heidelberg–Karlsruhe 1980, p. 276.

[18]Petersen, *op. cit.*, p. 41.

the courts.[19] When they were challenged by supporters of the *Republikanischer Richterbund*, the Conservatives retorted that what their Liberal-Left colleagues were demanding was the politicisation of the administration of justice.[20]

What worried many Liberals and Leftists were the authoritarian traditions, reactionary values and political loyalties of most judges.[21] Robert Kuhn suggests that a majority of judges and state attorneys supported the DNVP, who were monarchists and anti-democratic.[22] Is it any wonder that Right-wing Putschists, members of the "black" *Reichswehr*, Nazis and the like, who engaged in violent activities against the state, were looked upon by many courts as merely "misguided" patriots, whereas Communist revolutionaries were deemed to be committing high treason for simply writing plays about the class struggle?[23] Rosenbaum suggests that the values of most judges were linked to their homogeneous social provenance.[24] Kirchheimer believed that judges, in their hatred of the new Republic, embraced the political Right because it attacked the "traitors of 1918" and promised a return to an authoritarian state.[25] It was for this reason that "(e)xploiting the notion of judicial independence for all its worth, the majority of the judicial corps acted with some consistency as the benevolent protectors of the so-called patriotic forces of society".[26]

Even a cursory treatment of the cases upon which the negative assessment of the record of the administration of criminal justice in the Weimar Republic was made is beyond the limits of this paper. Nevertheless, a very brief summary of some of the cases will provide the reader with an understanding of the nature of the problems.

[19]"Die Richter . . . unterscheiden, wie Jasper ausführt, zwischen dem Wesen des Staates, dem die ganze Treue galt und der zufällig auswechselbaren Staatsform. Und eben sie als Richter und nicht die 'zufällige' Regierung konnten beurteilen, was dem Staat zu schulden sei. Was links stand, und mochte es auch 'nur' die SPD sein, gehörte zu den potentiellen Landesverrätern." Rasehorn, *op. cit.*, pp. 160–161.

[20]See the summary of the debate between Gustav Radbruch and Otto Liebmann which took place in the pages of *Die Justiz* and the *Deutsche Juristenzeitung* in Rasehorn, *op. cit.*, pp. 144–145. Otto Kirchheimer suggested that Right-wing judges could retreat to the letter of the law when under attack for allowing their political colours to show. See Otto Kirchheimer, *Political Justice. The Use of Legal Procedure for Political Ends*, Princeton 1961, p. 212.

[21]Reinhard Bendix, in the biography of his father, Ludwig Bendix, who had been active in legal reform and the *Republikanischer Richterbund* during the Weimar Republic, echoed these concerns. See Reinhard Bendix, *From Berlin to Berkeley. Jewish-German Identities*, New Brunswick–Oxford 1986, pp. 89–94.

[22]Kuhn, *op. cit.*, p. 17.

[23]See Petersen, *op. cit.*, pp. 97–108; Hattenhauer, *Die geistesgeschichtlichen Grundlagen des deutschen Rechts*, *op. cit.*; Rasehorn, *op. cit.*, p. 147.

[24]Rosenbaum. *op. cit.*, pp. 104–105.

[25]". . . the judicial apparatus set out to grant respectability and protection – at least initially against the wishes of and sometimes in open conflict with the authorities of the day – to lawless behavior by people identified with patriotic goals.

Patriotism in this context meant anything directed toward expunging the instruments and the consequences of the 1918 defeat and the resurrection of a strong state authority. This inclination brought the judiciary into the spiritual neighborhood of the political right." Kirchheimer, *op. cit.*, pp. 211–212.

[26]*Ibid.*, p. 213.

The Case of Rothardt. Rothardt, a newspaper editor, wrote an article in 1922 accusing President Ebert of having committed treason in the closing stages of the First World War by joining a strike committee of munitions' workers in Berlin. Ebert proved that he joined the strike committee only to help bring a speedy end to the strike. The court nevertheless found that Ebert had "committed treason in the legal sense". The judges were considered heroes by Nationalist forces.[27]

The Case of the Borkum Song. Borkum, an island in the North Sea which was a popular resort was known throughout Germany as inhospitable to Jews. The local orchestra played a popular German tune and the guests at the spa delighted in the singing of an antisemitic doggerel to the music.[28] This practice created a scandal which forced the local authorities to order the band not to play the song. But this order was quashed by the Prussian High Court of Administration arguing that the orchestra was not responsible for the content of the songs whose music it played. No criminal charges were laid under Section 130, incitement to violence.[29]

The Fechenbach Case. Felix Fechenbach, former secretary of Kurt Eisner, gave a copy of the Ritter telegram (sent in July 1914) to a Swiss writer in April 1919. He also gave information concerning secret Rightist organisations to the British. Even though the telegram could do no harm to post-war Germany and the statute of limitations had elapsed, Fechenbach was sentenced to eleven years hard labour. Two of the judges who reviewed the case for the Bavarian government and found no difficulty with the verdict were participants in the Beer Hall Putsch. One was killed, the other sentenced to five years imprisonment.[30]

The Haas Case. A bookkeeper for the firm of Haas in Magdeburg was murdered. A young National Socialist, Schröder, arrested for fraud and questioned about the murder (Schröder possessed a revolver) implicated Rudolph Haas who was a Jew with Leftist sympathies. The investigating judge, Kölling, had Haas arrested. But intervention by high SPD officials in Magdeburg and cooperation with the Berlin police led to Schröder's arrest. When confronted, Schröder confessed. Kölling and the director of the

[27]Rasehorn, *op. cit.*, pp. 179–181.
[28]"An Borkums Strand nur Deutschtum gilt,
Nur deutsch ist das Panier,
Wir halten rein den Ehrenschild
Germanias für und für.
Doch wer dir naht mit platten Füßen,
Mit Nasen krumm und Haaren kraus,
Der soll nicht deinen Strand genießen,
Der muß hinaus! Der muß hinaus!
Hinaus!"
In Rasehorn, *op. cit.*, p. 179; Cf. Erich Eyck, *Die Krisis der deutschen Rechtspflege*, Berlin 1926, p. 24; Hamburger and Hamburger-Drück, *op. cit.*, pp. 209–210; Beer, *Die Juden, op. cit.*, pp. 191–196.
[29]Rasehorn, *op. cit.*, p. 178.
[30]*Ibid.*, pp. 175–176.

provincial court, Hoffmann, did everything they could to interfere with the investigation. Kölling refused to set Haas free even after Schröder had confessed. Both judges faced disciplinary hearings.[31]

The Case of Carl von Ossietzky. In March 1929, Carl von Ossietzky published an anonymous article in *Die Weltbühne*, 'Windiges aus der deutschen Luftfahrt', in which he pointed to the rebuilding of the *Luftwaffe* which was forbidden by the Treaty of Versailles. He was found guilty of *Landesverrat* by the *Reichsgericht* on 23rd November 1931 and sentenced to six months in prison. There was a public outcry. His lawyer, Max Alsberg, the most celebrated defence attorney in Germany commented: He [Alsberg] "would not have believed that there were judges in Germany who would brand a political opponent as a common criminal by means of a criminal trial".[32]

The battle between the Liberal-Left and Conservative jurists was fought out largely along ideological lines. Since many Conservatives were ready to admit that there had been problems, especially in the area of criminal law, the debate really revolved around the academic question: how many misjudgements and judicial errors constitute a crisis? One person's "problem" is another person's "crisis". The question which must be assessed is not a semantic one concerning the definition of the word "crisis", but the seriousness of the problems besetting the administration of the criminal law in Weimar Germany.

JEWISH LEGAL DISTRESS: THE VIEW OF THE CENTRALVEREIN

The question of a Jewish state of distress with regard to the criminal law has both a subjective and objective side. Both Niewyk and Beer have suggested that there was a general perception by the staff of the Legal Defence Department of the C.V. that, by and large, justice had been done. In opposition to these two scholars I maintain that there is a *prima facie* case against such a position, as a cursory reading of the *C.V.-Zeitung* will show. And even those rare articles, such as the one by Kurt Alexander approvingly cited by Beer, admit to the existence of problems.

The following examples could be multiplied. They express over and over again the same sense of outrage by Jewish jurists at the failings of the German criminal justice system.

In an article entitled 'Man darf Judenrepublik sagen! Ein merkwürdiges Reichsgerichtsurteil', the author lamented:

". . . the distressing thought cannot be suppressed that the emotional dislike of Jewish fellow citizens which is fed by prejudices of all kinds has found a place even in the circles of the highest judges; this must cause every real friend of the Fatherland deep concern".[33]

---

[31] *Ibid.*, pp. 182–183.
[32] *Ibid.*, pp. 205–206.
[33] 'Man darf Judenrepublik sagen! Ein merkwürdiges Reichsgerichtsurteil', in *C.V.-Zeitung*, V (1926), p. 165.

In another article dealing with the work of the *Centralverein* in the courts, the author makes the following charges:

> "Surely we are the ones who in this cause have the most to complain . . . Now it is true that the *laws* have often failed; but worse than this failure is the *failure of the administration of justice*, which the Jew sees with different eyes than the rest of the population . . . If a Jew today would write about the Christian religion would it be possible in Germany, for such an 'impertinence' to remain unpunished? . . . Notwithstanding a few hopeful things we have experienced in recent times, the fact is that the *courts have often viewed serious abuses and insults of Jews with the greatest leniency*."[34]

In describing a case of serious insult of Jews upon the occasion of a Zionist meeting in Breslau, the *Centralverein* protested the blatant antisemitism of the State Attorney, Speer. In objecting to the finding of the court, the story in the *C.V.-Zeitung* stated: "The judgement of the court shows once again that German Jews are still being given over to the attacks of the antisemites practically without protection."[35]

Niewyk and Beer both admit that the situation concerning the administration of justice was poorer in Bavaria than in other German provinces. In the following passage from an article in the *C.V.-Zeitung* we can see precisely how this view is reflected therein:

> "These are no longer isolated cases. *The terror*, which is practised by Mr. Streicher and his comrades through defaming judges and state attorneys under the indulgent tolerance of the justice administration, *touches the foundation of the administration of justice*. Judicial judgement is no longer free. The judge, the state attorney who makes a sharp grab at a National Socialist, must expect to be attacked in the press, in the provincial parliament, to have his personal and official honour stomped into the dirt, without finding the protection which he could have expected on account of his person and his office, or better yet *on account of the law*."[36]

In a 1926 article demanding equal protection from the law for every citizen, the *C.V.-Zeitung* gave vent to the feelings of most German Jews represented by the *Centralverein*:

> "The *crisis of trust* which the German administration of justice is enduring has reached the point that it is necessary to go beyond the merely critical consideration to positive demands and suggestions . . .
> The lack of trust of broader elements of the population in the German administration of justice is justified *in the case of the German Jews to a very large extent and more than anywhere else*. Whoever follows with interest the stories in the columns of this newspaper will hear nothing new when the assertion is made that the feelings of the German Jews in a majority of cases have not been treated justly, have reached the point that they feel themselves positively *without rights*."[37]

Finally, in a presentation of the legal defence work undertaken by the *Centralverein*, the *C.V.-Zeitung* draws this conclusion from two recent cases: "The two cases which we are reporting today, are a clear proof for the *layman* as well

[34]'Winterarbeit im C.V.', in *C.V.-Zeitung*, V (1926), p. 26.
[35]'Die Ratschläge der "Rabbiner Abraham und Kareski". Leichte Sühne schwerer Beleidigung', in *C.V.-Zeitung*, III (1924), p. 144.
[36]'Bayerische Rechtsnot', in *C.V.-Zeitung*, VI (1927), p. 480.
[37]'Gleicher Schutz allen Staatsbürgern!', in *C.V.-Zeitung*, V (1926), pp. 499–500.

that the term *legal distress of the German Jews* is not a phrase, but rather a burden which continually rests upon us."[38]

The examples above are typical expressions of the sentiments portrayed in the pages of the *C.V.-Zeitung*. Combined with the publications of the *Philo Verlag*, such as Foerder's *Antisemitismus und Justiz* and the papers from the conference of jurists organised by the *Centralverein* in June of 1927 – *Deutsches Judentum und Rechtskrisis*, they serve to show beyond doubt that the German-Jewish community was deeply disturbed by the way in which the administration of justice in the Weimar Republic was being executed.

Even if it were true that the sentiments expressed in the *C.V.-Zeitung* did not accurately reflect those of the German-Jewish population at large, they would reflect those of the leadership of the organisation. There can be no doubt that the great majority of C.V. leaders shared the following view expressed by Alfred Wiener in relation to the conference of jurists organised by the C.V. in Berlin:

> "That here and there the basis of a verdict came, suspiciously, too close to the so-called science of race, did not escape them. They had also read in these pages highly unusual interpretations of paragraph 166 of the *Reich*'s Criminal Code, which removed legal protection from the Jewish religion. But they were astounded, yes, they were shaken by the *great extent of such material*, of such low estimation of Jews and Jewry . . . they all felt that the numerous reported cases of misjudgements, of actual errors of reasoning were not lapses of an individual, but rather often systematic consequences *of a frightening lack of knowledge, even misunderstandings of Jewish life and Jewish views of the world*.
>   . . . One may or may not wish to speak of a Jewish legal distress – the protection of Jews and Jewry through the laws is not sufficient, it breaks down."[39]

Frequent references by Foerder, Eyck, Holländer, Reichmann, Weil and many others leave no doubt in the reader's mind that the generally accepted view of the leadership of the *Centralverein* in relation to the administration of justice was a critical one. The rejection of this view by Conservatives such as Kurt Alexander stand out as clear exceptions to the reader of the *C.V.-Zeitung*. True, as both Niewyk and Beer point out, the situation in Prussia was far better than in Bavaria or East Prussia and the practices of the civil courts were certainly more favourable than those of the criminal justice system.[40] But the general picture which emerges is of a Jewish community which has lost confidence in the administration of justice in general. Thus, Beer's claim, that "those in charge of the C.V. Legal Defence Department, too, declared themselves satisfied by the judicial decisions of the German courts"[41], simply cannot be accepted.[42]

But if there were no condition of legal distress for Jews in the Weimar Republic

---

[38]'Rechtsschutzarbeit des C.V.', in *C.V.-Zeitung*, VI (1927), p. 14.

[39]Alfred Wiener, 'Die Juristentagung des C.V. Überblick – Ablauf – Ergebnis', in *C.V.-Zeitung*, VI (1927), pp. 353–355.

[40]Cf. Niewyk, 'Jews and the Courts', *loc. cit.*, pp. 101–102.

[41]Beer, 'The Protection', *loc. cit.*, p. 175.

[42]Beer himself admits that the record of the courts in cases of group libel was less than impressive: "Mit Ausnahme des Bereichs der Kollektivbeleidigung gelang es den Verletzten fast immer, in höheren Instanzen ihr Recht zu finden." *Die Juden, op. cit.*, p. 254. But Niewyk points out that clearly half of the cases that he gathered concerned libel (individual and group) and this represented by far the largest category of cases before the courts. Cf. Niewyk, 'Jews and the Courts', *loc. cit.*, p. 101.

why do so many of the C.V. legal experts continually refer to such a condition? I think that Beer correctly sensed the answer to this when he wrote that "the question of a specific Jewish state of distress in respect of law and justice arose in connection with the wider debate on the "crisis of confidence besetting justice", initiated among others by Erich Eyck."[43]

A majority of German Jews supported the *Deutsche Demokratische Partei* until 1930.[44] Jewish support for the DDP was especially strong in Berlin. Ludwig Holländer, the undisputed head of the *Centralverein* was a member of the DDP. Most of the leadership of the C.V. were either members or sympathisers of the Left-Liberals. As such they would have been close to the *Republikanischer Richterbund*, the League of Republican Judges which, as we have seen, carried the fight against the one-sided practice of justice in the Weimar Republic.

Time and again the legal minds of the C.V. indicated that the Jewish concern for justice was part of a larger German concern. Alfred Wiener expressed this when he wrote: "*Impartial justice* – only this is Dr. Eyck's demand, not only for the sake of Jewish Germans, but indeed for the great German Fatherland . . ."[45] No issue demonstrated the close identification between the Liberal, Democratic Weimar Republic and the Jews more than the defamation of the Republic as the *Judenrepublik* – the "Jew-Republic". In reporting a case in which a speaker to a group of 60–70 members of a *völkisch* group in the town of Gotha exclaimed: "We don't need the Jew-Republic, fie on the Jew-Republic!", the *C.V.-Zeitung* expressed outrage at this united attack upon the republican democracy and upon the Jews. The fact that the Supreme Court did not see a clear insult here, increased the anger of the Jewish paper.[46]

Why Beer has not addressed the Liberal character of the C.V. leadership and linked their views on Jewish legal distress to it more forcefully, is not clear. A more straightforward approach would be to describe the dominant view and then to discuss the dissenting opinions of men like Max Hachenburg and Kurt Alexander along political lines. Instead of denying the existence of a general crisis of law in the Weimar Republic, Beer should have explicitly informed the reader of his intention. That the leadership of the *Centralverein* felt that there were serious problems and gaps in the administration of justice, especially in the criminal courts – regardless of what one chooses to call it – cannot be denied.

The crisis of law concerning the Jews was founded on the following considerations: (1) the unequal treatment of Jews from time to time by the justice system; (2) the acceptance by the courts at times of unreasonable arguments advanced by antisemites and/or the rejection of reasonable arguments made by

---

[43]Beer, 'The Protection', *loc. cit.*, p. 176. In fact, the first major treatment of the crisis of law was Foerder's pamphlet published by the *Philo Verlag* in 1924. Allusions to the crisis are found in the pages of the *C.V.-Zeitung* and examples of miscarriages of justice appeared in *Im deutschen Reich* the newspaper which preceded the *C.V.-Zeitung* (which first appeared in 1922).

[44]See Ernest Hamburger and Peter Pulzer, 'Jews as Voters in the Weimar Republic', in *LBI Year Book XXX* (1985), p. 48; Arnold Paucker, 'Jewish Self-Defence', *loc. cit.*, p. 58.

[45]Wiener, 'Die Juristentagung', *loc. cit.*

[46]This was yet another example of the courts' retreat to the letter of the law. Jewish commentators did not accept the apparent impartiality at face value. See 'Man darf Judenrepublik sagen!', *loc. cit.*

Jewish plaintiffs; (3) the narrow interpretations of the law in some cases involving Jews; (4) the free rein accorded prominent antisemites in some court proceedings in haranguing and badgering their accusers; (5) the occasional direct antisemitic remark made by a court clerk, state attorney or judge during a trial. The following examples are based on reports in the *C.V.-Zeitung* or other publications of the *Centralverein*.

Time precludes a detailed presentation of examples which illustrate the grievances of the German-Jewish community, but a few poignant cases can be outlined. Here is an example reported by the *C.V.-Zeitung* of a court case involving only two individuals: A physician sent a note to three neighbours who had called upon another doctor for their medical needs instead of the note sender. The overlooked practitioner inquired whether his Nationalist activity – he was the local leader of a *völkisch* group – was the reason for their not calling on him or whether they simply preferred the services of a Jewish physician (the popular colleague in question was a Christian from a mixed marriage). The latter charged the former before an *Ehrengericht* (court of honour). But the note sender was found not guilty because the court saw no reason why the doctor should not inquire about the reasons why his neighbours were not using his services. This caused the C.V. to write cynically: "Geht es um die Kasse, benutzt man auch die Rasse! (If it's a question of money, race is used as well!)"[47]

Another case involved repeated insults to a German-Jewish landlord by a French tenant. The latter was in the habit of calling the former by the term "German pig". The Jewish landlord initiated proceedings against the tenant. But the judge in the Berlin court ruled against the plaintiff arguing: "The plaintiff is not libelled about his citizenship [and] according to his descent is not a person who is reckoned as German in common parlance."[48] Eyck points out in this connection that the judge is incapable of feeling just how upsetting such insults are to members of the Jewish community.

Jewish complaints were not only directed at the failures of the system of justice to protect Jewish rights and interests, they were also voiced in regard to what was widely perceived as a double standard in applying the law. One area of deep concern involved the response of state attorneys to Jewish complaints. It was the prerogative of the state attorneys in cases of delicts concerning libel, coercion, threats, and bodily harm to recognise a public interest in the prosecution. Very often Jewish complainants were told that there was no public interest in the case and hence they were advised either to pursue the charges by means of a private action or simply to drop the matter. Foerder describes the advantages in having a case prosecuted by the state attorney:

[47]'Neugierige Fragen an einen Gutsbesitzer: eine Ehrengerichtliche Entscheidung', in *C.V.-Zeitung*, III (1924), p. 431.
[48]Eyck, *op. cit.*, p. 23. A reference to the same case is found in an 'Offener Brief an Herrn Dr. Otto Liebmann, Herausgeber der Deutschen Juristen-Zeitung.Von Reichsjustizminister a.D. Dr. Gustav Radbruch, ordentl. Professor der Rechte an der Universität Kiel', in *Die Justiz*, Band I, Berlin 1925/1926, p. 196. Cf. Rasehorn, *op. cit.*, p. 169.

"The practical consequences of these different treatments is shown above all in the fact that the aggrieved is a party in the private action [and] thus cannot be called as a witness; and, therefore, under certain circumstances in relation to the denials of the accused and in the absence of other witnesses cannot offer any proof for the substance of his accusation. Furthermore, he must pay certain costs in advance. Moreover, when he must prosecute the case himself, he has no access to the state attorney, the organs of the police for, say, the necessary investigations. But beyond this an entirely different moral effect of course is worked upon the delinquent when he sees that the state attorney's office immediately takes the part of the aggrieved and helps him to achieve satisfaction."[49]

Here are several examples of cases rejected by state attorneys for not being of public interest:

A Jewish woman was hit over the head with a walking stick by a leading antisemite without provocation so that she suffered a severe nervous shock.

An old Jewish man who was cursed in the crudest way and threatened with death by a young overseer at the *Kurplatz* in Salzbrunn.

A young Jewish man who was attacked and beaten up by five antisemitic rowdies on a public street at night.

A Jewish salesman whose display windows were smashed by a member of a respectable student organisation. The student declared upon his being questioned by the police: "When I smash the windows of a semite, that does no harm."[50]

In contrast to these cases, however, the state attorneys seemed to have no problem in seeing a public interest in the prosecution of cases brought by antisemites against Jews for forcibly removing their swastika pins. Sometimes these cases were treated as theft. Erich Eyck also criticised this double standard when he wrote: ". . . that the same ideas which show themselves to be insufficient to count as libel of Jews, in another case go so far that criminal prosecution results".[51] And Ludwig Holländer, director of the C.V., pointed out on many occasions that the public outcry would be extremely intense should a Jewish author libel the Christian religion in ways which are done repeatedly by antisemites in relation to the Jewish religion.

JUSTICE SERVED OR JUSTICE DENIED?

Having examined both the subjective and objective sides of the discussion concerning the question of legal distress and lack of trust in the administration of Weimar justice it now becomes possible to analyse the works of Niewyk and Beer who hold that, in spite of some exceptional cases, justice was served by the Weimar judiciary.

[49]Ludwig Foerder, *Antisemitismus und Justiz*, Berlin 1924, p. 16.
[50]Foerder goes on to say that the rejection by the state attorneys in these cases was appealed and in some cases all the way to the Ministry of Justice. *Ibid.*
[51]Eyck, *op. cit.*, p. 53.

Niewyk, writing in the United States, adopts the sociological approach of quantifying the problem. Gathering the court cases available in the published records and classifying the cases in terms of verdict and extent of penalty assessed, he concludes that in only about 7% of the cases studied can a legitimate complaint against the courts be supported.[52] Beer follows Niewyk in this quantitative approach with respect to the degree of severity of punishments imposed by the courts.[53] Beer also cites with favour the conservative view of Kurt Alexander which was by no means representative of the leadership of the *Centralverein*:

> "First of all it is *factually* false to arrive at a *general* opinion on the basis of a series of *single* cases. Even if the number of decisions, on whose account we feel injured in our constitutional right to equal treatment, appears to be large, it is in actuality very small in relation to the decisions issued by German courts generally and which affect the interests of citizens of the Jewish faith. It is still the rare exception to which our complaints should be directed."[54]

The counter-position to this within the *Centralverein* was represented by Erich Eyck, one of those who delivered papers at the conference of jurists investigating the question of the state of legal distress. A member of the Left-Liberal DDP and the *Republikanischer Richterbund* he contributed to C.V. publications and was active in the debate concerning the general crisis of law in the Weimar Republic. He explicitly took issue with the quantitative approach to assessing the problem of the administration of justice in a pamphlet dealing with the general issue:

> "Now it is often said that these mistakes which have come to light, which are not in themselves contested, are insufficient to justify a general accusation against the administration of justice. For one they represent only a *small number* of the total sum of cases handled by our state attorneys and judges. Moreover, what is involved here are primarily cases with a *political twist* and thus an idiosyncracy which is not a determining factor for the whole of the administration of justice. To the first point it may be objected that in the first instance the total sum of dubious cases, of which I can only discuss a small part, is nevertheless still far too great to be overlooked; however, above all *one* apparent fault can of course destroy more trust in the system of justice than a thousand good and healthy judgements are capable of reconstructing."[55]

This criticism of the quantitative approach is strengthened when we consider that the dubious cases which had come to public attention were often spectacular ones involving grievous actions on the part of judges and state attorneys. And the fact that in many cases the grievances were addressed and righted by the higher courts, could not undo the original damage.[56]

[52]Niewyk, 'Jews and the Courts', *loc. cit.*, pp. 106.
[53]*Ibid.*, pp. 107–108; Beer, *Die Juden, op. cit.*, pp. 247–248.
[54]Dr. Kurt Alexander, 'Wir – und die Justiz', in *C.V.-Zeitung*, V (1926), pp. 557–558.
[55]Eyck, *op. cit.*, p. 30.
[56]Alan Borovoy, general legal counsel for the Canadian Civil Liberties' Association, has forcefully argued that the fact that legitimate dissenters, artists, non-conformists and the like have in the end been exonerated by the courts, which tried them on charges resulting from the violation of anti-hate laws, does not ameliorate the pain and suffering which "innocent" defendants had to endure by going through trials, appeals, possible terms in jail, etc. See Alan Borovoy, *When Freedoms Collide*, Toronto 1988. In the case of the Weimar administration of justice it is clear that unjust decisions by the lower courts could not simply be rectified by rulings of the Supreme Court, as Beer emphatically suggests. See Beer, *Die Juden, op. cit.*, p. 254, 302; *idem*, 'The Protection', *loc. cit.*, p. 174.

Even if one were to accept the validity of a statistical treatment of the court cases without looking at their qualitative significance, Niewyk's method of paring down the number of objectionable verdicts must be closely scrutinised. He gives several examples of verdicts which were objected to by C.V. lawyers, but he justifies them by appealing to the emotional state of the judges to show that their intentions were honourable:

> ". . . noting Fritsch's advanced age and the fact that he had been fined and jailed repeatedly in forty years of anti-Jewish agitation, the judge commented *stoically* [my emphasis – C.L.] that a tougher penalty would teach him nothing. In a similar libel case, a judge in Nuremberg chose to fine rather than to jail one of Julius Streicher's co-workers because, as he *sneeringly* [my emphasis – C.L.] put it, the man was so 'mired in fanaticism' that no sane person would take him seriously. In the unsettled early years of the Republic a Munich judge let a Judeophobe off with a light fine and the *sorrowful* [my emphasis – C.L.] observation that extremist rhetoric had become a general bad habit in those overheated times."[57]

The fact that Jewish observers at the time imputed different emotions or motives to these same judges is not mentioned by Niewyk.

In my view Niewyk similarly misinterprets the motives of judges in other cases as well. For example, he runs the risk of turning the largely Rightist and Nationalist judiciary into civil libertarian defenders of freedom of expression guaranteed by the Weimar constitution, the very constitution which so many of them ignored. Where the legal counsel for the C.V. suspected other than noble motives in the verdicts rendered in cases dealing with the public use of the term "Jew Republic" (not "Jewish Republic" which in Niewyk's rendering becomes too "sanitised") Niewyk writes:

> "The issue of free speech impinged directly upon prosecutions of antisemites who used the term 'Jewish Republic' to describe the Weimar system. Brought to trial under the terms of the 'Law for the Protection of the Republic', they were exonerated whenever they could persuade the courts that their contention that Jews dominated the Republic was legitimate political criticism rather than subversive rhetoric. In cases such as these, Weimar jurists affirmed the healthy principle that courts ought not to endorse or condemn any political ideology."[58]

This insufficient awareness of the differences in the views of spokesmen for the C.V. on Niewyk's part is further demonstrated in his lumping together of Kurt Alexander, Hans Reichmann and Erich Eyck in arguing that "Jewish lawyers engaged in self-defense activities themselves acknowledged that miscarriages of justice . . . were isolated occurrences that in no way typified the attitudes of German courts towards Judeophobes".[59] Desisting from investigating the differences within the legal defence apparatus of the C.V. is an approach Niewyk shares with Beer. We shall return to this shortly.

Beer seeks to strengthen his thesis that there was no condition of legal distress

---

[57]Niewyk, 'Jews and the Courts', *loc. cit.*, p. 103.

[58]*Ibid.*, p. 105. It is more than a little odd that Niewyk cites three articles in the *C.V.-Zeitung* each of which is critical of the courts and none of which mentions freedom of speech. In fact, we have here good examples of conservative judges retreating to the letter of the law when it suits their purposes. Beer, on the other hand, recognises that the SPD favoured the abolition of the blasphemy section of the criminal code, not out of a concern with freedom of expression in general, but on the basis of its own political ideology. See Beer, *Die Juden*, *op. cit.*, p. 253. But, at the same time, Beer defends the 'positivism' of the conservative judges, *ibid.*, p. 214.

[59]Niewyk, 'Jews and the Courts', *loc. cit.*, p. 106.

facing the Jews in the Weimar Republic by pointing to the fact that there was little written by Jewish jurists about specifically Jewish issues in either the mainstream legal journals such as the *Deutsche Juristenzeitung* and the *Juristische Wochenschrift* or in the organ of the *Republikanischer Richterbund, Die Justiz*. Beer claims that there was only one article published in *Die Justiz* which relates to a specifically Jewish matter.[60]

In the first instance, there were actually several articles which concerned themselves with Jewish matters in *Die Justiz*. The article by Canditt on the case of the banning of the Borkum song,[61] the discussion of the case of Ludwig Haas by Henriette Fürth,[62] and the anonymous article concerning the case of Police President of Berlin Grzesinski called a "Jew-Bastard" by the National Socialist,[63] can be seen as dealing directly with Jewish concerns. But it must be understood that Beer's differentiation between strictly Jewish issues and general German issues is based upon anachronism. It is the understanding of the Jewish communities in the post-*Shoah* world. As Zwi Bacharach has pointed out:

> "The Jews as staunch Republican Germans often assessed racist antisemitism as being more of a threat to the Republican order (in which they were rooted) than as a threat to their very existence . . .
> Now when Jews set out to protest against the racist doctrine, they did so not first of all as Jews to whom injury had been done – for 'it is not merely a Jewish matter that concerns us here, but also a German matter' – they reacted to racism as Germans by presenting opposition thereto in the character of enlightened Germans."[64]

This unity of interest between the Jewish and general German cause was well-expressed by Julius Brodnitz in his welcoming remarks to the delegates to the conference of jurists hosted by the C.V. in 1927:

> "We, consciously German, Jews are given the duty, in this realm as well, in the fine words of Ranke, 'to represent the general cause in one's own' . . . The united Jewish jurists at the conference do not sequester themselves only to *deal with a purely Jewish task*; the labour serves, rather, an extremely meaningful general *German* task to whose solution we are called upon to contribute on the basis of our own distress. May the serious labour not only serve *German*

---

[60]See Ludwig Foerder, 'Die "Judenrepublik"in der Rechtsprechung', *Die Justiz*, vol. I, No. 2 (1925/1926), pp. 519–540. See Beer, *Die Juden, op. cit.*, pp. 207–208.
[61]See Hugo Canditt, 'Das Oberverwaltungsgericht und das Borkumlied', *Die Justiz*, vol. I, No. 1 (1925), pp. 79–88.
[62]See Henriette Fürth, 'Laiengedanken und Forderungen zu den Fällen Haas-Schröder und Flessa', *Die Justiz*, vol. II, No. 1 (1926), pp.10–18.
[63]See 'Calumniare audacter! Neuer Gebrauch eines alten Rezeptes', *Die Justiz*, vol. VIII, No. 2/3 (1932/1933), pp. 106–122.
[64]Walter Zwi Bacharach, 'Jews in Confrontation with Racist Antisemitism, 1879–1933', in *LBI Year Book XXV* (1980), p. 210. Many historians of Weimar Jewry have testified to the intertwining of Jewish interests with those of general German ones. The leaders of the C.V. claimed time and again that they were carrying on their fight against antisemitism not only for the protection of Jewish interests but for the well-being of the German Fatherland. But this well-being depended upon a Democratic Germany which upheld Liberal values. This tied the Jews firmly to the Republican camp. Peter Pulzer made the following observation in this regard: "What Jews did appreciate was that antisemitism was also anti-liberal and anti-democratic. The assault on the Jews was also, perhaps primarily, an assault on the Republic. It was therefore more important to defend the Republic than to identify specific enemies." Peter Pulzer, 'The Beginning of the End', in *Die Juden im Nationalsozialistischen Deutschland, op. cit.*, p. 23.

Jewry, but rather bear valuable fruit for the *German Fatherland* which cannot be separated from it."[65]

If this is the case then it is pointless to draw lines between the Jewish and the German cause. In fact, *most* of what was written in the pages of *Die Justiz* was related to the common Jewish/German cause of Democracy and tolerance.

CONCLUSION

As we have seen, there was a widespread feeling among the jurists involved in legal defence at the C.V. that there was a serious problem and a growing disenchantment with the administration of justice in the Weimar Republic.* Arnold Paucker, in a private communiqué to the author, has confirmed that his many discussions in the past with those centrally involved in this legal defence work confirm precisely these views. [66] Furthermore, there were good grounds for these jurists to be concerned both as Jews and as Germans. Why the Liberal position in the C.V. is underemphasised both by Niewyk and Beer is not clear. That they themselves have adopted the position of the conservatives within the organisation – a position which did not represent the views of the majority of the leadership – is never made clear.

But there is a danger in this of inadvertently assisting those who would whitewash the past. As Germany gropes its way to an uncertain future it may attempt to build on a misinterpretation of the past. If the Weimar Republic can be seen to have offered its Jewish citizens justice until the Nazi beasts descended from their spaceships to terrorise the population of Germany into submission, then there is no reason for Germans to examine their own history to understand the events of 1933–1945. If the comparison is made between Weimar and Nazi justice then Weimar justice appears in an excellent light. But if Democratic standards are applied to test the administration of justice then the Weimar Republic stands before history with a serious blemish.

This is not to suggest that the courts could have prevented the Nazi takeover. As Beer so rightly points out: "emotionally motivated mass movements cannot be stemmed by courts of law".[67] The Weimar Republic was a Democracy, but it was only a tentative Democracy. It was a Democracy born of national disaster, a Democracy which represented national betrayal to large segments of the population. Historians of the period refer to it as "the improvised Democracy"[68] as a "Democracy without Democrats".[69] Known also in extreme Nationalist

[65]Justizrat Dr. Julius Brodnitz, 'Unserer Juristentagung zum Gruß!', *C.V.-Zeitung*, VI (1927), pp. 337–338.
*With regard to court decisions in boycott cases, where the C.V. felt that it was more successful, see the preceding essay by Sibylle Morgenthaler, 'Countering the Pre-1933 Nazi Boycott against the Jews', in this volume of the Year Book – (Ed.).
[66]Dr. Arnold Paucker in a letter to the author, London, 25th May 1990.
[67]Beer, 'The Protection', *loc. cit.*, p. 175.
[68]Theodor Eschenburg, *Die improvisierte Demokratie*, Munich 1963.
[69]Paul Loebe, *Der Weg war lang*, 3rd edn., Berlin 1954, p. 95.

circles as the "Jew Republic" the fate of the German Jews was the shared fate of the Weimar Democracy. But there was a legal system which offered Jews some protection under law, as imperfect and as flawed as that system might have been. Had the administration of justice in the Weimar period functioned perfectly and had all the draft amendments to the Criminal Code been enacted, extending the legal protection further, it is hard to see what difference this would have made in a political culture which was to a significant degree anti-Democratic. The defence of the Jews depended entirely upon the defence of the Republic and that depended primarily upon the political and economic and not upon the legal struggle.[70]

[70]The author wishes to express his thanks to the following individuals for providing helpful suggestions which went to strengthening the final draft of this article: Nachman Ben-Yehuda, Alan Borovoy, Howard Brotz, Irwin Cotler, Bruce Elman, Louis Greenspan, Ben Kayfetz, Michael Marrus, Arnold Paucker, William Shaffir and Hesh Troper.

Germans and German Jews

Jewish Lawyers in Germany, 1848–1938
The Disintegration of a Profession

BY KONRAD H. JARAUSCH

In the summer of 1933 a remarkable article in the *Deutsche Juristenzeitung* asked "talented and energetic Jews for [professional] restraint".[1] Surprisingly, this warning was not issued by an antisemitic zealot, but by one of the leading Jewish lawyers, Max Hachenburg.[2] This assimilated liberal attorney and board member of the German Attorney Association (*Deutscher Anwaltverein*, DAV) took much pride in the contribution of Jewish scholars like Paul Laband to "German legal life". But because of "a few embarrassing abuses in big cities" he was "not surprised that a reaction is now emerging against the excessive employment of Jews in public positions".[3] Risking collegial resentment and racist exploitation, this self-criticism was intended as a call for moderation in the disbarring of Jewish attorneys: "The restriction might have an educational effect on the Jewish intelligentsia. But it should not go further than necessary, at least not in such a general way." By accepting some reduction of over-representation in the legal profession, Hachenburg sought to avoid a wholesale purge. Appealing to Conservative nationalism and Christian compassion, he vainly tried to turn the mandatory law into a "discretionary rule . . . This would avoid driving most honest men who only consider themselves German to despair" and suicide.[4] Reflecting a tradition of caution under persecution, such impassioned pleas were unable to prevent the complete expulsion of Jews from the German legal profession.

With its tragic end, the German-Jewish symbiosis has left a trail of misunderstanding. Due to its seeming futility, thinking about Jewish assimilation in Germany requires exceptional "empathy as well as factuality".[5] In general German histories antisemitism almost appears to have triumphed posthumously, since Jews are marginalised as an ethnic sub-category without much bearing on other developments.[6] These difficulties in appreciating the Jewish

---

[1]The author wishes to thank Fred Grubel for proposing the topic, Frank Mecklenburg for archival assistance at the Leo Baeck Institute, and Gerhard Weinberg for helpful suggestions.

[2]Article in *Deutsche Juristenzeitung*, 38 (1933), pp. 608ff., reprinted in Kurt Pätzold (ed.). *Verfolgung, Vertreibung, Vernichtung. Dokumente des faschistischen Antisemitismus 1933 bis 1942*, Leipzig 1984, pp. 69f.

[3]*Ibid*. Cf. also Max Hachenburg, *Lebenserinnerungen eines Rechtsanwalts und Briefe aus der Emigration*, ed. by Jörg Schadt, Stuttgart 1978, p. 94. Already in the original 1927 edition of his memoirs, Hachenburg had advised reserve.

[4]*Ibid*., p. 61.

[5]Fritz Stern, 'The Burden of Success. Reflections on German Jewry', in his *Dreams and Delusions. The Drama of German History*, New York 1987, pp. 97ff.

[6]The collections by Geoff Eley, *From Unification to Nazism*, Boston 1986; David Blackbourn, *Populists and Patricians*, London 1987, and Thomas Nipperdey, *Nachdenken über die deutsche Geschichte*, Munich 1987, contain no essays on this topic. An exception is Hermann Graml (ed.), *Nach Hitler. Der schwierige Umgang mit unserer Geschichte. Beiträge von M. Broszat*, Munich 1987.

current within the stream of German history might perhaps be overcome by focusing on paradigmatic developments such as the dramatic rise and fall of Jewish lawyers. Unfortunately, extant accounts are of only modest help. During the Second World War, the Nazis gloated about "expiating a hundred-and-forty-year-old guilt" by freeing the judiciary of Jews.[7] Among surviving Jewish lawyers, a bitter-sweet impulse to recapture a lost world while explaining their outrageous expulsion inspired many moving memoirs and autobiographies.[8] Though lawyers were individually and collectively recognised as leaders within the Jewish community, they were rarely numerous enough to attract much scholarly attention of their own.[9] Even if conscious of the importance of Jewish colleagues, general histories of the legal profession either subsumed them under other Germans or were uncertain about what to make of them.[10] Only recently have Left-Wing attorneys succeeded in re-awakening the memory of their suffering and in restoring some sense of the Jewish contribution to professional development.[11] Since "the history of Jewish jurists among attorneys has yet to be written", the following, based on general research on German attorneys, can only provide a preliminary sketch of their legal position and social situation.[12]

In the current post-modern uncertainties, how is a historian to address such an emotional and complex subject? In some ways the outcome of the *Historikerstreit* seems to have reaffirmed the accepted narrative of German peculiarity, teleologically fixated on 1933.[13] But the post-structuralist impulse, originating in French debates, is gradually reaching the politically and diplomatically orientated field of German history and beginning to fracture accepted master plots.[14] In spite of all efforts to hold the line, the impetus towards a critical historicisation of the Third *Reich*, which puts Hitler's rule into temporal context without

[7]Sievert Lorenzen, *Die Juden und die Justiz*, Berlin 1943, is a Nazi polemic. But since the text is based upon the files of the Justice Ministries of the *Reich*, Prussia, and the smaller German states, it contains interesting material, not accessible elsewhere.

[8]See the Leo Baeck Institute catalogue under "lawyers".

[9]Ernst J. Cohn, 'Three Jewish Lawyers in Germany', in *LBI Year Book XVII* (1972), pp. 155–178. Cf. Günter Plum, 'Wirtschaft und Erwerbsleben', in Wolfgang Benz, *Die Juden in Deutschland, 1933–1945. Leben unter Nationalsozialistischer Herrschaft*, Munich 1988, pp. 280ff.

[10]Fritz Ostler, *Die deutschen Rechtsanwälte, 1871–1971*, Essen 1982, rev. edn.; and Dietrich Rüschemeyer, *Juristen in Deutschland und in den USA. Eine vergleichende Untersuchung von Anwaltschaft und Gesellschaft*, Stuttgart 1976.

[11]Udo Reifner, 'Die Zerstörung der freien Advokatur im Nationalsozialismus', *Kritische Justiz*, 17 (1984), pp. 380ff.; Gerhard Jungfer, 'Die Vertreibung der jüdischen Juristen', *Anwaltsblatt*, 1989, pp. 10–14. See also Stefan König, *Vom Dienst am Recht. Rechtsanwälte als Strafverteidiger im Nationalsozialismus*, Berlin 1987; and Kritische Justiz (ed.), *Streitbare Juristen*, Baden-Baden 1988.

[12]Reifner, *loc. cit.*, p. 390. While the German term *Juristen* includes all legally trained personnel, the following remarks will focus on attorneys as lawyers in the liberal professions, only occasionally referring to administrative officials, judges and university professors.

[13]Richard Evans, 'The New Nationalism and the Old History: Perspectives on the West German *Historikerstreit*', *Journal of Modern History*, 49 (1987), pp. 761ff.; Geoff Eley, 'Nazism, Politics and Public Memory. Thoughts on the West German *Historikerstreit*, 1986–1987', *Past and Present*, 121 (1988), pp. 121ff.

[14]Georg G. Iggers, *The Social History of German Politics: Critical Perspectives in West German Historical Writing Since 1945*, Leamington Spa 1985; cf. also Thomas Childers's reflections on 'The Social Language of Politics in Germany', *American Historical Review*, 95 (1990), pp. 331–358.

relaxing its moral condemnation, appears to be growing as well.[15] At the same time the *Gesellschaftsgeschichte* synthesis of the Bielefeld school has come under increasing pressure from historians of every-day life (*Alltagsgeschichte*), inspired by anthropological perspectives.[16] By eroding the established grand narratives, these methodological impulses are breaking down accepted boundaries of German and Jewish history and suggesting fresh explorations of groups caught inbetween. The legal profession provides an interesting example of the fragmented nature of the Central European experience, since it reflects the many conflicts between practitioner aspirations, bureaucratic traditions, professorial pronouncements and client desires. Probing the fate of the Jewish minority among German attorneys requires going beyond the official legislative record into tracing every-day social interactions and changing patterns of cultural prejudice. Though the legal career virtually remained a male preserve in this period, the case of attorneys should shed fresh light both on problems of Jewish emancipation and limits of German professionalism.[17]

Within the gradual emergence of an independent attorney occupation, the admission of Jewish practitioners proved to be an especially embattled process. In their "professionalisation from above", Central European advocates became quasi-civil servants during the late eighteenth century, called *Justizkommissare* in Prussia. The strong hand of the state meant that lawyers were subject to the same requirements of legal education, religious affiliation and national reliability as ordinary public officials.[18] Though the *Aufklärung* spirit suggested the removal of civil restrictions, Isaac Itzig had to convert before he was admitted to the judiciary in 1799, going on to an illustrious legal career. Since Hardenberg's emancipation edict of 1812 failed to guarantee admission of Jews to the judiciary as state office, Liberals had to continue to agitate for overcoming religious and ethnic prejudice in the *Vormärz*. While some states like Hamburg allowed individual exceptions such as Gabriel Riesser, only Baden, Württemberg and Hesse regularly appointed Jews as attorneys (10 of 94 Frankfurt lawyers were Jewish in 1837). In Prussia rising parliamentary pressure prompted the passage of a compromise in 1847 which maintained exclusion from justice, police or executive, but implied that Jews could "be appointed as *Justizkommissarien* and advocates". Finally, the progressive Revolution of 1848 abolished all religious restrictions and allowed the unbaptised Jew, Dr. Jonas, to be approved as

[15]See the exchange on 'Historisierung des Nationalsozialismus', between Martin Broszat and Saul Friedländer in *Die Zeit*, 29th April 1988, and Konrad H. Jarausch, 'Removing the Nazi Stain? The Quarrel of the German Historians', *German Studies Review*, 11 (1988), pp. 285ff.

[16]Geoff Eley, 'Labor History, Social History, *Alltagsgeschichte*: Experience, Culture and Politics of the Everyday', *Journal of Modern History*, 61 (1989), pp. 297ff.; and D. Crew, 'Form Content and Meaning: *Alltagsgeschichte*, a New Social History "From Below"?' (MS, Austin 1989).

[17]Misogynist prejudice among jurists was so strong that by January 1932 there were only 79 female lawyers. Cf. Konrad H. Jarausch, *The Unfree Professions. German Lawyers, Teachers and Engineers, 1900–1950*, New York 1990, pp. 35f.

[18]Hannes Siegrist, 'Public Office or Free Profession? German Attorneys in the Nineteenth and Early Twentieth Centuries', in Geoffrey Cocks and Konrad H. Jarausch (eds.), *German Professions 1800–1950*, New York 1990, pp. 66ff.

judicial trainee over the resistance of the Berlin *Kammergericht*. But the restoration cabinets used the requirement of swearing a Christian oath to limit full Jewish equality in the judicial bureaucracy and deflect aspirants into a private career.[19]

After the breach of the legal walls, the struggle over Jewish entry into the legal profession shifted to the administrative realm. In 1857 Prussian Justice Minister Louis Simons used overcrowding as pretext for "putting a temporary stop to the further influx of Jewish candidates", but public outrage forced the rescinding of this exclusion in 1861. The reactionary Bismarck cabinet focused on barring entry to the judiciary, until the more flexible Minister of Justice Gerhard Leonhardt abandoned opposition and the North German Confederation decreed full equality on 3rd July 1869. In spite of such bureaucratic discrimination, 75 of the 2,480 attorneys and notaries in Prussia were Jewish by 1871.[20] During the Liberal founding decade of the Second *Reich*, the Lawyer Code of 1878 reconstituted attorneys as members of a completely liberal profession. At the same time the number of Jewish judges expanded rapidly from 3 to 124.[21] But the *Schlesische Volkszeitung* ridiculed "the Jewish law trainee" as either "impudent" or "slimy", while Court Chaplain Stoecker ranted in the Prussian Lower House about "Jewish advocates invading an entire profession with their competition". Due to the ensuing slow-down of appointments to the judiciary, there were only 2.82% (200) Jewish judges in 1914, in contrast to a larger number of Jewish *Referendare* at 13.34% (824) and *Assessoren* at 8.36% (251). Academic antisemitism and administrative discrimination deflected Jewish lawyers into the only accessible career - the *freie Advokatur*. During the 1880s, the Jewish share of Prussian attorneys rose impressively from 7.3% (146 of 1,991) to 20.4% (586 of 2,870) and continued to grow to 23.4% in 1893 and 27.4% in 1904! Due to their "strong-willed self-assertion, struggle for emancipation and political involvement", non-baptised Jews constituted over one-quarter of the Prussian legal profession within a single generation.[22]

Though facilitated by the liberal lawyer spirit, the rise of Jewish attorneys was

---

[19]Sievert Lorenzen, 'Das Eindringen der Juden in die Justiz vor 1933', *Deutsche Justiz* (1939), pp. 731–740; and Monika Richarz, *Der Eintritt der Juden in die akademischen Berufe. Jüdische Studenten und Akademiker in Deutschland 1678–1848*, Tübingen 1974 (Schriftenreihe wissenschaftlicher Abhandlungen des Leo Baeck Instituts 28), pp. 172ff. Cf. Ernest Hamburger, *Juden im öffentlichen Leben Deutschlands. Regierungsmitglieder, Beamte, und Parlamentarier in der monarchischen Zeit 1848–1918*, Tübingen 1968 (Schriftenreihe wissenschaftlicher Abhandlungen des Leo Baeck Instituts 19), pp. 8ff.; and Adolf Weissler, *Geschichte der Rechtsanwaltschaft*, Leipzig 1905, pp. 436ff.

[20]Lorenzen, *Juden in der Justiz, op. cit.*; and 'Das Eindringen', *loc. cit.*, pp. 768–777. Cf. Hamburger, *Juden, op. cit.*, pp. 40ff.; and Jacob Toury, *Soziale und politische Geschichte der Juden in Deutschland 1847–1871*, Düsseldorf 1977, pp. 93f.

[21]Kenneth Ledford, *A Social and Institutional History of the German Bar in Private Practice, 1878–1930*, unpubl. Diss., Johns Hopkins Univ., 1988. Earlier research underestimates the importance of the Jewish debate for the establishment of the *Freie Advokatur*.

[22]Peter Pulzer, 'Religion and Judicial Appointments in Germany, 1869–1918', in *LBI Year Book XXVIII* (1983), pp. 191f.; Lorenzen, 'Das Eindringen', *loc. cit.*, pp. 956–961; and Richarz, *Eintritt, op. cit.*, pp. 172ff. Cf. Norbert Kampe, *Studenten und 'Judenfrage' im Deutschen Kaiserreich*, Göttingen 1988; and *idem*, 'Jews and Antisemites at Universities in Imperial Germany (I) – Jewish Students: Social History and Social Conflict', in *LBI Year Book XXX* (1985), and 'Jews and Antisemites at Universities in Imperial Germany (II) – The Friedrich-Wilhelms-Universität of Berlin: A Case Study on the Students' "Jewish Question" ', in *LBI Year Book XXXII* (1987).

never easy. To overcome prejudice, many Jewish *Anwälte* worked harder. Württemberg Minister of Justice Faber quipped, in this job "the public does not ask, if one is Christian or Israelite, it only goes to the most capable".[23] Stemming from a culture steeped in talmudic reasoning, Jewish attorneys also benefited from the uneven economic distribution of their co-religionists, since much legal business derived from commercial transactions in which they could use their family ties and social connections. In spite of increasing competition, professional relations with non-Jewish colleagues were usually correct. But considerable social distance remained, fed by prejudice against "inherited Jewish defects". Especially in the smaller towns, Jewish jurists and businessmen associated with one another, but rarely had family contacts with Gentiles.[24] Since old biases died hard, relations with "Aryan" clients were somewhat ambivalent. Superior competence did eventually overcome discrimination. Notably in legal scholarship, Jewish authors made substantial and acknowledged contributions.[25] But unusual legal cleverness, rhetorical ability or financial wizardry often reawakened older fears, making them congeal in a new stereotype of the "Jewish Shyster lawyer" (*jüdischer Rechtsverdreher*). While prominent Jewish lawyers were elected to professional offices (DAV board membership) and Progressive Party leadership positions, the stigma of "irremovable difference" continued to haunt their lives. In the *Kaiserreich* much of the success of Jewish lawyers centred on the business provided by their own community, with talented attorneys only gradually dealing with Christian colleagues and clients as a matter of course.[26]

During the Weimar Republic, the integration of Jewish lawyers into the wider profession accelerated. Distinguished service during the First World War demonstrated the patriotism of Jewish attorneys even to Conservative sceptics who could no longer deny decorated veterans national respect.[27] Prompted by Jewish attorneys such as Otto Landsberg and Eugen Schiffer who became Ministers of Justice, the Weimar Constitution reaffirmed legal equality without a debate: "The enjoyment of civic and public rights as well as the admission to public offices are independent of religious affiliation." Moreover, the long-range

---

[23]Robert Hirsch, 'Erinnerungen', reprinted in Monika Richarz (ed.), *Jüdisches Leben in Deutschland*, vol. II, *Selbstzeugnisse zur Sozialgeschichte im Kaiserreich*, Stuttgart 1979, Veröffentlichung des Leo Baeck Instituts, pp. 283ff.

[24]S. Feuchtwanger, *Die Freien Berufe*, Munich 1922, pp. 165ff.; Weissler, *Geschichte der Rechtsanwaltschaft*, *op. cit.*, pp. 603; Hachenburg, *Lebenserinnerungen, op. cit.*, pp. 68ff.; and Siegfried Neumann, *Nacht über Deutschland*, Munich 1978, pp. 66ff.

[25]Hugo Sinzheimer, *Jüdische Klassiker der deutschen Rechtswissenschaft*, Frankfurt a. Main 1953; Cohn, 'Jewish Lawyers', *loc. cit.*, pp. 157ff.; Reinhard Bendix, *Von Berlin nach Berkeley. Deutsch-jüdische Identitäten*, Frankfurt a. Main 1985, pp. 83ff.

[26]F. Philipp, *Lebenserinnerungen*, Altona 1917, pp. 14f.; Alfred Apfel, *Behind the Scenes of German Justice*, London 1935.

[27]Friedrich Solon, 'Mein Leben in Deutschland vor und nach dem 30. Januar 1933', reprinted in Richarz, *Jüdisches Leben*, vol. II, *op. cit.*, pp. 435ff. Cf. Neumann, *Nacht über Deutschland, op. cit.*, pp. 16ff.; and Werner T. Angress, 'Das deutsche Militär und die Juden im Ersten Weltkrieg', *Militärgeschichtliche Mitteilungen*, 19 (1976), pp. 77–146; and *idem*, 'The German Army's "Judenzählung" of 1916. Genesis – Consequences – Significance', in *LBI Year Book XXIII* (1978), pp. 117–137.

secularisation of the Jewish community brought educated Jews into the German mainstream and reduced the visible ethnic distinction to a less perceptible religious difference.[28] As a result of these developments, the number of Jewish judges in the *Reich* rapidly increased to 796 in 1932 (except in Bavaria). In Prussia the ranks of Jewish attorneys continued to swell to 3,370 in 1933, amounting to an astounding 28.5%, with another 1,215 practising in other German states. Among notaries public the proportion of 2,051 Jewish practitioners was even higher, reaching 32.9%.[29] These burgeoning numbers suggest that Jewish lawyers were beginning to be accepted by non-Jewish colleagues and clients without a second thought. Not infrequently, the bigger metropolitan law firms had both Jewish and Gentile partners, functioning apparently quite well before 1933.[30] Not that in the smaller towns and in traditional circles antisemitic prejudices had entirely vanished. But the liberalisation of administrative practice and the evident success of Jewish competence had reduced bias to the social level. In spite of some racist resentment against "rapid Jewification", the progress of Jewish integration into the German legal profession suggested to experienced observers like Max Hachenburg the hope "that the distinctions will gradually disappear".[31]

The grounds for such optimism about further integration were both individual and collective. Since the DAV publications did not mention whether attorneys were Jewish, it is difficult to piece together solid indicators. But impressive examples indicate that "Jewish attorneys formed a certain elite within the German legal profession". It was not superior talent, but rather exclusion from the bureaucracy which pushed the best and the brightest Jewish law graduates into *freie Advokatur* while the most promising Gentile students chose public services careers.[32] Were not the most celebrated defenders of the Republic in headline criminal or political trials Jewish attorneys like Alfred Apfel, Max Alsberg or Erich Frey? Even German Nationalists who had run foul of Republican laws sometimes hired such famous court-room stars.[33] Were not some of the most respected legal commentators, such as Albert Pinner, Martin Drucker or Ludwig Bendix, Jewish attorneys? Even Conservative jurists turned

[28]Lorenzen, *Juden und Justiz, op. cit.*, pp. 151ff., also mentions attorneys Kurt Rosenfeld (Prussia) and Dr Ludwig Marum (Baden) as Socialist ministers. Cf. Cohn, 'Jewish Lawyers', *loc. cit.*, pp. 176ff.; and George L. Mosse, *German Jews Beyond Judaism*, Bloomington 1985.

[29]Cited in Lorenzen, 'Eindringen', *loc. cit.*, pp. 963ff.

[30]Paul Ronge, *Im Namen der Gerechtigkeit. Erinnerungen eines Strafverteidigers*, Munich 1963, pp. 139ff.

[31]Lorenzen, *Juden und Justiz, op. cit.*, pp. 165f.; Hachenburg, *Lebenserinnerungen, op. cit.*, pp. 94f.; Curt Riess, *Der Mann in der schwarzen Robe. Das Leben des Strafverteidigers Max Alsberg*, Hamburg 1965, pp. 23ff.; and Adolf Heilberg, 'Erinnerungen 1858–1936', in Richarz, *Jüdisches Leben*, vol. II, *op. cit.*, pp. 289ff.

[32]Hans Kilian, 'Die jüdische Rechtsanwaltschaft im "dritten Reich"', *Deutsche Freiheit*, 12th September 1934, is an exceptionally perceptive portrait of German-Jewish lawyers by a former insider.

[33]Apfel, *German Justice, op. cit., passim*; Riess, *Alsberg, op. cit.*, pp. 209ff.; Erich Frey, *Ich beantrage Freispruch*, Hamburg 1959; and Robert M. W. Kempner, *Ankläger einer Epoche. Lebenserinnerungen*, Frankfurt a. Main 1986, pp. 32ff.

time and again to the writings of such accomplished interpreters.[34] Were not the best known spokesmen for the legal profession, such as Adolf Heilberg, Max Hachenburg or Max Friedländer, Jews? Even traditionalist practitioners paid much attention to the suggestions of these experienced professionals.[35] Due to their energy and dedication, it should not be surprising that eleven of the twenty-five board members of the DAV in 1933 were Jewish! Similarly, the editor of the professional journal of attorneys, the internationally respected *Juristische Wochenschrift*, was the Jewish lawyer Julius Magnus. In Berlin twenty of the thirty-three members of the combined Lawyers' Chamber board (*Anwaltskammer*), elected on 7th February 1933, were Jews.[36] Finally, in antisemitic cases, the Weimar courts, though nationalistic, proved surprisingly fair. Jewish attorneys like the DAV chairman Martin Drucker gained such professional success during the Weimar Republic that some observers claimed that they "achieved an intellectual and economic preponderance among German lawyers".[37]

Lingering problems, nevertheless, created noticeable irritations. Though abating, the perceived over-representation of Jewish students aggravated the academic overcrowding of the 1920s. Though Jewish enrolment declined from 9.4% in 1894/1895 to 4.7% in 1932/1933 due to fewer births, it was still five times larger than the .91% share of Jews in the Prussian population. Jewish law matriculations ran somewhat counter to the trend, rising to 10.2% in 1911/1912 and only dropping to 5.8% by the end of the Republic.[38] Moreover, the unusual concentration of Jewish attorneys in certain cities made them highly visible to frustrated competitors. In metropolitan Berlin 48.3% of lawyers were Jewish, in Frankfurt a. Main 45.3% were Jews and in Breslau their share amounted to 35.6%. In contrast the rural districts of Kiel, Celle or Naumburg averaged 10% or less.[39] Prompted by their urban environment, many Jewish attorneys could be found at the innovative edge of the profession. All too openly embracing the Republic like the lawyers in the *Republikanischer Richterbund* or proposing Left-wing solutions to the occupational crisis, like Sigbert Feuchtwanger and Ludwig Bendix, did not exactly endear them to more traditionally-minded small-town

[34]Berliner Anwaltverein (ed.), *Festschrift Herrn Rechtsanwalt und Notar Justizrat Dr. jur. h. c. Albert Pinner*, Berlin 1932; and Julius Magnus (ed.), *Festschrift Martin Drucker*, Leipzig 1934, reprinted with a new introduction by Fred Grubel, Aalen 1983. M. Drucker was a second generation Protestant, but his racist enemies considered him Jewish. These *Festschriften* are rolls of honour for the scholarly and professional contributions of Jewish attorneys.

[35]Heilberg, 'Erinnerungen', *loc. cit.*, pp. 289ff.; Hachenburg, *Lebenserinnerungen*, *op. cit.*, pp. 184ff.; and for Friedländer see Robert Heinrich, *100 Jahre Rechtsanwaltskammer München*, Munich 1979, pp. 160f.

[36]Ostler, *Die deutschen Rechtsanwälte*, *op. cit.*, pp. 229ff.; and Jarausch, *Unfree Professions*, *op. cit.*, p. 118. In Munich the figure was one-third.

[37]Donald L. Niewyk, 'Jews and the Courts in Weimar Germany', *Jewish Social Studies*, 37 (1975), pp. 99ff. Kilian, 'Die jüdische Rechstanwaltschaft', *loc. cit.*, speaks of a "well earned reputation". Cf. Reifner, 'Die Zerstörung der freien Advokatur', *loc. cit.*, pp. 390ff.

[38]Hartmut Titze (ed.), *Das Hochschulstudium in Preussen und Deutschland, 1820–1944*, Göttingen 1987; Kampe, *Studenten und Judenfrage*, *op. cit.*, p. 78; and Michael Kater, *Studentenschaft und Rechtsradikalismus in Deutschland, 1918–1933*, Hamburg 1975, pp. 218f.

[39]Ministry of Justice table on lawyer purge, reprinted in Lothar Gruchmann, *Justiz im Dritten Reich, 1933–1941*, Munich 1988, pp. 151f.

practitioners.[40] Similarly, the abandonment of the Liberal tradition in favour of Socialist or even Communist involvement by some well-known lawyers such as Curt Rosenberg or Paul Levi created fears of radicalism.[41] Finally the flaunting of success by stars like Max Alsberg and the occasional representation of questionable criminals by defenders like Erich Frey aroused envy among non-Jewish colleagues and attracted unfavourable publicity among clients. In Fritz Stern's felicitous phrase, Jewish attorneys were in many ways "the victims of their own success", with envy arising from spectacular advance.[42]

Spawned by neo-Conservative and *völkisch* resentment, the political onslaught against Jewish lawyers came from a new Nazi association which emerged during the Depression. When Adolf Hitler needed a defence counsel in the frequent political trials, the NSDAP turned to a young assistant at the Technical University of Munich, Dr. Hans Frank, who had become an enthusiastic Nazi in June 1919 and joined the Party and SA in 1923. Since the case-load of defending NS-ruffians grew too heavy for one person to handle alone, on 1st November 1928 twenty-nine lawyers who belonged to the Party founded a League of NS German Jurists (*Bund NS Deutscher Juristen*, BNSDJ) for "the advancement of the general aims of the NSDAP". Working towards the seizure of power was complemented by professional goals of the renewal of law in general: "The plight of German law is a vital question for our time and a task in the forefront of our Party activity." According to Hitler's founding charge, the BNSDJ had a monopoly in legal Party matters and demanded academic standing as well as Party membership as prerequistites for joining. As Party auxiliary, the BNSDJ was run according to the *Führer*-principle with essential powers reserved for Hans Frank who delegated them to *Gauobmänner* in the Party districts.[43] In spite of Hitler's notorious dislike for lawyers, the BNSDJ slowly began to grow after the Party's public commitment to legality. In 1929 there were only sixty to eighty NS-lawyers; a year later League membership crept up to 233; in 1931 numbers expanded to 701; by 1932 members doubled to 1,374; and by April 1933 there were roughly 1,624 NS-jurists. The danger in the new organisation lay less in its attracting the "best racial and professional talent" than in the rising power of the NSDAP.[44]

The programme of the BNSDJ was a curious blend of antisemitic with more general anti-Liberal and anti-Marxist resentments, making it difficult to sort out their relative salience. After its October 1930 and March 1931 conferences in

[40]Birger Schulz, *Der Republikanische Richterbund, 1921–1933*, Frankfurt a. Main 1982; Feuchtwanger, *Freie Berufe, op. cit.*, pp. 168f.; and examples in Jarausch, *Unfree Professions, op. cit.*, chapters I–IV.

[41]Curt Rosenberg, 'Jugenderinnerungen', and Philipp Löwenfeld, 'Memoiren', reprinted in Richarz, *Jüdisches Leben*, vol. II, *op. cit.*, pp. 298–324; and Kritische Justiz, *Streitbare Juristen, op. cit.*, pp. 131ff.

[42]Riess, *Alsberg, op. cit.*, pp. 200ff.; Kempner, *Ankläger, op. cit.*, pp. 38ff. Cf. also Stern, *Dreams and Delusions, op. cit.*, p. 112.

[43]Hans Frank, *Im Angesicht des Galgens*, Munich 1953; 'Aufruf!', *Völkischer Beobachter* (13th November 1928); 'BNSDJ', *Bayern-Kurier*, both in BA, NS 16, No. 112. Cf. Niklaus Frank, *Der Vater. Eine Abrechnung*, Munich 1987, pp. 27ff.; and Kenneth Willig, *The Theory and Administration of Justice in the Third Reich*, unpubl. Diss., Philadelphia 1975, pp. 334ff.

[44]Frank, *Angesicht, op. cit.*, pp. 70, 84ff.; membership list of 1st January 1931, Bundesarchiv Koblenz (BA), NS 16, No. 112; Rechtspolitische Abteilung to Gregor Strasser, 2nd July 1932, BA, NS 16, No. 112. Other figures from Willig, *op. cit.*, pp. 335f. Not all jurist Party members joined the League.

Leipzig, the BNSDJ expanded its *Völkischer Beobachter* supplement into a new journal, called *Deutsches Recht* so as to "prepare, in the service of Adolf Hitler's movement, the way for the idea of German law, without which the Third *Reich* cannot exist". In the first issue Hans Frank rhapsodised programmatically about the "awakening of German law". Castigating the revaluation decision, abortion *cum* divorce practices, and the protection of the Republic law, he played on traditionalist aversion to materialism, politicisation, immorality, lack of honour and excessive individualism. Claiming that "German man is deeply alienated from his law", he held, in a classic summation of the antisemitic stereotype, the "rootless, Asiatic-oriental, crooked, intriguing, lying, sensationalist decadence-lawyers" responsible for the legal decline. Long on hatred, Frank was short on prescriptions, beyond asserting: "Whatever benefits the *völkisch* community shall be law", even if saving German ideals required the re-introduction of the death penalty, forced sterilisation and other "brutal, yes even partly inhumane" cures. For NS-lawyers such as the opportunist and racist Walter Luetgebrune, intellectual renewal implied the elimination of Jewish corruptions such as material "greed", empty formalism, and alienation from the popular sense of justice. Since antisemitism was embedded into a wider crusade against the Liberal or Socialist spirit of the Weimar regime, anti-Jewish appeals combined shameless financial envy with protestations of sincere idealism.[45]

Which lawyers were willing to follow this murky creed and become BNSDJ fanatics? A list of the first 211 League members who joined by 31st December 1930 indicates the character of the founding cohort when compared to the structure of non-NS lawyers in 1932. Surprisingly there were 2.5% noblemen and 1.4% women, considerably higher proportions than among attorneys in general! Geographically the BNSDJ founders hailed disproportionately from Bavaria (due to Frank's influence) as well as from Saxony and Thuringia, with Prussia under-represented. Early activity centred on Munich, Dresden, Berlin, and Leipzig, i.e. metropolitan areas with enough Party members to found a special professional group. The NS-jurists were surprisingly well-educated, with over one-half possessing a doctorate. Moreover, 8.1% were in higher positions, revealing some penetration of the elite, while only 5.2% held employment that was questionable for university graduates. Though some were dispersed in commerce and industry, over half of the League's founders were in the liberal professions, two-fifths officials and one-seventh still in training. With 53.6%, lawyers were the strongest single group, followed by trainees with 14.2%, judges with 10.8%, higher officials with 10% and businessmen with 4.8%. A second list of 1st October 1931 contains 253 names of only lawyers and notaries. While the possession of doctorates and superior court positions by two-thirds indicates modest success, these lawyers were less likely to be DAV members and held virtually no professional offices. The early Jurists' League grew out of the

---

[45]M. Reiter, 'Zur Einführung', *Deutsches Recht*, 1 (1931), pp. 1f.; Hans Frank, 'Erwachen des dt. Rechts', *ibid.*, pp. 3ff.; Ferdinand Mössmer, 'Eherecht', *ibid.*, pp. 20ff.; 'Stellenvermittlung', *ibid.*, p. 152; Georg Lind, 'Dt. Rechtsnot', *Deutsches Recht*, 2 (1932), pp. 9ff.; '3. Reichstagung des BNSDJ', *ibid.*, pp. 225ff. Cf. H. Heydeloff, 'Staranwalt der Rechtsextremisten', *Vierteljahrshefte für Zeitgeschichte*, 23 (1984), pp. 373ff.; and Reifner, *loc. cit.*, pp. 383ff.

"hatred of many intellectually and economically hampered 'Aryan' " attorneys rather than the resentment of bureaucrats: "They were utterly looked down upon as loudmouths, ordinary demagogues, empty windbags and virtually complete incompetents", driven by the basest of material motives.[46]

The Nazi *Machtergreifung* presented these outsiders with the chance to purge the profession by ruthlessly delicensing racially or politically undesirable competitors. Rabid NS lawyers saw the victory of "the National movement" as an opportunity for settling old scores by peremptory arrest of defence attorneys such as Alfred Apfel, Hans Litten, Hugo Sinzheimer or Martin Drucker.[47] Shouting "Juden raus", on 11th March 1933 SA troops stormed the Breslau courts and chased Jewish judges and attorneys into the streets, badly injuring two lawyers. Under pressure from the police chief, the Appellate Court president informed local attorneys five days later that he would henceforth admit only seventeen Jewish lawyers, setting a dangerous precedent by disbarring three hundred and fifty others! Though Hitler ordered "a stop to the disruption of the administration of justice", such "spontaneous" assaults spread to other towns like Munich and Kassel, leading to the beatings and murders of several prominent lawyers who were political opponents.[48] Prodded by the BNSDJ, new Rightist groups such as a *"Christlichnationaler Anwaltverein"* of one hundred Breslau attorneys "demand[ed] an immediate solution because of the preponderantly un-German legal-chamber". On 23rd March 800 Berlin jurists founded a similar *Bund nationaler Rechtsanwälte und Notare*, which immediately called for the exclusion of Jewish colleagues.[49] Claiming that "the arrogant behaviour of Jewish attorneys has created special outrage", Prussian Commissar Hanns Kerrl on 31st March ordered the chambers "that only certain Jewish attorneys shall practise, generally corresponding to the proportion of Jews in the rest of the population". According to press reports, only thirty-five of two thousand Berlin Jewish lawyers would be left! In anticipation of the national boycott of Jewish stores, non-Aryans could no longer represent clients and be deputised as poor-law defenders or as mandatory counsels. In Bavaria, Frank similarly ordered that "Jewish attorneys are forbidden to enter the courts until further notice".[50]

[46]'BNSDJ Mitgliederverzeichnis per 1. Jan. 1931', BA, NS 16, No. 112; 'BNSDJ Mitgliederverzeichnis vom 1. Oktober 1931', on microfilm, Parteikanzlei. Cf. Kilian, 'Jüdische Rechtsanwälte', *loc. cit., passim.*

[47]Jungfer, 'Die Vertreibung der jüdischen Juristen', *loc. cit.,* pp. 11f. Cf. also *Streitbare Juristen, op. cit.,* pp. 193ff., 282ff.

[48]Material in Geheimes Staatsarchiv Preussischer Kulturbesitz (PrGStA) Da, Rep 84a, No. 35; description of attorney Ludwig Foerder in Benz, *Die Juden in Deutschland, op. cit.,* pp. 284f.; and Heinrich, *100 Jahre Rechtsanwaltskammer, op. cit.,* pp. 106f. Cf. Horst Göppinger, *Juristen Jüdischer Abstammung im "Dritten Reich". Entrechtung und Verfolgung,* Munich 1990 (2nd rev. edn.), pp. 49–55 and 62–64; Gert Buchheit, *Richter in roter Robe. Freisler, Präsident des Volksgerichtshofs,* Munich 1968, pp. 24ff.; König, *Dienst am Recht, op. cit.,* pp. 54ff.; and Gruchmann, *Justiz im Dritten Reich, 1933–1940, op. cit.,* pp. 125f.

[49]Rebiztki to Prussian Justice Ministry, 17th March 1933, PrGStA Da, Rep 84a, No. 35; *Bericht des Vorstands der Anwaltskammer zu Berlin 1933* and König, *Dienst am Recht, op. cit.,* pp. 55f. For estimates of the figure of Jewish lawyers cf. PrGStA Da, Rep 84a, No. 75.

[50]Schlegelberger to cabinet, 10th March 1933, BA, R 43 II, No. 1534; Kerrl circular, 31st March 1933, PrGStA Da, Rep 84a, No. 35; and 'Die Liste der Berliner Anwälte', *Frankfurter Zeitung,* 9th April 1933. Cf. Lorenzen, *Juden und Justiz, op. cit.,* pp. 176ff.; König, *Dienst am Recht, op. cit.,* p. 56; Gruchmann, *Justiz, op. cit.,* pp. 127f. and Göppinger, *Juristen, op. cit.,* pp. 56–60.

Temporary suspension was, however, not enough for Nazi fanatics. Though increasingly excluded from court-rooms, Jewish attorneys were still legally free to practise. Hence many colleagues began to shun them (in Naumburg), local associations expelled them (in Magdeburg) and Christian-Nationalist organis-ations argued that it was unethical to substitute for them (in Düsseldorf). For Prussia, Kerrl forbade the preparation of legal briefs by "not-admitted" attorneys and reiterated his other prohibitions on 4th April.[51] When the states were trying to make the antisemitic boycott permanent, *Reich* Justice Minister Franz Gürtner forestalled complete exclusion by drafting a more moderate national law which aimed at a twisted kind of compromise. Spurred by reports in the *Manchester Guardian* and London *Times*, fear of an uproar abroad exerted some restraining influence.[52] Hitler asked the cabinet on 7th April, "only to regulate what is necessary at this time. For attorneys a solution similar to the law on the restoration of the professional civil service ought to be found", while doctors were to remain free. Rejecting a general *numerus clausus*, the government also extended disbarment to "non-Jewish attorneys, if these have been active as Communists". The law on "admission as attorney" revoked credentials for Jews, but on Field-Marshal Hindenburg's insistence excepted those who, like Siegfried Neumann, had been admitted during the *Kaiserreich*, fought in the war or had fathers or sons who were killed at the front. During disbarment proceedings, attorneys were suspended so as to drive away their clients, even if they might eventually be readmitted. From April on the chambers purged their membership, fuelled by "Aryan" resentment against the "dominant position" of their Jewish competi-tors. In spite of Jewish warnings against over-reaction, expulsions concentrated on those cities where Nazis deemed "the disproportion quite unbearable", but spread also to smaller towns:

TABLE I

Purge of Jewish Lawyers in Prussia, 1933–1934

Oberlandesgericht district	Lawyers	Jewish		Purged		Remainder	
		No.	%	No.	% of Total	No.	% of Jewish
Berlin	3,890	1,880	48.3	721	18.5	1,159	61.6
Frankfurt	607	275	45.3	121	19.9	154	56.0
Breslau	1,056	378	35.6	145	13.7	233	61.6
Königsberg	375	90	24.0	47	12.5	43	47.8
Others	5,886	750	12.7	330	5.6	420	56.0
Total	11,814	3,373	28.6	1,364	11.5	2,009	59.6

[51]Kerrl, 4th April 1933, and other material in PrGStA Da, Rep 84a, No. 75. Cf. Bohn's memorandum on the need to purge all Jewish attorneys and notaries, 4th April, *ibid.*; and König, *Dienst am Recht*, *op. cit.*, pp. 64f.

[52]See *The Manchester Guardian* reports of 13th March, 1st April and 7th April as well as *The Times* stories on 2nd and 5th April in the clipping file of the Wiener Library.

Barring another 399 attorneys in the rest of the *Reich*, the purge deprived 38.5% of Jewish advocates (9.1% of the total) and 58.5% of Jewish notaries (19.3% of the total) of their livelihood![53]

When it became known that exceptions permitted three-fifths of the Jewish lawyers to continue their practice, mobs in Celle, Frankfurt a. Main, Hanover and Duisburg once again used their fists to "cleanse" the courts. Though Jewish attorneys had to prove in a humiliating procedure that they fitted one of the special clauses, Nazi fanatics were incensed about their being re-admitted at all. Over the protests of the *Reichsbund jüdischer Frontsoldaten* (RjF) and Conservative jurists, the board of the Berlin chamber on 23rd May 1933 forbade "any professional association" with disbarred or still legal Jewish attorneys, such as joint offices (*Sozietät*), help in circumventing expulsion or taking over case-loads. Since zealots like Kerrl and Frank disbarred as many attorneys as possible, the first implementation order defined the exceptions more broadly. When Jewish lawyers' leaders demanded that the Prussian Ministry protect their remaining rights, Roland Freisler had to agree that admitted lawyers were fully equal, but the purged DAV and Chamber leadership rejected any compromise as "interference in the internal matters of a Party organisation".[54] Rampant confusion about what remained permissible forced the *Reich* Ministry to clarify the situation in negotiations with the state ministries during the summer. On 1st October, the second implementation instruction assured that "Jewish attorneys remaining in office retain the full enjoyment of their professional rights and can demand that respect which they are owed as members of their professional community". But at the same time, the BNSDJ excluded all Jews from the lawyers' professional association, depriving them of a collective voice, of listing in the annual directory, consigning them to inferior status.[55]

Formally still free to practise, Jewish lawyers, listed in a separate guide, were squeezed out economically. Systematic "chicanery, humiliation and economic pressure" instituted a veritable "boycott by fear". While "astonishingly many 'Aryan' individuals and firms remained loyal" to their Jewish advocates, opportunistic desertion by other clients gradually eroded the basis of most legal practices. From official city affairs and important business dealings, legal work

---

[53]'Auszug aus der Niederschrift über die Ministerbesprechung vom 7. April 1933', BA, Rep R43 II, No. 1534, *Wolffs Telegraphen-Bureau* (*WTB*) releases of 10th April and 12th May 1933. Treated as civil servants, 804 *Referendare* were purged. Otto Palandt, 'Die grosse juristische Staatsprüfung in Preussen', *Deutsche Justiz*, 96 (1934), p. 252; Max Hachenburg, *ibid.*, 95 (1933), No. 9; and 'Übersicht über die Zahl der am 1. Mai zugelassenen arischen und nichtarischen Rechtsanwälte und Notare', *ibid.*, p. 950. Cf. *Die Juden in Deutschland*, Munich 1935, 2nd edn., pp. 33ff., 45ff; Göppinger, *Juristen, op. cit.*, pp. 69–72, 90–91; Neumann, *Nacht, op. cit.*, pp. 84f.; Heinrich, *100 Jahre Rechtsanwaltskammer, op. cit.*, pp. 110ff.; and Gruchmann, *Justiz, op. cit.*, pp. 135ff.

[54]Freisler to Gürtner, 15th May 1933 versus Oelze to Papen, 4th April 1933; Löwenstein to Justice Minister, 25th April 1933; and 'Niederschrift der Besprechung' of 7th and 11th July 1933, in PrGStA Da, Rep 84a, No. 75. Cf. Göppinger, *Juristen, op. cit.*, pp. 89–90; Gruchmann, *Justiz, op. cit.*, pp. 140ff.; and Michael H. Kater, *Doctors under Hitler*, Chapel Hill 1989, chap. VI.

[55]'Bericht über die Referentenbesprechung im Reichjustizministerium', 20th June 1933; '2. Durchführungsverordnung' for the 7th April law, 1st October 1933, *Reichsgesetzblatt* 1933, 1, p. 699; Rudolf Schraut (ed.), *Deutscher Juristentag*, Berlin 1933, pp. 11f. Cf. Gruchmann, *Justiz*, pp. 158ff. and the clippings in the Wiener Library file on lawyers.

shifted towards "the politically persecuted and many Jewish people, even those who only were declared to be Jewish by the Nazis". Expulsion from non-Jewish buildings usually forced lawyers to move their premises to less attractive locations and the difficulties of hiring "Aryan" personnel made it hard to keep competent staff. The continuation of "administrative and judicial principles of the destroyed legal order" of the Weimar Republic and the impossibility of imagining the suffering to come militated against overt political resistance, prohibited by Nazi terror. But the tightening repression of the SS state pushed many Jewish lawyers into a covert oppositional stance, seeking to subvert as many Nazi measures as possible. It took much sagacity and luck to escape repeated *Gestapo* provocations with fake clients. Working for organisations such as the *Jüdischer Hilfsverein* restored the original legal ethos of helping the persecuted escape and emigrate. But in spite of individual heroism, the psychological pressure proved unbearable in the long run. Through constant harassment, "thousands of professional men . . . together with their families and their employees, were faced with certain ruin".[56]

Instead of merely reducing Jewish presence, the Nazification of the professions aimed at a complete racial purge. Nazi zealots like Freisler promoted the disenfranchisement of the remaining Jewish veterans or old practitioners and the rescinding of their pensions. Considering Jews "utterly unfit" for rendering German justice, Minister Franz Gürtner conceded that the selection of poor-law attorneys "will have to depart from the consideration that an Aryan party expects the appointment of an Aryan lawyer".[57] The Nuremberg laws of 15th September 1935 discriminated further against Jewish professionals by limiting citizenship to racial Germans. The creation of two inferior classes of mixed descent, pejoratively known as *Mischlinge,* and Jews (of at least one-half Jewish birth and religion) effectively excluded "all Jewish officials with their pension", thereby purging the last judges who had escaped so far. The stripping of citizenship rights also meant "that notaries who are Jews in this sense must resign".[58] On 6th February 1936 the Justice Ministry permitted German attorneys to refuse representing Jewish clients because it was incompatible with "their duties as Party members" or BNSDJ leaders. When some "three-quarter German" attorneys of mixed descent protested against their professional

[56] *Verzeichnis nichtarischer Rechtsanwälte Deutschlands,* Berlin 1934; Max Hermann Maier, *In uns verwoben, tief und wunderbar,* Frankfurt a. Main 1972; Apfel, *Behind the Scenes, op. cit.,* p. 172; Beer, Berkowitz, *op. cit.,* pp. 55f.; Kilian, 'Die jüdische Rechtsanwaltschaft', *loc. cit., passim;* Fred Grubel, 'Martin Drucker', *loc. cit.,* pp. xiiff.; Fritz Ostler, 'Rechtsanwälte in der NS-Zeit', *Anwaltsblatt,* 1983, pp. 52ff.

[57] Kilian, 'Jüdische Anwälte', *loc. cit.,* part 2; 'Juden in der dt. Rechtspflege?', *Hakenkreuzbanner,* 18th July 1935; Gürtner to the KG presidents, 18th February 1935; note on "Beiordnung von nichtarischen RA als Armenanwälten arischer Parteien', 2nd November 1935, BA, R 22, No. 263; 'Die Auswahl von Armenanwälten, Pflichtverteidigern, Konkursverwaltern u. dergl.', *Deutsche Justiz,* 97 (20th December 1935). Cf. *Der gelbe Fleck. Die Ausrottung von 500 000 deutschen Juden,* Paris 1936, pp. 126–132.

[58] Wilhelm Stuckart, 'Die völkische Grundordnung des dt. Volkes', *Deutsches Recht,* 5 (1935), pp. 557ff.; Dr. Günter Vollmer, 'Die jüdischen Notare', *Deutsche Justiz,* 98 (1936), p. 28. Cf. Raul Hilberg, *The Destruction of European Jews,* New York 1979 edn., pp. 46ff.; and Pätzold, *Verfolgung, Vertreibung, Vernichtung, op. cit.,* pp. 84ff., 108ff.

declassification, the minister intimated that they might still serve as court-appointed defenders, but refused to reinstate them in general. To eliminate the 2,552 solicitors remaining on 1st January, 1936, a "scholarly" conference resolved that "in the future it shall be impossible for Jews to speak in the name of German law". The Justice Ministry compiled a list of authors whose books were to be removed from all law libraries, since "Jewish views have nothing in common with German legal scholarship". In the wake of the Nuremberg Laws, the revised Lawyer Code of December 1936 allowed the Ministry to reject the admission of "non-Aryan" attorneys without additional justification, thereby cutting off the influx of fresh "non-Aryan" professionals, defined as racially inferior.[59]

Not content with gradual attrition, *NS Rechtswahrer Bund* (NSRB) lawyers continued to demand the complete elimination of the last 1,753 legally admitted Jewish competitors in the Nazi press. In 1938 *Reich Rechtsanwaltskammer* (RRAK) president Reinhard Neubert enviously complained about "the relatively high number of Jewish lawyers with high incomes", even if "Aryan" attorneys in Berlin earned almost twice as much in 1936 (14,795 *vs* 7,963 Mk). Though the ministry resisted NSRB pressure, an exploratory discussion of April 1938 between Justice officials and lawyers' leaders reached "full agreement that Jews in the sense of the Nuremberg laws . . . are to be excluded from the legal profession as soon as possible". Licensing a limited number of "Jewish client representatives" could both support disbarred colleagues from its proceeds and provide the Jewish population with legal protection.[60] Since only 479 of the 2,153 Viennese lawyers were "Aryan", the Austrian *Anschluss* provided further impetus for disbarment and a meeting on the 4th of May settled on the term "legal consultant" for Jewish defenders. On 28th June 1938 the *Reich* Justice Ministry sent a draft exclusion law to the *Führer*'s Deputy Hess for approval, arguing that "as in the medical occupations, the final clarification of the Jewish problem in the legal profession appears ready for a solution . . .". Ten days later, Martin Bormann officially agreed. But the remaining Jewish lawyers protested this renewed injustice through Dr. Julius Fliess. Invoking the guarantee of equality of 1st October 1933, these veterans and old attorneys "opposed any regulation which . . . would limit the practice of a part of the lawyers or create distinctions in the legal position of attorneys".[61]

[59]Gürtner circular, 6th February 1935; K. and R. Eder to Gürtner, 14th and 26th March; Gürtner to OLG president Breslau, 7th April 1936, all in BA, R 22, No. 264; and Erwin Albert, *Verzeichnis jüdischer Verfasser juristischer Schriften*, Stuttgart 1937, 2nd edn. See also Göppinger, *Juristen, op. cit.*, pp. 92–93, 153–163; König, *Dienst am Recht, op. cit.*, pp. 181f.; and Heinrich, *100 Jahre Rechtsanwaltskammer, op. cit.*, pp. 134f.

[60]See the articles in *Angriff*, 11th November 1937, *Stürmer*, 4th March 1938 and the *Völkischer Beobachter*, 5th April 1938. Neubert, 'Aufstellung', 16th February, 1938, ZStA Po, Rep 30.01, No. 8518; Jonas, 'Vermerk' on negotiations of Schlegelberger with RRAK and NSRB representatives, 8th April 1938; 'Ausgangspunkte für die Versorgung der jüdischen Anwälte', 6th April 1938; and Kritzinger, 'Vermerk', 12th April 1938, BA, R 22, No. 253. Cf. Gruchmann, *Justiz, op. cit.*, pp. 174ff.

[61]Jonas, 'Vermerk', 6th May 1938; 'Vermerk', 1st June 1938; Gürtner to Frick, 28th June, and to Hess the same day; Bormann to Gürtner, 8th July 1938; Julius Fliess to Gürtner, 30th June 1938; 'Vermerk' on Jewish *Frontkämpfer*, 28th July 1938, in BA, R 22, No. 253. Cf. Gruchmann, *Justiz, op. cit.*, pp. 176ff.

Unimpressed, the Ministry continued drafting exclusionary rules that flatly asserted: "The legal profession is closed to Jews." But on the basis of the common "war experience", the ancient Field-Marshal August von Mackensen pleaded with the Ministry to stop "destroying the existence of veterans, even if they are Jewish". When the medical leadership delicensed Jewish physicians in July, NSRB spokesman Erwin Noack emphatically demanded that "we also 'cleanse' ourselves of Jews". On 28th August Franz Gürtner forwarded the final copy of the 5th decree of the *Reich* citizenship law to Hitler for his official signature.[62] Incredulous, Jewish attorneys could only ask "that the appointment of Jewish consultants be speeded up as much as possible". On 9th September, Gürtner informed the cabinet of the pending suspension of the remaining Jewish attorneys, except for 172 legal consultants whose special designation would mark them as Jews. Though Hitler signed the order on 27th September Bormann asked for a postponement of the announcement "for the duration of the present high international tension". On 15th October the *Deutsches Nachrichtenbüro* finally released the headline: "No more Jewish attorneys!" With one stroke of the pen another 10% of lawyers lost their livelihood. Exceptionally zealous, the Munich *Gestapo* arrested "about half of the Jewish attorneys", confiscated their papers and sent many to the Dachau concentration camp. When on 19th December 1938 Rudolf Hess forbade any Party or affiliate member to represent "non-Aryan" clients, the persecuted Jewish minority was left virtually without defence. Oblivious to foreign opinion, NSRB fanatics crowed: "Long hatched by the lawyers' section, the plan of the final elimination of Jewish attorneys has become a reality."[63]

Bereft of their jobs, the political and racial victims of "Germanisation" faced a terrible choice: either they could struggle on, trusting that the storm would blow over, or they could emigrate into an unknown and often unfriendly outside world. Veterans like Horst Berkowitz, who had shed their blood for the fatherland, or intellectuals like Siegfried Neumann, who felt culturally German, were especially reluctant to leave, thinking of the Nazis as a passing aberration. Some older practitioners with sufficient means, like Eugen Schiffer, could simply retire and prepare their memoirs. But professionals in the prime of life could only practise under incredible difficulties. Primarily chosen from among wounded veterans, legal consultants had to return up to 90% of their earnings over 300 Mk per month to subsidise disbarred colleagues, carry special identification and

---

[62]'Entwurf I' of the 'fünfte Verordnung zum Reichsbürgergesetz', n.d; Hueber to Gürtner, 14th July 1938; Mackensen to Gürtner, 30th July 1938; Noack to Pohle, 5th August 1938; Gürtner to Frick, 27th August 1938, BA, R 22, No. 253.

[63]Note on 'Ausscheiden der Juden aus der Rechtsanwaltschaft', 31st August 1938; 'Vermerk', 5th September 1938; Gürtner to Hess, 9th September 1938; Bormann to Gürtner, 29th September 1938; 'Keine jüdischen Rechtsanwälte mehr!', *Dt. Nachrichtenbüro*, 15th October 1938, BA, R 22, No. 254; and 'Fresh Campaign against Jews', *Sunday Times*, 16th October 1938. Cf. 'Vertretung von Juden in Rechtsangelegenheiten', *Mitteilungsblatt des NSRB*, 15th January 1939; 'Rechtsanwälte', *Deutsches Recht*, 9 (1939), p. 141; and Lorenzen, 'Eindringen der Juden', *ibid.*, pp. 956–966. Cf. Gruchmann, *Justiz, op. cit.*, pp. 178ff.

must not hire "Aryan" secretaries under the age of forty-five.[64] To make ends meet, Jewish professionals in some larger cities organised aid committees for their suffering colleagues. The more unfortunate practitioners like Robert Kempner were displaced into lesser occupations, such as running an emigration service. Carrying on in a reduced but related job could prove dangerous, since the lawyers' chambers prosecuted unauthorised legal advisers such as Ludwig Bendix. In most cases waiting for a better day meant economic privation and social isolation, since "Aryan" associates and clients all too quickly turned away. Bureaucratic chicanery and intermittent police brutality made life difficult, while few long-standing colleagues showed any solidarity. The lawyer-play-wright Siegfried Neumann quipped bitterly: "The racial question [*Rassenfrage*] has turned out to be a financial question [*Kassenfrage*]." Jewish professionals were systematically restricted to representing Jewish clients, even if such business disappeared with compulsory Aryanisation. The decreasing size of the Jewish community and the continual escalation of Nazi persecution made staying on at best a temporary solution.[65]

With fewer tangibles and intangibles to lose, younger professionals preferred to emigrate, since they were vigorous enough to build up a new existence elsewhere. "After the seizure of power, I considered it as my main task to provide legal protection for Jews", attorney Kurt Sabatzky recalled his attempt "to find holes in the tight Party and *Gestapo* net through which Jews could escape". When they could no longer bear organised contempt, the women especially urged: "We must get out, whether we want to or not. If not for our own sake, then for the children." Often flight was precipitated by threatening arrest, SA plunder, *Gestapo* beatings, or necessitated as condition of release from a concentration camp. A first wave of academics left directly after the seizure of power, because, like Alfred Apfel or Franz Neumann, they were marked as political enemies. A second group of university jurists such as Rudolf Isay or Rudolf Callmann fled after the Nuremberg Laws, resentful of the growing racial harassment and aware that their future looked bleak. A third cohort, containing such famous laywers as Max Hachenburg and Ernst Fraenkel, escaped after the *Kristallnacht* pogrom in November 1938 dispelled the last illusions about so-called legality. Even if they saved their lives, experts found emigration especially difficult, since their skills and credentials were largely untransferable. Only a few attorneys such as Heinrich Kronstein repeated their training in another system and succeeded in passing the bar examination. Versed in business affairs, other émigré lawyers

[64]Erwin Noack, 'Die Entjudung der dt. Anwaltschaft', *Juristische Wochenschrift*, 67 (1938), pp. 2796f.; 'Durchführungsbestimmungen zu Par. 5 und 14 der 5. VO zum Reichsbürgergesetz', *ibid.*, pp. 2797f.; 'Angelegenheiten der jüdischen Konsulenten', *ibid.*, pp. 2798ff.; and 'Angelegenheiten der Konsulenten', *Deutsches Recht*, 9 (1939), p. 1427. Cf. Berkowitz, *Versehrt, op. cit.*, pp. 39ff.; Göppinger, *Juristen, op. cit.*, pp. 94–97.

[65]Neumann, *Nacht, op. cit.*, pp. 84ff.; Kempner, *Ankläger, op. cit.*, pp. 119ff.; Bendix, *Von Berlin, op. cit.*, pp. 197ff.; and Göppinger, *Juristen, op. cit.*, pp. 97–111, with many heart-rending individual examples. Cf. Ernst Loewenberg, 'Mein Leben in Deutschland', in Richarz, *Jüdisches Leben in Deutschland, op. cit.*, vol. III, p. 247; and *Die Juden im Nationalsozialistischen Deutschland/The Jews in Nazi Germany 1933–1943*, herausgegeben von Arnold Paucker mit Sylvia Gilchrist und Barbara Suchy, Tübingen 1986 (Schriftenreihe wissenschaftlicher Abhandlungen des Leo Baeck Instituts 45).

flocked into para-legal jobs such as real-estate, financial advising and the like. Some of the younger attorneys drew upon their broad cultivation and became well known as historians, such as Hans Kohn, Erich Eyck or Robert Kann. Another energetic group of advocates worked in US intelligence jobs and in the military government of their former home. Finally, after the war many émigré lawyers could apply a measure of their expertise in restitution cases. In spite of the surprisingly successful adaptation, the trauma of expulsion and new beginning was severe.[66]

Far more tragic than deprivation or expulsion were incarceration and death. After the shock of the Nazi seizure of power, some leading professionals like the star defender Max Alsberg committed suicide. Many practitioners who had aroused the enmity of Nazi potentates were "beaten to death", like lawyer Dr. Max Plaut. Others who could not believe the indignities, such as the attorney Bruno Marwitz, "died from a broken heart". Those former professional leaders who died from natural causes, like Adolf Heilberg, remained publicly unlamented and unmourned so as to obliterate their contributions. Hundreds of opposition or Jewish professionals like the former editor of the *Juristische Wochenschrift* Julius Magnus were intermittently locked up in camps where many perished. More than their colleagues who were disbarred in 1933, the war veterans and long-standing professionals who continued to practise until November 1938 were caught up in the final Holocaust from 1940 on. Committed to fighting for their clients, legal consultants and community leaders like Otto Hirsch, the former Director of the *Reichsvertretung der deutschen Juden* died in the concentration camps.[67] When "Aryan" practitioners observed the disappearance of their Jewish colleagues, most excused persecution as an "unfortunate incident" or a "regrettable exception", instead of understanding it as typical of general Nazi attitudes. Even if it were possible to compile exact figures for all the ruination, expulsion, incarceration and killing, the human suffering perpetrated in the name of "Aryanisation" remains immeasurable and indescribable. As a result of the racial purge, the Nazified law profession was not only smaller, but legally insecure and intellectually impoverished.[68]

---

[66]Ronge, *Gerechtigkeit, op. cit.*, pp. 186f.; Apfel, *Behind the Scenes, op. cit.*, pp. 167f.; Hachenburg, *Lebenserinnerungen, op. cit.*, pp. 12f.; Göppinger, *Juristen, op. cit.*, pp. 265–324; and Kurt Sabatzky, 'Meine Erinnerungen an den Nationalsozialismus', in Richarz, *Jüdisches Leben, op. cit.*, vol. III, pp. 293ff. For prominent attorneys see Herbert A. Strauss (ed.), *Biographisches Handbuch der deutschsprachigen Emigration nach 1933*, Munich 1980ff. On the fate of average practitioners cf. the study by Frank Mecklenburg, 'Deutsche emigrierte Juristen in den USA', forthcoming in 1990.*

*On Great Britain see now Kurt Lipstein, 'The Contribution to Law by German-Jewish Refugees in the United Kingdom', in Werner E. Mosse *et al.* (eds.), *Second Chance. Two Centuries of German-speaking Jews in the United Kingdom*, Tübingen 1991 (Schriftenreihe wissenschaftlicher Abhandlungen des Leo Baeck Instituts 48) – (Ed.).

[67]Riess, *Mann in der schwarzen Robe, op. cit.*, pp. 331f.; Bendix, *Von Berlin, op. cit.*, pp. 187ff.; Göppinger, *Juristen, op. cit.*, pp. 230–265; and *Der gelbe Fleck, op. cit.*, pp. 254ff. The standard histories pay too little attention to this frightful toll. Cf. Ostler, 'Rechtsanwälte in der NS-Zeit', *loc. cit.*, pp. 54f. *vs.* Reifner, 'Die Zerstörung der freien Advokatur', *loc. cit.*, pp. 62ff.

[68]Reifner, 'Die Zerstörung der freien Advokatur', *loc. cit.*, pp. 389ff.; Jungfer, 'Vertreibung', *loc. cit.*, pp. 7ff. Cf. Kater, *Nazi Doctors, op. cit.*, chap. 6. Bernt Engelmann, *Germany Without Jews*, Toronto 1984, does not treat lawyers.

Half a century removed, the Jewish-German symbiosis in the legal profession seems as remarkable for its rapid rise as for its tragic break-down. By opening opportunities for the study of jurisprudence while barring bureaucratic careers, Imperial Germany's combination of formal equality and administrative preju-dice propelled Jewish law graduates into becoming attorneys. After the middle of the nineteenth century their Liberal outlook made many Protestant lawyers receptive to the influx of new colleagues of a different faith. In later decades, secularisation reduced the salience of religious distinctions from a public affair to a private matter, so that many Jewish jurists, though proud of their heritage, no longer actively practised their creed.[69] In contrast to government servants, attorneys had a special interest in protecting civil rights, since the very mission of the *freie Advokatur* as a liberal profession consisted of limiting the arbitrary exercise of power of the State. Because they were fighting both for their own emancipation and social progress in general, Jewish lawyers found their calling congenial and rapidly embraced its Liberal ethos. Unlike Catholic practitioners who demanded equal representation via a quota system, Jewish attorneys championed the abolition of all restrictions on equality and thereby became the spokesmen for ethnic minorities as well as for unpopular political viewpoints. The astonishing influx of Jews not only fuelled the extraordinary numerical growth of attorneys, but also made outstanding practical and theoretical contributions to the progressive outlook of German lawyers between 1879 and 1933. Not surprisingly, many of the leaders of the Liberal Parties, such as Eduard Lasker, were Jewish attorneys. In the rise of Jewish lawyers, the dynamics of emancipation, Liberalisation and professionalisation combined into a potent whole.[70]

Though the process of integration was never complete, the extent of the antisemitic back-lash, unleashed by Hitler's hordes, came as a grim surprise to liberal practitioners. In contrast to apologetic accounts, anti-Jewish measures were not forced upon lawyers from the outside by an all-powerful Nazi Party. Instead, the ever-escalating repression from March 1933 on was spearheaded by a minority of discontented colleagues from within, organised in the antisemitic BNSDJ.[71] The founders of the *Bund* were imbued with the corrosive social prejudices, nurtured by academic antisemitism of the 1880s in the *Vereine Deutscher Studenten* and spreading thereafter like poison throughout the student corporations and associations.[72] The professional crisis of the 1920s, marked by hyper-inflation, overcrowding and impoverishment of one-third of practitioners

[69]Hachenburg, *Lebenserinnerungen, op. cit.*, pp. 11ff.; Heilberg, 'Erinnerungen', *loc. cit.*, pp. 289ff.

[70]James F. Harris, *Eduard Lasker, 1829–1884. A Study in the Theory and Practice of German Liberalism*, Boston 1984; Konrad H. Jarausch, 'The Decline of Liberal Professionalism: Reflections on the Social Erosion of German Liberalism, 1867–1933', in *idem* and Larry E. Jones (eds.), *In Search of a Liberal Germany*, Oxford 1990, pp. 261–286. The literature of the traditional professions pays too little attention to minorities.

[71]Jürgen Borck, 'Einführung', *Anwaltsblatt*, 1989, pp. 7f. in contrast to Ostler, *Deutsche Rechtsanwälte*, pp. 229ff.

[72]Konrad H. Jarausch, *Students, Society and Politics in Imperial Germany. The Rise of Academic Illiberalism*, Princeton 1982, pp. 265ff.; and now also Kampe, *Studenten und "Judenfrage", op. cit., passim.*

to below the subsistence level, made desperate attorneys grope for neo-Conservative solutions such as a *numerus clausus* and listen to *völkisch* promises of a racial or gender purge. The inadequacy of self-help measures and of government support during the Great Depression generally eroded the faith of the majority of practitioners in the tradition of the *freie Advokatur*. In the final crisis, many threatened lawyers repudiated career integration and deserted both the Liberal Parties and the Republic.[73] But it still required the political seizure of power by the NSDAP in order to sanction the professional pogrom of the minority of antisemitic zealots by endowing it with the force of law. Not just legal disenfranchisement, but the desertion of German clients and the strangulation of Jewish business forced out the Jews among the attorneys. The post-1933 separation of Jewish and German advocates was especially painful for participants, since during the preceding two generations integration had become so close.

The consequences of the break-up of the professional symbiosis were disastrous both for Jewish and other German lawyers. Clearly, the suffering of Jewish victims was dramatic and heart-rending. For professionals, losing their licence not only meant the destruction of their livelihood, but also the annihilation of their self-esteem. While economic hardship was bad enough, expulsion from their career robbed accomplished practitioners of their purpose in life. Since profession had come to mean more than a job, namely a secular calling endowed with a higher ethical purpose, the deprivation of such self-realisation caused an enormous shock, often misunderstood. In spite of valiant resistance and Jewish self-help, forced emigration or even ultimate death seemed to many lawyers only the logical conclusion of this initial injustice.[74] Though less apparent, the negative impact on the remaining German lawyers was also calamitous. While bringing fewer material benefits than expected, collaboration with Nazi crimes eventually exacted not only an ethical but also a physical price. Hopes for the restoration of a Germanic law soon turned into illusions with the rise of the *Unrechtsstaat* of legalised injustice of SS, Party and bureaucracy.[75] Though all too few resisted openly, the more perceptive attorneys soon realised that Nazi erosion of training, manpower deficits, material and social reversals, corruption of practice, corrosion of ethics and loss of self-government led to a profound *de-professionalisation*. In trying to save their callings by abandoning their Jewish colleagues with their Liberal legacy, Nationalist professionals succeeded in destroying their careers, their families and even their country. In the final

[73]For more detail see Jarausch, *Unfree Professions, op. cit.*, pp. 78–111; and Larry E. Jones, *German Liberalism and the Dissolution of the Weimar Party System, 1918–1933*, Chapel Hill 1988.

[74]Cf. Jarausch, 'The German Professions in History and Theory', in Cocks and *idem* (eds.), *German Professions, op. cit.* The psychological dimension is underestimated by the literature of both the Holocaust and the professions.

[75]Reinhard Rürup (ed.), *Topographie des Terrors*, Berlin 1989, 7th edn.; and Bundesjustizministerium (ed.), *Justiz und Nationalsozialismus*, Cologne 1989, pp. 89ff. Cf. also Geoffrey Cocks, *Psychotherapy in the Third Reich. The Göring Institute*, New York 1985.

analysis, the Nazi inspired "restoration of racial cleanliness" destroyed justice itself.[76]

The tragic story of German-Jewish lawyers has profound implications for understanding the tangled Central European past. While taking pride and recalling sorrow, Jewish historians might want to break out of the self-isolation of debates about identity and see their history as a partial merging with and painful removal from German development.[77] At the same time, German historians ought to conceptualise their subject as a problematic coalescence of disparate fragments rather than as a paradigm of unity. Even after the unification of its remnants, the disasters of the Bismarckian state suggests dissolving the national narrative not only territorially but also ethnically, religiously and in terms of gender. The curious fate of the German-Jewish symbiosis implies that the very categories of analysis need to be re-thought. The richness and diversity of Central European experiences become apparent only when they are seen as an ensemble of overlapping and conflicting histories.[78]

[76]Lorenzen, *Juden und Justiz, op. cit.*, p. 196. Cf. also Kater, *Doctors Under Hitler, op. cit., passim*; Jarausch, 'Die unfreien Professionen. Überlegungen zu den Wandlungsprozessen im deutschen Bildungsbürgertum 1900–1950', in Jürgen Kocka (ed.), *Bürgertum im 19. Jahrhundert. Deutschland im europäischen Vergleich*, Munich 1988, vol. II, pp. 124ff.

[77]Michael Ignatieff, 'The Rise and Fall of Vienna's Jews', *New York Review of Books*, 29th June 1989, pp. 21ff. Cf. also Peter Gay, *Freud, Jews and Other Germans*, New York 1978, pp. 3ff.

[78]These reflections were stimulated by the conference on post-modern predicaments in the writing of German history at the University of Chicago, October 1989. Its papers will be published in a special issue of *Central European History*, edited by Michael Geyer and Konrad H. Jarausch.

Partners and Pariahs: Jews and Medicine in Modern German Society

BY GEOFFREY COCKS

On 2nd October 1936, a headline in an English newspaper announced: 'Hitler Needs Jewish Doctors'. The short article underneath claimed that there was such a shortage of doctors in Germany that the Nazi regime was offering an "amnesty" to émigré Jewish physicians who would return for training with the army medical corps.[1] As we shall see, this particular report and others like it in the foreign press before and during the war were surely far from accurate. Jews did continue to play a role in German medicine even after 1933, primarily of course as victims of a longstanding cultural bias raised to deadly virulence by the newer racism of the Nazis. But the place and image of Jews in German medicine even in the Third *Reich* was also determined by historical factors that had helped shape the reality of Jewish and non-Jewish doctors and patients in Germany during the late nineteenth and early twentieth centuries. Chief among these factors were the professionalisation of medicine and the evolving social dynamics of illness and health. Actual attempts by agencies in Nazi Germany to exploit Jewish medical expertise, efforts fabricated, exaggerated, and distorted abroad between 1936 and 1944, thus assume importance not as meaningful modifications of Nazi policy or of diminution of the historical significance of German antisemitism, but as part of the ongoing social history of medicine in Germany, a history in which Jews had served as partners as well as pariahs.

Almost half a century before, on 12th January 1881, pathologist and medical reformer Rudolf Virchow spoke to a gathering of Liberal politicians in Berlin on the dangers to Germany posed by the growing antisemitic movements of the day. In spite of what he saw as the gravity of the situation, Virchow closed his address on an optimistic note: "I have spoken candidly and have, I think, caused as little damage as possible, just like a doctor in examining a wound. But I believe a thorough examination is vital and will bear fruit."[2] This speech was reprinted in 1936 in the *Internationales Aerztliches Bulletin*, the journal of German Socialist

[1]'Hitler Needs Jewish Doctors', *Daily Herald*, 2nd October 1936, PC 4, reel 45, Wiener Library, London. This article is a revised version of a paper entitled 'Anti-Semitism, National Socialism, and the Medical Profession in Germany', presented on 29th December 1989 at a session of the American Historical Association Meeting in San Francisco co-sponsored by the Leo Baeck Institute. I am grateful to Fred Grubel and to Fritz Stern for their helpful comments on this essay. Research for this article was made possible by grants from the National Endowment for the Humanities, the International Research and Exchanges Board, the American Historical Association, and Albion College.
[2]'Rudolf Virchow: Gegen den Antisemitismus', *Internationales Aerztliches Bulletin*, 3 (1936) p. 16.

physicians exiled to Prague,[3] as part of that organisation's attempts to combat the Nazi regime by revealing the atrocities and absurdities of the Third *Reich*'s medical and health policies. Of course the editors of the *Aerztliches Bulletin* could not know what we know about the ultimate result of the Nazi campaign against the Jews. The Holocaust justly and inevitably throws a deep shadow across any history of the Jews in the lands of Central Europe during the last two centuries, but in so doing poses problems of teleology for historians. As Michael Ignatieff has put it: "In no field of historical study does one wish more fervently that historians could write history blind to the future."[4] This is a problem generally for historians of modern Germany, creating a view of German history, in the words of Richard Evans, "from Hitler to Bismarck".[5] While such a view is fruitful in terms of exploring certain of the continuities in German history, it also characterises the problem of teleology created by the shattering impact of the Nazi era. And finally, as Henry Friedlander has recently observed, the special need for commemoration of the victims of Nazi genocide threatens in some instances to become a substitute for rigorous historical investigation of the subject.[6]

When it comes to the subject of antisemitism and the medical profession in Germany, one finds the optimism of Virchow ultimately unfounded. An investigation into the history of antisemitism in the German medical profession from the late 1800s to 1945 does not, however, reveal a simple augmentation of undifferentiated prejudice but rather a set of complex dynamics congruent with the view of German history won by the most recent studies in the history of German society both before and after 1933. Certain crucial "peculiarities" of German history also persisted within the ranks of doctors. Thus while this history instructs us in the "illiberal" features of Liberalism (in the case of medicine the consequences of "interventionism" in social problems), it also reminds us of the effects of the special tradition of "illiberalism" in Germany. As Fritz Stern has put it in the case of antisemitism in the German officer corps: "In Germany there was no Dreyfus Affair because there was no Dreyfus."[7] Moreover, the history of antisemitism in the medical profession is not only a

[3]*Internationales Aerztliches Bulletin. Zentralorgan der Internationalen Vereinigung Sozialistischer Aerzte*, *Jahrgang I–VI (1934–1939) Reprint*, Beiträge zur Nationalsozialistichen Gesundheits- und Sozialpolitik, 7, Berlin 1989.

[4]Michael Ignatieff, 'The Rise and Fall of Vienna's Jews', *New York Review of Books*, 29th June 1989, p. 21.

[5]Richard J. Evans, 'From Hitler to Bismarck. "Third Reich" and Kaiserreich in Recent Historiography', *The Historical Journal*, 26 (1983) pp. 485–497, 999–1020.

[6]Henry Friedlander, comment, 'How to Remember. The Reichskristallnacht', German Studies Association, Milwaukee, 7th October 1989.

[7]Fritz Stern, 'The Burden of Success: Reflections on German Jewry', in *idem, Dreams and Delusions: The Drama of German History*, New York 1987, p. 108. See also George L. Mosse, *Germans and Jews. The Right, the Left, and the Search for a "Third Force" in Pre-Nazi Germany*, New York 1970, pp. 34–115. A subtext of my paper is the mutual support that older and newer modes of interpretation can provide in illuminating the history of Germany, just as, for example, Heinrich Mann's portrait of Diederich Hessling in *Der Untertan* (1918) as a national type is given new dimension by Thomas Kohut's recent psycho-historical analysis of Wilhelm II. See Kohut, 'Mirror Image of the Nation. An Investigation of Kaiser Wilhelm's Leadership of the Germans', in *The Leader*, ed. by Charles B. Strozier and Daniel Offer, New York 1985, pp. 179–229.

history of the nature, degree, and incidence of a widely held prejudice, but it is also the history of Jews and their involvement in the medical profession in Germany as doctors, patients, and fellow citizens or, after 1933, non-citizens. In turn, any account of the members of the medical profession must be placed in the context of the social history of health and illness. This is especially the case, as we shall see, with the Third *Reich*, not only because the 1930s and 1940s were decades of crucial change in the social place of medicine, health, and illness in Germany and elsewhere, but also because of both the charged absence and presence of Jews in this context as reality and as image, both Nazi and otherwise.

While antisemitism has been a consistent feature of Western Civilisation, its ferocity has ebbed and flowed. It was particularly strong in Europe between 1880 and 1945 due to a number of conditions, chief among which was the force of Nationalism and which in Germany assumed a reactionary *völkisch* cast. The change prompted the Jewish ophthalmologist Julius Hirschfeld, who was born in Potsdam in 1843, to recall from a twentieth-century vantage point his youth as a time "when antisemitism had not yet been invented".[8] Whatever discrimination Jews had faced before the late nineteenth century that revealed the cultural majoritarian bias of the emancipation effected during the Enlightenment, the first half of the new century in particular was to manifest a pervasiveness of discrimination and virulence of hatred against the Jews perhaps unparalleled in all of history. That this development was accompanied and to a significant degree accelerated by unprecedented Jewish assimilation and success in many fields, especially in Germany, is a particularly important factor to keep in mind when studying antisemitism in the professions.

To characterise this period as one of increased antisemitic prejudice is not to say that the antisemitic attitudes and policies of the Nazis were the logical, much less inevitable, outcome of this trend. Recent research has revealed the great variety of approaches to the "Jewish problem" in Germany, views falling basically into three groupings, those favouring assimilation, those advocating segregation, and those espousing expulsion. Although there is division over the question of a fundamental dichotomy between the traditional Christian bias of the majority and that of the racist minority or whether there were more complex connections across the borders of the three basic groupings, there is now widespread agreement that antisemitism in Germany was a complex phenomenon not reducible to the notion of it as a "rehearsal for destruction".[9] As Peter Gay has put it in terms of Theodor Fontane's description of German cultural attitudes toward Jews, "evidence was . . . mixed: favourable in large part,

[8]Werner Friedrich Kümmel, 'Jüdische Aerzte in Deutschland zwischen Emanzipation und "Ausschaltung"', in *Richard Koch und die ärztliche Diagnose*, ed. by Gert Preisser, Hildesheim 1988, p. 23.
[9]Uriel Tal, *Christians and Jews in Germany. Religion, Politics, and Ideology in the Second Reich, 1870–1914*, Ithaca 1975; See the paper by Donald Niewyk, 'Rehearsal for Destruction? Continuity and Change in German Anti-Semitism, 1871–1945', German Studies Association, Milwaukee, 8th October 1989; and now published in great detail as 'Solving the "Jewish Problem". Continuity and Change in German Antisemitism 1871–1945', in *LBI Year Book XXXV* (1990), pp. 335–370.

ominous in small details".[10] At the same time, however, one, of course, cannot argue that previous bias was unrelated to the versions of antisemitism displayed by Hitler and the Nazis.[11] Indeed, the very pervasiveness and variety of antisemitic attitudes among the German populace would allow for acquiescence in or indifference to, if not wholehearted support for, the antisemitic policies of the Nazis, especially since the Nazis were adept at presenting vague and flexible promises that appealed to the complaints and ambitions of a wide variety of individuals across the social and political spectrum. And the crises after 1914 served to shake up the already somewhat murky waters of German social morality, tragically depositing the sediment at the top.

Not only was antisemitism socially pervasive as well as variable in its origins and forms, it was always coupled with other concerns or discontents specific to the individual or group involved. Its occasion and virulence was also situational, as with the search for scapegoats during hard times or, as in the case of the opportunistic psychotherapists who in 1933 emphasised their alleged independence from "Jewish" psychoanalysis in the face of attacks from rival psychiatrists,[12] manipulated for protection or advantage. The professions in general were an important arena for these attitudes, since it was during the late nineteenth and twentieth centuries that professions emerged alongside class and caste as powerful elements in a modernising German society and economy. And Jews played a particularly important role in this realm, especially in the "free professions" such as law and medicine which, unlike the traditional Christian strongholds of the officer corps, the high judiciary, and the bureaucracy, were open to Jews. Like the English Dissenter and the French Protestant, the German Jew "filled the function which society abandoned to him".[13] The same principle applied to the concentration of Jews in medical specialities such as dermatology and internal medicine which grew in technical sophistication and thus in importance and came to be in increasing demand in the urban centres of Germany.[14]

Although the number of Jews entering the medical profession declined at the end of the nineteenth century and their advancement on university medical

[10]Peter Gay, *Freud, Jews and Other Germans. Masters and Victims in Modernist Culture*, New York 1978, p. 113.

[11]Otto Dov Kulka and Paul R. Mendes-Flohr (eds.), *Judaism and Christianity under the Impact of National Socialism*, Jerusalem 1987.

[12]Geoffrey Cocks, 'The Professionalization of Psychotherapy in Germany, 1928–1949', in *German Professions, 1800–1950*, ed. by Geoffrey Cocks and Konrad H. Jarausch, New York 1990, p. 314. Bias could mix with strategically expressed philosophical conviction, as in a preference for Jung over Freud: Paul Feldkeller, 'Geist der Psychotherapie', *Deutsche Allgemeine Zeitung*, 5th October 1937; or be exploited directly: "Schuld an dem Konflikt ist der Jude Strauss", Matthias Heinrich Göring to Herbert Linden, 9th November 1939; REM 2954, Zentrales Staatsarchiv, Potsdam.

[13]Herbert Lüthy, *La banque protestante en France*, Paris 1959, vol. I, p. 90; quoted in Erwin Ackerknecht, 'German Jews, English Dissenters, French Protestants: Nineteenth-Century Pioneers of Modern Medicine and Science', in *Healing and History, Essays for George Rosen*, ed. by Charles E. Rosenberg, New York 1979, p. 88.

[14]Kümmel, 'Jüdische Aerzte', *loc. cit.*, p. 20.

faculties remained hindered,[15] Jews were over-represented in medicine by a factor of ten: in 1933 Jews of Mosaic faith constituted 0.76 percent of the *Reich* population, about 10 percent of the physicians in Germany, and between 30 and 40 percent of the doctors in Berlin.[16] After the First World War, doctors faced a series of "very specific dislocations",[17] including an oversupply of medical students, the lack of state acknowledgment as a profession, and the depredations of "socialised medicine" seen by many doctors as oppressive, inefficient, politicised, and Leftist. Jews tended to be prominent in the health insurance (*Krankenkasse*) system and in Socialist politics in general due to their general commitment to social justice, their predominantly urban location, and, once again, the function of a type of *Lückentheorie* in terms of social and professional opportunity.[18] Thus Jews tended to become both specific and general targets of disaffected doctors caught in changing social, economic, and political conditions. One fateful result of all of this was the membership after 1933 of as many as 45 percent of all physicians in the Nazi Party.[19] This is one instance of what Fritz Stern has called the German Jews' "burden of success".

But the German medical profession was susceptible to the blandishments of the Nazis for other reasons as well, reasons which, if anything, were even more fateful, especially for Jewish doctors and Jews in general, in terms of the policies of the Third *Reich*. The most dangerous trend within medicine and the biological sciences in Germany and the West as a whole during this era was that of "biologism"; the certainty that human problems could be definitively solved by the application of ruthless biological principles.[20] Social Darwinism and the eugenics movement were symptoms of a way of thinking that was strengthened in Germany by the *völkisch* movement. Coupled with the growing sophistication, influence, and power of the scientific professions and the tendency of doctors in particular to engage in "the generalization of expertise",[21] this trend aggravated the tendency of professionalism to exalt expertise at the expense of ethics. This,

---

[15]Michael H. Kater, 'Professionalization and Socialization of Physicians in Wilhelmine and Weimar Germany', *Journal of Contemporary History*, 20 (1985), p. 689; David L. Preston, 'The German Jews in Secular Education, University Teaching, and Science. A Preliminary Inquiry', *Jewish Social Studies*, 38 (1976) pp. 110–111, 114–116.

[16]Michael H. Kater, 'Hitler's Early Doctors. Nazi Physicians in Predepression Germany', *Journal of Modern History*, 59 (1987), p. 35, note 35; Karl A. Schleunes, *The Twisted Road to Auschwitz. Nazi Policy Toward German Jews 1933–1939*, Urbana 1970, p. 41. Nazi racial definitions raised the percentage of Jewish physicians in Berlin to around 60 percent: see, 'Die Juden in der Berliner Aerzteschaft', *Deutsches Aerzteblatt*, 66 (1936), p. 1046.

[17]Michael H. Kater, 'The Nazi Physicians League of 1929. Causes and Consequences', in *The Formation of the Nazi Constituency 1919–1933*, ed. by Thomas Childers, London 1986, p. 147.

[18]Donald W. Light, Stephan Leibfried, and Florian Tennstedt, 'Social Medicine vs Professional Dominance. The German Experience', *American Journal of Public Health*, 76 (1986), p. 79; Robert W. Proctor, *Racial Hygiene. Medicine Under the Nazis*, Cambridge, Mass. 1988, pp. 251–281; Doron Niederland, 'The Emigration of Jewish Academics and Professionals from Germany in the First Years of Nazi Rule', in *LBI Year Book XXXIII* (1988), pp. 294–295.

[19]Kater, 'Hitler's Early Doctors', *loc. cit.*, p. 36, note 35.

[20]Proctor, *Racial Hygiene, op. cit.*, pp. 213, 286, 293, 297, 306; Stephen Jay Gould, *The Mismeasure of Man*, New York 1981.

[21]Robert M. Veatch, 'Scientific Expertise and Value Judgments. The Generalization of Expertise', *Hastings Center Studies*, I, No. 2 (1973), pp. 29–40.

according to Rainer Baum, is "the nature of modern sin, the withdrawal of moral concerns from public roles in our lives".[22] Moreover, there was a long tradition in Europe of associating Jews, in particular, with both healing and illness.[23] Psychiatry was especially prone to the vague categorisations that cultivated prejudice,[24] although it resembled medicine in general in its emphasis on the relatively "quick fix" of individual treatment instead of the more complex gradualism of social reform. With the "medicalisation" of society in the late nineteenth century, doctors became "a social group under the greatest possible pressure to emphasize the useful".[25] This technical orientation towards the problems and responsibilities of the individual was attractive to political forces of both Left and Right committed to crash programmes in the spirit of the "culture of impatience".[26] Finally, as Susan Sontag has argued, during the nineteenth century disease became a powerful metaphor for the "unnatural",[27] which in the twentieth century combined with racial antisemitism to produce an especially noxious pattern of thought and action. One has only to look at the disease imagery that oozes over the pages of *Mein Kampf* to appreciate the danger inherent in this turn.

We do not yet have detailed studies of the relative incidence of antisemitism within the various branches of medicine or of the relevant mixes of religious, regional, generational, or social and economic backgrounds among doctors. We also do not know with precision the differences in attitudes between city and countryside. While collaboration and competition with the many Jewish medical practitioners in the large cities, especially Berlin, could, in general, lead either to resentment or admiration, rural provincialism and ethnocentrism were probably aggravated as the spread of the transportation and media networks in Germany generated impressions, even in advance of the propaganda of the Nazis, of urban life as corrupt, debilitating, and embodied in the figure of the Jew.[28] Case studies will go some way towards filling this gap, since antisemitism varied within a shared cultural context in nature, degree, and function from individual to individual, as, for example, Peter Loewenberg has shown in his psycho-historical analysis of Heinrich Himmler.[29]

What a majority of German physicians displayed at the advent of the Third *Reich*, however, was ambition, a fear of de-professionalisation as a result of the economic and political woes of Weimar, and a specifically strong German

[22]Rainer C. Baum, *The Holocaust and the German Elite*, Totowa, N.J. 1981, p. 266; quoted in Peter Hayes, *Industry and Ideology. IG Farben in the Nazi Era*, Cambridge 1987, p. 382.

[23]Sander L. Gilman, 'Jews and Mental Illness. Medical Metaphors, Anti-Semitism, and the Jewish Response', *Journal of the History of the Behavioral Sciences*, 20 (1984), p. 150.

[24]Jan Goldstein, 'The Wandering Jew and the Problem of Psychiatric Anti-Semitism in Fin-de-Siècle France', *Journal of Contemporary History*, 20 (1985), pp. 521–552.

[25]Sherry Turkle, *Psychoanalytic Politics. Freud's French Revolution*, New York 1978, p. 49.

[26]Susan Gross Solomon, 'David and Goliath in Soviet Public Public Health. The Rivalry of Social Hygienists and Psychiatrists for Authority over the *Bytovoi* Alcoholic', *Soviet Studies*, 41 (1989), p. 269.

[27]Susan Sontag, *Illness as Metaphor*, New York 1978, p. 74.

[28]*Ibid.*, p. 76.

[29]Peter Loewenberg, 'The Unsuccessful Adolescence of Heinrich Himmler', in *idem, Decoding the Past. The Psychohistorical Approach*, New York 1983, pp. 209–239.

tradition of illiberalism. This last element, combined with the powerful force of a German Nationalism characterised by a bellicosity born of particularist doubt and geopolitical anxiety, had for a long time torn at the liberal qualities associated with professional culture and had produced the "unpolitical" disdain for representative government[30] that accompanied their very real political activity on the level of their own professional interests. These motives played an important role in the activities of doctors under National Socialism, since, as recent research has shown, *Gleichschaltung* was very often a process of "self-Nazification" pursuant to advantage or protection within a polycentric power system.[31] Thus antisemitism was one element among many determining the attitudes and actions of physicians in Nazi Germany. It was an important element, however, since there is evidence to suggest that denunciations of Jews, while common throughout the social spectrum,[32] were most common among the members of the new middle classes and especially those groups of ambitious people with much to lose and much to gain.[33]

Since the record of doctors in abandoning and persecuting their Jewish colleagues and patients is a well known and dismal one and the involvement of doctors in the euthanasia programme and the Final Solution has become increasingly well understood, it is my purpose here to concentrate on a specific issue in an area of life in the Third *Reich* where factors other than murderous intent played important roles. Although this subject matter is minor when compared with the role of doctors in tolerating and effecting the Nazi policy of genocide against the Jews, it is not simply a matter of recording exceptions and anomalies, such as the odd case of risky patient loyalty to a Jewish physician[34] or IG Farben's use of the name of a famous Jewish medical researcher, Paul Ehrlich, in its advertising abroad.[35] Rather my concern is with what may have been attempts on the part of a number of agencies between 1936 and 1944 to employ Jewish physicians, both full Jews and so-called *Mischlinge*, to treat German soldiers and civilians and the possible part such a policy might have played in the shaping of both the image and reality of the Jewish physician in the context of the larger social history of health and illness in Nazi Germany.

Although by September 1938 all doctors who were full Jews or Mosaic half-Jews had been taken off the register, the army in particular continued to worry about the shortage of physicians in the event of war. As we have seen, there was at least one foreign report of this as early as 1936. Just after the outbreak of the war the *Manchester Guardian* reported that Jewish doctors had already been

[30]Fritz Stern, 'The Political Consequences of the Unpolitical German', in *idem*, *The Failure of Illiberalism*, London 1972, pp. 3–25.

[31]Konrad H. Jarausch, 'The Crisis of German Professions 1918–33', *Journal of Contemporary History*, 20 (1985), p. 394.

[32]Robert Gellately, 'The Gestapo and German Society. Political Denunciation in the Gestapo Case Files', *Journal of Modern History*, 60 (1988), p. 686.

[33]Martin Broszat, 'Politische Denunziationen in der NS-Zeit', *Archivalische Zeitschrift*, 73 (1977), p. 225.

[34]*Deutschland-Berichte der Sozialdemokratischen Partei Deutschlands (Sopade)*, Salzhausen 1980, 6 (1939), pp. 926–927.

[35]'Geschäftsgeist in Nazi-Deutschland', *Internationales Aerztliches Bulletin*, 5 (1938), p. 20.

drafted into the German army and that the appeal for Jewish doctors, in particular specialists, to return had been renewed.[36] While these particular reports may reflect a distorting concern over the pre-war influx of Jewish physicians into Great Britain,[37] there is documentary evidence from at least one German source for the *Wehrmacht*'s worries. According to surgeon Siegfried Ostrowski, who worked until 1939 at the Jewish Hospital in Berlin, around the time of the Munich crisis in 1938 army medical officials were discussing the return of Jewish physicians to civilian duty to replace doctors called up for military service and, if necessary, even the drafting of Jewish doctors into the army.[38]

It is not far-fetched to give some credence, therefore, to renewed reports from abroad in 1942 that the German military again was wrestling with the worsening consequences of a shortage of medical specialists among whom Jews had been numerous.[39] It was also reported that an ill-defined demand by the Army Chief of Medical Personnel to *Reichsgesundheitsführer* Leonardo Conti for the "release and deployment" of Jewish doctors was effected by Conti for civilian hospitals,[40] although it is not at all clear who was to be released from where. In 1944 the United States Office of Strategic Services reported that "Jewish nurses and doctors . . . have been accepted by official health organizations"[41] and Conti himself was apparently the source for the self-serving post-war claim in the United States Strategic Bombing Survey report on German war-time medical services that "by 1943 all physicians of 50 per cent Jewish ancestry were reinstated to full medical practice, and in the summer of 1944 when the air raid casualties increased in alarming proportions all physicians of 100 per cent Jewish ancestry were reinstated to full medical practice".[42]

Even though Conti had a long record of vehement antisemitism,[43] in his career he also occasionally displayed a frame of mind that marked him off from some of the more volatile of his Nazi brethren. We do not know what Conti thought of the Final Solution (he committed suicide at Nuremberg) and the pressures of the war in his realm might have compelled him to seek some sort of systematic employment of Jewish physicians. In any case, as Michael Kater has suggested, these policies could have issued in mid-1942 from Hitler's new plenipotentiary

[36]'Jewish Doctors Now Wanted', *The Manchester Guardian*, 15th September 1939, PC 5, reel 106, Wiener Library.

[37]Andrew Sharf, *The British Press and Jews under Nazi Rule*, London 1964, pp. 161, 168–169.

[38]Siegfried Ostrowski, 'Vom Schicksal Jüdischer Ärzte im Dritten Reich. Ein Augenzeugenbericht aus den Jahren 1933–1939', in *Bulletin des Leo Baeck Instituts*, Nr. 24 (1963), pp. 335–336.

[39]'German Medical Services. Army's Difficulties', *The Manchester Guardian*, 12th January 1942, PC 5, reel 106, Wiener Library; Proctor, *Racial Hygiene, op. cit.*, pp. 154, 156.

[40]'Dr. Conti – Reichs-Totengräber', *Die Zeitung*, 20th February 1942, PC 5, reel 106, Wiener Library.

[41]United States Office of Strategic Services, Research and Analysis Branch, *Notes on Air-Raid Damage and Health in Germany*, R & A No. 1801, 10th March 1944, p. 2, Hoover Library, Stanford University.

[42]United States Strategic Bombing Survey, Morale Division, *The Effect of Bombing on Health and Medical Care in Germany*, 2nd edn., January 1947, p. 162a, Hoover Library.

[43]Michael H. Kater, 'Doctor Leonardo Conti and His Nemesis. The Failure of Centralized Medicine in the Third Reich', *Central European History*, 18 (1985), pp. 302–303.

for health, Karl Brandt.[44] Although such actions would not have had to have been based on legal exceptions to the 1938 decree expanding the *Reich* Citizenship Law to prohibit the practice of medicine by Jews on non-Jews,[45] it is the case that decrees in 1939, 1940, and 1941 implementing and amending the *Reichsärzteordnung* of 1935 allowed for the possibility of exceptions that *could* have been used to readmit Jews, at least Mosaic half-Jews, to practise on non-Jews.[46] Some *Mischling* doctors of the second degree had already been drafted into the army.[47]

But is it likely that full Jews were readmitted to practice, as Conti claimed? It seems extremely unlikely, although, according to Raul Hilberg, in some cities in Hungary in 1944 Jewish doctors were exempt from deportation because of domestic need and foreign pressure.[48] In Germany Jewish doctors, designated as *Krankenbehandler*, and nurses who treated Jews were protected only until August of 1942.[49] Thus Conti's claim for 1944 could only have involved full Jews in mixed marriages since all other full Jews had already been deported. Although in the occupied territories the army regularly fought with the SS over Jewish workers,[50] by 1944 the SS was ruthlessly exploiting Jewish medical labour in the camps and so, for practical as well as ideological reasons, would have not been willing to part with them. Only when the camps were abandoned with the German retreat did some Jewish doctors end up in Germany treating slave labourers.[51] In any case, it is likely that Hitler would have stopped any such programme cold.[52] We know only of the occasional accidental exceptions: Christopher Browning has told of a Jewish doctor deported to Poland from Stettin in 1940, who worked throughout the war as a physician and who after 1942 would only have been treating Germans or Poles.[53]

---

[44]Michael H. Kater, *Doctors Under Hitler*, Chapel Hill 1989, p. 205.

[45]*Reichsgesetzblatt*, 2nd August 1938, pp. 969–970. According to Article 2, the Interior Minister was empowered to restore the right to practise upon recommendation of the *Reichsärztekammer*. It is not clear that this could have been used to allow practice by Jews on non-Jews. At any rate, there is at the least some degree of potential ambiguity throughout the legislation regarding the possibility of the future practice of medicine by Jews, an ambiguity not in evidence, by contrast, in the legislation excluding Jews from the practice of law. Article 1 of that decree is a model of ruthless clarity: "Juden ist der Beruf des Rechtsanwaltes verschlossen." *Reichsgesetzblatt*, 14th October 1938, p. 1403. It seems arguable that especially with the outbreak of the war the Nazis had a much greater need for Jewish doctors than for Jewish lawyers.

[46]*Reichsärzteordnung*, Berlin 1943, pp. 107, 139, 149.

[47]Kater, *Doctors Under Hitler*, op. cit., p. 205.

[48]Raul Hilberg, *The Destruction of the European Jews*, rev. edn., New York 1985, vol. III, pp. 834, 850. There are also reports of Jewish doctors being spared by *Einsatzgruppen* in the East, presumably for service in the ghettos and camps. Richard Breitman, personal communication, 29th December 1989.

[49]Mrs. A., 'Jewish Hospital Berlin', File 02/29, Yad Vashem Archives, Jerusalem.

[50]Henry Friedlander, personal communication, 10th May 1989.

[51]Gisella Perl, *I Was a Doctor in Auschwitz*, New York 1948, pp. 152–153.

[52]David Bankier, 'Hitler and the Policy-Making Process on the Jewish Question', *Holocaust and Genocide Studies*, 3 (1983), pp. 1–20.

[53]Christopher Browning, personal communication, 31st May 1989. Jewish doctors were also active on behalf of the resistance to Nazism; see, for example, the account of a Jewish physician treating partisans in Russia in Nechama Tec, *In the Lion's Den. The Life of Oswald Rufeisen*, New York 1990, pp. 190–191.

Official exceptions were made by Conti for *Mischlinge*.[54] And beginning in 1941 the Ministry of the Interior and the *Wehrmacht* asked regional medical officers to include Jewish physicians in their annual survey of medical personnel,[55] while as early as 1941 the *Reich* Education Ministry was scouring university clinics for doctors who could serve the civilian population at large in an emergency capacity. The need was so great, the Ministry averred, that even "jüdische Mischlinge" and "jüdisch versippte" physicians (related by marriage) were needed for emergency service.[56] Although the university archive consulted reveals none of the results of this query,[57] we do know that the Nazi regime was faced with a desperate shortage of doctors, especially on the home front. This was of course a problem that only worsened as the war intensified both at the front and over the cities of Germany. The basically misogynist Nazi regime was even compelled to allow women to become doctors in order to replace the Jews who had been forced out of the profession and the "Aryan" doctors who had been drafted into the military. When, for example, in 1944 the *Gestapo* was rounding up conspirators in the wake of the 20th of July attempt on Hitler's life, three of the four von Bredow girls were arrested, but not Marguerite, who was a doctor in a hospital.[58] And when Horst Eberhard Richter, now a psycho-analyst in Germany, landed in a Berlin military hospital in late 1942 after contracting post-diptherial polyneuritis on the Eastern front, he was attended by a young half-Jewish physician.[59]

Even had this practice been more extensive than it apparently was, it would have little historical meaning in terms of overall Nazi racial policy. It is not as policy that this phenomenon is potentially important, but as part of a broader social history of illness in the Third *Reich*. Doctors in Germany found themselves in the middle of significant social change, being courted and challenged both from above and below. During the Third *Reich* "Aryan" physicians confronted both the promise of professionalisation, as embodied in the 1935 decree recognising medicine as a profession rather than as a trade, but also the concomitant "de-professionalisation" resulting from the imposition of political

---

[54]H. G. Adler, *Der verwaltete Mensch. Studien zur Deportation der Juden aus Deutschland*, Tübingen 1974, p. 302. The Nazi policy and legislation affecting "Mischlinge" has been dealt with recently in depth by Jeremy Noakes in his 'The Development of Nazi Policy towards the German-Jewish "Mischlinge" 1933–1945', in *LBI Year Book XXXIV* (1989), pp. 291–354.

[55]Reichsminister des Innern to Regierungspräsident Frankfurt a.d. Oder, 23rd August 1941, p. 3, Pr. Br. Rep. 3 B Nr. 178, Staatsarchiv Potsdam. It was due to the shortage of doctors that in 1942 Conti opposed the plan of the Interior Ministry's Stuckart to sterilise all first degree *Mischlinge*. See Uwe Dietrich Adam, *Judenpolitik im Dritten Reich*, Düsseldorf 1979, p. 323, note 100. Conti's motive here was to prevent already overworked doctors from being burdened with sterilisations, but he also *might* have had in mind the deleterious effects on the future supply of doctors of the flight underground of half-Jewish physicians escaping sterilisation.

[56]Kölnische Gesellschaft für Christlich-Jüdische Zusammenarbeit, *Heilen und Vernichten im National-sozialismus*, Cologne 1985, p. 126. This particular request would seem to exclude full Jewish doctors in mixed marriages.

[57]UA 9/684, Universitätsarchiv der Universität zu Köln.

[58]Marie Vassiltchikov, *Berlin Diaries 1940–1945*, New York 1987, p. 224.

[59]Horst-Eberhard Richter, *Die Chance des Gewissens. Erinnerungen und Assoziationen*, Hamburg 1987, p. 37.

control, the deterioration of educational standards, and the perversion of professional ethics.[60] At the same time, the modern trend towards physician monopoly of health care and dominance over the patient was both advanced and challenged from below in Germany between 1933 and 1945, especially as a result of war-time exigencies. The increasing importance of doctors was most evident in the demand for prescription drugs, a demand that as early as 1936 was described by an alarmed city medical director from Oberhausen as an "Arzneihunger".[61] The regime sought to encourage prescriptions to heighten productivity, especially of those stimulants one pharmacologist rather boldly labelled "the chemical whip".[62] On the other hand, by 1941 the SS Security Service was complaining about the deleterious effects of the flood of advertising ("Reklame-flut") issuing from the drug companies.[63] But the use of the large number of drugs coming onto the market for the first time in the 1930s tended as well to decentralise medical care by often reducing increasingly overworked doctors to conduits for prescriptions. The difficult living conditions brought on by the war, the increasing political surveillance of doctors and patients, and the shortages of both doctors and drugs only encouraged the treatment or endurance of illnesses without recourse to a physician.

This pattern of behaviour was especially common under a war-time regime characterised by a mix of coercion and chaos. People, within the limits imposed by the nature of their situation and their government, were often left to their own devices in dealing with the difficulties of life under National Socialism. Recent research has suggested that the Nazis failed to create the type of solidarity displayed by their propaganda, but that the propaganda itself permeated the society, "remaining as an insistent background noise to daily life".[64] The result was an exercise in what the sociologist de Certeau has called "antidiscipline" or "subversion". This was not a process of conscious political choice but rather the active transformation of the conditions of life by means of the "polytheism of scattered practices"[65] against the imposition of systems by the powerful. And while patriotic support for Hitler and the regime remained strong throughout German society, such personal preservative "strategies" add a further dimension to the recent delineation by Martin Broszat of the ascending categories of popular *Opposition, Resistenz*, and *Widerstand* to the Nazi dictatorship and are, as de Certeau himself argues, particularly relevant in the more general social realm

---

[60]Konrad H. Jarausch, 'The Perils of Professionalism. Lawyers, Teachers, and Engineers in Nazi Germany', *German Studies Review*, 9 (1986), pp. 107–137.

[61]"Auszug aus der Niederschrift über die 7. Sitzung der Rheinischen Arbeitsgemeinschaft für Wohlfahrtspflege am 4. Juli 1936 im Kreissparkassengebäude zu St. Goar", RW 53/455, Nordrhein-Westfälisches Hauptstaatsarchiv, Düsseldorf.

[62]F. Eichholtz, 'Ermüdungsbekämpfung. Ueber Stimulantien', *Deutsche medizinische Wochenschrift*, 67 (1941): 56.

[63]'Meldungen aus dem Reich', 20th February 1941, microcopy T-175, reel 260, frame 3286, National Archives, Washington, D.C. The entire series has been published as: *Meldungen aus dem Reich*, ed. by Heinz Boberach, Herrsching 1984.

[64]Jane Caplan, *Government Without Administration. State and Civil Service in Weimar and Nazi Germany*, Oxford 1988, p. 190.

[65]Michel de Certeau, *The Practice of Everyday Life*, transl. by Steven Rendall, Berkeley 1984, p. 47.

of health and illness where professionalised medicine intruded more deeply and regularly into people's lives than other professions, thus occasioning greater popular reaction. For example, the more the Nazis required doctors' attestations for work absences and supplemental rations, the more people made use of such documents.[66] A somewhat atypical yet illustrative instance of this type of "coping" was Heinrich Böll's regular exploitation, with the help of the family doctor, of a sinus infection to avoid onerous Nazi youth group activities.[67] While it would be easy to overstate the effects of these actions, they also cannot be ignored, especially in our age of popular political assertion.

What role did Jewish doctors play in this history? At present the answer to this question consists almost entirely of further questions. How did Germans react to Jewish doctors? How did Jewish physicians balance personal survival, hatred for the regime and its soldiers and citizens, and observance of the Hippocratic oath? Were restrictions imposed, such as a ban on the recruitment of women or treatment of the opposite sex? And, especially in the case of *Mischlinge*, to what extent would patients have been officially or perceptually aware of the "racial" difference?

Since the presence of Jews after 1938 was in any case limited, it also makes sense to speak more generally of the presence of an absence. This was particularly the case in terms of the shortages of qualified doctors, especially those left over for the civilian population. Doctors tended to be towards the old and exhausted or, especially in the hospitals, the young and inexperienced, prompting a scramble by factories and agencies to secure their own doctors and drug supplies.[68] Despite widespread antisemitism aggravated by Nazi propaganda, individual Jewish doctors certainly must have been missed by patients and colleagues, especially since Jewish physicians remained an important part of German life even between 1933 and 1938. In the case of specialists the loss of Jewish practitioners often simply could not be borne: even Nazi leaders relied on them.[69] Just as importantly, members of the lower classes of society, to whatever degree they thought of it in these terms, suffered from the absence of the many Jewish doctors who staffed the clinics run by the state health insurance system, a system that the Nazis purged of its most dedicated functionaries, plundered to pay for rearmament, and restructured to "encourage" people to stay well and on the job. An extreme example of the price paid for Nazi policy came from the SS Security Service itself. On 4th August 1941 it reported that in Banat, the German enclave in the Balkans, a possible health catastrophe loomed because, unlike the

---

[66]Amt für Volksgesundheit to Ärztekammer Cologne, 22nd August 1944, Reg. Aachen 21308, Nordrhein-Westfälisches Hauptstaatsarchiv; 'Doctors Warned', *Daily Herald*, 29th March 1940, PC 5, reel 106, Wiener Library.

[67]Heinrich Böll, *What's To Become of the Boy? Or: Something to Do with Books*, transl. by Leila Vennewitz, New York 1984, pp. 39, 44–45, 68.

[68]"VO z. Sicherstellung der ärztlichen Versorgung der Zivilbevölkerung" [draft], 1942, R 18/5576, Bundesarchiv, Koblenz; Reich Interior Ministry to Reich War Ministry, 22nd July 1942, Reg. Düsseldorf 54364III, Nordrhein-Westfälisches Hauptstaatsarchiv.

[69]Such as the Nazi Mayor of Stuttgart; Eric Kohler, personal communication, 9th June 1989.

Jewish doctors who had treated the uninsured poor for free, non-Jewish doctors demanded payment.[70]

The image of the Jewish doctor in the minds of Germans during the Third *Reich* is even more difficult to assess. Resentment against Jewish doctors could have been strengthened by the growing dissatisfaction over the impersonality of "modern" medicine, a trend that accelerated after the war in all the nations of the West.[71] At the same time, it was of course non-Jewish doctors who became the focus for popular discontent in Germany after 1933, which might have undercut traditional and Nazi-inspired stereotypes about Jewish doctors. And while people grumbled about medical treatment, they continued to flock to physicians so that badly needed treatment by a Jewish doctor might well have created trust in any number of individual instances. The war, however, most probably brought with it an intensification of the Nazi image of "the Jew" as a source of contagion from the East. This image built upon earlier prejudices against the *Ostjuden* who had come in large numbers to Central Europe during the nineteenth century.[72] The perceived threat to an increasingly bourgeois society preoccupied with high standards of personal hygiene was revived by the growing danger of the incidence and spread of diseases like typhus brought in from the East by war prisoners, slave labourers, and German soldiers.[73] Unlike the First World War, epidemics did not occur. But this fear, added to the other difficulties brought on by the war, rather than creating a sense of shared – though incomparable – suffering, probably tended to harden people's attitudes towards outsiders in general. And the particular association between Jews and disease promoted by Nazi film and print would have been strengthened by any knowledge or rumour of the increasingly high incidence of disease actually visited upon the Jews by the Nazis in the ghettos and camps.[74]

Even before the war the Nazis had created a general anxiety in the populace about the social consequences of ill health and especially about hereditary illness. The law designed to prevent the reproduction of so-called "degenerates" spawned what the *Reich* Interior Minister called "an almost psychotic fear"[75]

[70]'Meldungen aus dem Reich', reel 261, frame 4481.

[71]Edward Shorter, *Bedside Manners. The Troubled History of Doctors and Patients*, New York 1985.

[72]Jack Wertheimer, *Unwelcome Strangers. East European Jews in Imperial Germany*, New York 1987. Jews from the East were widely viewed as a source of uncleanliness and disease: see *idem*, ' "The Unwanted Element" – East European Jews in Imperial Germany', in *LBI Year Book XXVI* (1981), p. 26. Jewish organisations, however, established medical facilities for the immigrants: Trude Maurer, *Ostjuden in Deutschland 1918–1933*, Hamburg 1986, pp. 542–543. See also Wertheimer, 'The "Ausländerfrage" at Institutions of Higher Learning – A Controversy over Russian-Jewish Students in Imperial Germany', in *LBI Year Book XXVII* (1982), pp. 187–218, and also his essay in *LBI Year Book XXVIII* (1983); and S. Adler-Rudel, *Ostjuden in Deutschland 1880–1940*, Tübingen 1959. (Schriftenreihe wissenschaftlicher Abhandlungen des Leo Baeck Instituts 1).

[73]Lohner to Conti, 4th March 1943, microcopy T–315, reel 17, frames 128–131, National Archives; Hauptarzt WBK, 3rd September 1942, NSDAP Kreisleitung Eisenach, Folder 00014a, Myers Collection, University of Michigan; Deutscher Gemeindetag Berlin to Deutscher Gemeindetag Düsseldorf, 1st September 1942, RW 53/466, Nordrhein-Westfälisches Hauptstaatsarchiv.

[74]Leonardo Conti, 'Stand der Volksgesundheit im 5. Kriegsjahr', (1944), p. 6, Reg. Aachen 16486, Nordrhein-Westfälisches Hauptstaatsarchiv. Films like *Der ewige Jude* in fact utilised footage from the ghettos to emphasise to the German public the "unhygienic" habits of Jews.

[75]R 18/5585, Bundesarchiv.

among the people, a fear heightened by the war-time programme to kill off mental patients.[76] The war of course sharpened concerns about physical and mental well-being, feelings made more brittle not only by Nazis claims for the vigour of the "Master Race," but also by ongoing health problems, often aggravated by Nazi youth group activities, traceable to the First World War, the inflation of 1923, and the Depression.[77] And while some Nazi officials argued that employment of severely wounded soldiers would be an inspiring example of heroism, some army medical officers worried that such a policy would have a depressing effect on the populace.[78] Damage to the "secret narcissistic illusion of intactness"[79] occasioned by injury or illness often leads to feelings of rage against the outside world. It is possible that this reaction was generalised among Germans and that it helped increase animosity against the image of Jews and Jewish doctors. In any case, the ferocity of the fighting in the East and its hastening approach towards the homeland would (*pace* Hillgruber's notion of a "heroic" struggle) have increased the general xenophobia of the population. The *Wehrmacht* itself had from the beginning fought a different war in the East than it did in the West. Whereas Jewish prisoners of war in the West generally "enjoyed relative immunity",[80] in the East (where the rules of the Geneva Convention were not observed) the army co-operated with the SS by identifying and handing over Jewish POWs.[81]

Although professional and occupational groups could serve as sanctuaries for Jewish members, as was the case with bureaucrats in the *Reich* Interior Ministry,[82] the medical profession proved to be no safe haven for Jews. The bulk of German physicians turned against or away from their Jewish colleagues (and patients) out of ambition, prejudice, and fear, while many of them served prominently in the Nazis' war against the Jews of Europe. German Jews likewise found little effective help among the populace as a whole after 1933. The Germans by and large responded to the persecution of Jews with favour, indifference, or at best resignation. The image of the Jewish doctor in particular remained coloured in the minds of many Germans by ancient associations with

[76]Christa Wolf, *Patterns of Childhood*, transl. Ursule Molinaro and Hedwig Rappolt, New York 1980, pp. 149, 195–198.

[77]Wehrwirtschafts-Inspektion VII (Munich), 1937, microcopy T–77, roll 248, frames 824–828, National Archives; Gesundheitsamt Düsseldorf, 'Jahresgesundheitsbericht', 28th February 1933, Reg. Düsseldorf 54708, Nordrhein-Westfälisches Hauptstaatsarchiv; Peter Loewenberg, 'The Psychohistorical Origins of the Nazi Youth Cohort', in *Decoding the Past, op. cit.*, pp. 240–283.

[78]Dr. Wolff, 'Die Betreuung unserer Schwerverletzten', *Deutsches Aerzteblatt* 47/48 (1941), microcopy T-78, roll 191, frames 677–682; Kommandeur, Sanitäts-Abteilung Chemnitz, 'Arbeitsbehandlung in den Res. Lazaretten', 6th March 1943, *ibid.*, roll 189, frame 1409, National Archives.

[79]Richter, *Chance des Gewissens, op. cit.*, p. 37.

[80]Hilberg, *Destruction, op. cit.*, vol. II, p. 627; David A. Foy, *For You the War Is Over. American Prisoners of War in Nazi Germany*, New York 1984, pp. 128–131. And see now also Yoav Gelber, 'Central European Jews from Palestine in the British Forces', in *LBI Year Book XXXV* (1990), pp. 327–328.

[81]Omer Bartov, *The Eastern Front, 1941–45. German Troops and the Barbarisation of Warfare*, New York, 1986, p. 109; Christian Streit, 'The German Army and the Policies of Genocide', in *The Policies of Genocide. Jews and Soviet Prisoners of War in Nazi Germany*, ed. by Gerhard Hirschfeld, London 1986, pp. 1–14.

[82]Adam, *Judenpolitik, op. cit.*, pp. 342–343.

mystery and disease. And this image was intensified by Nazi propaganda and the real and imagined threats to physical well-being occasioned by the war. Any deployment of Jewish physicians would by and large have served to mitigate this prejudice, but the extent of such contact between Jewish doctors and "Aryan" patients is still uncertain.

Yet the matter of German antisemitism since 1945, including such phenomena as the "inability to mourn",[83] would seem to be complex since instances or absences of it were probably in many cases related to specific experiences within the social contexts created by Nazism. We simply need to know more about what happened in the realms of illness and health between 1933 and 1945 and the resultant effects on attitudes towards Jews. Antisemitism remained a significant force in Germany during the post-war period. In 1952 polling in West Germany found that 37 percent of the population felt that it was better to have no Jews in the country.[84] Although antisemitism has declined in the West with the passing of generations, new targets of prejudice and discrimination, such as the large Turkish community in West Germany, have emerged. And among professionals in West Germany, doctors and lawyers counted the largest minorities still expressing antisemitic views.[85] This fact is especially troubling given the ever greater prestige, power, and technical capacity, even if compromised by institutional constraints and popular reaction, possessed by doctors in particular. The recent *Bundesärztekammer* projections for the 1990s of 40–50,000 unemployed doctors are therefore particularly unsettling, because West German doctors enjoyed prosperity between 1945 and 1990 and because economic hard times were a major factor in doctors' anti-democratic and racist radicalisation before 1933.

---

[83]Alexander and Margarete Mitscherlich, *The Inability to Mourn. Principles of Collective Behavior*, transl. by Beverley R. Placzek, New York 1975.

[84]Axel Schildt, 'Popular Political Consciousness in Germany (after 1945)', paper presented at the University of Michigan, 27th October 1989.

[85]Frederick Weil, 'The Imperfectly Mastered Past. Anti-Semitism in West Germany Since the Holocaust', *New German Critique*, 20 (1980), p. 143.

Academics in Germany: German and Jew
Some Preliminary Remarks

BY FRITZ K. RINGER

The university professors were of course a particularly influential group in nineteenth- and early twentieth-century Germany. In the Anglo-American context, one can see professionalisation as the strategy of a private association to control the qualifications for membership in it and thus also to protect the market for its specialised competence. For France, Germany, and other Continental European countries, one has to give more attention to the role of the state in setting professional standards. In either case, however, professionalisation has been inseparably linked to the development of higher education. The universities have not only created, systematised and transmitted specialised knowledge; they have also controlled access to a growing range of professions and social positions by means of elaborate systems of academic qualifications. The imposition of academic standards has been justified by an emphasis upon "merit" and "achievement" that is one of the forms of modern middle-class ideology. As the current interest in the professions and in professionalisation deepens, the role of higher education as an autonomous source of middle-class self-definitions and outlooks will be ever more clearly understood.

Nowhere has this autonomy of higher education been more important than in nineteenth-century Germany. Because educational modernisation there came relatively early and full industrialisation relatively late, I argued some years ago and still believe, an educated upper-middle class emerged as a particularly prominent social group. The "mandarins", members of the university-educated or "academic" professions, made up an educated stratum that was more a status elite than an economic class in Max Weber's terms. The social prestige of the educated, their style of life and their outlook were based more on their learning than on aristocratic birth on the one hand, or on wealth and economic power on the other. Their close ties to the monarchical civil service gave them a degree of political influence, at least during a transitional period in German history, and they claimed a broader cultural leadership as well. Institutionally, it was the revitalisation of the German universities during the late eighteenth and early nineteenth centuries that secured their position, together with the early emergence of a system of academic entitlements. The pre-eminent place of the German university professors and the outstanding achievements of German scholarship during the nineteenth century were built on these social foundations. I called the German academics "mandarin intellectuals" in part because they were the most prominent representatives of the "mandarin elite" as a whole. But they also controlled the standards of access to that elite, and they acted as its natural spokesmen. They articulated its social and cultural aspirations, its "ideology".

The central element in "mandarin ideology" was the immensely influential notion of "cultivation" (*Bildung*), the vision of learning as personal self-fufilment through interpretive interaction with venerated texts. Having recently completed a book on French academic culture around 1900, I am more convinced than ever that the distinctive ideal of *Bildung* decisively shaped the German intellectual and scholarly tradition of the nineteenth century. It established the dominant hermeneutic direction in German philological and historical scholarship. It engendered a distrust of instrumental or "utilitarian" knowledge and thus indirectly affected the prevalent conception of academic freedom as well. It implied personal and evaluative insight (*Weltanschauung*), rather than causal intervention in the physical and social world. At a more directly political level, the mandarin ideals of the "legal" and "cultural" state eventually gave rise to a revulsion against modern "interest" politics.

From around 1890 on, the social position and cultural leadership of the German mandarin intellectuals came under pressure from changes within the educational system as well as in the larger environment. Intensive industrialisation, once it came, proceeded swiftly. It was accompanied by particularly threatening concentrations of entrepreneurial power on the one hand, and by the rapid advance of working-class organisation on the other. Money and "the masses" confronted each other in undisguised conflicts of material interest; the emerging high capitalist "class" society made traditional status conventions appear irrelevant, and technological "civilisation" threatened to overwhelm the inherited norms of humanist "culture". In secondary and higher education, increased enrolments and the rise of "realistic" studies raised the spectres of "massification" and "utilitarianism", while the inexorable advance of disciplinary specialisation threatened to sever the tie between *Wissenschaft* and *Weltanschaung* in the idealist philosophy of *Bildung*. In response to these converging pressures, a creative minority of German academic "modernists" sought to "translate" vital elements of their heritage to ensure their continued relevance. But the large majority of "orthodox" mandarins took up a strictly defensive, anti-democratic and anti-modernist stance that took on irrationalist dimensions, under the impact of defeat, revolution and inflation, during the Weimar period. In any case, references to an existing "crisis of culture" began to appear in German academic literature about 1890, and by 1920, a "crisis of *Wissenschaft*" was widely perceived as well.

Against this general background, I wish to report briefly upon some quantitative work done by my doctoral student, David Vampola. Of course I do not mean to anticipate the completion of his dissertation, the working title of which is 'The Characteristics of the German Professoriate 1860–1938' or to publish his findings prematurely. Instead, I will simply give notice of some of the results we anticipate, in very broad terms, where they pertain to the topic here.

Essentially, Vampola has recodified and re-analysed biographical and career data on German academics initially collected during the mid-1950s by a team of Göttingen sociologists led by Helmuth Plessner. The Göttingen group developed an extensive file of data cards for all faculty who taught at German universities and university-level institutions at approximately ten-year intervals between 1864 and 1953. Various handbooks, encyclopedias and other biographical sources were used to produce remarkably complete records of each faculty member's date of birth, father's occupation, religion, year of doctorate and of "habilitation", university position by institution, faculty, subject, academic rank and date of appointment to that rank. The team's main findings were initially presented in a monograph by Christian von Ferber that is still the only source on the survey.[1] Focusing on the period through 1938, Vampola has carefully reconstructed and recodified the major variables; he has to some extent "purified" the sample by excluding such marginal fields as agriculture and veterinary science, along with sports and language teachers, teaching assistants and others not considered full members of the academic teaching faculty. Beyond that, the Göttingen group was handicapped by the very incomplete development of data processing techniques during the 1950s. Progress in that area during the last 35 years has enabled Vampola to carry out analytical programmes that were impossible earlier. Much of his work deals with the growth of the various disciplines, with the academic standing and subject specialisation of particular universities, with waiting periods between promotions and other indicators of "opportunity" or "openness" in various subject areas at various times.

Instead of discussing all of these matters, however, I want to concentrate on the two topics that seem most pertinent in the present context, namely father's occupation and religion. Indeed, under the first of these headings, I will ignore the social make-up of particular disciplines or universities and look only at the social origins of all faculty members at German universities who appeared in the sample for the first time during specific years surveyed between 1864 and 1938. Even more conclusively than Ferber's initial tabulation, these data point to the extraordinary degree to which German university faculty members, even after the middle of the nineteenth century, came from "mandarin" family backgrounds. Thus, between 1864 and 1890, roughly two-thirds of the fathers of new German university academic staff were members of the educated upper middle class: university professors, high officials, lawyers, doctors or members of other educated professions, Protestant clergymen and secondary teachers. An additional 6–9 percent of the parents were members of a non-economic lower middle class of middle and lower officials and teachers that traditionally served as the most important channel of upward mobility into the professoriate. This left only about 25 percent, or one-quarter, for the entire range of economic occupations in agriculture, commerce and industry. During the period 1864–1890, agriculture in fact accounted for some 5–8 percent of German academics; an economic lower middle class of small independents and employees added another 12–15 percent, and the working class was virtually excluded at 1–2 percent.

Above all, the economic upper middle class of industrialists, large merchants

[1]Christian von Ferber, *Die Entwicklung des Lehrkörpers der deutschen Universitäten und Hochschulen 1864–1954*, Göttingen 1956.

and executive-level employees was very poorly represented among the fathers of German university faculty members, between 1864 and 1890, at only about 3–6 percent. Obviously, these figures should be promptly cited whenever anyone expresses surprise that there should have been so little trace in the German intellectual tradition of the ideologies commonly associated with the commercial and industrial "bourgeoisie", especially in the Anglo-American context. In Germany until late in the nineteenth century, there was a sharp separation between two middle-class hierarchies: one of these encompassed the educational system and the civil service; the other included the artisanal, commercial and industrial occupations.

Vampola's new figures further indicate a rather abrupt change between 1890 and 1900. During that interval, the percentage of new German university faculty's fathers in the educated upper middle class declined from about 63 percent to about 55 percent. It then continued to fall to around 50 percent by 1910, and it remained in that neighbourhood upto and including 1938. As in comparable distributions for university students, part of the ground thus vacated was taken up by the non-economic lower middle class, which increased its representation by several percentage points between 1890 and 1910, and by serveral more during the inter-war period. The percentages for the economic lower middle class also rose a little, hovering between 16 and 19 percent from 1900 to 1938, while those for agriculture and for the working class changed very little.

The other really significant shift was in the representation of the entrepreneurial upper middle class, which jumped from about 6 percent in 1890 to nearly 10 percent in 1900, and to some 11–13 percent between 1910 and 1931. For German conditions, this was a remarkable increase. It was due in part to a lengthening of the probationary period that young scholars spent as poorly paid *Privatdozenten* before obtaining permanent faculty appointments. Wealth was tending to become a condition of membership in the German academic elite. Yet this "plutocratic" shift in German faculty recruitment probably had broader causes too. Advanced education was starting to serve as a prerequisite for access to leading positions in industry as well; the separation between the educational and the economic occupational system was breaking down. Here was another objective symptom of the "cultural crisis" that began to emerge as a theme in German academic literature at just about that time.

But I want to move on to the religious affiliation of German university faculties. While the Göttingen sample unfortunately includes large percentages of unknowns on the variable of religion, the share of "knowns" increased from some 20 percent for 1864, and around 25 percent between 1873 and 1890, to roughly 35 percent from 1900 to 1938. With all due caution, it is certainly worth looking at the results, which are very interesting indeed. One predictable result that emerges from the distribution of the "knowns" is the relative under-representation of Catholicism. Catholics made up 36 percent of the German population in 1900. Their share of university teachers, however, declined from some 24–25 percent of "knowns" between 1864 and 1873, to a low of 16–18 percent between 1880 and 1900, presumably as a result of the *Kulturkampf*.

Though the proportion of Catholics recovered a little thereafter, it never moved far from 20 percent during the first third of the twentieth century. Protestants, by contrast, were generally represented somewhat above their share of the total population, most markedly from 1890 on.

Meanwhile, academics of the Jewish faith were about 9 percent of those of known religion among teachers at German universities as of 1864. Their share of the "knowns" entering the Göttingen sample for the first time at subsequent intervals reached a remarkable high of 16–17 percent in 1873 and 1880, declined sharply to about 12 percent by 1890 and, even more steeply, to around 7.5 percent in 1900 and 1910. The loss of representation thus begun in the 1880s and accelerated in the 1890s continued into the inter-war period, with figures near 7 percent in 1920, 5 percent in 1931, and of course 0 percent in 1938.

Given the fact that Jews were roughly 1 percent of the German population as of 1900, one has to begin by noting the very considerable over-representation they achieved during the later 1860s and 1870s, which, moreover, was not without precedent in earlier decades. To understand this at all, one has to recall that Jews in nineteenth-century Germany were especially numerous in socio-occupational groups that sent relatively high proportions of their sons to the universities. Beyond that, one would have to look to aspects of the Jewish cultural tradition in ways that unfortunately surpass my competence. At the same time, one cannot avoid the hypothesis that, despite certain intellectual antecedents and official restrictions, antisemitism was not a significant presence in the German academic community before the late 1870s at the earliest. Even if one looks at the whole period from 1864 to 1938, as a matter of fact, Jews accounted for 13 percent of German university faculty members in the field of medicine, and for nearly 17 percent of those in law, despite their virtual exclusion from the higher civil service. These are striking symptons of cultural vitality on the one hand, and of cultural openness on the other. I wonder what we would find if we had similar data on American colleges and universitites before the Second World War?

The reverse side of the coin, of course, is that some form of antisemitism demonstrably arose and deepened at the German universities almost exactly in phase with other symptoms of the perceived "crisis" of culture and of learning. The changes in the indicators from 1880 on are unmistakable, abrupt, and persistent, right up to the catastrophe of the 1930s. Some data collected by a Jewish organisation for 1909–1910 strongly suggest that at that time, the antisemitic sentiments of German university professors were directed primarily against Jews who refused to convert to Christianity. In 1909–1910, almost 12 percent of *Privatdozenten* but less than 3 percent of full professors at German universities were of the Jewish religion. At the same time, Jewish converts to Christianity (*Getaufte*) accounted for an additional 7 percent of *Privatdozenten* and 4 percent of full professors.[2] We do not know just when German academics began to expect their Jewish colleagues to convert to Christianity; the decline in the representation of those of Jewish religion at German universities from 1880 on

[2]Bernhard Breslauer (ed.), *Die Zurücksetzung der Juden an den Universitäten Deutschlands*, Berlin 1911.

could conceivably disguise a rise in the representation of converts. We simply cannot say.

I have written elsewhere about the antisemitic arguments of certain orthodox German university professors during the Weimar period, in which the Jews characteristically stood for modernity and for the destructive potential of critical reason.[3] At the same time, I have suggested that few German academics truly identified with the rabid antisemitism of the student majority, or with the biological racism of the National Socialists. I believe that the German mandarins' responsibility for the rise of Hitler lay less in what they did than in what they failed to do and say to safeguard reason and democracy. But I cannot address these issues here. Instead, I want to conclude by urging others to investigate some of the questions raised by the fascinating but incomplete religious data collected by the Göttingen group and analysed by David Vampola. A study of entries for academics in the *Neue deutsche Biographie,* for example, could confirm, disprove or extend the findings I have described here.

[3]Fritz K. Ringer, 'Inflation, Antisemitism and the German Academic Community of the Weimar Period', in *LBI Year Book XXVIII* (1983), pp. 3–9. See also Fritz K. Ringer, *The Decline of the German Mandarins. The German Academic Community 1890–1933*, Cambridge, Mass. 1969, pp. 435–439.

The German Professionals and their Jewish Colleagues
Comments on the Papers of Konrad Jarausch, Geoffrey Cocks and Fritz K. Ringer

BY FRITZ STERN

First of all it seems to me that all three papers suggest – both by what is present and by what is absent – the importance of the comparative element of history.* There is not only the Europe of 1992, there was also the Europe of 1882, by which I mean to say that the comparative element is particularly important for German history and to some extent, of course, for the history of antisemitism.

Put very crassly: Hitler was a *Sonderweg* – a special pathway – this has been much debated among German historians of late, but the earlier periods were obviously marked by similarities and dissimilarities with the rest of Europe, particularly Western Europe. In every period of German history – as with every history – there was an awareness of the contemporary world. People knew what was going on in France, England, Holland etc. and therefore we must attempt to recapture what they knew, what they feared, and try to live in their period. We cannot read German history backwards from the present to the past, but rather the other way round: we should make a real moral and intellectual effort not to see history with the end as a kind of inevitable conclusion or evolution, but try to rediscover what they themselves knew.

Thus I was struck, in Fritz Ringer's paper by the reference to the German mandarin revulsion against interest politics; but that revulsion against interest politics existed in most parliamentary countries at the same time. I think here in the United States of Veblen or Henry Adams, of the Progressives, in general. That is to say there was also a revulsion in France, in Germany and the United States at the end of the nineteenth century against so-called interest politics.

Certainly antisemitism in Germany at the end of the nineteenth century became virulent – or more virulent – than in the period up to the 1870s, in the 1870s particularly so. And thus all the more astounding is the success in those visible and humanly important fields that we see in Germany and which is stressed in these papers. In what other countries did Jews constitute so important a presence in medicine, law and teaching? And these are areas that touch people directly and in a very human fashion. The pre-eminence in some professions, others could have been adduced, obviously, from the commerical

*The following remarks at the 104th Annual Meeting of the American Historical Association in a session sponsored by the New York Leo Baeck Institute on 29th December 1989 in San Francisco, were taken from a transcript of an informal talk.

and economic world, was conditioned by exclusion from other fields, that is to say that this pre-eminence had to do to a large extent with exclusion from public service and so on. But there still remains an awesome disproportion if one thinks only, for instance, of the fact of 48% of Berlin lawyers being Jewish. Secondly I would stress to all of you the need for the broadest context with regard to the culture of Germany in order to understand the particular subject that we are addressing. I was struck by Fritz Ringer's remarks, with which on the whole I entirely agree, about *Bildung* and how important that concept was, but I would say that it was not an invention of the universities but rather sprang from a profound cultural movement, from a literary imagination, from Goethe and Schiller and indeed from the generation of the German reformers.

It is wrong to assume that it was entirely a monopoly of the German universities. They certainly institutionalised it, but it arose from elsewhere.

What did Germans think of sickness and of health? This makes me think, as did all these papers, of a contention of Ralf Dahrendorf many years ago that Germans thought pain was ennobling. And there was a certain brutality in German hospitals. The Jewish doctors in their great predominance, their numerical disproportion, did they have the same notions? Were they perhaps more solicitous? Would one benefit from considering a work of fiction such as Arthur Schnitzler's *Professor Bernhardi*, and so on?

The third point that I want to make is that I am uncomfortable with the lure of the quantitative. The quantitative is no doubt useful because it gives among other things the impression of factuality, of certainty. But does it not facilitate the forgetting of some of the most important elements, i.e. the human psychological elements? The *mentalité*? What did men think, what did their wives think? What was life really like in the Jewish milieu, among Jewish converts to Christianity, on the Gentile side? How did lawyers, doctors and academics about whom we have heard think, feel and define themselves?

Numbers alone tell us something, but they are only the beginning. It is useful to have the quantitative but the quantitative should not be substituted for the qualitative.

A final general observation. As I read some of the papers, I recalled the statement made by Max Weber when, in 1919, he warned his young German students who wanted to become *Privatdozenten* against entering the profession, and what he says about academic life in Germany at the time (and which can be applied to some extent to our own life and to the United States); it is a fairly grim picture that he drew. He warns his students: do you really want to embark on a career where chance plays such a role, where mediocrity tends to triumph? He says: when it comes to my Jewish students, I tell them at once to abandon all hope. Thus Max Weber in 1919.

On the one hand, then, in 1919, when things were much more open for Jews, and when Jews already had the kind of presence which Fritz Ringer has described, Weber said abandon all hope, and yet we see historically the pre-eminence that, in fact, they had. And therefore, as I once said before, there was a kind of unique measure in Germany of both hospitality and hostility, and I suspect that both were needed for the spectacular presence and success that Jews achieved. At the same time this hostility obviously presented the feeling of victimisation amongst the Jews, before 1933; most Jews accepted antisemitism and some even shared it. I recently came across an unpublished letter of Einstein dated 1909, in which he complained bitterly about German Jews, particularly in academic life. Why such fawning before the State? Why is it that a competent artisan is so much more impressive, is so much more a real person than a careerist academic? Was Jewish self-criticism always Jewish self-hatred? I would say that one should listen to voices and opinions such as these of Einstein. Let me also say that the careers of even the greatest German-Jewish scientists made clear that there was antisemitism at every stage, that they took it for granted and overcame it as well as they could in most cases; and among the best of them there obviously was a very strong scientific ethos. Fritz Ringer mentioned the cultural factors that one has to take into consideration as to why they came to be so disproportionately represented. I would suggest that one element was that which we have come to call, since the end of the nineteenth century, the scientific ethos was particularly strong among many Jews.

It is perfectly clear that the Jews did have a pre-eminent place, that they therefore added a competitive element in a society that was competitive yet did not wish to be so, having as an ideal a more harmonious society. Competitive, yes, I wondered as I wrote the words, whether to a competitive element they did not also add a compassionate element, and this particularly in the medical field.

I found the paper of Konrad Jarausch extremely informative and suggestive, casting the question in admirably broad terms, making the effort of not reading history backwards. Let me come back to the 48% of Jewish lawyers. It reminded me of a letter that Eleanor Roosevelt wrote to Franklin Roosevelt, when the latter was at Columbia Law School and she wrote "How many Jew boys are there in your class?" And this from a woman of whom we think, rightfully as a magnificent fighter for all the values we cherish. And the reason for the letter – two actually came to mind on the same theme – was that the prejudice against Jews in the professions was extraordinarily strong and it was not limited to Germany. As Fritz Ringer already mentioned in passing, there was no such disproportion of Jews in American higher education before the First World War and not before the Second World War, so that that has to be reckoned with, and the pervasive prejudice in America has to be taken into account as well. At some point Jarausch noted the superior competence of the lawyers did eventually overcome discrimination. Was it only competence or was it something to do with the theme that I mentioned in the case of the doctors – compassion; was it perhaps a particular kind of solicitude? Of course eventually this specific quality did not overcome prejudice but fell victim to it.

Geoffrey Cocks's paper raises the question of why Jews did so well in the sciences. Given the original title of Geoffrey Cocks's paper, I was surprised that there was relatively little analysis of the lives and careers of Jewish doctors between 1933 and August 1938 when they were deprived of the right to treat so-called "Aryan" patients. Let me here interpolate a remark that I meant to make earlier. The Nazis, following their ideology, issued the law for the "restoration" of the civil service (*Gesetz zur Wiederherstellung des Berufsbeamtentums*) and thus deprived themselves of some of their most eminent scientists, thereby really doing extraordinary harm to their own scientific effort. On the other hand, for a long time, from 1933 to 1938 they allowed a degree of normality for the rest of the Jewish population – doctors, lawyers and businessmen – that was really quite extraordinary. But the life of the Jewish doctor, whether converted or not, would have shown the extraordinary interplay that existed in the early years of the Third *Reich* between astounding normality and exclusion, elimination and terrible hardship. Jewish doctors were indeed excluded from public clinics and insurance cases, but in the private sector they continued to practise and there was a good deal of persisting "Aryan" patronage of Jewish doctors, despite all the propaganda, particularly from *Der Stürmer* and other publications about the possibility of sexual abuse and the like. There was a fair amount of "Aryan" co-operation with Jewish doctors on the basis of consultation, as well as a great deal of "Aryan" rejection. All of this has to be kept in mind.

There is a regrettable current controversy over the opinions and the standing of the famous neurologist Karl Bonhoeffer, the father of Dietrich Bonhoeffer, who is now suddenly the subject of attack over remarks written in the late 1920s on eugenics which seem to bear out what Cocks said about brutality, but which had nothing to do with antisemitism itself. Brutality in eugenics, brutality in the very notion of dealing with racial or degenerate types. And it seems to me unfortunate that someone who played as heroic a role as Bonhoeffer should now become a target in this way. One final observation on Geoffrey Cocks's paper; I do wonder about the reliability of evidence about the use of Jewish doctors after 1938 on the basis of foreign reports. Why would the *Manchester Guardian* or the *Daily Herald* know anything about Nazi policy with regard to Jewish doctors? In any case after 1938, how many were left? To the best of my knowledge there may have been thoughts or hopes on the part of the German army that one could use these Jewish doctors after 1938, but I do not think this was ever done.

Let me say, in reference to David Vampola's work; one speaks of the educated upper middle class, there I think one would want further division. That is a very broad category. I would be particularly interested in how important over a period of time was the Protestant clergy. As you remember, it was Nietzsche who said that they were the fathers of academic life. That Catholics were discriminated against, of course we know. What of their economic condition? Was their economic condition not also disproportionately worse than that of their Jewish confrères? What about Catholic representation in Catholic states such as Bavaria? And was it only discrimination about which Max Weber wrote, or was it something about Catholic parental expectations and schooling? Finally, let me again stress that I found the whole question of Jewish over-representation in Fritz Ringer's paper very revealing: that there was a constant hostility after the 1870s and yet acceptance particularly in certain fields. And there one would wish that although he mentioned law and medicine there was more specificity even within those categories. Law was where Jews were reluctantly given opportunities and where Jews became pre-eminent in so many different ways.

Let me conclude by stating what is obvious from the three papers which you have heard. Our subject – German-Jewish history – is exceptionally complex, rich and fraught with tragedy. So much of the drama of history was played out there; the life of German Jewry was central to it and still is controversial, is still surrounded by taboos and anxieties. On the one hand I think our field is rich in archives, including the archive of the Leo Baeck Institute. It is rich in talent; in so many countries there are so many historians working in it. And there are, of course, many different approaches, as was made clear here. But I think all approaches, whichever one you may take, need empathy, breadth and humanity. You cannot leave the subject to the distorting and simplifying media. You cannot leave it to the novelists, because there is no Dickens, no Balzac. Therefore we have our own task, made the more compelling by very recent events, but above all because we have obligations not only to our discipline but also to posterity.

One of Wagner's Jewish Friends
Berthold Auerbach and his Unpublished Reply to Richard Wagner's Antisemitism (1881)

BY PAUL LAWRENCE ROSE

"The first Jew with whom I could discuss the whole subject of Judaism with a hearty lack of inhibition" was how Richard Wagner remembered Berthold Auerbach, the best known German-Jewish writer of the nineteenth century after Heine.[1] When Auerbach and Wagner first met at Dresden in 1846 their discussions of Judaism had doubtless been amicable and something of a revelation for the curious, not yet obsessed, composer. Auerbach had made it his mission to promote a new understanding of Judaism as a humane and humanitarian religion. It was a vindication intended to justify the Jewish religion in the eyes of the German world and at the same time to raise the self-esteem of the Jews themselves. These ideas might have fallen on interested ears in 1846, but after his conversion in 1848 to a new revolutionary kind of Jew-hatred Wagner could only have regarded them as repellent and absurd. Auerbach for his part came to regard Wagner as the epitome of the barbarous Jew-hatred which emerged in German public life in the 1870s to afflict the last decade of his own life. Saddened and angered by the rise of Wagnerian antisemitism, Auerbach fell into an intellectual paralysis and showed himself powerless to react publicly to Wagner's rantings. More than once, as we shall see, he considered writing a rejoinder to Wagner and yet, when he finally did so, he failed to publish it. In this impotent fascination with the *Meister* Auerbach suffered from a syndrome common to others of the Wagnerian circle of Jewish friends – and perhaps also of a wider segment of Jewish cultured society of the Second Empire. But the case is

---

[1]Richard Wagner, *My Life* (=MLE), transl. by Andrew Gray, Cambridge 1983, p. 325, from the German text *Mein Leben*, ed. by Martin Gregor-Dellin, Munich 1963. Literature: Anton Bettelheim, *Berthold Auerbach. Der Mann, sein Werk, sein Nachlass*, Stuttgart–Berlin 1907; idem, 'Der Nachlass Berthold Auerbachs in Schwäbischen Schiller-Verein', *Schwäbischer Schillerverein: 6. ter Rechenschaftsbericht*, 1902, pp. 3–53; idem, 'Berthold Auerbach', *Allgemeine deutsche Biographie*, XLVII (1903), pp. 412–419; Moses Zwick, *Berthold Auerbachs sozialpolitischer und ethischer Liberalismus*, Stuttgart 1933; S. Liptzin, *Germany's Stepchildren*, Philadelphia 1944, ch. 5. Margarita Pazi, 'Berthold Auerbach and Moritz Hartmann. Two Jewish writers of the Nineteenth Century', in *LBI Year Book XVIII* (1973), pp. 201–208; idem, 'Berthold Auerbach und seine revolutionäre und literarische Tätigkeit', in *Revolution und Demokratie in Geschichte und Literatur. Festschrift für Walter Grab*, ed. by J. H. Schoeps and I. Geiss, Duisburg 1979, pp. 355–374. For a superb account of Auerbach's perceptions of Germans and Jews see Jacob Katz, 'Berthold Auerbach's Anticipation of the German Jewish Tragedy', *Hebrew Union College Annual*, LIII, 1982, pp. 215–240. See now also David Sorkin, 'The Invisible Community. Emancipation, Secular Culture and Jewish Identity in the Writings of Berthold Auerbach', in Jehuda Reinharz and Walter Schatzberg (eds.), *The Jewish Response to German Culture*, Hanover, NH 1985, pp. 100–119; Paul Lawrence Rose, *Revolutionary Antisemitism in Germany from Kant to Wagner*, Princeton 1990, chapter 13.

also interesting from the viewpoint of Wagner since it nicely exposes the composer's typical exploitation of his so-called Jewish friends and highlights the viciousness which the manipulative Wagner usually tried to conceal in his dealings with those friends.[2]

Wagner's relations with Auerbach – as with all his Jewish friends and most of his Gentile ones besides – pursued an unhappy course. In a contemporary letter from the days of his first conversations with Auerbach in 1846, Wagner remarked that "with Auerbach I several days ago struck up a warm friendship. He read us his new tale and I recited to him my *Tannhäuser* for the first time. He is a splendid fellow."[3] At this time Wagner was on his best behaviour and remained so for as long as Auerbach could be of service to him. In 1848, for example, he sought Auerbach's aid in publishing one of his revolutionary poems[4] and in 1859 Wagner asked his friend Pusinelli to forward a manuscript of the poem of the *Ring* to Auerbach ("I attach much importance to your fulfilling this request").[5] Wagner followed this up with a direct request for an opinion from his "most honoured friend" Auerbach, no doubt in the unexpressed hope that some Jewish influence might be exercised on behalf of the poem.[6] This was not to be.

The disappointed Wagner did not bare his fangs publicly until the reissue of *Judaism in Music* in 1869, but already in 1865–1867 he was committing privately to paper some of his now nasty thoughts about the unfortunate Auerbach. It is worth quoting these poisonous pages from the memoirs *in extenso* to convey the jaundiced view which Wagner had conceived of a man whose sincerity and good intentions were well known to all around him. Describing his disillusionment with the artistic crowd at Dresden in the 1840s, Wagner recalls in *Mein Leben* how he had come into contact with Auerbach.

> "This short, burly, Jewish peasant lad, as he was pleased to represent himself, made an entirely winning impression; it was only later that I learned the by no means innocent significance of his green jacket, and above all, his green hunting cap, which lent him the looks of an authentic author of Swabian peasant stories. The Swiss poet Gottfried Keller later once told me in Zürich that Auerbach, after deciding to take Keller under his wing and help him get his literary products into circulation and make some money, had advised him above all else to

[2] On Wagner's Jewish friends (on which subject an apologetic exhibition was mounted at Bayreuth in 1984) see my paper, 'The Noble Anti-Semitism of Richard Wagner', *The Historical Journal*, XXV (1982), pp. 751–763. For further details see Rose, *Revolutionary Antisemitism in Germany, op. cit.*, chapt. 20 and my forthcoming *Wagner-Race and Revolution*, London 1991. The important study of Jacob Katz, *Richard Wagner. Vorbote des Antisemitismus*, Königstein 1985 (English transl. *The Darker Side of Genius. Richard Wagner's Anti-Semitism*, Hanover, NH 1986), which appeared after the completion of this article, discusses Auerbach at pp. 47f., 95f.

[3] Wagner to Alwine Frommann (who had commended Auerbach), 9th October 1846, in Richard Wagner, *Sämtliche Briefe* (=SB), Leipzig 1970. (Pazi, 'Auerbach and Hartmann', *loc. cit.*, p. 212, errs in stating that Auerbach and Wagner were acquainted in Dresden in "1855–1859", but they did meet in Zürich in August 1852 (SB, IV, p. 448)). In a letter of 1846 Auerbach describes his warm impressions of the energetic Wagner. See Hans Knudsen, 'Berthold Auerbach in Dresden', *Neues Archiv für Sächsische Geschichte und Altertumskunde*, Dresden 1919, p. 374, cited by Katz, *Richard Wagner, op. cit.*, p. 47. See also Berthold Auerbach, *Briefe an seinen Freund Jakob Auerbach. Ein biographische Denkmal*, Frankfurt a. Main 1884, I, pp. 55, 62, 72.

[4] MLE, p. 362.

[5] *The Letters of Richard Wagner to Anton Pusinelli*, ed. by E. Lenrow, New York 1932, p. 112 (12th December 1859).

[6] Wagner to Auerbach, 2nd April 1860, printed in Bettelheim, *Auerbach. Der Mann, op. cit.*, p. 424.

procure a similar jacket and cap, on the grounds that he, Keller, was also not handsome and tall, and thus would be well advised to give himself a rather rustic and quaint appearance; Auerbach had then adjusted the cap on his, Keller's, head in such a way as to make him look a bit rakish. But at first I didn't see anything affected about Auerbach; he had assimilated so much of the folkways and colloquialisms of the people, and with such skill, that one could only wonder why, with these delightful qualities, he nonetheless moved in entirely antipodal spheres with the greatest ease. At any rate, he always seemed to be in his element precisely in those circles which one would have thought antipathetic to those characteristics he continually emphasised; there he stood in his green coat, a bit crude, but sensitive and open, surrounded by members of polite society who flattered him, delighting to display letters from the Hereditary Duke of Weimar to him, together with his replies, and all the time observing things from the standpoint of a Swabian peasant nature, which nonetheless suited him so well.

What especially attracted me to him was that I found in him the first Jew with whom I could discuss the whole subject of Judaism with a hearty lack of inhibition. He seemed to be particularly anxious, in fact, to remove in an agreeable manner any prejudices on this score, and it was touching to hear him talk of his childhood, when it seemed to him that he was the only German who had got through Klopstock's *Messias* in its entirety. He had read this, it seemed, secretly in his humble village home, and had one day been late to school on that account, for which he was greeted by the teacher when he finally arrived in the classroom with the words: 'You god-damned Jew-boy. Where have you been? Lending money again?' Such experiences had only made him melancholy and reflective, but had not embittered him, and he had, as he asserted, even managed to feel pity for the crudity of those who tormented him. These were qualities that I found very estimable; yet in the course of time I began to be somewhat concerned that he didn't get beyond his pre-occupation with similar ideas and relationships, so that it appeared to me as if the world and its history boiled down for him solely to the problem of what to do about Judaism. One day I turned to him in an amiably intimate way and advised him simply to let the whole Jewish question go hang; there were, after all, a number of other standpoints from which to judge the world. Curiously enough, he lost all his ingenuousness at that point, adopted what struck me as a not entirely authentic tone of whimpering emotion, and assured me he could never do that, as Judaism still contained too much that demanded his complete sympathy. Later I could not help recalling this surprising obsessiveness I had noticed in Auerbach when I learned that he had contracted in the course of time a series of Jewish marriages, of which the only favourable result that came to my ears was that they had brought him a fortune. When I saw him again in Zürich after a number of years, I found his countenance changed in a disconcerting manner; he looked extraordinarily common and dirty; his former refreshing liveliness had turned into the usual Jewish fidgetiness, and every word he spoke came out in such a way that one could see he regretted not having saved it for a newspaper article.

During that time in Dresden, however, Auerbach's warm support for my artistic intentions, even though it was offered from his Jewish-Swabian standpoint, did me a lot of good."[7]

One suspects that some of this new venom was due to Wagner's being irked at Auerbach's friendship with Meyerbeer who in 1856 had provided melodic settings for his *Black Forest Tales*.[8] But it was perhaps what he perceived as Auerbach's failure to promote the *Ring* poem which really inspired this attack, or so it seems from the *Explanations* which Wagner appended to *Judaism in Music* in 1869. Here seemingly circumspect remarks evince his usual capacity to cloak a vicious personal attack in terms of moral rectitude and truth-telling. In this case,

[7]MLE, pp. 324f. (*Mein Leben*, pp. 337ff.). In 1879 Wagner alluded to Auerbach's hints to Keller. See Wagner, *Gesammelte Schriften und Dichtungen* (=GSD), Leipzig 1888, X, p. 141. (*Prose Works of Richard Wagner* [=PW], transl. by W. A. Ellis, London 1892–1899, VI, p. 137.)

[8]Giacomo Meyerbeer, *Briefwechsel und Tagebücher*, ed. by H. and G. Becker, Berlin 1975, III, pp. 350, 576. Auerbach had known Meyerbeer since at least 1841 and the friendship continued until the composer's death. See Auerbach, *Briefe, op. cit.*, I, p. 200; *ibid.*, II, p. 410 (27th October 1879), remembers him as a "creator of greatness".

Wagner's moral point is that the Jewish collective conspires to intimidate any individual enlightened Jew from supporting such outspoken enemies of Judaism as Richard Wagner. As an example of this repression he cites Auerbach's case. (Auerbach is not named but would have been recognised immediately by any reader from the phrases describing him).

> "To give you an idea of the tyranny (of the Jewish clique), let one instance serve for many. An undoubtedly very gifted, truly talented and intellectual writer of Jewish origin, who seems to have almost grown into the most distinctive traits of German folk-life, and with whom I had long and often debated Judaism in all its bearings – this writer made the later acquaintance of my poems *The Ring of the Nibelung* and *Tristan and Isolde*. He expressed himself about them with such warm appreciation and clear understanding, that he certainly laid to heart the invitation of my friends, to whom he had spoken, to publish openly his views about these poems that had been so astonishingly ignored by our own literary circles. *This was impossible to him!*"[9]

This is clearly a reference to Wagner's submission of the *Ring* poem to Auerbach in 1859–1860; obviously Auerbach had been unable to oblige Wagner with a publicity puff and in this rebuff may be seen the real motive for Wagner's sudden turning against his friend in *My Life* in 1865–1867.

Wagner's tone in the new edition of *Judaism in Music* in 1869 was almost enough to provoke Auerbach to a public rejoinder; but he restricted himself to private expressions of distaste. Auerbach wrote thus to his cousin on 12th March 1869: (considering that he had not seen Wagner's acidulous remarks in the manuscript of *My Life*, Auerbach's perception of the viciousness underlying the composer's fine public comments is most astute).

> "I don't know what I should do. I cannot be at ease. I would like to give Richard Wagner a public answer and I believe I could give him a blow which he would not lightly get over. But that would be for me really pointless . . . Even more astonishing than the tenacious preservation of the Jews in history are the tenacity and changing themes of Jew-hatred. One thing that must be allowed Wagner is that he knows how to mix true with un-true, and that is why the matter is more dangerous and poisonous than it seems and therefore cannot simply be brushed aside. What Wagner has written only through venom and envy will pass. But there will remain something which must be fully recognised and dragged out. I personally have a special reason for a rejoinder. On page 55 Wagner speaks of me. You know that in Dresden we were often and much together and also corresponded later. He speaks now certainly very well and back-slappingly of me, but even there I may still be of use to him. He lies in what he says, perhaps unintentionally. I have for a witness Eduard Devrient. And then I might finally say to him: There are many Jews who on account of the non-recognition of their unpleasant personality, their half-talent, their arrogance and so forth might say, 'Alas, I am rejected and unappreciated because I am a Jew'. But Wagner says: My music is publicly discredited by a secret band of Jewish writers acting under a secret Jewish command; one insults me, another equally attacks me by passing over me in silence, and all this happens to me because I am a non-Jew, because I am a Christian.' What can one do with this home-fiddling? Why is there no longer a Börne?
> I believe I must speak out, but one cannot always keep up with one's duty. I stand on the roof-beams of my current book and must put out the decorations, giddy though I may often be. I cannot undertake anything else. I am not styled for polemic, I am too sensitive and vulnerable and take no joy in war. And yet this affair leaves me no peace and takes up all my thought."

To demonstrate how Wagner is able to mix elements of truth with general falsehood, Auerbach cites Wagner's treatment of Mendelssohn.

[9] *Aufklärungen* to *Judaism in Music* (1869) (GSD, VIII, pp. 285f.; PW, III, p. 120).

"It was a fitting nemesis that Mendelssohn should have been portrayed by Wagner as the incarnation of Jew-music . . . In 1845–46 I had much to do with Mendelssohn at Leipzig . . . I found him to be utterly averse to anything that was to do with the Jews . . . And now Mendelssohn has to represent Jew-music! What Wagner said about Mendelssohn's music, I have in part always found to be true myself. It is so refined and mannered that it lacks natural feeling and naturalness. Only in the *Walpurgisnight* and *Midsummer Night's Dream* is it to my mind individual and fresh. That Meyerbeer also creates things which are not fresh in feeling is also true; but there are colourists in art and also in music who out of pure desire for colour, paint and compose."[10]

In Auerbach's mind, Wagner was right in criticising the lack of inner life in the music of Mendelssohn and Meyerbeer, but he was grievously and mischievously wrong in attributing that defect to the Jewishness of the two composers.

A more pessimistic letter followed on 21st March.

"In this Richard Wagner history one can learn to recognise something which still is hidden secretly in the world. In the *National-Zeitung* there is an article by Gumprecht, one of its regular music critics, and he invokes Wagner's authority for the claim that productive genius is absent among the Jews. Is that not revolting? To say that of the people that created the Bible and has enlightened and advanced the whole world until now and who knows for how much longer! I wish I could resign myself and shake loose the whole rebellion which ever and ever excretes a stock of coarseness and arrogance. One must check oneself in order not to despair of the world when one sees how a poisonous tree, which one believed to have been chopped down finally, again strikes new roots. And all this calls itself (*variously*) Christian love, free-thought, beautiful humanity!

On all sides I am oppressed. And I oppress myself in speaking of this business, yet I can no other."[11]

Auerbach's paralysed response to Wagner's attack of 1869 should be contrasted with that of the writer's non-Jewish friend, the novelist Gustav Freytag, who in an outspoken magazine article that year resolutely rejected Wagner's libels.[12] Auerbach preserved what he thought was dignified silence although it must have been tested when he found himself in 1871 in the company of Wagner's niece and in October of that year shared a carriage with Countess Muchanoff to whom, he remembered, "Wagner had dedicated the Jew-booklet" in whch he had been mocked.[13] Meanwhile, Wagner continued his carping in private. In 1869 he discussed with Cosima "the stories of Gottfried Keller, how much more significant they are than Auerbach's!" The following year Cosima notes:

[10]Auerbach, *Briefe, op. cit.*, I, pp. 392f. Other grains of truth in Wagner seem to be the existence of a "Jewish form of speech" (though it is cultural in origin), *ibid.*, I, p. 101 (5th April 1856), and the "demonic power of gold in the world of culture". The latter is portrayed in the novel, *Das Landhaus am Rhein* (1867–1869), but it is not taken to be specifically Jewish. There seems to be a reference to the Leipzig conversations (PW, VI, p. 250; GSD, X, p. 251) in which Auerbach's liberal opinions displeased Mendelssohn.

[11]Auerbach, *Briefe, op. cit.*, I, pp. 394f.

[12]Gustav Freytag, *Gesammelte Werke*, Leipzig 1898, XVI, pp. 321–326, quoted by Alfred Low, *Jews in the Eyes of the Germans. From the Enlightenment to Imperial Germany*, Philadelphia 1979, pp. 338f. Freytag had been a guest at Auerbach's synagogue wedding. Though they later quarrelled, Freytag magnanimously published his regrets for having made injurious remarks against his friend. See also George L. Mosse, *Germans and Jews. The Right, the Left, and the Search for a "Third Force" in Pre-Nazi Germany*, New York 1970, pp. 61–76, for details.

[13]He already knew the countess, according to the letter of 2nd October 1891, in Auerbach, *Briefe*, II, p. 78. Cf. Bettelheim, *Auerbach der Mann*, pp. 326f., for Frau Jachmann, Wagner's niece.

"An article by Berthold Auerbach (no such genius he!) about the woods is printed in the newspaper. Richard says he found it unreadable on account of its affected closeness to nature. 'These fellows (the Jews) are a real nuisance'."[14]

During the 1870s Auerbach observed Wagner's rising career with disquiet. In 1871 he found the city of Mannheim gripped by Wagner-fever while the Master was conducting there. "There is clearly something in Wagner which genuinely springs from the renewal of art, but one may despair of people for making such a fuss of it."[15] A year later:

"I am always disturbed when there is so much talk of Richard Wagner. Wagner is clearly a significant creative power. But what he does well is still melody in the old fashion, and what he achieves that is new or what he really seeks for is not good. The man perverts a good portion of the new enthusiasm for the fatherland to the ends of his violent prophesying."[16]

Wagner's bombastic disregard of the "legitimate boundaries" of art and taste excluded him from the company of Beethoven and Mozart.

"(As with Hebbel's *Judith*) I hope that it will be the case with Richard Wagner that one will soon find it incomprehensible how any store could have been set by this kind of stuff. Both Hebbel and Wagner have daring and a technical gift, but because they lack the natural rhythm of melody, they now preach and prove through their works that the straight and the healthy are just nonsense. Always the colossal! – that's their motto. Their men are always swaggering and their women are a mixture of sensual frenzy and philosophical madness."[17]

Auerbach's reactions to the *Ring* première of 1876 are not known, but he certainly understood the *Nibelungenlied* in a contrasting way to Wagner. The Germans, remarked Auerbach, are an ancient historical people, but their long history might as well have happened to another race. "Like our literature before Lessing, so our political life before Frederick the Great has no living power." From the *Nibelungenlied*, Wagner deduced notions of Germanic race; but in Auerbach's mind the ancient epic suggested rather a fatal paradox in German history.[18] To promote a continuity between medieval German literature and the modern German mind was not only misconceived, but potentially disastrous. Continuities which in other nations are not only healthy but productive become dangerous in the case of Germany.

From 1869–1882 Auerbach's feelings about the place of the Jews among the German *Volk* fluctuated wildly between despair and complacency. His assurance was tested severely and painfully by the series of incidents marking the rise of a new respectable antisemitism in German politics – the Billroth and Treitschke

[14]Cosima Wagner, *Die Tagebücher* (ed.) by Martin Gregor-Dellin and Dietrich Mack, Munich 1976–1977. Translations from *Cosima Wagner's Diaries* (=CWD), London 1978–1980, I, pp. 125, 224 (14th July 1869, 29th May 1870). On Keller and Auerbach see also GSD, X, p. 141. PW, VI, p. 137. MLE, p. 324.

[15]Auerbach, *Briefe, op. cit.*, II, p. 95 (21st December 1871).

[16]*Ibid.*, II, p. 104 (7th April 1872).

[17]*Ibid.*, II, p. 277 (7th April 1876). Cf. II, p. 259 (10th October 1875). On 21st March 1876 Auerbach mentions a discussion of *Tristan* (II, p. 276). Wagner is omitted from Auerbach's notes on great musicians, e.g. in II, pp. 95, 241, 422.

[18]Auerbach, *Briefe, op. cit.*, II, p. 309 (7th April 1877).

affairs and the Antisemitic Petition of 1880–1881.[19] It was precisely at the peak of the agitation aroused by the Antisemitic Petition that Wagner came back to haunt Auerbach who now immediately recognised in the Master the spiritual source of the new Jew-hatred.

"Schopenhauer extirpated all idealism in young hearts . . . From him youth learned that all idealism, humanity and care for mankind is humbug. In minds trained thus only baseness could make way and so Jew-baiting is now a merry sport for our students. Richard Wagner also had his effect in this. For he was the first to acknowledge himself as a Jew-hater and he proclaimed Jew-hatred to be quite compatible with culture [*Bildung*]. So flowed together many different currents, to which were added the anxieties of the sons of minor officials lest the Jews gain access to those official careers reserved previously for themselves."[20]

The great Berlin *Ring* cycle of May 1881 mounted by the Jewish impresario Angelo Neumann brought Auerbach's agonising about Wagner to a head. Rehearsals began with Wagner himself participating on 1st May and at the première on 5th May the composer made a speech on-stage. The public patronage by Berlin Jews of the notorious Jew-hater was simply too much for Auerbach, who finally took up the challenge to pen a polemic against Wagner which he had evaded in 1869. The manuscript *Richard Wagner and the Self-Respect of the Jews* (see Appendix), is dated 2nd May 1881, but yet again Auerbach's nerve was to fail him and he was to leave the essay unpublished among his papers.[21] Its main thrust, typically of the altruistic Auerbach, is not against Wagner (whose antisemitism is taken as given) but against those Jews who fool themselves into attending Wagnerian performances by claiming that it is all for their own self-improvement. Jewish self-respect should not permit Jews to honour Wagner and his operas, asserted Auerbach, for the man is inseparable from his Jew-hating ideology. The article is, however, more a cry of anguish than a serious analysis and unfortunately fails to address the central problem of how far Wagner's Jew-hatred is embedded in the operas and whether this is somehow communicated subconsciously to the audience. A connexion between the operas

[19]Cf. Peter J. Pulzer, *The Rise of Political Anti-Semitism in Germany and Austria*, revised edition, London 1988, p. 243; Michael Meyer, 'Great Debate on Antisemitism. Jewish Reaction to New Hostility in Germany, 1879–1881', in *LBI Year Book XI* (1966), pp. 137–140. Walter Boehlich, *Der Berliner Antisemitismusstreit*, Frankfurt a. Main 1965.

[20]Auerbach, *Briefe, op. cit.*, II, p. 443 (6th December 1880). R. S. Levy, *The Downfall of the Anti-Semitic Parties in Imperial Germany*, New Haven 1975, pp. 21ff, comments that the idea of the Petition came to Förster during the Bayreuth Festival of August 1880; but Wagner, it should be noted, was approached on the matter by Förster by 6th July of that year, i.e. before the Festival began (CWD, II, p. 506). For Wagner's reasons for refusing to sign the Petition see my 'Noble Anti-Semitism of Richard Wagner', *loc. cit.*, pp. 759ff.

[21]*Richard Wagner und die Selbstachtung der Juden*, manuscript (5 pp.) in the Auerbach–Nachlass, Deutsches Literaturarchiv, Schiller-Nationalmuseum, Marbach am Neckar. The title is listed in Bettelheim, 'Nachlass', *loc. cit.*, p. 52, but no other reference has appeared in the literature. Pazi, 'Auerbach and Hartmann', *loc. cit.*, p. 212, states that "his answer to Wagner was never published or even drafted". (This may be true of the intended reply of 1869 to which Pazi is referring.) I am grateful to Mrs Lisl Mathew of the James Cook University of North Queensland for her kind help in reading the hand of the manuscript. Auerbach's low opinion of the artistic value of Wagner's work was doubtless reinforced by conversations with the critic Eduard Hanslick at Marienbad in 1879 (Auerbach, *Briefe, op. cit.*, II, p. 404; 13th June 1879).

and the hatred would have been the strongest possible reason for Jews not to attend or patronise performances of Wagner.

Auerbach's essay does show how fully he had grasped the Master's evil influence on the antisemitic campaign, despite Wagner's self-righteous pretence of having stood apart from the vulgar Jew-baiters, as he termed them. (He preferred a more enlightened kind of Jew-hatred, as he wrote elsewhere.) As Auerbach well understood there could be no common ground between himself and Wagner for each man had a fundamentally opposed concept of the "humanity" which they both preached. The Russian pogroms of Jews of April 1881, in which hundreds were murdered, elicited reactions which show how distressingly different were Wagner's and Auerbach's ideas of "humanity". Thus Auerbach a fortnight after his essay against Wagner:

> "I cannot tell you how the Jew-baiting in Russia makes me despair, and especially the constant threats. What a grim riddle is posed by the renewal of this abominable vulgarity. I mean, that such an epidemic, such a poisoning of souls, has never yet been seen . . . The intellect can remain calm, but not so the heart."[22]

Contrast Wagner's delighted approval of the pogroms as an "expression of the strength of the [Russian] people".[23]

Auerbach's religion of humanity was a genuine expression of brotherly love, not, like Wagner's, a pretext for racial hatred. In *What is Humanity?* (1880) he insisted:

> "Humanity is the acknowledgement of human worth in every fellow man. General human rights are independent of descent, state, religion and social place. The equality of rights of all men is thus determined."[24]

Nevertheless the events of 1880–1881 remorselessly forced Auerbach to acknowledge that Heine's mistrust of the Germans had after all been well placed. In those years Auerbach had to concede with grief in his heart that the Germans did not want to share their fatherland with the Jews and he had to admit that – for all his own personal successes – his public effort to promote co-operation between Jews and Germans had been a general failure. Auerbach had placed his hopes for the redemption of the Jews in their solidarity with the German people of whom he devoutly believed the Jews were part. A century of emancipation, however, had not vindicated this conviction. The farther emancipation progressed, the more abrupt and incensed became the opposition to the Jews and the more proclaimed their allegedly irreducible apartness from the Germans. The road to redemption had turned into a cruel deception. Auerbach died at Cannes, far from his homeland, on 8th February 1882. He died in the awareness that the self-styled "noble" antisemitism of Richard Wagner had defeated his search for redemption through the German *Volk*.

---

[22] Auerbach, *Briefe, op. cit.*, II, p. 458 (15th May 1881). Cf. II, pp. 456, 459. In 1879 Auerbach had reacted to reports of a blood libel pogrom with a piece entitled *Cannibal Easter*. See Zwick, *Auerbach, op. cit.*, pp. 109f.

[23] CWD, II, p. 705 (14th August 1881).

[24] Quoted in Zwick, *Auerbach, op. cit.*, p. 57.

APPENDIX

Richard Wagner und die Selbstachtung der Juden

Da niemand das Wort ergreift, so will ich es tun. Man hört jetzt sagen, es war immer in den Gemüten ein ruhender Widerspruch gegen die Juden, der nun erst zu Bewegung und Ausdruck gekommen ist. Niemand kann behaupten oder auch bestreiten, dass ein ruhender, ein unbekannter Widerspruch ein wirklicher ist. In der Welt der Erscheinungen ist eben nur das wirklich, was zu Erscheinung und Ausdruck kommt. Angenommen indes, aber nicht zugegeben, es habe sich mit Bildung und rechtschaffenem Denken vertragen, dass ein Widerspruch gegen die Juden in den Seelen ruhte, so ist doch tatsächlich, dass eben der Gebildete und Rechtschaffene sich schämte, solchen ruhenden Gegensatz kund zu geben. Dieses Schamgefühl war der deutlichste Beweis, dass man ein ererbtes oder anerzogenes [unerzogenes?] Vorurteil für unberechtigt und unwürdig hielt.

Wer war es nun, der zuerst die Stirn hatte, in den Sphären der Bildungswelt offen und geradezu zu auszusprechen, er empfinde eine Idiosyncrasie gegen die Juden? Wer war es, der den Juden das Recht und die Fähigkeit, in einem bestimmten Kunstgebiete sich schaffend zu erweisen, absprach?

Es war Richard Wagner!

Er begann den kühnen Frevel an der Bildung und Humanität. Nach seinem Vorgange legten andere die sittliche Scham, sich offen zu Vorurteil, zu Hass und Verfolgung zu bekennen.

[Margin] Noch hat kein Künstler seinen Namen mit absolutem Judenhass befleckt, und so gewiss Richard Wagner in der Geschichte stehen wird, freilich anders als er meint, so gewiss wird sich mit seinem Namen die traurige Kunst verbinden, die dazu gehört, der Vernunft und der Humanität ins Gesicht zu schlagen.

Richard Wagner war noch ehrlich genug einzugestehen, dass er noch besondere Gründe für seinen Hass und seine Verfolgung habe, denn Juden seien es gewesen, die vormals, noch bevor er eine ganz neue Form der Kunst geschaffen hat, ihn hinderten und herabsetzten. Als ihm die absolute Grundlosigkeit dieses Vorwurfs bewiesen wurde, hielt er sich nicht für verpflichtet, denselben zurückzunehmen.

[Margin] Und was die Juden und Jüdinnen seiner Zeit? Sie waren so gebildet, dass sie gar nicht entbehren konnten, durch Richard Wagner noch gebildeter zu werden.

Das ist nun so. Man hält es für moralisch gestattet, einen widerlegten Vorwurf gegen die Juden stillschweigend oder offen aufrecht zu erhalten.

Nun schuf Richard Wagner seine neuen Werke, wonach alles Vergangene nur Chaos gewesen sein sollte; erst jetzt kam Licht, kam Organisation und Schönheit.

Ich getraue mir keine Berechtigung zu, über den Wert und Bestand der sogenannten Zukunftsmusik zu urteilen, das aber muss doch jeder gebildete Deutsche sagen: versetze das Verfahren und den Anspruch Richard Wagners auf ein anderer geistiges Gebiet – ich nehme zunächst das der Poesie. Denken wir uns also, es träte ein Mann auf der da sagte, alles was bisher als Dichtung angesehen wurde, – zunächst als deutsche und zunächst unsere klassische Periode, Lessing, Schiller, Goethe – alles ist nichtig, verkehrt und falsch, nur etwa Goethes Faust zweiter Teil kann als ein Anfang betrachtet werden, ähnlich wie Beethoven's neunte Symphonie, und auf dieser Grundlage baue ich weiter und schaffe Euch eine ganz neue Kunst, die mit der vergangenen und was darin galt, gar nichts mehr zu tun hat; ich bin der neue Schöpfer, mit mir beginnt der neue Tag.

Was würde man zu solcher Unmasslichkeit sagen? Jeder Denkende müsste erwidern, die Kultur aller Völker, und nun zunächst die von uns Deutschen ist eine Kontinuation, aus welcher Neubildungen hervorgehen, die aber unablöslich sind von den Errungenschaften der Vergangenheit. Was sich als eine ganz neue Welt auftun will, hat keinen Halt in sich, denn die Geschichte leugnen, das Erbe der Vergangenheit vernichten ist so frevelhaft als eitel.

Es ist keine Frage, dass ohne eine geniale Begabung ein Mann mit seinen Arbeiten nicht zu Ansehen und Anhang kommen kann, wie wir das vor uns sehen. Wir halten in der Literatur ein ähnliches Beispiel. In Friedrich Hebbel war eine entschiedene dichterische Kraft erschienen, aber es war Wahnwitz von ihm mit seiner Erscheinung eine ganz neue Geistesepoche datieren zu wollen, ja nicht einmal eine Epoche, sondern eben den Weltbeginn. Ähnlich verhält es sich mit Richard Wagner. Seine grössere oder geringere Bedeutung mag von Berechtigten definiert werden.

Nun aber komme ich auf meinen Ausgangspunkt zurück. Verträgt es sich auch nur mit einem kleinen Rest von Ehrgefühl, dass die Juden sich zu den Darstellungen Richard Wagnerscher Werke herandrängen?

Zuerst antworten manche, ich habe das Recht und die Pflicht zur Vervollkommnung meiner Bildung mich mit allen Erscheinungen im Bereich des Geistes bekannt zu machen. Gewiss. Sind aber die Männer und die Frauen, die so sprechen immer und allwege darauf bedacht, ihren Bildungstand lückenlos zu erhalten?

Und wäre es auch. Der Besuch einer von dem Komponisten geleiteten und ihm zu Ehren gemachten Aufführung seines Werkes ist eine persönliche Huldigung. Wäre der Verfasser eines Werkes in der Ferne oder nicht mehr am Leben, so gälte die Teilnahme dem Werke. So lange er lebt, hasst und verachtet, ist er eins mit seinem Werke, und wer ins Theater geht, huldigt ihm.

Nein, wird hier erwidert, vergiss nur den Verfasser von seinem Werke, ich frage gar nicht danach, was er denkt, ich lasse mir von ihm nichts vormachen, und weiter geht er mich nichts an! [Margin] Hand aufs Herz, oder auf die Noten, wo es sein soll!

Das ist nur Selbsttäuschung, denn Ihr wollt es nicht eingestehen, dass es Euch doch nur um ein Amüsement zu tun ist, und wenn Ihr ehrlich seid, könnt Ihr nicht leugnen, dass Ihr Euch in eine Gesellschaft drängt, von der Ihr wisst, dass Ihr verachtet und . . . [word illegible] hinaus geworfen seid, – es ist also gerade aus Genusssucht, es ist Stolzsucht, es ist das lässliche Verlangen, auch dabei zu sein, auch gesehen zu werden, auch zu sehen, an dem . . . [word illegible] teilzunehmen, die Juden und Jüdinnen gestattet, sich zur Aufführung der Wagner-Trilogie hier anzudrängen, und sie sollten doch das Gefühl haben, dass es der Nachbar und die Nachbarin wagen kann, gewiss er denkt; Pfui, über diese Bildungsprahlerei, die sich mit allerlei schmückt, aber den einzigen Schmuck nicht hat, und der heisst Ehre.

Berlin, 2. Mai 1881   Berthold Auerbach

Social Democracy on the Ambiguous Ground between Antipathy and Antisemitism: The Example of Wilhelm Hasenclever

The Jews of the Diaspora used the word *Rish'ut* (i.e. wickedness, pronounced *Rish'es* in the Yiddish vernacular), in order to express the feelings of the Gentile world towards them. This is the same feeling which Leon Pinsker named "Judophobie" in his book *Auto-Emancipation* – the feeling of antipathy which he thought was felt by every Gentile towards the Jews, whether or not this was shown. Obviously, the Jews developed parallel emotions, which also failed to find frequent expression.

In the European languages, *Rish'es* is usually translated as "antisemitism"; it is the purpose of this article to challenge this tendency. The *Rish'es* of the Gentiles could reach the point of killing Jews, and it could indeed find its expression in antisemitism, or worse. However, one must oppose this generalised rendering of the term, since part of the antisemitism was merely verbal, and affected the Jews less than the *Rish'es*.

The distinction is necessary in order to separate two phenomena, similar in their background, but equating them may lead to a confusion of concepts that would turn any collective hostility towards Jews into "antisemitism, and worse". The Holocaust, for example – an extreme case of antisemitism – loses its uniqueness when it is perceived as no more than an extreme form of *Rish'es*, which can be discussed along with any other collective hostility. It is therefore necessary to distinguish between *Rish'es*, antisemitism, and the aspiration to annihilate Jews and Judaism.

Rish'es of the Gentiles itself is as old as the Diaspora, and so is the Jewish response to it; modern antisemitism and its terminology is the result of Jewish emancipation following the French Revolution, and its goal is to curtail or abolish the legal, economic, and social accomplishments of this emancipation. The annihilation of the Jews is indeed antisemitism's final logical conclusion, implicit in it from the very beginning and expressly deduced by the end of the nineteenth century, but no one considered the actual realisation of this conclusion at that time. Antipathy, a feeling of loathing or even hatred towards Jews, is a pre-condition for the *Rish'es* of Judeophobia: antisemitism, however, can exist without it. The case of the antisemite Eichmann, who was not motivated by *Rish'es*, is famous. He was an antisemite by principle, out of a *Weltanschauung*. The equation of *Rish'es* and antisemitism creates in his case a distorted perception, according to which there is a uniform desire on the part of the Gentile world to confine the Jews in an isolated ghetto, if not indeed to

229

annihilate them. The only aspiration of *Rish'es*, however, was that the Jews disappear through assimilation, a goal that was also supported by the friends of the Jews who supported emancipation. Only consistent antisemites – and they were a minority – dreamt of Madagascar as the ghetto for World Jewry.

Antisemitism was a constant and persevering theory, *Rish'es* was a selective, capricious and elusive practice, therefore difficult to eradicate. In our generation it has been temporarily muted because of the association with the Holocaust, but it is by no means dead.

All the post-revolutionary, Conservative, Clerical, Liberal, Democratic and Socialist circles, dealt with Judeophobia and antisemitism, and their attitude towards both phenomena was hesitant and inconsistent from the start. Only with the consolidation of their positions in the German *Reich* did they decide: the Conservatives opted for antisemitism, the Liberals against it; the Clericals and Democrats maintained their Judeophobia, but opposed antisemitism. Only the Socialists remained in the ambiguous ground between both, in an ideological no-man's land. They shared with the Clericals and the Democrats a popular heritage of traditional *Rish'es* – as preached from the pulpits of the church and the universities, and like the antisemites, they tended to consider the Jews a corrupting capitalist element. In their propaganda they ascribed to the antisemites the potential of undermining capitalism, and for this reason they considered them partial partners in the struggle to purge society from capitalism.

In the *Allgemeiner Deutscher Arbeiter-Verein* (ADAV) workers' union, founded by Ferdinand Lassalle, the ambivalent attitude towards antisemites was expressed in the union's official publication, the *Social-Demokrat*.[1] in the rival movement of the *Sozialdemokratische Arbeiterpartei* (SDAP), led by August Bebel and Wilhelm Liebknecht, the philosopher Eugen Dühring had a temporary similar influence, encouraging an anti-capitalistic sympathy for antisemitism.[2]

It is at this point that Wilhelm Hasenclever,[3] the last president of the Lassalleans, becomes relevant. Using a pseudonym, Hasenclever published in 1881 a pamphlet entitled *Respect for Truth. A Contribution Regarding the Jewish Question in Germany*.[4]

This was the first German Social Democratic pamphlet in forty years to deal with the Jewish Question. The very first was written by Karl Marx, who published a double article *Zur Judenfrage* in 1844. This article became scarce in the

---

[1] *Social-Demokrat*, 1865–1871; *Neuer Social-Demokrat*, 1871–1875; On the antisemitic tendency of both publications see Arno Herzig, 'The Role of Antisemitism in the Early Years of the German Workers' Movement', in *LBI Year Book XXVI* (1981), pp. 243–259, esp. pp. 251–253.

[2] Eduard Bernstein, *Sozialdemokratische Lehrjahre*, Berlin 1928, chapter 10: 'Dühring-Bewegung und der Mohrenklub', pp. 52–59.

[3] Wilhelm Hasenclever, *Reden und Schriften*, edited by Ludger Heid, Klaus-Dieter Vinschen and Elisabeth Heid, Bonn 1989; introduction by Ludger Heid, ' " . . . gehört notorisch zu den hervorragendsten Leitern der sozialdemokratischen Partei' '. Wilhelm Hasenclever in der deutschen Arbeiterbewegung', pp. 15–68 (biography and evaluation). Henceforth quoted as Heid, *loc. cit.*

[4] Wilhelm Revel (i.e. W. Hasenclever), *Der Wahrheit die Ehre*, subtitled: *Ein Beitrag zur Judenfrage in Deutschland*, Nuremberg 1881, pp. 181–199.

original edition,[5] but was republished twice, once in the *Social-Demokrat* mentioned above, and once in 1881, in a paper of the same name, the *Sozialdemokrat*, edited by Eduard Bernstein[6] – thus showing that the workers' movement was incapable of dealing with the Jewish Question on a theoretical level independently. Perhaps it was this insecurity that lead Hasenclever to publish under a pseudonym: after all, the time had come to deal with this difficult issue from a fresh perspective, which would take into account the Socialist outlook, but would also be acceptable to the general public, which had reservations about Jews, shared by the author himself.

Both essays, the one by Marx as well as Hasenclever's, are imbued with antipathy towards the Jew as a type, but oppose antisemitism. This was due to the fact that both considered emancipation of every kind a basic, and thus uncontestable premise. It is possible that the re-publication of Marx's pamphlet encouraged Hasenclever to write his own, but the difference in their intellectual level and long-term influence makes any comparison impossible: Marx's article was indeed forgotten for a while, but after its re-publication it was the basis for any discussion of the Jewish Question within the Marxist camp for generations to come. We know nothing about the impact of Hasenclever's pamphlet, especially because the identity of the writer was unknown till the present time, when Ludger Heid and his co-editors published and annotated it.[7] However, it is not the impact of the pamphlet that concerns us here, but the testimony it bears to the level on which a man – considered till his dying day an ideal representative of the workers' movement – dealt with the fundamental question of emancipation. Since the merging of both currents of the workers' movement – the Lassallean and Bebelian, called in its time the "Eisenachian" Party – in 1875, Hasenclever was considered number two (or three) in the unified Party, along with Wilhelm Liebknecht and August Bebel.[8] Regarding the accomplishment of unification, he was considered number one.[9]

In every photograph of the Party's leaders in Hasenclever's generation, he appears next to Bebel and Liebknecht, his stature increased, just below Marx and Lassalle, whose dimensions are also exaggerated. The opinion of such a man on the Jewish Question, which was a relevant issue in both Germany and Russia

[5]This essay by the young Karl Marx was published in the only issue of the *Deutsch-Französische Jahrbücher*, confiscated immediately after its delivery at the end of February 1844.
[6]The tendentious synopsis in the *Neuer Social-Demokrat* of 20th September and 8th November 1872; the full version in *Sozialdemokrat* (Zürich), Nos. 27 and 28, 30th June and 7th July 1881.
[7]See note 3, Heid, *loc. cit.*, esp. pp. 53–57. Note 89, *ibid.*, describes the way in which the editors of Hasenclever's *Reden und Schriften, op. cit.* came to publish the pamphlet which had practically disappeared by that time.
[8]Liebknecht disregarded Marx's and Engels's warning against the unification, but Bebel was also aware of their negative attitude towards the ADAV; they both hoped that the unification would also lead to the taking over of the ADAV, and thus shared the enthusiasm of the mass of rank and file members to a limited degree only.
[9]Tölcke strongly urged for the unification of the parties from 1874. However, because of his previous animosity towards the "Eisenacher", he was viewed with suspicion, and the appeasing Hasenclever was preferred. About this issue see Arno Herzig, *Der Allgemeine Deutsche Arbeiterverein in der deutschen Sozialdemokratie. Dargestellt an der Biographie des Funktionäre Carl Wilhelm Tölcke (1817–1893)*, Berlin 1979, chap. 8: 'Einigung und Integration', pp. 294–341.

in 1881, in the year his pamphlet was published, is important to the historian. The significance of his response to the Jewish Question does not depend on our evaluation of him as a Party leader and theorist, but as the representative and spokesman of his Party's mood, whether or not this was his intention.

Among the three leaders of the unified Party, Hasenclever was the one who best expressed the opinion and mood of the rank and file member – better than Liebknecht, who claimed authority as Marx's representative, and better than Bebel, who relied heavily on Friedrich Engels, and aspired to become the integrative figure of the party.

Like Bebel, Hasenclever had a worker's past (as a tanner),[10] and like him, he was the man of letters in the Lassallean wing of the united Party, which had been impoverished in literary talent since the removal of Johann Baptist von Schweitzer from the office of president in 1871.[11]

The editors and authors of the book here under discussion, Ludger Heid, Klaus-Dieter Vinschen and Elisabeth Heid, have compiled the best of Hasenclever's articles and poems, together with the pamphlet on the Jewish Question with which we are concerned. His articles, poems and political essays,[12] reflect the Workers' Party in his generation, its intellectual horizons as well as its organisational and cultural accomplishments. This is of importance for a correct evaluation of the status of the Jewish Question within the emerging workers' movement.

Hasenclever's way to the workers' movement was similar to that of many other Liberal-Democrats from Western Germany, such as Friedrich Albert Lange and Carl Wilhelm Tölcke.[13] He started as an oppositionist in the *Nationalverein*,[14] and like others, he despaired about its lack of initiative concerning the question of German unification and the solution of the social problem of his day. When Lassalle appeared on a propaganda tour in the Rhineland he joined him.[15] He served in the Prussian army in the wars against Denmark (1864) and Austria (1866), and returned a staunch enemy of militarism. From 1866 on he served in

[10]Note the typical title of one of his essays of 1869 – 'Ich bin ein Gerber von der Feder', Hasenclever, *Reden und Schriften, op. cit.*, pp. 149–151. See notes there on the subject of the worker as writer.
[11]He owed his election as Schweitzer's follower to his courageous stand both against the continuation of the war after Sedan, and in this role as Duisburg's deputy in the *Reichstag*. See Heid, *loc. cit.*, pp. 27–30.
[12]Hasenclever, *Reden und Schriften, op. cit.*, chap. 1: Hasenclever als Parteipolitiker (pp. 72–92); als Parlamentarier (pp. 98–125); als Publizist (pp. 141–216) – this chapter also includes the essay on the Jewish Question; als Literat (pp. 218–310) – including the essay 'Glückliche Ehen', further discussed below.
[13]Joachim H. Knoll und Julius H. Schoeps (eds.), *Friedrich Albert Lange. Leben und Werk*, Duisburger Forschungen, vol. 21, 1975; papers by Peter Irmer, Shlomo Na'aman and Ludger Heid on the early publicist Lange; on Tölcke's democratic period, Herzig *op. cit.*, section: 'Tölckes Entwicklung zum Sozialisten', pp. 37–46, whch also mentions Hugo Hillmann, who, like Hasenclever, was one of the radical West Germans who came to the workers' movement through the *Nationalverein*.
[14]Heid, *loc. cit.*, esp. pp. 22–26 and the essay 'Über die Beeinflussung des Arbeiterstandes durch die gegenwärtige Presse', Hasenclever, *Reden und Schriften, op. cit.*, pp. 141–147, and the illuminating notes on pp. 147–148.
[15]This refers to Lassalle's second appearance in the Rhineland, which has become famous for his Ronsdorf speech of 22nd May 1864. Heid, *loc. cit.*, pp. 23.

leading positions in the ADAV, and from 1869 he was elected the ADAV's candidate for the electoral area of Duisburg.[16] In 1871 he was voted President of the ADAV instead of Schweitzer, who resigned. As President he started negotiations with the Eisenachians regarding the unification of the workers' parties, which was carried out in 1875.[17] Like other Socialist leaders, he became a candidate for the *Reichstag* elections, edited the rapidly growing party publications, and occasionally served the ensuing prison terms. From the date of the *Sozialistengesetz* – (enactment of the law against Socialism, 1878) and until his death, he was also harassed with expulsions from various German cities. He died in 1889, after a period of mental illness.[18]

The course of his life is that of the Socialist Democrat, anti-clerical and anti-militarist. He was a Socialist for whom Socialism meant the fulfilment of Liberalism in all domains, according to the original Latin meaning of the word. From Lassalle and Marx he took whatever supported this view: thus, he identified himself with the insurrectional Paris commune of 1871 backed by Marx.[19] The evolvement of society towards Socialism was for him a natural expression of human progress. He subscribed to Engels's view of the glorious Socialist future,[20] but the dialectics of this theorist, which he did not comprehend, held no attraction for him.

Engels, who labelled other Lassalleans "scoundrels", considered him simply an "ass".[21] He personified the ideal post-unification Social Democrat – a believer, confident in the political way he had chosen, a legalist as long as Liberals and rulers also upheld law and legality. His acquaintance with Jews and their problems was that of any ordinary citizen, no more. He felt as much antipathy towards them as did others. Along with all the Democrats, he criticised their arrogant, ambitious behaviour. It did not occur to him that Jews might also harbour criticism of their neighbours.

This criticism of Jews was formulated by Marx before him, in the pamphlet mentioned above (especially in the second part of this double article). Hasenclever's new point of criticism, was that the Jews, though persecuted in the past,

---

[16]*Ibid.*, pp. 21ff. The ground for the remarkable victory in this industrial electorate on 15th February 1869, was laid by the persons mentioned in note 13.

[17]See note 9.

[18]Heid, *loc. cit.*, p. 63, note 120. It is interesting to note, that in this new edition of Hasenclever's *Reden und Schriften, op. cit.*, which also includes a re-evaluation of his work, Hasenclever's mental illness is dealt with very discreetly, as though it were shameful. The latest publishers of his works conclude the chronological table with a quote from Osterroth's biographical dictionary, which only states quite simply that on the eve of the repeal of the law against Socialists, Hasenclever died (p. 312).

[19]Heid, *loc. cit.*, pp. 29–34. See Hasenclever, *Reden und Schriften, op. cit.*, where the article from *Vorwärts*, No. 76 (1st July 1877) is quoted, which begins with the words: "Nieder mit der Republik!", pp. 155–159.

[20]Hasenclever, *Reden und Schriften, op. cit.*, 'Staatssozialismus' (1877), pp. 160–164. This is in the same vein as Hasenclever's support of Bebel's "treffliche Schrift", *Die Frau und der Sozialismus*, in his essay 'Pfui der Schande!'; see pp. 165–168.

[21]Werner Blumenberg (ed.), *August Bebel. Briefwechsel mit Friedrich Engels*, Den Haag 1965. Engels's letter to Bebel dated 10th May 1883, p. 158: the 1875 agreement in Gotha had saddled them with "einem Esel und für eine Zeitlang auch einem Schuft". It is undisputed, that "Esel" refers to Hasenclever, and "Schuft" to Hasselmann.

now supported the law repressing Socialism in the *Reichstag* and in the press. His writings mention the Liberal Eduard Lasker and the Democrat Leopold Sonnemann, but not the Socialist Jews such as Paul Singer who maintained solidarity with their comrades. According to Hasenclever's view, as long as there existed a law against Socialists, even the discussion of discrimination against the Jews was a display of favouritism. The urgent repeal of this law was the only relevant issue at the present.

Antisemitism, which the public tends to consider relevant, is merely verbal. The antisemites have not reached the point of action, and it is therefore unnecessary to deal with them. He ascribes no importance to the *Antisemiten-Petition*, the antisemitic petition in the Prussian parliament in 1881, but the fact that the large majority of parliament sided against the Jews is considered by him as a sign that something is indeed amiss – *vox populi* being, as known, *vox dei*.[22]

Hasenclever finds that the passionate concern for the Jewish Question is artificial, and its purpose is to serve as a distraction from the injustice embodied in the law against Socialism. In the final account, it is part of a capitalist conspiracy against Socialism – which others called philosemitism. Indeed, if the German public is appalled by the 1881 pogroms in Russia after the assassination of the Tsar, this is also a distraction from the issue of the law against the Socialists.[23]

The Jewish Question is thus divided into two issues: in the West, including Germany, it is an artificial one, because the environment there exercises a civilising effect on the Jews, and they cannot exercise their talents for profiteering – the nations there are developed, and all that is called for, is Jewish self-restraint.[24] We may conclude, that Hasenclever believes that the Jews will disappear if they restrain their evil inclinations, as indeed Marx predicted. The East presents a different problem: there the Jews are stronger than their environment, and thus they prosper and do not opt for emigration, in spite of persecution.[25] Hasenclever has nothing further to say about Eastern Jews, but according to this line of thought, the popular claim that the Jews in the East were exploiting the nations among which they lived – upheld by Karl Kautsky years later[26] – was justified. This also implies that the German government was justified in preventing the immigration of Eastern Jews into Germany.

Thus, the problem of German Jews is their lack of self-restraint, as seen in the

---

[22]Revel (Hasenclever), *Der Wahrheit die Ehre, op. cit.*, section VIII, cited here from Hasenclever, *Reden und Schriften, op. cit.*, pp. 195–197 and p. 187.

[23]*Ibid.*, section II, pp. 183–186.

[24]*Ibid.*, pp. 185ff.

[25]*Ibid.*, p. 184, ". . . trotzdem wandern die Juden nicht aus nach den gesegneteren Ländern der Freiheit und Zivilisation".

[26]Karl Kautsky, 'Das Massaker von Kischeneff und die Judenfrage', *Die Neue Zeit*, 1903, vol. II, pp. 303–309, in which the very same argument as Hasenclever's is presented. The Jews are charged with the exploitation of the population, and are advised to behave inconspicuously and to assimilate speedily. The crisis of Eastern Jewry in 1881/1882, when Hasenclever's essay appeared, had a tremendous international impact, but it was harmless in comparison with the crisis of 1903. It is easy to understand Hasenclever's ignorance of the crisis which occurred in his own day. However, one cannot excuse the arrogant theorist Kautsky, who wrote the essay in the capacity of the Polish party's counsellor, as indeed he pointed out proudly.

attacks of the press, influenced by Jews, on the antisemites – attacks which create false and provocative propaganda. This is the reason for the slogan of "anti-Philosemitism", supported by Hasenclever. It is directed against what he describes as the "Philosemitische Hetze" (incitement) against antisemites, and will be discussed below.[27]

At the end of the pamphlet Hasenclever presents a revealing comparison: persecution has refined the Social Democrats but corrupted the Jews. There is an obvious lesson to be learned as far as the Social Democrats are concerned, and also one regarding Liberalism, which is identified with Jewry.

Hasenclever's opposition to antisemitism is mild, but he is quite determined about the negation of philosemitism.

The pamphlet ends with the words: "Equal rights and equal laws for *everyone* in the German *Reich*." This applies to the Jews as well, and thus affirms that the article is not antisemitic. However, the emphasised "for everyone" refers primarily to the Socialists, who do not enjoy legal equality, and suffer under a discriminating and repressive law. The conclusion is: Do not worry about the Jews, who can manage well enough, but about the mistreated Socialists.

The pamphlet is addressed to the citizens in general. Its intention is to decrease the importance of the Jewish Question and increase that of anti-Socialist repression, and for this reason it was published under a pseudonym: it is a citizen who speaks, not an interested party. Thus, lively concern with the Jewish Question is undesirable. If one were to elicit a conclusion from the content itself, it is that *antisemitism* is insignificant, though undesirable, while *antipathy* – the criticism of the Jewish way of life and a loathing for Jews' behaviour – is a justified and healthy response that will persist until the time when the Jews are assimilated within the German nation, and have disappeared completely.

Antisemitism is nothing; antipathy – everything.

In order to confirm this harsh sentence, we shall turn to one of the Hasenclever's literary sketches, published in 1877, under the title 'Happy Marriages'.[28] This is a description of the corruption of the nation's morals by the Jewish plutocracy, and is presented as a folkloristic tale by the renowned Democrat Franz Ziegler (here called "Z"), Lassalle's intimate friend in the days when he first began agitation among the workers.[29]

Ziegler is no antisemite either. In all his works, there is not a single word against Jewish emancipation. But he certainly felt an antipathy towards Jews. The crucial sentence in his narrative is: "Money does not reek, not even of garlic." To the Germans, as is well known, garlic symbolises the Jew. The protagonists of the story – *Kommerzienrat* Weinberg and his son-in-law Traut-

[27]Hasenclever, *Reden und Schriften*, *op. cit.*, pp. 184–185.

[28]*Ibid.*, 'Glückliche Ehen', pp. 304–310.

[29]On Franz Ziegler, see the introduction to the fifth volume of: Gustav Mayer (ed.), *Ferdinand Lassalle. Nachgelassene Briefe und Schriften*, Berlin 1925, pp. 2–10; in the same text see Ziegler's numerous letters to Lassalle, which cast a significant light on the background of his 'Offenes Antwortschreiben'. Ziegler also wrote the first version of the ADAV's statute. An attentive reading of the letter's explicit Judeophobia, makes it obvious that "Z" could only refer to Ziegler.

mann, both manufacturers and tradesmen, as well as Weinberg's beautiful and desirable daughter Rebekka – are Jews.[30]

The aged Ziegler concludes, that it requires a Hercules to clean this Augean stable, and Hasenclever states his belief that it is the Socialists who are destined for this Herculean task.

Did Hasenclever accurately portray relations between Socialists and Jews until the end of the First World War? Did he indeed, like the proverbial blind chicken, find the grain of truth – namely that antisemitism was unimportant to the Socialists? Or was antipathy the secret? 1881, the year in which the essay in question was published, will not supply us with a clear answer. The year 1891 will.

In 1881 the Social Democrats feared the antisemitic movement's possible electoral successes at their expense. Antisemitic propaganda was directed primarily towards the working class, especially in Berlin, in addition, the law curtailing Social Democracy's propaganda was already in force, and it was unclear how it would affect the elections. For this reason, the *Sozialdemokrat* edited by Eduard Bernstein in Zürich, directed much of its attention to the antisemites' rallies, and so did the Party, which was operating under clandestine conditions. It was not love for Jews, but rather their hatred towards the government, that led them to do so. The motive for this course of action was selfish (though that does not negate the historical value of their position). A book about the history of the Workers' Party in Berlin written many years later by Bernstein (1907), presents his great interest in antisemitism in the context of the Party's electoral prospects.[31]

The first united congress of the Second International convened in Brussels in 1891 in a different atmosphere: the fear of suppression had gone, but when Abraham Cahan from New York proposed a denunciation of antisemitism as opposed to the courageous Jewish struggle against the Tsar, a heated discussion arose in the committee which prepared the debates. The representatives of Latin countries claimed that such a position was impossible, since the Jews were the main representatives of capitalism. A verbal compromise was finally found, typical of this forum – to denounce jointly antisemitism and philosemitism. The congress therefore denounced both antisemitic and philosemitic agitation.[32]

From that moment on, following the resolution against antisemitism, the Socialists no longer described capitalism as a result of Jewish activities; but what

---

[30]'Glückliche Ehen', *loc. cit.*, p. 305; "Geld riecht nicht, auch nicht nach Knoblauch".

[31]Eduard Bernstein, *Die Geschichte der Berliner Arbeiter-Bewegung*, vol. II, Berlin 1907, second chapter, 'Des Sozialistengesetzes zweite Phase. Vergebliches Mühen des sozialen Bauernfanges', pp. 59–126.

[32]*Congrès International ouvrier socialiste. Histoire de la IIe Internationale*, vol. 8, 'La question juive', pp. 41–44; the resolutions of the eighth session in German on pp. 15–16, in French, pp. 43–44. The crucial point in the German version reads: "Verurteilung der antisemitischen und philosemitischen Hetzereien", and in French – "condamnant les excitations antisémitiques et philosémitiques".

Police dissolve a Socialist meeting
attended by Wilhelm Liebknecht and
Wilhelm Hasenclever

The Second Congress of the Social Democratic Workers Party in 1871

about the denunciation of "philosemitic incitement"? Was this only meant to express opposition to the apologetics of capitalism, or was this mainly an indirect expression of antipathy towards the Jews? For public opinion all over the world did consider the Jews controllers of the literary and journalistic market, and as such, the apologists of capitalism.

This is what Ziegler and Hasenclever thought at the time, and likewise it was the opinion of the workers' representatives from France and Belgium at the congress in Brussels.

Was this the very antisemitism forbidden to Socialists, rearing its "ugly" head under the guise of "opposition to philosemitism"? Simply viewed, with no attention to delicate nuances, the declaration of war on philosemitism indeed seems to be no more than disguised antisemitism. Antisemitism, removed through the front door, but, it would seem, let in by the back.

Within German society a moderate antipathy towards Jews was prevalent. In Austria it was more aggressive, in Russia less explicit, in the Ukraine more overt. In Italy it was less noticeable, in France and Belgium more so. In all these countries, the Socialists refrained from dealing with the Jewish Question. The two-fold decision in Belgium reflected hesitation and confusion. The solution was to avoid the issue. Only when remote regions such as the "Oriental countries" or the Ukraine were discussed, did the Socialists feel confident enough to denounce antisemitic pogroms. This confusion led them to make frequent mention of the resolution against antisemitism in their propaganda, while a silence was kept on the simultaneous declaration against philosemitism. At the same time, they were careful not to upset the anti-Jewish sentiment prevalent within the public and the Party, claiming that there was also a committment to struggle against philosemitism. This claim was frequently used by the Poles in various regions of divided Poland. At the same time, the Jews in the Party refrained from mentioning any Jewish issues, fearing that this would raise the problem of philosemitism.

The balance required between the philo- and antisemitic issues, was theoretically and practically discussed by the German Party's most brilliant man of letters – Franz Mehring – who joined the Party in 1891, when the law against Socialism was repealed. In many ways, Mehring reminds one of Franz Ziegler. Like him, he was a Democrat from trans-Elbian Prussia, and like him he had imbibed an intense anti-Jewish sentiment in his parental home. Like Ziegler, he spent a long time in the outer circles of the Socialist Party. Unlike Ziegler, however, he finally did join the Social Democrats. Mehring proved his opposition to antisemitism by copying Engels's article against it from the Austrian Socialist Party organ[33] for the *Volkszeitung* of Berlin, the Leftist Liberal

---

[33]Mehring's hostile attitude towards Social Democracy in his work '*Die deutsche Sozialdemokratie, ihre Geschichte und ihre Lehre*, 1879, on the eve of the introduction of the law against Socialists, was not yet forgotten and it decreased his influence.

publication of which he was the Acting Editor.[34] This was a positive line of action, which also benefited him, since this publication, whose Editor-in-Chief was Aaron Bernstein (Eduard's uncle), was the symbol of philosemitism. Engels's article further cemented the Liberal-philosemitic position of the paper. After joining the Social Democrats, however, Mehring energetically strove for a different balance between anti- and philosemitism in his writing: in many articles he proved the hypocrisy and adverse effects of philosemitism, while his opposition to antisemitism was expressed in a very mild manner.

Articles such as 'Anti- und Philosemitisches', or 'Kapitalistische Agonie', are self-explanatory. Others require some interpretation, such as 'Mönch und Rabbi', with the main characters representing anti- and philosemites, "both stinking", as Heine had put it at the end of his famous 'Disputation' in the *Hebräische Melodien*, or 'Drillinge' (Triplets), which was written to pillory the philosemitic capitalist, the antisemite and the anarchist, who jointly represent the powers of evil.[35]

The question of whether it is permissible to support the struggle of the philosemitic Liberals against the antisemites, who represent – in their own way – a Socialist rebellion, is typical of Mehring's outlook. Instead of answering directly, he says that the formulation of the question already implies the answer, and this means that it is negative; he could of course claim that the opposite was meant, as this was said regarding the elections to the Prussian diet, where the Liberals were weak and the antisemites strong: a sphinx-like attitude indeed.

Mehring is thus opposed to antisemitism, when it is perceived in a most narrow and formal sense, as a movement competing with the Socialist Party in the elections, and when it restricts the meaning of capitalism to Jewish capitalism alone. The entire emotional content which accompanies antisemitic propaganda, is transferred by Mehring to the realm of antipathy towards Jews, permitted also to Socialists. In order to explain what it was that he considered antisemitism and what as permissible antipathy, he added to his articles (those given above, as well as many which cannot be mentioned here), an important and influential literary enterprise: the publication of unknown or forgotten articles by the founders of modern Socialism – Marx, Engels and Lassalle. The first volume of this posthumous publication appeared in 1902,[36] and included Marx's article on the Jewish Question. With the exception of the publication of Marx's work by the aging Engels, this was the most important literary enterprise for the inculcation of what was then called "the doctrine of scientific Socialism". The publication was a scientific paradigm at the time, and had world-wide

[34] *Marx-Engels-Werke* (MEW), East Berlin 1956–1968, vol. XXII, pp. 49–51, and Friedrich Engels on antisemitism, *Volks-Zeitung*, XXXVIII, No. 110 (13th May 1890), quoted in: Thomas Höhle, *Franz Mehring. Sein Weg zum Marxismus, 1869–1891*, Berlin 1956, p. 265.

[35] Franz Mehring, 'Anti- und Philosemitisches', *Die Neue Zeit*, 1890–1891, vol. II, pp. 585–588; 'Kapitalistische Agonie', *Die Neue Zeit*, 1891–1892, vol. II, pp. 545–548; his 'Mönch und Rabbi', *Die Neue Zeit*, 1892–1893, vol. I, pp. 841–844; and his 'Drillinge', *Die Neue Zeit*, 1893–1894, vol. II, pp. 577–582.

[36] Franz Mehring, *Aus dem literarischen Nachlass von Karl Marx, Friedrich Engels und Ferdinand Lassalle*, vol. I, *Gesammelte Schriften von Karl Marx und Friedrich Engels, von März 1841 bis Mitte 1844*, Stuttgart 1902.

influence. This enterprise served Mehring as an opportunity to promote his view of philo- and antisemitism, with Marx's texts as a basis:[37] the Jews' right to legal equality is the same as any capitalist's right, i.e. in as much as the capitalists enjoy their rights and privileges, so should the Jews. However, the antipathy towards Jews is also justified, because, trade and speculation form their world and are inherent in them. The Jewish Socialists like Marx and Lassalle showed the right way: they assimilated within their environment and were no longer recognisable as Jews. Mehring concludes that the *petite bourgeoisie* has no choice but to become Socialist, and the same is true of the Jews: the philosemites will not save them.

From the founders of Socialism, and through Mehring, the orthodox Marxists such as Rosa Luxemburg, Leo Trotsky, Lenin and Stalin, learnt the doctrine of philo- and antisemitism. Thus, antipathy towards the Jews is for Mehring the ambiguous ground between anti- and philosemitism, and the same is true for the epigones.[38]

These ambiguous grounds between antipathy and antisemitism, were a comfortable area for all the covert antisemites among the workers and the Party functionaries, whose freedom of action had been curtailed from above by the Party's resolution. This is generally true for many European countries, and emphatically so of Eastern Europe.

It would be a distortion to say that Mehring was an overt or covert antisemite, and that he intended to provide this ambiguous ground. If we substitute for the term "antisemite" *Rish'es* or "antipathy" as defined here, we will have a better understanding of his attitude. At the same time, his position will no longer be perceived as a personal whim, but as a reflection of the general public attitude, which is thus of historical meaning. However, the results of his approach would have surprised Mehring, because when the antisemites gained power in the second decade of our century, it was easy for them to lead the inhabitants of this swamp of antipathy towards whatever degree of antisemitism they desired, including the annihilation of the Jews. Only a single step separated antipathy from antisemitism. Ordinary citizens – Socialists as well as the bourgeoisie – who constantly expressed their detestation of Jewish flaws, had always considered themselves quite removed from the vulgarity, fanaticism, and simplifications of the antisemites; they thought that between themselves and these antisemites there was not a small step but a vast distance. And yet, only three years elapsed

[37]Mehring's introduction to the chapter 'Aus den Deutsch-Französischen Jahrbüchern' in the posthumous edition, gave him the opportunity to present his own position regarding the Jewish Question, through the favourable interpretation of Marx's essays on that question. Also *ibid.*, 'Gesellschaft und Staat', pp. 341–352, followed by 'Die Judenfrage', pp. 352–356. His view impacted on the first generation of Marxists, and influenced Lenin as well.

[38]The shift from Judeophobia to antisemitism and then to the concept of the extinction of the Jews is most evident in Stalin's case. In his theoretical writing on *Marxism and the National Question* in 1913, he held the traditional Marxist view regarding the Jewish Question, which he did not believe to be a national question at all. Indeed, it would disappear with their assimilation following the social upheaval. Yet he ended with the preparation for the doctors' trial, which aroused the fear of pogroms among the Jews.

between the seizure of power by the Nazis in 1933, and the display in the 1936 Olympics of the people's rebirth which was almost contemporaneous with the Nuremberg Laws, thus revealing how easy it was to turn antipathy into antisemitism.

Ziegler and Mehring grew up in Eastern Germany; Hasenclever in the West. But their attitude towards the Jewish Question was the same: both in their rejection of antisemitism and in their antipathy towards Jews. The first two belong to the intellectual elite; Hasenclever and his friend Tölcke were less sophisticated, but they all shared the same antipathy towards Jews (which was indeed felt by Marx himself). Part of their arguments impressed the emancipated Jews, but most of them only aroused surprise and ridicule, then as now. Marx's proof of the inferiority of Jews based on the prayer said upon leaving the lavatory, Hasenclever's argument against Jewish cemeteries, or Mehring's claims about the inferiority of Yiddish, all testify to their persistent wallowing in the Judeophobic swamp, or else to a deprecation of the Jewish problem, something which they would never have allowed themselves when discussing the problems of any other nation. Among all those mentioned here, the most interesting is Hasenclever. Not because he is the most important, but rather because he was the most popular among them, and believed he would be able to persuade the public at large – under the guise of a pseudonym – to oppose the discrimination against Jews professed by antisemites, and at the same time to uphold the antipathy towards the Jews, which the philosemites were trying to diminish – without success.

A man like Hasenclever reveals the nature of the relations between Socialists and Jews in a clearer and more explicit fashion than do the more illustrious representatives of the Socialist cause. The thousands of activists in the labour unions and the Social Democratic Party, and thousands of editors who developed in the atmosphere created by Hasenclever and his colleagues, led sections of the working class from the ambiguous ground of antipathy towards Jews, to active antisemitism.

Like Mehring, Hasenclever would have been surprised by the results of his historical impact; he too, would claim that this was not the result he had intended. No doubt, the parity between the impacts of antisemitism and philosemitism as posed by Hasenclever and Mehring, as well as the mass of members of the International, was merely the result of some analytic carelessness. Eduard Bernstein made this clear in his article, 'Das Schlagwort und der Antisemitismus' (The Slogan and Antisemitism),[39] but unfortunately, errors sometimes go down in history as intentional misdeeds. I believe, that the Socialist stand on the Jewish Question is one outstanding example.

There is one more point to be remembered, namely, that such errors exist not only in the camp of Hasenclever or Mehring, but on the Jewish side as well.

---

[39]Eduard Bernstein, 'Das Schlagwort und der Antisemitismus', *Die Neue Zeit*, 1893–1894, vol. II, pp. 228–237f.

Nazi Domination

The End of Emancipation and the Illusion of Preferential Treatment: German Zionism, 1933–1938

BY FRANCIS R. NICOSIA

In the midst of the political crisis in Germany in 1932, the *Jüdische Rundschau* carried an editorial entitled 'Forderungen und Aufgaben für den Fall eines Nationalsozialistischen Sieges' (Challenges and Tasks in the event of a National Socialist Victory) on 12th August.[1] It predicted the complete collapse of the "jüdisches Assimilationsgedanken" (the idea of Jewish assimilation) in Germany should Hitler become *Reich* Chancellor, and called on all Jews, as the Zionist movement had done in the past, "sich auf eine neue Wirklichkeit umzustellen" (to adapt themselves to a new reality). In a letter dated 15th June 1932, to Chaim Weizmann of the World Zionist Organisation, Kurt Blumenfeld, President of the *Zionistische Vereinigung für Deutschland* (ZVfD), wrote: "Die deutschen Juden gleiten in eine neue Situation hinein, ohne sich über die grundlegenden Veränderungen voll Rechenschaft zu geben . . ." (The German Jews are slipping into a new situation without taking completely into account the fundamental changes . . .); he further asserted that the deepening economic crisis might be the primary motivation for future converts to Zionism from among the Jews of Germany.[2] In his speech to the delegates to the 24th *Delegiertentag* of the ZVfD in Frankfurt a. Main on 11th September 1932, Blumenfeld outlined the grim prospects for all Jews in Germany in the near future, and the absolutely essential nature and the undeniable correctness of the Zionist alternative for all German Jews.[3]

In these and other references to the ever deepening political and economic crisis in Germany and its likely impact on the Jewish community during the half year or so before the National Socialist *Machtübernahme*, the German Zionist movement did not dwell on the specific form that Nazi persecution of Jews in Germany might take; nor did it really concern itself with activities designed to work against a Nazi political victory. This is not surprising in view of the traditional Zionist emphasis on Palestine with its concomitant and relative de-

---

[1] *Jüdische Rundschau*, 12th August 1932, reprinted in Jehuda Reinharz, *Dokumente zur Geschichte des deutschen Zionismus 1882–1933*, Tübingen 1981 (Schriftenreihe wissenschaftlicher Abhandlungen des Leo Baeck Instituts 37), Nr. 210, pp. 528–530.

[2] Kurt Blumenfeld, *Im Kampf um den Zionismus. Briefe aus fünf Jahrzehnten*, Stuttgart 1976, Veröffentlichung des Leo Baeck Instituts, p. 122. Just five months before, in another letter to Weizmann dated 5th January 1932, Blumenfeld seemed to doubt that Hitler and National Socialism realistically stood any chance of coming to power. See *ibid.*, pp. 114–117.

[3] *Jüdische Rundschau*, 16th September 1932, as reprinted in Reinharz, *Dokumente, op. cit.*, Nr. 211, pp. 530–542.

emphasis of the need for *Abwehr* against antisemitism in Germany.[4] Instead, it focused with alarm on the correctness of the traditional Zionist message, the failure of most German Jews to heed that message in the past and the singular importance of its role in the upheaval that was coming. This editorial approach was also taken time and again by the *Jüdische Rundschau* during the early weeks of the Nazi regime.[5] As it contemplated the gathering storm in 1932 and its own critical role in the coming crisis in Jewish life in Germany, the ZVfD did not imagine that the nature of Nazi antisemitism and its consequent policies towards the Jewish community as a whole might deprive it of an environment conducive to effective Zionist work. This was, of course, the environment of Jewish emancipation as it existed in the Weimar Republic. If emancipation was not, in the Zionist view, a feasible or desirable solution to the Jewish Question, it was nevertheless the essential, if rapidly disappearing, means to the fulfilment of Zionist ends.[6]

It is true that there was a certain convergence of Nazi and Zionist interests in the removal of Jews from Germany. Theodor Herzl had annunciated a fundamental premise of political Zionism that National Socialism simply could not reject, namely that Jewish emancipation and assimilation, rather than being the solution to the Jewish Question, were the causes of modern antisemitism.[7] It is also true that Hitler's regime, in its determination to remove Jews from Germany, undertook specific measures designed to facilitate Zionist work in Germany and the promotion of Jewish emigration.[8] However, what appeared on the surface to be a symbiosis of Zionist and Nazi aspirations in Germany was in fact much more complicated and problematical: it was, rather, a relationship in which the all-powerful Nazi state exploited Zionism and the German Zionist movement against a backdrop of coercion and brutality towards all Jews. As Jews, Zionists in Germany were generally not exempt from the brutality of political, economic and social disenfranchisement that the Nazi regime meted out to the entire Jewish community after 1933. Thus, Zionist work in the Third *Reich*, unlike in the Weimar Republic, was rendered extraordinarily difficult and dangerous. With the end of Jewish emancipation in 1933, the respective means

---

[4]For the ambiguous relationship between the ZVfD and the idea of defence against antisemitism in Weimar Germany, see Arnold Paucker, *Der jüdische Abwehrkampf gegen Antisemitismus und Nationalsozialismus in den letzten Jahren der Weimarer Republik*, Hamburg 1968, pp. 39ff.; Jehuda Reinharz, 'The Zionist Response to Antisemitism in Germany', in *LBI Year Book XXX* (1985), pp. 105–140.

[5]See for example *Jüdische Rundschau*, 31st January, 29th March 1933.

[6]This idea is touched upon briefly in Francis R. Nicosia, 'Ein nützlicher Feind. Zionismus im nationalsozialistischen Deutschland 1933–1939', *Vierteljahrshefte für Zeitgeschichte*, 37 (Juli 1989), pp. 367–400. For an excellent account of the larger implications of the end of emancipation for Jews in Germany during the 1930s, see Reinhard Rürup, 'Das Ende der Emanzipation. Die antijüdische Politik in Deutschland von der "Machtergreifung" bis zum Zweiten Weltkrieg', in *Die Juden im Nationalsozialistischen Deutschland/The Jews in Nazi Germany 1933–1943*, herausgegeben von Arnold Paucker mit Sylvia Gilchrist und Barbara Suchy, Tübingen 1986 (Schriftenreihe wissenschaftlicher Abhandlungen des Leo Baeck Instituts 45), pp. 97–114.

[7]See for example Theodor Herzl, *Der Judenstaat. Versuch einer modernen Lösung der Judenfrage*, in Julius Schoeps (Hrsg.), *Wenn Ihr wollt, ist es kein Märchen*, Königstein/Ts 1985, pp. 209–211.

[8]See Francis R. Nicosia, *The Third Reich and the Palestine Question*, Austin–London 1985, chapts. 2, 3, 4, 7, 8.

with which Zionism and National Socialism in Germany hoped to achieve the common end of Jewish emigration proved to be very different. The brutal liquidation of German Jewry after 1933, notwithstanding the dramatic increase in German-Jewish immigration into Palestine, could never be a desirable condition for effective Zionist work in Germany.

I. MEANS AND ENDS IN ZIONIST POLICY

Before the First World War, most German Zionists, themselves emancipated and highly assimilated Jews, did not reject Jewish life in the Diaspora altogether, and viewed Zionist emigration to Palestine as a phenomenon exclusively for the masses of Eastern European Jews.[9] This gave way, however, after the First World War to a focus on Palestine and the idea of ultimate emigration for German Jews as well.[10] Nevertheless, German Zionism continued to assume that the conditions of Jewish life created by Jewish emancipation during the Wilhelminian and Weimar periods would have to prevail as the essential environment for effective Zionist work for as long as Jews remained in Germany. The *Jüdische Rundschau* greeted the revolution in Germany in November 1918, with the words: "Die Demokratie und die Gerechtigkeit, in deren Zeichen das deutsche Volk in die neue Zeit eintritt, sind uns starke, unüberwindliche Helfer. Wir begrüssen die Revolution!"[11] (Democracy and Justice, under whose sign the German people are entering the new era, are strong and unconquerable helpers for us. We welcome the revolution!) The 15th *Delegiertentag* of the ZVfD of 25th–27th December 1918, clearly stressed the twin goals of building up the Jewish National Home in Palestine and the complete equality of Jews in Germany and in other countries.[12] As late as 21st October 1932, the *Jüdische Rundschau* published a statement to all Zionists by Kurt Blumenfeld, President of the ZVfD, reminding them of the resolution on the direction of Zionist policies in Germany, recently passed at its convention in Frankfurt, which authorised the leadership of the ZVfD: ". . . den Kampf für die Durchsetzung unserer Forderungen – Wahrung der vollen Gleichberechtigung und Freiheit der Entfaltung unserer Eigenart – mit ganzer Kraft zu führen"[13] (. . . to lead with all of its strength in the struggle for the attainment of our demands – protection of full equality and freedom of development of our own uniqueness). However National Socialism intended to eliminate all Jewish rights and equality in Germany and the German Zionist movement, notwithstanding its usefulness to the authorities, was really

[9]See Jehuda Reinharz, *Fatherland or Promised Land. The Dilemma of the German Jew*, Ann Arbor 1975, pp. 119–120.

[10]See Reinharz, 'The Zionist Response', *loc. cit.*, p. 138.

[11]*Jüdische Rundschau*, 15th November 1918, as cited in Werner T. Angress, 'Juden im politischen Leben der Revolutionszeit', in *Deutsches Judentum in Krieg und Revolution 1916–1923*. Ein Sammelband herausgegeben von Werner E. Mosse unter Mitwirkung von Arnold Paucker, Tübingen 1971 (Schriftenreihe wissenschaftlicher Abhandlungen des Leo Baeck Instituts 25), p. 146.

[12]'Protokoll des XV. Delegiertentages der Zionistischen Vereinigung für Deutschland', Berlin, den 25.–27. Dezember 1918, reprinted in Reinharz, *Dokumente, op. cit.*, Nr. 116, pp. 245–254.

[13]*Jüdische Rundschau*, 21st October 1932.

not to be exempt from the brutality of the Nazi liquidation of Jewish life in Germany after 1933. Its interests and activities, like those of other non-Zionist and anti-Zionist Jewish organisations, would suffer enormously with the end of Jewish emancipation in Germany while its central role in the regime's efforts to secure rapid Jewish emigration from Germany did little to protect it from the overall Nazi onslaught against the Jewish community.

In his essay 'Entscheidungsjahr 1932', published in 1966, Robert Weltsch, the former editor of the *Jüdische Rundschau*, observed that in 1932 and for a while thereafter many Zionists maintained the illusion that some sort of altered but mutually acceptable relationship between a Nazi state and German Jews was possible.[14] On a number of occasions in 1933, the ZVfD attempted to convince the authorities of the need to maintain suitable conditions for Jewish life in Germany, at least until the process of dissimilation and emigration ran its course. It set out to secure what it considered to be the appropriate means in Germany for the common end of Jewish emigration. On 21st June 1933, the ZVfD addressed a formal declaration to Hitler expressing its desire to work for the resolution of the Jewish Question in Germany in a manner that would be in the best interests of both the German and the Jewish peoples. Entitled 'Äusserung der Zionistischen Vereinigung für Deutschland zur Stellung der Juden im neuen deutschen Staat' (Statement of the Zionist Federation for Germany on the Position of the Jews in the New German State), the statement rejected emancipation and assimilation as solutions to the Jewish Question; it further endorsed Germany's national rebirth under National Socialism and the principles of *Abstammung, Religion, Schicksalsgemeinschaft* and *Artbewusstsein* that were its foundations and that were, moreover, the foundations of Zionism as the expression of the national rebirth of the Jewish people.[15] Besides outlining Zionist plans for Jewish emigration from Germany to Palestine and condemning international anti-German propaganda and boycott efforts, the statement suggested a protected, minority status for the Jewish community while the process of emigration was under way:

"Worum es uns geht, ist die Schaffung einer Lebensmöglichkeit für die Gesamtheit unter Wahrung unserer Ehre, die uns das höchste Gut ist. Wir wollen auf dem Boden des neuen Staates, der das Rassenprinzip aufgestellt hat, unsere Gemeinschaft in das Gesamtgefüge so einordnen, dass auch uns, in der uns zugewiesenen Sphäre, eine fruchtbare Betätigung für das Vaterland möglich ist."

("Our concern here is in securing a possibility for living for the entire community based on the protection of our honour, which is our greatest possession. We want so to arrange our community in its entirety on the soil of the new state, which has raised the principle of race, that for us too a fruitful field of activity for the fatherland in our own sphere is possible.")

[14]Robert Weltsch, 'Entscheidungsjahr 1932', in *Entscheidungsjahr 1932. Zur Judenfrage in der Endphase der Weimarer Republik*. Ein Sammelband herausgegeben von Werner E. Mosse unter Mitwirkung von Arnold Paucker, Tübingen 1966, 2. Auflage (Schriftenreihe wissenschaftlicher Abhandlungen des Leo Baeck Instituts 13), p. 557.
[15]Politisches Archiv des Auswärtigen Amts/Bonn (hereafter PA): Inland II A/B, 83–21, Bd. 1, 'Äusserung der Zionistischen Vereinigung für Deutschland zur Stellung der Juden im neuen deutschen Staat', Berlin, 21. Juni 1933.

If the statement of 21st June was vague about the specific conditions under which German Jews should live in the new Germany, a general memorandum of 13th September 1933, from Martin Rosenblüth of the ZVfD, shortly before he emigrated to England, addressed that question with considerable clarity and detail.[16] Rosenblüth reasoned that German Zionism had little choice but to seek conditions that would best ensure orderly Jewish emigration, and that those conditions, especially the matter of the assets of the emigrants in the process, were possible only with the co-operation and support of Nazi authorities. He defined a specific status for Jews in the new Germany, one that the ZVfD hoped would prevail during the process of removing Jews and at least some of their assets from Germany in an orderly, humane and mutually beneficial manner. He reasoned thus:

> "Die deutsche Zionisten . . . glauben, dass die Neuregelung des Status der deutschen Juden davon ausgehen muss, dass die deutsche Judenheit eine deutlich erkennbare festumrissene Gruppenminorität gegenüber einer nummerisch mehr als 100x so starken Staatsnation darstellt."
>
> (The German Zionists believe that the new regulations governing the status of Jews must be based on the assumption that German Jewry constitutes a clearly recognisable and well-defined minority group in the midst of a nation that is numerically 100 times as large).

He further argued that since the German *Staatsnation* was determined to identify as closely as possible the concepts of *Volk* and *Staat*, it was unrealistic to expect the old ideas and formulae for Jewish life in Germany to continue. Instead he suggested that entirely new approaches had to be found, ". . . um ein *modus vivendi* für eine solche Minoritätengruppe innerhalb des neuen Staates zu schaffen" (in order to establish a *modus vivendi* for such a minority group within the new state).

Rosenblüth elaborated on the conditions that he hoped would characterise the existence of Jews as a recognised national minority in the new Germany. He called for the civil and legal equality of Jews with other citizens and the avoidance of any restrictions on their economic livelihood. He also appealed for support from the state for the occupational training and retraining of German Jews in order both to ensure a livelihood while they remained in Germany and to prepare them for a new life in Palestine. Protection for autonomous Jewish religious institutions, schools, sports organisations, welfare agencies and emigration offices was also suggested, and particular emphasis was placed on the need to allow the free emigration of at least half of German Jewry with its assets over the following ten years. In short, Rosenblüth and the ZVfD hoped that the means to the common end of Jewish emigration would be characterised by conditions of Jewish life in Germany similar in some respects to those that prevailed before 1933. Notwithstanding the reality that both the ZVfD and the Nazi state generally agreed that the Jews constituted a distinct *Volksgemeinschaft*, and that it was desirable to promote Jewish emigration from Germany, the antisemitism of the regime would preclude much of Rosenblüth's programme,

---

[16]PA: Ref. D., Po5 NE adh 6, Nr. 4, Bd. 2, 'Zusätzliche Bemerkungen zur deutschen Judenfrage', 13. September 1933.

and impose extraordinarily difficult conditions on German Zionism in its efforts to secure an orderly and economically viable departure of Jews from Germany.

By the end of 1933, the ZVfD along with most other Jewish organisations in Germany generally came to rely on their own resources and to look to Jewish organisations rather than to the authorities for whatever relief or assistance that was necessary under the circumstances.[17] Appeals and complaints to the government seemed increasingly hopeless as the realisation that Hitler and National Socialism were not simply passing phenomena, and that Jewish life in Germany was about to come to an end became increasingly prevalent. The state was no longer an instrument for the protection of Jews in Germany against antisemitic excesses; it had become itself the instrument of those excesses.

II. VULNERABILITY, DEPLETION AND ISOLATION

In 1933, in spite of some clear signs that the authorities were inclined to "favour" Zionism and the German Zionist movement as primary instruments in promoting Jewish emigration, the ZVfD was as much the target of Nazi brutality and violence as the non-Zionist and anti-Zionist Jewish organisations in Germany; its functions and activities were often severely threatened.[18] In March 1933, two

---

[17]See Avraham Barkai, *From Boycott to Annihilation. The Economic Struggle of German Jews, 1933–1943*, transl. by William Templer, Hanover, N.H. 1989, p. 39. An example of this, of course, is the formal establishment of the *Reichsvertretung der deutschen Juden* in September, in which the ZVfD played an important role along with non-Zionist organisations. See Max Gruenewald, 'The Beginning of the "Reichsvertretung"', in *LBI Year Book I* (1956), pp. 57–67; Friedrich Brodnitz, 'Die Reichsvertretung der deutschen Juden', in Hans Tramer (ed.), *In Zwei Welten. Siegfried Moses zum fünfundsiebzigsten Geburtstag*, Tel-Aviv 1962, pp. 106–113; and Hugo Dahn, 'Die Gründung der Reichsvertretung', *ibid.* pp. 97–105.

[18]The clear signs included, of course, the *Haavara* Transfer Agreement, concluded on 28th August between the German government and Zionist officials from Germany and Palestine, as well as the policies of the Foreign Ministry, the Economics Ministry, the Ministry of the Interior and the *Reichsbank*. See Nicosia, *Third Reich, op. cit.*, chaps. 3 and 4; and Werner Feilchenfeld, Dolf Michaelis and Ludwig Pinner, *Haavara-Transfer nach Palästina und Einwanderung deutscher Juden 1933–1939*, Tübingen 1972 (Schriftenreihe wissenschaftlicher Abhandlungen des Leo Baeck Instituts 26). For more on the actions of the authorities against the ZVfD, see Hans Mommsen, 'Dokumentation. Der nationalsozialistische Polizeistaat und die Judenverfolgung vor 1938', *Vierteljahrshefte für Zeitgeschichte*, 10 (1962), pp. 77–78; and Martin Rosenblüth, *Go Forth and Serve. Early Years and Public Life*, New York 1961, pp. 247–250. See now also Avraham Barkai, 'German Interests in the Haavara-Transfer Agreement 1933–1939', in *LBI Year Book XXXV* (1990), pp. 245–266. Though Barkai and I seem to agree on the motives and aims of the Nazi regime in the matter of the *Haavara*-Transfer Agreement, as well as on the larger question of the role of Zionism in Nazi Jewish policy, he is mildly critical of what he perceives as my view of German Zionists as ". . . a passive, though unwilling instrument in the hands of the Nazis" (note 10). In my book I do not really draw conclusions about German Zionism during the 1930s, but focus instead on the Nazi regime, its motives and objectives in its over-all policies on Jewish emigration and Zionism, and the coercive nature of these policies. Since then I have been writing about the impact of those policies on German Zionism. I stress the limited option of all German Jews (including Zionists) in the face of the Nazi onslaught and the absence of any degree of compatibility or symbiosis with Nazi policy. My research reveals a picture of German Zionists (indeed, of all Jews in Germany) as vulnerable and unwilling, but certainly not passive. After reading Barkai's fine essay, however, I remain somewhat puzzled by his concern about the Zionist side of *Haavara* on the one hand, and his continuing focus on the German side on the other.

confidential reports were filed in London by un-identified German Zionists with the Political Department of the Jewish Agency for Palestine. The first report, dated 24th March, painted a rather bleak picture of the situation confronting the ZVfD after two months of Nazi terror.[19] The report told of raids by storm troopers on the ZVfD headquarters in which telephone wires were cut, cupboards forced open, petty cash and postage stamps stolen, and lists of East European Jews and other documents taken away. While the police claimed no knowledge of these raids, the report warned that Zionist officials in Germany were in danger of "preventive arrest" or worse. The report went on to describe the harshly anti-Zionist tone of recent articles in the *Völkischer Beobachter* which included a violent attack on Chaim Weizmann of the World Zionist Organis-ation. After describing other ominous developments, the report articulated the following fear:

> "The closing down of the Zionist Organisation in Germany would be a calamity. Apart from other disadvantages, Palestine emigration would be paralysed, for there would no longer exist a body which can be officially entrusted with certificates; collections and propaganda would also stop."

The second report, dated 26th March, also told of anti-Zionist articles in the press, particularly a virulent one in the *Lokal-Anzeiger* under the headline 'Zionist Agitation Against Germany', and warned that "the position of the Zionist Federation has been gravely threatened".[20]

Both reports stressed that these actions did not appear to be part of a co-ordinated campaign by the government to undermine the work of the ZVfD, and implied that the perpetrators were probably local Nazis and members of the SA acting on their own initiative. Indeed, the authors of the reports had little choice but to accept the protestations of the police that the authorities knew nothing of the raids or of their perpetrators. However this was of little consolation because the problem faced by the Zionists was the reality that even if the regime did not sponsor specific acts of violence against the Zionist movement, it nevertheless did promote a virulent antisemitic hate campaign against all Jews, one which of course did not admit the existence of "good Jews", and thus did not exempt any Jews from its wrath. In May, the *Hashomer Hazair* lamented the negative impact of the government's anti-Jewish propaganda and policies on Zionist work.[21] In a telegram to Rabbi Stephen Wise of the American Jewish Congress on 27th March 1933, the World Zionist Organisation in London articulated this problem and the dangerous reality it produced in Germany with the following words:

> ". . . But it should be added that responsibility for these excesses still falls on instigators antisemitic campaign conducted many years and attention directed to fact that while attempts now being made to stop individual acts of physical violence government has still not

---

[19]Central Zionist Archives/Jerusalem (hereafter CZA): S25/9703, 'Confidential Report on the Zionist Situation in Germany', London, 24th March 1933.
[20]CZA: S25/9703, 'Confidential Message from the Zionist Federation of Germany', London, 26th March 1933.
[21]See Jehuda Reinharz, 'Hashomer Hazair in Germany (II). Under the Shadow of the Swastika, 1933–1938', in *LBI Year Book XXXII* (1987), p. 194.

taken effective measures stop wild antisemitic propaganda its own press pamphlets posters where Jewish plots against Hitler ritual murder plots etc. freely alleged . . ."[22]

Even as Zionist fears and the potential for violence against the German Zionist movement subsided somewhat towards the end of 1933 and through 1934 with a brief relaxation of anti-Jewish violence,[23] other problems began to arise which further complicated the work of the ZVfD. In September, for example, the police authorities observed with satisfaction that Zionist ideology, espoused in the past only by the ZVfD and its affiliated organisations, was being embraced by Jewish organisations previously opposed to it, such as the *Centralverein deutscher Staatsbürger jüdischen Glaubens* (C.V.).[24] This reflected, of course, the reality that in the new Germany, emigration was the only political option for the Jewish community permitted by the state. Yet the new pre-eminence of Zionism in the Jewish community in Germany, after decades of relative unacceptability, brought with it still greater problems which impeded effective Zionist work. The ZVfD, while noting the significant growth in membership and the prominent role of the ZVfD in the recently established *Reichsvertretung der deutschen Juden*, nevertheless fretted over the difficulties caused by the combination of rapid growth and the anti-Jewish measures of the regime.[25] One such problem was the loss of Zionist leaders and activists who emigrated to Palestine in ever greater numbers after 1933, at a time when they were needed even more in Germany to cope with the sudden growth of the Zionist movement. In 1933 alone, prominent Zionist leaders such as Kurt Blumenfeld and Georg Landauer emigrated to Palestine and Martin Rosenblüth to England. The ZVfD described this problem in greater detail in a circular letter to all Zionist *Ortsgruppen* in February 1934, in the following manner:

"Die Gefahr dieser raschen Vorwärtsentwicklung auf zahlreichen Gebieten darf nicht verkannt werden. Die Kerngruppe des deutschen Zionismus ist durch die Abwanderung sehr stark zusammengeschmolzen. Demgegenüber steht eine sehr starke Peripherie, die nicht genügend zionistisch geprägt ist . . . Die Organisation, so gross sie geworden ist, befindet sich heute in einem amorphen Zustand. Unsere Hauptaufgabe wird es weiter sein, neue Menschen für die Führung unserer Ortsgruppen zu gewinnen. Nur wenn die Bildung einer neuen 'Elite' gelingt, kann eine durchgreifende zionistische Erziehung und eine Neuformierung unserer Organisation Erfolg haben."[26]

(The danger of this sudden progress in many areas should not be missed. As a result of emigration, the core of German Zionism has dwindled considerably. Against this there is a very strong periphery that is not Zionist enough . . . The organisation, as large as it has become, nevertheless finds itself today in an amorphous condition. Our main task will continue to be to recruit new people for the leadership of our *Ortsgruppen*. Only if we are

[22]CZA: S25/9703, Telegram from the World Zionist Organisation, London, to Rabbi Stephen Wise, American Jewish Congress, 27th March 1933.
[23]See Uwe Dietrich Adam, *Judenpolitik im Dritten Reich*, Düsseldorf 1972, pp. 85ff.; Karl Schleunes, *The Twisted Road to Auschwitz. Nazi Policy Toward German Jews, 1933–1939*, Urbana, Ill. 1970, pp. 116ff.
[24]CZA: F4/100, Württembergisches Innenministerium und Württembergische Politische Polizei an das Reichsministerium des Innern, Nr. 3/1376/33a, 4. September 1933.
[25]See for example CZA: S7/93, Zionistische Vereinigung für Deutschland an die Zionistischen Ortsgruppen und Vertrauensleute, 24. Oktober 1933.
[26]CZA: L13/138, Zionistische Vereinigung für Deutschland an die Zionistischen Ortsgruppen und Vertrauensleute, 8. Februar 1934.

successful in building a new "Elite" can a thorough Zionist education and a recasting of our organisation meet with success.)

This difficulty would only intensify as the decade wore on and more and more Zionist officials emigrated. In December 1935, Robert Weltsch, editor of the *Jüdische Rundschau*, wrote with regret from Berlin to Kurt Blumenfeld in Jerusalem that:

"Die völlige Entblössung von leitenden zionistischen Personen wirkt sich sehr übel aus. Die Frage, ob die neue Generation und die Neuzionisten überhaupt in die Arbeit hereinwachsen können, ist völlig ungeklärt. Ich bezweifle das. Jedenfalls wird die Tradition gebrochen sein, und auch die Kenntnisse können sich die Leute niemals erwerben. Wir müssen also damit rechnen, dass die ganze Bewegung sehr bald ein völlig neues Gesicht bekommt."[27]

(The departure of leading Zionist personalities is having a negative impact. The question whether the new generation and the new Zionists are capable of doing the job is not entirely clear. I doubt they can. In any case the tradition will be broken and they can never obtain the experience. We must therefore accept that the entire movement will very soon have an entirely new face.

In May, 1938, shortly after the decree of April 26th making it compulsory for Jews to register their property holdings in Germany and abroad with the authorities, the ZVfD in Berlin reported unusually large numbers of Jews at its *Palästina-Amt* in Berlin and the impossibility of effectively serving these prospective emigrants due to shortages of personnel and resources.[28] It became a particularly acute problem after the *Kristallnacht* pogrom of November 1938, as Benno Cohn, the president of the ZVfD reported in a letter from Berlin to Georg Landauer in Jerusalem: "Sehr schwierig sind wieder die Personalia der leitenden Menschen. Alles [sic] will zur Zeit weggehen, und man kann kaum die Verantwortung übernehmen . . ."[29] (Once again the problem of personnel and the leading people is very difficult. At this time all want to leave and there is hardly anyone to take over . . .)

There were other problems that grew out of the ever worsening conditions of Jewish life in Germany during the 1930s which had negative consequences for the work of the ZVfD. Periodic arrests of Jewish leaders by the authorities, a common occurrence in Germany during the 1930s, often included prominent members of the ZVfD as well as those of the non-Zionist organisations. In reporting the release from police custody of Zionist leaders Franz Meyer and Benno Cohn in early October, 1936, Martin Rosenblüth of the London Office of the Central Bureau for the Settlement of German Jews in Palestine expressed his frustration over never being quite sure of the reasons that prompted such arrests, notwithstanding Zionist cooperation in matters relating to the *Haavara* Transfer

---

[27]CZA: A222/98, Robert Weltsch, Berlin, an Kurt Blumenfeld, Jerusalem, 6. Dezember 1935.
[28]CZA: S7/689, Martin Rosenblüth an Werner Senator, London, 6. Mai 1938. Rosenblüth was reporting on a conversation he had had earlier that day with Walter Tempel, formerly of the *Palästina-Amt*, who had just returned to London from Berlin. Tempel also reported that the personnel problem was only compounded by the prohibition that the authorities had imposed earlier on foreign Jews entering Germany to assist Jewish organisations.
[29]CZA: S7/902, Benno Cohn, Berlin, an Georg Landauer, Jerusalem, 22. November 1938.

Agreement and emigration policy.[30] Moreover during the *Kristallnacht* in November 1938, Zionist officials and others connected with the *Palästina-Amt* in Berlin were arrested along with thousands of other Jews, although they were released by the police shortly thereafter and helped to re-open the office in order to maintain the flow of Jewish emigration from Germany to Palestine.[31]

Contact between the ZVfD and the Jewish Agency in London and Jerusalem became more infrequent and difficult to maintain after 1936. Of course, the ZVfD, like all Jewish organisations in Germany, were under constant surveillance by the police, particularly after 1935, and thus exposed to considerable potential danger from any exchange of correspondence between Germany and the outside world. In October 1936, the ZVfD complained to the Executive of the Jewish Agency for Palestine in Jerusalem that German Zionism was virtually cut off from information concerning political activities in Palestine and in the larger Zionist movement world-wide, which impeded the effectiveness of Zionist work.[32] In July 1938, Franz Meyer of the ZVfD wrote to the Executive of the Jewish Agency in London: "Mit besonderem Bedauern muss ich erneut feststellen, wie mangelhaft der Kontakt zwischen Ihnen und den in Deutschland arbeitenden Zionisten ist."[33] (With regret I must once again state how deficient the contact is between you and Zionists working in Germany.) Meyer lamented the fact that the views of the ZVfD were not solicited for the formal memorandum submitted by the Jewish Agency for Palestine to the international conference on refugees at Evian-les-Bains in 1938. Later that month, Meyer reiterated the concern of the ZVfD over being isolated in another letter to the Jewish Agency in London. After expressing his understanding for the difficulties of communication between Germany and the outside world, he insisted nevertheless: "Ich bitte Sie wirklich sehr, in Zukunft dafür zu sorgen, dass trotz der bestehenden Hindernisse nicht verabsäumt wird, alles erforderliche Material hierher gelangen zu lassen."[34] (I beg you to make every effort in the future, in spite of the existing impediments, not to desist from sending us all necessary materials.)

III. COMMUNAL CONFLICT

The National Socialist *Machtübernahme* tended to aggravate rather than neutralise some of the long-standing conflicts between the ZVfD and other

---

[30]CZA: S7/493, Martin Rosenblüth, London, an Nahum Goldmann, Paris, 6. Oktober 1936. The Central Bureau for the Settlement of German Jews in Palestine was established by the World Zionist Organisation and the Jewish Agency for Palestine at the Eighteenth Zionist Congress in Prague in August–September 1933, with offices in London and Jerusalem.

[31]See Institut für Zeitgeschichte/Munich: Beweisdokumente, Eichmannprozess, Nr. 742, interview with Dr. Kurt Jacob Ball-Kaduri by Hans Friedenthal, March 1957.

[32]CZA: S5/2194, ZVfD, Berlin, an die Executive der Jewish Agency for Palestine, Jerusalem, 13. Oktober 1936.

[33]CZA: S5/432, Franz Meyer, Berlin, an das Büro der Exekutive der Jewish Agency for Palestine, London, 13. Juli 1938.

[34]CZA: S5/432, Franz Meyer, Berlin, an die Jewish Agency for Palestine, London, 29. Juli 1938.

Jewish organisations in Germany. Traditional differences and rivalries were placed in an entirely different and much more dangerous context as the state declared all Jews to be the enemy of Germany and of necessity forced the various Jewish organisations together to create a single Jewish response. The Nazis believed that all Jews, without exception, were the embodiment of evil, notwithstanding the usefulness of Zionism and the Zionist organisation in the pursuit of a *"judenrein"* Germany; as such they constituted a relatively uniform target in the application of Jewish policy and of consequence this created pressures that naturally threw Jewish organisations closer together as they responded to the radically new conditions of Jewish life in the new Germany. However their closer proximity did not necessarily mean that the vulnerability and danger shared by all, Zionists, non-Zionists and anti-Zionists alike, would automatically resolve traditional conflicts. In some instances, those conflicts were exacerbated.[35]

The rather tenuous and difficult relationship between the ZVfD and the *Centralverein* that existed before 1933[36] continued more or less thereafter. Notwithstanding the obvious dependence of the *Reichsvertretung* on the cooperation of the C.V. and the ZVfD, the mounting pressures on the non-Zionist C.V. to support the Zionist preoccupation with Palestine, visible even during the Weimar years, did not at all reflect any inclination to accept Zionist ideology as the salvation of German Jews, let alone Zionist leadership in Jewish affairs. The C.V. criticised what it believed were the efforts of the ZVfD to direct Jewish emigration to Palestine at the expense of other suitable destinations.[37] Moreover, the fundamental aim of Nazi Jewish policy to promote the emigration of Jews from Germany naturally resulted in a larger role and a higher profile for the ZVfD in the Jewish community, particularly in the *Reichsvertretung*; this also meant, of course, a relative decline from pre-eminence for the C.V. as Jewish emigration became the only permissible option, causing further tension in its relationship with the ZVfD.[38]

The relationship between the ZVfD and the anti-Zionist *Reichsbund jüdischer Frontsoldaten* (RjF) was also characterised by a grudging and uneven cooperation. At times, the new realities in Jewish life in Germany after 1933 threw the two into open conflict that reflected all of the animosity and bitterness of the traditional Zionist-Liberal/Assimilationist struggle among Jews in Germany.[39] Of course many in the non-Zionist C.V. had long since accepted the idea of Zionist work in

[35]For a general account of the internal politics among German-Jewish organisations during the 1930s, particularly the ongoing rivalries among the Zionists, non-Zionists and anti-Zionists in the *Reichsvertretung*, see Jacob Boas, 'German-Jewish Internal Politics under Hitler 1933–1938', in *LBI Year Book XXIX* (1984), pp. 3–25.
[36]For the complexities of the relationship between the ZVfD and the C.V. during the Weimar Republic, see Paucker, *Der jüdische Abwehrkampf, op. cit.*, pp. 39ff. See also Kurt Loewenstein, 'Die innerjüdische Reaktion auf die Krise der deutschen Demokratie', in *Entscheidungsjahr 1932, op. cit.*, pp. 380–383.
[37]See for example *C.V.-Zeitung*, 13th October 1935.
[38]Boas, 'German-Jewish Internal Politics', *loc. cit.*, pp. 23–25.
[39]For the history of the RjF see Ulrich Dunker, *Der Reichsbund jüdischer Frontsoldaten 1919–1938. Geschichte eines jüdischen Abwehrvereins*, Düsseldorf 1977.

Palestine for the benefit of the *Ostjuden* and other persecuted Jewish refugees, while always rejecting Zionism as anything remotely relevant to the situation of Jews in Germany. The RjF, although neutral in internal Jewish politics before the *Machtergreifung* and generally content to defend the sacrifices of Jewish veterans at the front for Germany during the First World War, was forced to emerge as a political force among Jews in Germany after 1933. While it supported Zionist efforts to create a refuge for a small number of Jews as well as for Jewish religious traditions in Palestine, the RjF would not countenance any form of or rationale for nation-building abroad by any German-Jewish organisation.[40] The RjF's abandonment of its former neutrality in Jewish affairs in 1933 placed it on a collision course with the ZVfD in determining the appropriate response of the Jewish community to the Nazi "New Order".[41]

In July 1934, Captain Leo Löwenstein, Chairman of the RjF, prepared a rather lengthy report on his organisation's relationship with German Zionism.[42] Entitled 'Zionisten und R.J.F. insbesondere ihre Mitarbeit in der Reichsvertretung der deutschen Juden' (Zionists and RjF, especially their cooperation in the *Reichsvertretung der deutschen Juden*), Löwenstein outlined the continuing conflict between the RjF and the ZVfD, complained about recent Zionist efforts to discredit and denounce the RjF in the *Jüdische Rundschau* and the inability of the *Reichsvertretung* to stop it. The report outlined the ideological differences between the RjF and the ZVfD; it emphasised the former's rejection of a Zionist "politisch-nationale jüdische Gemeinschaftsbildung" (building of a political-national Jewish community) re-affirmed its "über ein Jahrtausend alte Gefühlsbindung an die deutsche Heimat" (ties of more than a thousand years to the German homeland) and asserted that it "setzt sich dafür ein, dass die deutschen Juden aus dieser Tatsache die innere Kraft zur Überwindung ihrer Lage gewinnen" (supported the effort of German Jews to find the inner strength to overcome their situation). Although Löwenstein described the willingness of his organisation, in spite of everything, to cooperate with the ZVfD and the C.V. in the creation of the *Reichsvertretung* in 1933 as a unified Jewish response to the altered conditions of Jewish life in Germany, the RjF and the ZVfD would remain in fundamental conflict over the nature and form of that response.

Of course this was not a new ideological rift in the Jewish community in Germany. However under the circumstances of the Nazi "New Order" and the vulnerable position of the Jewish community in Germany after 1933, the traditional Zionist/non-Zionist/anti-Zionist tensions of the past took on a decidedly different, much more dangerous and certainly more harmful character in an environment in which all Jews were the targets of humiliation, disenfranchisement, pauperisation and deportation. The RjF's goals for the future of Jews in Germany, articulated by Löwenstein in an earlier speech in Cologne and repeated in his July 1934, report, included:

---

[40]See for example *Der Schild*, 1st June 1934.
[41]See Boas, 'German-Jewish Internal Politics', *loc. cit.*, pp. 10ff.
[42]CZA: A142/47/7, 'Zionisten und R.J.F. insbesondere ihre Mitarbeit in der Reichsvertretung der deutschen Juden', von Leo Löwenstein, 23. Juli 1934.

"Ehrenhafte Regelung und Befriedung unseres Verhältnisses in unserer deutschen Heimat und zu unserem deutschen Volke im Rahmen des heutigen nationalen deutschen Staates. Erziehung unserer jungen Generation zu dieser Auffassung, besonders auch durch Arbeitsdienst und wahrhafte Ertüchtigung. Ablehnung jeglicher politischer Ziele jenseits der deutschen Grenzen und aller Bestrebungen, die uns aus der deutschen Nation hinausführen wollen, wie nationale Minorität und dergl. Seit Generationen und auf Generationen verwurzelt mit unserer deutschen Heimat sowie unseren Pflichten und unseren Rechten, die sie uns gab, im stolzen Bekenntnis zu jüdischen Stamm und Glauben."[43]

(Regulation with honour and pacification of our relations in our German homeland and to our German people within the framework of today's national state. Education of our young generation in this attitude, especially through work and true physical training. Rejection of every political endeavour beyond the borders of Germany and of all efforts to lead us out of the German nation, such as national minority status and so on. For generations deeply attached to our German homeland as well as to our rights and duties which it gave to us, in proud communion with our Jewish origins and faith.)

This view, reflective of a lingering sentiment among some Jews to hold on in Germany, was utterly at odds with the policy and goals of the Nazi state. In the end, the continued existence of "deutschnationale" sentiments among Jews in Germany could only make Zionist work more difficult. They would be seen as part of a natural effort by Jews to thwart the Jewish policy of the regime, as responsible for the slow progress of current Jewish emigration policies, and thus would indirectly contribute to the much harsher nature of dissimilation and deportation policies adopted by the police authorities in 1938, which included, of course, the dissolution of the ZVfD.[44]

The open conflict between the ZVfD and the RjF continued until the spring of 1937 when even the latter felt compelled by the course of events in Germany to change its view of Zionist work in Palestine to a more positive one. In a letter to the members of its *Landesvorstand* on 26th April 1937, the ZVfD reported:

"Wie Ihrer Aufmerksamkeit nicht entgangen sein wird, hat sich die Stellungnahme des Reichsbundes jüdischer Frontsoldaten zu den Fragen des Palästina-Aufbaus in der letzten Zeit gewandelt. Sein Organ 'Der Schild' hat von jeder aggressiven Note gegen den Zionismus schon seit geraumer Zeit abgesehen und den Fragen des Palästina-Aufbaus, wenn auch unter gewissen, dem Reichsbund jüdischer Frontsoldaten nahe liegenden Gesichtspunkten, sein Interesse zugewandt."[45]

(As you have probably noticed, the position of the *Reichsbund jüdischer Frontsoldaten* on the questions relating to development work in Palestine has recently changed. Its publication "*Der Schild*" has for some time now desisted from aggressive words against Zionism and has

---

[43] *Ibid.*

[44] For example, the police authorities expressed alarm over continuing assimilationist tendencies among Jews in Germany early in 1935. In a note to all *Staatspolizeistellen* in Germany on 10th February, Reinhard Heydrich observed: "In letzter Zeit mehrt sich die Zahl der Vorträge in jüdischen Organisationen, in denen Propaganda für das Verbleiben in Deutschland getrieben wird. Da ohnehin die Versammlungstätigkeit der Juden derart rege ist, dass eine ordnungsgemässe Überwachung nicht gewährleistet ist, ordne ich mit sofortiger Wirkung an, dass sämtliche jüdischen Versammlungen, soweit in ihnen Propaganda für das Verbleiben in Deutschland gemacht werden soll, bis auf weiteres zu verbieten sind." See Bundesarchiv/Koblenz (hereafter BA), R/58–276, Geheimes Staatspolizeiamt an alle Staatspolizeistellen, II 1 B2–60934/J.191/35, 10. Feb. 1935. For more on the turn of events in Nazi Jewish policy in 1938, see Adam, *Judenpolitik, op. cit.*, pp. 159ff.; Schleunes, *Twisted Road, op. cit.*, pp. 214ff.

[45] CZA: L142/47/7, ZVfD, Berlin, an die Mitglieder des Landesvorstandes der ZVfD, 26. April 1937.

shown some interest in the questions relating to development work in Palestine, albeit within the context of certain viewpoints always held by the *Reichsbund jüdischer Frontsoldaten*.)

The letter requested from the members of the *Landesvorstand* approval of a draft of an agreement between the ZVfD and the RjF in which the following points were settled: the RjF agreed that all Jewish war veterans were welcome in its ranks, regardless of their political or religious inclinations; the ZVfD rescinded its declaration of 6th June 1934, which had made membership in the RjF incompatible with membership in the ZVfD; the RjF recognised the positive aspects of Zionist work in Palestine; and both organisations pledged themselves to friendly cooperation.[46]

Perhaps the most bitterly contentious relationship of the ZVfD before 1933 was with the Revisionist Zionist movement in Germany;[47] this remained so after the remnants from the split in Revisionist ranks in Germany after 1931 were forced by the Nazi assumption of power to come together in April 1934, in the new *Staatszionistische Organisation (Vereinigte Revisionisten Deutschlands)* under the controversial Georg Kareski.[48] The Revisionists had failed to gain control of the Zionist movement in Germany from within the ZVfD during the Weimar years, and formally seceded in October 1931. After 1934, the re-constituted *Staatszionistische Organisation* worked independently of and usually in opposition to the ZVfD in an effort to establish its own separate relationship with the authorities, control over the Zionist movement in Germany and by extension over the affairs of the Jewish community as a whole. In order to do this, the *Staatszionisten* sought to accommodate themselves publicly to the policies of the Nazi regime. This was a rather difficult and delicate task in view of the policies and activities of the larger Revisionist movements outside of Germany, the Jewish State Party and the New Zionist Organisation, which openly supported the international economic boycott against Germany, opposed the *Haavara* Transfer Agreement and supported the immediate creation of a large independent Jewish state in Palestine. After 1934, the *Staatszionistische Organisation* proclaimed its complete independence from those organisations, its opposition to the international anti-German boycott and its support for the *Haavara* agreement; after 1937, with the Nazi regime's first formal rejection of an independent Jewish state in Palestine in the wake of the recommendations of the Royal Commission (Peel Commission) for Palestine, the *Staatszionisten* dropped their public support for immediate Jewish statehood.[49]

The renewed Revisionist struggle against the ZVfD was officially launched at

---

[46]The text of this agreement can be found in CZA: L142/47/7.

[47]See Francis R. Nicosia, 'Revisionist Zionism in Germany (I). Richard Lichtheim and the Landesverband der Zionisten-Revisionisten in Deutschland, 1926–1933', in *LBI Year Book XXXI* (1986), pp. 209–240.

[48]See Yehoyakim Cochavi, 'Georg Kareski's Nomination as Head of the Kulturbund. The Gestapo's First Attempt – and Last Failure – to Impose a Jewish Leadership', in *LBI Year Book XXXIV* (1989), pp. 227–246; Herbert S. Levine, 'A Jewish Collaborator in Nazi Germany. The Strange Career of Georg Kareski, 1933–1937', *Central European History*, 8 (1975), pp. 251–281; and Francis R. Nicosia, 'Revisionist Zionism in Germany (II). Georg Kareski and the Staatszionistische Organisation, 1933–1938', in *LBI Year Book XXXII* (1987), pp. 231–267.

[49]See Nicosia, 'Revisionist Zionism in Germany (II)', *loc. cit.*, pp. 251ff.

the new organisation's first national conference in October, 1934.[50] In fact, the ZVfD was already sufficiently alarmed over the activities of the *Staatszionisten* in July when, in a circular letter to all of its *Ortsgruppen*, it noted that Revisionist activities ". . . die Aufmerksamkeit aller Mitglieder der ZVfD verdient und uns zu einer entschiedenen Gegenaktion zwingt".[51] (deserves the attention of all members of the ZVfD and forces us to take decisive counter-action). The main points of the Revisionist attack against the ZVfD beginning in 1934 included many of the old arguments from its struggle with the ZVfD leadership during the 1920s, as well as some new political themes. Among those points, three stand out for their intensity, their controversial nature and their centrality in the Revisionist campaign for pre-eminence in the Jewish community between 1934 and 1938: that the ZVfD promoted Jewish assimilation in Germany, that it was a thoroughly Marxist organisation, and that it opposed the creation of an independent Jewish state in Palestine. While these themes were not entirely new, they were significantly different in emphasis and intensity, and possessed far more significant and dangerous implications for the ZVfD in the dangerous environment of National Socialism. In particular, public charges against any Jewish organisation that it counselled Jews to remain in Germany and to assimilate, or that it was Marxist, were dangerous in light of the ideological convictions and the Jewish policy of the Nazi regime.[52]

In their bid to assume leadership over German Jewry, Kareski and the *Staatszionisten* sought to by-pass both the ZVfD and the *Reichsvertretung* by establishing their own relationship with the police authorities. In Kareski's public statements throughout 1935, he alluded to the assimilationist tendencies of other Jewish organisations, including the ZVfD, and offered himself and his organisation to the police authorities as the only effective instrument that could guarantee the liquidation of German Jewry and its rapid emigration from Germany.[53] In the summer of 1935, he made his own emigration proposals to the authorities, including a recommendation that the state appoint him as *Auswanderungskommissar* with the full authority to undertake all necessary measures to secure the emigration of a half million Jews from Germany.[54] Moreover, Kareski

---

[50]For a complete account of the proceedings, see CZA: Z4/3296, Reichskonferenz am 13. und 14. Oktober 1934 (no date). See also *Jüdische Rundschau*, 19th October 1934.

[51]CZA: A142/47/7, ZVfD, Berlin (Meyer), an die Zionistischen Ortsgruppen und Vertrauensleute, 26. Juli 1934.

[52]For instance, the Jewish Agency reported in the spring of 1937 that the Nazi press constantly characterised Jews as Communists, and that Jews in Germany demanded action to counter this kind of propaganda. See CZA: L22/383, Fritz Ullmann, Jewish Agency z.Zt. in Karlsbad, an Nahum Goldmann, Jewish Agency/Geneva, 21. März 1937.

[53]See Cochavi, 'Georg Kareski and the Kulturbund', *loc. cit.*, pp. 234ff.

[54]The proposal was made public in an editorial by Max Schulmann in *Der Staatszionist*, the official newspaper of the *Staatszionistische Organisation*, on 25th August 1935, at precisely the time that the *Gestapo* and the SD were demanding a greater role in the emigration process and more effective and rapid emigration procedures. Schulmann also sent a lengthy proposal to the German Foreign Office several weeks later offering the services of the *Staatszionistische Organisation* in the process of removing German Jews from Germany to Palestine; in this proposal, Schulmann once again suggested the appointment of a Jewish *Auswanderungskommissar*. See PA: Inland II A/B, 83–21, Bd. 3, Max Schulmann an das Auswärtige Amt, 11. September 1935.

and the *Staatszionisten*, often with support from the Berlin Jewish community, broadened their target to include the *Reichsvertretung* as a whole. For example, in a speech on 25th May 1937, Kareski publicly called for the elimination of the *Reichsvertretung*; at the same time, he held out the possibility of a radically reorganised body.[55] In attacking the *Reichsvertretung*, dominated as it was by the ZVfD, the *Centralverein* and the *Reichsbund jüdischer Frontsoldaten*, as a suitable representative body for German Jewry, Kareski was able to lump the ZVfD together with those organisations that represented liberal and assimilationist traditions among German Jews which were the antithesis of Nazi Jewish policy. At a time when the main agencies of the SS, namely the *Gestapo* and the *Sicherheitsdienst* (SD), were assuming a leading role in the formulation and execution of a Jewish policy that was determined to obliterate assimilationist tendencies among German Jews and to focus its resources on a more effective and rapid Jewish emigration, any doubts about the effectiveness of the existing emigration process, not to mention the commitment of the ZVfD to rapid and total Jewish emigration, were potentially dangerous.

IV. THE ECONOMIC IMPACT

In his book *Der Judenstaat*, Theodor Herzl envisioned a planned and orderly migration of the Jewish people to Palestine. At the very centre of this process was the assumption that Jews would be able to bring with them their assets, which would play an important role in the development of the Jewish state. Implicit in this assumption was the notion that Jews would continue to live in political and economic freedom so long as they remained in the Diaspora, until their emigration to Palestine. A "Jewish Company" was to be established which would act as an "Übergangsinstitut". About the task of this company Herzl wrote: "Die Jewish Company hat zunächst die Aufgabe, die Immobilien der abziehenden Juden zu liquidieren."[56] (The Jewish Company has the task of liquidating the possessions of the departing Jews.) However the world economic crisis of the 1930s coupled with the Nazi assumption of power in 1933 precluded this scenario for Zionist emigration from Germany to Palestine. In 1931, the Brüning government imposed a ban on the removal of capital from Germany; the Nazi regime maintained this policy after 1933 out of the same economic necessity as well as the traditional ideological conviction that considered all Jewish property and wealth as stolen.

The transfer of Jewish assets to Palestine along with Jewish emigrants from Germany, which was possible during the Weimar Republic before 1931, remained a Zionist wish after 1933. In his memorandum of 13th September 1933, referred to above,[57] Martin Rosenblüth outlined the necessary economic conditions for Jews in the new Germany as follows: "Auf wirtschaftlichem Gebiet

---

[55]CZA: S7/493, S. Adler-Rudel, London, an Georg Landauer, Jerusalem, 10. Juni 1937.
[56]Herzl, *Der Judenstaat*, *op. cit.*, p. 215.
[57]See above, note 16.

erfolgen keine Einschränkungen der Betätigungsmöglichkeit für Juden in Handel, Industrie, Handwerk und Gewerbe" (In the economic sphere there should be no limitations on the activities of Jews in commerce, industry, the trades and business). He then called for the organised and systematic emigration of one half of the German-Jewish community over the course of the next ten years which would entail ". . . dass den auswandernden Juden ein gewisser Teil ihres Vermögens zwecks sofortiger Transferierung freigegeben und ihnen der Restbetrag in einem allmählichen, über mehrere Jahre sich erstreckenden Liquidationsprozess in ihrer neuen Heimat zur Verfügung gestellt wird" (that a certain portion of their assets for immediate transfer be made available to emigrating Jews and the remaining amount be made available to them in their new homes in a gradual process of liquidation that may take several years). Clearly Rosenblüth had in mind something more than the recently concluded *Haavara* Transfer Agreement which allowed for the transfer to Palestine of a very small portion of an individual's assets in the form of German exports; he was looking instead for the eventual transfer of virtually all Jewish assets when he referred to *Haavara* in the following manner: "Eine gewisse vorläufige Regelung der Frage, die aber den Bedürfnissen einer grossen Auswanderung kaum gerecht werden dürfte, ist durch den kürzlich veröffentlichten Runderlass des Reichswirtschaftsministers getroffen worden." (A certain temporary regulation of the question, albeit one which can hardly suffice for the needs of a large emigration, has been accomplished in the recently published circular letter of the *Reich* Minister of Economics). But the economic condition that Zionists considered necessary for the effective emigration of Jews from Germany to Palestine would not be possible under the Third *Reich*.

The spate of anti-Jewish legislation between 1933 and 1938, designed to achieve the political, social and cultural dissimilation of the Jewish community, had obviously severe negative economic repercussions as well. Indeed, one cannot discount the economic motivations behind virtually every facet of Nazi Jewish policy, from the civil service law of 7th April 1933, to the "Aryanisation" of Jewish businesses, to the Four-Year Plan of 1936, to the economic sanctions against Jews after the *Kristallnacht* pogrom in 1938, to the formal "Ausschaltung aus der Wirtschaft" in 1938 and 1939, to the "final solution" during the Second World War.[58] The negative economic consequences of the anti-Jewish legislation and the "Aryanisation" of Jewish businesses during the 1930s included unemployment and loss of livelihood for thousands of Jews, which meant, of course, a growing dependence on Jewish welfare agencies both inside and outside of Germany.[59] While exceptions were made for Jewish war veterans at least until

---

[58]This view regarding Nazi Jewish policy during the 1930s is articulated by Barkai, *From Boycott to Annihilation, op. cit.*, pp. 13–17. See also Helmut Genschel, *Die Verdrängung der Juden aus der Wirtschaft im Dritten Reich*, Göttingen 1966.

[59]See S. Adler-Rudel, *Jüdische Selbsthilfe unter dem Naziregime 1933–1939. Im Spiegel der Berichte der Reichsvertretung der Juden in Deutschland*, Tübingen 1974 (Schriftenreihe wissenschaftlicher Abhandlungen des Leo Baeck Instituts 29), pp. 177ff. See in particular the *Denkschrift* from the *Reichsvertretung* to Hans Heinrich Lammers, the State Secretary in the *Reichskanzlei*, of January 1934, in which the disastrous economic consequences of unemployment and loss of livelihood among Jews is described. The *Denkschrift* is reprinted *ibid.*, pp. 188–191.

the Nuremberg racial laws of September 1935, there were none made for the Zionists, notwithstanding their central role in the emigration policy of the regime. That the activities of Zionist and other Jewish organisations in Germany had always depended on the financial support of their members goes without saying; obviously the steady pauperisation of the entire Jewish community after 1933, coupled with the dramatic growth in membership, activity and responsibility, created enormous and unprecedented new strains and burdens for the German Zionist movement.

The steady erosion of the economic position of Jews in Germany was in many ways the most difficult burden with which the ZVfD and other Jewish organisations had to deal, even with the extraordinary self-help efforts of the entire Jewish community.[60] In a letter to Martin Rosenblüth in London in October 1933, Michael Traub, the Director of the *Keren Hayesod* (Palestine Foundation Fund) in Germany and a member of the *Reichsvertretung* observed:

> "Über die allgemeine Situation in Deutschland lässt sich in einem Briefe nur sagen, dass schlimmer als alle Gewalttakte (die in letzter Zeit anscheinend seltener vorkommen) der wirtschaftliche Entwurzelungsprozess ist, der unerbittlich und systematisch durchgeführt wird. . . . Und da dieser Prozess nicht nur die grossen Unternehmungen umfasst . . . sondern auch die mittleren Geschäfte, ist in wenigen Monaten mit einem sehr starken Rückgang des jüdischen 'Nationalvermögens' in Deutschland zu rechnen."[61]

> (Regarding the situation in Germany, it can only be said in a letter that the process of economic deprivation which is inexorably and systematically being pursued is worse than all acts of violence (which have recently subsided) . . . And since this process encompasses not only large concerns . . . but also medium sized ones, we must face a very strong decline in Jewish wealth in the next few months.)

By the end of October 1937, a comprehensive report on the position of Jews in Germany compiled by the Central Bureau for the Settlement of German Jews in Palestine (London and Jerusalem) opened with the observation: "Das Ziel des Nationalsozialismus bleibt die völlige wirtschaftliche und moralische Vernichtung der ca. 375,000 Juden, die in Deutschland noch leben."[62] (The goal of National Socialism remains the total economic destruction and loss of morale of the approximately 375,000 Jews who still live in Germany.)

The economic disintegration of the Jewish community during the 1930s constituted an enormous impediment to effective Zionist work in Germany. Of course all of the anti-Jewish measures of the Nazi state between 1933 and 1939, particularly the "Vertreibung aus der Wirtschaft" (expulsion from the economy), were designed to encourage Jews to leave Germany,[63] albeit under conditions that made effective Zionist work in Germany extraordinarily difficult. By the end of 1935, Salomon Adler-Rudel of the ZVfD and the *Reichsvertretung* reported on the negative impact of the growing economic crisis of the Jewish community on

---

[60]For a complete account of the Jewish self-help efforts in response to the disastrous economic impact of Nazi Jewish policy, see Adler-Rudel, *Jüdische Selbsthilfe, op. cit.* See also Barkai, *From Boycott to Annihilation, op. cit.*, pp. 39–53.
[61]CZA: S7/93, Michael Traub, z. Zt. Paris, an Martin Rosenblüth, London, 21. Oktober 1933.
[62]CZA: S7/689, 'Die Lage der Juden in Deutschland', Ende Oktober 1937.
[63]See Adam, *Judenpolitik, op. cit.*, pp. 172ff.

Zionist activity in Germany.[64] He observed that the growing pauperisation of the Jewish community was contributing to the emigration of those with means and, in general, to the flood of prospective emigrants at the *Palästina-Amt*, realities which placed enormous burdens on the *Gemeinden*, the Zionist movement, and in general on the various relief efforts in the Jewish community:

> "Die nur kurz skizzierten Verhältnisse haben eine ungeheure Steigerung des Auswanderungs-bedürfnisses der Juden zur Folge und zwar sind es jetzt nicht nur die jüngeren und wenig bemittelten Menschen die sich zur Auswanderung entschliessen, sondern auch die sehr wohlhabenden und heute noch gut fundierten Familien sehen sich zur Auswanderung gezwungen . . . Die Palästina-Ämter sind von Auswanderungswilligen derart überlaufen, dass sie die Anzahl der ihnen zuströmenden Menschen kaum bewältigen können . . . Der wirtschaftliche Niedergang, die Steigerung der Zahl der Hilfsbedürftigen, erfordern von den jüdischen Gemeinden grösste Anstrengung und grösste Opfer, um den enormen Bedarf an Hilfsmitteln aufbringen zu können."

> (These factors which have been outlined briefly have resulted in an enormous increase in the emigration requirements of the Jews, and it is now not only the younger and poorer people who have decided to emigrate, but also the well-off and prosperous families see themselves as forced to leave . . . the Palestine Offices are so flooded with people willing to emigrate that they can hardly manage the numbers streaming to them . . . The economic collapse, the increase in the number of the needy, demand from the Jewish communities the greatest effort and sacrifice in order to be able to satisfy the enormous need for relief.)

The emigration of leaders and other personnel at the ZVfD, a problem referred to above, was in part naturally generated by the ever-worsening economic condition for all Jews. In a letter to Georg Landauer in Jerusalem of 3rd August 1938, Benno Cohn of the ZVfD characterised the emigration of Zionist leaders since 1933 in the following manner: "Diese sehr anarchische Abwanderung wird grosse Nachteile mit sich bringen."[65] (This very anarchistic emigration will have grave consequences.) Cohn referred to the economic crisis of German Jewry as a natural cause of this problem and warned of the far greater difficulties that would soon result from the coming Nazi onslaught on the remaining Jewish stake in the economy:

> "Wir stehen angesichts der neuen Gewerbegesetze vor einer Massenerwerbslosigkeit im Winter, die man auf 30 000 Verdiener, also etwa 100 000 Familienmitglieder schätzt. Wir werden daher mit den bisherigen Methoden der sozialen Arbeit nicht auskommen können . . ."

> (In view of the new economic measures, we face massive unemployment in the winter, which is estimated to be 30,000 wage earners, thus effecting about 100,000 family members. Therefore we will not be able to get by with previous methods of social work . . .)

The *Haavara* Transfer Agreement, concluded between the German government and Zionist officials from Germany and Palestine in August 1933, did represent a very small degree of relief from the contradictory realities of economic disenfranchisement and the requirements of effective and orderly emigration.[66] Among the almost 60,000 Jews who were able to emigrate from Germany to Palestine between 1933 and 1939, many were able to take a small

---

[64]CZA: S7/357, Aufzeichnung von S. Adler-Rudel, z.Zt. in Genf, über die Lage der Juden in Deutschland, 29. November 1935.

[65]CZA: S7/689, Benno Cohn, Berlin, an Georg Landauer, Jerusalem, 3. August 1938.

[66]See: Werner Feilchenfeld *et al.*, *Haavara-Transfer*, *op. cit.*; Nicosia, *Third Reich*, *op. cit.*, chapt. 3.

portion of their assets with them to Palestine via the *Haavara* system. From the beginning of the *Haavara* system in November 1933, until its end in December 1939, more than RM100 million in Jewish assets were transferred to Palestine. Without *Haavara*, those assets, along with many of the Jews who were able to get to Palestine via the *Haavara* system, would undoubtedly have been lost to the Nazi drive to liquidate Jewish life in Germany. But *Haavara* was relatively small compensation for the disastrous economic consequences of Nazi Jewish policy on all Jews, including Zionists, during the 1930s; nor did it represent a significant portion of those assets which were lost to the Nazi state that might otherwise have been transferred to Palestine. Zionists had always envisioned a peaceful, orderly emigration of Jews with their assets to Palestine, requiring the mainten-ance of political and economic freedom in the Diaspora, or, in other words, of the conditions of Jewish emancipation. The Nazi state, on the other hand, pursued a policy of forced emigration that was based on political, economic, social and cultural disenfranchisement, on harassment, coercion, humiliation and impover-ishment. Jews were to leave penniless and *Haavara* was perhaps the only exception, however small, to the requirements of Nazi ideology and policy.

V. CONCLUSION

Zionism and the German Zionist movement were never more than convenient tools in the eyes of the National Socialist state in the implementation of its Jewish policy before the "final solution". The encouragement that the various govern-ment and Party agencies gave the ZVfD during the 1930s was by no means a reflection of Nazi respect for or solidarity with the philosophy and aims of Zionism. It meant neither the acceptance of Zionism as a positive force in Jewish life with the national rebirth of the Jewish people, nor of the related objective of an independent Jewish state in Palestine as the focus of that national rebirth. From the early years of the Nazi movement through the 1930s, there was a clear and consistent Nazi policy towards Zionism which was based on a rejection of the substance of Zionist ideology, a view that Zionism was but another arm of the international Jewish conspiracy, and an acceptance of Zionism merely as a useful instrument in the quest to make Germany *"judenrein"*.[67] The idea of Zionists offering themselves to, or being regarded by, the Nazi state as allies in the pursuit of common ends, as entertained by Georg Kareski and the *Staatszionisten*, was simply impossible in a system that required only "useful" Jews, and in a *Weltanschauung* that condemned all Jews as inferior and evil.

In a little known memorandum to the *Stellvertreter des Führers*, the Ministry of the Interior and the Propaganda Ministry of 30th October 1934, Foreign Minister Konstantin von Neurath stated that the German Foreign Office opposed any agreements with Jewish organisations inside or outside of Germany in which Germany did not in effect work from a position of strength and dictate

[67]See Nicosia, *Third Reich, op. cit.*, chapts. 2, 3, 4, 7, 8.

the terms.[68] This memorandum was the work of *Referat-Deutschland*, the thoroughly Nazified department in the German Foreign Office responsible for Jewish policy and its impact on foreign policy, and was a response to overtures made by leaders of the anti-German economic boycott movement to the German Embassy in London in September to halt the boycott in return for the restoration of Jewish rights in Germany. The memorandum observed:

> "Ein Verhandeln oder Paktieren mit irgendwelchen jüdischen Organisationen oder jüdischen representativen Körperschaften in der Judenfrage, sei es im Inland oder im Ausland, kommt nicht in Frage. Wenn eines Tages an der Judenfrage gerührt werden sollte, so dürfte eine solche Geste lediglich einen Ausdruck der Stärke und nicht der Schwäche darstellen."

> (Dealings or agreements with any Jewish organisations or representative Jewish bodies regarding the Jewish Question, either inside the country or abroad, are out of the question. If some day it should come to such contact on the Jewish Question, such a gesture should appear as an expression of strength and not of weakness.)

This policy made no exceptions for the Zionists. It reflected a larger overall approach in which the interests and goals of the Nazi state mattered while those of the Jewish community were deemed irrelevant, and a determination to pursue Jewish policy solely on Nazi terms. The *Haavara* Agreement, and not much more, was compatible with such an approach.

The ZVfD was indeed encouraged in its efforts to promote Jewish emigration from Germany to Palestine from 1933 through 1938. This did not entail, however, any form of preferential treatment, satisfaction of Zionist requirements for effective Zionist work in Germany or ideological meeting of the minds between Zionism and National Socialism with regard to the solution of the Jewish Question in Germany. The attitude of the National Socialist regime towards Zionism is perhaps best outlined in a report on the Zionist movement in Germany put together by Adolf Eichmann and Herbert Hagen of section II/112 in the *Sicherheitsdienst* (SD) on 20th October 1936.[69] As part of the increasingly active role of the SS in the formulation and execution of Jewish policy, the report argued:

> ". . . dass sich die 'Zionistische Weltorganisation' im Ausland in sehr eindeutige Gegnerschaft zum Nationalsozialismus gestellt hat. Wenn sich die ZVfD – als innerhalb der Reichsgrenzen bestehende jüdische Organisation – eine Zurückhaltung auferlegt hat, so ist der Grund nicht etwa in einer freundlicher Haltung dem Staat gegenüber zu suchen, sondern in der Erkenntnis, dass jede jüdische Organisation, gleich welcher Art, ein 100%er Gegner des Nationalsozialismus sein muss. Die ZVfD ist als Landesverband der Zionistischen Weltorganisation . . . ein tätiges Mitglied des weltanschaulichen Gegners 'Judentum'."

> (. . . that the World Zionist Organisation abroad has placed itself in clear opposition to National Socialism. If the ZVfD, as an existing Jewish organisation within the borders of the *Reich*, has demonstrated caution, the reason for this cannot be found in a friendly attitude towards the state but in the knowledge that every Jewish organisation must be a 100 per cent

---

[68]BA: R43 II/602, Auswärtiges Amt, Berlin, an Stellvertreter des Führers, Reichsministerium des Innern und Reichsministerium für Volksaufklärung und Propaganda, 83–63 17/10, 30. Oktober 1934.

[69]BA: R/58–955, Bericht 'Die Zionistische Weltorganisation', II/112, 20. Oktober 1936. Department II/112 in the SD was responsible for the Jewish Question, with section II/112–3 responsible for Zionism.

opponent of National Socialism. The ZVfD is, as the German branch of the World Zionist
Organisation . . . an active member of the enemy "Jewry".)

The report also pointed to the unacceptable Zionist quest for an independent
Jewish state in Palestine and to the fundamental incompatibility of Zionism and
National Socialism with the observation that:

> "Die Arbeit der 'Zionistische Weltorganisation' – indirekt auch die der ZVfD – birgt neben
> der schon vorhandenen eine weitere sich verstärkende Gefahr: Ein starkes jüdisches
> Palästina. Das Weltjudentum wird für alle Zeiten, bedingt durch die klare Haltung des
> Nationalsozialismus, für Deutschland als Gegner bestehen; ein starkes jüdisches Palästina
> könnte ein wesentlicher Faktor seines Kampfes sein."

> (The work of the World Zionist Organisation – indirectly that of the ZVfD as well – hides a
> further growing danger: a strong Jewish Palestine. World Jewry will always be an enemy for
> Germany given the clear position of National Socialism; a strong Jewish Palestine could be an
> important factor in its struggle.)

In its conclusion, the report indicated quite clearly the rationale for Nazi policy
towards Zionism and the extent to which the German Zionist movement would
be tolerated: "Der ZVfD wird solange Bewegungsfreiheit in beschränktem
Masse gewährt als durch ihre Förderung in der Auswanderung sichtbare Erfolg
zu verzeichnen sind." (The ZVfD will be permitted freedom of movement in a
restricted way for as long as its promotion of emigration demonstrates visible
success.) German Zionism remained "useful" to the needs of Nazi Jewish policy
until the end of 1938, and not beyond. After the *Kristallnacht* pogrom of
November 1938, the SS took control of the emigration process in the *Altreich* from
the government ministries that had previously controlled the process, particularly the Interior and Economics Ministries, based on the brutal deportation
model established by Eichmann and the SD in Vienna after March 1938. This
radical transformation of emigration procedures effectively transferred responsibility for organising and effecting Jewish emigration from the Jewish community,
particularly from the Zionists, to the SS. Whatever semblance of order and
legality that might have existed in the emigration process before November 1938,
gave way to the stepped-up pace of rounding up Jews, seizing their assets and
simply deporting them regardless of whether they possessed entry visas to other
countries.[70] These methods, coupled with the final legislation eliminating the
Jewish role in the German economy in 1938 and 1939, removed whatever basis
for Zionist work had existed in Germany since 1933. Accordingly, the ZVfD
along with all remaining Jewish organisations were dissolved by the authorities
in the wake of the *Kristallnacht* in November 1938.[71]

Both the legal and illegal emigration of Jews from Germany to Palestine and
other destinations continued to be encouraged by the police authorities within
the context of their brutal deportation policies; but organised Zionist activity

---

[70]See Adam, *Judenpolitik, op. cit.*, pp. 204ff.
[71]The *Staatszionistische Organisation* was formally dissolved by the SD on 31st August, 1938, primarily
because it was never able to convince the authorities that it was entirely independent of Revisionist
organisations outside of Germany which were actively involved in the international boycott against
Germany. For more on SD suspicions of the Revisionists and their connections abroad, see BA: R/
58–544, II–112, Aktennotiz betr. Einzelfälle, 26. April 1938.

and official Zionist participation in the emigration process came to an end. With the exception of the continued functioning of the *Palästina-Amt* in the old headquarters of the ZVfD in the Meinekestrasse in Berlin, which simply distributed immigration certificates for Palestine, the process of Jewish emigration became the exclusive preserve of the SS; with much of the pre-1933 Jewish population still in Germany and an annexed Austria, the Zionist movement had for all practical purposes ceased to function in Germany. If the end of emancipation from 1933 through 1938 had severely impeded the effectiveness of Zionist work in Germany, the final assault on what was left of Jewish life in Germany between 1939 and 1941 destroyed German Zionism along with the entire Jewish community altogether.

Early but Opposed – Supported but Late
Two Berlin Seminaries which Attempted to Move Abroad

BY CHRISTHARD HOFFMANN AND DANIEL R. SCHWARTZ

Berlin's two rabbinical seminaries, located on the same street, one Orthodox and one Liberal, faced, along with the rest of Germany Jewry, quite a dismal present in the 1930s, and as time went on could expect a more and more dismal future. However, they also looked back at quite a respectable past: since their foundation in the early 1870s, they had been among the central institutions of *Wissenschaft des Judentums*, and had produced generations of scholars, rabbis and teachers. Thus, it was only natural for their pilots to begin to think of transferring the institutions abroad. Indeed, both did try, one in 1933 and the other in 1939, but neither plan came to fruition. Although many of the individuals involved did emigrate, the institutions stayed in Berlin and died there. In this paper, we have attempted to reconstruct the two projects and the reasons they failed.*

I. ON LITHUANIAN PATRONS, GERMAN CLIENTS, AND THE 1933 ATTEMPT TO TRANSFER THE HILDESHEIMER SEMINARY TO PALESTINE

A. *Introduction*

The 1933 plan to move Berlin's *Rabbinerseminar für das Orthodoxe Judentum* ("the Hildesheimer Seminary")** to Palestine was very shortlived: the balloon was

*The two studies presented in this essay have been prepared within the context of a larger project on 'Wissenstransfer durch Emigration' sponsored by the *Zentrum für Antisemitismusforschung der Technischen Universität Berlin*. Christhard Hoffmann, who is responsible for the second part of this contribution, is on the *Zentrum*'s staff; Daniel Schwartz, who has written the first part, is on that of the Department of Jewish History at the Hebrew University Jerusalem. Both authors wish to express their thanks to the *Zentrum*'s director, Professor Herbert A. Strauss, for his encouragement and advice, and to the *Deutsche Forschungsgemeinschaft* which has generously supported the general project. The section written by Christhard Hoffmann was translated from the original German by Belinda Cooper, and the author would like to thank the *Zentrum* for assuming the costs of the translation. Further thanks for valuable comments and additions are due to Professors Raphael Loewe, London, and Herbert Strauss, who read an early draft of this part of our contribution.
**Thanks are due to Dr. Meir Hildesheimer of Bar-Ilan University, and to Mr. Marc Shapiro of Harvard University (who is completing a monograph about Rabbi Jechiel Jacob Weinberg), for their comments on a first draft of this part of the essay, and for various details which they supplied. Transliteration of Hebrew generally follows the practice of the 1971 English *Encyclopedia Judaica*, wherein articles may be found regarding most of the individuals and topics mentioned. Three abbreviations for collections of Hebrew letters:
Ahiezer = Ch. O. Grodzenski, *Ahiezer. Collected Letters*, vols. I–II, ed. by A. Surasky, Bnai Brak, 1970. (Not to be confused with his *Responsa Ahiezer*.)
Iggerot LaReiya = *Iggerot LaReiya. Collected Letters From the Great Rabbis of his Generation to . . . Rabbi Abraham Isaac HaKohen Kook*, Jerusalem 1985/1986.

launched in mid-September 1933 and grounded within four months. Moreover, although the episode did attract attention during those few months, for understandable reasons the principals involved usually preferred not to leave to posterity anything more than hints about the project and the way it was scuttled.[1] It is only by ferreting through contemporary newspapers and letters than the episode may be pieced together. So it is not suprising that it has received very little attention.[2] However, it sheds important light on the ambivalent and embattled situation of German Orthodoxy in its final generation. In a more general way, furthermore, precisely because of its circumscribed nature it provides a very clear example of a dynamic known from elsewhere in the history of human relations, wherever one group places its collective soul and fate in the hands of another which enjoys the trust and honour, and reciprocates responsibly, but, when push comes to shove, cannot possibly save its dependents if that would entail allowing them to join its own ranks.

There are three main figures in the story. The protagonist was Rabbi Dr. Meier Hildesheimer, the son of the Seminary's founder, in his seventieth and what turned out to be his last year in 1933/1934.[3] After a lifetime of service in various capacities in the world of German Orthodoxy, and especially in the separatist *Adass Jisroel Gemeinde* in Berlin, in the last few years of his life he devoted much of his energies to fundraising and other efforts on behalf of the *Rabbinerseminar* which his father had founded in 1873, the financial situation of which was catastrophic, although the number of its students (*ordentlich* and *ausserordentlich*) had risen to

---

Seridei Esh = J. J. Weinberg, *Seridei Esh* (collected responsa and studies), 4 volumes, Jerusalem 1961–1969. All translations in this section and its appendixes are by Daniel Schwartz.

[1] The attempt to avoid the real reason the project was scotched is evident as early as January 1934 – see our Appendix IV. Similarly, Moses Auerbach deliberately avoided, in his memoirs, all topics which involved polemics; see *The Memoirs of Rabbi Moses Auerbach*, Jerusalem 1981/1982, p. 7 (in Hebrew). (These memoirs were originally published in successive issues of *HaMaayan 21–22* [1981–1982]; in the one-volume edition, from which we shall cite, the pagination is new but the footnotes are numbered as in the original.)

[2] The most detailed accounts known to me are those in Auerbach, *op. cit.*, pp. 66–67, note 116 and in Isi Jacob Eisner, 'Reminiscences of the Berlin Rabbinical Seminary', in *LBI Year Book XII* (1967), p. 49. Among other references to the affair, especially worthy of note is a passing reference in connection with the tensions between the Polish *Agudath Israel* and its German counterpart: M. Friedman, *Society and Religion. The Non-Zionist Orthodox in Eretz-Israel, 1918–1936*, Jerusalem 1977, p. 223, note 23 (in Hebrew). Most recently, the episode was recalled in the course of a general 1986 address by the Chancellor of the Jewish Theological Seminary of America, entitled 'Shaping the Image of the Modern Rabbi', Ismar Schorsch, *Thoughts from 3080. Selected Addresses and Writings*, (n.p., n.d. [New York 1988?]), pp. 19–20. For general orientation and *personalia* concerning the *Rabbinerseminar*, see Eisner's article, *loc. cit.*, pp. 32–52, also E. G. Lowenthal, 'In seinen Hörern noch lebendig . . . Das Rabbiner-Seminar zu Berlin', *Emuna*, 9 (1974), pp. 103–111.

[3] On him, see Joseph Carlebach, *Dr. Meier Hildesheimer zatzal zum Gedenken* (n.d., n.p. [1934?]), 13 pages; W. S. Jacobson, 'Rabbiner Dr. Meier Hildesheimer', in M. Sinasohn (ed.), *Adass Jisroel Berlin. Entstehung, Entfaltung, Entwurzelung, 1869–1939,* Jerusalem 1966, pp. 84–87. Typically, neither of these pieces refers at all to the Palestine plan, although Jacobson specifically underlines Hildesheimer's many trips "durch ganz Deutschland, Oesterreich-Ungarn, die Schweiz, Holland, Belgien und Frankreich, nach Südafrika und Amerika" (p. 86)! On the Hildesheimer circle and its institutions see, most recently, Mario Offenberg (ed.), *Adass Jisroel, die jüdische Gemeinde in Berlin (1869–1942). Vernichtet und Vergessen*, Berlin n.d. [1986?].

about ninety in 1933.[4] Add to the financial troubles the rise of Nazism, on the one hand, and, on the other hand, the retirement of one of the few longtime faculty members[5] and the pressure to return to Palestine by another who had spent many years there earlier in the century,[6] and it is not difficult to understand the genesis of the idea of moving the institution to Palestine.

The main antagonist, who more or less singlehandedly buried the plan, was Rabbi Chaim O. Grodzenski of Vilna, one of the most influential Lithuanian rabbis of the twentieth century and one who – in contrast to some other Torah sages – was willing to engage in practical decision-making and therefore consented to act in official capacities. In 1933 he was not only the most prominent rabbi in Vilna ("Jerusalem of Lithuania"), and the moving force of the *Va'ad Hayeshivot* – the organisation which cared for the *yeshivot*, which were to feel threatened by the plan to move the *Rabbinerseminar* to Palestine[7] – but also president of the rabbinic board ("Council of Torah Sages") of the world organisation of extreme Orthodoxy, the *Agudath Israel* (which he had helped found two decades earlier).[8] He was, moreover, one of the prime advocates of the notion of *daat Torah* ("Torah opinion"), i.e., the notion that great rabbinic sages such as himself are endowed with a capacity for delivering true guidance, of *halakhic* authority, even beyond their usual judicial capacity of resolving *halakhic* questions on the basis of the relevant sources.[9] And he was opposed to the thought of moving the *Rabbinerseminar* to Palestine.

[4]For the number of students, see V. Unna's piece on the *Rabbinerseminar* in a triad of articles on Germany's seminaries: *Israelitisches Gemeindeblatt* (Mannheim), 14th March 1933, p. 8. As for the Seminary's financial situation, suffice it to note that its *Jahres-Berichte*, which had indeed appeared annually until the First World War, appeared after 1919 only in 1924, 1928 and 1938. As their prefaces explain, this was due to the institution's grave financial difficulties. Cf., 'Die Not der Rabbinerhochschulen in Deutschland', *Der Israelit*, 30th June 1932, p. 6; 'Jüdische Wissenschaft in Not', *Israelitisches Gemeindeblatt* (Mannheim), 14th December 1932, pp. 8–9. Hence, for example, Hildesheimer's extended trip to South Africa in 1929/1930, devoted to fundraising for the Seminary (according to his grandson, M. Hildesheimer, *HaMaayan*, 17/2 [Tevet 1976/1977], p. 7 note 18 [in Hebrew]). According to J. J. Weinberg, Hildesheimer actually rescued the Seminary from disaster (*Lifrakim*, Warsaw 1936, p. 264 [in Hebrew]).

[5]Ill health forced Joseph Wohlegemuth to retire from the Seminary in 1931; he had been on its staff since 1894.

[6]Moses Auerbach. He had spent 1909–1917 in Palestine and throughout the 1920s had been making attempts to return; see note 117 of his memoirs (above, note 1).

[7]See note 46.

[8]On Grodzenski, see, most recently, S. Finkelman, *Reb Chaim Ozer. The Life and Ideals of Rabbi Chaim Ozer Grodzenski of Vilna*, Brooklyn 1987; further bibliography listed *ibid.*, p. 271; and see especially, A. Surasky, *Giants of Jewry*, I, New York 1982, pp. 275–331. Most of this literature is inevitably hagiographic. As for *Agudath Israel* and its Council of Torah Sages, see G. C. Bacon, *Agudath Israel in Poland, 1916–39. An Orthodox Jewish Response to the Challenge of Modernity*, dissertation, Columbia University, 1979. Note the organisational chart on p. 101, showing the Council's hegemony. For the remarkable willingness of some modern Lithuanian rabbis to assume decision-making responsibility for World Jewry, as opposed to most of their predecessors and contemporaries who confined their practical decision-making to their own communities, see S. Y. Zevin, *Ishim Veshitot*, Tel-Aviv, 1951/1952, pp. 196–197; Rabbi Grodzenski is the most recent of the examples cited here.

[9]The concept, or at least its aggressive assertion, was a new one: it has been traced back only to one of Grodzenski's Lithuanian contemporaries, Rabbi Israel Meir Ha-Kohen Kagan (the "Hafetz Hayyim"). See Bacon, *op. cit.*, pp. 53–60, also *idem, 'Daat Torah* and Birthpangs of the Messiah. The Ideology of *Agudath Israel* in Inter-War Poland', *Tarbiz*, 52 (1982/1983), pp. 497–508 (in Hebrew). An article on the concept and its history, by Dr. Dov I. Frimer, will appear in a forthcoming issue of

The very notion of a rabbinical seminary, it should be understood, was repugnant to traditional circles in Eastern Europe, where Jewish learning was confined to *yeshivot*. The latter differed from rabbinical seminaries in that they were not professional training schools, but rather places where the Torah was – ideally – studied for its own sake, and in that they did not include any secular subjects, much less encourage their students to study in universities as well. The *Rabbinerseminar*'s curriculum included various "secular" subjects and its students studied at the university also; Grodzenski once compared the combination of university and talmudic studies to the admixture of poison to pure water (Appendix II).[10] Correspondingly, Eastern European scorn for German *Rabbiner Doktoren* was widespread, as was the conception that the level of Torah scholarship among German rabbis could not begin to compare with that usual in the East.[11] Therefore, while Lithuanian sages, such as Rabbi Grodzenski, might grudgingly admit that there was some justification for the foundation of an Orthodox rabbinical seminary in Germany, so as not to leave the field totally to the Reformers, they were horrified by the thought of such an institution opening in the Holy Land as well.[12]

Tradition. For a definition of *daat Torah* in an *Agudath Israel* publication, see B. Weinberger, 'The Role of the Gedolim', *The Jewish Observer*, 1/2 (October 1963), pp. 11–12, 20: "It assumes a special endowment or capacity to penetrate objective reality . . . a form of 'Ruach Hakodesh' [= Holy Spirit, D.R.S.] as it were, which borders if only remotely on the periphery of prophecy" (p. 11). Weinberger's only named examples of individuals endowed with this capacity are Grodzenski, Kagan and a third Lithuanian rabbi, the "Hazon Ish" (Rabbi Abraham Karlewitz). Weinberger's statement has been cited and criticised in another American Orthodox journal: L. Kaplan, 'Rabbi Isaac Hutner's "Daat Torah Perspective" on the Holocaust. A Critical Analysis', *Tradition*, 18 (1979/ 1980), pp. 245–248.

[10]For the *Rabbinerseminar*'s curriculum, which included not only Talmud and legal codes – the main fare of the *yeshivot* – but also such topics as Bible (*mirabile dictu*), history, Jewish literature, philosophy, homiletics, pedagogy and even social work, see its annual reports, also *Studien- und Prüfungsordnung des Rabbiner-Seminars zu Berlin*, Berlin 1928. For a statement of its rationale, which contrasts it with that of the Lithuanian *yeshivot*, see Moses Auerbach, 'Ziel und Weg der heutigen Rabbinerausbildung', in *Der Israelit* for 15th, 22nd and 29th September 1932. Cf. Weinberg's articles on Hirsch, quoted below, note 16.

[11]With regard to the *Rabbinerseminar* and its students, this conception is best represented by Reuven Katz, quoted p. 280, and by the material collected in I. Etkes, *Rabbi Israel Salanter and the Beginning of the "Musar" Movement*, Jerusalem 1982, pp. 304–309 (in Hebrew). Similarly, Unna's 1933 article on the *Rabbinerseminar* (above, note 4) concentrated on the problem that about half of the *Seminar*'s students were Polish. They would not be allowed to accept positions in Germany, and prospects in Poland too were dim: ". . . die Gemeinden dort sich gegen Rabbiner mit Hochschulbildung wehren . . ." As for Grodzenski, it is enough to note his organisation of the opposition to the introduction of secular studies for rabbinical candidates in Russia, and the report that, when once approached on behalf of an academically-trained Torah scholar, he replied that "Poland is not in need of rabbis with doctorates", Finkelman (above, note 8), p. 66, and p. 205, note *. In general, compare, for two examples, Eli Ginzberg's report of how his father, upon arriving in Berlin from Lithuanian *yeshivot*, mocked "Rabbiner Doktor" Esriel Hildesheimer, the founder of the *Rabbiner-seminar*, in *Keeper of the Law. Louis Ginzberg*, Philadelphia 1966, pp. 40–41; and the memoirs of Bernard Drachman, a German-American rabbi and scholar, who acknowledged the Eastern European prejudice but nevertheless professed wonder at his not having been allowed to teach Talmud at Yeshiva College, in *The Unfailing Light. Memoirs of an American Rabbi*, New York 1948, p. 368.

[12]See Appendixes I–II, where Grodzenski clearly states both sides of this attitude. (Grodzenski monotonously repeated the theme in his next two letters to Rabbi Kook [*Iggerot LaReiya*, pp. 214– 216], because he thought the first one had not arrived.) For similar appreciations of the

Caught in the middle between the two main actors was the third, Rabbi Dr. Jechiel Jacob Weinberg, Rector of the *Rabbinerseminar*, a bit of Lithuania in Berlin.[13] Weinberg who had enjoyed a reputation as a genius in the Lithuanian *yeshivot* of his youth, saw a rabbinical career in Lithuania interrupted by a family tragedy, in the wake of which he moved to Germany. After a short period teaching in Berlin, he – as several other Jewish scholars in the period between the world wars – was taken under Paul Kahle's wing, and spent a few years in university work.[14] When, however, in 1924 the central position – teaching Talmud and rabbinics – at the *Rabbinerseminar* became open due to the sudden demise of another young Lithuanian scholar there, Weinberg was invited to take up the position.[15] He was to remain there, and eventually at the *Seminar*'s helm, until the end.

Thus, in the struggle between Hildesheimer and Grodzenski, Weinberg was caught in the middle. On the one hand, by 1933 Weinberg had been associated with the *Seminar* for a decade and could in no way share Eastern European scorn for it or be nonchalant about its future.[16] On the other hand, however, there was no way that Grodzenski could be ignored. Not only was Weinberg himself, as a

---

Rabbinerseminar's function as competition for Reform in Germany, see the 1879 letter by Rabbi Y. E. Spektor of Kovno published by M. Hildesheimer in *HaMaayan*, 14/2 (Tevet 1973/1974), pp. 34–35 (in Hebrew), and some other testimonials assembled by Hildesheimer, *ibid.*, pp. 35–37, note 87.

[13] Marc Shapiro of Harvard University is currently completing a volume about Weinberg. In the meantime, see, *inter alia*, Auerbach, *op. cit.* (see note 1), pp. 57–59, note 105 (with bibliography); M. Pineas (Pinkus) in Sinasohn, *op. cit.* (see note 3), pp. 175–177; and Eliezer Berkovits, 'Rabbi Yechiel Yakob Weinberg *zatzal*. My Teacher and Master', *Tradition*, 8/2 (Summer, 1966), pp. 5–14. For another very insightful account of Weinberg, see A. Surasky's introduction to Weinberg's *It is My Brothers that I am Seeking*, Bnai Brak 1966, pp. 17–42 (in Hebrew). Isidor Grunfeld, 'The "Ba'al Seride Esh"', in *The Torah Personality. A Treasury of Biographical Sketches* (collected from the pages of *The Jewish Observer*), ed. by N. Wolpin, Brooklyn 1980, pp. 99–105, is not as much pure hagiography as many of the other essays in that anthology; Grunfeld died before he could complete his volume about Weinberg (mentioned *ibid.*, p. 105). A collection of autobiographical references in Weinberg's writings may be found in *HaMaayan*, 6/3 (Nisan 1966), pp. 56–66 (in Hebrew).

[14] Note Kahle's acknowledgement of the assistance rendered by Menachem Zulay, A. Sperber, Rafael Edelmann and Weinberg: Paul Kahle, *Masoreten des Westens*, II (1930), p. vi and p. 3, note 1.

[15] On Rabbi Abraham Elijahu Kaplan (1889–1924) and his replacement by Weinberg, see *Jahres-Bericht des Rabbiner-Seminars zu Berlin für 1924 (5684)*, pp. 8, 27–28; Auerbach, *op. cit.* (see note 1), p. 56, note 103.

[16] According to Leo Jung, in Sinasohn, *op. cit.* (see note 3), p. 113, "Dr. Weinberg war einer der wenigen Gedolim [= great sages] osteuropäischer Abstammung, der die hervorragenden Eigenschaften der deutschen thoratreuen Juden voll anerkannte." For two strident expressions of Weinberg's respect for German Orthodox rabbis, see his *Seridei Esh*, II, p. 53, note * (where he emphasises that they cared little for their academic titles which were mere window-dressing for external consumption), and pp. 14a, 16b–17a (where he sets out their virtues and educational successes in contrast to Eastern European failures). See also his 'Rabbi Samson Raphael Hirsch *zatzal*', *Nach^alat Z'wi*, 7 (1936/1937), pp. 130–139 (with a defence of the *Rabbinerseminar* on p. 134), and *idem*, 'Zur Auseinandersetzung über S. R. Hirsch und seine "Thora im Derech Erez" Devise', *ibid.*, pp. 186–193. Note also the reference to "The Gaon, the Zaddik, our Master, Rabbi Esriel Hildesheimer", in a 1949 *responsum* (*Seridei Esh*, II, p. 236); this titulature – which omits "Dr."! – goes well beyond what is required and usual in the usual inflation of honorifics. For other similar Eastern European expressions of high respect for this Hildesheimer, see M. Hildesheimer's biographical introduction to *Responsa of Rabbi Esriel on Orach Chaim and Yoreh Deah*, Tel-Aviv 1968/ 1969, pp. 24–26 (in Hebrew). In this long florilegium of complimentary references to Esriel Hildesheimer and openings of letters to him, none refers to his doctorate. Cf. our notes 11 and 57, also the excerpt from *Seridei Esh*, II, No. 123, quoted in the text below.

Lithuanian Jew, bound by all that was dear to him to accept Grodzenski's authority,[17] more basically, the fact was that Lithuanian rabbis were the legitimators of German Orthodoxy, which was beleaguered in its own land. Whether in Berlin, Frankfurt a. Main or elsewhere, the separatist Orthodox communities looked to Lithuanian models and authorities. Having seceded from the general Jewish communities of Germany, they attached themselves to Vilna as best they could: they sent their *halakhic* questions to Rabbi Grodzenski and his colleagues, they collected money for Lithuanian *yeshivot*, they sent their children to the latter to study for shorter or longer periods, and they featured the affairs of the Lithuanian *yeshivah* world very prominently in the pages of their press.[18] The problem was, as we shall see, that the respect and feeling of community was not reciprocated with the same fervour and sincerity. The Lithuanians, that is, while content to enjoy the allegiance and support of the Germans, and while even willing to undertake responsibility for their spiritual wellbeing, seem nevertheless to have viewed the German Orthodox more as poor cousins than as partners. In the crunch, that position would become clear.

B. *The Hildesheimer Circle and Eastern European Jewry ca. 1933*

Before turning to the specifics of the Palestine-transfer plan and its defeat, we should mention three minor episodes and two affairs of more abiding importance

[17]It is characteristic that even in his defence of Hirsch, Weinberg somewhat tactlessly "proudly emphasises" that he is an *Ostjude*, and claims – in the journal of a Frankfurt society dedicated to Hirsch's memory – that *Ostjuden* better understood Hirsch than the Germans did, because for *Ostjuden* the *yeshivah* was "Heimatboden", not only a place for "eine Episode der schwärmerischen Aufwallung" (p. 133 of his 1936/1937 article quoted in the preceding note).

[18]For the acceptance of Lithuanian models and authority, see, for a characteristic example, Weinberg's reference to "in all the lands of the East not a single rabbi . . ." in *Seridei Esh*, II, No. 123 (quoted at length in the text below). For another of our protagonists, see Grodzenski's 1913 'Letter Concerning the Communities in Germany', published in the *Memorial Volume for . . . J. J. Weinberg, Head of the Berlin Rabbinical Seminary*, ed. by E. Hildesheimer and Kalman Kahane, Jerusalem 1969, pp. 1–4 (in Hebrew) = *Ahiezer*, I, pp. 240–245. Here, Grodzenski explains that the issue in question (whether or not the Orthodox should secede from the general Jewish community) is not a *halakhic* question *sensu strictu*, and is one which the local rabbis, most familiar with local politics, are best qualified to decide. It is this special nature of the question which explains the anomaly that earlier German rabbis – contrary to their usual practice – had not asked Lithuanian sages for a decision. This same orientation underlies the fact that the *Rabbinerseminar*, as we have seen, took one Lithuanian after another for its central talmudic position; cf. Alexander Carlebach, *Men and Ideas. A Jewish Miscellany*, Jerusalem 1982, p. 64. On this Lithuanian hegemony over German Orthodoxy in its final fifteen years, see J. A. Wolf (one of the last instructors at the *Rabbinerseminar*), *The Period and its Problems*, Bnai Brak 1964/1965, pp. 111–113 (in Hebrew). Cf. Joseph Carlebach's series of articles on a trip to the East sponsored by German *Agudath Israel*'s *Keren Hathora* (fund for supporting *yeshivot*), in *Der Israelit* of 8th, 15th, 22nd and 29th December 1932 and 5th January 1933 (with a photograph of Rabbi Grodzenski in the centre of p. 4 of the third instalment), also – on an earlier trip – Alexander Carlebach, 'A German Rabbi Goes East', in *LBI Year Book VI* (1961), pp. 60–121. In general, for some more samples from 1932–1933, see articles in *Der Israelit*, 6th October 1932, p. 6 and 13th October 1932, p. 6 (Lithuanian appeals for financial support; former by Rabbis Grodzenski and Kagan); 10th March 1932, pp. 2–3, 8th September 1932, p. 10, 3rd November 1932, p. 6 and 15th December 1932, p. 6 (life in the Lithuanian *yeshivot*); and 20th and 27th September 1933 and 2nd November 1933 (large front-page stories upon the deaths of Rabbi Kagan and Rabbi Meir Shapira of Lublin).

of the same approximate period. They all testify to, and probably contributed to, the atmosphere and type of relationship between Berlin and Lithuania which were to determine the outcome of the Seminary-transfer plan.

Of the three episodes, the first came in 1928/1929, when an interesting *halakhic* conundrum and terrible human problem put Weinberg at loggerheads with one of the foremost Lithuanian *halakhic* authorities, Rabbi Joseph Rosin of Dvinsk ("the Rogotchover"), and Meier Hildesheimer found himself in the middle. The question was, whether a widow whose husband had died without leaving children might be freed to marry someone else, in accordance with the law of Deuteronomy XXV: 5–10, by a brother-in-law who had converted to Christianity. In this case, the question was complicated by the fact that the deceased husband was survived by another brother, who was not an apostate, but only a non-believer; he was also practically inaccessible – in Soviet Russia. Weinberg ruled that only the non-believer could release the widow, which, due to his inaccessibility, meant that the woman had to remain an *agunah* (unable to marry). The Rogotchover, in contrast, ruled that the apostate was no worse than the non-believer, and so ruled that the apostate could release the woman for remarriage. It may be remarked that this case shows the Lithuanian taking a position more lenient than that upheld by the Berlin rabbi; in the cases to be discussed below, the positions were reversed, as might have been expected. What is important for us, here, is that the Lithuanian peremptorily brushed aside Weinberg's objections in very strident, not to say insulting, terms, circumvented Weinberg and "ordered" (the term is Weinberg's) the Berlin rabbinical court to arrange the proper ceremony with the apostate brother, who lived in Germany. Weinberg had no choice but to instruct Meier Hildesheimer to follow Rabbi Rosin's orders.[19]

This episode showed Weinberg – the Seminary's Lithuanian credentials, so to speak – being treated highhandedly by a Lithuanian rabbi as if he were a virtually negligible German rabbi. The next case illustrates the other side of the coin. By the early twentieth century, cremation had become so popular among free-thinking German Jews that Rabbi Meier Lerner of Altona had seen fit to

[19]On this episode, see *Seridei Esh*, III, pp. 152–165; Weinberg sets out the story on p. 157, and on pp. 157–158 prints his own letter to Meier Hildesheimer, instructing him to follow Rabbi Rosin's directions but taking umbrage at the latter's tone. (It seems that it is this second letter from Rosin to M. Hildesheimer which is printed in Rosin's *Responsa Tzafenat Paaneach*, I, Dvinsk 1940, No. 80, p. 68. However, unfortunately – although perhaps not accidentally? – the end of the letter, which apparently contained the nasty language to which Weinberg referred, is missing.) What especially angered Weinberg was the way Rabbi Rosin ignored the great modern and early modern decisors (*Aharonim*) upon whom Weinberg had depended, referring to Weinberg as having "ferreted out late nobodies (*liqqet nemushot*)". Such independence was typical of the Rogotchover; see Zevin, (above, note 8), pp. 79–80, 109–126. To complete the story, we may note that Weinberg, although he instructed Hildesheimer to follow Rosin's "orders", nevertheless sent his discussion to several other rabbinical authorities, asking for their opinions. Of the six published responses – four published in *Seridei Esh*, III, pp. 158–165 and two referred to *ibid.*, p. 157 – all but one agreed with Rosin (albeit with varying degrees of certainty); the one who agreed with Weinberg suggested that he ask Rabbi Grodzenski to influence Rabbi Rosin to back down – *ibid.*, p. 165. Is it only a coincidence that the five sages who supported Rosin against Weinberg were all in Lithuania or Palestine, while the one who agreed with Weinberg was Rabbi Yishayahu Fürst of Vienna?

publish a booklet in which he collected the opinions of all the great rabbis of the day. They condemned the practice and imposed the strongest penalty available to them: it is forbidden, they agreed, to bury in a Jewish cemetery the ashes of people who had been cremated at their own behest.[20] Nevertheless, by late 1930 the question was being raised in Orthodox circles. The matter was referred to Weinberg, whose response begins as follows:[21]

> "To the Rabbi, the Gaon Dr. M. Schlesinger (may he live long and well) . . . Concerning *Rabbiner* Dr. P's [or: F's – it is impossible to distinguish between these unvocalised Hebrew initials] questions as to whether the urns containing ashes of those cremated after death may be buried in a Jewish cemetery alongside the other graves – it is totally clear and obvious that it is forbidden, and God forbid that something like this happen among the Jews. And I may testify that in all the lands of the East not a single rabbi would ever allow this . . . Now, *Rabbiner* Dr. Hoffmann in Frankfurt also agrees that it is forbidden, but in the continuation of his discussion he tends to argue in favour of a lenient decision . . . But this argument is very strange, and I will not deny that had I not seen his own signature (may he live long and well) I would not have believed that the words were his . . ."

That is, Weinberg saw here a suggestion which no real rabbi could possibly consider. Real rabbis were in the East; indeed, for the clear and straightforward rejection of the suggestion, by Rabbi Grodzenski, see his *Responsa Ahiezer*.[22] The German rabbis who asked the question, and wanted a lenient response, are only *Rabbiner Doktoren*. While after the war Weinberg, in a retrospective and martyrological context, could assert that the Orthodox rabbis of Germany "hid their academic titles and used them only in their dealings with the government and in their wars against the assimilationist non-religious",[23] here – in 1930 – we see that he too seems to have shared something of the usual Lithuanian disdain for the type of rabbi his own institution was producing. This did not bode well for his ability or willingness to defend the *Seminar* against its Lithuanian detractors. Three years later, as we shall see,[24] it was Weinberg himself who told Rabbi Grodzenski of the plan to move the Seminary to Palestine, following which Grodzenski immediately expressed his disapproval. Given the attitude towards German *Rabbiner Doktoren* evinced here by Weinberg, it is difficult to imagine that he put up much of a fight on behalf of the plan.

The third passing episode came in 1932. After Rabbi Dr. Felix Goldmann of Leipzig published an attack on the traditional marriage laws which at times result in suffering (inability to marry or to remarry), tradition was defended on the front page of Breslau's *Jüdische Zeitung* by a Jewish layman, Arnold Wiener of Beuthen, who defended the Orthodox tradition. In doing so, however, Wiener

---

[20]See M. Lerner, *Chaye Olam*, Berlin 1905; the German title-page of this Hebrew booklet reads *Gutachten Rabbiner aller Länder über Exhumierung und Aschenurnebeisetzung auf jüdischen Friedhöfen*, I. For references to numerous polemical pieces in the German-Jewish controversy over cremation in the late nineteenth and early twentieth centuries, see the bibliography concluding M. Higger's discussion of the matter in his *Halachot VeAggadot*, New York 1932, pp. 161–183 (in Hebrew). For its growing acceptance in Berlin in the 1930s, see 'Religiös-liberale Tendenzen im Bestattungswesen der Berliner Gemeinde', *Jüdisch-liberale Zeitung*, 15th September 1932, Beilage.

[21]*Seridei Esh*, II, No. 123, p. 278.

[22]Chaim O. Grodzenski, *Responsa Ahiezer*, III, New York [2]1946, No. 72d, p. 139.

[23]*Seridei Esh*, II, p. 53, note *.

[24]See note 121.

argued that the tradition itself allowed for adjustment so as to alleviate such human suffering. This brought forth protests in the press by two rabbis who were Hildesheimer graduates: Rabbi Dr. Saul Kaatz of Hindenburg and Rabbi Dr. J. Merzbach of Darmstadt. Until this point, in the spring of 1932, all was more or less as to be expected, although Wiener was hurt to discover that the Orthodox were criticising him for defending them. However, the fat hit the fire when another Hildesheimer graduate, Rabbi Dr. Marcus Melchior (later of Copenhagen), who was rabbi of Beuthen, stepped to his congregant's defence. Melchior published an article showing to his own satisfaction that the possibilities of Reform within the *Halakhah* were indeed greater than Kaatz and Merzbach had admitted. This elicited a new attack in *Der Israelit*, by Rabbi Dr. Hermann Klein of Berlin. But when Melchior persisted, and even won the support of another *Rabbinerseminar alumnus*, Rabbi Dr. Chaim Lauer of Mannheim, rabbi and teacher at the *Klaus* and *yeshivah* in Mannheim, Klein and Merzbach asked Grodzenski himself to intervene. Grodzenski wrote letters, and composed a formal *responsum* as well; Klein published it in 1933, and this stage of the matter apparently died out.[25] Melchior moved to Denmark the next year.

This episode, which preceded by only a few months the Seminary-transfer plan, is important for two reasons. First, quite obviously, it reinforced Rabbi Grodzenski's standing as the arbiter for German-Jewish Orthodoxy. Secondly, it is likely that this affair contributed to a general exasperation, in his mind, with Western rabbis. For in the very recent past, in the wake of the large number of

---

[25]For the preceding paragraph, see A. Wiener, 'Über jüdische Ehegesetze', *Jüdische Zeitung* (Breslau), 5th February 1932, pp. 1–2; S. Kaatz, 'Über jüdische Ehegesetze', *ibid.*, 12th February 1932, p. 2 (with short response by Wiener); J. Merzbach, 'Vorschläge über jüdische Ehegesetze', *Der Israelit*, 3rd March 1932, pp. 3–4 and 10th March 1932, p. 4; M. L. Melchior, 'Über jüdische Ehegesetze: Arnold Wiener und seine Kritiker', *Jüdische Zeitung*, 8th July 1932, p. 2 (so late because first submitted to *Der Israelit*, which after a long delay refused to publish it); H. Klein, 'Beuthener Ehereformer', *Der Israelit*, 25th August 1932, pp. 4–5; and 'Reformer?' (signed by "F."), *Jüdische Zeitung*, 9th September 1932, p. 3. (According to Wiener, *loc. cit.*, Goldmann's article which sparked the controversy appeared in Breslau's *Jüdisch-liberale Zeitung* in January 1932 – I have not been able to verify this.) For Melchior's persistence and continued protestation of adherence to tradition, see 'Verband der Rabbiner Oberschlesiens', *ibid.*, 16th December 1932, p. 3 (= *Der Israelit*, 15th December 1932, p. 6). And for yet another attack on Wiener, see the long and anonymous 'Modernes Sadduzäertum', *Der Israelit*, 12th January 1933, p. 4. (For Melchior's rabbinate in Beuthen, and his relations with Wiener, see Marcus Melchior, *A Rabbi Remembers*, New York 1968, pp. 117–120; *ibid.*, pp. 67–77 on his studies at the *Rabbinerseminar*, 1915–1918.) As for Rabbi Grodzenski's involvement, note that already the second instalment of Merzbach's response had consisted mainly of quotes from 'kein Geringerer als der Wilnaer Raw'', Grodzenski. For Grodzenski's letters to Klein and Merzbach, see *Ahiezer*, I, pp. 32–34. It is in Grodzenski's letter to Merzbach, where he calls Melchior only "Dr." (not "Rabbi"), that we find reference to "Dr. Lauer" (Professor Simon Lauer of Lucerne, Chaim's son, has kindly confirmed that it was indeed his father who was involved). On Lauer, see Shlomo Rülf, 'The Mannheim Klaus in its Final Years', in *For the Sake of Unity and Uniqueness. The Life Work and Teachings of Rabbi Isak Unna*, Jerusalem 1975, pp. 152–155 (in Hebrew). For Grodzenski's *responsum*, which is in Hebrew, see H. Klein, 'Zwei Gutachten zur Frage der Ehereform', *Nachᵃlat Z'wi*, 3 (1932/1933), pp. 289–297 (mostly reproduced in Grodzenski's *Responsa Ahiezer*, III, No. 23, pp. 53–54). As a matter of fact, the issue did not die out. In a couple of years the new front on this issue would be in America. See the collection of protests, headed by Rabbi Grodzenski's and by that of Chief Rabbi Kook of Palestine, published by the Union of Orthodox Rabbis of the USA and Canada: *LeDor Aḥaron*, Brooklyn 1936/1937.

agunot created by the First World War, there had been at least two other attempts to reform the Jewish marriage laws – one in England, one in New York – and Rabbi Grodzenski had spent much energy, in 1928–1929, in organising vocal opposition.[26] In 1930, however, he saw to the publication of a collection of letters written earlier in the century in opposition to a similar reform which had been urged by French rabbis, and he apparently thought that should settle the matter. Thus, his exasperation, in 1933, to find himself once again forced to deal with this problem, this time in Germany, may be well imagined, and may be read easily through the lines of one of his published letters on the topic. Indeed, Rabbi Klein himself, who corresponded with Grodzenski and published his *responsum*, admitted, in wonder and exasperation, that those who supported the proposed reforms included "pious" Orthodox Jews (*yereim*).[27] But this means that, early in 1933, Grodzenski was forced to deal with traditionalist rabbis in Germany – including two Hildesheimer *alumni* – who were willing to violate the most basic of Jewish traditions, and to realise that the defenders of the true faith in Germany – including other Hildesheimer graduates – were incapable of doing so, even in their own home court. So it is all the less likely that Grodzenski and his colleagues would approve of that type of rabbi being allowed authority in the Holy Land, when the question came up a few months later.

We may now turn to the two more lasting episodes on the agenda of German Orthodoxy in the very same months as the *Seminar*-transfer issue. The first had to do with the movement, on behalf of World Jewry – especially in the USA and Poland – to impose an economic boycott against Germany and German products in retaliation for German anti-Jewish measures and, especially, the German anti-Jewish boycott of the 1st April 1933 (which was originally planned to continue indefinitely). Such a Jewish boycott could result in reprisals against German Jews, and was, therefore, a source of debate and anxiety. Nevertheless, Jewish national self-respect seemed to require it. German Orthodoxy, however, which in the nature of things tended to play down the nationalistic aspect of Jewry in favour of Judaism being a religion alone, and to prefer quiet diplomacy to confrontationalist activism, came out strongly against the move, as did some

---

[26]See *Ahiezer*, II, pp. 337–341; cf. Rosin's *responsa* (above, note 19), No. 116, p. 90.

[27]See *Ein Tnai Benisuin*, ed. by A. Waronowski (Grodzenski's secretary), Vilna 1929/1930. (This booklet reproduces the material first collected in 1907/1908 by Rabbi Judah Lubetzky of Paris. Rabbi Grodzenski wrote the first and the last pages of the volume; see also his 1907 letter on p. 16. These three are reprinted in *Ahiezer*, II, pp. 329–331, 342–344). For Grodzenski's exasperation in 1932, see *Ahiezer*, I, p. 35: "As for conditional marriage, and also concerning (the giving of a conditional) *get* (writ of divorce immediately) after marriage – [these are] matters of falsehood with which it is not worthwhile to deal, and we have already published the booklet *Ein Tnai Benisuin*." For Klein's dismayed admission that the Reformers included pious Jews, see the introduction to his 'Zwei Gutachten' (above note 25). Compare another Lithuanian's exasperation at Germans' need to call him in to deal with the heretical options published earlier in the century by another *Rabbinerseminar* alumnus, R. Leszynsky: "I shall have to respond, for there is none among the Orthodox [here in transliteration, which is a pejorative alternative to Hebrew words for "pious" – DRS], who can answer – let the heavens tremble! . . . let all mankind know that the Orthodox are bankrupt . . ." (*The Letters of Rabbi Yitzhak Isaac Halevy, Author of Dorot HaRishonim*, ed. by A. Reichel, Jerusalem 1972, p. 203 [letter of late 1912, in Hebrew]). (For Halevy's close association with Grodzenski, see *ibid*, p. 7, also Finkelman [above, note 8], pp. 59–68.)

Lithuanian rabbis including Grodzenski himself.[28] But when Meier Hildesheimer went to Warsaw in September 1933 in an attempt to dissuade the Jewish
community there from imposing the boycott, he failed miserably. The day after
his arrival, banner headlines in one of the Yiddish Socialist dailies "revealed"
that Hildesheimer had in fact been sent by Hitler: "Berlin Rabbi – Hitler-Agent.
Came Yesterday To Warsaw Community Council. The Shameful Hitler-Agent
Must Be Driven Out Of Warsaw."[29] And even the more sympathetic view
expressed by another Warsaw Jewish newspaper assumed that it was the fear of
"shameful" incarceration in a concentration camp which in fact motivated
Hildesheimer and his colleagues.[30] While Hildesheimer succeeded in convincing
the Warsaw rabbis not to impose a religious ban upon German products, his
attempt to convince the Jewish community not to boycott was not received
favourably, and he left Warsaw the next day. And within a month or two even
the Polish *Agudath Israel*, despite Grodzenski's protest, had been forced by public
opinion to go along with the boycott.[31] Thus, in the autumn months of 1933 the
world of Eastern European Jewry took a step which directly affected German
Jews despite the pleas of Hildesheimer and his colleagues. They, in turn, were
left willy-nilly playing the role of kow-towers to Hitler.

The other episode, which began around the same time and was played out in
parallel to the *Seminar*-transfer plan, concerned an eminently *halakhic* problem
and, therefore, centred around Weinberg, the *Seminar*'s great *halakhic* authority.
In April 1933 the Nazi government – ostensibly out of mercy to animals –
decreed that animals be stunned electrically prior to slaughter. This raised a
severe problem, for Jewish law forbids the consumption of animals maimed prior

---

[28]For Orthodox opposition to the boycott, see *Der Israelit*, 14th September 1933, p. 5; 20th September
1933, p. 9; and 9th November 1933, p. 5; also Grodzenski's letter to Eliezer Silver (on whom see A.
Rakeffet-Rothkoff, *The Silver Era in American Orthodoxy. Rabbi Eliezer Silver and his Generation*,
Jerusalem–New York 1981, esp. pp. 46–48 and 155–161 on his ties with Grodzenski), in *Ahiezer*, II,
pp. 296–297 (No. 182); also 'Rabbi Benjamin' (see below, note 43) in *HaHed*, 9/2 (Heshvan 1933),
pp. 6–8. Similarly, a year earlier, Hildesheimer and Grodzenski had opposed the organisation of
activist protests by World Jewry against Russian persecutions; see Grodzenski's letter in *Iggerot
LaReiya*, p. 192.

[29]See *Naje Folkscajtung*, 16th September 1933, p. 1. On this episode, see Jacobson (above, note 3), p.
86, also in his *Memoirs*, Jerusalem 1952/1953, p. 62 (in Hebrew). Indeed, according to Jacobson, the
immediate impetus for Hildesheimer's trip was a *Gestapo* demand, accompanied by threats of
reprisal, that the German Orthodox dissuade the Polish rabbis from excommunicating those who
violated the boycott; Hildesheimer left for Poland the same day. One wonders what the editors of
the *Folkscajtung* knew and what they only guessed. On this *Bundist* newspaper, see J. S. Hertz,
'*Folkszeitung*. A Jewish Socialist Daily', in *The Jewish Press That Was. Accounts, Evaluations and Memories
of Jewish Papers in Pre-Holocaust Europe*, ed. by Arie Bar, Tel-Aviv 1980, pp. 113–121. As Hertz notes
(p. 115), "the main adversaries with whom the writers constantly debated were the Zionists and the
Orthodox". While in this case it is difficult to term such a headline "debate", it is nevertheless the
case that, with regard to the boycott, Hildesheimer and his colleagues had subscribed to a view held
by the Zionist leadership as well, due to fears that the boycott would sabotage its efforts to transfer
Jewish property out of Germany. See Yoav Gelber, 'On Zionist Policy and the *Haavara* Agreement,
1933–1945', *Yalkut Moreshet*, 17 (January 1974), pp. 126–127 (in Hebrew).

[30]*Haynt*, 17th September 1933, p. 7 (comment added at end of interview with M. Hildesheimer). On
the same page there is also a short article about Hildesheimer and his visit.

[31]For this reversal, see Grodzenski and "Rabbi Benjamin", above, note 28. For one of the foremost
supporters of the boycott among *Agudah* ranks, see Judah Leib Zirelson (1860–1941), *Lev Yehudah*,
Jerusalem 1960/1961, pp. 70–80 (in Hebrew).

to slaughter. Does electric stunning constitute maiming? Weinberg held it was possible to justify a negative answer to this question, thus allowing the meat, and, in September 1933, he went to Poland and Lithuania to attempt to convince his mentors there that this was the case. According to Weinberg, he spent many hours with Grodzenski, and the latter asked him to compose a detailed *responsum* justifying his position. He did so, and, in the winter of 1933/1934, the *Kashruth* commission of *Adass Jisroel* sent the *responsum* – nearly 100 closely-printed pages – to numerous Eastern European rabbis, asking for their approval.[32]

Weinberg's discussion is, of course, very technical. The truth must be said, however, that besides the technical questions involved the real battlefield on which this issue was debated was defined by two non-technical considerations. Those who supported allowing the meat held that, if the stringent view were adopted and the meat forbidden, thus requiring Jews either to abstain from meat or to pay exorbitant prices for imported kosher meat (if it could be had), multitudes of Jews would not survive the challenge and would, instead, begin to consume non-kosher meat. Moreover, some Orthodox leaders expressed the fear that non-Orthodox rabbis would declare the pre-stunned meat kosher. If Orthodox rabbis proclaimed the meat unkosher, the result would be not only that many would eat unkosher meat, but also the impression would be given that Orthodox opposition was not a result of truly *halakhic* objections: that it was rather only either a product of reactionary intransigence or a misuse of religious authority for political purposes.[33] Thus, those who would permit the meat held that technical doubts notwithstanding, broader communal considerations required a permissive decision.

As for those who would forbid the meat, among whom Rabbi Grodzenski took the lead,[34] they not only took the more stringent line regarding the doubts concerning the technical *halakhic* point: they too had wider communal considerations. First of all, many held that the Nazi decree was a measure intended to force Jews to violate their own law, and, as such, any concession would be repugnant. Indeed, even if they were allowed to eat such meat under other circumstances, they would be forbidden to do so due to it being a German demand – in the classic formulation, in times of decrees against Judaism it is even forbidden to change the colour of one's shoelace.[35] Secondly, they feared that if

---

[32]On this episode, see Robert Kirschner, *Rabbinic Responsa of the Holocaust Era*, New York 1985, pp. 38–50 (with English version of Weinberg's retrospective preface to the *responsum*). For the *responsum*, see *Seridei Esh*, I, pp. 4–106 (text), 107–172 (sixteen responses). *Ibid.*, pp. 370–371, Weinberg published a winter 1933/1934 memorandum on his conversations with Polish rabbis, and pp. 371–392 contain a fair amount of related correspondence. For Rabbi Grodzenski's letters and statements on the subject, see *Ahiezer*, I, pp. 94–98; II, pp. 374–378. In general, much interesting material concerning European and especially German struggles concerning ritual slaughtering may be found in Michael L. and Eli Munk, *Shechita. Religious and Historical Research on the Jewish Method of Slaughter*, Jerusalem 1976, and in the companion Hebrew volume, *Eduth Néemana, Part I. Responsa on Halachic Problems Arising out of the Defence of Shechita in Europe. Taken from the Archives of the Central Office of Shechita Affairs in Berlin*, Jerusalem 1974, wherein numerous letters on the subject may be found.

[33]Indeed, a German letter by Weinberg quoted in the Munks' English volume (above, note 32, pp. 64–65) shows that such an assumption had become widespread.

[34]See note 32.

[35]See Babylonian Talmud, *Sanhedrin* 74a–b, cited, for example, in Rabbi H. Y. Jeruchem's letter reprinted in *Seridei Esh*, I, pp. 171–172. (On Jeruchem, see *Meorei Galicia. Encyclopedia of Galician*

German Jews were allowed to compromise, other countries might follow suit. And this was not merely theoretical: in Lithuania itself, the legislature was soon to be very near to adopting a law virtually prohibiting kosher slaughtering.[36]

The latter view carried the day. After Weinberg's *responsum* was sent out, several German rabbis begged their Eastern colleagues to approve,[37] but almost every one of the latter who responded complimented Weinberg for his learning but refused to support his conclusion. And when Grodzenski delivered his *daat Torah* against Weinberg's *responsum*,[38] the matter was closed, apart from a few aftershocks and complaints. As with the boycott affair, in other words, so too regarding the kosher slaughtering question, the Hildesheimer circle had been exhibited to the Jewish world as one too willing to compromise upon what was dear to Judaism. Thus, just as with the three more circumscribed episodes of 1928–1933 with which we began, so too in these two larger affairs of late 1933, the impression had been reinforced that the affairs of Orthodox Germany Jewry may – must – be decided for it in the Eastern European heartland.[39]

C. *The Rabbinerseminar's Palestine Plan and its Burial*

"Die inneren Erregungen, die mit der Problematik dieser Reise verbunden waren . . . ihn doch aufs tiefste erschütterten, werfen einen Schimmer der Tragik über dieses letzte Jahr seines Lebens."[40]

This affair transpired between September 1933 and January 1934 and is easily summarised. Given the bad, and deteriorating, situation of German Jewry in general and the *Rabbinerseminar* in particular, Meier Hildesheimer decided to investigate the possibility of moving the institution to Palestine. Rabbi Grodzenski heard of this from Weinberg during the latter's visit to Vilna in September 1933, and immediately asked that Hildesheimer be informed of his *daat Torah* against the plan (see Appendixes I and II). Hildesheimer, however, did not give up the plan, but instead went to Palestine to investigate the prospects there. He

---

Rabbis and Scholars, III, Jerusalem 1986, cols. 277–282 [in Hebrew].) The applicability of this approach to the stunning issue was denied by some German rabbis who pointed out, perhaps somewhat disingenuously, that the Nazi decree was not directed against Jews alone. See *Seridei Esh*, I, p. 139 (E. M. Lassmann) and p. 387 (Isak Unna). Similarly, in a sensitive article 'Zur Frage der elektrischen Betäubung', in *Der Israelit*, 8th March 1934, pp. 1,3–4 (the author's name is noted *ibid.*, 15th March 1934, p. 5), E. Munk's review of the considerations pro and con which the rabbinical authorities must consider tactfully ignores this type of consideration.

[36]See *Ahiezer*, II, pp. 358–374. In general, cf. the Munk volumes (above, note 32).

[37]See especially Esriel Munk's letter to Grodzenski cited in the Munks' Hebrew volume (above, note 32), p. 123 (a defence of his article cited in note 35), and Jakob Hoffmann's emotional appeal to Grodzenski, in *Seridei Esh*, pp. 121–123. In the latter, pp. 122–123, Hoffmann reports a rumour that great rabbis in Galicia had concluded that stunning was technically allowable but nevertheless to be forbidden lest their government be encouraged to impose similar regulations.

[38]See *Ahiezer*, I, pp. 94–95, No. 46 (16th October 1934), also reprinted in *Seridei Esh*, I, p. 379. Note also E. Munk's publication of another somewhat later statement by Grodzenski, reprinted *ibid.*, p. 386.

[39]It should perhaps be reiterated that German Orthodoxy's and Weinberg's acceptance of the Lithuanian hegemony was not applicable only in cases where the Lithuanians held to the more stringent position, while the Germans were willing to compromise. In the levirate marriage case with which we began, the positions were opposite.

[40]From *Der Israelit*'s long obituary for M. Hildesheimer, 26th July 1934, pp. 6–7.

first tried Jerusalem, but got a very cold and hostile shoulder from the Orthodox there: a long article in the *Agudath Israel* weekly, *Kol Yisrael*, told him to stay away, and *Agudath Israel* spokesmen took care to inform the newspaper that the organisation was not associated with the project and that, indeed, all the great rabbis opposed it.[41] In the more modern Tel-Aviv, however, Hildesheimer did much better, receiving the support of the city's Chief Rabbis and Religious Community Council (*Va'ad Ha-Kehillah*).[42] And the editor of the Orthodox monthly *HaHed*, Yehoshua Radler-Feldmann (known to all as "Rabbi Benjamin"), came out with two back-to-back articles in the Teveth (December 1933/ January 1934) issue: the first attacked the Palestinian rabbinate as being isolated from modernity and therefore unable to communicate with the multitudes of modern and non-religious Jews in the country, and the second praised the Berlin *Rabbinerseminar* for producing rabbis who were precisely the opposite. Therefore, Rabbi Benjamin called for support for Hildesheimer's plan.[43]

Grodzenski, however, was not to be ignored. He wrote to numerous rabbis in Palestine, calling upon them to stymie Hildesheimer,[44] and he also wrote to Hildesheimer himself, in Palestine, in the strongest terms (see Appendix I), laying down his *daat Torah* against the move. Correspondingly, Rabbi Reuven Katz, the Chief Rabbi of Petach Tikva, published a scathing attack on the *Rabbinerseminar* in the next month's issue of *HaHed*.[45] Katz caricatured the *Rabbinerseminar* as an institution where the title "Rabbi" was more important than Torah, where Torah study was really ancillary and university studies were the main concern, an institution on a par with elementary-school level *yeshivot* in Palestine, etc., and he also expressed the fear that the Seminary, in Palestine, would compete with the *yeshivot*. And Katz, who had been a close student of Grodzenski's, specifically cited the latter's opposition.[46]

---

[41] See *Kol Yisrael*, 30th November 1933, p. 2 and 14th December 1933, p. 4. Hildesheimer's failure in Jerusalem is also mentioned in the letter in our Appendix I. Indeed, "Rabbi Benjamin" stated that anyone with any sense knew that the idea had no chance in Jerusalem: *HaHed*, 9/4 (Teveth 1933/ 1934), p. 4.

[42] For this support, see Eisner (above, note 2), p. 49; "Rabbi Benjamin" in *HaHed*, 9/5 (Shevat 1934), pp. 10–11; also our Appendixes III–IV.

[43] See *HaHed*, 9/4 (Teveth 1933/1934), pp. 1–4. On Rabbi Benjamin, see Getzl Kressel, *Cyclopedia of Modern Hebrew Literature*, II, Tel-Aviv 1967, cols. 831–833 (in Hebrew). The fact that Rabbi Benjamin had studied in Berlin, and had been a neighbour of Moses Auerbach (see his testimonial to the latter in *HaHed*, 9/5 [Shevat 1934], p. 11), probably contributed to his sympathetic approach to Hildesheimer's plan. In this connection, it is interesting that just before the *Rabbinerseminar* transfer plan caused a furor M. Auerbach published in *HaHed* (9/1 [Tishri, 1933], pp. 15–16) an article on 'Eretz-Israel and the Orthodox in Germany', which called for the development of westernised education in Palestine so as to facilitate the emigration of Orthodox Jews from Germany. Was this the beginning of Rabbi Benjamin's campaign?

[44] For these letters, see *Ahiezer*, II, Nos. 289 (to Rabbi Abraham Karlewitz [the "Hazon Ish"]; this letter refers to others as well), 291 (to Joseph Zevi Duschinsky, Chief Rabbi of the Orthodox community of Jerusalem), and 293 (mentions his letter to Rabbi Abraham Isaac Kook, Chief Rabbi of Palestine – see below, note 48). For Grodzenski's letter to Shlomo Aronson, the Ashkenazic Chief Rabbi of Tel-Aviv, see note 131. It seems assured that Grodzenski wrote to Reuven Katz as well; see beow.

[45] 9/5, Shevat 1934, pp. 1–3.

[46] For the ever-present fear that students might leave the *yeshivot*, see for example, the long alarmist article on pp. 2–3 of the 4th January 1934 issue of *Kol Yisrael*, at the height of the *Rabbinerseminar* debate. Grodzenski himself may not have expressed the fear that *yeshivah* students would defect to

This Lithuanian attack carried the field. Although Rabbi Benjamin and a former *Rabbinerseminar* student answered Katz in *HaHed*, and although Chief Rabbi Kook tried to mediate by suggesting that the *Seminar* might be allowed to open house in Palestine as a seminary for teachers, rather than for rabbis, and despite a few appeals by Meier Hildesheimer to Grodzenski himself, the latter was adamant, and his opinion was final. At the very same time that he was publishing a moving appeal to the Jews of Poland and Lithuania to support German Jewry financially and in its attempts to emigrate to Palestine,[47] he vociferously argued, in numerous letters, that moving the *Seminar* – a "rabbi-factory"! – to the Holy Land would be to "make crooked that which could not again be made straight" (= an irretrievable error; Ecclesiastes I:15), comparable to the abomination of bringing a sacrifice at the wrong time and the wrong place (quoting Leviticus XIX:7); "it would be a foreign plant in the vineyard of the House of Israel in the Holy Land, planting there the German culture which has already struck many dead, and we saw what it brought them".[48] By late December 1933, even before these articles in *HaHed* had been published, Grodzenski's efforts had forced Chief Rabbi Aronson of Tel-Aviv, who had supported the project, to write to Hildesheimer and urge him to back down (Appendix III).[49] The *Seminar's* *Kuratorium* formally decided to remain in Berlin,[50] the faculty put the best

---

the *Rabbinerseminar*. He does seem to have argued that if the seminary moved to Palestine, its graduates would receive positions which otherwise would have been given to *yeshivah* graduates; see Appendix III, first paragraph; On Katz's links to Grodzenski, see the former's *Shaar Reuven*, Jerusalem 1952, pp. 5–6, 216–222, also Rakeffet-Rothkoff (above, note 28), p. 47.

[47]*Dos Vort* [Vilna], 8th December 1933, p. 5.

[48]For the rejoinders in *HaHed*, see 9/5 (Shevat 1934), pp. 10–11; 9/7 (Nisan 1934), p. 12; and 9/9 (Sivan 1934), p. 12. Grodzenski's opinions cited in this paragraph are from his three letters to Rabbi Kook, reprinted in *Iggerot LaReiya*, pp. 213–216 (all within a few weeks before or after his letter to Hildesheimer quoted in Appendix I). In the last-quoted passage, from p. 215, note that "struck many dead" apparently compares the wiles of German culture to those of a loose woman (Proverbs VII:26). For the first of these letters, see our Appendix II. On "rabbi-factory", see below, note 124. Kook's attempt to mediate came in a letter to Rabbi Katz, which the latter mentions in *HaHed*, 9/5, pp. 9–10 and also reported to Rabbi Grodzenski; Grodzenski alluded to it in a letter of 21st February 1934 to Kook (*Iggerot LaReiya*, p. 219), after the affair had blown over. Kook's response to Grodzenski's first letter was published in his *Da'at Kohen*, Jerusalem 1969, No. 223, p. 419; however, it deals only with another issue raised in Grodzenski's letter, and makes no mention of Hildesheimer or the Seminary. It may be noted that Kook was quite ill during the winter of 1933/1934, and also that his letters to Grodzenski did not arrive (so Grodzenski, in *Iggerot LaReiya*, p. 219). However, it may be doubted that things would have been different had Kook been healthy and had his letters arrived. As for Hildesheimer's letters to Grodzenski, which apparently emphasised Rabbi Kook's support, I have not located them, but they are mentioned by Grodzenski, *ibid.*

[49]We may also note that after Aronson died little more than a year later, in March 1935, he was replaced by another close student of Grodzenski: Rabbi Mordechai Avigdor Amiel. See Rakeffet-Rothkoff (above, note 28), p. 47. Indeed, although some names have as usual been expunged by the scrupulous editor, it seems obvious – due to the timing and the reference to the "Kehillah" – that a letter from Grodzenski to the Hazon Ish, sent a mere three weeks after Aronson died, already began the campaign for Amiel's appointment. For the letter, see *Ahiezer*, II, pp. 433–434, where it is reprinted from the Hazon Ish's collected letters (*Kovetz Iggerot*, II, ed. by S. Greinemann, Bnai Brak 1955/1956, pp. 175–177).

[50]According to Weinberg (above, note 4), p. 271 (his farewell speech to Auerbach, who moved back to Palestine early in 1935; reprinted in Auerbach [above, note 1], p. 113); the decision is also mentioned in a letter from Grodzenski to Kook of 21st February 1934 (*Iggerot LaReiya*, p. 219).

possible face on the decision (Appendix IV), and that was that. Although neither Hildesheimer nor Weinberg totally gave up the hope of moving to Palestine,[51] the next few months – the last of Hildesheimer's life – were to see him resuming his former course of travelling around the Jewish world seeking money for his treasured institution in Berlin.[52] He died on *Tishah Be'Av* (22nd July 1934), the eulogist in *Der Israelit*, quoted at the outset of this section, surmising that his defeat in Palestine had broken him and hastened his death. In a long front-page obituary in the Vilna weekly published by *Va'ad Hayeshivot*,[53] however, there was not a word about the affair, only praise for him and for the *Seminar* which he had built into an important institution, which trained strictly Orthodox rabbis and leaders for Germany and elsewhere.

The end of the story is just as simple and just as tragic. The *Rabbinerseminar* continued to hobble along in Berlin, and Weinberg continued to submit his *halakhic* decision to Rabbi Grodzenski's approval.[54] In 1938, shortly after the "*Kristallnacht*", the teachers of the *Rabbinerseminar* wrote to Yeshiva College in New York and the Hebrew University in Jerusalem (perhaps elsewhere as well), inquiring about the chances of sending students.[55] While these appeals apparently had no general results, many students and almost all of the teachers, apart from Weinberg, did manage to emigrate as individuals.[56] The outset of the war found Weinberg in Warsaw, where he stayed until he was deported to a

---

[51] A hope repeated in speeches in 1934/1935, reprinted in Weinberg (above, note 4), pp. 258, 266, 271–272. The persistence of the hope of moving is bemoaned in a Grodzenski letter of 6th June 1934 (in Weinberg, *Seridei Esh*, I, p. 379). Note that both Moses Auerbach and Samuel Grünberg, Weinberg's two main colleagues at the institution, visited Palestine in the spring of 1934 (according to Weinberg [above, note 4], p. 258). However, Auerbach's account of the trip (above, note 1, pp. 67–68) indicates that he was seeking a position for himself alone, not resuscitating the *Seminar*-transfer plan.

[52] For some details about his fundraising trip to London a few weeks before he died, see the *Jewish Chronicle*'s obituary for him on p. 10 of its issue of 27th July 1934.

[53] *Dos Vort*, 27th July 1934.

[54] See Berkovits (above, note 13), p. 10.

[55] For the former, see A. Rothkoff, *Bernard Revel. Builder of American Jewish Orthodoxy*, Philadelphia 1972, p. 209 (where a 22nd December 1938 letter by Revel on the matter is quoted). As for the Hebrew University, a 23rd November 1938 letter from the *Rabbinerseminar*'s faculty to Salman Schocken, head of the University's *Kuratorium*, has been preserved in file 2051 of the J. L. Magnes papers in the Central Archives for the History of the Jewish People, Jerusalem.

[56] For the *Rabbinerseminar*'s seven teachers and forty-nine regular students in 1937/1938, see pp. 14–15 of its 1938 *Jahres-Bericht*. Of the teachers, Jacob Freimann died a natural death in Berlin in 1937; Alexander Altmann emigrated to England; and Samuel Grünberg, Esriel Hildesheimer and [J.] Abraham Wolf went to Palestine. They were all able to pursue their careers, although not in rabbinical schools (Hildesheimer's 1938 letters to Alexander Marx of the Jewish Theological Seminary, New York, in an unsuccessful bid for a position in the Seminary Library, are preserved in that seminary's archives [where they were found by Dr. Hoffmann.]) On Weinberg, see below. Letters in the Yeshiva University archives (Records 13/3) show that the seventh *Rabbinerseminar* teacher, the historian Dr. Maximilian Landau, attempted – with Ismar Elbogen's support – to find a position at Yeshiva or at Dropsie College in 1939. These letters put Landau in the The Hague in January 1939 and in Warsaw in June of that year; I have been unable to trace him thereafter. As for the students, I have so far ascertained that at least twenty emigrated, ten of them to Palestine/Israel. For a last-minute plan to move the *Rabbinerseminar* to Palestine, hatched in October 1938 and dashed a few weeks later by the "*Kristallnacht*", see Z. Wahrhaftig, *Refugee and Survivor. Rescue Efforts during the Holocaust*, Jerusalem 1988, pp. 270–271.

detention camp in Germany; after the war, he lived his last two decades with a former student at the *yeshiva* in Montreux, Switzerland. Although that was a very provincial setting for an authority of his stature, he had few options. As I was told by the son of another rabbi who knew him well, Weinberg assumed that if he were to move to Israel the bastions of Orthodoxy there, centring around the *yeshivot* of Bnai Brak (near Tel-Aviv) which are still known as "Lithuanian *yeshivot*", would greet him only as "noch ein daytscher Doktor" . . .[57] As for Rabbi Benjamin, he was to be more successful two decades later, when he took an active role in the propaganda on behalf of founding Bar-Ilan University, an Orthodox University near Tel-Aviv.[58] Bar-Ilan, however, does not train rabbis. Dr. Meir Hildesheimer, the grandson of our protagonist, now teaches in its Department of Jewish History.

In 1966, the year Weinberg died, admirers published a Hebrew version of a small volume he had originally published in Yiddish. While the Yiddish original (1922) had been entitled *The Way to Reconciliation with the Orthodox*, the Hebrew version is somewhat pathetically entitled *It is My Brothers that I am Seeking*. The title was borrowed from the biblical story of Joseph (Genesis XXXVII:16). Indeed, the 1933 attempt to move the *Rabbinerseminar* to Palestine seems to illustrate the brotherless situation of the Jews of separatist Orthodoxy in Germany. Like Joseph in Egypt, they would not be full brothers to those of the impure environment in which they lived. However, like Joseph in Canaan, those whose brothers they wanted to be did not really accept them as such. So, like Joseph, Weinberg lived out his life in exile, and was to be allowed only a burial in the Holy Land. And rabbis of his style, of the *Rabbinerseminar* style, have yet to find a place in Israel.

II. THE PLANNED TRANSFER OF THE HOCHSCHULE (LEHRANSTALT) FÜR DIE WISSENSCHAFT DES JUDENTUMS TO CAMBRIDGE IN 1939

From the end of 1937, the opportunities for Jews to earn a living in National Socialist Germany were additionally limited by a new wave of regulations and violent measures. National Socialist Jewish policy aimed ever more clearly at forcing all German Jews to emigrate. The institutions of Jewish studies which

---

[57] Although it may be noted that Rabbi Katz, in a 1934 letter to Weinberg (reprinted in *Seridei Esh*, I, pp. 381–382) concerning the controversy on stunning, carefully addressed him with a long list of honorific rabbinic titles but made no reference to his doctorate. At the end of his letter, in contrast, Katz added regards for Weinberg's Berlin colleagues, "the great sage Rabbi Dr. Munk", "Rabbi Dr. Hildesheimer", and "Rabbi Dr. Wohlgemuth", and mentioned having heard from "Rabbi Dr. Auerbach". Weinberg, apparently, was still in a different class. Correspondingly, during the first years of the war he was to serve as a chief rabbinical authority in Warsaw. Again, when Weinberg died the funeral cortège in Jerusalem, which had originally set out to bury him near leading Western-style rabbis, was diverted by Lithuanian-style *yeshiva* students so that he could be buried near their great Torah authorities. For this episode see Wahrhaftig, *op. cit.*, p. 273.
[58] See A. Ben-Yosef, 'The Beginning of Bar-Ilan University', *Bar-Ilan*, 4–5 (Decennial Volume, 1955–1965) [1967], esp. pp. 12–13 (in Hebrew).

still existed were also endangered, even when teaching apparently continued and in fact, as in the case of the *Hochschule*, experienced a sort of revival in the form of new professors dismissed from the universities and the establishment of a general academic department.[59] In this situation, two projects existed to save German-language Jewish studies through transfer to English-speaking countries: the "College-in-Exile Project" of the Hebrew Union College (HUC) in Cincinnati, and a plan by the Cambridge Judaist Herbert Loewe to transplant the *Hochschule* to Cambridge (England) as a Jewish Academy. Both projects were modelled after examples that had already been followed successfully in the history of academic emigration in various countries after 1933. Julian Morgenstern, president of the HUC, had in mind the "University in Exile" created by Alvin Johnson as a graduate faculty at the New School for Social Research in New York when, in October 1938, he suggested a project for taking on twenty-five (later, in reality, nine) refugee scholars from Central Europe at the HUC. Herbert Loewe perhaps was thinking of the successful transfer of the *Kulturwissenschaftliche Bibliothek Warburg* moved in 1933 from Hamburg to London complete with staff, when, early in 1939, he drafted a plan to transfer the *Hochschule* to England. Through Michael Meyer's detailed study,[60] we are well informed about the relatively successful HUC project in which eight German-speaking Judaists found a new home in Cincinnati. On the Loewe project, which failed completely, there has until now been only a short summary presentation by Richard Fuchs,[61] who as a former member of the *Kuratorium* of the *Hochschule* was for a time himself involved in the project and the development of the plan after his emigration to England. On the basis of additional source material,[62] we will attempt here to reconstruct in detail Loewe's plan, the steps taken towards its realisation and the causes of its failure.

[59]See Herbert A. Strauss, 'Die letzten Jahre der Hochschule (Lehranstalt) für die Wissenschaft des Judentums, Berlin 1936–1942', in Julius Carlebach (ed.), *Wissenschaft des Judentums – Schulen und Lehren* (forthcoming).

[60]See Michael A. Meyer, 'The Refugee Scholars Project of the Hebrew Union College', in Bertram W. Korn (ed.), *A Bicentennial Festschrift for Jacob Rader Marcus*, New York 1976, pp. 359–375.

[61]See Richard Fuchs, 'The "Hochschule für die Wissenschaft des Judentums" in the Period of Nazi Rule. Personal Recollections', in *LBI Year Book XII* (1967), pp. 3–31, esp. pp. 27ff.

[62]Unfortunately, only fragments remain on the planned transfer of the *Hochschule*. The documents from Herbert Loewe's papers have apparently been lost. Based on personal recollection and knowledge of the documents from his father's papers, Professor Raphael Loewe gave a detailed account of the events in a letter to the author of 24th August 1987 (cited in the following as Raphael Loewe Letter (RLL)). We thank Professor Loewe for permission to use this description in our reconstruction. A copy of this letter can be found in the archives of the *Zentrum für Antisemitismusforschung der Technischen Universität Berlin* as well as in Professor Loewe's personal archives. Dr. Maria Leschnitzer kindly placed at our disposal several documents from the papers of Adolf Leschnitzer, who was also involved in the project. Additional important information comes from the papers of Hans Liebeschütz (the letters from Ernst Grumach and Arnold Berney) as well as Ismar Elbogen (letters of Adolf Leschnitzer and Herbert Loewe), both in the possession of the Archives of the Leo Baeck Institute, New York (LBI Archives) and the papers of Ernst Grumach, in the possession of his daughter Dr. Irene Shirun in Jerusalem. We thank Dr. Shirun for providing access to these documents and for permission to cite her father's letters. Finally, the papers of the Society for the Protection of Science and Learning (SPSL), deposited in the Bodleian Library, Oxford, Dept. of Western Manuscripts, also contain references to the Loewe plan.

The beginnings of the plan to transfer the *Hochschule* are unclear. It cannot be said with any certainty whether plans for *in corpore* transfer already existed before November, 1938. The concept of an international academy for Jewish studies had already been laid out in the many projects drafted since 1933 by Eugen Täubler for the rebuilding of Jewish studies – for example, a Bible institute at the Hebrew University in Jerusalem. In autumn 1938, Täubler considered transferring the *Hochschule* to Jerusalem (in particular the library) and restructuring it as a research institute with branches in Jerusalem and New York. However, he never took concrete steps to realise his far-reaching plans.[63] In addition, there were already discussions among individual professors at the *Hochschule* about whether it would be promising to seek a new domicile in England or whether only the USA could be considered as a place of refuge.[64]

The plan for transfer of the entire institution may have first come about at the end of 1938 after the November Pogrom. In any case, only then did it take on concrete form. Among the professors at the *Hochschule*, Hans Liebeschütz already had close contact, dating back to the twenties, with the Warburg Library. He certainly knew details of its transfer to London in 1933, and it may be assumed that he recommended this successful project to Leo Baeck and other colleagues as a model for the *Hochschule*. During one of his visits to England – at the end of 1938 or beginning of 1939 – Leo Baeck may have spoken with various people about the idea of transferring the *Hochschule*, among others with Herbert Loewe. Loewe took up the idea and worked out a concrete plan that was completed in March, 1939, at the latest.[65]

Herbert Martin James Loewe (1882–1940) was one of the most distinguished Judaists in England. He was a Reader in Rabbinics at Cambridge University. After reading Oriental Studies and (Christian) Theology, he first taught Rabbinic Hebrew at Oxford after the First World War, before coming to Cambridge in 1931. Because of his profound erudition, Loewe was considered in England's academic world to be *the* representative of Jewish Studies of his generation. He had varied connections with Christian theologians, and in 1939 even became president of the English Society for Old Testament Study, a position which made it possible for him to approach relief organisations and

---

[63]Täubler to Magnes, 2nd September 1938, Nachlaß Täubler, E IV 023, Universitätsbibliothek Basel; Täubler to Elbogen, 14th November 1938, Elbogen Papers, LBI Archives, New York, See also Selma Stern-Täubler, 'Eugen Täubler and the "Wissenschaft des Judentums"', in *LBI Year Book III* (1958), pp. 40–59, here 55ff.; for Täubler's reaction to Loewe's transfer plan, see Grumach to Liebeschütz, 27th March 1939, Liebeschütz Papers, LBI Archives: "The idea of communal living has a lot to be said for it, even if only because it is cheaper, but also has its dangers. One need only think of Professor T., who once again wants special favours and pours his wrath out upon our poor heads because we supposedly stole his projects, for whose realisation he certainly, God knows, did little enough, nevertheless . . . however would like to be counted in after all."

[64]Liebeschütz to Grumach, 30th August 1938, Grumach Papers (Dr. Irene Shirun, Jerusalem): "In my opinion, in regard to England, one must approach things so as to attempt to ensure that the English Jews also take part in accommodating scholars from the Judaistic institutes (without distinction and accentuation of the colour of these institutes) . . . I myself am very interested in England."

[65]Grumach to Liebeschütz, 27th March 1939, *loc. cit.*

contributors quasi-officially, and to promote the transfer of the *Hochschule* within British academia.[66]

Loewe's plan envisioned rebuilding the *Hochschule* in close association with Cambridge University – if not at first institutionally, at least in spatial proximity. A selection of the *Hochschule*'s teaching staff, to be determined more exactly, would live together in a house in Cambridge, and together with the also-transferred library of the *Hochschule* would form the foundation of a Jewish academy. Loewe hoped that this academy would achieve quick recognition in Great Britain's academic world by continuing the *Monatsschrift für Geschichte und Wissenschaft des Judentums* and other projects, and that perhaps some of the distinguished scholars at the *Hochschule* could find parallel teaching positions at the University as well.

To obtain public support for his plan and investigate financial assistance, Loewe sent out a circular letter, with an accompanying memorandum formulated by Leo Baeck, to a number of scholars in England from related disciplines (theology, oriental studies, history). The response was entirely positive. Well-known Christian theologians such as the professors Herbert Danby, George A. Cooke, Godfrey R. Driver, David C. Simpson, J. Vernon Bartlet (Oxford), J. O. F. Murray, A. C. Moule, John S. Whale (Cambridge), and also other professors such as Hersch Lauterpacht (Cambridge) and D. S. Margoliouth (Oxford) sent expressions of sympathy. For example, Professor Danby wrote:[67]

> "The suggestion of transferring the *Lehranstalt* and the *Monatsschrift* to England provokes a devout hope that the transference may be made a fact. The Science of Judaism has an intense and far-reaching importance which would in any case make a centre for its cultivation welcomed by the English academic world. But another aspect is worth pointing out. In the English-speaking world of theological study non-Jewish students have profited greatly from Jewish scholars (of the type of Schechter, Montefiore, Israel Abrahams and certain others) in the fields where Christian and Jewish studies coincide. The effect is seen in a heightened respect and an open sympathy on the part of Christian scholars for Jewish scholars and Jewish studies, an assurance to Jewish scholars that their labours are not purposeless, and, in non-academic circles, a more comprehending friendliness among Christians toward Jews.
>
> If this can be traced to the efforts of just a few solitary Jewish students over a space of fifty years, one is tempted to expect still more impressive results from a band of scholars like the staff of the *Lehranstalt*, working in an environment which must prove congenial to them and at the same time assure them of a considerable public of non-Jewish readers and sympathizers."

One might ask why Loewe turned first and foremost to Christian colleagues and the general academic public, but not to Jewish circles in England, to gain moral support and financial assistance for the transfer plan.

Quite obviously, he had to expect that the project of transferring the *Hochschule* could not count on undivided approval among all Jewish circles and movements; in fact, it would run into doubts and resistance especially on the part of the Chief Rabbi. Chief Rabbi Dr. Joseph Herman Hertz (1872–1946) was a strong personality, an energetic advocate of Orthodoxy, an equally decisive opponent of the liberal religious school of thought within Judaism, and a sympathiser with

---

[66]On Loewe, see *Encyclopedia Judaica*, vol. 11, p. 447; *RLL*, pp. 1f.
[67]Quoted from 'Preliminary List of Letters Received in Support of the Transfer of the Lehranstalt', *Leschnitzer Papers* (Dr. Maria Leschnitzer).

Zionism.[68] Hertz had shown himself in no way indifferent to the persecution of Jews under National Socialist Germany and to the increasingly numerous Jewish refugees from Central Europe. Following the November Pogrom of 1938, a relief organisation was founded in his name, the Chief Rabbi's Religious Emergency Council, which functioned until 1950 and took responsibility for the rescue and support of rabbis and Jewish religious officials from the areas under Nazi control.[69] Through the assumption of guarantees, a number of German-speaking rabbis could be brought to England and thus rescued. Hertz had also supported individual Jewish students with stipends (for example I. O. Lehmann, who had previously studied at the *Hochschule* in Berlin), and thus given them the opportunity to live in England.[70] Thus he used his best efforts to assist all Jews, regardless of affiliation, in emigrating from Germany. But the transfer of an entire institution of Jewish studies, including all its teaching staff, was another matter. Hertz could hardly sympathise with this plan, although, naturally, he did not express his doubts publicly in the political climate of 1938/1939. Despite its official "super-confessional" orientation, the Berlin *Hochschule* was considered a representative of liberal Reform Judaism; it could become competition for the Orthodox Jews' College in London, which was under the direct influence of the Chief Rabbi. For the same reason, Hertz viewed with scepticism and a certain envy the creation of Judaic chairs at the universities which were removed from his influence. His relationship with Herbert Loewe, the most important representative of academic Judaic studies in England at this time, was also personally rather tense.[71] Thus it seems understandable that Loewe first attempted to win the support of wide academic and non-Jewish circles, in order then to neutralise the existing internal Jewish resistance with their prestige. It is also in keeping with this that Loewe wanted to establish the new institution not, as originally planned by the representatives of the *Hochschule*,[72] in London, that is in direct proximity to the Chief Rabbi, but in Cambridge, closely associated with Loewe's university.

To the refugees from Germany, who came to England at the beginning of 1939 and worked in cooperation with Loewe on the transfer plan, such as Richard Fuchs,[73] Hans Liebeschütz and Adolf Leschnitzer, the frictions and rivalries within Anglo-Jewry were above all unfamiliar and in any case a hindrance. Some of them had been in Nazi prisons and concentration camps before their emigration to England, and, therefore, for them the important thing was to put the transfer plan into action as quickly as possible. Thus they also immediately wanted to enlist financial support from *all* Jewish circles. They learned only

---

[68]See *Encylopedia Judaica*, vol. 8, pp. 397f.; *Joseph Herman Hertz. In Memorium*, London 1947.
[69]See Ernst G. Lowenthal, 'Bloomsbury House. Flüchtlingsarbeit in London 1939–1946. Aus persönlichen Erinnerungen', in Ursula Büttner (ed.), *Das Unrechtsregime. Internationale Forschungen über den Nationalsozialismus*, vol. 2: *Verfolgung – Exil – Belasteter Neubeginn*, Hamburg 1986, pp. 267–308, this reference p. 271.
[70]Grumach to Liebeschütz, 1st June 1939, *loc. cit.*
[71]*RLL*, p. 4f.
[72]Fuchs mentions only "Attempts to transfer the Hochschule to *London*", Fuchs, *loc. cit.*, p. 27.
[73]On Fuchs see also note 118 below.

gradually that they had to be very careful "not to estrange, by approaching one group, the sympathy of others".[74] The danger of "slipping through the extremes"[75] always existed. Thus there were misunderstandings, for example even with Loewe, when at the beginning of April, 1939 representatives of the *Hochschule*[76] held a long discussion with the Chief Rabbi, in which he was even said to have promised support from his Religious Emergency Council for one or two *Hochschule* scholars.[77] The motives behind such a meeting with the Chief Rabbi are clear from a letter that Max Wiener and Ernst Grumach wrote to Liebeschütz:[78]

> "Tomorrow we have . . . a discussion in which we will push for greater standardization and demand that the Loewe line be followed unconditionally. In addition the old man [Leo Baeck is meant, C.H.], with whom we spoke already, felt that the long discussion with Hertz can in no way have been disadvantageous, as he is very probably to be considered a negative factor to be dealt with through friendliness, which was apparently achieved by the discussion; of course we will not take advantage of the assistance offered. Perhaps you will be so kind as to emphasize in your coming discussion with Lowe [sic] that the conversation with Hertz aimed only to eliminate or neutralize him, and that all those involved consider his way (sc. Lowe's) to be the right one. We hope for the participation of other circles only from a financial point of view, and must leave it to his and Fuchs' negotiating skills to achieve the most possible in this regard without hindrance from us and disturbance of the Lowe line."

Despite his officially sympathetic behaviour towards the transfer project, Chief Rabbi Hertz then apparently did try to place obstacles in the path of the enterprise. At a meeting of the Manchester Jewish community at the beginning of May, 1939, at which Loewe solicited financial support for the transfer plan, Alexander Altmann (formerly of the Hildesheimer Seminary), who had only become communal rabbi in Manchester in 1938, had spoken out clearly against moving the *Hochschule*, and himself thus encountered dissent from other members of the community. It is to be assumed this opposition was requested of Altmann by the Chief Rabbi and that, given his still new position among English Jewry, he saw no other way out but to obey this request.[79] Apparently, however, Altmann's opposition could not seriously harm the project.

The plan to transfer the *Hochschule* entered its decisive phase in June, 1939, when Leo Baeck visited England and could speak directly with Loewe about the details. Fine tuning of the content orientation and academic profile of the

[74]See Fuchs, *loc. cit.*, p. 28.

[75]Grumach to Liebeschütz, 27th March 1939, *loc. cit.*

[76]It is not clear who held these discussions with the Chief Rabbi.

[77]Grumach to Liebeschütz, 7th May 1939, *loc. cit.*

[78]Wiener and Grumach to Liebeschütz, 9th April 1939, *loc. cit.*

[79]This was already seen this way by contemporaries, cf. Fuchs to Liebeschütz, 11th May 1939: "I have just received a letter from Loewe, with copies of his discussion with people in Manchester. There was argument there; Altmann opposed our plan – supposedly at the instigation of the Ch. R. [. . .]." Grumach to Liebeschütz, 1st June 1939: "You have probably heard that the Chief Rabbi is supposed to be behind Altmann, Manchester." Cf. also Raphael Loewe, *loc. cit.*, pp. 4f.: ". . . I remember seeing a letter from my father, to Altmann in Manchester, gently reproving him for public opposition to the project . . . I showed the letter to Altmann many years later, and he smilingly said that much had changed since then. My private construction of his opposition is that he was in effect "directed" by Hertz to rally oppostion to the scheme, and that because of his recent arrival and as yet unconsolidated position he had no option but to cooperate."

planned Jewish academy had not yet occurred, which had given rise to rumours and misunderstandings among some members of the *Hochschule*.[80] Now most individual questions, above all organisation and financing, could be settled. The most important changes, as compared with the original plan, involved the fact that the academy to be created would not only take on professors from the *Hochschule*, but also scholars from the already-closed Jewish theological seminaries in Breslau and Vienna.[81] Such an expansion presented itself for various reasons: inclusion of the seminaries in Breslau and Vienna could made it clear to the outside world that it was not a question of the transfer of one particular institution and a particular (liberal) school of thought, but of the rescue of Central European Jewish studies and its academic heritage in general. Possible resistance by the Chief Rabbi or Jewish sponsors to the *Hochschule*'s philosophical orientation could thus be defused. The impetus for this expansion may have been provided by the fact that Samuel Krauss of the *Israelitisch-Theologische Lehranstalt* in Vienna was already in Cambridge as a result of Loewe's mediation. Thus he could easily be included in the Jewish academy.[82] Otherwise, however, only the transfer of the *Hochschule* remained the central aim of the effort, as almost all the lecturers from the already-closed seminaries in Breslau and Vienna had by now emigrated. Theoretically, therefore, they could easily be included without increasing the burden.

With regard to organisation, a committee had been constituted, under the leadership of the Cambridge historian Ernest Barker, which was to form the future governing body of the Jewish academy. In addition to Barker as chairman, members included Professor David Winton Thomas as treasurer, Rev. C. H. Dyer as secretary, the Master of St. John's College (E. A. Benians), Dr. Coulton, Professor Michael Postan as well as representatives from Oxford, London, Manchester and Glasgow and finally two representatives of the English Jewish community.[83]

Loewe had already found a large piece of garden property in Cambridge, near the colleges (at the corner of Grange Road and Madingley Road), with a house that could house at least six fellows (and if necessary their families), and possibly the *Hochschule*'s library. It was thought to make available a yearly salary of £200 at the start for each fellow. The first of October was decided upon as the possible day the academy would open.[84]

To what extent financing for the fellows and the house was secured can be judged only with difficulty from the material available. When Leo Baeck returned to Berlin in mid-June, 1939, he reported to Ernst Grumach that the pledges he had received were enough not for two, but for twelve people, "not counting some private pledges of indeterminate amount".[85] Later, A. J. Makower of the Jewish Professional Fund promised to take on two people for

[80]See Grumach to Liebeschütz, 7th May 1939 and 16th May 1939, *loc. cit.*
[81]See the Memorandum "Transfer of the Central European Jewish Institutes", Appendix V.
[82]*RLL*, p. 2.
[83]Ernest Barker to D. C. Thomson (SPSL), 25th June 1939 (Mss. SPSL 161/2).
[84]Grumach to Liebeschütz, 20th June 1939, *loc. cit.*
[85]*Ibid.*

three years, Manchester one and Cambridge three. The Rockefeller Foundation had promised to double the amounts pledged and every sum subscribed afterwards.[86] This account of Baeck's to Grumach is – for whatever reason – obviously far too positive. In the Rockefeller Foundation Archives there are no documents on such a promise; in fact, there is not even a reference to the entire project.[87] If they existed at all, they could only have been oral promises.

Ernest Barker, who turned to the Society for the Protection of Science and Learning (SPSL) on 25th June 1939 to inquire about possible stipends for Ernst Grumach,[88] Hans Liebeschütz and Eugen Mittwoch (as future fellows of the planned Jewish academy), mentioned then that at that point £700 (that is, stipends for $3\frac{1}{2}$ people) had been definitely assured.[89] A similar amount can be found in one of the memoranda drawn up about the project in this period (June, 1939).[90] Adolf Leschnitzer, who worked with Loewe in Cambridge, informed Ismar Elbogen on 4th July 1939 that "the financing [of the academy is] at the moment 80% certain; the remaining fifth should be covered in the near future".[91] It cannot be determined from this how many fellows this financial plan included; it is possible that six fellows were expected as a foundation, because the house could hold that many scholars. Even if one cannot achieve absolute clarity on this point, and even if one takes into account that some of these details were somewhat coloured for tactical reasons, one must nevertheless assume that the financial basis was solid enough in June–July 1939 to allow the opening of the Jewish academy – possibly with only four or five fellows at first – to seem realistic.[92]

---

[86]Grumach to Liebeschütz, 4th July 1939, *loc. cit.*

[87]Letter from E. Levold, archivist of the Rockefeller Archive Center, to the author, 12th April 1989.

[88]In his letter to D. C. Thomson (SPSL), 25th June 1939, Barker actually wrote: "Bernays, a Hellenist scholar, still in Berlin, but to be transferred to the new institute". This is obviously wrong, as the famous Hellenist Jacob Bernays lived in the nineteenth century. It seems likely that Barker meant Ernst Grumach, who was a Hellenist scholar "still in Berlin" at that time. It is not impossible that he meant Arnold Berney, but he was not a Hellenist and he already lived in Jerusalem in 1939.

[89]*Ibid.*

[90]See Appendix VI.

[91]Leschnitzer to Elbogen, 4th July 1939, Elbogen Papers, LBI Archives.

[92]Raphael Loewe was more sceptical about the chances of success (*RLL*, p. 4): "I have to give you my opinion, for what it is worth, that had the scheme not been overtaken by the war the necessary finance would not have been forthcoming, and with great regret it would have been 'postponed', and in effect abandoned." In a letter to the author, 29th January 1990, Professor Loewe further described his doubts: "You mention the possibilities of a few fellows receiving stipendia of £200 a year. In 1939 this figure would have sufficed a very careful single person provided that he did not have to consider what we call in English the "overheads" – local rates, electricity etc.; and it would not have been enough for a married couple. There would also have been the cost of furnishing the house. I do not recollect that these problems were ever thought out – it would perhaps have seemed premature; but I do not think that my mother, who was closely involved and who had a much better sense of economic realities than my father had, would have allowed them to be forgotten. My father possibly thought that, if matters suddenly gathered momentum, he could persuade friends to contribute beds, etc., and have persuaded one of the big Jewish businesses to find from stock what could not be thus assembled. For this reason I do not believe that October 1939 was ever seriously contemplated as an opening date, even though for propaganda purposes it might have been appropriate to flourish it. Given one more year, it is just possible that these problems might have been overcome, but not during the midsummer months of 1939."

An additional important point that was worked out during Baeck's stay in England in June 1939 concerned the profile on the content of the future academy. As the institute was to have no teaching responsibilities, but was to constitute itself only as a research institute, it was important to formulate overriding research aims. In two project sketches[93] which were probably formulated in early summer, 1939 by Loewe, perhaps together with Baeck and others, as short pieces of information for interested scholars and potential sponsors, the new institute's responsibilities were described as follows:

1. Important periodicals, source collections and large academic projects in German-language Jewish studies were to be continued in England. This concerned above all the *Monatsschrift für Geschichte und Wissenschaft des Judentums* and the *Zeitschrift für die Geschichte der Juden in Deutschland*, which were to be combined and published as an English-language quarterly; in addition the *Monumenta Talmudica* (a series of academic treatises, of which five volumes had already appeared from 1913 to 1923), and the *Germania Judaica*, an alphabetical index of all parts of Germany in which Jewish settlements had existed, as well as an inventory of the sources relating to each. The second part of the first volume had appeared in 1934. (It was reprinted by the Leo Baeck Institute in 1963 and the second volume was published by the Institute in 1968.)

2. The main emphasis of the academy's work was to be research on the "history of the Jews in the various lands of their dispersion". Contemporary Jewish history was to be included. The old plan for a *Cambridge Jewish History* which Ismar Elbogen and Israel Abrahams had worked out even before the First World War was recalled. It was hoped that Elbogen himself would come to Cambridge from the USA in order to take over as head of the history department.[94]

3. In the area of Oriental studies, the treasures of the Cambridge *Genizah* collection would be used to benefit various aspects of Jewish studies (Bible and *Massorah*, history of language, history of literature).

4. The institute would be especially devoted to preserving the traditions of German-speaking Jewry, in view, not least, of a possible return to Germany following the end of Nazi rule.

5. Finally, it was thought that the academy would also contribute to the dissemination of Jewish knowledge among schoolchildren, students and teachers, *inter alia* by publishing text books.

The Jewish academy would be defined above all by its research subjects, not by the religion of its members. Christian scholars were also expressly invited to participate – an essential prerequisite for integrating the institute into English academic life.

The cited points of the research programme show that those involved were still

---

[93]See Appendixes V and VI.
[94]Leschnitzer to Elbogen, 4th July 1939; Loewe to Elbogen, 27th August 1939, *loc. cit.*

far removed from concrete academic planning, and that everything was written down that was imaginable and desirable, without consideration of the possibilities of realisation. Only the *historical* orientation is clear as a specific area of emphasis. On the whole, however, the results of Baeck's visit to England in June 1939 were entirely positive. Through Loewe's untiring efforts, it was possible within a few months to clarify the most important organisational and financial issues to the point where opening the academy as early as October, 1939 seemed to be within the bounds of possibility.

But this was not to be. The outbreak of war between Great Britain and Germany on 3rd September 1939 dashed all hopes. Emigration of German citizens to England became impossible. As the surviving documents of the time show, none of those involved in the transfer project had imagined that war was so near at hand. Nevertheless, one might have expected that, following successful conclusion of the talks between Baeck and Loewe, practical steps towards the transfer of individual fellows from Berlin to Cambridge would have got underway quickly. Yet nothing of the sort occurred. In the eleven weeks that passed between Baeck's visit to England and the outbreak of war, one observes a slowing of the pace, even a remarkable passivity among the main persons involved. The project faltered even before it collapsed with the outbreak of war. The applications made to the SPSL for three fellows, for example, were not pursued further, although the SPSL had signalled its basic willingness to support the three scholars.[95] The *Hochschule* professors involved, impatiently awaiting the beginning of the transfer, felt the sudden delay especially harshly. Grumach's letters to Liebeschütz clearly document the process of disillusionment and growing doubt. While Baeck had still said, upon his return from England, that the pledges would be sufficient for twelve fellows and that it depended only on when Grumach wished to begin,[96] later all that was said was that one could not rush things, and that at the start no more than "five, and if possible at first even fewer"[97] people could be considered. Naturally, doubt grew about the credibility of Baeck's statement as a result of such inconsistencies. This is especially clear in a letter from Grumach to Liebeschütz of 4th of July 1939:[98]

> "Dear Herr Liebeschütz! I would like to help you, but I don't expect very much from speaking with your old boss [Leo Baeck is meant, C.H.]. For months I have been asking him to do something for a friend who urgently needs help, and he promises me the moon without doing anything. I don't reproach him for this: he is so overburdened with other things that he cannot worry about individual issues; only in that case he shouldn't make promises, but he doesn't have the heart to say no to me . . . Unfortunately, the same attitude also appears in his

[95]Thomson (SPSL) to Barker, 3rd July 1939 (Mss. SPSL 161/2): "The Executive Committee learnt last week with interest of the development in connection with the Hebrew Institute in Cambridge. They will be interested to learn of further stages in this development and their Cambridge members undertook to report at the next meeting. There are not before us at the moment any applications for grants on behalf of any of the three names you mention but needless to say the Committee will be only too delighted should the Institute provide in effect academic hospitality or research facilities for Jewish scholars whom they consider worthy of grants, and would be only too pleased to pay the grants through you in such cases." There was no further correspondence following this letter.
[96]Grumach to Liebeschütz, 4th July 1939, *loc. cit.*
[97]Grumach to Liebeschütz, 10th July 1939, *loc. cit.*
[98]Grumach to Liebeschütz, 4th July 1939, *loc. cit.*

handling of our matter, and we are almost afraid that here, too, many things have been portrayed all too rosily. Although B. still holds to his account. According to him, Macower is definitely to take on two people, Manchester one, Cambridge three, and the Rockefeller Foundation has promised to double this sum (and every one later subscribed), and a sort of committee is to work on gaining further support. After that we naturally expected that there would be no further hesitation, but that at least a permit application would already have been made for one or another, above all for Wiener, who has completed his preparations for emigration and thus is in a predicament. But now they say that it could take a long time, that one must not push, etc., without the reasons for this being understandable to us. In fact, B. even advised Wiener at least to go to Cinc[innati], although with the somewhat strange justification of possibly freeing up the funds there, something which could of course also be taken care of by mail. You will understand that we are very disconcerted and dejected, and Wiener in particular, with whose knowledge I am writing, is extremely depressed. It would mean a lot to know how things really look and whether anything can be done to speed things up . . . I just remembered further that after his return, B. let fall the remark: 'It depends only on you, when you want to begin. If you want, on October 1', and I believe also to have recently mentioned this date. This makes his present behaviour even stranger. The rub is that one can never speak to him in peace and that he is so burdened that he himself no longer comes to important discussions.''

Grumach's letter brings up the question of the background to Baeck's contradictory statements and the causes of the sudden hesitation. An absolutely certain answer to this question probably cannot be found on the basis of the available material. Nevertheless, it seems in my opinion that several data support the view that the project faltered due to a double dilemma faced by Leo Baeck:

1. He had to make a decision about the make-up of the academy's personnel – and could not do it. 2. He knew that his presence in Cambridge was necessary for the success of the project, but he did not want to abandon his community in Berlin.

In the negotiations with Loewe, the question of personnel was at first excluded. Because the means available at first were apparently sufficient only for five fellows,[99] a choice became unavoidable. The decision, as to which of the *Hochschule* scholars was to be taken on as a fellow of the academy and which was not, was to rest with Baeck alone[100] – a decision that, considering the political situation in Germany, must have been inhumanly difficult. For understandable reasons, it was important to Loewe to establish the academic prestige of the re-established *Hochschule* on a high level with famous names having good reputations in Jewish studies and beyond. Only in this way could the promised funds be assured. In addition, the line-up of fellows was to occur according to the disciplinary priorities of the research programme, that is, it was to reflect the academy's planned primarily historical orientation. In April Loewe had already emphasised to Baeck that only "first class scholars" were to be selected for the institute, and as far as possible, no unnecessary "duplications" were to occur. Those who could not be taken on would have to be helped in other ways.[101]

Thus for Baeck, a dilemma arose from which only the outbreak of war would free him. He knew that a decision on acceptance or non-acceptance meant much

[99]Grumach to Liebeschütz, 16th May 1939 and 10th July 1939, *loc. cit.*
[100]Loewe to Elbogen, 27th August 1939, *loc. cit.*
[101]Grumach to Liebeschütz, 20th April 1939, *loc. cit.*

more to those affected than simply a question of future academic work. In this situation of persecution, in which rescue of life and limb had to take precedence, purely academic standards could not be applied. Thus, however, the decision Baeck was saddled with on the selection of fellows became a problem. He could not make the decision. Even when he had a choice in mind – for example, he clearly wanted to include Täubler[102] – he could not make it public as long as all the others were not "taken care of".[103] He knew of the great hopes and expectations of his colleagues in Berlin and of those who, like Arnold Berney[104] or Hans Liebeschütz, had already emigrated: they all wanted to be part of the re-established *Hochschule*, and Baeck was not one who could say "No". The HUC offer would relieve some of the burden, and thus Baeck advised all those affected, perhaps with the exception of Täubler, to accept the invitation to Cincinnati.[105] Otherwise, his statements and behaviour seem contradictory, as at first – presumably to encourage his colleagues and raise their spirits, maybe also out of the understandable desire to escape his dilemma – he gave a much too positive depiction of the financial situation which he then had to retract. Apparently he could speak with no one about his dilemma. For these very understandable reasons which are to be respected, Baeck did not make a decision about the choice of fellows. Only a week before the outbreak of war, on 27th August 1939, Loewe wrote to Elbogen: "The choice of the members [of the institute] rests with Baeck."[106] Apparently, Baeck hoped that the situation would ease by itself through the emigration of some of his colleagues (for example to Cincinnati) and the acquisition of more funding. But valuable time was lost through this waiting.

A further motive for Baeck's dilatory treatment of the transfer plan could lie in the fact that at this point he still considered the *Hochschule*'s responsibility, as an institution for rabbinical training, to be in Berlin. For his part, he felt a duty not to leave Germany as long as Jews still lived there.[107] This also endangered the transfer plan, because Loewe considered Baeck's presence in Cambridge indispensable for the success of the project. Only with Leo Baeck at its head did the Jewish academy have a chance of success. At the meeting in June, Baeck

---

[102]Grumach to Liebeschütz, 16th May 1939, *loc. cit.*

[103]In the summer term of 1939, in addition to Baeck the following lecturers taught at the *Hochschule* (not including the language and physical education teachers): Ernst Grumach (classical philology, ancient history), Eugen Täubler (Bible studies and history), Max Wiener (Bible studies and philosophy of religion), Alexander Guttmann (Talmud), Arthur Spanier (Jewish literature). Of the previous lecturers who had already left the *Hochschule* in the summer of 1939, the following had no position: Moses Sister (Bible studies and linguistics), Arnold Berney (modern history), Hans Liebeschütz (medieval history), Franz Rosenthal (Oriental studies), Moses D. Goldmann (Islamic studies), Maximilian Landau (Eastern European history), Ismar Freund (history of the emancipation), Gustav Ormann (Bible studies, linguistics), Fritz Friedlander (philosophy).

[104]See the letters of Berney to Liebeschütz, Liebeschütz Papers, LBI Archives, Baeck informed Berney in July, 1939 that the new institute in Cambridge would open in autumn 1939, Berney to Liebeschütz, 20th July 1939, *loc. cit.*

[105]Grumach to Liebeschütz, 10th July 1939, *loc. cit.*

[106]Loewe to Elbogen, 27th August 1939, *loc. cit.*

[107]See Leonard Baker, *Hirt der Verfolgten. Leo Baeck im Dritten Reich*, Stuttgart 1982, pp. 330ff. In the original English edition: *Days of Sorrow and Pain. Leo Baeck and the Berlin Jews*, New York – London 1978, pp. 246–248.

could not make up his mind to emigrate to England, and in diplomatic fashion refused to abandon his Berlin community. At most, he was prepared to compromise by living in England for several months (one term) per year, and he wanted to try to have the German authorities "give him a double residency", which was hardly possible in 1939.[108] Loewe seems to have accepted this compromise.[109] He then made an effort, together with Leschnitzer, to bring Ismar Elbogen to Cambridge on a similar basis (at least one term a year).[110]

The outbreak of war destroyed all these hopes. It is futile to speculate in retrospect whether the building of the Jewish Academy in Cambridge would have succeeded given a few more months. The *Hochschule* remained in Berlin and could continue instruction until July 1942, before it too was closed and those last members who were not able to escape, deported to the concentration and extermination camps.[111]

After the outbreak of war, there was no longer anyone who could continue to pursue the old plan. Loewe died in 1940, probably not least as a result of his exhausting commitment to the project. Shortly before the end of the war, in January, 1945, Eugen Täubler turned to Hermann Berlak, Leo Baeck's son-in-law living in London, with the suggestion of taking up the pre-war plan once again and creating a Leo Baeck Library intended as a research institute, in Cambridge.[112] This proposal was as little capable of realisation as Täubler's later plan to annex the *Hochschule* to the chair for Jewish history at Columbia University in New York as the Leo Baeck Library.[113]

In the fifties, however, refugee scholars in England founded three separate and independent institutions, each of which wanted to contribute to the rebuilding of Jewish studies, which had been destroyed in Central Europe, and thus in a certain sense were to be considered moral successors of the *Hochschule*.

In 1953, Alexander Altmann founded the Institute of Jewish Studies in Manchester, which took on the responsibility of promoting academic research and education on Jews and Judaism. Despite Altmann's opposition to the transfer plan before the war, Leo Baeck, who lived in England after the war, was immediately prepared to support the institute and to help with fund-raising.[114] The institute also received a small part of the *Hochschule* library. After Altmann left for the USA in 1959, the institute was transferred to London and joined to the Hebrew department of University College in London, where it still exists today.[115]

[108]Dr. Maria Leschnitzer to the author, 5th January 1989; Fuchs, *loc. cit.*, p. 28.

[109]See Fuchs, *op. cit.*, p. 28.

[110]Loewe to Elbogen, 27th August 1939, *loc. cit.*

[111]See Fuchs, *loc. cit.*, pp. 29ff.; Strauss, *loc. cit.*

[112]Täubler to Berlak, 4th January 1935, *Nachlass E. Täubler*, E IV 006, Universitätsbibliothek Basel.

[113]Täubler to Baeck, 11th September 1946, *Nachlass Eugen Täubler*, E III, 002, Universitätsbibliothek Basel.

[114]*RLL*, p. 5.

[115]See Raphael Loewe, 'The Contribution of German-Jewish Scholars to Jewish Studies in the United Kingdom', in Werner E. Mosse *et al.* (eds.), *Second Chance. Two Centuries of German-speaking Jews in the United Kingdom*, Tübingen 1991 (Schriftenreihe wissenschaftlicher Abhandlungen des Leo Baeck Instituts 48), pp. 437–462.

In 1955, the Leo Baeck Institute came into being, taking as its task research into German-Jewish history from the Emancipation. With its working centres in Jerusalem, London and New York, the Leo Baeck Institute initiated a new phase of German-Jewish studies and led to the revitalisation and re-establishment of the scholarly tradition of German-Jewish historiography, which had been terminated so brutally in Germany.[116]

Finally, in 1956, the year Baeck died, the Leo Baeck College for the Study of Judaism and the Training of Ministers and Teachers was founded in London to serve as a training centre for rabbis, teachers of religion and social workers of the Reform movement.[117]

Thus, in the name of and with the support of Leo Baeck, after the war the tradition of German-Jewish studies was taken up in England after all. Of course, the situation had completely changed following the Holocaust. There was also no continuity of personnel, aside from Leo Baeck (who died within a year or two of the formation of the three institutes) and Hans Liebeschütz.[118] Therefore it seems inadequate to interpret these new institutions as later realisations of the unsuccessful pre-war plans.

---

[116]See Herbert A. Strauss, 'Die Leo Baeck Institute und die Erforschung der deutsch-jüdischen Geschichte', in *Geschichte und Gesellschaft*, 9, 1983, pp. 471–478; Christhard Hoffmann, 'Deutsch-jüdische Geschichtswissenschaft in der Emigration – das Leo-Baeck-Institut', in Herbert A. Strauss *et al.* (eds.), *Die Emigration der Wissenschaften*, München 1991.

[117]See 'The Leo Baeck College after 30 Years', in *European Judaism*, vol. 19/20 (Winter 1985/Summer 1986), pp. 4ff.

[118]Hans Liebeschütz (1893–1978) was to make a signal contribution to the work of the Leo Baeck Institute for over two decades. He was one of the guiding spirits of the Institute during the first phase of its existence. Many essays in the *LBI Year Book* and his monographs in the Institute's *Schriftenreihe* bear witness to his scholarly involvement. Richard Fuchs (1886–1970) likewise took a decisive part in the work of the Leo Baeck Institute. Both men served on the Institute's London Executive until their deaths.

APPENDIX

I

Letter of Rabbi Chaim Oser Grodzenski of Vilna[119]

Third day of Chanukah, 5694 [15th December 1933]

To his Excellency, my dear and esteemed friend, the perfect sage and man of total virtue, our teacher and rabbi Dr. Meier Hildesheimer, in the Holy Land (may it soon be restored):

With best wishes, etc. During the Ten Days of Repentance[120] I was visited by our friend, the great sage, our rabbi and teacher . . .[121] and he told me of his Excellency's suggestion and desire to travel to our Holy Land and transfer to it the Berlin Seminary. I told him, and asked him to pass on to your Excellency and your colleagues, *daat Torah* that this should not be done under any circumstances. But later I heard that his Excellency went to the Holy Land and is attempting to fulfil his desire, and that he is attempting to do so in Tel-Aviv after they did not agree to it in Jerusalem, the Holy City, and he wants to found the seminary there with the excuse that [it would benefit] the Sephardic Jews of the eastern cities.[122] So I find myself obliged to turn to you in this letter.

Now when your respected father, the rabbi and sage and pious man, established the Berlin Seminary, he meant it for the sake of Heaven. For the Reformers had grown strong and had taken over the Jewish communities, the Torah was frequently forgotten and they elected freethinking "bad-sons"[123] with higher education. So when your respected father (a saint's memory is a blessing) founded the Orthodox community "Adass Jisroel" he needed to compete with the Reformers, and so it was necessary, in that place and time, that the Orthodox communities too should have rabbis with degrees in higher education. That was why he founded the seminary, the students of which study in the university as well, and that was in Germany, which was then a cultured land.

---

[119]For Hebrew original, see *Ahiezer*, II, pp. 443–444. The text is taken from the collected letters of the Hazon Ish, to whom Grodzenski sent a copy the same day; see the latter's collected letters (note 49), II, pp. 171–173. For another English translation of the central portion of the letter, see Schorsch (note 2), p. 20. There, the letter is mistakenly dated to Chanukah of 1934.

[120]I.e., 21st–30th September 1933. For Weinberg's visit to Grodzenski during this period, see *Seridei Esh*, I, pp. 370–371, §d.

[121]Weinberg's name is discreetly omitted in the published version of this letter, but may still be read in the first and third of Grodzenski's letters to Chief Rabbi Kook printed in *Iggerot LaReiya*, pp. 213 and 215; the former is translated in our Appendix II.

[122]I have not found this idea elsewhere.

[123]A deliberate and pejorative misspelling of the Hebrew word for "rabbis" (*rabbanim*), so as to derive it from *ra* ("bad") and *banim* ("sons").

But how can one even consider opening a rabbi-factory[124] in the Holy Land, where there are great yeshivot and great rabbis, great in Torah and piety – (how could anyone think that there one might) choose new rabbis for whom the profession is the main thing and the Torah is ancillary? Nor do the Sephardic Jews of the eastern cities need rabbis like this: they are not competent to serve the pious, and the left-wingers do not need Berlin-style rabbis. So the move would not help anything, but only bring disaster for the Holy Land and disgrace for the Torah.

And I am shocked that my friend dared to do so without first consulting with [*Agudath Israel*'s] Council of Torah Sages or other greats of Torah and piety, especially after he heard there was opposition. I cannot believe that my friend would on his own initiative do something so dangerous without the approval of the great sages of the Diaspora and the great sages of Jerusalem the Holy City. My friend knows our long friendship and love, but the truth is more beloved than anything. So I therefore pronounce to him a public rebuke, out of private love. And let him consider well before doing anything, for I shall not rest and I shall not be silent in this matter, for anyone who can protest must do so and see that that which has been opened against be closed.

. . .[125] I hereby close with a great blessing for my friend, that he return home safely, from one whose soul is linked to his and who wishes him all the best,

Chaim Oser Grodzenski

II

Letter from Rabbi Grodzenski to Rabbi Abraham Isaac Kook, Chief Rabbi of Palestine[126]

1 Kislev 5694 [19th November 1933]

To His Excellency the famous and great etc. Rabbi and Gaon, our Master, Abraham Isaac HaKohen Kook (may he live long and well).

May God bless him.

With best wishes, etc. His honoured letter arrived after the Day of Atonement [30th September 1933], and I thank Your Honour for the blessings from his pure heart. Due to the sanctity of the holidays and the post-festival duties I was unable to answer until now. – Please give regards, in my name, to Rabbi Meier Hildesheimer (our master and teacher). Although I already informed him, through the Rabbi and Gaon Jechiel Jacob Weinberg (our master and teacher),

---

[124]This is quite a strong term to use, and its authenticity has been questioned; in a letter Grodzenski sent to M. Hildesheimer about three weeks later (22 Teveth 5694), Dr. Meir Hildesheimer (II) has kindly informed me, the parallel passage reads merely "how can one even consider founding a rabbinical seminary in the Holy Land . . ." However, Grodzenski did use the same term for the *Rabbinerseminar* – behind Hildesheimer's back, to be sure – in a letter he wrote to Chief Rabbi Kook only two days after the one translated here (*Iggerot HaReiya*, p. 214), just as *Responsa Ahiezer*, IV, No. 45, p. 51 (ca. 1928 = *Seridei Esh*, II, p. 251), where Grodzenski characterises an overly-liberal rabbi as running a "conversion-factory", shows that this type of invective was familiar. And note with Eisner, *loc. cit.*, p. 35, that the founder of the *Rabbinerseminar* in his 1873 inauguration speech already felt the need to emphasise that the Seminary was not to be a "rabbi-factory"; even then, apparently, the barb was a popular one.

[125]Some text is apparently omitted in the published version of the letter.

[126]*Iggerot LaReiya*, pp. 213–214.

who heads the Berlin Seminary, that it is totally impossible to move that institution to the Holy City, here I repeat, that what was proper in Berlin, so as to give a little knowledge of Talmud to Germans,[127] which was the way his [Hildesheimer's] father (the pious rabbi and gaon, of blessed memory) found to compete with the Reformers, is not proper for Jerusalem, the Holy City. And it is self-understood that studying in the university in the Holy City, together with rabbinical duties, is a match doomed to failure – mixing a cup of poison in the waters of the Talmud. And for people like you it is enough to be brief. I do not know precisely what he [Hildesheimer] wants to do, apart from what I heard from His Excellency the Rabbi and Gaon Weinberg. That is the topic concerning which I wished to urge [you to take action].

[The rest of the letter concerns ritual slaughter in Johannesburg; and the latter is the only topic dealt with in Rabbi Kook's published response to this letter][128]

III

Letter of Rabbi Solomon Aronson, Ashkenazic Chief Rabbi of Tel Aviv[129]

11 Teveth 5734 [29th December 1933]

To my friend, the great scholar and glory of his congregation, our teacher, Rabbi Meier Hildesheimer:

Lately, there has developed great unrest and a violent storm of opposition to the idea of bringing this seminary.[130] All of the directors and students of the *yeshivot*, all the religious institutions are vigorously protesting the introduction of the Berlin Seminary to our land. The storm and wrath are especially great abroad, in Poland and Lithuania, and the great sage Rabbi Chaim Oser Grodzenski of Vilna has gone to war with wrathful vigour against the idea of introducing it into the Land of Israel, which is full of advanced *yeshivot*. The only hope of the students of the latter is to be chosen, in the course of time, to be rabbis in the various settlements which are being built and which will be built – and here, suddenly, comes new competition from abroad.

The cup of wrath and protest has been poured out upon me as well.[131] Therefore, I have considered it obligatory to inform His Excellency, so that he might reconsider if it is possible and desirable to take this step, of uprooting this important institution and bringing it hither, at a time when virtually all of the religious in Israel absolutely oppose it with all their strength and energy. After all, the life of Torah and tradition does not draw its strength from the marginal intelligentsia, and if [by bringing the Seminary] we would encounter not love and support among the faithful, but rather hatred and great hostility and great zeal, there will be no hope for normal life. True, I will be very sorry if my hope to live

[127]In his letter to Kook of 27th December 1933 (*Iggerot LaReiya*, p. 215), Grodzenski states of the *Rabbinerseminar* students that "their knowledge of all the rabbinical disciplines is generally meagre".

[128]See above note 48.

[129]Hebrew original published in Y. Alfasi, *HeHakham HaMufla. Rabbi Shlomo Ha-Kohen Aronson, the Chief Rabbi of Tel-Aviv. His Life and Work*, Tel-Aviv 1985, pp. 116–117 (in Hebrew).

[130]A change of one letter (HNH instead of HZH) would yield "bringing the seminary hither", which appears preferable.

[131]In a letter of 26th December 1933 reprinted in *Ahiezer*, II, p. 445, Rabbi Grodzenski referred to his letter to Aronson as similar to the one to Hildesheimer brought above as Appendix I.

together with you and your colleagues in our city will not be fulfilled. But I may not ignore the truth, and the obvious truth, lately, is that *almost all** of religious Jewry opposes bitterly the bringing of the Seminary into the Land, and we [who support it] remain *truly few*,* so it is impossible. Especially great here is the influence of Rabbi Chaim Oser Grodzenski of Vilna, who is making the whole world cry out and himself thunders[132] against the plan.

Therefore, my friend and honoured companion, with a torn and broken heart I advise His Excellency not to do anything for the present, and not to pursue the step which was decided upon when he visited. For if it is difficult in any case to swim against the stream, this is especially difficult when the stream consists of *our own brothers*,* those with whom we fully agree concerning Judaism and its values.

> With best respects and great love,
> Shlomo Ha-Kohen Aronson

* original emphasis

IV

Letter of the Faculty ("Dozentenkollegium") of the Rabbiner-Seminar[133]

Sunday, 5 Shevat 5694 [21st January 1934]

Let the mountains greet the great rabbis, shepherds of Israel, etc, our teacher Rabbi S. Aronson and our teacher Rabbi B. Z. Ouziel, the Chief Rabbis of the holy community of Jaffa–Tel-Aviv.

With best wishes and proper respect. The report which Rabbi Dr. Meier Hildesheimer, who is a member of our *Kuratorium*, gave us upon his return from our Holy Land, and his account of the loving reception which was accorded him by the chief rabbinate, and of the expressions of goodwill which were made by broad circles among our brethren in Tel Aviv concerning the idea of transferring our great seminary to our Hebrew city, brought great joy to our hearts, and we blessed and thanked God who has kept us in life and sustained us so as to hear such news from the Holy Land. We feel a special emotional need to express to your excellencies, and to all those who take refuge in your shadow, our deep thanks. And it goes without saying that we here in the Diaspora aspire and yearn with all our hearts and all our souls to immigrate and dwell in our Holy Land which is returning to life.

To our sorrow, the proper time has not yet come for the fulfilment of this heartfelt desire, and we may not yet return to the home of our fathers. The Jews of this country are in difficulty and depression, and they have no other consolation apart from the spiritual institutions which they created in the good days of the past. For more than six decades, our great Seminary has been a spiritual centre for all the Jewish exiles in this country and the neighbouring lands. From it, Torah and light and pure Judaism have gone out, faithful shepherds and energetic leaders, champions of Judaism and bearers of its standard.

---

[132]Literally: "screams like a crane" (borrowed from the Babylonian Talmud, *Kiddushin*, 44a).

[133]The Hebrew original may be found in the archives of the *Va'ad Ha-Kehillah* of Tel-Aviv, now in the Historical Archives of the Municipality of Tel-Aviv-Jaffa, Section 8, File 767. Despite protracted searching, I was unable to find in these archives any more material relating to this episode.

Herbert Loewe
(1882–1940)

'Naje Folkscajtung', Warsaw, 16th September 1933
The headlines denounce M. Hildesheimer as an agent of
Hitler and call for his expulsion from Poland

So how could we now leave to themselves our fellow Jews, who have been overtaken by suffering and daily worry? We cannot act too early. We believe that we are obliged first to care for the spiritual needs [of the Jews] in this country, and to fill the vacuum which will be created by our Seminary's departure.

Of course, we never give up the thought of our redemption, our return to the desired land. All of our words and thoughts are with the Holy Land, which is being built with God's help before our eyes in God's mercy upon us, in His great mercy upon His people which is scattered and downtrodden throughout the Diaspora: its only light is in Zion, [its only] hope is in the land of our past and our future. We are here but our heart is there.

Once again, then, we express to you, and all those who are with you, our sincere thanks for the loving invitation to return to the land of our fathers. It is our prayer that God, who is good, will visit His people with salvation and mercy, so we may all be worthy of the coming of the righteous redeemer, and the return of all the sons to their border[134] speedily in our days.

With all feelings of respect and esteem, from a heart full of thanks and blessing,
[signed:]
Moses Auerbach, Jechiel Jacob Weinberg, Samuel Ha-Kohen Grünberg

V[135]

Transfer of the Central European Jewish Institutions

Political developments in certain European countries have dealt a shattering – and in some cases a fatal – blow at Jewish research and teaching.

It will be an achievement of historical importance if the present plan succeeds: an effort is being made to transfer the leading Jewish scientific institutes to England and incorporate them in a new body, so that they may continue their programme of work which has been interrupted.

Three institutes are at the moment under consideration on account of the high standard which they maintained for many years, and which they can continue to maintain in a new environment. These three institutes are:
(a) The Lehranstalt in Berlin, (b) the Israelitisch-Theologische Seminar in Vienna, and (c) the Jüdisch-Theologische Seminar in Breslau.

In addition to the institutes themselves and their future work in common, it is proposed to foster the publications with which these institutes had previously been connected, (a) the Monatsschrift, (b) the Zeitschrift and (c) certain publications such as Monumenta Talmudica, Germania Judaica, etc.

It seems advisable (1) to create a new body as a successor to these three institutes, to be called the Jewish Academy; (2) that the two journals should be combined in a new quarterly, and (3) to take measures to see that the literary undertakings which have hitherto been carried on by these institutes are continued.

This proposed Jewish Academy would occupy an important and distinctive position in the Jewish scientific world.
(1) It will in the first instance be a place of research. How far the members of the Academy should engage in teaching cannot now be estimated.
(2) The work of the Academy will extend in general to all Jewish studies, but in

---

[134]See Jeremiah XXXI:16(17).
[135]The documents reproduced in Appendix V and VI are from the Leschnitzer papers (Dr. Maria Leschnitzer, New York).

particular it will care for the history of Jews in the various lands of their dispersion. Note will be taken not only of activity in the past but of the history and development of Jewish culture in present circumstances.

(3) It will further devote particular attention to the preservation of the traditions and culture of German Jewry with a view to preparation for a return when political conditions change.

(4) Finally, the Academy will not limit itself to pure research, but will seek to provide for the needs of Jewish elementary and secondary education, and will endeavour to promote the writing of text-books suitable for students, teachers and children.

The Academy will therefore have more than a local interest: it is hoped that it will become a centre in the Diaspora for Jewish studies.

What has been said in another leaflet about the Lehranstalt holds good with regard to the enlarged scope of the proposed Academy. The process of extension is not complete; financial and other considerations will decide what members of other institutes are to be incorporated, but the independence of the Academy will be assured, and if the proposed scheme at Cambridge is realised there will be opportunity for Jews of all shades of religions opinion to collaborate without compulsion to conformity, but without offence to the convictions and practices of any of its members.

VI

Memorandum on the Transfer of Jewish Studies from Central Europe to England

The nineteenth century was of paramount importance in the history of Jewish studies, for it saw the rise of a new school of thought which introduced a scientific method of approach to these studies. As a result of the influence of men like Zunz and Geiger, various Institutes – notably the Seminar at Breslau (founded in 1854), the Lehranstalten at Berlin (1872) and at Vienna (1893) – were set up with the object of promoting what has been termed the "science of Judaism" (Die Wissenschaft des Judentums). From these parent bodies have sprung other centres of learning in Europe and America, notably in Budapest, New York and Cincinnati. In all of them the same objective spirit has prevailed and their influence has been world-wide. They are able to count among their alumni such eminent scholars as Schechter, the late Reader in Talmudic in Cambridge; Büchler, Friedländer and Claude Montefiore of London. These are names that will, perhaps, be better known to people in England. Specialists, however, will be as familiar with the names of Hermann Cohen and Steinthal, philosophers; the brothers Darmesteter, philologists; David Kaufmann, Wilhelm Bacher, H. Torczyner, Jacob Barth, Lidzbarski, D. H. Müller, M. Friedman, orientalists; Jacob Bernays, Jacob Freudenthal, classicists. Amongst the alumni and teachers still living are to be counted the present President, Dr Leo Baeck, himself a distinguished theologian and philosopher; Professor Samuel Krauss, who has written extensively on linguistic, Talmudic, Synagogal and archaeological subjects; Dr I. Elbogen, the liturgiologist and historian; Professor Mittwoch the Arabist, and Professor E. Täubler, the historian.

The names already mentioned suggest to some extent the range of subjects covered by the activities of these three Institutes. They cover indeed the whole field of learning – History, Law, Language, Literature, Theology, Bible, Liturgy, Archaeology – which we in this country are accustomed to describe as the

"Humanities". For well over 80 years the work initiated in these Institutes has been carried on continually, and, as their publications indicate, successfully.

The life of these Institutes, and with these Institutes the accumulated traditions which they represent, must cease unless a new centre can be found for them. Two Institutes have, in fact, been closed already. The Institutes would find in Great Britain, with its appreciation of the old Humanities and its objective spirit of free enquiry, a most appropriate milieu, and if it were possible to transplant these Institutes to the near neighbourhood of a University, such a step would be of great reciprocal value.

For several reasons it has been considered expedient not to re-establish the three Institutes separately, but to combine them in a new organisation and under a new name. It has, moreover, seemed particularly desirable that the home of this new organisation should be in Cambridge. The choice of Cambridge is determined largely by two considerations in connection with future work. The Institutes contemplate several projects. One of these was planned in Cambridge so far back as 1912 by the late Israel Abrahams, Reader in Talmudic, and Dr I. Elbogen: it was a systematic history of the Jews, under the editorship of Cambridge historians and according to the Cambridge plan. Such a work is badly needed. The position of the Jews in universal history has often been wrongly depicted, in a Judaeo-centric manner, neglecting the environment of the Jews and the mutual relation of the Jews and the environment. On the Jewish side, the outside world is too often left out of account. On the other hand, the failure of the Victoria County Histories to draw upon Jewish sources for recovering place-names, the ignoring of Jewish influences in such institutions as Mortgage, the writ of Elegit, the separate examination of the wife in Final Concords, has several times been noted.

Another project, on the Oriental side, is the proper utilisation of the Cambridge Genizah in several directions: the study of the Bible and Massora; the study of the Jewish dialect of Arabic; the study of the Genizah material for literary and historical purposes, are obvious instances.

The tasks which the new organisation hopes to undertake include the continuation of the Monatsschrift, which has been in existence for 82 years. In spite of grave difficulties at the present time, an issue is actually now impending, but it will not be possible to maintain publication of this highly important periodical in Germany for much longer. Among other works still incomplete, mention must be made of the Monumenta Talmudica, the Germania Judaica, the publications of the Kohut Foundation, and the important series of essays which were issued regularly by the Institutes in conjunction with their annual reports. Above all, note must be taken of the new edition, by Professor Samuel Krauss, of Kohut's Arukh, the oldest complete Rabbinic lexicon. In some cases it will be necessary, for purposes of index and similar reasons, to continue the use of German in those undertakings which are in process of publication. But all future work will be in English.

It is to be anticipated that the activity hitherto carried on by these institutes will come to an end unless this project succeeds. If the scholars whom it is proposed to re-unite are absorbed as individuals by teaching institutions maintained by Jewish communities, their corporate labours will hardly be possible. Whether this proposed Institute will eventually undertake teaching must be left to the future. The present scheme is limited purely to academic research: it is not devised, in the first instance, to afford relief to refugees. But it is proposed that the scholars shall live in common and in this way the cost of their maintenance will be largely reduced.

It need hardly be reiterated that the new Institute will be completely independent of all political and religious bodies. Its members may be drawn from any school of thought and Christian scholars will be as welcome as Jewish; the sole criterion will be objective scholarship. But it will definitely be a Jewish Institute.

There will be a governing body on which several distinguished Cambridge scholars have already consented to serve. The President of the Berlin Lehranstalt, Dr Leo Baeck, and Professor Mittwoch, would be available to carry over the old traditions into the new home, and Professor Samuel Krauss is already settled in Cambridge. A suitable house has been offered and will, it is hoped, be secured. It is estimated that the annual cost per Fellow, including, if married, his wife and family, will be £200. Besides Professor Krauss, already mentioned, funds for three Fellows have already been promised. It is hoped that other fellowships may be provided by combinations of Cambridge Colleges.

The experimental period which is visualized is seven years; first, so as to obtain the benefit of the Covenant system, and secondly, because such a period should suffice to give the new Institute time to establish and justify itself and to find benefactors who would place it on a permanent foundation.

Loyalties in Conflict:
French Jewry and the Refugee Crisis, 1933–1935

BY VICKI CARON

The attitude of French Jewish elites towards their refugee co-religionists in the 1930s has long been an issue of considerable controversy.* During the decade itself, refugee groups together with several French sympathisers frequently accused the native French Jewish establishment of having abandoned them. Most recently this view has been reiterated in Maurice Rajsfus's scathing polemic *Sois Juif et tais-toi*! as well as in the more subdued article by Jean-Baptiste Joly, 'L'Aide aux émigrés juifs: Le Comité National de secours'.[1] Not only did the Jewish refugee committees fail to provide adequate philanthropy, these critics maintain, but, more importantly, they refused to press the French government to pursue more liberal refugee policies. Indeed, according to this view, French Jewish elites, fearful of an antisemitic backlash and desiring to prove that they placed French national loyalties above Jewish ones, even went so far as to pressure the French government to close the borders. Most historians who have studied the issue, however, including David Weinberg, Paula Hyman, and most recently Catherine Nicault, have been more circumspect. While conceding that French Jews may not have accomplished a great deal on the political front, these scholars insist that in reality there was little choice. From their perspective it was the French government which set the limits – which by 1935 had become very narrow indeed. They argue that French Jews had control over one aspect of the refugee question only –

*Research for this article was supported by grants from the National Endowment for the Humanities and the Memorial Foundation for Jewish Culture. I would also like to thank Michael Miller for alerting me to several documents located at the Archives of the *Préfecture de Police* in Paris, as well as Nancy Green and Paula Hyman for their helpful comments.
[1]Maurice Rajsfus, *Sois Juif et tais-toi!: 1930–1940. Les français "israélites" face au nazisme*, Paris 1981; and Jean-Baptiste Joly, 'L'Aide aux émigrés juifs. Le Comité National de secours', in Gilbert Badia, *et al.* (eds.) *Les Bannis de Hitler: Accueil et luttes des exilés allemands en France (1933–1939)*, Paris 1984, pp. 37–64. Among the most prominent French Jews critical of the attitudes of the native establishment's refugee committees were the Zionist poet, André Spire; the Left-wing Zionist activist Wladimir Rabinovitch (Rabi); and Léon Blum, the Prime Minister of France during the Popular Front. On Spire see Paula Hyman, *From Dreyfus to Vichy: The Remaking of French Jewry, 1906–1939*, New York 1979, p. 221; Spire, 'Face à Hitler', in *Revue Juive de Genève*, 2ème année, No. 1 (October 1933), p. 5. On Rabi, see David H. Weinberg, *A Community on Trial. The Jews of Paris in the 1930s*, Chicago 1977, p. 90; Rajsfus, *op. cit.*, pp. 149, 151–152; Rabinovitch, 'Charles Péguy. Témoinage d'un Juif', in *Esprit* (1st June 1939), pp. 321–332; Rabi, 'Le Scandale des Comités', in *Samedi*, 4th February 1939, p. 4. On Blum see 'M. Léon Blum et la question juive', in *L'Ordre*, 27th November 1938, p. 3; 'Le Discours de Léon Blum', in *Droit de Vivre*, 3rd December 1938, p. 6; Rabi, 'De 1906 à 1939', in Bernhard Blumenkranz (ed.), *Histoire des Juifs en France*, Toulouse 1972, p. 384.

philanthropy. And, with regard to that endeavour, these scholars maintain, French Jewry probably accomplished as much as could be expected.[2]

In this paper I would like to re-examine this debate in light of some new archival evidence. My chronological focus will be on the period 1933 to 1935 – the first stage of the refugee crisis in France and a crucial period in terms of laying the groundwork for refugee policies for the rest of the decade. To be sure, the attitudes of native French Jewish elites towards the refugees evolved noticeably during the 1930s. Nevertheless, considerable evidence suggests that with respect to these early years the harsh assessment put forth by those critical of the Franco-Jewish establishment, is, on the whole, correct. Despite the very real constraints imposed upon Jewish leadership as a result of government policy, I believe it can be shown that even within the parameters imposed, French Jewish leaders could have done a good deal more, both politically and even in terms of providing philanthropy. Contrary to the view that they merely responded to government pressures, it is clear that several individuals within the Franco-Jewish establishment played a far more active role. In particular, Jacques Helbronner, whose activities during these years have strangely been ignored, not only lobbied incessantly for a more restrictive refugee policy in his capacity as Jewish spokesman – he was Vice-President of the Central Consistory as well as a member of the executive committee of the *Comité National de secours aux réfugiés allemands victimes de l'antisémitisme*, the principal relief committee between 1933 and 1935 – but, more importantly, he even held key posts in the government that enabled him to exert a direct influence over the formulation of official refugee policy itself. Most significantly, Helbronner, who was already a *Conseiller d'Etat*, was appointed in 1934 to serve as France's delegate to the League of Nations High Commission for Refugees, the international agency created in late 1933 to deal specifically with the German refugee question. Certainly, the hard-line views espoused by Helbronner and his supporters were not shared by all native French Jews involved in refugee work. Indeed, Helbronner's most outspoken opponent within the Jewish establishment was Raymond-Raoul Lambert, the General Secretary of the *Comité National* and from 1934 on the Editor-in-Chief of the *Univers israélite*, the major journal of French Jewry.[3] Lambert, as we shall see,

---

[2]Weinberg, *op. cit.*; Hyman, *op. cit.*, esp. chapter 8, pp. 199–232; Catherine Nicault, 'L'accueil des Juifs d'Europe centrale par la communauté juive française (1933–1939)', in mimeographed Proceedings of the Colloquium, *Réfugiés et Immigrés d'Europe Centrale dans le Mouvement Antifasciste et la Résistance en France (1933–1945)*, Institute d'Histoire du Temps Présent, Centre National des Recherches Scientifiques (CNRS), 17th–18th October, 1986. Although a much abbreviated version of this essay with the same title has been published in Karel A. Bartosek, René Gallissot, Denis Peschanski (eds.), *De l'exil à la résistance. Réfugiés et immigrés d'Europe Centrale en France, 1933–1945*, Paris 1989, pp. 53–59, all citations below refer to the longer version.

These three historians vary considerably in the degree to which they are critical of the native French Jewish establishment. Weinberg is decidedly the most critical while Nicault is the most sympathetic. Nevertheless, even Weinberg takes into account the external limitations imposed by French government policy.

[3]For biographical sketches of Lambert see Richard I. Cohen, *Carnet d'un Témoin, 1940–1943*, Paris 1985, introduction, pp. 13–62; Cohen, 'A Jewish Leader in Vichy France, 1940–1943. The Diary of Raymond-Raoul Lambert', in *Jewish Social Studies*, vol. XLIII (Summer–Fall 1981), pp. 291–310.

consistently put forth a far more moderate position, one significantly more sympathetic to the refugees themselves. Nevertheless, during the first phase of the refugee crisis, it was Helbronner's views that prevailed – a situation which had disastrous repercussions for those refugees who had found asylum in France. The proposition that France would serve only as a *gare de triage*, a half-way house for refugees en route to final destinations elsewhere, was, therefore, not simply a policy foisted upon an unwilling French Jewish community by an increasingly restrictionist government. Rather, it was a goal embraced quite willingly by at least one very important and influential sector of the native Jewish establishment itself.

To understand better the emergence of these positions, it is useful to look back at the early history of the Jewish relief effort. In the first months following Hitler's rise to power, there were few signs of the difficulties soon to emerge. France, in sharp contrast to most other Western nations, at first warmly welcomed the German refugees. Camille Chautemps, Minister of the Interior, together with Foreign Minister Joseph Paul-Boncour, issued directives to the French embassy and consulates in Germany to waive visa requirements for those fleeing. Border police were instructed to allow refugees to enter freely, and it was proclaimed that the German émigrés would be granted special status.[4] As a result, 25,000 of the approximately 60,000 refugees who fled Germany in 1933 flocked to France, 85 percent of whom were Jews.[5] The generosity of the French stemmed not only from the country's long-standing tradition of affording political asylum. Diplomatic factors, too, were at stake. Hitler's triumph and the ensuing crackdown on Jewish and political dissidents offered France a bittersweet diplomatic victory, fully vindicating the hard-line anti-German policy France had tenaciously pursued since the Treaty of Versailles. Providing asylum to the martyrs of "Teutonic barbarism" seemed

[4]See especially *Journal Officiel* (JO), Chambre des députés, 5th April 1933, p. 1893; Ministry of Interior Circular No. 222, 20th April 1933, in Archives, Préfecture de Police, Paris (APP) BA 407 P 13.112–3. For summaries of the various circulars and edicts dealing with French refugee policy in 1933 see especially, Police report, 'Renseignments concernant les réfugiés d'Allemagne', 10th November 1933, in APP, BA 407P 13.112–1; Police report, 'Résumé des instructions ministérielles concernant les réfugiés d'Allemagne', 27th November 1933, *ibid.*

[5]Official sources estimated that between 60–65,000 refugees left Germany in 1933. See Michael R. Marrus, *The Unwanted European Refugees in the Twentieth Century*, New York 1985, p. 129; 'L'aide aux réfugiés allemands', in *Le Temps*, 6th December 1933; Rita Thalmann, 'L'immigration allemande et l'opinion publique en France de 1933 à 1936', in *La France et l'Allemagne, 1932–1936*, Paris 1980, p. 150. Although it is usually estimated that there were 25,000 German refugees in France in December 1933, there may have been as many as 40,000 during the summer and early autumn of the year. See 'Les réfugiés allemands en France', in *Le Matin*, 5th August 1933, cutting in Archives Nationales, Paris (AN) F⁷ 13431; French ambassador, London, to the British Foreign Office, 14th September 1933, in Public Records Office, London (PRO) FO 371/16757. C8149.

On the percentage of Jews among all German refugees, see 'Report of Bernhard Kahn submitted to the [Joint Distribution Committee] Executive Committee Meeting', 4th January 1934, Joint Distribution Committee Archives, New York (JDC) No. 160; Marrus, *The Unwanted*, p. 129; Marcel Livian, *Le Parti Socialiste et l'immigration*, Paris 1982, p. 12; and '60,000 have fled from Nazis' Reich', *New York Times* (NYT), 6th December 1933, p. 18.

but a small price to pay for the tremendous harvest of international good will and support France hoped to reap now that world opinion had been brought face to face with the German terror.[6]

French Jewry warmly welcomed the government's generous policies, and in these early months of the refugee influx made every effort to ensure that the good will continued. Throughout March and April of 1933, French Jewish leaders engaged in a veritable flurry of activities on behalf of the refugee cause. Prominent Jewish journalists such as Henri Prague, Editor-in-Chief of the *Archives israélites*, actually encouraged German Jews to come to France. France, he declared, would become their "veritable Eldorado", and he predicted that the influx of newcomers would rejuvenate French Jewish institutions.[7] Simultaneously, Jewish groups sponsored mass rallies and demonstrations throughout the spring of 1933 to protest against Nazi antisemitism and to win popular support for the refugee cause. In fact it was primarily the immigrant led groups – *La Ligue internationale contre l'antisémitisme* (LICA) and the *Fédération des sociétés juives de France* (FSJF) that took the initiative in organising these events together with Liberal and Left-wing allies.[8] Nevertheless, despite some initial reluctance, native elites, including the most prominent representatives of the French rabbinate, soon joined in.[9] Perhaps most importantly, the major institutions of native French Jewry – the Central Consistory and the *Alliance*

---

[6]The French ambassador in London vividly related this shift in British opinion. Reporting to Foreign Minister Joseph Paul-Boncour in the spring of 1933, he wrote: "Qu'il en vienne donc, leur présence [that of German-Jewish refugees] développera parmi les Anglais des sentiments de méfiance à l'égard de l'Allemagne dont, hier, j'ai recueilli moi-même une manifestation significative.

Après un dîner chez Sir Austen Chamberlain, j'avais fait remarquer que 'la France avait abandonnée, à la requête de la Grande-Bretagne, l'occupation de la région rhénane; elle aurait légalement le droit d'y être encore et, si nos troupes s'y trouvaient à l'heure actuelle, les Juifs allemands ne seraient pas inquiétés ni maltraités'. Tous les Anglais ont acquiescés." M. de Fleuriau, French Ambassador to Great Britain, to Paul-Boncour, 6th April 1933, in *Documents Diplomatiques Français*, Tome 3, (17th March 1933–15th July 1933), p. 175. See also French Ambassador, Belgium, to Paul-Boncour, 30th March 1933, Archives, Ministère des Affaires Etrangères, Paris (MAE) Z (Europe 1930–1940) 710, pp. 6–7; A. Kammerer, French Ambassador in Brazil, to Paul-Boncour, 1st April 1933, in MAE SDN I E 446, pp. 25–27; NYT, 21st July 1933, p. 5.

[7]Prague, 'Une Histoire qui recommence!', in *Archives israélites* (AI), 16th March 1933, p. 41. See also Prague's other articles: 'Le Reveil', 22nd June 1933, p. 93; 'Les Leçons de l'histoire', 6th July 1933, pp. 101–102; 'Un Autre Foyer', 3rd November 1932, p. 173, all in the AI.

[8]Hyman, *op. cit.*, pp. 217–218; Rajsfus, *op. cit.*, p. 106; Thalmann, 'L'immigration allemande', p. 157; Thalmann, 'L'émigration du IIIe Reich dans la France de 1933 à 1939', in *Le Monde Juif*, No. 96 (October–December, 1979), p. 133; 'Les Protestations dans le monde', in AI, 4th May 1933, p. 70; 'La Protestation de la France contre les persécutions antisémites', in *Tribune Juive*, No. 49, 6th December 1933, pp. 843–844; 'L'antisémitisme', in *Le Temps*, 13th April 1933, p. 2; 'Nazis Menace World Say Paris Speakers', in NYT, 11th May 1933, p. 13; 'A Lyon, M. Herriot s'élève contre la persécution des Juifs', in *L'Aube*, 9th–10th April 1933, p. 3; and the numerous police reports and press clippings in APP BA/1814 241.155–1–C; APP BA/1815 241.155–1–B; APP BA/1813 241.155–C; AN F7 13430; AN F7 13432; AN F7 13433.

[9]Police report, 14th April 1933, in APP BA/1815 241.155–1–B; 'L'Assemblée Consistoriale', in AI, 8th June 1933, p. 86; 'Une protestation des rabbins français contre les persécutions dont sont victimes les juifs allemands', in *Journal d'Alsace et de Lorraine*, 3rd May 1933, cutting in Archives départementales du Bas-Rhin, (ADBR) D 460 paq. 5(36).

Israélite Universelle – jumped into the fray with respect to organising a refugee relief campaign.[10] Admittedly, they were not the only ones: throughout the early spring of 1933, no less than 15 refugee committees – some sponsored by one of the many Jewish organisations, others by a wide range of political groups – cropped up in Paris alone to assist refugees on a wide range of problems including housing, food, job placement, emigration possibilities and legal and juridical advice.[11] Still, it was the committee created by the French Jewish establishment, initially called the *Comité d'Aide et d'Accueil aux Victimes de l'antisémitisme en Allemagne*, and later reorganised and renamed the *Comité National*, that emerged as the most important source of refugee assistance and was ultimately recognised by the government as the chief spokesman on refugee issues.[12] To ensure that the borders stay open, the *Alliance Israélite*

[10]Consistoire Israélite de Paris, report, April–September, 1933, in Archives, Consistoire Israélite de Paris (ACIP) B 135 bis; ACIP, Report, August and September, 1933, ACIP B 128; 'Un Appel de M. Israel Lévy', in *Univers israélite* (UI), 21st April 1933, p. 52; 'Une protestation des rabbins français contre les persécutions dont sont victimes les juifs allemands', cutting from *Journal d'Alsace et de Lorraine*, 3rd May 1933, in ADBR D 460 paq. 5 dos. 36; 'Appel aux Juifs de France en faveur des victimes de l'antisémitisme allemand', 9th June 1933, Leo Baeck Institute Archives, New York (LBI Arch.) AR–C 1698/4099; Edmond de Rothschild, *Appel au judaisme français. Discours prononcé à la réunion du 11 juillet 1933*, Paris 1933.

[11]Joseph L. Cohen, 'Report on HICEM and on the French National Committee for German refugees', 8th August 1933, in JDC No. 617. According to a report dated 13th November 1935 of the *Service Juridique pour les réfugiés allemands* there were as many as 20 committees. (in JDC No. 602.) For a description of major Jewish committees see Nicault, *loc. cit.*, *passim*. The two most important Left-wing refugee committees were the Matteoti Committee, affiliated with the Socialist Party, and the *Secours rouge*, affiliated with the Communist Party. On the work of the other committees, see Jacques Omnès, 'L'aide aux émigrés politiques (1933–1938)', in Badia, *et al.* (eds.), *Les Bannis de Hitler*, pp. 65–104; Joly, 'L'Assistance des quakers', *ibid.*, pp. 105–116; Walter F. Peterson, *The Berlin Liberal Press in Exile. A History of the Pariser Tageblatt-Pariser Tageszeitung, 1933–1940*, Tübingen 1987, pp. 69–71; Ruth Fabian and Corinna Coulmas, *Die deutsche Emigration in Frankreich nach 1933*, Munich 1978, pp. 38–45; Jean-Michel Palmier, *Weimar en exil. Le Destin de l'émigration intellectuelle allemande antinazie en Europe et aux Etats-Unis* (2 vols.), Paris 1988, vol. I, pp. 278–283, 364–365, 401–408; Ralph Schor, *L'Opinion française et les étrangers*, Paris 1985, p. 614.

[12]The *Comité National* was actually a federation of pre-existing refugee relief committees. It was created primarily to avoid needless duplication of services and interventions with government authorities, but another goal of its founders was to concentrate authority in the hands of native Jews associated with consistorial circles. Among its sponsors were many prominent non-Jews. Its first honorary president was former Minister Paul Painlevé, who was succeeded after his death in late 1933 by Senator Henri Bérenger. Other sponsors included Senator Justin Godart; Edouard Herriot, Radical Party deputy; Senator André Honnorat; Deputy François Piétri; Georges Risler, President of the *Musée Social*; Baron Edmond de Rothschild, President of the *Consistoire Central*; Israel Lévi, the Chief Rabbi of France; and Sylvain Lévi, Professor at the *Collège de France* and President of the *Alliance Israélite Universelle*. The Committee's Executive Committee in 1933 included: Robert de Rothschild, Acting President; Albert Cahen; Jacques Helbronner, Sylvain Lévi; Jacques Sée; Pierre Dreyfus; Maurice Stern; Maurice Rueff, Albert Manuel; Bernard Melamède and Raymond-Raoul Lambert.

  On the creation of the *Comité d'Aide et d'Accueil* and later the *Comité National* see Nicault, *loc. cit.*, pp. 4–5; Joly, 'L'Aide aux émigrés juifs', pp. 37–64; Joseph C. Hyman to Henry Wienman, 16th October 1933, in JDC No. 601; 'The Activity of the HICEM for the Jewish Emigrants from Germany', reports for March, 1933 to October 1934 and July to August, 1934, in JDC No. 674; Joseph L. Cohen, 'Report on HICEM and on the French National Committee for German refugees', 8th August 1933, in JDC No. 617; 'Aide Mémoire concernant la Réunion du Comité de Liaison du 28 mai', 2nd June 1933, in Archives of the *Alliance Israélite Universelle*, Paris (AIU) X D 56; Minutes of meeting regarding the creation of the *Comité National*, n.d. [22nd or 23rd June 1933],

Universelle even promised the authorities that it would undertake full financial responsibility for the refugees, guaranteeing that they would not become public charges.[13] Thus, during these first weeks, French Jewry gave every appearance of having made a wholehearted and long-term commitment to the refugee cause.

By the summer of 1933, however, this wave of optimism and good will was rapidly giving way to deep-seated apprehensions. To a large extent, the problem was a financial one. No one – neither the government nor the official representatives of French Jewry – had expected an exodus of the magnitude or duration of that which took place in 1933. Despite the *Alliance*'s assurances that the refugees would not become public charges, the task of having to sustain a prolonged fund-raising campaign proved beyond the endurance of French Jewish institutions. By June of 1933, the *Comité d'Aide et d'Accueil* was caring for 5,799 refugees in Paris alone. No fewer than 400 persons per day knocked on the committee's door for some sort of assistance, and of these approximately 125 each day were first-time clients.[14] Expenses mounted quickly – by the summer of 1933 the Committee's budget was approaching 900,000 francs per month.[15] Unfortunately, the French Jewish community of the 1930s was ill equipped to meet these demands. Nevertheless, there were several very wealthy families, most notably the Rothschilds, who were able to pour huge sums into refugee relief; indeed, they paid a full third of all the Committee's expenses in 1933.[16] Yet, nearly one-half of France's total Jewish population of about 260,000, were of recent immigrant origin themselves and could barely

LBI Arch. AR–C 1698/4099; Raymond-Raoul Lambert, 'L'accueil de la France', in *Revue Juive de Genève*, No. 8 (May 1933), pp. 348–351; AI, 22nd June 1933, p. 99.

On official recognition of the *Comité National* as the sole spokesman on refugee matters see letter from Chautemps to [Robert de Rothschild] President of the *Comité National*, 19th July 1933, attached to *Comité National* circular No. 1, 13th August 1933, in MAE, SDN I E 451; 'Création du "Comité National Français de Secours aux émigrés Allemands victimes de l'antisémitisme"', in UI, 30th June 1933, pp. 349–352.

The *Comité-National* also had important provincial branches, the principal one being the *Fédération des Comités de Secours de l'Est de la France*, headquartered in Strasbourg. See 'Conférence régionale à Metz des Comités de Secours pour les réfugiés', in *Tribune Juive*, No. 46, (17th November 1933),
p. 793; 'La Fédération des Comités de Secours de l'Est', in *Tribune Juive*, No. 47 (24th November 1933), p. 809; 'Metz. Pour les fugitifs d'Allemagne', in UI, 17th November 1933, p. 293.

[13]Police report, 5th April 1933 in APP BA/1814 241.155–1–C. See also MAE, Contrôle des Etrangers, to the British ambassador in Paris, 12th April 1933, in MAE Z 710, pp. 51–52.

[14]Comité d'Aide et d'Accueil, 'Compte rendu, No. 2, Activité du Secrétariat Général du 20 au 30 mai 1933', in AIU X D 56; 'Compte rendu, No. 3, Activité du Secrétariat Général du 1er au 10 juin, 1933', *ibid.*; 'Compte rendu, No. 4, Activité du Secrétariat Général du 10 juin–30 juin, 1933', in MAE SDN I E 451.

[15]Israel Lévi, the Chief Rabbi of France and Sylvain Lévi, the president of the *Alliance Israélite Universelle*, sent a desperate telegram to Cyrus Adler on 2nd June 1933: "Need instant help. Five thousand Jewish refugees. Number constantly growing. Daily expense thirty thousand francs. Funds threaten exhaustion." in JDC, No. 617. See also Comité d'Aide et d'Accueil, 'Compte rendu, No. 2, Activité du Secrétariat Général du 20 au 30 mai 1933', in AIU X D 56; 'L'Organisation des secours pour les réfugiés allemands', in AI, 6th July 1933, p. 105.

[16]Joseph L. Cohen, 'Report on HICEM and on the French National Committee for German Refugees', 8th August 1933, in JDC No. 617; Mr. Harvey, British embassy, Paris to J. V. Perowne, 10th January 1934, in PRO FO 371/17698/C308.

afford major donations.[17] In response, French Jewish leaders began a desperate search for outside funding. France's Chief Rabbi, Israel Lévi, organised a fund-raising campaign in the United States and warned potential American donors that, "A catastrophe is at the gate".[18] At the same time, the *Comité National*, despite its earlier promises, began to appeal directly to the French government for assistance. Indeed, no sooner had the Committee been created in July of 1933 than its acting president, Robert de Rothschild, notified Minister of Interior Chautemps that it was teetering on the verge of bankruptcy. Without an immediate infusion of public funds, Rothschild threatened, the Committee would be forced to close, throwing the 3,500 refugees currently on relief out on to the streets. And, he warned, deprived of food and shelter "these unfortunates in their distress risk disturbing the public order".[19] Such desperate appeals had the desired effect. The *Comité National* found a major American donor: the Joint Distribution Committee.[20] And the French government, although refusing any direct financial assistance, did offer the use of abandoned hospitals and military barracks to serve as temporary refugee housing, supplementing the use of hotels.[21] Thus, the worst case scenarios predicted by Lévi and Rothschild were, at least for the moment, averted.

[17]On the size of the French Jewish population in the mid-1930s see Jacques Adler, *The Jews of Paris and the Final Solution. Communal Response and Internal Conflicts, 1940–1944*, New York 1987, p. 5. The FSJF was actually the first Jewish organisation to establish a relief committee for the refugees, but it had to abandon these efforts due to lack of funds. See Weinberg, *op. cit.*, p. 111; Hyman, *op. cit.*, p. 208; Jacques Biélinky, 'FSJF', in UI, 15th December 1933, p. 421; Joseph L. Cohen, 'Report on HICEM and on the French National Committee for German Refugees', 8th August 1933, in JDC No. 617.

[18]At the behest of Lévi, Edward Mamelsdorf, Bernard J. Shoninger, Karl Hirschland and Ludwig Lewisohn formed a committee in the United States to raise money for the French campaign. See their appeals to Justice Irving Lehman, 22nd June 1933 and Mamelsdorf to Lehman, 2nd June 1933, both in JDC No. 617. Robert de Rothschild also appealed to Stephen Wise for financial assistance in July 1933. See Jacques Biélinky, 'Deux manifestations du Comité français pour le Congrès mondial juif', in UI, 28th July 1933, pp. 487–88.

[19]Rothschild to Chautemps, 26th July 1933, in APP BA 407 P 13.112–1. See also [*Comité National*] 'Note pour M. le Président du Conseil', 20th July 1933, in LBI Arch. AR–C 1698/4099; 'Procès verbal de la 2ᵉᵐᵉ séance tenue par la Commission Interministérielle des réfugiés israélites allemands', 16th October 1933, in MAE Z 711, pp. 39–40.

The 3,500 refugees mentioned by Rothschild were only those receiving assistance. According to police estimates from late 1933, there were close to 10,000 refugees from Germany in the Department of the Seine alone, 7,304 of whom had actually registered with the Préfecture de Police in Paris. Police report, 28th November 1933 [attached to Police report 'Renseignements concernant les réfugiés d'Allemagne', 10th November 1933,] in APP BA 407ᴾ 13.112–1.

[20]In 1933, the JDC covered 20 percent of the *Comité National*'s budget. See Yehuda Bauer, *My Brother's Keeper. A History of the American Jewish Joint Distribution Committee, 1929–1939*, Philadelphia 1974, p. 141. By the late 1930s the JDC was contributing a far heavier share: in 1937 it adopted the principle of giving the newly created French Jewish relief committee, the *Comité d'Assistance aux Réfugiés* (CAR), a sum equal to that collected in France. By 1938–1939, the JDC was subsidising 90–100 percent of the CAR's budget. France regularly received the largest allotment of JDC funds of all refugee-receiving countries. See Morris Troper to Robert de Rothschild and A. Lévy, CAR, 14th February 1940, in JDC No. 617.

[21]The government offered these facilities in July of 1933. In October of 1933, about 700 refugees in the Paris region were housed in these barracks, while 1,700 continued to be housed in hotels. See Police reports, 10th October 1933, in APP BA/1814 241.155–1–A; 'Les réfugiés Allemands dans la région parisienne', November 1933, in APP BA/1814 241.155–1–A. See also Comité National, 'Compte rendu, Activité du Secrétariat Général du 16 octobre au 31 décembre 1933', in AIU

Budgetary factors alone, however, were not the Committee's sole source of concern. Cultural and political problems also plagued the relief effort. One particularly thorny issue was the all too visible Germanness of the refugees. According to journalist Janine Auscher many French Jews, fiercely patriotic, were reluctant to give money to the relief campaign since the refugees in their eyes were "above all . . . Germans, thus our former enemies".[22] Moreover, French Jewish elites repeatedly reproached their wealthy German co-religionists for refusing to carry their share of the relief burden. According to one well known journalist, Jacques Biélinky, himself of Eastern European immigrant background, wealthy German Jews, brought up in a Prussian culture which had done little to inculcate the virtue of charity "had opposed all [the *Comité National's*] solicitations with an icy refusal".[23] Jacques Helbronner, too, railed against those German Jews who were gambling away their fortunes on the Riviera while their French co-religionists back in Paris slaved away on behalf of the less fortunate victims of Nazi persecution.[24] Attempts at persuasion ultimately gave way to force: according to a report in the *Tribune Juive*, the major organ of Strasbourg Jewry, the *Comité National* actually petitioned the government to expel one wealthy German banker who had repeatedly refused to make a contribution.[25]

East European Jews were scarcely more sympathetic. Resentful of the fact that they had been looked down upon by their German co-religionists, some were not

France, XD 56 (226); 'Procès verbal de la 2ème séance tenue par la Commission Interministérielle des réfugiés israélites allemands', 16th October 1933, MAE Z 711, p. 40; 'Procès verbal de la 4ème séance tenue par la Commission Interministérielle des réfugiés israélites allemands', 11th November 1933, in MAE Z 711, pp. 99–100; Joly, 'L'Aide aux émigrés juifs', pp. 53–54. On the refusal of the government to offer further assistance see Police report, 'Réunion à la Présidence du Conseil des réprensants des diverses départements et services intéressés [aux réfugiés allemands]', 23rd September 1933, in APP BA 407ᴾ 13.112.1. Similar facilities had been made available in Mulhouse. See 'L'Assemblée Consistoriale', in AI, 8th June 1933, p. 87.

[22] Janine Auscher, 'L'Oeuvre du Comité d'Aide et d'Accueil aux réfugiés allemands', in UI, 28th July 1933, p. 481. Similarly, Jacques Helbronner explained the delay in the organisation of French Jewish refugee work saying: "C'est que les français de religion israélite sont français avant d'être juifs et que nous avons eu du mal à oublier ce que les juifs allemands ont été pendant la guerre." Minutes, Meeting to discuss the creation of the *Comité National*, 22nd or 23rd June 1933, p. 11, in LBI Arch. AR–C 1698/4099. See also 'Création du 'Comité National Français . . .', in UI, 30th June 1933, p. 351; Biélinky, 'Paris Hospitalier', in UI, 22nd December 1933, p. 440; F. W., 'France: La question de l'immigration allemande', in UI, 3rd May 1935, p. 526.

[23] Biélinky, 'Deux réunions en faveur des réfugiés', in UI, 26th January 1934, p. 606; Biélinky, 'Les victimes de Hitler en France', in *Kadimah*, 5ème année, No. 11 (28th September 1934), p. 14.

[24] Minutes of meeting regarding the creation of the *Comité National*, 22nd or 23rd June 1933, in LBI Arch. AR–C 1698/4099. Rothschild obviously complained to his friend Felix Warburg about this problem since at a meeting with the High Commissioner of Refugees Warburg proclaimed: "Then there is a small number of Jews who foresaw what was coming and who got some of their funds out of Germany, and they are rather noisy and objectionable in the cafés, in the public places in Paris. And they make the life of the Jews in Paris difficult and have a tendency to spread antisemitism. They have not contributed to any great extent to the relief funds. And they will be made to do so even if they are unwilling, but the process is painful and slow . . . The refugees in France are slow and disagreeable, and the effect has been that antisemitism is growing in France by leaps and bounds." Refugee Committee Meeting called by James G. McDonald, 25th February 1934, in JDC No. 404. For other examples of this resentment see Ernest Ginsburger, 'Tribune des lecteurs', in UI, 3rd November 1933, p. 218; Pierre Lévy, letter to the editor, in UI, 1st September 1933, p. 654; 'Nos Echos. Ouvert le samedi', in UI, 16th February 1934, p. 692.

[25] 'La disparition de Comité de Secours aux réfugiés', in *Tribune Juive*, No. 10 (9th March 1934), p. 185.

altogether displeased that the tables had now turned radically. As one journalist noted:

> "Many German Jews, extremely patriotic and extremely conscious of their dignity, rose up not long ago against the immigration of East European Jews who might have harmed their considerable social standing and reinforced the impact of anti-Jewish propaganda. Today, they are the ones harming the situation of their co-religionists and reinforcing the antipathy against Jews that exists in the country where they seek to settle. Thus, the hostile attitude taken by German Jews against the immigrants has now suddenly turned against themselves."[26]

Summing up the whole dilemma, another journalist declared:

> "At the beginning, it's true, German Jews found a warm and generous welcome. But since then a good deal has changed. French Jews complain that the newcomers have brought with them the particular faults of the Germans. Too noisy, too convinced of the superiority of German civilisation. In brief – veritables 'Boches'.
>
> Immigrant Jews from Eastern Europe, for their part, always mistrustful of the 'Yekkes' [German Jews] have at times reproached them for their lack of solidarity. Moreover, people often distinguish, just as many antisemites do with respect to Jews in general, between each individual considered separately and the group to which he belongs. People admit that there may be 'chic types' among the German Jews; none the less, they retain a [negative] opinion of them as a whole."[27]

Political tensions drove yet another wedge into relations between the native French Jewish elites and the refugees. Already in April of 1933, Chief Rabbi Lévi had counselled Jews to abstain from mass demonstrations to protest against Nazi antisemitism.[28] Ostensibly motivated by the fear that such demonstrations might inspire an even harsher Nazi crackdown against those Jews who remained in Germany, there is little doubt that Lévi had domestic considerations in mind as well. The strongly Left-wing cast of the protest rallies and demonstrations was quickly making many French Jews, who frequently attributed the rise of antisemitism directly to the disproportionate influence of Jews in the Socialist and Communist parties, extremely uncomfortable and fearful of an antisemitic backlash.[29] Many in the Jewish establishment therefore felt compelled to warn

---

[26]L.D., 'Que faut-il penser de l'immigration d'éléments indésirables?', in *Tribune Juive*, No. 28 (9th July 1937), p. 1.

[27]Martin, 'Ce qui se passe chez nous. Les émigrés d'Allemagne en France et la question juive', in *La Terre retrouvée*, 25th March 1936, p. 10, also reprinted as, 'Les émigrés d'Allemagne en France et la question juive', in UI, 24th April 1936, pp. 485–486. See also 'Billet Strasbourgeois', in *Tribune Juive*, No. 12 (25th March 1933), p. 262; L. D., 'Ce que nous apprennent les nouveaux immigrés', in *Tribune Juive*, No. 10 (6th March 1936), pp. 145–46.

[28]Hyman *op. cit.*, p. 218; 'Contre l'antisémitisme hitlérien', in *L'Oeuvre*, 7th April 1933, cutting in APP BA/1814 241.155–1–G; 'Rabbi asks French not to annoy Nazis', NYT, 7th April 1933, p. 12. See also Lambert, 'Tendons la main aux savants allemands juifs persécutés!', in UI, 15th December 1933, p. 406.

[29]In June of 1933 Helbronner, for example, declared: "Ces groupements [Left-wing refugee committees] sont en train de causer à ces réfugiés allemands d'une part et aux français israélites d'autre part, des dangers que l'on ne soupçonne pas; que des gens qui ont des préoccupations politiques prennent pour continuer leur politique l'arme de l'antisémitisme, c'est leur affaire, mais il est indispensable que les français israélites et que les autres personnalités de religion non israélite . . . n'aient pas l'impression qu'on veut se servir d'eux dans un but politique. Or il a été mis sous nos yeux des tracts et des journaux de ces groupements qui sont en train d'exciter les passions pour reprendre plus tôt des sentiments d'antisémitisme." Minutes, Meeting to discuss the creation of the *Comité National*, 23rd June 1933, p. 10, in LBI Arch. AR–C 1698/4099. See also Assemblée Générale, Meeting of the Central Consistory, 27th May 1934, in ACIP B 132⁵ (affaires administratives); Dr.

the refugees that they had better behave. Expressing the irritation felt by many native French Jews, Rabbi Ernest Ginsburger declared: "It seems that they [the refugees] apparently do not understand that they must observe a reserve, a discretion, I'd dare say even a prudence of which they should not make a spectacle. Who knows whether this effacement, this modesty would not have been better for their cause?" Even "the Pollaks," he maintained, had conducted themselves better. Although they too had been persecuted, they had found in France a happy and peaceful refuge "without meetings, without grandiloquent appeals to justice, to humanity, to history, to the universal conscience. Reduced almost entirely to their own devices", these Poles, he continued, "knew how to create an honourable position; they acquired for themselves esteem and consideration, engaged in economic and social philanthropic activities, and, conscious of their debt, at the time of danger, as fearless volunteers of war, they gave their blood to France. Couldn't their conduct and their economic activities serve as examples to the new refugees or must we call into question their much vaunted capabilities, their intelligence, their science, their initiative?"[30]

Political discord surfaced even at the *Comité National* itself, to the dismay of the native elites. As a result of the ever-growing volume of demands for assistance, Lambert reinforced security at the Committee in the spring of 1933 to prevent disorder from erupting among the impatient crowds that gathered daily outside on the street; in July, he even requested a police presence to help maintain order.[31] Incidents nevertheless broke out. According to Lambert, in late May two refugees "whose incorrect behaviour, threats and revolutionary remarks, have created unrest in the street" ultimately assaulted several employees of the Committee. Following a police investigation, these troublemakers were deported.[32] In the autumn of 1933, a far more serious incident occurred. At the Andral Hospital, one of the sites donated by the government to house the refugees, a full-fledged demonstration against the Committee broke out. The

---

Jean Sterne, 'Judaisme et opinions politiques', in UI, 24th April 1936, pp. 483–484; Rabi, 'De 1906 à 1939', p. 382. On the political activities of the émigré community, see Fabian and Coulmas, *op. cit.*, pp. 50–61; Peterson, *op. cit.*, *passim*; Palmier, *op. cit.*, *passim*; Ursula Langkau-Alex, *Volksfront für Deutschland? Vorgeschichte und Gründung des Ausschusses zur Vorbereitung einer deutschen Volksfront, 1933–1936*, vol. I, Frankfurt a. Main 1977.

[30]Ernest Ginsburger, 'Tribune des lectures', in UI, 3rd November 1933, pp. 218–219.

[31]Comité d'Aide et d'Accueil, 'Compte rendu, No. 2, Activité du Secrétariat Général du 20 au 30 mai 1933', in AIU X D 56; [Lambert], Comité National, 'Note pour M. le Préfecture de Police', 25th July 1933, in APP BA 407[P] 13.112–1.

[32]Comité d'Aide et d'Accueil, 'Compte rendu, No. 2, Activité du Secrétariat Général du 20 au 30 mai 1933', in AIU X D 56. R.C., a German refugee who worked for the *Comité National* described the tense conditions there as follows: "La plupart de ceux qui travaillaient n'avaient pas la formation professionnelle requise, ce qui explique qu'il y ait eu tant d'incapables au comité. Les émigrés s'en plaignaient et reprochaient aux employés, bien souvent réfugiés eux-mêmes, leur attitude de fonctionnaires bornés. L'ambiance était unimaginable: nous étions sans cesse débordés par des montagnes de courrier par le monde qui se pressait dans la salle d'attente et qui faisait parfois la queue dans la rue depuis la veille au soir. Il faut avoir l'esprit bien trempé ou le coeur insensible pour arriver à vivre et travailler au milieu de tant de misères." R.C., 'A Vichy, dans la gueule du loup', in Gilbert Badia, *et al.*, *Exilés en France, Souvenirs d'antifascistes allemands émigrés (1933–1945)*, Paris 1982, p. 124. See also Peterson, *op. cit.*, p. 73; Joly, 'L'Aide aux émigrés juifs', pp. 50–51.

Left-wing protesters charged that the Committee had betrayed every promise it had ever made to the refugees. The food was disgusting, the pocket money woefully inadequate, and the Committee's personnel mean-spirited. But the Committee's worst crime was having herded the refugees into military barracks, which, the protesters and their Communist supporters alleged, were no better than Nazi-style concentration camps. "The administration of the Committee", their tracts proclaimed, "has lost our confidence and has shown itself to be from the lowest to the highest-level functionary a band of swindlers". Robert de Rothschild's response was swift and sharp. He demanded that the police expel the ringleaders who "not having the least recognition for the hospitality offered by our country, continue to engage in propaganda of a clear Communist tendency".[33]

By the end of 1933, the relationship between the refugees and the *Comité National* was thus sorely strained. Refugees deeply resented what they perceived to be diminishing financial support, and the patronising and condescending tone of those in charge of relief. French Jewish elites, for their part, expressed shock and anger at the impertinence and above all at the ingratitude of the newcomers. As Ernest Ginsburger again pointed out, French Jewry had certainly done their humanitarian duty, but, he asked, had the refugees done theirs?[34] If they truly appreciated the hospitality offered them, it was now time that they show more tact and discretion – that they give up what Lambert called, "that gregarious mentality, that need to band together in the service of slogan-brandishing associations".[35] Or as Robert de Rothschild matter-of-factly put it: "If they are

[33]Police report, 'au sujet de distribution de tracts dans les bastions des réfugiés allemands', 21st November 1933, in APP BA/1814 241.155–1–A. Aside from this agitation, which, according to the police ended in failure, the police reported that conditions in the camps were relatively good and that the refugees were well behaved. For various police reports on the camps see reports of 4th October 1933, in BA/1815 241.155–1–D; G. Oudara, Directeur, Commissaire Spécial de Police (Renseignments généraux), 19th October 1933, in BA/1814 241.155–1–A; October 1933, in BA/1813 241.155–B; 'Les réfugiés allemands dans la région parisienne', November 1933, in BA/1814 241.155–1–A, all in APP.

For less sanguine descriptions of conditions in these barracks see Hanna Schramm and Barbara Vormeier, *Vivre à Gurs: Un camp de concentration français, 1940–1941*, transl. by Irene Petit, 1979, p. 197; Madeleine Misard, 'Comment la France absorbe-t-elle l'immigration judéo-allemand?', in *L'Excelsior*, 22nd January 1934, cutting in APP BA/1815 241.155–1–G; Margaret Hess, 'Little Germany in Paris gives a haven to Exiles', NYT, 15th April 1934, sec. IX, p. 11; Georges Imann, 'Chanaansur Seine', in *Je Suis Partout*, 25th January 1934, cutting in AIU, Ms. 650, Boite 15 (50); and the sharply critical assessment of the High Commissioner for Refugees, 'Texte du discours de Sir James G. McDonald, Ht. Commissaire pour les réfugiés (juifs et autres) radiodiffusé par les stations de TSF de la National Broadcasting Co.', 14th January 1934, in LBI Arch. AR–C 1638/4099.

[34]Ernest Ginsburger, 'Tribune des Lectures', in UI, 3rd November 1933, p. 219.

[35]Lambert, 'L'avenir de l'émigration allemande et l'opinion française', in UI, 12th October 1934, p. 65. William Oualid similarly warned the refugees to abstain from all political activities in the wake of the Stavisky affair street demonstration of February 1934 during which five Communist German émigrés were arrested. Oualid, 'Une tendance à laquelle il faut savoir résister', in UI, 9th March 1934, p. 93. See also Peterson *op. cit.*, p. 76. The most blatant example of the paternalism of native Jews towards the refugees was the Manual put out in 1938 by the CAR. Its six-point programme was: "1) Ne faites pas de politique, puisque les lois de notre pays vous l'interdisent; 2) Surveillez votre tenue; 3) Soyez polis et discrets; 4) Soyez modestes. Ne vantez pas les qualités du pays que vous venez de quitter, et qui vous semblent manquer en France. 'Chez nous, tout allait mieux' est une formule qui choquera les Français qui vous écoutent; 5) Apprenez vite à vous exprimer en français. Ne parlez pas à haute voix et, si vous parlez une langue étrangère, évitez de le faire en

not happy here, let them leave. They are guests whom we have warmly received, but they should not go about rocking the boat".[36]

Yet all of these problems, troublesome as they were, could have, and probably would have been surmounted had it not been for the single most difficult challenge that confronted the *Comité National* in this period – the severe job shortage which resulted from the Depression and the government's ensuing retreat from its formerly liberal position.[37] Indeed, no sooner had the refugees begun to arrive than a host of pressure groups began to raise the hue and cry that the refugees presented a grave economic threat. French workers were none too eager to see yet another group of foreigners snatching up jobs which, in their opinion, belonged first and foremost to the French. Although legislation had already been passed in 1932 setting quotas on the numbers of foreigners who could work as salaried employees in a wide range of industries, labour unions nevertheless remained vigilant.[38] Already in May of 1933, the *Comité d'Aide et d'Accueil* noted that "a certain opposition is manifesting itself among the ranks of organised labour against the granting of work authorisations to our refugees because certain émigrés might accept work at substandard wages and for more than an 8-hour day".[39] And, according to Emile Farinet, a Socialist Party militant, the refugee crisis could only be solved by an "exodus [of the émigrés] to our fertile French provinces".[40] Small business owners, especially in Alsace and Lorraine, were in an even greater uproar, fearing competition from refugees who had already begun to create new businesses and industries in the region. Their lobbying efforts, organised by the local chambers of commerce and tinged with a heavy dose of antisemitism, were so successful that the central government eventually closed the border provinces altogether to further refugee settlement.[41]

public, dans la rue, dans un transport en commun, à la terrasse d'un café; 6) Respectez toutes nos lois et toutes nos habitudes." See Rajsfus, *op. cit.*, p. 139; *La Juste Parole*, No. 38 (20th July 1938), p. 17.

[36]Original draft of Rothschild's speech to the General Assembly of the Consistory of Paris held on 26th May 1935. According to Weinberg, this statement was deleted from the subsequent printed versions of the speech. Weinberg, *op. cit.*, p. 76; Hyman, *op. cit.*, p. 204.

[37]On the impact of the Depression see Michael R. Marrus and Robert O. Paxton, *Vichy France and the Jews*, New York 1981, pp. 34–35; Schor, *L'Opinion française*, pp. 547–611. By the end of 1934, the number of unemployed was 356,000. See 'Le problème de chômage et de la main d'oeuvre étrangère', in *Le Temps*, 18th November 1934, p. 8. For a stimulating discussion of the impact of economic depressions on xenophobia in general from the late nineteenth century until today see Gérard Noiriel, *Le Creuset français. Histoire de l'immigration xix*ᵉ*-xx*ᵉ*-siècles*, Paris 1988.

[38]For the provisions of the 1932 law see *Journal Officiel*, Lois et décrets, 22nd October 1932, p. 11310; Schramm and Vormeier, *op. cit.*, p. 212; Livian, *op. cit.*, pp. 10–11; Marrus and Paxton, *op. cit.*, pp. 54–55; Schor, *L'Opinion française*, pp. 588–596.

[39]Comité d'Aide et d'Accueil, 'Activité du Secrétariat Général du 20–30 mai, 1933', in AIU X D 56. See also Thalmann, 'L'immigration allemande', p. 158; Schor, *L'Opinion française*, pp. 559–579. According to Victor Basch, President of the *Ligue des droits de l'homme*, "Beaucoup d'ouvriers sont refoulés parce que, parfois, la CGT [*Confédération Générale du Travail*] elle-même le demande, par suite de la surabondance de la main-d'oeuvre française dans certaines corporations . . ." 'Le Congrès international des Ligues de droits de l'Homme', in *Les Cahiers des Droits de l'Homme* (CDH), 20th January 1933, p. 29.

[40]Emile Farinet, 'Appel aux militants du Parti. Venez en aide aux exilés allemands qui cherchent du travail et des amitiés', in *Le Populaire*, 3rd August 1933, cutting in APP BA/1814 241.155.1-G.

[41]On xenophobia among merchants and artisans in general during periods of depression, see Noiriel, *op. cit.*, p. 272; Schor, *L'Opinion française*, pp. 597–600. On Alsace and Lorraine in particular, see

Members of the liberal professions, especially lawyers and doctors, were no less protectionist. Their powerful national syndicates pressed relentlessly to reinforce already stringent legislation restricting the number of foreigners practising their professions. Ultimately, they succeeded in pushing through laws that discriminated not only against foreigners, but, for the first time in French history, against naturalised French citizens as well. In 1934 naturalised foreigners were legally barred from practising the profession of law for a full ten years following the receipt of their French citizenship. In 1935, in the aftermath of a wave of mass demonstrations and strikes at French universities protesting the "unfair competition" posed by foreign medical students, many of whom were Central and East European Jews (in one case a Jewish medical student was actually lynched), a similar law was passed that stipulated a five-year waiting period on the practice of medicine by naturalised doctors.[42]

Faced with this shrill protectionist onslaught, it is not surprising that the government began to retreat from its extremely liberal policy. Already by the summer of 1933 it implemented a number of piecemeal measures to narrow down the category of those who could be considered eligible for political asylum. The most important of these was the refusal to grant entry visas or residence permits to any refugee not possessing either German citizenship or an International Nansen passport. This directive had serious repercussions since nearly 50

'Procès verbal de la Ière séance tenue par la Commission Interministérielle des réfugiés allemands', 27th May 1933, in MAE Z 711, p. 94; Président du Conseil, Ministre de la Guerre (Direction Général des Services d'Alsace et de Lorraine) et Ministre de l'Intérieur, Sûreté Nationale (signed by Chautemps and Guy de la Chambre) to the Prefects of Bas-Rhin, Haut-Rhin and Moselle, 1st July 1933, APP BA 407 P 113.112–1; Foreign Ministry (Europe), Note, 18th July 1933, in MAE Z 710, pp. 196–197; J. Morize to Paul-Boncour, [20th] July 1933, in MAE Z 710, p. 207; Police report, 'Réunion à la Président du Conseil des représentants des divers départements et services intéressés [aux réfugiés allemands]', 23rd September 1933, in APP BA 407[P] 13.112–1; 'L'installation des réfugiés allemands en France et particulièrement dans les départements recouvrés', in *Les Dernières Nouvelles de Strasbourg*, 10th December 1933, clipped in ADBR D460 paq. 5/36; 'Les réfugiés allemands en France', in *Le Matin*, 5th August 1933, cutting in AN F[7] 13431; Emil Lengyel, 'Refugees from Hitlerism', *New York Herald Tribune, Magazine*, 19th November 1933, pp. 9–10; Thalmann, 'L'immigration allemande', pp. 162–163.

Roland-Marcel, Prefect of Bas-Rhin warned that as a result of these economic complaints, "Il est indiscutable qu'un certain antisémitisme se reveille ici et qu'il nous faut y prendre garde." Prefect Bas-Rhin, Cabinet, 'Note pour M. le Secrétaire Général', 30th June 1933, in ADBR D 460 paq. 5/36. The situation had become so serious that Israel Lévi, the Chief Rabbi of France, actually met with Roland-Marcel to discuss ways to diminish antisemitism. See 'L'installation des réfugiés allemands dans les départements recouvrés', in *Le Matin*, 17th August 1933, cutting in ADBR D 460 paq. 5/36; 'Les réfugiés allemands dans l'est', in *Le Figaro*, 18th August 1933, cutting in ADBR D 460, paq. 5/36; and 'La question des réfugiés allemands', in *Tribune Juive*, 25th August 1933, p. 565.
[42]The legislation regarding lawyers was passed on 19th July 1934; that regarding doctors on 26th July 1935. See Noiriel, *op. cit.*, pp. 284–287; Schor, 'L'Opinion française', pp. 31–32; *idem, L'Opinion française*, pp. 601–611; Livian, *op. cit.*, p. 49; Jean-Charles Bonnet, *Les Pouvoirs publics français et l'immigration dans l'entre-deux-guerres*, Lyon 1976, pp. 201–235, 283–284; Etienne de Véricourt, 'Le Problème des étrangers dans le cadre de la profession médicale', in *Les Etudes*, No. 5 (5th May 1935), p. 351; Jean Pécout, *L'Etude et l'exercise de la médecine par les étrangers*, Paris 1939, introduction and pp. 40–46; Maurice Mordagne, 'La situation des étudiants en médecine et médecins juifs allemands dans les facultés de Médecine', in *Le Concours Médical*, 2nd September 1934, pp. 2453–2456; Emile Sergent, 'Etudiants et médecins étrangers en France', in *Revue des Deux Mondes*, 15th April 1935, pp. 814–828.

percent of all the refugees who entered France from Germany were of East European origin, mainly Poles. Most of these people had lived in Germany for many years – the majority had even been born there – but either they had never acquired German citizenship, or they had been stripped of it by Nazi decree. The French government now declared that those individuals still holding East European passports would be considered "economic" rather than "political" refugees, and as such, they were to be repatriated to Eastern Europe.[43] Still, despite this and other measures, the flow of refugees into France continued, and in October of 1933 Interior Minister Chautemps formally declared an end to the liberal regime for German refugees. German refugees would still be allowed to enter France, but they would no longer be treated in a privileged manner. Henceforth, like all other foreigners, they would have to secure an entry visa in advance, a procedure which was becoming ever more difficult.[44] In November France announced that she would no longer serve as the world's "dumping ground".[45] At best, she would act as a *gare de triage* – a transit station – for émigrés en route to final destinations elsewhere. As Senator Henry Bérenger, France's

[43] A police report of 30th June 1933 claimed that of the 4,900 refugees who had arrived in Paris as of March, 1933, 50 percent were German Jews, 40 percent Poles, and 10 percent stateless. This report noted: "suivant les dernières instructions reçues, les soi-disant réfugiés israélites polonais font l'objet d'une mesure de refoulement lorsque leurs passeports n'ont pas été visés par les autorités français en Allemand". In APP BA/1814 241.155–1–A. Of a total of 5,600 Polish and stateless Jews in France as of December 1933, it was estimated that only 1,190 or 21 percent had been born in Poland. See M. Kramarz, 'Les Juifs polonais réfugiés d'Allemagne', in UI, 29th December 1933, p. 477.

According to Ministry of Interior, *Sûreté Nationale*, Circular No. 40 of 1st April 1933, if France were to accept these "non-Allemands sans ressources et sans papiers . . . il ne sera plus possible par la suite de [les] refouler vers l'Allemagne". In ADBR D 460 paq. 5 (36). Similarly, Guy de la Chambre, the Under-Secretary of State for the President of the Council, noted that "de nombreux israélites polonais qui s'étaient fixés en Allemagne sont entrés en Alsace par la Sarre; il y aurait lieu de s'entendre avec la Pologne pour permettre leur repatriement". 'Procès verbal de la Ière séance tenue par la Commission Interministérielle des réfugiés allemands', 27th May 1933, in MAE Z 711, p. 94. On refugees with Nansen passports see Minister of Interior, Sûreté Générale, to the Prefect of Bas-Rhin, 22nd June 1933, in ADBR D 460, paq. 5/36; Ministry of Foreign Affairs (Europe), Note, 18th July 1933, in MAE Z 710, pp. 196–197. Speculating on the motives behind this hostility towards East Europeans, Bernhard Kahn pointed out that France was particularly wary of granting work permits to these refugees since, according to reciprocal treaties held with several East European nations, they would have been eligible for unemployment insurance after six months on a job. Kahn to Stephany, 25th July 1935, in JDC No. 602. There is also little doubt that antisemitism directed specifically against Eastern European Jews, who were frequently depicted as the most undesirable of all immigrants, played a role as well. See for example: Blanchet, 'Note pour la Sous-Direction des Chancelleries et du Contentieux', 21st March 1931, in MAE Z 433, pp. 36–37; Police report, 24th October 1933, in APP BA/1814 241.155–1–A; A. Mallet, to the Director of the *Sûreté Nationale*, Cabinet, 24th May 1933, in ADBR D 460 paq. 5/36. To defend their interests East European refugees even formed the *Comité pour les juifs polonais réfugiés d'Allemagne*. See Biélinky, 'La situation des 'Ostjuden' réfugiés en France', in UI, 27th October 1933, pp. 186–187; Biélinky, 'Deux réunions en faveur des réfugiés: A l'association des Juifs polonais réfugiés d'Allemagne', in UI, 26th January 1934, p. 607; Comité pour la défense des droits des israélites en Europe centrale et orientale, *La défense des droits et de la dignité des réfugiés et apatrides israélites et non-israélites en France, 1934, 1935, et 1936*. Paris [n.d.], pp. 8 and *passim*.

[44] 'Procès-verbal de la 3ème séance tenue par la Commission Interministérielle des réfugiés allemands', in MAE Z 711, p. 70. See also Schor, *L'Opinion française*, p. 616.

[45] Marrus, *The Unwanted*, p. 147.

first delegate to the newly created League of Nations High Commission for Refugees (and the honorary president of the *Comité National*) proclaimed in December of 1933, "the refugees that France has received must not remain on its soil, but must be re-distributed among other countries further away and more suited to receive them . . ."[46]

The question that needs to be raised with regard to French Jewish elites is not simply how they reacted to this shift in policy, but whether and to what degree they may have even played a direct role in bringing it about. To be sure, the Depression imposed very real and severe limitations on relief work – for it was clear that work permits for the refugees would be allocated only on a very minimal basis.[47] Whether the new immigrants were truly harmful to the French economy was then, as today, a matter of considerable debate. Yet, that there existed a strong popular perception that they constituted a serious economic threat is beyond a doubt. French Jewish elites felt, therefore, that if they were to avoid the charge of being unpatriotic, of placing their Jewish interests above their commitments to the French people as a whole, they had best address these concerns. In a speech of 30th June 1933 announcing the official opening of the *Comité National*, Robert de Rothschild proclaimed that French Jews were bound by a double obligation. Not only did "the most simple duties of humanity command" them "to welcome them [the refugees], [and] to help them secure new means of existence". But, no less important, he declared, was the duty French Jews owed to the French people who had so graciously offered their hospitality: "There is at this moment in our country an unemployment crisis which we must take care not to aggravate, since French opinion would not support – and rightly so – that these Germans, no matter how worthy they are of being treated with kindness, become an object of preferential treatment here."[48] Thus, Fernand Corcos, a prominent French Zionist and member of the League for the Rights of Man and Citizen, maintained that: "If French workers were to run up against jobs taken without discernment by Germans, the most regrettable misunderstandings could arise."[49] Similarly, Senator André Honnorat, director of the *Comité des savants*, which supervised the placement of refugee intellectuals, deemed it "dangerous to welcome too many German Jews in France"; to do so "would provoke a backlash of jealousy among unemployed French intellectuals".[50]

[46]'Suisse: La conférence pour les réfugiés allemands', in *Havas*, 8th December 1933, cutting in MAE Z 711, p. 131.

[47]See the pessimistic outlook expressed already in Comité d'Aide et d'Accueil, 'Compte rendu No. 2, Activité du Secrétariat Général du 20 au 30 mai, 1933', in AIU X D 56.

[48]'Création du *Comité National Français de Secours aux émigrés allemands victimes de l'antisémitisme*', in UI, 30th June 1933, p. 351.

[49]Corcos, 'L'inéluctable devoir', in UI, 27th October 1933, p. 179. See also 'Une lettre de M. Henry Bernstein', in UI, 24th November 1933, pp. 308–309; Julien Weill, 'Servir Dieu', in UI, 13th April 1934, p. 54.

[50]Minutes, Meeting to discuss the creation of the *Comité National*, 22nd or 23rd June 1933, p. 20, in LBI Arch. AR-C 1698/4099. See also Police report, 24th October 1933, in APP, BA/1814 241.155–1–A. The *Comité des Savants* was essentially a branch of the *Comité National* and was heavily subsidised by the *Alliance Israélite Universelle* and the Rothschilds.

The range of possibilities available to the *Comité National* was thus narrowing considerably. Nevertheless, French Jews still had choices and continued to exercise some influence over government policy – for the government conferred with the Committee at every step of the way. The dilemma was how to use this influence and how to balance the dual obligations to which Robert de Rothschild had alluded. To be sure, achieving this reconciliation would be no easy matter, for it was not at all clear which side of the balance would be stressed. Contrary to prevailing opinion, native French Jews did not speak with a single voice, and, it was precisely over this issue of how to balance these conflicting obligations that a major dispute arose within the ranks of the Committee. Essentially, two viable options were available. Either the Committee could adopt a hard-line position, abandoning altogether its commitment to the refugees so as to opt for what it perceived to be the best interests of France. Or it could pursue a more moderate path, striving to arrive at a true accommodation between the interests of the refugees, on the one hand, and those of the French public, on the other. These two positions crystallised around two of the central figures within the Committee: Jacques Helbronner, who represented the hard-liners, and Raymond-Raoul Lambert, the *Comité National*'s General Secretary, who represented the more moderate path.[51] The outcome of the battle between these two would have profound repercussions, influencing not only the nature of the relief effort, but, more significantly, the formulation of French official refugee policy itself.

As foremost spokesman for the hard-line position, Helbronner, whether he represented the *Comité National* or the French government at the League of Nations High Commission for Refugees, never failed to put forth the most extreme, anti-refugee position possible. From his point of view there was no question of conflicting loyalties. French Jews had one obligation, and one obligation only, and that was to France. In June of 1933, at a meeting of Jewish organisations, he demanded of his colleagues: "What do you plan to do with these masses [of refugees]? We're in a period of unemployment, we cannot encumber our [liberal] professions, nor are there jobs in factories or in commerce for this influx of labour that has descended upon us." He then went on to add:

> "France, like every other nation, has its unemployed, and not all the Jewish refugees from Germany are people worth keeping . . . If there are 100 to 150 great intellectuals who are worthy of being kept in France since they are scientists or chemists who have secrets our own chemists don't know . . . these we will keep, but the 7, 8 or perhaps 10,000 Jews who will come to France, is it really in our best interest to keep them?"[52]

Several years later he reiterated this position, openly bemoaning the fact that the borders had been too open in 1933. From his perspective, France had received too many of "the riff-raff, the rejects of society, the elements who could not

[51]Helbronner's closest ally was Louis Oungre, President of the Jewish Colonization Association; Lambert's was William Oualid, Professor in the Faculty of Law at the University of Paris, a member of the Executive Committee of the *Comité National* in 1934, and President of the *Comité Central d'assistance aux émigrants Juifs*, the French branch of the international Jewish emigration agency, HICEM.
[52]Minutes of the Meeting regarding the creation of *Comité National*, 22nd or 23rd June 1933, p. 12, in LBI Arch. AR–C 1698/4099.

possibly have been of any use to their own country . . ." These individuals, he declared, were simply "a bunch of nonentities of no use to any human agglomeration".[53]

Given Helbronner's utter disdain for the refugees, it is not surprising that he made use of every opportunity to press the government to take the most restrictive policy possible. At a series of interministerial meetings convened in the autumn of 1933 to discuss strategies for dealing with the Jewish refugee question, Helbronner – who represented the *Comité National* there together with one of the Rothschilds, most often Robert de Rothschild – lobbied the government vigorously to close the borders as tightly as possible, and he vetoed every proposal which would have enabled Jewish refugees to have remained in France. When one minister suggested that the refugees should be sent to industrial centres outside Paris where they might find better job opportunities, Helbronner objected. In light of their grievances, he argued, they would be ripe for Communism.[54] Furthermore, although initially willing to consider the settlement of refugees in rural France, by 1934 he adamantly opposed this proposal as well. France, he maintained, was not a country of colonisation. When the Joint Distribution Committee tried to persuade French Jews at least to investigate the possibilities of agricultural placement, Helbronner protested vehemently:

> "From the political point of view, the projects envisioned likewise raise serious objections: whether it's a question of settlements in small groups or in large masses, it's to be feared that, due to the special conditions under which these settlements will be undertaken, [and] due also to the language, the particular customs of the elements to be settled, these projects would only create an atmosphere of hostility in the designated regions and among the French peasants that could degenerate into a more or less blatant antisemitism . . ."[55]

For Helbronner, there was only one solution to the dilemma: emigration. As the French government's delegate to the League of Nations High Commission for Refugees, Helbronner never failed to put forth in the most unequivocal terms the view that France could serve as a transit country only – a *gare de triage*. France, he repeatedly insisted, had done her duty; it was now time for the international community, and particularly the League of Nations, to do theirs. Even the vast majority of those refugees already in France (with the exception of the 100–150

---

[53]'Réunion commune du Bureau et des représentants du Comité Exécutif du Comité pour la défense des droits des israélites en Europe centrale et orientale avec le bureau et la Commission des Affaires Extérieures de l'Alliance Israélite Universelle', 24th March 1936, in LBI Archives AR–C 1698/4099. Also cited in *Comité pour la défense* . . . , *op. cit.*, p. 71.

[54]'Procès verbal de la 3ᵉᵐᵉ séance tenue par la Commission Interministérielle des réfugiés allemands', 23rd October 1933, in MAE Z 711, pp. 70–74.

[55]'Note Confidentielle de M. Helbronner: Quelques considérations concernant l'établissement agricole en France de réfugiés allemands', July 1934, in LBI Arch. AR–C 1698/4099. See also: 'Réunion commune du bureau et des représentants du Comité Exécutif du Comité pour la Défense des Droits des Israélites en Europe centrale et orientale avec le Bureau et la Commission des Affaires Extérieures de l'Alliance Israélite Universelle', 24th March 1936, in LBI Archives AR–C 1698/4099; 'Summary of the Meeting of the Advisory Council of the High Commission [for Refugees] held in Paris', 18th June 1934, in JDC No. 250. On JDC plans for agricultural settlements, see Kahn to Major Frank Goldsmith, 25th October 1933, in JDC No. 617.

intellectuals he considered useful) would, he insisted, have to go.[56] Helbronner's attitude, it should be noted, infuriated both James G. McDonald, the High Commissioner for Refugees, and Bernhard Kahn, the European Director of the Joint Distribution Committee, both of whom were firmly convinced that in light of the bleak prospects of finding new immigration possibilities, the countries of first asylum would have to make a considerable effort to absorb a significant portion of their refugees. As Kahn put it: "The idea that the majority of these refugees are only temporary visitors must be radically changed if the refugee problem were ever to be solved." Indeed, the Joint was so eager to see refugees settled in France, that it even offered to pay the *Comité National* five pounds for every refugee successfully placed in a job.[57] Unfortunately, by mid-1934 such constructive solutions were becoming increasingly difficult to find, a problem Kahn attributed in no small measure to the influence of the hard-liners in the Committee. These people, he charged, had wanted from the beginning only "to get rid of the refugees", and to achieve their goal they "disapprove [of] every attempt to help the refugees constructively, no matter what the project may be".[58] Madeleine Coulon, General Secretary of the *Comité pour la Défense des Droits des Israélites en Europe centrale et orientale*, also known as the Gourevitch-Dreyfus Committee, similarly pointed her finger straight at Bérenger and Helbronner. Those who "should have boldly defended the refugees' rights of residence and work" had instead used their governmental positions to "push to the extreme the theory that France serve as a simple transit country for Jewish refugees, and that, with the money collected in France and abroad to save the lives and the dignity of the refugees, they had steered them, so as to get rid of them all, to Paraguay . . ."[59]

[56]For Helbronner's hard-line policy at the League of Nations see Helbronner to the Foreign Minister, Report 'au sujet de la IIIe session du conseil d'administration pour les réfugiés provenant d'Allemagne', 5th November 1934, in MAE Z 313, pp. 13–17; Minutes, High Commission for Refugees, 'Summary report of the Meeting of the Advisory Council of the High Commission, London, 15th July 1935', p. 8, in JDC No. 251; 'Notes on discussions of Advisory Council of the High Commission', 18th June 1934, in JDC No. 260; Bernhard Kahn to Paul Baerwald, 6th November 1934, in JDC No. 601; High Commissioner for Refugees, 'Compte rendu de la session du Comité Consultatif du Haut-Commissariat tenue à Londres, 29–30 Octobre, 1934', in JDC No. 250; Helbronner to the Foreign Minister, 5th November 1934 and 15th February 1935, in MAE SDN I E 448, pp. 241–245; pp. 248–252.

[57]Kahn, 'Report on the Activities of the AJDC with special Attention to the last five months', 16th April 1934, pp. 13, 16, in JDC No. 160.

[58]Kahn to Max Warburg, 16th October 1934, in JDC No. 617. See also Bauer, *op. cit.*, pp. 150–153.

[59]Cited in *Comité pour la défense . . .*, *op. cit.*, p. 3. This committee, also known as the *Comité pour la Défense des droits des israélites en Europe centrale et orientale*, was founded in August 1933 and had as its directors Boris Gourevitch, a former Menshevik refugee in Paris, and Pierre Dreyfus, the son of Captain Alfred Dreyfus. The Gourevitch Committee did not provide relief. Rather, it was essentially political in nature and lobbied the government on a wide range of issues dealing with refugees and antisemitism in Central and Eastern Europe as well as in France itself. Among its sponsors were many prominent non-Jews, including: Anatole DeMonzie; Pierre-Etienne Flandin; Justin Godart; Paul Reynaud; and Edouard Daladier, who became its honorary President in the late 1930s. See Nicault, *loc. cit.*, p. 5; Hyman, *op. cit.*, p. 222–223; 'Paris Committee formed to Aid Jews in Europe', in NYT, 13th August 1933, p. 24; Report on the 'Comité pour la défense des droits des israélites en Europe centrale . . .', n.d., [1933], in ACIP B 127; and *Comité pour la défense . . .*, *op. cit.*, *passim*.

Helbronner, to be sure, was not the sole spokesman for the Committee, and his most outspoken opponent was the most prominent representative of the younger generation of French Jewish leaders – Raymond-Raoul Lambert. Ironically, Lambert has been the figure in the French Jewish community most vilified by the critics of the native Jewish establishment, and especially by Rajsfus.[60] In reality, however, there is no convincing evidence to support this point of view. Indeed, Lambert was probably more sensitive than any of his colleagues to the plight and needs of the refugees, perhaps because of his profound familiarity with the German language and with German culture.[61] Throughout the 1930s he worked tirelessly to bring about a true accommodation between the needs of the refugees and what he perceived to be the best interests of France. In sharp contrast to Helbronner, who consistently rejected every attempt to find constructive solutions to the refugee problem, Lambert worked indefatigably throughout 1933 to 1935 to find job opportunities for the refugees that would have permitted them to remain in France. Indeed, in the spring of 1933, he outlined one of the most extraordinarily liberal positions put forth by anyone in France. In an article that appeared in *La Revue Juive de Genève*, Lambert proclaimed:

> "There is a difficult but admirable project to be realised. There are those who object that unemployment is raging, that the employment possibilities are extremely limited, that the Depression has necessitated in every enterprise a reduction of personnel. We, however, will by no means despair. We will enlighten opinion and those higher up will not fail to lessen the severity of certain prescriptions. The presence in France of new technicians, of new scientists, of new artists could bolster the productive force of the country and perhaps give rise to useful industries. Just the other day someone mentioned to me a plan for the agricultural colonisation of a vast domain in the South of France; someone else told me of a study by an entrepreneur who wants to create toy workshops so as to compete with Nuremberg; another declared the possibility of establishing the fur trade in Paris to take the place of Leipzig. Perhaps these are exaggerations or wild fantasies; but all this at least goes to prove the existence of certain possibilities which we mustn't scorn."[62]

Lambert quickly realised that this task would not be so simple; nevertheless, throughout the summer and autumn of 1933 he lobbied the Minister of Labour ceaselessly to secure as many work permits as possible.[63] Even in November of 1933, facing a severe shortage of funds and an increasingly reluctant govern-

---

[60]See Rajsfus, *op. cit., passim.*; as well as *idem, Des Juifs dans la collaboration: l'UGIF (1941–1944)*, Paris 1980, *passim.*

[61]Lambert's sympathy for the refugees may have been due in part to his extraordinary familiarity with German culture. He spoke German fluently, and in the early 1920s he served as the assistant to the High Commissioner of the Territory of the Rhineland in Bonn. See Cohen, *Carnet*, p. 18; 'Raymond-Raoul Lambert fera la première conférence de la *Tribune Juive*', in *Tribune Juive*, No. 4 (26th January 1934) p. 71.

[62]Lambert, 'L'accueil de la France', in *Revue Juive de Genève*, 1ère année, No. 8 (May 1933), pp. 349–350.

[63]On Lambert's efforts to secure jobs for the refugees see Comité d'Aide et d'Accueil, 'Compte rendu No. 2, Activité du Secrétariat Général du 20–30 mai, 1933', in AIU X D 56; Biélinky, 'Les victimes de Hitler en France', in *Kadimah*, 28th September 1934, pp. 12–15; [Lambert], 'Note pour M. le Président du Conseil', 20th July 1933, in LBI Arch. AR-C 1698/4099; Joly, 'L'Aide aux émigrés juifs', p. 55. Despite his efforts, Lambert was not terribly successful. Between 1933 and mid-1935, only 2,403 refugees were successfully placed, primarily in domestic service and agriculture. On the problem of work permits see also 'Le problème des réfugiés allemands', in *L'Europe Nouvelle*, 17th February 1934, pp. 171–172; Schramm and Vormeier, *op. cit.*, pp. 209–216.

ment, he declared: "Let's be done with the period when one thinks solely of feeding and lodging the unfortunates." It was now time to labour seriously to bring about constructive solutions, particularly in agriculture and industry.[64] Moreover, unlike Helbronner, who had categorically ruled out all agricultural settlements, Lambert was willing to give the question some consideration. Nevertheless, he too vehemently opposed mass colonisation, fearing that the creation of unassimilated ethnic enclaves would prevent the successful integration of the refugees and would offend French sensibilities.[65] Nevertheless, Lambert was more than willing to support the small-scale settlement of refugees in rural areas, and he endorsed the creation of agricultural training centres to ensure that refugees eligible for this type of work be carefully selected and receive proper training.

Indeed, Lambert's commitment to the refugees even led him to criticise the government when he felt it had reneged on its original promises. According to a report of the British embassy in Paris:

> "The committee [there is no doubt that the writer is referring to Lambert's role here] is stated to be very dissatisfied with the attitude of the French authorities, who originally, for political reasons welcomed the refugees, but now make it virtually impossible for any of them to obtain work here. When with great difficulty the committee finds some opening, the French authorities refuse to grant a 'permis de travail' or waste so much time about it that the job has been filled by someone else meanwhile."[66]

In January of 1934, when the authorities began for the first time to expel refugees whose papers were not in order, Lambert sent off a sharply-worded protest to the government: "After the splendid effort offered by France in favour of the unfortunates", he declared, "it would be unjust if excessively severe measures were to come and destroy so considerable an achievement that has contributed to enhancing the prestige of hospitable France throughout the world."[67] But perhaps the strongest testimony to Lambert's efforts is the fact that he won the praise of the refugees themselves. In an article of July 1934, sharply critical of the *Comité National*, the *Pariser Tageblatt*, the foremost émigré newspaper, went to great lengths to exempt Lambert from its scathing attack:

> "The power of his work within the relief organisation is as great as his goodness of character and his affability towards the émigrés seeking assistance. Naturally, he can do nothing to counteract the bitter necessity of empty coffers; however, even those who suffer a refusal, those who are turned away by him, will always retain the feeling of having spoken to a humane and obliging man. Unfortunately, one cannot say as much for a good number of employees and

---

[64]"Conférence régionale à Metz des Comités de secours pour les réfugiés', in *Tribune Juive*, No. 46 (17th November 1933, p. 793; Lambert, 'L'émigration allemande et la Société des Nations', in UI, 3rd November 1933, p. 210.

[65]Lambert, 'L'émigration allemande et la Société des Nations', in UI, 3rd November 1933, pp. 210–11; Lambert, 'De l'orientation morale', in *Les Cahiers du Renouveau*, No. 1 (December 1934), p. 25; Lambert to Jacques Fouques-Duparc, League of Nations section, Foreign Ministry, 21st March 1934, in MAE SDN I E 448, p. 164.

[66]Mr. Harvey, British embassy, Paris, to J. V. Perowne, 10th January 1934, PRO FO 371/17698/C308.

[67]Comité National, 'Note sur la situation légale des réfugiés d'Allemagne en France', n.d. [early 1934], in LBI Arch AR–C 1698/4099.

even directors of *Comité National* services, even when they are German émigrés themselves . . ."[68]

To be sure, Lambert was by no means an extreme radical on refugee matters. There were other groups, most notably the Gourevitch-Dreyfus Committee, which pushed much further than Lambert both in terms of criticising government policies publicly and with regard to advocating more innovative proposals for refugee settlement, including mass colonisation schemes, either in France itself, or in French colonies, or the idea that the government ought to allocate 8,000 to 10,000 work permits to the refugees, in return for the equivalent number of jobs created for French workers by refugee-owned firms.[69] It must also be said that Lambert accepted certain government policies, such as the weeding out of East European refugees and the attempts to distinguish between "economic" and "political" refugees, without much protest.[70] Moreover, he even concurred with Helbronner that a major priority of the *Comité National* should be emigration and repatriation.[71] And finally, Lambert, like nearly all native spokesmen, never ceased to admonish the refugees to assimilate as quickly as possible. In December 1934 Lambert excoriated those German émigrés "still incapable of constructing a French sentence" and who stubbornly refused "to renounce any of their former habits". And, he went on: "It is better to change oneself than to try to reconstruct a world which is not dependent upon us."[72] Still, the fact remains that Lambert fought valiantly for constructive solutions to the refugee problem, and this effort set him apart sharply from his hard-line colleagues.

Unfortunately, by early 1934, Helbronner had clearly gained the upper hand. Emigration and repatriation became the sole priorities of the *Comité National*, and relief, to the extent that it would continue, was now to be allocated on a short-

[68]'Les Pauvres réfugiés: Accusation au lieu d'aide', translation of 'Die armen Flüchtlinge', in *Pariser Tageblatt* (PT), No. 225, 25th July, 1934, p. 3, in LBI Arch AR–C 1698/4099.

[69]See *Comité pour la défense . . . , op. cit., passim.* On the Gourevitch Committee see note 59 above.

[70]As early as May 1933 the Committee instituted a rigorous selection process, whereby the refugees were divided into three categories: "A. les véritables proscrits politiques et confessionnels; B. les proscrits politiques douteux C. les émigrants qui profitent dans circonstances pour chercher dans un autre pays la fortune qui ne leur saurait plus depuis longtemps en Allemagne." In late May 1933, 50 percent of Category "A" was comprised of Germans and the other half of Poles, Stateless and others; 59 percent of category "B" was comprised of Poles, Stateless, and others; and 68 percent of category "C" was comprised of these groups. Comité d'Aide et d'Accueil, 'Compte Rendu, No. 2, Activité du Secrétariat Général du 20 au 30 mai 1933', in AIU X D 56. See also Joly, 'L'Aide aux émigrés juifs', p. 47; Nicault, *loc. cit.*, p. 7; R.C., *loc. cit.*, p. 124.

[71]As of the summer of 1933, the 3 main policies of the *Comité National* were: 1) repatriation of refugees who could be sent back to their country of origin (i.e., East Europeans); 2) overseas emigration with the assistance of international Jewish emigration associations; and 3) the settlement of "productive" elements in France, without harming unemployed French workers. See Comité National, 'Compte rendu de l'Activité du Secrétariat Général du 1er juillet jusqu'au 1er octobre, 1933', in MAE SDN I E 451, pp. 111–112; 'Comité National, Compte rendu de l'Activité du Secrétariat Général du 11 mai 1933 jusqu'au 16 octobre 1933', in AIU, France, X D 56.

[72]Lambert, 'De l'orientation morale', in *Les Cahiers du Renouveau*, No. 1 (December 1934), p. 25. This article also appeared as 'Die moralische Anpassung der Emigration', in PT, 12th December 1934, p. 5, cited in Peterson, *op. cit.*, p. 73.

term basis only, simply to tide the refugees over until they could depart. According to the *Comité National*'s financial report for 1933–1934: "After having fed the refugees", the most urgent task was "to evacuate them to those countries of immigration capable of receiving them – Palestine, Brazil . . . etc, so that our labour market, already so anaemic as a result of the Depression, is not overburdened by this influx of foreign workers."[73] Most significantly, the *Comité National* even began to ship the refugees back to Germany. As one *Comité National* employee noted: "At the beginning of 1934, the emigration service of the *Comité* received a strict order to get rid of the refugees by sending them wherever: to Africa, to America, or even to Germany. We 'repatriated' even those people who no longer possessed anything, we paid for their railway ticket and sent them back to Germany."[74] This policy was by no means undertaken surreptitiously; Robert de Rothschild announced it publicly in January of 1934: "We must likewise expect to repatriate certain elements to their countries of origin. Conditions even in Germany are improving and atrocities are, for the moment, non-existent. Besides, life in this country, too – as everywhere – is difficult due to the Depression."[75] The time had therefore come to renounce constructive solutions once and for all.[76]

In light of this single-minded emphasis on emigration, there seemed, at least to the hard-liners in the Committee, no compelling reason to continue the relief effort any longer. Indeed, to do so would only encourage further waves of refugees to seek asylum in France. As a result, in the spring of 1934 the Committee announced plans to liquidate those charity cases still on the books, and in July it closed its doors altogether to further requests for material assistance. One year later it shut down even its administrative and juridical services. Accurately assessing the situation, a police report of October 1934 noted: "M. Robert de Rothschild, Vice-President of the Jewish Consistory of Paris, who has contributed abundantly towards the assistance programme for the German émigrés is now said to have declared that he no longer wishes to continue that effort."[77] Clearly, the French Jewish establishment was giving up all efforts to reconcile its competing loyalties and obligations to the refugees and to France. In this struggle, French interests, or at least what the hard-liners within the committee considered to be French interests, dominated. The refugees were, quite simply, to be abandoned.

The émigré community was up in arms. Both the *Pariser Tageblatt* and the *Pariser Haynt*, the major organ of the Yiddish immigrant press, launched scathing

---

[73]Comité National, 'Rapport financier, Exercice 1933–1934', in LBI Arch. AR–C 1698/4099.
[74]R.C., *loc. cit.*, p. 124.
[75]As paraphrased by Biélinky in 'Deux réunions en faveur des réfugiés', in UI, 26th January 1934, p. 606.
[76]Robert de Rothschild's speech of 23rd July 1935 reported in 'Assemblée générale du Comité National de Secours', in UI, 2nd–9th August 1935, p. 729.
[77]Police report, 9th October 1934, in MAE Z 711, p. 237; see also note 76 above.

attacks on the policies of the *Comité National*.[78] A. Halperin, the *Pariser Haynt*'s leading editorial-writer, charged that the Committee's claim to have successfully liquidated the refugee problem by the summer of 1934 was, to put it mildly, ludicrous:

> "Is it possible to find anyone to affirm that there is no longer a need for the Committee? That all the refugees are satisfied? We know exactly what this liquidation signifies – get out and go wherever we shove you. It's not surprising that the list of those on assistance has dropped to 500. What will become of all the other refugees? Better not ask!"[79]

Georg Bernhard, the editor of the *Pariser Tageblatt* and the president of the *Fédération des Emigrés d'Allemagne en France*, was no less outraged. In a speech he delivered in October 1934 he thanked the French government for its hospitality but then proceeded to excoriate "the attitude of his French co-religionists, who, with the exception of a small number, including the Baron de Rothschild, have not made the necessary effort to come to the assistance of the Jewish refugees".[80] Indeed the anger and fear of the future were so great that 200 refugees, including the well-known writer Egon Erwin Kisch, staged a demonstration outside the *Comité National* in late July 1934 to protest the closing. According to a police report, the demonstrators "criticised the functioning of the *Comité National*, which they accuse of having squandered the money that, according to them, was entirely of foreign origin. The French Jews, they claimed, had done nothing to help their co-religionists and had never made the least effort to facilitate their stay in France."[81]

The refugees were by no means alone in their harsh denunciations of the *Comité National*'s irresponsibility and indifference. The Joint Distribution Committee and the High Commissioner for Refugees seconded these attacks. Ironically, it was the Joint that had initially proposed the liquidation scheme. However, it had something altogether different in mind. Indeed, according to Bernhard Kahn, the Joint had promised in late 1933 to continue subsidising the *Comité National* only on the condition that the Committee lobby the government as vigorously as possible to keep the borders open and make every conceivable effort to place

---

[78]Throughout late July and early August of 1934 the PT carried a series of articles sharply critical of the policies of the *Comité National*, several of which are abstracted and translated in LBI Arch. AR–C 1698/4099. These articles infuriated Helbronner, and may have determined the timing of the closure of the committee. According to one report, "Après un échange de vues avec M. Louis Oungre et après lecture des articles parus dans le *Pariser Tageblatt*, M. Helbronner décide d'accord avec M. Louis Oungre de fermer la rue de la Durance le 1er août et de liquider immédiatement." Comité National, Executive Committee Meeting of 25th July 1934, in LBI Arch. AR–C 1698/4099.

[79]*Pariser Haynt* (PH), 3rd June 1934, translated in ACIP B 129 (PH).

[80]'Conférence de M. Georg Bernhard', 11th October 1934, in AN F7 13433. For a history of Bernhard and the PT, see Peterson, *op. cit.*

[81]Police report, 'au sujet des émigrés juifs', 30th July 1934, in APP BA/1815, 241.155–1–B. See also Heinz Liepmann, 'The Refugee People', in *The Jewish Forum* (February 1935), pp. 19–20, cutting in JDC No. 617.

refugees in constructive employment.[82] But, as we have seen, Kahn believed the hard-liners in the Committee had systematically undermined these goals, and when the Committee announced its intended closing, he was up in arms. On 25th July 1934, he cabled the New York office that the "French liquidation plan had not [had the] full results expected. This failure entirely due to [the] attitude of [the] French Committee." On 1st August, he cabled again "desperate refugees threatening with desperate acts".[83] McDonald had similarly lost all patience with the Committee. Indeed, he paid an unannounced visit to the Committee's office just prior to its closing, and, to the chagrin of several administrators, he even addressed the delegation of refugee protesters.[84] In early 1935, he told Louis Oungre, the French director of the Jewish Colonization Association and Helbronner's closest ally, that he "did not agree with Dr. Oungre's idea that the more that is done in France, the less will be the chances of the League's assuming responsibility. No efforts should be spared to obtain concessions for the refugees from the French government and the governments of the other countries. They must be shown clearly that there is no sense in shoving refugees from one frontier to the other. A plan of emigration should be proposed for those who can emigrate and who are really not desired in France. For the others *cartes de travail* should be stubbornly demanded, calling on France's tried and true hospitality. As to further emigration", McDonald maintained, "it must be admitted that the opportunities at the present time are very meagre".[85] Even the Paris Consistory, whose Vice-President was none other than Robert de Rothschild himself,

[82]On 20th October 1933 Kahn cabled Paul Baerwald of the JDC in New York: "Our negotiations with French Committee rather successful. While French government cannot give any financial aid to refugees they will do everything to absorb many hundreds more by giving Carte Travaille. Government also favors our settlement plan [to create agricultural settlements]. Under these circumstances am ready to assist French Committee with three hundred thousand francs. Told government and French Committee assistance dependent on not closing borders." Confidential cablegram, in JDC No. 617. On the JDC's persistent efforts to persuade the *Comité National* to adopt a more constructive approach see J. C. Hyman, 'Draft Statement of Observations on Conditions of the Refugees in France and on Organizational Problems of the Jewish Communities in Germany', December 1933, in JDC No. 617; B. Kahn, 'Report on the Activities of the AJDC with special attention to the last five months', 16th April 1934, in JDC No. 160; 'Brief Report on the Work in Germany and on the Situation of the Refugees', 22nd August 1934, in JDC No. 404.

[83]Kahn to Baerwald, 25th July 1934 and 1st August 1934, both in JDC No. 617. See also Bauer, *op. cit.*, pp. 149–151.

[84]'Le Commissaire pour les réfugiés MacDonald à Paris', transl. of 'Flüchtlingskommissar MacDonald in Paris', in PT, No. 226 (26th July 1934), p. 3, in LBI Arch. AR–C 1698/4099. See also Joly, 'L'Aide aux émigrés juifs', p. 62.

[85]'Minutes of Meeting with the High Commissioner for Refugees', 29th January 1935, Enclosure 3, p. 10, in JDC No. 161. McDonald similarly complained that the premature liquidation of the *Comité National*'s relief activities constituted a "threat of starvation to hundreds of Jewish refugees, including many children, [and] is an indictment of Jewish leadership and of the High Commission . . ." McDonald to Paul Baerwald, 28th July 1934, in JDC No. 617. On Oungre's hard-line position see, High Commissioner for Refugees, Minutes, Meeting of Advisory Council, 29th January 1934, in LBI AR 7162, Box 5; 'Minutes of Meeting with the High Commissioner for Refugees, held at JDC offices, Paris', 29th January 1935, p. 5, in JDC No. 161.

expressed grave concern. The Consistory's general secretary, Albert Manuel, himself a member of the *Comité National*'s executive committee, informed Rothschild in June of 1934 that, as a result of the Committee's planned closing, desperate refugees were flocking to the Central Synagogue to demand assistance. The Consistory, Manuel pointed out, was in no position to take on this financial burden, and he begged Rothschild to reconsider the Committee's closing in light of the disastrous impact it would have on other Jewish institutions.[86]

These protests, unfortunately, proved to be of no avail and the doors of the Committee remained firmly shut. The great tragedy of this period was still to come, however, since beginning in the autumn of 1934 the Right-wing governments of Pierre-Etienne Flandin and Pierre Laval initiated the harshest antiforeign crackdown to date. Following the assassination of King Alexander of Yugoslavia and the French Foreign Minister Barthou by a foreign terrorist in October, French authorities, seeking to rid their country of the hordes of "undesirables", resorted for the first time to a policy of mass expulsion. Residence permits were increasingly denied and requests of refugees who had entered France either without papers or on short-term visas were now routinely rejected. According to new decree laws announced in November 1934, all foreigners not in possession of residence permits would now be forcibly expelled.[87] At the same time, the government was making it more difficult than ever to acquire a work permit; even those permits already in circulation were to be renewed only in exceptional circumstances. In 1935, the Laval government pushed through yet another series of decree laws sharply limiting, for the first time, the right of foreigners to engage in artisan trades and peddling. These laws did not only touch refugees, but threw out of work thousands more immigrants, many of whom had been in France for years, including large numbers of East European Jews employed in the garment trades.[88] Without a work permit, it was

---

[86]A. Manuel to Robert de Rothschild, 4th June 1934, in ACIP B 129 (Emigrants).

[87]Minister of Interior, Sûreté Nationale, Circular No. 257, 6th November 1934 and 4th December 1934 in APP BA 64 (Provisoire) 51343–5. On the crackdown beginning in late 1934 see Bonnet, *op. cit.*, p. 302; Schramm and Vormeier, *op. cit.*, pp. 203–204; Marrus and Paxton, *op. cit.*, p. 55; Bauer, *op. cit.*, pp. 152–153; Peterson, *op. cit.*, p. 76–77; Schor, *L'Opinion française*, pp. 552–554; Fabian and Coulmas, *op. cit.*, p. 31–33; 'Paris Police Seize Hundreds in Café Raids in Drive to Rid City of Undesirable Aliens', in NYT, 6th November 1934, p. 6; 'Paris Raids Continue', in NYT, 27th November 1934, p. 10; *Comité pour la défense* . . . , *op. cit.*, pp. 1–2, 27, 47 and *passim.*

[88]On the decree laws regulating foreign artisans, see *Journal Officiel* (JO), Lois et Décrets, April 12, 1935, pp. 4101–4116; August 9, 1935, pp. 8699–8700. See also Bonnet, *op. cit.*, p. 220; Marrus and Paxton, *op. cit.*, p. 57. On the laws regulating ambulatory commerce, see JO, Lois et Décrets, October 31, 1935, pp. 11490–11491. The government also planned to levy a tax on all employers whose foreign workforce constituted more than 5 percent of the total workforce. See, 'Défendons les travailleurs immigrés', in *Humanité*, 6th November 1934, cutting in APP BA/1814 241.155–1–G.

Although the 1935 decree laws did not single out Jewish immigrants, the law of 9th August claimed that the greatest abuses had been caused by foreigners involved in home work, "façonniers le plus souvent". The great majority of these were East European Jews in the garment industry.

impossible to acquire a residence permit, and, as we have seen, without the residence permit, foreigners faced the very real threat of expulsion.[89]

This government crackdown provided the occasion for the last and final round in the battle between the hard-liners and the moderates in the Committee. Not surprisingly, the position put forth by Helbronner was that Jewish organisations had no right whatsoever to intervene with the government. According to one report: "Mr. Helbronner insists on the general character of the problem of the stateless refugees and upon the necessity of not turning it into a Jewish Question . . . Given the evolution of the issue at present, any intervention in favour of the stateless refugees from the Jewish side could only compromise the programme undertaken by Viscount Cecil [of the League of Nations High Commission for Refugees] regarding a more general plan."[90] Helbronner even went so far as to remind Jewish organisations that Jewish refugees were in fact a "privileged" category of foreigners, and they therefore had no cause to complain.[91] There is no doubt, however, that Helbronner's remarks regarding the High Commission were inspired by bad faith, since McDonald himself had already protested to the French government against the policy of expulsion, and he had encouraged Jewish organisations, including the *Comité National*, to do the same.[92] Bernhard Kahn similarly warned the Committee not to act as the government's "sheriff" with regard to the execution of expulsion orders. American Jews, he threatened, would halt all further contributions to the French relief campaign once they discovered the abominable policies their money was actually supporting.[93]

Once again, Lambert took a diametrically opposed position. As he saw it, the government's crackdown amounted to a direct assault against Jewish refugees in particular, an assault which he warned would have dangerous and long-lasting repercussions. In two important articles that appeared in late 1934 and early 1935, Lambert lashed out against both French official policy and the passivity of

---

[89]In November, Bernhard Kahn spoke of the French government's plans for "wholesale expulsion". Kahn to Paul Baerwald, 6th November 1934, in JDC No. 601. See also Vormeier, 'La Situation administrative des exilés allemands en France (1933–1945): Accueil-Repression-Internement-Déportation', in *Revue d'Allemagne*, vol. XVIII, No. 2 (April–June 1986), pp. 187–188; Badia, 'La France découverte par les émigrés', *ibid.*, pp. 176–177; Schramm and Vormeier, *op. cit.*, pp. 215–221; Luigi Camplonghi, 'La Grande pitié des émigrés et des proscrits', in CDH, 30th November 1934, p. 749; 'La Question des étrangers devant la chambre', in CDH, 10th December 1934, pp. 771–775; Victor Basch, 'Lettre ouverte au Président du Conseil', in CDH, 20th February 1935, pp. 102–103; Maxime Piha, 'Reprends ton baton . . . et marche', in *Cahiers Juifs*, No. 13 (January–February 1935), pp. 3–5.

[90]'Réunion Biennale des Associations Juives', 7th July 1935, in LBI, AR-C 1627/4078.

[91]Minutes, High Commission for Refugees, 'Summary report of the Meeting of the Advisory Council of the High Commission', London, 15th July 1935, p. 8, in JDC No. 251.

[92]On McDonald's protests see McDonald to D. Tetreau, Ministry of Foreign Affairs, 15th November 1934, Papers of James G. McDonald, Lehman Collection, Columbia University, NY (MP): H2; 'McDonald Reports on Refugee Plight', NYT, 29th November 1934, p. 31; McDonald, 'Note' to the Ministry of Foreign Affairs, 1st February 1935, pp. 246–247, in MAE SDN I E 448.

[93]Kahn to Baerwald, 6th November 1934, in JDC No. 601.

French Jewry.[94] Contrary to Helbronner's appeal that Jewish organisations remain silent, Lambert proclaimed: "The situation must preoccupy our organisations and our official representatives, since the considerable number of Jewish immigrants in France turns this question of foreigners into a specifically Jewish Question. The first victims of the new measures are the Jewish refugees, from Germany, Poland and Romania, for whom the associations are seeking possibilities to establish them in new countries." If the government truly desired the refugees to emigrate, he pointed out, these new measures were making that goal illusory. The problem was that once a refugee failed to obey an expulsion order, he was in infraction of the law and thus began to amass a criminal record. Under these circumstances, no country could be expected to grant that refugee an entry visa. Lambert therefore proclaimed:

> "It's necessary that the authorities no longer refuse to grant departure extensions [to those expelled] and that they understand the tragic problem of the stateless refugees . . . These uprooted unfortunates, whom war, successive migrations or political upheavals have caused to lose their nationality of origin (Polish, Russian or Romanian), find themselves physically unable to obey an expulsion order. No country will grant them an entry visa; they are thus subject to the sad obligation of remaining in France illegally, if the negotiations of the charitable organisations which care for them are not successful in steering them towards Palestine or South America."

Lambert then went on to discuss the fact that, "the new measures hit the immigrant Jews established in France for many years of whom several even have French children. Some are artisans, others entrepreneurs, and it is no exaggeration to say that more than 5,000 persons in Paris find themselves in these straits." If Jewish garment workers were to lose their work permits as well, thousands more desperate individuals would, he predicted, fall into the hands of the relief committees. He thus implored "the authorities not [to] ignore the tragic destiny of the stateless foreigners for whom no frontier can be opened".[95]

Lambert then turned his attention to the pathetic role of French Jewry itself. French Jews, he charged, had all too readily believed the popular myth that foreigners stole jobs from French workers and thus created unemployment. In reality, he argued, "unemployment was not the cause of the Depression, but rather its consequence" and Jewish organisations, he suggested, had been wrong to "submit themselves docilely to the pressure of every political party, without exception, which demands more severe protective measures for our national work force, whether it be the Radical Party at its last Party Congress or the labour unions which protect their own unemployed". It was now time to wake

---

[94]Lambert, 'Le Statut des étrangers', in UI, 12th December 1934, pp. 209–210; Lambert, 'L'émigration juive d'Allemagne', in *Revue juive de Genève*, 3ème année, No. 4 (January 1935), p. 143. All quotes in the following two paragraphs are from 'Le Statut' except when otherwise indicated. On the favourable reception of these articles by the Yiddish press, see PH, 16th December 1934, transl. in ACIP B 129 (PH 1934); PH, 1st–3rd February 1935, trans. in ACIP B 131 (1935). For Rajsfus's very different interpretations of these passages see Rajsfus, *Sois juif, op. cit.*, pp. 124–125.

[95]Lambert, 'L'émigration juive d'Allemagne', in *Revue juive de Genève*, 3ème année, No. 4, (January 1935), p. 143. On similar condemnations of the government crackdown by native Jewish leaders see Oualid, 'Rapport du Comité Central d'assistance aux Emigrants Juifs', in *Les Cahiers du Renouveau*, No. 5 (April 1935), pp. 156–158; *idem*, 'Les étrangers en France', in UI, 8th February 1935, p. 314; Nicault, *loc. cit.*, note 36, p. 25.

up, he proclaimed, and he called upon the Central Consistory and the *Alliance Israélite Universelle* "to prove to the immigrant Jews that French Judaism will not refuse to comprehend its imperative duty". "If one allows this storm to pass over simply by bowing one's head", he continued, "who will be able to affirm that in several years, one might try to remedy an even more severe economic depression by revising those naturalisations which were granted after the war?". Contrary to prevailing opinion at the time, Lambert was convinced that the situation of German Jewry remained grave despite the apparent calm.[96] Most immediately, he feared that a pro-German vote in the forthcoming Saar plebescite, scheduled for mid-January 1935, would provoke yet another surge of refugees seeking asylum in France.[97] Lambert therefore warned French Jews that they had no alternative but to prepare for worse times ahead: "In so doing, we will have greater authority and more facilities to receive those unfortunates the future holds in store for us . . ."

Lambert apparently won a short-term victory – the *Comité National* ultimately joined other major Jewish organisations – including the FSJF, and the Gourevitch Committee – in protesting the decree laws and calling on the government to honour France's long-standing tradition of political asylum.[98] None the less, by the spring of 1935, for reasons that are not entirely clear, Lambert beat a retreat.[99] In a *Comité National* report which appeared in early 1935 he proclaimed that emigration, not constructive solutions, would be the sole function of the Committee. He even went on to praise the French government's policies: "They [the government authorities] have never failed to give us the most valuable encouragement and to facilitate our task to the greatest degree possible." While it

[96]Lambert, Confidential Report, 'La Situation des Juifs en Allemand, January 1936', to Flandin, 15th February 1936, in MAE Z 705, p. 50. Indeed, Lambert repeatedly chastised the French press for not paying adequate attention to antisemitism in Germany. See for example the articles by Lambert, 'L'agonie du judaisme allemand', 1st August 1933, pp. 541–542; 'L'avenir du judaisme allemand', 29th December 1933, pp. 465–466; 'Le IIIème Reich et les Juifs', 26th April 1935, all in the UI.

[97]According to Marrus, about 7,000 refugees fled to France from the Saar after the plebiscite, of whom between 38–40 percent were Jews, *The Unwanted*, p. 133. The Prefect of the Moselle, however, claimed that 12,603 Saar refugees had sought asylum in France as of 12th March 1935, although 586 of them had already been deported back to the Saar. See Prefect de la Moselle to MAE, 13th March 1935, in MAE Z 314.

[98]On the *Comité National*'s protest see Oualid, 'Rapport du Comité Central d'assistance aux Emigrants Juifs', in *Les Cahiers du Renouveau*, No. 5 (April 1935), pp. 157; 'Minutes of Meeting with the High Commissioner for Refugees', 29th January 1935, Enclosure 3, in JDC No. 161. On the protests of the FSJF and the Gourevitch-Dreyfus committee, see 'M. Flandin et les Juifs étrangers', in AI, 10th January 1935, p. 4; *Comité pour la défense* . . . , *op. cit.*, pp. 22–23; 'Une mémoire de la Fédération des Sociétés Juives', in UI, 25th January 1935, p. 310; 'Le mémoire de la Fédération des Sociétés juives de France', in UI, 1st February 1935, p. 326; Memorandum, 'Extraits de lettres en réponse à l'envoi du mémoire concernant la situation particulière des juifs établis en France et faisant l'objet de mesures prises contre les étrangers', 1935, in ACIP B131 (FSJF); Hyman, *op. cit.*, p. 209.

[99]The most probable reason for Lambert's shift is that the *Comité National* apparently received assurances from the Interministerial Committee on Immigration, directed by Edouard Herriot, that the rights of political refugees would be protected. Herriot nevertheless stood fast against granting political refugees the right to work. Foreign Ministry, 'Note pour M. le Secrétaire Général', 8th February 1935, in MAE Z 314, pp. 109–110.

was true that "the general measures, taken since October of 1933 with regard to foreigners, have rendered the stay and the establishment of refugees in France more difficult", it was nevertheless the case, he argued, that these measures "have not hit the refugees any more cruelly than other foreigners in France". "Moreover", he added, "the authorities have never dreamt of denying a right of asylum which conforms to our tradition. But, in light of the barriers created against the emigration from Germany by every country, France finds itself obliged to make its policy conform to the necessity in which our country finds itself, that is, to remain with respect to this immigration only a *gare de triage*. The only elements that will be permitted to settle definitively are those whose political refugee status can be proven and who bring to our country's economy undeniable talents that cause no harm to our national labour force."[100]

Whatever the reasons for Lambert's capitulation, there are signs that he felt deeply uncomfortable with having to articulate the hard-line position. Indeed, in the wake of the Nuremberg Laws in the autumn of 1935, he openly expressed a sense of extreme frustration and helplessness. In an article entitled 'Appeal to the Grand Rabbis of Europe', Lambert admitted that "we can no longer expect any action from Geneva, where religious and political persecutions are passed off as questions of secondary importance". The only hope, he claimed, was that "those large Jewish organisations, those that are not in a state of lethargy, obstinately continue, each one within its own domain, the positive action that attenuates miseries, that holds out hope to the young, and might, little by little, save those families who have already fled or may still be able to flee the Hitlerian hell". But, cognisant of the woeful inadequacy of this prescription, Lambert felt it necessary to offer another consolation: "One must now act in the spiritual realm", he proclaimed. This would be a job for the rabbis, not for the beleaguered relief organisations.[101] Lambert's point was unmistakable. In the absence of both emigration possibilities and opportunities for constructive settlement in the countries of first asylum, what could World Jewry do for the future victims of Hitlerian antisemitism but offer prayers and spiritual guidance.

Lambert's defeat and the *Comité National*'s subsequent withdrawal from the scene had dire consequences for those 15,000 to 17,000 refugees who still remained in France at the end of 1934.[102] According to a report of the German Commission, a refugee-directed committee that handled juridical and administrative assistance:

---

[100]Assemblée générale du Comité National de Secours', in UI, 2nd–9th August 1935, p. 730. See also Comité National, 'Rapport sur l'Activité du Comité National du 1er janvier 1934 jusqu'au 31 décembre 1934', in AIU X D 56.

[101]Lambert, 'Appel aux Grand-Rabbins d'Europe', in UI, 18th October 1935, p. 49.

[102]On the figure of 15,000–17,000 see Kahn to Baerwald, 6th November 1934, in JDC No. 601. The consequences were especially severe since all the other committees were collapsing as well. See Bauer, *op. cit.*, p. 153.

"There can be no divergence of opinion with respect to the present situation. The misery is frightful and the despair of the people unutterable. The cases of suicide have multiplied during the last weeks. The refugees, driven to the depths by hunger and despair, threaten to cede to provocations of crime and corruption. We are constantly being told by those to whom assistance has been refused, that they find themselves before the alternatives of stealing or begging. Thefts, and what is more frequent, cases of petty larceny, are the consequence of this state of affairs, and serve only to injure the cause of immigration and of Jewry in general . . . Never, since the beginning of the immigration, has the distress of the refugees been so poignant." [Italics in text][103]

Another report dating from late 1934 noted that as a result of the complete absence of job opportunities, even many middle-class refugees, who previously had been able to support themselves, were becoming "entirely proletarianised and reduced to living in the poorest quarters of Paris". Prostitution was on the rise, and the majority of the refugees "are restless, undernourished and terribly nervous . . . The uncertainty of their future is constantly haunting them."[104] In the spring of 1935 the *Jüdische Rundschau*, one of the principal organs of German Jewry, published letters from several young German refugees who complained bitterly of "the moral isolation and the quasi-total solitude in which they suffer, above all in France. The first year, the mass of refugees received at least some material assistance. At present, this assistance has dried up, and the majority now find themselves in a frightful situation, without means, without friends."[105] So intolerable had the situation become that many refugees were even requesting to be sent back to Germany.[106] As one of the Joint's representatives put it, with no prospect of a better future in France, "they would rather go back to Germany and suffer among their friends".[107]

I do not in any way wish to imply that French Jewry alone was entirely responsible for the deplorable and desperate state in which the refugees found themselves by the end of 1934. Indeed, the primary responsibility for the radical

[103]'Report of the German Commission of the National Committee', 27th June 1934, in JDC No. 601. This report was signed by Hugo Simon, the President of the German Commission, Georg Bernhard, Dr. Sammy Gronemann, Dr. Oscar Cohn, Dr. W. Friedländer, L. Aron, Dr. M. Strauss, Fritz Wolff. On the dire conditions see also Walter Friedländer, Director of the *Service Social pour les réfugiés allemands*, and representative of the *Comité Allemand*, 'Report of the Condition of the German Refugees in France, as of the early part of 1936', 31st March 1936, in JDC No. 602. On the split between the *Comité National* and German Commission see Lambert to Hugo Simon, 29th June 1934, in JDC No. 601.

[104]Paula Kurgass, Germany Emergency Committee Report, 'Extracts from a Study of the Situation of the German Refugees in Paris by Paula Kurgass', October 1934, in JDC No. 617.

[105]Cited in, 'Pour le Pessah des réfugiés', in *Journal Juif*, No. 14 (5th April 1935), p. 8.

[106]Police report, 'Situation actuelle de l'immigration juive allemande dans le département de la Seine', February 1934, in APP BA/1814 241.155–1–A. Some refugees had already requested to be repatriated to Germany as early as June 1933. See Comité d'Aide et d'Accueil, Compte rendu, No. 3, 1st–10th June 1933, in AIU X D 56.

[107]Morris C. Troper, 'Summary Report of Trip (24th October, 1934 to 13th December, 1934)', p. 18, in JDC No. 160. On the desperate conditions see also, 'Excerpt of letter from Melvin M. Fagen to Mr. Waldman', London, 16th November 1935, in JDC No. 617; Manès Sperber, *Ces temps là. Au delà de l'oubli*, Paris 1979, pp. 77, 104–105; *Comité pour la défense . . .* , *op. cit.*, pp. 16, 20; Bauer, *op. cit.*, p. 151; Badia, 'La France découverte par les émigrés', in *Revue d'Allemagne*, vol. XVIII, No. 2 (April–June 1986), p. 174.

retreat from the liberal policies of the spring of 1933 rests overwhelmingly with the French government. Nevertheless, one sector of French Jewry – those I have called the hard-liners – played an influential and very direct role in the formulation of official policy itself, pressing the government at every step of the way to pursue the most restrictionist policy possible. These Jewish leaders, in weighing what they perceived to be their mutually contradictory obligations to the refugees, on the one hand, and to the French government and people, on the other, felt compelled to opt entirely for the latter. The refugees, as a result, were left virtually defenceless. As David Wyman has shown with regard to the American case during the period of the Holocaust in *The Abandonment of the Jews*, the role of native Jewish elites, while not the primary determinant of refugee policy, nevertheless remains a factor that cannot be discounted.[108] Indeed, due to Helbronner's pivotal position at the League of Nations High Commission for Refugees, French Jews were perhaps in a better position to influence the actual determination of refugee policy in these early years than their co-religionists elsewhere in the West. Obviously, the response of people like Helbronner and his allies must be assessed against the background of growing antisemitism during this period. Yet, their tendency to blame antisemitism entirely on the refugees and the immigrants betrays a serious misunderstanding. As some French Jews, including Lambert, were beginning to realise, the existence of antisemitism had little to do with Jewish behaviour, whether it be the behaviour of the refugees themselves, or that of Left-wing Jews like Léon Blum.[109] Nevertheless, many French Jews could not accept this proposition and felt that their own well-being and acceptance into French society was being seriously undermined by an ever-swelling foreign Jewish presence.

Moreover, it is clear that French Jewish elites, at least during this period, did not do everything possible to provide philanthropic assistance to the refugees. The closing of the *Comité National* had nothing to do with government pressure. Rather, it reflected a conscious decision undertaken independently by the hard-liners within the Committee. Indeed, as we have shown, philanthropy itself became highly politicised. To be too generous, according to Helbronner and his allies, would only have encouraged greater numbers of refugees to have sought asylum in France. Moreover, the hard-liners feared that if French Jewry appeared overly solicitous regarding the fate of the refugees, antisemitic resentment and charges of dual loyalty would inevitably result. Consequently, from the hard-liners' point of view, it was simply easier to abandon all efforts on behalf of the persecuted victims of Nazism. To do so would prove once and for all that French Jews always put their French above their Jewish interest.

[108]David S. Wyman, *The Abandonment of the Jews. America and the Holocaust 1941–1945*, New York 1984, esp. chaps. 8–9, pp. 143–177.
[109]On Lambert, see his article, 'Nos Griefs', in UI, 26th October 1934, p. 98.

This analysis of French Jewish responses to the refugee crisis between 1933 and 1935 also suggests that the native-immigrant paradigm that has dominated the historiography of twentieth-century French Jewry may not be entirely adequate for understanding the wide range of native Jewish opinion. The native Jewish establishment was, as we have seen sharply divided over issues such as the refugee crisis, and these differences ultimately resulted in the implementation of vastly divergent policies. Indeed, the tensions between Lambert and Helbronner that had been simmering throughout the 1930s exploded fully during the Vichy period. At the end of 1941, Xavier Vallat, Vichy's newly appointed General Commissioner on Jewish Questions, appealed to Helbronner to assume the leadership of the soon-to-be-created Jewish Council, the *Union Générale des Israélites de France* (UGIF). Helbronner refused, less because he perceived the dangerous political ramifications of the organisation than because he deeply resented Vichy's attempt to lump native and immigrant Jews together. Lambert, on the other hand, accepted Vallat's mandate and became the leading force behind the UGIF in the unoccupied zone. Of course, Lambert was motivated in part by personal ambitions, and Helbronner was quick to chastise him for breaking ranks with Consistorial leadership. "It is inconceivable", Helbronner complained, "that this individual acts as if he were the Chief Rabbi of France, the President of the Central Consistory, and the Vice President of the Welfare Organisations, all in one".[110] But, as Richard I. Cohen has recently shown, Lambert's motives were by no means entirely personal. According to Cohen, Lambert was inspired above all by a very real and deeply felt commitment to the immigrant Jewish community. As Lambert saw it, the major function of the UGIF would be to provide desperately needed relief to those Jews now interned in the camps, and he vigorously fought what turned out to be a losing battle with Vallat to ensure that the UGIF's sphere of action be limited exclusively to social work to avoid any taint of political collaboration. Tragically, it was Lambert's long-standing commitment to refugee relief that ultimately led him down the slippery slope of co-operating with the Vichy regime.[111]

But, to return to the 1930s, a brief postcript is in order. With the rise of the

---

[110]Richard I. Cohen, *The Burden of Conscience. French Jewry's Response to the Holocaust*, Bloomington, Ind. 1985, p. 61. Cohen suggests that Lambert's break with Consistorial circles during Vichy was sudden. (See Cohen, *Carnet*, p. 36.) However, throughout the 1930s Lambert often used his position at the UI to criticise the native Jewish establishment.

[111]On Vallat's negotiations with both Helbronner and Lambert see Adler, *op. cit.*, chap. 5, pp. 81–106. Cohen, *Burden*, pp. 52–67; *idem, Carnet*, pp. 33–41; *idem*, 'The Jewish Community of France in the Face of Vichy-German Persecution: 1940–44', in Frances Malino and Bernard Wasserstein (eds.), *The Jews in Modern France*, Hanover, NH 1985, pp. 190–94; Marrus and Paxton, *op. cit.*, pp. 108–110. On Helbronner's xenophobia, see Adler, *op. cit.*, pp. 84–85; Cohen, *Burden*, pp. 58, 177; *idem, Carnet*, p. 42. Both Lambert and Helbronner were ultimately deported by the Germans in 1943. For an excellent review article on the role of French Jewish leadership during the Vichy period see Marrus, 'Jewish Leadership and the Holocaust. The Case of France', in Jehuda Reinharz (ed.), *Living with Antisemitism. Modern Jewish Responses*, Hanover, NH 1987, pp. 380–396.

Popular Front in 1936, the situation changed radically.[112] Government policy became considerably more lenient towards the refugees, and the *Comité National* was reconstituted, under pressure by the Joint Distribution Committee, as an entirely new entity. To sever all negative associations with its predecessor, the new committee was renamed the *Comité d'Assistance aux Réfugiés* (CAR), and the dominant force here was undeniably Lambert. Indeed, Helbronner was, at least for the moment, out of the picture; Léon Blum refused to send him back to the League of Nations High Commission for Refugees,[113] and the Joint Distribution Committee refused to allow any of the Committee's former personnel, with the exception of Lambert and Robert de Rothschild, to play any role whatsoever in the CAR.[114] Thus, Lambert's defeat in 1935 proved to be a temporary one, and, in the long run he emerged as the major voice in Franco-Jewish relief work. Under his influence, French Jewry, with the support of the French government, renewed its commitment to finding constructive employment opportunities, at least for those refugees already in France.[115]

Unfortunately, however, the situation took a dramatic turn for the worse in 1938 and 1939 when thousands more Jewish refugees arrived on French soil as a result of the *Anschluss*, the *Kristallnacht*, the Munich Crisis, and the deteriorating political and economic situation in Eastern Europe. According to one report, there were no fewer than 57,500 Jewish refugees in France by 1st January 1939, a figure that did not even include refugees of East European origin. Another 13,400 would arrive during the first seven months of that year.[116] Confronted with this "invasion of undesirables" the government of Radical Party leader,

[112]On the policies of the Popular Front see Livian, *op. cit., passim*; Schor, L'Opinion française, pp. 33–35; Peterson, *op. cit.*, pp. 78–79; Timothy Maga, *The United States, France and the Refugee Problem, 1933–1947*, unpubl. dissertation, McGill University, Montreal 1981, pp. 83–87; Bonnet, *op. cit.*, pp. 315–328. For more negative assessments see Schor, *L'Opinion française*, pp. 639–652; Thalmann, 'L'immigration allemande', pp. 171–172.

The Popular Front's refugee policy was to grant an amnesty to all refugees from Germany in France as of 5th August 1936, thus regularising the status of those who had come illegally after October 1933. However, it was clearly stipulated that no further refugees from Germany would be allowed to enter unless they had authorised visas. See Ministry of the Interior (Salengro) Circular No. 312, 14th August 1936 and Circular No. 314, 23rd September 1936, both in APP BA/1814, 241.155–1–A. Efforts were also made to allow those refugees in France to obtain work permits. See R.S., 'Le Problème international des réfugiés', 2nd October 1936, in UI, p. 53; 'L'Activité juridique de la Ligue', in CDH, 30th June–10th July 1936, p. 490; 'Le Statut des réfugiés allemands en France', 7th–14th August 1936, in UI, p. 749.

[113]M. Moch, 'Note sur les réfugiés d'Allemagne', 2nd July 1971, in AIU, CDV, Ms. 650, Boîte 12, dossier 44.

[114]JDC, 'Aid to Jews overseas. Report on the activities of the AJDC for the Year 1936', NY, 1937, in JDC, No. 156, p. 43; Kahn to J. C. Hyman, 11th May 1936, in JDC No. 617; Kahn to J. C. Hyman, 15th July 1936, in JDC No. 617.

[115]On the CAR's commitment to constructive solutions see: 'Le Statut des réfugiés allemands en France', in UI, 7th–14th August 1936, p 732; and *ibid.*, p. 749; Kahn to J. C. Hyman, 15th July 1936, and attached Minutes, 'Réunion préparatoire pour l'organisation de l'assistance aux réfugiés', 7th July 1936, in JDC No. 617; 'Appel du Comité d'Assistance aux Réfugiés', in UI, 17th December 1937, p. 250.

[116]'Intercommittee for the Work of Assistance for Refugees in France. The Situation of the Refugees in France', n.d. [August/September 1939], in JDC No. 617. It is difficult to arrive at a precise estimate of the number of Jewish refugees since many entered France illegally.

Edouard Daladier, and his Minister of Interior Albert Sarraut not only resumed the harsh policies of 1934 and 1935, but pushed through yet another series of anti-foreign decree laws, making it virtually impossible for newly arrived refugees to regularise their legal status and remain in France.[117] The policy of mass expulsion was reinstated, and those refugees now unable to leave were either imprisoned or ultimately interned. Ironically, the CAR now refused to abandon its commitment to the refugees, despite this fierce government crackdown. It continued to search for constructive solutions, and, for the first time, it displayed a willingness to consider even such radical alternatives as mass agricultural settlements in South-Western France and in French colonies.[118] Tragically, however, it was simply too late. Whatever opportunities had existed in 1933 and 1934 to lay the foundations for such schemes were now being washed away by the relentless tide of international events.

[117]On government policies in 1938–1939 and the rise of antisemitism generally in this period see Caron, 'Prelude to Vichy. France and the Jewish Refugees in the Era of Appeasement', *Journal of Contemporary History*, vol. XX, No. 1 (January 1985), pp. 157–176. Timothy Maga, 'Closing the Door. The French Government and Refugee Policy, 1933–1939', in *French Historical Studies*, vol. XII, No. 3 (1982), pp. 424–442; Marrus and Paxton, *op. cit.*, pp. 34–71; Bonnet, *op. cit.*, pp. 341–357; Schor, *L'Opinion francaise*, pp. 653–672, 699–709.

[118]On some of these schemes see Bauer, *op. cit.*, pp. 193–194, 237, 264–265; Marrus and Paxton, *op. cit.*, pp. 57, 60–62; Nicault, *loc. cit.*, pp. 14–15; Schor, *L'Opinion francaise*, p. 646.

British Policy Towards German Crimes Against German Jews, 1939–1945

BY PRISCILLA DALE JONES

At the end of the Second World War, thousands of Germans and other Axis nationals stood trial in a variety of Allied courts, charged with committing war crimes in German-occupied territory against Allied civilians or military personnel.* British military courts, for example, adjudicated 357 cases involving German, Italian and Austrian nationals. Three hundred and fourteen of these trials involved 989 German nationals or those in German employ.[1] But German brutality was not confined to war-time acts committed against Allied nationals outside Germany. The scope of pre-war and war-time Nazi cruelties against German Jews, against stateless persons and against nationals of states allied with Germany was vast and unprecedented. These acts of violence, later known as crimes against humanity, did not constitute breaches of the laws and usages of war as traditionally defined – war crimes *stricto sensu* – and, therefore, presented a particularly difficult political and legal challenge to the Allies.

From the outbreak of the war, officials of Allied governments-in-exile based in London were eager to publish declarations condemning Nazi atrocities and pledging to exact legal retribution. Nazi Germany was waging a cruel and savage battle against the early victims of Nazi aggression, such as Poland or Czechoslovakia, ignoring the established laws of warfare, and violating various international conventions to which Germany had given her signature concerning the rights of victors towards inhabitants of occupied territories.

But Allied countries such as Great Britain, which did not experience first-hand the rigours of German occupation, were, on the whole, very reluctant to make any public statements concerning German atrocities. British Foreign Office officials wished, particularly, to avoid commenting on German crimes against German nationals, specifically, German Jews. Later, as pressure mounted from the Polish, Czech and other Allied governments for war crimes policy statements from the British government, Foreign Office officials carefully distinguished between atrocities against German Jews and war crimes committed in occupied countries. Foreign Office officials were hesitant to recommend British investi-

---

*Crown-copyright material in the Public Record Office is reproduced by permission of the Controller of Her Majesty's Stationery Office. The writer wishes to thank Warren Jones for proof reading and Jeffery A. Rudd for his assistance in the preparation of this article. In spite of his own academic obligations, Mr. Rudd read the manuscript and made many editorial suggestions, for which the author is very grateful.
[1] These statistics are compiled from the following War Office files: Public Record Office, Kew (hereafter PRO), WO 235/1–198, 200–96, 301–499, 501–89. The WO 235 series in the Public Record Office consists of transcripts of war crimes trials conducted by British military courts in Germany and elsewhere.

gation and prosecution of Germans for war crimes against Allied, even British, victims. They were even more reluctant to consider trying Germans for atrocities against German Jews.

The British government was, initially, disinclined to view Nazi misconduct as considerably worse than that of aggressors in past wars. British scepticism as to the accuracy of Allied reports of German atrocities in Germany and occupied Europe only reinforced these doubts. Considered an almost routine war tactic, most atrocity stories were met with disbelief in official quarters. Foreign Office and other British government officials treated them with scepticism: non-British, particularly Jewish, sources of atrocity reports were thought to be hysterical and prone to exaggeration. A Foreign Office counsellor, Reginald Leeper, remarked in May 1940 that "as a general rule the Jews are inclined to magnify their persecutions".[2] Russian sources were also distrusted. In early October 1941, reports arrived at the Foreign Office about the discovery of a massacre on the outskirts of Kiev. This was the 29th–30th September 1941 shooting to death of 33,771 Jews by SS troops at Babi Yar ravine.[3] William Cavendish-Bentinck, the Acting Counsellor and Head of the Dominions and Intelligence Department in the Foreign Office who commented on these Russian broadcasts of "masses of horrors", had "a feeling that many of these are the product of Slav imaginations". Besides, even the British government "put out rumours of atrocities and horrors for various purposes", and he had "no doubt that this game is widely played".[4] Admitting that "many, if not most" of the atrocity reports received by the British government "may be correct", Cavendish-Bentinck nevertheless believed that his government did not possess – except in certain isolated instances – sufficient evidence to be able to determine their veracity.[5] Roger Allen of the Dominions and Intelligence Department, who was responsible for keeping track of enemy war crimes, particularly against British victims, was equally "sceptical of unsubstantiated stories".[6] Allen agreed

---

[2]PRO, FO 371 24472 C5471/116/55, Leeper, 21st May 1940, minute. A Central Department official had remarked earlier that "Jewish sources are always doubtful". PRO, FO 371 24472 C5471/116/55, illegible signature, 16th April 1940, minute.

[3]'Operations Situation Report, Einsatzgruppe C', 7th October 1941, quoted in Lucy S. Dawidowicz (ed.), *A Holocaust Reader*, New York 1976, pp. 84, 89–90.

[4]PRO, FO 371 26540 C11999/287/18, William Cavendish-Bentinck, 16th October 1941, minute to Cadogan. It was Cavendish-Bentinck's task to evaluate the accuracy of such reports from Nazi-occupied Europe. Martin Gilbert, *Auschwitz and the Allies*, New York 1981, p. 150. The atrocity "game" had been "widely played" during the First World War, to the eventual embarrassment of the British government. This contributed to Foreign Office doubts as to the accuracy of atrocity reports during the Second World War. As Cavendish-Bentinck recalled: "One remembered, I remember, during the first war, all sorts of stories were put out, and we believed them, we used them, in propaganda, and they were completely untrue, and . . . that propaganda . . . rebounded on us. So I was a bit sceptical." On-camera interview with Cavendish-Bentinck, included in 'Auschwitz and the Allies', a BBC-TV Production, based on Gilbert, *op. cit.*

[5]PRO, FO 371 26540 C11999/287/18, Cavendish-Bentinck, 11th November 1941, minute.

[6]PRO, FO 371 26540 C11999/287/18, Permanent Under-Secretary of State Sir Alexander M. G. Cadogan, 17th October 1941, minute. At the beginning of the war, it had been decided, at the suggestion of the Attorney-General, that Cavendish-Bentinck's department should follow Axis war crimes against British victims. Roger Allen was appointed to carry out the task, PRO, FO 371 26540 C11999/287/18, Cavendish-Bentinck, 16th October 1941, minute to Cadogan.

with the general Foreign Office view that the government should avoid taking any responsibility for the accuracy of Allied atrocity reports.[7]

Foreign Office officials generally questioned the accuracy of Allied and Free French atrocity reports, and whether – "apart from certain cases" – the British government possessed "sufficient evidence to be able to sift those which are based on fact from those which are untrue". When it was possible to "confirm the atrocities", evidence came from sources which had to remain secret.[8] Nevertheless, they had contact in official files with widely-accepted reports of Nazi brutality in occupied countries. Cavendish-Bentinck acknowledged on 10th October 1941 that there was "no doubt" that the Germans were "committing far worse atrocities than they did in the last war". He believed, however, that it would be difficult to prove many of these atrocities until the war had ended, investigations were made and eyewitness testimony had been presented.[9]

The ambivalent attitude of the Foreign Office towards Allied atrocity reports is clearly shown in two documents from the autumn of 1941. In a lengthy minute dated 15th November 1941 and entitled 'Collection of Information Regarding German Atrocities in Occupied Territories', Frank K. Roberts, a first secretary in the Central Department of the Foreign Office, pointed out that, because nearly all German atrocities had been committed against Allied and not British nationals, information regarding crimes could be supplied only by the Allied governments. Neither the Allies nor Britain had any control over the accuracy of such atrocity reports.[10] But while the Foreign Office may have doubted specific atrocity reports, an undated Foreign Office memorandum, prepared in late autumn 1941 and entitled 'German Methods of Warfare and of Occupying Foreign Territory', made it clear that there was no doubt about widespread Nazi breaches of the laws of war. According to this memorandum, the Germans had "on no occasion shown the slightest regard for the lives of wounded or non-combatants". The Germans divided conquered populations into "Germanic" groups, which the Nazis turned "into extensions of Nazi Germany", and "non-Germanic" groups, which the Nazis used "as working slaves" or murdered outright. In "non-Germanic" countries like Poland or Czechoslovakia, "murder, torture and robbery" were "supplementary Nazi instruments". The object of German aggression "had been fully stated" by various German officials: "The German race has higher rights than all others; it must have more bread, clothes and living room than Poles or Jews." The Allied governments-in-exile had on several occasions reported on "German atrocities in their respective countries". There was at present "no time" for British officials "to attempt to sift these reports". However,

[7]PRO, FO 371 26540 C11999/287/18, R. Allen, 11th November 1941, minute.

[8]Cavendish-Bentinck charged that: "Various Allied Governments and the Free French" used and "embroidered" atrocity "tales . . . for propaganda purposes", PRO, FO 371 26540 C11999/287/18, Cavendish-Bentinck, 11th November 1941, minute.

[9]PRO, FO 371 26540 C11999/287/18, Cavendish-Bentinck, 10th October 1941, minute to Deputy Under-Secretary of State Sir Orme G. Sargent.

[10]PRO, FO 371 26540 C11999/287/18, Frank K. Roberts, First Secretary in the Central Department of the Foreign Office, 15th November 1941, minute.

"It has [been] . . . fully established, and photographs have been published, of Yugoslav hostages who have been taken and killed in public by slow . . . strangulation. There is no doubt about the shooting of indiscriminate hostages in Poland . . . We know that as the German troops have advanced into Russia, the police battalions that followed in their train have, in individual districts, killed literally tens of thousands of civilians within a few days."[11]

In addition to the uncertain reliability of Allied atrocity reports, there were two additional reasons for Foreign Office reserve and hesitation regarding war crimes and crimes against humanity. First, the Foreign Office believed that no precedent existed for interference in another nation's treatment of its own nationals. The idea of "crimes against humanity" was not, however, unknown. In the Fourth Hague Convention of 1907, "the usages established among civilised peoples", "the dictates of the public conscience" and the "laws of humanity" were referred to as three sources of international law.[12] The expression "laws of humanity" was meant here "in a non-technical sense", and was not intended to mandate the creation of a new body of law separate from laws pertaining to the prosecution of war crimes *stricto sensu*.[13]

The term "crimes against humanity" was used in a non-technical sense for the first time in a declaration issued on 28th May 1915 by the governments of Britain, France and Russia concerning Turkish massacres of Armenians at the beginning of the First World War. This declaration denounced the massacres as "crimes against humanity and civilisation", for which all members of the Turkish government and its agents would be held responsible.[14] After the First World War, the Preliminary Peace Conference of Paris decided in January 1919 to create a Commission on Responsibilities, composed of fifteen representatives from ten nations, including Britain, and charged with "inquiring into the responsibilities relating to the war".[15] On 29th March 1919, the Commission submitted its Majority Report, along with dissenting reports by the American and Japanese members, to the Preliminary Peace Conference.[16] The Majority Report concluded that Germany and her Allies carried on the war "by barbarous or illegitimate methods in violation of the established laws and customs of war and the elementary laws of humanity". The Commission recommended that all enemy nationals, "without distinction of rank . . . who have been guilty of offences against the laws and customs of war or the laws of humanity, are liable

[11]PRO, FO 371 26540 C11999/287/18, Foreign Office unsigned [corrections by Cavendish-Bentinck], undated [late autumn 1941], memorandum entitled 'German Methods of Warfare and of Occupying Foreign Territory'.

[12]Fourth Hague Convention of 1907, quoted in *History of the United Nations War Crimes Commission and the Development of the Laws of War* [henceforth *History of the UNWCC*] compiled by the UNWCC, with a foreword by Lord Wright, London 1948, p. 25.

[13]*History of the UNWCC*, pp. 25–26, 188–189.

[14]The full text of the declaration is quoted in the 'Armenian Memorandum' presented by the Greek Delegation to the Commission on Responsibilities, Conference of Paris, 1919. *History of the UNWCC*, pp. 35–36, 189.

[15]Britain, the United States, France, Italy and Japan had two representatives each; Belgium, Greece, Poland, Romania and Serbia had one delegate each. *History of the UNWCC*, p. 32.

[16]*Violations of the Laws and Customs of War. Reports of Majority and Dissenting Reports of the American and Japanese Members of the Commission on Responsibilities, Conference of Paris, 1919* (henceforward *Report of the Majority of the Commission on Responsibilities*), Carnegie Endowment for International Peace, Division of International Law, Pamphlet No. 32, cited in *History of the UNWCC*, p. 33.

to criminal prosecution".[17] In its Memorandum of Reservations presented to the Commission, American delegates objected to the references to the "laws and principles of humanity" included in the Majority Report. The Americans maintained that, unlike the laws and customs of war, the laws and principles of humanity were not "a standard certain" upon which experts in international law were in agreement. Rather, they "vary with the individual, which, if for no other reason, should exclude them from consideration in a court of justice, especially one charged with the administration of criminal law".[18]

The Commission concluded its task by drafting provisions for treaties with enemy governments. However, in the Treaty of Versailles, Articles 228–230, signed on 28th June 1919, and in the Peace Treaties with Austria, Hungary and Bulgaria,[19] the American view prevailed, and all references to "laws of humanity" were deleted. The Treaty of Sèvres, the first treaty of peace with Turkey, signed on 10th August 1920, did contain a provision, Article 230, by which the Turkish government undertook to deliver to the Allies those responsible for massacres committed during the war on Turkish territory. This article was intended to cover Turkish offences against its own nationals, specifically those of Armenian or Greek descent. However, the Treaty of Sèvres was not ratified, and was replaced by the Treaty of Lausanne, signed on 24th July 1923. This treaty had no provisions for the punishment of war crimes or crimes against humanity, and was accompanied by a "Declaration of Amnesty" for all offences committed between 1st August 1914 and 20th November 1922.[20]

A second reason for Foreign Office reluctance to try enemy war criminals was the disastrous experience of war crimes trials at Leipzig after the First World War. These trials of German nationals, conducted by a German court, were largely a superficial formality in which the convicted few soon escaped from prison or were released after serving perfunctory sentences.

After the First World War, Article 228 of the Treaty of Versailles gave the Allies the right to try Germans for violations of the laws and customs of war. A list of 896 German war criminals wanted for trial by six countries – Britain, Belgium, France, Italy, Poland and Romania – was prepared in 1919,[21] and was presented to Baron Kurt von Lersner, the German ambassador in Paris, on 3rd February 1920.[22] Following von Lersner's public threat to resign rather than to allow the listed men to be handed over to the Allies for trial, the German government proposed a compromise, which an Allied-appointed commission

---

[17] *History of the UNWCC*, pp. 36, 38, quoting the *Report of the Majority of the Commission on Responsibilities*.
[18] "Memorandum of Reservations" presented by the Representatives of the United States to the Report of the Commission on Responsibilities, 4th April, 1919', contained in Annex II to the *Report of the Majority of the Commission on Responsibilities*, quoted in *History of the UNWCC*, p. 36.
[19] Peace Treaties of Saint-Germain-en-Laye (Articles 173–176), Trianon (Articles 157–159) and Neuilly-sur-Seine (Articles 118–120), cited in *History of the UNWCC*, p. 43.
[20] Treaty of Lausanne, 'Declaration of Amnesty' and the attached Protocol, 24th July 1923, cited in *History of the UNWCC*, p. 45.
[21] *History of the UNWCC*, p. 46.
[22] James F. Willis, *Prologue to Nuremberg*, London 1982, p. 120. According to Willis, the six countries listed in the text plus Yugoslavia submitted 854 names of suspects. The total was 854 because a few names appeared on more than one list.

declared compatible with Article 228: German authorities would conduct the prosecutions before the Supreme Court of the Empire (the *Reichsgericht*), without any Allied interference, but with the reservation that the Allies could re-try any accused before their own courts if they were dissatisfied with the outcome.

The Allies then presented the German government with a revised list of forty-five suspects charged with the gravest offences; seven of the names were contributed by the British government. Investigators encountered serious difficulties in collecting evidence against the accused: many suspects had disappeared, and witnesses could not be traced or were unable or unwilling to testify. Nevertheless, the trials opened before the *Reichsgericht* on 23rd May 1921.

Allied indignation at the conduct of the trials, the number of acquittals, and the leniency of the sentences mounted steadily until January 1922, when Allied governments withdrew their observers in protest. In June 1922, the Court decided to continue the trials in the absence of any Allied representatives. The outcome of these trials was no more satisfactory than those conducted before the Allied withdrawal. Of 901 allegations, some 861 had been dismissed by 1925. The final results of the Leipzig trials were indeed unimpressive:

> ". . . out of a total of 901 cases of revolting crimes brought before the Leipzig Court, 888 accused were acquitted or summarily dismissed, and only 13 ended in a conviction; furthermore, although the sentences were so inadequate, those who had been convicted were not even made to serve their sentence. Several escaped, and the prison warders who had engineered their escape were publicly congratulated."[23]

The British government made a major public statement dealing specifically with German crimes against German nationals in a White Paper published shortly after Britain declared war against Germany on 3rd September 1939. This Paper was published primarily to counter "shameless" and "unscrupulous" German propaganda about British atrocities committed in South Africa forty years earlier: "Before the war and ever since its outbreak", the German government had "almost daily" been issuing reports "accusing Great Britain of atrocities in South Africa". The Paper was published only secondarily to publicise the acts of violence committed by the German government against its own nationals: defending Britain's image was, apparently, more important than condemning German atrocities against German Jews and other German nationals. The White Paper recorded evidence held in British government files of German atrocities against German nationals in Germany between 1938 and 1939. Much of the official correspondence annexed to the report dealt with the persecution of Jews, particularly the treatment of Jewish prisoners at Dachau concentration camp, and included statements of former prisoners about conditions at Buchenwald concentration camp. The British government had not previously published the documents for fear of embittering Anglo-German relations, and – even after the outbreak of the war – for fear of "inspiring hatred" between the two countries. The White Paper read in part:

---

[23] *History of the UNWCC*, p. 46–48 and Willis, *op. cit.*, p. 146 (quoted).

"In view of this shameless [German] propaganda, which is wholly devoid of any foundation, His Majesty's Government think it opportune to publish some of the reports they have received of the treatment accorded in Germany itself to German nationals ... These documents were not written for publication, and, indeed, so long as there was the slightest prospect of reaching any settlement with the German Government it would have been wrong to do anything to embitter relations between the two countries. Even after the outbreak of the war His Majesty's Government felt reluctant to take action which might have the effect of inspiring hatred. But the attitude of the German Government and the unscrupulous propaganda which they are spreading compels His Majesty's Government to publish these documents so that public opinion both here and abroad may be able to judge for itself."[24]

The first suggestion that Britain should concern herself with German war crimes came from the Polish government-in-exile. The Polish embassy in London approached the Foreign Secretary, Viscount Halifax, on 31st January 1940 about a proposed Anglo-Franco-Polish declaration. The embassy submitted a first draft of the declaration to the British and French governments in early February. The draft called for the punishment "according to the full force of the law" of those Germans guilty of war crimes.[25]

But, with the exception of Sir Robert G. Vansittart, Chief Diplomatic Adviser at the Foreign Office, Foreign Office officials like the Permanent Under-Secretary of State Sir Alexander M. G. Cadogan, Roger M. Makins of the Central Department, Assistant Under-Secretary of State William Strang, and the Foreign Secretary, Halifax, were disinclined to commit the British government to punishing German war criminals.[26]

After several drafts and counterdrafts, a Franco-Polish draft declaration was approved by the War Cabinet on 12th April 1940. The Cabinet requested, however, and received, a formal assurance from the Polish government that the Poles considered the declaration a statement of principle, not a contractual obligation.[27] The declaration, signed by Britain, France and Poland, charged that the conduct of the German authorities and occupation forces in Poland constituted war crimes. By this declaration the governments of Britain, France and Poland protested "to the conscience of the world against the action of the German Government and of its agents", and reaffirmed "the responsibility of

[24]ZHC 1 8746/12, Command Paper 6120 of 1939, *House of Commons Accounts and Papers*, vol. XXVII, 1938–1939. Documents were dated 3rd March 1938 to 18th February 1939, and included letters from Sir Neville Henderson (Berlin) to Foreign Secretary Viscount Halifax; Consul-General Gainer (Vienna) to Halifax; Consul-General Carvell (Munich) to Halifax; and Sir G. Ogilvie-Forbes (Berlin) to Halifax.

[25]PRO, FO 371 24422 C2544/2026/18, Polish Ambassador Count Edward Raczynski, 31st January 1940, letter to Halifax. Enclosed unsigned undated Polish draft declaration.

[26]PRO, FO 371 24422 C2901/2026/18, Vansittart, 26th February 1940, minute to Halifax and 1st March 1940, minute; PRO, FO 371 24422 C3612/2026/18. Vansittart, undated [about 9th March 1940], minute; PRO, FO 371 24422 C2901/2026/18, Cadogan, 28th February 1940, minute; PRO, FO 371 22422 C3040/2026/18, Makins, 26th February 1940, minute, Strang, 27th February 1940, minute; PRO, FO 371 22422 C3612/2026/18, Strang, 9th March 1940, minute and Cadogan, 9th March 1940, minute; PRO, FO 371 22422 C4103/2026/18, Makins, 15th March 1940, minute.

[27]PRO, FO 371 24423 C5591/2026/18, Extract from War Cabinet Conclusions 89(40), 12th April 1940.

Germany for these crimes and their determination to right the wrongs thus inflicted on the Polish people".[28]

The Foreign Office faced "an almost insoluble" problem: how, on the one hand, to give encouragement to those under Nazi domination; and, how, on the other hand, to avoid committing the government too far to the principle of exacting retribution for war crimes.[29] Throughout 1941, most British officials attempted to follow the Foreign Office precedent of 1940 of expressing sympathy for the plight of peoples under German occupation, but, at the same time, of avoiding any public statement that might be construed as an obligation to prosecute Nazi war criminals. Meanwhile, the Poles, Czechs and other Allies increased pressure on the Foreign Office for a war crimes policy statement.[30] Churchill's public statements in June and October 1941 on German atrocities in occupied territory and on the need to punish Nazi war criminals also helped to undermine the non-committal attitude of the Foreign Office.[31]

Most Foreign Office officials agreed that Britain "must at all costs avoid saying anything which would commit us to the policy of making lists of war criminals for subsequent trial". In the autumn of 1941, Allied governments-in-exile pressed the Foreign Office for a joint declaration along just these lines. The Foreign Office feared, however, that British acquiescence would limit Britain's freedom to repudiate that policy at a later date. The Foreign Office believed that none of the Allied governments acting alone or corporately would be able to enforce the proposed joint declaration. In their view only Britain "could give it any reality".[32]

Foreign Office efforts to maintain a detached attitude towards Nazi war crimes began to crumble with the publication of the St. James's Palace Declaration of 13th January 1942. Here Belgium, Czechoslovakia, Greece, Luxembourg, the Netherlands, Norway, Poland, Yugoslavia and the French National Committee condemned Nazi atrocities in the occupied territories and declared that the trial and punishment of Nazi war criminals would be one of their "principal war aims".[33] A direct result of the St. James's Declaration was that, for the first time, officials outside the Foreign Office expressed an interest in formulating a war crimes policy. At the end of January 1942, the Attorney General, Sir Donald B. Somervell, and the Solicitor General, Sir David Maxwell Fyfe, sought permission to investigate British war crimes policy in order to assist

[28]PRO, FO 371 24423 C5454/2026/18, Foreign Office, 17th April 1940, telegram to the Governments of Canada, Commonwealth of Australia, New Zealand and the Union of South Africa.

[29]PRO, FO 371 24422 C4248/2026/18, Strang, 21st March 1940, minute.

[30]PRO, FO 371 26540 C11442/287/18, Roberts, 13th October 1941, minute about Czech-Polish draft resolution condemning German atrocities in occupied territory.

[31]Churchill, 22nd June 1941, broadcast, quoted in *The Times* of 23rd June 1941. PRO, FO 371 26540 C11987/287/18, Churchill, 25th October 1941, in which the Prime Minister stated that: "Retribution for these crimes must henceforward take its place among the major purposes of the war."

[32]PRO, FO 371 26540 C12833/287/18, Deputy Under-Secretary of State Sir Orme G. Sargent, minute.

[33]PRO, FO 371 26540 C13050/287/18, final draft of 13th January 1942 St. James's Palace Declaration.

in the formulation of that policy. The Foreign Office Legal Adviser, Sir William Malkin, the Permanent Under-Secretary of State, Alexander Cadogan, and the Foreign Secretary, Anthony Eden, all supported the Law Officers' proposal. In early February Eden invited Somervell and Fyfe to study the problem of war crimes policy.[34]

The resulting study, a memorandum of 15th April 1942, was the first systematic, official discussion of the legal aspects of war crimes. Somervell and Fyfe assumed that international law would be applied; thus, only war crimes *stricto sensu* would be prosecutable offences. Germans would eventually face charges before British military courts of atrocities against Allied nationals in occupied Europe; German atrocities against German nationals did not constitute war crimes, and were, therefore, beyond the scope of British military courts.[35]

Throughout the spring and summer of 1942, news of the suffering and death of civilians, particularly Jews, in occupied Europe continued to reach London, and by October 1942, the detached attitude of the Foreign Office towards war crimes was under fire on every front. Faced with intensifying pressure from the British public, from Parliament and from the Allies – including the Soviets, who openly declared that war criminals should be tried – many Foreign Office officials came to believe that a war crimes policy statement would soon be necessary.

That statement was the Anglo-Soviet-American declaration of 17th December 1942. Britain, the Soviet Union and the United States with Belgium, Czechoslovakia, Greece, Luxembourg, the Netherlands, Norway, Poland, Yugoslavia and the French National Committee condemned "in the strongest possible terms" the Nazis' "bestial policy of cold-blooded extermination" of European Jewry. They also re-affirmed "their solemn resolution to ensure that those responsible for these crimes shall not escape retribution, and to press on with the necessary practical measures to this end".[36]

Churchill's involvement in the making of war crimes policy grew as news of Nazi atrocities continued to reach London. In October 1943, the Cabinet approved his recommendation that the foreign ministers of Great Britain, the United States and the Soviet Union issue a new declaration.[37] Roosevelt and Stalin accepted Churchill's draft, which became the Moscow Declaration of 1st November 1943. This declaration pledged that those responsible for German atrocities should be returned to the countries where their crimes were committed, and then judged and punished "on the spot by the peoples whom they have outraged". The Moscow Declaration added that "most assuredly the three Allied Powers will pursue [war criminals] . . . to the uttermost ends of the earth and will

[34]PRO, FO 371 30914 C1466/61/18, Malkin, 3rd February 1942, minute; Cadogan and Eden, 3rd February 1942, minutes; Malkin, 4th February 1942, letter to Somervell.
[35]PRO, FO 371 30916 C4049/61/18, Law Officers of the Crown, 15th April 1942, memorandum; Somervell, 15th April 1942, letter to Malkin.
[36]Eden, 17th December 1942, House of Commons statement, quoted in PRO, CAB 66/50, Annex No. 4 to Lord Chancellor Simon's 2nd June 1944 Cabinet Memorandum (W. P. [44]294).
[37]PRO, FO 371 34374 C11981/31/62, War Cabinet, 8th October 1943, Conclusions (W.M. [43] 137).

deliver them to their accusers in order that justice may be done".[38] The prosecution of war criminals where their crimes were committed meant that Britain would not bear exclusive responsibility for their trial. Churchill feared that Britain "would be incapable of carrying out mass executions for any length of time, especially as we have not suffered like the subjugated countries".[39]

On 21st November 1944, the Cabinet decided that British military courts, established in Germany or elsewhere, should try cases of war crimes committed against British subjects in British territory.[40] Drafting of the Royal Warrant, which became the statutory basis for British military courts, began in late 1944. The Royal Warrant was finally published in mid-June 1945. British military courts were given the jurisdiction to try those German and Japanese war criminals not tried by the four-power International Military Tribunal at Nuremberg. Provision was also made "for the trial and punishment of violations of the laws and usages of war committed during any war in which . . . [Britain] may have been or may be engaged at any time after the second day of September nineteen hundred and thirty-nine".[41] The class of offences prosecutable in British military courts was limited to war crimes *stricto sensu*. All German and Japanese atrocities committed before the outbreak of the war, and all acts of violence which the Axis powers committed against their own nationals were, therefore, beyond the scope of British war crimes courts.[42]

From the time of the Law Officers' memorandum of 15th April 1942 until the publication of the Royal Warrant on 14th June 1945, the proper scope of jurisdiction of British war crimes courts would be much discussed in British official circles. As the war progressed, revealing the nature and extent of Nazi criminality, the British government came under increasing pressure to broaden the category of justiciable war crimes to include German offences against the German Jews and other non-Allied civilians. Foreign Office officials, who were generally opposed to *ad hoc* law and tribunals, viewed this possibility with considerable trepidation.

During a debate in the House of Lords on 7th October 1942, the Lord Chancellor, John Simon, announced an American- and Allied-backed proposal to establish a United Nations Commission for the Investigation of War Crimes. The Commission's terms of reference would be limited to investigating Axis war crimes against Allied nationals, recording available evidence and testimony and reporting periodically to the governments concerned. At a meeting held at the Foreign Office just over a year after Simon's statement, on 20th October 1943,

---

[38]Moscow Declaration of 1st November 1943 in PRO, CAB 66/50, Annex No. 5 to Lord Chancellor Simon's 2nd June 1944 Cabinet Memorandum (W.P. [44] 294).

[39]PRO, FO 371 34378 C13458/31/62, Churchill, 9th November 1943, Cabinet paper (W.P. [43] 496); and War Cabinet, 10th November 1943, Conclusions (W.M. [43] 152).

[40]PRO, FO 371 39008 C16362/14/62, War Cabinet, 21st November 1944, Conclusions (W.M. [44] 152).

[41]14th June 1945 Royal Warrant, Army Order 81/1945, Regulations for the Trial of War Criminals, quoted in Sir David Maxwell Fyfe (ed.), *War Crimes Trials*, vol. V, London 1949, p. 233.

[42]*History of the UNWCC*, p. 216.

seventeen Allied nations constituted the Commission under the name of the United Nations War Crimes Commission (UNWCC).[43]

In early October 1942, Leon Rosengarten, secretary of the Zürich-based Jewish Aid Committee for Emigration, wrote to Prime Minister Churchill about Simon's statement of 7th October 1942 that every crime against members of the United Nations would be punished. Rosengarten wondered if Simon's warning applied to atrocities against stateless persons who were formerly German, Austrian, and Romanian Jews. Roger Allen of the Foreign Office Dominions and Intelligence Department listed the "considerable" problems which Rosengarten's suggestion entailed. Allen believed that most, if not all, offences committed against these groups were

> ". . . not in any sense war crimes. To consider them would involve extending the scope of the [United Nations War Crimes] Commission, and it might mean creating a body of ad hoc law. The question is in fact surely too big for the Commission: it is nothing less than a question of indicting Nazi internal policy during the whole period of the regime. This is a political, not a legal, issue, and should be dealt with as such."

He added that those accused of war crimes investigated by the UNWCC would probably be tried by military courts in the countries where their crimes were committed. Allen found it difficult to envisage an appropriate tribunal to judge cases of crimes against Jewish and non-Jewish German nationals.[44] He feared that the question of such tribunals would become a recurrent and difficult problem for the British government because of the scope of Nazi atrocities against German Jews and other enemy nationals.

A meeting of Foreign Office legal experts convened by the Lord Chancellor on 10th August 1943 considered the jurisdiction for offences committed against stateless persons in German-occupied territory. Those present, including the Attorney General, Somervell; Foreign Office Legal Adviser, Sir William Malkin; Sir Cecil Hurst (the United Kingdom Representative Designate on the UNWCC); Treasury Solicitor, Sir Thomas Barnes and Judge Advocate General (JAG), Sir Henry MacGeagh, agreed that "a special scheme would be required if indeed the matter was to be covered". The Lord Chancellor argued that "it was particularly important that HMG should protect the interests of stateless persons".[45] Malkin maintained that "offences against German Jews are not war crimes".[46]

---

[43]PRO, FO 371 30919 C9669/61/18, Lord Simon, House of Lords statement, 7th October 1942. *History of the UNWCC*, pp. 2–3. The Foreign Office was never an enthusiastic supporter of the UNWCC. Legal Adviser Sir William Malkin admitted that there was "some useful material in some of the Committee's documents", but added that "it has been a stamping ground for every crank in . . . [Britain]", and concluded that he would "not be disposed to pay too much attention to its products". PRO, FO 371 38990 C14/14/62, Malkin, 5th January 1944, minute. The Under-Secretary of State for Foreign Affairs, Richard Law, regarded the UNWCC "as a great bore, & probably a great mistake". Britain was, nevertheless, "committed to it". PRO, FO 371 39007 C15546/14/62, Law, 19th November 1944, minute.
[44]PRO, FO 371 30920 C10560/61/18, Rosengarten, 9th October 1942, letter to Churchill; R. Allen, 9th November 1942, minute. British officials often referred to the Allies as the "United Nations".
[45]PRO, FO 371 34371 C9532/31/62, meeting of legal experts, 10th August 1943.
[46]PRO, FO 371 34369 C8796/31/62, Malkin, 6th August 1943, minute.

At a meeting on 16th March 1944 of Committee No. III, one of the new UNWCC subcommittees, the American representative, Herbert Pell, proposed extending the definition of war crimes to cover offences against German Jews in Germany. Foreign Office minutes concerning Pell's proposal reveal some confusion and disagreement over what exactly Britain and the Allies had promised regarding retribution for war crimes.[47] Denis Allen of the Central Department noted that concerned Allied governments had affirmed their determination to ensure that those responsible for German crimes against Jews in general should not escape retribution. He added, however, that the Foreign Office regarded German crimes against German Jews as "an internal German affair, punishable under German law". Allen recommended that Allied governments "should be very wary of assuming any far reaching commitments as to the ways and means of carrying out such punishment . . . [the Allies] will have enough to do without involving themselves in responsibility for executing retrospective justice in Germany", Most Foreign Office officials considered it inappropriate for the UNWCC to deal with such cases. Allen concluded that "we must, I think, try to secure acceptance of the view that the whole question should as far as possible be left to be dealt with, if at all, by the Germans after the war and that the United Nations Govts. should not assume any advance responsibility in the matter".[48] John M. Troutbeck, a counsellor in the Foreign Office, argued that it would be difficult for the Allies to leave punishment for such crimes to the Germans or others who committed them. He wrote, "we are so far committed to ensuring that people responsible for crimes against Jews in their own countries receive retribution that we shall have difficulty in taking the line that this can be left to the Germans (or Hungarians etc. as the case may be)".[49] Malkin disagreed with Troutbeck's interpretation of Britain's public resolutions and maintained that the three-power statement of 17th December 1942 read "as if it were intended to be confined to atrocities against Jews in occupied territories . . . The trouble about these eloquent declarations, at any rate from the point of view of the lawyer, is that it is frequently uncertain exactly what they are intended to apply to."[50] But if, as Troutbeck suggested, the British or Allied governments had "gone on record in favour of the punishment of offences committed against Jews in Germany", Malkin wished "very much . . . to see what has been said". As far as he was concerned, the question could be resolved only "by a political decision, probably at a high level". Until such a decision was taken, Malkin would follow Foreign Office policy, which held that the UNWCC were "not in a position to take on this subject of their own notion, or in particular

---

[47]PRO, FO 371 38992 C3567/14/62, Herbert Pell proposal at 16th March 1944 meeting of UNWCC Committee No. III.

[48]PRO, FO 371 38992 C3567/14/62, D. Allen, 20th March 1944, minute.

[49]Troutbeck concluded that "The words 'if at all' in Mr. Allen's minute seem in particular to be out of keeping with our public statements." PRO, FO 371 38992 C3567/14/62, Troutbeck, 21st March 1944, minute.

[50]This was not a surprising observation, since Foreign Office lawyers had had an active hand in drafting "these eloquent" but rather vague declarations.

by extending their definition of war criminals, and that if they want to deal with it they must ask for an extension of their terms of reference".[51]

Jews and Jewish refugees created difficulties for other Foreign Office departments. The head of the Refugee Department, A. W. G. Randall, feared that British trials of suspected war criminals on charges of crimes against Jews would make it more difficult for Jews to return to their native countries after the war. He wrote:

> "[The] Refugee Dept's interest in this business is that nothing should be done to make it more difficult for Jews to return to their former countries of residence. This can be effected by our securing the abolition of all discriminatory legislation and the restitution of German citizenship etc. I should have thought the punishment of crimes against Jews only would favour continued racial segregation and increase thus the difficulty of fitting any substantial number of Jews into the framework of German national life."[52]

In a broadcast on 24th March 1944, President Roosevelt also voiced the hope that the oppressed might return to their homelands after "the tyrant" was driven out. Roosevelt, however, was more sensitive than Randall to the possibility that there might not be a substantial number of Jews surviving at the war's end to fit into the framework of the life of any European nation. Roosevelt condemned "the systematic torture and murder of civilians, men, women, and children, by the Nazis and the Japanese", which continued "unabated", and the "slaughters of Warsaw, Lidice, Kharkov, and Nanking", as "startling examples of what goes on day by day year in year out, wherever the Nazis and Japs are in military control – free to follow their barbaric purpose". Roosevelt then turned to the murder of European Jewry:

> "In one of the blackest crimes of all history – begun by the Nazis in the day of peace and multiplied by them a hundred times in time of war – the wholesale schematic murder of the Jews of Europe goes on unabated every hour. As a result of the events of the last few days hundreds of thousands of Jews who while living under persecution have at least found a haven from death in Hungary and the Balkans, are now threatened with annihilation as Hitler's forces descend more heavily upon these lands. That these innocent people, who have already survived a decade of Hitler's fury, should perish on the very eve of triumph over the barbarism which their persecution symbolizes, should be a major tragedy."

Roosevelt again proclaimed the determination of the United States that

> ". . . none who participate in these acts of savagery shall go unpunished. The United Nations have made it clear that they will pursue the guilty and deliver them up in order that justice be done . . . All who knowingly take part in the deportation of Jews to their death in Poland or Norwegian and French to their death in Germany are equally guilty with the executioner. All who share the guilt shall share the punishment."[53]

Reporting to Congress on 12th June 1944 about the steps taken by the United States government to provide a refuge for the victims of German brutality, Roosevelt stated that "the Nazis, in spite of the fact that they faced certain defeat, were determined to complete their 'programme of mass extermination' of minorities". The President believed that this systematic persecution "was but

[51]PRO, FO 371 38992 C3567/14/62, Malkin, 21st March 1944, minute.
[52]PRO, FO 371 38992 C3567/14/62, A. W. G. Randall (head of Refugee Department, Foreign Office), 22nd March 1944, minute.
[53]PRO, FO 371 38995 C8144/14/62, Roosevelt, declaration of 24th March 1944.

one manifestation of Hitler's intention to salvage from military defeat a victory for Nazi principle".[54]

On 28th June 1944, the War Cabinet approved a memorandum by the Lord Chancellor reviewing the work of the UNWCC. Simon thought that the Commission had defined their terms of reference too narrowly, as a result of which their work had suffered. The UNWCC should, he suggested, be pressed to take a broader view of their functions. He added that Britain should agree to an extension of the Commission's terms of reference to include crimes committed against Italians and Danes, and that the Commission should collect evidence of German atrocities perpetrated in occupied countries against Jews.[55] German crimes against German Jews in Germany, however, were not war crimes.[56] The Cabinet approved these propositions, subject to discussion by Eden and Simon of certain minor points.[57] The British government consistently maintained that German crimes against German nationals could not be considered war crimes, however compelling the need for their punishment might be.

The problem of the types of cases which the UNWCC should consider arose again in mid-August 1944. Malkin thought that the Commission could deal with cases of non-Allied nationals moved to Allied territory under German occupation and mistreated there by Germans.[58] In spite of Malkin's "clear expression of opinion" that the UNWCC could consider such cases, it was still unclear to the Foreign Office whether these cases constituted war crimes. Patrick Dean, a legal adviser in the Foreign Office, expressed that uncertainty when he wrote in August 1944:

> "The basis of jurisdiction to try [cases involving] German and Hungarian Jews who are moved into Poland and other Allied territory and there maltreated or murdered by the Germans would presumably be that the crime has been committed in Allied territory and . . . would be justiciable before the courts of the Allied territory concerned. It is a little difficult to say whether such action by the Germans amounts to a war crime or not . . ."[59]

Con O'Neill, a Central Department adviser on Germany, agreed that atrocities committed against enemy nationals on racial, religious, or political grounds in enemy territory could not be dealt with under war crimes procedure. He argued, nevertheless, that Britain should take steps to punish these "vile" crimes. Besides "the moral issue", he saw "two practical advantages" to be gained. First, "The men who committed [these crimes] . . . would be from all points of view, not least our own as occupying authorities, better put away than left running round free in Germany." Second, it would relieve the "very strong pressure" which was "already taking very visible shape" both in Britain and in the United States "to see that some sort of amends are made to German Jews".

---

[54]Roosevelt, 12th June 1944 statement, quoted in *The Times*, of 13th June 1944, in PRO, FO 371 38995 C8144/14/62.

[55]PRO, FO 371 38996 C8667/14/62, Simon, 2nd June 1944, War Cabinet memorandum (W.P. [44] 294).

[56]PRO, FO 371 38999 C9971/14/62, D. Allen, paper of 17th July 1944.

[57]PRO, FO 371 38996 C8667/14/62, War Cabinet, 28th June 1944, Conclusions (W.M. [44] 83).

[58]PRO, FO 371 38999 C10561/14/62, D. Allen, 14th August 1944, minute.

[59]PRO, FO 371 38999 C10561/14/62, P. Dean, 16th August 1944, minute.

Those "amends" could take the form of "compensation for lost property" or of "punishment of those who inflicted the injuries". O'Neill preferred the latter because, "Personal remedies are simpler than property remedies". Although unstated, O'Neill clearly feared a revival of antisemitism in Germany as a result of Jewish financial restoration. The punishment of those guilty of crimes against Jews would probably be resented less by the German people "than the taking of elaborate steps to restore to Jews, in a starving country, their pre-Nazi financial status". Punishing the culprits was, however, no simple matter. O'Neill thought the accused would have to be tried in German courts and under German law. He predicted that the United Nations would "be in a very strong position to bring pressure to bear on the German authorities on a matter of this sort. And the readiness of the latter to do something about it would provide a valuable test of the genuineness of their repudiation of Nazi principles and practises [sic]."[60]

G. W. Harrison, an Acting First Secretary in the Central Department, agreed with O'Neill; he had, in fact, "always thought that the best way of handling this thorny problem is to bring pressure to bear on the successor govt. in Germany (and in Hungary and other satellites too for that matter), if there is one". The execution of Mussolini in Italy suggested that a successor government could be "quite zealous" in dealing with this type of crime. The harder British public opinion pressured the British government on this question, the more pressure the British government could "bring to bear" on Germany. Harrison thought however, that it would be impractical to pursue this issue without a successor government in Germany.[61]

On 17th July 1944, Denis Allen submitted a paper written in consultation with the German Advisory Section and Malkin concerning crimes committed on racial, political, or religious grounds in German-occupied territory. In accordance with its terms of reference, the UNWCC had hitherto confined its investigations to cases involving breaches of the laws of war committed against members of the Allied forces or against inhabitants of Allied territory occupied by the enemy. The UNWCC had been aware for some time of British and American public pressure that they should also investigate cases involving atrocities committed by the enemy against non-Allied nationals, in particular, German crimes against Jews in Germany and in other enemy countries. The Foreign Office had several objections to this view. First, in many cases, the offences in question were in all probability not crimes under German law as it then stood. Second, even if the offences were contrary to German law, they were not contrary to the laws and customs of war under international law; the Allies, therefore, could not prosecute. Third, the Allies could not take responsibility for enforcing "universal retrospective justice" in Germany. Any attempt to deal with these offences would raise difficult practical questions of how far back to go – since there was no essential difference between crimes against Jews before the war and those committed in its course – and what type of crime should be punished.

[60] PRO, FO 371 38998 C8992/14/62, O'Neill (Central Department, German Advisory Section; later in German Department), 13th July 1944, minute.
[61] PRO, FO 371 38998 C8992/14/62, G. W. Harrison (Central Department), 15th July 1944, minute.

Those who advocated retribution for crimes against Jews in enemy satellite countries, such as Hungary, found support in the Allied declaration of 17th December 1942 about the mistreatment of Jews in occupied Europe; in Eden's declaration of 31st March 1944 which was aimed primarily at satellite governments, warning them against complicity in German persecution of the Jews; and in Eden's statement of 5th July 1944 about the deportation of Jews from Hungary to Poland. Allen argued, however, that none of these declarations appeared to involve the British government in an "inescapable commitment" to try perpetrators of crimes against Jews and others in enemy countries. This extended even to crimes in German concentration camps.

> "The crucial fact in all of these cases is that there is a clear distinction between offences in regard to which the United Nations have jurisdiction under international law, i.e. war crimes, and those in which they have not. Atrocities committed on racial, political or religious grounds in enemy territory fall within the latter category. It follows that the United Nations cannot themselves assume any formal obligation in regard to the punishment of those responsible for such atrocities."

On a practical level, formal commitments might be difficult if not impossible to fulfil. Allen's paper concluded with two recommendations. First, Britain should object to UNWCC consideration of atrocities committed on racial, political, or religious grounds in enemy territory. Second, the Allies should be prepared to exert pressure upon successor governments in enemy countries to ensure that criminals were brought to justice. The Allies would not, however, assume any formal commitment to try the culprits or impose upon the enemy any formal obligation to try them or surrender them for trial.[62]

Malkin and the Central Department agreed that the Foreign Office should continue to draw the "firm distinction" noted in Allen's paper between atrocities against Allied nationals or in Allied countries and those against enemy nationals, and that this second category should not be brought under the heading of war crimes. In response, however, to meet "strong public feeling", Britain should exert "the strongest pressure" upon post-war governments in enemy countries to prosecute those responsible for atrocities against enemy nationals.[63] The Permanent Under-Secretary, Cadogan, also believed that these were "the inevitable conclusions" to be drawn from Allen's paper.[64] Eden was not so sure: "May be. But am I not pledged in some of my numerous statements about Jewish persecutions to punish those responsible and is it possible to square this with conclusions in . . . [Allen's] paper?"[65] Foreign Office officials, however, assured Eden that his declarations were consistent with the concept of war crimes *stricto sensu*. While admitting that the Foreign Secretary's declarations obliged the government "to do all in their power to ensure that those responsible for crimes against Jews in German-occupied Europe shall not escape retribution", Denis Allen pointed out that "official statements in this regard had always been worded in very general terms". Malkin argued further that "nothing in these declarations

[62]PRO, FO 371 38999 C9971/14/62, D. Allen, paper of 17th July 1944.
[63]PRO, FO 371 38999 C9971/14/62, Roberts, 18th July 1944, minute.
[64]PRO, FO 371 38999 C9971/14/62, Cadogan, 18th July 1944, minute.
[65]PRO, FO 371 38999 C9971/14/62, Eden, 22nd July 1944, minute.

. . . [constituted] an inescapable commitment on the part of HMG to bring to trial the perpetrators of crimes against Jews and others in *enemy* territories". In his view, the "inescapable" conclusion was that "the action which HMG and the other United Nations Governments can themselves usefully take must be limited to the case of war crimes in the strict sense of the term. The Department do not consider that such a limitation would be inconsistent with anything that has been said in the Secretary of State's declarations."[66] Eden, apparently reassured, sent a copy of Allen's 17th July paper to the Lord Chancellor and to the Attorney General on 5th August.[67]

In November 1944, G. G. Fitzmaurice, the Third Legal Adviser of the Foreign Office, expressed his reservations about the possibility of including a clause in the draft armistice with Germany compelling the Germans to establish a tribunal to try those accused of atrocities against Jews and others in Nazi concentration camps. The execution of such a clause would lead to great difficulties. "The main trouble is that, however morally indefensible these actions may have been, they were presumably legal under German law as it then stood." If so, the accused[68] "could not be indicted for having done anything illegal in the technical sense. If therefore it is a German court of law which is to try him, it will be necessary to cause the German authorities to introduce retrospective legislation which would make all these actions *ex post facto* illegal." Fitzmaurice opposed United Nations participation in any German tribunal. He feared that if the Allies participated they would have to share some responsibility for what the tribunal did. As a result the British government might, in the eyes of world opinion, bear responsibility for decisions they could not influence. Fitzmaurice concluded that if no solution could be found, this type of clause should not appear in the armistice. The most Britain could hope for would be "to bring some indirect pressure on the Germans to take on their own initiative such action as it might be found possible to take under existing or amended German law".[69]

Foreign Office officials G. W. Harrison of the Central Department, and Frank Roberts agreed with Fitzmaurice about inserting such a clause in the armistice with Germany. Noting that there would "no doubt be some pressure here and in the USA, to get these people punished", Harrison acknowledged the great difficulty of this problem. He was "very reluctant", however, to see a special clause inserted into the armistice: "It is so very much a domestic German affair." He believed that "very strong pressure" could be brought to bear on a post-war German government – if there was one. He doubted whether Britain should go as far as "insisting"; he did not, however, imagine that Britain would have to threaten sanctions against Germany. If there was no German government, this problem would "be even more uncertain". Referring to Eden's old idea of a sword of revenge being wielded by survivors, Harrison concluded: "One could only

[66]PRO, FO 371 38999 C9971/14/62, D. Allen, 25th July 1944, minute, emphasis in original.
[67]PRO, FO 371 38999 C9971/14/62, Eden, 5th August 1944, letter to Lord Chancellor and Attorney General.
[68]The accused, in Fitzmaurice's hypothetical example, was a camp commander arraigned before a tribunal "for beating a Jew".
[69]PRO, FO 371 39069 C116/116/18, Fitzmaurice, 19th November 1944, minute.

hope that the injured parties, where they have survived, or their relatives would take matters into their own hands."[70] Frank Roberts agreed with Harrison, fearing that: "We shall be confronted with more than enough awkward problems in regard to war criminals guilty of acts against one or other of the United Nations [i.e., the Allies] without wandering off into the by-paths of executing retrospective justice within Germany itself."[71]

Foreign Office Counsellor John M. Troutbeck responded to the anxieties of Harrison and Roberts by noting that "the passing of new retrospective legislation" would not be necessary. The cancellation of "some special Nazi [amnesty] laws or decrees", which were the source of the "legality of the acts perpetrated in concentration camps" would be sufficient. Troutbeck acknowledged that: "The whole question is of course charged with political lightning", and predicted that the Cabinet would eventually decide the issue.[72]

Members of Parliament were also interested in the question of German crimes against German nationals. During a debate in the House of Commons on 10th November 1944, the Labour MP George R. Strauss referred to the murder of about 7,000 anti-Nazi German nationals at Buchenwald. Strauss wanted Britain to consult with the Allies to widen the category of war crimes to include crimes in German territory against German nationals. He asked the Commons whether the perpetrators of this mass murder should go free, and if the Allied governments would wash their hands just because of the victims' nationality.

> "Are not these crimes every bit as vile, whether they are perpetrated in German territory or in any other territory, or whether the victims are German nationals or the nationals of any other country? There is no distinction at all between the vileness of the crimes, either on territorial or national grounds . . .
>
> This is not a national war; it transcends frontiers and national conceptions. It is essentially a war of ideas."

Decent behaviour and individual freedom were pitted against tyranny and lies. The government spokesman George Hall, who was Under-Secretary of State for Foreign Affairs, questioned Strauss's belief that an Allied declaration might stop atrocities. Hall reminded Strauss that, in spite of the many declarations summoning Germans to cease their inhuman treatment and massacres, the brutality still continued.[73]

On 31st January 1945, Strauss asked Eden for a new statement about the intention of the government to treat as war criminals those responsible for the murder or ill-treatment of anti-Nazi Germans in concentration camps or elsewhere in Germany. Replying for the government, the Minister of State, Richard Law, stated:

> "As my right hon. Friend the Foreign Secretary informed my hon. Friend in reply to a question on 4th October, crimes committed by Germans against Germans are in a different

---

[70]PRO, FO 371 39069 C116/116/18, Harrison, 20th November 1944, minute.

[71]PRO, FO 371 39069 C116/116/18, Roberts, 20th November 1944, minute.

[72]PRO, FO 371 39069 C116/116/18, Troutbeck, 19th November 1944, minute.

[73]At this point, Captain A. S. Cunningham-Reid, MP (Conservative, St. Marylebone) pointed out that there was not a quorum (forty members) present, and the Commons adjourned. PRO, FO 371 39007 C15594/14/62, House of Commons debate, 10th November 1944.

category from war crimes and cannot be dealt with under the same procedure. But in spite of this, I can assure my hon. Friend that His Majesty's Government will do their utmost to ensure that these crimes do not go unpunished. It is the desire of His Majesty's Government that the authorities in post-war Germany shall mete out to the perpetrators of these crimes the punishments which they deserve."[74]

Law was pressed by the Labour MP R. Moelwyn Hughes, who asked if "the authorities in post-war Germany" meant occupying Allied authorities or German authorities. Law answered that, "The authorities to which I refer are the authorities who will be in control in Germany when the war comes to an end. I think I can leave it to my hon. and learned Friend to imagine who those authorities will be."[75] Law's reply to Moelwyn Hughes met with the approval of Con O'Neill of the Foreign Office Central Department. In a departmental minute commenting on this exchange in the House of Commons, O'Neill wrote that Law had "succeeded in maintaining an ambiguity which, in view of the difficulties now cropping up, may prove useful".[76]

On 20th March 1945, the House of Lords debated the progress of the UNWCC and steps to secure the punishment of war criminals on a motion by Lord Addison. Addison referred to the war's unprecedented "scientific and organized cruelty" and to "the attempted extirpation of whole populations, without any regard to any share which they have taken in the war . . . People have been taken by train-loads to be murdered, and the machinery of murder has been constructed beforehand." Arguing that, "we cannot . . . pass over what has happened in Germany with regard to the Jews", Addison maintained that "we shall all agree that those who order the deportation by the train-load of German Jews for the purposes of massacre should not go unpunished". He inquired "whether arrangements are in contemplation for dealing with offenders of this class". Commenting on Law's statement of 31st January in the House of Commons, Addison was sceptical of "a German authority being set up in Germany that will deal with these people", and hoped that "if any authority is to be set up in Germany to deal with them it will be set up by the United Nations". The Lord Chancellor interrupted at this point to say that the Allies, not the Germans, would establish the tribunals which would try the criminals: "The statement of Mr. Law does not contemplete [sic] that they will be German tribunals: it contemplates that upon the defeat of Germany the Allies will set up the organization and the tribunals under which such process might take place." Simon's purpose here was to dispel what he considered to be the false notion that the Germans themselves would try the perpetrators of such crimes. For the government, Lord Simon then spoke of the horrible cruelties against the Jews, which fell "strictly outside what may be called war crimes" and were "not war crimes in the strict sense".[77]

---

[74]In the first draft of this answer, the last sentence began: "It is the intention of His Majesty's Government . . ."

[75]PRO, FO 371 46795 C464/63/18, Strauss, MP (Labour, Lambeth), 31st January 1945, parliamentary question; Law reply; Moelwyn Hughes, MP (Labour, Carmarthen) supplementary question.

[76]PRO, FO 371 46795 C398/63/18, O'Neill (German Department), 6th February 1945, minute.

[77]PRO, FO 371 46795 C1205/63/18, House of Lords debate, 20th March 1945.

The Lord Chancellor's intervention during the House of Lords debate concerned some Foreign Office officials who still hoped to pursue a policy of ambiguity towards war crimes trials. After commenting that, "Crimes of the 'dog eating dog' order, that is, those committed by Germans against their own nationals are now the concern of German Dept.", Wardrop noted that the phrase "authorities in post-war Germany" used by Law in his statement of 31st January "was deliberately ambiguous, as was the supplementary answer in which Mr Law said that he could leave it to the House to imagine who those authorities would be". Wardrop grudgingly supposed that the Lord Chancellor was correct in saying that the British government would be responsible for establishing the trial organisation. But even if this were so, Wardrop believed, the tribunals would "be *German tribunals*". Lord Simon's statment had "none of the happy ambiguity of Mr Law's", and could only "be interpreted as meaning what is not the case. The satisfaction with which Lord Addison received it leaves no doubt as to the way in which he, at any rate, interpreted it."[78] O'Neill agreed that Simon's statement was "a bit awkward as our present idea is that either Allied Military Government Courts or (when suitably purged) German or Austrian Courts should try these people, as may at any time seem most convenient. In either case trials would have to be under German law."[79]

General A. V. Anderson of the War Office questioned Foreign Office opposition to Allied trials of Germans for crimes against German nationals. Anderson believed that Britain should consider such trials if German courts did not properly try and punish those accused of such crimes. Anderson suggested that the Allies should consider assuming the jurisdiction to try the accused. Although this would be a matter for the War Cabinet to consider, he thought that Britain should welcome the assumption of Allied jurisdiction if this became necessary in the interests of justice. Anderson admitted that: "Such a step would no doubt involve a departure from all precedent but on the other hand it would appear morally justifiable since experience suggests that the only alternative is to let these miscreants escape scot free."[80]

Andrew Clark of the Legal Division of the Control Commission for Germany (CCG), recommended that Britain should not pressure a post-war German government to try Germans for crimes against German nationals. Clark argued that it would be disastrous to pressure the Germans when Britain could not compel them to act. German success in resisting this pressure would undermine British authority in Germany and, possibly, nullify all the work of the CCG. Clark feared "a repetition of the Leipzig trials farce" unless British pressure took "the form of a direct order". The question of where "to draw the line", as to the identity of the atrocity victim and of the date of the commission of the atrocity, troubled Clark: "If we once embark upon a policy of enforcing retribution for atrocities committed by Germans against their own Nationals where are we to

[78]PRO, FO 371 46795 C1481/63/18, Wardrop (employed temporarily at Foreign Office, October 1944–May 1945), undated [approximately 25th–26th March 1945], minute, emphasis in original.
[79]PRO, FO 371 46795 C1481/63/18, O'Neill, 26th March 1945, minute.
[80]PRO, FO 371 46795 C265/63/18, General A. V. Anderson (War Office), 17th January 1945, letter to Troutbeck (Head of German Department).

draw the line? Presumably it is not suggested that we are only to concern ourselves with cases in which the victim was a Jew." It was neither feasible to investigate crimes committed as early as January 1933, nor possible to collect satisfactory evidence "in respect of such ancient history". Clark proposed that "somewhere about 1938 is as far back as it is practicable to go". Why he chose 1938 as opposed to any other date is not explained. He also opposed the introduction of retroactive legislation and argued:

> "Legislation which purports to make a past act which was legal at the date of its commission into a presently punishable crime [is] contrary to every concept of equity and natural justice [and is] one of our serious grounds of complaint against the Nazi regime. Surely at a time when we are endeavouring to restore the rule of law to Germany we should not deliberately tar ourselves with the same brush."

Nevertheless, if German atrocities against Germans were, in fact, crimes under German law, the accused could then be tried under German law in Allied military courts after the defeat of Germany. Such atrocities were not, however, war crimes. Clark concluded with the recommendation that Britain should be content "with preparing such lists of names and collecting such evidence as our existing resources of manpower permit and limit ourselves in Germany to a policy of 'encouraging' the Germans to try their own criminals and affording them every facility for so doing, but without bringing any pressure to bear".[81] Ivone A. Kirkpatrick, of the Control Commission for Germany (British Element) (CCG [BE]), generally agreed with Clark because it was in his "experience . . . bad policy to bring pressure to bear on the Germans unless one is ready with practical plans for enforcing one's will in the event of German evasion".[82]

O'Neill of the Foreign Office agreed with Anderson and Clark that Britain should consider trying the perpetrators of crimes against German nationals, rather than waiting for the German courts to do so under Allied pressure. O'Neill wanted Britain to "grasp the bull by the horns now rather than later". But he disagreed with Clark about "retrospective legislation":

> ". . . there is no valid objection to amendment or repeal with retrospective effect in such cases. The fundamental question is whether an act is or is not, by (so to speak) natural law, a crime. To convert something which was not a natural crime into a legal one by retrospective legislation or judicial decision, which is the Nazi practise [sic], is odious. To convert something which was a natural, but not a legal, crime into a legal crime with retrospective effect by similar means, which was our proposal, is just."

The best solution would thus be the assumption of jurisdiction to try these crimes under German law in British military courts. As for the date from which crimes should be investigated, O'Neill argued that "the *point de départ* must be either the beginning of the Nazi regime or the beginning of the war. The latter has much to be said for it; but we shall be exposed to strong [Allied] political pressure in favour of the earlier date." O'Neill concluded that, because of British and

---

[81]PRO, FO 371 46795 C398/63/18, Andrew Clark (Legal Division, CCG), 26th January 1945, letter to General Kirby. The Control Commission for Germany, composed of representatives of Britain, the United States, France and the Soviet Union, exercised joint authority over Germany during the occupation period.

[82]PRO, FO 371 46795 C398/63/18, Kirkpatrick (CCG (BE)), 2nd February 1945, letter to Troutbeck.

American commitments to act on this matter, Anderson was right to argue that Britain should seize the initiative. O'Neill rejected Clark's final recommendation as "clearly wrong" and advised that Kirkpatrick be so informed.[83]

The Attorney General, Donald Somervell, was uneasy about the subject of German crimes against German nationals and agreed with Clark about retrospective legislation. He regretted British commitments on this subject, because of the "legal and . . . considerable practical difficulties" involved.[84] Troutbeck, now Head of the German Department, suggested that: "The crux of the matter is that we and the U.S.G. [United States Government] are committed up to the hilt to seeing that effective steps are taken to punish these people, and means must be found."[85] Acting First Secretary John G. Ward, of the Reconstruction Department, was sure that public opinion would "force" Britain "to take action at least against the most notorious offenders who fall into our hands". He predicted "an outcry" in Britain and the United States if British military courts distinguished between victims on the basis of nationality. He concluded by noting the relationship between war crimes *stricto sensu* and atrocities against German nationals. Ward, who had recently reviewed a report on Buchenwald concentration camp, noted "that war crimes and atrocities v. Germans are hopelessly mixed up". An eyewitness, a German deserter, "described mass executions in which Poles, Russians and German Jews & Communists were indiscriminately involved".[86]

The Attorney General chaired a meeting of Foreign Office and War Office officials on 2nd March 1945 on the punishment of Germans and Austrians for crimes against their own nationals. Attending officials described these offences

[83]PRO, FO 371 46795 C398/63/18, O'Neill, 6th February 1945, minute.
[84]PRO, FO 371 46795 C540/63/18, Somervell, 1st February 1945, letter to Malkin.
[85]PRO, FO 371 46795 C398/63/18, Troutbeck, 7th February 1945, minute. In mid-January 1945, the American State Department and other United States governmental agencies were considering whether the Allies had jurisdiction to try, as war crimes, offences committed against neutral nationals or stateless persons in enemy territory. PRO, FO 371 51009 U359/29/73, Lord Halifax (British Ambassador in Washington), 13th January 1945, telegram to Foreign Office. On 1st February, United States Acting Secretary of State Joseph Grew held a press conference and revealed that Roosevelt's latest war crimes proposals "provide for the punishment of German leaders and their associates for their responsibility for the whole broad criminal enterprise . . . including offences wherever committed against the rules of war and against minority elements Jewish and other groups and individuals". PRO, FO 371 46795 C540/63/18, Grew 1st February 1945 statement. Halifax informed the Foreign Office the next day that:

> "After issuing a first edition of statement Grew was pressed very hard to admit that United States Government was prepared to insist that Germans be punished for war crimes against Germans. He attempted to explain off record that this would in fact be so but that it was not desired to put this in statement for the present. Correspondents persisted with the result that after withdrawal for consultation (no doubt with Hackworth [Green Hackworth, the legal adviser at the State Department]) Grew authorised insertion in last sentence of words 'wherever committed'."

PRO, FO 371 46795 C540/63/18, Halifax, 2nd February 1945, telegram to Foreign Office. Grew had made it "clear" that the United States was now committed to the punishment of Germans for crimes committed in Germany against Jews and others on racial, religious, or political grounds. What was not clear, however, was whether the United States government thought that the Allies should have direct jurisdiction, or from what starting point crimes should be punished. PRO, FO 371 46795 C398/63/18, O'Neill, 6th February 1945, minute.
[86]PRO, FO 371 46795 C398/63/18, Ward (Reconstruction Department), 8th February 1945, minute.

as "atrocities other than war crimes". Somervell, who argued strongly against retroactive legislation, believed that such legislation would in any case be unnecessary in view of what was then known about Nazi atrocities. Those attending agreed that Hitler's will may have been absolute under present German law, and for that reason "the most atrocious crimes against Jews could not be punished". It was agreed, however, that, before considering retroactive legislation, Britain should determine first if Hitler's will was absolute. Opinion was divided over whether German or Allied courts should conduct trials for these offences. The Control Commissions for Germany and Austria and the War Office tended to favour trials by Allied courts; the Attorney General preferred trials by native courts until such a course proved unsatisfactory. He agreed to prepare a memorandum on the legal position, on the basis of which the Foreign Office would have to redraft their directive for submission to the Official Committee on Armistice Terms and Civil Administration (ACAO).[87]

The general view of those at the 2nd March meeting, and of Somervell's memorandum a few days later, was that it was "unlikely (or at any rate we cannot assume now) that there would at the time be German courts which could be trusted to deal with the cases though the situation may become different later". If so, British authorities "on the spot should have authority to try cases which were ready in the Allied military courts".[88]

The War Cabinet's ACAO met at the War Office on 2nd May 1945. The Committee considered a Foreign Office memorandum on the punishment of Germans and Austrians for crimes against their own nationals and a draft directive to the Allied Commanders-in-Chief.[89] The ACAO invited the Foreign Office to revise, yet again, their draft directive.[90]

On 30th May, Field Marshal Sir Bernard Montgomery issued his first proclamation to the German people since his appointment as British representative on the Allied Control Commission. He stated that the British government had appointed him to "command and control the area occupied by the British Army in Germany" and that: "Those who have committed war crimes according to international law will be dealt with in a proper fashion."[91]

On 19th June 1945, a directive from the Combined Chiefs of Staff to the Supreme Commander Allied Expeditionary Force (SCAEF) finally removed the previous restriction on the trial of persons charged with war crimes. That directive read: "Whether offences were committed before or after occupation by your Forces and regardless of nationality of victim, you may proceed with such

---

[87]The meeting was attended by Colonel Bacon (Legal Adviser to the Civil Affairs Directorate, War Office) and Lieutenant Colonel Arnold from the War Office, Lord Schuster of the Control Commission for Austria, Clark and Sir A. Brown of the CCG, and Malkin, P. S. Falla (Reconstruction Department), Wardrop and O'Neill from the Foreign Office. PRO, FO 371 46795 C755/63/18, O'Neill, 2nd March 1945, minute. The ACAO was composed of Foreign Office and War Office officials, and was concerned with detailed planning for the occupation period.
[88]PRO, FO 371 46795 C931/63/18, Malkin, 8th March 1945, letter to Somervell.
[89]PRO, FO 371 46795 C1741/63/18, Joint Secretaries, 24th April 1945, note ACAO/P(45)43.
[90]PRO, FO 371 46796 C2121/63/18, minutes of ACAO, 2nd May 1945.
[91]PRO, FO 371 46732 C3057/24/18, Field-Marshal Sir Bernard Montgomery, proclamation of 30th May 1945.

trials in Military Courts under your Command."[92] German offences against British or Allied victims were defined as war crimes; German atrocities against German Jews were "crimes of violence other than war crimes", and, therefore, beyond the scope of British military courts.

This limitation on the scope of British military courts was pointed out during the first of the concentration camp trials conducted by the British, that of the Bergen-Belsen commandant, Josef Kramer, and the staffs of Bergen-Belsen and Auschwitz. Proceedings against forty-eight defendants opened on 17th September 1945. The accused were charged with committing war crimes, and faced one or both of two counts. The first charge alleged that staff members of Bergen-Belsen, "responsible for the well being of the persons interned there, in violation of the laws and usages of war were together concerned as parties to the ill treatment . . . causing the deaths of . . . Allied nationals . . . and physical suffering to other . . . Allied nationals". The second charge made the same allegations, but with regard to Auschwitz. In his opening statement, prosecution counsel Colonel T. M. Backhouse, of the Legal Staff, Headquarters, British Army of the Rhine, submitted that the acts mentioned in the two charges constituted war crimes, because the persons interned in Auschwitz and Belsen included Allied nationals. He expressly noted that "we are not, of course, concerned in this trial with atrocities by Germans against Germans".[93]

On 5th November 1945, the Lord Chancellor, the Attorney General, the Treasury Solicitor, Colonel Bradshaw of the War Office, Colonel Betts – the United States Judge Advocate General at Frankfurt – and other British officials met to discuss the problem of German crimes against Germans or against stateless persons. These offences were now described as "crimes against humanity". After a long discussion, officials agreed that "crimes against humanity, i.e. crimes committed by Germans against Germans or against stateless persons mostly before the war, would be dealt with, in the first place, in the most notorious cases before British Military Government Courts". It was hoped that "as soon as an example and a precedent of sentences had been set . . . German Courts, with or without, a British observer, would be found capable of

---

[92]R. A. Beaumont noted at the end of June 1945 that this directive was "very late in coming forward". The Royal Warrant had been published already, and courts in the British zone could "now presumably function". PRO, FO 371 51027 U5011/29/73. Combined Chiefs of Staff, 19th June 1945, telegram to SCAEF; Beaumont, 30th June 1945, minute.

[93]Sir David Maxwell Fyfe (gen. ed.), *War Crimes Trials*, vol. II, edited by Raymond Phillips, London 1949, p. vii; p. 15, quoting Colonel Backhouse. Forty-eight defendants were listed on the charge sheet, including the commandment, Josef Kramer. Three defendants named were unable to stand trial. A fourth was taken ill during trial; he was withdrawn, and the Court recorded no finding against him. PRO, WO 235 12. British authorities had decided to accept responsibility for the Belsen trial for two reasons. First, Britain controlled this zone of Germany and had custody of the defendants. Second, there was a problem of multiple jurisdiction; because the victims were of ten different Allied nationalities, it would have been impossible to form a workable Court if all these nationalities had demanded representation. United Nations War Crimes Commission (ed.), *Law Reports of Trials of War Criminals*, London 1947–1949, vol. II (1947), p. 8. The conduct of defence counsel (see Chap. VII) and the leniency of the sentences passed in the Belsen case (see Chap. VIII) were to provoke great controversy.

dealing with these crimes". The Americans acted similarly in their zone of occupation.[94]

On 20th December 1945, the CCG passed a law concerning the trial of those responsible for war crimes, crimes against humanity and crimes against peace. This enactment, known as Control Council Law No. 10, was passed "to establish a uniform legal basis in Germany for the prosecution of war criminals". Crimes against humanity were defined as follows:

". . . atrocities and offences, including but not limited to murder, extermination, enslavement, deportation, imprisonment, torture, rape or other inhumane acts committed against any civilian population, or persecutions on political, racial or religious grounds whether or not in violation of the domestic laws of the country where perpetrated".

Control Council Law No. 10 thus applied to offences committed before and during the war.[95]

In accordance with Control Council Law No. 10, British officials in the British zone of occupation in Germany issued Ordinance No. 47, which granted jurisdiction to German ordinary courts in all cases of crimes against humanity committed by Germans against Jewish and non-Jewish Germans or stateless persons.[96] The German courts were authorised to try cases of crimes against humanity under either the German Penal Code or under Control Council Law No. 10.[97]

CONCLUSION

Throughout the war the Foreign Office resisted any commitment to British trials of Nazi and Japanese war criminals. The Foreign Office was even more hesitant to become involved in trying Germans for crimes against humanity committed against Jewish and non-Jewish German nationals. As the war progressed, reports of German atrocities, particularly those committed against European Jewry, and news of Japanese atrocities, particularly against British prisoners-of-war or civilians in occupied British territory, aroused British parliamentary and public opinion and undermined the non-committal war crimes position of the Foreign Office. While Foreign Office officials continued to question specific allegations of atrocities, particularly from Jewish or Soviet sources, they could no

[94]Coldstream of the Lord Chancellor's Office and Patrick Dean of the Foreign Office were also present. PRO, FO 371 50992 U8830/16/73, P. Dean, 6th November 1945, minute. On 9th September 1945, the ACAO Committee had agreed in principle that "a few sample [crimes against humanity] cases should be tried by [British] Military Government Courts so as to afford precedent for the way such cases should be handled thereafter". The remaining cases, involving German or stateless victims, "should be tried by the ordinary German Courts". PRO, FO 371 70822 CG3936/ 34/184, General Brian H. Robertson, Military Governor (Headquarters, CCG[BE], Berlin), 29th September 1948, letter to Foreign Secretary Ernest Bevin.

[95]Control Council Law No. 10, *Military Government Gazette, Germany, British Zone of Control*, No. 5, p. 46, quoted in *History of the UNWCC*, pp. 212, 213.

[96]Ordinance No. 47, published in *Military Government Gazette, Germany, British Zone of Control*, No. 13, p. 306, cited in *History of the UNWCC*, p. 214.

[97]PRO, FO 371 70824 CG4446/34/184, undated, unsigned paper (for Overseas Reconstruction Committee) on Trial of Cases of Crimes Against Humanity and Certain War Crimes in the British Zone of Germany.

longer doubt that Germans were committing widespread breaches of the laws and usages of war. The aggressive war crimes policy of Britain's allies, particularly Poland and Czechoslovakia, and Churchill's forceful statements on Nazi atrocities and the need to punish culprits stole the initiative from the Foreign Office in formulating war crimes policy. As a result of this pressure, and in an effort to maintain what the Foreign Office optimistically considered Britain's lead in the war crimes question, the Foreign Office was compelled to develop a more active war crimes policy and modify its reserved attitude towards the possible trial of Axis war criminals .

Almost from the outset of discussion about the legal aspects of war crimes, the Foreign Office view was that war crimes committed against Allied nationals should be adjudicated by the national courts of the victims' country, and that war crimes committed against British nationals should be tried by British military courts. The Foreign Office and other British officials generally agreed that international law provided the legal foundation for these courts which could try only breaches of the laws and usages of war, that is, war crimes *stricto sensu*. Foreign Office and other officials thus argued that the *point de départ* for war crimes should be the outbreak of the war in September 1939; all Axis offences before that date were, therefore, beyond the permissible scope of war crimes courts. This meant that German atrocities committed in Europe, Italian atrocities committed in Ethiopia and Japanese atrocities committed in China before September 1939 were outside the jurisdiction of British war crimes courts. Axis offences against their own nationals, stateless persons and nationals of states allied with the Axis, whether committed before or after the war, were also to be outside the jurisdiction of British war crimes courts.

Several factors contributed to the conservative and legalistic view of the Foreign Office: a general resistance to British involvement in the war crimes morass; an intense fear of "getting hopelessly bogged down, with a final dismal repetition of. . . [the Leipzig trial] fiasco"; a distrust for *ad hoc* law and tribunals; and a limited expectation that war crimes trials would provide "a kind of rough & ready, and above all, rapid justice".[98]

Most Foreign Office officials, along with the Lord Chancellor and the Cabinet, firmly believed that German atrocities committed against Jewish and non-Jewish German nationals and stateless persons were not in any sense war crimes. The Foreign Office generally opposed extending the definition of war crimes to cover these offences, which were considered an internal German affair, punishable, if at all, only by the Germans under German law. The Foreign Office generally made a clear distinction between war crimes, over which the Allies had jurisdiction under international law, and atrocities committed on racial, political or religious grounds in enemy territory, over which the Allies had no jurisdiction.

The view of the Foreign Office Refugee Department regarding war crimes was that nothing should be done to make it more difficult for Jews to return to their former homes in Europe after the war. Wishing to avoid a post-war influx of Jews into Palestine, the Refugee Department feared that British trials of Germans on

[98]PRO, FO 371 30924 C12380/61/18, R. Allen, 18th December 1942, minute.

charges of crimes against humanity committed against Jews would make it harder for Jews to return to their native countries after the war.

While officials inside and outside the Foreign Office generally agreed that German atrocities against German Jews did not constitute war crimes, opinion was strongly divided over whether Britain should take steps to ensure the punishment of the perpetrators. Several Foreign Office officials were concerned about the very strong public and parliamentary pressure in Britain to ensure that amends of some sort were made to German Jews. The question thus arose whether Britain should exert pressure upon a post-war government in Germany to try, in German courts under German law, those responsible for atrocities against German Jews.

Parallel to this discussion was the question of whether the UNWCC should extend its terms of reference to allow it to investigate German crimes against Jews in Germany and in other enemy countries. The official Foreign Office view was, first, that the offences in question were in all probability not crimes under German law as it then stood; second that even if the offences were contrary to German law, they were not contrary to international law and did not, therefore, constitute prosecutable war crimes; and, third, that the Allies could not take responsibility for enforcing retrospective justice in Germany.

Foreign Office opinion was divided as to whether the draft armistice with Germany should have a clause compelling the Germans to establish a tribunal to try those accused of atrocities against Jews and others in Nazi concentration camps. Some Foreign Office officials opposed a special clause. They maintained that, however morally indefensible, these actions were presumably legal under German law; post-war German authorities would, therefore, have to introduce retrospective legislation to make these actions *ex post facto* illegal. Other officials opposed inserting a special clause into the armistice because they considered German mistreatment of German nationals to be a domestic German affair. The second group believed, however, that Britain could apply very strong pressure on a post-war German government to prosecute these cases, otherwise survivors or their relatives could take matters into their own hands.

Some Foreign Office officials argued that retrospective legislation was unnecessary because the post-war authorities in Germany would need only to cancel Nazi laws or decrees which allegedly legalised the barbarous acts committed in concentration camps. Others suggested that Britain should assume jurisdiction to try these crimes under German law in British military courts because they feared a public outcry in Britain and the United States if British military courts distinguished between victims on the basis of nationality.

The War Office believed that the Allies should assume jurisdiction to try these cases. This was, admittedly, a departure from all legal precedent. The War Office argued that such action would be morally justifiable because the only alternative would be to let the culprits escape without trial of any kind.

Representatives of the CCG maintained that, if these atrocities were in fact crimes under German law, the accused could then be tried in Allied military courts under German law after the defeat of Germany. Such atrocities were not, however, war crimes. The CCG wanted Britain to encourage post-war German authorities to try their own criminals, but not to pressure the Germans unless

Britain was prepared to enforce her will in the event of German evasion. CCG officials predicted disastrous ramifications for British authority in Germany, and for the work of the CCG, if Britain could not compel the Germans to act and the Germans successfully resisted British pressure.

The War Office and the CCG tended to favour trials by Allied courts; the Attorney General preferred trials by native German courts until such a course proved unsatisfactory. By March 1945, the general view of British government officials, including Somervell, was that Britain could not assume that post-war German courts could be trusted to deal with these cases, though the situation might become different later. By the end of the war there was a general consensus in Britain that British authorities in Germany should have the authority to try Germans for crimes of humanity against German nationals, and that these cases would be turned over to German courts as soon as precedents regarding sentences had been set.

From the outset of discussions about German atrocities against Allied and German nationals, the majority of Foreign Office officials consistently believed that any British trials of war criminals should be limited to British military court trials of Germans charged with war crimes against Allied or British nationals. German atrocities against Jewish and non-Jewish German nationals did not constitute war crimes, and were justiciable, if at all, only by German courts. The Foreign Office view prevailed, and, as a result, British military courts never tried Germans for crimes against humanity against Jewish and non-Jewish German nationals.

In conclusion it is interesting to note the result of Britain's decision to leave to German courts cases of German crimes of humanity committed against German Jews and non-Jews. By the summer of 1948, German courts in the British zone of occupation were trying defendants accused of crimes against humanity committed against German nationals; British Control Commission courts, having superseded British Military Government courts in Germany on 1st January 1947, were trying defendants accused of crimes against humanity committed against non-German nationals.[99] By March 1949, German courts had tried 2,180 defendants on charges of crimes against humanity committed against German nationals or stateless persons. Of this total, 866 accused had been acquitted; four had been sentenced to death; 1,249 had been sentenced to terms of imprisonment shorter than life; and sixty-one had been fined. No defendant had been sentenced to life imprisonment.[100] By April 1949, none of the four men sentenced to death had been executed. One had escaped, one case was pending appeal, one case was pending confirmation of the Clemency Authority and the sentence of the fourth had been commuted to life imprisonment.[101]

[99]PRO, FO 371 70821 CG3440/34/18, Lorna K. Newton (German Section), 26th August 1948, minute. PRO, FO 371 77052 CG976/15/184, Lubbecke, 25th March 1949, telegram to Foreign Office (German Section).

[100]PRO, FO 371 77052 CG1008/15/184, Under-Secretary of State for Foreign Affairs, Christopher Mayhew, 28th March 1949, reply to Eric Fletcher, MP (Labour–Islington East) parliamentary question.

[101]PRO, FO 371 77053 CG1075/15/184, Lubbecke, 6th April 1949, telegram to Foreign Office (German Section). Foreign Office statistics concerning sentences shorter than life imprisonment do not specify the length of these sentences.

The Jewish Press under the Nazi Regime
Its Mission, Suppression and Defiance
A Memoir

BY ARNO HERZBERG

The press in a totalitarian state is an instrument of the government which gives outright orders or issues prepared guidelines for what is "fit to print". In every case the totalitarian state uses news as a weapon with the declared aim of influencing the morale of the people and forming their conception and their picture of current events by featuring certain news or by withholding reports of facts which might contradict government policies; by preparing the public for future developments in foreign or domestic policies; by featuring stories which describe the nature and character of adversary or friend; and, above all, by compelling the press to submit to a tight control and to give unconditional support to the regime by observing any guidelines issued by the authorities, printing editorials distributed by a propaganda centre and discarding any criticism or withholding any detrimental news item from the public.

It is somewhat ironic that the Jewish press was subjected to these rules commensurate with the concept and framework the Nazis had established for the treatment of the Jewish community.[1] But it was still more strange that the Jewish editor had to observe some of these rules himself in order to build up and maintain the morale of his readers. On the one hand, we were the object of government interference; on the other hand, we had to employ some of the guiding principles of a totalitarian regime to select the news that would be fit to print from our point of view.[2]

As far back as May 1934 I defined the task of the Jewish editor in a lengthy article in *Der Morgen*:[3]

---

[1]The Jewish press in Nazi Germany has featured in quite a number of publications, many sponsored by the Leo Baeck Institute, others elsewhere. We single out here the four essays by Jacob Boas published in *LBI Year Books XXVII, XXIX, XXXI* and *XXXIV* (1982, 1984, 1986 and 1989) which were based on a previous doctoral dissertation; Herbert Freeden, *Die jüdische Presse im Dritten Reich*, Frankfurt a. Main 1987, Veröffentlichung des Leo Baeck Instituts; two essays by Margaret T. Edelheim-Muehsam in *LBI Year Books I* and *V* (1956 and 1960); Herbert A. Strauss, 'Haitonuth hayehudit beGermaniah bishnim 1918–1938', in Yehuda Gothelf (ed.), *Itonuth Yehudit shehayta*, Tel-Aviv 1973 (in Hebrew). Specific reference to some of these studies will be made below.

[2]For the purpose of this essay I have drawn on my article on the 'Last Days of the German-Jewish Press', in *Contemporary Jewish Record*, April 1942; and my memoirs of the period, including my press activities, which are kept by Yad Vashem, Jerusalem (a condensed version was written for the Research Institute for the Jewish Press of Tel-Aviv University).

[3]Arno Herzberg, 'Jüdischer Journalismus heute', in *Der Morgen*, 10. Jahrgang, Heft 2 (May 1934), pp. 49–52; quotation on p. 51.

"The Jewish newspaper is today an instrument of adult education and spiritual guidance which should be positive. Statements of fact must not be considered pessimism. A Jewish newspaper does not fulfil its task unless it presents realities with an almost stubborn insistence on the facts confronting us".

For almost four years, in my capacity as manager and editor of the Jewish Telegraphic Agency in Berlin from 1934 to 1937, I had the unique opportunity of applying these guidelines to almost every news item published by the Jewish press. It was a nerve-wracking undertaking, but any hardships were offset by the instinctive urge to keep up the spirit of our people, to maintain our own mental equilibrium and, most of all, to defy the odds that we might be flattened by the Nazi steamroller. To adjust to the ever-changing scene in the Nazi state required something like a sixth sense, a combination of intuition and an instinctive feel for an analysis of the situation and the ability to deduce from seemingly unimportant events or utterances the outlines of a policy that, as the years went by, became for us a matter of life and death.

THE FIRST SUPPRESSIONS

From 1933 to 1938 Nazi policies were aimed at isolating German Jews from the German public and at curbing Jewish influence in all fields of human endeavour. There were numerous by-products of these policies indicating a desire of the Nazi authorities to let Jews live their own lives. But there was an obsession that all signs of Jewish life had to be concealed from the eyes of the ordinary German. This applied to Jewish newspapers.

There was a time when these newspapers could be bought at news-stands, especially in Berlin. It was quite a sight and very stimulating to see them on display all along the Kurfürstendamm. But as early as 1934 this was prohibited. Jewish newspapers could reach their readers only by subscription. Non-Jews could not subscribe to them.

There was, for example, never an outright prohibition of photographing Nazi officials present at Jewish gatherings. But we could deduce it from the behaviour of a *Gestapo* agent at one of these meetings. He seized all the photographs taken because he might have been included in one of them.

Similarly, no order was ever issued forbidding the mention of Purim, with all its historical background. We discovered that somebody might find a certain resemblance between Haman and Hitler himself.[4] It would not have been clever to "insult" the *Führer* by emphasising the story of Purim and Haman's ignominious end. This would have contradicted, too, the "enlightening" articles the Nazi press published about Purim. Their "historians" discovered that the Persians were pure Aryans who had been murdered by Jews.

All these occurrences were more or less pinpricks in the first year of the regime. It was a different story when for instance I went too far and provoked the first

---

[4]See for example Arnold Paucker, *Jüdischer Widerstand in Deutschland. Tatsachen und Problematik*, Beiträge zum Widerstand 1933–1945, Gedenkstätte Deutscher Widerstand, Heft 37, Berlin 1989, p. 6. (An expanded English version will be published in 1991.)

suspension of a Jewish newspaper for three months. (I had published an article in the *C.V.-Zeitung* in which I showed that some Nazi slogans showed a similarity with certain remarks of a Jewish author in the twenties.)[5] This suspension occurred in 1935, at a time when we still could probe how sensitive the regime was to any challenge. It proved to be a valuable lesson.

Such a lesson should have already been learned in 1933 after an outright confrontation between the Jewish press and the Nazi authorities.

In the Summer of 1933, a new American Ambassador, William E. Dodd, was sent to Germany. Upon his arrival in Hamburg he granted an interview to the Jewish Telegraphic Agency which was distributed to all Jewish newspapers in Germany. He did not hide the fact that President Roosevelt, newly elected at that time, had asked him to keep a watchful eye on developments that might adversely affect German Jews.[6]

With only moderate hindsight it is not difficult to realise that this was not the interview of a diplomat knowledgable in the ways of a totalitarian state. He did not know that such a regime hates nothing more than an indication of any interference in its internal affairs, and resents nothing more than news emanating from a source it cannot control. When Jewish newspapers published the interview with the American Ambassador, reaction was swift and thorough. The Jewish Telegraphic Agency had to retract the story and state that the interview never took place. Jewish newspapers had to print the retraction on their front page. At this stage the Nazi authorities, the *Gestapo* and the Propaganda Ministry, were inclined to close down all operations of the Jewish Telegraphic Agency. They were particularly incensed that the interview appeared in the foreign press. But at this time in 1933 the regime was still concerned with its image abroad and the Foreign Office especially was not sure how a suspension would reflect on Nazi efforts to project the image of a government of reason and reliability. There was also the question whether it was advisable at this stage to violate the German-American Commerce Treaty. After prolonged negotiations in which the American Consul took part, the Nazi authorities arrived at a compromise which gave them control over the news distributed in Germany, but made it difficult to send news out of Germany. The Jewish Telegraphic Agency (JTA) was allowed to distribute news to Jewish newspapers and subscribers inside Germany, but was prohibited from transmitting news to any of their offices abroad. Up to that time the Berlin office had cabled or airmailed news to the JTA offices in London, New York, Paris, Prague and Warsaw. All these offices were owned by an American citizen; it was all so to say in the same family. Final negotiations resulted in a concession. The Nazi authorities permitted us to mail our daily bulletin to other JTA offices. In return, these offices, except New York, were permitted to send us their daily bulletins by airmail.

---

[5]The *C.V.-Zeitung* was suspended from 27th June to 29th September 1935 (inclusive). My article was unsigned.
[6]See in this connection, Deborah E. Lipstadt, 'The American Press and the Persecution of German Jewry. The Early Years 1933–1935', in *LBI Year Book XXIX* (1984), pp. 48ff.

The JTA office in Berlin was organised as a German corporation with all its shares in the hands of an American citizen. Its founder, Jacob Landau, could not have foreseen in 1927 how valuable the simple fact of this arrangement would become some day. The company could claim protection under the American-German Commerce Treaty in effect at that time and the American Consul General, Mr. Geist, could intervene if we were not able to function as a commercial enterprise.

The news bulletin of the Berlin JTA was published five times a week except on Jewish and public holidays. It appeared in a simple mimeographed form, extending from four to ten pages, depending on the volume of news that was available. It had to be mailed in the afternoon in order to reach subscribers the next morning.

It was not an easy task to put a daily bulletin together. As the days and months went by and the Nazis tightened their hold over the German people; as the extent of the persecution became clearer and clearer and our very existence became tenuous and insecure, the challenge grew.

THE NEWS AS A WEAPON

There were two areas where news developments required attention and concern. The German scene with its rapidly changing conditions as they affected Jews and Jewish affairs both inside and outside Germany, and the Jewish scene abroad in its reaction to Nazi policies and the pursuit of their own noteworthy interests and happenings. It might sound strange, but the Nazi press was our main source of information for how and where the war against the Jews was waged. For the Nazis, the news was a weapon to be used to keep adherents in line, frighten adversaries and destroy the morale of enemies. It took a long time before Jews and non-Jews in Germany and the democratic countries realised this nature of every news item coming out of Germany. Each one served a purpose. Each one was addressed to a specific audience.

It was easy for me to recognise that the Nazi press in the capital of the *Reich* was different from the newspapers appearing under the control of local functionaries outside Berlin. Here we would register the biting comments and vile insults that poured from these pages day after day. Here we could find speeches by local Nazi leaders which provided a preview of things to come. Such papers as the *Fränkische Tageszeitung* in Nuremberg and the *Rheinisch-Westfälische Zeitung* of Essen spared no gory details to describe the fate in store for Jews. They foretold the killing of Jews in large numbers. They predicted their being made penniless and chased out of the country. These local papers were the first ones to demand that Germany become free of Jews. They did not hesitate to paint a picture which, with some hindsight we can now say, was not so entirely different from actual events after 1938.[7] This was a long, long time before Auschwitz and

---

[7]For details see Herzberg, 'Last Days of the German-Jewish Press', *loc. cit.*, p. 145.

Treblinka. This was 1936 and 1937. Nobody wanted to believe that such things could ever happen.

One daring editor, Fritz Neuländer in charge of the community paper in Cologne,[8] took it upon himself to defy the threats that were being brandished in these Nazi newspapers. Again and again he would show how the German trait of thoroughness could border on the ridiculous. When the Association of Chimney Sweeps expelled Jews from their ranks, it was too tempting for him to point out that there were no Jewish chimney sweeps in Germany and that the Jews had no intention of invading this dirty trade after they had been thrown out of so many others.

These and other sarcastic comments delighted his readers, but his aggressive writing got him into serious trouble. He was arrested, sentenced to six months imprisonment; his licence was revoked and his paper was suspended for several months.[9]

Nothing, not one word, was published about all these troublesome events in the Jewish press. Neither could we report a significant demonstration that took place for several years on Purim in synagogues all over the country. It continued until the *Gestapo*, the secret police, caught on to its meaning and prohibited it.

The Feast of Purim, which commemorates the unsuccessful attempt to annihilate the Jews of Persia, provided an opportunity to release the pent-up frustrations people had accumulated for many months. People felt history was repeating itself. They came in large numbers to hear the *Megillah* read. Whenever the reader mentioned Haman's name, the crowd stamped their feet. It was an ancient custom long forgotten, but revived now under the most trying circumstances. The deafening roar of defiance of those stamping feet did a world of good. It gave a badly needed lift to people. The trouble was that we could not report it. Many times there were more news items on our desks that we could not report than news that was "fit to print". It was a basic requirement not to report news which could be classified as "atrocity stories". This was prohibited by law. But it was an ambiguous law; it could be stretched by the imagination of a *Gestapo* agent and it was severe enough to silence the most persistent violator. And besides, in the Nazi *Reich* laws had of course no real meaning at all. What the *Gestapo* found in the "interest of the Party and the State" was the unwritten law of the land. This we found out again and again. These pages are a demonstration of this fact.

If we were concerned with maintaining the morale of our people, we had to consider the fact that every day placed a thousand hardships on every Jew, and posed a thousand questions for which there were no ready answers. The Jewish press was the only means to get information, to view the world and to find sense and meaning in life as a Jew. The general press, completely Nazified and

---

[8]Fritz Neuländer was the editor of the *Gemeinde-Blatt Köln-Ehrenfeld*, founded in 1931. It was published four times a week with an edition of 3,000.
[9]Editors and key employees of Jewish publishing houses had to obtain licences from the Nazi authorities. This was later extended to all their employees.

appalling in its uniformity, was no longer a source ordinary Jews could rely on. Most Jews stopped reading these papers.

The result was that the Jewish papers doubled and tripled their circulation. The number of subscribers to the *Jüdische Rundschau*, the semi-weekly organ of the Zionist Organisation, jumped from less than 10,000 to 37,000. The *C.V.-Zeitung*, weekly organ of the *Centralverein deutscher Staatsbürger jüdischen Glaubens* (C.V.), formed in 1893 to defend Jewish rights and interests, had the highest paid circulation, about 50,000. The *Israelitisches Familienblatt*, the only unaffiliated newspaper, increased its circulation to over 36,000. *Der Schild*, organ of the war veterans of the *Reichsbund jüdischer Frontsoldaten* (RjF) had just under 20,000 readers.[10] In the cities with larger Jewish populations, the *Gemeindeblätter*, monthly or semi-monthly publications were circulated without charge by the local communities; the largest, in Berlin, had a circulation of 46,000 in 1934. We can safely conclude from these figures that every Jew read two or three Jewish newspapers every week. Although the news reported was almost uniform in all these papers – the papers received them from the news service of the JTA – the editorials were enlightening and did much to maintain morale.[11] Under these circumstances every suppression of a paper for several months deprived its readers of a valuable source of information and it was at the same time a financial loss for the publishing house and the many people who worked for a living in the editorial offices or in the distribution centre.

All these possible side effects added to the responsibility each editor had to bear. It was no matter to trifle with. It weighed heavily on each one of us. It was necessary to ponder the repercussions of every news item not only in view of the disguised censorship we had to face, but, most of all, how it would affect the morale of our people. If we published too many shocking stories, it might depress all those who hoped that a kind of normalcy would prevail in the end. At the same time, it could augment the feeling of being trapped, and could induce many to flee the vice that was closing around them. Whatever we did, events might prove us wrong. Whatever we did not do might turn out to be an omission that could harm our people. This was a predicament no one could solve and no one could escape from.

CENSORSHIP AND ITS REPERCUSSIONS

Every day we had to send our bulletin "free of charge" to four different authorities:

The Ministry of Propaganda,
The Commissioner of Jewish Affairs in the Propaganda Ministry,

[10]Figures from Freeden, *Die jüdische Presse, op. cit.*, p. 36. These figures are authoritative. They amount to a total of 142,850 for 1934 for four of the five largest Jewish papers in Germany Freeden gives earlier, p. 32, a slightly higher figure (143,800) for these four "political" papers but this is an insignificant discrepancy. Of course there was a gradual decline of circulation after 1934 in view of emigration, but in 1938 they still totalled 106,400. The *Berliner Gemeindeblatt* (see below) actually increased its circulation after 1934 and still published an edition of 40,000 in 1938.

[11]Cf. for instance one of the four essays by Jacob Boas (note 1), 'Countering Nazi Defamation. German Jews and the Jewish Tradition, 1933–1938', in *LBI Year Book XXXIV* (1989), pp. 205–226.

The Jewish Section of the *Gestapo* (Eichmann's Office),
The Office of the *Gestapo* in Berlin.

All these offices exercised a type of surveillance which was different in kind from
the censorship that we associate with this word. Censorship, it is assumed, is
applied before publication; newspapers and magazines have to be submitted to
the censor before they are printed and circulated to the public. Nazi censorship
did not work in this manner. It was applied *after* publication. The editor had to
take responsibility for every word after his bulletin, newspaper or magazine was
printed and in the hands of subscribers. Approval prior to printing and mailing
was not required.

The fact that we had to deal with several censors introduced another
uncertainty and insecurity into our daily routine. We were more or less at the
mercy of the ever-present, bitter rivalries of the different bureaucracies. After
posting our printed matter, we just had to sit and wait for a reaction, for a 'phone
call or for a letter. It was like looking into an abyss.

One day the telephone rang in our office. A clipped voice identified itself:
"This is *Sturmbannführer* Eichmann speaking. We do not like the news item you
published about the meeting of the Board of Deputies of British Jews in London.
It would be better if it were not to appear in the Jewish press." Then the phone
went dead.

This was one of the rare occasions when we were informed about objections to
an item before it could appear in the Jewish papers. Eichmann's telephone call
had to be taken seriously and conveyed to all concerned. I telephoned the editors
of the papers published in Berlin and sat down and wrote to each editor in the
provinces asking them not to publish this particular item. "I deem it advisable",
I wrote, "not to publish it." It was obvious what the letter meant – it did not
require any explanation.[12]

I had to follow the same procedure when Kuchmann,[13] of the *Judenreferat* in the
Berlin *Gestapo*, called. He objected to a news item from London which described
the heart-warming reception of a small group of Jewish children, who had come
from Germany to England (a forerunner of the large transports after the
"*Kristallnacht*"), and were the lucky ones who had reached safety. Obviously, it
would have been too much of a comfort to the parents of those children sent
abroad if they had read about it in print; their morale would have been
strengthened and this was not desirable.

Censorship did not only apply to a news item as such, it included headlines
and advertisements, especially death notices. It might seem somewhat far-
fetched to speak about death announcements, but this was, in fact, what
happened. That someone died suddenly and unexpectedly – as was the habit to
say in the announcement – might indicate that he had died in a concentration

---

[12]See my article 'Last Days of the German-Jewish Press', *loc. cit.*
[13]The *Gestapo* inspector Kuchmann appears in connection with Kareski (see below) in Yehoyakim
Cochavi, 'Georg Kareski's Nomination as Head of the Kulturbund . . .', in *LBI Year Book XXXIV*
(1989), p. 236, and in other studies of the *Judenreferat*.

camp. This would not have been consonant with the official version that the concentration camps did not actually exist.

At first such headlines as 'Tragt ihn mit Stolz den gelben Fleck' in the *Jüdische Rundschau* and 'Wir wollen leben' in the *C.V.-Zeitung* were permitted. But this changed after the Nuremberg Laws were decreed in 1935. Honour and pride could no longer be claimed by Jews. No such telling and morale raising headlines were allowed.

It was after these Laws were promulgated that the campaign against the Jews took on a different perspective and aim. To force emigration of Jews became part and parcel of Nazi policy. Jews were never allowed to raise their voices against this policy. I remember a speech delivered by the *Staatskommissar für jüdische Angelegenheiten* Hans Hinkel.[14] He had invited himself to address a gathering of Jewish leaders in Berlin and laid down the law: no participation of Jews in any activities outside the Jewish sphere, with the one final aim: emigration. This was in 1937. (After the war this same Hinkel was "denazified" and like many a Nazi official lived out his life in peace and comfort.)

Anyway, the *Gestapo* barred any adverse discussion of Nazi policies by warning Jewish leaders individually that any violation of this verbal order would impel them to take "proper measures". The Jewish press could never report the meeting at which Hinkel spoke and it could never report the change in Nazi policies concerning emigration. We were only allowed to point to the economic necessity of looking for a new home abroad.

It was pure luck that a *Gestapo* agent did not choose to interpret references to emigration as an attack on government policy. A friend of mine spoke at a meeting in a small town. The supervising *Gestapo* man happened to be drunk and my friend was promptly reported as having said something not in favour of emigration although he had not uttered a single word in this respect. Nevertheless, upon his return to Berlin he was summoned by the *Gestapo*, his passport was confiscated and he was forced to sign a statement accepting imprisonment in a concentration camp if he should ever again utter any anti-emigration sentiments.

Whenever I spoke in meetings arranged by the *Preussischer Landesverband* in cities and towns all over Germany, a *Gestapo* agent was always present. Many times the agent introduced himself, warned me of his power to stop the meeting, and sat down right in front of me, most of the time in the first row. It was not a pleasant atmosphere to be faced with. It was more than intimidating to see how the man took his notes, looking up straight into your face, motionless and emotionless, but enough to let you know, through his very presence, that your days could be numbered. There was always the chance that this man's notes would wind up in Eichmann's office in Berlin and, worse, that his superior reading the report might knock at my hotel door and take me away forever. In the final analysis, every speaker and every editor was dependent on the whims of

---

[14]For Hinkel see a.o. *ibid.*, pp. 228ff. His role has been examined in a number of studies of the Nazi period.

a low-level bureaucrat who might have only a limited knowledge of what was going on, but could do you the utmost harm. And this was the crucial point.

Since *Gestapo* agents were present in the large synagogues of Berlin, it happened that they reported sermons that were plainly beyond their understanding. But the result was that the *Gestapo* "invited" some rabbis and threatened them with a "vacation" in a concentration camp unless they mended their ways.

One well-known rabbi, Emil Bernhard Cohn, was put on trial before a special court in Berlin which actually judged only "crimes against the regime" and was notorious for the severe sentences it handed out. It was a public trial. A member of the Presidium of the Jewish community of Berlin and of the *Reichsvertretung*, Adolf Schoyer, and I were the only spectators. A *Gestapo* agent testified that the rabbi had "incited" his listeners and had made remarks that could be interpreted as being hostile to the Nazi regime. The Prosecutor asked for a prison sentence, but the Court, for unknown reasons, acquitted the rabbi. This did not prevent the *Gestapo* from arresting him some time later. When he was finally released – once he got out of jail in order to take part in his son's Bar Mitzvah – the Jewish community was instrumental in spiriting him out of the country. There was not much time to lose. He was in mortal danger. We could not report this trial.

We could not report on any anti-Jewish groups and their activities abroad. Most were financed by the Nazi government. To reveal that German rifles and ammunition were found among the Arabs in Palestine after the outbreak of the disturbances in 1936 would have been an invitation to suicide. We could never write anything about the boycott of German goods and anti-Nazi activities in the West, especially in America. Any report of demonstrations against Nazi policies was quite impossible. Anyone connected in a leading capacity with anti-German activities could never be mentioned by name. This even included Winston Churchill. We had to pretend that men like Einstein or Stephen S. Wise just did not exist. Any emigrant from Germany was a non-person if he was active in the anti-Nazi movement abroad or previously connected with the political life of the Weimar Republic.

As the years went by, restrictions and restraints increased again and again. But in spite of all the difficulties the large newspapers devoted twenty and more pages to political articles and news, and Jewish art and literature; there were special sections for the Jewish woman, Palestine, emigration economic questions, and sport and hobbies. According to the guidelines of the Propaganda Ministry Jewish publications had to deal only with those events and cultural developments in which Jews were directly involved. Under this restriction any discussion, activity and even mere advertisements mentioning Goethe, Schiller, Beethoven or Bach were banned.

In the summer of 1937 specific topics were prohibited. *Staatskommissar* Hinkel, issued a decree listing the subjects which could no longer be dealt with in articles or news. These topics included news normally printed without hesitation in a Jewish paper. To criticise the anti-Jewish policies of the Polish Government was out of the question. Italian aspirations towards Palestine or the Italian colonial policy in general were taboo. Quotations from Nazi newspapers were no longer allowed. Speeches of foreign statesmen praising Jews and their achievements were forbidden. It was a formidable list. It included subjects about which I myself had said much more than was prudent.

In 1938 I again provoked the suspension of the *C.V.-Zeitung* for a month because I had published articles on the Romanian government led by the vicious antisemite Professor Goga.[15] I cited his anti-Jewish measures, one after the other, exactly as reported in the German press. When the editor, my friend Dr. Alfred Hirschberg,[16] sought a reason for the suspension, he was told, as a special favour, that such a survey might have led Jews to believe that they were still well off in Germany and had no need to emigrate into a hostile world. Furthermore, to publish a summary like this could be taken as implied criticism of a government friendly to Germany.

It was not surprising to find contradictions or reasons bordering on the ridiculous in rulings of the Propaganda Ministry and the *Gestapo*. I hesitated to release a resolution of the Zionist Congress in 1937 which condemned the persecution of Zionists in Russia because it contradicted Nazi propaganda allegations that Russia was dominated by Jews. I plucked up the courage to phone an official of the Propaganda Ministry to ask for a ruling. He promised to call me back the next day, but when he failed to do so, I approached him again. "It is forbidden to print this story", he declared. But the editor of the *Jüdische Rundschau*, who had no idea that I had contacted the Ministry, printed the resolution and got away with it.[17]

PREVENTIVE MEASURES

Events like this made it necessary to co-ordinate steps taken or not taken, or to assess bad and good news. Every Friday morning the editors of the papers published in Berlin assembled in the *Reichsvertretung der deutschen Juden (Juden in*

[15] *C.V.-Zeitung*, XVII, Nr. 1 (6th January 1938), contained a first article, 'Was wird aus Rumäniens Juden?' (signed "o.e."), followed by two unsigned articles, 'Die Judenfrage in Rumänien' and 'Zur Lage der Juden in Rumänien', in *C.V.-Zeitung*, XVII, Nrs. 2 and 3. Four issues were banned and the paper reappeared with Nr. 8.

[16] On the *C.V.-Zeitung* editor and *Centralverein-Syndikus* Alfred Hirschberg see a.o. Arnold Paucker, *Der jüdische Abwehrkampf gegen Antisemitismus und Nationalsozialismus in den letzten Jahren der Weimarer Republik*, Hamburg 1969 (2nd edn.), *passim*. He was one of the most active functionaries of the C.V. and figures in much of the literature on Jewry in the Weimar Republic and under the Nazi regime. Hirschberg succeeded in emigrating to Brazil. He was a prolific writer. See also his essay, 'Ludwig Hollaender, Director of the C.V.', in *LBI Year Book VII* (1962), pp. 39–74. Hirschberg died in 1971.

[17] Robert Weltsch, Editor-in-Chief of the *Jüdische Rundschau*, has himself written a great deal about his own brushes with the Nazi authorities and we cannot quote all this copious literature here. As far as this Year Book is concerned see his two illuminating essays 'A Goebbels Speech and a Goebbels Letter', in *LBI Year Book X* (1965), pp. 280–286, and 'Looking Back over Sixty Years', in *LBI Year Book XXVII* (1982), in particular pp. 384–385. See now also Herbert A. Strauss, 'Robert Weltsch und die Jüdische Rundschau', a paper delivered at a 'Kafka Symposium' on *Der Prager Kreis* on 10th November 1988 at the *Freie Universität*, Berlin (publication in German and possibly in English, forthcoming).

Deutschland). Under the chairmanship of Otto Hirsch,[18] its Director, they received information about developments within and without the Jewish community about measures to speed up emigration, about the state of education in Jewish schools and everything that might be or become news. Most of it was for background information only, not for publication. It was a gathering of not more than ten people, all of whom had known each other for a long time. The small circle and the goodwill that brought us together guaranteed a working relationship that was consonant with the personal dangers each one of us faced every day. These meetings gave us the opportunity to exchange information, emanating mostly in an unofficial way from the Nazi authorities, about what would and would not pass. It was here that agreement was reached not to publish certain news. It was here that we heard of the conflicting views of Nazi authorities about the Jewish Question and decided how to steer clear of them or wondered what to expect of them. If e.g. the Ministry of Economics had recommended not forcing a radical elimination of Jews from the economic life of the country – a move the Nazi Party wanted – it was instructive to know that discussions like these were going on, who had heard of them and whether this source of information was reliable. In those years, until 1938, there were still some connections each one of us had with former Gentile friends and acquaintances. Many times I received some guarded information about developments in the economic sector from a student friend of mine who held a responsible position in a large bank and had connections to the Minister of Economics, Hjalmar Schacht. I heard about Nazi indoctrination of the school system from one of my former teachers. All this was gathered at occasional meetings, most of them out of the public eye, in homes or during walks in fields and forests, and was intended to circumvent the conspiracy of silence, to penetrate the wall that was building up around us.

ISOLATION AND IN THE FANGS OF THE GESTAPO

To look over the wall, to observe the currents of international diplomacy, to judge the situation abroad became more difficult as the months and years went by. The import of Jewish newspapers, especially from New York, was already prohibited in the summer of 1933.[19] By a quirk of fate we still received those papers from New York and Warsaw which came bundled up and without a return address. I read them with a keen sense of urgency, with the knowledge that I could look over the wall, but with the distinct awareness that these papers were dangerous merchandise. I tried to stop further deliveries by informing an emissary of the London office of the danger we were in.

It took many months before I succeeded. In the meantime, a trusted employee

---

[18]Otto Hirsch's life and work has been the subject of a book by Paul Sauer, *Für Recht und Menschenwürde. Ein Lebensbild von Otto Hirsch (1885–1941)*, Gerlingen 1985 and an essay by the same author, 'Otto Hirsch (1885–1941). Director of the Reichsvertretung', in *LBI Year Book XXXII* (1987), pp. 341–368. Hirsch died in Mauthausen concentration camp.
[19]16th August 1933.

had the task of tearing up these newspapers, shredding them and discarding the remains among the rubbish. At that time there were no incinerators in Berlin and papershredders were not yet invented. There was no other way to get rid of them.

But reading these papers gave me an opportunity to find out what was going on within Jewish organisations, especially in America, how far the concentration on fund-raising had progressed, to what degree German-Jewish leaders could still count on a flow of cash from abroad to keep welfare services intact. There was the matter of public opinion abroad, the inroads German propaganda made, the attitude of the foreign press which was far too impressed with Nazi attainments and much too little concerned about their victims. Every few weeks I went to see Dr. Leo Baeck, President of the *Reichsvertretung*. I sat in his small office alone with him, briefing him about developments that were not to be found in German newspapers, answering his questions and concerns and admiring his towering intellect. Of the the many losses of documents and data every emigrant has to suffer, one item stands out. For a number of years I attended the lectures of Leo Baeck, listened to sermons he delivered and speeches he made. He spoke slowly. I could record every word in shorthand. But all these notes were lost and so was a personal letter he wrote to me when I left Germany. With an overriding sense of duty and dedication he and so many others stood at their posts, fearlessly and persistently, without hesitation and without question.

Many things are now held against them. The fact that in 1933 Jewish leaders tried to stop the boycott movement against German goods in America and Europe has all too often been castigated in retrospect.[20] It is of course a fact that the Presidium of the Berlin Jewish community sent a cable to the American Jewish Committee asking them to stop the spread of atrocity stories and the boycott of German goods. It is forgotten, however, that this cable and other communications were sent after Hermann Göring himself had summoned Jewish leaders on 26th March 1933 and ordered them to take this action – or else. From a participant of that meeting I heard the amazing story that the Jewish leaders did not take this lying down, but actually dared to talk back to Göring. It did not mean much to him. He dismissed them all with a wave of his hand.

I remember the speech of a Vice President of the C.V., Bruno Weil, who, about this time, proclaimed his opposition to a boycott of German goods. He, too, did not mean what he said. It was just window dressing.

As far as that cable is concerned, Jewish leaders in America were informed via other channels about the true origin of this communication. Those who sent the cable certainly did not subscribe to its contents. The boycott of German goods was seen as the only way to harm Nazi Germany and to reduce the pressures on German Jewry.

There was one man who pursued his own policies and provided his own solutions to problems. Georg Kareski, member of the Presidium of the Berlin

---

[20]There have, of course, been many arguments on the role of the Jewish leadership in Germany; one of which made the headlines in the Jewish press in the USA in 1982. And this is not the place to deal with the controversies on the *Haavara*-Transfer agreement and the phase of the deportations.

Jewish community, was for years a questionable figure and viewed with keen suspicion.[21] We all knew that he had connections with the *Gestapo* which used him, a radical Zionist, and his paper, *Der Staatszionist*, to obtain information about what was going on among the Jewish leaders. Once the *Gestapo* even attempted, unsuccessfully, to replace Leo Baeck with Kareski. I had never talked to him until we met on a guided tour conducted by the Berlin community to review educational and welfare facilities. He engaged me in a prolonged conversation, at the end of which he said: "Whenever you have difficulties with the *Gestapo*, just let me know; I might be able to straighten things out." Of course, I never availed myself of this offer.

The members of the Presidium of the Berlin Jewish community were very concerned about the activities of their fellow member and his ties to the *Gestapo*. I am not so sure now that we did not exaggerate matters in this respect. I remember talking to Dr. Alfred Klee, a famous defence lawyer, and he complained about Kareski. I suggested that members of the Presidium should get together in someone's home to discuss any sensitive matters not for the ears of Kareski. This would prevent any leaks. He took up my proposal with his fellow members and they excluded Kareski from certain proceedings.

I was able to convey my thoughts about Kareski to Boris Smolar, Chief Correspondent of the JTA. He saw to it that the facts about Kareski were made known the world over. On an earlier visit to Palestine, prior to his emigration, crowds assembled in the streets and followed Kareski wherever he went. Eventually he was forced off the street and, finally, he had to leave Palestine. We were never able to print a word about what had happened.[22]

On the other hand, there were events that were so tightly guarded and kept from the public by Nazi censorship that getting close to the story was virtually impossible. The famous painter, Max Liebermann, died in 1935. He had been President of the Berlin Academy of Arts until ousted by the Nazis. He was a celebrated portraitist and his death was an event which concerned art-lovers all over the world. Naturally, news of his death was not carried by the Nazi press. As far as they were concerned, he had only been a Jew degrading German art and his death was to be ignored.

A member of the Presidium of the Berlin community telephoned me to say that he found Max Liebermann's name in the list of those to be buried in its cemetery. But he did not know the time and place of the funeral.

It was obvious that the *Gestapo* was afraid that this funeral could be used by people to congregate in great numbers and be turned into a demonstration of their concern and affliction. The *Gestapo* made sure that the time and place of the funeral was set by them and kept from reporters of the Jewish and foreign press.

---

[21]The suspect role of Georg Kareski has been the subject of a number of studies, first by Herbert S. Levine: 'A Jewish Collaborator in Nazi Germany. The Strange Career of Georg Kareski, 1933–1937', *Central European History*, 8 (1975); and more recently by Francis R. Nicosia, 'Revisionist Zionism in Germay (II). Georg Kareski and the Staatszionistische Organisation, 1933–1938', in *LBI Year Book XXXII* (1987), pp. 231–267, and Cochavi, 'Georg Kareski's Nomination as Head of the Kulturbund . . .', *loc. cit.* pp. 227–246.

[22]On Kareski's "trial" after his final emigration to Palestine see the literature quoted above (note 21).

Even the President of the Berlin community, Heinrich Stahl, told me that he did not know when and where the funeral would take place; it might be hours or days away.

It was impossible to get in touch with Liebermann's home as it had an unlisted telephone number and nobody knew how to obtain it. Finally, I remembered that an aunt of mine was a close friend of the Liebermanns. The artist had painted my uncle's portrait and hers. I managed to get the telephone number from her and telephoned the Liebermanns' house on the famous square in front of the Brandenburger Tor. When Mrs. Liebermann heard who I was, she came to the 'phone. She assured me that she did not know when the funeral would take place, but she wanted me to be present. I should speak to Stahl the next morning; by then the time and place of the funeral would be cleared.

It seemed almost uncanny how very few people attended the service in the hall at the cemetery. Had it not been for the professional pallbearers and the few members of the family, there would not even have been a *minyan*. A trio of sad-faced musicians played Handel's "Largo". The moment was tragic and solemn.

Leo Baeck finished speaking his historic eulogy and we rose from our seats. Turning round, we saw about a dozen *Gestapo* agents sitting at the rear of the hall, who later positioned themselves a few hundred feet from the graveside. This was a symbol of frightening clarity. The exponent of a cultural era with a highly visible Jewish participation was dead. The heritage he represented was destroyed. And there stood the bullying thugs of a new "order" with all its cruel aggressiveness. The sight was unforgettable.

We could publish only a brief account of the death of the great artist – nothing about the events surrounding his funeral and only a short outline of the eulogy. It was better to forego a detailed recounting of what had really transpired.

TO KEEP UP MORALE

All these restrictions and restraints harboured within them the danger of ghettoisation and isolation. The question was always how to overcome this danger without violating professed Nazi policies and winding up with a suspension or ending up in a concentration camp.

At the same time, we had to face the clear dilemma of what to present to the Jewish public and how to prepare our readers for yet more trying times to come. The question of how a story might affect the morale and mental stability of our readers was a decisive factor in editorial presentations. This was especially true of information relating to emigration; and here again we had to suppress a great deal of news.

Any story telling of a trickle of emigration to South America or elsewhere might have resulted in an avalanche of visa applicants and closed any possible escape route. It was bad enough that Jews had to go from consulate to consulate to inquire about visas. It was bad enough that the queues, especially in front of the American Consulate, were becoming longer every day. But publishing anything that might have resulted in a stampede of visa applicants would not have been a morale-building factor. It was up to the appropriate Jewish organisation to publish news of this sort. We would gladly print it, but we simply could not take the responsibility for releasing it on our own volition.

We tried again and again to keep up the spirit of the Jews in a way that made any news item a tool for maintaining morale under the most trying circumstances.[23] There was a host of good news to search for. Any achievement of a Jew in any country, any decoration or elevation of an individual Jew provided a lift of the spirit to readers. Jewish Nobel-prize winners boosted morale and were a source of pride at a time when the Jews were being told every day how inferior they were.

There were stories of developments of Jewish communities abroad. From Europe to Australia, from Asia, Africa and America, there were many events that could be reported in order to give readers a positive outlook. Developments in the *Yishuv* in *Eretz Israel* could be a source of hope and even the riots of 1936 could not detract from the positive effect of building up a country for ourselves. This offset Nazi propaganda that Jews could not accomplish anything and lived on the sweat of others.

In 1937 I wrote a series of articles for the *C.V.-Zeitung*, dealing with the organisational structure of Jewries all over the world. My intention was to acquaint readers with the names of organisations and leading personalities in different countries in case they emigrated. It happened that I had to interrupt the series and to our surprise Adolf Eichmann, asked the editor of the paper, Alfred Hirschberg,[24] when the series would be continued. This immediately aroused my suspicion. What business had Eichmann with Jewish leaders in foreign countries? Since I always had a hunch that the Nazis would expand their reach and invade neighbouring countries, I omitted, as much as I could, an analysis of those countries. I could never (to this day) overcome the feeling that my writings might have helped Eichmann to seize Jewish leaders and organisations when the Germans invaded country after country all over Europe. I will never know whether this actually happened. It showed the danger that perfectly legitimate, and from the Jewish point of view necessary, information could be used by the Nazis for thir own sinister purposes.

Again and again a decisive attempt was made to derive from the past a measure of benefit for the present; to reach out to the great minds of the past. There was an abundance of cultural treasures, stories of Jews past and present and their accomplishments. There were novels and short stories written by amateurs and by professionals. There was a desire to go back to one's "roots".

Many a story invited parallels with the present. Many a quotation from the Scriptures showed strength, presistence and perseverence in the face of tribulation. Many a Psalm could provide solace and could acquire new meaning. But

---

[23]Cf. Boas, 'Countering Nazi Defamation', *loc. cit.*; *idem*, 'The Shrinking World of German Jewry, 1933–1938', in *LBI Year Book XXXI* (1986), pp. 241–266; and Margaret T. Edelheim-Muehsam, 'Reactions of the Jewish Press to the Nazi Challenge', in *LBI Year Book V* (1960), pp. 308–329.

[24]Alfred Hirschberg (see note 16) braved many Nazi threats, intimidations and arrests.

here, too, we had to be selective. It would have been impossible to quote Psalm CXL:

> "Deliver me, O Lord from the evil man: Preserve me from the violent man; Which imagine mischiefs in their heart; Continually are they gathered together for war. They have sharpened their tongues like a serpent; Adders' poison is under their lips . . . Let not an evil speaker be established in the earth;".

All the quotations and many more amounted to a kind of subtle criticism of the regime and served to remind our people that these dark days would not last for ever. It was many months before the Nazi censors caught on to the true meaning of some of these stories, whereupon they made it clear that they did not like them.

One prayer that caused problems was the prayer for the welfare of the government. It was an integral part of the prayerbook, but it had lost its meaning. It would have been more than hypocrisy to pray for the most vicious enemy the Jewish people had ever had. We could safely leave this to the churches. On the other hand, to omit it completely might be interpreted as disrespect and as an expression of displeasure with the government. It was impossible to discuss this in any forum, or in any newspaper column. But it attests to the common sense of Jewish leaders that this prayer was gradually abandoned[25] without comment. In the end, the *Gestapo* relieved hesitant souls of their objections. The prayer was prohibited.

RUMOUR AND WIT

And then there was more news we just could not publish, again and again an accumulation of facts had simply to be ignored. It is remarkable how the human mind reacts to the uniformity of news, as found in the Nazi press, and to the suppression of news, which was a hallmark of the Jewish press. In a totalitarian state, word of mouth dispenses certain news the government wants to withhold from the public. Rumour is the unavoidable result of such policy. During all the Hitler years, rumour after rumour floated around – and naturally this was not restricted to Jewish circles. Everyone had a story to tell, everybody heard it from "reliable sources". It was instructive to see how fast rumours could travel and how much they became distorted in the process. But there was always the strange fact that any rumour had a kernel of truth in it. There was always something behind it. It did not come out of the blue. But to sift the facts from what was sometimes wishful thinking or an accumulation of meaningless data was an endeavour that could easily lead to a dead-end. One had to realise again and again that rumour was a defence mechanism of the news-hungry mind, a way to beat the censor and a means of keeping a precarious mental balance. It could easily be overdone and we took note of this. Editorials condemning rumour-mongering were written, and facts calculated to encourage readers were provided. But this was no more than a gesture. The spreading of rumours continued.

[25]For an adaptation of the Jewish prayer for the beloved fatherland see Paucker, *Jüdischer Widerstand in Deutschland, op. cit.*, p. 6.

And there was another defence mechanism that had its place in those difficult times but which could not be mentioned in the Jewish press. The political joke or the joke with political overtones was taboo in the strictest sense of the word. It had developed to a fine art. The joke circulating from mouth to mouth was used to keep up spirits, to generate some kind of affirmative attitude in the midst of insecurity: it was an expression of the will to endure and to overcome: it cut an adversary down to size and robbed him of the aura of invincibility: it was an escape hatch for the spirit. But it could be exaggerated and it could contribute to an unrealistic attitude. We will never know how far it actually raised the spirits of the story-tellers themselves.

We could not pay much attention to this expression of Jewish wit. We were concerned with the almighty, unpredictable figure of the censor with his power over life and death, suppression and suspension. Many a time we had to select modes of expression that were so subtle that they bordered on the obscure. Many a time we had to brood over delicate shades of meaning in the hope that the reader would understand while the censor would not be provoked to interpret an expression as hostile. The word "democracy" seemed to be rather unpopular with the censor although the Nazis, at times, maintained that theirs was the only truly democratic system. So we replaced it with the word "self-government" or described it as "a development prevailing in certain countries". Anti-Nazi demonstrations and publicity abroad could never be mentioned by name or author. So they were listed as "expressions of Jewish concern". This was a play on words; one had to learn it and be ambitious enough to be good at it.

BRINGING NEWS OUT OF GERMANY

My telephone was tapped. Every time I lifted the receiver I heard the familiar click of a recording device, but I never knew whether somebody would call and say something that would give a hint of some forbidden activity. Even calling from a public telephone had its dangers; I did not know whether the phone at the other end was tapped.

My incoming mail was opened although the envelopes did not show any sign of having been tampered with. But I could detect the interception if a line was extended over the flap of the envelope by the sender and the lines were no longer matching when I received the letter. Letters usually delivered overnight were delayed for days. The "love letters" the censor read spoke of wonderful days ahead while, in my mind, the future was a senseless blank; one lived from day to day.

In such an atmosphere the need to escape, to breathe the air of freedom even for a few days or weeks became, often, a matter of urgency. To take a trip abroad was a wholesome experience for unsteady nerves and a means to regain one's mental balance. Whenever I could, I took advantage of it. At the same time, I could hit back at our oppressors. I could make use of the facilities of the Jewish Telegraphic Agency abroad to tell the truth about the situation inside Germany.

In the year before the Olympic Games of 1936, which were to take place in Berlin, the Nazis proceeded to assemble an elaborate display and make Germany a showplace. All the signs "Juden unerwünscht" disappeared from the entrances of villages and towns. The signs "Jews not admitted" adorning shops and offices were quietly taken away. The Nazi press did its utmost to tone down anti-Jewish propaganda. The hundreds of thousands of foreign tourists who then flocked to the Berlin Games saw a happy, united and peaceful Germany, no sign of atrocities and no indication of rearmament. They could see a seemingly complete devotion to the peaceful pursuit of sports and the glamorous and well-organised activities of non-political social gatherings. This was indeed a significant transformation of a hideous regime. It was natural that, in such an atmosphere, foreigners and the foreign press were inclined to belittle as mere propaganda all the atrocity stories they had heard and read.

To the well-meaning observer these stories just could not be true. To counter all these lies of a hated regime was, therefore, worth the effort and the danger.

I sat in the little hotel of the small Polish town. A few streets away stood the house where I was born. Many generations of my family had lived and died in this town. After the First World War it was handed over to Poland. Its name was changed – Filehne became Wielun. The birthplace of the founders of the famous Filene's Department Store in Boston was no longer on the map. The border divided the town right down the middle. A few hundred feet away was Germany.

I had crossed the border on a valid German passport issued before 1933 showing my former profession as a member of the judiciary. The German border guards let me pass without question. They did not stamp my passport after I told them I wanted to visit the graves of my family. The Germans had no record of my having been to Poland.

Years had passed since I had stood in the cemetery on a hill at the end of town. The entrance door still squeaked as I had remembered it. It still left me with the same uneasiness I had felt as a child. The bees were still buzzing and the shadows were still dancing over the resting place of countless generations. But there was no longer anyone to take care of the graves. The road and the paths were covered with overgrown weeds. The graves were buried under grass. There was silence all around. No one came here to visit. Those who cared lived hundreds and thousands of miles away. There was only a handful of Jews left in the town; suddenly it dawned on me that the same deterioration, the same loneliness was in store for all the Jewish cemeteries in Germany. After our dispersal all over the globe, after all of us had disappeared, who would come to visit the graves?

In the hotel I wrote by hand a news report to the London office of the Jewish Telegraphic Agency. It gave a vivid picture of the loss of life and livelihood that had become the German Jews' fate. It described, for the first time, the terror Jews in small towns were subjected to by their German neighbours. They could not buy medicine when ill. They and their children were constantly taunted. They did not dare to leave their houses. They were forced to move to larger cities in the hope that from there they would be able to emigrate. The report revealed details of the desecration of cemeteries, of synagogues, of the destruction of Jewish property and the hopelessness that had overcome the Jews. German Jewry was bound to be wiped out. It was only a matter of time.

I gave the letter to the owner of the hotel. She had known me since I was a child. I did not dare to go to the post office to buy stamps, nor did I want to be seen posting a letter. Although, at that time, the mails were not censored in Poland, I addressed the letter to the home of an employee of the London office, whose address I had memorised. In an accompanying note I asked the London editor to keep the story "under wraps" for about two weeks and dateline it Amsterdam. I had not been there for years.

When the story was published in the Jewish press in the Western countries, it served as a vivid reminder that the war against the Jews had not been called off, that it was, at best, suspended. But my story served a more obvious purpose. The *New York Times* and the *Associated Press* asked their Berlin correspondents to write articles about German Jewry. News agencies in England and France featured this dispatch and headlined it. It was put out on the news wires all over the world. This was a setback for the Nazi regime. Again and again, whenever I went abroad I sent stories to the London office to keep the German-Jewish Question in the headlines. In the winter of 1937 I went to Czechoslovakia. I arranged to meet Michael Wurmbrand, the JTA correspondent in Prague, in a small winter resort so full of people that we could be part of the crowd. We spent hours walking and talking. There was a lot to tell of the true state of affairs and there was a warning to convey: Czechoslovakia was no longer a safe haven. The Jews should prepare for the worst.

During those decisive years after 1933 Jewish leaders in Germany were hoping that a different attitude would result from spreading the truth all over the world. They felt that the dissemination of news abroad was absolutely essential and part of the last-ditch effort to save as many as possible. They were hoping that reaction in the Western countries might provide some relief from a relentless persecution and a breathing spell which could be used to proceed with an orderly emigration and they trusted that the Western democracies and the rest of the world would not tolerate an expansionist regime that was undermining their own interests and the basic order they had established after the First World War.

In fact, the outside world could have gauged the German preparations for war by the way they treated the Jews.[26] The process was gradual, beginning with intimidation and ending in murder. The more the Germans rearmed, the bolder they became in their mistreatment of the Jews. Every success of their foreign policy, every retreat of the Western powers served as a new incentive to accelerate and intensify anti-Jewish measures and to ignore any repercussions they might have abroad. The Western democracies gave the Nazis every reason to believe that they had a free hand in everything they wanted to do with the Jews. This was a despicable failure on the part of the Western World, a breakdown of values for which the democracies were to pay dearly.

The reason for this failure can be attributed (at least partly) to the lack of

---

[26]This thesis has been well expounded by Herbert A. Strauss, 'The Drive for War and the Pogroms of 1938 . . .', in *LBI Year Book XXXV* (1990), pp. 267–278. I had advanced it years ago in several articles.

intensive reporting by Western correspondents and the hidden or even overt resistance of their editors to reveal the true nature of Nazism.[27] For them it was still a question of those in power and those out of power. Journalists knowledgeable of conditions in the thirties testify today to the shortcomings of the general American press in those decisive years. It left its mark on Jews and non-Jews, on policy makers and on the ordinary citizen.

I talked to several leading personalities after I left Germany and went to the United States in September 1938. My objective was to inform them about the crucial changes coming in Germany for Jews and for the world. I told them that it was only a matter of weeks and months before devastating blows would fall on German Jews and that emigration had become a matter of life or death. I had given the same urgent news when I passed through Amsterdam on my way to the States. The President of the Jewish community assembled a number of prominent Jews in his house. They listened attentively, asked questions and responded to my warnings. Some of them went to Canada before Holland was invaded.

It was another story in New York. Every time I left one of those prominent people I felt a keen disappointment. I was shaken by the narrowness of their views and all I could muster was a feeling of desperation.

The reaction of Rabbi Stephen S. Wise, leader of the American Jewish Congress, was typical. "We know everything that is going on in Germany", he told me, and he dismissed me with a wave of his hand. His faith in the American press was boundless. Obviously, he had never heard of restrictions placed on news-gathering in a totalitarian state. He thought American journalists could overcome it. He and other Jewish leaders shared a lack of understanding of a different and completely alien regime. He was taken in by his views of a world that had changed beyond his conception. He and other Jewish leaders knew only part of the story. I sometimes wondered whether they wanted to know it all. The news coming out of Germany during the Hitler regime was, actually, sporadic and anything but systematic. Even Jewish newspapers published in America and wide parts of the world treated events in Germany in a superficial fashion. Not one of them maintained a permanent correspondent in Germany. Although these publications were banned in Germany, correspondents would have been accredited by the Foreign Office just to maintain good foreign relations. These correspondents might have been the subject of harassment and, occasionally, might have been expelled, but the outside world would have become acquainted with the true nature of the regime. No Jewish leader or organisation in America felt the necessity to pour money into such a news service. Their pre-occupation with internal matters, with the obvious necessity for organising themselves, prevented them from seeing the true picture. Hardly any of them came to Berlin during those crucial years. It was enough for them to read the papers.

In view of the arrangements with the Nazi authorities the Berlin office of the

---

[27]See Lipstadt, 'The American Press', *loc. cit.*, pp. 27–55; and for England, Andrew Sharf, *The British Press and Jews under Nazi Rule*, Oxford 1964.

JTA could not cable or send any news for consumption abroad. Several times a year the New York office – always short of money – sent Boris Smolar, Editor-in-Chief and roving European correspondent to Berlin. He stayed for weeks at a time, sometimes for months. Then his duties would summon him to other countries and a vital area of news remained without coverage. We supplied him with news, made contacts for him to see Jewish leaders and saw to it that he received an accurate picture of things to come. Once in a while, New York sent other correspondents who were more of a liability than an asset. They did not have much of an idea of the restrictive climate in which they had to gather news. They had not learned about it in the Schools of Journalism that they had attended. We took care of these people in spite of the fact that we violated German law.

There were some underground correspondents in Berlin who served Jewish newspapers abroad. One of them, by the name of Fink, worked without accreditation for some length of time. He sent his handwritten articles in Yiddish to a cover in New York. They appeared under a pen-name. He thought that no one could read his letters, and that no one could trace the source. But one day in 1937 he was arrested. We never heard of him again.

Strange as it may sound I enlisted the help of Nazi authorities to provide money for the support of temporary correspondents of the Jewish Telegraphic Agency. German currency restrictions made it impossible to transfer money out of the country or to hand it to foreigners inside Germany. With the help of an oral message transmitted by a correspondent I persuaded the London office to write a letter threatening to discontinue the delivery of news unless some of our debts were paid.

I dared to go to the *Reichspressekammer* with this letter. Referring to the German-American Commerce Treaty, I proposed that I would send every month a certain amount of marks to the account of the *Reichspressekammer* to be kept in trust until such time as a JTA correspondent would come to Berlin and would withdraw the money for living expenses. In this manner, not a single German mark would have to go abroad and harm the German balance of payments. To my surprise, my proposal was approved. The result was that the Nazis actually helped finance what was, in effect, anti-Nazi news and propaganda.

How these correspondents could be financed was always on our minds and it concerned, too, some of our Jewish leaders who were interested in maintaining a flow of news to the public outside Germany. One of them, with whom I shared more than just the initials of our names, gave me cash from his organisation to be used to support a JTA correspondent stationed in Berlin. For tax purposes I had to give a receipt with a false name and false address showing the delivery of paper and stationery.

This simple act violated so many Nazi laws that it would have been enough to put us away for good. We broke these laws by giving money to a foreigner. We violated the law against the spreading of "atrocity stories" because I would give precisely such stories to a correspondent of a foreign news service. I would be violating German tax laws by diverting money to a purpose not sanctioned by

German law. To top it all, I had given a false receipt and I had used the money of a Jewish organisation for unlawful purposes. This alone would have been sufficient to dissolve the organisation. Hundreds would have been thrown out of work.

We were aware of the danger each day brought. But we remained objective enough to see that the violation of laws could and would have repercussions on the moral fibre of our people. We discussed this question many times. I brought it up in one of my conversations with Leo Baeck. He was absolutely in favour of obeying Nazi laws, especially the currency laws. He was afraid that a different attitude would lead to a lessening of moral standards among our people. I wondered that he could take this position when he knew that what I was reporting to him and what I was doing was not exactly sanctioned by German law. I argued that we were at war with a vicious regime and that we had to do our best to overcome its assault on our lives and use every means at our command to defend ourselves, even at the risk of disobeying German laws. I said if our people ever saw normal times again, they would be aware that they have to maintain their probity.

And there were other questions that touched on the fundamentals of our existence, and were still more complex and more urgent. We asked ourselves: were all these efforts against insurmountable odds really worthwhile? Did it make any sense to risk life and limb in pursuit of an ever elusive goal? And in the end, would we not be as expendable as any other Jew?

We had an eventful summer in 1937; every day brought its share of questions. Then, one day in the autumn of 1937 it really was all over. Early one morning I was alone with one secretary in our office. The door bell rang; in stormed a horde of men, pushing the girl to the wall and entering my office demanding that I did not leave the room. Like vultures they grabbed every piece of paper, pored over each cable or telegram, whether they understood English or not, turned over wastepaper baskets and read abandoned news items. Then they left us an order from the *Gestapo* closing the offices and threatening everybody who might try to resume operations. And out they went. I wondered why they had left without taking me into custody.

We went to the American Consulate. Mr. Geist composed a cable to the State Department giving a coded report of the action taken against us. Days and weeks went by. In spite of all the efforts of the Consulate the office was never reopened. It was significant how secure the Nazis felt. The German-American Commerce Treaty was nothing but a useless piece of paper.

The closing of the JTA office was a serious blow to the Jewish press. The larger papers tried to replace our service with their own sources of news from abroad. But whatever they did was nothing but a stop-gap measure. November 1938 came and with it the liquidation of all Jewish newspapers. The isolation of German Jewry was complete.

Forced Labour of German Jews in Nazi Germany

BY KONRAD KWIET

In autumn 1941, when genocide in the East was already under way and the mass deportation of German Jews was introduced, a remarkable event took place in the control centres of the Nazi system. In his capacity as *Reichskommissar* for the *Ostland*, Hinrich Lohse suspended a series of "wild" executions in the Latvian port of Libau. Lohse took this step not because he was opposed to a radical "solution of the Jewish Question", but because he had taken exception to the manner of its implementation. This interference by the highest civilian authority aroused indignation in SS headquarters, in Riga and Berlin alike. The *Reichs-sicherheitshauptamt* (*Reich* Security Central Office, or RSHA) made a complaint and requested further information via the *Reichsministerium für die besetzten Ostgebiete* (Ministry for the Occupied Territories in the East).[1] In a short letter of 15th November 1941, Lohse justified his ban. Furthermore, unaware of the killing directive which had been issued to the SS *Einsatzgruppen* some weeks before, he asked for further information as to whether "all Jews in the East are to be liquidated?" Lohse added: "Is this to occur without regard for age and sex and economic interests (e.g. that of the *Wehrmacht* in skilled workers in armaments factories)? Of course the cleansing of the East of Jews is an urgent task, but its solution must be reconciled with the needs of the war economy."[2] At the end of December the answer arrived. The *Reichskommissar* was instructed to contact the appropriate Higher SS and Police Leader in future. As far as the Jews were concerned, he was informed by Berlin: "In the Jewish Question, meanwhile, the matter should be settled by verbal discussions. Economic concerns are not to be taken into consideration in the settlement of this problem."[3]

This issue has been the subject of much debate among researchers, always against a background of controversy. Then as now, at the heart of the question are problems of theory and interpretation, the classification and historicisation of Nazism in general and Nazi persecution of the Jews in particular.[4] The international *Historikerstreit* (now apparently on the wane) revealed the great difficulty encountered by some historians in dealing with the German murder of the Jews. One typical feature is that much of the running has been made by noted "outsiders" such as Ernst Nolte and Arno Mayer, rather than by the experts.

---

[1]Nürnberger Dokument (Nbg.) Dok. PS–3663. Brief Reichsministerium für die besetzten Ostgebiete (RMfdbO) an Reichskommissar für das Ostland (RKO), 31st October 1941.

[2]*Ibid.* Brief RKO an RMfdbO, 15th November 1941.

[3]*Ibid.* Brief RMfdbO an RKO, 18th December 1941.

[4]An excellent critical survey of the historical interpretations and controversies can be found in Ian Kershaw, *Der NS-Staat*, Reinbek 1988; see also Dan Diner (ed.), *Ist der Nationalsozialismus Geschichte? Zu Historisierung und Historikerstreit*, Frankfurt a. Main 1987. See now Richard Breitman's seminal study, *Himmler. Architect of Genocide*, New York 1991. I am grateful to him for having provided me with two relevant documents for this article (see notes 57 and 76).

These historians have formulated judgements and concepts which frequently disregard historical reality and end in speculation and apologia. The approaches of Susanne Heim and Götz Aly have also met with fierce opposition. Both are concerned to attribute a "rationality" to Nazi policies of annihilation and to work out the concept of an "economy of the Final Solution". Basically, their theory holds that it was not racial hatred which led to genocide but that it was prepared and implemented by a group of the "planning intelligentsia" – consisting of "economists, agricultural scientists, population experts, labour force specialists, regional planners and statisticians".[5] Such thinking has been rejected as untenable by Ulrich Herbert,[6] Christopher Browning,[7] and Dan Diner.[8]

The present contribution addresses a theme which is touched on in all these debates but not made a central feature, since attention has been focused primarily on Nazi rule in the East.

Unlike the situation in the occupied territories, the Jews in Germany were drawn back into the production process as forced labourers. By the beginning of 1939 at the latest, the destruction of their economic existence had left behind an army of impoverished and jobless Jews, which threatened to become a burden on the German *Reich*. In taking steps to remove this burden from society, the Nazis could count on the agreement of wide circles of the population and the vigorous support of the economic and military elites. The granting of priority to material interests recommended the use of forced labour as a means of re-incorporating the Jews into economic life, at least until the "Final Solution" was agreed upon and the gaps in the workforce could be filled by the forced recruitment of workers from other sources. Until then the Jews could cling to the hope that their continued existence was guaranteed by their labour. The Nazis exploited this belief by disguising the road to the extermination camps with the familiar euphemisms of "evacuation" and "resettlement".

Jewish forced labour in Germany has been very little researched until now. It is included in some descriptions of the history of the German Jews.[9] Some description and documentation can also be found in regional studies, in the history of individual firms, in personal accounts and in literature on the concentration camps. Important as trail-blazers are the works of Ulrich Herbert,[10] who argues that, with the decision of autumn 1941 to use Soviet

[5]Susanne Heim and Götz Aly, 'Sozialplanung und Völkermord', in *Konkret*, 10 (1989), p. 82. See also *idem*, 'Die Ökonomie der "Endlösung". Menschenvernichtung und wirtschaftliche Neuordnung', in *Sozialpolitik und Judenvernichtung*, Berlin 1987.

[6]Ulrich Herbert, 'Rassismus und Rationalität', in *Konkret*, 12 (1989), pp. 56–60.

[7]Christopher R. Browning, 'Vernichtung und Arbeit', in *Konkret*, 12 (1989), pp. 64–69.

[8]Dan Diner, 'Die Wahl der Perspektive', in *Konkret*, 1 (1990), pp. 68–72.

[9]Avraham Barkai, *Vom Boykott zur "Entjudung". Der wirtschaftliche Existenzkampf der Juden im Dritten Reich 1933–1943*, Frankfurt a. Main 1988, pp. 173–181; see also Konrad Kwiet, 'Nach dem Pogrom. Stufen der Ausgrenzung', in *Die Juden in Deutschland 1933–1945. Leben unter nationalsozialistischer Herrschaft*, ed. by Wolfgang Benz, Munich 1988. Parts of this contribution have been adapted for this Year Book article.

[10]Ulrich Herbert, *Fremdarbeiter. Politik und Praxis des "Ausländereinsatzes" in der Kriegswirtschaft des Dritten Reiches*, Berlin–Bonn 1985; and *idem*, 'Arbeit und Vernichtung. Ökonomisches Interesse und Primat der "Weltanschauung im Nationalsozialismus"', in *Ist der Nationalsozialismus Geschichte?, op. cit.*, pp. 198–236.

prisoners-of-war as forced labourers more intensively than before, the Nazi regime was free to push on with a programme of genocide based on racial ideology because the exploitation of the Jewish workforce was no longer essential. Military representatives of the war economy were involved in this change of direction. Their strategies for the "solution of the Jewish Question" will be revealed in this essay.

Initially, responsibility for the central military management of the war economy lay with the *Wehrwirtschaft- und Rüstungsamt* under General Thomas in the *Oberkommando der Wehrmacht*.[11] In the large military areas the *Rüstungsinspektionen* (armaments inspectorates) were created, while *Rüstungskommandos* (*RüKdos*) emerged in the government districts. After the outbreak and spread of the Second World War, this apparatus was extended to the occupied territories. Everywhere, and from the beginning, the military experts regarded the exploitation of Jewish labour as extremely important. They were present at every scene where the programme of the "Final Solution" was implemented. Some military representatives were dismayed by the murder actions; on occasion they offered criticism or made protests, sometimes in strong language. In so doing they always referred to "economic interests" or the "requirements of the war economy", and submitted statistics and calculations to show the "losses" and "disadvantages" resulting from the "withdrawals of Jews". A clash with the SS was inevitable. The conflict was particularly intense where there was a large potential force of Jewish workers which the military were unwilling to lose. It would seem that the conflicts were triggered less by the rival concepts of "work" and "extermination" than by a tactical question – how to determine the time when extermination should take place. In all the battles over interests and authority, there was constant evidence of one basic attitude: like the military as a whole, the military representatives of the war economy were not attempting to put a stop to the murder programme, but only to delay the "withdrawal" of Jewish forced labour until the vital "replacement question" was settled.

Measures to exploit the Jewish labour force in Germany were undertaken after the November Pogrom of 1938. The method chosen was the pseudo-legitimate route of official decree.[12] As in the other areas of repression and persecution, the complex and dynamic Nazi system of rule created a multiplicity of "offices" responsible for the introduction, organisation, supervision and liquidation of Jewish forced labour. These institutions represented the "power blocks" of State, Party and SS, of the *Wehrmacht* and the economy – at central, regional and local level. Among the participants in the discussions and decisions were the key

---

[11]See here Rolf-Dieter Müller, 'Die Mobilisierung der deutschen Wirtschaft für Hitlers Kriegführung', in Bernard R. Kroener, Rolf-Dieter Müller and Hans Umbreit (eds.), *Das Deutsche Reich und der Zweite Weltkrieg*, vol. V/1, Stuttgart 1988, pp. 349–689; also 'Die Mobilisierung der Wirtschaft für den Krieg – eine Aufgabe der Armee? Wehrmacht und Wirtschaft 1933–1942', in *Der Zweite Weltkrieg*, ed. by Wolfgang Michalka, Munich 1989, pp. 349–362; Georg Thomas, *Geschichte der deutschen Wehr- und Rüstungswirtschaft (1918–1943/1945)*, ed. by Wolfgang Birkenfeld, Freiburg-Boppard 1966.

[12]Joseph Walk (ed.), *Das Sonderrecht für die Juden im NS-Staat. Eine Sammlung der gesetzlichen Massnahmen und Richtlinien – Inhalt und Bedeutung*, Heidelberg 1981.

authorities and subordinate authorities of the Plenipotentiary for the Four Year Plan, the Plenipotentiary for *Reich* Administration, the Plenipotentiary for the Labour Supply, the *Reichsarbeitsministerium*, the *Reichsfinanzministerium*, the *Reichswirtschaftsministerium* or the *Reichsministerium für Bewaffnung und Munition*, the Office of the *Führer*'s Deputy and the Party Chancellery, as well as the war economic offices of the *Wehrmacht* and the representatives of industry and trade. The SS and police apparatus asserted its claim to leadership in the issue. It also press-ganged the representatives of the remaining Jewish community. Thus the *Reichsvereinigung der Juden in Deutschland* and *Kultusgemeinden* were forced to pass on orders and provide administrative assistance. As in the other "registration actions", they were compelled to collaborate with the introduction and organisation of Jewish forced labour.

The prelude was a decree of 20th December 1938, in which the President of the *Reichsanstalt für Arbeitsvermittlung and Arbeitslosenversicherung* ordered the labour exchanges to assign all unemployed Jews who were fit to work to jobs, and "with the utmost speed". This approach was linked with a desire to divert non-Jews "to priority, politically important projects". However, a further directive was dispatched to the local authorities and firms concerned. These were to have regard to racial doctrine and take care to set the Jews to work in "self-contained" units, "separated from the main body" of workers.[13] It was obvious that only carefully chosen hard and difficult work was to be done by the Jews. Building sites, road and motorway work, rubbish disposal, public toilets and sewage plants, quarries and gravel pits, coal merchants and rag and bone works were regarded as suitable. Some fanatical Nazis were less than enthusiastic, particularly when work was assigned which threatened to undermine the dogma of "strict separation" of Germans and Jews. There was much annoyance when Jews appeared on farms, in bakeries and in other foodstuff factories. However, these reproaches died away after the outbreak of the Second World War, when the issue was seen as one of forcing Jews to work for the German war effort. There were a number of reasons for this change.

Workers, especially skilled workers, were already in short supply in 1939.[14] As more men were called up to the *Wehrmacht*, the number of unfilled vacancies rose dramatically. One result was "anarchy" in the labour market, against which the Nazis waged a vain battle. From a very early stage, German military experts in the war economy recognised that, as the war dragged on, the major problem lay less in the supply of raw materials than in the "deployment of the human labour force". The alternatives were: "Either supply new forces or curb orders".[15]

---

[13]Nbg. Dok. PS–1720. Arbeitseinsatz der Juden, 20th December 1938.

[14]Bundesarchiv Militärarchiv (BA/MA) RW 20–3/9.Geschichte der Rüstungsinspektion (RüIn) III, Heft 1, 1st September 1939–30th September 1940, p. 29; see also BA/MA RW 20–3/12. Lagebericht RüIn III, Heft 1, 21st September 1939–11th January 1940; see also the vital contribution by Bernhard R. Kroener, 'Die personellen Ressourcen des Dritten Reiches im Spannungsfeld zwischen Wehrmacht, Bürokratie und Kriegswirtschaft', in *Das Deutsche Reich und der Zweite Weltkrieg*, vol. V/1, *op. cit.*, pp. 693–989.

[15]BA/MA RW 20–3/10 Geschichte der RüIn III, Heft 2, 1st October 1940–31st December 1941, p. 15.

Following Hitler's order for intensified efforts in armament production, they worked with the other authorities responsible for the workforce in an attempt to keep the shortage of workers within bounds. Priorities were established, based on the needs of the armament programmes. In concrete terms, this meant that firms concerned with civilian or less urgent military manufacturing were constantly examined and "combed through" so that the workers "set free" could be distributed to firms on the priority list. This redistribution of existing workers was called the "inter-firm adjustment". In addition, there were rationalisations, closures of firms, retraining schemes, introduction of the 60-hour week, increased temporary exemptions from front-line service, and the deployment of *Wirtschaftsurlauber* (soldiers seconded to "urgent" work in the factories during periods of leave). These efforts met with little success. In October 1940 the military experts in Berlin claimed that 29,400 workers were needed in the metal industry alone, with the shortage of skilled workers estimated at 15,700.[16] It became even more important to recruit new workers. The reservoir of women workers and *"Fremdarbeiter"* (foreign workers), of prisoners-of-war and Jews, was tapped to exhaustion. Public and private businesses now rushed to demand Jewish workers. Thus in October 1940 the *Oberkommando des Heeres* asked the *Reichsarbeitsministerium* for 1,800 Jews for work in the railway administration at Oppeln, Breslau and Lublin. The Lower Saxony labour exchange offered between 1,000 and 2,000 Jews to the *Hermann-Göring-Werke* in Watenstedt-Salzgitter. At the beginning of 1941 the *Siemens-Halske-Werke* in Berlin demanded 400 workers for an "urgent manufacturing programme in communications" on behalf of General Fellgiebel; here Jewish women were put to work as forced labourers.[17]

At this stage, a total of some 30,000 Jews had already been conscripted as forced labourers, approximately 20% of the remaining Jewish community of Germany. It was not long before the decision was taken to conscript all Jews between the ages of 15 and 65 years who were fit to work. On 4th March 1941 the *Reichsarbeitministerium* ordered the introduction of general forced labour.[18] The *Rüstungsinspektion* calculated an increase of 73,000 Jews, 42,000 of whom were men and 31,000 women. For *Wehrkreis* Kassel some 5,000 workers were planned. *Rüstungsinspektion IX* noted: "It remains to be seen what the effect of the action will be in regard to the overall labour market in the area, since the accommodation and deployment of the Jews still cause especially great difficulties."[19]

Meanwhile, it had become known that Jewish workers were not only to be kept "separate from the main body of workers", but were "if possible" to be housed in self-contained camps. Only a few authorities followed this suggestion; there were barrack camps in Essen and Salzgitter, Dresden and Munich. Though the intention in early 1939 was to quarter all German Jews – in case of war – in special camps, classified as "Arbeitsdienstlager", this was not done, partly

---

[16]BA/MA RW 20–3/15. Lageberichte der RüIn III, Heft 4, Lagebericht von 15th October 1940, p. 1.
[17]BA/MA RW 20–3/15. Lageberichte der RüIn III, Heft 4. Lagebericht von 15th January 1941, p. 6.
[18]Walk, *op. cit.*, p. 174.
[19]BA/MA RW 20–9/25. RüIn IX, Lagebericht, 15th January 1941–15th May 1941, p. 19. On the deliberations before the outbreak of the war as to how to utilise Jewish labour see Appendix.

because the limited building capacity was required for other mass accommodation. In many areas, barracks were hastily erected to accept the ever-
increasing number of foreign workers and prisoners-of-war, all of whom required
"self-contained" accommodation. In Berlin, where Jewish forced labourers were
concentrated, firms limited themselves to setting up *"Judenabteilungen"*, *"Juden-
gruppen"*, or *"Judenschichten"* (Jewish detachments, groups or shifts). In October
1941 the *Rüstungsinspektion* registered 21,000 Jews employed in firms involved
with the war economy, including approximately 11,000 in the metal industry.
About half of them were women.[20] The *Reichsvereinigung* also gave a figure of
21,000 at the end of 1941, when some 33,450 *Sternträger* (wearers of the Yellow
Star) were left behind after the first wave of deportations. Approximately 2,000
still had a job in the Jewish administrative apparatus. The rest were divided
among groups who were protected from forced labour: children, the seriously ill,
the seriously disabled, and Jewish partners in so-called "privileged mixed
marriages".[21] At the beginning of 1943 – when Jewish forced labour in Germany
was approaching its end – the SS statistician Dr Richard Korherr gave his
notorious "interim balance" in his report on 'The Final Solution of the European
Jewish Question'. Here he noted that there were still 21,659 Jews engaged in
"work of importance for the war effort" in the German *Reich*.[22]

Jewish forced labour required the clarification of legal issues relating to work
and pay. There were long discussions between the various departments and
offices in order to develop the new *"Sonderrecht"*. This was finished when the
planned deportations got under way. The *Verordnung über die Beschäftigung der
Juden* (decree on the employment of Jews) came into force at the beginning of
October 1941.[23]

Defined as *"Artfremde"* (ethnic aliens), Jewish workers were refused acceptance
into the "works community" and therefore denied all the rights to which other
members could lay claim. Jewish forced labourers received no family and child
allowances, no maternity and marriage allowances, no extra payments on
Sundays and holidays, no money at Christmas, no death benefits, no bonuses or
loyalty payments. They received no paid holidays and no wages in the event of
sickness. They were denied protection against unlawful dismissal, were not
covered by safety regulations, and were not entitled to unemployment benefit or
old age pension schemes. The underlying principle was that "Jewish employees
have a claim to remuneration only for work actually done". Firms were provided
with a charter giving them the right to virtually unlimited exploitation of their
Jewish workers. For a maximum of work they had to pay a minimum in wages.[24]
In the forced labour ghettos and concentration camps, it became standard
practice to transfer this pay to the special accounts of the exploiters.

As a rule Jewish forced labourers were placed on the lowest wage scale.
Thanks to the *Finanzamt*, taxes were deducted from their earnings at the highest

---

[20]BA/MA RW 20–3/15. Lageberichte, RüIn III, Heft 4, 15th July 1940–15th August 1941, p. 6.
[21]Barkai, *Vom Boykott zur "Entjudung"*, *op. cit.*, p. 176.
[22]BA Koblenz, NS 19 neu/1570.
[23]*Reichsgesetzblatt*, 1941 I, p. 675.
[24]Raul Hilberg, *Die Vernichtung der europäischen Juden*, Berlin 1982, p. 110.

rate. The *Finanzamt* also supervised the "blocked accounts" containing the remaining proceeds from the forced sale of Jewish businesses, property and other possessions, and from which only a monthly "free allowance" of up to RM 250 could be taken. At the end of 1940 a special tax was imposed on the Jews; this removed 15% from their wages and declared it to be a "social compensation payment". Other "aliens" – Polish forced labourers and gipsies – also had to pay this tribute. The average hourly pay of a German workers in 1939 was just RM 0.90. Jewish forced labourers, on average, received less than half that. One young cemetery worker and gravedigger in Fürstenwald earned RM 0.16.[25] A 15½ year old unskilled worker in a Berlin factory making uniforms received hourly pay of RM 0.30 for her day and night shifts; when she reached the age of 16 the pay rose to RM 0.34.[26] The *Siemens-Schuckert-Werke* paid its women assemblers RM 0.50 per hour.[27] One forced labourer who had been trained as a lathe operator in the *Deutsche Waffen- und Munitionsfabrik* in Berlin-Borsigwalde received RM 0.90.[28] As time passed, firms and authorities grew anxious to save wages. Municipal administrations thus preferred to employ Jewish "work columns" to sweep the streets and, in winter, to shovel the snow. The *Reichsvereinigung* was then obliged to pay welfare support. One Munich building firm took on 450 Jewish workers in spring 1941 to establish a self-contained "Jewish settlement" in the Milbersthofen area – without pay, but with the task of doing their work "in the interests of the Israelite religious community and its members".[29] Anyone evading "voluntary" deployment was threatened with transfer to the nearby Dachau concentration camp.

For many forced labourers, the pay was not sufficient to cover their cost of living. Rents had to be paid, for small, often squalid rooms where they had been forcibly quartered shortly before. As part of the *"Entjudung"* of the German residential areas, local authorities, estate agents and house-owners had pushed through the physical separation of Germans and Jews and thereby taken an essential step on the road to the envisaged "Final Solution of the Jewish Question". The seizure of desirable Jewish homes also offered a way of easing the strain on the housing market. After the outbreak and extension of the war, the general housing shortage reached catastrophic proportions. And the greater the need, the louder became the appeals from wide circles of the population for the "gathering together" and – if that did not suffice – the expulsion of the Jews. Such sentiments found their expression in the establishment of "Jewish houses" and barracks, and in the organisation of "evacuation" to the East. During this short waiting period of uncertainty and fear, of isolation and loneliness, Jewish forced labourers continued to seek extra sources of income. On top of their forced labour, some found illegal work in small firms in the major cities, especially Berlin, where concern with regulations and paper-work was rather less exact. Profound weariness and exhaustion were the consequences.

[25]Hans Rosenthal, *Zwei Leben in Deutschland*, Bergisch-Gladbach 1980, p. 45.
[26]Wiener Library (WL) P IIIe, No. 1185.
[27]Jochen Klepper, *Unter dem Schatten deiner Flügel*, Stuttgart 1956, pp. 922 and 1136.
[28]WL P IIId, No. 1141.
[29]Peter Hanke, *Zur Geschichte der Juden in München zwischen 1933 und 1945*, Munich 1967, p. 339.

Hunger became an important factor in the suffering of Jewish forced labourers. Step by step, the authorities reduced their nourishment by continually cutting down their share of rationed foods. Jews had to go without meat and fish, eggs and fruit, chocolate and cakes, coffee and tea, wine and alcohol. The *Ernährungsämter* withdrew the special supplements for pregnant women and breast-feeding mothers, children and old people, the sick and disabled. What remained was a vestige of basic foodstuffs, relief packages which were still arriving from abroad and were deducted from the rations, the foodstuffs obtained by mutual aid or on the "black market". The *Ernährungsämter* also thought it appropriate to cancel the special rations for forced labourers. The following is taken from a report from the Berlin *Rüstungsinspektion III* in August 1941 on the "nutrition of Jewish workers":[30]

> "The *Haupternährungsamt* Berlin reports that Jewish workers may no longer receive extra cards for long, heavy and very heavy labour. Non-Aryans also may not receive the same food as the Aryan workers in a munitions firm. For the care of the Aryan workforce, the *Haupternährungs-amt* of the city of Berlin supplies the works canteens of the munitions factories with supplementary foodstuffs such as rice, noodles, bacon, margarine etc. in order to make the meals tastier and more nourishing. But there is no objection if hot meals are prepared for the Jewish workers in a special kitchen solely on the basis of their food ration cards. Special cooking facilities can also be made available to non-Aryans for their own preparation. However, it is not permissible for Jews to eat in the same canteens or mess halls as the Aryans."

To hunger was added the strain of travelling to and from work. It often took forced labourers hours to reach their place of work or their homes. After the November Pogrom of 1938, motor vehicles and drivers' licences had been confiscated; bicycles were requisitioned in 1942. Jewish forced labourers could only use buses or trams, underground trains or municipal railways if they had a special pass. This privilege was granted if the distance from home to work was more than 7 km. or over an hour's walk. *Sternträger* were allowed to sit on public transport only when all the Germans had found a seat. Enforced detours were frequent, since a *Judenbann* meant that Jews could not travel through designated roads, squares or parks.

Once at work, the Jewish forced labourers had to obey the company's "Jewish regulations". Instructions on "security" issued by the Berlin electricity works in 1941 contained the following "disciplinary regulations for the surveillance of Jews":[31]

> "1. Jews must be collected by the gate-keeper before starting their work, be brought by security to their changing-room and handed over to the foreman of their work crew.
> 2. The Jews may only move about the works property under supervision. They may never stay within the works alone. Work will be undertaken by them in self-contained crews which must be under the leadership of an Aryan member of the company.
> 3. After the end of work, the Jews are to be taken by security in the same way, as a self-contained group to the exit to works property."

[30]BA/MA RW 20–3/15. Lagebericht der RüIn III, Heft 4, 15th July 1940–15th August 1941, p. 8.
[31]Quoted from Konrad Kwiet and Helmut Eschwege, *Selbstbehauptung und Widerstand. Deutsche Juden im Kampf um Existenz und Menschenwürde 1933–1945*, 2nd edn., Hamburg 1986, p. 255.

Jewish forced labourers (1) and (3) from left taking a break with German workers

From Günter B. Ginzel, 'Jüdischer Alltag in Deutschland', Düsseldorf 1984, and by courtesy of Abraham Pisarek-Archiv, Berlin

Jewish martyrs of the Anti-Nazi resistance
(who had worked as forced labour in Berlin factories)
executed or murdered in 1942/3
Above: Siegbert Rotholz
Below: Herbert Baum, Hella Hirsch, Ismar Zöllner

It was not easy for German Jews to get used to their new places of work under such conditions. Their social origins and professional training had prepared them for a world very different from the one into which they were now thrust. Vivid evidence of this is provided by the personal accounts of Jewish forced labourers.[32]

One furrier – expelled from his business – was forced to report to the Jewish labour exchange in Berlin at the end of 1939.

"Together with a senior teacher, a factory owner and a painter, I was sent to the Lehrter station . . . to clean the toilets of the incoming trains. We were set to work with only a cloth and scouring sand. I asked humbly for a scrubbing brush. At that Herr B. became furious and yelled: 'You Jews are quite used to wallowing in filth so get to the sh . . ! Anyone here who rebels will make a real discovery. Do you know where I can send you?' "[33]

In 1940, a lawyer, whose practice in Gleiwitz had been confiscated, was sent to a sewage farm "where 30 Jews in all had to work . . . Work lasted from 7.00 until 17.00 with a short break at lunchtime, under civilian supervision and *Gestapo* control. Over the years I lost 30 pounds doing this work. I had to cultivate the humus and shovel it onto wagons, up to 150 cwt. on many days."[34] Better prepared for arduous labour was the owner of a lamp factory who had been very active in sport, including judo, in his spare time. He was dispatched to a Berlin building firm: "We had to do heavy roadwork, such as breaking up stones, carting stones and sand, and fetching the stones for the pavers. The work did not break me so much, but there were some workers among us who literally collapsed under it. When the first bombs fell, we had to tear down the badly damaged houses, which caused us many accidents."[35]

As a rule the forced labourers had to work a ten-hour day. One graduate of the by then closed Berlin *Lehranstalt für die Wissenschaft des Judentums* was employed examining and cleaning greasy shells in the *Deustsche Waffen- und Munitionsfabrik* in Berlin-Borsigwalde.[36] A woman from an upper-middle-class family which had converted to Christianity was forced to peel 6 cwt. of potatoes every day in a tiny, windowless room in the *Zeiss-Ikon-Görtz* factory in Berlin-Zehlendorf.[37] Approximately 200 workers formed the *Judenabteilung* which did piece-work manufacturing fuses and timers for U-boats in the *Dresden Göhle Werke* of *Zeiss-Ikon*. One woman forced labourer, classed as a *Mischling*, recalled: "This work required great concentration, manual dexterity and good eyesight. My eyes suffered very much from the effects of this precision work, as we worked continuously each day in artificial light using magnifying glasses and tweezers."[38] The *IG-Farben Konzern* was especially known and feared for the harsh treatment it meted out.

[32]Kwiet, 'Nach dem Pogrom', *loc. cit.*, pp. 581–589; see also Monika Richarz (ed.), *Jüdisches Leben in Deutschland*, Bd. 3. *Selbstzeugnisse zur Sozialgeschichte*, Stuttgart 1982, Veröffentlichung des Leo Baeck Instituts.

[33]WL P IIIb, No. 616.

[34]WL P IIa, No. 90.

[35]WL P IIId, No. 1097.

[36]WL P IIId, No. 1141.

[37]Robert A. Kann, *Erinnerungen von Valerie Wolffenstein aus den Jahren 1891–1945*, Vienna 1981, p. 37.

[38]Michael Brenner, *Am Beispiel Weiden. Jüdischer Alltag im Nationalsozialismus*, Würzburg 1983, p. 99.

One Jewish woman was sent to a Berlin factory specialising in silk for parachutes:[39]

"For ten hours we had to ensure that the thread on the rotating spindles did not get tangled or snap, and that the spindles did not run empty. The room was hot, the work hard and tiring. The noise made any conversation with one's colleagues impossible. During the break in the breakfast room there was only one theme: how can we get out of here? Women who had been there some time told of the harassment to which they had been subjected. Some succeeded in obtaining their release. Gynaecological illness was one reason which was accepted, we heard; this made it impossible to stand at the machine for hours on end."

Women suffered more than men from these demands and privations. In addition to the factory shifts, they also had to face their housework and the need for long and exhausting trips for food. Many women had to look after a family, and many were still caring for parents and grandparents. Mothers sent their children to kindergartens run by the Jewish community during their working hours. On occasion, they came back after work to find only empty rooms; during their absence a *Kindertransport* had been sent to the East.

Among many young Jewish people, a feeling of hopelessness set in. Banned from schools and other centres of education, they had been degraded to the level of unskilled workers without any prospect of working their way up as apprentices or journeymen. However, some young people attempted to break out of the cycle of demoralisation and isolation. In the *Hachscharah* – agricultural estates described by the Nazis as "living communities for Jewish forced labourers" in 1941 and liquidated in 1943 – Jewish and Zionist ideals survived and found expression in the will to emigrate and the longing for a new life in *Eretz Israel*.[40] Groups were also formed in munitions factories. In many cases, social barriers first had to be overcome before new friendships could be made. This problem was most severe for young people who had grown up in an upper-middle-class environment. In the factories and firms, many of them made their first-ever contacts with their companions in suffering from working-class Jewish families. There were some who found the strength and courage to embark on political resistance. For instance, the two *Judenabteilungen* in the electric motor works of Siemens contained many of the young forced labourers who formed the Herbert Baum group, an organisation with a proud place in the history of Jewish resistance and German anti-fascism.[41]

The personal accounts also reflect the experiences of the forced labourers with their supervisors. It is possible to suggest a typology of attitude and treatment which covers the various forms and levels encountered. Firstly, there were the

[39] Inge Deutschkron, '*Ich trug den gelben Stern*', Cologne 1978, p. 75.

[40] Joel König (Esra Ben-Gershom), *David. Aufzeichnungen eines Überlebenden*, Frankfurt a. Main 1979; Anneliese Ora Borinski, *Erinnerungen 1940–1943*, Ms. in Institut für Zeitgeschichte (IfZ) ZS 43/2; see also Werner T. Angress, 'Auswandererlehrgut Gross-Breesen', in *LBI Year Book X* (1965), pp. 168–187; and *idem, Generation zwischen Furcht und Hoffnung, Jüdische Jugend im Dritten Reich*, Hamburg 1985.

[41] See Kwiet/Eschwege, *op. cit.*, pp. 114–139; Eric Brothers, 'On the Anti-Fascist Resistance of German Jews', in *LBI Year Book XXXII* (1987), pp. 369–382. On the current state of research see Arnold Paucker, *Jüdischer Widerstand in Deutschland. Tatsachen und Problematik*. Beiträge zum Widerstand 1933–1945, Gedenkstätte Deutscher Widerstand, Heft 37, Berlin 1989. (A revised and enlarged English version, published by the *Gedenkstätte*, is now in print.)

supervisors who made no bones about their anti-Jewish feelings and who took every opportunity to torment and degrade their slave labourers and even to hand them over to the *Gestapo*. The forced labourers knew that even the slightest infringement of the "Jewish regulations" could be interpreted as sabotage and result in draconian punishment. Employees were instructed to notify their superiors of any incidents that occurred. Some were more than happy to do so. They observed every move the forced labourers made, eavesdropped on conversations, and inspected bread brought in during short breaks to see whether forbidden foods were being eaten. Alongside complaints and denunciation came verbal attacks, ranging from minor incidents to wholesale and furious attacks. Everywhere the Jewish workers faced loud commands, dressings down, bullying demands for work. These modes of speech were even adopted by people who were not fully committed either to Nazism or to antisemitism.

However, Jewish forced labourers sometimes came into contact with fellow-workers who tried to alleviate their hard conditions or to make up the deficiencies in their rations. These people had the courage to greet and encourage *Sternträger*, to help them get easier work, or to show them other, smaller kindnesses. Secretly, they might hand over sandwiches, fruit, slices of meat, tobacco, sweets or tablets. Such gestures of sympathy, compassion and help occurred frequently, and those who made them were dubbed "decent Germans" by the survivors. From their ranks was drawn the small band of Germans who went one vital step further – and began to try and save Jews. The survivors have also left accounts of such conduct; they show that forced labour offered an opportunity for the re-establishment of social contacts. After their social exclusion and banishment to a "ghetto without walls", Jewish forced labourers became acquainted with Germans who were ready to resist and, knowing that they were risking their own lives, to keep Jews out of the clutches of the *Gestapo*. Visits by the *Gestapo* were notified in advance and Jews forced to "go underground". Some Germans offered hiding places and helped to safeguard the lives of the illegal existence of the Jews underground.

From a distance, Jewish forced labourers also became aware of the existence of foreign slave labourers and prisoners of war. Some pitied these "utterly ragged figures"[42] and noted how they "searched through the canteen waste buckets after the meal break".[43] On occasion individual Jews would break out of the separate *Judenabteilung* to make contact with the "foreign workers' camp". On these journeys the Jews would take the remains of their own starvation rations for distribution among the Poles or Russians. But contact with these foreign workers also made the Jews more aware of the threat to themselves. As the army of foreign workers grew larger, some Jewish forced labourers became afraid that they would be replaced by Poles and Russians at work.

Hitler and Himmler were always determined that the use of Jewish workers – in Germany as in the occupied territories – was only a transitional solution. From autumn 1941 at the latest they made it clear that the "exemptions" from deportation or liquidation in the East were "temporary" and could be "retracted

[42]WL P IIId, No. 1141.
[43]WL P IIId, No. 26.

at any time". The civilian and military authorities took note of the directives and adapted to the losses involved. When the first *"Rüstungsjuden"* ("armament" Jews) were "withdrawn" in October 1941, the military representatives of the war economy complained that they had not been given an opportunity to state their views. In every report there were references to the losses in production and demands for "immediate replacements". The *Kriegstagebuch* of *Rüstungsbereich* Frankfurt a. Main contains the following entry for 20th October 1941:[44]

> "Several armaments firms, including *Voltohm Seil- und Kabelwerke AG* . . . *Radio Braun* report that in a sudden transportation of *Jews* from Frankfurt/M to the *Generalgouvernement* on Sunday 19th October 1941, without the prior agreement of the *RüKdos*, a number of their Jewish workers had been withdrawn, the consequence of which was to damage the *Wehrmacht* manufacture involved since replacement workers could not be supplied immediately."

In Berlin the first "withdrawal" endangered the "manufacture of insulation for billets in the East".[45] At once, contact was established with the labour exchanges and the *Gestapo* in an effort to come to an arrangement. The interests of the *Rüstungsinspektion* involved "preventing the withdrawal of Jewish workers . . . from armaments and special firms as far as is absolutely possible". There was sympathy for this appeal within the Berlin labour exchange. Its "Jewish expert", Eschhaus, let it be known that Jewish workers would not be withdrawn for the present. Even the deportation office of the *Gestapo* was ready to co-operate. On 28th October 1941, the *Kriegstagebuch* of *Rüstungskommando III* noted:[46]

> "It was decided in discussion that state police headquarters does not want to ignore the needs of the armament economy in any way and will examine doubtful cases in an accommodating manner. Basically the *RüKd* must get in touch with the technical specialist *Kommissar* Stübs, and *Regierungsrat* Dr. Kunz is personally available for important questions. The *Kommando* is instructed . . . to send the lists of its Jewish workers with an appropriate covering letter, in which the indispensable workers are indicated with a red cross . . . Basically it is to be noted that evacuations which have already taken place cannot be called off."

What was to be co-ordinated at local level had already been laid down within the central leadership. On 25th October 1941 the *Wirtschaft-Rüstungsamt* in the *Oberkommando der Wehrmacht* dispatched a memorandum to the *Rüstunginspektionen* containing the RSHA "guidelines" for the implementation of deportations. Account was taken of the needs of the war economy. Jewish forced labourers were among those whose deportation was "temporarily" postponed. Exemption would be granted only if proof was provided that "resettlement" would endanger the "carrying out of urgent armament orders on schedule".[47] *Rüstungskommandos* and firms set to work to compile the lists of names and to send them to the *Gestapo*

---

[44]BA/MA RW 21–19/9 RüKdo Frankfurt/M *Kriegstagebuch* (KTB) No. 8, p. 10.

[45]BA/MA RW 21–4/8 RüKdo Berlin III KTB 8, 23rd October 1941, p. 12.

[46]*Ibid.*, 28th October 1941, p. 14.

[47]Heydrich's guidelines on deportation of October 1941 have – to the best of the author's knowledge – not yet been located. References to them can be found in the "circulars" issued by regional state police headquarters and in a KTB entry of the Frankfurt *Rüstungskommando* on 22nd November 1941: BA/MA RW – 19/9. KTB No. 8, p. 13. Similarly, in the later, surviving deportation guidelines issued by the RSHA, "temporary exemption . . . of Jewish workers in work of importance to the war effort" is permitted. See H. G. Adler, *Der verwaltete Mensch. Studien zur Deportation der Juden aus Deutschland*, Tübingen 1974, p. 188.

and labour exchanges. In Frankfurt a. Main a list of 360 names was compiled with a request to delay transportation until "replacement workers" were available.[48] Such lists and reasons were provided everywhere. But the *Gestapo* promise to examine these requests "benevolently" was not always fulfilled. "Withdrawals" of Jewish forced labourers were recorded constantly. At the end of November 1941 the Berlin labour exchange would no longer accept responsibility for preventing the deportation of Jews working in the metal industry. "A non-withdrawal of Jewish armaments workers", explained the director of the labour exchange, "would only be possible if the *Gestapo Sippenlisten* (genealogical lists) were at its disposal at the correct time and if the *Gestapo* was to guarantee that only non-Aryans examined by itself [i.e. the labour exchange] are sent to the transport."[49] The labour exchange faced considerable difficulties, not only in supplying "replacements" in view of the acute labour shortage, but also in selecting the Jewish forced labourers to be deported. The *"Sippenlisten"* were long in coming. The head of the labour exchange felt it essential "as before . . . to let employees from his office participate in the measures in the synagogues, in order to obtain reliable documents on the non-Aryans affected by the evacuation".[50] However, the *Rüstungskommandos* confided that the agreements made would be kept and that the "indispensable armaments Jews" would be the last Jewish group to be deported. There was full information on the scale and timetable of the deportations. On 15th November 1941, *Rüstungsinspektion III* wrote a report:[51]

> "The transporting of about 75,000 Jews away from Berlin, of whom around 20,000 are employed in important jobs – about 10,000 in the metal sector alone – also affects the question of the supply of replacement workers. A replacement in the shape of German workers through the labour exchanges is out of the question. By 4th December 1941 a further 15,000 Jews, and then from February 1942 the remainder, are to be evacuated. The Jews working in the armaments industry are, if possible, to be removed from the firms at the end of the evacuation measures."

Another report summarised experiences in the period from October 1940 to December 1941:[52]

> "The Jews who had previously worked individually in firms were collected into self-contained groups, sections in a firm, or Jewish shifts. Here they worked separate from the Aryan workforce. They were supervised only by Aryan masters or foremen. At various levels the results were very good, e.g. in the chemical and textile economy and especially in the electrical industry, where Jewish women proved to be highly skilled winders etc. . . . . In October 1941 there suddenly began – without the *Rüstungsinspektion* having a chance of stating its own position beforehand – a resettlement of Jews to the East. Jews engaged in urgent production were not to be evacuated for the time being. On the other hand, as the deportation was, for various reasons, to be carried out on the basis of kin, important workers were nevertheless caught up in the process in increasing numbers and lost to the armaments firms. Because of a lack of replacement skilled workers and a shortage of transport capacity, the planned further resettlement of Jews was halted at the beginning of 1942."

[48]BA/MA RW 21–19/9 RüKdo Frankfurt/M KTB No. 8, 2nd November 1941, p. 13.
[49]BA/MA RW 21–4/8 RüKdo Berlin III, KTB No. 8, 29th November 1941, p. 32.
[50]*Ibid.*, p. 33.
[51]BA/MA RW 20–3/16, RüIn III, Heft 5, 15th September 1941–15th February 1942, p. 9.
[52]BA/MA RW 20–3/10, RüIn III, Heft 2, 1st October 1940 – 31st December 1941, p. 15.

When the *Reichsbahn* trains were available once more and the extermination camps and gas wagons were ready for operation, the wave of deportations began anew.

Once again the military representatives of the war economy were confronted with the "Jewish Question" and the old debates revived. These arguments now took place against the background of a distinct power shift. To an increasing extent, the *Wirtschaft-Rüstungsamt* under General Thomas had lost influence: it was clear that Albert Speer as *Reichsminister für Bewaffnung und Munition* was building an empire and assuming control over the *Rüstungskommandos*. In fact, one vital decision had already been taken in occupied Poland. This illuminates the strategy which was developed by the leading military and war economy authorities for the solution of the "replacement problem". In September 1942 the *Oberkommando der Wehrmacht* was quite prepared to relinquish control of armament firms in the *Generalgouvernement* to the *Reichsministerium für Bewaffnung und Munition*. Field Marshal Keitel freely admitted that Speer was now solely responsible for debating "with the SS about of the removal of Jewish workers".[53] He expressly forbade all military offices to continue "placing themselves protectively . . . in front of the Jews".[54] Indeed such protection no longer appeared necessary – Keitel announced the deployment of Polish workers.

When the "replacement" issue was due to be settled in the *Generalgouvernement Wehrkreiskommandant* General Freiherr von Gienanth made his own position clear. On 18th September 1942 he sent a memorandum to the *Oberkommando der Wehrmacht*. It included the following comments:[55]

> "If work of vital importance for the war effort is not to suffer, the Jews can only be released after the training of the replacements step by step. This task can only be undertaken locally, but must be centrally directed by *one* office [emphasis in original] in cooperation with the Higher SS and Police Leader.
> It is requested that the decree be implemented in this form. The guideline should be to exclude the Jews as quickly as possible without damaging work of vital significance for the war effort."

In the *Oberkommando der Wehrmacht* this request fell on deaf ears, and General von Gienanth was put on the retired list. On 10th October 1942 his successor was informed "that the Jews employed by the *Wehrmacht* in auxiliary military services and in the armaments industry are to be replaced immediately by Aryan workers".[56] The instruction gained the approval of *Reichsführer SS* Himmler, who had advanced his claims to leadership after reading the Gienanth memoran-

---

[53]On the arguments with the SS see Albert Speer, *Der Sklavenstaat*, Stuttgart 1981 (an account with a pervasive tone of apologia); for criticism see Matthias Schmidt, *Albert Speer. The End of a Myth*, London 1985. Typical of Speer was his attempt to exert his influence to delay the withdrawals of Jews. An entry of the KTB, Chef WI Amt of 22nd September 1942 contains the following: "Speer wants to speak to the *Führer* because of the withdrawals of Jews from the industrial economy. His proposal concerns creating self-contained *Juden-Betriebe* (firms made up of Jews) until further notice." BA/MA RW 19/186.

[54]BA/MA RW 19/186. KTB Chef Wi Amt, 12th September 1942.

[55]Quoted from Helge Grabitz and Wolfgang Scheffler, *Letzte Spuren*, Berlin 1988, pp. 310–312.

[56]Grabitz/Scheffler, *op. cit.*, p. 312.

dum[57] and, on 9th October 1942, had submitted a stage-by-stage plan proposing the liquidation of Jewish forced labourers.[58] The penultimate step involved "amalgamating" them in a number of "*KL-Großbetrieben*", large concentration-camp firms in the East of the *Generalgouvernement*.[59] The ultimate aim was stated in the final sentence: "However, here too, corresponding to the wish of the *Führer*, the Jews are to disappear one day." The military were also made aware of the programme of the "Final Solution". The *Oberkommando der Wehrmacht* passed on the Himmler order and simply added that "after this it [is] the task of the military offices responsible for the firms to fix the implementation of the above guidelines with the appropriate SS and Police Chief".[60]

In the *Altreich* too, the decision to remove all Jews from the armaments factories had been taken. On 22nd September 1942 Adolf Hitler gave the order to Sauckel, who was responsible for labour supply.[61] Goebbels noted triumphantly in his diary:[62]

> "The *Führer* once again expresses his firm determination to get the Jews out of Berlin at all costs. Even the comments of our economic experts and industrialists, to the effect that they cannot do without so-called Jewish precision work, do not impress him. Suddenly the Jews are being praised absolutely everywhere as workers of the highest quality. This argument is repeatedly used against us in order to plead leniency for them. But they are not as indispensable as our intellectuals make them out to be. It will not be too difficult, in view of the fact that in Berlin alone we have 240,000 foreign workers, to replace the remaining 40,000 Jews – of whom only 17,000 are active in the production process – with foreign workers as well. As things stand the Jewish precision worker is becoming a constant argument of intellectual philosemitic propaganda. Here we see again that we Germans are only too easily inclined to be too just, and to judge questions of political necessity with emotion but not with cool intellect."

Some weeks passed before the "*Entjudung*" of the armaments factories was achieved. On 20th October 1942 the deportation experts of the Berlin *Gestapo* again offered the assurance that the "*Rüstungsjuden*" would be the last group to be deported;[63] on 13th November 1942 they announced that "within the next six months the Jews would be completely removed [and replaced] by Poles".[64] Firms were exhorted to offer the "utmost collaboration" and reminded of their duty to provide accommodation for the "replacement workers". Within the firms there was widespread regret at the withdrawal of the Jews. In October 1942 the Berlin *Rüstungskommando* reported:[65]

> "The Jews have been described by all the works managers as excellent workers, on the same level as skilled workers. The evacuation of the Jews is settled. The replacement is to be provided by Poles, whose training requires many weeks. The works managers fear that they

[57]NA Washington T 175 roll 22–2527369.
[58]Grabitz/Scheffler, *op. cit.*, p. 179.
[59]On the establishment of "forced labour camps for Jews (*Zwangsarbeitslager*=ZAL{J}) in the *Reichskommissariat* 'Ostland' " see Alfred Streim, 'Konzentrationslager auf dem Gebiet der Sowjet-union', in *Dachauer Hefte*, 5 (1989), pp. 174–187.
[60]Grabitz/Scheffler, *op. cit.*, p. 179.
[61]Speer, *op. cit.*, pp. 349–350.
[62]IfZ ED 83/2. Joseph Goebbels, *Tagebuch*, 30th September 1942.
[63]BA/MA RW 21–4/12, RüKdo Berlin II, KTB No. 12, 1st October 1942–31st December 1942, p. 19.
[64]*Ibid.*, p. 17.
[65]BA/MA RW 21–3/2 RüKdo Berlin II, KTB, 1st October 1942–31st December 1942, p. 19.

will have to set on two Poles for each Jew in order to achieve the same results. The order that the armaments firms are to be spared until last in the evacuation of the Jews has not always been put into practice. As the Jews are evacuated by family, there have been repeated instances where Jews employed in armaments firms have also been removed prematurely. This has caused a certain unrest in the *Judenabteilungen*. The works managers generally regret that the original proposal to retain the Jews as workers, and to this end to quarter them and to transfer them to camps exactly like foreign workers, has not been implemented."

Some individual works managers tried to obtain further exemptions from the labour exchange or the *Gestapo*. An end was put to such intervention in January 1943. Special circulars were sent by the *Rüstungskommandos*[66] to inform the firms that all applications or visits would be "futile". Petitions could be submitted to the *Rüstungskommandos* only if they included detailed figures on the expected fall in production. These instructions also stipulated that the labour exchange must be informed of the disappearance of Jewish workers and applications for replacements directed to them. Finally, the firms also had a duty to inform the *Gestapo* immediately of every "Jew being released from manufacturing or becoming dispensable in any way whatsoever".

At the end of February 1943 the *Gestapo* was finally in a position to strike the decisive blow against the "*Rüstungsjuden*". On 27th February the so-called "factory actions" began. Approximately 7,000 Jews were seized in arrests and raids on firms, on the streets, and on homes. The manhunt lasted for several days. In Berlin, it triggered a unique protest demonstration after Jews who were living in "privileged mixed marriages" were among those seized during the mass arrests. "Aryan" wives arrived at the assembly point in the Rosenstrasse and began to chorus demands for the release of their husbands, supported by passers-by who took the side of the demonstrators. Shocked by this wholly spontaneous and large-scale resistance, the *Gestapo* gave way and began to release the Jewish husbands step by step. The successful result of the public protests inevitably led to speculation that similar actions might have changed the course of Nazi policy towards the Jews. *Reichsminister* Goebbels was highly dissatisfied with the course of the "factory action". His diary contains the following entry for 2nd March 1943:[67]

"We are now removing the Jews from Berlin at last. They were gathered together suddenly last Saturday and will now be shifted to the East in the shortest time possible. Unfortunately it emerges yet again that the better circles, especially the intellectuals, do not understand our Jewish policy and are placing themselves in part on the side of the Jews. As a consequence [news of] our action has been betrayed prematurely so that a whole crowd of Jews has slipped through our hands."

In the war diaries and reports of the *Rüstungskommandos* there were no more expressions of criticism or regret. The only factors thought worthy of mention related to the "disruption" caused and the "replacements" in the firms. In view of the army of millions of slave labourers and prisoners of war which had now been

---

[66]BA/MA RW 21–4/13 RüKdo Berlin III, KTB No. 13, Sonderrundschreiben No. 2 of 20th January 1943.
[67]IfZ München Fa 246/2. Goebbels, *Tagebuch*, 2nd March 1943.

brought to Germany, the fate of Jewish forced labourers was no longer considered important.

In Berlin the *Rüstungskommandeur* ordered an entry to be made in the service diary:[68]

> "On 27th February, suddenly and abruptly, there occurred the withdrawal of all Jews still involved in the labour process, 11,000 of whom were in the armaments sector. As in many cases the Jews were put to work in self-contained units, sometimes on important programmes, every attempt had to be made to find extensive replacements. This was only possible by calling up all the Western workers who arrived in the first half of March exclusively for this purpose, as well as other workers who became available, especially as a result of the compulsory registration action and as a result of closures. Thus the shutdown of specific manufactures could be prevented and there were merely certain interruptions caused by the initial training period of the new workers."

Such "interruptions" occurred in the *Elektro-Motorenwerk* of *Siemens Schuckert Werke*, where the disappearance of the Jews caused problems "in the deliveries for the U-boat programme, particularly of converters and control motors for fire-control facilities".[69] As was reported by *Rüstungskommando I*, the *Oberkommando der Marine* immediately applied for the assignment of "20 lathe operators, 10 fitters, 18 electrical mechanics and 20 women". *Rüstungskommando III* in Berlin reported that "the complete removal of the Jews . . . in the Adolf Hitler tank programme" had caused a number of difficulties. To ensure the manufacture of tanks on schedule, the labour exchange promised "to provide a replacement supply of 100% in smaller and medium-sized firms, and of at least 50% in larger firms, within 48 hours".[70]

In the area covered by Berlin *Rüstungskommando V*, the "last Jews [were] removed without immediate supply of replacement". Disruption was recorded only in those firms with "a particularly high percentage of Jews working in them".[71] *Rüstungskommandos* in other German regions were hardly affected by the "factory actions". Jewish forced labourers had disappeared from many areas long before. The remainder were in individual armaments concerns or with firms making their contribution to the war effort by collecting and re-cycling rags and scrap. For example, a report came in from the *Rüstungsbereich* Düsseldorf:[72]

> "On the basis of an order of the RSHA all Jewish workers had to be removed from the firms by 27th February 1943. There was no possibility of objecting. For the armaments concerns this measure was of little significance. It was somewhat greater for rag-sorting institutions, scrap dealers and similar firms."

The "factory action" pointed the way to the end of Jewish forced labour in Germany. Further *Gestapo* decrees ensured that all firms became "Jew free". Only a few forced labourers remained and these, in accordance with Himmler's programme for the Final Solution, were put to "self-contained work which is revocable at any time".[73] Still tolerated and exploited were the "non-Aryan"

---

[68]BA/MA RW 21–2/3 RüKdo Berlin I, KTB, 1st January 1943–31st March 1943, p. 17.
[69]BA/MA RW 21–2/3 RüKdo Berlin I, KTB, 1st January 1943–31st March 1943, p. 7.
[70]BA/MA RW 21–4/13 RüKdo Berlin III, KTB No. 13, 27th February 1943, p. 29.
[71]BA/MA RW 21–6/1 RüKdo Berlin V, KTB, 28th February 1943, p. 15.
[72]BA/MA RW 21–16/12 RüKdo Düsseldorf, KTB, p. 20.
[73]Walk, *op. cit.*, p. 481.

workers who were protected by having non-Jewish spouses or by classification as a *Mischling*.

After being dismissed without notice from their firms, the forced labourers and their families were given the *Gestapo*'s "place on the list" for "resettlement" in the East. Their interim and final destinations were the compulsory ghettos of Theresienstadt, Lodz and Warsaw, Riga and Kovno, Minsk and Izbica, and the extermination camps of Chelmno and Belzec, Treblinka and Auschwitz. In all these places of organised mass murder German Jews – who had already suffered all the preceding stages of defamation and victimisation – were confronted with a reality which was terrible beyond their imagination. In this de-humanised world of barbarisation and death, they shared their fate with other Jews. Their encounters with the *Ostjuden*, their "brothers and sisters" from Eastern Europe, have recently been impressively described by Avraham Barkai.[74] The slave labourers were "selected" on the loading platforms of the extermination camps. Usually it was young women and men, fit for work, who were recruited once again for forced labour on the building sites, in the camp factories and firms of the SS, the *Wehrmacht*, industry or trade. There they were exploited by a system which adopted the maxim of "destruction through labour".

In the occupied territories of the East, the military representatives of the war economy at first tried to retain the potential of Jewish labour until adequate replacements were guaranteed. This guideline permitted them to make interventions and protests, but prohibited mass resistance or refusal to obey. When the *Rüstungsinspektionen* and *Rüstungskommandos* found themselves unable to decide the timing of "withdrawals" or even to ensure the arrival of new workers, they – like other military offices – accepted the inevitable "losses"; the attitude they adopted was "to shrug their shoulders and look the other way".[75] This approach was demonstrated to perfection in a report written at the beginning of 1943 by the Baranowicze branch office and sent to the Minsk *Rüstungskommando*. The head of the branch – a *Rittmeister* – reported that the last "Jewish action" had taken place on 17th December 1942 and had ended with the "final removal of all Jews from the firms". He continued:[76] "The fact that all Jewish skilled workers have also disappeared in this way, making up about 50% of the workforce, is regrettable in the interests of production but cannot be helped."

The absolute priority accorded by Nazi racial fanatics to the extermination of the Jews ultimately clashed once again with the material interests of the system. As the military and economic situation deteriorated, there was increasing pressure to retain the economic potential of those Jewish slave labourers who were still "available" in the concentration camps. Moreover, demands were even made for them to be sent back to work in a Germany which was now almost completely "*judenfrei*". In April 1944 the *Eichmann-Referat* opposed any "so-called open deployment of labour in firms in the *Reich* . . . , as it would . . . contravene

---

[74]Avraham Barkai, 'German-Speaking Jews in Eastern European Ghettos', in *LBI Year Book XXXIV* (1989), pp. 247–266; see also *idem*, 'Between East and West. Jews from Germany in the Lodz Ghetto', in *Yad Vashem Studies, XVI* (1984), pp. 271–332.

[75]Klaus-Jürgen Müller, *Das Heer und Hitler*, Stuttgart 1969, p. 45.

[76]NA Washington T 77 R 1159 141. Aussenstelle Baranowicze, RüKdo Minsk, p. 9.

the *Entjudung* of the *Reich* which has been largely completed in the meantime".[77] But this veto was overridden. The reservoir of non-Jewish workers was virtually exhausted. Though almost 7.7 million foreign workers and prisoners-of-war had been harnessed to the German war effort, they were not enough. Jewish workers were now required to cover the shortfall. While the gassings and shootings continued and the last centre of European Jewry was destroyed with the deportation of the Hungarian Jews, both Jewish and non-Jewish concentration camp inmates were deported to the *Altreich* from early summer 1944. Once more the SS, businesses and factories hired out their slaves. Some of these weak, emaciated and half-starved women and men, girls and boys, were crammed into accommodation provided by the firms, which often resembled conditions in the camps themselves; others were forced to march to work from the numerous satellite and permanent camps. Once again their routes and workplaces could be seen by the German people, though these – with few exceptions – took little notice of the survivors of the "Final Solution". Even today, the material "compensation" for the victims is a matter of dispute.

The vast majority of Jewish forced labourers in Germany, in the event, shared the fate of their co-religionists in countries occupied by the Nazis. Their harsh exploitation for the German war effort had been, at best, no more than a temporary reprieve. The extermination of Jews included the slave labourers in Germany as soon as – and often even before – replacements, in the shape of foreign workers and prisoners-of-war, could be found for them. Appeals for "exemptions" from deportation for skilled or essential workers had small hope of success in a system based on irrationality, racial hatred and mass murder, and geared to the enslavement of a whole continent. Forced labour in the Nazi war machine was only another step along the path of destruction for the Jews in Germany.

---

[77]Quoted from Ulrich Herbert, 'Von Auschwitz nach Essen', in *Dachauer Hefte*, 2 (1986), p. 18.

APPENDIX

The following document, hitherto totally unknown and published here for the first time, is an historical key-document, revealing as it does the considerations, plans and perspectives of the bureaucratic *Leitzentralen* (Ministry of the Interior, Security Police, Regular Police, army and concentration camp administration) after the *caesura* of the November Pogrom and with reference to the outbreak of war. The archival history of the document is equally staggering: captured by the Russians, it was deposited at the "Special Archives" in Moscow, from where a copy was sent to the GDR authorities in the late fifties, but instead of being transferred to the *Zentrales Staatsarchiv*, Potsdam it remained in the hands of the State Security Police (*Stasi*), together with thousands of other Nazi records. All this material (amounting to a source complex of some 9,000 metres) was finally handed over to the *Zentrales Staatsarchiv* against the background of the collapse of the GDR. An annex to the *Staatsarchiv* has now been established in the former administration building of the *Stasi* in Berlin and this material is housed there. The document printed here can be located as: Bestand ZR, Nr. 912 4. 13, Bl. 20–23, Zentrales Staatsarchiv, Außenstelle Berlin, Freienwalder Straße.

Abschrift

DER CHEF DER SICHERHEITSPOLIZEI   Berlin, den 1. März 1939
S–V 8 Nr. 152^{III}/38–553–1–g.   SW 11, Prinz-Albrechtstr. 8

Geheim
Abschrift.

Vermerk:

Am 28.2.1939 fand bei der Abteilung I des Reichsministeriums des Innern unter Vorsitz von Ministerialrat Dr. *Loesener* und der Beteiligung von Vertretern des Oberkommandos der Wehrmacht, des Hauptamtes Sicherheitspolizei (Ministerialrat Dr. *Zindel*, Reg. Ass. *Hülf* – S–PP II –, Reg. Rat Thorn), des Hauptamtes Ordnungspolizei (Hauptmann *Sehrt*) und des Leiters der Konzentrationslager, Gruppenführer *Eicke*, eine Besprechung darüber statt, wie die Dienstleistung der Juden im Kriegsfalle zu regeln ist. Eine besondere Regelung der Dienstleistungspflicht der Juden im Kriege wurde dadurch erforderlich, daß nach Abänderung der Musterungs- und Aushebungsverordnung durch das OKW die Juden nicht mehr für die Ersatzreserve II beordert und von dem Dienst bei der Wehrmacht vollständig ausgeschlossen werden.

1): *Frage der Erfassung der Juden*:

Es war die Vorfrage zu klären, in welchem Umfange die Juden zu geeigneten Dienstleistungen heranzuziehen sind. Es bestand Einigkeit, daß ein besonderer Einsatz der jüdischen Frauen und Kinder in keinem Verhältnis zu dem erforderlichen Aufwand an Arbeitskräften (Überwachung) und Mitteln stehen würde. Arbeitsmäßig ist von dem Einsatz der jüdischen Frauen und Kinder kein Erfolg zu erwarten. Da die Juden in erster Linie für öffentliche Straßenarbeiten herangezogen werden sollen, muß für ihren Einsatz der Maßstab der Wehrtauglichkeit zu Grunde gelegt werden. Entsprechend der Wehrerfassung der männlichen Bevölkerung im Alter von 18–55 Jahren in Ostpreußen erschien eine Altersbegrenzung von 18–55 Jahren angebracht. Bei einer Gesamtzahl von ca. 600.000 Juden muß man schätzungsweis mit 200.000 Juden, die für eine Dienstleistung im Kriege in Frage kommen, rechnen.

Wenn auch ein Arbeitseinsatz nur bei den wehrtauglichen 45–55 jährigen Juden in Frage kommt, erscheint eine Beschränkung der Erfassung auf diese Jahrgänge der männlichen Juden nicht zweckmäßig. Eine besondere Gesamterfassung sämtlicher Juden unter dem Gesichtspunkt einer besonderen Verwendung im Kriege wurde allgemein für praktisch gehalten. Maßgebend für diese Auffassung war die Betrachtung, daß im Kriege unter Umständen von Fall zu

Fall bestimmte sicherheitspolizeiliche Maßnahmen (z.B. besondere Überwachung) gegen die gesamte Judenschaft erforderlich werden, für die die friedensmäßige Gesamterfassung der Juden die Möglichkeit gibt.

Es ist vorgesehen, diese Erfassung der Juden dadurch zu regeln, daß ihnen im Wege einer Reichspolizeiverordnung eine polizeiliche Anmeldepflicht auferlegt wird (analog der Wehrerfassung der Wehrtauglichen). Die Regelung dieser Frage wird im einzelnen zwischen den Sachbearbeitern des OKW und des Hauptamtes Ordnungspolizei besprochen und vorbereitet.

2): *Für welche Arbeiten sollen die Juden herangezogen werden?*

Ministerialrat Dr. *Loesener* führte aus, daß die Juden kolonnenmäßig, getrennt von den deutschblütigen Arbeitskräften zu beschäftigen sind. Sie dürften sich in erster Linie für eine Verwendung bei Straßenbauten und Beschaffung des hierfür erforderlichen Materials (Steinbrucharbeiten) eignen. Infolge des großzügigen Straßenbauprogrammes des Führers und der besonderen Inanspruchnahme des gesamten Straßennetzes im Kriege ist an eine Beschäftigung sämtlicher arbeitsfähigen Juden mit dieser Art von Arbeiten zu denken.

3): Von der Art ihrer Beschäftigung hängt wiederum die Frage ihrer *Unterbringung* ab. Da die Behandlung der Juden im Kriege das besondere Interesse der Bevölkerung erregen wird, ist von dem Grundsatz auszugehen, daß die Juden im Kriege in ihrer Lebensführung nicht besser gestellt sind, als die deutschblütigen Volksgenossen. Ihr arbeitsmäßiger Einsatz ist der Ersatz für die Ableistung von Wehrdiensten, zu denen sie wegen ihrer Rassenzugehörigkeit nicht herangezogen werden können. Ihre Beschäftigung und Unterbringung muß deshalb auch in militärischer Form gelöst werden. Die Bevölkerung hätte zweifellos kein Verständnis dafür, wenn die Juden ohne eine besondere Änderung ihrer Lebensbedingungen im Kriege ihren zivilen Berufen nachgehen könnten, während die deutschblütigen Volksgenossen an der Front und in der Heimat ihrer Wehrdienstpflicht für das Vaterland genügen. Deshalb dürfte auch ihre Unterbringung in besonderen Lagern, die mit den Arbeitsdienstlagern zu vergleichen sind, angebracht sein. Verwendungsmöglichkeit der Arbeitsdienstlager für diese Zwecke wird Gegenstand einer besonderen Anfrage beim Reichsarbeitsministerium sein.

4): *Frage der Errichtung von Lagern*:

Es ist sodann die Frage zu klären, wem die Errichtung der Lager zufällt, wieviele Lager und wo sie zu errichten sind, wie die Lager überwacht werden müssen. Da die Arbeitsdienstpflicht an die Stelle einer Wehrdienstleistung tritt, erscheint die Schaffung der geeigneten Unterbringungsmöglichkeiten für die Juden ebenso wie ihre Erfassung eine Aufgabe der Wehrmacht zu sein. Die Vorbereitung und Durchführung dieser Aufgaben durch die Wehrmacht dürfte auch deshalb zweckmäßig sein, weil die erforderlichen Geldmittel als besondere Mob. – Ausgaben von der Wehrmacht aufzubringen sind. Wenn die Schaffung dieser Lager dem Leiter der Konzentrationslager, Gruppenführer Eicke, übertragen würde, müßten von dem Verwaltungsamt der SS schon jetzt die erforderlichen Mittel bei der Anmeldung des besonderen Mob. – Geldbedarfs berücksichtigt werden. Für die Anmeldung dieses Postens fehlen aber zur Zeit noch die erforderlichen Unterlagen. Bevor die Frage entschieden wird, wer der Träger für die Einrichtungen für die geeignete Unterbringungen der Juden zu schaffen hat, kommt eine Berücksichtigung bei der Anmeldung des besonderen Mob. – Geldbedarfs für die Sicherheitspolizei überhaupt nicht in Frage.

Das Ergebnis der Besprechung wurde von Ministerialrat Dr. *Loesener* wie folgt zusammengefaßt:

1) Erfassung der Juden auf Grund der Einführung einer besonderen Melde-
pflicht bei den Polizeibehörden. Bei der Erfassung ist die Arbeitsdienstun-
fähigkeit zu prüfen. Die Prüfung erfolgt durch die Vorlage eines Attestes eines
jüdischen Arztes. Die von den jüdischen Ärzten nicht arbeitsfähig geschriebe-
nen Juden werden einer besonderen Nachuntersuchung unterzogen. Nach der
Erfassung findet eine weitere ärztliche Untersuchung nicht mehr statt. Die
endgültige Feststellung der Arbeitsfähigkeit erfolgt erst im Lager.
Diese Gesichtspunkte sind zweckmäßigerweise in einer besonderen Reichspolizeiverordnung zusammenzufassen. Vorbereitung und Regelung der
Erfassung erfolgt durch das Hauptamt Ordnungspolizei und das Oberkommando der Wehrmacht im beiderseitigen Einvernehmen.
2) Für die Begründung der Arbeitsdienstpflicht bedarf es keiner besonderen
gesetzlichen Regelung, da die Heranziehung der Juden auf Grund des
Kriegsleistungsgesetzes oder der Notdienstverordnung erfolgen kann. Für die
Heranziehung genügt eine allgemeine Verwaltungsanordnung (auf Grund
des Notdienstgesetzes Anweisung an die einzelnen Bedarfsträger).
3) Über die Frage, mit welchen Arbeiten die Juden im Kriege zu beschäftigen
sind und wie sie unterzubringen sind, ist zunächst die Stellungnahme der
Reichsanstalt für Arbeitslosenversicherung und Arbeitsvermittlung einzu-
holen, die den beteiligten Ressorts als Grundlage für die von ihnen vorzubrin-
genden Gesichtspunkte zugeleitet wird. Der Vertreter des Gruppenführers
Eicke ist ferner gebeten worden, eine Mitteilung der Auffassung des Gruppenführers Eicke über die Frage der Unterbringung zu veranlassen. Regierungs-
assessor Rülf (S–PP II B) wird die vom sicherheitspolizeilichen Standpunkt
besonders beachtlichen Gesichtspunkte und erforderlichen Maßnahmen
zusammenstellen und den Referenten S–V 1 und S–V 8 zuleiten.

An
a) das Referat S–V 2
    z.Hd. von Herrn Oberregierungsrat Dr. Siegert
         oder Vertreter im Amt
   im Hause.
b) das Referat S–V 1
    z.Hd. von Herrn Ministerialrat Dr. Zindel
         oder Vertreter im Amt
   im Hause.
c) das Referat S–PP II B
    z.Hd. von Herrn Regierungsrat Lischka
         oder Vertreter im Amt
   im Hause.
d) die Abteilung I des Reichsministeriums des Innern
    z.Hd. von Herrn Ministerialdirektor Dr. Danckwerts
         oder Vertreter im Amt
   in Berlin.

Abschrift übersende ich mit der Bitte um Kenntnisnahme. Um baldige
Zuleitung der dortigen Stellungnahme gemäß letzter Absatz des Vermerks wird
gebeten.

                                        In Vertretung:
                                        gez. Dr. Best.

Gentiles and Jews after 1945

Restitution and Legitimacy in Post-War Austria 1945–1953

I

The *Anschluss* unleashed on Austria's Jews a storm of elemental ferocity.* Physical assault and psychological humiliation went hand-in-hand with an unprecedented "trail of looting".[1] In both Vienna and the provinces personal and household possessions, businesses, legal and medical practices, private flats and properties became the targets for the cupidity of sections of the non-Jewish population. Over the following months the authorities attempted – with only limited success – to regulate this "wild Aryanisation". The *Vermögensverkehrstelle* was set up in April by *Reichskommissar* Bürckel to supervise the orderly transfer or liquidation of Jewish businesses and to appoint temporary directors (*Kommissarische Leiter*). In doing so it sought to deflect the disappointed "utopian" aspirations of those supporters who had worked "underground" for the illegal National Socialist Party, to implement a "substitute for social policy"[2] – especially in housing, while at the same time "rationalising" the small business and shopkeeping sector and, not least, increasing state revenue. Property was sold by intimidated or panic-stricken owners for a fraction of its value, and most

*For an earlier version of some of the arguments advanced here and fuller German documentation see Robert Knight (ed.), *"Ich bin dafür, die Sache in die Länge zu ziehen"*. *Die Wortprotokolle der österreichischen Bundesregierung von 1945 bis 1952 über die Entschädigung der Juden*, Frankfurt a. Main 1988, (henceforth Knight, *Wortprotokolle*); I would like to thank Dr. Friederich Weckerlein for his help in preparing this article and to express special thanks for the valuable help of Dr. Georg Weis, whose efforts, as administrator of the collection agencies (*Sammelstellen*) and the *Hilfsfonds*, in implementing restitution deserve considerable recognition.

[1]Helmut Genschel, *Die Verdrängung der Juden aus der Wirtschaft im Dritten Reich*, Göttingen 1966 (Göttinger Bausteine zur Geschichtswissenschaft, vol. 38), p. 165. See also in particular; Hans Safrian and Hans Witek, *Und Keiner war dabei. Dokumente des Alltäglichen Antisemitismus in Wien 1938*, Vienna 1988. p. 15; Jonny Moser, *Die Judenverfolgung in Österreich, 1938–1945*, Vienna–Frankfurt a. Main–Zürich 1966; Herbert Rosenkranz, *Verfolgung und Selbstbehauptung. Die Juden in Österreich 1938–1945*, Munich 1978, pp. 26–30, 60–75, 126–136; Gerhard Botz, 'The Jews of Vienna from the *Anschluss* to the Holocaust', in Ivar Oxaal, Michael Pollak and Gerhard Botz (eds.), *Jews, Antisemitism and Culture in Vienna*, London–New York 1987, pp. 185–204; Georg Weis, 'Arisierungen in Wien', in *Wien 1938 Vienna 1978* (Forschungen und Beiträge zur Wiener Stadtgeschichte, vol. II), pp. 183–189; Gerhard Jagschitz, 'Von der "Bewegung" zum Apparat. Zur Phänomenologie der NSDAP 1938 bis 1945', in Emmerich Tálos, Ernst Hanisch and Wolfgang Neugebauer (eds.), *NS-Herrschaft in Österreich 1938–1945*, Vienna 1988, pp. 487–516; Hans Witek, ' "Arisierungen" in Wien. Aspekte nationalsozialistischer Enteignungspolitik 1938–1940', *ibid.*, pp. 199–216; for eye-witness accounts see the classic account G.E. R. Gedye, *Fallen Bastions*, London 1939; the autobiographical account by George Clare, *Last Waltz in Vienna. The Destruction of a Family 1842–1942*, London 1981; and the presumably autobiographical novel by Leopold Ehrlich-Hichler, *"1938" – Ein Wiener Roman*, Vienna 1956; for journalistic accounts see Reinhard Engel, 'Wirtschaft ohne Juden', *Trend*, March 1988, pp. 119–141; and Erika Wantoch, 'Freuds Ende. Ein Protokoll', *Profil*, Nos. 18–21 (2nd–22nd May 1989).

[2]Botz, *loc. cit.*, pp. 188–189.

of the price paid was used to pay discriminatory taxes.[3] What remained was transferred to blocked bank accounts and subject to considerable restrictions.

By the time of the November Pogrom the experience accumulated in the *Ostmark*, in achieving the speediest possible transfer of property and emigration with minimum loss of foreign exchange, provided a useful model for the authorities in Berlin.[4] As the 60,000 remaining Jews (out of a total population of about 200,000) were taken away to their deaths in 1942 a series of decrees dotted the legal "i"'s on the expropriation of what had been one of Europe's richest Jewish communities; all property of Jews who had lost their citizenship through emigration or death was taken over by the state.[5]

It is difficult to state accurately how much property changed hands as a result. Up to about 10,000 businesses which were probably transferred immediately after the *Anschluss* were not included in the 26,000 officially recorded as having been taken over. Of these about 21,000 were "liquidated".[6] In addition there were 60–70,000 flats, nearly all in Vienna, thousands of leasehold and freehold properties,[7] personal effects,[8] household possessions, securities,[9] insurance policies and mortgages. Estimates of the total value of this property at the time of the *Anschluss*, of how much was taken out before the war and how much survived it are equally uncertain. The figure produced by the compulsory registration of Jewish property (above the value of 5,000 Reichsmark) at the end of April 1938, 2,041,828 Reichsmark, was certainly too low.[10]

[3] Above all *"Reich* flight tax" (*Reichsfluchtsteuer*) and "Jewish property levy" (*Judenvermögensabgabe*) which, according to Austrian official sources amounted to 328 million Reichsmark. See Blair (British Embassy, Vienna) to Thomas (Foreign Office [FO]), 11th October 1956, Public Record Office (PRO), FO 371/124114/RR1461/5.

[4] Safrian and Witek, *op. cit.*, pp. 42, 97–98; see also introduction to Tálos *et al.* (eds.), *op. cit.* p. XII; and Genschel, *op. cit.*, p. 151; cf. Kurt Schmid and Robert Streibel (eds.), *Der Pogrom 1938. Judenverfolgung in Österreich und Deutschland*, Vienna 1990.

[5] Eleventh and Thirteenth executive order to the Reich Citizenship Law (*Verordnung zum Reichsbürgerschaftsgesetz*), 25th November 1942 and 7th July 1943.

[6] Cf. report by the *Staatskommissar in der Privatwirtschaft*, 1st February 1939 cited in Witek, *loc. cit.*, p. 213; *Bericht über Jüdisches Erbloses Vermögen in Österreich*, (unpublished report for the Vienna *Kultusgemeinde*), Georg Weis, 1st December 1952, for which I am most grateful to Dr. Weis; the figures for "Aryanisation" files held by the post-war Finance Ministry (*Bericht über die Tätigkeit des Wiedergutmachungsreferates (der Kultusgemeinde) bis Dezember 1950* (Archiv der Israelitischen Kultusgemeinde, Wien, File Wiedergutmachung 1948–1952) roughly tally with these (200 export houses, 10,000 trading firms [*Handelsbetriebe*], 1,000 taxi firms, 5,000 small businesses (*Gewerbetreibende*), 80 banking houses, 1,500 industrial firms, 17,000 liquidated firms). The high figure of 50,000 commercial businesses (*gewerbliche Betriebe*) "in Jewish hands" given by Bürckel to Göring in November 1938 (cited in Safrian and Witek, *op. cit.*, p. 186) may be explained by Bürckel's wish to exaggerate the "achievement" of "Aryanisation" and the extent of "Jewish influence".

[7] The estimate of 30,000 houses (*Bericht über die Tätigkeit, op. cit.*) may include leasehold property. According to the same report there were about 10,000 properties in Vienna and 3,000 in Lower Austria; Rosenkranz (*op. cit.*, p. 70) gives a figure of 2,000 for properties in the Burgenland.

[8] Estimated by Weis at 31 million Reichsmark, *op. cit.*, p. 12.

[9] Estimated by Weis (*ibid.*, p. 17) at nearly 266 million Reichsmark.

[10] The memorandum presented by the Executive Committee for Jewish Claims on Austria to the Austrian Government at the start of its negotiations in June 1953 ('Überblick der materiellen Verluste der Juden in Österreich', Archive of the Israelitische Kultusgemeinde, Vienna [IKGA] File Wiedergutmachung 1948–1952) used the *Gestapo* registration figure as a basis for its calculations to estimate the total value at the *Anschluss* at about 3 thousand million Reichsmark or (on the basis of the official 1938 exchange rate) about 1,200 million dollars.

The policies adopted by governments of the Second Austrian Republic in the face of this situation raise a number of historical, legal and moral issues. In one sense the restitution of "Aryan" property was no more than the technical problem of tracing and returning property – albeit one of unprecedented magnitude. But it was also a competition for political and economic power in which the victims of "Aryanisation" faced the gainers – ranging from individual inhabitants of flats, lawyers or small peasants who had taken over part of real estate to banks or finance houses which had supplied mortgages on "Aryanised" property.[11] Thirdly, and this is the main concern here, restitution raised questions about the legitimacy of the newly-founded Second Republic.

At this point it is important to note the special relevance for Austria of the distinction between restitution and compensation.[12] Restitution is the reversal of "the expropriation or forced transfer of objects or rights",[13] where possible in their original condition, while compensation is generally a payment arising from a liability for damages to people or property.[14] On the level of the state the two operations may be considered two sides of the same coin – both demonstrate the degree to which one state distances itself from actions which took place on its territory[15] – and in practice, too, the border between the two categories is often blurred. Nevertheless the distinction is important in its implications for Austria's legitimacy as the "first victim of Nazism". This had been laid down – albeit more ambivalently than sometimes maintained – in the Moscow Declaration of November 1943.[16] The legal argument – the validity of which is not of concern here – entailed the view that the *Anschluss* had been an illegal occupation, not a legally recognised annexation and that the Second Republic was not the legal successor of the Third *Reich*. On that basis post-war governments were to deny all legal liability towards victims of Nazi oppression.[17] Those payments which

[11]The exclusion of "altruistic Aryanisers" who took possessions from friends or neighbours into safekeeping is not meant to imply that they did not exist (though their importance was exaggerated after the war) but merely that they were largely irrelevant for the purpose of this article since – almost by definition – they took no part in the post-war political dispute over restitution.

[12]See Ludolf Herbst's introduction to Ludolf Herbst und Constantin Goschler (eds.), *Wiedergutmachung in der Bundesrepublik Deutschland*, Munich 1989, pp. 9ff (Schriftenreihe der Vierteljahrshefte für Zeitgeschichte: Sondernummer); Walter Schwarz, 'Die Wiedergutmachung nationalsozialistischen Unrechts durch die Bundesrepublik Deutschland. Ein Überblick', *ibid.*, pp. 33–54.

[13]"Wiedergutmachung des Unrechts am Vermögen, der Wegnahme oder erzwungenen Weggabe von Sachen und Rechten." Walter Schwarz, *Rückerstattung nach den Gesetzen der Alliierten Mächte*, Munich 1974 (*Die Wiedergutmachung nationalsozialistischen Unrechts durch die Bundesrepublik Deutschland*, vol. I), p. 1.

[14]See Georg Weis, *Restitution through the Ages*, London 1962 (Noah Barou Memorial Lecture), p. 7.

[15]Both are encompassed by the German word "Wiedergutmachung" although, as Herbst points out (Introduction to Herbst and Goschler (eds.), *op. cit.*, pp. 9–10) confusion is created by the application of the term "Wiedergutmachung" to either or both of the two sub-categories of compensation or restitution.

[16]See Robert Keyserlingk's "revisionist" study, *Austria in World War II; an Anglo-American Dilemma*, McGill 1988.

[17]See i.a. Stephan Verosta, *Die Internationale Stellung Österreichs*, Vienna 1947; Robert E. Clute, *The International Legal Status of Austria 1938–1955*, den Haag 1963; Ewald Wiederin, 'März 1938 – staatsrechtlich betrachtet', in Ulrike Davy *et al.* (eds), *Nationalsozialismus und Recht. Rechtssetzung und Rechtswissenschaft in Österreich unter der Herrschaft des Nationalsozialismus*, Vienna 1990, pp. 226–265; Keyserlingk, *op. cit.*, *passim*; and for an attempt to place these arguments in a historical context Robert Knight, 'Besiegt oder Befreit? Eine völkerrechtliche Frage historisch betrachtet', in Günter

were made were thus not paid as "compensation" but variously as "relief" (*Opferfürsorge*), "aid" (*Hilfsfonds*) or, most recently, "donation of honour" (*Ehrengabe*). A willingness to pay compensation would have undermined the Austrian state's "victim thesis".

Restitution, by contrast, followed logically from it. It was an administrative move, reversing an illegal act, – at no major cost to the exchequer and with no admission of Austrian liability for the act itself. Restitution is thus in a sense a less demanding "test" for the validation of the "victim thesis" than compensation. More importantly, it highlights more graphically the tensions which arose between that thesis and the social and economic reality of Austria during the *Anschluss*.

Source limitations mean that this tension will be traced here largely on the level of "high politics". The social or individual psychological dimensions of restitution cannot be covered. On the other hand the *verbatim* minutes of the Austrian cabinet for the post-war period provide an unusually vivid insight into the thinking of the political leadership of the country.[18]

II

The policies adopted by the provisional State Government, set up under Soviet auspices in Eastern Austria in April 1945, cannot be isolated from the wider context of Austrian attitudes towards National Socialism and Jews after eight years of *Anschluss*. On the surface the first denazification measure, passed on 8th May was draconian, laying down penalties up to and including death and selecting former members of the illegal Nazi Party for specially harsh treatment.[19] In fact, as the records of cabinet show, there was from the start resistance

Bischof and Josef Leidenfrost (eds.), *Die Bevormundete Nation: Österreich und die Alliierten 1945–1949*, Innsbruck 1988 (Innsbrucker Forschungen zur Zeitgeschiche, vol. IV) pp. 75–91.

[18]On the methodological and source problems surrounding the study of West German restitution and compensation see Ludolf Herbst's introduction in Herbst and Goschler (eds.), *op. cit.* The files of the Austrian Restitution Commissions do not appear to be available for research though August Walzl uses some from the Graz *Oberstes Landesgericht* in *Die Juden in Kärnten und das Dritte Reich*, Klagenfurt 1987, pp. 307–318; see also the (unreliable) study by Dietmar Walch, *Die jüdischen Bemühungen um die materiellen Wiedergutmachungen durch die Republik Österreich*, (Veröffentlichungen des historischen Instituts der Universität Salzburg, vol. I) Vienna 1971; for eye-witness accounts of the negotiations between the Claims Committee and the Austrian Government, see Gustav Jellinek, 'Die Geschichte der österreichischen Wiedergutmachung', in Josef Fraenkel (ed.), *The Jews of Austria. Essays on their Life, History and Destruction*, London 1967, pp. 395–426; Nahum Goldmann, *Mein Leben als Deutscher Jude*, Munich – Vienna 1980, pp. 448–453; the recent brochure of the official Austrian Press Service (*Bundespressedienst*), *Massnahmen der Republik Österreich zugunsten bestimmter politisch, religiös oder abstammungsmässig Verfolgter seit 1945*, Vienna 1988, is tendentious and inaccurate; Walther Kastner, 'Entziehung und Rückstellung', in Davy *et al.* (eds.), *op. cit.*, pp. 191–199, is legalistic, and misleading. For Austrian restitution in an international context see above all Walter Schwarz, *Rückerstattung, op. cit.*, pp. 329–330; see also Nina Sigi, *German Reparations. A History of the Negotiations*, Jerusalem 1980, pp. 205–211.

[19]*Staatsgesetzblatt*, (StGBl.), Nr. 13, 4th June 1945 ('Verfassungsgesetz über das Verbot der NSDAP'); for denazification see i.a. Sebastian Meissl, Klaus-Dieter Mulley, Oliver Rathkolb (eds.), *Verdrängte Schuld – Verfehlte Sühne. Entnazifizierung in Österreich 1945–1955*, Vienna 1986; also, Dieter Stiefel, *Entnazifizierung in Österreich*, Vienna 1981.

to radical measures. Much of this came from Socialist ministers in whose memories the repression by the pre-war "clerico-fascist" regime bulked large. The Socialist Chancellor Karl Renner, who had enthusiastically endorsed not only the *Anschluss* but also the incorporation of the "Sudetenland" after the Munich agreement, had a personal interest in glossing over the immediate past. From the start he put all his considerable authority behind a policy of "reconciliation". On 30th April, only three days after the official declaration of Austrian independence, he told a meeting of officials of the new administration:

> "We . . . will have a hard task keeping atonement within the bounds of the law and making it as mild as possible . . . Those who played a leading part in one of the two fascist movements [the clerico-fascist or the Nazi – RK] and acted in a vicious fashion to everyone else cannot expect to be re-admitted to public service. But that does not apply to those who in passionate joy and in the expectation that the *Anschluss* would [in any case-RK] come about, went along with the rest because they could not foresee what an adventure this policy would plunge our people into. They can all go peacefully back to their normal life and they will all be able to carry on quietly in their jobs . . ."

In particular exceptions should be made for indispensable experts and those who showed loyalty to the new State.[20] Renner's empathy with the small Party members led him to conjure up the danger of a backlash against denazification at a stage when hardly any denazification had yet taken place. Characteristically, he masked his own inability to empathise with the victims with a historico-philosophical gloss; in reply to calls for more radical measures he warned of the danger of the return of

> "people who think they've lost out, who want to have positions made free for them to occupy. We must beware of doing the same as the Nazis did. If we do the same thing once again and simply carry on calling for persecution and revenge there is the danger that the mood will swing round; all we will achieve – from the viewpoint of future Austrian history – will be to replace one act of vengeance with another. We'll have to be very careful in how we go about this. I am in favour of severely punishing the real war criminals – though I cannot support such an extensive use of the death penalty for purely verbal crimes."

He concluded that "we will not be so casual (*leichtfertig*) in applying [the death penalty] as the Nazis were and we won't at some later date give another regime the chance to hang our People's judges".[21]

Renner was generally supported by his Socialist colleagues, in particular Adolf Schärf, (Chairman of the *Sozialistische Partei Österreich* (SPÖ), later Vice Chancellor and President) and Oskar Helmer, who as Interior Minister (1945–1959) was to be a prime mover of the rehabilitation of former Nazi Party members.

Resistance within the government came mainly from the Communists. Their arguments – that only rapid and effective action by the government could stem the eruption of an enraged patriotic anti-Nazi "Volksseele" – may appear less realistic than Renner's view that denazification would cause the mood to swing

---

[20]'Rede des Staatskanzlers an die Beamtenschaft', 30th April 1945, cited in Knight, *Wortprotokolle, op. cit.*, p. 80.
[21]Kabinettsratsprotokoll (KRP) 12, 12th June 1945, Archiv der Republik, Vienna (AdR); Knight, *Wortprotokolle, op. cit.*, p. 97; on Renner's ability to clothe opportunism with philosophy see Anton Pelinka, *Karl Renner zur Einführung*, Vienna 1989.

against the population, but they did at least seem to have recognised some of the dimensions of the problem posed by the Nazi catastrophe.[22] They were in part supported – in an improbable alliance – by those People's Party leaders who had personally suffered from Nazi persecution. Both Leopold Figl, who in December 1945 was to become Austria's first Chancellor and Felix Hurdes, later Minister of Education, warned against the slow pace of denazification.

Nevertheless by the summer of 1945 denazification had already effectively ground to a halt. The pattern was to be often repeated: draconian-seeming legislation perforated with loopholes which could only be exploited by those with personal or political patronage. This is the sense in which Renner's judgement that the government had "already taken care of this problem" should be understood.[23]

A discussion of the continuity of antisemitism in post-war Austria cannot be undertaken here except to make two points: firstly, there is sufficient empirical evidence for that continuity to put the onus of proof firmly on the proponents of a "discontinuity thesis": secondly, that although the social function of antisemitism in post-war Austria is clearly different from that of the First Republic, that difference does not involve any significant tension between "the fascist-tending consciousness of the majority of Austrians" and a "ruling anti-fascist minority".[24]

Renner, at any rate, displayed a blithe imperviousness to Jewish suffering, in stark contrast to his concern for the "small Nazi":

> "I think that in dealing with the Nazi problem we are getting into a critical situation . . . at the time of the *Anschluss* all these little officials, these small citizens and businessmen did not have far-reaching aims at all – at the most to do something to the Jews – but above all they were not thinking of sparking off a world war. If these people are now severely punished and lose their position they will appeal to people's sympathy and their sense of justice and it may be that the mood will swing round."[25]

On this issue however – unlike the question of denazification – Renner did not meet with any substantial disagreement from Communists or People's Party politicians. For the Communists the seizure and nationalisation of *Reich* German capital was of more importance than the restoration of Jewish property.

This basic configuration was reflected in the measures taken by the State Government. They were largely aimed at curtailing the widespread plundering of unclaimed or heirless property in the chaos of the immediate post-war period. The first measure to register "Aryanised" property came to cabinet early in

[22]See for example Fischer's comments on 12th June 1945, KRP 12, AdR; Knight, *Wortprotokolle, op. cit.*, pp. 87–91; cf. Ernst Fischer, *Das Ende einer Illusion*, Vienna 1973, p. 103. The connection between Fischer's anti-fascist sensibility and his acceptance of Stalinism raise biographical and psychological questions which cannot be discussed in this context.

[23]Report by Edgar Johnson (Office of Strategic Services) of a conversation with Renner, 17th August 1945, cited in Oliver Rathkolb (ed.), *Gesellschaft und Politik am Beginn der zweiten Republik. Vertrauliche Berichte der US-Militäradministration aus Österreich 1945 in englischer Originalfassung*, Vienna – Cologne – Graz 1985, p. 115.

[24]Bernd Marin, 'Antisemitism before and after the Holocaust', in Oxaal *et al.* (eds.), *op. cit.*, pp. 216–233, here p. 227.

[25]KRP 28, 29th August 1945, AdR; Knight, *Wortprotokolle, op. cit.*, p. 114.

May. Helmer at once raised the Socialists' claims for compensation and restitution of property confiscated by the Dollfuss regime in 1934. Renner took up the point and linked it to his continuation in office:

> "I consider it self-evident that a law [returning the Socialists' property – RK] has to be passed. After all it would be quite incomprehensible if every small Jewish salesman or hawker is compensated for his loss while a movement, to which 47 per cent of the population belong, can simply have the result of its hard-earned fund-raising and organisational work taken away with impunity and without compensation, without the law providing redress. But I don't want to link that with this law; however I do declare that I will make my continuance in office as State Chancellor absolutely dependent on such a law being decreed. I hereby declare that I would not be in a position to continue to direct affairs of state if the injustice of 1934 was not redressed. I ask you, Gentlemen, not to forget that I also have a personal reputation to uphold and that my prestige in the whole state and to a large extent in the population depends on this injustice being redressed. I could not carry on affairs with the blot (*Makel*) of having upheld the rights of 7% of the population as being so sacrosanct that I made an extraordinary law for them while neglecting the rights of the other, far larger part."

In the final version of the law the reference to property taken from "Jewish, part-Jewish, Jewish-related or other owners" ("jüdischen, teiljüdischen oder jüdisch versippten [sic!] oder anderen Eigentümern") was replaced by one to property which had been taken "for so-called racial, national or other reasons in connection with the National Socialist seizure of power".[26] The amendment and Renner's comments pointed the direction of future Austrian policy; a playing-down of Jewish persecution to the advantage of a more generalised vague definition of victims and, as a part of this, equating it with the persecution of the Socialist movement under Dollfuss and Schuschnigg. The point is underscored by the two other laws passed in the same session. The "repatriation" law (*Repatriierungsgesetz*) and "Administrators" Law were passed to register and control "*Reich*" German property.[27] Significantly, whereas Schärf later praised Renner's initiative in securing "altösterreichisches Eigentum" for the new state and in regularising the administration of abandoned firms he referred to "restitution" only in connection with trade union, co-operative and church property confiscated by "fascism". In the case of "Aryanised" property he referred only to precautions (*Vorsorgen*) which had to be taken to secure and in some cases to nationalise it.[28] This basic discriminatory attitude emerges even more clearly from an exchange in Cabinet which took place several months later when the government sought to nationalise this property taken over from the Nazis. The State Secretary for Religious Affairs asked for an assurance that church property seized by the Nazis would not be included in the planned nationalisation. In response Renner recalled that, as far as he remembered, it had indeed been decided to exempt it. Karl Waldbrunner, the Socialist Undersecretary for Industry, Business, Trade and Transport confirmed this with the

[26]KRP 5, 10th May 1945, AdR; Knight, *Wortprotokolle, op. cit.*, pp. 82f.; StGBl., Nr. 10, 10th May 1945 ('Gesetz über die Erfassung arisierter und anderer im Zusammenhange mit der national-sozialistischen Machtübernahme entzogenen Vermögenschaften').

[27]StGBl., Nr. 9 (Verwaltergesetz); StGBl., Nr. 11 (Repatriierungsgesetz), 10th May 1945.

[28]Adolf Schärf, *Österreichs Wiederaufrichtung 1945*, Vienna 1960, pp. 195–196.

revealing comment that the exception had not been laid down in the law, in order
to avoid triggering "all sorts of claims, in particular from the Jews".[29]

Renner's empathy with the "small Nazi" extended to restitution as well. He
condemned "the mass of arbitrary measures (*Willkürlichkeiten*) which have been
spreading throughout the various district town halls (*Bezirksbürgermeisterämter*) in
Vienna and with housing allocations. These arbitrary housing allocations cause
much more bad blood than the whole Nazi business."[30] He was concerned by the
spread of the "most unacceptable legal situation" (unleidlichsten Rechtsverhält-
nisse) and the political problems which would arise when Nazis returned to find
their property taken.[31]

The four months between April and September 1945, when the Renner
government had a relatively free hand on this issue brought virtually no concrete
measures of restitution beyond the declaratory law of May.[32] The time limit for
registration of "Aryanised" property was twice extended and about 4,000 public
administrators and supervisors (*Aufsichtspersonen*) many of them Socialist appoin-
tees were put in charge of all kinds of heirless property.[33] More fundamentally, it
is likely that if it had been left to its own devices the government would have
taken no further legislative action at all and that Austrian restitution would have
been limited to the thorny path of individual claims in the civil courts.[34]

III

The Soviet authorities had not shown any particular interest in restitution, nor
exerted any pressure on the Renner government to implement it. The Western
occupation authorities, on the other hand, and the Americans in particular, were

[29]"Diese Ausnahme wurde jedoch nicht im Gesetz verankert, um nicht Ansprüche wachzurufen, weil
sich sonst allerhand Ansprüche, namentlich der Juden melden würden." KRP 28, 29th August
1945, AdR; Knight, *Wortprotokolle, op. cit.*, p. 81.
[30]"Diese eigenmächtigen Wohnungszuweisungen machen viel mehr böses Blut als die ganze
Nazisache", KRP 12, 12th June 1945, AdR; Knight, *Wortprotokolle, op. cit.*, p. 98.
[31]KRP 28, 29th August 1945, AdR; Knight, *Wortprotokolle, op. cit.*, pp. 113–115.
[32]See the complaints of the provisional leader of Vienna's Jewish community, David Brill, *Der Neue
Weg*, Nr. 1/2 (1945).
[33]OSS Intelligence Summary, No. 29, 27th November 1945, cited in Rathkolb (ed.), *Gesellschaft und
Politik, op. cit.*, p. 101.
[34]Renner made this clear when he told the Anglo-American Palestine Committee in February 1946:
"Whatever the Government may do . . . the Jewish community can never recover. . . . 1945 is the
final and complete end of the old Austro-Hungarian Empire. With it has gone the basis of Jewish
commerce. Most of the Jews have been exterminated and their assets throughout eastern Europe
have been seized as German property. Under Russian influence nationalised economies are being
built up which will leave no room for Jewish family business. And even if there were room . . . I do
not think that Austria in its present mood would allow Jews once again to build up these family
monopolies. Certainly we would not allow a new Jewish community to come in from eastern
Europe and establish itself here when our own people need work."
  Cited in Richard Crossman, *Palestine Mission*, London 1946, pp. 102–103. But see the
contradictory statement in the *New York Times* (21st February 1946). Thomas Albrich, *Exodus durch
Österreich, Die jüdischen Flüchtlinge 1945–1948* (Innsbrucker Forschungen zur Zeitgeschichte, vol. I)
Innsbruck 1987, pp. 93–94, quotes from Crossman's other conversations, but unaccountably fails
to mention Renner's statement.

strongly committed to it. In the London Declaration of January 1943 the "United Nations" (including the Soviet Union) had proclaimed their intention "to do their utmost to defeat the methods of dispossession practised by the governments with which they are at war against the countries and peoples who have been so wantonly assaulted and despoiled". The declaration had, admittedly – in line with orthodox international law – been directed to "external restitution", i.e. property taken from states, but the explicit mention of transfers or dealings "apparently legal in form, even when they purport to be voluntarily effected" clearly applied to the pseudo-legal methods adopted in "Aryanisation". Even if Western authorities did show more interest in the economic interests of their own nationals, they also included in their sphere of activity restitution of expropriated German or Austrian property.[35] With the establishment of the Allied Commission in September 1945 this was extended to the whole country.[36]

Austrian officials had already anticipated this. In August 1945 officials of the legal department of the Ministry of Foreign Affairs (formally a department of the State Chancellory) produced a long memorandum on the subject of restitution and compensation. After sketching out the expropriation which had followed the *Anschluss* it pointed out that there was no *Judenstaat* which might put forward claims, in accordance with international law:

> "Nevertheless the Jews play a major role in foreign policy, firstly because a large part of the press is in their hands, which enables them to exert their influence on world opinion and secondly because they have succeeded in getting the governments of other states to take up their demands. They succeeded in this all the more easily because a large part of international finance capital was in Jewish hands . . . It is not without reason that Jewry has been termed the fifth world power, on whose enmity Hitlerite Germany foundered".

In view of this it was recommended "if possible to avoid everything which might bring Jewry itself and hence indirectly world opinion against Austria". Although Austria's financial means were limited, and in any case it would be unfair to treat Jews better than Christian victims of Nazism, the possibility of obtaining financial support for Austria from the financial world made it "not appropriate (*wenig angezeigt*) to upset them by being too petty in the compensating of their co-religionists". Legally, the memorandum argued, Austria as a victim of the Third *Reich* was not obliged to compensate its former citizens but as the occupation powers were unlikely to accept this argument it was essential to negotiate a compromise. There were also "certain moral considerations" to take into account. One of these was the fact that indigenous antisemitism in Austria had

---

[35]Cf. Foreign Office minutes interpreting the declaration by (legal adviser) Patrick Deane, 18th January and Ward, 23rd January 1943, PRO, FO 371/36365/W1861; criticism of this formalistic view by Schwarz, *Rückerstattung, op. cit.*, p. 15; text of the 'Inter-Allied Declaration Against Acts of Dispossession Committed in Territories Under Enemy Occupation or Control', 5th January 1943, in *Foreign Relations of the United States* (FRUS) 1943, vol. I, Washington 1963, pp. 443–444; British Property Control Branch (Carinthia), Weekly report, 26th May 1945, PRO, FO/1020/2873; Walzl, *op. cit.*, pp. 308ff.

[36]The former Austrian refugee Albert Löwy played a prominent part as an official in the American Legal Division. His papers, though not catalogued, are available to researchers in the *Institut für Zeitgeschichte*, Vienna (henceforth IfZ, Vienna, Löwy PP).

been much stronger than in Germany and many antisemitic measures had gained the applause of the Viennese population. It would seem "odd" if "the Vienna government of all governments" ("gerade die Wiener Regierung") were to oppose compensation with the argument that the Austrians and the Viennese in particular had had nothing to do with this persecution. It would also be "unacceptable" for "Aryanised" property to remain with its present owners. Even where the property was in private hands restitution was the only acceptable "foreign policy solution".[37]

This curious mix of morality, opportunism, realism and veiled antisemitism suggests unresolved tensions within both the author and the "official mind". On one point, at any rate, its judgement was accurate enough – as the activities of the American element of the Allied Commission in Vienna after September 1945 showed. At the end of January 1946 Peter Krauland, Minister of Property Control and Economic Planning (*Vermögensicherung und Wirtschaftsplanung*, BMfVSWP) reported to Cabinet that the American authorities had peremptorily demanded that the "Administrator Law" of the previous May be immediately rescinded in order to safeguard "Jewish property, which America is interested in". He added – without going into details – that some "quite inept" (*recht ungeschickt*) notes had been sent by Austrian authorities.[38] Despite resistance from Waldbrunner und Kraus (Minister of Agriculture and Forestry) and from business and labour interests the American demand was complied with and a new law passed.[39] Though the change was resented by Austrian ministers[40] in practice it does not seem to have made much difference. As the Cold War intensified Western authorities became increasingly reluctant to press even their own economic claims against the Austrian government, for fear of offering ammunition to the Russians.[41] The Ministry set up under Krauland to control heirless and unclaimed property, which according to Figl "has been created specifically and on our own initiative to seize and preserve all property that the Nazis have stolen"[42] became a by-word for corruption. In 1949 it was incorporated

[37]'Die aussenpolitische und die völkerrechtliche Seite der Ersatzansprüche der jüdischen Naziopfer' [n.d.] (probably early in August 1945), AdR, BKA AA, Abteilung Politik 2 (Box 6) 1070–J/45.

[38]MRP 5, 29th January 1946, AdR; Knight, *Wortprotokolle, op. cit.*, p. 121.

[39]MRP 6, 30th January 1946, AdR; BGBl., Nr. 75, 1st February 1946 ('Bundesgesetz über öffentliche Verwalter und öffentliche Aufsichtspersonen').

[40]Cf. Adolf Schärf, *Österreichs Erneuerung 1945–1955. Das erste Jahrzehnt der zweiten Republik*, Vienna 1957, pp. 126–127.

[41]For example the decree calling on the population to register United Nations property (see *Wiener Zeitung*, 25th May 1946) was evidently widely ignored, and even sabotaged, but this did not provoke any Western protest; see minutes of the monthly meetings of the Four Power Reparations, Deliveries and Restitution Division of the Allied Commission, RDR/P (47) 4, 25th March 1947, PRO, FO1020/2561; Western support of oil interests, which has been taken as evidence of an economically motivated policy (for example by Reinhard Wagnleitner, 'Die britische Österreich-planung', in Anton Pelinka and Rolf Steininger [eds.], *Österreich und die Sieger; 40 Jahre 2. Republik – 30 Jahre Staatsvertrag*, Vienna 1986, pp. 67–78 here pp. 73–74) in fact suggests the reverse – *viz.* the primacy of politics. Cf. Robert Knight, *British Policy towards Occupied Austria 1945–1950*, Ph.D. Diss., London University 1986, pp. 38–39, 49–51, pp. 100–101.

[42]*New York Times*, 21st February 1946. Figl was speaking to the Anglo-American Palestine Committee (see above note 34).

into the Finance Ministry after a scandal over blocking the return of the "Aryanised" Guggenbach Paper Factory in return for a political donation.[43]

As important as the need to accommodate American concerns was the way the logic of Austria's opposition to Soviet claims to "German assets" was leading it towards some form of restitution legislation. The Soviet claims – damaging for Austria though they undoubtedly were – were not, as has often been argued, an exercise in legal sophistry designed to justify the seizure of Austrian economic goods and promote the Sovietisation of Austria. On the contrary, they arose squarely from the Moscow Declaration and the involvement of many Austrians in the war, whether in the depredations of the *Wehrmacht* and SS or in the form of the considerable German investment made in Austria in support of the war effort. The decision of the Potsdam conference of August 1945 to concede to the Soviet Union German external assets lying in their zone of Austria (and elsewhere in Eastern Europe) was thus neither a Western "blunder" nor a Soviet "trick" but in essence a recognition by the West that the Soviet Union had a better claim to German investment in Austria than Austria itself.[44] The problem was not, as usually argued, that "German assets" had not been clearly defined but that on any definition Austria stood to lose many capital assets.

This became clear for the first time in September when the Soviet authorities vetoed an Austrian law nationalising key industries including some German assets. Renner protested to the Soviet political adviser that "we no longer feel that this expression 'liberated country' is quite being reflected in our treatment".[45] He saw, correctly, that Austria's only hope of resisting the Soviet claims was to establish her legitimacy as a "counter-victim" of Nazi Germany. Though this was, admittedly, a fairly obvious line for a pragmatic politician to argue, some earlier statements had not entirely rejected all responsibility.[46] Now Renner sought to launch Austria's rehabilitation. He saw an early chance for doing so in August 1945 when the United Nations Rehabilitation and Relief Administration (UNRRA) decided to grant Austria the same relief as she was giving to the United Nations. This decision he explained to Cabinet "says more than has ever been said before: that we were not a belligerent state, that we are innocent and have the right to be supplied like all the others". The Austrian response welcoming the decision should be "the first part of a campaign, which Austria should begin at appropriate occasions in front of world opinion (*vor der Weltöffentlichkeit*)".[47]

[43]Krauland was arrested in 1949 and put on trial together with his leading officials in 1954. He was found not guilty.
[44]For a more detailed discussion see Robert Knight, *British Policy, op. cit.*, pp. 42–52; Reinhard Bollmus, 'Ein kalkuliertes Risiko? Grossbritannien, die USA und das "Deutsche Eigentum" auf der Konferenz von Potsdam', in Bischof and Leidenfrost (eds.), *op. cit.* pp. 107–127.
[45]KRP 29, 5th September 1945, AdR; Knight, *Wortprotokolle, op. cit.*, p. 35.
[46]The Declaration of Independence of 27th April for example had explicitly cited "in pflichtgemässer Erwägung" the last paragraph of the Moscow Declaration; cf. also the comments of the Minister of Justice Gerö that, "Erst später habe man sich entschlossen, die Okkupationstheorie als die für Österreich günstigere These zu vertreten." Justice Ministry, Cabinet Paper, 27th April 1948, Annex to MRP 109, AdR.
[47]KRP 27, 24th August 1945, AdR; Knight, *Wortprotokolle, op. cit.*, p. 35; cf. Wilfried Mähr, *Der Marshallplan in Österreich*, Graz – Vienna – Cologne 1989, p. 31.

The defence of German assets impinged on the restitution of "Aryanised" property in the following way: if the Austrian state were recognised as a liberated victim of Nazi Germany rather than as a quasi-belligerent then all transfers of property which had become German between 1938 and 1945 would be illegitimate because of the "general coercion" arising from the *Anschluss*. The Soviet Union would then have to prove in each individual case that the transfer had been legitimate rather than the other way round. The argument, in other words, made German take-overs of Austrian property analogous with "Aryanisation".[48] Early in 1946 some Austrian officials and politicians latched onto the 1943 London Declaration as one way of advancing this claim. By moving retrospectively into the "magic circle" of the declaratory powers, it could argue that German take-overs in Austria were as invalid as in other occupied countries. They would not be an aspect of "internal" German policy but, in international law, the result of an illegal action by a foreign country. Foreign Minister Gruber made it clear that he saw Austrian adherence to the declaration as a useful "political instrument" for strengthening his hand over German assets, because it provided a legal basis which "none of the four powers could reject because they had already signed it".[49]

However, the instrument had two edges. If all transfers were to be considered *ipso facto* coerced, "Aryanisation", which was coercion *par excellence*, would also have to be dealt with.[50] Some ministers saw the danger; Schärf continued to argue that any measures beyond the existing civil procedure were superfluous, and might even hinder restitution. Finance Minister Zimmermann pointed out that the declaration would open the floodgates for claims for the "entjudeten Vermögen" [sic!]. Gerö, the Minister of Justice, warned of the dangers of rigorously applying the principle of "forced transfers" to all transactions completed between 1938 and 1945. It would, he said create an unprecedented legal uncertainty ("eine Rechtsunsicherheit in unerhörtem Ausmass").[51] If these and other objections from interest groups were eventually overruled one reason was probably the deepening crisis over German assets. In February and April the Soviet authorities took over more land and factories. The culmination came early in July when the "Kurasov order" led to over 250 firms moving under Soviet administration.

By now Parliament had formally passed a "Nullification Law", declaring Austria's adherence to the London Declaration. Detailed provisions were to

---

[48]The way this process on the level of property transactions tied in with the more widespread tabuisation of antisemitism and trivialisation of the Holocaust cannot be discussed here.

[49]MRP 9, 22nd February, AdR; Knight, *Wortprotokolle, op. cit.*, pp. 129, 132.

[50]It is probably no accident that many of the Red Army take-overs of land in February were of "Aryanised" property. Report by Finanzamt, Korneuburg to Finanzlandesdirektion für Wien, Niederösterreich und Burgenland, 16th February 1946 (copy forwarded to Foreign Ministry) 100.559, AdR, BKA AA, Wirtschaftspolitische Abteilung, Box 3 (Finanzen 7 Generalia); conversely the argument was often advanced that Soviet confiscations stood in the way of a settlement of the "heirless property" fund.

[51]See above (note 49); see also MRP 10, 26th February 1946; Knight, *Wortprotokolle, op. cit.*, pp. 129–130.

follow.[52] But the tactical hopes placed in the declaration were soon disappointed. Even Western officials were not ready to endorse a blanket presumption of a "general coercion" for all transactions between 1938 and 1945. Instead they merely sought to exclude assets where it could be shown specifically that pressure had been applied.[53] The Soviet defence of their take-overs brought up this point:

> "The Nazis had abolished the Austrian State true enough, but they had not abolished private property. Private owners had had full freedom of action and hence their sale had to be recognised unless in individual cases something else could be proved."[54]

The most obvious refutation of this argument (apart from state assets) was "Aryanisation". It was no accident that immediately after the "Kurasov order" Figl cited several Jewish property owners in support of his thesis that after March 1938 everything took place under force and duress ("ab März 1938 [ist] alles unter Zwang und Druck geschehen".) Yet at the same time to illustrate the economic damage the Soviet take-overs would do he chose three firms or sectors which had been on the other side of the fence – having either gained from "Aryanisation" or expanded enormously as part of the Nazi war economy.[55]

Restitution at all events – as a by-product of the government's policy – now had to be tackled. On 26th July Parliament passed the first Restitution Law covering the relatively small number of cases where property had been taken over by the federal or provincial authorities.[56] The Second Law concerned property which had fallen to the state as a result of other measures, including denazification.

The real political hot potato was the restitution of property which had come into private or corporate hands. An early indication of the strength of opposition to a full-scale restitution had already come in the course of the parliamentary debate over the "Nullification Law" as Ernst Kolb, a deputy of the *Österreichische Volkspartei* (ÖVP), and later Minister of Trade, argued that Austria had nothing to make good since it had done nothing wrong. On the contrary it had prior claim to *Wiedergutmachung* since a considerable part of the property which had to change hands had belonged to the state. The word "Aryanisation" had been used in order to conceal the fact that the majority of the confiscated property had been withdrawn not for racial but for political reasons".[57] A comparison between the final version of the Third Restitution Law and the draft discussed in cabinet in

---

[52]BGBl. N. 106, 25th May 1945 (Bundesgesetz über die Nichtigkeiterklärung von Rechtsgeschäften und sonstigen Rechtshandlungen, die während der deutschen Besetzung Österreichs erfolgt sind).

[53]Clark to Kurasov, 10th July 1946, FRUS 1946, vol. V, Washington 1969, pp. 353–354.

[54]Meeting between Gruber and the Soviet Deputy Political Director, Koptelov, 13th July 1946, Alfons Schilcher, *Österreich und die Grossmächte 1945–1955*, Vienna–Salzburg 1980, document 53, pp. 107–109.

[55]The three were Zistersdorf Oil, the Danube Steam Shipping Company and the banking conglomorate Schoeller-Bleckmann, MRP 30, 6th July 1946, AdR. Figl's comments that Jewish property, such as that taken over by the Red Army, should be put in the hands of the "österreichische Ansiedlungsgesellschaft" until the legal questions were "cleared up" also suggests a less than clear-cut commitment to restitution; see above and AdR, MRP 30, 6th July 1946.

[56]BGBl., Nr. 156, 26th July 1946 (Erstes Rückstellungsgesetz).

[57]*Wiener Zeitung*, 16th May 1946.

November shows that such viewpoints carried weight. In compromising between domestic and international considerations the law was, on balance, more favourable to the former.[58] The first three paragraphs appeared to provide an absolute commitment to restitution of all property which had been "acquired" (*entzogen*) "in connection with the National Socialist take-over of power". Several of the paragraphs which followed, however, substantially weakened the force of this.

Firstly, personal effects, household goods, as well as bearer shares and bonds were excluded, unless the claimant could trace them. This made it less effective than the equivalent German legislation, which required merely that property had to be identified as having been seized. As a result the scope of restitution was, for all practical purposes, restricted to real estate and businesses.[59]

Secondly, the presumption of a "general coercion" was undermined by concessions made in the case of those transfers where the rules of fair trade (*redlicher Verkehr*) were considered to have been complied with "in other respects" (*im übrigen*). A leading government lawyer spoke of rewarding "relative decency" (*relative Anständigkeit*).[60] If the Restitution Commission thought fit, the original owner might be required to pay not merely for investments made on the property, charges, taxes, mortgages repayments and an "appropriate recompense" ("eine angemessene Vergütung seiner Tätigkeit") for the activity of the "acquirer" (*Erwerber*).[61] He could even be ordered by the Commission to return the purchase price – even if he had not been able to dispose of it freely. In other words the fact that property had been sold to pay for discriminatory taxes would not be taken into consideration.[62]

Thirdly, meeting some objections of agricultural interests, the Commission had discretion to limit the restitution of large estates which had been subdivided and used for land settlement. If restitution was contrary to "an overwhelming

[58]MRP 45, 12th November 1946, AdR; Knight, *Wortprotokolle, op. cit.*, pp. 147–157 and Appendices 8 and 9; BGBl., Nr. 54, 6th February 1947 (Bundesgesetz über die Nichtigkeit von Vermögensentziehungen [Drittes Rückstellungsgesetz]); cf. the 12-page submission from the *Österreichischer Sparkassen- und Giroverband* to the *Kammer für Handel, Gewerbe und Industrie*, 10th October 1946; and the minutes of the parliamentary subcommittee for property control, 29th January 1947, Dokumentationsarchiv des österreichischen Widerstands, Vienna, Akt. 6200b (Ludwig Nachlass). Kastner's view in Davy *et al.* (eds.), *op. cit.*, pp. 194–195, that the law attempted "die beiderseitige Interessenlage zu berücksichtigen" is undermined by the evidence presented here.

[59]See 'Claims of Jews from Austria', by Dr F. R. Bienenfeld (WJC), September 1952 (unpublished report), p. 9, IfZ, Vienna. Löwy PP.

[60]Willhelm Rauscher, 'Probleme des Dritten Rückstellungsgesetzes', *Österreichische Juristenzeitschrift*, 2, No. 18 (26th September 1947), p. 387.

[61]Kastner (*loc. cit.*, p. 195) considers it "bemerkenswert" that no allowance was made for the devaluation of currency when calculating these payments to be made to the "acquirer". Whether this really brought "wesentliche Vorteile" to the owner, who was generally resident abroad, and was faced by both considerable practical obstacles and currency restrictions in realising his asset in view of the post-war fall in land prices is doubtful.

[62]Art. 6 (1); in the negotiations for the fulfilment of Article 26 of the State Treaty Gottfried Klein, the leading expert of the Finance Ministry, estimated the value of *Reichsfluchtsteuer* and *Judenvermögensabgabe* levied in Austria as about 328 million RM. Cf. Blair (British Embassy, Vienna) to Thomas (FO), 11th October 1956, PRO, FO 371/124114/RR1461/5. Cf. note 3 above.

public interest" the Commission could restrict restitution to a basic recognition of the claim.[63]

Fourthly, the fact that the Restitution Commissions were allowed substantial discretion brought into play the social and political interests seeking to restrict the scope of restitution. Apart from the examples already mentioned the Commission could, in the enforcement of payment of charges on the original owner, restrict his or her right to dispose of property and even ("in especially urgent cases") order it to be taken as security. Furthermore the professional judges in the Commissions were to be outweighed by two expert lay judges ("fachmännische Laienrichter").[64]

Finally, two of the thorniest restitution questions were left out of the law altogether – the restitution of tenancies and leaseholds and the establishment of a fund out of "heirless property".[65]

In short, the Third Restitution Law, far from being the application of the London Declaration involved a series of concessions to the subjective "normalcy" of "Aryanisation" and the widespread Austrian perception that it had been legitimate. Compared to both West Germany under direct military government and those former occupied Western countries like Holland or Norway with which the Austrian government sought to be equated the Law was favourable towards the "Aryaniser".[66]

IV

As the Law entered its final stages, in February the first discussions about an Austrian treaty had just started in London. These discussions have generally been viewed one-dimensionally as a struggle to prevent a real or imagined Soviet take-over of the country. This obscures an important aspect of Austrian policy – the use of its position as a Western bulwark against the Soviet Union to assert its claim as a "collective victim" of the Third *Reich*. In line with this it denied all claims on it arising from Austrian complicity in Nazi policy and even sought, at least on paper, to advance claims of its own against Germany.[67] Foreign Minister Karl Gruber left for London in January 1947 aiming "in the light of the London Declaration to have the principle laid down that all legal transactions completed after March 1938 were void because there had been general coercion". This was coupled with a defensive aim: to avoid commitment to compensating victims of the Third *Reich* by referring them to Germany. The compensation claims of dismissed public employees alone, it was feared, could amount to 1.5 thousand million Schillings.[68]

[63]3rd RG, Art. 23 (4).
[64]3rd RG, Arts. 23 (2), 16 (4).
[65]3rd RG, Arts. 14 (1), 30 (2).
[66]Schwarz, *Rückerstattung, op. cit.*, pp. 329–340.
[67]For background see the standard work Gerald Stourzh, *Geschichte des Staatsvertrages 1945–1955*, Vienna 1980.
[68]MRP 52, 14th January 1947, AdR; Interministerielle Konferenz, 4th January 1947, AdR, BKA AA (Österreichische Botschaft London), Box 4 (Diverses), zu Zl. 105.139–pol–47.

The provisions for compensation for damage to property of United Nations citizens[69] – though primarily intended to assert Western pre-war claims to commercial and industrial interests – seemed to the Austrian government to raise the spectre of Austrian refugees who had become citizens since leaving Austria making similar claims.[70] Gruber argued to the Foreign Office that this would bring the danger "of arousing afresh the embers of antisemitism in Austria, while it would also appear unfair that these Austrians who had escaped should receive better terms than those who had remained and been placed in concentration camps".[71] Krauland warned, ominously, that the Austrians would probably be forced to introduce a special tax to finance any special treatment for Jews.[72] On the other side of the political spectrum the Austrian Socialist press *attaché* in London, Walter Wodak, lobbied his Labour Party contacts with anti-capitalist arguments. The compensation provisions, he warned, would mean handing over Austria to American capital.[73] In the defensive words of the *Ballhausplatz* report on the results of the first round of negotiations:

> "The Jewish organisations organised an extensive offensive . . . The relevant submissions of the 'Jewish World Congress' [sic] are couched in spiteful tones [in gehässiger Tonart vorgetragen] and demand bluntly [unverblümt] that Austria be burdened with responsibility for her participation in the war."[74]

Western officials were generally sympathetic to Austrian arguments. The Americans were not prepared to discriminate against citizens accepted since 1938, but they were ready to lower the level of compensation for damage to that given by Austria to its own citizens, that is none at all. British officials, for their part, accepted the arguments that Jewish victims should not be given "special treatment" both on grounds of "equity" and because such treatment would, allegedly, encourage antisemitism. Though some of his officials continued to battle for British commercial interests Ernest Bevin signalled his readiness to accommodate the Austrians in the "Judenfrage" (sic).[75]

On restitution proper Gruber had little alternative to committing himself to a full extent. Shortly after his arrival he told journalists that although there were still problems about property without heirs, Austria was ready to guarantee *"Wiedergutmachung"* to every Austrian who had lost his property under Nazi laws, without distinction. If Jewish organisations demanded compensation for indi-vidually named Jews Austria would not oppose this. When these comments were

---

[69]Article 42 in the 1947 draft, article 25 in the final version.

[70]See Knight, *British Policy, op. cit.*, pp. 102–105.Both Stourzh, *op. cit.*, pp. 30–31, and Wagnleitner, 'Walter Wodak in London oder die Schwierigkeit, Sozialist und Diplomat zu sein', in Gerhard Botz *et al.* (eds.), *Bewegung und Klasse: Studien zur österreichischen Arbeitergeschichte*, Vienna 1978, pp. 217–242, neglect this aspect. Wagnleitner in particular accepts uncritically the SPÖ version that there was a threat from American capital.

[71]Meeting between Gruber and Oliver Harvey (Deputy Undersecretary, Foreign Office), 11th February 1947, PRO, FO 371/63955/C2941.

[72]Note of a conversation between Krauland and the French diplomat de Lavergne, 28th March 1947, AdR, BKA AA (Österreichische Botschaft London), Box 10, Zl.31-StV/47.

[73]Wagnleitner, 'Walter Wodak', *loc. cit.*; see also Knight, *British Policy, op. cit.*, pp. 101–103.

[74]'Bericht über die Ergebnisse der Londoner Konferenz', 4th March 1947, PRO, FO 371/63963/C6532.

[75]'Zusammenfassung der Aussprachen mit BEVIN etc.' [n.d.], AdR, BKA AA, Politik II, Box 41 (Staatsvertrag), Zl. 77–StM/47.

relayed home they were cautiously welcomed by the head of the Jewish community, but led Peter Krauland to complain in Cabinet that Gruber had made a "180 degree" switch in the agreed policy. If Gruber had been correctly reported, the government now owed the public an explanation.[76] The disposal of heirless property seems to have caused special concern to Krauland, whose ministry controlled it. He reported that it was "not pleasant to hear that he would have to set up a fund for every minority group, especially as there is no guarantee on who would be in charge of running it and because the question of Aryan or non-Aryan [sic!] is still open."[77] In fact behind the scenes the Austrian delegation succeeded in blunting the effect of Jewish lobbying.[78] The final version of the clause protecting the "property, rights and interests of minority groups"[79] included the concession that the details were to be worked out "in agreement with" the Austrian government not merely "in consultation" with them as originally suggested.[80] The long negotiations over the establishment of the fund after the State Treaty came into force showed that the difference was not negligible.

These discussions did not attract much publicity compared to the dispute over German assets, which appeared to be the cause of the deadlock in which the talks ended on 24th April. Yet, as already suggested, this question needs to be viewed in a wider context in which restitution also has its place. For at its heart was not the technical definition of what was or was not a German asset or even the Western wish to block an outrageous or sinister Soviet demand. It was the fact that German investment and "normal" non-coercive activity in Austria after 1938 had been so extensive that by any definition the Potsdam decision gave the Soviet Union a legitimate claim to a sizeable economic enclave in Eastern Austria. The point was that the West and in particular the United States were now no longer ready to accept the risks of such an enclave.

Their problem was that they could not argue this on the merits of the reality of the (non-Jewish) Austrian experience of the *Anschluss*. The wearisome investigations of the Austrian Treaty Commission over the summer of 1947 confirmed this. They showed in detail what had already emerged in outline in Moscow – that many of the properties claimed by the Russians as "German assets" had indeed become German in a normal, or quasi-normal, commercial way.[81] Any

[76]MRP 54, 25th January 1947, AdR. Knight *Wortprotokolle, op. cit.*, p. 167.

[77]MRP 64 a(usserordentlich), 17th April 1947, AdR; Knight, *Wortprotokolle, op. cit.*, p. 171.

[78]See British Foreign Office minutes on the representations made by the World Jewish Congress early in February, PRO, FO 371/64060/C2896/C2897.

[79]Article 44 in the 1947 version, Article 26 in the final version.

[80]Text in Stourzh, *op. cit.*, p. 289.

[81]And the most "copper-bottomed" cases of coercive transfers had been cases of "Aryanisation". Out of 43 larger firms with over 50% German interest 20 had been German in March 1938, 6 had been acquired as a result of "Aryanisation", 7 had been normal purchases from the United Nations or Austrians; Out of 172 medium sized firms the figures were 92, 51 and 6 (the other cases involved bank transactions), Vienna to Foreign Office, 3rd August 1947, PRO, FO 371/63985/C10416; Memorandum of US Delegation to the Austrian Treaty Commission, German Assets in Austrian Industry, CFM/ATC (47)56, 6th August 1947, also French Statement of French Delegation, CFM/ATC (47) 65, 13th August 1947, paragraph II, 1, American Records of the Austrian Treaty Commission, IfZ, Vienna.

agreement would simply have to by-pass altogether the problem of defining
"coercion". The proposal presented by General Cherrière in October 1947
attempted to do just that by offering to buy out the Soviet Union from Austria
with a combination of oil assets, Danube shipping assets and US Dollars.[82] Seen
in the wider context outlined here this was not merely an ingenious scheme – it
was an American offer to buy the Austrians out of the debt they had incurred to
the Russians through their involvement in the Third *Reich*.

V

By the time restitution proper began in the second half of 1947 its foreign policy
aspect had become much less important.[83] The crude statistics of the restitution
which took place over the following years are easily told; by 1955, when the
Restitution Commissions had virtually ceased work 48,795 claims had been dealt
with under the terms of the first three laws, the overwhelming majority (34,750)
under those of the third. Of these 30,298 had been resolved.[84] About a quarter of
these claims had been granted without qualification, about a third had been
"settled" in some form or other.[85] In the absence of information about the details
of the judgements, in particular about what payments were involved in the
"settlements" the statistics are difficult to interpret, but one point can be made
with some measure of certainty; since restitution was largely restricted to real
estate there was a strong disincentive for plaintiffs, often living far away, to
pursue a long and complex legal case for property which they often did not intend
to maintain. The settlement therefore often revolved around the question of how
much more the "acquirer" should pay the original owner on top of the original
price.[86]

   By contrast the politics of restitution, which are the main concern here, are
relatively transparent. Though complaints were voiced almost from the start

---

[82]See Stourzh, *op. cit.*, p. 185; Knight, *British Policy, op. cit.*, p. 136.
[83]See the unsuccessful lobbying by Jewish organisations of the Foreign Office in 1948; PRO, FO 371/70410/C239; 1949, PRO, FO 371/76436/C1610, FO 371/76439/C2936.
[84]*Wiener Zeitung*, 25th May 1955; the figures given by Chancellor Julius Raab in a radio speech shortly before (*Wiener Zeitung*, 8th March 1955) need to be treated with scepticism. For example the figure of 43,000 he gave for positive decisions included 15,000 settlements and rejected claims. Cf. Malcolm (British Embassy, Vienna) to Young (Foreign Office), 9th March 1955, PRO, FO 371/117850/RR1571.
[85]'Status of Restitution of Alienated Property', Gottfried Klein for the Minister (of Finance), 21st May 1952; (copy, IfZ, Vienna, Löwy PP). The figures up to and including April 1952, (excluding cases dealt with by the *Oberste Rückstellungskommission*) show that 29,406 claims had been submitted, 4,490 withdrawn, 1,276 transferred, 9,168 settled, 6,635 granted, 2,590 denied and 5,247 were still pending. See also Walch, *op. cit.*, Annex 1/1.
[86]Raab put the value of all restituted property including "settlements" at 2,000 million Schillings (but see note 84 above). Two years earlier the "Claims Committee" had estimated that in all the value of all property (excluding property of the Jewish Community) saved after 1938 or returned after 1945 was 780 million RM out of 3,000 million RM (see note 10 above). The decisions of the Restitution Commissions are difficult to interpret in isolation from the details of the cases; see the compilation in Ludwig Heller and Wilhelm Rauscher (eds.), *Die Rechtsprechung der Rückstellungskommissionen* (Neue Folge), Wien 1949ff.

that the Commissions were favouring the "Aryanisers",[87] within Austria they were soon drowned by increasingly vociferous protests against both existing and possible future restitution legislation. This opposition received considerable impetus in May 1948 when voting rights were restored to "less implicated Nazis", many of whom had been beneficiaries of "Aryanisation". Their increased assertiveness is shown by the founding in June 1948 of a *Verband der Rückstellungs-betroffenen* (League of Restitution Victims). Its freely distributed magazine *Unser Recht* proclaimed its aim as the redress of what was described as the "monstrous injustice" created by the restitution legislation. More important than its mixture of thinly veiled antisemitism, distortion of the reality of "Aryanisation" and pose of martyrdom is the resonance it found in a broader political spectrum. By appeals to "common sense", self-evident "fairness", and a high-flown invocation of Western legal traditions, above all that of "equality before the law" it was able to gain the moral high ground.[88] Like denazification, restitution legislation now began to be increasingly portrayed as an Allied *Diktat*.

As early as the summer of 1948 first consideration was given in Krauland's Ministry of Property Control and Economic Planning (BMfVSWP) to a revision of the restitution law or, alternatively, to setting a time limit for the submission of restitution claims. The Minister of Agriculture Kraus, was the chief mover, given shifting support by Krauland but opposed by Minister of Justice Gerö, who feared that a revision would impose an impossible administrative burden on a judiciary already under great stress.[89] At a cabinet meeting early in November 1948 Kraus successfully opposed extending the deadline for restitution applications.[90] The decision provoked an uproar among Vienna's Jewish community. A 9-point resolution was passed calling for the government not only to extend the time-limit, but also to grant restitution of flats and take action on heirless property. Perhaps most decisive of all was the intervention of the American legal official Albert Löwy.[91] Shortly after Figl tried to placate Kraus: "we know that these measures are hard for agriculture sector. But international policy (*Weltpolitik*) is forcing us to take them and there is no need for us to make enemies for ourselves in the world." Graf complained that the language used by the protest meeting showed that those "whom it depends on are not contributing to making peace". It was agreed to extend the limit for another six months.[92] The controversy over the law raged in the press and pamphlets. Löwy judged that

[87]Cf. minute by Sir Alfred Brown (Legal Adviser, FO) on complaints by the Anglo-Jewish Association, 13th November 1947, PRO, FO/371/64060/C14911; see also *Wiener Zeitung*, 3rd March 1948.

[88]Cf. the series of articles on the restitution laws in the *Wiener Zeitung*, 16th and 30th December 1948; 6th, 8th, 9th and 12th January 1949.

[89]MRP 130, 26th October 1948, AdR.

[90]MRP 132, 9th November 1948, AdR; Knight, *Wortprotokolle, op. cit.*, pp. 195–198.

[91]*Die Gemeinde*, No. 4 (December 1948); Confidential Memo, 22nd November 1948, IfZ, Vienna, Löwy PP.

[92]MRP 135, 30th November 1948, AdR; Knight, *Wortprotokolle, op. cit.*, p. 200; see also *Die Gemeinde*, No. 4 (December 1948), p. 3.

"the emasculation of the restitution laws" was "so popular a course of action" that the Government would not reverse it without American intervention.[93]

In March 1949 the *Verband der Unabhängigen* (VdU) was formed to attract the former Nazi members and their families. One of its leaders Fritz Stüber described the restitution laws as "Austria's genuflection of contrition (*Bussfall*) in front of foreign capital".[94] The VdU was formed under the active patronage of the Socialist Interior Minister Helmer, who hoped to split the Conservative vote. Part of the ÖVP, on the other hand, tried to woo former Nazis directly. Julius Raab, head of the industrialists' wing (Chancellor 1953–1961), one of the main instigators, was sympathetic to the arguments of the "restitution victims".[95] Another, Alfons Gorbach, who later succeeded Raab as Chancellor (1961–1964), in spite of having been a (Catholic) political prisoner in Dachau had more sympathy with the former soldiers than Jewish refugees, as a speech in the 1949 election campaign made clear:

> "Nowhere in the events of recent years was there so much genuine decency, so much self-denying fulfilment of duty as with the soldiers of this war . . . The emigrant gentlemen may inject as much moralistic acid (Moralinsäure) as they will; those who held their own out there in the toughest test know better what decency is than those who took themselves abroad into safety at the first ripple of the blue ocean . . . I deny the emigrants any right to take part in the discussion of the Nazi question."[96]

After the success of the VdU in the October 1949 election, which gave them 15 seats in Parliament, the pressure to amend the restitution law increased. Early in the new session Gorbach put forward an amendment to the restitution bill and he was quickly followed by the VdU in the new year.[97] Detailed discussions then began between the two coalition parties. They were opposed both by the United States High Commissioner Geoffrey Keyes[98] and by Gerö's successor as Minister of Justice Otto Tschadek, who forecast that it would mean re-opening about 70% of the restitution cases already decided.[99] But Tschadek was not supported by many in the SPÖ and the failure of the State Treaty negotiations at the end of

[93]'Latest Developments in Restitution Legislation in Austria', US Legal Division, Löwy, 19th January 1949, IfZ, Vienna, Löwy PP.
[94]Fritz Stüber, *Ich war Abgeordneter. Die Entstehung der Freiheitlichen Opposition in Österreich*, Graz–Stuttgart 1974, pp. 144f. Max Riedlsperger, *The Lingering Shadow of Nazism. The Austrian Independent Party Movement since 1945* (Eastern European Monographs 92), New York 1978, ignores this and other unsavoury aspects of the VdU.
[95]Cf. *Wiener Montag*, 25th June 1951,
[96]"Nirgendwo im Geschehen der letzten Jahre hat es so viel echte Anständigkeit, so viel selbstverleugnende Pflichterfüllung gegeben wie eben bei den Soldaten dieses Krieges . . . Da mögen die Herren Emigranten noch soviel Moralinsäure verspritzen; jene, die draussen in härtester Prüfung ihren Mann gestanden haben, wissen besser, was anständig ist, als jene, die sich beim ersten Kräuseln des blauen Ozeans auf Übersee in Sicherheit gebracht haben . . . Ich spreche den Emigranten auch das Recht ab, in der NS-Frage mitzureden." *Salzburger Volkszeitung*, 2nd June 1949 cited in Manfred Rauchensteiner, *Die Zwei. Die Grosse Koalition in Österreich, 1945–1966*, Vienna 1987, pp. 134–135, who, remarkably, does not find these words worthy of any other comment than the preface that Gorbach "sprach sicherlich vielen [ehemaligen Soldaten] aus der Seele" (sic!).
[97]Löwy Memoranda, 19th January 1950, B–48122, and 23rd February 1950, B–48122, IfZ Vienna, Löwy PP.
[98]Keyes to Figl, 23rd March 1950; Knight, *Wortprotokolle, op. cit.*, p. 221.
[99]Blair (British Embassy, Vienna) to Porter (FO), 20th April 1950, PRO, FO 371/84969/C2756.

1949 meant that foreign policy considerations carried less weight than before. Minister of Finance Margaretha told an American official that the ÖVP "couldn't tolerate the continuance of injustices created by the existing law . . . The Austrians had been told by the occupying powers that they couldn't have a treaty unless they passed the law and now they have no treaty and only a law which creates injustices."[100]

On 13th July 1950, the final day of the parliamentary year, a bill was introduced with the support of both major parties. It proposed a number of amendments to the benefit of the "acquirer". The most important one would allow restitution cases to be re-opened in cases where the firm had been insolvent or heavily in debt or where landed or wooded estates had been divided up. It also determined that agricultural property should go back to the "acquirer" if the claimant failed to prove a qualification for operating it, or where the next owner had himself been a victim of the Nazis. Perhaps the most radical feature was the proposal to use "heirless property" to alleviate the hardship of four groups including those who had acquired "Aryanised" property in good faith and who themselves had been subject to political persecution or bought property to assist political victims. This tied in with the widespread claim of the "restitution victims" that they had bought Jewish property out of altruistic motives, above all to help Jews escape.[101]

When the bill was introduced in the Autumn session of the Austrian Parliament the Americans, especially the Legal Division, took up a stronger stand against the law than the government had expected. According to a British observer the American attaché Dowling "was particularly concerned that if the Austrians were permitted to get away with so brazen a violation of one of the Treaty terms it would serve as an indication of Austrian readiness to violate any other provisions of the Treaty without compunction".[102] Keyes complained formally to Figl that the proposed law was in contradiction to the draft article of the State Treaty and a radical departure from the 1946 "Nullification Law", and he repeated earlier protests at the failure to implement further restitution measures and the "heirless property" fund. In Cabinet Tschadek saw his warnings against the law proved right, Schärf described the American intervention as outrageous (*unerhört*) and Figl complained that "the Jews are besieging us." ("Die Juden rennen uns die Tür ein".) But ministers were not willing to force the issue. They were also in a sense hoist by their own legal petard. The Americans considered the proposed law to be in violation of the London Declaration. Though the cabinet committee set up to review the situation now (tentatively) queried Austria's obligation to a law which was "not a generally recognised rule of international law to which Austria . . . would be bound", and

---

[100]Memorandum by EM (= Edward Magg, Legal *Attaché* at the American Legation), 17th April 1950, PRO, FO 371/84969/C2756.

[101]'Entwurf eines Bundesgesetzes über den Härteausgleich in Rückstellungsachen', *Wiener Zeitung*, 29th June 1950. Dowling (US *Chargé*) to State Department, Vienna 97, 27th July 1950 (Copy), Löwy PP, IfZ, Vienna. For portrayals of "altruistic Aryanisations" see *Unser Recht, passim*.

[102]Memorandum by Jerome Jacobson (BDBJ) to Beckelman (Joint), 4th September 1950, Board of Deputies of British Jews Archive, Folder C11/8/1/3.

to which Austria had not been a party,[103] it had been invoked too often in the past in Austria's interests to be simply thrown overboard. In December the proposed law was dropped, amid angry reaction from the VdU.

The pressure to revise the restitution law needs to be seen in connexion with a basket of measures aimed at hastening the re-integration of Nazis, providing amnesties for those still affected (such as those returning from Soviet imprisonment), dismantling the remaining denazification measures and indemnifying those affected for the penalties they had suffered. One aspect of this was that the remnants of the anti-fascist leadership of the ÖVP, like Education Minister Hurdes and Chancellor Figl, found themselves increasingly on the defensive while the business circles surrounding Raab gained the upper hand. Hurdes now commented plaintively on the way former Nazi civil servants were being restored their pension rights, presenting his case, significantly, in the form of a negative argument – that Nazis should not be given privileged treatment:

> "The principle of compensation for damages is applied to the Nazis but not to the victims of the Nazis. This is, repeatedly, creating ill-will. The Nazi victims are continually told: the poor State cannot pay. But with the National Socialist the State can pay. This is surely applying double standards. I don't want to put pressure on (hetzen), but if the State points to its financial condition with regard to the Nazi victims it might be worth considering if the National Socialists couldn't be treated in the same way."[104]

Hurdes's voice carried little weight and the success of the VdU presidential candidate in 1951 increased the competition for the former Nazi votes even more. After much manoeuvring there came a further initiative in 1952. This time the government ignored American objections and parliament passed a *"Wiedererwerbsgesetz"* which allowed "Aryanisers" under some circumstances to regain property they had lost through restitution. Another law, submitted simultaneously, allowed Nazis who had lost property as a result of denazification to regain it. In a rare display of unanimity both measures were vetoed by the Allied Council.[105] But in any case much of what they had meant to achieve – aside from the retroactive effect – was now probably being accomplished by the Restitution Commissions exercising their discretionary powers[106] in combination with the credit institutes. Wilhelm Krell administrative director (*Amtsdirektor*) of Vienna's Jewish community described the situation as "catastrophic". Nearly everyone to whom property had been transferred was now regarded as having dealt decently and fairly (*redlich*) so that the full purchase price had to be returned. Since 99% of Jewish claimants did not have the means and were unable to get credit from the

---

[103]Keyes note to Figl, 1st September 1950 (official Austrian translation) and MRP 216, 5th September 1950, AdR; Knight, *Wortprotokolle, op. cit.*, pp. 229–234.

[104]MRP 212, 18th July 1950, AdR; Knight, *Ministerratsprotokolle, op. cit.*, pp. 225f.

[105]*Wiener Zeitung*, 19th August 1952; Figl appears to have made a linkage with the question of an amnesty for returning prisoners of war, most of whom had been accused as war criminals, and the release of "heirless property". Cf. Rauchensteiner, *op. cit.*, pp. 174–175, who, however, wrongly implies that Figl's proposal to transfer "heirless property" in return for American compromise on the "Spätheimkehreramnestie" was a fresh initiative on his part to break the deadlock, in response to which "die Amerikaner blieben hart".

[106]See above, p. 427.

credit houses the results were either settlements in favour of the "Aryaniser" or compulsory auction of the property.[107] The law passed by parliament in 1954 two years later (*"Vermögensrückübertragungsgesetz"*) aimed at handing back property forfeited as a result of denazification was also vetoed by the Allied Council. The American High Commissioner complained that it contravened the London Declaration and called on the victims to be given priority over former Nazis.[108] After the State Treaty of May 1955, though restitution was placed on a new legal footing, the dismantling of denazification and the compensation for damages incurred through it was rapidly completed.[109]

VI

The American authorities had thus successfully blocked the attempts to revise the restitution legislation formally, but they were not able or willing to force the Austrian government to take any further steps; in particular on the two most controversial issues: the establishment of a fund from "heirless" property[110] and the restitution of tenancy and leasehold rights.

The fund from "heirless property" could perhaps be supported by the argument that the property should not go to the government but to the victims. The line adopted, internally, by Austrian official circles was subtly different, however. As early as August 1945 the *Ballhausplatz* had suggested that rather than have "very distant relatives . . . who normally would never have come into possession of concrete properties" inheriting, it would be wiser to restrict the right of inheritance and "to use the property which had become heirless to compensate the other victims of the Nazis".[111] In line with this the rights of inheritance in the restitution laws were restricted to "spouse, forbears (immediate) and descendants, siblings and their children and other legal heirs who had shared a household".[112] Both this exceptional over-ruling of the normal principles of the civil code and even the application of a fund raised from overwhelmingly Jewish property to include political victims might theoretically be justified – if the funds were indeed made available as soon as possible. In fact it soon became clear that the authorities, above all Krauland's Ministry, which had the responsibility for "heirless property", were determined to delay it.

In Spring 1948 impatience grew among the American Jewish organisations

[107]Wilhelm Krell (*Amtsdirektor*) to Fred Reiss, 28th February 1951, IKGA, Vienna, File Externa 1951.

[108]*Wiener Zeitung*, 14th August 1954; Minutes of the Allied Council for Austria, 224th Session, 13th August 1954.

[109]Stiefel, *op. cit.*, p. 314; Articles 8 to 10 of the State Treaty impose some formal obligations on Austria, i.a. to maintain denazification legislation, but they do not seem to have ever been the subject of international interest.

[110]The term included "unclaimed" property. For the German practice see Schwarz, 'Wiedergutmachung', *loc. cit.*, pp. 37–38; and Hockerts, 'Anwälte der Verfolgten. Die United Restitution Organisation', in Herbst and Goschler (eds.), *op. cit.*, pp. 249–271.

[111]See note 37 above, p. 422.

[112]Second Restitution Law, Art. 2 (2); Third Restitution Law Art. 14 (2).

and the Jewish community in Vienna, which was only being kept financially above water by means of massive American aid. Harold Trobe, the representative of the chief benefactor the community, the American Joint Distribution Committee, now pushed for a fund to be set up. He described the wretched condition of those Jews who had returned or had survived – some of them forced to stay in temporary camps – and proposed a 25 million Schilling advance.[113] His proposal was discussed at the Cabinet meeting of 9th November mentioned earlier.[114] The discussion it sparked off graphically encapsulated the tension between antisemitism, political pragmatism and post-war legitimacy, already noted; the Minister of Agriculture Kraus strongly opposed the suggestion. It would be contrary to the constitution, he argued, for "one race" to receive special privileges: since "others, who did not go away are not receiving any support but the Jews are to get some". The Minister of Transport added that the *Bundesbahn* had 82 million Schillings in unpaid bills. Krauland tried to "complete the picture" by pointing out that the 9,000 Jews living in Vienna were living in wretched conditions and should be helped "if it is necessary". The influence of the Jews in America also had to be taken into account. When the Minister of Trade Ernst Kolb responded with the by now conventional thesis of Austria's collective innocence he was rebuffed in cynical fashion by Helmer:

> "Kolb: "Austria received none of these assets and the injustice done to the Jews was not done by Austria. Austria and the Greater German *Reich* are two different things.
> Helmer: What was taken away from the Jews can't be put down to the 'Greater German *Reich*'. A large part comes down to our dear fellow citizens right enough. That is a statement which corresponds to the facts. But on the other hand . . . everywhere I can see only Jewish expansion, among the doctors and in commerce – especially in Vienna. But we can't implement a special scheme (eine Separataktion). But the question is also a political one. In 1945 the Nazis also had everything taken away from them and we can now see a situation in which even a National Socialist *Akademiker* has to work on a building-site . . . we are no longer living in 1945. The English are now fighting the Jews: the Americans have not kept their obligations. The atrocities of the Jews in the Palestine war have had an effect . . . I would be in favour of dragging things out (dass man die Sache in die Länge zieht). Just consider it, we should say . . . we have to take different things into consideration. There are people who understand that alright. The Jews will understand that themselves when they realise that a lot of people are opposed to them. We should simply say to him, [Trobe] We'll see about it. (Wir werden schon schauen)."

Helmer was supported by Figl. An advance to the Jewish community would not only produce domestic and foreign problems; it would make an unfair distinction to the disadvantage of National Socialists. But, on the other hand, he cautioned, "at present we cannot afford to say 'no' either. We'll have to say, 'give us time to get our budget straight and see where and how we can help you . . .' "[115]

Two months later Max Isenbergh of the American Jewish Committee also approached ministers about an advance but was rebuffed with a variety of more or less specious arguments. The most significant was the oft-repeated cynical

---

[113]'Memorandum über die Probleme der Juden in Wien', Trobe, 12th March 1948; Trobe to (US Political Adviser) Erhardt, 16th July 1948, Archive of the Israelitischen Kultusgemeinde, Vienna, File Berichte und Protokolle, 1948–1956.
[114]See above, p. 431.
[115]MRP 132, 9th November 1948, AdR; Knight, *Wortprotokolle, op. cit.*, pp. 195–198.

objection that a loan to the Jews would be special treatment for Jews and thus a perpetuation of Nazi racial discrimination. Helmer was more open when he asked why the Jews could not "earn their own living like everyone else in Austria". Isenbergh concluded, more charitably than the situation justified, that "regardless of whether they may privately favour just treatment of Nazi victims, they are primarily concerned, in view of the coming elections, to avoid any legislation inimical to the interests of former Nazis, who, with their families and friends, constitute a strong voting bloc".[116] Gerhard Riegner from the World Jewish Congress (WJC) Geneva office followed Trobe and Isenbergh, but made no more progress.[117]

It took an intervention from the American legation to shift the Cabinet. Helmer maintained his opposition to the state intervening "one-sidedly". State Secretary of the Interior Ferdinand Graf complained of blackmail and money-making motives and wished to abstain from the vote. But Gruber's judgement that it would be "unwise" (*unklug*) to offend the Americans proved decisive. It was decided to offer an advance of 5 million Schillings – a fifth of the amount requested. On no account should the press be told.[118] This was not the end of the story, however. The Finance Ministry not only applied to the Americans to re-imburse them out of Marshall Aid, it also demanded security for the advance from the *Kultusgemeinde* itself! Even so, at the start of October it was still blocking implementation of the loan. After some expression of resentment the *Kultusgemeinde* accepted the loan, which was used for repair and upkeep of buildings and educational projects.

The increased self-confidence of the government since 1945 was demonstrated by the way further pressure on the fund question was simply ignored. When an American note – one of several – came to the Cabinet early in 1952 Schärf made it clear that the fund would only be set up under compulsion:

> "On the basis of the assertion that it's a question of heirless property (herrenloses Gut) we can't let anything be taken away from us unless . . . we are forced to by the State Treaty (können wir uns nichts wegnehmen lassen, wenn wir nicht . . . durch den Staatsvertrag dazu gezwungen sind)."

He added that he was convinced that the number of Jews killed was relatively small – "most of them really did get over the border". Figl endorsed him: "The biggest *Judenmassaker* only began in 1942 and by then our Jews were gone – usually with some luggage, a ship's ticket and 200 RM [sic!]."[119] Neither this nor a further US note of June 1952 was apparently answered.[120] When the Jewish community asked for a further advance – this time of 15 million Schillings – from

---

[116]Records of Isenbergh's conversations, presumably by Robert James, legal *attaché* of the US Embassy, who was present, can be found in the Institut für Zeitgeschichte, Vienna, Löwy PP; 'Latest development of restitution legislation in Austria', B–48045, 18th April 1949, IfZ, Löwy PP; cf. Knight, *Wortprotokolle, op. cit.*, pp. 208–210.

[117]*Wiener Zeitung*, 15th February 1949; *Die Gemeinde*, No. 2 (March 1949).

[118]MRP 160, 8th June 1949, AdR; Knight, *Wortprotokolle, op. cit.*, pp. 211–214.

[119]MRP 275, 8th January 1952, AdR; Knight, *Wortprotokolle, op. cit.*, p. 240.

[120]See draft note by US Legal Division, 13th May 1953, No. 205, IfZ, Vienna, Löwy PP.

the future "heirless property" fund, it was blocked.[121] Figl appears to have attempted to make the payment conditional on US agreement to soften their stance over the "late returners (*Spätheimkehrer*)".[122] In negotiations with the Jewish Claims Committee between 1953 and 1955 the Austrian Government stuck to its position that it could not discuss a matter which had already been settled in the draft State Treaty – an argument which was not merely legally incorrect, but inconsistent with attempts to amend restitution legislation in 1950.

Nearly as controversial as "heirless property" was the restitution of tenants' and leaseholders' rights.[123] In post-war Vienna, where the housing shortage was acute, any decision about 60,000 flats and thousands of business premises, doctors' and lawyers' practices – the majority of which were presumably relatively intact – would be controversial. That they had belonged to Jews made it more so. In an ironically circular argument the fact that the inheritors were living abroad was taken as evidence that they would "unfairly" sell, lease or sublet any premises returned to them before returning abroad. Yet at the same time the fact that there was no legal basis for regaining their accommodation or leased premises was a major disincentive to those – admittedly probably a minority – who might be contemplating return. In the early months of the occupation when the Russians and the Communists held sway in Vienna and many Nazis had fled, several thousand flats, some of which had belonged to Jews, were given to resistance fighters or Nazi victims.[124] But the legal position was unclear and the attitude of the housing authorities to returning refugees does not seem to have been sympathetic.[125] Though the Third Restitution Law provided for legislation at a later date, the political cost involved grew.[126] A law was drafted in 1947, agreed in Cabinet in May 1948 but referred back to a parliamentary sub-committee. The Americans saw this "unconscionable procrastination" as "part of its effort to curry the favour of former Nazis".[127] According to the Jewish community it was so drafted that it would only result in the restitution of at the most 50 homes.[128] As time went on the chances of a law coming into force faded and it seems unlikely that even Keyes believed that his insistent call in September 1950 for "speedy measures" would have much effect. In Cabinet Tschadek described the demand as "an absolute danger" (*eine absolute*

---

[121]Kultusgemeinde to Figl, 2nd May 1952, IfZ, LN.

[122]See Rauchensteiner, *op. cit.*, pp. 174–175.

[123]The other restitution laws which were passed covered relatively minor areas: the question of firms' names (4RG); the property of juridical persons who had lost their legal personality (*Rechtspersönlichkeit*) (5RG); trade protection rights and patents (*gewerbliche Schutzrechte*) 6RG, and claims arising from revoked or unfulfilled conditions of service (*Dienstverhältnisse*) in the private economy (7RG).

[124]Adolf Schärf, *Zwischen Demokratie und Volksdemokratie. Österreichs Einigung und Wiederaufrichtung im Jahre 1945*, Vienna 1950, p. 99, puts the number at 18,000; cf. Knight, *Wortprotokolle, op. cit.*, p. 139.

[125]See letter from the Chief Commandant Vienna to the Chairman of the Executive Committee of the Allied Council, 30th July 1946, concerning the living quarters of Jewish returnees, PRO, FO 1020/2360.

[126]Article 23 (2), 3RG ('Besondere Regelung für Bestandverhältnisse').

[127]Present Status of Restitution Legislation in Austria, US Legal Division, 27th October 1948, IfZ, Vienna, Löwy PP.

[128]Keyes to Figl, 21st June 1949; Keyes to Figl 23rd March 1950, appended to MRP 163 and MRP 198, AdR; Knight, *Wortprotokolle, op. cit.*, pp. 216–219, 221–223.

Gefahr) which would create "serious unrest" (*eine unbedingte Beunruhigung*).[129] Soon afterwards the bill was put into cold storage and – apart from a short-lived revival three years later – it remained there until the State Treaty came into force.[130]

VII

The State Treaty brought Austria the restoration of sovereignty and the departure of Allied authorities. Her status as a "collective victim" of the Third *Reich* was confirmed both by the adoption of the term "State Treaty" (in preference to Peace Treaty) and by the last-minute removal of a reference in the preamble to "responsibility" arising from its participation in the war. The Relief Fund (*Hilfsfonds*) agreed to shortly afterwards, following the two-year long negotiations between the Federal Government and the Claims Committee under Nahum Goldmann's chairmanship, was in line with this policy. It was, as the government had consistently argued, neither restitution nor compensation but an *ex gratia* payment made not to Jewish victims specifically, but to "former Austrians who reside abroad, and who are in need of assistance irrespective of their religion". Payments of between 10,000 and 40,000 Schillings were made to the neediest cases of Jewish refugees living abroad.[131] The total sum available over an eleven-year period was 550 million Schillings (in fact the fund was used up by 1959).[132]

After some prevarication by the Austrian government the restitution called for in Article 26 (1) of the State Treaty was settled by a lump payment of 6 million dollars and 10% for administration costs (about 170 million Schillings). Over 11,000 claims were made, most of them against discriminatory taxes.[133] The tracing and realising of "heirless property" was carried out between 1957 and 1961.[134] In all over 320 million Schillings were collected (over 38 million of which

[129]MRP 216, 5th September 1950, ADR; Knight, *Wortprotokolle, op. cit.,* p. 232–233.

[130]Krell and Heiter (IKG) to Bundesministerium für soziale Verwaltung, 27th December 1953; Krell to Beckermann, 1st July 1953, IKGA, Vienna, File Wiedergutmachung 1948–1952.

[131]'Fonds zur Hilfeleistung an Politisch Verfolgte, die ihren Wohnsitz und Ständigen Aufenthalt im Ausland haben' (Hilfsfonds). For the negotiations which twice broke down see Goldmann, *op. cit.,* pp. 448–451.

[132]*Wiener Zeitung,* 20th July 1955.

[133]'Fonds zur Abgeltung von Vermögensverlusten politisch Verfolgter (Abgeltungsfonds)', Georg Weis, 13th February 1964, unpublished report kindly given to me by Dr Weis. The areas covered were bank accounts, securities, mortgages, life assurance, discriminatory taxes, cash and municipal and state pension rights. The figure of 6 million Dollars was considerably lower than the amount the Austrians expected to pay under a "category solution" initially adopted, which they estimated would cost 200 to 250 million Schillings. See Blair (British Embassy, Vienna) to Swann (FO), 20th September 1957, PRO, FO 371/130304/RR1481/9. The restoration of tenant rights was not included. Austrian officials argued that the restoration of tenancy rights was "not possible" in the sense of Article 26 (1), a phrase clearly meant to apply to property which had been destroyed or was not traceable.

[134]The delay in setting up the fund (according to the State Treaty to be within 18 months of ratification) and the use of Jewish property for the 20% of payments to "political victims" were two respects in which this solution, in the British view, violated the terms of the State Treaty, see Tripp (British Embassy, Vienna) to Barnes (FO), 15th April 1959, PRO, FO 371/144908/RR1481/20.

came from the Federal Republic on the basis of the Bad Kreuznach agreement of 1961). As with the earlier restitution the largest single category was real estate. The settlements of claims concerning 3,896 properties raised over 83 million Schillings. The bulk of the payments – 80% of them to *Glaubensjuden* within Austria – were made between 1961 and 1969.[135]

VIII

The history of Austrian restitution is not just an illustration of the banal truth that in politics expediency will generally triumph over humanity. It shows the problem post-war Austria faced in establishing its legitimacy as a collective victim of the Third *Reich* when its social and economic entanglement in that regime had been extensive, nowhere more so than in its racial persecution. This continuing tension between officially propagated myth and authentic experience makes it doubtful whether in Austria restitution had the kind of cathartic or educative effects claimed for it for the German Federal Republic by Walter Schwarz.[136] It seems more likely – on the basis of an admittedly impressionistic examination of the press coverage of the issue – that it strengthened existing antisemitic clichés. The reduction of the question of responsibility in the Holocaust to material aspects may have facilitated this and intensified the tendency to repress unpalatable memories of lives destroyed and misery inflicted, while the very fact that most of the survivors had fled Austria transmuted the question from one of self-responsibility into a conflict between Austria and "abroad".[137] Finally, restitution highlights the problems arising from the claim of the modern state to have replaced direct violence by the laws of the market, guaranteed by the principles of the bourgeois civil code.[138] For the

[135]Sammelstellen A und B, Schlussbericht, 1957–1969, Georg Weis, kindly made available to the author and now in his possession.

[136]Schwarz, *Rückerstattung, op. cit.*, pp. 375–376.

[137]On public attitudes and the press see Hilde Weis, *Antisemitische Vorurteile in Österreich*, Vienna 1987; John Bunzl and Bernd Marin, *Antisemitismus in Österreich. Sozialhistorische und soziologische Studien* (Vergleichende Gesellschaftsgeschichte und politische Ideengeschichte der Neuzeit, vol. III), Innsbruck 1983; espec. pp. 204ff.; and most recently on the press Ruth Wodak *et al.*, *"Wir sind alle Unschuldige Täter!" Studien zum antisemitischen Diskurs im Nachkriegsösterreich*, unpublished MS, Vienna 1989 (2 vols.), kindly shown to the writer; cf. the autobiographical, Anton Pelinka, *Windstille, Klagen über Österreich*, Vienna–Berlin 1985, p. 3; apart from these historians have not done much to counter prejudices; Rauchensteiner (*op. cit.*, pp. 424–425) shifts the date of the 12th *Opferfürsorgegesetznovelle* back from 22nd March 1961 to before the summer of 1960 to support his conclusion that unlike the Americans the Jewish organisations "waren freilich nicht so rasch [sic!] zufriedenzustellen und setzten Österreich . . . [im Sommer 1960] neuerlich unter Druck". In a similar distortion Ludwig Steiner simply jumps over two and half years of fruitless negotiations when he writes, in Alois Brusatti and Gottfried Heindl (eds.), *Julius Raab: eine Biographie in Einzeldarstellungen*, Linz 1986, p. 232: "Raab wollte dieses Problem möglichst rasch [!] einer Lösung zuführen. Er lud dazu Nahum Goldmann . . . zu einem Gespräch am 12. Februar 1956 nach Wien ein."

[138]Jürgen Habermas, *Strukturwandel der Öffentlichkeit*, Berlin 1962, pp. 96ff.; David Blackbourn and Geoff Eley, *The Peculiarities of German History. Bourgeois Society and Politics in Nineteenth-Century Germany*, Oxford–New York 1984, pp. 190–194.

outburst of 1938 was not merely an exercise in unrestrained greed, it was a revolt against capitalist exchange itself,[139] which shattered the "bourgeois freedoms" with which Jewish emancipation had been intimately bound up. The inability of the post-war Austrian state to redress significantly the resulting state of affairs highlights the depth of the crisis. It was not that restitution deviated from the principles of the civil code (*Bürgerliches Recht*) in favour of the Jews, but that it could not deviate enough to satisfy natural justice. It was more than a bitter irony that the bourgeois principles of "equality before the law" and "security of contract" could be harnessed so effectively by the same people who had ruthlessly violated both seven years before, and that the breaches allegedly made in them on behalf of the victims, rather than the victims' plight itself, could be successfully portrayed as the real problem.

[139]Detlev Claussen, *Grenzen der Aufklärung. Zur gesellschaftlichen Geschichte des modernen Antisemitismus*, Frankfurt a. Main 1987, esp. pp. 32, 35.

The Attitude towards Jews in Bavaria after the Second World War

BY CONSTANTIN GOSCHLER

In May 1947, two years after the end of Nazi rule in Germany, Rabbi Philip S. Bernstein, the Jewish Adviser to the American Military Governor, made a speech to the UN Commission for Palestine in the Bavarian capital of Munich. The scenario he depicted was bleak:[1] "Gentlemen, if the United States Army were to withdraw tomorrow, there would be pogroms on the following day." This comment throws a harsh light on the problem of German attitudes towards the Jews after the collapse of Hitler's rule. Was Bernstein dramatising the situation in an attempt to impress his audience, or were his fears justified by actual developments? Did conditions in Bavaria on this issue differ from those in other regions of Germany? The following essay will investigate the course of events, paying particular attention to the vital and turbulent years between the end of the war and the beginning of the 1950s.

The first answers to these questions can be obtained by assessing a number of surveys of public opinion. On the basis of interviews with approximately 3,400 people in its occupation zone and in West Berlin during 1946, the American Military Government for Germany produced a report on antisemitism in the U.S. Zone on 3rd March 1947. The survey distinguished five groups: "those with little bias (20%), nationalists (19%), racists (22%), antisemites (21%), and intense antisemites (18%)".[2] The Military Government came to the alarming conclusion that antisemitism had actually increased in recent months.[3] If the categories of racists, antisemites and intense antisemites are amalgamated, then 59% of interviewees in Bavaria fell into that group. In the *Länder* of Hesse (63%) and Württemberg-Baden (65%), which were also part of the American Zone, the proportion was even higher, while in West Berlin it was comparatively low at 45%.

Dislike of the Jews was not equally distributed among all social groups. Communists showed least antipathy towards them; dislike increased as the educational level declined; Protestants were to be found among the antisemites more frequently than Catholics, although in both denominations it was the regular churchgoers who showed greater hostility; the agricultural population

---

[1]Thomas P. Liebschütz, *Rabbi Philip S. Bernstein and the Jewish Displaced Persons*, Diss., Cincinnati 1965, p. 105, quoted in Juliane Wetzel, *Jüdisches Leben in München 1945–1951, Durchgangsstation oder Wiederaufbau?*, Munich 1987, pp. 356–357.

[2]Report No. 49 (3rd March 1947): 'Antisemitism in the American Zone', in Anna J. Merritt and Richard L. Merritt (eds.), *Public Opinion in Occupied Germany. The OMGUS Surveys, 1945–1949*, London 1970, p. 146.

[3]*Neue Zeitung*, 5th May 1947, 'Steigender Antisemitismus. Die Ergebnisse einer Umfrage der Nachrichtenkontrolle', p. 2.

was more hostile than the urban population, but Munich provided a much greater percentage of antisemites than other cities; women were more prejudiced than men, a factor which was probably connected to their lower level of education.[4]

A full year later the investigation in the U.S. Zone was repeated in order to detect how attitudes had developed in the interim. The overall share of the prejudiced groups – intense antisemites, antisemites and racists – remained virtually the same in April 1948. The first two of these categories had actually declined somewhat, but that of the racists had increased.[5]

Any attempt to follow the course of developments over time is hampered by problems with the available data, since both the regions covered and the questions asked were different in later polls. In these circumstances no direct comparison is possible. However, it is clear from investigations conducted in the territory of the U.S. Zone under the auspices of the American High Commissioner, and from data gathered by a German opinion research institute and covering the whole of the Federal Republic, that negative attitudes towards the Jews remained widespread even after the beginning of the 1950s. In December 1946, 48% of those questioned in the American Zone took the view "that some human races are more fit to rule than others"; by October 1949, after some swings above and below, the figure was still 44%.[6] A study covering the entire Federal Republic even detected a clear increase in negative attitudes towards the Jews between 1949 and 1952.[7] In the following decades the extent of antisemitic views declined strongly, though without ever disappearing completely.[8]

What these figures show is that antisemitism – or at least negative attitudes towards Jews – affected a considerable proportion of the German population in the first decade after the Second World War. This is certainly shocking but, in view of recent history, not altogether surprising. What do the figures mean when applied to Bavaria, our own area of inquiry? Insofar as the figures allow distinctions or comparisons to be made with other German regions, they reveal a gradual though not a fundamental difference in the prevalence of such attitudes. However, the potential peculiarities of the Bavarian example are not apparent if the investigation is confined to opinion research data. It is, therefore, necessary

[4]See 'Antisemitism in the American Zone', *loc. cit.*
[5]See Report No. 122 (22nd May 1948): 'Prejudice and Antisemitism', in Merritt and Merritt (eds.), *Public Opinion in Occupied Germany, op. cit.*, pp. 239–240.
[6]See Report No. 1 (30th December 1949): 'The State of German Nationalism following the Founding of the West German Republic', in Anna J. Merritt and Richard L. Merritt (eds.), *Public Opinion in Semisovereign Germany. The HICOG Surveys, 1949–1955*, Urbana–Chicago–London 1980, pp. 53–54.
[7]To the question "What is your attitude toward Jews?", in August 1949 15% of those sampled in West Germany gave ambivalent answers and 23% of answers were clearly antisemitic. In December 1952 these responses were 18% and 34% respectively. See Elisabeth Noelle and Erich Peter Neumann (eds.), *Jahrbuch der öffentlichen Meinung, 1947–1955*, Allensbach 1956, p. 128.
[8]The proportion of people believing that no Jews should live in Germany declined from 37% in December 1952 to 19% in March 1965. See Elisabeth Noelle and Erich Peter Neumann (eds.), *Jahrbuch der öffentlichen Meinung 1965–1967*, Allensbach–Bonn 1967, p. 96. In October 1981 14% were against working with Jewish colleagues or living together in the same house. The responses for black people were 23% for both. See Elisabeth Noelle-Neumann and E. Piel (eds.), *Allensbacher Jahrbuch der Demoskopie 1978–1983*, Munich–New York–London–Paris 1983, p. 79.

to analyse specific problem areas which will enable us to clarify details of developments in Bavaria.

First and foremost, it is essential to recall the situation and composition of the Jewish community in Bavaria after the end of the Nazi persecutions. There are two crucial factors to be taken into account. Firstly, between 1945 and 1950 more Jews were living in Bavaria than in the whole of the rest of Germany. Secondly – and closely connected with the first point – there was hardly any continuity of Bavarian Jewish life before the destruction of the Jewish communities in Hitler's Germany and after the end of Nazi rule.

After the war, there were two very different spheres of Jewish life in Bavaria. One of them, the remnant of the Bavarian Jewish communities, began to reorganise in many localities. The example of Munich is typical. In 1933 the Munich Jewish community had numbered approximately 9,000 people. By the end of June 1945 there were 430 Jews there, forming the core of a new Jewish community. Of these 84 were so-called "full Jews" who had managed to go into hiding in the Nazi years; over 300 were baptised Jews or those living in "privileged mixed marriages", who had been protected from deportation; and there were a number of survivors returning home from Theresienstadt and other camps. By spring 1946 the Jewish remnant in Munich had grown to around 700 people, including a number of re-emigrants from abroad.[9]

Alongside the small number of surviving German Jews in Bavaria, however, there was a significant concentration of Jewish people from a different background. In numerical terms this group was far more important. These were the Jewish Displaced Persons (DPs). According to Allied definition the DPs were "civilians outside the national boundaries of their countries by reason of the war", who needed assistance to return or to resettle.[10] They included Jews who had been liberated from Nazi concentration camps and forced labour camps, as well as people who had poured into the Western occupation zones, particularly the American Zone, only after the end of the war. In 1946 alone, when the influx reached its high point, more than 100,000, mainly Polish Jews, crossed into the American Zone – mostly into Bavaria – where they were given DP status.[11] One reason for this influx of East European Jews lay in post-war Polish antisemitism; another was the attempt of Jewish organisations to create a mass problem in the American Zone in order to intensify the pressure for the opening of Palestine to

[9]See Juliane Wetzel, ' "Mir szeinen doh". München und Umgebung als Zuflucht von Überlebenden des Holocaust 1945–1948', in Martin Broszat, Klaus-Dietmar Henke and Hans Woller (eds.), *Von Stalingrad zur Währungsreform. Zur Sozialgeschichte des Umbruchs in Deutschland*, Munich 1988, pp. 334, 340.

[10]See Supreme Headquarters, Allied Expeditionary Force (SHAEF), Administrative Memorandum No. 39 (revised – 16th April 1945), subparagraph 5b, Archiv des Instituts für Zeitgeschichte, München (IfZ–Archiv), Fi 01.06.

[11]See Wolfgang Jacobmeyer, 'Die Lager der jüdischen Displaced Persons in den deutschen Westzonen 1946/47 als Ort jüdischer Selbstvergewisserung', in Micha Brumlik *et al.* (eds.), *Jüdisches Leben in Deutschland seit 1945*, Frankfurt a. Main 1986, p. 37.

Jewish immigrants.[12] As far as Bavaria was concerned, the result was that the number of Jewish DPs increased from approximately 25,000 in spring 1946 to around 80,000 by the end of the year.[13] Due to the subsequent emigration of Jewish DPs, the total then declined rapidly until the beginning of the 1950s.

The vast majority of these DPs lived in camps. These were administered by the American Military Government for a transitional period, before coming under the control of the United Nations Relief and Rehabilitation Administration (UNRRA) and later the International Refugee Organisation (IRO). Most Jewish DPs in the camps were waiting for the chance to emigrate, usually to Palestine/Israel or the USA. In their own view, they were completely outside German society. For a short period Jewish life blossomed in the camps, though this came to an end as most of the Jewish DPs left the country.[14] By the beginning of the 1950s the majority of camps were closed, and the remaining few thousand Jewish DPs were transferred to German responsibility in mid-1951.

However, a smaller proportion of Jewish DPs settled outside the camps and integrated into German society and the economy. There they became members of the newly established Jewish religious communities, the structure of which was thereby changed in a fundamental way. After a short time the old-established German Jews were frequently in the minority in these communities, a fact which inevitably led to cultural, political and religious tensions. In part this was the result of the contrast between the *Ostjuden* – much more traditional in religious matters – and the old-established German Jews. The tendency was intensified by the fact that, as a consequence of the Nazi persecutions, it was the Jewish partners in mixed marriages who had been much more likely to survive – the very people who were already on the periphery of, or even outside, the Jewish faith.

The composition of the Jewish religious community in Bavaria at the end of the 1950s can be described with some accuracy. In Munich there were 1,800 former DPs and approximately 400 German Jews, while the proportion of DPs to German Jews was generally similar among the 850 Jews who were scattered among seven other Bavarian Jewish religious communities.[15] While the gathering of tens of thousands of DPs in UN-administered camps had been a passing – though highly significant – phenomenon of the early post-war years, the

---

[12]See Wolfgang Jacobmeyer, 'Jüdische Überlebende als "Displaced Persons". Untersuchungen zur Besatzungspolitik in den deutschen Westzonen und zur Zuwanderung osteuropäischer Juden 1945–1947', in *Geschichte und Gesellschaft*, 9 (1983), pp. 434–435.

[13]IfZ-Archiv, Fi. 01.30–01.34, ITS-Arolsen; see also Wetzel, 'München und Umgebung als Zuflucht', *loc. cit.*, p. 349.

[14]See Abraham J. Peck, 'Jüdisches Leben in Bayern nach 1945. Die Stimme von She'erit Hapletah', in Manfred Treml and Josef Kirmeier (eds.), *Geschichte und Kultur der Juden in Bayern. Aufsätze*, Munich–New York–London–Paris 1988, pp. 505–516; Wetzel, 'München und Umgebung als Zuflucht', *loc. cit.*, pp. 352–354.

[15]Nuremberg (43 former DPs, 164 German Jews), Regensburg (84 former DPs, 88 German Jews), Augsburg (85 former DPs, 64 German Jews), Würzburg (25 former DPs, 80 German Jews), Straubing (79 former DPs, 9 German Jews), Bamberg (65 former DPs, 10 German Jews), Amberg (60 former DPs, 9 German Jews). See Harry Maòr, *Über den Wiederaufbau der jüdischen Gemeinden in Deutschland seit 1945*, Mainz 1961, pp. 29–30.

fundamental restructuring of the Jewish communities was a factor of lasting importance. Nowhere was the change so radical as in Bavaria.

The "DP question" was also a factor in shaping Bavarian attitudes towards the Jews in the early post-war period, even though the DPs included other groups. In this respect the attitude of the American Military Government, which had custody of the camps during this period, is also significant. At first no distinction was made between Jewish and non-Jewish DPs. This could lead to situations in which the Jews were accommodated alongside their former persecutors, since the DPs clearly included people who had collaborated with the Germans or who had actually taken an active part in the persecutions.[16]

In these circumstances the conduct of the first American Military Governor for Bavaria, General George S. Patton, was notorious. It was Patton who ensured that the DP camps were surrounded with barbed wire and watch towers and were generally ill-equipped to give their inhabitants any sense of liberation. The Jewish DPs were often physically and spiritually shattered by their experiences, which inevitably had a damaging effect on social standards in many cases; consequently, they made a much less favourable impression on Patton and some other Americans than the physically clean, well-turned out Germans.[17]

Measures were taken to remedy the situation in August 1945, after the Americans were appalled by the results of a commission of investigation under Earl G. Harrison, the former American Immigration Commissioner. In his report Harrison had concluded:[18]

> "As the matter now stands, we appear to be treating the Jews as the Nazis treated them except that we do not exterminate them. They are in concentration camps in large numbers under our military guard instead of S.S. troops. One is led to wonder whether the German people, seeing this, are not supposing that we are following or at least condoning Nazi policy."

Patton regarded these reproaches as the result of a Jewish conspiracy in Washington. He wrote in his diary: "Harrison and his ilk believe that the Displaced Person is a human being, which he is not, and this applies particularly to the Jews who are lower than animals."[19]

Eisenhower acted to remove Patton, as well as the barbed wire. Moreover, the Jewish DPs were now accommodated in separate camps. From then on, the American occupying power adopted a positive attitude towards the Jewish DPs in Bavaria as elsewhere. To this end the post of "Adviser on Jewish Affairs to the Military Governor" was created and appointments made on the suggestion of the big American Jewish organisations. One such Jewish Adviser was Rabbi Bernstein, whose remarks opened this essay.

The Military Government also adopted a positive approach to the German Jews living outside the camps. At the same time, the Americans took care that

---

[16]Leonhard Dinnerstein, *America and the Survivors of the Holocaust*, New York 1982, pp. 17–24.
[17]See *The Patton Papers: 1940–1945*, ed. by Martin Blumenson, Boston 1974, pp. 750–755.
[18]See Earl G. Harrison Report to President Truman on 'The Plight of the Displaced Jews in Europe', August 1945, p. 12, reprinted in Dinnerstein, *op. cit.*, Appendix B.
[19]*The Patton Papers*, *op. cit.*, p. 751.

antisemitic tendencies did not emerge in Bavarian politics, and it was a major contribution of the American Military Government that antisemitism ceased to be socially acceptable in any form. In October 1945 the American Military Government also instructed the Bavarian government to give preferential treatment to the Jews.[20] Subsequently the Bavarian government established a *Staatskommissariat zur Betreuung der Juden* (state commission for the care of the Jews). At first this was headed by Hermann Aumer, an *"Achteljude"* ("one eighth Jew") according to the definition of the Nuremberg Laws. His task was "to take all necessary measures in order to give all necessary assistance to the Jewish population of Bavaria [which had been] persecuted on racial grounds". At the same time he was also to ensure "that the Jewish part of the population of *Land* Bavaria again becomes a healthy factor in the Bavarian economy".[21]

After the dismissal of Aumer for corruption, a *Staatskommissariat für rassisch, religiös und politisch Verfolgte* (state commission for the victims of racial, religious and political persecution) was created by amalgamating Aumer's organisation with the *Staatskommissariat für die politisch Verfolgten*, which had been created in the interim. At its head was appointed Philipp Auerbach, a member of an old-established Hamburg Jewish family. He had spent four and a half years in German prisons and concentration camps and, after liberation, had initially worked for the government of North Rhine Province in the care of victims of persecution and refugees. After the British Military Government had dismissed him over political differences, Auerbach had worked as Chairman of the zonal office of the Jewish communities in the British Zone and as Vice President of the *Zentralkomitee für die befreiten Juden* in the British Zone.[22]

Before Auerbach took office in Bavaria, the main principles of his work were outlined by his future boss, the Social Democratic Minister of the Interior, Josef Seifried. Firstly, good will must be demonstrated to the Americans; "but at the same time we have to help the DPs to move on, because more refugees are already pressing behind them".[23] This was a reference to the German expellees from the East whose presence, indeed, was creating a source of intense social rivalry.

In June 1947 the Bavarian *Ministerrat* discussed the mass influx of Jews from the East into Bavaria. *Ministerpräsident* Hans Ehard of the *Christlich-Soziale Union* (CSU) predicted that it could lead to the rise of antisemitism in a previously unknown form. State Secretary Gentner poured oil onto the flames by declaring that of the 600 Polish Jews in his *Landkreis*, only two were willing to work while all the others were involved in the black market. "The consequence was a hatred of

---

[20]See Bayerischer Ministerrat, 24th October 1945, IfZ-Archiv, Sl Hoegner, ED 120, folder 354.

[21]Bestallungsurkunde für Hermann Aumer, 26th October 1946, signed Wilhelm Hoegner, Bayerisches Hauptstaatsarchiv, München (BayHStA), MA 114 262.

[22]See Constantin Goschler, 'Der Fall Philipp Auerbach. Wiedergutmachung in Bayern', in Ludolf Herbst and Constantin Goschler (eds.), *Wiedergutmachung in der Bundesrepublik Deutschland*, Munich 1989, pp. 78–79.

[23]See testimony of Josef Seifried, 31st August 1951, Archiv des Bayerischen Landtags, München (Archiv-BayLT), Protokoll der 6. Sitzung des Untersuchungsausschusses zur Untersuchung der Vorgänge im Landesentschädigungsamt, p. 106.

Jews which was previously completely unknown."[24] The fact that the German police had no right to enter the DP camps was a particular source of irritation.

While the German Jews in Bavaria came under the control of the Bavarian authorities, these had no rights where the DP camps were concerned. Persistent friction was the result. Because of their experience, the Jewish DPs in the camps were overwhelmingly hostile towards the Germans and regarded their stay as no more than a temporary stop.[25] Naturally enough there was some law-breaking amongst the Jewish DPs and, as a result of the persecution they had suffered, scarcely any feeling that injustice was being done to the German population. Yet the criminal element among the DPs was very small.[26] Nevertheless, Jewish participation in the black market and other crimes specific to the post-war situation was often highlighted. Stories on the subject were eagerly circulated among the Bavarian population and became part of the inventory of a new generation of prejudices. Symbol of the trend was Munich's *Möhlstraße*, which until 1949 was a well-known centre both of Jewish life and also of the black market.[27] Another fertile breeding ground for antipathy was the fact that Bavaria had to pay considerable sums to finance the DPs, over and above the occupation costs.[28] One particular stumbling block was created when German homes had to be evacuated to accommodate DPs, a process which inevitably caused hardship.[29] Furthermore, the German side felt scarcely any responsibility or obligation regarding the Jews from Eastern Europe, who had come into the area only after the end of the war.

In attitudes towards the Jews in Bavaria as a whole, however, some distinctions were made. Typical of this is a comment made at the beginning of 1947 by Josef Baumgartner, the Bavarian *Landwirtschaftsminister* and later chairman of the *Bayernpartei*. In a closed political discussion of the CSU he remarked:[30]

> "Without the Jews and particularly the Jewish businessmen in the USA and the rest of the world we will never manage: We need them for the resumption of our old trade relations! As regards the many *Ostjuden* here in Bavaria I am of a different opinion: Gentlemen! I was unfortunately compelled to take part in the Jewish congress in Reichenhall: The one pleasing thing at the meeting for me was the resolution which was unanimously adopted: 'Out of Germany'! (Laughter)".

[24]See Bayerischer Ministerrat, 20th June 1947, IfZ-Archiv, N1 Hoegner, ED 120, folder 364.
[25]See Peck, *loc. cit.*, p. 505.
[26]See Jacobmeyer, 'Jüdische Überlebende als "Displaced Persons"', *loc. cit.*, pp. 439–441.
[27]See Wetzel, 'München und Umgebung als Zuflucht', *loc. cit.*, pp. 354–355.
[28]See Institut für Besatzungsfragen, *Das DP-Problem. Eine Studie über die ausländischen Flüchtlinge in Deutschland*, Tübingen 1950, pp. 87–91.
[29]See 'Mündlicher Bericht des Ausschusses für Sozialpolitik zu den Anträgen des Abgeordneten Stock und Genossen betreffend Freigabe der von der UNRRA beschlagnahmten Arbeitersiedlung "Kaltherberge" in München', *Verhandlungen des Bayerischen Landtags*, Stenographische Berichte, 45th meeting on 16th January 1948, pp. 576–581.
[30]Josef Baumgartner on 4th March 1947 at the "Dienstag-Club", in Klaus-Dietmar Henke and Hans Woller (eds.), *Lehrjahre der CSU. Eine Nachkriegspartei im Spiegel vertraulicher Berichte an die amerikanische Militärregierung*, Stuttgart 1984, p. 122. Baumgartner is referring to the second congress of liberated Jews at Bad Reichenhall in 1947.

In an attitude with echoes dating from the 1920s – for example the expulsion of *Ostjuden* from Bavaria ordered by *Generalstaatskommisar* von Kahr in 1923[31] – the Jews from the East were regarded as more or less undesirable elements. By contrast, the German Jews tended to be seen as important helpers in the re-establishment of international trade relations.

This contrast between the German Jews and the *Ostjuden* also coincided with tensions within the Jewish community itself. From the point of view of foreign Jewish organisations, the Jewish communities in Germany were acting as virtual collaborators for a time, in so far as they did not follow the goal of their own disbandment. In 1948 the World Jewish Congress in Montreux had decided that there should be no new Jewish society on the "blood-soaked soil" of Germany. This attitude was changed only gradually.[32] On the other side, the German Jews continued to harbour traditional resentments against their co-religionists from the East.[33]

The post-war Jewish communities in Bavaria were thus in a quandary. On the one hand – at least until the beginning of the 1950s – they were looked at askance by the vast majority of foreign Jewish organisations and the Jewish DP organisations. On the other, they lived in an environment which was bound to seem highly insecure. When post-war antisemitism flared up again from 1947 it appeared even more threatening now that it was no longer encouraged and exacerbated from above as in the Nazi years, but bore the character of an "indigenous" antisemitism with its roots in popular sentiment.

Alongside the difficulties arising from the DP problem, this antisemitism was associated mainly with the fact that most of the Jews were now completely without means and in need of support. Though the privileges granted to them were really very modest, they aroused envy amongst the Bavarian population. Other needy groups, such as the victims of political persecution and the German refugees and expellees, also felt the force of this resentment. However, the last of these had one major socio-psychological advantage; since the Germans were not directly to blame for the injustices they suffered, this group could ultimately count on greater sympathy.

A dangerous brew had been created by the mixing of traditional prejudices against the Jews with resentment at privileged treatment as compensation for their sufferings under Nazism and their supposed massive participation in the black market. At the beginning of 1948 the CSU deputy Georg Stang told the Bavarian *Landtag* that he detected a "spontaneously increasing wave of antisemitism". He continued:[34]

---

[31]See Reiner Pommerin, 'Die Ausweisung von "Ostjuden" aus Bayern 1923. Ein Beitrag zum Krisenjahr der Weimarer Republik', in *Vierteljahrshefte für Zeitgeschichte*, 34 (1986), pp. 311–340.

[32]See Hendrik George van Dam, 'Die Juden in Deutschland nach 1945', in Franz Böhm und Walter Dirks (eds.), *Judentum. Schicksal, Wesen und Gegenwart*, vol. II, Wiesbaden 1965, p. 896.

[33]See Maòr, *op. cit.*, pp. 25ff.

[34]See *Verhandlungen des Bayerischen Landtags*, Stenographische Berichte, 52nd meeting on 6th February 1948, p. 834.

"I am sorry for the decent Jews who must now suffer in the judgement of the people for the bad performance of many of those of their race . . . I think that there is no need to stir up antisemitism, which we all rigorously reject, artificially; the flame [will] rise up on its own if things go on as before with many members of the Jewish race."

In view of such tensions, *Staatskommissar* Auerbach had already published an appeal to the Jewish communities in Bavaria in March 1947. Here he had called on them not to behave in a provocative manner in public. In particular, Auerbach urged the Jews not to make unjustified attacks on people as "German pigs" or as Nazis on public transport or in the street; nor should they provoke people by a "public display, on trains and in trams, of foodstuffs and luxuries which are not accessible to the general population". Incidents of this kind, he thought, had contributed to the spread of an antisemitism previously unknown in Bavaria.[35] This appeal brought Auerbach sharp criticism in the New York journal *Aufbau*.[36]

However, when Auerbach let it be known through the press and radio that the Jews in Bavaria were to be granted more favourable rates of exchange in the currency reform of June 1948, the result was the spread of numerous rumours about the preferential treatment of the Jews, in which the antisemitic undertones were unmistakable. There were other more aggressive reactions. The American Military Government reported "attempted student demonstrations before American Joint Distribution Committee Agencies and rumors of a march of Bavarians upon the home of Dr. Auerbach".[37] Eventually the Americans debated whether Auerbach's tactically unwise public statements had been responsible for stirring up antisemitism, and whether he should consequently be dismissed. However, they came to the following conclusion regarding Auerbach's comments: "If they have roused anti-semitism that is evidence of a hangover of Nazism in the Bavarian mind, rather than the fault of Dr. Auerbach."[38]

One of the most striking symptoms of increasing post-war antisemitism was an extensive series of desecrations of Jewish cemeteries. From the beginning of 1948 there were fresh reports of such attacks each week in the newspaper, especially in Franconia. The incidents developed into a wave, which lasted for months before ebbing once again. But it was not limited to Bavaria; similar incidents occurred in other German *Länder*. Though deliberate antisemitic conduct did not lie behind every single attack, the incidents were nevertheless only the tip of the iceberg. Beneath them lay a wide range of attitudes towards the Jews and their places of worship, ranging from indifference to outright hostility.

After protests from Auerbach and others, the Bavarian *Ministerrat* debated

[35]See Philipp Auerbach, 'An alle Jüdischen Gemeinden', 7th March 1947, IfZ-Archiv, Nl Hoegner, ED 120, folder 138.
[36]See *Verhandlungen des Bayerischen Landtags*, Stenographische Berichte, 45th meeting on 16th January 1948, p. 578.
[37]OMGB, Monthly Report for Period Ending 30 June 1948. Education and Cultural Relations Division. Religious Affairs Branch, IfZ-Archiv, MF 260, OMGUS-By, 10/51–3/3.
[38]Louis G. Kelly, Chief/OMGUS-Displaced Persons Branch, 28th July 1948, IfZ-Archiv, MF 260, OMGUS-CAD, 3/173–1/19.

whether an appeal to the population – of the kind issued by the governments of Hesse and North Rhine-Westphalia – was a suitable method of stopping the incidents. But *Ministerpräsident* Ehard and his ministers believed that such a step would only attract unwanted attention. Their main fear was that Bavaria would be depicted in foreign press headlines as the stronghold of antisemitism. The *Ministerrat* eventually agreed "that these destructions of cemeteries were not a sign of antisemitism, but provocative acts by terrorist circles".[39]

In reality, the problem could not be overcome by adopting an ostrich-like policy of this kind. Complaints about the ineffectiveness of the Bavarian police grew more frequent. With the argument that "this news and the commentaries associated with it [are] . . . liable to do considerable damage to the reputation of Bavaria abroad",[40] a question was asked in the Bavarian *Landtag* in July 1948 regarding the desecration of Jewish cemeteries. *Innenminister* Willi Ankermüller defended the *Landpolizei* under his control against the charge that it had not intervened sufficiently or been successful in hunting for the perpetrators. He indicated that of 21 desecrations which had been notified, 15 cases had been cleared up. Of these, seven were attributed to "natural processes of decay" and in six more the perpetrators had been "children and youths playing". In only two cases had criminal offences been attributable to adults, and in one of these the perpetrator had been trying to demonstrate the need for a permanent watch on the cemetery. (In fact, mounting a guard was not an entirely effective method: in Regensburg shortly before, an auxiliary policeman given the job of protecting the Jewish cemetery had himself been responsible for desecrating it.[41]) Referring to the fact that numerous Christian cemeteries had also been desecrated during the same period, Ankermüller rejected the view "that the damage done to the Jewish cemeteries had been the affair of a Nazi underground movement. All these occurrences must be seen much more as symptom of a general brutalisation caused by the Nazi dictatorship and the war."[42]

In the background to this debate was an attack in the press by *Regierungsrat* Bachmann of the *Innenministerium* against the President of the Bavarian *Landpolizei*, *Freiherr* von Godin. Bachmann was himself a Jew who had survived the Nazi period by spending a number of years underground. He had reacted with bitter sarcasm to the publication of the *Landpolizei* findings that the destruction in Jewish cemeteries could be attributed to the weather and to children at play, and to the refusal to perceive any signs of antisemitism in these developments. His letter to the Franconian *Main-Post* contained the following remarks:[43]

---

[39]See minutes of the meeting of the Bayerischer Ministerrat, 16th April 1948, Bayerische Staatskanzlei, München.

[40]See Interpellation der Abgeordneten Dr. von Prittwitz und Gaffron und Hausleiter und Genossen betreffend Schändung israelitischer Friedhöfe (Beilage 1615), *Verhandlungen des Bayerischen Landtags*, Stenographische Berichte, 79th meeting on 22nd July 1948, p. 1650.

[41]See *Süddeutsche Zeitung*, 6th July 1948, 'Neue Schändungen jüdischer Friedhöfe'; *Verhandlungen des Bayerischen Landtags*, Stenographische Berichte, 81st meeting on 28th July 1948, p. 1756.

[42]See *Verhandlungen des Bayerischen Landtags*, Stenographische Berichte, 79th meeting on 22nd July 1948, pp. 1748–1749.

[43]See *Verhandlungen des Bayerischen Landtags*, Stenographische Berichte, 81st meeting on 28th July 1948, p. 1752. Bachmann was alluding to the US-financed "Hoover Program", which provided extra food rations for German schoolchildren.

"It is thus clearly established who is guilty of these scandalous incidents, and that is none other than the American government. It appears that German children have eaten their fill of school meals to such an extent that they are now capable of overturning hundreds of heavy gravestones."

In the Bavarian *Landtag*, Bachmann's comments provoked a storm of indignation which had much wider implications than its original cause, namely the desecration of Jewish cemeteries. The CSU deputy Hans Hagn argued furiously:[44]

"No person in this house approves when memorials to the dead are damaged in any way. But we must not go so far as artificially to create an atmosphere in which our efforts to achieve a good understanding with previous victims of racial persecution are seriously impaired simply because of the effects of the climate or the stupidity of little children."

Bachmann was marked out as a "calumniator", his comments as a tasteless gaffe which damaged Bavaria's reputation in the world. The Bavarian *Landtag* was unanimous in its judgement (even *Staatskommissar* Auerbach agreed); amid applause, *Innenminister* Ankermüller announced the "disciplinary assessment" of the *Regierungsrat*, who was now regarded as a man who had fouled his own nest.[45]

In many ways this episode is symptomatic of Bavarian relations with Jews and antisemitism after the war. Of course none of the deputies approved of the desecration of Jewish cemeteries – this was sheer common sense. But at the same time, hardly anyone was ready to get to grips with the potential antisemitism which these acts expressed. The existence of such sentiments was freely admitted in other circumstances, and could even be used as a political argument. For example, during efforts to block unwanted measures concerning the DPs there were constant references to the danger of encouraging the growth of antisemitism.[46] It is thus more than an unfortunate coincidence that the Bavarian *Landtag* showed its greatest resolution in reprimanding Bachmann for breaking the silence about the deeper causes behind the desecration of Jewish cemeteries.

Neither the harsh Bavarian climate nor the games of Bavarian children, however, could be used as an excuse in August 1949, when the liberal *Süddeutsche Zeitung* published a reader's letter signed "Adolf Bleibtreu". The letter included the following remarks:[47] "I am employed by the Amis and many of them have already said that they forgive us everything except for one thing, and that is that we did not gas them all, for now America is blessed with them." The letter had been chosen from many with a similar content and published without comment.

Next day, following a protest meeting, some 600 Jewish demonstrators gathered with banners expressing their anger and tried to make their way to the *Süddeutsche Zeitung*. Their route was barred by the German police. The attempt to disperse this unauthorised demonstration led to bitter street fighting in which demonstrators hurled paving stones in response to the use of police truncheons. One policeman – in self-defence, according to the commission of enquiry – fired

[44] *Ibid.*
[45] *Ibid.*,p. 1757.
[46] See *Verhandlungen des Bayerischen Landtags*, Stenographische Berichte, 45th meeting on 16th January 1948, p. 577.
[47] *Süddeutsche Zeitung*, 9th August 1949, 'Leserbriefe'.

his gun and severely wounded two demonstrators. Order was finally restored only with the help of the American military police.[48]

The publication of this letter and the subsequent conduct of the German police were both bitterly criticised, particularly by the Jewish press abroad. Nevertheless, the Munich Jewish religious community made a full apology to the German guardians of order.[49] The American High Commissioner, John J. McCloy, who had to consider possible proceedings against the *Süddeutsche Zeitung*, decided to accept its editor's excuse that the matter had been a regrettable oversight:[50]

> "It appears to me to be far better to allow the free democratic forces in Germany and the reaction of a vigorous public conscience to rebuff and combat Nazi and antisemitic sentiments wherever they appear, than to intervene with arbitrary Military Government action in every instance of this sort and thereby discourage the initiative and sense of responsibility of the German public."

The publication of the "Bleibtreu letter" had drawn clear attention to the existence of antisemitic attitudes in the Bavarian and German population. However, it was highly significant that its publication had met with the unanimous condemnation of the German media. The American High Commissioner, who regarded the resolution of problems between Jews and Germans as the litmus test of German democracy, placed his hopes for the future on the process of change which this development reflected, proceeding more or less from the top down.[51]

At the beginning of the 1950s, however, Bavaria was still making the headlines. A series of events there culminated in a sensational trial which many Jews regarded as an attempt to make new antisemitic propaganda. On 10th March 1951, the President of the Bavarian *Landesentschädigungsamt* (compensation office) was arrested in Munich. The man was Philipp Auerbach, who was also a board member of the *Zentralrat der Juden in Deutschland* founded in 1950.[52] He was accused of a whole series of offences committed while in office, some of which were ill-founded, but the fundamental argument was that Auerbach and others had enriched themselves from the reparations for the victims of Nazi persecution. Accused along with Auerbach was the Bavarian *Landesrabbiner* Aaron Ohrenstein, who had compared his position with that of a bishop. In consequence, the two most prominent representatives of post-war Bavarian Jewry were taken before a Bavarian court.

Before Auerbach's arrest the police had occupied the Bavarian *Landesentschädigungsamt*, which was responsible for organising reparations in Bavaria, in January 1951. This action was described by a furious Auerbach as a "frontal

---

[48]See Murray D. van Wagoner to C. Montieth Cilpin, 26th August 1949, IfZ-Archiv, MF 260, OMGUS-By 13/144–2/7; *Neue Zeitung*, 11th August 1949, 'Schwere Tumulte in München. Antisemitischer Leserbrief verursacht Straßenschlacht'.

[49]See van Wagoner to Cilpin (as note 48).

[50]John J. McCloy to Murray D. van Wagoner, 3rd September 1949, IfZ-Archiv, MF 260, OMGUS-By 13/134–3/11.

[51]See Kurt Grossmann, *Germany's Moral Debt. The German-Israel Agreement*, Washington D.C. 1954, p. 14.

[52]See Goschler, *loc. cit.*, pp. 77–98.

attack on reparation and Jewry".[53] The trial, in 1952, was seen by foreign observers in particular as a test case for German attitudes towards the Jews. Seven years after the end of Nazi rule, was a German court now to pass judgement on two Jews, when three of its five judges had been associated with the Nazi Party in some way?

The Bavarian *Justizministerium* showed a lack of sensitivity in dealing with questions of this kind. Its response to reproaches was as follows:[54] "I fully concur with you when you reject all collective discrimination, e.g. of racial or religious kind. But I must dismiss equally resolutely the attempts to discriminate against a judge because he was once a member of the Nazi Party, for this too is a matter of a collective prejudice." The presiding judge, *Landgerichtsdirektor* Mulzer, contributed a large number of maladroit observations during the trial. When Auerbach's defence counsel, Klibansky, asked for the postponement of the trial because it coincided with a Jewish festival, Mulzer interrupted him to say that he could not be expected to listen to endless details of Jewish rites. Klibansky replied that his client had spent five years in a concentration camp waiting for the chance to state his views, to which Mulzer responded by referring to his own "period of waiting" as a prisoner-of-war of the Russians.[55] While there is no need to read overt antisemitism into these exchanges, at the very least they reveal a profound lack of sympathy for the Jewish situation. However, there was another major indication that this was no normal or unpolitical trial, and that was the active propaganda made against Auerbach by *Justizminister* Müller during the entire investigation.

When judgement was finally given on 14th August 1952, the main elements of the original accusation had collapsed. Nevertheless, the court sentenced Auerbach to $2\frac{1}{2}$ years' imprisonment and a fine of DM 2,700 for using the title "Dr." when he was not entitled to do so (which Auerbach admitted), and for a number of other offences which he continued to deny.[56] Auerbach talked of a "terror sentence" and protested that a second Dreyfus case had been created.[57] But the appeal he had lodged never took place: three days after sentence was passed, Auerbach committed suicide.

Had a Jew been driven to his death by an antisemitic judiciary, as many observers suspected?[58] To provide at least some answers to this question, it is necessary to look into the background of the trial. Through his work for Jewish and other victims of Nazi persecution, Auerbach had acquired an extremely

[53]See *Süddeutsche Zeitung*, 29th January 1951, 'Entschädigungsamt unter Polizeibewachung'.

[54]Dr. Koch (Under Secretary at the Bayerisches Staatsministerium der Justiz) to Bruno Weil, 22nd September 1952, Archives of the Leo Baeck Institute, N.Y. (LBIA), Axis Victims League Inc. (Siegfried Moses) – box 1 (47/3).

[55]See Committee on Fair Play for Auerbach, April 1952, LBIA, Axis Victims League Inc. (Siegfried Moses), box 1 (47/3), *Neue Zeitung*, 27th April 1952, 'Gefahrvolle Entwicklungen', by Eberhard Körting.

[56]See Urteil in der Strafsache gegen Auerbach und drei Andere, ausgefertigt am 5.12.1952, Akten der Staatsanwaltschaft München I, Az. 2 KLs 1/52.

[57]See *Neue Zeitung*, 16th August 1952, 'Gericht begründet das Urteil gegen Auerbach und Ohrenstein'.

[58]See for example Rabbi D. Wilhelm Weinberg, 'Randbemerkungen zum Freitode Auerbachs', (1952), LBIA, Kurt Grossmann Collection.

influential position in Bavaria. In the process he had also acquired enemies. His main opponent was the Bavarian *Justizminister* and deputy *Ministerpräsident* Josef Müller, known as *"Ochsen-Sepp"*. Müller told the press that Auerbach was behaving like a *Gauleiter*;[59] about Hendrik George van Dam, later Secretary General of the *Zentralrat der Juden in Deutschland*, he said that Bavaria had no desire to be ruled by a Jewish "king".[60] Various earlier attempts by Müller to destroy Auerbach had failed because Auerbach initially had considerable support, not only from the victims of racial and political persecution but also from the Bavarian government itself. The latter was particularly pleased that Auerbach had managed to accelerate the emigration of the Jewish DPs to a considerable degree. By linking the payment of reparations to DPs with emigration, he was said to have persuaded 80,000 Jewish DPs to leave Bavaria. Not all the measures he adopted were irreproachable from a bureaucratic point of view, but the authorities had been more than willing to tolerate them; for the Bavarian government, the main thing was that the DPs left Bavaria.[61]

Auerbach's balancing act between the interests of the Jewish and other victims of persecution on the one hand, and the Bavarian state on the other, became increasingly difficult to maintain. After he had broken away from the increasingly Communist-dominated *Vereinigung der Verfolgten des Naziregimes* (VVN), many victims of political persecution began to oppose him. To the German Jews his behaviour was often "too ostentatiously Jewish", too little *"deutsch korrekt"*. By contrast, the Jewish DPs were frequently disturbed by his closeness to the German state.[62] Among his bitterest opponents was the Jewish Restitution Successor Organisation (IRSO) because Auerbach, in the struggle between the post-war German-Jewish communities and the IRSO for the inheritance of the destroyed Jewish communities, had energetically espoused the cause of the German Jews. In this conflict the IRSO gained a valuable ally in Benjamin Buttenwieser, the deputy American High Commissioner, a Wall Street man and himself a Jew. Only when the Jewish organisations had signalled to Auerbach's arch rival Müller that they were no longer ready to protect him, and indeed would even be interested in an action against him, could Müller inaugurate a political action which led to the accusation against Auerbach.[63]

In fact, from a purely judicial point of view Auerbach was not an entirely innocent victim. Once action was taken, the judiciary had no alternative but to investigate the matter and to pass judgement accordingly. A search through the extensive documentation of the trial reveals no indications that the investigating

[59]See *Neue Zeitung*, 14th October 1948, 'Auerbach heftig angegriffen'.

[60]See minutes of a meeting of *Landgerichtsrat* Aman and van Dam, 27th July 1951, Staatsanwaltschaft München I, Akten des Prozesses gegen Auerbach und drei Andere, Az. 2 KLs 1/52.

[61]See testimony of von Gumppenberg, 1st February 1952, Archiv-BayLT, Protokoll der 18. Sitzung des Untersuchungsausschusses zur Untersuchung der Vorgänge im Landesentschädigungsamt, p. 18.

[62]See report of Paul W. Freedman (American Jewish Committee), 'The Philipp Auerbach Tragedy', 17th September 1952, p. 31, Archives of the YIVO, New York, N.Y., RG 347, AJC, records, GEN–10, box 36.

[63]See report of Paul W. Freedman, 'Auerbach Jailed', 20th March 1951, pp. 18ff., YIVO, RG 347, AJC records, GEN–10, box 36.

authorities and the judges were motivated by hostility to Jews in the course of their work. On the contrary, Auerbach's co-defendent (and rival) Ohrenstein was actually able to make tactical use of his status as a Jewish rabbi during the trial.[64]

The real problem lies in the decision to take action at all. It was an open secret that Auerbach's work was not all done "by the book". But under the special circumstances of the post-war years such idiosyncracies were quietly tolerated. Otherwise it would have been impossible for him to achieve the truly extraordinary results that he did, to the benefit of the persecuted and the Bavarian state alike. One commission of enquiry established by the Bavarian *Landtag* declared:[65] "Such tasks were not to be solved by normal means nor by individuals who were used to working faithfully to the letter of the law but would have been somewhat helpless in face of the extraordinary situation confronting them." These arguments receded into the background only after the creation of the disparate coalition of interests described above. The Stuttgart lawyer Benno Ostertag, himself a Jew, put the matter well:[66] "Auerbach was the broom of his government who could be stuck in the corner whenever it suited his government and used again whenever they wanted it."

What significance did the trial have for attitudes towards the Jews? Undoubtedly the effect was negative, partly because the *Justizminister*'s public campaign created the impression that something was seriously amiss in the question of reparations and the Jews. Such opinions only confirmed and strengthened prevailing prejudices. For this reason the *Zentralrat der Juden in Deutschland* became anxious to distance itself from Auerbach and to treat the issue as an ordinary criminal trial.[67] It must be said, however, that the trial was not the anti-Jewish tribunal that Auerbach and his defenders liked to claim.

Nevertheless, the issue involved a number of circumstances which make talk of a political trial appear justified. These include matters relating to attitudes towards the Jews in Bavaria. In this affair, Jews were to be found on both sides – that of the victim and that of the wire-pullers – though the dominating image is the tragic fate of Auerbach himself. For our purposes, the vital point is that his entire conduct cannot be understood without taking into account attitudes towards the Jews in Bavaria, including the problem of a powerful post-war antisemitism. To this Auerbach reacted with aggressive counter-measures on one hand, but with efforts to reduce the conflict – particularly by encouraging the emigration of Jewish DPs – on the other. Auerbach tried to combine resolute advocacy of the rights of Jews in post-war German society with strong loyalty

[64]See Staatsanwaltschaft München I, Akten des Prozesses gegen Auerbach und drei Andere, Az. 2 KLs 1/52.
[65]Schlußbericht des Untersuchungsausschusses zur Prüfung der Vorgänge im Landesentschädigungsamt (LEA) vom 10.12.1953, *Verhandlungen des Bayerischen Landtags*, 1953/54, Beilage 5128, p. 15.
[66]Benno Ostertag, 'Auerbach und die bayerische Regierung', in *Allgemeine Wochenzeitung der Juden in Deutschland*, 22nd February 1952.
[67]See report of Paul W. Freedman, 20th March 1951, pp. 18–20 (as note 63).

towards the Bavarian state. The complexities of his conduct demonstrate the
exceptionally complicated situation facing the German Jews after the end of Nazi
rule.

In 1965, Hendrik George van Dam claimed that the continued existence of
potential antisemitism in the German people was "basically an antisemitism
without Jews".[68] As we have seen, at least in the first years after the war,
conditions in Bavaria were different: here there was an antisemitism *with* Jews.
The exceptional concentration of Jewish people in Bavaria in the early years
after Nazi rule was not repeated to the same extent anywhere else in Germany. In
Bavaria there were conditions which, together with the profound legacy of anti-
Jewish prejudices from the Nazi era, created the foundations for a distinct post-
war antisemitism. This was notably *volkstümlich*, while at the level of official
policy – partly due to the influence of the American Military Government – it
was no longer acceptable.

Decisive for the post-war development of attitudes towards the Jews was the
disappearance of the political conditions in which undoubted latent anti-Jewish
or antisemitic sentiments could have made a breakthrough. Equally, in
politically responsible circles in Bavaria after the war there is evidence of
attitudes which, though not overtly antisemitic, nevertheless reflected group
dislikes and prejudices and frequently resulted in unsympathetic or narrow-
minded modes of conduct and speech. Later, particularly from the 1960s, this
gave way to a somewhat awkward rapprochement.[69]

Antisemitic attitudes in the population declined slowly, in a process which will
not be investigated further here. There were setbacks throughout, and these
attitudes have not entirely disappeared even today. This can clearly be seen in
the development of the internationally famous Oberammergau Passion Play,
which despite several revisions of the text, still contains anti-Jewish passages,
and which, therefore, regularly comes under attack from Jewish critics.[70]
Criticism of this kind were also made on the occasion of the most recent
performance in 1990.[71] Such local incidents aside, Bavaria – once the exceptional
situation of the post-war years had ceased to exist – was no longer different from
other German regions as regards attitudes towards the Jews.[72]

[68]See van Dam, *loc. cit.*, p. 912.
[69]See *ibid.*, p. 913.
[70]See Hans Lamm, 'Und wieder: Traditionsreiches Oberammergau . . . Neuer Bürgermeister und
neuer Geist?', in *Münchener Jüdische Gemeindezeitung*, No. 28 (1984), pp. 13–14.
[71]See *Abendzeitung* (Munich), 15th June 1990, 'Neue Kritik an Oberammergaus frommen Spielen:
Judenfeindlicher Ballast'.
[72]With reference to the general developments in both the *Bundesrepublik* and the former *Deutsche
Demokratische Republik*, see a.o., Monika Richarz, 'Jews in Today's Germanies', in *LBI Year Book
XXX* (1985), pp. 265–274.

Franz Rosenzweig

A Life of Contradiction
The Philosopher Franz Rosenzweig and his
Relationship to History and Politics

BY STEFAN MEINEKE

I

In the summer of 1938 the historian Friedrich Meinecke received a visit that greatly surprised him.* The caller was Ernst Simon, a convinced Zionist who had emigrated to Palestine as early as 1928. Simon took the occasion of a visit to his gravely ill father to meet his former professor, who had been forced by the National Socialists to give up the various representative functions he had performed within the academic community.[1] Meinecke and Simon had a long discussion in which they tried to fathom the political situation they lived in, and the fate of German culture. It was in this context that the conversation turned to Franz Rosenzweig. Rosenzweig, who had died in 1929, had written under Meinecke's guidance, in 1912, an exceptional doctoral dissertation on Hegel's concept of the state. After the First World War, however, Rosenzweig resolutely refused to continue his academic career and committed himself, in theory and practice, to serving Judaism, the faith of his ancestors which he had only recently come to affirm.

In his conversation with Ernst Simon, Meinecke pointed out that he saw in Rosenzweig's course a paradigmatic significance for an understanding of the entire war generation born around 1890: the thinking of that generation had been driven by a desire for the original and for the natural; as such it was clearly opposed to the Idealist Protestant cultural heritage of the nineteenth century.[2]

Taking Meinecke's remark as a point of departure, I intend to evaluate to what degree Rosenzweig's intellectual development must in fact be considered characteristic of that entire generation of intellectuals. The focal point of this investigation will be Rosenzweig's relationship to history and politics, since such relationship would seem to demonstrate most clearly the specific nature of his thinking. In contrast to the general Rosenzweig research, which mostly exhibits

*My investigation is based on, in part, as yet unpublished letters by Rosenzweig, which Mr. Rafael Rosenzweig kindly allowed me to make use of. I am indebted to him, as well as to Professor Paul Mendes-Flohr (Jerusalem), and also to Ernst Schulin, my professor at Freiburg, for their valuable criticism of my manuscript. I would further like to thank my translator, Barbara Mahoney, for all her efforts in putting a thoroughly German text with all its intricacies into idiomatic English. But the English translation would not be what it is without the most gracious help that came from Marianne Berta in giving the essay a final revision.

[1] In 1934, the *Historische Reichskommission*, presided over by Meinecke, was dissolved by the Nazi regime. One year later Meinecke was forced to give up his position as editor of the *Historische Zeitschrift*. For a detailed account of the events leading up to his resignation see: Helmut Heiber, *Walter Frank und sein Reichsinstitut für die Geschichte des neuen Deutschlands*, Stuttgart 1966.

[2] A protocol of the discussion by Ernst Simon is deposited in The Jewish National and University Library, Jerusalem, Arc. Ms. Var. 350.

a strong preference for arguing within the context of the history of philosophy and which is thus interested both in a systematic and system-bound interpretation of his writings, it is the intention of this paper to understand Rosenzweig's thinking as the expression of a singular historical situation.[3]

II

Franz Rosenzweig, born December 1886, in Kassel, grew up in a family which had, in nearly every aspect, adapted itself to the conventions of German bourgeois circles. His father, a successful businessman, belonged to the well-respected city notables, being a National Liberal representative of the city council as well as a member of numerous institutions and foundations.[4] In regard to Franz, his only and sheltered child, he entertained, from early on, great hopes that his son might follow in his footsteps. As a result of the pressure from his father, the sensitive young man developed a decidedly rebellious attitude. This was so much the case that a friend of the family later remarked that Franz had spent his youth "in permanent opposition".[5] In the final analysis, however, it remains unclear what role exactly his resistance to paternal authority played in awakening his interest in the Jewish tradition.

In any case, and in marked contrast to the assimilated atmosphere within the family, the son, it seems, often attended Sabbath services and on occasion observed the fast of the Day of Atonement. It was his great-uncle Adam Rosenzweig, a strongly religious man, who very much encouraged him in this respect. Adam Rosenzweig lived in the attic of the Rosenzweig's home and was considered by Franz's parents to be a rather odd sort of recluse.[6] Nonetheless, it is probably safe to say that Franz saw in his own religious affiliation nothing more than a statistical entry; the matter did not seem to have bothered him unduly. The strained relations between him and his father seem to have been aroused above all else by his father's pragmatic orientation towards success, in consequence of which the son felt under pressure to comply with the necessity of conforming for career's sake. In sharp contrast to any such intention, however, Franz Rosenzweig made it the very maxim of his life to choose, wherever possible, the nonconformist way of the greatest degree of resistance.[7]

[3]For a general idea of the state of the Rosenzweig research see Carsten Schwoon, 'Die wissenschaftliche Rezeption', in *Juden in Kassel 1808–1933. Eine Dokumentation anläßlich des 100. Geburtstages von Franz Rosenzweig*, Kassel 1986, pp. 274–277, as well as the reports, edited by Wolfdietrich Schmied-Kowarzik in *Der Philosoph Franz Rosenzweig (1886–1929). Internationaler Kongress Kassel 1986*, 2 vols., Freiburg-München 1988.

[4]See Franz Rosenzweig, *Briefe und Tagebücher (Gesammelte Werke I)*, edited by Rachel Rosenzweig and Edith Rosenzweig-Scheinmann in collaboration with Bernhard Casper, Den Haag 1979, p. 1, henceforth referred to as C(ollected) W(orks) 1.

[5]*Ibid.*

[6]See *ibid.*, p. 2 as well as the letter to Gertrud Frank, 29th September 1901, *ibid.*, pp. 4–5.

[7]Interesting references to the social background and the commonness in Franz Rosenzweig's generation of such an attitude to life will be found in Hans D. Hellige, 'Generationskonflikt. Selbsthaß und die Entstehung antikapitalistischer Positionen im Judentum. Der Einfluß des Antisemitismus auf das Sozialverhalten jüdischer Kaufmanns- und Unternehmersöhne im Deutschen Kaiserreich und in der k. und k.-Monarchie', in *Geschichte und Gesellschaft*, 5 (1979), pp. 476–518.

After attending the *Friedrichs-Gymnasium* in the city of his birth, Kassel, where he already showed notable distinction, he entered medical school in the summer of 1905. He continued his studies through the first general exams (*Physikum*, or intermediate pre-clinical exam), taken in the autumn of 1907. He wanted to prove to his father that he was quite capable of a *Brotstudium*. In the winter semester of 1908 he pursued studies in history and philosophy at Freiburg, which were very much more in accord with his genuine intellectual interests. With Meinecke as his supervisor, he earned his doctor's degree *summa cum laude* in 1912. In his evaluation of his doctoral dissertation, Meinecke left no doubt about his student's exceptional talent, which he hoped to promote in the future.[8]

Upon receiving his doctorate, Franz Rosenzweig was obliged to confront the more and more pressing problem of having to choose which direction, in principle, his life should take. There were two questions which particularly occupied him. On the one hand, he reflected upon his own relationship to history and to academically established science in general. On the other hand, he was toying with the suggestion a friend had made: that he should complete the assimilation process already effected by his parents by converting to Christianity.

Initially he answered the second question with a "yes". He accepted his friend's suggestion on the condition that he might first give his inherited Judaism another careful inspection. But the more sceptical he grew as to the sense it made to continue a career in academics, the greater became his fascination with Judaism. So in the end, Rosenzweig abandoned his plans for the future completely: instead of taking the "simple and straight path"[9] of an academic career, he gave up all academic ambition in order to "become a Jew" with all the consequences.

Rosenzweig's abrupt departure from academic life proved to be final. Even when Meinecke, in 1919, repeatedly offered him *Habilitation* and in 1921 invited him to work regularly on the *Historische Zeitschrift*, Rosenzweig invariably refused.[10] Of course, his intransigence implied no animosity towards Meinecke; it was actually an expression of a deep-seated rejection of academics. In 1923, when asked by representatives of the Jewish community of Frankfurt to habilitate *pro forma* in order to enhance the status of the *Freies Jüdisches Lehrhaus*, which he directed, Rosenzweig refused just as uncompromisingly as he had when rejecting Meinecke's previous offers. In a letter to Martin Buber he reported that he had turned down the community's proposal "with a scornful laugh", since he was "totally free" from any "Universitätsfimmel".[11]

Although at first incomprehensible to those who knew him, Rosenzweig's rejection of an academic career was not the result of a momentary mood but rather the solution to a problem he had given long consideration. As early as 1906 he had, in a diary entry, defined academic research as something which

---

[8]Friedrich Meinecke's evaluation of Rosenzweig's doctoral dissertation, to be found in *Archiv der Philosophischen Fakultät der Albert-Ludwigs-Universität Freiburg*.
[9]Letter to Friedrich Meinecke, 30th August 1920, in *CW 1*, p. 679.
[10]Unpublished letter to Margrit Rosenstock, 3rd February 1921.
[11]Letter to Martin Buber, 12th January 1923, in *CW 1*, p. 879.

could not grasp the reality of the world but, on the contrary, led the way out of reality.[12] So academic triumphs rated on a par with sports records for him: they were nothing but purely artificial successes, impressive in their acrobatics, but not related in any way to what he understood to be the reality of human life. Cultivation of science was therefore a luxury, and scholarly pride the expression of egocentricity, only possible to members of an institution whose sole function is to revolve around itself. He often lamented the "unreality" of university activity, which he countered from the very first with "self-reliance and rejection".[13] Such unreality manifested itself, according to Rosenzweig, in the inability of the arts and sciences to provide an answer to concrete problems associated with man's attitude towards life. Wherever the ethical question as to the right way of life presented itself to human beings, the arts and sciences remained inept. They could offer possibilities, but they could not set norms. In Rosenzweig's opinion, therefore, the whole process of acquiring scientific knowledge was characterised by its inherent negativity: the insight it generated in regard to the historical determinedness and relativity of all moral standards undermined the validity of ethical traditions without offering something in its place. For the increasingly dynamic development in the arts and sciences made it impossible to give an explanation of the world that could in turn have served as a starting point for a new tradition. In fact, it was the very progress that was taking place in the arts and sciences which created the cultural crisis. With the loss of common sense, the demand for a new intellectual orientation became increasingly important for society as a whole.

This crisis first manifested itself in the German Empire from the turn of the century: in the intensive debate over culture; in the appearance of numerous alternative, renewal and reform movements; and in the public esteem enjoyed by various popular philosophers (Rudolf Eucken, Ernst Haeckel) and their works. The social dominance of bourgeois National Liberalism began to weaken and found itself confronted with the pluralism of disparate private *Weltanschauungen*.[14]

Franz Rosenzweig's intellectual transformation must be understood in terms of this cultural background. His wholehearted reversion to the Jewish tradition was perfectly in accord with the general dialectic of a loss of faith in science and a readiness to affirm religious belief. Since the study of history had none other than itself as its objective and was thus incapable of perfecting human individuality, it became, as Rosenzweig wrote in a letter to Meinecke, an

> "insatiably curious, ever voracious ghost totally consuming the man whom it holds in its grip until nothing is left of his humanness" [unersättlich neugieriges unstillbar gefräßiges

[12]Diary entry, 20th November 1906, in *CW 1*, p. 65.
[13]Letter to his parents, 20th September 1917, in *CW 1*, p. 446.
[14]A complete representation of this process of disintegration culminating in the *Geist der zwanziger Jahre* is not yet available. Still interesting, though problematical in its judgements, is Georg Steinhausen's *Deutsche Geistes- und Kulturgeschichte von 1870 bis zur Gegenwart*, Halle 1931. Among the many more recent investigations are Fritz Stern, *Kulturpessimismus als politische Gefahr* (originally in English: *The Politics of Cultural Despair*, Berkeley 1961), München 1986; Gerhard Kratzsch, *Kunstwart und Dürerbund*, Göttingen 1969; Hermann Lübbe, *Politische Philosophie in Deutschland*, München 1974; Ulrich Linse, 'Die Lebensreformbewegung', in *Archiv für Sozialgeschichte*, 17 (1977), pp. 538–543; Corona Hepp, *Avantgarde. Kulturkritik und Reformbewegungen nach der Jahrhundertwende*, München 1987.

Gespenst, das den, den es besessen hält, aufzehrt bis von seiner Menschlichkeit nichts mehr übrigbleibt].[15]

The relativity of every single academic achievement, demonstrated by the insatiable and dubious progress of research in the field of history, proved to Rosenzweig the irrelevance of any such achievement for the present. In this he diagnosed the self-destruction of historical thinking, since it not only demonstrated the relativity of tradition but also the arbitrariness of its own scientific interests, methods, and results.[16]

So what could offer an escape from the enervating dilemma of historical thinking must by necessity come from beyond history. It could only be the non- and supra-historical that man might rightfully define as his "innermost property"; and only the supra-historical could give him the power and strength to orientate himself in the present and answer the vital questions concerning him in his "innermost self". Ever since the summer of 1913, Rosenzweig believed that it was Judaism that furnished the source of eternal, absolute truth. For, by complying with the religious rituals and moral standards of Judaism, the believer took part in the Covenant made by God with Israel at the beginning of all time. Beyond the anarchy of cultural values and the dubious nature of scientific knowledge, the changeless world of eternity opened itself up to Rosenzweig in the world of the Jewish religion.

Fascinated by this experience, he saw Judaism defined above all else by its timelessness and its seclusion from the world. Judaism's distance from history and the present – the condition necessary for its infinite nature – proved to be not its deficit but, rather, its unique distinction: since the Jewish people did not attempt to anchor themselves in the world, they could outlive all other nations. By their participation in the liturgy, rituals and laws of the synagogue, they transcended the present and entered the timeless world granted by God. Thus it was Rosenzweig's conviction that the true Israel should be nothing more than a "kingdom of priests".[17]

His extreme interpretation of the timelessness of Judaism directly determined his attitude towards the social world. Compared to the eternity of Judaism, the world faded to a mere "intermediate kingdom" (*Zwischenreich*)[18] about which he was led to say:

[15]Letter to Friedrich Meinecke, 20th August 1920, in *CW 1*, p. 681.

[16]For a general account see Thomas Nipperdey, 'Sich an der Geschichte orientieren?', in *idem*, *Der Mensch als Orientierungswaise? Ein interdisziplinärer Erkundungsgang*, Freiburg 1982, pp. 107–144.

[17]A fundamental depiction is Alexander Altmann, 'Franz Rosenzweig on History', in *The Philosophy of Franz Rosenzweig*, edited by Paul Mendes-Flohr, Hanover 1988, pp. 124–137.

However, Alexander Altmann does not refer at all to the crisis of historicism, which exercised an important influence on Rosenzweig's early thinking. A contribution to this problem give Paul Mendes-Flohr and Jehuda Reinharz, 'From Relativism to Religious Faith. The Testimony of Franz Rosenzweig's Unpublished Diaries', in *LBI Year Book XXII* (1977), pp. 161–174, as well as Paul Mendes-Flohr, 'Franz Rosenzweig and the Crisis of Historicism', in *The Philosophy, op. cit.*, pp. 138–161. Furthermore Steven T. Katz, 'On Historicism and Eternity. Reflections on the 100th Birthday of Franz Rosenzweig', in *Der Philosoph Franz Rosenzweig, op. cit.*, vol. 2, pp. 745–770, as well as Stéphane Mosès, 'Politik und Religion. Zur Aktualität Franz Rosenzweigs' (originally in French 1982), *ibid.*, pp. 855–875, here pp. 865–871.

[18]Letter to Hans Ehrenberg, 11th May 1918, in *CW 1*, p. 560. Here also the quotation: "The Christian relationship to the intermediate kingdom is affirmative; the Jewish one negative."

"The entire history of the world, of nations, wars and revolutions loses, for the Jew, its seriousness and importance."[19]

Accordingly, Rosenzweig found the believing Jew's way of thinking to be characterised by a disinterest in all evolving history. On the other hand this also meant for him that a Jew who believed in the importance of the social world or who even became actively engaged in it had failed to understand his religious duty. Consequently, he condemned the attempts of the Zionists and the assimilated Jews to establish themselves in the world through money or power.[20] For he was convinced that every involvement with social reality diminished what he believed was the true advantage of Judaism: its meta-historical, timeless nature. Preserving this nature, therefore, meant in Rosenzweig's opinion real self-assertion of Judaism.

Nonetheless, it would be completely wrong to conclude from Rosenzweig's concept of Judaism that he wanted to reduce the religious existence solely to its spiritual inner dimension. On the contrary, Rosenzweig insisted that faith must prove itself in the practice of everyday life. Because he understood the world as God's creation, it was a quite logical consequence for him to define devotion to the world as a claim derived directly from the first commandment. Thus he concluded:

"The love of God must find expression in the love of one's neighbour."[21]

In the light of this, he referred to the type of mystic as "fundamentally amoral" who, in "proud withdrawal", despised the world because he "strives for nothing else but to be God's darling".[22] In the same manner, theological disputes over "God in heaven" should be deemed "rather negligible issues" as long as the believer would only succeed, by thought and action, in becoming one with the reality of life.[23] Statements of this kind, of which there are several, lead Emmanuel Lévinas to conclude that Rosenzweig maintained, above and beyond any search for truth, the "priority principle of active love".[24] However, it was only in a rather restricted sense that the first commandment of love could be a guiding principle for action in the present. For, if Judaism was characterised by

[19]Cited in Karl Löwith, 'Martin Heidegger and Franz Rosenzweig. Ein Nachtrag zu "Sein und Zeit"', in *idem, Gesammelte Abhandlungen. Zur Kritik der geschichtlichen Existenz*, Stuttgart 1960, pp. 68–92; quotation, p. 87.

[20]Letter to Gertrud Oppenheim, 1st May 1917, in *CW 1*, pp. 398–402. See also Stéphane Mosès, *System und Offenbarung. Die Philosophie Franz Rosenzweigs* (originally in French: *Système et révélation. La philosophie de Franz Rosenzweig*, Paris 1982), München 1985, pp. 162–168.

[21]Franz Rosenzweig, *Der Stern der Erlösung (Gesammelte Werke 2)*, edited by Reinhold Mayer, Den Haag 1976, p. 239. Henceforth referred to as C(ollected) W(orks) 2. Translation into American English by William W. Hallo on the basis of the German second edition of 1930, New York 1971; paperback edition, Boston 1972. English edition in *The Littman Library of Jewish Civilization*, London 1971; reprint Notre Dame, Indiana: Notre Dame Press, 1985.

[22]*CW 2*, pp. 231–232.

[23]Letter to Gertrud Oppenheim, 31st May 1917, in *CW 1*, p. 414.

[24]'Judentum und Christentum nach Franz Rosenzweig. Ein Gespräch', in *Zeitgewinn. Messianisches Denken nach Franz Rosenzweig*, edited by Gotthard Fuchs and Hans H. Henrix, Frankfurt a. Main 1987, p. 175. See also, above all Bernhard Casper, 'Zeit – Erfahrung – Erlösung. Zur Bedeutung Rosenzweigs angesichts des Denkens des 20. Jahrhunderts', in *Der Philosoph Franz Rosenzweig, op. cit.*, vol. 2, pp. 553–566.

timelessness and a seclusion from the world, its commandments could, naturally, only refer to that which also was timeless. Hence Rosenzweig's thinking was bound not only "to take as a starting point" but also to stop short before "naked man in his finite existence, as he precedes all levels of culture".[25]

On the other hand, if a dimension of social criticism was to be opened up in the commandment of love, a political concept of order would be required to render the social implications concrete. Such historisation, however, was absolutely incompatible with Rosenzweig's assertion of the ahistorical nature of Judaism. So the authority of the commandment of love remained limited to a non-social dimension. The service to mankind which Rosenzweig hoped to accomplish with his thinking was not complemented by an involvement with society. His theory of history surely did grant him the greatly desired access to a timeless mode of life. Such gain, however, turned out to be a loss at the same time; for the new standpoint to which his thinking had brought him dramatically narrowed his view of the social world and thus promoted a fatalistic acceptance of history in its concrete manifestations. Rosenzweig's conception of an ahistorical Judaism secluded from the world enabled him to escape and to overcome, by aiming at a timeless and religious mode of existence, the paralysing force of relativism and scepticism which had more and more burdened him during his historical studies. In this way, the young Rosenzweig was a striking proof of Nietzsche's prognosis that a historical thinking which leads to nihilistic consequences need not only be a "malaise", but also a "virtue", since it could work as a release from all the inhibitions and any sense of duty as dictated by convention, thus enabling man to make his own decisions in complete personal autonomy. Hence, when in October 1913 he discovered the spiritual power of Judaism, Rosenzweig realised that historical thinking had been for him but the "doorstep leading to something totally new and unfamiliar".[26]

III

It was not until the First World War came to a close that Rosenzweig found time to give formal voice to his theory of history. Later this would become a part of his *opus magnum*, *Der Stern der Erlösung*, which he actually completed within the short period of merely half a year in February of 1919. Nonetheless, his correspondence indicates that already during the war he had tried to practise that which he later proclaimed in *Der Stern* as his ideal: that the faithful Jew must refrain from involvement in worldly affairs.

When in 1914 war became reality, the attitudes of the different social groups toward this event were highly dependent upon the perspectives they took in regard to the future. In general, research has well established that the German

---

[25]Already stated by Karl Löwith with reference to Heidegger as well as to Rosenzweig: Löwith, 'Heidegger', *loc. cit.*, p. 70.

[26]Friedrich Nietzsche, *Fröhliche Wissenschaft* (Musarion Edition), München 1922, p. 247.
  Details are in Karl Schlechta, 'Nietzsches Verhältnis zur Historie', in *idem*, *Der Fall Nietzsche*, München 1958, pp. 42–70.

Jews had seen the war as an opportunity to achieve completely equal social standing by leaving no doubt about their loyalty to the nation. The *Kaiser's* famous proclamation of 4th August 1914 – "For me there are no longer any parties, only Germans" – is assumed to have been left open to such interpretation, and it certainly evoked storms of enthusiasm amongst German Jews. Further, it has been stated that the Jews were quite prepared to heed the call of the *Centralverein deutscher Staatsbürger jüdischen Glaubens* and to prove their loyalty to the German nation "beyond the normal measure to be expected from a citizen".[27] However, this does not hold true for Rosenzweig. Of course there is the fact that he voluntarily signed up for military service in April 1915, but he had very private reasons for doing so. Just because he was perfectly aware that he, an awkward and fearful man,[28] could be almost anything except a good soldier, he deliberately chose – "since the home reserves *[Landsturm]* have been called up" – to give up his position with the Red Cross and to face the dangers of the front line.[29] His military combat service thus served him as a sort of personal test, but beyond that he did "not expect to gain anything whatsoever from the war" certainly not the achieving of complete emancipation for which the *Centralverein* hoped.[30]

From the very beginning of war, Rosenzweig emphasised in letters to his parents "how repugnant all the butchery is to me"[31] and how he did not in any way "feel myself to be a German".[32] In his attitude towards the state he was "merely performing my duty".[33] He dismissed any attempt to deny the historical nature of national identity by creating unchangeable national characteristics for the sake of interpreting war as a conflict of moral principles. Although he found himself in agreement with the widespread opinion that Western European culture had nothing more to offer,[34] there did not exist for Rosenzweig a "Germanness" *[deutsches Wesen]* whose enforcement upon the world could cure the latter of social decadence and foreign corruption. A Germanic metaphysics of this kind, which in the final analysis went as far as making the nation's right to exist conditional on the fulfilment of its assumed historical mission to the world,[35] was certainly far from Rosenzweig's mind. For what he had had to

---

[27]Cf. Egmont Zechlin, *Die deutsche Politik und die Juden im Ersten Weltkrieg*, Göttingen 1969. See also Arnold Paucker, 'Zur Problematik einer jüdischen Abwehrstrategie in der deutschen Gesellschaft', in *Juden im Wilhelminischen Deutschland*. Ein Sammelband herausgegeben von Werner E. Mosse unter Mitwirkung von Arnold Paucker, Tübingen 1976 (Schriftenreihe wissenschaftlicher Abhandlungen des Leo Baeck Instituts 33), pp. 479–548, especially pp. 545–548.

[28]Cf. the anecdote, transmitted by Gertrud Oppenheim in *CW 1*, p. 181.

[29]Letter to his parents, 15th April 1915, in *CW 1*, p. 180. Compare also the reference of Bertha Badt-Strauß, *ibid.*, p. 174.

[30]Letter to Hans Ehrenberg, October 1916, in *CW 1*, p. 243.

[31]Letter to his parents, 9th September 1914, in *CW 1*, p. 174.

[32]*Ibid.*

[33]Letter to Eugen Rosenstock, 8th November 1916, in *CW 1*, p. 286. Furthermore: letter to his parents, 29th December 1916, in *CW 1*, pp. 325–326.

[34]Cf. the letter to Hans Ehrenberg, 10th May 1917, in *CW 1*, pp. 405–407, esp. p. 407.

[35]Thus, for instance, the social philosopher Paul Natorp: "If the German . . . became untrue to his innermost calling, it would indeed be time to erase his name from [the face of] the earth.", in 'Die Seele des Deutschen', in Paul Natorp, *Deutscher Weltberuf*, Jena 1918, quotation p. 202.

realise above all, as a historian, was the determination underlying all cultural phenomena. And in regard to the German culture, too, he had in fact been long convinced that it was nothing other than the mere expression of a number of sociological facts and that the rise of the working class would bring a new culture into being which would know nothing of Goethe.[36] Hence, given such historical thinking, it was impossible for him to consecrate war or even proclaim it, as Rudolf Eucken had, "the world's ultimate test of the soul of Germany" (*Weltbewährungsprobe deutscher Innerlichkeit*).

Although Rosenzweig could not bring himself to celebrate the war as a dispute of moral principles, he did not disapprove of the war either. In his eyes, war was neither good nor bad. Rather it should be understood as a fundamental and inescapable fact of human life. War, then, was not a product of human madness: it belonged to human nature – just as much as the arts and sciences. To live as a human being and to fight wars was one and the same. True peace could therefore only be granted through God's act of redemption at the end of all time. Hence Pacifism became for him a highly "profligate attitude" since it was based on the absurd claim that man will be able to achieve peace by his own strength.[37] If, however, war was always to remain a potential human cause, then the State must take measures accordingly. Hence Rosenzweig asserted:

> "It remains the foremost task to keep the constitution . . . in excellent condition not only for times of peace but times of peace and war. For it is through both, peace and war, that the life of a nation unfolds."[38]

Given this distance from all enthusiasm for war, he yet consented to accept war as "essentially necessary".[39]

After the outbreak of the war, Rosenzweig had not only striven to avoid any identification with German Nationalism elated with the certainty of victory; he

---

[36]Diary entry, 17th June 1906, in *CW 1*, p. 49.

[37]Letter to his parents, 17th August 1916, in *CW 1*, p. 204. Concerning his views on Pacifism see also his letter to his parents, 1st September 1916, *ibid.*, pp. 210–214, as well as the letter to Eugen Rosenstock, 2nd October 1917, *ibid.*, pp. 461–463.

[38]'Die Reichsverfassung in Krieg und Frieden' (written 1917), now to be found in Franz Rosenzweig, *Zweistromland. Kleinere Schriften zu Glauben und Denken*, edited by Reinhold and Annemarie Mayer (*Gesammelte Werke 3*), Dordrecht 1984, pp. 253–255. Quotation p. 255. Henceforth referred to as C(ollected) W(orks) 3.

[39]Letter to his parents, 4th October 1916, in *CW 1*, p. 238. It is therefore misleading when Rosenzweig is associated with Pacifism, an impression created by Rivka Horwitz in one of her essays. Rosenzweig's " 'non-German' feelings" (see Horwitz, p. 249) were directed simply against the German philistine's war euphoria. But his criticism of "the inferior and average" [*die Minderwertigen und Durchschnittlichen*], fed as it was by the intellectual aristocrat's feelings of resentment, was by no means reason enough for Rosenzweig to reject German war politics, or even dismiss war as a means for politics. Since Horwitz leaves out of account the entire bulk of Rosenzweig's political writings as well as his letters written in 1918–1919, her interpretation must necessarily remain unsound in this respect. When, in footnote 66, she quotes a statement of Rosenzweig's ("The Jew is . . . the only genuine 'Pacifist' "), her conclusions are wrong because she fails to recognise the fact that Rosenzweig placed the crucial term between inverted commas. For Rosenzweig, the Jew is a "Pacifist" for the very reason that he is enabled by his religion to overcome both the anxieties and hopes that have their roots in the world – including, of course, matters of "political" Pacifism. Cf. Rivka Horwitz, 'Voices of Opposition to the First World War among Jewish Thinkers', in *LBI Year Book XXXIII* (1988), pp. 233–259; as to Rosenzweig, especially pp. 249–253.

went still further inasmuch as he tried to deny his war experience any impact at all on his thinking. For him, the Jew, who could play no greater part in world history than that of a "handyman" (*Handlanger*),[40] the war must not acquire any existential significance. Thus in 1917 he vigorously asserted his opinion in a letter to his parents:

> "I deny that war makes any real impact on any man. In my case, it would be particularly absurd [to assume such impact]."[41]

And again in October of the same year he acknowledged without disappointment that the war manifested itself "as nothing but a gap" in his life.[42]

Already at that point in time, however, this conclusion was no longer unreservedly true.[43] Rosenzweig, stationed at the quiet Balkan front, gave way, in the course of 1917, to writing several essays attempting to interpret the war in terms of universal history.[44] One consideration was central to all his thoughts: a war that brought the entire world into a clash of such an unheard-of intensity must have in its wake a new and supra-national political order. In very much the same way as Friedrich Naumann,[45] Rosenzweig saw the German Empire as predestined to develop such guiding forms of cooperation in South-Eastern Europe. To Rosenzweig, the goal of ensuring to Germany a long-term influence in South-Eastern Europe seemed to be the natural objective of German war politics. In 1917, when he still conceived of a German victory as obvious, Rosenzweig declared it should "not be deemed of first importance to weaken the beaten enemy, but to enhance one's own strength".[46]

Accordingly, he saw territorial annexation justified only inasmuch as the enemy's vital interests were not directly endangered. In this sense he considered himself to be a supporter of a "negotiated peace" (*Verständigungsfrieden*).[47] While the German Empire was to maintain the *status quo* in the West in order to keep a mutually acceptable settlement with France and Belgium open, it should turn to South-Eastern Europe with a view to directing the "political wasteland" of the

---

[40]Letter to Hans Ehrenberg, 8th November 1916, in *CW 1*, p. 285. For a fundamental view on this problem see George L. Mosse, *The Jews and German War Experience 1914–1918* (Leo Baeck Memorial Lecture 21), New York 1977.

[41]Letter to his parents, 29th May 1917, in *CW 1*, p. 411.

[42]Letter to W.H., 5th October 1917, in *CW 1*, p. 468.

[43]See Paul Mendes-Flohr, 'Historicism', *loc. cit.*, p. 146, who emphasises that Rosenzweig followed the events during the war very intensively.

[44]These essays, some of which are previously unpublished, are now available in *CW 3*, chapter: 'Zur Politik', pp. 241–368. With the exception of Paul Mendes-Flohr's 'Historicism', *loc. cit.*, pp. 145–154, research on Rosenzweig until now has failed to take notice of them.

[45]Friedrich Naumann, *Mitteleuropa*, Berlin 1915. Rosenzweig wanted to dedicate one of his political essays to Naumann, "The herald of the concept of *Mitteleuropa*", see the letter to his mother, 13th October 1918, in *CW 1*, pp. 612–613.

[46]'Das Kriegsziel' (written 1917), in *CW 3*, pp. 297–299, quotation p. 299.

[47]'Nordwest und Südost' (first edition 1917), now in *CW 3*, pp. 301–307, in which he differentiates between "Annexionists and 'Central Europeans'" [*Mitteleuropäern*] (p. 303). It would be unwarranted to conclude from this that he would have denounced the annexation of the Balkan Region. When, in the Autumn of 1917, a realisation of *Mitteleuropa* seemed plausible to him, he rejected categorically the anti-annexation movement of the *Unabhängige Sozialdemokratische Partei Deutschlands (USPD)*. See an unpublished letter to Margrit Rosenstock, November 1917.

Balkan region towards its "universal task": that of being a bridge between East and West.[48] Rosenzweig saw the existence of the Balkan states wholly in terms of this one function; for if they could not live "by their own inner resources" they must, in the future as well, remain "servants to, not masters of" their fate.[49] But this of course meant that Rosenzweig thereby created an absolute "historical law"[50] out of historically determined and thus changeable political dependencies. Consequently, German expansion in the South-East was, *a priori*, given historical legitimisation: it would mean nothing but the execution of what Rosenzweig regarded as the Balkan States' historical fate. The fascination which the notion of *Mitteleuropa* held for him was ultimately based upon his being able to surround a pure power struggle with an aura of conducting a cultural mission. He saw Germany's involvement in the Balkan region as a supra-national responsibility because it was an effort to ensure a lasting influence of occidental culture. The "distinction" of the German Balkan imperialism as postulated by Rosenzweig consisted in its ostensible freedom from all *Realpolitik*.[51] Not least, he hoped that such a policy, which would combine territorial with moral conquests, would in turn have a positive effect on the mentality of the Germans, enabling them – as the leading members of a commonwealth which would spread out as far as the Orient – to free themselves from the *raison d'état* of the Prussian bureaucratic military state and to acquire finally "the openness of mind which belongs to a 'universal people' (*Weltvolk*) that fully trusts in its universal historical significance".[52]

When in 1917 Rosenzweig spoke of the German *Reich*'s significance for *Mitteleuropa* and brooded over the "host of spiritual and political tasks" which such significance implied, he had already revised the quietist point of view he had taken at the outbreak of the war.[53] As one can see from his "euphoria for *Mitteleuropa*", he only possessed a sense of politics inasmuch as he could spiritualise it into a battle of ideas. Hence it was not the hard political reality – Max Weber's "slow and steady drilling of tough boards"[54] – that interested Rosenzweig, but, and quite exclusively so, its ideal superstructure. According to his own cultural elitism, he demanded an ethical imperialism without recognis-

---

[48]'Die neue Levante' (first edition 1917), in *CW 3*, pp. 309–312, quotations pp. 310 and 311.
[49]*Ibid.*, p. 311.
[50]*Ibid.*, p. 310.
[51]'Nordwest', in *CW 3*, p. 306.
[52]*Ibid.*, p. 305.
  This goal had already been given expression when he criticised Hegel in his doctoral dissertation. See his foreword to *Hegel und der Staat*, now to be found in *CW 3*, pp. 45–52. There p. 51: "Hegel's hard and limited concept of the state" should be replaced so that Bismarck's state "may expand and become an empire breathing free and universal air" (*freie Weltluft atmendes Reich*). See Wolfdietrich Schmied-Kowarzik, 'Der Philosoph Franz Rosenzweig (1886–1929). Eine Vergegenwärtigung', in *Juden in Kassel, op. cit.*, pp. 87–96, here pp. 87–89.
[53]'Realpolitik' (first edition 1917), in *CW 3*, pp. 261–265, quotation p. 265.
  What needs correction is Rivka Horwitz's view that Rosenzweig took little notice only of the war-time events. Her conclusion may be tenable, at best, if restricted to certain periods of time. Cf. Horwitz, 'Voices of Opposition', *loc. cit.*, pp. 250–251.
[54]Max Weber, 'Der Beruf zur Politik' (first edition 1919), in *Max Weber. Soziologie, Universalgeschichtliche Analysen, Politik*, edited by Johannes Winckelmann, 5th edition, Stuttgart 1973, p. 185,

ing that every "attempt at moralising politics" brings about, as Hermann Lübbe has observed, "the reverse effect of politicising morals".[55] Unwilling to grant politics its inner law, the writer Rosenzweig got more and more lost in the clouds of his romantic political sentiments.

On the one hand, Rosenzweig wanted to see politics in the service of abstract ideals, as becomes evident in his rejection of Bismarck's pragmatic foreign policy as an expression of "reckless egoism";[56] on the other hand, however, he was fully aware that a political practice based on ideals could have fatal consequences. He himself even took the view that it was only through her enthusiastic *Nibelungentreue* in relation to Austria-Hungary that Germany became involved in the war. Notwithstanding this, he believed that a politician of Bismarck's stamp in all probability could have avoided a general war by letting the Danubian Monarchy fall.[57] But despite having seen this alternative, he leaned decidedly towards politics of principle which demanded conflict. In this respect he remarked in an essay written in the spring of 1917 that politics should not exist for "the purpose of improving one's [respective] overall political situation", but, rather, "purely for its own sake".[58] Rosenzweig's rigorous ethical convictions, which were "not to be subdued either by fear or by egoism", dismissed all concessions to the reality.[59] Accordingly, Rosenzweig judged the political actor not by his success but solely by the intentions he presumably had. In this respect he held a point of view which stood in direct and radical conflict to that of the responsible politician: for whoever wanted to shape the reality of the world must be expected to take into due consideration the potential consequences of his actions. Since it was just this that Rosenzweig refused to accept, he reveals to us how much and how thoroughly his thinking remained unpolitical. His very underestimation of the facts, which found expression in his alienation from politics, caused him to praise the unworldly, scholarly type of politician. Thus he entertained an enthusiasm for Bethmann Hollweg, *Reichskanzler* from 1909–1917, so singular that it could hardly be outdone. This enthusiasm was brought about by Bethmann's speech to the *Reichstag* on 4th August 1914, in which he declared the German invasion of Belgium to be against international law. This admission of guilt Rosenzweig considered a "singular deed unprecedented in all history",[60] "in which God acts directly through one individual man".[61] Even when Bethmann – on 2nd December 1914 under pressure from various interest groups

[55]According to Hermann Lübbe in his analysis of German philosophy during the First World War, *Politische Philosophie in Deutschland, op. cit.*, p. 193.

[56]'Ökumene' (written 1917), now in *CW 3*, pp. 314–348, quotation p. 344.

[57]*Ibid.* Rosenzweig does not say this directly; nonetheless, this conclusion must be drawn from his remarks: "It is hard to conceive of anything that is farther away from the spirit of Bismarck's politics than the policy that led to Germany's entry into the war."

[58]'Realpolitik', in *CW 3*, p. 264.

[59]This well-known saying of Heinrich Heine's in its original context refers to Fichte. See Heinrich Heine, 'Zur Geschichte der Religion und Philosophie in Deutschland' (first edition 1834), in the 8th part of the Complete Works, edited by Paul Beyer *et al.*, Leipzig, no date, p. 253.

[60]Letter to his parents, 5th August 1914, in *CW 1*, p. 174.

[61]Letter to his parents, 18th August 1917, in *CW 1*, p. 431.

– revoked his statement,[62] Rosenzweig's sympathy did not waver. As late as February of 1917, he wrote to his parents:

> "If he (and what he stands for) did not exist, it would be no ignominy if Germany lost. But being as it is, we can be sure that there is still a future for Goethe's people."[63]

In light of this, Rosenzweig was given much cause to grieve as the "Bethmann politics of ideals"[64] came to an end in July of 1917.

> "I am inconsolable . . . for does this not mean that Germany will have to do without its future for the period of time up to the next war? I had been spellbound by this man to a degree that I took interest in a matter with which I have, strictly speaking, nothing to do – but this is all over now . . ."[65]

What renders Rosenzweig's hero-worship for Bethmann problematic is the fact that it was not grounded in political effectiveness but, rather, in the *Reichskanzler*'s undoubtedly faultless moral character. The mere fact that Bethmann, who was referred to in public as the "philosopher from Hohenfinow", ran the Government, could hardly be reason enough to be in any way certain about the course of German war-time politics.[66] Evidently this is exactly what Rosenzweig did: for him Bethmann's personal integrity was, time and again, proof enough to maintain faith in the German "love of peace".[67]

That the *Reichskanzler* "will never resort to cunning and brutal force out of trust in such force" and thus remains in his innermost being open to understanding,[68] was for Rosenzweig evidence of "the very eminence of the historical role Germany plays in this war".[69] Nonetheless, with the declaration of unconditional submarine warfare (1st February 1917), he should at least have realised how unfounded his enthusiasm for Bethmann was. But his idealist concept of politics,[70] which mistook political intentions for political realities, prevented him from seeing the fatal dynamics of an historical process which had long parted ways from the *Reichskanzler*'s aims. Thus, his political judgement became alienated from reality: after all, what it referred to were merely possibilities, while the reality of German politics was left unconsidered.

---

[62]Peter Graf Kielmannsegg, *Deutschland und der erste Weltkrieg*, 2nd edition, Stuttgart 1980, p. 265.
[63]Letter to his parents, 17th February 1917, in *CW 1*, p. 350.
[64]Letter to Rudolf Ehrenberg, 24th December 1916, in *CW 1*, p. 322.
[65]Letter to his parents, 20th July 1917, in *CW 1*, p. 422.
[66]With respect to the problematic concept of Bethmann Hollweg, see Klaus Hildebrand, *Bethmann Hollweg. Der Kanzler ohne Eigenschaft? Urteile der Geschichtsschreibung*, Düsseldorf 1970.
[67]'Realpolitik', in *CW 3*, p. 264. Also see, letter to Rudolf Ehrenberg, 24th December 1916, in *CW 1*, p. 322.
[68]With these words Rosenzweig circumscribed his view of "decent politics". Letter to Ernst Simon, dated "beginning" of June 1923, in *CW 1*, p. 909.
[69]Letter to Rudolf Ehrenberg, 24th December 1916, in *CW 1*, p. 322.
[70]Cf. his views on Pacifism: "Pacifism is such a profligate attitude of mind for the very reason that it assumes that the good or the bad consist in the outer state of things instead of the inner states of men." Letter to his parents, 17th August 1916, in *CW 1*, p. 204. Upon the entry of Bethmann's successor, Michaelis, of whom he disapproved, Rosenzweig writes: ". . . everything in fact depends on individuals". Letter to his parents, 18th August 1917, in *CW 1*, p. 431.

His extraordinary willingness to admire Bethmann struck Rosenzweig as well. Two months after the *Reichskanzler*'s resignation he wrote:

"I myself, it is true, did not realise until Bethmann's fall how strongly my view of politics had been encapsulated in hero-worship . . . I do believe that it was the lack of a genuine relationship to the German people which somewhat induced me to cling to a sort of personal representative. Just as in general, surely, Germany to me means Schiller and Goethe and nothing else – not, that is to say, Müller or Schulze."[71]

The feeling that, both as Jew and as intellectual, he had nothing more than a peripheral social standing, evoked an even stronger desire for leadership by an intellectual elite. In this context he saw the duty of the *Reichskanzler*, an office reached through appointment by the Emperor and not through party allegiance, to be the protector of an imperialism kept free from the direct influence of group interests. In that Bethmann seemed to fulfil such requirement, Rosenzweig concluded that Bethmann gave Germany something "which its creator, Bismarck, had failed to bestow: a genuine soul".[72] Only from that point on Germany could conceive of itself as a united nation and would feel for certain that it could be more than an amalgamation of Prussian militarism and "new-German industrialism" which had been building up since 1871. Bethmann was irreplaceable for Rosenzweig because the highly-educated *Reichskanzler* symbolised Rosenzweig's hope for a radically new, unpolitical politics which would reconcile intellectually all political and social antagonisms. Perhaps even more than his vision of a *Mitteleuropa* Rosenzweig's enthusiasm for Bethmann proved thus to be of an unrealistic character. And the interpretations by which Rosenzweig tried to understand the fall of his "hero" accordingly have to be seen in the light of the expectations Rosenzweig entertained with regard to Bethmann's chancellorship:

"The fact that everybody is railing at Bethmann proves perfectly what a low sort really the average German is."[73]

Accordingly, when the elected representative of the Centre Party, Matthias Erzberger, proclaimed in his sensational speech before the *Reichstag* on 6th July 1917, the end of the Bethmann era,[74] Rosenzweig had sharp criticism:

"Erzberger's 'feat' amounted to just what politics is supposed not to be; it was nothing else but a revolution of the narrow-minded German philistine (*des deutschen Spießers*)."[75]

In his speech Erzberger left no doubt about the misdirected and messed-up military situation and demanded from Parliament a peace resolution with no stipulations on annexations in order to pave the way for a negotiated peace which he now deemed necessary. The Left-wing parties added their support, and the

---

[71]Letter to Hans Hess, 30th September 1917, in *CW 1*, pp. 452–453.
[72]'Realpolitik', in *CW 3*, pp. 264–265.
[73]Letter to his parents, 17th July 1917, in *CW 1*, p. 422.
[74]For the political context see Klaus Epstein, *Matthias Erzberger und das Dilemma der deutschen Demokratie* (originally in English: *Matthias Erzberger and the Dilemma of German Democracy*, Princeton 1959), Frankfurt a. Main 1976, pp. 204–228.
[75]Unpublished letter to Margrit Rosenstock, 6th August 1917.

Reichstag was able to pass the resolution on 19th July with the votes of the Centre, Progressive, and Majority Socialist parties.

Rosenzweig, who did not accept this sceptical diagnosis of Germany's war-time prospects,[76] saw these events only as evidence of a "war-time psychosis".[77] The fact that it was the Left-wing parties which had brought Bethmann down led Rosenzweig to entertain strong doubts as to whether democracy, by its nature, might not always be apt to facilitate the coming to power of unscrupulous demagogues.[78] In this light, Bethmann's fall seemed to him a dark omen; and it brought to the surface anti-democratic sentiments that had been latent in Rosenzweig since the pre-war period.[79] Such sentiments became particularly evident in December of 1917 when he worked out a rudimentary constitutional model which strictly disapproved of making the *Reichskanzler*'s power dependent on a parliamentary majority. And it was indeed in consequence of his concept of leadership by an intellectual elite that he wanted the *Reichskanzler* to be completely dissociated from any sort of interest politics as represented by political parties. Inevitably, Rosenzweig was thus compelled to declare consti-tutional monarchy in its essentials sacrosanct.[80]

With Bethmann's fall Rosenzweig's political enthusiasm disappeared. How-ever, upon recovery from the initial shock, his interest in politics returned with surprising speed. As early as the middle of November he declared himself to be "happy about politics".[81] When, at the beginning of the same month, *Graf* Hertling[82] was appointed *Reichskanzler* this went rather well with Rosenzweig's hope for leadership by an intellectual aristocracy.[83] And the fall of Russia even led him to consider that the realisation of his concept of a *Mitteleuropa* might be imminent.[84] Hence, when, at the close of the year, Rosenzweig tried to strike some sort of political balance, he came to the bold conclusion that "the war has decided matters in favour of Germany".[85]

[76]See, for example, his essay written at the turn of the year 1917–1918, 'Vox Dei? Die Gewissensfrage der Demokratie', now in *CW 3*, pp. 267–282, particularly pp. 279–280.
[77]Unpublished letter to Margrit Rosenstock, 6th August 1917.
[78]Cf. the letter to Margrit Rosenstock, 14th December 1917, in *CW 1*, p. 488; and the letters to Eugen Rosenstock, *ibid.*, p. 489 (written 15th December 1917) and p. 494 (written 19th December 1917).
[79]See the diary entries of 22nd May and 25th May 1906, now in *CW 1*, pp. 44 and 45–46.
[80]Rosenzweig explains his rather inconsistent ideas on constitution in an as yet unpublished letter to Eugen Rosenstock, dated 1st December 1917. See also Rosenzweig's letter to Ernst Baumann, 25th October 1917, in *CW 1*, p. 477 and esp. the letter to Hans Ehrenberg, 4th May 1918, in *CW 1*, pp. 551–553.
[81]Letter to Ernst Baumann, 25th October 1917, in *CW 1*, p. 477, in which he also wrote: ". . . as a matter of fact, I do not care about politics now, after Bethmann's fall, and I must almost force myself into thinking of it" [i.e. politics].
[82]Letter to his parents, 14th November 1917, in *CW 1*, p. 479.
[83]For information on Georg von Hertling see Winfried Becker, *Georg von Hertling*, Mainz 1981. The one-time leader of the Centre Party was a professor of philosophy and as such was one of the founders and also the president of the *Görres-Gesellschaft*. Bethmann recommended him as his successor; von Hertling was a Right-wing member of his party.
[84]Unpublished letter to Margrit Rosenstock, beginning of November 1917.
[85]'Vox dei?', in *CW 3*, p. 280.

IV

It was a natural consequence of his optimistic view of the military situation that
Rosenzweig was utterly unable to comprehend the events of the last year of war.
"I never" – he confessed to his mother in October of 1918 – "up to this year, really
took into consideration military defeat; some sort of a *Hubertusburg* at the most,
perhaps, meaning some sort of non-victory, with the results achieved by
Bismarck quite unimpaired."[86] But the catastrophic situation which actually
came about, inconceivable in its dimensions, threw Rosenzweig into a bottom-
less pit of doubts and despair, which manifested itself in his complete dismissal of
all new political developments. And even more so than had been the case in the
previous year, following Bethmann's fall, he proved unable now to avoid being
seized by the problems of the "intermediate kingdom" (*Zwischenreich*). When the
Germans sued for an armistice on 4th October, Rosenzweig, too, realised that
the war was drawing to its final solution. Having been so burdened by various
demands[87] since the beginning of the new year, he had hardly bestowed any
attention on the as yet undramatic events of the day; but, when Prince Max von
Baden became *Reichskanzler*, Rosenzweig found the imminent parliamentari-
sation of the *Reich* "exceedingly interesting" and "exciting".[88] But what, soon
after, became far more fateful and important was the necessity of bringing the
war to a close, rendered urgent by Germany's petition for armistice; and it was of
course this question which henceforth was to command Rosenzweig's attention.
Although he suspected that peace was to be had only under "bad conditions", it
was nevertheless his desire that the conflict might be brought to an end
"whatever the costs", since "a Christian nation" ought "not to conduct a
senselessly heroic war of total destruction".[89] The end of the war, close at hand
now, filled Rosenzweig initially more with joy for the coming peace, rather than
with any anxiety about the uncertain future. For indeed he visualised that future,
despite the pessimism that may also be found in his writings, in much too
promising a light, the preservation of the Monarchy, perhaps even that of the
Hohenzollern, with Alsace becoming a neutral state and German-Austria
becoming united with the German Empire – all of this seemed to Rosenzweig to
be still in reach even under the conditions of a very "unfavourable" peace
settlement as he understood it.[90] So when, at the same time, he complained "that
we are going to lose everything that can be lost . . ." he proved – just as his

[86]Letter to his mother, 19th October 1918, in *CW 1*, p. 614.
[87]In particular: the death of his father on 19th March; an officer-candidates' training course in
Rembertow, near Warsaw, from May through July; stay in military hospital in Leipzig from the
middle of July through August; end of August he began to write *Der Stern der Erlösung*; stay in
military hospital at the end of September in Belgrade.
[88]Letters to his mother, 2nd October 1918, in *CW 1*, p. 610, and 6th October 1918, *ibid.*, p. 611.
[89]Unpublished letter to Margrit Rosenstock, 13th October 1918.
[90]His unrealistic expectations are documented in two unpublished letters to Margrit Rosenstock,
11th and 28th October 1918, as well as in two published letters to his mother, 13th and 19th
October 1918, both in *CW 1*, p. 613 and p. 614.

contemporaries – how very much mistaken he was about the meaning this statement was bound to acquire.[91]

With the publication of Wilson's second letter on 16th October Rosenzweig's hopes plunged. The tone and tenor of the letter, in which Germany was accused of having waged a barbaric war and in which the *Kaiser* was called an arbitrary despot, destroyed all his hopes for an honourable settlement. While he had still believed in the second week of October he was getting used to "this new climate of a defeated Germany", he was now haunted by a feeling of real disaster.[92] The letters which he wrote on 19th October clearly document his frame of mind as he wavered between desperation and protest.

> "I, in particular, am beginning to realise only now, when destruction shows fully its ugly face, that it was dearer to me than I admitted to myself. It was, really, the world (as such) which one put trust in simply because it existed. The mystery of God's will makes itself really felt only in the event of defeat; for in victory, people take things simply as natural. And what is most curious is how everything converges into the distress one feels about the House of Hohenzollern. I had no idea, actually that I am that much of a monarchist at heart. I feel completely outraged at the prospects of a President [sic] Scheidemann or an Emperor Max . . ."[93]

Now that the *Kaiser* as representative of Prussian militarism was being held responsible for the length and severity of the war and his abdication became a political necessity, Rosenzweig discovered that he had a liking for him.

> "I did not discover until now, in my grief over Wilhelm, to what degree I am really a monarchist. I want to have a king, the end is terrible; Wilhelm falls, and not a finger is lifted for him."[94]

Again and again in the first weeks of November he thought of the *Kaiser* and "his awful and deplorable exit".[95]

> "I have never liked to shout hurray for the *Kaiser*, but now I would give a great deal if I had an opportunity to do so again."[96]

And suddenly it seemed difficult even for him, the civilian *par excellence*, "to take off his uniform", since that meant saying goodbye to another part of the past.[97] And when, on 17th November, he found himself a spectator to the retreat of the Freiburg troops, he felt "absolutely sick", for "one could not help feeling how things should have developed, and how they have turned out now".[98]

The sentimentality with which Rosenzweig grieved over the disintegration of the old was reflected in the resentment he felt towards the new. As for himself, he believed it to be "most natural, normal and inevitable . . . to be in the reactionary camp",[99] since "a monarchist at heart just cannot allow himself to mix with the

---

[91]Letter to his mother, 19th October 1918, in *CW 1*, p. 614.
[92]Unpublished letter to Margrit Rosenstock, 12th October 1918.
[93]Unpublished letter to Margrit Rosenstock, 19th October 1918; similarly: letter to his mother, sent on the same day, now in *CW 1*, p. 614.
[94]*Ibid.*, letter to his mother.
[95]Unpublished letter to Margrit Rosenstock, 9th November 1918.
[96]Unpublished letter to Margrit Rosenstock, 11th November 1918.
[97]Letter to his mother, 12th November 1918, in *CW 1*, p. 617.
[98]Unpublished letter to Margrit Rosenstock, 17th November 1918.
[99]Unpublished letter to Margrit Rosenstock, 8th November 1918.

Republicans, or a warrior with the Pacifists".[100] Because he needed to remain true to his old convictions, he declared his sympathy for the counter-revolution,[101] which he described in his letters as a "hopeless" but for that very reason all the more admirable cause.[102] He was an eyewitness to the Revolution in Freiburg, where it began on 9th November, "still taking a rather quiet course".[103] What, in his opinion, particularly seemed to be missing was the strength and momentum of a great and genuinely fascinating idea. In its place Rosenzweig diagnosed the mere presence of "a mixture of force and chaos".[104] Thus the Revolution had no creative meaning for him: he considered it a military revolt run wild and which, although it managed to destroy the old order at a moment in history when this was possible, was nonetheless unable to bring anything convincingly new in its place. Destruction, then, was the Revolution's only effect. Its appalling lack of ideas was evident for him in the calibre of politicians now gaining influence. The Left Socialist leaders impressed him as cliché-ridden "simpletons and peacemongers" (*Naivusse und Pacificusse*),[105] who owed their power only to the street-terror of packs of "15–18 year-old loafers playing soldier" (*Munitionslümmeln*).[106] And come to that, he feared a general "advance of the *Hermann Michel* sort",[107] which caused him some anxiety particularly with regard to his own precarious social standing. The fact that the *Rat der Volksbeauftragten*, constituted exclusively by the two strongest workers' parties, did not come about as a result of general elections he denounced as a disregard for, and violation of, the right to political participation as already guaranteed by the constitution of the *Kaiserreich*.[108] And indeed, the degree of political freedom already reached during the *Kaiserreich* made any form of one-class rule seem like a step backwards.[109] In order to protest against the political monopoly of the workers' parties, Rosenzweig even went as far as contemplating membership of the National Liberal Party.[110]

Above and beyond such criticism, however, a further breakthrough manifested itself in the form of Rosenzweig's strict refusal to accept any facts created by the Revolution. The politicisation of the masses was quite simply absolutely incompatible with his ideal of leadership by an intellectual aristoc-

[100]Unpublished letter to Margrit Rosenstock, 9th November 1918.
[101]In addition to three unpublished letters to Margrit Rosenstock, 9th, 12th and 13th November 1918, cf. the letter to his mother of 13th November 1918, in *CW I*, p. 618. There he writes, however, that a "monarchist-democratic reaction, originating in Baden, against the Bolshevik republic . . . would not be entirely hopeless". Rosenzweig apparently saw the situation in Berlin and in the *Reich* differently.
[102]Unpublished letter to Margrit Rosenstock, 12th November 1918.
[103]Unpublished letter to Margrit Rosenstock, 9th November 1918.
[104]Unpublished letter to Margrit Rosenstock, 11th November 1918.
[105]Unpublished letter to Margrit Rosenstock, 12th November 1918.
[106]Letter to his mother, 13th November 1918, in *CW I*, p. 618.
[107]Unpublished letter to Margrit Rosenstock, 11th November 1918.
[108]Letter to his mother, 13th November 1918, in *CW I*, p. 618.
[109]See Heinrich A. Winkler, *Die Sozialdemokratie und die Revolution von 1918/19*, 2nd edition, Bonn 1980, pp. 11–20.
[110]Letter to his mother, 13th November 1918, in *CW I*, p. 617. Before Rosenzweig could carry out his decision, the party had already begun to dissolve itself.

racy. As far back as 1906 he had entrusted to his diary that "it needs a weakling to live in a really democratic way";[111] now, in view of present events, he went on to state:

> "I believe I'll never be a democrat again! It is a thing just as impossible as Pacifism. In every time there will be rule, and there will be war. Freedom and peace I expect to be something that lies – beyond."[112]

In the name of ahistorical laws he dismissed the reality of concrete, historical events and dispensed with any attempt to understand such reality in its genesis. Consequently, Rosenzweig decidedly disapproved of all those who, in search of an explanation for the military defeat, did not hesitate to bestow severe criticism on the *Ancien Régime*. For those who in the moment of defeat looked for someone to blame were, in his opinion, unworthy renegades always aligning themselves with historical success and therefore unable to surrender themselves heroically to the "mysteriousness of God's will".[113] As far as he was concerned, the renegade mood, which assumed that "all the dead have been killed for nothing", was the "really disastrous mark of our defeat". Every attempt at a new orientation appeared to him, from that point of view, as blasphemous.

> "And now the journalists come crawling out of their Swiss holes [in the sense of 'comfortable retreats'] and, with a 'Here we are', they take the helm like *wahre Jakobs*."[114]

The political activism which broke out in 1918 did not seem merely undignified to Rosenzweig but naive as well. For it had been the events of the past four years, which had especially proven to him that history could be neither created nor prevented, just impotently endured. "Prophets of doom", who drew general attention to the truth of this, were therefore much more necessary than the fickle "helper" (*Helfer*), since in an emergency situation "everybody is apt to help himself first" (*jeder sich selbst helfen will*).[115] The tragic nature of the events of the time, making all political activity questionable, proved itself above all else in the catastrophe of the First World War, a catastrophe which he believed to have been unpreventable. And the various pre-war crises he saw as evidence for the inevitability of the events as, gradually escalating, they preceded the First World War. This view of history led him to dismiss all criticism of German pre-war diplomacy.

> ". . . if such policies in leading to war, had an unhappy ending, this does not alter the fact that they had been the perfectly right ones."[116]

---

[111]Cf. *CW 1*, p. 46.
[112]Unpublished letter to Margrit Rosenstock, 11th November 1918.
[113]Unpublished letter to Margrit Rosenstock, 19th October 1918.
[114]All quotations taken from an unpublished letter to Margrit Rosenstock, 12th November 1918.
[115]All quotations taken from an unpublished letter to Margrit Rosenstock, 11th November 1918.
[116]Unpublished letter to Margrit Rosenstock, 12th November 1918. As to the outbreak of war, see also the following essays, 'Realpolitik' (Spring of 1917), now in *CW 3*, pp. 261–265; 'Vox Dei?' (1917–1918), and pp. 267–282; and the unpublished letter to Margrit Rosenstock, November 1917, in which he analyses the British pre-war policy.

Rosenzweig's way of thinking culminated in the proposition that the Germans would only have been able to avoid the war at the price of self-renunciation.[117] As discussion over who was responsible for war proved in this light to be a moral and scientific impossibility, the problem arose all the more as to whether the war could have been militarily or politically successful. With regard to the discussions of the war-time goals, which had been in full force since the *Reichstag* peace resolution, it seemed to Rosenzweig as early as October 1917 that the power-political consciousness of the Germans was rather uncultivated. As opposed to the *demos* of Britain, the Germans lacked a "natural imperialist will".[118] In a way very similar to Oswald Spengler's pamphlet entitled *Preußentum und Sozialismus*, published three years later, Rosenzweig also held "Bismarck's spoon-feeding" (*Bismarcks Bevormundungssystem*) responsible[119] for this situation. After the collapse of the *Reich*, Rosenzweig concluded in November 1918 that since its founding the *Reich* had failed to be more than a "mere artificial image" (*nur ein künstliches Bildwerk*), because there had "never been" such a thing as a German people, in the sense of a politically unified whole with a capacity to act.[120]

By persuading himself that defeat could primarily be traced to the disintegration of a self-assertive national will, Rosenzweig defended the conduct of war, for which the Supreme Army Command had been responsible, against every fundamental criticism. What remained unrecognised in its central meaning was the role of military-strategic thinking, which found first expression in the violation of Belgian neutrality and grew fatally dominant from then on. So Rosenzweig's interpretation tended to suppress the causes of the catastrophe rather than to attempt to analyse and understand them. The painful burden of events, brought about by the situation, prevented him from making a realistic and unemotional account of the events of war.

The conditions of the armistice, made public on 11th November and generally deemed Draconian, again left him livid. What especially outraged him was the commitment imposed on Germany to return all allied prisoners of war, with no basis of reciprocity.

> "One has reason for hatred here. No such thing could ever have come from 'Prussian militarism'. For this would have been incompatible with the residue of chivalrous tradition which was, surely, still there."[121]

On the same day he stated that he had learned belatedly to feel himself "to be not only a German", but "even a Prussian".[122] The more clearly he realised the consequences of defeat the more he saw himself as part of a national destiny comprising all Germans. But for that very reason he was gripped by a "dread of the future".[123] While he had, as late as 1917, still nourished his vision that a new

---

[117]*Ibid.*
[118]Letter to Eugen Rosenstock, 18th October 1917, in *CW 1*, p. 470.
[119]*Ibid.*
[120]Unpublished letter to Margrit Rosenstock, 16th November 1918.
[121]Unpublished letter to Margrit Rosenstock, 11th November 1918.
[122]*Ibid.*
[123]Letter to his mother, 12th November 1918, in *CW 1*, p. 617.

German Empire, to be created after the war, might find the way to a supranational culture of the future, Rosenzweig stated in the middle of October:

> "The fact that Germany remains undevastated will hardly contribute much to the country's comeback; what is really bad is that the nation is tied up like a parcel, while the others divide up the world among themselves. This will still reinforce the characteristic constriction (*Engigkeit der Herzen*) that governed German hearts even before the war."[124]

For the morally outlawed, powerless Germany, deprived of her possibilities for economic growth, Rosenzweig prophesied a "tremendously venomous time" for inner-German affairs too.[125] Germany was "not mature, not strong enough" for the punishment thrust upon it, which is why, in his opinion, it would "simply be broken in spirit and become subject to real degeneration".[126] Rosenzweig had no doubts whatever that a further decline of virtues like tolerance and an ability to compromise, already underdeveloped in the Germans, would hit the Jews the hardest. Burdened by both the trauma of defeat and of revolution, the German people "had a special need . . . to avail itself of the services of all the world's favourite scapegoat" (*hat den "allgemeinen Sündenbock der Völker . . . ganz besonders nötig"*).[127] Therefore he expected, in common with other public voices of the time,[128] that the accumulated despair of the Germans would result in persecution of the Jews. Whatever the new political order would turn out to be, Rosenzweig believed that an increase in antisemitism was inevitable.[129] Nothing, therefore, seemed more certain to him in spring of 1919 than that "the insecurity of life [is] rather greater now than it was in the war".[130]

What he had still regarded in 1906 as a bold flight of fancy – that there would in the future be a German culture which would know nothing of Goethe – now appeared to be close at hand:

> "The 'culture' that was ours will be destroyed even in our lifetime . . . Something new will take its place, of course. But it will not be ours."[131]

That culture presupposed security; and after the "world of unchallenged authoritarian order, of secured and unsecured rights and privileges"[132] had come to an end, Rosenzweig concluded that there was no longer a future for German culture. He felt compelled therefore to expect for himself an "end of things",

---

[124]Letter to his mother, 13th October 1918, in *CW I*, p. 613.
[125]Unpublished letter to Margrit Rosenstock, 12th November 1918.
[126]Unpublished letter to Margrit Rosenstock, 19th October 1918.
[127]Unpublished letter to Margrit Rosenstock, 12th November 1918: "After all, what else is a revolution in Germany bound to end up in but Jew-baiting."
[128]Cf. the comments collected by Zechlin in his *Deutsche Politik, op. cit.*, pp. 550–552. On the scapegoat-myth, pp. 559–561. See furthermore Werner T. Angress, 'Juden im politischen Leben der Revolutionszeit', in *Deutsches Judentum in Krieg und Revolution 1916–1923*. Ein Sammelband herausgegeben von Werner Mosse unter Mitwirkung von Arnold Paucker, Tübingen 1971 (Schriftenreihe wissenschaftliche Abhandlungen des Leo Baeck Instituts 25), pp. 137–315, here pp. 144–145; Eva G. Reichmann, 'Der Bewußtseinswandel der deutschen Juden', *ibid.*, pp. 511–612, here p. 537.
[129]Letter to his mother, 13th October 1918, in *CW I*, p. 613.
[130]Unpublished letter to Margrit Rosenstock, 7th April 1919.
[131]Unpublished letter to Margrit Rosenstock, 11th November 1918.
[132]Eberhard Kolb, Introduction to Eberhard Kolb (ed.), *Vom Kaiserreich zur Weimarer Republik*, Köln 1972, p. 10.

which was "not, however, the end of the world".[133] He seemed particularly impressed by the sombre historical prophecy of Oswald Spengler, who had, as far as Rosenzweig could see, succeeded in his work entitled *Der Untergang des Abendlandes* in bringing to light the true dimension of the disaster. Rosenzweig praised the work of this "fatal fatalist" (Thomas Mann) as the "greatest *Geschichtsphilosem* . . . since Hegel".[134]

The collapse of the monarchy consequently meant much more to Rosenzweig than merely a change in the political system. It marked the beginning decline of a culture of which he understood himself to be a member.[135] Such diagnosis presented Rosenzweig with the distressing consequence "that our whole generation has simply been put on the scrap heap".[136] The destructive progress of history, in which all accreted connections are annihilated, left him, then just over thirty, with the feeling that he was an epigone.

Only reluctantly did he think of the approaching publication of his dissertation on Hegel's concept of the state,[137] which he now dismissed as anachronistic. The events of November 1918, which he took to be the beginning of the disintegration of all aspects of life, threw him into a state of deep resignation.[138]

The intensity of his apocalyptic mood found expression in the relentlessness with which he tried to conquer the crisis intellectually. If indeed "everything had gone" and the familiar world was simply "no longer there", then the last remaining place of refuge was the timeless religious sphere.[139] When, on armistice day, Rosenzweig and Siegfried A. Kaehler visited the Freiburg cathedral, he became fully aware of this certainty:

> "Tonight, after the conditions had been made public, I was, for a minute, in the cathedral together with Kaehler. There we saw plainly what had been before and what will remain after. There were people moving through the chancel behind the screen. They were carrying lights, and one had the feeling that they were pursuing there, protected from the collapse of the world, their eternal business, their [very own] business. What else are such cathedrals but a stone-embodied 'Nevertheless' against the world in the world."[140]

In view of his personal war-time experience, Rosenzweig was completely convinced that he had been right in his decision, taken in the summer of 1913, to live out the rest of his life according to religious tradition. Because the loss of the

---

[133]Unpublished letter to Margrit Rosenstock, 16th November 1918.

[134]Letter to Rudolf Ehrenberg, 5th May 1919, in *CW 1*, pp. 628–629. Also see the three unpublished letters to Margrit Rosenstock, 30th April, 2nd May and 6th May 1919.

[135]Unpublished letter to Margrit Rosenstock, 11th November 1918: "The 'culture' that was ours will come to an end even in our lifetime . . ." [*Die 'Kultur', die unser war, wird noch zu unseren Lebzeiten untergehen . . .*]

[136]Unpublished letter to Margrit Rosenstock, 16th November 1918.

[137]Already in: letter to his parents, 1st September 1917, in *CW 1*, p. 434. Also: letter to Gertrud Oppenheim, 4th May 1919, *ibid.*, p. 628. Letter to Rudolf Ehrenberg, 14th May 1919, *ibid.*, p. 630.

[138]The assumption that Rosenzweig was unaffected by the outcome of the war, a view sometimes maintained by the Rosenzweig research, must certainly be corrected. Cf. Altmann, *History, op. cit.*, p. 234, note 75, and Reinhold Mayer, *Franz Rosenzweig. Eine Philosophie der dialogischen Erfahrung*, München 1973, p. 25.

[139]Letter to his mother, 19th October 1918, in *CW 1*, p. 614.

[140]Unpublished letter to Margrit Rosenstock, 11th November 1918.

"power-protected soulfulness" (*machtgeschützte Innerlichkeit* – Thomas Mann) struck him deeply, he now needed to strive all the more energetically to preserve in his Judaism something of unconditional permanence. In the rapid change of things only the timeless could, for him, be timely.

V

Just because Rosenzweig was greatly alarmed by the military defeat and disturbed by the Revolution, he made himself, paradoxically, a promoter of another sort of revolution, an intellectual one, by the publication of his main philosophical work, entitled *Der Stern der Erlösung* and published in 1921. According to his convictions, the constructionist and system-related thinking of German Idealism ought to be broken down ruthlessly for the sake of paving the way towards a new response to the fundamental problem of human existence, which now made itself powerfully felt: the question of the possibility of a proper and successful life. Consequently, philosophy ought not to continue in narcissistic speculation, debating as to whether or not a timeless being can be abstracted from the wealth of appearance. In contrast, philosophy ought to orientate itself to the reality of human existence. Philosophy must become empirical in order to become effective in a practical sense: which would mean that everyday man with his everyday sufferings must be taken seriously.

Rosenzweig's intended revolution of philosophy was legitimised in his mind by its reformative goal. Because such "new thinking" dedicated itself to the problem of leading a fruitful life, it restored to philosophy a question which in fact always had been considered by common sense to be of first and foremost importance.[141] In this sense his "new thinking" introduced nothing which in itself was new; it represented, rather, an attempt to get at the roots of the present intellectual crisis, and to bring the latter to a close.

In order to reach this goal, however, Rosenzweig thought it necessary to overcome German Idealism completely. So the task of destroying this manner of philosophising had to be carried out first; for only then could a new way of thinking come in. The intended restitution of philosophy therefore necessarily coincided with the "*reductio ad absurdum*" of philosophy.[142] As was the case for so many intellectuals of his generation, the loss of security which he had experienced created a drive in him to attempt solutions which, uncompromising as they were, provoked exactly what they ought to have avoided: the collapse of all remaining orientations.[143]

[141]Rosenzweig enjoyed stressing that his "new thinking" meant nothing else than a "philosophy of common sense". See 'Das neue Denken' (1st edition 1925), in *CW 3*, p. 140. Cf. 'Anleitung zum jüdischen Denken' (written 1921), now in *CW 3*, p. 598.

[142]Cf. 'Das neue Denken', in *CW 3*, p. 142. As to his devastating critique of German Idealism: *Der Stern* (*CW 2*), introduction to the first part, 'Über die Möglichkeit, das All zu erkennen', pp. 3–24.

[143]This demonstrates at the same time the main problem of conservative thinking during the Weimar Republic. It had to become revolutionary, because it found nothing worth preserving in and of the present. On this aspect, principally: Martin Greiffenhagen, *Das Dilemma des Konservatismus in Deutschland* (paperback edition), Frankfurt a. Main 1986, pp. 241–256.

True to the demand he had made in *Der Stern*, that the philosopher must risk taking a step "into the world" (*ins Leben*),[144] Rosenzweig, late in 1916, already expressed his wish to pursue an educational activity as soon as the war came to an end.[145] *Der Stern*, which was, according to his own words, "nothing more than a book" (*eben doch nur ein Buch*), ought to be not only the culmination of his own philosophical thinking but also its final manifestation.[146] As the head of the *Lehrhaus*, Rosenzweig had, in the summer of 1920, witnessed the realisation of his personal goal: the practical field lay wide open to the theorist now. The institute, located in Frankfurt, was from its outer appearance designed to be a kind of Jewish adult education centre. For the most part topics of the classical Jewish tradition were dealt with in open lecture series and study groups.[147] The founding of the *Lehrhaus* counteracted the fast-spreading religious indifference among Jews during the Weimar Republic, evidence of their final emancipation.[148] By providing education, lecturers hoped to compensate for the weakness of Judaism and Jewish knowledge in the Jewish home and synagogue. Against the apparently boundless tendency towards assimilation, the *Lehrhaus* made an effort to preserve the Jewish identity. Not only on Holy Days but also every day, the student was encouraged "to experience everything as a Jew" ([alles] sich jüdisch begegnen zu lassen).[149] The unity of thinking and being, destroyed in modern man, should be restored to a harmonious unity in the Jewish way of life. Inspired by this vision, Rosenzweig directed the *Lehrhaus*, which extended itself much beyond the specific Jewish element to cultural problems in general, until the summer of 1922. After that, an incurable illness, which was to torture him for nearly eight years, forced him to retreat from all public activities.[150]

---

[144]These are the meaningful last two words of *Der Stern*. See *CW 2*, p. 472.

[145]Letter to Rudolf Ehrenberg, end of February 1916, in *CW 1*, p. 185.

[146]Letter to Friedrich Meinecke, 30th August 1920, in *CW 1*, p. 680: "The author of *Der Stern der Erlösung* . . . is of another calibre than the one of *Hegel und der Staat*. But after all, the new book is nothing more than – a book. I do not attach too great importance to it myself."

[147]On the Frankfurt *Lehrhaus* there is a wealth of literature. Fundamentally: Ernst Simon, 'Franz Rosenzweig und das jüdische Bildungsproblem' (1st edition 1931), in *idem, Brücken. Gesammelte Aufsätze*, Heidelberg 1965, pp. 393–406, and *idem, Aufbau im Untergang. Jüdische Erwachsenenbildung im nationalsozialistischen Deutschland als geistiger Widerstand*, Tübingen 1959 (Schriftenreihe wissenschaftlicher Abhandlungen des Leo Baeck Instituts 2), pp. 9–16. Nahum N. Glatzer, 'The Frankfurt Lehrhaus', in *LBI Year Book I* (1956), pp. 105–122. More recent publications: Wolfgang Schivelbusch, 'Das Frankfurter Jüdische Lehrhaus', in *idem, Intellektuellendämmerung. Zur Lage der Frankfurter Intelligenz in den zwanziger Jahren*, Frankfurt a. Main 1982, pp. 33–51. Further essays in the collected volumes of: *Lernen mit Franz Rosenzweig*, edited by Werner Licharz, Frankfurt a. Main 1984, as well as *Der Philosoph Franz Rosenzweig, op. cit., (1886–1929)*, here vol. 1, chapter entitled 'Das Freie Jüdische Lehrhaus', pp. 303–395.

[148]For a general idea of the status of the Jews in the Weimar Republic see, Monika Richarz (Hrsg.), *Jüdisches Leben in Deutschland. Selbstzeugnisse zur Sozialgeschichte 1918–1945*, Stuttgart 1982. Veröffentlichung des Leo Baeck Instituts; Trude Maurer, *Ostjuden in Deutschland 1918–1933*, Hamburg 1986. Maurer's investigation goes far beyond the subject matter indicated in the title.

[149]'Bildung und kein Ende' (1st edition 1920), now in *CW 3*, pp. 491–503, quotation p. 499.

[150]The exact medical diagnosis of Rosenzweig's illness was "amyotrophic lateral sclerosis" (failure of muscle control due to progressive deterioration of the nerves that control movement). Generally the disease leads to death within two to three years. See now Martin G. Goldner, 'Franz Rosenzweig in seiner Krankheit', in *Der Philosoph Franz Rosenzweig, op. cit.*, vol. 1, pp. 327–335.

In view of the central goal of the *Lehrhaus*, the educational work actually carried out could be nothing but the means to the end. For Rosenzweig, though, this was not a negative conclusion. On the contrary, if it was the very progress of science which demonstrated that the world and history cannot be subject to a final explanation, then education was only worthwhile in so far as it helped to fortify a *Weltanschauung* that could serve those who chose it as a means of self-assertion. He explained this connection by drawing upon his war experiences. In the trenches, "a good many learned philosophers" came to realise that the naive "*Weltanschauungen* of the uneducated . . . were far less apt to be shaken than the scholar's 'proud book-learning' could ever have given him reason to believe".[151]

For Rosenzweig the value of an educational concept manifested itself less in its content than by its effectiveness in bringing about the autonomy of individuals or social groups. Hence, in terms of German Judaism, the task of education in present times could be defined in a valid sense as the 're-creation of a common and genuine Jewish identity" and as "educating coming generations, making them self-reliant Jews".[152]

In other words, the *Lehrhaus* was not at all supposed to resemble the type of the German adult education centre (*Volkshochschule*). The basis of its work was not the intellectual unprejudicedness of its teachers but, on the contrary, their being rooted in a common Jewish *Weltanschauung*.[153] For the truth of Judaism could not be revealed through any rational method of inference and conclusion: it could only be revealed in the moment of experience.

As early as 1916, Rosenzweig had asserted:

> "The sort of 'conviction' that, if any, may find expression in a conversion to Judaism must simply and solely be seen in the fact that one discovers a taste for 'Jewish family life'; there can be no such conviction as underlies a conversion to Christianity . . ."[154]

Hence the *Lehrhaus* should not spread a canon of established Jewish knowledge; still more to the point, it ought not to talk at all *about* Judaism. Instead, Rosenzweig attempted to reawaken "the very Jewishness of Jewish man" ["die Jüdischkeit des jüdischen Menschen"] through human intercourse.[155]

Convinced that Judaism could not be set against "other 'humannesses' " (*andre Menschlichkeiten*), Rosenzweig did not attempt at all to define its essence. Programmatically, he wrote to one of his fellow workers at the *Lehrhaus*:

> "What we begin with is actions. Some time in the future, may the principles governing them be found by us or by others . . . Judaism is not a law. It makes law. But it is not identical with such law. Rather, it means 'being' Jewish."[156]

To Rosenzweig being Jewish meant first and foremost bringing to life an attitude or life style that is not governed by a fixed set of laws, but is in accord

---

[151]'Die Wissenschaft und das Leben' (written in March 1918), now in *CW 3*, pp. 483–489; quotation p. 485.
[152]*Ibid.*, p. 488.
[153]Franz Rosenzweig in an unpublished letter to Margrit Rosenstock, 13th June 1919.
[154]Letter to his parents, 21st July 1916, in *CW 1*, p. 201.
[155]'Bildung und kein Ende', in *CW 3*, p. 492.
[156]Letter to Rudolf Hallo, 27th March 1922, in *CW 1*, p. 761.

with the commandment of love, making man responsible for the fate of his neighbour. As a didactic method, therefore, the *Lehrhaus* was left with nothing but a "principle of unprincipledness" (*Rezept der Rezeptlosigkeit*).[157] According to Rosenzweig, he who wanted to further Jewishness in a Jew could "give him nothing but the empty forms of preparedness" ("nichts geben als die leeren Formen des Bereitseins").[158] In this sense the *Lehrhaus* was supposed to be an "existential meeting place" (*existenzieller Ort der Begegnung*), where human contacts could help bring about crucial religious experiences.[159]

Rosenzweig's hope of bringing new strength to German Judaism through the *Lehrhaus* was not fulfilled. Even at the time of his greatest success no more than four per cent of the Jewish community were attracted.[160] His religious existentialism had the effect of alienating the assimilated Frankfurt bourgeoisie. The intellectual who was deeply moved by the eternal nature of Judaism and the Jewish citizen rooted in the German daily life could not come to terms with each other.

As the limited success of the *Lehrhaus* concept proves, Rosenzweig's ideas of a Jewish renewal reflected something insurmountably esoteric. While he had revolted against the systematic thinking of Idealism in the name of man hungry for meaning, he in his turn, also failed to develop more than a very limited understanding of the real concerns of his Jewish fellow human beings. His hope of learning "by starting with life and going back to the Torah" ("aus dem Leben . . . zurück in die Tora" [sic]), thus "leading everything back to Jewishness",[161] could not be fully realised. Modern society with its own set of conceptions could not as a whole be subsumed under the mission of the Torah. A religious tradition understood as timeless could obviously offer no solutions to current political and social problems. It is not surprising, therefore, that the *Lehrhaus* made no effort to join in the controversial discussion that was going on within German Jewry as regards the political issues of the time.[162] So what also becomes apparent here is Rosenzweig's inability to identify and align himself with any of the inner-Jewish fractions. His statement to the effect that

> "the liberal German-Jewish position, which had been a meeting ground to almost the whole of the German Jewry for nearly a century, has obviously dwindled to the size of a pin-point, so that just one man – I, that is – can occupy it."

reveals how deeply separated he felt from *all* the main currents of contemporary Judaism.[163] Again and again he criticised the liberal "*Centralvereins-Judentum*" for

---

[157]'Bildung und kein Ende', in *CW 3*, p. 500.
[158]*Ibid.*
[159]Schivelbusch, *Intellektuellendämmerung, op. cit.*, p. 50.
[160]*Ibid.*, p. 49. Also see, letter to Rudolf Hallo, beginning of December 1922, in *CW 1*, pp. 849–872.
[161]'Neues Lernen' (written 1920), in *CW 3*, pp. 505–510, quotations pp. 507–508.
[162]See Richard Koch's 'Einführung in das Programm des Lehrhauses', in *CW 1*, p. 689: "The *Lehrhaus* is not concerned with political polemics. Here there is no flying at each other between the Orthodox and Liberal, between the Zionists and *Staatsbürger jüdischen Glaubens*. Such differences we left behind. Let everyone take care of this matter as he likes."
[163]Letter to Gertrud Oppenheim, July 1924, in *CW 1*, p. 980.

its failure to act as the trustee of the Jewish tradition.[164] In May 1922, he wrote, with some resignation, that representatives of any stature amongst German Jews were almost exclusively Zionists.[165] Therefore, admiring them as the "healthier" and "better" Jews,[166] he actually did admit that it was they who made a real effort to take "being a Jew" (*Judesein*) seriously. Despite statements of this kind, Zionism as a secular political movement remained nonetheless completely alien to him. As late as in the year of his death, he referred to the non-Zionists' cooperation with the Jewish Agency as "drinking tea with the devil" (*Teetrinken mit dem Teufel*),[167] justifiable only by the acuteness of the crisis situation. But contrary to what he had thought before 1920, he was no longer willing to exclude the possibility that an intellectually purified, aristocratic Zionism could in its own way renew Judaism.[168] This now gave him an opportunity to arrive at a more pragmatic judgement of Zionism. Regardless of its political goals, he decided to judge Zionism by what it achieved for religious life in Palestine.[169]

For no other reason than the religious values Zionism promised to promote, Rosenzweig was willing to modify his previous dogmatic rejection. At the same time, however, he made it very clear that, despite the admiration he entertained for the readiness to make sacrifices which was so conspicuous in the Zionist movement, he could only respect its way but not share it.[170] As a "non-Zionist", as he referred to himself, Rosenzweig thus maintained, throughout his last years as well, his belief in the validity of his theory of history as postulated in *Der Stern*.[171] In his private life also he hardly commented any more on the events of the day. In the crisis year of 1923, when the fall of the Republic seemed imminent and its citizens were burdened by the inflation, he wrote to his academic mentor Meinecke:

---

[164]See letter to Hugo Sonnenfeld, 10th May 1922, in *CW 1*, pp. 780–781. Letter to his mother, 22nd May 1924, in *CW 1*, p. 964.

[165]Letter to Hugo Sonnenfeld, 10th May 1922, in *CW 1*, pp. 780–781.

[166]Letter to Rudolf Hallo, end of January 1923, in *CW 1*, p. 886, and letter to Benno Jacob, 15th May 1927, in *CW 1*, p. 1144.

[167]Letter to his mother, 5th June 1929, in *CW 1*, p. 1215.

[168]See diary entry of 12th April 1922, in *CW 1*, p. 774, and report from Richard Koch, *ibid.*, p. 1011.

[169]Letter to Benno Jacob, 23rd May 1927, in *CW 1*, pp. 1148–1150. Also see letter to Benno Jacob, 10th May 1927, *ibid.*, pp. 1140–1141.

[170]Letter to Gertrud Oppenheim, 9th June 1924, in *CW 1*, pp. 968–969. Cf.: "I am certainly not going to become a Zionist – just to prevent such misunderstanding. I shall not be what I cannot be. But I regret my inability. (Not being able to – not only in consequence of my illness, but not able, also, if I had remained in good health.)" *Ibid.*, p. 969.

[171]See letter to Martin Buber, 18th August 1929, in *CW 1*, p. 1227. Stéphane Mosès, undoubtedly one of the most knowledgeable Rosenzweig experts, gives in many respects a convincing analysis (see note 20, above). However, his attempt in several essays to postulate a return to politics in Rosenzweig's later thinking – which he interprets as a drive towards Zionism – remains questionable, because it does not account for a number of statements Rosenzweig made to the contrary; therefore Mosès's interpretation that Rosenzweig finally renounced the theory of history he proposed in *Der Stern* must be considered subjective. See Stéphane Mosès, 'Franz Rosenzweigs letztes Tagebuch', in Licharz (ed.), *Lernen mit Franz Rosenzweig, op. cit.*, pp. 136–154, esp. pp. 145–148, and from the same author, 'Hegel beim Wort genommen. Geschichtskritik bei Franz Rosenzweig', in Fuchs and Henrix (eds.), *Zeitgewinn, op. cit.*, pp. 67–89, in particular pp. 81–83, and 'Politik und Religion. Zur Aktualität Franz Rosenzweigs', in *Der Philosoph Franz Rosenzweig, op. cit.*, vol. 2, pp. 855–875.

"My premonitions of the present course of things date back indeed to the sweeping and total resignation I experienced in November of 1918 . . . Now even such towers of mind which used to rise high like islands are engulfed by the flood. Anything which could not manage to get into an ark that will keep above water by its own strength can have no hope of survival and of ever getting on ground again in days to come, and planting the young vine in the old ground."[172]

Friedrich Meinecke's old claim[173] – to develop the state and society in order to ensure the individual an existence worthy of a human being – was given up by Rosenzweig. Without hope that the world might ever be tuned to reason through political activity, all that remained for the individual to do was to retreat to the "ark" of a religious belief turned away from the world. Thus Germanness and Jewishness were, in his mind, completely autonomous domains of reality;[174] and it was just because of their unconnectedness that he saw no difficulties in the coexistence of both.[175] Such an interpretation doubtless implies that for Rosenzweig the continued existence of German Jewry was, in principle, not to be questioned. So while he expected, as early as 1924, the beginning of a new "era of persecution" against which nothing could be done "either by us or the well-meaning Christians" he also expressed his hope "that this era of persecution will be one of dialogue between religions".[176]

However, for more he dared not hope. He believed that truth could be experienced only through personal intercourse, which meant that the possibility of leading a fruitful, successful life was dissociated by Rosenzweig from all social conditions and shifted entirely into the private sphere. As a Jew, Rosenzweig felt released from any task of setting a positive goal for the development of society as a whole. For the laws of the Torah could only be lived and observed in personal intercourse. History, in consequence, had to be left to itself.

When one looks at Rosenzweig's intellectual development as a whole, the resulting impression is that he made a continuous effort to free himself from the burden of history. From the beginning of his development, his protest against a historical consciousness, which uprooted its own base, had already been present. This attitude was overwhelmingly confirmed by the outcome of the war, which Rosenzweig experienced as the "end of the world".[177] This history seemed to him

[172]Letter to Friedrich Meinecke, 17th September 1923, in *CW 1*, p. 924.

[173]Cf. Friedrich Meinecke, 'Kausalitäten und Werte in der Geschichte' (written 1925), now in Friedrich Meinecke. *Zur Theorie und Philosophie der Geschichte*, (Werke 4) 2nd edition, Stuttgart 1965, pp. 61–89, here p. 87.

[174]In addition to many other documents, see also 'Der Jude im Staat' (written 1920), now in *CW 3*, pp. 553–555. Here Rosenzweig maintains the traditional alienation from politics as a decisive characteristic of Jewry.

[175]Compare, for example, letter to Helene Sommer, 16th January 1918; and particularly, the letter to Rudolf Hallo, end of January 1923, both in *CW 1*, pp. 505–506, and pp. 885–888, as well as Reinhold Mayer, 'Vorbemerkungen', in *CW 3*, p. xvi.

[176]Letter to Martin Buber, 19th April 1924, in *CW 1*, p. 947. One cannot, therefore, assert that Rosenzweig "has never taken notice of the hydra of non-religious racist antisemitism", as Michael Brocke does in his essay, 'Franz Rosenzweigs Briefe und Tagebücher', in Licharz (ed.), *Lernen mit Franz Rosenzweig, op. cit.*, pp. 257–270; quotation, p. 265. For a general understanding of the development of antisemitism during the Weimar Republic see Heinrich A. Winkler, 'Die deutsche Gesellschaft der Weimarer Republik und der Antisemitismus', in Bernd Martin and Ernst Schulin (eds.), *Die Juden als Minderheit in der Geschichte*, München 1981, pp. 271–289.

[177]Unpublished letter to Margrit Rosenstock, 16th November 1918.

to become simply a totally destructive power. But the horror generated by history can be lessened through re-consideration of a Judaism which Rosenzweig defined as being independent of time and social relations. Rightly seen, however, this rescue attempt is an act of desperation. For his desire to achieve within Judaism an Archimedean standpoint, beyond all history, necessarily resulted in a diminished perception of social reality and ultimately led him into political apathy. But no doubt this question presented Rosenzweig with a dilemma: for if one desired to be politically effective in Germany, one needed to become involved with German politics. This meant assimilation. So involvement in politics would have destroyed exactly what Rosenzweig wished to reconstruct: the wholeness of Jewish man. Furthermore, the reader of Spengler had lost all faith in the capacity of political activity to find solutions. The decline of European culture was in his eyes an inevitable reality – it could no longer be prevented, it could only be endured.

Since the situation was, as he understood it, inescapable, Rosenzweig chose the only way possible: accepting the religious, he tried to fortify the strength of the human in a civilisation which he saw in an ever-deepening process of dehumanisation. In view of this process, Rosenzweig could declare to friends that some time in the future his way of thinking could contribute to the necessary revitalisation of European culture.[178]

The very radicality, however, with which he intended to overcome the crisis reveals the degree to which his thinking was in fact the expression of such crisis. Rosenzweig's desire to preserve in a timeless religiousness the last remnant of security, at a time when everything had become political and thus subject to change, finds an explanation in the extremity generated by the historical era through which he lived. Nonetheless, he who gives way to a yearning for the constant as radically as he did does not overcome history, but only surrenders to it. Martin Buber, Rosenzweig's friend and companion, found a pithy formula which goes to the heart of the problems expressed in Rosenzweig's thinking.

> "The catastrophes of historical realities often are, at the same time, crises of man's relation to reality. As to the special way in which our time has been given knowledge of this, I could not think of a greater and more telling example than that provided by Franz Rosenzweig."[179]

---

[178]Letter to Rudolf Hallo, 4th February 1923, in *CW 1*, pp. 888–890.
[179]Quote according to Paul E. Pfuetze, 'Martin Buber und der amerikanische Pragmatismus', in Paul A. Schilpp and Maurice S. Friedman (eds.), *Martin Buber*, Stuttgart 1963, pp. 448–478, quotation pp. 452–453.

Two Centenaries

BY WILLIAM W. HALLO

The years 1986—1988 marked the centenaries of the birth of two men whose intellectual development described — for a time — very similar trajectories, and whose encounter proved fateful and fruitful to both. Franz Rosenzweig was born in 1886 in Kassel (Germany) and died in Frankfurt a. Main in 1929 after an intensely productive career as philosopher, theologian and pedagogue — a career cut short by amyotrophic lateral sclerosis (Lou Gehrig's disease). His published *oeuvre* has been catalogued under 84 entries beginning with a student-study published in 1917 and ending with the French translation of his *magnum opus* (1982); the catalogue appears at the end of the latest re-edition of his *Gesammelte Schriften* (1976—1984).[1]

Eugen Rosenstock-Huessy was born in Berlin in 1888 and died in Hanover, New Hampshire, in 1973, after leaving an even more prolific legacy of publications as well as other activities and initiatives. Some 457 published items, dating from the doctoral dissertation of 1910 to the posthumous re-publication of a letter to Rudolf Ehrenberg in 1987 are listed in the Comprehensive Bibliography of his works compiled by Lise van der Molen.[2] In addition, a massive edition of his unpublished American lectures — some 11,000 manuscript pages in all — is planned by the Eugen Rosenstock-Huessy Fund.

The Rosenzweig Centenary was observed in a number of ways, most notably in his native city of Kassel, whose university (*Gesamthochschule*) sponsored an international congress at which some seventy specialists addressed a sizeable audience on all aspects of Rosenzweig's life and thought (7th—11th December 1986). The results were edited by the organiser of the congress, Wolfdietrich Schmied-Kowarzik, in two stately volumes.[3] For the occasion, the city of Kassel also sponsored, concurrently, an exhibition documenting Jewish life in Kassel. A substantial catalogue provided a permanent record of the exhibition;[4] like the conference itself, its motto was Rosenzweig's exclamation/explanation: "Ich bleibe also Jude."[5] Among many other contributions about Rosenzweig, it includes a biography and numerous photographs of himself, his family and his colleagues. And it is probably more than coincidence that a major study on the names and fates of the Jews of Kassel during the Nazi period appeared in the same year.[6]

[1] Franz Rosenzweig, *Der Mensch und sein Werk. Gesammelte Schriften*, IV/2, Doordrecht-Boston-Lancaster 1984, pp. 309–324. Cf. now also L. Anckaert and B. Casper, *Franz Rosenzweig. A Primary and Secondary Bibliography*, Leuven 1990.

[2] 'The writings of Eugen Rosenstock-Huessy', in George Allen Morgan, *Speech and Society. The Christian Linguistic Social Philosophy of Eugen Rosenstock-Huessy*, Gainesville, Florida 1987, pp. 155–196.

[3] *Der Philosoph Franz Rosenzweig (1886–1929). Internationaler Kongress – Kassel 1986*, 2 vols., München 1988.

[4] *Juden in Kassel 1808–1933. Eine Dokumentation anlässlich des 100. Geburtstages von Franz Rosenzweig*, Kassel 1986.

[5] See below notes 30f.

[6] Beate Kleinert and Wolfgang Prinz (eds.), *Namen und Schicksale der Juden Kassels 1933–1945: ein Gedenkbuch*, Kassel 1986.

More modest commemorations were held elsewhere to mark the centenary. In New Haven, Yale's biennial Franz Rosenzweig lectureship, established by a grant of the late Arthur A. Cohen, devoted its 1986 meeting to the theme of 'Franz Rosenzweig's Lehrhaus: its Significance and Position in Judaism' (8th—10th April 1986). The featured speaker was Nahum N. Glatzer.[7] In New York, the Leo Baeck Institute sponsored a one-day conference (15th February 1987), some of the papers of which were published in its Year Book.[8]

The centenary of Rosenstock-Huessy was observed with a conference at the college where he had taught for more than twenty years, Dartmouth (15th—19th August 1988). A large and enthusiastic group of former students, colleagues and admirers from all over the world participated in the numerous panels, sessions and excursions. Many of the resulting papers will be published in *Stimmstein* and other outlets in the near future. What follows is based on my own remarks at the meeting.

A highlight of the Kassel conference was the revelation that a corpus of some 1,500 unpublished letters of Rosenzweig (mostly dating to the period 1917—1922) had survived in the estate of Margrit Rosenstock-Huessy and that they had been entrusted for publication to Harold M. Stahmer, of the University of Florida, who had previously introduced the English edition of the letters between Rosenzweig and Rosenstock-Huessy.[9] The new corpus consists almost entirely of Rosenzweig's letters to Margrit Rosenstock-Huessy, Eugen's wife, and even in the absence of her answers (which have not survived), they vastly outnumber the published letters exchanged between Eugen and Franz.[10] It is not, however, only their number that promises to give them crucial importance, but also their content. As the husband of Eugen and Margrit's granddaughter, Stahmer has understandably avoided revealing the more personal aspects of the letters. But his remarks at the conference, subsequently published in this Year Book,[11] allow us to see the, literally, daily accounting which they provide in regard to Rosenzweig's writing *The Star of Redemption* (completed February 1919). The hitherto perceived notion of that process was that it took place exclusively or primarily at the front-lines of the Balkan theatre of operations in the First World War, and that it was communicated, as often as not, by postcard to Adele Rosenzweig, his mother. Now it appears that a much more nuanced process was

---

[7]Nahum Glatzer died on 26th February 1990.

[8]*LBI Year Book XXXIV* (1989), pp. 357–384; cf. the Preface by Arnold Paucker, p. IX.

[9]Eugen Rosenstock-Huessey (ed.), *Judaism Despite Christianity. The "Letters on Christianity and Judaism" between Eugen Rosenstock-Huessy and Franz Rosenzweig*, University of Alabama 1969; New York 1971, 'Introduction' by Harold Stahmer, pp. 1–25.

[10]*Judaism Despite Christianity* features English translations of twenty-one letters exchanged between them, including nine from Franz Rosenzweig. The new edition of his letters includes these and fourteen more to Eugen Rosenstock-Huessy (Nos. 370, 439f., 445, 457, 459, 464, 466, 469, 1032, 1036, 1059, 1197, 1211). See Franz Rosenzweig, *Briefe und Tagebücher = Gesammelte Schriften, I*, 2 vols., Den Haag, 1979.

[11]Harold M. Stahmer, 'Franz Rosenzweig's letters to Margrit Rosenstock-Huessy, 1917–1922', in *LBI Year Book XXXIV* (1989), pp. 385–409. My thanks to Professor Stahmer for sending me a copy of his paper in advance of publication.

at work, in which Margrit often served as sounding-board for his ideas.[12] We can count on eventually seeing two pages of description of the thought behind the writing for every page of writing itself – all in the author's immediate words. He has, as it were, furnished us with a running commentary on his own most important book – and it goes without saying that future interpretation of Rosenzweig will have to take the new evidence into account.

A highlight of the Yale conference was a roundtable workshop on the original *Lehrhaus* conducted by surviving participants. Glatzer was joined in this workshop by Martin Goldner,[13] Gertrude Hallo,[14] and Rudolph F. Stahl, and both audio- and videotapes were made of the occasion.[15] Goldner took the occasion to show his copies of the *Festschrift* originally prepared by him and offered to Franz Rosenzweig on the occasion of his fortieth birthday, sixty years earlier. This departure from the usual format of an anniversary volume consisted of forty-six handwritten contributions, limited to one folio-size page each, but unlimited as to medium. In addition to 38 letters, short essays in German or (in three cases) Hebrew, translations and commentaries, it featured six poems (including one by Karl Wolfskehl), a dramatic fragment, and a drawing by Ludwig Alfred Jonas. The volume, or "Mappe" as it was known from its format, was familiar enough to the participants in the workshop, all of whom were represented in it. But it was a revelation to the audience, for it had never been published,[16] and it was Goldner's heartfelt desire to see this happen. With the material support of Ernst L. Frank (New York), the result appeared in 1987 as a limited edition in three hundred numbered copies and in the original folio format. It includes facsimiles of the original contributions as well as Goldner's transcriptions and translations. The title page reads: "Franz Rosenzweig zum 25. Dezember 1926: Glückwünsche zum 40. Geburtstag/Congratulations to Franz Rosenzweig on his 40th Birthday 25 December 1926. Published on the Centenary of Franz Rosenzweig's birth by the Leo Baeck Institute–New York."

Out of all the contributions to the volume, I would like to single out here just one, No. 32, by Eugen Rosenstock-Huessy. Taking his text from Rosenzweig's introduction to Hermann Cohen's writings on Judaica,[17] Rosenstock developed, in five hundred well-chosen words, a concept of "determination" that is both grammatical and philosophical, or theological. The combination is in line with

---

[12]This seems especially to be the case with Part 2, Book 2, culminating in its "grammatical analysis of the Song of Songs".

[13]Martin Goldner died on 13th April 1987.

[14]Gertrude Hallo died on 18th April 1986.

[15]Available from the author.

[16]Individual items from it have, however, occasionally appeared in print in the interim. Cf. e.g. No. 16: Rudolf Hallo, 'Der Tempel Salomos', for which see Rudolf Hallo, *Schriften zur Kunstgeschichte in Kassel. Sammlungen-Denkmäler-Judaica*, ed. by Günter Schweikhart, Kassel 1983, pp. 663f.

[17]*Hermann Cohens Jüdische Schriften* mit einer Einleitung von Franz Rosenzweig, vol. I, Berlin 1924, pp. xiii–lxiv; reprinted in F. Rosenzweig, *Zweistromland*, Berlin 1926, pp. 185–239; *Kleinere Schriften*, Berlin 1937, pp. 299–350; *Gesammelte Schriften*, III, Dordrecht 1984, pp. 177–233. The passage in question occurs on p. liv of Cohen's work, on p. 229 of the 1926 edition and pp. 213f. of the 1984 edition.

Rosenstock-Huessy's lifelong pre-occupation with problems of speech and language.[18]

Rosenzweig developed his "new thinking" in acknowledged dependence on and reaction to Rosenstock's ideas.[19] This has been demonstrated repeatedly by a number of commentators, most emphatically and most recently by Stahmer in 1984.[20] He bases himself not only on the crucial encounter of 7th July 1913, but on the "speech-letters" exchanged in 1916.[21] And he deplores that, in the new edition of Rosenzweig's letters, this correspondence is no longer kept intact as a self-contained unit (as the two authors intended) – a view in which he is not alone.[22] It may be noted in this connection that Bernhard Casper, who is otherwise more inclined to trace Rosenzweig's ideas to Heidegger or even Wittgenstein,[23] admits that Heidegger's turn to "Sprachdenken" is derivative from Rosenzweig and Rosenstock.[24]

Rosenzweig himself only once (and then casually) used the term "speech-thinking" in print, and only twice the term "speech-thinker"[25] – but then to make it clear that he equated it with what he preferred to call "the new thinking".[26] Thus Rafael and Rachel Rosenzweig were probably justified in entitling the final volume of the *Gesammelte Schriften* 'Sprachdenken im Übersetzen', as was Anna Bauer in writing of "Rosenzweigs Sprachdenken".[27] But by whatever name, Rosenstock's short essay fairly resonates with this "speech-thinking", with the love of language exemplified in his own writings and in

---

[18]Stahmer, *loc. cit.* (note 9) p. 19. For a recent summary of his work, especially as a "Sprachdenker", see Morgan, *op. cit.*, esp. ch. 1.

[19]Rosenzweig, 'Das neue Denken', *Der Morgen*, 1 (1925), pp. 426–451. The acknowledgement in question occurs on pp. 440f. Latest reprinting: *Gesammelte Schriften*, III (1984), p. 152. English translation in Nahum N. Glatzer, *Franz Rosenzweig. His Life and Thought*, New York 1953, pp. 190–208, esp. p. 200. French translation in Olivier Mongin *et al.*, *Franz Rosenzweig* (=Les Cahiers de *La Nuit Surveillée*, No. 1, 1982), pp. 39–63, esp. p. 53.

[20]Stahmer, '"Speech-letters" and "speech-thinking". Franz Rosenzweig and Eugen Rosenstock-Huessy', *Modern Judaism* (1984), pp. 57–81. Cf. *idem*, *"Speak That I May See Thee"*. *The Religious Significance of Language*, New York 1968, chs. 3, 4, 7.

[21]Above, note 10.

[22]In my mother's copy of *Gesammelte Schriften*, I/1, I found (on the same day that I first read Stahmer's article) the following slip in her handwriting: "I find the disruption of the Rosenzweig–Rosenstock correspondence *very* disturbing, & Eugen's reasons for keeping them separate very convincing. He was still alive when this edition was in its first stages. Was he asked & did he consent?"

[23]Cf. also Ranjit Chatterjee, 'Freedom upon the Tablets. Wittgenstein, Rosenzweig and Language', Paper presented to the Jewish Studies Workshop, The University of Chicago, 4th February 1988 (iii+48 pp.), esp. pp. 35ff. I am indebted to Dr. Chatterjee for a copy of his paper.

[24]Bernhard Casper, 'Zur Einführung', introduction to Rosenzweig, *Gesammelte Schriften*, I, pp. ix–xxiii, esp. p. xvii; cf. Stahmer, '"Speech-letters . . ."', *loc. cit.*, pp. 60f. Cf. also Steven S. Schwarzschild, 'Franz Rosenzweig and Martin Heidegger. The German and the Jewish Turn to Ethnicism', in *Der Philosoph Franz Rosenzweig*, II, 1988, pp. 887–889.

[25]In 'Das Neue Denken', first published in *Der Morgen*, 1 (1925), pp. 426–451; latest republication in *Gesammelte Schriften*, III (1984), pp. 139–161. For "Sprachdenken" see pp. 442 and 152, for "Sprachdenker" pp. 440 and 151 respectively. For (the absence of) other references to the concept, see the exhaustive index in *Gesammelte Schriften*, IV/2 (1984), pp. 325–361, esp. p. 352.

[26]In the (partial) English translation (above, note 19), "Sprachdenker" appears as "speaking thinker" (Glatzer, *op. cit.*, p. 199).

[27]*Der Philosoph Franz Rosenzweig*, II, *op. cit.*, pp. 903–912.

Rosenzweig's "grammatical analysis" of the Song of Songs and other classic Jewish texts.[28]

Rosenzweig first met Rosenstock in 1912 at a conference in Baden-Baden and then, more extensively, at the beginning of 1913, attending the latter's first lectures in law at Leipzig.[29] A deep friendship ensued, and by July, Rosenstock had almost persuaded Rosenzweig to follow his example and convert to Christianity. But Rosenzweig's move to Berlin in the middle of the High Holydays coincided with his decision to remain a Jew. "Ich bleibe also Jude!" as he put it in his famous letter to Rudolf Ehrenberg,[30] which became, as we have seen, the motto of the Kassel Conference.[31]

In Berlin, Rosenzweig came under the influence of Hermann Cohen, recently arrived from Marburg, who combined a profound understanding of Greek and German philosophy with an active involvement in Jewish life and thought, lecturing at the *Lehranstalt* (later *Hochschule*) *für die Wissenschaft des Judentums*. Rosenzweig attended his lectures during the academic year 1913–1914, and acknowledged their great impact on him.[32] A decade later, he was to provide a long and learned introduction to Cohen's writings on Judaica.[33]

It was from this introduction that Rosenstock took the title and point of departure of his brief essay, entitled 'Der Geist des Menschen ist der heilige Geist'.[34] If this is, as Rosenstock claims, an actual quotation from Hermann Cohen, it must come from Rosenzweig's memory or notes of the 1913–1914 lectures, for it is not present in the published version of the lectures, which appeared in 1915,[35] where the nearest equivalent is "Gott hat seinen heiligen Geist dem Menschen gegeben. Der menschliche Geist ist daher selbst zum heiligen geworden".[36] Nor is it to be found in the article on 'The Holy Spirit' which Cohen published in the same year.[37] What we find there, rather, are more nuanced formulations such as "So ist der Geist der Heiligkeit bei Gott zugleich der Geist der Heiligkeit im Menschen;"[38] "Der heilige Geist, von Gott dem Menschen gegeben, bildet den unzerstörbaren *Charakter* des Menschen;"[39] "Aber

---

[28]Cf. above, note 12.

[29]*Gesammelte Schriften*, I/1 (1979), pp. 124f.

[30]*Ibid.*, p. 133.

[31]See also the cover of *Juden in Kassel* (above, note 4), and the Introduction by Ingrid Kräling, *ibid.*, pp. 10–12.

[32]Glatzer, *op. cit.*, pp. 29f. See Rosenzweig, *Zweistromland* (1926), p. 219 = *Gesammelte Schriften*, III, p. 205. For the impact of Cohen's lectures at the *Lehranstalt* three years later, see the contribution by Gertrude Hallo (No. 15) in the "Mappe".

[33]Above, note 17.

[34]Collation of the facsimile suggests a number of minor corrections to Goldner's transcription. In line 5, "Zehn" is capitalised (as in line 6). Line 6 appears to begin a new paragraph. Lines 16–17: This sentence seems to have been squeezed in secondarily by the author. Line 30: instead of "Entscheidung", the word (divided over two lines) seems to read "Er-schleichung". For a new transcription and translation see Appendix.

[35]Hermann Cohen, *Der Begriff der Religion im System der Philosophie* (= *Philosophische Arbeiten*, X/1, 1915).

[36]*Ibid.*, p. 104.

[37]'Der heilige Geist', *Festschrift zum siebzigsten Geburtstage Jakob Guttmanns* (= *Schriften . . . der Gesellschaft des Judentums*, 1915), pp. 1–12; reprinted in *Hermann Cohens Jüdische Schriften*, vol. III, pp. 176–186.

[38]P. 2 of the original article = p. 177 of the reprint.

[39]P. 15 = p. 189.

der heilige Geist ist die Verbindung des Menschen mit Gott;"[40] "Der Geist ist dem Menschen gemeinsam mit Gott und die Heiligkeit ist dem Menschen gemeinsam mit Gott;"[41] "So ist der heilige Geist der Geist Gottes und der Geist der Menschheit."[42] In his most famous work, *Die Religion der Vernunft aus den Quellen des Judentums*, published posthumously in 1919,[43] Cohen devoted a whole chapter to 'Der heilige Geist', rewriting his earlier article considerably, but the closest approximation to our sentence occurs elsewhere in the book as "Der heilige Geist ist der Menschengeist".[44] (This is precisely a formulation which, as we will see, will *not* admit of Rosenstock's exegesis.)

What Rosenzweig apparently did, then, was to sum up the essence of all these formulations in one memorable theologem. And Rosenstock based his exegesis of Cohen on Rosenzweig's theologem.

Rosenstock begins by pointing out that the spirit of the prophet (*in casu*: Moses) is "the holy spirit" because he imparts God, literally shares God with humanity, and because he is a fore-teller and a forth-teller. These last terms are not Rosenstock's. They attempt to translate the noun "Künder" which Martin Buber and Rosenzweig regularly use to translate the biblical term normally rendered "prophet" in English. Rosenstock himself used (with emphasis) the verbal form "er *kündete*".

But Rosenstock himself develops this point further by insisting on the definite article in the theologem. The holy spirit is the spirit of the human being, yes, but only of "the definitive human being", definitively minted like a coin, and as different from a human creature in general as a coin from a gold ingot (a metaphor Rosenstock used elsewhere as well).[45]

Rosenstock's linguistic and theological speculation is at once reminiscent of Rosenzweig's discussion of the "Grammar of the Logos".[46] For Rosenzweig, the definite article completes the process of answering "what" a thing is. "Determination by whatever means it may be expressed" allows the thing to be directly apprehended, to be "recognised as this individual thing".[47] But one of the means of determination other than the definite article is the proper noun, or name; to acquire individuality, this named entity "has to legitimate itself as a member of a plurality".[48] And in the "grammatical appendix" to the "Logic of Revelation", the proper name is the focus of the discussion: "With the summons by the proper name, the word of revelation entered the real dialogue . . . That which has a name of its own . . . is incapable of utter absorption into the category for there can be no category for it to belong to; it is its own category".[49] Thus the

---

[40]P. 15 = p. 190.
[41]*Ibid.*
[42]P. 21 = p. 196.
[43]Hermann Cohen, *Die Religion der Vernunft aus den Quellen des Judentums*, Leipzig 1919, chapter VII.
[44]*Ibid.*, p. 302.
[45]Stahmer, ' "Speech-letters" ', *loc. cit.*, p. 75 and note 48.
[46]Rosenzweig, *The Star of Redemption*, translated by William W. Hallo, Notre Dame, Indiana 1985, pp. 124–131 = *Gesammelte Schriften*, II (1976), pp. 138–145.
[47]*Star of Redemption*, p. 128.
[48]*Ibid.*
[49]*Ibid.*, pp. 186f. = *Gesammelte Schriften*, II, p. 208; cf. Bauer, 'Rosenzweigs Sprachdenken', *loc. cit.*, p. 904.

prosopographically determined individual shares with the substantive, determined by the definite article, its membership in and yet its distinction from a larger class or type.

What Rosenstock did in his brief essay was to take Rosenzweig's concept of grammatical determination and use it to refine the interpretation of Rosenzweig's theologem. What could have become a bone of contention between the two thus serves instead as a suitable tribute from the Christian to the Jewish theologian. Thirty-five years later, Rosenstock still praised Rosenzweig as "a great man of Calvin's stature and suffering".[50]

The one page which is thus added to the published *oeuvre* of Rosenstock pales in significance beside the massive augments promised by the Eugen Rosenstock-Huessy Fund, and equally beside the 1,500 letters from Rosenzweig to Eugen and especially to Margrit Rosenstock-Huessy which still await publication. But it may be appropriate to recall that Rosenzweig's own scholarly career began, not with the massive study on *Hegel und der Staat* which had been his doctoral dissertation, but with an article about a single folio page. At the threshold of the First World War, he edited a Hegel autograph newly acquired by the Royal Library in Berlin and showed that it was in actuality Hegel's copy of a programmatic statement by Friedrich W. Schelling.[51] Thus we have, in a sense, come full circle: from a folio page which launched Rosenzweig's publishing career (1917) to a folio page dedicated to him by Rosenstock-Huessy and published seventy years later (1987).

---

[50]Eugen Rosenstock-Huessy, 'The Generations of Faith', *The Hartford Quarterly*, I, No. 3 (1961).

[51]Rosenzweig, *Das älteste Systemprogramm des deutschen Idealismus. Ein handschriftlicher Fund* (=Sitzungsberichte der Heidelberger Akademie der Wissenschaften phil.-hist. Klasse, Jahrgang 1917, 5. Abhandlung). The manuscript was submitted in 1914; its publication was delayed by the War. Republished most recently in *Gesammelte Schriften*, III, pp. 3–44.

APPENDIX I

„Der Geist des Menschen ist der heilige Geist."

Franz Rosenzweig Zweistromland (1926), 229.

Als ich diesen Satz Hermann Cohens im Bericht Franz Rosenzweigs las, entfuhr mir der Ausruf: Ja hat denn je ein Mensch etwas anderes geglaubt! Alsbald fiel mir eine mehrfache Diskussion ein, zwischen dem Berichterstatter und mir, die sich auf die Zehn Gebote bezog. Auf sie schien mir Licht durch jenen Satz zu fallen.

Gott hat die Zehn Gebote gegeben. Einverstanden? Wem hat er sie gegeben? dem Volke Israel. Durch wen hat Gott sie übersetzt ins menschliche Wort? Mitteiler war der Mund Moses und seine Hand.

War nun Moses Geist nicht kraft dieses Eid-Mitteilers Gottes heilig? Ich sehe keine Möglichkeit, diese Frage anders als mit Ja zu beantworten. Aber nur weil Moses sie mitteilte, weil er den Widerstand des Volkes wagte und überwand, nicht weil er „dachte", sondern weil er hinderte, war der Geist des Menschen Moses heilig. Der Eintritt allein bewährt die Heilkraft.

Die Juden aber hatten Gottes Rat, vor lauter Moses den heiligen Geist nicht zu vernehmen. Der menschliche Geist „des" Menschen verstellt also den „heiligen" Geist. Die christliche Überlieferung war nichts anderes über den Hlg. Geist zu sagen.

Es ist einfach wahr, dass der heilige Geist der Geist des Menschen ist. Wessen sonst? Die Teilung, die interessiert, ist nicht, ob Gottes Geist oder des Menschen Geist heilig sei, da der heilige Geist die göttliche Eid-Mitteilung im Menschen ist. Denn brennend ist nur die Deutung des Wörtleins „des" in der Fügung: „der Geist des Menschen."

Überall, wo man von dem „Arbeiter, dem Philosophen, dem Menschen" spricht, pflegt man Entscheidung zu treffen. Der bestimmte Artikel erhebt die Menschenart, von der die Rede ist, zur Endgültigkeit. Diese Endgültigkeit kommt den ihr zugezählten Menschenkindern nicht zu. Menschenkind und „der Mensch" sind wie Goldbarren und Münze, zweierlei.

Selbstverständlich also, dass dies ist: Der heilige Geist ist der Geist des endgültigen Menschen. Wo immer Menschenart endgültig geprägt wird, ist Gott, in jedem Opfer, jeder Wandlung, jeder selbstgrauen Hingabe, die das geliebte Menschenkind sich vollenden lässt. Kuppen: wo geprägte Art fort und weitergelebt wird, im Alltag, Brottag, Ehetag – da ist des Menschen Geist nicht heilig, weil der Mensch nicht gegenwärtig ist, sondern nur ein oder mehrere Menschenkinder, die der heilige Geist wohl verklären kann, doch ohne sie zu begeistern, selbst wenn sie gut und heilig denken.

Denn heilige Gedanken sind wie heiliger Geist. Heiliger Geist ist nur im Entäussern. Um hinein des Glaubens zu hören zum heiligen Geist immer der Ausgang in die gefahrvolle Menschenkinderwelt, um aus Kindern Menschen zu wandeln, um Kinder Israels anzureden und sie über ihre angeborene Art emporzureissen. Sonst lohnt es nicht, vom heiligen Geist zu reden. Denn sonst befinden wir uns nicht am Tage der Geschichte Gottes in dem Menschen, am Urtag der Schöpfung des Menschen.

Eugen Rosenstock-Huessy

APPENDIX II

„Der Geist des Menschen ist der heilige Geist."
Franz Rosenzweig, Zweistromland (1926), 229.

Als ich diesen Satz Hermann Cohens im Bericht Franz Rosenzweigs las, entfuhr mir der Ausruf: Ja hat denn je ein Mensch etwas anderes geglaubt? Alsbald fiel mir eine mehrfache Diskussion ein, zwischen dem Berichterstatter und mir, die sich auf die Zehn Gebote bezog. Auf sie scheint mir Licht durch jenen Satz zu fallen. Gott hat die Zehn Gebote gegeben. Einverstanden? Wem hat er sie gegeben? dem Volke Israel. Durch wen hat Gott sie übersetzt in menschliche Rede? Mitteiler war der Mund Mosis und seine Hand.

War nun Mosis Geist nicht kraft dieses Sich-Mitteilens Gottes heilig? Ich sehe keine Möglichkeit, diese Frage anders als mit Ja zu beantworten. Aber nur weil Moses sie mit-teilte, weil er den Widerstand des Volkes wagte und überwand, nicht weil er „dachte", sondern weil er *kündete*, war der Geist des Menschen Mosis heilig. Der Einbruch allein bewährt die Heilkraft.

Die Juden aber hatten Gottes Recht, vor lauter Moses den heiligen Geist nicht zu vernehmen. Der menschliche Geist „des" Menschen verstellt seinen „heiligen" Geist. Die christliche Überlieferung weiss nichts anderes über den Hlg. Geist zu sagen.

Es ist einfach wahr, dass der heilige Geist der Geist des Menschen ist. Wessen sonst? Die Teilung, die interessiert, ist nicht, ob Gottes Geist oder des Menschen Geist heilig sei, da der heilige Geist die göttliche Sich-Mitteilung in Menschen ist. Sondern brennend ist nur die Deutung des Wörtleins „des" in der Fügung: „der Geist des Menschen".

Überall, wo man von „dem" Arbeiter, dem Philosophen, dem Menschen spricht, pflegt eine Erschleichung zu stecken. Der bestimmte Artikel erhebt die Menschenart, von der die Rede ist, zur *Endgültigkeit*. Diese Endgültigkeit kommt den ihr zugezählten Menschenkindern nicht zu. Menschenkind und „der" Mensch sind wie Goldbarren und Münze, zweierlei.

Selbstverständlich also, dass dies ist: *Der heilige Geist ist der Geist des endgültigen Menschen.* Wo immer Menschenart endgültig geprägt wird, ist Gott, in jedem Opfer, jeder Wandlung, jeder selbstvergessenen Hingabe, die das geliebte Menschenkind sich vollenden lässt. Hingegen: wo geprägte Art fort und weitergelebt wird, im Alltag, Berufstag, Ehetag – da ist des Menschen Geist nicht heilig, weil „der" Mensch nicht gegenwärtig ist, sondern nur ein oder mehrere Menschenkinder, die der heilige Geist noch verklären kann, doch ohne sie zu begeistern, selbst wenn sie gut und heilig denken.

Denn heilige Gedanken sind nie heiliger Geist. Heiliger Geist ist nur im Entäussern. Im Sinne des Glaubens gehört zum heiligen Geist immer der Ausgang in die gefahrvolle Menschenkinderwelt, um aus Kindern Menschen zu wandeln, um Kinder Israels anzusprechen und sie über ihre angeborene Art emporzureissen. Sonst lohnt es nicht, vom *heiligen Geist* zu reden. Denn sonst befinden wir uns nicht am Tage der Geschichte Gottes in den Menschen, am Urtag der Schöpfung des Menschen.

Eugen Rosenstock-Hüssy

APPENDIX III

"The spirit of the human being is the holy spirit."
Franz Rosenzweig, *Zweistromland*, 1926, p. 229.

When I read this sentence of Hermann Cohen's in the report of Franz Rosenzweig, an exclamation escaped me: Well, has ever anyone believed otherwise? Soon I was reminded of a frequent discussion between the rapporteur and me which had reference to the Ten Commandments. This appears to me to be illuminated through that sentence. God gave the Ten Commandments. Agreed? To whom did he give them? To the people of Israel. Through whom did God translate them into human discourse? The imparter was the mouth of Moses and his hand.

Now was not the spirit of Moses holy, thanks to God's thus imparting himself? I see no possibility of answering this question otherwise than with a yes. But the spirit of the human being Moses was holy only because Moses im-parted them (i.e., the Ten Commandments) (literally: shared them), because he risked the opposition of the people and overcame it, not because he was "thinking", but because he was *foretelling/forthtelling*. Only the collapse confirms the healing power.*

The Jews, however, had the God-given right *not* to become aware of the holy spirit in the face of so much Moses. The human spirit of "the" human being displaces/misplaces his "holy" spirit. Christian tradition has nothing but this to say about the Holy Ghost.

It is a truism that the holy spirit is the spirit of the human being. Of whom otherwise? The distinction which is of interest is not whether it is the spirit of God or the spirit of the human being that is holy, since the holy spirit is the divine self-imparting in human beings. Rather, it is only the interpretation of the little word "the" in the phrase "spirit of the human being" that is crucial.

Wherever and whenever one speaks of "the" worker, the philosopher, the human being, there tends to lurk something surreptitious. The definite article elevates the human type under discussion to *definitiveness*, to finality. This definitiveness does not apply to the human creatures subsumed under the type. Human creature and "the" human being are as distinct as gold ingot and coin.

It thus goes without saying that the fact is: *The holy spirit is the spirit of the definitive human being.* Wherever human type is definitively minted, there God is — in every offering, every transformation, every selfless sacrifice that allows the beloved human creature to perfect itself.

On the other hand: where the minted type is absent and life goes on, in the every-day, the work-a-day, the wedding day — there the spirit of the human being is not holy, because "the" human being is not present but only one or more human creatures whom the holy spirit can still transfigure but without inspiring/inspiriting them, even if they think in good and holy fashion.

For holy thoughts are never holy spirit. Holy spirit exists only in parting with something. In the sense of faith, the holy spirit always involves going out into the perilous world of the children of men, in order to turn children into men, in order to address the children of Israel and to raise them forcibly above their innate type. Otherwise it is not worthwhile to speak of the *holy* spirit. For otherwise we do not find ourselves at the day of God's history in human beings, on the primal day of the creation of the human being.

Eugen Rosenstock-Huessy

* To judge by the facsimile, this sentence was added as a kind of afterthought.

Post-War Publications on German Jewry

A Selected Bibliography of Books and Articles 1990

Compiled by
BARBARA SUCHY and ANNETTE PRINGLE

Leo Baeck Institute
4 Devonshire Street
London W.1.

CONTENTS

BIBLIOGRAPHY 1990

I. HISTORY

A. General

26924. ABRAHAMSON, GLENDA, ed.: *The Blackwell companion to Jewish culture: from the eighteenth century to the present.* Oxford: Blackwell, 1989. 853 pp., illus. [Incl. writers, scholars, artists; many German-Jewish.]

26925. ASSOR, REUVEN: *The German-language Jewish press in Europe.* [In Hebrew, with English summary]. [In]: Qesher, No. 7, Tel-Aviv, May 1990. Pp. 61–65.

—— BARKAI, AVRAHAM: *German interests in the Haavara-Transfer Agreement 1933–1939.* [See No. 27562].

26926. BATTENBERG, FRIEDRICH: *Das europäische Zeitalter der Juden: zur Entwicklung einer Minderheit in der nichtjüdischen Umwelt Europas.* Bd. 1–2. Darmstadt: Wissenschaftliche Buchgesellschaft. 1990. 2 vols. Bd. 1: Von den Anfängen bis 1650. XVI, 307 pp., illus., bibl. notes (263–277), index of names, index of subjects, map. Bd. 2: Von 1650 bis 1945. XIII, 361 pp., illus., bibl. notes (311–328), index of names, index of subjects, map.

—— BIECHELE, WERNER: *Jüdische Intellektuelle im Spannungsfeld von bürgerlichem Demokratie-Verständnis und antisemitischen Rassenwahn.* [See No. 27730.]

26927. BRENNER, MICHAEL: *The Jüdische Volkspartei – national-Jewish communal politics during the Weimar Republic.* [In]: LBI Year Book XXXV, London 1990. Pp. 219–243, illus., tabs., notes.

26928. BURMEISTER, KARL HEINZ: *Der Würfelzoll – eine Abart des Leibzolls auf Juden.* [In]: Steuerliche Vierteljahresschrift, 1990. Herne, 1990. Pp. 232–236, notes.

26929. *Fin-de-siècle and its legacy.* Eds.: Mikulas Teich, Roy Porter. Cambridge; New York: Cambridge Univ. Press, 1990. 345 pp., illus., facsims., tabs., notes. [Incl.: Nationalism, anti-semitism, socialism and political Catholicism, as expressions of mass politics in the twentieth century (Enzo Collotti, 80–97, notes). Also passim on Jewish contributions to culture, film, painting, theatre.]

26930. FREIMARK, PETER: *Davidschild und Brauerstern: zur Synonymie eines Symbols.* [In]: Jahrbuch 1990 der Gesellschaft für die Geschichte und Bibliographie des Brauwesens, Berlin 1990. Pp. 13–33, illus., notes.

26931. FRIESEL, EVYATAR: *Atlas of modern Jewish history.* Oxford; New York: Oxford Univ. Press, 1990. 159 pp., maps, bibl. [Covers Jewish history, demography, and intellectual developments from the 17th century to the 1980s. Incl. Germany, as well as the evolution of antisemitism.]

26932. FUCHS, KONRAD: *Ein Konzern aus Sachsen: das Kaufhaus Schocken als Spiegelbild deutscher Wirtschaft und Politik 1901 bis 1953.* Eine Veröffentlichung des Leo Baeck Instituts. Stuttgart: Deutsche Verlags-Anstalt 1990. 344 pp., illus., notes, bibl., chronology, index. [Cf.: Unternehmens – Geschichten (Henry Marx) [in]: Aufbau, Vol. 57, No. 5, New York, March 1, 1991, pp. 7, 12–13.]

26933. GROSSMAN, AVRAHAM: *The way to Ashkenaz.* [In Hebrew, title transl.]. [In]: Eit-mol, No. 84, Tel-Aviv, Dec. 1990. Pp. 11–13.

26934. HAUMANN, HEIKO: *Geschichte der Ostjuden.* Orig.-Ausg. München: Dt. Taschenbuch-Verl., 1990. 212 pp., maps, notes, bibl. (195–206). (dtv, 4549.) [Refers also to Jews in Bohemia and Moravia, Galicia and Hungary.]

26935. HERZIG, ARNO: *Zur Problematik deutsch-jüdischer Geschichtsschreibung.* [In]: Menora, Bd. 1, München, 1990. Pp. 209–234, notes.

26936. HILDESHEIMER, ESRIEL: *Bishop of the Jews.* [In Hebrew, title transl.]. [In]: Sinai, Vol. 105, Jerusalem, Kislev-teveth 5750 [= Dec. 1989/Jan 1990]. Pp. 142–165. [On the title and function called "Bishop of the Jews" or "Judenbischof" bestowed by Christian authorities to Jewish communal leaders in the Middle Ages; deals with Germany (pp. 159–161), and compares England with Germany (pp. 161–165).]

26937. HILDESHEIMER, ESRIEL: *The provision against gentile courts in late medieval Ashkenaz: halacha and practice.* [In Hebrew]. [In]: Proceedings of the Tenth World Congress of Jewish Studies, Jerusalem 1989. Division C, Vol. 1, ed. by David Assaf. [In Hebrew]. Jerusalem: World Union of Jewish Studies, 1990. Pp. 217–224.

26938. HORCH, HANSS OTTO: *'Auf der Zinne der Zeit': Ludwig Philippson (1811–1889) – der 'Journalist' des Reformjudentums.* Aus Anlaß seines 100. Todestages am 29. Dezember 1989. [In]: Bulletin des LBI, 86, Frankfurt am Main, 1990. Pp. 5–21, notes.

26939. *Die jüdische Welt von gestern: 1860–1938.* Text- und Bild-Zeugnisse aus Mitteleuropa. Hrsg. von Rachel Salamander. Wien: Brandstätter, 1990. 321 pp., 425 illus., bibl., index of persons. [Cont. the sections: Literatur, Wissenschaft und die Künste; Nationale und politische Identifikationen; Die mitteleuropäische Katastrophe. Incl. the essays: Aussenseiter und Provokateure (Marcel Reich-Ranicki, 166–169). Mit der einen Hand die Emanzipation (Julius Schoeps, 248–251). Rauch, Grab der Millionen (Joachim Riedl, 282–285). Ch'hob gesejn a Barg/Ich habe einen Berg gesehen (Moische Schulstein, übertr. aus dem Jiddischen von Rachel Salamander, 308–309).]

26940. IANCU, CAROL, ed.: *Bleichröder et Crémieux: le combat pour l'émancipation des Juifs de Roumanie devant le Congrès de Berlin; correspondance inédite (1878–1880).* Montpellier: Université Paul Valéry, Centre de recherches et d'études juives et hébraïques, 1987. 264 pp., illus., ports., facsims., map. (Collection Sem.) [Documentation.] [See also No. 26971.]

26941. LIBERLES, ROBERT: *From toleration to Verbesserung: German and English debates on the Jews in the eighteenth century.* [In]: Central European History, Vol. 22, No. 1, Atlanta, Ga., March 1989, pp. 3–32, notes.

26942. KARADY, VICTOR: *Le renouveau des travaux socio-historiques sur les juifs du Centre-Est européen.* [In]: Actes de la recherche en sciences sociales, No. 83, Juin 1990. [15 pp.]. [Refers also to the LBI Year Books.]

——— KAUFMANN, URI: *The impact of the French Revolution on rural Jewry in Alsace, Baden, and Switzerland; a comparison.* [See No. 27099.]

26943. KOCHAN, LIONEL: *Survival or renaissance: (recent developments in academic Jewish studies).* [In]: Times Literary Supplement, London, April 20–26, 1990, pp. 425–426. [Covers many recent studies on German-Jewish history.]

26944. KOCHAN, LIONEL: *Jews and idols and messiahs: the challenge from history.* Oxford: Blackwell, 1990. 231 pp., notes, glossary, bibl. (207–224). [Author argues that Jewish history should be understood in terms of the conflict between the messianic theme and developing communities. This is illustrated by comparing the communities of London and Berlin in the 17th and 18th centuries.]

26945. LOTTER, FRIEDRICH: *The scope and effectiveness of Imperial Jewry law in the High Middle Ages.* [In]: Jewish History, Vol. 4, No. 1, Haifa, Spring 1989. Pp. 31–58, tabs, notes. [Incl. lists of charters for German towns, e.g. Bamberg, Cologne, Nuremberg, Speyer, Worms; also charter for Vienna.]

26946. MAURER, TRUDE: *Variations on the theme of 'Einigkeit und Recht und Freiheit': Jewish Obituaries of German heads of state 1888–1925–1934.* [In]: LBI Year Book XXXV, London 1990. Pp. 153–188, illus., notes.

26947. MEYER, MICHAEL A.: *Recent historiography on the Jewish religion in modern Germany.* [In]: LBI Year Book XXXV, London 1990. Pp. 3–16, notes.

——— MEYER, MICHAEL A.: *Jewish identity in the modern world.* [See No. 27526.]

26948. MIRON, DAN: *Modern Hebrew literature and the pre-modern German-Jewish experience.* New York: Leo Baeck Institute, 1989, 48 pp., notes (44–46). (Leo Baeck Memorial Lecture, 33.)

26949. MISHOR, MORDECHAY: *Ashkenazi traditions: toward a method of research.* [In Hebrew, with English summary]. [In]: Massorot: studies in language traditions and Jewish languages, Vol. 3–4, Jerusalem, 1989. Pp. 87–127.

26950. NAVÉ-LEVINSON, PNINA: *Was wurde aus Saras Töchtern? Frauen im Judentum.* Gütersloh: Mohn, 1990. 192 pp., illus. [Incl. German-Jewish women, e.g. Glückel von Hameln, Bertha Pappenheim, Jeanette Wolff.]

26951. NIPPERDEY, THOMAS: *Deutsche Geschichte 1866–1918. Bd. 1: Arbeitswelt und Bürgergeist.* München: Beck, 1990. 834 pp. Special chap. on the Jews in Germany.]

26952. MOSSE, WERNER E.: *Integration through apartheid: the Hirschs of Halberstadt 1780–1930.* [In]: LBI Year Book XXXV, London 1990. Pp. 133–150, ports., notes.

26953. RICHARZ, MONIKA, ed.: *Bürger auf Widerruf: Lebenszeugnisse deutscher Juden 1780–1945.* München: Beck, 1989. 609 pp. (Eine Veröffentlichung des Leo Baeck Instituts New York.) [For details and contents see No. 25958/YB XXXV.] *Reviews* (continued): Diskriminierung, Aufstieg, Vernichtung (Christine Brinck) [in]: Süddeutsche Zeitung, Nr. 150, München, 3. Juli 1990, p. 12. Besprechung (Rüdiger Görner) [in]: Schweizer Monatshefte, Jg. 70, H. 3, Zürich, März 1990, pp. 258–262.

26954. RICHARZ, MONIKA: *Landjuden – ein bürgerliches Element im Dorf?* [In]: Idylle oder Aufbruch? Das Dorf im bürgerlichen 19. Jahrhundert: ein europäischer Vergleich. Hrsg. von Wolfgang Jacobeit [et al.]. Berlin: Akademie-Verl., 1990. Pp. 181–190.

26955. RICHARZ, MONIKA: *Viehhandel und Landjuden im 19. Jahrhundert: eine symbiotische Wirtschaftsbeziehung in Südwestdeutschland.* [In]: Binnenhandel und wirtschaftliche Entwicklung. Hrsg. von Sándor Gyimesi. Budapest: Akademisches Forschungszentrum für Mittel- und Osteuropa an der Karl Marx Universität für Wirtschaftswissenschaften Budapest, 1989. (Studia Historiae Europae Medio-Orientalis, 2.) Pp. 292–315. [Paper read at a conference in Budapest; also publ. in]: Menora, Bd. 1, München, 1990. Pp. 66–88, notes.]

26956. RÜRUP, REINHARD: *An appraisal of German-Jewish historiography.* [In]: LBI Year Book XXXV, London, 1990. Pp. XV–XXIV. [See No. 27160.]

26957. RÜRUP, REINHARD: *Integration und Identität: Probleme der jüdischen Sozialgeschichte in Deutschland seit dem 18. Jahrhundert.* [In]: Berliner Wissenschaftliche Gesellschaft, Jahrbuch 1989. Berlin 1991. Pp. 93–108.

26958. SACHAR, HOWARD M.: *The course of modern Jewish history.* New rev. edn. New York: Vintage, 1990. XVIII, 891 pp., maps, bibl. [First publ. in 1958, this edn. has four new chaps. It incl. German-Jewish history from the enlightenment; also antisemitism, Nazi persecution and Holocaust.]

26959. SCHMITZ, DIETMAR: *Sie waren Freiwild für die Stadträte: Vertreibung von jüdischen Gemeinden aus deutschen Städten im 15. Jahrhundert.* [In]: Tribüne, Jg. 29, H. 113, Frankfurt am Main, 1990. Pp. 194–215, illus, notes.

26960. SCHOEPS, JULIUS H.: *Leiden an Deutschland: vom antisemitischen Wahn und der Last der Erinnerung.* Orig.-Ausg. München: Piper, 1990. 211 pp. (Serie Piper, Bd. 1220.) [Collection of essays arranged under the headings: *Vom Scheitern einer Hoffnung* (13–66; cont. the essays, titles condensed): Die missglückte Emanzipation (13–30). Antisemitismus im deutschen Alltag (31–39). Vertreibung und Ausbürgerung im NS-Staat (40–54). Der deutsche Protestantismus und der Mord an den Juden (55–66). *Vergangenheit, die nicht vergeht* (67–115; incl.): Treitschke redivivus? Ernst Nolte und die Juden (84–95). Zur Situation der Juden in der Bundesrepublik Deutschland (96–115). *Begegnungen und Erfahrungen* (116–196; cont. review articles on Max Brod & Hans-Joachim Schoeps; Hans Blüher; Theodor Lessing; Max Liebermann; Betty & Gershom Scholem).]

26961. SCHRECKENBERG, WILHELM: *Literaturbericht: Das Judentum in Geschichte und Gegenwart.* Teil 1.– 3. [In]: Geschichte in Wissenschaft und Unterricht, Jg. 41, H.4; 5; 12, Stuttgart 1990. Pp. 240–256; 312–320; 776–798, bibl. notes.

26962. SCHREINER, KLAUS: *Von der Judentoleranz zur Judenemanzipation.* [In]: Geschichtliche Grundbegriffe: historisches Lexikon zur politisch-sozialen Sprache in Deutschland. Bd. 6. Hrsg. von Otto Brunner [et al.]. Stuttgart: Klett-Cotta, 1990. Pp. 573–578, notes.

26963. SHATZMILLER, JOSEPH: *Shylock reconsidered: Jews, moneylending, and medieval society.* Berkeley: Univ. of California Press, 1990. VIII, 255 pp., bibl. [Incl. Germany. Author concludes that Jewish moneylenders were often respected and admired members of the community.]

26964. SHMUELI, EFRAIM: *Seven Jewish cultures: a reinterpretation of Jewish history and thought.* Transl. from Hebrew by Gila Shmueli. Cambridge; New York: Cambridge Univ. Press, 1990. XV, 293 pp., notes. [Incl. German-Jewish culture, Graetz, Mendelssohn, Rosenzweig, Scholem.]

26965. SORKIN, DAVID: *Emancipation and assimilation: two concepts and their application to German-Jewish history.* [In]: LBI Year Book XXXV, London 1990. Pp. 17–34, notes.

26966. STEMBERGER, GÜNTER, ed.: *Die Juden: ein historisches Lesebuch.* Orig.-Ausg. München: Beck, 1990. 348 pp., illus., bibl. (339–347). (Beck'sche Reihe, 410.) [Collection of essays and texts from various sources illustrating Jewish history from its beginning to 1948].

26967. TA-SHEMA, ISRAEL M.: *Rabbi Joseph Karo: between Spain and Germany.* [In Hebrew, with English summary]. [In]: Tarbiz, Vol. 59, No. 1–2, Jerusalem, Oct. 1989–March 1990. Pp. 153–170.

26968. TOURY, JACOB: *Flickers of crisis consciousness amongst German Jewry during the Weimar Republic (1924–1928).* [In Hebrew, with English summary]. [In]: Yalkut Moreshet, No. 48, Tel-Aviv, April 1990. Pp. 9–32.

26969. VIERHAUS, RUDOLF: *Die Landjudenschaften in Deutschland als Organe jüdischer Selbstverwaltung in der Frühen Neuzeit bis zur Emanzipation.* [In]: Nachrichten der Akademie der Wissenschaften in Göttingen: I. Philologisch-Historische Klasse, Jg. 1989, Nr. 4, Göttingen, Juni 1990. Pp. 155–159. [Recommendation to publish posthumously the collection of source material of the same title by Daniel Cohen (Nov. 12, 1921 Hamburg – Sept. 19, 1989 Jerusalem).]

26970. VOLKOV, SHULAMIT: *Jüdisches Leben und Antisemitismus im 19. und 20. Jahrhundert.* Zehn Essays. München: Beck 1990. 234 pp., notes. [Cont.: 1. Antisemitimus als kultureller Code (for original version in English see LBI Year Book XXIII/1978, pp. 25–46). 2. Zur sozialen und politischen Funktion des Antisemitismus: Handwerker im späten 19. Jahrhundert. 3. Das geschriebene und das gesprochene Wort: über Kontinuität und Diskontinuität im deutschen Antisemitismus. 4. Antisemitismus und Anti-Zionismus: Unterschiede und Parallelen. 5. Antisemitismus als Problem jüdisch-nationalen Denkens und jüdischer Geschichtsschreibung. 6. Die Verbürgerlichung der Juden in Deutschland als Paradigma. 7. Jüdische Assimilation und Eigenart im Kaiserreich. 8. Soziale Ursachen des jüdischen Erfolges in der Wissenschaft. 9. Die Dynamik der Dissimilation: deutsche Juden und die ostjüdischen Einwanderer. 10. Selbstgefälligkeit und Selbsthass.] [Cf.: Juden ohne Judentum (Peter Honigmann) [in]: Frankfurter Allgemeine Zeitung, Nr. 288, 11. Dez. 1990, p. L 25.]

26971. WELTER, BEATE: *Die Judenpolitik der rumänischen Regierung 1866–1888.* Frankfurt am Main: Lang, 1989. 317 pp. (Menschen und Strukturen; historisch-sozialwissenschaftliche Studien, Bd. 5.) [Deals also with the intervention of European states in favour of the emancipation of Romanian Jewry and with the relations between Western and Eastern Jews.] [See also No. 26940.]

26972. WERSES, SHMUEL: *The French Revolution as reflected in Hebrew literature.* [In Hebrew.] [In]: Tarbiz, Vol. 58, No. 3–4, Jerusalem, Apr.-Sept. 1989 [publ. in Aug. 1990]. Pp. 483–521. [From late 18th through 19th century, in Haskalah literature and in Jewish newspapers, particularly in Germany.]

26973. ZIMMERMANN, MOSHE: *Jewish history and Jewish historiography: A challenge to contemporary German historiography.* [In]: LBI Year Book XXXV, London 1990. Pp. 35–52, notes.

26974. ZIMMERMANN, MOSHE: *'Die aussichtslose Republik': Zukunftsaussichten der deutschen Juden vor 1933.* [In]: Menorah, Bd. 1, München, 1990. Pp. 152–183, notes.

Linguistics/Western Yiddish

26975. AVENARY, HANOCH: *Orale judendeutsche Volkspoesie in der Interaktion mit literarischer Überlieferung.* [In]: Bulletin des LBI, 87, Frankfurt am Main, 1990. Pp. 5–17, append. & notes (12–17).

26976. FRAKES, JEROLD C.: *The politics of interpretation: alterity and ideology in old Yiddish studies.* Albany: State Univ. of New York Press, 1989. XV, 283 pp. [Deals also with the German roots of Yiddish and the negative attitude of German Jews towards Yiddish during the Enlightenment. Cf.: Review essay (Dovid Katz) [in]: Journal of Jewish Studies, Vol. 41, No. 1, Oxford, Spring, 1990, pp. 140–144

26977. FRIDERICHS-BERG, THERESIA: *Die 'Historie von dem Kaiser Octaviano': überlieferungsgeschichtliche Studien zu den Druckausgaben eines Prosaromanes des 16. Jahrhunderts und seiner jiddischen Bearbeitung aus dem Jahre 1580.* Hamburg: Buske, 1990. XII, 431 pp., illus. (Jiddische schtudies, Bd. 3.)

26978. *Jiddistik-Mitteilungen: Jiddistik in deutschsprachigen Ländern.* Nr. 3 & 4. Hrsg. von der Jiddistik im Fachbereich Sprach- und Literaturwissenschaften der Universität Trier (Postfach 3825, D-5500 Trier). Red.: Gabriele Brünnel. Trier, Apr. & Nov. 1990. 2 issues, notes, bibl. [See also No. 26983.]

26979. LÖTZSCH, RONALD: *Jiddisches Wörterbuch.* Leipzig: Bibliographisches Institut, 1990. 202 pp. [Cont. more than 8,000 entries.]

26980. MAMPELL, KLAUS: *Jiddisches in unserer Sprache.* [In]: Sprachspiegel, 45, Nr. 4, Luzern, 1989. Pp. 120–121.

26981. MÜLLER, HERMANN-JOSEF: *Eulenspiegel bei den Juden: zur Überlieferung der jiddischen Eulenspiegel-Fassungen.* [In]: Eulenspiegel-Jahrbuch 1990, Bd. 30, Frankfurt am Main 1990. Pp. 33–50, illus., notes.

26982. *Oksforder Yidish.* A yearbook of Yiddish studies. [In Yiddish]. 1. Ed. by Dovid Katz. In cooperation with the Oxford Centre for Postgraduate Hebrew Studies. Chur; London [et al.]: Harwood Academic Publ., 1990. 401 pp. [Incl.: Yiddish in Yiddish (Dovid Katz, 1–2). [Jekuthiel] Blitz and [Josef] Witzenhausen: new aspects of an old conflict (Marion Aptroot, 3–38). On the origins of Ashkenaz and Yiddish (Shmuel Hiley, 107–114). Irony in Arthur Schnitzler and Lamed Shapiro (Dafna Clifford, 253–269). Remnants of Yiddish in the German of Schopfloch (Haddassah Shy, 333–355). In memoriam: Florence Guggenheim-Grünberg (387–389).]

26983. RÖLL, WALTER: *Ein antijüdisches Flugblatt von 1670 als sprachliche Quelle.* [In]: Jiddistik-Mitteilungen, Nr. 4, Trier, Nov. 1990. Pp. 1–4, notes. [See also No. 26978.]

26984. ROSENFELD, MOSCHE N.: *'Eine schöne Historie': ein jiddisches Lied, das in Fürth im Jahre 1739 gedruckt wurde.* [In]: Nachrichten für den jüdischen Bürger Fürths, Isr. Kultusgemeinde Fürth (Blumenstr. 31), Sept. 1990. Pp.43–46, facsims. [Facsimile reproduction and German transcription of a hitherto unknown Yiddish song.]

26985. SHMERUK, CHONE: *Yiddish adaptations of children's stories from world literature.* [In]: Studies in Contemporary Jewry, Vol. 6, Oxford, 1990. Pp. 186–200. [Refers also to Western-Yiddish literature.]

26986. WEXLER, PAUL, ed.: *Studies in Yiddish linguistics.* Tübingen: Niemeyer, 1990. IX, 216 pp. [Incl.: Freud and the family drama of Yiddish (Christopher Hutton, 9–22). Methodologies and ideologies: the historical relationship of German studies to Yiddish (Gabriele L. Strauch, 83–101). References and bibliography of Yiddish linguistics 1979–1988 (189–216).]

B. Communal and Regional History

1. Germany

26987. ALTENA. HÖTTLER, KURT: *Erinnerungen an jüdische Mitbürger: auch ein Kapitel Stadtgeschichte.* [In]: Altena: Beiträge zur Heimat- und Landeskunde. Altena: Heimatbund Märk. Kreis, 1988. Pp. 66–70, illus.

26988. ANSBACH. SCHUBSKY, KARL W./SÜSS, HERMANN, eds.: *Geschichte der Juden im ehemaligen Fürstentum Ansbach* von S. Haenle. Vollständiger Original-Nachdruck der Ausgabe von 1867, bearbeitet und mit einem Nachwort versehen von Hermann Süss. 8016 Feldkirchen: Hainsfarther Buchhandlung, 1990. 240, XVI pp. (Bayerische jüdische Schriften, Bd. 1.) [Cf.: Chronik jüdischen Lebens (Georg Schwinghammer) [in]: Tribüne, Jg. 29, H. 116, Frankfurt am Main, 1990. Pp. 187–188.]

—— BADEN. [See also No. 27127.]

—— — KAUFMANN, URI: *The impact of the French Revolution on rural Jewry in Alsace, Baden, and Switzerland: a comparison.* [See No. 27099.]

—— — RICHARZ, MONIKA: *Viehhandel und Landjuden im 19. Jahrhundert: eine symbiotische Wirtschaftsbeziehung in Südwestdeutschland.* [See No. 26955.]

26989. — WETTERICH, SUSANNE: *Davids Stern an Rhein und Neckar: Ausflüge auf den Spuren jüdischen Lebens in Baden-Württemberg.* Stuttgart: Silberburg-Verl., 1990. 263 pp., map. (Mit dem Fahrrad, mit dem Auto.) [Covers also the Nazi period.]

26990. — ZEILE, CHRISTINE: *Baden im Vormärz: die Politik der Ständeversammlung sowie der Regierung zur Adelsfrage Grundentlastung und Judenemanzipation, 1818–1843.* München: Kyrill & Method, 1989. IV, V, 311 pp., bibl. (280–311).

26991. BAVARIA. BRENNER, MICHAEL: *Vor 70 Jahren wurde der Verband Bayerischer Israelitischer Gemeinden gegründet: die erste demokratische Vereinigung der Juden im Deutschen Reich.* [In]: 'Allgemeine', Nr. 45/30, Bonn, 26. Juli 1990. P. 3 & [slightly altered] in: Aufbau, Vol. 56, No. 17, New York, Aug. 17, 1990, pp. 5–6.

26992. BAYREUTH. WIRTH, WERNER: *Die Bayreuther Synagoge wird renoviert.* [In]: Nordbayerischer Kurier, Bayreuth, 25. Juni 1990.

26993. BERLIN. ALBERT, C./BALTZER, B.: *Jüdische Assimilation im Spiegel der Grabsteine auf dem Friedhof Berlin-Weissensee.* [In]: Zeitschrift für Semiotik, Bd. 11, H. 2–3, Tübingen, 1989.

26994. — BÄHTZ, DIETER: *Die jüdischen Salons in Berlin zu Beginn des 19. Jahrhunderts in der antisemitischen Historiographie der Faschisten.* [In]: Tradition und Traditionssuche des deutschen Faschismus, Protokollband 2. Poznań, 1988. Pp. 163–172.

—— — DESAI, ANITA: *Baumgartners Bombay.* [See No. 27905.]

26995. — JERSCH-WENZEL, STEFI/JOHN, BARBARA, eds.: *Von Zuwanderern zu Einheimischen: Hugenotten, Juden, Böhmen, Polen in Berlin.* Berlin: Nicolaische Verlagsbuchhandlung, 1990. 804 pp., illus., tabs. [Incl.: Einleitung (Stefi Jersch-Wenzel, 7–11). Juden in Berlin (Brigitte Scheiger, 154–488, illus., facsims.; cont. the following chapts.): I. Koordinaten jüdischen Lebens in Berlin – die ersten Generationen (1671–1750). II. Vom Schutzjuden zum Staatsbürger – die Berliner Judenschaft im Spannungsfeld zwischen Ausgrenzung und Integration (1671–1812). III. Organisation und Aufgabenfelder der jüdischen Gemeinde

Berlin bis zur Emanzipation (1812). IV. Zwischen Emanzipation und Restauration. V. Die Jüdische Gemeinde in Berlin (1847–1914).]

26996. — *Nachrichtenblatt des Verbandes der Jüdischen Gemeinden in der Deutschen Demokratischen Republik.* Red.: Siegmund Rotstein [et al.]. Dresden, März; Juni; Sept. 1990. 3 issues, illus. [Final issues, publication suspended. *März 1990* incl.: Das Königstädtische Reform-Realgymnasium zu Berlin: seine jüdischen Mitschüler und Lehrer (Günter Müller, 5–7; incl. the Nazi period). *Sept. 1990*: Der Anteil jüdischer Kinder an der Schulgeschichte Berlins bis zum Jahr 1945 (Rudi Racho, 10–13; abridged version of an essay planned to be publ. by the 'Stadtarchiv der Hauptstadt' der DDR in its periodical 'Berliner Geschichte', H. 12, Berlin, 1991). Erinnerungen an die Synagoge Ryke-Strasse, 1928–1931 (Selig Auerbach, 13–14). Further contributions are listed according to subject.]

——— — VÖLKER, HEINZ-HERMANN: *Die Hochschule für die Wissenschaft des Judentums in Berlin, 1900–1942.* [See No. 27522.]

——— — WOLFF, RAYMOND: *Oberkantor Frommermann: Musik in der Jüdischen Brüdergemeinde Neukölln.* [See No. 27561.]

26997. BIELEFELD. RÖHS, KARL-WILHELM: *'Der gute Ort': die jüdischen Friedhöfe in Bielefeld.* Bielefeld: Garten-, Forst- u. Friedhofsamt; Bielefeld: Deutsch-Israel. Arbeitsgemeinschaft, 1987. 43 pp.

26998. BORNHEIM. *Bornheimer Beiträge zur Heimatkunde.* H. 3, Heimat- und Eifelverein Bornheim, 1989. 140 pp., illus., facsims., ports. [Incl. three articles on Jews in Bornheim.]

26999. — *Juden in Bornheim.* Ausstellung 1989. (Bearb.: Hildegard Heimig; wiss. Beratung: Heinrich Linn.) Bornheim: Der Stadtdirektor, 1989. 74 pp., illus., ports. [Incl.: Der Untergang der jüdischen Gemeinde Bornheim unter der NS-Diktatur 1933–1945 (pp. 33–41).]

27000. BREMEN. GRUBER, INGE: *Spurensuche: die jüdische Gemeinde in Bremen von den Anfängen bis heute.* Ergebnisbericht der Arbeitsgemeinschaft 'Spurensuche' unter der Leitung von Inge Gruber (1988/1989). Bremen, 1990. 246 pp., illus., charts, facsims., plan, ports., tabs., bibl. (Schriftenreihe des Kippenberg-Gymnasiums, Bd. 3.)

27001. BREMERHAVEN. WEIHER, UWE: *Die jüdische Gemeinde an der Unterweser: vom 'deutschen Staatsbürger jüdischen Glaubens' zum 'Feind im eigenen Land'.* Bremerhaven: Stadtarchiv, 1989. 72 pp., illus., ports., facsims., bibl. (Kleine Schriften des Stadtarchivs Bremerhaven, 7.)

27002. BRESLAU. *Breslauer Juden 1850–1945.* Katalog zur Ausstellung. Hrsg. im Auftrag der Hist. Kommission für Schlesien und des Ludwig Petry-Instituts für ostdeutsche Landes- und Volksforschung Mainz von Josef Joachim Menzel. St. Augustin: Konrad-Adenauer-Stiftung, 1990. 167 pp., illus., maps, bibl.

27003. — LAGIEWSKI, MACIEJ: *Der alte jüdische Friedhof von Breslau.* [In Polish, title transl.] Wroclaw: Muzeum Architektury, 1986. 59 pp.

27004. — MASER, PETER: *Breslauer Judentum im Zeitalter der Emanzipation.* [In]: Jahrbuch der Schlesischen Friedrich-Wilhelms-Universität zu Breslau, 29, Sigmaringen, 1988. Pp. 157–176, notes.

27005. — *Mitteilungen des Verbandes ehemaliger Breslauer in Israel.* Hrsg.: Richard Prager [et al.] No. 54. Tel-Aviv 61035 (P.O. Box 3591), 1990. 20 pp. [Incl.: Heinrich Zwi Graetz, 1817–1891 (Egon Israel Löwenstein, 2–3). Breslau 1929 – Wroclaw 1989 (Joseph Walk, pp. 4 & 17). Ein Besuch in Wroclaw (Jehuda Ben-Avner, 9). Erinnerungen an meine Alija (Ernst Tichauer, 13). Hebräische Steingravuren vor dem Ohlauer Tor: die Geschichte des ersten jüdischen Friedhofs in Breslau (Horst G. W. Gleiss, 16–17).]

27006. BÜCHENBACH. SCHOLZE, BRUNHILDE: *Die Auswanderung von bayerischen Juden nach Nordamerika: aufgezeigt am Beispiel des Hajum Fleischmann aus Büchenbach.* [In]: Erlanger Bausteine zu Fränkischen Heimatforschung, Bd. 38, Erlangen, Heimatverein, 1990. Pp. 147–172, illus.

27007. — SCHOLZE, BRUNHILDE: *Das jüdische Schulwesen in Büchenbach im 19. Jahrhundert.* [In]: Erlanger Bausteine zur Fränkischen Heimatforschung, Bd. 37, Erlangen, Heimatverein, 1989. Pp. 47–64.

27008. COBURG. FROMM, HUBERT: *Die Coburger Juden: Geschichte und Schicksal.* (Mit einem Beitrag von Rainer Axmann). Coburg: EBW, 1990. XI, 353 pp., illus., plan, facsims., ports., bibl. [Incl.: Namensverzeichnis: Juden in Coburg zwischen 1933 und 1942 mit Angabe der letzten Wohnung (319–324).]

27009. COLOGNE. CORBACH, DIETER: *Die Jawne zu Köln: zur Geschichte des ersten jüdischen Gymnasiums im Rheinland und zum Gedächtnis an Erich Klibansky, 1900–1942.* Gedenkbuch zur

Ausstellung [Nov. 1990]. Köln: Scriba, 1990. 303 pp., illus., facsims., ports., tabs, bibl. (Spurensuche jüdischen Wirkens, 4.) [Introduction transl. into English by Anette Corbach and Jonathan Corrall (p. 263–300).]

27010. — ELIAV, MORDECHAI: *The dispute surrounding the organ in Köln: (a Zionist-orthodox coalition against reform).* [In Hebrew, with English summary.] [In]: Zion, Vol. 54, No. 4, Jerusalem, 1989. Pp. 437–459. [Dispute over the introduction of the organ into the new synagogue of Cologne, ca. 1900–1906.]

27011. DESSAU. SCHARFENBERG, GERD: *Zur Verleihung des Herzoglich Anhaltischen Hausordens 'Albrechts des Bären' an den Dessauer Hofbankier Moritz Cohn.* [In]: Nachrichtenblatt des Verbandes der Jüdischen Gemeinden in der DDR, Dresden, Juni 1990. pp. 11–14.

27012. DÜREN. MÜLLER, REGINA: *Um Heimat und Leben gebracht: zur Geschichte der Juden im alten Landkreis Düren 1830–1945.* Düren: Hahne & Schloemer, 1989. 212 pp., illus.

27013. DÜSSELDORF. SUCHY, BARBARA: *Juden in Düsseldorf: ein geschichtlicher Überblick von den Anfängen bis zur Gegenwart.* Hrsg.: Landesbildstelle Rheinland (Medienstelle des Landschaftsverb. Rheinland). Düsseldorf: Landschaftsverb. Rheinland/Landesbildstelle Rheinland, 1990. 24 Dias & Beiheft (70 pp., illus.).

27014. EMDEN. LOKERS, JAN: *Die Juden in Emden 1530–1806: eine sozial- und wirtschaftsgeschichtliche Studie zur Geschichte der Juden in Norddeutschland vom ausgehenden Mittelalter bis zur Emanzipationsgesetzgebung.* Aurich: Ostfriesische Landschaft, 1990. 259 pp., illus., tabs., notes. (Abhandlungen und Vorträge zur Geschichte Ostfrieslands 70.) [Cf.: Besprechung (Dieter Berg) [in]: Das Historisch-Politische Buch, Jg. 39, H. 2, Göttingen, 1991, p. 43.]

27015. EMMERICH. KÜNZL, HANNELORE: *Die Synagoge zu Emmerich von 1812.* [In]: Trumah, 1, Wiesbaden, 1987. Pp. 213–222, notes.

27016. ERLANGEN. MÜNCHHOFF, URSULA: *Jüdische Schüler des Gymnasiums Fridericianum Erlangen 1815–1861.* [In]: Erlanger Bausteine zu Fränksichen Heimatforschung, Bd. 37, Erlangen, Heimatverein, 1989. Pp. 65–92. [Title condensed.]

27017. ESSEN. *Gestern Synagoge – 'Alte Synagoge' heute: Geschichte im Spiegel von 75 Jahren Baugeschichte.* Text und Auswahl der Bilder: Edna Brocke und Michael Zimmermann. Hrsg.: 'Alte Synagoge' Essen. Essen, 1988. 27 pp., illus.

27018. — *Stationen jüdischen Lebens: von der Emanzipation bis zur Gegenwart.* Katalogbuch zur Ausstellung 'Stationen jüdischen Lebens' in der Alten Synagoge Essen. Hrsg.: Alte Synagoge Essen. Text u. Bildauswahl.: Edna Brocke u. Michael Zimmermann. Bonn: Dietz, 1990. 336 pp., illus., facsims., bibl. [Cont. the chapts.: Tradition und Assimilation. Eine jüdische Gemeinde vor 1933. Entrechtung und Selbstbehauptung. Austreibung und Auswanderung. Das Jahr 1938. Shoah (incl.: list of Nazi victims: Die Essener Opfer der Shoah). Nach 1945. Sechs Schicksale und eine Rede.]

27019. FRANCONIA. *Im Oberen Maintal, auf dem Jura, an Rodach und Itz: Landschaft – Geschichte – Kultur.* Zum 150jährigen Bestehen der Kreissparkasse Lichtenfels hrsg. von Günter Dippold in Zusammenarbeit mit Josef Urban. Lichtenfels, 1900. 1 vol., illus., ports., facsims., notes. [Incl.: Als aus Juden Nachbarn und aus Nachbarn Juden wurden: jüdische Gemeinden im 19. und 20. Jahrhundert (Joseph Motschmann, 303–335). Anfänge und Entwicklung der Industrie vom 18. Jahrhundert bis 1914 (Günter Dippold, 143–196; deals passim with the factories and firms founded by Jews).]

27020. — TANNEBAUM, WILLIAM ZVI: *From community to citizenship: the Jews of rural Franconia.* Ann Arbor, Mi.: Univ. Microfilms International, 1989. XIII, 363 pp., tabs., bibl. (342–363). Stanford, Stanford Univ., Thesis, 1989.

27021. FRANKFURT am Main. BEN-AVNER, YEHUDA: *On the controversy regarding the rabbinate in the Adass Jeshurun of Frankfurt am Main in the 1920s.* [In Hebrew, title transl.]. [In]: Sinai, Vol. 106, Jerusalem, Nissan-Iyar 5750 [Apr./May 1990]. Pp. 72–79. [On the 'Israelitische Religionsgesellschaft']

27022. — MAYER, EUGEN: *The Jews of Frankfurt: glimpses of the past.* Transl. and revised by his son Israel Meir (Mayer). Frankfurt am Main: Kramer, 1990. 72 pp., illus. [For German edn., 1966, see No. 5631/YB XII.] [E.M., July 4, 1882 Zweibrücken – Dec. 27, 1967 Jerusalem, jurist, journalist, editor of the Frankfurter Israel. Gemeindeblatt, emigrated in 1933 to Palestine.]

27023. — *Museum Judengasse: Fundamente, Geschichte, Börneladen: eine Dependance des Jüdischen Museums.* Frankfurt am Main: Stadt Frankfurt am Main, 1990. 9 leaves in folder.

27024. — SCHLOTZHAUER, INGE: *Das Philanthropin 1804–1942: die Schule der Israelitischen Gemeinde in Frankfurt am Main.* Frankfurt am Main: Kramer, 1990. 132 pp., illus., bibl.

27025. — SCHLOTZHAUER, INGE: *Ideologie und Organisation des politischen Antisemitismus in Frankfurt am Main, 1880–1914.* Frankfurt am Main: Kramer, 1989. 327 pp., illus., ports., facsims., tabs., bibl. (312–322). (Studien zur Frankfurter Geschichte, 28.) Frankfurt am Main, Univ. Diss., 1987/1988, revised version.

27026. — *Writings from the Archive of the Frankfurt a.M. community on the rabbinate in the year 5519 (=1759).* [In Hebrew]. [In]: Tzfunot: Tora quarterly, Vol. 2, No. 4, Benei-Beraq, Tammuz 5750 [=June/July 1990]. Pp. 105–108. [Gives the text of three letters from 1759.]

27027. FRIEDRICHSTADT. *Juden in Friedrichstadt*: Katalog zur Ausstellung [Nov. 1988.]. Hrsg.: Gesellschaft für Friedrichstädter Stadtgeschichte. Friedrichstadt: 1988. 1 vol.

27028. — HEINZ, H./STOLZ, GERD: *Auf jüdischen Spuren in Deutschland: ein Vierteljahrhundert in Frieden gelebt.* [In]: Aufbau, Vol. 57, No. 5, March 1, 1991. Pp. 16–17.

27029. FÜRTH. HEYMANN, WERNER J., ed.: *Kleeblatt und Davidstern: aus 400 Jahren jüdischer Vergangenheit in Fürth.* Emskirchen: Mümmler, 1990. 240 pp., illus., ports., facsims, plan, bibl. (236–240). [Incl., titles condensed: Talmudschule und jüdische Erziehung in Fürth (Mosche N. Rosenfeld, 80–93). Der Rabbiner Dr. Isaak Loewi (Barbara Ohm, 99–111). Gabriel Löwenstein: Gründer der Fürther Sozialdemokratie (Gerd Walther, 112–115). David Morgenstern, 1814–1882: der erste jüdische Landtagsabgeordnete in Bayern (Ilse Sponsel, 116–125). Die Juden im Fürther Wirtschaftsleben (Gerd Walther, 158–166). Jüdische Vereine in Fürth (Brigitte Schmitt, 186–199). Jüdische Wohltäter (Siegfried Ziegler, 200–213). Die Stifterfamilie Krautheimer (Horst Gemeinhardt, 214–229).]

27030. — *Nachrichten für den jüdischen Bürger Fürths.* Hrsg.: Isr. Kultusgemeinde Fürth. Red.: Ruben J. Rosenfeld. Fürth (Rosenstr. 31), Sept. 1990. 46 pp., illus. [Incl.: 'Festsetzung allgemeiner Normen über Grösse und Umfang der Grabsteine auf dem Jüdischen Friedhof': ein Streitfall aus dem Jahre 1842 in Fürth (Brigitte Schmitt, 18–19). Der israelitische Religionsverein Fürth und die Mortara-Angelegenheit: eine unbekannte Akte aus dem Jahre 1858 (Ruben J. Rosenfeld, 20–23). Fürther Jüdische Kalender, Teil 2: Wandkalender, 1740–1825 (Mosche N. Rosenfeld, 24–29, facsims.; for pt. 1 see No. 26020/YB XXXV). Die jüdischen Gefallenen von 1914–1918 aus Fürth (Günther H. Seidl, 40–42). Further contributions are listed according to subject.]

27031. GÖPPINGEN. BAR-GIORA-BAMBERGER, NAFTALI: *Memor-Buch: die jüdischen Friedhöfe Jebenhausen und Göppingen.* Göppingen, 1990. 346 pp., illus., facsims., plans, tabs., bibl. (Veröffentlichungen des Stadtarchivs Göppingen, Bd. 24.)

27032. GROSSMANNSDORF. BRAUN, JOACHIM: *Geschichte der ehemaligen jüdischen Gemeinde von Grossmannsdorf a. M.* Ochsenfurt, n.p., 1988. 48 pp., illus., facsims., ports.

27033. GÜTERSLOH. GATZEN, HELMUT: *Jüdische Friedhöfe: zur Erinnerung ein Stein aufs Grab.* [In]: Gütersloh (Kreis): Heimat-Jahrbuch 1989 (1988). Pp. 140–143, illus.

27034. HALDENSLEBEN. ENGELCKE, DETLEV: *Die Geschichte der Juden in Haldensleben: Anfang und Ende einer ausgelieferten Minderheit.* Magdeburg: Synagogengemeinde Magdeburg, 1989. 1 vol. [Available in the library of the Jüdische Gemeinde Berlin, Oranienburger Strasse 28.]

27035. HAMBURG. KLOETZEL, C. Z.: *Eine jüdische Jugend in Hamburg vor dem Ersten Weltkrieg.* Hamburg: Verl. Verein für Hamburgische Geschichte, [1988?]. 52 pp., illus. [Kloetzel's revised memoirs, previously publ. in 3 parts [in]: Hamburgische Geschichts- und Heimatblätter, Bd. 11, H. 5; 9; 11–12 (1984–1987).] [Cheskiel Zwi Kloetzel, orig. Chaskel Zwi Klötzel, Feb. 8, 1891 Berlin – 1951, journalist, author of travel and children's books, emigrated to Palestine.]

27036. — VIETH, HARALD: *Von der Hallerstraße 6/8 zum Isebek und Dammtor: jüdische Schicksale und Alltägliches aus Harvestehude-Rotherbaum in Hamburg seit der Jahrhundertwende.* Hamburg: Harald Vieth (Hallerstr. 8, 2000 Hamburg 13), 1990. 112 pp., illus., facsims., notes, bibl.

27037. — *Wegweiser zu ehemaligen jüdischen Stätten im Stadtteil Rotherbaum (II).* Hrsg.: Deutsch-Jüdische Gesellschaft Hamburg. (Bearb.: W. Mosel). Hamburg: DJG Hamburg, 1989. 236 pp., notes, bibl., index of names. (Wegweiser zu ehemaligen jüdischen Stätten in Hamburg, H.3.) [Obtainable from Deutsch-Jüdische Gesellschaft, 2000 Hamburg, Esplanade 14.]

27038. HAMM. ASCHOFF, DIETHARD: *Streiflichter auf die mittelalterliche Geschichte der Juden in Hamm.* [In]: Jahrbuch des Vereins für Orts- und Heimatkunde in der Graftschaft Mark, 86, Witten, 1988. Pp. 125 ff.

27039. HANAU. ROSENFELD, MOSCHE N.: *Ein jüdischer Wandkalender für das Jahr 5386 (1625–1626): Fragment eines Hanauer Wandkalenders.* [In]: Nachrichten für den jüdischen Bürger Fürths, Isr. Kultusgemeinde Fürth (Blumenstr. 31), Sept. 1990. Pp. 31–32, facsims.

27040. HANOVER. *Georg Steinberg: Gedenkausstellung anlässlich des 150. Geburtstages des jüdischen*

Kaufmanns, Soldaten und Schriftstellers Georg Steinberg (1840–1919). (Verantwortlicher Leiter: Rainer Sabelleck.) Göttingen: Kreisvolkshochschule, 1990. 31 pp., illus., ports., facsims., bibl. (28–31). [At head of title]: Leben und Schreiben in der Hannoverschen Provinz.

27041. HEILBRONN. SCHWINGHAMMER, GERHARD, ed.: *Heilbronn und Hans Franke, Publizist, Dichter und Kritiker, 1893–1964*. Ein Lesebuch von Texten von und über Hans Franke. Heilbronn: Verlag Heilbronner Stimme, 1989. 80 pp., illus., ports., facsims. (Heilbronner Stimme, Buchreihe, Bd. 3.) [At head of title]: Das schreibende Gewissen der Stadt. [Reflects the history of the Jews of Heilbronn.]

27042. HERBERN. FARWICK, JOSEF: *Beiträge zur Geschichte der jüdischen Gemeinde in Herbern*. Herbern: Farwick, 1988. [19] pp., illus.

27043. — FARWICK, JOSEF: *Der jüdische Friedhof in Herbern*. Herbern: Farwick, 1988. 6 pp.

27044. HOFGEISMAR. *'Suchet der Stadt Bestes': die jüdische Gemeinde Hofgeismars zwischen Assimilation und Untergang*. Hrsg. von Helmut Burmeister und Michael Dorhs. Hofgeismar: Verein für Hessische Geschichte und Landeskunde, Zweigverein Hofgeismar, 1990. 80 pp., illus.

27045. HOHENLIMBURG. FRITSCH, ARWED: *Reflexionen – Mutmaßungen – Annäherungen an ein Haus in Hohenlimburg*. [In]: Hohenlimburger Heimatblätter für den Raum Hagen, 49 (1988). Pp. 309–313. [Refers to the synagogue.]

27046. HORN-BAD MEINBERG. CAPELLE, WALTER E.: *Juden in Horn-Bad Meinberg: eine Dokumentation über die vergangenen 150 Jahre, 1837–1987*. Eine authentischer Bericht. [Title condensed]. Horn-Bad Meinberg, 1988. 31 pp., facsims., bibl. [Available in the LBI New York.]

27047. JÜLICH. SCHULTE, KLAUS H.S.: *Sozial- und Wirtschaftsgeschichte der Juden im Herzogtum Jülich*. In zwei Teilen. Neuss: K.H.S. Schulte, 1988. 2 pts. in 1 vol. *Teil A: Die Geleitpolitik im Herzogtum Jülich seit dem 16. Jahrhundert*. XIII, 175 pp. *Teil B: Dokumentation der Bescheidpraxis der Jülicher Gerichte im heutigen Selfkant während des 17. und 18. Jahrhundert*. V, 147 pp. [Mimeog.]

27048. KONSTANZ. MAURER, HELMUT: *Konstanz im Mittelalter. 1: Von den Anfängen bis zum Konzil*. Konstanz: Stadler, 1989. 1 vol. (Geschichte der Stadt Konstanz, Bd. 1.) [Incl. chap. on the persecution of the Jews during the 14th century.]

27049. KORBACH. TREMMEL, ERICH: *Jüdische Musikleben in Waldeck im frühen 19. und frühen 20. Jahrhundert: Versuch einer Rekonstruktion am Beispiel Korbachs*. [In]: Geschichtsblätter für Waldeck, 77, Arolsen, 1989. Pp. 209–216.

27050. LAMBSHEIM. KINKEL, KURT: *Die Juden in Lambsheim.*. [In]: Heimatjahrbuch 1985, Landkreis Ludwigshafen, [1985]. Pp. 95–102, illus., tabs.

27051. LEMGO. *Juden in Lemgo und Lippe: Kleinstadtleben zwischen Emanzipation und Deportation*. Bielefeld: Verlag für Regionalgeschichte, 1988. 300 pp., illus. (Forum Lemgo, Heft 3.) [Incl. (titles condensed): Porta Westfalica Judaica (Arie Walter Sternheim-Goral, 187–201; on the Sternheim family). Juden in Lemgo im 19. Jahrhundert (Jürgen Scheffler, 28–62, illus., tabs.). Die jüdische Schule in Lemgo (Klaus Pohlmann, 63–86). Erinnerungen an Lemgo: die Großeltern Lenzberg und die Emigration (Kurt May, 159–164). Erinnerungen eines 81jährigen (Willy Hochfeld, 114–136). Kindheitserinnerungen (Ernst Hochfeld, 137–153, illus.) Jüdisches Kleinstadtleben in Deutschland und Polen (Karla Raveh, 154–158). Jüdische Schicksale in Bad Salzuflen und Schötmar (Jörg Höhn, 254–258). Echternstraße 70 (Hanne Pohlmann, 259–270; on the Frenkel family).]

27052. — WAGNER, EDITH: *Erinnerungen einer Emigrantin*. [In]: Lemgoer Hefte, 42, Jg. 11, 1988. Pp. 6–7.

—— LEIPZIG. [See also No. 27595.]

27053. — UNGER, MANFRED/LANG, HUBERT, comps.: *Juden in Leipzig*. Eine Dokumentation zur Ausstellung anlässlich des 50. Jahrestages der faschistischen Pogromnacht im Ausstellungszentrum der Karl-Marx-Universität Leipzig, vom 5. Nov. bis 17. Dez. 1988. Leipzig, 1988. 239 pp., illus., ports., facsims. [Incl. the Nazi period.]

27054. LEVERKUSEN. *Juden in der Geschichte der Stadt Leverkusen*. Hrsg. im Auftrag der Stadtgeschichtlichen Vereinigung Leverkusen von Rolf Müller. Leverkusen, 1988. 126 pp., illus.

27055. LINZ am Rhein. RINGS, ANTON & ANITA: *Die ehemalige jüdische Gemeinde in Linz am Rhein: Erinnerung und Gedenken*. (Hrsg. von der Stadt Linz am Rhein.) Linz am Rhein, 1989. 228, XX pp., illus., ports., facsims., diagrs., plans, tabs., bibl.

27056. LUCKENWALDE. GOLDSTEIN, WERNER: *Luckenwalde ohne Juden*. [In]: Neues Deutschland, Berlin, 2. Nov. 1990. P. 9, port. [Also on the author's experience in Luckenwalde between 1934 and 1938 when he was imprisoned in the concentration camp Sachsenhausen and on the local pastor Detlev Riemer who researches the history of the Jews of Luckenwalde.]

27057. MECKLENBURG. Borchert, Jürgen: *Des Zettelkastens anderer Teil: Fundstücke und Lesefrüchte.* Rostock: Hinstorff Verl., 1988. 190 pp., index of persons. [Also on the history of the Jews in Mecklenburg, incl. the Nazi period. Cf.: Jüdische Spuren in Mecklenburg von Rostock bis Büstrow (Ernst G. Lowenthal) [in]: 'Allgemeine', Nr. 45/2, Bonn, 11. Jan. 1990, p. 11 [&]: (Albrecht Schreiber) [in]: Nr. 45/4, 25. Jan. 1990 [&]: (Adolf Diamant) [in] Nr. 45/35, 30. Aug. 1990, p. 8.]

27058. METELEN. *Jüdische Gemeinde Metelen von den Anfängen bis zur Vertreibung.* (Nachdruck d. Ausg. von 1987. Vorwort von Gertrud Althoff.) Metelen, 1990. 47 pp., illus., facsims.

27059. MÖNCHENGLADBACH. *Besuch der ehemaligen jüdischen Bürger in Mönchengladbach [1989].* Dokumentation. Hrsg.: Stadt Mönchengladbach, Der Oberstadtdirektor. Mönchengladbach: Presse -und Informationsamt, 1989. 294 pp., illus., facsims., ports.

27060. MÜHLHAUSEN/Thuringia. Liesenberg, Carsten: *Juden in Mühlhausen: ihre Geschichte, Gemeinde und bedeutende Persönlichkeiten.* Selbstverlag C. Liesenberg, 1989. 218 pp., illus., ports., facsims., plans., notes (170–184). [Mimeog., available in the LBI New York.] [Incl. statistical material, various lists, a.o., deportation lists.]

27061. MUNICH. Kilian, Hendrikje: *Die jüdische Gemeinde in München 1813–1871: eine Großstadtgemeinde im Zeitalter der Emanzipation.* München: Uni-Druck, 1989. V, 386 pp. (Miscellanea Bavarica Monacensia, Bd. 145.) (Neue Schriftenreihe des Stadtarchivs München.) Zugl. München, Univ. Diss., 1988.

27062. NAUMBURG. Onasch, Martin: *Spuren jüdischer Kultur in Naumburg.* [In]: Nachrichtenblatt des Verbandes der Jüdischen Gemeinden in der DDR, Dresden, März 1990. Pp. 10–11.

27063. NIEDERWERRN. Grossmann, Karlheinz: *Die Niederwerrner Juden 1871–1945.* Mit einem Vorwort von Peter v. Heusinger. Würzburg: Königshausen & Neumann, 1990. 272 pp., illus.

27064. NUREMBERG. Mahr, Helmut: *Die Edikt 'Die Verhältnisse der jüdischen Glaubensgenossen in Bayern betreffend' vom 10. Juni 1813: seine Zielsetzung und seine Auswirkung auf die Niederlassung von Juden in den Landgerichten Nürnberg und Cadolzburg.* Teil 2. [In]: Nachrichten für den jüdischen Bürger Fürths, Isr. Kultusgemeinde Fürth (Blumenstr. 31), Sept. 1990. Pp. 33–35, facsims. [For pt. 1 see No. 26076/YB XXXV.]

27065. OFFENBACH. Ruppel, Hans G./Werner, Klaus: *Die erste Erwähnung von Juden in Offenbach am Main.* [In]: Alt-Offenbach, N.F., H. 20, Offenbach, 1989. Pp. 15–16, notes.

27066. OLDENBURG. Schrape, Joachim: *Neue Forschungsergebnisse über die Frühzeit der Oldenburger Judenschaft und ihre erste Synagoge.* [In]: Oldenburger Jahrbuch, Bd. 89, Oldenburg, 1989. Pp. 41–54, illus., notes.

27067. OSTERODE. Ballin, Gerhard: *Die jüdischen Geschäfte am Kornmarkt und an der Marientorstrasse in Osterode.* [In]: Heimatblätter für den Südwestlichen Harzrand, Nr. 45, Osterode, 1989. Pp. 61 ff.

27068. PALATINATE. Kuby, Alfred Hans, ed.: *Juden in der Provinz: Beiträge zur Geschichte der Juden in der Pfalze zwischen Emanzipation und Vernichtung.* 2., durchgesehene Aufl. Neustadt a.d. Weinstrasse: Verlag Pfälzische Post, 1989. 325 pp., illus., bibl. (242–322). [For contents see No. 25107/YB XXXIV.]

27069. PFORZHEIM. Brändle, Gerhard/Zink, Wolfgang: *Jüdische Gotteshäuser in Pforzheim.* Pforzheim: Stadtverwaltung, 1990. 104 pp., illus., ports., facsims., plans. [Covers the history of the Jews in Pforzheim, also the Nazi period and deportations to Gurs and Auschwitz.]

27070. RECKLINGHAUSEN. Möllers, Georg/Mannel, Georg: *Zwischen Integration und Verfolgung: die Juden in Recklinghausen.* (Eine Sammlung ausgewählter Dokumente). Recklinghausen: Winkelmann, 1988. 10 pp., [30] pp. in folder, illus. (Dokumentenmappe zur Kirchen- und Religionsgeschichte des Ruhrgebiets, 2).

27071. RHEURDT. Mäschig, Theo: *Die Rheurdter Juden [1848–1942].* Rheurdt: Gemeinde Rheurdt, 1988. 111 pp., illus.

27072. RHINELAND. *Jüdische Gedenkstätten im Rheinland.* Dokumentation über Reste jüdischer Kultur und heutiges Gedenken. Im Auftrag der Evangelischen Kirche im Rheinland durchgeführt vom Auschuss für Kirchliche Zeitgeschichte (Vorsitz: Prof. Dr. Günther van Norden), bearbeitet von Gottfried Abrath. [In]: Monatshefte für die Evangelische Kirchengeschichte des Rheinlandes, Jg. 37/38, Köln/Bonn, 1988/1989. Pp. 621–650, bibl.

27073. — Kastner, Dieter: *Der Rheinische Provinziallandtag und die Emanzipation der Juden im Rheinland, 1825–1845.* Eine Dokumentation. 1–2. Köln: Rheinland-Verl.; Bonn: Habelt [in Kommission], 1989. 2 vols., 988 pp., facsims., tabs., bibl. references, index of places &

persons. (Archivberatungsstelle Rheinland, Rheinprovinz, 2, 1–2.) [Incl.: Einführung (7–81) dealing with the social and economic history of the Rhineland Jews and the historical background to the emancipation.]

27074. — LANSER, GÜNTER [et al.]: *Jüdische Friedhöfe am Niederrhein.* [In]: Neues Rheinland, 32, Nr. 11, Pulheim, 1989. P. 4.

———— — ROHRBACHER, STEFAN: *Volksfrömmigkeit und Judenfeindschaft: zur Vorgeschichte des politischen Antisemitismus im Katholischen Rhineland.* [See No. 27872.]

———— — ROHRBACHER, STEFAN: *Ritualmord-Beschuldigungen am Niederrhein: christlicher Aberglaube und antijüdische Agitation im 19. Jahrhundert.* [See No. 27871.]

27075. ROTHENBURG. KÜNZL, HANNELORE: *Die mittelalterliche Mikwe von Rothenburg ob der Tauber.* [In]: Trumah, 1, Wiesbaden, 1987. Pp. 213–222, notes.

27076. — KWASMAN, THEODORE: *Die jüdischen Grabsteine in Rothenburg ob der Tauber.* [In]: Trumah, 1, Wiesbaden, 1987. Pp. 7–138, notes.

27077. — MERZ, HILDE: '*Mit bittere Seele eine bittere Klage . . .*'. [In]: Trumah, 1, Wiesbaden, 1987. Pp. 1–6, illus. [On the rediscovery and identification of the memorial to the pogrom of Jews in 1298 in Rothenburg.]

27078. SALZUFLEN. RAU, HERMANN GÜNTHER/ROTHE, HARRY: *Der jüdische Friedhof von Salzuflen.* [And]: Wallbaum, Kurt: *Aus der Geschichte der Synagogue zu Schötmar.* [In]: Stadtmagazin Bad Salzuflen, 4, 1988, H. 5, pp. 62–63 [&] h. 8, pp. 6–8.

27079. SAUERLAND. BÖDGER, JOHANNES: *Geschuldete Erinnerung: Ereignisliteratur kann die historisch fundierte Aufarbeitung des Schicksalsweges der Juden im Sauerland nicht ersetzen.* [In]: Sauerland, 1988. Pp. 122–123.

27080. — VRIES, ILSE DE: *Schwarze glänzende Stiefel: Erinnerung.* [In]: Sauerland, 1988. Pp. 87–89, illus. [On persecution of Jews.]

27081. SCHERMBECK. KAMMEIER, ANDREA/BORNEBUSCH, WOLFGANG: *Die Geschichte der jüdischen Gemeinde in Schermbeck.* [In]: Wesel (Kreis): Heimatkalender, 9 (1988). Pp. 122–129, illus.

27082. — NEUHEUSER, HANNS PETER: *Die früheste Liste der jüdischen Einwohner der Gemeinde Schermbeck.* [In]: Mitteilungen der Westdeutschen Gesellschaft für Familienkunde, Bd. 34, Nr. 3, Neustadt a.d. Aisch, 1989. Pp. 75 ff.

27083. SCHWABEN. RÖMER, GERNOT, ed.: *Schwäbische Juden: Leben und Leistungen aus zwei Jahrhunderten in Selbstzeugnissen, Berichten und Bildern.* Augsburg: Presse-Druck- und Verlags GmbH, 1990. 248 pp., illus., ports., facsims., bibl.

27084. SPANDAU. POHL, JOACHIM: *Juden in Spandau in der frühen Neuzeit.* [In]: Jahrbuch für Brandenburgische Landesgeschichte, 39, Berlin, 1988. Pp. 97–115.

27085. SPEYER. *Frauen in Speyer: Leben und Wirken in zwei Jahrtausenden.* Ein Beitrag von Speyerer Frauen zum Jubiläumsjahr. Hrsg. von der Stadt Speyer. Speyer, 1990. 359 pp. [Incl.: Edith Stein: eine Skizze zu ihrer Speyerer Zeit (Maria Adele Herrmann, 99–106). Vom Leben jüdischer Frauen 1. Im Mittelalter 2. In der liberalen jüdischen Gemeinde, Schicksale in der NS-Zeit (Siegrun Wipfler-Pohl, 146–175). Sara Lehmann, 1891–1976 (Siegrun Wipfler-Pohl, 240–248; S.L., social worker).]

27086. STEINHEIM. WALDHOFF, JOHANNES: *Sabbatlampe und Sederschale.* [In]: Steinheimer Kalender, 1989 [1988]. Pp. 46–48, illus.

27087. STUTTGART. SAUER, PAUL: *Jüdische Industriepioniere und Sozialreformer: hervorragende Leistungen für die Wirtschaftsentwicklung Stuttgarts zur Gründerzeit.* [In]: Beiträge zur Landeskunde, Jg. 6, Stuttgart, 1989. Pp. 1–9.

27088. THORN. NOWAK, ZENON HUBERT: *Zur Geschichte der Thorner Juden in der ersten Hälfte des 19. Jahrhunderts.* [In]: Bulletin des LBI, 87, Frankfurt am Main, 1990. Pp. 19–28, notes.

27089. TRIER. NOLDEN, REINER: *Nachlese zur Ausstellung 'Juden in Trier'.* [In]: Landeskundliche Vierteljahresblätter, Jg. 35, Nr. 1, Trier, 1989. Pp. 33 ff. [Refers to Nos. 25135–25136/YB XXXIV.]

27090. ULM. LANG, P.: *Die Reichsstadt Ulm und die Juden 1500–1803.* [In]: Rottenburger Jahrbuch für Kirchengeschichte, Jg. 8, Sigmaringen, 1989. Pp. 39–48.

27091. WALDECK. BERBÜSSE, VOLKER: *Geschichte der Juden in Waldeck: Emanzipation und Antisemitismus vor 1900.* Wiesbaden: Kommission für die Geschichte der Juden in Hessen, 1990. 297 pp., notes, bibl. (Schriften der Kommission für die Geschichte der Juden in Hessen, 11).

27092. — BERBÜSSE, VOLKER: *Gleichstellung und Judenfeindschaft: die Bedeutung der Juden für das Fürstentum Waldeck im 18. und 19. Jahrhundert und die Abwehrhaltung gegen ihre Emanzipation.* Dargestellt am Beispiel einer politischen Karikatur. [In]: Geschichtsblätter für Waldeck, 77, Arolsen, 1989. Pp. 189–207, illus.

27093. — STEINER, GÜNTER: *Waldecks Weg ins Dritte Reich: gesellschaftliche und politische Strukturen eines ländlichen Raumes während der Weimarer Republik und zu Beginn des Dritten Reiches.* Kassel: Verlag Gesamthochschulbibliothek, 1990. 327 pp., illus., facsims., map, tabs., bibl. (320–327). (Nationalsozialismus in Nordhessen; Schriften zur regionalen Zeitgeschichte, H. 11) [Refers passim also to Jews.]

——— WESTPHALIA. [See also Nos. 27178 and 27410.]

27094. — TERHALLE, HERMANN: *Ein bisher unbekanntes Judengeleit aus dem Jahre 1673.* [In]: Unsere Heimat, (Borken), 1988. Pp. 249–252.

27095. WÖRLITZ. ALEX, REINHARD: *Erdmannsdorffs Judentempel im Landschaftsgarten Wörlitz.* [In]: Nachrichtenblatt des Verbandes der Jüdischen Gemeinden in der DDR, Dresden, Sept. 1990. Pp. 4–7, illus., plan, notes. [Synagogue, constructed by Friedrich-Wilhelm von Erdmannsdorff in 1789/90, damaged during the November 1938 Pogrom, now restored. Article deals also with the situation of the Jews in Wörlitz in the 18th century.]

27096. WOLBECK. EVERS, STEFAN: *Geschichte der Juden in Wolbeck.* (Hrsg.: SPD-Ortsverein Wolbeck). Münster: SPD-Ortsverein Wolbeck, 1988. 52 pp. (Veröffentlichung zur Wolbecker Ortsgeschichte, 2.)

——— WÜRTTEMBERG. RICHARZ, MONIKA: *Viehhandel und Landjuden im 19. Jahrhundert: eine symbiotische Wirtschaftsbeziehung in Südwestdeutschland.* [See No. 26955.]

——— — WETTERICH, SUSANNE: *Davids Stern an Rhein und Neckar.* [See No. 26989.]

1a. Alsace

27097. FRITZ-VANNAHME, JOACHIM: *Sollte euer Hass Teil eures Erbes sein? Der erste Christdemokrat: Henri Abbé Grégoire und sein Kampf für die Judenemanzipation.* [In]: Die Zeit, Nr. 5, Hamburg, 26. Jan. 1990. P. 36, port. [H. Abbé Grégoire, Dec. 4, 1750 Lorraine – May 27/28, 1831 Paris, Catholic clergyman, led the campaign for the civic emancipation of the Jews before and during the French Revolution; presented the delegation of Alsace-Lorraine Jews to the National Assembly on Oct. 14, 1789, influential also in the emancipation of German Jewry.]

27098. GERSON, DANIEL: *Die Ausschreitungen gegen die Juden im Elsaß 1848.* [In]: Bulletin des LBI, 87, Frankfurt am Main, 1990. Pp. 29–44, notes.

27099. KAUFMANN, URI: *The impact of the French Revolution on rural Jewry in Alsace, Baden, and Switzerland: a comparison.* [In]: Proceedings of the Tenth World Congress of Jewish Studies, Division B, Vol. II, Jerusalem, 1990. Pp. 239–242, notes.

2. Austria

27100. ADLER, KURT H.: *'Wegen veränderter Umstände ad acta . . .': wie Oberst d.R. Salomon Adlers Erhebung in den k.u.k. Adelsstand scheiterte.* [In]: Tribüne, Jg. 29, H. 116, Frankfurt am Main 1990. Pp. 138–144, illus. [On the procedures for the ennoblement of Jews in Austro-Hungary.]

27101. *The Austrian Jewish Museum.* With contributions of Kurt Schubert [et al.]. Transl. from the German by Elisabeth Sorantin. Eisenstadt: Österreichisches Jüdisches Museum, 1989. 85 pp., [40 pp. of] illus.

27102. DEAK, ISTVAN: *Jewish soldiers in Austro-Hungarian society.* New York: Leo Baeck Institute, 1990. 31 pp., notes (27–29). (Leo Baeck Memorial Lecture, 34.)

27103. DON, YEHUDA/KARADY, VICTOR, eds.: *A social and economic history of Central European Jewry.* New Brunswick, N.J.: Transaction Publ., 1990. VIII, 262 pp., notes. [Cont.: 1. The identity of post emancipatory Hungarian Jewry (Jacob Katz, 13–32). 2. Central European Jewry between East and West (Nethaniel Katzburg, 33–46). 3. The Jewish position in interwar Central Europe: a structural study of Jewry at Vienna, Budapest, and Prague (William O. McCagg Jr., 47–82). 4. Demography and social mobility: historical problem areas in the study of contemporary Jewry in Central Europe (Victor Karady, 83–120). 5. Patterns of Jewish economic behaviour in Central Europe in the twentieth century (Yehuda Don, 121–154). 6. Why was the Viennese liberal Bildungsbürgertum above all Jewish (Steven Beller, 155–178). 7. Jews among Vienna's educated middle class elements at the turn of the century (Gary B. Cohen, 179–190). 8. Orthodoxy and the Kultusgemeinde in interwar Vienna (Harriet Pass Freidenreich, 191–206). 9. In search of identity: Slovakian Jewry and nationalism 1918–1938 (Yeshayahu A. Jelinek, 207–228). 10. The ethnic composition of the economic elite in Hungary in the interwar period (György Lengyel, 229–248). 11. Lawyers against the current anti-semitism and liberal response in interwar Hungary (Mária Kovács, 249–256).]

27104. GOVRIN, NURIT: *His Highness the Kaiser [Franz Joseph], king of the Jews.* [In Hebrew, title transl.]. [In]: Eit-mol, No. 94, Tel-Aviv, Dec. 1990. Pp. 3–5.

27105. *Handbuch zur Geschichte der Juden in Österreich.* Reihe B. Bd. 1 ff. Wien: Böhlau, 1990 ff. *Reihe B, Bd. 1:* LOHRMANN, KLAUS: *Judenrecht und Judenpolitik im mittelalterlichen Österreich.* [See No. 27109.]

—— HAUMANN, HEIKO: Geschichte der Ostjuden. [See No. 26934.]

27106. HOFMANN, PAUL: *The Viennese: splendor, twilight and exile.* New York: Doubleday/Anchor, 1988. 346 pp., illus., ports., notes. [Incl. Jewish contribution to cultural, economic and social life; also on Viennese antisemitism, as well as a chap. 'Waldheim's Vienna'.]

27107. *Juden in Österreich.* [In]: Zeitgeschichte, Jg. 15, H. 11/12, Wien, Aug./Sept. 1988. [Cont.: Vater-Sohn-Konflikt und das Problem der nationalen Identität: österreichisches Fin de Siècle (Rudolf G. Ardelt). Die Austritte aus dem Judentum in Wien 1868–1944 (Peter Honigmann). 1938 – der Anschluss und seine Folgen (Günter Fellner). Österreichs Juden im Spiegel der neueren Geschichtsliteratur (Jonny Moser). Jüdisches Volks- und Geschichtsbewußtsein (A. Blumenfeld/M. Drill).]

27108. *Jüdisches Denken und Wirken als Teil österreichischer Identität.* Von Angelo Ara [et al.]. Wien (Tivoligasse 73): Karl v. Vogelsang-Institut zur Erforschung der Geschichte der Christlichen Demokratie in Österreich, 1989. Pp. 119–246, bibl. (Christliche Demokratie, Jg. 7, H. 2.)

27109. LOHRMANN, KLAUS: *Judenrecht und Judenpolitik im mittelalterlichen Österreich.* Wien: Böhlau, 1990. 354 pp., illus., bibl. (312–335). (Handbuch zur Geschichte der Juden in Österreich, Reihe B, Bd. 1.)

27110. LOWER AUSTRIA. WAPPELSHAMMER, ELISABETH: *Jüdische Geschichte – jüdische Kultur in Niederösterreich: Erinnerungen ans Mittelalter und seine Folgen.* Wien (Rembrandtstraße 26/1): Verein Kultur im Alltag, 1990. 47 pp., illus., facsims., plans, bibl.

27111. SALZBURG. ALTMANN, ADOLF: *Geschichte der Juden in Stadt und Land Salzburg: von den frühesten Zeiten bis auf die Gegenwart.* Weitergeführt bis 1988 von Günter Fellner u. Helga Embacher. Salzburg: O. Müller, 1990. 396 pp., illus., bibl. (361–367). [Orig. publ. in 2 vols., Berlin, Lamm, 1913 & Frankfurt am Main, Selbstverlag A. Altmann, 1930, covering the period up to 1911, now carried on until 1988. Incl.: Biographischer Überblick über das Leben von Adolf Altmann (Manfred Altmann, 11–18). Zur Geschichte der Juden in Salzburg von 1911 bis zum Zweiten Weltkrieg (Günter Fellner, 363–373). Nach dem Holocaust – Jüdische Mitbürger/innen in Salzburg (374–394). Literatur über Adolf Altmann (395–396).] [A. Altmann, Sept. 8, 1879 Hunsdorf – 1944 Auschwitz, rabbi, historian, emigrated to the Netherlands in 1938, imprisoned in the concentration camp Westerbork, deported, together with his wife, to Theresienstadt and Auschwitz.]

27112. SEEWANN, HARALD: *Zirkel und Zionsstern: Bilder und Dokumente aus der versunkenen Welt des jüdisch-nationalen Korporationswesens.* Ein Beitrag zur Geschichte des Zionismus auf akademischem Boden. Text- und Begleitband. Graz: Harald Seewann (A – 8011 Graz, Postfach 358), 1990. 2 vols. (283; 372 pp.) illus., facsims, notes. [On National-Jewish student organisations, a.o., Vienna, Graz, Bukowina, Prague, Preßburg, Brünn; the Begleitband cont. chiefly illustrations and facsims.].

27113. STEINBERG, MICHAEL P.: *The meaning of the Salzburg Festival: Austria as theatre and ideology, 1890–1938.* Ithaca, N.Y.: Cornell Univ. Press, 1990. XVII, 353 pp., illus., bibl. [Salzburg Festival, co-founded by Max Reinhardt, inaugurated in 1920 with 'Jedermann' by Hugo von Hofmannsthal; many Jewish artists have participated in the Festivals; book also discusses the relationship of Jews to Austrian Catholic culture.]

27114. VIENNA. WOLFF, LARRY: *Postcards from the end of the world: an investigation into the mind of fin-de-siècle Vienna.* London: Collins, 1989. 275 pp., bibl. (259–263). [Also on Jews and antisemitism.]

27115. — *Eine zerstörte Kultur: jüdisches Leben und Antisemitismus im Wien seit dem 19. Jahrhundert.* Hrsg.: Gerhard Botz, Ivar Oxaal, Michael Pollak. Buckloe: Obermayer, 1990. 420 pp., illus., notes. [Cont.: Probleme und Perspektiven (Einleitung der Herausgeber, 9–28). Die Juden im Wien des jungen Hitler: historische und soziologische Aspekte (Ivar Oxaal, 29–60). Soziale Schicht, Kultur und die Wiener Juden um die Jahrhundertwende (Steven Beller,

61–82). Kulturelle Innovation und soziale Identität im Wien des Fin de siècle (Michael Pollak, 83–102). Die Wiener Kultur und die jüdische Selbsthass-Hypothese; eine Kritik (Allan Janik, 103–120). Spezifische Momente und Spielarten des österreichischen und des Wiener Antisemitismus (Peter Pulzer, 121–139) Nuancen in der Sprache der Judenfeinde (Sigurd Paul Scheichl, 141–168). Sozialdemokratie, Antisemitismus und die Wiener Juden (Robert S. Wistrich, 169–180). Die Politik der jüdischen Gemeinde Wiens zwischen 1890 und 1914 (Walter R. Weitzmann, 181–220). Politischer Antisemitismus im Wien der Zwischenkriegszeit (Bruce F. Pauley, 221–246). Katholischer Antisemitismus in der Ersten Republik (Anton Staudinger, 247–270). Die assimilierte jüdische Jugend im Wiener Kulturleben um 1930 (Richard Thieberger, 271–284). Die Ausgliederung der Juden aus der Gesellschaft: das Ende des Wiener Judentums unter der NS-Herrschaft, 1938–1943 (Gerhard Botz, 285–312). Fluchtpunkt Schanghai (Françoise Kreissler, 313–324). Ein historisch neuartiger 'Antisemitismus ohne Antisemiten'? (Bernd Marin, 325–348). Letzter Walzer in Wien – ein Nachtrag (George Clare, 349–356). Ilusionen und Kompromisse: Zur Identität der Wiener Juden nach 1945 (Ruth Beckermann, 357–364).]

27116.   — LE RIDER, JACQUES: *Modernité et crises de l'identité.* Paris: Presses Universitaires de France, 1990. 432 pp., notes. (Perspectives critiques.) [Also German edn.]: *Das Ende der Illusion: die Wiener Moderne und die Krisen der Identität.* Übers. aus dem Franz. von Robert Fleck. Wien: Österr. Bundesverl., 1990. 496 pp., bibl. [Incl. section on the crisis of Jewish identity which discusses the situation of the assimilated Viennese intellectual Jews, Sigmund Freud and Theodor Herzl, Karl Kraus, the cultural Zionism of Richard Beer-Hofmann; deals also with Otto Weininger.]

27117.   — *Schmelztiegel Wien – einst und jetzt: zur Geschichte und Gegenwart von Zuwanderung und Minderheiten.* Aufsätze, Quellen, Kommentare. Hrsg. von Michael John und Albert Lichtblau. Einleitung von Erich Zöllner. Wien: Böhlau, 1990. X, 487 pp., illus., tabs., diagrs. [And]: *Didaktisches Beiheft* von Waltraud Weisch und Hildegard Bruckner. 104 pp., illus., tabs., maps.

3. Czechoslovakia

——   DON, YEHUDA/KARADY, VICTOR, eds.: *A social and economic history of Central European Jewry.* [See No. 27103.]

——   HAUMANN, HEIKO: *Geschichte der Ostjuden.* [See No. 26934.]

27118.   PRAGUE. FIALA-FÜRST, INGEBORG: *Das jüdische Prag.* [In]: Mnemosyne, Nr. 8, (Ed.: Armin A. Wallas, Rennsteiner Str. 118, A–9500) Villach, Mai 1990. Pp. 7–27, notes.

27119.   JÄHN, KARL-HEINZ, ed.: *Das Prager Kaffeehaus: literarische Tischgesellschaften.* (Aus dem Tschechischen von Reinhard Fischer [et al.].) 2. Aufl. Berlin: Verlag Volk und Welt, 1990. 335, [32] pp., illus., ports., facsims. [Incl. text by Egon Erwin Kisch, refers also to German-speaking Jewish writers.]

27120.   *Review of the Society for the History of Czechoslovak Jews.* Vol. 1: 1986–87; Vol 2: 1988–89. Ed.: Lewis Weiner. New York: Society for the History of the Czechoslovak Jews, 1987 & 1989. [Obtainable from Joseph Abeles, 102–30 62nd Road, Forest Hills, N.Y. 11375.] [*Vol. 1 1986–87* incl.: Jewish physicians in Old Prague (Guido Kisch, 16–28). Joachim Gans of Prague: America's first Jewish visitor (Gary C. Grassl, 53–90). Max Brod's life in music (Zdenka E, Fischmann, 101–120). Rabbi and statesman: Samson Raphael Hirsch, Landesrabbiner of Moravia, 1847–51 (Gertrude Hirschler, 121–149). Recollections of Czech Jewry (Nahum Goldmann, 160–166). The Jews of Slovakia: some historical and social aspects (Yehoshua Robert Büchler, 167–176). *Vol. 2: 1988–89*: The Jews of Bohemia and Moravia during the 18th and 19th centuries: their daily life in memoirs and documents (Wilma Iggers, 33–52). Further contributions are listed according to subject.]

27121.   SADEK, VLADIMIR: *Rabbi Löw und sein Bild des Menschen.* [In]: Judaica Bohemia, Vol. 26, No. 2, Prague 1990. Pp. 72–83, notes.

27122.   STÖLZL, CHRISTOPH: *Kafkas böses Böhmen: zur Sozialgeschichte eines Prager Juden.* Ungekürzte, korrigierte Ausg. Frankfurt am Main: Ullstein, 1989. 147 pp. (Ullstein-Buch, Nr. 34546.) [Orig. publ. 1975. Incl. history of antisemitism in Bohemia 1850–1920.]

27123.   WLASCHEK, RUDOLF M.: *Juden in Böhmen.* München: Oldenbourg, 1990. 220 pp. (Veröffentlichungen des Collegium Carolinum, Forschungsstelle für die böhmischen Länder, Bd. 66.)

[Incl. the Nazi period.] [Cf.: Juden, Tschechen, Deutsche (Reuven Assor) [in]: Tribüne, Jg. 29, H. 116, Frankfurt am Main, 1990, pp. 188–190.]

4. Hungary

—— DEAK, ISTVAN: *Jewish soldiers in Austro-Hungarian society.* [See No. 27102.]
—— DON, YEHUDA/KARADY, VICTOR, eds.: *A social and economic history of Central European Jewry.* [See No. 27103.]
—— HAUMANN, HEIKO: *Geschichte der Ostjuden.* [See No. 26934.]
—— ISAACSON, JUDITH MAGYAR: *Seed of Sarah: memoirs of a survivor.* [See No. 27303.]
—— KATZ, JACOB: *An unclarified episode in the life of the Hatam Sofer: the Alexandersohn affair.* [In Hebrew]. [See No. 27462]
—— KLEIN, R. L.: *The scent of sunflowers: a chronicle of faith, hope, and survival in war-ravaged Budapest.* [See No. 27299.]
27124. KORBULY, DEZSÖ: *Im Zeichen 'rassischer Notwehr': politischer Katholizismus und Antisemitismus in Ungarn (1890–1944).* [In]: Tribüne, Jg. 29, H. 116, Frankfurt am Main, 1990. Pp. 125–137, notes.
27125. LÖWENHEIM, AVIGDOR: *The leadership of the Neolog Jewish Congregation of Pest in the years 1914– 1919: its status and activity in the Jewish community.* [In Hebrew, with English summary]. Jerusalem, Hebrew University, Diss., Jan. 1990. 349, X pp.
27126. LUKACS, JOHN: *Budapest um 1900: Ungarn in Europa.* (Übers. aus dem Amerikan. von Renate Schein und Gerwin Zohlen). Wien: Kremayr u. Scheriau, 1990. 302 pp., illus. [Transl. of No. 26154/YB XXXV.]
27127. WAHLE, HEDWIG: *Die Juden in Ungarn.* Wien (Burggasse 35): Informationszentrum im Dienste der Christl.-Jüd. Verständigung, 1990. 23 pp. (IDCIV-Vorträge, 27.)

5. Switzerland

—— KAMIS-MÜLLER, AARON: *Antisemitismus in der Schweiz 1900–1930.* [See No. 27879.]
—— KAUFMANN, URI: *The impact of the French Revolution on rural Jewry in Alsace, Baden, and Switzerland: a comparison.* [See No. 27099.]
27128. MARCUS, MARCEL: *Swiss Jewry.* [In]: European Judaism, Vol. 23, No. 1, London, Spring 1990. Pp. 45–49, appendix, tab., notes. [Author, French born, grew up in post-war Germany, is now Rabbi in Bern.]

C. German Jews in Various Countries

27129. BERNSTEIN, SAUL, ed.: *Jubilee: our first fifty years Synagogue Adath Yeshurun.* Kew Gardens, N.Y.: Synagogue Adath Yeshurun, 1990. 192 pp., illus., ports., facsims. [Synagogue was founded by German-Jewish immigrants.]
27130. BÖHM, GÜNTER: *Deutsche Juden in Peru im 19. Jahrhundert.* [In]: Trumah, 1, Wiesbaden, 1987. Pp. 159–174, notes.
27131. CESARANI, DAVID, ed.: *The making of modern Anglo-Jewry.* Oxford: Blackwell, 1990. 222 pp. [Also on Jewish immigrants from Germany and Austria. Incl.: The acculturation of the children of immigrant Jews in Manchester, 1890–1930 (Rosalyn Livshin, 79–96).]
27132. DIETHARDT, ULRIKE/LUNZER, HEINZ [et al.], eds.: *Leben mit österreichischer Literatur: Begegnung mit aus Österreich stammenden amerikanischen Germanisten, 1938/1988.* Elf Erinnerungen. Wien (Gumpendorfer Str. 15): Dokumentationsstelle für Neuere Österreichische Literatur; Wien: Österr. Gesellschaft für Literatur, 1990. VII, 143 pp., bibl. (Zirkular, Sondernummer, 20.)
27133. ECKMAN, JULIUS. STAMPFER, JOSHUA: *Pioneer Rabbi of the West: the life and times of Julius Eckman.* Portland, Or. (P.O. Box 751): Institute of Judaic Studies, [1989]. XII, 201 pp., bibl. [Julius Eckman, 1805–1877, came from Posen to America and eventually became rabbi in Portland, Or.]
27134. EXILE. ARONSFELD, C. C.: *Von den ehemals deutschen Juden in England.* [In]: MB, Jg. 58, Nr. 61/62, Tel-Aviv, Aug./Sept. 1990. P. 9.

27135. — *Exilforschung*. Ein internationales Jahrbuch. Hrsg. von Thomas Koebner [et al.]. *Bd. 8: Politische Aspekte des Exils*. München: Edition Text und Kritik, 1990. 243 pp.

27136. — FREYERMUTH, GUNDOLF S.: *Reise in die Verlorengegangenheit: auf den Spuren deutscher Emigranten (1933–1945)*. Hamburg: Rasch & Röhring, 1990. 339 pp. [Based on interviews with Jewish and non-Jewish emigrés, a.o., Paul Falkenberg, Paul Hohner, Grete Mosheim, Hans Sahl; refers also to contemporary Germany and its attitudes towards the Nazi period and the persecution of the Jews.]

27137. — FUNKE, HAJO: *Die andere Erinnerung: Gespräche mit jüdischen Wissenschaftlern im Exil*. Unter Mitarbeit v. Hans-Hinrich Harbort. Frankfurt am Main: Fischer-Taschenbuch-Verl., 1989. 470 pp, illus. (Fischer-Taschenbücher, 4610.)

——— — GOLDSCHMIDT, MANUEL R.: *Mein Bruder Peter 1923–1987*. Eine biographische Skizze. [See No. 27773.]

27138. — GRAUL, BERND A. K.: *'Freiheit tu ich euch offenbaren': jüdische Emigranten im brasilianischen Urwald* [in Rolandia]. [In]: 'Allgemeine', Nr. 45/1, Bonn, 4. Jan. 1990. P. 5.

27139. — GREEN, JONATHAN, comp.: *Them: voices from the immigrant community in contemporary Britain*. London: Secker & Warburg, 1990. [Incl. taped depositions of three former German-Jewish refugees (i.a. Sir Claus Moser); also incl. list of interviewees with biographical details.]

27140. — HARPPRECHT, KLAUS: *Die deutschen Juden in Buenos Aires*. [In]: Frankfurter Allg. Zeitung, Magazin Nr. 563, 14. Dez. 1990. Pp. 22–35, 80, ports., illus.

——— — MAURITIUS. [See No. 27367.]

——— — PAUCKER, ARNOLD: *History in exile: writing the story of German Jewry*. [See No. 27162.]

27141. — ROJER, OLGA ELAINE: *Exile in Argentina, 1933–1945: a historical and literary introduction*. New York; Bern: Lang, 1989. XXII, 250 pp., bibl, (239–254). (American university studies: Ser. 22, Vol. 3.)

27142. — *Sociedade Israelita Brasileira de Cultura e Beneficiencia SIBRA, 1936–1986*. Porto Alegre: SIBRA, 1986. 78, [16] pp., illus., ports., facsims., tabs. [Also on German- and Austrian-Jewish émigrés.]

27143. — TRAHTEMBERG, LEON: *Vida Judia en Lima y en las provincias del Peru*. Un recuento historico documentado sobre la presencia judia en el territorio del Peru en el siglo XX. Lima: Union Israelita del Peru, 1989. 261 pp., illus., maps. [Incl. refugees from Nazi Germany.]

27144. — WALTHER, PETER THOMAS: *Von Meinecke zu Beardt? Die nach 1933 in die USA emigrierten deutschen Historiker*. Ann Arbor: University Microfilm International, 1990. IV, 411 pp., English summary (372–408), bibl. Buffalo, State Univ. of New York, Diss., 1989.

——— HEAVENRICH, MARIAN BLITZ: *Recollections*. [See No. 27775.]

27145. HELD, LEWIS ISAAC: *Held family history. Vol. 1: From antiquity to Irving I. Held*. N.p., 1990. 1 vol., illus., ports., facsims, geneal. tables, bibl. [Mimeog., available in the LBI New York.] [Family came from Bavaria to the USA in 1846.]

27146. JAY, MARTIN: *Permanent exiles: essays on the intellectual migration from Germany to America*. New York: Columbia Univ. Press, 1990. XXII, 328 pp., notes. [Paperback edn. of No. 22001/YB XXXI.]

27147. KAHN-FREUND. LUTHARDT, WOLFGANG: *Arbeit, Recht und Gerechtigkeit: zur Erinnerung an Otto Kahn-Freund (1900–1979)*. [In]: Internationale wissenschaftliche Korrespondenz, Jg. 26, H. 2, Berlin, Juni 1990. Pp. 181–190. [Sir O.K., professor of comparative law at Oxford and Cambridge, barrister, specialist in labour law, data see No. 16588/YB XXV.]

27148. KRIEGSHABER, VICTOR H. BAUMAN, MARK M: *Victor Kriegshaber, community builder*. [In]: American Jewish History, Vol. 79, No. 1, Waltham, Ma., Autumn 1989. Pp. 94–110. [V.H.K., 1859–1934, born in Louisville, Kentucky, of German-Jewish parents from Hesse-Darmstadt, studied in Frankfurt and Darmstadt, became city engineer and urban planner in Louisville.]

27149. LIEDTKE, RAINER: '. . . *deutsche Geistescultur zu fördern': deutsch-jüdische Immigranten und die Schiller-Anstalt in Manchester*. [In]: Tribüne, Jg. 29, H. 116, Frankfurt am Main, 1990. Pp. 146–153, notes.

27150. LIPMAN, V. D.: *A history of the Jews in Britain since 1858*. Leicester: Leicester Univ. Press, 1990. 274 pp., illus., ports., facsims., maps, glossary, notes, bibl. (XI–XVI). [Incl. Section 'Nazism and the refugees' (190–198); also deals with earlier Jewish immigration from Germany and its influence on religious practices.]

27151. LUEBKE, FREDERICK C.: *Germans in the New World: essays in the history of immigration*. Champain: Univ. of Illinois Press, 1990. XXII, 198 pp. [Incl. German-Jewish immigrants.]

27152. POLSTER, GARY EDWARD: *Inside looking out: the Cleveland Jewish Orphan Asylum, 1868–1924*.

Kent, Oh.: Kent State Univ. Press, 1990. XIV, 240 pp., illus., bibl. [Examines the efforts of the German Jews of Cleveland to 'Americanise' and remove from Yiddish culture the children of the orphan asylum.]

—— ROTHMUND, DORIS: *Lion Feuchtwanger und Frankreich*. [See No. 27662.]

27153. SARNA, JONATHAN D./KLEIN, NANCY H.: *The Jews of Cincinnati*. Cincinnati, Oh. (3101 Clifton Ave.): Hebrew Union College, 1989. IX, 190 pp. illus., bibl. [First German-Jewish settlers came to Cincinnati in 1817. Incl. also German-Jewish refugees in the 1930s and the refugee scholar project of Hebrew Union College.]

—— SCHOLZE, BRUNHILDE: *Die Auswanderung von bayerischen Juden nach Nordamerika*. [See No. 27006.]

27154. STRAUS FAMILY. PAUL, ROLAND/STEINEBREI, HANS: *Die Brüder Straus – Kaufleute, Politiker und Philanthropen*. [In]: Globus, Jg. 22, H. 2, Bonn, März/Apr. 1990. Pp. 21–22, illus., ports. [On Lazarus Straus, born 1809 in Otterberg, Palatinate, emigrated to the USA in 1852, and his three sons: Isidor, co-owner of Macy's department store, the philanthropist Nathan, and the politician Oscar.]

27155. WENGER, BETH S.: *Congregation and community: the evolution of Jewish life at congregation Mishkan Israel, 1840–1990*. New Haven, Ct.: Congregation Mishkan Israel, 1990. 68 pp., illus., ports., facsims, bibl. references incl. in notes (63–68). [Congregation founded by German-Jewish immigrants from Bavaria.]

II. RESEARCH AND BIBLIOGRAPHY

A. Libraries and Institutes

27156. DEUTSCHES LITERATURARCHIV, Marbech am Neckar. *Jahrbuch der Deutschen Schillergesellschaft*. Jg. 34. Im Auftrag des Vorstands hrsg. von Wilfried Barner [et al.]. Stuttgart: Kröner, 1990. VIII, 520 pp., notes. [Incl.: Der Briefwechsel Martin Heideggers mit Elisabeth Blochmann: Bemerkungen zur Edition (Joachim W. Storck, 453–463). Erinnerung [an Heidegger 1933/1934] (Hans-Georg Gadamer, 464–468).]

27157. HOCHSCHULE FÜR JÜDISCHE STUDIEN, Heidelberg: *Trumah*. 1. Hrsg. von Moshe Elat, Martin S. Cohen und Theodore Kwasman. Wiesbaden: Reichert, 1987. X, 368 pp., illus. [Contributions relevant to German-Jewish history are listed according to subject.]

27158. —— CARLEBACH, JULIUS. *The Hochschule für jüdische Studien in Heidelberg*. [In]: Christian Jewish Relations, Vol. 22, Nos. 3–4, London, Autumn/Winter 1989. Pp. 100–102.

27159. LEO BAECK INSTITUTE. *Bulletin des Leo Baeck Instituts*. Nr. 86–87. Hrsg. von Joseph Walk, Jacov Guggenheim und Itta Shedletzky, unter Mitarbeit von Tamar Laakmann. Frankfurt am Main: Hain, 1990. 81; 79 pp., notes. [2 issues.] [Individual contributions are listed according to subject. Issue Nr. 85/1990 with the indexes for Nos. 50 (1974) – 84 (1989) will be published later.]

27160. —— *Leo Baeck Institute Year Book XXXV*. German Jewry: integration – self-questioning – catastrophe. Post-war historiography. Ed.: Arnold Paucker. London: Secker & Warburg, 1990. XXIV, 616 pp., illus., parts., facsims., tabs., notes, bibl. [493–589], index. [Cont.: Preface (Arnold Paucker, VII–XIII; incl. obituaries for Solomon A. Birnbaum, p. XII; for Daniel J. Cohen, pp. XII–XIII; for Steven S. Schwarzschild, p. XIII). An appraisal of German-Jewish historiography; introduction to Year Book XXXV (Reinhard Rürup, XV–XXIV). Individual contributions are listed according to subject.]

27161. —— *Selected reviews*. LBI Year Book XXXV: Jubiläum im Leo Baeck Institut in London: das 35. Leo Baeck Institut Year Book (Deutsche Welle, Radio Köln, Red.: Dr. Kluge, 23. Okt. 1990). Besprechung (Kurt Gräubig) [In]: deutschland-berichte, Jg. 26, Nr. 12, Bonn, Dez. 1990, pp. 91–92. LBI Year Book XXXIV: Besprechung (Kurt Gräubig) [in]: deutschland-berichte, Jg. 26, Nr. 9, Bonn, Sept. 1990, pp. 20–21

27162. —— LBI London. PAUCKER, ARNOLD: *History in exile: writing the story of German Jewry*. A paper delivered at a Symposium on 'German-speaking exiles in Great Britain' held at the University of Aberdeen, Sep. 24 –26, 1990. 20 pp. [To be published in 1991; typescript available at the LBI London.] [Deals with the Leo Baeck Institute London and the generation of its 'founding fathers'.]

27163. —— LBI New York. *Library and Archives News*. Ed.: Gabrielle Bamberger. No. 29. New York: Leo Baeck Institute, Winter 1990. 8 pp.

27164. — — *LBI News.* Ed.: Gabrielle Bamberger. No. 58. New York: Leo Baeck Institute, Summer 1990. 16 pp., front illus., illus., ports., facsims. [Incl.: The LBI launches major history project: a four volume collaborative history of the Jews in German-speking lands since the 17th century (pp. 3–8). Reports on the LBI New York events and on its collections in library and archives. Obituaries: Fred W. Lessing 1915–1990, chairman of the board and treasurer of the New York LBI for over 25 years (p. 2, port.; see also No. 27544). Nahum N. Glatzer 1903–1990, scholar, member of the board and fellow of the New York LBI (p. 12).]

27165. — — LOWENTHAL, ERNST G.: *Hervorragender Mitarbeiter des LBI: zum 100. Geburtstag von Ernest Hamburger.* [In]: MB, Jg. 58, Nr. 65, Tel-Aviv, Dez. 1990, p. 10. [E. Hamburger, Socialist politician, political scientist, emigrated to France in 1933, to the USA in 1940.]

27166. SALOMON LUDWIG STEINHEIM-INSTITUT FÜR DEUTSCH-JÜDISCHE GESCHICHTE, Universität Duisburg. *Menora.* Jahrbuch für deutsch-jüdische Geschichte. Bd.I.Im Auftrag des 'Salomon Ludwig Steinheim-Instituts für deutsch-jüdische Geschichte' hrsg. von Julius H. Schoeps in Verbindung mit Arno Herzig und Hans Otto Horch. Red.: Ludger Heid. München: Piper, 1990. 368 pp., illus., notes. (Serie Piper, Bd. 1221.) [Cont.: Einführung (Julius H. Schoeps, 7–14). Individual contributions are listed according to subject.]

27167. WIENER LIBRARY, London. THE WIENER LIBRARY NEWSLETTER. Ed.: A. J. Wells. No. 15, (Summer 1990) [&] No. 16 (Winter 1990–1991). London, 1990. 2 issues (8 pp. each), illus. [*No. 15* incl.: Fred Lessing, 1915–1990 (Walter Laqueur/Hans Feld, pp. 1 & 8; see also No. 27544). Art in Terezin: Peter Kien (Kaethe Fischel, 2). Reports on Wiener Library events.]

27168. YAD VASHEM, Martyrs' and Heroes' Remembrance Authority. *Yad Vashem Studies.* 20. Ed. by Aharon Weiss. Jerusalem: Yad Vashem, 1990. 1 vol. [Contributions pertinent to German Jewry are listed according to subject.]

—— ZENTRUM FÜR ANTISEMITISMUSFORSCHUNG der Technischen Universität Berlin. [See No. 27884.]

B. Bibliographies and Catalogues

27169. *The Blackwell companion to Jewish culture: from the eighteenth century to the present.* Ed. by Glenda Abrahamson. Oxford: Blackwell, 1989. 853 pp., illus. [Incl. entries on many German- and Austrian-Jewish personalities, and articles on Jews in, a.o., film, theatre.]

27170. CENTRAL BRITISH FUND FOR JEWISH WORLD RELIEF. *Archives of the Central British Fund for Jewish World Relief, 1933–1960. Series 1: The Jewish people from Holocaust to nationhood.* Reading (Berkshire RG1, 50 Milford Road): Research Publication Ltd., [1990?]. 77 microfilm reels. [The CBF was founded in 1933, initially to cope with the Jewish refugees from Germany and provide assistance to those left under Nazi rule. Cf.: Refugees on record (David Cesarani) [in]: Times Literary Supplement, London, Jan. 11, 1991.]

27171. COLE, HELENA: *The history of women in Germany from medieval times to the present.* Bibliography of English-language publications. [Compiled] with the assistance of Jane Caplan and Hanna Schissler. Washington, D.C.: German Historical Insitute, 1990. 102 pp. (Reference guide of the German Historical Institute, No. 3.) [Incl. many Jewish women, e.g. Rahel Varnhagen.]

27172. DUSCHKEWITZ, WOLFGANG, ed.: *Selbständig erschienene Werke österreichischer Autoren jüdischer Herkunft seit 1848.* Forschungsprojekt des Jubiläumsfonds der Österreichischen Nationalbank Nr. 3183. Abschlussbericht. Redaktion: Wolfgang Duschkewitz [et al.]. Wien: Österreichische Nationalbank, 1988. 53 pp.

27173. *Encyclopedia of the Holocaust.* Ed. in chief [and preface]: Israel Gutman. Foreword by Elie Wiesel. Transl. by Mordechai Shalev. English edn. ed. by Geoffrey Wigoder. New York: Macmillan; London: Collier Macmillan, 1990. 4 vols., XLIX, 1905 pp., illus., ports., facsims., maps, tabs., bibl., glossary, chronology, appendix: major Jewish organisations in Germany 1893–1943. [Cont. about 950 signed, original articles. A German edn. is in preparation by Piper, Munich, scheduled to appear in autumn 1992.]

—— FEINSTEIN, BEN-ZION, ed.: *A guide to the archive of Hechalutz and youth movements in Germany.* [In Hebrew]. [See No. 27541.]

—— FREUDENHEIM, TOM L.: *Books on art and the Jewish tradition.* [See No. 27553.]

—— *Handbuch zur Geschichte der Juden in Österreich.* [See No. 27109.]

27174. *Index of articles on Jewish studies (and the study of Eretz Israel).* Vol. 29: 1987. Comp. and ed. in 'Kiryat Sefer', the Jewish National and University Library. Ed. board: Bitya Ben-Shammai, Susie Cohen [et al.] Jerusalem: The Jewish National and Univ. Library Press, 1989.

XXXVI, 352 pp., author & subject indexes. [A selective bibliography, incl. articles on German-speaking Jewry.]

27175. *Das Jüdische Museum in Budapest.* Hrsg.: Ilona Benoschofsky [et al.] Aus dem Ungar. von Ruth Futaky; Fotos: László Szelényi. [Budapest]: Corvina, Wiesbaden 1989. 245 pp., 249 illus. [Catalogue of the Jewish museum in Budapest.]

—— KOBER, ADOLF. MÜLLER-JERINA, ALWIN: *Adolf Kober (1879–1958): Versuch einer Bio-Bibliographie.* [See No. 27500.]

27176. *Leo Baeck Institute New York. Catalog of the archival collections.* Ed. by Fred Grubel in cooperation with Alan S. Divack, Frank Mecklenburg, Michael A. Riff and Nusi Sznaider. Tübingen: Mohr, 1990. XIII, 409 pp. (Schriftenreihe wissenschaftlicher Abhandlungen des Leo Baeck Instituts, 47). [Cont.: Preface (Fritz Stern). Introduction (Fred Grubel). Major collections: alphabetical listing with descriptions (1–156). Index of names, places, subjects to major collections (159–187). Small collections (alphabetic listing coded for contents (191–409).] [The second volume of the LBI New York catalogue. For first vol., listing Jewish communal history; newspapers, periodicals, serials, alamanacs; the LBI's memoir collection, see No. 8517/YB XVI.]

27177. *Post-war publications on German Jewry: a selected bibliography of books and articles 1989.* Compiled by Irmgard Foerg and Annette Pringle. [In]: LBI Year Book XXXV, London, 1990. Pp. 491–589.

27178. REININGHAUS, WILFRIED: *Quellen zur Geschichte der Juden im Westfälischen Wirtschaftsarchiv Dortmund.* [In]: Westfälische Forschungen, Jg. 39, Münster 1989. Pp. 359 ff.

27179. SELAVAN, IDA COHEN: *A survey of bibliographies of Jewish interest 1980–1990.* [In]: Jewish Book Annual, Vol. 48 (1990–1991), New York, 1990. Pp. 89–105. [Incl. bibls. on antisemitism; Holocaust; Martin Buber and other German Jews.]

27180. YALE UNIVERSITY LIBRARY. *Guide to Yale University Library Holocaust video testimonies. Vol. 1. Fortunoff Video Archive for Holocaust testimonies.* New York: Garland Publishing, 1990. XIII, 116 pp. [The archive opened in 1982; incl. more than 1,400 videotaped interviews with Holocaust survivors. Vol. 1 incl. summaries of 255 of those interviews.]

—— ZENTRUM FÜR ANTISEMITISMUSFORSCHUNG. *Bibliographie zum Antisemitismus: die Bestände der Bibliothek des Zentrums für Antisemitismusforschung der Technischen Universität Berlin.* [See No. 27884.]

III. THE NAZI PERIOD

A. General

—— GENERAL. Communal & regional Histories referring to the Nazi period and fully listed in other sections: Berlin (No. 27522). Bornheim (No. 26999). Bremerhaven (No. 27001). Breslau (No. 27002). Düren (No. 27012). Düsseldorf (No. 27013). Essen (No. 27017, 27018). Franconia (No. 27034). Friedrichstadt (No. 27027). Haldensleben (No. 27034). Herbern (No. 27042). Horn-Bad Meinberg (No. 27046). Lemgo (No. 27051, 27052). Luckenwalde (No. 27056). Mecklenburg (No. 27057). Mühlhausen (Thuringia) (No. 27060). Niederwerrn (No. 27063). Leipzig (Nos. 27053, 27595). Palatinate (No. 27068). Pforzheim (No. 27069). Recklinghausen (No. 27073). Rheurdt (No. 27071), Sauerland (No. 27079). Speyer (No. 27085). Waldeck (No. 27033).

—— — NOVEMBER Pogrom 1938: All publications dealing specifically with the November Pogrom are combined under this heading without additional cross-reference in section IIIA under the name of the places or regions.

27181. AHRWEILER. *Kreis Ahrweiler unter dem Hakenkreuz.* (Hrsg.: Landkreis Ahrweiler. Schriftleitung: Ignaz Görtz.) Meckenheim: Warlich, 1989. 416 pp., illus., bibl. (404–414.) (Studien zur Vergangenheit und Gegenwart, Bd. 2.) [Incl.: Die Verfolgung der Juden im Kreis Ahrweiler während der nationalsozialistischen Gewaltherrschaft 1933–1945 (Leonhard Janta, 215–265).]

27182. AMÉRY, JEAN: *At the mind's limits: contemplations by a survivor on Auschwitz and its realities.* Transl. from the German by Sidney and Stella P. Rosenfeld. Foreword by Alexander Stille. New York: Schocken, 1989. 144 pp. (paperback). [First German edn. See No. 6118/YB XII.] [J.A., (orig. Hanns Mayer) Oct. 1912 Vienna – Oct. 17, 1978 Salzburg.]

27183. AUERBACHER, INGE: *Ich bin ein Stern.* Aus dem Amerikan. von Mirjam Pressler. Mit einer

Zeittafel von Franz Josef Schütz. Weinheim: Beltz & Gelberg, 1990. 79 pp., illus., map [Orig. title: 'I am a star'. Account for young readers of I.A., born 1934 in Southern Germany, on the persecution of the Jews by the Nazis and her imprisonment in Theresienstadt 1942–1945.]

27184. AURICH. REYER, HERBERT, ed.: *Aurich im Nationalsozialismus*. Im Auftrag der Stadt Aurich hrsg. Aurich: Ostfriesische Landschaft, 1989. 525 pp., illus. (Abhandlungen und Vorträge zur geschichte Ostfrieslands, Bd. 69.)

27185. AUSCHWITZ. CZARNECKI, JOSEPH: *Last traces: the lost art of Auschwitz*. Introd. by Chaim Potok. New York: Atheneum Publ., 1989. XV, 175 pp., illus. [Photographs of paintings, drawings, and graffiti left behind by the inmates of Auschwitz. Also incl. commentaries with information, where known, about the artists.]

——— — AMÉRY, JEAN: *At the mind's limits: contemplations by a survivor on Auschwitz and its realities*. [See No. 27182.]

——— — AUGUST, JOCHEN: *Erinnern oder verweigern: das schwierige Thema Nationalsozialismus*. [See No. 27457.]

27186. — *Kunst zum Überleben – gezeichnet in Auschwitz*. Ausstellung von Werken ehemaliger Häftlinge des Konzentrationslagers Auschwitz aus d. Besitz d. Staatl. Gedenkstätte Oswiecim-Brzezinka (veranstaltet vom Verb. Bildender Künstler Württemberg), [Red. d. Katalogs: Sybille Goldmann et al.] Ulm: Südtt. Verl.-Ges., 1989. 94 pp., [mostly illus.]

27187. — MEYER, ALWIN: *Die Kinder von Auschwitz*, Göttingen: Lamuv, 1990. 240 pp. [13 personal accounts of survival in Auschwitz and life thereafter.]

27188. — STEIN, HERBERT: *Wie die Welt vom Holocaust erfuhr. Schweigen in Düsseldorf über einen Gerechten der Völker*. [In]: Tribüne, Jg. 29, H. 115, Frankfurt am Main, 1990. Pp. 159–160. [On Eduard Schulte, German industrialist, who tried to inform the Allies about mass extermination of Jews in Auschwitz.]

27189. — WOHL, TIBOR: *Arbeit macht tot – Eine Jugend in Auschwitz*. Mit einem Vorwort von Hermann Langbein, hrsg. von Benjamin Ortmeyer. Frankfurt am Main: Fischer Taschenbuch Verlag, 1990. 191 pp. [T.W., 1923 Prague, deported to Theresienstadt, in October 1942 to Auschwitz, from where he escaped in January 1945.]

27190. — WOHL, TIBOR. *Das Gebet des Rabbi Elieser:* Vorabdruck eines Kapitels aus dem Auschwitz-Buch 'Arbeit macht tot'. [In]: Tribüne, Jg. 29, H. 115, Frankfurt am Main, 1990. Pp. 129–132.

27191. — ZIMMERMANN, MICHAEL: *Kunst zum Überleben*. Ausstellung in der Alten Synagoge Essen: Zeichnungen von Auschwitz-Häftlingen. [In]: Tribüne, Jg. 29, H. 114, Frankfurt am Main, 1990. Pp. 63–65, illus.

27192. AUSTRIA. BOTZ, GERHARD: *Die Ausgliederung der Juden aus der Gesellschaft: das Ende des Wiener Judentums unter der NS-Herrschaft (1938–1943)*. [See No. 27115.]

27193. — *Dokumentationsarchiv des Österreichischen Widerstandes. Jahrbuch 1990*. (Red.: Siegwald Ganglmair) Wien: Österreichischer Bundesverlag [1990]. [6], 147 pp., illus., ports., notes. [Incl. an essay on the author Else Feldmann.]

27194. — *Fünfzig Jahre Danach – der 'Anschluss' von innen und aussen gesehen*. Hrsg.: Felix Kreissler. Beiträge zum Internationalen Symposium von Rouen 29. Feb. – 4. März 1988. Veranstaltet vom Centre d'Etudes et de Recherches Autrichiennes (CERA) der Universität Rouen, in Zusammenarbeit mit dem österreichischen Kulturinstitut Paris. Wien; Zürich: Europaverlag, 1989. 286 pp. [Incl.: Die neue Etappe der faschistischen Judenverfolgung und der Ausbruch des Antisemitismus in Wien 1938 (Kurt Pätzold, 189–201, notes). Von der Annexion im März 1938 zur Reichskristallnacht am 10. November 1938: einige Gedanken zu den Folgen und Auswirkungen des Antisemitismus in Österreich (Herbert Steiner, 202–215, notes.). Terror und Selbstmord in Wien nach der Annexion Österreichs (Eckart Früh, 216–226, notes).]

27195. — KRISS, SUSANNE [et al.]: *Wien – Belgien – Retour?* Bearbeitet und eingeleitet von Erika Thurner. Wien: Geyer Edition, [1990.] 236 pp., plans, map. [Autobiographical account of three Jewish women from Vienna, two of them active in the Communist resistance movement (S. K. and Hertha Fuchs-Ligeti) who emigrated to Belgium, and survived deportation to Theresienstadt (Susanne Kriss), to Auschwitz-Birkenau via Malines (Hertha Fuchs-Ligeti) and arrest by the German army in Brussels (Gundl Herrnstadt-Steinmetz).]

——— — RATTNER, ANNA/BLONDER, LOLA: *1938 – Zuflucht Palästina: zwei Frauen berichten*. [See No. 27581.]

27196. — ROSENKRANZ, HERBERT: *Entrechtung, Verfolgung und Selbsthilfe der Juden in Österreich, März bis Oktober 1938.* [And comment]: Bemerkungen zu dem Beitrag von Herbert Rosenkranz (Peter Pulzer) [In]: Österreich, Deutschland und die Mächte; internationale und österreichische Aspekte des 'Anschlusses' vom März 1938. Hrsg. von Gerald Stourzh und Birgitta Zaar. Wien: Verlag der österreichischen Akademie der Wissenschaften, 1990. Pp. 367–418 [& comment]: pp. 419–422.

27197. BAD DÜRKHEIM. FELDMANN, G.: *Die Bedrängnisse der Bad Dürkheimer Juden in der Nazizeit und die Ereignisse in der 'Kristallnacht' 1938.* [In]: Pfälzer Heimat, 41, Speyer, 1990, pp. 25–27.

27198. BADEN. FREI, ALFRED/RUNGE, JENS, eds.: *Erinnern – Bedenken- Lernen: das Schicksal von Juden, Zwangsarbeitern und Kriegsgefangenen zwischen Hochrhein und Bodensee in den Jahren 1933 bis 1945.* Sigmaringen: Thorbecke, 1990. 226 pp., illus., facsims., maps, plans, ports. bibl.

———— — WETTERICH, SUSANNE: *Davids Stern an Rhein und Neckar.* [See No. 26989.]

27199. —— WIEHN, ERHARD R., ed.: *Oktoberdeportation 1940: Gedenkschrift und Dokumentation zur Deportation der badischen und saarpfälzischen Juden nach Gurs und andere Vorstationen von Auschwitz.* Konstanz: Hartung-Gorre, 1990. 1024 pp.

———— BAECK, LEO. FRIEDLANDER, ALBERT H.: *Leo Baeck. Leben und Lehre.* [Also on L.B.'s role during the Nazi period.] [See No. 27463.]

27200. BAKER, RON: *The refugee experience: communication and stress, recollections of a refugee survivor.* [In]: Journal of Refugee Studies, Vol. 3, No. 1, Oxford, 1990. Pp. 64–71, notes. [Author of German-Jewish background, came to Britain at the age of 8.]

27201. BARKAI, AVRAHAM: *Vom Boykott zur 'Entjudung': der wirtschaftliche Existenzkampf der Juden im Dritten Reich 1933–1943.* Frankfurt am Main: Fischer, 1988. [For details see No. 25257/YB XXXIV] Review: (Moshe Zimmermann) [in]: Historische Zeitschrift, Bd. 251, H. 1, München 1990. Pp. 209–211.]

27202. BARTOSZEWSKI, WLADYSLAW: *Von der Pogromnacht 1938 bis zur Endlösung der Judenfrage.* Anmerkungen eines christlichen Europäers. [In]: Zeitschrift für Württembergische Landesgeschichte, Jg. 48 (1989), Stuttgart, 1990. Pp. 375–390.

27203. BELLON, BERNARD P.: *Mercedes in peace and war: German automobile workers, 1903–1945.* Irvington, N.Y.: Columbia Univ. Press, 1990. XV, 356 pp., illus., ports., tabs., bibl. (325–346). [Incl. Mercedes's involvement with Nazism and its use of slave labour, recruited both from concentration camp inmates and prisoners of war.]

27204. BENZ, WOLFGANG: *Herrschaft und Gesellschaft im nationalsozialistischen Staat: Studien zur Struktur- und Mentalitätsgeschichte.* Orig.-Ausg. Frankfurt am Main: Fischer, 1990. 215 pp. (Fischer-Taschenbücher, 4435.) [Incl. 4 studies on the persecution of German Jews, the November Pogrom 1938, the deportation of Bavarian Jews.]

———— BERLIN. [See also No. 26996.]

27205. —— *'Als wäre es nie gewesen': Menschen, die nicht mehr entkamen – Fotografien aus den letzten Jahren des jüdischen Gemeindelebens in Berlin bis 1942.* Austellung zum Gedenken an den 50. Jahrestag der Pogrome vom November 1938. Veranstaltet von der Jüdischen Abt. des Berlin Museums im Martin Gropius-Bau, Nov.1988/Jan. 1989. (Ausstellungskonzeption: Nicola Galliner. Bildtexte im Katalog: Helmuth F. Braun.) Berlin: Samson Verl., 1989. 105 pp., illus., ports.

27206. —— *Direkt vor der Haustür: Berlin Lichtenrade im Nationalsozialismus.* Hrsg.: Geschichtswerkstatt Berlin-Lichtenrade. Berlin (Jebenstr. 1): Aktion Sühnezeichen/Friedensdienste, 1990. 368 pp., illus. [Also on the persecution of the Jews in Lichtenrade.]

27207. —— JOCHHEIM, GERNOT: *Protest in der Rosenstrasse.* Stuttgart: Hoch, 1990. 191 pp., illus., ports., facsims. [A book for young readers based on documents and autobiographical accounts: on the fate of the Berlin Jews and those living in mixed marriages during the Nazi period, and on the successful protests of women in March 1943 against the imprisonment of their Jewish husbands and children.]

———— — GALLUS, MANFRED, ed.: *Kirchengemeinden im Nationalsozialismus.* [See No. 27223.]

27208. —— *Kreuzberger antifaschistisches Gedenktafelprogramm 1985 bis 1990 und Gedenkzeichen an den Orten des jüdischen Gemeinde- und Kulturlebens vor 1941.* 2., durchgesehene und erweiterte Aufl., Berlin (Mariannenplatz 2): Kunstamt Kreuzberg, 1990. 50 pp., illus., plan.

27209. —— KROCH, URI: *Die jüdische Waldschule 'Kaliski', Berlin.* [In]: MB, Jg. 58, Nr. 56/57, Tel-Aviv, März/Apr. 1990. P. 15, port. [Report on a meeting of former students of the Private Jüdische Waldschule Kaliski in New York, Nov. 1989, attended also by Lotte Kaliski who lives in New York. For the history of the school see Nos. 23221–23222/YB XXXII.]

27210. —— METCALFE, PHILIP: *Berlin 1933: das Jahr der Machtergreifung. Lebensläufe zu Beginn des Nationalsozialismus.* (Aus dem Amerikan. übertr. von Marie-Luise Gutbrodt unter Mitarb. von Gabriele Dick.) Stuttgart: Bonn aktuell; München: Moderne Verlagsgesellschaft, 1989.

360 pp., illus., bibl. (349–356). [The situation in Berlin in 1933 as experienced by five prominent personalities, incl. Bella Fromm, society columnist for 'Vossische Zeitung'.] [B.F., Dec. 21, 1900 Nuremberg – Feb. 9, 1972 New York, journalist, emigrated to New York in 1938.]

27211. BERMAN, AARON: *Nazism, the Jews and American Zionism, 1933–1948.* Detroit: Wayne State Univ. Press, 1990. 238 pp., notes (185–216), bibl. (217–229). [The American Zionist response to the Nazi persecution of Jews, their help for refugees, incl. German Jews.]

27212. *Between rescue and annihilation: studies in the history of German Jewry 1932–1938.* [In Hebrew]. Ed. by Yad Vashem; The Institute of Contemporary Jewry; Leo Baeck Institute. Jerusalem: 'Daf Noy' Press, 1990. 316 pp. [Collection of about 20 essays.]

27213. BIRGER, TRUDI (zusammen mit Jeffrey M. Green): *Im Angesicht des Feuers: wie ich der Hölle des Konzentrationslagers entkam.* Aus dem Englischen von Christian Spiel. München; Zürich: Piper, 1990. 215 pp. [Born 1927 in Frankfurt am Main, the author emigrated with her parents in 1933 to Lithuania, imprisoned in 1941 in the Ghetto of Kovno, later deported to the concentration camp Stutthof and freed by the British; now lives in Jerusalem.]

27214. BLACKWELL, CAROLYN S.: *German-Jewish identity and German-Jewish response to National Socialism 1933–1939.* West Lafayette, Ind., Purdue Univ., Phil. Diss., 1988. 317 pp.

27215. BLASIUS, DIRK: '*Bürgerlicher Tod': Der NS-Unrechtsstaat und die deutschen Juden.* [In]: Geschichte in Wissenschaft und Unterricht, H. 3, Seelze, 1990. Pp. 129–144, notes.

27216. BRESLAU. ANDREE, CHRISTIAN: *Die Ausschaltung jüdischer Mediziner der Universität von Breslau und die Gleichschaltung der Ärzteschaft durch den Reichsärzteführer Gerhard Wagner.* [In]: National-sozialismus und Widerstand in Schlesien. Ed. by Lothar Bossle [et al.] Sigmaringen: Thorbecke, 1989. (Schlesische Forschungen, Bd. 3.) Pp. 105–120, notes, index of names.

27217. BRUNSWICK. *Erinnern und nicht verdrängen! Zum Gedenken an die Verdienste, an die Diskriminierung und an die Verfolgung jüdischer Juristen.* Dokumentation der Gedenkveranstaltung am 7. Nov. 1988 in Braunschweig. (Hrsg.: Der Präsident des Oberlandesgerichts [et al.].) Wolfenbüttel: Druckerei der Arbeitsverwaltung, 1989. 38, [17] pp., facsims., bibl. [Incl. lecture on the fate of Jewish jurists in Brunswick during the Nazi period (Dieter Miosge, 23–33).]

27218. — MIOSGE, DIETER: *Die Braunschweiger Juristenfamilie Mansfeld.* [In]: Justiz im Wandel der Zeit: Festschrift des Oberlandesgerichts Braunschweig. Hrsg.: Rudolf Wassermann. Braunschweig: Joh. Heinr. Meyer Verl., 1989. Pp. 328–348, notes. [On members of the partly Jewish family Mansfeld, Protestants from 1826, and their fate during the Nazi period.]

27219. — ROLOFF, ERNST AUGUST [et al.]: '*Kristallnacht' und Antisemitismus im Braunschweiger Land.* Drei Vorträge im November 1988. Büddenstedt-Offleben: Küssner, 1988. 69 pp. (Arbeiten zur Geschichte der Braunschweigischen Evang.-Lutherischen Landeskirche im 19. und 20. Jahrhundert, Nr. 6.) [Cont.: Die Pogromnacht im Braunschweiger Land (Dietrich Küssner). Lebensschicksale jüdischer Mitbürger im Bereich der Pauligemeinde Braunschweig 1933–1945 (Ernst August Roloff). Antisemitismus und Verfolgung der Juden im Salzgittergebiet (Bernhild Vögel).]

27220. BUCHENWALD. HAMMER, ERWIN: *Das 'klassische' KZ. Berliner Ausstellung über das Konzentrationslager Buchenwald.* [In]: Tribüne, Jg. 29, H. 114, Frankfurt am Main, 1990. Pp. 60–63.

27221. BÜNDE (Westphalia). SAHRHAGE, NORBERT: *Bünde zwischen 'Machtergreifung' und 'Entnazifizierung': Geschichte einer westfälischen Kleinstadt von 1929 bis 1953.* Bielefeld: Verl. für Regionalgeschichte, 1990. 368 pp., illus. [Cont. also sections on the destruction of the Jewish community and restitution after 1945.]

——— CHURCH. [See also No. 27356.]

27222. — *Christian confrontation with the Holocaust.* [In]: Holocaust and Genocide Studies, Vol. 4, No. 3, Oxford, 1989. Pp. 261–340. [Collection of six essays incl.: Christology and the First Commandment (Eberhard Bethge, 261–272), 1934: pivotal year of the Church struggle (F. Burton Nelson, 283–297). On the impossibility and necessity of being a Christian: post Holocaust reflections based on the thought of Jean Améry and Emil Fackenheim (John K. Roth, 299–310). German Christian nationalism: its contribution to the Holocaust (Arlie J. Hoover, 311–322).]

27223. — GALLUS, MANFRED, ed.: *Kirchengemeinden im Nationalsozialismus: sieben Beispiele aus Berlin.* Berlin: Edition Hentrich, 1990. 249 pp. [Deals with the Protestant Church; incl. the attitude towards the persecution of the Jews and the consequences of the Nuremberg Laws within the Protestant communities.]

27224. — Gotto, Klaus/Repgen, Konrad, eds.: *Die Katholiken und das Dritte Reich.* 3., erweiterte u. überarb. Aufl. Mainz: Matthias-Grünewald-Verl., 1990. 224 pp. [Augmented edn. of No. 21063/YB XXX. Also questions whether or not the Catholic Church failed with regard to the persecution of the Jews.]

27225. — Prolingheuer, Hans: *Jundennot und Christenschuld. Eine evangelisch-kirchenhistorische Erinnerung aus Anlaß des Gedenkens an die Novemberpogrome 1938.* [In]: Opfer und Täter. Zum nationalsozialistischen und antijüdischen Alltag in Ostwestfalen-Lippe. Pp. 127–146. [See No. 27410.]

27226. — Schreiber, Matthias: *Friedrich Justus Perels: ein Weg vom Rechtskampf der Bekennenden Kirche in den politischen Widerstand.* München: Kaiser, 1989. 263 pp. (Heidelberger Untersuchungen zu Widerstand, Judenverfolgung und Kirchenkampf im Dritten Reich, Bd. 3.) [F. J. Perels, of Jewish descent, jurist, from 1936 legal adviser of the 'Bekennende Kirche', murdered by the Nazis on Apr. 22./23, 1945 in Berlin.]

27227. — Smid, Marikje: *Deutscher Protestantismus und Judentum 1932/33.* München: Kaiser, 1990. XXX, 547 pp., bibl. (495–522). (Heidelberger Untersuchungen zu Widerstand, Judenverfolgung und Kirchenkampf im Dritten Reich, Bd. 2.)

27228. — Stegemann, Wolfgang, ed.: *Kirche und Nationalsozialismus.* Unter Mitarbeit von Dirk Acksteiner [et al.]. Stuttgart: Kohlhammer, 1990. 176 pp. [Incl.: Evangelische Kirche und 'Endlösung der Judenfrage' (Kurt Meier, 75–95, notes). Christliche Judenfeindschaft und Neues Testament (Wolfgang Stegemann, 131–163, notes).]

——— Cochavi, Yehoyakim, ed.: *The Zionist youth movements in the Shoah.* [See No. 27535.]

27229. Cohn, Frederick G.: *Signals: a young refugee's flight from Germany in the thirties.* Penzance: United Writers Pubications, 1990. 284 pp., map. [Autobiographical narrative of two brothers' escape from Nazi Germany (via Czechoslovakia, Poland, Sweden, Norway) to England.]

27230. CZECHOSLOVAKIA. Frankova, Anita: *Zusammensetzung der direkt nach dem Osten abgesandten Transporte tschechischer Juden (1939–1944).* [In]: Judaica Bohemiae, Vol. 26, No. 2, Prague, 1990. Pp. 65–71, notes.

27231. — Büchler, Yehoshua Robert: *Jewish day schools in Slovakia during the Holocaust.* [And]: Lipscher, Ladislav: *Pastor Vladimír Kuna, rescuer of Jewish children in Slovakia during World War II.* [In]: Review of the Society for the History of Czechoslovak Jews, Vol. 2, New York, 1989. Pp. 53–64; 123–128.

27232. — Huller, Erwin: *Auswanderung in letzter Stunde. Die Flucht aus der alten und die ersten Jahre in der neuen Heimat.* [In]: Tribüne, Jg. 29, H. 115, Frankfurt am Main, 1990. Pp. 162–170.

27233. — Lipscher, Ladislav: *Die Verfolgung der Juden im slowakischen Staat 1939–1945.* [And]: Lipscher, Magdalena: *Jüdisches Schicksal in der Slowakei.* [In]: 1.9.39: Erinnerungen an den 2. Weltkrieg. Hrsg.: Walter Leimgruber. Zürich: Chronos, 1990. Pp. 199–216, notes; 217–225.

27234. — Lipscher, Magdalena: *Simon der Gerechte: ein jüdisches Familienschicksal.* (Mit einem Vorwort von Ralph Giordano.) Gerlingen: Bleicher, 1989. 229 pp., map. [On persecutions in Slovakia during the Nazi period.]

27235. — *München 1938: Ende des alten Europa.* Hrsg. im Auftrag der 'Deutsch-Tschechoslowakischen Gesellschaft für die Bundesrepublik Deutschland' von Peter Glotz [et al.]. Essen: Hobbing, 1990. 472 pp. [Papers presented at an international symposium, 1988, on the Munich agreement 1938, incl. the role of the German-Jewish refugees in Prague.]

——— Wlaschek, Rudolf M.: *Juden in Böhmen.* [See No. 27123.]

27236. DACHAU. *Dachauer Hefte.* Red.: Wolfgang Benz und Barbara Distel. Dachau: Verlag Dachauer Hefte. *Jg. 6, H. 6: Erinnern oder verweigern: das schwierige Thema Nationalsozialismus.* Nov. 1990. 239 pp.

27237. — KZ-Gedenkstätte Dachau, ed.: *Museum – Archiv – Bibliothek; Bericht für das Jahr 1989.* Dachau, 1990. 29 pp.

27238. Dobkowski, Michael/Walliman, Isidor, eds.: *Radical perspectives on the rise of fascism in Germany, 1919–1945.* New York: Monthly Review Press, 1989. 334 pp., bibl. essay (319–324). [Incl. antisemitism and chap.: From denazification to the 'Historiker-Debatte': reckoning with the past in the Federal Republic of Germany (Reinhard Kühnl, 267–288).]

27239. DÜSSELDORF. *The art of the Jewish children, Germany 1936–1941: innocence and persecution.* Ed. and transl. by Sybil Milton. New York: Philosophical Library, 1989. 158 pp., illus. [Transl.

of: '*Verjagt, ermordet: Zeichnungen jüdischer Schüler, 1936–1941*', ed. by Stadtmuseum Düsseldorf. Refers to the painter and art teacher Julo Levin, also to the history of the Düsseldorf Private Jüdische Volksschule, its teachers and students; for partial cont. see No. 25294/YB XXXIV.]

27240. — *Verfolgung und Widerstand in Düsseldorf 1933–1945.* (Katalog der Mahn- und Gedenkstätte Düsseldorf). Hrsg.: Landeshauptstadt Düsseldorf: Der Oberstandtdirektor. Konzeption und Redaktion: Angela Genger. Düsseldorf: Landeshauptstadt Düsseldorf, 1990. 202 pp., illus., bibl. [Incl: 'Kein Trost. Kein Vergessen': Juden in Düsseldorf (Bernd Rusinek, 134–158, notes.). Der 'Gekrümmte Gang': Erinnern – Wozu? (Ulrich Müller, 162–172, notes.). Gedenkstättenarbeit am Beispiel der Mahn- und Gedenkstätte Düsseldorf (Angela Genger, 178–188).]

27241. EICHMANN, ADOLF. MALKIN, PETER Z./STEIN, HARRY: *Eichmann in my hands.* New York: Warner Books, 1990. XIV, 272 pp., illus., ports., map, bibl.

27242. EMBKEN. BRANDENBURG, FRANZ-JOSEF: *Der Untergang der Embkener Synagogengemeinde.* [In]: Jahrbuch des Kreises Düren 1988. Pp. 48–54.

——— EMIGRATION. [See also Nos. 27571 and 27570.]

27243. — HELLER, ALFRED: *Dr. Seligmanns Auswanderung: der schwierige Weg nach Israel.* Hrsg. von Wolfgang Benz. München: Beck, 1990. 353 pp., illus. (Beck'sche Reihe, 414.) [A.H., 1886–1956, describes his emigration and life as a refugee until he finally, after 1945, reaches Palestine.]

——— ERLANGEN. *Juden und Judenpogrom 1938 in Erlangen.* [See No. 27347.]

27244. EXILE. KRÜGER, DIRK: *Die deutsch-jüdische Kinder- und Jugendbuchauthorin Ruth Rewald und die Kinder- und Jugendliteratur im Exil.* Frankfurt am Main: dipa, 1990. 350 pp. (Jugend und Medien, Bd. 21). Zugl. Wuppertal, Univ. Diss., 1990. [R. Rewald, data see No. 24880/YB XXXIII.]

27245. — STEINER, RICCARDO: *It is a new kind of diaspora.* [In]: International Review of Psycho-analysis, Vol. 16, Part 1, London, 1989. Pp. 35–78. [Deals with the politics of emigration of German- and Austrian-Jewish psychoanalysts during the Nazi period, based on the correspondence between Anna Freud and Ernest Jones. Excerpts from letters are included.]

27246. FINAL SOLUTION. FRIEDLÄNDER, SAUL: *The 'final solution': on the unease in historical interpretation.* [In]: History and Memory, Vol. 1, No. 2, Tel-Aviv, Fall-Winter 1989. Pp. 61–76, notes. [Incl. the historians' debate.]

27247. — DINER, DAN: *Historical experience and cognition: perspectives on National Socialism.* [In]: History and Memory, Vol. 2, No. 1, Tel-Aviv, Fall 1990. Pp. 84–110, notes. [Deals also with 'final solution'.]

27248. — GRABITZ, HELGA/SCHEFFLER, WOLFGANG, eds.: *Letzte Spuren: Fotos und Dokumente über Opfer des Endlösungswahns im Spiegel der historischen Ereignisse.* Berlin: Edition Hentrich, 1990. 337 pp., illus., [Incl.: Documents and numerous contemporary photos of Jewish slave workers at the firm of Fritz Emil Schultz in the Warsaw Ghetto (later in Treblinka); also on forced labour in the concentration camps of Trawniki, Lodz, Majdanek, Poniatowa and on the 'Aktion Erntefest' on Nov. 3/4, 1943, during which 42,000 Jews were executed.]

27249. — VÖLKER, HEINZ-HERMANN: *Zur Genesis der 'Endlösung'. Die Auswanderung als 'Lösung der Judenfrage'?* [In]: Tribüne, Jg. 29, H. 115, Frankfurt am Main, 1990. Pp. 88–104, notes.

27250. FLOOD, CHARLES B.: *Hitler: the path to power.* London: Hamish Hamilton; Boston: Houghton Mifflin, 1989. X, 686 pp., illus., bibl. (649–658). [Covers Hitler's early years from 1889–1925, incl. his antisemitism.]

——— FRAENKEL, DANIEL: *Between fulfilment and rescue: 'Hehalutz' and the plight of the Jews in Nazi Germany, 1933–1935.* [In Hebrew]. [See No. 27542.]

27251. FRANK, ANNE. *Anne Frank aus Frankfurt: Leben und Lebenswelt Anne Franks.* (Ausstellung des Historischen Museums Frankfurt am Main. Katalog: Jürgen Steen und Wolf von Wolzogen.) Frankfurt am Main: Historisches Museum, 1990. 176 pp., illus., ports., facsims.

27252. — LINDWER, WILLY: *Anne Frank: die letzten sieben Monate. Augenzeuginnen berichten.* Frankfurt am Main: S. Fischer, 1990. 255 pp., illus., facsims. [Cf.: Die letzten Monate der Anne Frank (Charlotte Petersen) [In]: Tribüne, Jg. 29, H. 115, Frankfurt am Main, 1990. Pp. 218–220.

27253. FRANKFURT am Main. FRIESE, JUDITH/MARTINI, JOACHIM: *Jüdische Musikerinnen und Musiker in Frankfurt, 1933–1942: Musik als Form geistigen Widerstandes* (Ausstellung in der Paulskirche Nov. 1990). Ausstellungsbegleitheft. Frankfurt am Main: Lembeck, 1990. 359, 76, 84 pp.

27254. FRECKENHORST. Löbbers, Heinrich (jun.): Die Juden in Freckenhorst und ihre Verfolgung im Dritten Reich. [In]: Freckenhorst 7, 1988. Pp. 63–71.

—— FREIBURG. Paepcke, Lotte: *Ein kleiner Händler der mein Vater war.* [See No. 27363.]

27255. FÜRTH. Rosenkranz, Bella: *Reise ins Ungewisse: Erinnerungen an die Aussiedlung der 'polnischen Juden' aus Fürth im Jahre 1938.* [In]: Nachrichten für den jüdischen Bürger Fürths. Hrsg.: Isr. Kultusgemeinde Fürth. Red.: Ruben J. Rosenfeld. Fürth (Blumenstr. 31), Sept. 1990. Pp. 16–17.

27256. Geary, Richard: *Hitler and Nazism.* London; New York: Routledge, 1990. 80 pp. (Lancaster pamphlets.) [Incl. persecution of the Jews.]

27257. *Geheimberichte aus dem Dritten Reich 1933–1935:* Der Journalist H. J. Noordewier als politischer Beobachter. Hrsg. von Paul Stoop. Berlin: Argon, 1990. 235 pp., illus., notes, bibl., index of names. [Abridged reprint of the confidential reports of the Dutch journalist Hendrik Jan Noordewier written from Berlin for the Nationaal Bureau voor Documentatie over Nederland. Reports mention also discrimination against and persecution of Jews.]

27258. Gellately, Robert: *The Gestapo and German society: enforcing racial policy 1933–1945.* Oxford: Clarendon Press; New York: Oxford University Press, 1990. 320 pp., maps.

27259. Ginzel, Günther B.: *'Unbesungene Helden' – Menschen, die Leben retteten.* Anmerkungen zu einem Forschungsprojekt. [In]: Opfer und Täter. [See No. 27410.]

27260. HAMBURG. Carlebach, Joseph. 1883–1942. *Jüdischer Alltag als humaner Widerstand: Dokumente des Hamburger Oberrabbiners Joseph Carlebach aus den Jahren 1939–1941.* Ausgewählt und kommentiert von Miriam Gillis-Carlebach. Hamburg: Verlag Verein für Hamburgische Geschichte, 1990. 118 pp., illus., facsims., ports. (Beiträge zur Geschichte Hamburgs, Bd. 37). [J. Carlebach, Jan. 30, 1883 Lübeck – March 26, 1942 in a concentration camp near Riga, pedagogue, Chief Rabbi of Lübeck, Altona and Hamburg.]

27261. — Freimark, Peter: *Juden an der Hamburger Universität.* [In]: *Hochschulalltag im 'Dritten Reich': Die Hamburger Universität 1933–1945.* Hrsg. von Eckart Krause [et al.]. Hamburg: Reimer, 1991 (Hamburger Beiträge zur Wissenschaftsgeschichte 3). Pp. 125–147, illus., notes. [On the unsuccessful Habilitation of the philologist Salomo Birnbaum in 1926–1927 and on the dismissal of Ernst Cassirer, Eduard Heimann, Theodor Plaut, Richard Salomon, William Stern, Erwin Panofsky, Walter Berendsohn et al.)

27262. — Freimark, Peter: *Promotion Hedwig Klein – zugleich ein Beitrag zum Seminar für Geschichte und Kultur des Vorderen Orients.* [In]: *Hochschulalltag im 'Dritten Reich': Die Hamburger Universität 1933–1945.* Hrsg. von Eckart Krause [et al.]. Hamburg: Reimer, 1991 (Hamburger Beiträge zur Wissenschaftsgeschichte 3). Pp. 852–864, notes.

27263. Heller, Alfred: *Dr. Seligmanns Auswanderung: der schwierige Weg nach Israel.* Hrsg. [und mit einem Nachwort] von Wolfgang Benz. München: Beck, 1990 (Beck'sche Reihe 414). 354 pp., illus. [Autobiographical account of the author's flight from Munich in 1939 to Palestine via Bratislava, Istanbul, Crete.]

27264. HERFORD. Brade, Lutz: *Die Achtung vor den Menschenrechten gegenüber der jüdischen Bevölkerung.* Beispiele aus Herford, Deutschland, Dänemark und Bulgarien zwischen 1933 und 1945. [In]: *Opfer und Täter. Zum nationalsozialistischen und antijüdischen Alltag in Ostwestfalen-Lippe.* Hrsg. von Hubert Frankemölle. (Im Auftrag der Gesellschaft für Christlich-Jüdische Zusammenarbeit, Paderborn. Bielefeld: Verlag für Regionalgeschichte 1990. Pp. 117–126. [See No. 27410.]

27265. Herzberg, Arno: *A Jewish editor in Nazi Germany: the personal story of the Berlin Jewish Telegraphic Agency editor and manager during the 1930s.* [In Hebrew, with English summary]. [In]: Qesher, No. 8, Tel-Aviv, Nov. 1990. Pp. 34–42.

27266. HISTORIOGRAPHY (Historians' Debate). *Gutachten zum "Historikerstreit"* (erarbeitet 1987 vom Ausschuß für Kirchliche Zeitgeschichte: Öffentlichkeitsausschuß und Ausschuß Juden und Christen der Landessynode der Evangelischen Kirche im Rheinland.) [In]: Monatshefte für die Evangelische Kirchengeschichte des Rheinlandes, Jg. 37/38, Köln/Bonn 1988/1989. Pp. 651–656.

27267. — Brockmann, Stephen: *The politics of German history.* [In]: History and Theory, Vol. 29, No. 1, Middletown, Ct., 1990. [On historians' debate.]

27268. — *Deutsche Geschichtswissenschaft nach dem Zweiten Weltkrieg (1945–1965).* Hrsg. von Ernst Schulin unter Mitarb. von Elisabeth Müller-Luckner. München: Oldenbourg, 1989. 303 pp. (Schriften des Historischen Kollegs, Kolloquien, Bd. 14.) [Papers presented at a colloquium, Munich 1986. Incl.: Die NS-Zeit in der westdeutschen Forschung 1945–1961. (Konrad Kwiet, pp. 181–198, bibl. notes).]

27269.　— HABERMAS, JÜRGEN: *The new conservatism: cultural criticism and the historians' debate.* Ed. and transl. by Shierry Weber Nicholsen. Introd. by Richard Wolin. Cambridge: Polity, 1989. XXXV, 270 pp.

——　— HERZIG, ARNO: *Zur Problematik deutsch-jüdischer Geschichtsschreibung.* [See No. 26935.]

27270.　— HEUSER, BEATRICE: *Museums, identity and warring historians – observations on history in Germany.* [In]: The Historical Journal, Vol. 33, No. 2, Cambridge, June 1990. Pp. 417–440. [Review essay incl. overview of the historians' debate and discusses the controversial plan to build a museum of German history in Berlin.]

27271.　— KUSS, HORST: *Aussonderung, Konzentration, Vernichtung: zur Geschichte der nationalsozialistischen Konzentrationslager und der Vernichtung des europäischen Judentums.* Ergebnisse und Fragen der zeitgeschichtlichen Forschung seit 1981. [In]: Neue Politische Literatur, Jg. 34, Stuttgart, 1989. Pp. 375–408.

27272.　— RÖMER, RUTH: *Sprachkritische Anmerkungen zum Historikerstreit.* [In]: Muttersprache. Bd. 100, H. 2–3, Wiesbaden, 1990. Pp. 259–265.

——　— SCHOEPS, JULIUS H.: *Leiden an Deutschland: vom antisemitischen Wahn und der Last der Erinnerung.* [See No. 26960.]

27273.　— WOLFFSOHN, MICHAEL: *Zahlenspiele mit den Auschwitzopfern?* Mit Wahrheit ist der Erinnerung am besten gedient. [In]: Frankfurter Allg. Zeitung, Nr. 7, 9. Jan. 1991. P. 10.

27274.　HILBERG, RAUL: *Die Vernichtung der europäischen Juden.* Durchgesehene und erweiterte Ausg. Bd. 1–3. Frankfurt am Main: Fischer, 1990. 3 Vols. (1354 pp.). (Fischer-Taschenbücher, 4417.) [Revised and augmented edn. of No. 19028/YB XXVIII in paperback; for American revised edn. see No. 22134/YB XXXI.]

27275.　HITLER, ADOLF. BURRIN, PHILIPPE: *Hitler et les juifs: genèse d'un génocide.* Paris: Edition du Seuil, 1989. 200 pp. (XXe siècle.)

27276.　— MADAJCZYK, CZESLAW: *Hitler's direct influence on decisions affecting Jews during World War II.* [In]: Yad Vashem Studies, 20, Jerusalem, 1990. Pp. 53–68.

27277.　— OESTERREICHER, JOHANNES: *Zur Genealogie von Hitlers Judenhass.* 1: Das Ausmass. Wien (Burggasse 35): Informationszentrum im Dienste der Christl.-Jüd. Verständigung, 1990. 27 pp., bibl. (IDCIV-Vorträge, 28.)

27278.　HOCH, GERHARD: *Von Auschwitz nach Holstein: der Leidensweg der 1200 jüdischen Häftlingen von Fürstengrube.* Hamburg: VSA-Verl., 1990. 197 pp., illus., map, plans, bibl.

——　HOLOCAUST. [See also No. 27318.]

27279.　— ADLER, DAVID A.: *We remember the Holocaust.* New York: Holt, 1989. XI, 147 pp., illus., bibl. [Personal accounts of survivors, incl. descriptions of Jewish life in pre-Hitler Germany.]

27280.　— AVISAR, ILAN: *Eduard Schulte — 'the mysterious messenger': an example of the responsibility, morality and courage of the bystander.* [In Hebrew, with English summary.] [In]: Nativ: a journal of politics and the arts, Vol. 3, No. 1, Tel-Aviv, Jan. 1990. Pp. 48–51. [On E.Sch. see No. 23318/YB XXXII.]

27281.　— BANKIER, DAVID: *The Germans and the Holocaust.* [In]: Yad Vashem Studies, 20, Jerusalem, 1990. Pp.69–98.

27282.　— BAUER, YEHUDA: *Is the Holocaust explicable?* [In]: Holocaust and Genocide Studies, Vol. 5, No. 2, Oxford, 1990. Pp. 145–155, notes.

27283.　— BAUMAN, ZYGMUNT: *Modernity and the Holocaust.* Ithaca, N.Y.: Cornell Univ. Press, 1989. XIV, 224 pp. [Explores the causes of the Holocaust, and the lessons it offers for contemporary society.]

27284.　— BRAHAM, RANDOLPH L., ed.: *Reflections of the Holocaust in art and literature.* New York: Columbia Univ. Press (distributor), 1990. VII, 166 pp. [Cont.: Etty Hillesum: A story of spiritual growth (Irving Halperin, 1–16). German-Jewish writers on the eve of the Holocaust (Diane R. Spielmann, 55–77). Women writers and the Holocaust (Ellen S. Fine, 79–96). Fictional facts and factual fictions: history in Holocaust literature (Lawrence L. Langer, 117–130). Ashes and hope: the Holocaust in second generation Americans (Alan S. Berger, 97–116). Holocaust and autobiography: Wiesel, Friedländer, Pisar (Joseph Sungolowsky, 131–146). Art of the Holocaust: a summary (Sybil Milton, 147–152). Jewish art and artists in the shadow of the Holocaust (Luba K. Gurdus, 153–164).]

27285.　— CENTER FOR HOLOCAUST STUDIES, Brooklyn, N.Y.: *We were children just like you.* [Exhibition catalogue.] Ed. by Yaffa Eliach. Brooklyn, N.Y.: Center for Holocaust Studies, Documentation and Research, 1990. 121 pp., illus., ports., facsims.

27286.　— CHALK, FRANK/JONASSOHN, KURT: *The history and sociology of genocide: analysis and case studies.* New Haven, Ct.: Yale Univ. Press, 1990. XVIII, 461 pp., illus., bibls. (publ. in cooperation with Montreal Institute for Genocide Studies). [Studies of genocide throughout history, incl. the Nazi Holocaust.]

27287. — *Encyclopedia of the Holocaust.* [See No. 27173.]

27288. — FLORSHEIM, STEWART J., ed.: *Ghosts of the Holocaust. An anthology of poetry by the second generation.* Foreword by Gerald Stern. Detroit: Wayne State Univ. Press, 1989. 190 pp., biographies (179–187). [Editor is of second generation German-Jewish background, as are many of the poets.]

——— — *Guide to Yale University Library Holocaust video testimonies.* [See No. 27180.]

27289. — HASS, AARON: *In the shadow of the Holocaust: the second generation.* Ithaca, N.Y.: Cornell Univ. Press, 1990. 178 pp., notes. [Children of Holocaust survivors, incl. German-Jewish.]

27290. — HELMREICH, WILLIAM B.: *The impact of Holocaust survivors on American society: a socio-cultural portrait.* [In]: Judaism, Vol. 39, No. 1, New York, Winter 1990. Pp. 14–27, notes. [Incl. relief organisations which helped rescue and resettle survivors.]

——— — HILBERG, RAUL: *The Holocaust today.* [See No. 27442.]

27291. — LANG, BEREL: *Act and idea in the Nazi genocide.* Chicago: Univ. of Chicago Press, 1990. XXII, 258 pp.

27292. — LEWIN, RHODA G., ed.: *Witnesses to the Holocaust: an oral history.* Introd. by David Cooperman and essay by Deborah Lipstadt. Boston: Twayne, 1990. XXIII, 240 pp., illus., glossary. [Sixty people talk about their experiences in the Holocaust, incl. German Jews.]

27293. — MILLER, JUDITH: *One by one: facing the Holocaust.* London: Weidenfeld & Nicolson; New York: Simon & Schuster, 1990. 319 pp. [Author examines current attitudes towards the Holocaust in six countries, incl. Germany.]. [Cf.: Edward Norden [in]: Commentary, Vol. 89, No. 2, New York, Aug. 1990, pp. 62–64.]

27294. — PERL, WILLIAM R.: *The Holocaust conspiracy: international policy of genocide.* New York: Shapolsky, 1989. 261 pp. [Author contends that Western powers did little to prevent Holocaust, but instead took deliberate action to support it. Also examines policies of Switzerland, the Soviet Union, Latin America, and the International Red Cross.]

27295. — TORY, AVRAHAM: *Surviving the holocaust: the Kovno Ghetto diary.* Ed. with introd. by Martin Gilbert. Textual and historical notes by Dina Porat. Transl. by Jerzy Michalowicz. Cambridge, Ma.: Harvard Univ. Press, 1990. XXIV, 554 pp., illus., facsims., ports., maps. [Incl. German Jews.]

27296. — UNITED STATES HOLOCAUST MEMORIAL COUNCIL: *'Remembering the voices that were silenced'.* Planning guide. Washington. DC., 1990. XI, 174 pp., illus., facsims., map. [At head of title]: Days of remembrance, April 22–29, 1990.

27297. — VITAL, DAVID: *Power, powerlessness and the Jews.* [In]: Commentary, Vol. 89, No. 1, New York, Jan. 1990. Pp. 23–28. [Based on lecture first delivered at an international conference on the meaning of the Holocaust, held at Northwestern Univ. Chicago in Nov. 1989. Deals in part with the apathy of Jewish leaders towards the Nazi victims.]

——— HUNGARY. BEN-TOV, ARIEH: *Das Rote Kreuz kam zu spät.* [See No. 27366.]

——— — BIBO, ISTVAN: *Zur Judenfrage: am Beispiel Ungarns nach 1944.* [See No. 27861.]

27298. — FRIEDMAN, BENEDIKT: *'Iwan, hau die Juden!' die Todesmärsche ungarischer Juden durch Österreich nach Mauthausen im April 1945.* St. Pölten (Dr. Karl Renner Promenade 22): Institut für Geschichte der Juden in Österreich, 1989. 66 pp., facsims. (Augenzeugen berichten, Schriftenreihe des Instituts für Geschichte der Juden in Österreich, H. 1.) [Incl. Die Protokolle: Augenzeugen berichten (32–64).]

27299. — KLEIN, R. S.: *The scent of sunflowers: a chronicle of faith, hope, and survival in war-ravaged Budapest.* New York: Feldheim, 1989. 519 pp., glossary. [Author tells of her experiences living as a Jew in Budapest, and of the Gentile couple who helped rescue her and her husband and other Jews.]

27300. — NOVACK, JUDITH MANDEL: *The lilac bush.* New York: Shengold Publishers, 1990. 110 pp. [Hungarian–Jewish author tells of her war-time experiences in Hungary and subsequently in Auschwitz. In 1947 she emigrated to the USA.]

27301. — WEINBERG, HARRY: *Against the tide.* New York: Shengold Publishers, 1990. 144 pp. [Hungarian Jewish author tells of his war-time experiences in slave labour and concentration camps. Emigrated to Israel in 1948 and to America in 1954.]

27302. *I came alone: the stories of the Kindertransports.* Ed. by Bertha Leverton and Shmuel Lowensohn. Lewes, Sussex: The Book Guild, 1990. 416 pp., illus., facsims. [Book is based on the reunion of Kindertransportees, organised by Bertha Leverton in June 1989 in Harrow, Middlesex.

Contains more than two hundred autobiographical accounts of those who escaped as 'unaccompanied children', from Germany, Austria and Czechoslovakia to Britain between December 1938 and the outbreak of World War II (Sept. 1939) with the help of Jewish and non-Jewish individuals and organisations.] [Cf.: Kinderlebenslieder (R.G.) [In]: AJR Information, Vol. XLV, No. 10, London, Oct. 1990.] [See also Nos. 27370; 27404.]

27303. ISAACSON, JUDITH MAGYAR: *Seed of Sarah: memoirs of a survivor.* Champaign: Univ. of Illinois Press, 1990. 200 pp., illus. [Author's memoir about pre-war life in Hungary, experiences in Auschwitz and subsequent rescue. Author lives now in U.S.]

27304. ITALY. *La legislazione antiebraica in Italia e in Europa.* Roma: Camera dei deputati, 1989. VIII, 353 pp., notes. [Papers delivered at a conference marking the fiftieth anniversary of the 1938 promulgation of racial legislation in Italy, sponsored by the Italian government, headed by Renzo De Felice; refers also to German-Jewish refugees living in Italy at that time.]

27305. JÄCKEL, EBERHARD/ROSH, LEA: *Der Tod ist ein Meister aus Deutschland: Deportation und Ermordung der Juden. Kollaboration und Verweigerung in Europa.* Hamburg: Hoffman & Campe, 1990. 317 pp., illus., chronol., bibl., maps. [Incl.: Von Berlin nach Wien (15–26).] Based on a four-part TV-film shown on ARD in Germany, Apr. 29–May 4, 1990.]

27306. JONG, LOUIS DE: *The Netherlands and Nazi Germany.* Foreword by Simon Schama. Cambridge, Ma.: Harvard Univ. Press, 1990. 75 pp. [First given as part of the Erasmus Lectures in 1988. Incl. the deportation of German-Jewish refugees.]

—— JURISPRUDENCE. [See Nos. 27217, 27396.]

—— DIESTELKAMP, BERNHARD/STOLLER, MICHAEL, ed.: *Juristen an der Universität Frankfurt am Main.* [See No. 27596.]

27307. —— GÖPPINGER, HORST: *Juristen jüdischer Abstammung im 'Dritten Reich': Entrechtung und Verfolgung.* 2., völlig neubearb. Auflage. München: Beck, 1990. 435 pp. [Cf.: Schandfleck der deutschen Justizgeschichte (Otto Gritschneider) [in]: Süddeutsche Zeitung, Nr. 24, München, 29. Jan. 1991. P. 30. First edn. published in 1963 under the title 'Die Verfolgung der Juristen jüdischer Abstammung durch den Nationalsozialismus', see No. 3772/YB IX.]

27308. —— KRACH, TILLMANN: *Die 'Gleichschaltung' der anwaltlichen Standesorganisationen in Preussen und ihre Folgen für die jüdischen Kollegen.* 1–2. [In]: Anwaltsblatt, Jg. 40, H. 6 & 7, Bonn, Juni & Juli 1990. Pp. 294–297; 352–357, notes.

27309. —— RAPP, GERTRUD: *Die Stellung der Juden in der nationalsozialistischen Staatsrechtslehre: die Emanzipation der Juden im 19. Jahrhundert und die Haltung der deutschen Staatsrechtslehre zur staatsrechtlichen Stellung der Juden im Nationalsozialismus.* Baden-Baden: Nomos, 1990. VII, 254 pp. (Nomos-Unischriften: Recht, Bd. 6.) Bayreuth: Univ. Diss. 1989.

27310. —— WÜLLENWEBER, HANS: *Sondergerichte im Dritten Reich: vergessene Verbrechen der Justiz.* Frankfurt am Main: Luchterhand-Literaturverl., 1990. 1 vol. [Refers also to trials of Jews.]

27311. KARLSTADT. GEHRING, ANDREA: *Die Karlstadter Juden unter dem Hakenkreuz. Analyse einer antisemitischen Politik: seine Auswirkungen und Folgen auf das Leben der Juden Karlstadts.* 2. Aufl. Karlstadt: Volkshochschule, 1985. 36, [15] pp., illus. (Beiträge zur Geschichte der Stadt Karlstadt und des Umlandes, H. 8.)

27312. KATER, MICHAEL H.: *Doctors under Hitler.* Chapel Hill: Univ. of North Carolina Press, 1990. XII, 426 pp., tabs., bibl. [Incl. doctors who participated in Nazi atrocities, also discusses the persecution of Jewish physicians.]

27313. KELMAN, SIDNEY: *Limits of consensus: unions and the Holocaust.* [In]: American Jewish History, Vol. 79, No. 3, Waltham, Ma., Spring 1990. Pp. 314–335. [On the response of American trade unions to Nazi Germany's treatment of the Jews, the boycott of German goods, their anti-Nazi statements, but also their unwillingness to help Jewish refugees.]

—— KOCHAVI, ARIEH: *British response to the involvement of the American Jewish Joint Distribution Committee in illegal Jewish immigration to Palestine.* [See No. 27370.]

—— KREISSLER, FRANÇOISE: *Fluchtpunkt Shanghai.* [See No. 27115.]

27314. KRONBERG (Hesse). KOPPER, CHRISTOPHER: *Das Hakenkreuz auf der Kornberger Burg.* Dortmund: Busche, 1990. 220 pp., bibl. (Incl. chap. on the persecution of Jews (213–220).]

27315. KULKA, ERICH: *Escape from a death train.* 1–2. [In]: Review of the Society for the History of Czechoslovak Jews, Vol. 1–2, New York, 1987 & 1989. pp. 179–202; 157–204.

27316. KULKA, OTTO DOV/MENDES-FLOHR, PAUL R., eds.: *Judaism and Christianity under the impact of National Socialism 1919–1945.* Jerusalem: The Historical Society of Israel, 1987. [For details and contents see No.23888/YB XXX.] Review: (Moshe Zimmermann) [in]: Historische Zeitschrift, Bd. 251, H. 1, München 1990. Pp. 206–209.]

27317. KUSHNER, TONY: *Politics and race, gender and class: refugees, fascists, and domestic service in Britain, 1933–1940.* [In]: Immigrants & Minorities, Vol. 8, Nos. 1–2, London, March 1989. Pp. 49–58. [Compares the role of Jewish refugee women who worked as domestic servants with that of women in the British Union of Fascists who were often recruited from the servant class.]

27318. LEE, BARBARA: *Heroic and shameful behavior in the Nazi concentration camp.* [In]: Journal of Psychology and Judaism, Vol. 14, No. 2, New York, Summer 1990. Pp. 109–124, notes. [Research on Holocaust survivors.]

27319. LEIPZIG. DIAMANT, ADOLF: *Gestapo Leipzig: zur Geschichte einer verbrecherischen Organisation in den Jahren 1933–1945.* Frankfurt am Main (Völckerstr. 9): A. Diamant, 1990. XV, 230 pp., illus., charts., facsims., tabs, bibl.

27320. — PLOWINSKI, KERSTIN: *Gedanken zur Intelligenz jüdischer Herkunft in Leipzig – ihre Rolle in den jüdischen Vereinen nach 1933.* [In]: Nachrichtenblatt des Verbandes der Jüdischen Gemeinden in der DDR, Dresden, März 1990. Pp. 8–10.

27321. LICHTENSTEIN, HEINER: *Zwischen Anpassung und Kollaboration: ein dunkles Geschichtskapitel: die Judenräte in der Nazi-Zeit.* [In]: Tribüne, Jg. 29, H. 115, Frankfurt am Main, 1990. Pp. 81–86. [On an international conference about 'Judenräte' held by the Evangelische Akademie (Arnoldshain) in May 1990.]

27322. LIMBERG, MARGARETTE/RÜBSAAT, HUBERT, eds.: *Sie durften nicht mehr Deutsche sein: jüdischer Alltag in Selbstzeugnissen 1933–1938.* Frankfurt am Main: Campus, 1990. 386 pp. [Cf.: Immer perfider drangsaliert. Jüdische Emigrantenberichte (Cornelia Rabitz) [in]: Süddeutsche Zeitung, München, Aug. 28, 1990, p. 7.]

27323. LODZ. ADELSON, ALAN/LAPIDES, ROBERT, eds. and comps.: *Lodz ghetto: inside a community under siege.* New York: Viking, 1990. 518 pp., illus. [Many German Jews were deported to Lodz. Cf.: Diarists of destruction (David Pryce-Jones) [in]: TLS, London, April 20–26, 1990, p. 423.]

27324. — *"Unser einziger Weg ist Arbeit": das Ghetto in Lodz 1940–1944.* (Red.: Hanno Loewy und Gerhard Schoenberner). Wien: Löcker, 1990. 288 pp. [Companion volume to an exhibition of the same title at the Jüdisches Museum Frankfurt am Main. Incl. essays by Jurek Becker, Wolfgang Scheffler, Florian Freund/Bertrand Perz, Karl Stuhlpfarrer, Dan Diner, Arnold Mostowicz, Shmuel Krakowski, Hanno Loewy. Cf.: Besprechung (Ludger Heid) [in]: Das Historisch-Politische Buch, Jg. 39, H. 1, Göttingen 1991. P. 22.; On the exhibition in Frankfurt: Im amtlichen Auftrag Fotografiert (Klaus Meier-Ude) [In]: Tribüne, Jg. 29, H. 114, Frankfurt am Main, 1990. Pp. 52–59, illus.]

27325. LÖRRACH. GÖCKEL, WOLFGANG: *Lörrach im Dritten Reich.* [In]: Das Markgräflerland, H. 2, Lörrach, 1990. Pp. 31–85. [Incl. persecution of the Jews (pp. 62–70).]

27326. MAASS, HANS: *Verführung der Unschuldigen: Beispiele judenfeindlicher Kinderliteratur im 3. Reich.* Karlsruhe: Evang. Presseverband für Baden, 1990. 31 pp. (Themen und Texte, 3.)

27327. MANNHEIM. KAHN, ROBERT B., ed.: *Reflections by Jewish survivors of Nazi persecution from Mannheim, Germany.* New York: Mannheim Reunion Committee, 1990. XVIII, 198 pp.

27328. MARGALIOT, ABRAHAM: *Between rescue and annihilation: studies in the history of German Jewry.* [In Hebrew]. [Cf.: Das wissenschaftiche Vermächtnis von Abraham Margaliot (Avraham Barkai) [in]: MB, Jg. 58, Nr. 65, Tel-Aviv, Dez. 1990, p. 7.] [A. M., historian, data see No. 25631/YB XXXIV.]

27329. MARIENFELDE. FABARIUS, HANS-WERNER: *Juden in Marienfelde: Schicksale im Dritten Reich.* Hrsg. vom Gemeindekirchenrat d. Evang. Kirchengemeinde Marienfelde. Berlin: Gemeindekirchenrat d. Evang. Kirchengemeinde Marienfelde, 1990. 100 pp., illus.

27330. MARIENMÜNSTER. GROTHE, EWALD [et al.]: *Verfolgt – vergast – vergessen: zur Geschichte der Juden in den Ortschaften der Stadt Marienmünster.* Bielefeld: Verl. für Regionalgeschichte, 1990. 60 pp., illus.

27331. MENDEN. HARTUNG, KARL: *Eine Ausstellung zur Geschichte der jüdischen Gemeinde Menden 1933–1945.* [In]: Der Märker, 38, Nr. 2, Altena, Westf., 1989. Pp. 81 ff.

27332. MILTON, SYBIL: *Menschen zwischen Grenzen: die Polenausweisung 1938.* [In]: Menora, Bd. 1, München, 1990. Pp. 184–206, illus., notes.

27333. MINDEN. NORDSIEK, HANS, ed.: *'Bitte vergessen Sie uns nicht': Briefe verfolgter und deportierter Juden von 1939 bis 1944.* [In]: Mitteilungen des Mindener Geschichtsvereins, 1988. 110 pp., illus., ports., facsims., plans, notes (105–109).

27334. MORGAN, TED: *An uncertain hour: the French, the Germans, the Jews, the Klaus Barbie trial, and the city of Lyon, 1940–1945.* New York: Wiliam Morrow, 1990. 416 pp., illus., map, notes. [Author recounts his boyhood wartime experiences in Lyon, incl. the persecution of the Jews and their deportation. He returned to the city to cover the Barbie trial.]

27335. MÜHLHAUSEN an der Unstrut. Theile, Manfred: *Im Schatten des gelben Sterns: zur Erinnerung an jüdische Bürger Mühlhausens.* Mühlhausen: Kreiskabinett für Kulturarbeit, 1990. 79 pp. [Cf.: Besprechung (Renate Kirchner) [In]: Nachrichtenblatt des Verbandes der Jüdischen Gemeinden in der DDR, Dresden, Sept., 1990., p. 28.]

27336. Müller, Wolfgang: *Moritz Rülf – ein jüdischer Lehrer in schwerer Zeit.* [In]: Opfer und Täter. Zum nationalsozialistischen und antijüdischen Alltag in Ostwestfalen-Lippe. Hrsg. von Hubert Frankemölle. [See No. 27710.] [M. R., Nov. 16, 1888, Kirchhain, deported in 1942, place and time of death unknown, teacher, 'Prediger' in Detmold from 1914 until 1937, director of the Israelitisches Kinderheim in Cologne from 1938 until 1942.]

27337. *'Mut zur Menschlichkeit'. Hilfe für Verfolgte 1933 bis 1945.* Presseecho: Berichte, Interviews. Pulheim: Landschaftsverband Rheinland, 1990. 153 pp., illus. [Mimeog. radio and newspaper reports of a conference organised by Günter B. Ginzel for the Forschungsprojekt 'Unbesungene Helden' and Landschaftsverband Rheinland at the Abtei Brauweiler (nr. Cologne) in October 1990. First international conference dealing with non-Jews individually aiding Jews in Nazi Germany.] [See also No. 27259.]

27338. Nelson, Burton F., ed.: *The Holocaust and the German church struggle.* San Francisco: The Edwin Mellen Press, 1990. 327 pp.

NOVEMBER POGROM 1938

—— — AMBERG. Laschinger, Johannes: *Judenpogrom in Weiden und Amberg 1938.* [See No. 27359.]

27339. — ARNSBERG. Sauer, Werner: *Die 'Reichskristallnacht' in Arnsberg, Neheim und Hüsten.* [In]: Das Hakenkreuz im Sauerland. Schmallenberg-Holthausen: Schieferbergbau-Heimatmuseum, 1988. Pp. 135–140. illus.

27340. — ASCHAFFENBURG. Körner, Peter: *Der Novemberpogrom 1938 in Aschaffenburg: ein Forschungsbericht.* [In]: Mitteilungen aus dem Stadt- und Stiftsarchiv Aschaffenburg, 2, Aschaffenburg, 1988. Pp. 170 ff.

27341. — — Spies, Hans-Bernd: *Die Reichskristallnacht im Spiegel der Aschaffenburger Presse.* [In]: Mitteilungen aus dem Stadt- und Stiftsarchiv Aschaffenburg, 2, Aschaffenburg, 1988. Pp. 192 ff.

27342. — BAVARIA. *Kristallnacht in Bayern: der Judenpogrom am 9. November 1938.* Eine Dokumentation. Hrsg. von Friedrich Kraft. München: Claudius Verl., 1988. 151 pp. (Sonntagsblatt Taschenbuch.)

27343. — BAYREUTH. *'Reichskristallnacht': das Schicksal unserer jüdischen Mitbürger.* Eine Gedenkschrift der Stadt Bayreuth von Sylvia Habermann [et al.] (2. überarb Aufl.) Bayreuth: Stadt Bayreuth, 1989. 50 pp., illus

27344. — Becker, Franziska/Jeggle, Utz: *Memory and violence: local recollections of Jewish persecution during the 'Reichskristallnacht'.* [In]: Yad Vashem Studies, 20, Jerusalem, 1990. Pp. 99–114. [For German orig. see pp 91–102 in No. 26912/YB XXXV.]

—— — BRUNSWICK. Küssner, Dietrich: *Die Pogromnacht im Braunschweiger Land.* [See No. 27219.]

27345. — Döscher, Hans-Jürgen: *Der Tod vom Raths und die Auslösung der Pogrome am 9. November 1938 – ein Nachwort zur 'Reichskristallnacht'.* [In]: Geschichte in Wissenschaft und Unterricht, H. 10, Seelze, 1990. Pp. 619–620, notes.

27346. — Döscher, Hans-Jürgen: *Zur Genesis der Pogrome am 9. November 1938. Ein Nachwort zur 'Reichskristallnacht'.* [In]: Zeitgeschichte 17, Wien 1990. Pp. 272–274.

27347. — ERLANGEN. *Juden und Judenpogrom 1938 in Erlangen.* Hrsg.: Stadtmuseum Erlangen. Red.: Christoph Friederich; Text: Ilse Sponsel; Mitarb.: Birke Griesshammer [et al.]. Erlangen, 1990. 101 pp. illus. (Veröffentlichung des Stadtmuseums Erlangen, 40.) [Revised and enlarged documentation for exhibition of the same title, shown at the Stadmuseum Erlangen in 1988.]

27348. — LIPPE. Bödeker, H./Furh, Kar: *Leben und Leiden der Juden in Lippe: zum Gedenken des 50. Jahrestages der Synagogenbrände in der Nacht vom 9. zum 10. November 1938.* [In]: Heimatland Lippe, 81 (1988). Pp. 290–298, illus.

27349. — Messmer, Willy, ed.: *Wir müssen jeden Tag sprechen . . .: die Reichspogromnacht und die Gedenkfeiern im Rückblick.* Mit einem beitrag von Margret u. Manuel Ruep. Östringen: Verl. der Jugendwerkstatt, 1990. 136 pp. illus.

27350.　— MIDDENDORF, WOLF: *Die 'Reichskristallnacht' in historischer und kriminologischer Sicht.* [In]: Zeitschrift des Breisgau-Geschichtsvereins, 107, Freiburg i. Br., 1988. Pp. 227–245.

27351.　— PEHLE, WALTER H, ed.: *November 1938: from 'Reichskristallnacht' to genocide.* Transl. by William Templer. Oxford: Berg, 1990. Ca. 265 pp, illus., ports. facsims., bibl. [For orig. German edn. and cont. see No. 25460/YB XXXIV.]

27352.　— RECKLINGHAUSEN. MÖLLERS, GEORG: *Pogrom am Polizeipräsidium: der 9./10. Nov. 1938 in Rechlinghausen.* [In]: Vestischer Kalender 60, 1989 (1988), Pp. 24–35, illus.

27353.　— RUHR. *'Kristallnacht im Ruhrgebiet': Dokumentierende Ausstellung.* Regional- und kirchenge- schichtliche Einblicke in den antisemitischen Alltag. Hrsg.: Verein zur Erforschung der Kirchen- und Religionsgeschichte des Ruhrgebiets e. V. Bochum: 1988. 79 pp., illus., facsims., bibl. [Obtainable through Ruhr-Universität Bochum, Abt. für Ev. Theologie, Postfach 150, 4630 Bochum 1.]

27354.　— SCHMALLENBERG. WIEGEL, JOSEF: *1938 – das Schicksalsjahr der deutschen Juden: 'Arisierung' und Novemberpogrom in Schmallenberg.* [In]: Das Hakenkreuz im Sauerland. Schmallenberg-Holthausen: Schieferbergbau-Heimatmuseum, 1988. pp. 119–134, illus.

27355.　— STRAUSS, HERBERT A.: *The drive for war and the Pogroms of 1939–testing explanatory models.* [In]: LBI Year Book XXXV, London, 1990. Pp 267–278, notes.

27356.　— TÖDT, HEINZ EDUARD: *Die Novemberverbrechen 1938 und der deutsche Protestantismus: ideologische und theologische Voraussetzungen für die Hinnahme des Pogroms.* [In]: Kirchliche Zeitgeschichte, 2, Göttingen, 1989. Pp. 14–37.

27357.　— VOLKOV, SHULAMIT: *The "Kristallnacht" in context — a view from Palestine.* [In]: LBI Year Book XXXV, London 1990. Pp. 279–296, notes.

27358.　— VREDEN. KREMER, GEORG: *Erinnerungen an die Pogromnacht 1938 in Vreden* [In]: Unsere Heimat (Borken), 1988. pp. 258–260.

27359.　— WEIDEN. LASCHINGER, JOHANNES: *Judenpogrom in Weiden und Amberg 1938.* [In]: Verhandlungen des Historischen Vereins für Oberpfalz und Regensburg, 128 (1988). Pp. 185–227.

27360.　OCHTRUP. *Geschichte der Jüdischen Gemeinde Ochtrup von den Anfängen bis zur Zerstörung und Vernichtung.* (Ausstellung 'Die Jüdische Gemeinde in Ochtrup vom Beginn bis zum Untergang' im Rahmen der Woche der Brüderlichkeit 1988/Arbeitsgemeinschaft Ge- schichte der Klassen 10, Jg. 1986/1987 d. Städtischen Realschule Ochtrup unter der Leitung von Gertrud Althoff). Ochtrup: Stadt Ochtrup, 1988. 148 pp., illus.

27361.　*Offene Wunden – brennende Fragen: Juden in Deutschland von 1938 bis heute.* Hrsg. von Günter Gorschenek und Stephan Reimers. Frankfurt am Main: Knecht, 1989. 174 pp.

27362.　PADERBORN. NAARMANN, MARGIT: *Christliches Kloster und Jüdisches Waisenhaus in Paderborn.* [In]: Opfer und Täter: zum nationalsozialistischen und antijüdischen Alltag in Ostwestfa- len-Lippe. Hrsg. von Hubert Franklemölle. (Im Auftrag der Gesellschaft für Christlich- Jüdische Zusammenarbeit, Paderborn.) Bielefeld: Verlag für Regionalgeschichte 1990. Pp. 87–116 [See No. 27410.]

27363.　PAEPCKE, LOTTE: *Ein kleiner Händler der mein Vater war.* Baden-Baden: Elster, 1989. 109 pp. [Personal account of the persecution in Freiburg i. Br. during the Nazi period, first publ. 1972.]

27364.　PAEPCKE, LOTTE: *Unter einem fremden Stern: ('Ich wurde vergessen').* Mit einem Nachwort 'Über die menschliche Würde und das Jude-Sein'. Moos; Baden-Baden: Elster, 1989. 139 pp. [Autobiographical account 1942–1945, first publ. 1952.] [L.P., born 1910 in Freiburg i. Br., married to a non-Jew, survived the Nazi period in Germany, now living in Karlsruhe.]

——　PALATINATE [See No. 27199.]

27365.　POHL, DIETER. *Polen und Juden unter deutscher Besatzung 1939–1945: zu einigen Neuerscheinungen.* [In]: Jahrbücher f. Geschichte Osteuropas 38, H. 2, Wiesbaden, 1990. Pp. 255–257, notes.

27366.　RED CROSS. BEN-TOV, ARIEH: *Das Rote Kreuz kam zu spät: die Auseinandersetzung zwischen dem jüdischen Volk und dem Internationlen Komitee vom Roten Kreuz im Zweiten Weltkrieg.* Zürich: Ammann, 1990. 511 pp. [Transl. of 'Facing the Holocaust in Budapest', see No. 25340/YB XXXIV.]

——　REFUGEE POLICY: [See also Nos. 27302 and 27404.]

27367.　— ANDERL, GABRIELE: *Statt Palästina Fluchpunkt Mauritius.* [In]: Aufbau, 56, No. 24, New York, Nov. 23, 1990. P. 16–17, 20, illus. [Final article of a five-part series on Jewish refugees from Czechoslovakia and Austria in Mauritius.]

27368.　— ARONSFELD, C. C.: *Unwelcome.* [In]: The Jewish Quarterly, Vol. 37 (137), London, Spring 1990. Pp. 43–45. [Deals with the lack of help that many countries showed to German-Jewish and other refugees from Nazi Germany. Author recounts his own experiences when coming to England in 1933.]

27369. — BERGHUIS, CORRIE K.: *Joodse vluchtelinge in Nederland 1938–1940.* Documenten betreffende toelating, uitleiding en kampopname. Met voorwoord van Dick Houwaart. Kok: Kampen, 1990. 240 pp., illus., facsims., notes (174–212), index of persons. [Cont. numerous Dutch documents related to refugee policy; also on the Jewish refugees from Nazi Germany who escaped to the Netherlands after the November Pogrom.]

27370. — KOCHAVI, ARIEH: *British response to the involvement of the American Jewish Joint Distribution Committee in illegal Jewish immigration to Palestine.* [In]: Immigrants and Minorities, Vol. 8, No. 3, London, Nov. 1989. Pp. 223–234, notes. [Incl. refugees from Austria and Germany.]

27371. — KONOVITCH, BARRY J.: *The fiftieth anniversary of the St. Louis: what really happened.* [In]: American Jewish History, Vol. 79, No. 2, Waltham, Ma., Winter 1989/1990. Pp. 203–209. [The story of the liner St. Louis which started from Hamburg in 1939 with 937 Jewish refugees and was refused permission to land in U.S., returned to Germany where most of the passengers eventually perished.]

———— — LIPMAN, V. D.: *A history of the Jews in Britain since 1858.* [See No. 27150.]

27372. — LOEBL, HERBERT: *Das Refugee Industries Committee: eine wenig bekannte britische Hilfsorganisation.* [In]: Exilforschung. Ein internationales Jahrbuch. Bd. 8: Politische Aspekte des Exils. Hrsg. von Thomas Koebner [et al.]. München: edition text und kritik, 1990. pp. 220–241, notes.

27373. — MULDER, DIRK/PRINSEN, BEN, ed.: *Uitgeweken: de voorgeschiedenis van kamp Westerbork.* Hooghalen: Herinnerungscentrum Kamp Westerbork, 1989. 116 pp., illus., bibl. (Herinnerungscentrum Kamp Westerbork: Historische reeks, 1.) [Collection of 8 essays, refers also to German-Jewish refugees.]

27374. — OFER, DALIA: *Personal letters in research and education on the Holocaust.* [In]: Holocaust and Genocide Studies, Vol. 4, No. 3, Oxford, 1989. pp. 341–355. [A case study on a group of German and Austrian-Jewish refugees stranded in Yugoslavia in 1939–1941.]

27375. — SCHMID, KLAUS-PETER: *Gefangen in der zweiten Heimat: Internierungslager – noch immer ein grosses deutsch-französisches Tabu.* [In]: Die Zeit, Nr. 22, Hamburg, 25. Mai 1990. Pp. 47–48, ports.

27376. — SNOEK, J. M.: *Die Nederlandse kerken en de Joden 1940–1945.* Kok: Kampen, 1990. 149 pp., illus. [Incl. the reaction of the church to Nazi antisemitism, and its attitude towards German-Jewish refugees.]

27377. — STRANGE, JOAN: *Despatches from the home front: the war diaries of Joan Strange 1939–1945.* Ed. by Chris McCooey. Eastbourne, Sussex (1 St. Anne's Road): Monarch, 1990 [1989]. 178 pp. [Joan Strange, a physiotherapist from Worthing, extended help to German- and Austrian-Jewish refugees.]

27378. — WEBSTER, PAUL: *Pétain's crime: the full story of French collaboration in the Holocaust.* London: Macmillan, 1990. 300 pp., illus., ports. [Incl. deportation of German-Jewish refugees from France. Cf.: The French Holocaust (Frederic Raphael) [in]: The Sunday Times, London, July 1, 1990.]

27379. REGENSBURG. WITTMER, S.: *Geschichte der Regensburger Juden von 1939 bis 1945.* [In]: Verhandlungen des Historischen Vereins d. Oberpfalz und Regensburg 129, (1989). Pp. 77–137. [Sequel to Nos. 25111/YB XXXIV; 26085/YB XXXV.]

———— RESISTANCE BY NON-JEWS. JOCHHEIM, GERNOT: *Protest in der Rosenstrasse.* [See No. 27207.]

27380. — SAHM, ULRICH: Rudolf von Scheliha 1897–1942: *ein deutscher Diplomat gegen Hitler.* München: Beck, 1990. 320 pp. [R.v. Scheliha informed the Swiss Carl Jacob Burckhardt of the Nazis' intention to murder the Jews.]

27381. RIEDSTADT. *Zum Beispiel Judenverfolgung: von der Entrechtung zum Völkermord: das Schicksal der jüdischen Gemeinden in Riedstadt.* (Autoren: Jugendgruppe der Jugendpflege Riedstadt & Jugendbildungswerk Gross-Gerau.) Gross-Gerau: Landratsamt, 1988. 53 pp.

27382. RÖHM, EBERHARD/THIERFELDER, JÖRG: *Juden, Christen, Deutsche: 1933–1945.* Bd. 1: 1933 bis 1935. Stuttgart: Calwer Verl., 1990. 451 pp.

———— RUHR. [See No. 27353.]

27383. SALZKOTTEN. WACKER, BERND/WACKER, MARIE-THERES: *. . . verfolgt, verjagt, deportiert: Juden in Salzkotten 1933–1942:* eine Dokumentation aus Anlaß d. 50. Jahrestages d. 'Reichskristallnacht' vom 9./10.11.1938. Hrsg. vom Arbeitskreis 'Juden in Salzkotten'. Salzkotten: Arbeitskreis 'Juden in Salzkotten', 1988. 188 & 33 pp., illus.

27384. SAMSON, META: *Spatz macht sich.* Hrsg. von Walter Lindenberg mit Illus. von Renate Schirrow. Berlin: Altberliner Verlag, 1990. 168 pp. [Meta Samson, a kindergarten nurse, wrote this story for her daughter during the Nazi period; printed in 1938 but not distributed, it now appears for the first time; a book for young readers.] [Meta and Marlene Samson were deported to Auschwitz in 1942.]

27385. SCHEURENBERG, KLAUS: *Überleben: Flucht- und andere Geschichten aus der Verfolgungszeit des Naziregimes.* Hrsg. von der Bruno- und Else-Voigt Stiftung. Red.: Kurt Schilde. Berlin: Edition Hentrich, 1990. 63 pp. (Stätten der Geschichte Berlins, Bd. 48.) [Author, who survived Theresienstadt and Wulkow/Sachsenhausen, describes experiences of young German Jews who successfully escaped from various concentration camps.] [K.Sch. died June 14, 1990 in Berlin at the age of 64, active member of the post-war Berlin Jewish Community; for his autobiography see No. 19071/YB XXVIII.]

27386. SCHLEUNES, KARL A.: *The twisted road to Auschwitz: Nazi policy towards German Jews.* With a new foreword by Hans Mommsen and an updated bibliographic essay by the author. Champaign: Univ. of Illinois Press, 1990. 290 pp. [Expanded paperback edn. of No. 9400/ YB XVII.]

27387. SCHMITT, HANS A.: *Lucky victim: an ordinary life in extraordinary times, 1933–1946.* Baton Rouge: Lousiana State Univ. Press, 1989. 254 pp., illus. [Author's experiences growing up as a 'Mischling' in Nazi Germany. Educated in Holland and England; later emigrated to America where he was reunited with surviving members of his family.]

—— SCHOEPS, JULIUS H.: *Leiden an Deutschland: vom antisemitischen Wahn und der Last der Erinnerung.* [See No. 26960.]

27388. SCHWARBERG, GÜNTHER: *Das Getto.* Göttingen: Steidl, 1989. 216, [6] pp., illus., plan, index of names. (Sonderheft für die Aktion Sühnezeichen/Friedensdienste.) [On Warsaw Ghetto.]

27389. *Schwestern, vergesst uns nicht: Frauen im Konzentrationslager: Moringen, Lichtenburg, Ravensbrück, 1933–1945.* Katalog zur Austellung: Frauen im Konzentrationlager (Bearb.: Barbara Bromberger). Frankfurt am Main: VAS, Verl. für Akad. Schriften, 1988. 106 pp., illus.

27390. SILESIA. KOWALSKY, INGE: *Oberschlesische Wurzeln: schlesisches Schicksal: eine Familie zwischen Kreuz und Davidstern.* Dülmen: Oberschlesicher Heimatverlag, 1986. 166, [18] pp., illus.

27391. SREBRNIK, HENRY: *The British Communist Party's national Jewish committee and the fight against anti-Semitism during the second World War.* [In]: Immigrants and Minorities, Vol. 8, Nos. 1–2, London, March 1989. Pp. 82–96, notes. [Incl. efforts on behalf of Jewish refugees and against the government's internment policy.]

27392. STEINDLING, 'DOLLY': *Vienna-France-Vienna: the story of a Jewish refugee and resistance fighter.* [In Hebrew, title transl.]. Ed. by Haim Avni. Transl. from the German manuscript by Bracha Freundlich. Jerusalem: Rubin Mass and the Institute of Contemporary Jewry, Hebrew University, 1989. 194 pp. [Autobiography, written during 1978–1980]. ['Dolly' Steindling, orig. Aharon Adolf, 1918 Wiener Neustadt – 1983 Vienna, escaped to France during the war; fought with the Resistance.]

27393. STOOP, PAUL, ed.: *Geheimberichte aus dem Dritten Reich 1933–1935: der Journalist H. J. Noordewier als politischer Beobachter.* Berlin: Argon, 1990. 235 pp. [Refers also to discrimination against Jews.]

27394. STORFER, BERTHOLD. ZARIZ, RUTH: *The riddle of the man who helped the devil.* [In Hebrew, title transl.]. [In]: Eit-mol, No. 93, Tel-Aviv, Oct. 1990. Pp. 9–11. [On B.S., Viennese financier, Jewish representative at Evian, director of the Overseas Emigration Bureau.]

27395. STRUM, HARVEY: *Jewish internees in the American South, 1942–1945.* [In]: American Jewish Archives, Vol. 42, No. 1, Spring/Summer 1990. Pp. 27–48, notes. [Incl. German and Austrian Jews who had escaped to Panama and were deported to the States and interned in camps in Florida, Georgia and Texas. Also deals with the State Department's attitude towards these refugees.]

27396. SWEENEY, ROBERT F.: *Where were the lawyers? German justice 1935–1945.* Baltimore: Hebrew University (Park Height Ave., Baltimore 21215), 1990. 12 pp. [Deals with the Nazi perversion of justice in regard to the Holocaust. First given as Yom Hashoah lecture, April 22, 1990.]

27397. SWITZERLAND. DIETZ, EDITH: *Den Nazis entronnen: die Flucht eines jüdischen Mädchens in die Schweiz.* Atuobiographischer Bericht 1933–1942. Vorwort von Micha Brumlik. Frankfurt am Main: dipa, 1990. 131 pp.

27398. THERESIENSTADT. BEN-ZION, SHMUEL: *Musy's train:* The negotiations with Heinrich

Himmler through the mediation of Dr. Jean-Marie Musy in order to rescue Jews from the concentration camps in Germany (autumn 1944–spring 1945). [In Hebrew, title transl.]. [In]: Dappim le-Cheker Tekufat ha-Shoah (Studies on the Holocaust Period), Vol. 8, Haifa, 1990. Pp. 135–163. [About a train with 1210 Jews from Theresienstadt which arrived at Kreuzlingen on February 7, 1945 thanks to efforts of J. M. Musy, Alt-Bundesrat of Switzerland.]

27399. — BONDY, RUTH: *'Elder of the Jews': Jacob Edelstein of Theresienstadt.* Transl. from the Hebrew by Evelyn Abel. New York: Grove Press, 1989. XIV, 476 pp., illus., ports., facsims., map, plan, bibl. [For Hebrew orig. and data on Jakob Edelstein, the first appointed 'Judenältester' in Theresienstadt, see No. 18153/YB XXVII.]

27400. — FRIESOVA, JANA RENEE: *The 'Girls Home' in Terezín.* [In]: Review of the Society for the History of Czechoslovak Jews, Vol. 2, New York, 1989. Pp. 13–24.

27401. — GROSSMAN, FRANCES GAEZER: *The art of the children of Terezín: a psychological study.* [In]: Holocaust and Genocide Studies, Vol. 4, No. 2, Oxford, 1989. Pp. 213–230.

27402. — NIETHAMMER, LUTZ: *Widerstand des Gesichts? Beobachtungen an dem Filmfragment 'Der Führer schenkt den Juden eine Stadt'.* [In]: Journal für Geschichte, 1989, H. 2, Weinheim, 1989. Pp. 34–47.

—— *Der Tod ist ein Meister aus Deutschland.* [See No. 27305.]

27403. TOUSSAINT, INGO, ed.: *Die Universitätsbibliotheken Heidelberg, Jena und Köln unter dem Nationalsozialismus.* München: New York: Saur, 1989. 406 pp. (Beiträge zur Bibliothekstheorie und Bibliotheksgeschichte, Bd. 2.) [Incl. boycott of Jewish booksellers, exclusion of Jewish library users, taking over of Jewish private libraries, removal of banned literature.]

27404. TURNER, BARRY: *. . . And the policeman smiled: ten thousand children escape from Nazi Germany.* London: Bloomsbury, 1990. VII, 292 pp., illus., bibl. (282–283). [On the 'Kindertransporte' organised by the Refugee Children's Movement of the Central British Fund which rescued German-Jewish and Austrian-Jewish children.]

27405. UNGER, ALFRED: *Als der Kulturbund zum Politbund wurde.* [In]: europäische ideen, Heft 71, Berlin, 1989. Pp. 20–24. [On the founding of the literary émigrés' 'Club 43' in London, which split away in protest from the Communist-dominated 'Kulturbund'. 'Club 43' consisted mainly of German- and Austrian-Jewish émigrés.]

27406. VECHTA. SCHIECKEL, HARALD/SIEVE, PETER: *Die Juden in Vechta: das Schicksal der Vechtaer Juden im Dritten Reich.* [In]: Beiträge zur Geschichte der Stadt Vechta. Vechta, 1988. Pp. 95–122, XII pp. of illus. [Incl. facsims., plan, ports.], bibl.

27407. *Verfolgung und Widerstand: Acta Ising 1988.* Hrsg.: Helmut Kreuzer und Dieter Zerlin (im Auftrag des Bayer. Staatsministeriums für Unterricht und Kultus.) München: Baer. Schulbuch-Verl., 1989. 112 pp., bibl. (Dialog Schule-Wissenschaft: Deutsch und Geschichte.) [Deals also with Nazi persecution of Jews.]

27408. WALKER, MARK: *German National Socialism and the quest for nuclear power 1939–1949.* Cambridge; New York: Cambridge Univ. Press, 1989. 290 pp., diagrs., notes (234–264), bibl. (268–283). [Incl. the exclusion of Jewish scientists and their work, particularly Einstein; also on Heisenberg's antisemitism.]

27409. WESTPHALIA. ASCHOFF, DIETHARD: *Holocaust in Augenzeugenberichten westfälischer Juden.* [And]: Unveröffentlichte jüdische Erinnerungen. [In]: Westfälische Forschungen, Bd. 38, Münster, 1988. Pp. 244–256; 257 ff.

27410. — *Opfer und Täter. Zum nationalsozialistischen und antijüdischen Alltag in Ostwestfalen-Lippe.* Hrsg. von Hubert Frankemölle. (Im Auftrag der Gesellschaft für Christlich-Jüdische Zusammenarbeit, Paderborn.) Bielefeld: Verlag für Regionalgeschichte 1990. 248 pp., illus. [Incl.: 'Das hat mir sehr weh getan'. Jüdische Jugend in Ostwestfalen-Lippe, Streiflichter 1933–1939. (Joachim Meynert, pp. 54–71, notes). Further contrib. are listed according to subject. Cf.: Unter den langen Schatten der NS-Zeit. [in]: 'Allgemeine', Nr. 46/6, Bonn, 21. Feb 1991. P. 9.]

27411. WIESBADEN. BEMBENEK, LOTHAR/ULRICH, AXEL: *Widerstand und Verfolgung in Wiesbaden 1933–1945.* Eine Dokumentation. Hrsg. vom Magistrat der Landeshauptstadt Wiesbaden, Stadtarchiv. Gießen: Anabas Verl., 1990. 456 pp., illus., notes, index of names. [Incl. a chap on discrimination against and persecution of the Jews, November Pogrom 1938, deportation (Pp. 274–312, ports.)]

27412. WILDUNGEN. GRÖTECKE, JOHANNES: *Bad Wildunger Juden und ihre Schicksale 1933 bis 1945.* [In]: Geschichtsblätter für Waldeck, 77, Arolsen, 1989. pp. 245–275.

27413. WOLF, KARLA: *Ich blieb zurück: die Überlebensgeschichte der Tochter einer christlichen Mutter und eines jüdischen Vaters im Nazideutschland und ihr Neuanfang in Israel.* Heppenheim: Evangelischer Arbeitskreis Kirche und Israel in Hessen und Nassau, 1990. 64 pp.

—— WÜRTTEMBERG. WETTERICH, SUSANNE: *Davids Stern an Rhein und Neckar.* [See No. 26989].

—— — GERBER, BARBARA: Jud Süß: *Aufstieg und Fall im frühen 18. Jahrhundert.* [See No. 27858.]

27414. ZEHDEN, WERNER A.: *Stacheldraht: ein Tagebuch.* Mit einer Einführung von Peter Steinbach. Passau (Neuburger Str. 106): Wissenschaftsverl. R. Rothe, 1990. 60 pp. (Kleine Rothe-Reihe, Bd. 2) [Autobiographical account of the author's committal to forced labour during 1944/1945 in Thuringia, how he survived and returned to Berlin.] [W.A.Z., born May 2, 1911, son of the lawyer Alfred Zehden and his non-Jewish wife.]

B. Jewish Resistance

—— CARLEBACH, JOSEPH. *1883–1942. Jüdischer Alltag als humaner Widerstand.* [See No. 27260].

—— DE CORT, BART: *'Was ich will, soll Tat werden'. Erich Kuttner 1887–1942: ein Leben für Freiheit und Recht.* [See No. 27710.]

27415. DIESENER, GERALD: *Friedrich Wolf und das Nationalkomitee "Freies Deutschland".* [In]: Zeitschrift für Geschichtswissenschaft, No. 8, 38, Berlin 1990. Pp. 689–699, notes. (Erweiterte Fassung eines Vortrags anläßlich des 100. Geburtstages von F.W. im Dez. 1988 in Neuwied.) [F.W., born 1888 in Neuwied, died 1953 in Berlin (East), Communist, physician, dramatist, writer.]

—— ELSAS, FRITZ: *Auf dem Stuttgarter Rathaus 1915–1922: Erinnerungen.* [See No. 27769.]

27416. GELBER, YOAV: *Central European and Austrian Jews from Palestine in the British forces.* [In]: LBI Year Book XXXV, London, 1990. Pp. 321–332, illus., notes.

27417. *Germans against Nazism: nonconformity, opposition and resistance in the Third Reich.* (Essays in honour of Peter Hofmann). Ed. by Francis R. Nicosia and Lawrence Stokes. New York; Oxford: Berg, 1990. XIV, 435 pp., illus., bibl., index. [Individual contributions are listed according to subjects.]

27418. JONCA, KAROL: *Jewish resistance to Nazi racial legislation in Silesia, 1933–1937.* [In]: Germans against Nazism: nonconformity, opposition and resistance in the Third Reich. [See No. 27417.]

27419. LUSTIGER, ARNO: *German and Austrian Jews in the International Brigade.* [In]: LBI Year Book XXXV, London, 1990. pp. 297–320, illus., ports., notes.

27420. MORAIS, FERNANDO: *Olga – the 'gift' to Hitler.* Transl. by Ellen Watson. London: Halban, 1990. 245 pp., illus., (124 plates) ports., facsims [Story of the German-Jewish Communist activist, Olga Benario, murdered in Ravensbrück in 1942.]

—— PAUCKER, ARNOLD: *Self-defence against fascism in a middle-class community: the Jews in Weimar Germany and beyond.* [See No. 27417.]

27421. PAUCKER, ARNOLD: *Jüdischer Widerstand in Deutschland: Tatsachen und Problemtik.* Überarbeiteter Text des am 3. November 1988 gehaltenen Vortrags in der Gedenkstätte deutscher Widerstand. [In]: deutschland-berichte, Jg. 26, Nr. 6, Bonn, Juni 1990. Pp. 25–35, notes (33–35). [Orig. publ. 1989, see No. 26554/YB XXXV.] [Reviews: Aufklärung gegen eine Legende (Otto Gritschneder) [in]: Der Landesverband der Israelit. Kultusgemeinden in Bayern, 43, Juni 1990 [& in]: Süddeutsche Zeitung, Nr. 133, München, 12. Juni 1990, p. 12. Besprechung (K. Nürnberg) [in]: MB, Jg. 58, Nr. 59, Tel-Aviv, Juni 1990, p. 7.]

27422. STEINBACH, PETER: *Widerstand gegen den Nationalsozialismus aus dem Exil? Zur politischen und räumlichen Struktur der deutschen Emigration 1933–1945.* [In]: Geschichte in Wissenschaft und Unterricht, H. 10, Stuttgart, 1990. Pp. 578–606, notes. [Also on Jewish refugees from Germany and Austria.]

—— STEINDLING, 'DOLLY': *Vienna-France-Vienna: the story of a Jewish refugee and resistance fighter* [In Hebrew, title transl.]. [See No. 27392.]

27423. WILHELMUS, W.: *Das Schicksal der jüdischen Kommunistin Adele Schiffmann.* [In]: Beiträge zur Geschichte d. Arbeiterbewegung, Jg. 32. Berlin (1990). Pp. 220–229.

Due to the wealth of studies in the history of German-speaking Jewry published in 1990, all the following sections have to be drastically curtailed – (Ed.).

IV. POST WAR

A. General

27424. ADELSON, LESLIE A.: *There's no place like home: Jeanette Lander and Ronnit Neumann's utopian quests for Jewish identity in the contemporary West German context.* [In]: new german critique, No. 50, Ithaca, N.Y., Spring/Summer 1990. Pp. 113–134, notes.

27425. *Antisemitismus in der politischen Kultur nach 1945.* Hrsg. von Werner Bergmann und Rainer Erb. Opladen: Westdt. Verl., 1990. 348 pp., bibl.

—— AUSTRIA. BECKERMANN, RUTH: *Illusionen und Kompromissee: zur Identität der Wiener Juden nach 1945.* [See No. 27115.]

—— — CLARE, GEORGE: *Letzter Walzer in Wien – ein Nachtrag.* [See No. 27115.]

27426. — KAINDL-WIDHALM, BARBARA: *Demokraten wider Willen? Autoritäre Tendenzen und Antisemitismus in der 2. Republik.* (Hrsg. vom Verein Krit. Sozialwissenschaft u. Polit. Bildung). Wien: Verl. f. Gesellschaftskritik, 1990. 231 pp., tabs. bibl. (225–231) (Österr. Texte zur Gesellschaftskritik, 40.)

27427. BENZ, WOLFGANG, ed.: *Legenden – Lügen – Vorurteile: Ein Lexikon zur Zeitgeschichte.* München-Gräfelfing: Moos & Partner, 1990. 222 pp. [Cf: Legenden – Lügen – Vorurteile (Georg Schwinghammer) [in]: Tribüne, Jg. 29, H. 116, Frankfurt am Main, 1990, pp. 190–191; Besprechung (Michael Salewski) [in]: Das Historisch-Politische Buch, Jg. 39, H. 2, Göttingen, 1991, p. 56.] [Lists and refutes the standard calumnies and prejudices of right-radical propagandists.]

27428. BAUMANN, ZYGMUNT: *Modernity and the Holocaust.* Cambridge: Polity Press, 1989. Pp. 224. [Cf.: Sociology, History and the Holocaust (Ivar Oxaal) [in]: Theory, Culture and Society, Vol. 8, London: Sage, 1991, pp. 153–166.]

—— BERGMANN, WERNER/ERB, RAINER, eds. *Antisemitismus in der politischen Kultur nach 1945.* [Refers to both parts of Germany and Austria] [See No. 27855.]

27429. BODEMANN, Y. MICHAL/OSTOW, ROBIN: *Federal Republic of Germany & German Democratic Republic.* [Report]. [In]: American Jewish Yearbook 1990, Vol.90, New York 1990. Pp. 356–370; 371–377 [Incl. Werner Nachmann scandal; Jenninger speech.]

27430. BOECKH, WOLFGANG: *Judentum in Deutschland (Ost): eine höchst differenzierte Entwicklung nach der politischen 'Wende'.* [In]: Tribüne, Jg. 29, H. 115, Frankfurt am Main, 1990. Pp. 6–11.

27431. DINER, DAN: *Deutschland, die Juden und Europa: vom fortschreitenden Sieg der Vernunft über die Vergangenheit.* [In]: Babylon. Beiträge zur jüdischen Gegenwart. H. 7. Hrsg.: Micha Brumlik [et al.]. Frankfurt am Main: Verl. neue Kritik, Sept. 1990. Pp. 96–104.

27432. ELSAESSER, THOMAS: *New German cinema – a history.* New Brunswick, N. J.: Rutgers Univ. Press, 1989. XVIII, 430 pp., illus. (British Film Institute cinema series.) [Incl. chap.: The impact of 'Holocaust'; also deals in general with cinema treatment of the Nazi period.]

27433. FACKENHEIM, EMIL L.: *Germany's worst enemy.* [In]: Commentary, Vol. 90, No. 4, New York, Oct. 1990. Pp. 31–34 [Author's misgivings about German reunification in the context of German-Jewish history.]

27434. FEDERAL REPUBLIC OF GERMANY. SANTNER, ERIC L.: *Stranded objects. Mourning, memory, and film in postwar Germany.* Ithaca, N.Y.: Cornell Univ. Press, 1990. 200 pp., illus., notes (163–195). [Deals with the impact of the Holocaust on German society, and how this is reflected in the films 'Our Hitler' by Syberberg and 'Heimat' by Reitz.]

27435. — FEINBERG, ANAT: *Wende, Umbruch oder Krise? Anmerkungen zum Jüdischen Leben in der Bundesrepublik.* [In]: Tribüne, Jg. 29, H. 114, Frankfurt am Main, 1990. Pp. 135–146, notes.

27436. GERMAN DEMOCRATIC REPUBLIC. AMMER, THOMAS: *DDR und Judentum 50 Jahre nach dem Novemberpogrom.* [In]: Deutschland-Archiv, Jg. 22, Nr. 1, Köln, 1989. Pp. 17 ff.

27437. — ESCHWEGE, HELMUT: *Die erneute Vertreibung der Juden: voller Angst verliess 1952/53 ein Drittel der jüdischen Gemeindemitglieder die DDR.* [In]: Leipziger Volkszeitung, 21./22. Juli 1990. [1 p.]

27438. — ESCHWEGE, HELMUT: *Unheimliche Begegnungen der diskriminierenden Art: Historiker Eschwege berichtet von persönlichen Erfahrungen.* [In]: 'Allgemeine', Nr. 45/17, Bonn, 26. Apr. 1990. P. 11. [H. E., born 1913 in Hamburg, emigrated in 1936 via various countries to Palestine, returned to the GDR after the war.]

27439. — HESSE, REINHARD: *Die zweite Schuld der Linken: Juden und Antisemitismus in der DDR*. [In]: Trans Atlantik, Nr. 5, München, Mai 1990. Pp. 19–28.

27440. — MERTENS, LOTHAR: *Der politische Umbruch in der DDR: bemerkenswerte Stellungnahmen der jüdischen Gemeinden*. [In]: Tribüne, Jg. 29, H. 113, Frankfurt am Main, 1990. Pp. 124–132. [Deals with the role of Jewish representatives in the former German Democratic Republic; all 4 issues (Nos. 113–116) of 'Tribüne' 1990 incl. reports on Jewish life in Germany today.]

27441. HERMLE, SIEGFRIED: *Evangelische Kirche und Judentum – Stationen nach 1945*. Göttingen: Vandenhoeck & Ruprecht, 1990. 422 pp. (Arbeiten zur kirchlichen Zeitgeschichte: Reihe B, Darstellungen; Bd. 16). [Cf.: Besprechung (Armin Boyens) [in]: Das Historisch-Politische Buch, 39/3, Göttingen, 1991. Pp. 92–93.]

27441. HERMLE, SIEGFRIED: *Evangelische Kirche und Judentum – Stationen nach 1945*. Göttingen: Vandenhoeck & Ruprecht, 1990. 422 pp. (Arbeiten zur kirchlichen Zeitgeschichte: Reihe B, Darstellungen; Bd. 16). [Cf.: Besprechung (Armin Boyens) [in]: Das Historisch-Politische Buch, 39/3, Göttingen, 1991. Pp. 92–93.]

27442. HILBERG, RAUL: *The Holocaust today*. [In]: Shofar, Vol. 8, No. 2, West Lafayette, Ind., Purdue Univ., Winter 1990. Pp. 8–15. [Incl. how the Holocaust is dealt with in present-day Germany.]

27443. HOLOCAUST TRAUMA. SUSANN HEENEN-WOLFF: *Psychoanalytische Überlegungen zur Latenz der Shoah*. [In]: Babylon. Beiträge zur jüdischen Gegenwart. H. 7. Hrsg.: Micha Brumlik [et al.]. Frankfurt am Main: Verl. neue Kritik, Sept. 1990. Pp. 84–95, bibl.

27444. KAUFFMANN, STANLEY: *Germany: remembrance of things past*. [In]: Partisan Review, Vol. 57, No. 1, Boston, Winter 1990. Pp. 89–96. [S.K., journalist of German-Jewish background recalls his impressions of visit to Germany and grandfather's hometown.]

27445. MAGONET, JONATHAN: *Brotherhood week sermon*, Koblenz, March 1989. [In]: European Judaism, Vol. 23, No. 1, London, Spring 1990. Pp. 3–6. [Rabbi M. is principal of the Leo Baeck College in London.]

27446. MANKOWITZ, ZE'EV: *The affirmation of life in 'She'erith Hapleita'*. [In]: Holocaust and Genocide Studies, Vol. 5, No. 1, Oxford, 1990. Pp. 13–21. [She'erit Hapleita (The Saved Remnant), organisation of Jewish D.P.s in the British and American Zones of Germany after World War II.]

27447. MANKOWITZ, ZE'EV: *The formation of 'She'erit Hapleita': November 1944–July 1945*. [In]: Yad Vashem Studies, 20, Jerusalem, 1990. Pp. 337–370. [Deals with Buchenwald and Dachau.]

27448. NICOSIA, FRANCIS R.: *The perils of publishing: scholars and publishers: a new twist to an old story*. [In]: German History, Vol. 8, No. 2, Oxford, June 1990. Pp. 217–222. [Deals with the author's experience of having his book 'The Third Reich and the Palestine question' (see No. 26546/YB XXXV) published by the German right-wing publisher Druffel without the author's consent and his subsequent fight to have this edition removed from the German market. For an abridged version in German see: Wissenschaftlicher und Verleger, eine neue Wendung in einer alten Geschichte? [in]: Vierteljahrsschrift für Zeitgeschichte 38, München 1990. Pp. 515–518.]

27449. PROSECUTION OF NAZI CRIMES. SCHWARBERG, GÜNTHER: *Die Mörderwaschmaschine*. Göttingen: Steidl, 1990. 144 pp., illus. [On the basis of 13 cases author accuses public prosecutors of the Federal Republic of Germany of too lenient prosecution of Nazi crimes. Cf.: Besprechung (Heinz Boberach) [in]: Das Historisch-Politische Buch, Jg. 39, H.2, Göttingen 1991, p. 55.]

27450. VITAL, DAVID: *The future of the Jews*. Cambridge, Ma.: Harvard Univ. Press, 1990. 161 pp., notes. [Author argues that world Jewry is fractured and divided; incl. German Jewry, Holocaust, German restitution.]

B. **Restitution**

——— ERB, RAINER: *Die Rückerstattung: ein Kristallisationspunkt für Antisemitismus*. [See pp. 238–252 in No. 27855.]

27451. FISCHER-HÜBNER, HELGA & HERMANN, eds.: *Die Kehrseite der 'Wiedergutmachung': das Leiden von NS-Verfolgten in den Entscheidungsverfahren*. Mit einem Vorwort von Hans Koschnick. Gerlingen: Bleicher, 1990. 232 pp. [Cf.: 'Friede mit den Tätern' statt Ausgleich gesucht (Matthias von Hellfeld) [in]: 'Allgemeine', 46/11, Bonn, 14. März 1991. P. 11.]

27452. Herbst, Ludolf/Goschler, Constantin: *Wiedergutmachung in der Bundesrepublik Deutschland.* München: Oldenbourg, 1989. Pp. 428. (Schriftenreihe der Vierteljahrshefte für Zeitgeschichte, Sondernummer). [Incl.: Der Fall Phillipp Auerbach. Wiedergutmachung in Bayern (77–98). Globalentschädigung für Israel und die Juden? Adenauer und die Opposition in der Bundesregierung (Michael Wolffsohn, 161–190, notes). Die SPD und die Wiedergutmachung gegenüber Israel (Shlomo Shafir, 191–213, notes). Anwälte der Verfolgten. Die United Restitution Organization (Hans Günter Hockerts, 249–271, notes). Der Wollheim-Prozeß Zwangsarbeit für I. G. Farben in Auschwitz (Wolfgang Benz, 303–339, notes). Die Entschädigung der jüdischen Gemeindebediensteten (Ernst G. Lowenthal, 341–350, notes). Die verkannten Opfer. Späte Entschädigung für seelische Schäden (William G. Niederland, 351–369, notes) Cf.: Review (Klaus Drobisch) [in]: Deutsche Literaturzeitung, Bd. 111, Berlin, Juni 1990. P. 508.]

27453. Jelinek, Yeshayahu A.: *Die Krise der Shilumim/Wiedergutmachungs-Verhandlungen im Sommer 1952.* [In]: Vierteljahrshefte für Zeitgeschichte, Jg. 38, H. 1, München, Jan. 1990. Pp. 113–139, notes.

27454. Jelinek, Yeshayahu: *Leo Baeck, Nahum Goldmann and the money from Germany. (A document.)* [In]: Studies in Contemporary Jewry, 5, Oxford Univ. Press, 1989. pp. 236–241, notes.

27455. Sahrhage, Norbert: *'Entnazifizierung' und 'Wiedergutmachung': das Umgehen mit nationalsozialistischen Tätern und jüdischen Opfern im Landkreis Herford nach 1945.* [In]: Opfer und Täter: zum nationalsozialistischen und antijüdischen Alltag in Ostwestfalen-Lippe. Hrsg. von Hubert Frankemölle. (Im Auftrag der Gesellschaft für Christlich-Jüdische Zusammenarbeit, Paderborn.) Bielefeld: Verlag für Regionalgeschichte 1990. Pp. 203–234. [See No. 27410.]

27456. Theis, Rolf: *Widergutmachung zwischen Moral und Interesse: eine kritische Bestandsaufnahme der deutsch-israelischen Regierungsverhandlungen.* Frankfurt am Main: Verl. für Akad. Schriften VAS, 1989. IV, 375 pp. Zugl. Hamburg, Univ. Diss., 1988.

C. Antisemitism, Judaism, Nazism in Education and Teaching

27457. August, Jochen: *Erinnern oder verweigern: das schwierige Thema Nationalsozialismus.* [In]: Dachauer Hefte, H. 6, 1990. Dachau: Verlag Dachauer Hefte, 1990. [On the international youth centre in Oswiecim founded in 1986.]

27458. *Christen und Juden: von den Wurzeln her verbunden. Leitlinien, Kriterien, Anregungen und Empfehlungen für die Verkündigung, die Erwachsenenbildung und den Religionsunterricht.* Hrsg.: Katechetisches Institut des Bistums Aachen, Institut für Religionspädagogik und Katechetik. Aachen: Hauptabteilung Erziehung und Schule im Bischöflichen Generalvikariat, 1989. 83 pp.

27459. Krosch, Anni: *Den Anfängen wehren: Verfolgung der Juden als Thema in der Grundschule.* [In]: Katechetische Blätter, Jg. 114, H. 9, München, 1989. pp. 673–676.

—— Suchy, Barbara: *Juden in Düsseldorf: ein geschichtlicher Überblick von den Anfängen bis zur Gegenwart.* [See No. 27013.]

27460. *Texte gegen Antisemitismus und Rassenwahn: Material der Gewerkschaft Erziehung und Wissenschaft im Deutschen Gewerkschaftsbund.* Hrsg.: Internationales Komitee von Erziehern zum Kampf gegen Rassismus, Antisemitismus und Apartheid. Frankfurt am Main: Bildungs-und Förderungswerk der GEW, 1989. 86 pp.

27461. Walter, Wolfgang: *Meinen Bund habe ich mit Dir geschlossen. Jüdische Religion in Fest, Gebet und Brauch.* Leipzig: St. Benno Verl., 1988. 221 pp. [On Jewish religion and ritual for the lay, non-Jewish reader, covers Orthodox practices in German countries, mainly 16th–18th century.]

V. JUDAISM

A. Jewish Learning and Scholars

27462. ALEXANDERSOHN, JONATHAN. Katz, Jacob: *An unclarified episode in the life of Hatam Sofer: the Alexandersohn affair.* [In Hebrew, with English summary]. [In]: Zion, Vol. 55, No. 1, Jerusalem, 1990. Pp. 83–126. [Jonathan Alexandersohn, of German origin, was appointed rabbi by the small Hungarian community Hejocsaba in 1833, accused of being unreliable in his halakhic decisions. Died as a wandering scholar in 1865 in Obuda near Pest.]. [Moses

Sofer, known as Hatam Sofer, 1762 Frankfurt am Main – 1839 Pressburg, rabbi, halakhic authority, and the leader of Orthodox Jewry.]

27463. BAECK, LEO. FRIEDLANDER, ALBERT H.: *Leo Baeck: Leben und Lehre.* Aus dem Engl. von Eva Gärtner. Mit einem Nachwort von Albert H. Friedlander u. Bertold Klappert. München: Christian Kaiser, 1990 (Kaisers Taschenbücher 84.) 350 pp. [Also on L.B.'s role during the Nazi period. Orig. publ. 1968 in the USA under the title: 'Leo Baeck: teacher of Theresienstadt' (No. 7044/YB XIV) and 1973 in England (No. 11238/YB XIX). The German translation, based on a revised new version of the original, appeared 1973 as a Veröffentlichung des Leo Baeck Instituts (No. 11237/YB XIX). Cf.: Ein Dissident der Geschichte (Elisabeth Endres) [In]: Süddeutsche Zeitung, München, Sept. 8, 1990.]

27464. — KURZWEIL, ZVI: *The relevance of Leo Baeck's thought to the mainstream of Judaism.* [In]: Judaism, Vol. 39, No. 2, New York, Spring 1990. Pp. 163–170, notes.

27465. — LOWENTHAL, ERNST G.: *Leo Baeck.* [In]: Berlinische Lebensbilder: Theologen. Hrsg. von Gerd Heinrich. Berlin: Colloquium, 1990. Pp. 262–275, notes., bibl.

27466. BARON, SALO WITTMAYER. *Obit.:* [In]: Jewish History, Vol. 4, No. 1, Spring [1989], Haifa 1990. Pp. 5–10. (Publ by Haifa Univ. Press, distrib. by E. G. Brill, Netherlands.) [S.W.B., Jewish historian, born May 26, 1895 in Tarnow, Galicia, died Nov. 24, 1989, New York.]

27467. BENDAVID, LAZARUS. BOUREL, DOMINIQUE: *Trois lettres inédites de Lazarus Bendavid.* [In]: Revue des Etudes juives, 149, 1–3, Jan.-Juin 1990. Pp. 129–135. [L.B., 1762, Berlin – 1832, Berlin, author, teacher, supporter of the Haskalah.]

27468. BERGMAN, S. HUGO: KLUBACK, WILLIAM: *The 'believing humanism' of Shmuel Hugo Bergman.* [In]: Review of the Society for the History of Czechoslovak Jews, Vol. 2, New York, 1989. Pp. 129–140. [S.H.B., data see No. 22300/YB XXXI.]

27469. BREUER, ISAAC. PELI, PINCHAS HACOHEN: *Isaac Breuer – Torah and derekh Eretz-Israel.* [In Hebrew, title transl.]. [In]: A kingdom of priests and a holy nation: a collection of articles in memory of David Cohen. Ed. by Yehuda Shaviv. [In Hebrew, title transl.] Jerusalem: The Family and Friends, 1989. Pp. 99–116. [Discusses Breuer's conflicting attitudes towards Zionism – for and against.]

27470. — MITTELMAN, ALAN L.: *Between Kant and Kabbalah: an introduction to Isaac Breuer's philosophy of Judaism.* Albany: State University of New York Press, 1990. 192 pp. [First full-length, systematic study in English of I.B. For data see No. 25606/YB XXXIV.]

27471. — SHALIT, DANIEL: *The relevance and importance of Rabbi Isaac Breuer.* [In Hebrew, title transl.]. [In]: Ha-Ma'yan, vol. 30, No. 4, Jerusalem, Tammuz 5750 [= June/July 1990]. Pp. 1–6.

27472. BUBER, MARTIN. BEN-CHORIN, SHALOM: *Martin Buber und die Nachfolge: Versuch eines Fazits zu seinem 25. Todestag am 13. June 1990.* [In]: Tribüne, Jg. 29, H. 114, Frankfurt am Main 1990, Pp. 147–151.

27473. — LEVY, ZE'EV: *Hermeneutik und Entmythologisierung: Rudolf Bultmann und Martin Buber.* [In]: Trumah, 1, Wiesbaden, 1987. Pp. 175–198, notes.

27474. — SCHORSCH, ISMAR: *Das Vermächtnis Martin Bubers.* Rede anlässlich des 25. Todestages [am 13. Juni 1990], gehalten am 18. Juni im Martin-Buber-Haus in Heppenheim. [In]: Aufbau, Vol. 56, No. 14, New York, July 6, 1990. Pp. 18–20.

27475. — SHAPIRA, AVRAHAM: *German romanticism as a source of Martin Buber's national theory.* [In Hebrew, with English summary]. [In]: Zionism, Vol. 15, Tel-Aviv 1990. Pp. 77–106.

——— — TAL, URIEL: Myth, solidarity and Zionist thought in the thought of Martin Buber. [And]: Two types of faith in the teaching of M. Buber. [In Hebrew, title transl.]. [See No. 27521.]

27476. — WELZEL, ULRIKE: *Das Erbe Martin Bubers: zum Gedenken an seinen 25. Todestag.* [In]: Das Jüdische Echo, Vol. 39, Nr. 1, Wien, Okt. 1990. pp. 208–214.

——— CARLEBACH, JOSEPH. *1883–1942. Jüdischer Alltag als humaner Widerstand.* [See No. 27260.]

27477. COHEN, HERMANN. SCHWEID, ELIEZER: *The influence of Maimonides in 20th-century Jewish thought.* [In Hebrew, with English summary] [In]: Mechkerei Yerushalayim be-Machshevet Yisrael (Jerusalem Studies in Jewish Thought). Vol. 9, Jerusalem, 1990. Pp. 293–324. [On Maimonides in the thought of Achad Ha-Am and Hermann Cohen.]

——— — ROTENSTREICH, NATHAN: *Between historical truth and religion of reason.* [See No. 27507.]

27478. — KLUBACK, WILLIAM: *Legacy of Hermann Cohen.* New York: Scholars Press, 1989. XII, 177 pp. (Brown Judaic Studies No. 167.)

27479. COHEN, SHAYE J.D./GREENSTEIN, EDWARD L., eds.: *The state of the Jewish studies.* Detroit: Wayne State Univ. Press 1990. 277 pp., notes, bibl. (A publication of the Jewish Theological

Seminary of America.) [Incl. 'Wissenschaft des Judentums', Fackenheim, Rosenzweig, Scholem.]

27480. DAN, JOSEPH: *Ashkenzai Hasidism in the history of Jewish thought.* [In Hebrew]. Tel-Aviv: The Open University, 1990. 12 units in 2 vols. (366; 290 pp.) [A textbook for Open University students.]

27481. EGER, AKIVA. FRIEDMAN, R.: *Prince of Torah and humility: The life and works of Rabbi Akiva Eger.* [In Hebrew, title transl.]. Jerusalem: Netivot, 5750 [=1990]. 445 pp. in 2 vols. [For children.] [A.E., data see No. 21259/YB XXX]

27482. EHRLICH, ERNST LUDWIG: *Christen und Juden auf meinem Weg.* Vortrag . . . anläßlich der Verleihung der Würde eines Honorarprofessors an der Berner Evangelisch-theologischen Fakultät. [In]: Judaica, Jg. 46, H. 1, Basel, März 1990. Pp. 1–11. [Incl. Leo Baeck, Martin Buber, Robert Raphael Geis; Karl Barth, Augustin Kardinal Bea, Karl Thieme.]

27483. ELBOGEN, ISMAR. STRAUSS, HERBERT A.: *Das Ende der Wissenschaft des Judentums in Deutschland: Ismar Elbogen und Eugen Taeubler.* [In]: Bibliographie und Berichte. Festschrift für Werner Schochow. Hrsg. von Hartmut Walravens. München; New York: Saur, 1990. Pp. 280–298. [See No. 27522.]

27484. EMDEN, JACOB: *Megillat Sefer: mémoires de Jacob Emden: l'anti Sabbatai Zewi (1697–1776).* Traduit [excerpt] de l'hébreu par M.R.H. [Maurice Ruben Hayoun]. [In]: La voix de la victoire, No. 13, Juin, 1990. P. 13–15. [J.E., Altona 1697–1776, rabbi, halakhic authority, anti-Sabbatian polemicist.]

27485. EPHRAIM BEN ISAAC (of Regensburg): *Hymnen und Gebete [von] Ephraim von Regensburg.* Hrsg., ins Deutsche übers. und erläutert von Hans-Georg von Mutius. Hildesheim: Olms, 1988. XI, 171 pp., bibl. (168–171). (Judaistische Texte und Studien, Bd. 10.) [E.b.I., 1110–1175, tosafist, member of the rabbinic court of Regensburg, the greatest of the liturgical poets of Germany.]

27486. FACKENHEIM, EMIL. SHULMAN, HARVEY: *The theopolitical thought of Emil Fackenheim.* [In]: Judaism, Vol. 39, No. 2, New York, Spring 1990. Pp. 221–231, notes.

27487. FEINER, SHMUEL: *Haskalah and history: the awareness of the past and its functions in the Jewish Enlightenment movement (1782–1881).* [In Hebrew, with English summary]. Jerusalem: Hebrew Univ., Diss., June 1990. 389, XIII pp. [On the Haskalah in Germany, Austro-Galicia, and Russia.]

——— FRIEDLÄNDER, DAVID: *Lesebuch für jüdische Kinder.* [See No. 27539.]

27488. GAMM, HANS-JOCHEN: *Das Judentum: eine Einführung.* Frankfurt am Main: Campus, 1990. 190 pp., map, bibl. (185–188). (Reihe Campus, Bd. 1031.) [Augmented paperback edn. of No. 16902/YB XXVI. Incl. antisemitism, German Jewry.]

27489. GEIGER, ABRAHAM: *Judaism and its history.* In two parts. Lanham, Md.: Univ. Press of America, 1985. VIII, 406 pp. (Brown classics in Judaica.) [Transl. of 'Das Judentum und seine Geschichte'.]

27490. GLATZER, NAHUM N. LOWENTHAL, ERNST G.: *Autor, Übersetzer und Gelehrter: Nahum Glatzer: vom Freien Jüdischen Lehrhaus Frankfurt bis nach Arizona.* [In]: 'Allgemeine', Nr. 45/12, Bonn, 22. März 1990. P. 8. [Further *obits.*: Nahum N. Glatzer 1903–1990, scholar, member of the board and fellow of the New York LBI [in]: LBI News, No. 58, New York, Leo Baeck Institute, Winter 1990, p. 12. Obituary note (Arnold Paucker) [in]: LBI Year Book XXXVI, London, 1991, p. XII.] [Glatzer, Nahum N[orbert], March 25, 1903 Lemberg – Feb. 27, 1990 Watertown, Ma., scholar, lived in Frankfurt am Main from 1920, emigrated to Palestine in 1933 and to the USA in 1938, professor of Judaic Studies at Boston Univ., of Jewish History at Brandeis Univ., member of the board of the New York LBI.]

27491. HELIN, RAPHAEL. SHISHA HALEVI, AVRAHAM: *A sketch of the character of Rabbi Raphael Helin of Glogau and his letter to the Hatam Sofer.* [In Hebrew, title transl.]. [In]: Moriah, Vol. 17, No. 1–4, Jerusalem, Shevat 5750 [=Feb. 1990]. Pp. 242–249. [On R.H. of Glogau, active in the 18th century in Eisenstadt.]

27492. HELLER, YOM TOV LIPMAN. DAVIS, JOSEPH MAURICE: *R[abbi] Yom Tov Lipman Heller, Joseph b. Isaac ha-Levi and rationalism in Ashkenazic culture 1550–1650.* Cambridge, Ma., Harvard Univ., Thesis, 1990. 544 pp., bibl. (527–543). [Yom Tov Lipman Heller, 1579 Wallerstein, Bavaria – 1654, rabbi in Prague, Vienna, Poland, commentator on the Mishnah; Joseph ben Isaac ha-Levi, 17th century.]

27493. HESCHEL, ABRAHAM JOSHUA. MOORE, DONALD J.: *The human and the holy: the spirituality of Abraham Joshua Heschel.* New York: Fordham Univ. Press, 1989. VII, 215 pp. [For data on A.H. see No. 21268/YB XXX.]

27494. — *To grow in wisdom: an anthology.* Ed. by Jacob Neusner with Noam Neusner. Lanham, Md.: Univ. Press of America, 1990, 272 pp.

27495. — FIERMAN, MORTON C.: *Leap of action: ideas in the theology of Abraham Joshua Heschel.* Lanham, Md.: Univ. Press of America, 1990. XVII, 291 pp., bibl.

27496. — PERLMAN, LAWRENCE: *Abraham Heschel's idea of revelation.* Atlanta, Ga.: Scholars Press, 1989. IX, 172 pp.

27497. HILDESHEIMER, ESRIEL. KAHANA, KALMAN: *Rabbi Esriel Hildesheimer and his rabbinical seminary.* [In Hebrew, title transl.]. [In]: Ha-Ma'yan, Vol. 29, No. 4, Jerusalem, Tammuz 5749 [=July 1989]. Pp. 1–8.

—— HIRSCH, SAMSON RAPHAEL. HIRSCHLER, GERTRUDE: *Rabbi and statesman: Samson Raphael Hirsch, Landesrabbiner of Moravia, 1847–51.* [See No. 27120.]

27498. — HEYMANN, CLAUDE: *Le rabbin S. R. Hirsch, un romantique?* [In]: Les Nouveaux Cahiers, 99, Paris, 1990. Pp. 17–22.

27499. KAUFMANN, JESEKIEL. KRAPF, THOMAS: *Exil und Fremde: ein Gedankenaustausch zwischen Jesekiel Kaufmann und Adolf Böhm in den dreißiger Jahren.* [In]: Bulletin des LBI, 87, Frankfurt am Main, 1990. Pp. 67–79, notes.

27500. KOBER, ADOLF. MÜLLER-JERINA, ALWIN: *Adolf Kober (1879–1958): Versuch einer Bio-Bibliographie anlässlich seines 30. Todestages.* [In]: Menora, Bd. 1, München, 1990. Pp. 278–296. [A. K., data see No. 21936/YB XXXI.]

27501. MAIMON, SALOMON, ENGSTLER, ACHIM: *Untersuchungen zum Idealismus Salomon Maimons.* Stuttgart-Bad Cannstadt: Frommann-Holzboog, 1990. 276 pp. (Spekulation und Erfahrung: Abt. 2, Bd. 16.) [S.M., ca. 1753 Sukóviboeg, Poland – Nov. 22, 1800 Niederesiegersdorf, Silesia, philosopher, one of the first followers of Kant; for his memoirs see No. 21274/YB XXX.]

27502. MENDELSSOHN, MOSES: *Hebräische Schriften II, 1–II, 5.* Bearb. von Werner Weinberg. Stuttgart: Frommann-Holzboog, 1989–1990. 5 vols. (Moses Mendelssohn: Gesammelte Schriften: Jubiläumsausgabe. Begonnen von Ismar Elbogen [et al.]. Fortgesetzt von Alexander Altmann in Gemeinschaft mit Fritz Bamberger [et al.]. Bd. 15, T. 1–2 – Bd. 18.) [For 'Hebräische Schriften' I & III see No. 12101/YB XX.]

27503. — ARKUSH, ALLAN: *The philosophical account of religion and Judaism in the thought of Moses Mendelssohn.* Ann Arbor: Univ. Microfilms International, [1990.]. 310 pp., bibl. (305–310). Waltham, Ma.: Brandeis Univ., Diss., 1988.

—— KLESSMANN, ECKART: *Die Mendelssohns.* [See No. 27789.]

27504. — LAUSCH, HANS: *Bemerkungen zu einer mathematischen Notiz Moses Mendelssohns.* (Paper No. 40) Clayton 3168, Vic., Australia: Department of Mathematics/Monash University, 1987. 10 pp., notes.

27505. — LAUSCH, HANS: *Moses Mendelssohn: 'Ja, was sage ich in der Mathematik?' Alexander Altmann (1906–1987) zum Gedächtnis.* Clayton 3168, Vic., Australia: Department of Mathematics/Monash University, 1988. 15 pp., notes. (Paper No. 41.)

27506. — ROSENBLOM, NOAH H.: *Theological impediments to a Hebrew version of Mendelssohn's "Phaedon".* [In]: Proceedings of the American Academy for Jewish research, Vol. 56, Jerusalem and New York, 1990. Pp. 51–81.

27507. — ROTENSTREICH, NATHAN: *Between historical truth and religion of reason.* [In Hebrew, with English summary]. [In]: Mechkerei Yerushalayim be-Machshevet Yisrael (Jerusalem Studies in Jewish Thought), Vol. 9, Jerusalem, 1990. Pp. 275–291. [Discusses Mendelssohn and Kant, and also Hermann Cohen.]

27508. — SCHOEPS, JULIUS H.: *Moses Mendelssohn: 2. Aufl.* Frankfurt am Main: Jüd. Verl. Athenäum, 1990. 194 pp., illus.

27509. — SLYMOVICS, PETER: *Mendelssohn and Locke – on tolerance.* [In Hebrew, with English summary]. [In]: Mechkerei Yerushalayim be-Machshevet Yisrael (Jerusalem Studies in Jewish Thought), Vol. 9, Jerusalem, 1990. Pp. 345–360.

27510. MENDES-FLOHR, PAUL: *Divided passions: Jewish intellectuals and the experience of modernity.* Detroit: Wayne State Univ. Press, 1990. 374 pp. [Collection of essays and articles, incl. some on Bloch, Buber, Scholem, Simon.]

27511. PELLI, MOSHE: *Struggle for change: studies in the Hebrew Enlightenment in Germany at the end of the 18th century.* [In Hebrew, title transl.]. Tel-Aviv: University Publishing Projects, 1988. 194, IX pp. [Analyses the works of Saul Berlin, Mendel Bresslau, Isaac Satanow, and Naphtali Wessely.]

27512. ROSENZWEIG, FRANZ. Amir, Yehoshua: *Der Platz der Geschichte bei Franz Rosenzweig.* [In]: Trumah, 1, Wiesbaden, 1987. Pp. 199–212, notes.

—— — Kern-Ulmer, Brigitte: *Franz Rosenzweig's 'Jüdisches Lehrhaus' in Frankfurt.* [See No. 27547.]

27513. — Zak, Adam: *Aufgeschobene Begegnung: Franz Rosenzweigs Konzeption der Beziehung zwischen Judentum und Christentum.* Aus dem Poln. übers. von Stefan Schreiner. [In]: Judaica, Jg. 46, H. 4, Basel, Dez. 1990. Pp. 195–207, notes.

27514. Rothschild, Fritz A., ed.: *Jewish perspectives on Christianity: the views of Leo Baeck, Martin Buber, Franz Rosenzweig, Will Herberg, and Abraham J. Heschel.* New York: Crossroad, 1990. X, 363 pp., illus., ports., bibl. (341–352).

27515. Rozenblit, Marsha L.: *Jewish identity and the modern rabbi – The cases of Isak Noa Mannheimer, Adolf Jellinek and Moritz Güdemann in nineteenth-century Vienna.* [In]: LBI Year Book XXXV, London 1990. Pp. 103–131, notes.

27516. Shavit, Uzi: *What is the 'Haskalah': an examination of the term 'Haskalah' in Hebrew literature.* [In Hebrew, with English summary]. [In]: Mechkerei Yerushalayim be-Sifrut Ivrit (Jerusalem Studies in Hebrew Literature). Vol. 12, Jerusalem, 1990. Pp. 51–83. [Deals with Jeiteles, Mendelssohn, Satanow and Wessely.]

27517. SCHOLEM, GERSHOM. Mosse, George L.: *Gershom Scholem as a German Jew.* [In]: Modern Judaism, Vol. 10, No. 2, Baltimore, May 1990. Pp. 117–133. [First delivered as a lecture at a conference on Scholem at Yale University.]

27518. STEINHEIM, SALOMON LUDWIG. Haberman, Joshua O.: *Philosopher of revelation: the life and thought of S.L. Steinheim.* Including an annotated translation, with a biographical and analytical introduction of the entire first volume of his four-volume work: 'The revelation according to the doctrine of Judaism – a criterion' and selections from volumes 2, 3, and 4. Philadelphia: Jewish Publication Society, 1990. XV, 332 pp. [Cf.: Philosopher of revelation: S. L. Steinheim on the occasion of the 200th anniversary of his birth. [in]: Modern Judaism, Vol. 10, No. 2, Baltimore, May 1990, pp. 135–145, notes.] [S.L.St. data see No. 21314/YB XXX.]

27519. — Shear-Yashuv, Aharon: *Salomon Ludwig Steinheim: ein deutsch-jüdischer Polyhistor im 19. Jahrhundert.* [In]: Menorah, Bd. 1, München, 1990. Pp. 47–65, notes.

27520. STRAUSS, LEO. Green, Kenneth Hart: *The return to Maimonides in the Jewish thought of Leo Strauss.* Waltham, Ma., Brandeis Univ., Phil. Diss., 1989. 341 pp. [L.St., data see No. 22721/YB XXXI.]

27521. TAL, URIEL: *Myth and reason in contemporary Jewry.* (Introd. by Amos Funkenstein.) [In Hebrew, title transl.]. Tel-Aviv: Sifriat Poalim; Tel-Aviv Univ., 1987. XVI, 280 pp. [Book planned by the author but publ. posthumously, cont. 11 essays arranged under the headings: A. Between myth and reason (incl. the essays): 1. Myth, solidarity and Zionist thought in the thought of Martin Buber (pp. 3–16; for German version, see No. 16238/YB XXV). 2. Two types of faith in the teaching of Martin Buber (17–26). 3. Reason, Judaism and Zionism in the thought of Albert Einstein (27–44). 4. M. Buber and A. Einstein – myth and reason in their national thought (45–53). B. Zionism, religious-Zionism and political Messianism (cont. 3 essays). C. Judaism and humanistic tradition (cont. 3 essays).] [U.T., data see No. 21316/YB XXX.]

—— TAEUBLER, EUGEN. [See No 27483.]

27522. Völker, Heinz-Hermann: *Die Hochschule für die Wissenschaft des Judentums in Berlin, 1900–1942.* [In]: Bibliographie und Berichte: Festschrift für Werner Schochow. Hrsg. von Hartmut Walravens. München; New York: Sauer, 1990. Pp. 196–230.

B. The Jewish Problem

—— Barnouw, Dagmar: *Visible spaces: Hannah Arendt and the German-Jewish experience.* [See No. 27610.]

27523. Ben-Chorin, Schalom: *Realismus und Innerlichkeit: Franz Werfel – Grenzgänger zwischen Judentum und Christentum.* [In]: Tribüne, Jg. 29, H. 115, Frankfurt am Main, 1990. Pp. 180–184.

27524. Hadomi, Leah: *Jüdische Identität und der zionistische Utopieroman.* [In]: Bulletin des LBI, 86, Frankfurt am Main, 1990. Pp. 23–66, notes.

—— Le Rider, Jacques: *Modernité et crises de l'identité.* [See No. 27116.]

27525. LESSING, THEODOR: *La Haine de soi: le refus d'être juif.* Traduit de l'allemand et présenté par Maurice-Ruben Hayoun. Paris: Berg, 1990. 172 pp. [German orig. publ. in Berlin 1930 under the title 'Der jüdische Selbsthaß'.]

27526. MEYER, MICHAEL: *Jewish identity in the modern world.* Seattle: Univ. of Washington Press, 1990. 120 pp., bibl. (The Samuel & Althea Stroum lectures in Jewish studies.) [Incl. German Jewry from the Enlightenment to today; also German antisemitism, the Nazi period, the Holocaust.]

27527. ROGASCH, WILFRIED: *Deutsche Juden oder jüdische Deutsche: Nachdenken über nationale Identität am Vorabend der Katastrophe.* [In]: Tribüne, Jg. 29, H. 113, Frankfurt am Main, 1990. Pp. 172–182, notes.

—— ROSENFELD, SIDNEY: *Denkmal für eine zerstörte Welt. Joseph Roths 'Hiob' und die Frage der deutsch-jüdischen Symbiose.* [See No. 27727.]

27528. WISTRICH, ROBERT S.: *Fateful trap: the German-Jewish symbiosis.* [In]: Tikkun, Vol. 5, No. 2, Oakland, Ca., March/April 1990. Pp. 34–38.

27529. WISTRICH, ROBERT S.: *The German-Jewish symbiosis in Central Europe.* [In]: European Judaism, Vol. 23, No. 1, London, Spring 1990. Pp. 20–30, notes.

27530. WOLF, SIEGBERT: *'Ich Denkender bin ein Jude': Gustav Landauer und seine Freundschaft mit Martin Buber.* [In]: Tribüne, Jg. 29, H. 114, Frankfurt am Main, 1990. Pp. 184–197.

C. Jewish Life and Organisations

27531. ADLER, KARL. RICHERT, FRITZ: *Karl Adler: Musiker – Verfolgter – Helfer: ein Lebensbild.* Stuttgart: Klett-Cotta. 88 pp., illus. (Veröffentlichungen des Archivs der Stadt Stuttgart, Bd. 46.) [K.A., Jan. 25, 1890 Buttenhausen – July 10, 1973 New York, director of music conservatory, conductor, active in Jewish communal and cultural life, assisted many Jews in obtaining emigration visas from 1933, emigrated to the USA in 1940.]

27532. BERLINER, CORA, LOWENTHAL, ERNST G.: *Gewinnende Persönlichkeit: Cora Berliner – ihre Laufbahn wurde 1933 abrupt beendet.* [In]: 'Allgemeine', Nr. 45/5, Bonn, 1. Feb. 1990. P. 7, port. [& in]: MB, Jg. 58, Nr. 55, Tel-Aviv, Feb. 1990, p. 4. [C.B., Jan. 23, 1890 Hanover – June 19, 1942 deported by the Nazis, date and place of death not known, social scientist, social worker. For biographical essay see No. 21332/YB XXX.]

27533. BRASSLOFF, MIRIAM: *Zedakah – Wohltätigkeit und Wohlfahrt: das soziale Denken im Judentum.* Wien (Burggasse 35): Informationszentrum im Dienst der Christl.-Jüd. Verständigung, 1989. 18 pp. (IDCIV-Vorträge, 23.)

—— BRENNER, MICHAEL: *The Jüdische Volkspartei – National-Jewish Communal Politics during the Weimar Republic.* [See No. 26927.]

27534. BRESLAUER, WALTER. LOWENTHAL, ERNST G.: *Lebensgeschichte als Zeitgeschichte. Erinnerungen an den Berliner Juristen Walter Breslauer (1890–1981).* [In]: Mitteilungen d. Vereins für d. Geschichte Berlins, 87. Jg., H. 1, Berlin Jan. 1991. Pp. 366–368. [W.B. July 3, 1890 Berlin – May 11, 1981 London, lawyer, active in Berlin Jewish community life, emigrated to England in 1936, studied law (Bachelor of Law), co-founder of the liberal Belsize Square Synagogue in London, of the AJR in Great Britain, board member of the Council of Jews from Germany.]

27535. COCHAVI, YEHOYAKIM, ed.: *The Zionist youth movement in the Shoah: a collection.* [In Hebrew, title transl.] Haifa: Institute for Research on the Holocaust Period of Haifa University and Beit Lochamei Haghetaot, 5749 [=1989]. 289 pp. [Incl. articles in Hebrew: The religious youth movements in Germany, 1933–1939 (Yaakov Isur, 73–79). 'Maccabi Hatzair' – the last Jewish youth movement in Germany (Chaim Schatzker, 81–103).]

27536. EIFERT, CHRISTIANE: *Symposion 'Arbeiterbewegung und Sozialarbeit'. Am 1. und 2. Dezember 1989 in Duisburg.* [In]: Internationale wissenschaftliche Korrespondenz zur Geschichte der deutschen Arbeiterbewegung, Jg. 26, H. 1, Berlin, März 1990. Pp. 75–79. [Incl. a seminar held by Ludger Heid 'Jüdische Wohlfahrtspflege und Proletariat'.]

27537. ELONI, YEHUDA: *The immortal 'Schlemiel'.* [In Hebrew, with English summary]. [In]: Qesher, No. 8, Tel-Aviv, Nov. 1990. Pp. 94–102. [On 'Schlemiel: illustriertes jüdisches Witzblatt', Berlin 1903–1905; then closed but reopened again a number of times up to 1925, mainly due to the efforts of its editor, the satirist Max Jungmann.]

27538. FRANK, JACOB. HOENSCH, J.: *Der 'Polackenfürst von Offenbach': Jacob Josef Frank und seine*

Sekte der Frankisten. [In]: Zeitschrift für Religions- und Geistesgeschichte, Jg. 42, H. 3, Köln, 1990. Pp. 229–244.

27539. FRIEDLÄNDER, DAVID: *Lesebuch für jüdische Kinder.* [Nachdruck der Ausgabe] Berlin: Voss, 1779; neu hrsg. und mit einer Einleitung und Anhang versehen von Zohar Shavit. Frankfurt am Main: dipa, 1990. 102 pp., bibl. (97–102). (Jugend und Medien, Bd. 18.) [Incl. facsimile, 46 pp., of 'Lesebuch für Jüdische Kinder.Zum Besten der jüdischen Freyschule'. Publ. 1779 in Berlin without Friedländer's name, with texts transl. by Moses Mendelssohn; only one original copy of this booklet is known to exist in Europe.]

27540. HECHALUZ. ESHKOLI, HAVA (WAGMAN): *The founding and activity of the Hehalutz-Histradrut Rescue Center in Geneva, 1939–1942.* [In]: Yad Vashem Studies, 20, Jerusalem, 1990. Pp. 161–210.

27541. — FEINSTEIN, BEN-ZION, ed.: *A guide to the archive of Hechalutz and youth movements in Germany which were connected with the Kibbutz Hameuchad, 1917–1946.* [In Hebrew, title transl.]. Kibbutz Lochamei Haghetaot: Beit Lochamei Haghetaot, Arkhion ha-Tenu'ah ha-Chalutzit, 1990. 196 pp. [Lists 392 entries with annotations regarding the contents of each file.]

27542. — FRAENKEL, DANIEL: *Between fulfilment and rescue: 'Hechalutz' and the plight of the Jews in Nazi Germany, 1933–1935.* [In Hebrew, with English summary]. [In]: Yahadut Zemanenu, Vol. 6, Jerusalem, 1990. Pp. 215–243. [On "Hechaluz" in Germany.]

27543. LACHMAN, FREDERICK R.: *Berufsentwicklung deutscher Juden.* T. 1–3: Vom Händler zum modernen Finanzier. T. 4: Wissenschaft und Kunst. [In]: Aufbau, Vol. 56, Nos. 13–16, New York, 1990, June 22 (p. 28); July 6 (p. 20); July 20 (pp. 20–21); Aug. 3 (pp. 20–21). [At head of title]: Was das Judentum dazu sagt.

27544. LESSING, FRED W. PAUCKER, ARNOLD: *Fred W. Lessing.* Address at the memorial gathering in honour of Fred W. Lessing, 24th July 1990 at the Wiener Library, London. [Manuscript, available in the LBI London and New York. Further addresses were delivered on this occasion by Walter Laqueur and Doris Wasserman. See also: *Obituaries*: Zum Tode von Fred W. Lessing: Verdienste um das LBI – Dienst an der Gemeinschaft. (Ernst G. Lowenthal) [in]: 'Allgemeine', Nr. 45/28, Bonn, 12. Juli 1990, p. 8. Fred W. Lessing 75jährig gestorben [in]: Aufbau, Vol. 56, No. 11, New York, May 25, 1990, p. 4. Fred W. Lessing 1915–1990, chairman of the board and treasurer of the New York LBI for over 25 years [in]: LBI News, No. 58, New York, Leo Baeck Institute, Winter 1990. p. 2, port. Obituary note (Arnold Paucker) [in]: LBI Year Book XXXVI, London, 1991. p. XII. Grosser Verlust für das Leo Baeck Institut: Fred W. Lessing gestorben (E. G. Lowenthal) [in]: MB, Jg. 58, Nr. 60, Tel-Aviv, Juli 1990, p. 6. Fred W. Lessing, 1915–1990 (Walter Laqueur); Fred Lessing (Hans Feld) [in]: The Wiener Library Newsletter, No. 15, London, Summer 1990, pp. 1 & 8. [F.W.L.: Feb. 15, 1915 Bamberg – May 6, 1990 Scarsdale, N.Y., industrialist, philanthropist, emigrated to England in 1934 and to the USA in 1942, associated with many Jewish organisations in the USA that reflect the German-Jewish legacy, chairman of the board and treasurer of the New York Leo Baeck Institute for over 25 years, chairman of the Wiener Library in London, benefactor of Tel-Aviv University.]

27545. PAPPENHEIM, BERTA. SEEMANN, BIRGIT: *'Von Unrecht zu schweigen . . .': Bertha Pappenheim – Jüdin, Sozialreformerin und Frauenrechtlerin.* [In]: Tribüne, Jg. 29, H. 115, Frankfurt am Main, 1990. pp. 185–193, notes.

27546. PRIJS, LEO: *Worte zum Sabbat: Über die jüdische Religion.* München: Beck, 1990. 117 pp. (Beck'sche Reihe 419) [Cont.: Chap. V: Erbauliches aus dem 18. Jahrhundert; chap. VI: Jüdisches Leben.]

27547. ROSENZWEIG, FRANZ. KERN-ULMER, BRIGITTE: *Franz Rosenzweig's 'Jüdisches Lehrhaus' in Frankfurt: a model of Jewish adult education.* [In]: Judaism, Vol. 39, No. 2, New York, Spring 1990. Pp. 202–214, notes.

27548. — MILLER, RONALD H.: *Dialogue and disagreement: Franz Rosenzweig's relevance to contemporary Jewish-Christian understanding.* Landham, Md.: Univ. Press of America, 1989. 234 pp. [Incl. correspondence with Hans Ehrenberg, cousin and close friend of F.R.]

—— SALAMANDER, RACHEL, ed.: *Die jüdische Welt von gestern, 1860–1938: Text- und Bildzeugnisse aus Mitteleuropa.* [See No. 26939.]

27549. SAMET, MOSHE: *Leaving the dead to lie unburied: towards the history of the debate concerning the determination of the time of death.* [In Hebrew, title transl.]. [In]: Ausfot: Annual for Jewish studies, Vol. 3, Jerusalem, 1989. Pp. 413–465. [Deals with 18th-century Germany, and particularly with the Duke of Mecklenburg and the Jews' refusal to obey his 1772 decree forbidding immediate burial of the dead.]

27550. SCHÄFER, PETER: *The ideal of piety of the Ashkenazi Hasidim and its roots in Jewish tradition.* [In]: Jewish History, Vol. 4, No. 2, Haifa, Fall 1990. Pp. 9–23. [On Hasidic Ashkenaz (ca. 1150–1250).]

27551. SELIGSOHN, JULIUS L. LOWENTHAL, ERNST G.: *Dr. Julius L. Seligsohn – ein Vergessener der Reichsvertretung.* [In]: MB, Jg. 58, Nr. 60, Tel-Aviv, Juli 1990. P.6. [J.L.S., May 7, 1890 Berlin – Feb. 28, 1942 Sachsenhausen, lawyer.]

27552. STERN, SHMUEL ELIEZER: *Decisions and customs of Mainz and Worms.* [In Hebrew, title transl.]. [In]: Tzfunot: Tora quarterly, Vol. 2, No. 4 (pp. 4–8), Vol. 3, No. 1 (pp. 4–9), Bnei-Beraq, Tammuz and Tishrei 1990.

—— VERBAND BAYERISCHER ISRAELITISCHER GEMEINDEN. [See No. 26991.]

D. Jewish Art and Music

—— [See also No. 27101.]

—— CZARNECKI, JOSEPH: *Last traces: the lost art of Auschwitz.* [See No. 27185.]

27553. FREUDENHEIM, TOM L.: *Books on art and the Jewish tradition.* [In]: Jewish Book Annual, Vol. 48 (1990–1991), New York, 1990. Pp. 106–119. [Incl. bibl. of books on Jewish art in Germany; German-Jewish artists; Holocaust.]

27554. FRIEDLAENDER, HENRI. LÖB, KURT: *Die Buchgestaltung Henri Friedlanders für die Amsterdamer Exil-Verlage Querido und Allert de Lange 1933–1940.* [In]: Philobiblon, Jg. 34, H.3, Hamburg 1990. Pp. 207–217, illus., notes, bibl.

27555. KÖLNISCHES STADTMUSEUM: *Judaica II.* (Bestandskatalog der Jüdischen Abteilung: Handschrift, Buchdruck, Graphik, Neuerwerbungen.) Bearb. von Liesel Franzheim. Köln: Kölnisches Stadtmuseum, 1990. 351 pp., mainly illus. [For volume I see No. 17346/YB XXVI.]

27556. LILIEN, EPHRAIM MOSES. FINKELSTEIN, HAIM: *E. M. Lilien: artist of the Zionist movement.* [In]: Ariel, No. 80, Jerusalem, 1990. Pp. 45–62.

27557. — FINKELSTEIN, HAIM: *E.M. Lilien, das Werden eines Künstlers.* [In]: Bulletin des LBI, 87, Frankfurt am Main, 1990. Pp. 55–66, notes.

27558. — GELBER, MARK: *E. M. Lilien und die jüdische Renaissance.* [In]: Bulletin des LBI, 87, Frankfurt am Main, 1990. Pp. 45–53, notes.

—— MILTON, SYBIL, ed.: *The art of the Jewish children.* [See No. 27239.]

27559. SCHÖNBERG. ARNOLD. RINGER, ALEXANDER: *Arnold Schoenberg: The composer as Jew.* Oxford: Clarendon Press; New York: Oxford Univ. Press, 1990. 272 pp., illus., ports. [Cf.: A Viennese interpretation of Moses: Arnold Schoenberg's Jewish identity (Alison Rose) [in]: Judaism, Vol. 39, No. 3, New York, Summer 1990, pp. 296–304, notes.]

27560. SULZER, SALOMON. PURIN, BERNHARD: *Komponist und Reformer: Über das Leben des Hohenemser Kantors Salomon Sulzer (1804–1890).* [In]: Neue Vorarlberger Tageszeitung, 5. Jan. 1990. Pp. 30–31, illus., port., facsim. [Cf.: Kunst des musikalischen Gebets (Dieter Adelmann) [in]: 'Allgemeine', Nr. 45/3, Bonn, 18. Jan. 1990, p. 7. Kantor und Sänger weltlicher Lieder: Salomon Sulzer zum Gedenken [in]: Aufbau, Vol. 56, No. 6, New York, March 16, 1990, p. 24.] [S.S., data see No. 22405/YB XXXI.]

27561. WOLFF, RAYMOND: *Oberkantor Frommermann: Musik in der Jüdischen Brüdergemeinde Neukölln.* [In]: Rixdorfer Musen, Neinsager und Caprifischer: Musik und Theater in Rixdorf und Neukölln. Hrsg. von Dorothea Kolland. Berlin: Edition Hentrich, 1990. Pp. 194–197. (Reihe Deutsche Vergangenheit: Stätten der Geschichte Berlins, Bd. 41.) [A.F., 1856 Zwanitz, Russia – 1924 Berlin, head cantor of the Jüdische Brüdergemeinde, Berlin-Neukölln, director of the Erste Internationale Cantorenschule zu Berlin, father of Harry Frommerman who founded the Comedian Harmonists.]

VI. ZIONISM AND ISRAEL

27562. BARKAI, AVRAHAM: *German interests in the Haavara-Transfer Agreement 1933–1939.* [In]: LBI Year Book XXXV, London, 1990. Pp. 245–266, notes.

27563. BEN-CHORIN, SCHALOM: *Oft fremd im eigenen Land: über Erfahrungen deutscher Juden in Israel.* [In]: Tribüne, Jg. 29, H. 116, Frankfurt am Main, 1990. Pp. 154–160.

27564. BERNSTEIN, PERETZ. HENNING, FRIEDRICH: *Ein Mitgestalter Israels: zum 100. Geburtstag von Friedrich (Peretz) Bernsteins.* [In]: Das Parlament, Nr. 23–24, Bonn, 1./8. Juni 1990. P. 17. [Also in]: Nachrichtenblatt des Verbandes der Jüdischen Gemeinden in der DDR, Dresden, Juni 1990, pp. 14–15. [P.B., orig. Friedrich/Fritz B., June 12, 1890 Meiningen – March 21, 1971 Jerusalem, publicist, Israeli politician, lived in Holland, settled in Palestine in 1936, active in politics under the name Peretz Bernstein.]

27565. BODENHEIMER, MAX. BODENHEIMER, HENRIETTE HANNAH: *Max Bodenheimer 1865–1940: politicial genius for Zionism.* Transl. by David Bourke. Edinburgh: The Pentland Press, 1990. IX, 125 pp., ports. [Transl. of: Max Bodenheimer – ein zionistisches Lebensbild.]

27566. BOHLMANN, PHILIP V.: *'The land where two streams flow': music in the German-Jewish community of Israel.* Champaign: Univ. of Illinois Press, 1989. XVIII, 257 pp. [On contributions by German Jews to all aspects of musical life in Israel.]

27567. BRENNER, MICHAEL: *The Jüdische Volkspartei – National-Jewish communal politics during the Weimar Republic.* [In]: LBI Year Book XXXV, London, 1990. Pp. 219–244.

—— BUBER, MARTIN. Shapira, Avraham: *German romanticism as a source of Martin Buber's national theory.* [In Hebrew]. [See No. 27475.]

—— COCHAVI, YEHOYAKIM, ed.: *The Zionist youth movements in the Shoah.* [See No. 27535.]

—— ELLERIN, BRUCE ELKIN: *Nietzche among the Zionists.* [See No. 27887.]

27568. FÖLLING, WERNER/MELZER, WOLFGANG: *Gelebte Jugendträume: Jugendbewegung und Kibbutz.* Witzenhausen: Südmarkverl. M. Fritz, 1989. 194 pp., illus., ports., facsims., bibl.

27569. FRANKEL, SIMON. LEVY, NISSIM: *Dr. Simon Frankel (1809–1880) – the first Jewish physician in Eretz Israel.* [In Hebrew]. [In]: Harefuah, Vol. 118, No. 8, Tel-Aviv, Apr. 15, 1990. Pp. 489–494. [S.F. 1809 Silesia – 1880 Jaffa, studied medicine in Munich, physician in Jerusalem from 1843 to 1858, thereafter temporarily in London, Germany, and New York before returning to Palestine.]

27570. GELBER, YOAV: *New homeland: immigration and absorption of Central European Jews 1933–1948.* [In Hebrew, title transl.]. Jerusalem: Leo Baeck Institute & Yad-Ben-Zvi, 1990. Ca. 650 pp., notes, bibl. [Cf.: Besprechung (Esriel Hildesheimer) [in]: MB, Jg. 58, Nr. 59, Tel-Aviv, Juni 1990. pp. 6–7.]

27571. GODENSCHWEGER, WALTER B./VILMAR, FRITZ: *Die rettende Kraft der Utopie: deutsche Juden gründen den Kibbuz Hasorea.* Frankfurt am Main: Luchterhand, 1990. 226 pp., illus. [Hasorea was founded in 1935.]

27572. HARTMANN, KARL JAKOB: *Aus der Wüste wurde ein Gartendorf: die schwäbische Mustersiedlung Shavey Zion zwischen Akko und Nahariya.* [In]: Tribüne, Jg. 29, H. 116, Frankfurt am Main, 1990. Pp. 162–166.

—— HECHALUZ. FRAENKEL, DANIEL: *Between fulfilment and rescue 'Hehalutz' and the plight of the Jews in Nazi Germany, 1933–1935.* [In Hebrew]. [See No. 27542.]

—— HELLER, ALFRED: *Dr. Seligmanns Auswanderung: der schwierige Weg nach Israel.* [See No. 27243.]

—— HERZL, THEODOR: *Briefe und Tagebücher.* [See No. 27776.]

27573. — BELLER, STEVEN: *Herzl.* London: Halban, 1990. 144 pp., bibl. (Jewish thinkers series.)

27574. — SHACHAR, DAVID: *The term 'ghetto' in the view of B. Z. Herzl.* [In Hebrew, title transl.]. [In]: Ha-Umma, No. 99–100, Tel-Aviv, Summer 1990. Pp. 447–453.

27575. JÜTTE, ROBERT: *Der Beitrag deutsch-jüdischer Einwanderer zum Aufbau eines Archivwesens in Israel.* [In]: Der Archivar, Jg. 43, H. 3, Siegburg, Juli 1990. Cols. 395–414, notes, bibl., (411–414). [Deals, a.o., with Alex Bein, Bernhard Brilling, Georg Herlitz, Joseph Meisl.]

—— KRAPF, THOMAS: *Exil und Fremde: ein Gedankenaustausch zwischen Jesekiel Kaufmann und Adolf Böhm in den dreißiger Jahren.* [See No. 27499.]

27576. MELZER, WOLFGANG: *Biographien jüdischer Palästina-Pioniere aus Deutschland: über den Zusammenhang von Jugend- und Kibbutzbewegung.* (Unter Mitarbeit von Werner Fölling.) Opladen: Westdt. Verlag, 1989. 268 pp. (Forschungsberichte des Landes Nordrhein-Westfalen, Nr. 3241.) [Based on biographical interviews with 10 former members of the 'Kibbutz Cheruth' movement, most of whom live in Givat Brenner.]

27577. MICHAELI, JACOB: *Kibbuz Hasorea: zur Geschichte einer von Juden aus Deutschland gegründeten Gemeinschaftssiedlung.* Durchgesehene u. erweiterte Aufl. Berlin: Fachbereich Politikwissenschaften der Freien Univ., 1987. 34 pp.

27578. OFER, DALIA: *The Israeli government and Jewish organisations: the case of the immigration of Jews from Shanghai.* [In]: Studies in Zionism, Vol. 11, No. 1, Tel-Aviv, Spring 1990. Pp. 67–80, notes. [About the 1949 rescue of the Shanghai Jewish community which mainly consisted of refugees from Germany.]

27579. OREN, AMIRAM: *Rassco's activities on behalf of immigrants of the fifth Aliyah (1934–1940).* [In

Hebrew, with English summary]. [In]: Cathedra for the History of Eretz Israel and its Yishuv, No. 55, Jerusalem, March 1990. Pp. 126–159. [Rassco = Rural and Suburban Settlement Co., founded in 1934 to help middle-class German immigrants settle in farming communities.]

—— PELI, PINCHAS HACOHEN: *Isaac Breuer – Torah and derekh Eretz-Israel.* [See No. 27469.]

27580. PORAT, DINA: *The blue and the yellow stars of David: the Zionist leadership in Palestine and the Holocaust 1939–1945.* Foreword by Saul Friedländer. Transl. by Jerzy Michalowicz. Cambridge, Ma.: Harvard Univ. Press, 1990. 344 pp., tabs. [Discusses whether the Jewish community of Palestine did everything in its power to rescue Jews in Nazi-occupied countries.]

27581. RATTNER, ANNA/BLONDER, LOLA: *1938 – Zuflucht Palästina: zwei Frauen berichten.* Bearb. u. eingeleitet von Helga Embacher. Wien: Geyer, 1989. 185 pp., illus., ports. facsims., bibl. (Erinnerungen aus Verfolgung und Widerstand 1938–1945.) [Materialien zur Zeitgeschichte, 6.) [Also on the persecution of Jews in Austria.]

27582. REINHARZ, JEHUDA: *Chaim Weizmann and German Jewry.* [In]: LBI Year Book XXXV, London, 1990. Pp. 189–218, ports., notes.

27583. ROSEN, PINCHAS. BONDY, RUTH: *Felix-Pinchas Rosen and his time.* [In Hebrew, title transl.]. Tel-Aviv: Zmora-Bitan, 1990. 633 pp. [P.R., orig. Felix Rosenblüth, data see No. 24593/YB XXXIII.]

27584. STAMPFER, JOSHUA, ed.: *Dialogue: the essence of Buber.* 2 vols. Portland, Or. (P.O. Box 751): Institute for Judaic Studies, [1989]. 74; 96 pp. [Essays first presented at a conference at Lewis and Clark College in 1987. Among the subjects discussed are 'Buber and Hebrew humanism', 'Buber in dialogue with Christianity', and 'The world of Hasidism'.]

—— TAL, URIEL: *Myth and reason in contemporary Jewry.* [In Hebrew, title transl.] [See No. 27521.]

—— THIELKING, SIGRID: *Auf dem Irrweg ins 'Neue Kanaan'? Palästina und der Zionismus im Werk Arnold Zweigs vor dem Exil.* [See No. 27759.]

27585. TOURY, JACOB: *The Jewish national press in Germany from its inception to the First World War.* [In Hebrew, with English summary]. [In]: Zionism, Vol. 15, Tel-Aviv, 1990. Pp. 9–33.

27586. UNNA, MOSHE: *Archetype: religious Zionism's training farm project in Germany at its beginning.* [In Hebrew, title transl.] Alon Shvut: Yad Shapiro, 1989. 112 pp. [Parts of this book appeared in 'Amudim' 1986–1987 (see No. 23661/YB XXXII); Bulletin des LBI 78 (1987) (see No. 24563/YB XXXIII, and 'Bishviley ha-Tchiah' (5748).]

—— VOLKOV, SHULAMIT: *The 'Kristallnacht' in context – a view from Palestine.* [In]: LBI Year Book XXXV, London 1990. Pp. 279–296. [See No. 27357.]

27587. ZIMMERMANN, MOSHE: *Das Gesellschaftsbild der deutschen Zionisten vor dem Ersten Weltkrieg.* [In]: Trumah, 1, Wiesbaden, 1987. Pp. 139–158, notes.

VII. PARTICIPATION IN CULTURAL AND PUBLIC LIFE

On the cuts in Section VII see the note before Section IV – (Ed.).

A. General

—— AUSTRIA. [See also No. 27717 and 27664.]

27588. BERLIN. WILHELMY, PETRA: *Der Berliner Salon im 19. Jahrhundert (1780–1914).* Berlin; New York: de Gruyter, 1989. 1028 pp., lists [of hostesses and guests, locations of the salons.], maps, diagrs., bibl. (Veröffentlichungen der Historischen Kommission zu Berlin, Bd. 73) [Refers also to the salons of Henriette Herz, Rahel Varnhagen and other Jewish women.]

27589. *Die Bukowina: Studien zu einer versunkenen Literaturlandschaft.* Hrsg. von Dietmar Goltschnigg und Anton Schwob. Tübingen: Francke, 1990. 465 pp. (Edition Orpheus, Bd. 3.) [Cont. 28 papers delivered at an international conference held at the Karl-Franzens-Universität Graz, Oct. 1987, covering, a.o., Rose Ausländer, Paul Celan, Karl Emil Franzos, Leo Katz, Alfred Margul-Sperber, Selma Meerbaum-Eisinger, Moses Rosenkranz.]

27590. EXILE LITERATURE. *Deutsche Bücherei, Leipzig: Die Sammlung der Exil-Literatur 1933–1945.* Überarb. Neudruck. Leipzig: Deutsche Bücherei, 1990. 5 pp. (Neue Mitteilungen aus der Deutschen Bücherei, Nr. 44.)

27591. —— *Deutschsprachige Exilliteratur seit 1933.* Bd. 2: New York. Hrsg. von John M. Spalek und Joseph Strelka. Teil 1–2. Bern: Francke, 1990. 1 vol. in 2 pts. (XXIX, 1817 pp.). [The third part of this Vol. 2, containing the bibliographies of the authors presented in the first two parts, will be published later.] [For Vol. 1: Kalifornien, publ. 1976, see No. 13701/YB XXII.]

——   — DIETHARDT, ULRIKE/LUNZER, HEINZ [et al.], eds.: *Leben mit österreichischen Literatur: Begegnung mit aus Österreich stammenden amerikanischen Germanisten, 1938/1988.* [See No. 27132.]

27592.   — *Exil. Forschung, Erkenntnisse, Ergebnisse.* Jg. 9, Nr. 2 & Jg. 10, Nr. 1. Hrsg. von Edita Koch. Maintal: E. Koch, 1989 & 1990. 2 issues, notes. [*Jg. 9, Nr. 2 (1989)* incl., (titles condensed): Verdecktes oder offenes Agieren? Strategien und Konflikte der Ossietzky-Kampagne 1933–1936 (Fritjof Trapp, 5–18; reflects the situation of exile writers, refers to German-Jewish emigrants). *Jg. 10, Nr. 1 (1990)*: Hilde Spiels historischer Roman 'Die Früchte des Wohlstands' (Waltraud Strickhausen, 27–42). Alice Rühle-Gerstels Exilroman 'Der Umbruch oder Hanna und die Freiheit' (Sonja Hilzinger, 43–52). Deutschsprachige jüdische Kinder- und Jugendbuchautoren im amerikanischen Exil (Elisabeth-Christine Mülsch, 65–73). Further contributions are listed according to subject.]

27593.   — *Schreiben nach Auschwitz.* Hrsg.: Peter Mosler. Köln: Bund-Verl., 1989. 152 pp. [Papers presented at a colloquium in Frankfurt am Main, 1988, by, a.o., Stefan Heym, Anna Loewy, Henry W. Katz, Hans Keilson, Ernst Loewy.]

27594.   — WOLFF, ILSE R., ed.: *Doch die Sprache bleibt . . . : eine Prosa-Anthologie des PEN-Zentrums deutschsprachiger Autoren im Ausland.* Gerlingen: Bleicher, 1990. 318 pp., biogr. notes (305–314). [Cont. autobiographical and fictional texts of 44 writers who left Germany for various reasons; incl. many German- and Austrian-Jewish émigré authors. Cf.: Eine rührige Schar. (Will Schaber) [In]: Aufbau, 65, No. 24, New York, Nov. 23, 1990, p. 6). The tongue in exile (Werner Rosenstock) [in]: AJR Information, Vol. 46, No. 4, London, Apr. 1991, p. 5.]

27595.   FELLMANN, WALTER: *Der Leipziger Brühl.* Leipzig: Fachbuchverl., 1989. 221 pp., illus., glossary, bibl. (Geschichte und Geschichten des Rauchwarenhandels.) [Also on the participation of Jews in the Leipzig fur trade from the 16th century and the liquidation of more than 400 fur-trade firms of Jews during the Nazi period.]

27596.   FRANKFURT am Main. DIESTELKAMP, BERNHARD/STOLLER, MICHAEL, eds.: *Juristen an der Universität Frankfurt am Main.* Baden-Baden: Nomos, 1989. 326 pp., ports., notes. [Incl. Frankfurt Jewish jurists, refers also to their elimination from the university during the Nazi period and the attitudes of their non-Jewish colleagues towards them.]

27597.   GIDAL, TIM N.: *Die Freudianer auf dem 13. Internationalen Psychoanalytischen Kongress 1934 in Luzern:* fotografiert von Tim N. Gidal. Texte: Tim N. Gidal/Volker Friedrich; Geleitwort: Heinz K. Henisch. München: Verl. Internat. Psychoanalyse, 1990, 184 pp., 150 illus. [Cf.: Freuds Ungeduld wuchs: Psychoanalyse und Nationalsozialismus: ein Photoband weckt Erinnerungen an eine heillose Zeit (Bernd Nitzschke) [in]: Die Zeit, Nr. 41, Hamburg, 5. Okt. 1990, pp. 46–47.] [T. N. Gidal, orig. Ignaz Nachum Gidalewitch, May 18, 1909, Munich, one of the pioneers of modern photo journalism, emigrated to Switzerland (1933), to Palastine (1936), 1947–1980 USA, lives in Jerusalem.]

27598.   GILMAN, SANDER L.: *Jewish writers in contemporary Germany: the dead author speaks.* [In]: Studies in Twentieth Century Literature, 13, Manhattan, Kansas, 1989. pp. 215 ff.

27599.   GUTTSMAN, WILHELM L.: *Worker's culture in Weimar Germany: between tradition and commitment.* Oxford: Berg, 1990. 332 pp., tabs., bibl. (318–327). [Author of German-Jewish background. Incl. many Jewish personalities, and their contributions to worker's culture, e.g. Wieland Herzfelde, John Heartfield, Willi Münzenberg, Rosa Luxemburg.]

27600.   HAMBURG. *Ich kann mich in so einer Welt nie mehr zurecht finden: jüdische Künstler der Hamburgischen Sezession.* [Ausstellung] Altonaer Museum in Hamburg, Norddeutsches Landesmuseum, 18. Okt. 1989 bis 14. Jan. 1990. Hamburg: Altonaer Museum, 1989. 20 pp.

27601.   SCHOCHOW, WERNER: *Die preussische Staatsbibliothek 1918–1914: ein geschichtlicher Überblick mit einem Quellenteil.* Köln: Böhlau, 1989. XII, 170 pp., tabs. (Veröffentlichungen aus den Archiven Preussischer Kulturbesitz, Bd. 29.) [Refers also to Jewish librarians at the Preussische Staatsbibliothek and their fate after 1933.] [Cf.: Die Verdrängung der jüdischen Staatsbibliothekare in Berlin (Ernst G. Lowenthal) [In]: 'Allgemeine', Nr. 45/19, Bonn, 10. Mai 1990, p. 10.]

27602.   SCHÖRKEN, ROLF/LÖWISCH, DIETER-JÜRGEN, eds.: *Das doppelte Antlitz: zur Wirkungsgeschichte deutsch-jüdischer Künstler und Gelehrter.* Paderborn: Schöningh, 1990. 219 pp. [Incl. essays on Einstein, Freud, Heine, Husserl, Marx, the Frankfurt School.]

27603.   SCHULTZ, HANS JÜRGEN, ed.: *Es ist ein Weinen in der Welt: Hommage für deutsche Juden unseres Jahrhunderts.* Stuttgart: Quell, 1990. Pp. 479. [Incl.: biographical essays on Sigmund Freud

(Johannes Cremerius, 11–34). Gustav Mahler (Hans Mayer, 35–52). Walther Rathenau (Ernst Schulin, 53–76). Else Lasker-Schüler (Käte Hamburger, 77–100). Rosa Luxembourg (Willy Brandt). Gustav Landauer (Harry Pross, 121–142). Max Reinhardt (Marianne Kesting, 143–168). Arnold Schönberg (Rudolf Stephan, 169–192). Martin Buber (Albrecht Goes, 193–216). Lise Meitner (Armin Hermann, 217–242). Albert Einstein (Robert Jungk, 243–262), Franz Kafka (Walter Jens, 263–284). Ernst Bloch (Jürgen Moltmann, 285–306). Walter Benjamin (Irving Fetscher, 307–330). Max Horkheimer (Alfred Schmidt, 331–360). Anna Freud (Uwe Henrik Peters, 361–382). Erich Fromm (Hans Jürgen Schultz, 383–406. Anna Seghers (Hans-Albert Walter, 407–430). Manes Sperber (Siegfried Lenz, 431–450). Hannah Arendt (Ria Endres, 451–472).]. [Cf.: Children of a loveless marriage (David Maier). [In]: AJR information, Vol. 46, No. 3, March 1991. Pp. 5–6.] [Book is based on a radio series of the Süddeutscher Rundfunk under the title 'Porträts zur deutsch-jüdischen Geistesgeschichte im 20. Jahrhundert'.]

—— STEINBERG, MICHAEL P.: *The meaning of the Salzburg Festival: Austria as theatre and ideology, 1890–1938.* [See No. 27113.]

27604. WEIMAR REPUBLIC. RITCHIE, J. M.: *Willett's Weimar theatre.* [In]: German Life and Letters, Vol. 43, No. 3, Oxford, April 1990. Pp. 218–233. [Review essay on No. 26744/YB (John Willett, The theatre of Weimar Republic); incl. also the German-Jewish exile theatre in England.]

B. Individual

27605. ADORNO, THEODOR W. REIJEN, WILLEM van: *Adorno zur Einführung:* mit Beiträgen von Peter Schiefelbein und Hans-Martin Lohmann. Überarb. Neuausg., 4., überarb. u. erweiterte Aufl. Hamburg: Edition SOAK im Junius-Verl., 1990. 124 pp., bibl. (108–120). (Zur Einführung, 56.)

27606. AICHINGER, ILSE. MOSER, SAMUEL ed.: *Ilse Aichinger: Materialien zu Leben und Werk.* Orig.-Ausg. Frankfurt am Main: Fischer, 1990. 293 pp., illus., bibl. (280–293). (Fischer-Taschenbücher, 6888: Informationen und Materialien zur Literatur.) [I.A., born Nov. 1, 1921 in Vienna, writer, of partly Jewish descent, survived the Nazi period in Germany.]

27607. ALTENBERG, PETER. BARKER, ANDREW: *Peter Altenberg: sein Einfluss auf die Literatur von Musil bis Kafka.* [In]: Literatur und Kritik, Jg. 1990, H. 241/242. Salzburg: Jan./Feb. 1990. Pp. 8–19. notes.

27608. AMÉRY, JEAN. HEIDELBERGER-LEONARD, IRENE, ed.: *Über Jean Améry.* Heidelberg: Winter, 1990. 130 pp., port. (Beiträge zur neueren Literaturgeschichte, Folge 3, Bd. 102.) [Incl.: Jean Amérys Selbstverständnis als Jude.] [J.A. (orig. Hanns Mayer, Oct. 1912 Vienna – Oct. 17, 1978 Salzburg, writer, essayist.]

27609. ANDERS, GÜNTHER. REIMANN, WERNER: *Verweigerte Versöhnung: zur Philosophie von Günther Anders.* (Deutsche Erstausg.) Wien: Passagen Verl., 1990. 185 pp., bibl. (181–185).

27610. ARENDT, HANNAH. BARNOUW, DAGMAR: *Visible spaces: Hannah Arendt and the German-Jewish experience.* Baltimore, Md.: Johns Hopkins Univ. Press, 1990. XVII, 319 pp., bibl. [Cf.: Speaking about modernity: Arendt's constructs of the political [in]: new german critique, No. 50, Ithaca, N.Y., Spring/Summer 1990. Pp. 21–39, notes.]

27611. —— ISAAC, JEFFREY C.: *At the margins: Jewish identity and politics in the thought of Hannah Arendt.* [In]: Tikkun, Vol. 5, No. 1, Oakland, Ca., Jan./Feb. 1990. Pp. 23–26, 86–92.

27612. —— MAY, DERWENT: *Hannah Arendt: eine bedeutende Repräsentantin deutsch-jüdischer Kultur.* (Aus dem Engl. übers. von Bernd Lenz.) München: Heyne, 1990. 195 pp., illus., bibl. (Heyne-Bücher: 12, Heyne Biographien.)

27613. AUSLÄNDER, ROSE: *Jeder Tropfen ein Tag: Gedichte aus dem Nachlass. Gesamtregister.* Hrsg. von Helmut Braun. Frankfurt am Main: Fischer, 1990. 419 pp. (Rose Ausländer: Gesammelte Werke in 7 Bänden, Nachtragsband mit dem Gesamtregister.) [Cont. more than 200 hitherto unpublished poems.] [R.A. née Rosalie Scherzer, May 11, 1901 Czernowitz – Jan. 3, 1988 Düsseldorf, poet, survived the Nazi period in hiding, emigrated to New York in 1946, lived in Düsseldorf from 1965. – Correction of data given in No. 24633/YB XXXIII.]

27614. —— BALEANU, AVRAM ANDREI: *Das Rätsel Rose Ausländer.* [In]: Menora, Bd. 1, München, 1990. Pp. 327–356, notes, bibl.

27615. BECKER, JUREK. HAGE, VOLKER: *Die Wahrheit über Jakob Heym: über Meinungen, Lügen und das schwierige Geschäft des Erzählens – eine Lobrede auf den Schriftsteller Jurek Becker.* [In]: Die Zeit, No. 12, Hamburg, 15. März 1991, p. 73.

27616.　BENJAMIN, WALTER. *Gesammelte Schriften. Bd. 7: Nachträge.* Hrsg. von Rolf Tiedemann und Hermann Schweppenhäuser. Frankfurt am Main: Suhrkamp, 1989. 2 vols. (1024 pp.) [Concluding volume of Benjamin's 'Gesammelte Schriften', 1972 ff.]

27617.　— BRODERSEN, MOMME: *Spinne im eigenen Netz: Walter Benjamin – Leben und Werk.* Bühl-Moos: Elster, 1990. 348 pp., 250 illus., ports.,

27618.　— BUCHELI, ROMAN: *Die Zuwendung zur Vergangenheit: zum 50. Todestag von Walter Benjamin (27. September).* [And]: HIRSCH, ALFRED: *Übergänge: zum Werk des Grenzgängers Walter Benjamin.* [In]: Neue Zürcher Zeitung, Nr. 220, Zürich, 22./23. Sept. 1990. Pp. 65–66, port.

27619.　— KLEEBERGER, PETER: *Walter Benjamin und der Spion: die Geschichte eines 'zerschlagenen' Buches aus den dreißiger Jahren.* [In]: Tribüne, Jg. 29, H. 113, Frankfurt am Main, 1990. Pp. 198–202. [On W.B.'s anthology 'Briefe', first published anonymously in 1931, republished under pseudonym in 1936 in Luzern, Switzerland, by the German journalist and spy Rudolf Rössler.]

27620.　—TIEDEMANN, ROLF [et. al.], eds. *Walter Benjamin 1892–1940:* eine Ausstellung des Theodor W. Adorno Archivs Frankfurt am Main in Verbindung mit dem Deutschen Literaturarchiv Marbach am Neckar. Marbach a.N.: Deutsche Schillergesellschaft, 1990. 559 pp., illus., ports., facsims., Berlin map appended. (Marbacher Magazin, 55.)

27621.　— WOOD, JAMES: *Art of darkness:* [In]: The Guardian, London, Oct. 4, 1990. P. 21 [Author traces B.'s final journey fleeing from Nazi-occupied Paris to the Spanish border where he committed suicide in Sept. 1940.]

27622.　BENYOETZ, ELAZAR: *Treffpunkt Scheideweg: Aphorismen.* München: Hanser, 1990. 197 pp. [E.B., data see No. 26790/YB XXXV.]

27623.　BERGNER, ELISABETH. *Elisabeth Bergner: das Leben einer Schauspielerin: ganz und doch immer unvollendet.* Hrsg.: Akad. d. Künste Berlin. (Bearb.: Klaus Völker). Berlin: Ed. Hentrich, 1990. 412 pp., illus. (Beiträge zu Theater, Film und Fernsehen aus dem Institut für Theaterwiss. der Freien Univ. Berlin, Bd. 4.)

————　BERMANN FISCHER, GOTTFRIED/BERMANN FISCHER, BRIGITTE: *Briefwechsel mit Autoren.* [See No. 27761.]

27624.　BERNSTEIN, EDUARD. HILDESHEIMER, ESRIEL: *The socialist Eduard Bernstein and Zionism.* [In Hebrew, title transl.]. [In]: Machbarot le-Machshava Sotsialistit, No. 14, Tel-Aviv, Summer 1990. Pp. 82–91 [Reprinted from 'Me'assef', Aug.9, 1977, pp. 81–96.]

27625.　BETTELHEIM, BRUNO: *Recollections and reflections.* London: Thames and Hudson, 1990. XI, 282 pp., bibl. [American edn. under the title: Freud's Vienna and other essays. New York: Knopf, 1990.] [Corrected entry of No. 26749/YB XXXV.] [Collection of 18 essays prepared for publication by the author shortly before his death, as substitute for an autobiography he did not wish to write. Also German transl. under the title: Themen meines Lebens: Essays über Psychoanalyse, Kindererziehung und das jüdisches Schicksal. Aus dem Amerikan. von Rüdiger Hipp und Otto Wilck, Stuttgart: Deutsche Verlags-Anstalt, 1990. 320 pp. Cf.: Hommage to Bettelheim (1903–1990) (David James Fisher) [in]: Partisan Review, Vol. 57, No. 4, Boston 1990, pp. 627–629. For B.B. data see No. 26749/YB XXXV.]

27626.　— ANGRES, RONALD: *Who, really, was Bruno Bettelheim?* [In]: Commentary, Vol. 90, No. 4, New York, Oct. 1990. Pp. 26–30. [Author, former pupil of B.B., alleges mistreatment by B., discusses his authoritarian personality.]

27627.　— *Obituaries. Bruno Bettelheim.* Ein Leben für Kinder: zum Tod von Bruno Bettelheim (Sabine Richebächer) [in]: Neue Zürcher Zeitung, Nr. 66, Zürich, 20. März 1990, p. 27. Der Reichtum der Empfindungen: in memoriam Bruno Bettelheim (Felix de Mendelssohn) [in]: Das Jüdische Echo, Vol. 39, Nr. 1, Wien, Oct. 1990. Pp. 195–198. For further obits. see No. 26749/YB XXXV.]

27628.　BIEBER, MARGARETE. BLAUERT, ELKE: *Der Archäologin Margarete Bieber zum Gedenken.* [In]: Nachrichtenblatt des Verbandes der Jüdischen Gemeinden in der DDR, Dresden, Sept. 1990. Pp. 15–16. [M.B., July 31, 1879 Schönau, Western Prussia – Feb. 25, 1978 New Canaan, Conn., archeologist, authority on Greek and Roman art, only female member of the faculty at the Univ. Giessen, dismissed in 1933, emigrated via England to the USA.]

27629.　BIRNBAUM, URIEL. *Uriel Birnbaum 1894–1956: Dichter und Maler.* [Ausstellung] Universitätsbibliothek Hagen, Jan./Feb. 1990. [Katalog] Hagen: Fernuniversität-Gesamthochschule, 1990. 142 pp., illus., ports., facsims., bibl. (114–117). (Veröffentlichungen der

Universitätsbibliothek Hagen, Bd. 1.) [Incl. Uriel Birnbaum: Anmerkungen zu Leben und Werk (Georg Schirmers, 1–36). 'Gläubige Kunst' – Zivilisationskritik als Gottes-Offenbarung: Bemerkungen zu Uriel Birnbaums Frühwerk (Armin A. Wallas, 37–82).] [U.B., Nov. 13, 1894 Vienna – Dec. 9, 1956 Amersfoort, Netherlands, (son of Nathan Birnbaum), author, painter, graphic artist, emigrated in 1939, survived in hiding in Amersfoort.]

27630. BLASS, ERNST. SCHUMANN, THOMAS B.: *'Zwischen Stahl und der Blume Viola': zum 100. Geburtstag des Lyrikers Ernst Blass.* [In]: Neue Zürcher Zeitung, Nr. 241, Zürich, 17. Okt. 1990. P. 27, port. [E.B., Expressionist writer, data see No. 17446/YB XXVI.]

27631. BOCK, CLAUS VICTOR: *Besuch im Elfenbeinturm: Reden, Dokumente, Aufsätze.* Würzburg: Königshausen & Neumann, 1990. XI, 223 pp. (Poesie und Philologie, Bd. 2.) [Incl. Karl Wolfskehl nach dreissig Jahren (45–59). Castrum Perigrini Amsterdam; ein Profil (210–221).] [C.V.B., Germanist, data see No. 22079/YB XXXI.]

27632. BORCHARDT, RUDOLF: *Prosa VI.* Stuttgart: Klett-Cotta, 1990. (Rudolf Borchardt: Gesammelte Werke in Einzelbänden. Hrsg. von Marie Luise Borchardt [et al.]). [Final volume of R.B.'s 'Gesammelte Werke', started in 1955 and comprising 14 volumes. For 'Prosa V' see No. 16449/YB XXV. Cf.: Im Widerstand gegen die zerrissene Zeit: zum Abschlussband von R.B.'s gesammelten Werken (Ernst Osterkamp) [in]: Neue Zürcher Zeitung, Nr. 102, Zürich, 4./5. Mai 1991.]

27633. BRESLAUER, WALTER. LOWENTHAL, ERNST G.: *Lebensgeschichte als Zeitgeschichte: Erinnerungen an den Berliner Juristen Walter Breslauer (1890–1981).* [In]: Mitteilungen d. Vereins für d. Geschichte Berlins, 87. Jg., H. 1, Berlin, Jan. 1991. Pp. 366–368. [W.B. July 3, 1890 Berlin – May 11, 1981 London, lawyer, active in Berlin Jewish community life, emigrated to England in 1936, studied law, co-founder of the liberal Belsize Square Synagogue in London, the AJR in Great Britain, board member of the Council of Jews from Germany.]

27634. BREUER, JOSEF. HIRSCHMÜLLER, ALBRECHT: *The life and work of Josef Breuer. Physiology and psychoanalysis.* Transl. by C. J. Lill. New York: New York Univ. Press, 1989. XIV, 514 pp., illus., ports., notes (325–418), bibl. (423–494). [This edn. is a rev. and updated version of a 1978 German publication; incl. material on Breuer's Jewish background and Viennese Jewry in the 19th century.] [J.B., Jan. 15, 1842 Vienna – June 25, 1925, Vienna, physician, collaborator with Freud, active in Jewish community affairs.]

27635. BROCH, HERMANN: AMANN, KLAUS/GROTE, HELMUT: *Die 'Wiener Bibliothek' Hermann Brochs: kommentiertes Verzeichnis des rekonstruierten Bestandes.* Wien: Böhlau, 1990. XXXI, 290 pp., illus., bibl. (Literatur in der Geschichte, Geschichte in der Literatur, 19.)

27636. BRUCKNER, FERDINAND: *Dramen.* Hrsg. und kommentiert von Hansjörg Schneider. (Mit einem Nachwort, Anmerkungen und einer Zeittafel des Herausgebers.) Wien: Böhlau, 1990. 680 pp. (F.B., orig. Theodor Tagger, data see No. 18406/YB XXVII.]

27637. BULLOCK, MARCUS PAUL: *Reading comes to grief: style and the philosophy of history in Martin Heidegger and Walter Benjamin.* [In]: The Germanic Review, Vol. 65, No. 4, Washington, D.C., Fall 1990. Pp. 138–149, notes.

27638. CANETTI, ELIAS.: *The play of the eyes.* Transl. by Ralph Manheim. London: André Deutsch, 1990. 329 pp. [Third vol. of autobiography covers the period 1931–1937 in Vienna. Cf.: Egotism before the tidal wave (Anthony Quinton) [in]: The Times Saturday Review, London, Aug. 25, 1990, p. 18.]

27639. CANETTI, ELIAS: *The secret heart of the clock: notes, aphorisms, fragments, 1973–1985.* Transl. by Joel Agee. New York: Farrar, Straus & Geroux, 1989. 151 pp.

27640. — PETERSEN, CAROL: *Elias Canetti.* Berlin: Colloquium, 1990. 93 pp., bibl. (87–89) (Köpfe des 20. Jahrhunderts, Bd. 114).

27641. — STIEG, GERALD: *Frucht des Feuers: Canetti, Doderer, Kraus und der Justizpalastbrand.* Wien: Edition Falter im Österr. Bundesverl., 1990. 237 pp., bibl.

27642. CASSIRER, BRUNO. ABELE, BERND: *Der Verlag Bruno Cassirer im Nationalsozialismus: 1933–1938.* [In]: Buchhandelsgeschichte, 1990/1, [Beilage zum] Börsenblatt für den Deutschen Buchhandel, Frankfurt am Main, 1990. Pp. B1–B18. [Incl. bibliography of books published by B.C. 1928–1936. For first pt. of article and B.C. data see No. 26753/YB XXXV.]

27643. CELAN, PAUL: *Werke: historisch-kritische Ausgabe.* Frankfurt am Main: Suhrkamp, 1990 ff.

27644. CELAN, PAUL: *Atemwende.* 1: Text; 2: Apparat. Hrsg. von Rolf Bücher. Frankfurt am Main: Suhrkamp, 1990. 2 vols. (144; 268 pp.). (Paul Celan: Werke: historisch-kritische Ausgabe. Abt. 1: Lyrik und Prosa, Bd. 7, 1–2.) [First volume of Celan's 'Historisch-kritische Ausgabe'.]

27645. — BOHRER, CHRISTIANE: *Paul Celan-Bibliographie.* Frankfurt am Main: Lang, 1990. 411 pp. (Literarhistorische Untersuchungen, Bd. 14.)

27646. — *Celan-Jahrbuch 3 (1989).* Hrsg. von Hans-Michael Speyer. Heidelberg: Winter, 1990. 214 pp. (Beiträge zur neueren Literaturgeschichte, Folge 3, Bd. 103.) [Incl.: Judentum, Antisemitismus, Verfolgungswahn: Celans 'Krise' 1960–1962 (James K. Lyon). Paul Celan: Auswahlbibliographie 1988–1989 (Christiane Bohrer).]

27647. — COLIN, AMY: *Paul Celan: holograms of darkness.* Bloomington: Indiana Univ. Press, 1990. 224 pp., illus., ports., notes (Incl. the influence of Yiddish literature on Celan's poetic development.]

27648. — DOR, MILO: *Auf der Suche nach der verlorenen Zeit: Erinnerung an Paul Celan.* [In]: Das Jüdische Echo, Vol. 39, Nr. 1, Wien, Okt. 1990. Pp. 183–190.

27649. — NOLAND, PETRA: *The legend of Paul Celan.* [In]: Present Tense, Vol. 17, No. 2, New York, Jan./Feb. 1990. Pp. 59–61.

27650. COHN, JONAS. MODEL, ANSELM: *'Ein deutsches Antlitz': zur Wertphilosophie und Ethik Jonas Cohns.* [In]: Freiburger Universitätsblätter, Jg. 29, H. 108. Freiburg: Juni 1990. Pp. 121–132. [J.C. Dec. 2, 1869 Görlitz – Jan. 12, 1947 Birmingham, philosopher, psychologist, emigrated in 1939 to Birmingham.]

27651. DILLY, HEINRICH, ed.: *Altmeister moderner Kunstgeschichte.* Berlin: Reimer, 1990. 295 pp., ports., notes, bibl. [Incl.: Erwin Panofsky, 1892–1968 (Renate Heidt-Heller, 165–187). Nikolaus Pevsner, 1902–1985 (Stefan Muthesius, 189–202). Aby Warburg, 1866–1929 (Martin Warnke, 117–139).]

27652. DRUCKER, MARTIN. *Martin Drucker: Gedenkveranstaltung aus Anlass seines 120. Geburtstages im Museum der Bildenden Künste zu Leipzig.* [In]: Anwaltsblatt, 1, Essen, 1990. Pp. 2–13. [Incl.: Martin Drucker: Anwalt des Rechts (Manfred Unger, 3–8). Also contributions by Fred Grubel, Gregor Gysi, Erhard Senninger.]

27653. EHRENZWEIG, ALBERT A. HESSEL, GABRIELE: *Albert A. Ehrenzweigs kollisionsrechtliche Lehren: Person und Werk.* Frankfurt am Main: Lang, 1990. XXII, 252 pp. (Europäische Hochschulschriften: Reihe 2, Bd. 927.) Münster i.W., Univ., Diss., 1989. [A.A.E., Apr. 1, 1906 Herzogenburg, Austria – June 4, 1964 Berkeley, Calif., professor of law, emigrated to England in 1939, to the USA in 1941.]

27654. EINSTEIN, ALBERT: *The collected papers of Albert Einstein.* Vol. 2: The Swiss years: 1900–1909. Ed.: John Stachel. [And compendium volume: comprising the English translation (Ann Beck, transl., Peter Havas, consultant). Princeton, N.J.; Oxford: Princeton Univ. Press, 1989. 2 vols., 656 pp., 62 facsims., indexes, bibl., (591–623); & compendium vol.: 399 pp. [All papers are presented in the original language; the compendium volume contains the English translation of all documents publ. in the main volume in other languages. For Vol. 1 see No. 24640/YB XXXIII.]

27655. — TAL, URIEL: *Reason, Judaism and Zionism in the thought of Albert Einstein.* [And]: *Martin Buber and A. Einstein.* [In Hebrew, title transl.]. [See No. 27521.]

—— — WALKER, MARK: *German National Socialism and the quest for nuclear power 1939–1949.* [See No. 27408.]

27656. — BANK, RICHARD D.: *Albert Einstein's humanism.* [In]: Midstream, Vol. 36, No. 7, New York, Oct./Nov. 1990. Pp. 23–28. [Incl. E. as Jew and Zionist.]

27657. — GRÜNING, MICHAEL, ed.: *Ein Haus für Albert Einstein: Erinnerungen, Briefe, Dokumente.* Berlin: Verl. der Nation, 1990. 583 pp., illus., ports., facsims., bibl. [Also on the architect Konrad Wachsmann.]

27658. ELIAS, NORBERT: NORBERT ELIAS ÜBER SICH SELBST. Frankfurt am Main: Suhrkamp, 1990. 196 pp., illus. (Erstausgabe, Edition Suhrkamp, 1590 = N.F.590.) [Cont.: Biographisches Interview (Norbert Elias [et al.]). Notizen zum Lebenslauf (Norbert Elias).] *Obituaries:* Ulrich Greiner [in]: Die Zeit, Nr. 33, Hamburg, 10. Aug. 1990, p. 36. A civilising Sociologist (Johann Gausblom) [in]: The Guardian, London, Aug. 6, 1990. 'Augenzeuge und Betroffener': zum Tode von Norbert Elias (Peter-Ulrich Merz-Benz) [in]: Neue Zürcher Zeitung, Nr. 179, 6. Aug. 1990, p. 15, port. Das Individuum und die Gesellschaft: zum Tode von Norbert Elias (Stephan Wehowsky) [in]: Süddeutsche Zeitung, Nr. 177, München, 3. Aug. 1990, p. 35.

27659. FEUCHTWANGER, LION. HOFE, HARALD VON: *Feuchtwangers angebliche Geschäftstüchtigkeit.* [And]: VILLARD, CLAUDIE: *Zwischen ästhetischem Anspruch und politischem Engagement: Lion Feuchtwangers Literaturkritik im Exil.* [In]: Exil, Jg. 10, Nr. 1, Maintal, 1990. Pp. 89–90, notes [&] 91–100, notes.

27660. — MILFULL, JOHN: *Geschichte und Auftrag des Judentums bei Lion Feuchtwanger.* [In]: Literatur und Geschichte 1788–1988. Hrsg. von Gerhard Schulz [et al.]. Bern: Lang, 1990. Pp. 241–249. (Australisch-Neuseeländische Studien zur deutschen Sprache und Literatur, Bd. 15.)

27661. — OTTO, EBERHARD: *Gegensätze und Gemeinsamkeiten. Leben und Werk der Schriftsteller Lion Feuchtwanger und Max Brod.* [In]: Tribüne, Jg. 29, H. 114, Frankfurt am Main, 1990. Pp. 166–171.

27662. — ROTHMUND, DORIS: *Lion Feuchtwanger und Frankreich: Exilerfahrung und deutsch-jüdisches Selbstverständnis.* Frankfurt am Main: Lang, 1990. 380 pp. (Europäische Hochschulschriften: Reihe 1, Bd. 1212.)

27663. FISCHER, LUDWIG/FISCHER, ROSY. *Expressionismus und Exil: die Sammlung Ludwig und Rosy Fischer, Frankfurt am Main.* Hrsg. von George Heuberger. Mit Beiträgen von Ljuba Berankova [et al.]. München: Prestel, 1990. 187 pp., illus., ports, facsims., bibl. [Companion-volume to an exhibition at the Jüdisches Museum, Frankfurt am Main, Aug.-Oct. 1990.] [Ludwig Fischer, 1860–1922; Rosy Fischer, 1869–1926; art dealers and collectors.]

—— FISCHER, SAMUEL. [See No. 27771.]

27664. FRANZOS, KARL EMIL. STEINER, CARL: *Karl Emil Franzos, 1848–1904: emancipator and assimilationist.* New York; Bern: Lang, 1990. X, 230 p. (North American studies in 19th century German literature, vol. 5.) [Covers also the history of German and European Jewry.]

—— FREUD, ANNA. STEINER, RICCARDO: *It is a new kind of diaspora.* [See No. 27245.]

27665. FREUD, SIGMUND: *Wir und der Tod.* Vortrag, gehalten in der Sitzung der 'Wien' [Loge B'nai B'rith] am 16. Februar 1915. [Introduced by]: NITSCHKE, BERND: *Wir und der Tod: ein Stück wiedergefundener Geistes-Geschichte.* [In]: Die Zeit, Nr. 30, 20. Juli 1990. Pp. 42–43. [A lecture by Freud, believed to be lost, now republished after 75 years.]

27666. — *Freud on women.* A reader. ed. and with introd. by Elisabeth Young-Bruehl. London: Hogarth Press, 1990. XII, 399 pp.

27667. — *The letters of Sigmund Freud to Eduard Silberstein.* Ed. by Walter Boehlich. Transl. by A. J. Pomerans. Cambridge, Mass.: Harvard Univ. Press, 1990. 288 pp., illus., ports. [Correspondence between F. and his childhood friend E.S. during their formative years, covering secondary school and university.]

27668. — BAKAN, DAVID: *Sigmund Freud and the Jewish mystical tradition.* New York: Columbia Univ. Press (distributor); London: Free Association Press, 1990. 365 pp. (paperback). [Orig. edn. Princeton, N.J.: Van Nostrand, 1958. 326 pp.]

—— BIANCOLI, ROMANO: *Erich Fromm und seine Kritik an Sigmund Freud.* [See in No. 27680.]

27669. — FRIEDEN, KEN: *Freud's dream of interpretation.* Albany, N.Y.: State Univ. of New York Press, 1990. 159 pp. [Explores the methods of dream interpretation in the Bible, the Talmud, and in the writing of Sigmund Freud.]

27670. — GAY, PETER: *Reading Freud: explorations and entertainments.* Hartford, Ct.: Yale Univ. Press, 1990. XVI, 204 pp., bibl. [Eight essays on aspects of Freud's life and thought, incl. his Jewishness and his attitude to antisemitism in Vienna. Cf.: Scholarly perils: Gay's Freud (Jeffrey M. Masson) [in]: Midstream, Vol. 36, No. 7, New York, Oct./Nov. 1990, pp. 29–32. (Review of No. 25752/YB XXXIV.]

—— GIDAL, TIM N.: *Die Freudianer auf dem 13. Internationalen Psychoanalytischen Kongress 1934 in Luzern.* [See No. 27697.]

27671. — GRESSER, MOSHE: *Sigmund Freud's Jewish identity: a study of his correspondence.* Chicago, Univ. of Chicago Divinity School, Thesis, 1990. V, 393 pp., bibl (385–393). [Available in the LBI New York.]

27672. — HESSING, JAKOB: *Jüdische Kritiken zu Sigmund Freud.* [In]: Neue Deutsche Hefte, Jg. 36, H. 2, Berlin, 1989. Pp. 285–288.

27673. — LEUPOLD-LÖWENTHAL, HARALD: *Freud und die Juden.* Wien (Burggasse 35): Informationszentrum im Dienste der Christl.-Jüd. Verständigung, 1988. 20 pp. (IDCIV-Vorträge, 19.)

27674. — PLÄNKERS, TOMAS: *Goethe contra Freud? Erinnerung an einen Streit um den Begründer der Psychoanalyse im Jahre 1930.* [In]: Frankfurter Allgemeine Zeitung, Nr. 197, 25. Aug. 1990.

27675. — STORR, ANTHONY: *Freud.* Oxford, New York: Oxford Univ. Press, 1989. 144 pp., illus., ports. (Paperback).

27676. FRIED, ERICH. MALINA, PETER: *'Zorn bleibt und Widerstand und kiene Ruhe': Erich Fried – ein österreichischer Dichter als Zeit-Historiker.* [In]: Das Jüdische Echo, Vol. 39, Nr. 1, Wien, Okt. 1990. Pp. 191–195.

27677. FRIEDLAENDER, SALOMO: *Die Lyrik Salomo Friedlaender/Mynonas:* Traum, Parodie und

Weltverbesserung. [Hrsg.]: Manfred Kuxdorf. Frankfurt am Main: Lang, 1990. IV, 201 pp. [S.F. (pseud.: Mynona), May 4, 1871 Gollantsch – Sept. 9, 1946 Paris, philosopher, expressionist writer under the pseud. Mynona, emigrated to Paris in 1933.]

27678. — KUXDORF, MANFRED: *Der Schriftsteller Salomo Friedlaender/Mynona:* Kommentator einer Epoche. Eine Monographie. Frankfurt am Main: Lang, 1990. II, 130 pp.

27679. FRIEDLAENDER-WILDENHAIN, MARGUERITE: *Ein Leben für die Keramik: die Handwerkskunst der grossen Keramikerin des Bauhauses.* (Fotos von Fran Ortiz. Übers.: Heinz Wachter.) Berlin: Verl. Neue Keramik, 1989. 224 pp., illus. [Orig. title: 'The invisible core'.] [M. F.-W., born Oct. 11, 1896 Lyons, France, potter, artist, emigrated with husband Frans Rudolf Wildenhain from Berlin to the Netherlands in 1933, and then to the USA, established a pottery and ceramics school in Guerneville, Calif.]

27680. FROMM, ERICH. *Wissenschaft vom Menschen = Science of man.* Bd. 1, Jahrbuch der Internationalen Erich-Fromm-Gesellschaft = Yearbook of the International Erich Fromm Society. Münster: Lit-Verl., 1990. 181 pp., bibl. [Contributions in German or English, with summaries in English, German, Italian & Spanish. Incl.: The humanistic science of man (& transl.): Humanistische Wissenschaft vom Menschen (Erich Fromm, 12–17; 5–11). Erich Fromms humanistische Philosophie einer Wissenschaft vom Menschen (Rainer Funk, 28–39). Erich Fromm und seine Kritik an Sigmund Freud (Romano Biancoli, 67–84).]

27681. — WEHR, HELMUT: *Fromm zur Einführung.* 1. Aufl. Hamburg: Edition SOAK im Junius-Verl., 1990. 145 pp., bibl. (136–140).

27682. GLASER, CURT. WALRAVENS, H.: *Curt Glaser (1879–1943): zum Leben und Werk eines Berliner Museumsdirektors.* [In]: Jahrbuch Preussischer Kulturbesitz, Bd. 26, Berlin, 1990. [C.G., 1879 Leipzig – 1943 New York, art historian, director of Staatliche Kunstbibliothek in Berlin until 1933, emigrated to France in 1933 and via various countries to the USA in 1940.]

27683. GRAUS, FRANTISEK. MORAW, PETER: *Zur Erinnerung an Frantisek Graus.* [In]: Historische Zeitschrift, Bd. 251, Heft 2, München, Okt. 1990. Pp. 283–290. [F.G., Dec. 14, 1921 Brünn – May 1, 1989, historian, medievalist, co-editor of 'Historische Zeitschrift'.]

27684. HAMBURGER, ERNEST. LOWENTHAL, ERNST G.: *Ein Absolvent des Kaiserin-Augusta-Gymnasiums in Charlottenburg: Professor Ernest Hamburger wäre unlängst 100 Jahre alt geworden.* [In]: Mitteilungen d. Vereins für d. Geschichte Berlins, 87. Jg., H. 1, Berlin Jan. 1991. Pp. 368–369.

27685. HECHT, JACOB & HERMANN. HERMAN, ZVI: *The river and the grain.* Transl. by Asher Goldstin. New York: Herzl Press, 1989. 496 pp., illus., ports., diagrs., maps, bibl. (478–484). [Hermann, H., March 13, 1877 Gondelsheim – Feb. 27, 1969, New York, ship-owner; Jacob H., June 25, 1879 Gondelsheim – Apr. 6, 1963 Basle, ship-owner. Founders, a.o., of the Rhenania Rheinschiffahrt, Mannheim, in 1908; also on Ruben H., son of Jacob, born 1909 in Antwerp, founder of the Dagon Company in 1951.]

27686. HEINE, HEINRICH. DAUBE, DAVID: *Heine's Belsazar.* [In]: Journal of Jewish Studies, Vol. 41, No. 2, Oxford, 1990. Pp. 254–258, notes.

27687. — FREDERIKSEN, ELKE: *Heinrich Heine und Rahel Levin Varnhagen. Zur Beziehung und Differenz zweier Autoren im frühen 19. Jahrhundert.* [In]: Heine-Jahrbuch 1990, Jg. 29, Hamburg, 1990, pp. 9–38.

27688. — HERMSTRÜWER, INGE: *Die van Geldern-Frauen.* Heines Familie mütterlicherseits. [In]: Der eigene Blick. Neuss 1989. Pp. 39–52.

27689. — HOLUB, ROBERT C.: *Heine and the New World.* [In]: Colloquia Germanica, Bd. 22, H. 2. Bern: 1989. Pp. 101–115, notes.

27690. — KRÖGER, UTE: *Der Streit um Heine in der deutschen Presse 1887–1914: eine Beitrag zur Heine-Rezeption in Deutchland.* Hrsg. von Helmut Schanze. Aachen 1989. 350 pp. Technische Hochschule Aachen, Diss., 1989. (Alano Medien 4)

27691. — LAMPING, DIETER: *Das 'sogenannte Persönliche' und die 'geistigen Erscheinungen': zur Problematik der literarischen Kontroverse um Personen am Beispiel des Streits zwischen Börne und Heine.* [In]: Zeitschrift für deutsche Philologie, Bd. 109, H. 2, Berlin, 1990. Pp. 199–217, notes.

27692. — LIPTON, LIANA P.: *A talent without character: a study of the unresolved conflicts in the work of Heinrich Heine.* (M.A. thesis) New York: Columbia University, 1990. [77] leaves.

27693. — LUTZ, EDITH H.: *Heines Beziehungen zum 'Verein für Cultur und Wissenschaften der Juden'.* Berlin, Freie Univ., Diss., 1989. 202 pp. [Typescript.]

27694. — PETERS, PAUL: *Heinrich Heine 'Dichterjude': die Geschichte einer Schmähung.* Frankfurt am

Main: Hain, 1990. 251 pp., notes. [On the origin and development of a negative reception to Heine by antisemitic and also Jewish authors. a.o., Karl Kraus, Theodor Adorno.]

27695. — WILLIAMS, A. F.: *Awakening – poetic role and critical intent in selected poems by Heine.* [In]: New German Studies, Vol. 15, No. 2, Hull, 1988/1989. Pp. 111–125, notes.

27696. HEINEMANN family. ST. JOHN, JOHN: *William Heinemann: a century of publishing, 1890–1990.* London: Heinemann, 1990. 689 pp., illus., ports., facsims., tabs., appendixes, bibl. (645–663). [Family of German-Jewish descent.]

27697. HERMANN, GEORG. GELBER, MARK H.: *Georg Hermann's late assessment of German-Jewish and Aryan-German writers.* [In]: Monatshefte für den deutschen Unterricht, deutsche Sprache und Literatur, Vol. 82, No. 1, Madison, Univ. of Wisconsin, 1990. Pp. 6–16.

27698. HERMLIN, STEPHAN. *Zum 75. Geburtstag von Stephan Hermlin.* [In]: Sinn und Form, H.2, Berlin, März/Apr. 1990. [Contributions by Hans Mayer (298–301); Walter Jens (301–303); Stefan Heym (303).]

27699. HERZ, MARKUS: *Betrachtungen aus der spekulativen Weltweisheit.* Hrsg. und eingeleitet von Elfriede Conrad [et al.]. Hamburg: Felix Meiner 1990. Pp. 141. Cf.: Wesentlicher Beitrag zur Kant-Erkennung (Willi Goetschel). [In]: Aufbau, Vol. 57. No. 5, New York, March 1, 1991, p. 12.

27700. HILFERDING, RUDOLF. SMALDONE, WILLIAM: *Rudolf Hilferding and the theoretical foundations of German Social Democracy.* [In]: Central European History, Vol. 21, No. 3, Atlanta, Sept. 1988. Pp. 267–299. [Refers also to H.'s Jewish background and his exile.]

—— KAFKA, FRANZ. [See also Nos. 27122, 27780.]

27701. — BORN, JÜRGEN: *Kafkas Bibliothek; ein beschreibendes Verzeichnis.* Mit einem Index aller in Kafkas Schriften erwähnten Bücher, Zeitschriften und Zeitschriftenbeiträge. Zusammengestellt unter Mitarb. von Michael Antreter [et al.]. Frankfurt am Main: Fischer, 1990. 256 pp., facsims. [Cf.: Leser im Labyrinth (Christoph von Wolzogen) [In]: Neue Zürcher Zeitung, Nr. 268, 17. Nov. 1990, pp. 67–68.]

—— — STÖLZL, CHRISTOPH: *Kafkas böses Böhmen.* [See No. 27122.]

27702. — *Franz Kafka: Schriftverkehr.* Hrsg. von Wolf Kittler und Gerhard Neumann. Freiburg: Rombach, 1990. 1 vol. [Incl.: Kartographien der Zerstreuung: Jargon und die Schrift der jüdischen Tradierungsbewegung bei Kafka (Bernhard Siegert, 222–247).]

—— KERR, ALFRED. MELLEN, PHILIP: *Gerhart Hauptmann and Alfred Kerr: a further consideration.* [See No. 27898.]

27703. KESTEN, HERMANN. TÄUBERT, KLAUS: *Besuch bei Hermann Kesten: zum 90. Geburtstag im Januar 1990.* [In]: europäische ideen, No. 73, Berlin, 1990. P. 20.

27704. KIRSCH, SARAH. MABEE, BARBARA: *Die Poetik von Sarah Kirsch. Erinnerungsarbeit und Geschichtsbewußtsein.* Amsterdam: Rodopl, 1989. 282 pp. (Amsterdamer Publikationen zur Sprache und Literatur, Bd. 83.) [German-Jewish author who deals also with Jewish themes, e.g. Holocaust.]

27705. KISCH, EGON ERWIN. WILLIAMS, KEIT: *The will to objectivity: Egon Erwin Kisch's 'Der rasende Reporter'.* [In]: The Modern Language Review, Vol. 85, Pt. 1, London, Jan. 1990. Pp. 92–106.

27706. — LEWIS, WARD B.: *'Egon Erwin Kisch beehrt sich darzubieten: Paradies America'.* [In]: German Studies Review, Vol. 13, No. 2, Tempe, Az., May 1990. Pp. 253–268, notes. [K.'s experiences during a tour of America in 1928/1929.]

27707. KOEBNER, RICHARD: *Geschichte, Geschichtsbewusstsein und Zeitwende*; Vorträge und Schriften aus dem Nachlass. Hrsg.: Inst. für Deutsche Geschichte der Univ. Tel-Aviv in Zusammenarbeit mit d. Richard-Koebner-Lehrstuhl für Deutsche Gesch. an d. Hebr. Univ. Jerusalem und H.D. Schmidt. Gerlingen: Bleicher, 1990. 299 pp.

27708. KRAUS, KARL. LESHEM, GIORA: *A Jew on the Great Wall of China: on Karl Kraus and his works.* [In Hebrew, title transl.]. [In]: Moznaim. Vol. 64, No. 6/7, Tel-Aviv, Feb./March 1990. Pp. 60–64.

27709. — SZASZ, THOMAS: *Anti-Freud: Karl Kraus' criticism of psychoanalysis and psychiatry.* Syracuse, N.Y.: Syracuse Univ. Press, 1990. 200 pp. [Incl. general introd. to K.'s life and work. For orig. publ. in 1976 see No. 13897/YB XXII.]

27710. KUTTNER, ERICH. DE CORT, BART: *'Was ich will, soll Tat werden'. Erich Kuttner 1887–1942; ein Leben für Freiheit und Recht.* Mit einem Geleitwort von Klaus Wowereit. Hrsg. vom Bezirksamt Tempelhof von Berlin, Abt. Volksbildung. Berlin: Edition Hentrich, 1990. 96 pp., bibl. (Reihe Deutsche Vergangenheit, Stätten der Geschichte Berlins, Bd. 42) [E.K.,

Socialist politician, writer, journalist. Lived in Berlin, in 1933 emigration to the Nether-lands, murdered in Mauthausen Oct. 6, 1942.]

—— LANDAUER, GUSTAV. WOLF, SIEGBERT: *'Ich Denkender bin ein Jude'. Gustav Landauer und seine Freundschaft mit Martin Buber.* [See No. 27530.]

27711. LASKER-SCHÜLER, ELSE. HESSING, JACOB: *Else Lasker-Schüler in Jerusalem: on 'Else', the play by Moti Lerner.* [In Hebrew]. [In]: Bamah: drama quarterly, No. 120, Jerusalem, 190. Pp. 36–40. [On the text of the play, recently staged in Israel.]

27712. —— ZIMROTH, EVAN. *The black swan of Israel.* [In]: Tikkun, Vol. 5, No. 1, Oakland, Ca., Jan./Feb. 1990. Pp. 35–39. [L.-S.'s Jerusalem period.]

—— LEVIN, JULO. *The art of the Jewish children, Germany 1936–1941: innocence and persecution.* [See No. 27239.]

27713. LEWALD, FANNY. RHEINBERG, BRIGITTA VAN: *Fanny Lewald: Geschichte einer Emanzipation.* Frankfurt am Main: Campus, 1990. 295 pp., illus. Tübingen, Univ., Diss., 1987.

27714. LUPRECHT, MARK: *'What people call pessimism': Sigmund Freud, Arthur Schnitzler, and nineteenth-century controversy at the University of Vienna Medical School.* Riverside, Sa.: Ariadne Press, 1991. 172 pp., bibl. (149–165). (Studies in Austrian literature, culture and thought.) [Deals with a medical-philosophical controversy between the above when both attended medical school in Vienna.]

27715. MARX, KARL. FISHMAN, ARYE: *The religious kibbutz: a note on the theories of Marx, Sombart and Weber on Judaism and economic success.* [In]: Sociological Analysis, Vol. 50, No. 3, Chicago, 1989. Pp. 281–290.

27716. —— GUTWEIN, DANIEL: *Marx's ideas on the relationship between Jews and capitalism: from Sombart to Weber.* [In Hebrew, with English summary]. [In]: Zion, Vol. 55, No. 4, Jerusalem, 1990. Pp. 419–447

27717. *Österreichisch-jüdisches Geistes- und Kulturleben.* Bd. 1–3. Hrsg.: Liga der Freunde des Judentums. Wien: Literas-Universitätsverl., 1988 (Bd. 1–2) & 1990 (Bd. 3). 144; 180; 118 pp.

27718. PICARD, MAX: *Die Welt des Schweigens.* Mit einem Vorwort von Franz Alt. München: Piper, 1988. 246 pp. (Serie Piper, 937.) [First edn. 1948.]

27719. RATHENAU, WALTHER. FREEDEN, HERBERT: *Der letzte der Rathenau-Mörder.* [In]: Tribüne, Jg. 29, H. 115, Frankfurt am Main, 1990. Pp. 50–54. [On Ernst Werner Techow, one of Rathenau's murderers, who turned into a fervent NS-opponent under the impact of a letter Rathenau's mother wrote to him after the assassination.]

27720. ROBINSON, PAUL: *The Freudian left: Wilhelm Reich, Geza Roheim, Herbert Marcuse.* With a new preface by the author. Ithaca, N.Y.: Cornell Univ. Press, 1990. XXI, 252 pp. (paperback).

27721. ROSENTHAL, BERTHOLD. KAUFMANN, URI: *Rosenthal, Berthold, Lehrer, Historiker.* [In]: Badische Biographien, Neue Folge, Bd. III. Hrsg. von Bernd Ottnad. Stuttgart: W. Kohlhammer, 1990. Pp. 225–227, bibl. [B.R., Jan, 17, 1875 Liedolsheim – Dec. 16, 1957, Omaha, Nebraska, teacher, historian, emigrated in 1940 to the USA via Portugal.]

27722. ROTH, JOSEPH: *Right and left.* Transl. by Michael Hodmann. London: Chatto & Windus, 1991. 224 pp.

27723. —— KEREKES, GABOR: *Der Teufel hieß Jenö Lakatos aus Budapest: Joseph Roth und die Ungarn.* [In]: Literatur und Kritik, H. 243/244. Salzburg: Apr./Mai 1990. Pp. 157–169.

27724. —— KESSLER, MICHAEL/HACKERT, FRITZ, eds.: *Joseph Roth: Interpretation – Kritik – Rezeption.* Tübingen: Stauffenberg, 1990. 476 pp. [Cont. about 40 papers delivered at an international symposium by the Akademie der Diözese Rottenburg-Stuttgart in 1989 in commemoration of the 50th anniversary of J.R.'s death.]

27725. —— MADL, ANTAL: *Zum Gedenken an Joseph Roth und Gerhard Fritsch.* [In]: Literatur und Kritik, H. 247/248. Salzburg: Sept./Okt. 1990. Pp. 335–339.

27726. —— REIBER, JOACHIM: *'Ein Mann sucht sein Vaterland': zur Entwicklung des Österreichbildes bei Joseph Roth.* [In]: Literatur und Kritik, H. 243/244. Salzburg: Apr./Mai 1990. Pp. 103–114, notes.

27727. —— ROSENFELD, SIDNEY: *Denkmal für eine zerstörte Welt: Joseph Roths 'Hiob' und die Frage der deutsch-jüdischen Symbiose.* [In]: Tribüne, Jg. 29, H. 116, Frankfurt am Main 1990. Pp. 175–185.

27728. —— TIMMS, EDWARD: *Doppeladler und Backenbart. Zur Symbolik der österreichisch-jüdischen Symbiose bei Joseph Roth.* [In]: Literatur und Kritik, H. 247/248. Salzburg: Sept./Okt. 1990. Pp. 318–324.

27729. — Voss, Oda: *'Hiob, Roman eines einfachen Mannes': Joseph Roth und das Ostjudentum*. [In]: Exil, Jg. 9, Nr. 2, Maintal, 1989. Pp. 19–41, notes.

27730. SCHNITZLER, ARTHUR. Biechele, Werner: *Jüdische Intellektuelle im Spannungsfeld von bürgerlichem Demokratie-Verständnis und antisemitischem Rassenwahn: Bemerkungen zu Arthur Schnitzlers 'Professor Bernhardi' und Friedrich Wolfs 'Professor Mamlock'*. [In]: Germanistisches Jahrbuch DDR-UVR [Ungarische Volksrepublik], 1989, Budapest, [1989?]. Pp. 77–90.

27731. SEGHERS, ANNA. Jens, Walter: *Anna Seghers*. [In]: Sinn und Form, H. 6, Berlin, Nov./Dez. 1990. Pp. 1165–1169.

27732. — *'Das siebte Kreuz' von Anna Seghers: Texte, Daten, Bilder*. Hrsg. von Sonja Hilzinger. Orig.-Ausg. Frankfurt am Main: Luchterhand, 1990. (Sammlung Luchterhand 918.) 223 pp., bibl. [Incl. autobiographical texts by A.S.]

27733. — Albrecht, Friedrich: *Gespräch mit Pierre Radvanyi*. [In]: Sinn und Form, H.3, Berlin, Mai/Juni 1990. Pp. 510–525. [Interview with P.R., the son of Anna Seghers, about his mother and their flight to France, and, via various countries, to Mexico.]

27734. — Stephan, Alexander: *Die FBI-Akte von Anna Seghers*. [In]: Sinn und Form, H. 3, Berlin, Mai/Juni 1990. Pp. 502–509.

27735. SEIDENBERG, HANS. Klein, Ingeborg/Licharz, Werner, eds.: *Juden und Christen – Juden in Deutschland: ein Leben für den Dialog*. (Zum Gedenken an Hans Seidenberg). Frankfurt am Main: Haag & Herchen, 1990. 39 pp., port. bibl. (Veröffentlichungen der Gesellschaft für Christlich-Jüdische Zusammenarbeit, Taunus). [Incl.: Blitzlichter aus der Geschichte der deutschen Juden (Hans Seidenberg, 3–16). Der Beitrag der Juden zur deutschen Kultur – Deutschland – Heimat der Juden (Werner Licharz, 17–39)] [H.S., Oct. 22, 1909 Breslau – Feb. 17, 1990 Frankfurt am Main.]

27736. SPIEL, HILDE. *Obituary Hilde Spiel*. A literary traveller between worlds. [In]: The Guardian, London, Dec. 6, 1990. [See also No. 27797.]

27737. TOLLER, ERNST. Dove, Richard: *He was a German: a biography of Ernst Toller*. With a preface by Frank Trommler. London: Libris, 1990. 320 pp., illus., bibl. [Cf.: Prison politics (William Sholto) [in]: Jewish Chronicle, London, Jan. 11, 1991, p. 34. Revival of a romantic revolutionary (John Willett) [in]: The Observer, London, Dec. 30, 1990.]

27738. TUCHOLSKY, KURT. *'Entlaufene Bürger': Kurt Tucholsky und die Seinen*. Eine Ausstellung des Deutschen Literaturarchivs im Schiller-Nationalmuseum, Marbach am Neckar. (Ausstellung und Katalog: Jochen Meyer in Zusammenarbeit mit Antje Bonitz.) Marbach: Deutsche Schillergesellschaft, 1990. 732 pp., illus., ports., facsims. (Marbacher Katalogue, 45.)

27739. — *Germany? Germany!: the Kurt Tucholsky reader*. Ed. by Harry Zohn. Transl. by Harry Zohn, Karl Ross, Louis Golden. Manchester: Carcanet, 1990. 256 pp., illus., ports., scores.

27740. UNGAR, HERMANN: *Das Gesamtwerk*. Hrsg. und mit einem Nachwort von Jürgen Serke. Wien: Zsolnay, 1989. P. 461.

27741. — *Der Bankbeamte und andere vergessene Prosa:* Erzählungen, Essays, Aufzeichnungen, Briefe. Mit einem Anhang herausgegeben von Dieter Sudhoff. Paderborn: Igel, 1989. Pp. 212.

27742. — *Krieg. Drama aus der Zeit Napoleons*. Mit einem Anhang herausgegeben von Dieter Sudhoff. Paderborn: Igel, 1990. P. 82.

27743. — Sudhoff, Dieter: *Hermann Ungar: Leben – Werk – Wirkung*. Würzburg: Königshausen & Neumann, 1990. 720 pp. illus. (Epistemata: Reihe Literaturwissenschaft, 55.) [Cf.: Das Werk als Ausdruck der Persönlichkeit (Hartmut Binder) [in] Neue Zürcher Zeitung, Nr. 257, 5. Nov. 1990, p. 36.]

——— VARNHAGEN, RAHEL. [See No. 27687.]

27744. WARBURG, ERIC M. Lowenthal, Ernst G.: *Hanseat und Brückenbauer: Eric M. Warburg gestorben*. [In]: 'Allgemeine', Nr. 45/29, Bonn, 19. Juli 1900. P. 12 & [slightly altered in]: Isr. Wochenblatt, Jg. 91, Nr. 35, Zürich, 31. Aug. 1990, p. 43. [See also: Eric M. Warburg gestorben [in]: Aufbau, Vol. 56, No. 15, New York, July 20, 1990, p. 4, port.] [E.M.W., Hamburg Apr. 15, 1900–July 9, 1990, banker, emigrated to the USA in 1938, returned to Hamburg in 1956.]

27745. WEININGER, OTTO: *Eros und Psyche: Studien und Briefe 1899–1902*. Hrsg. von Hannelore Rodlauer. Wien: Verl. der Österr. Akademie der Wissenschaften, 1990. 224 pp., illus. (Österr, Akademie der Wissenschaften, Philosophisch-Historische Klasse, Sitzungsberichte, 559.) [Publication of hitherto unknown texts and letters.]

27746. WERFEL, FRANZ. Abels, Norbert: *Franz Werfel*. Mit Selbstzeugnissen und Bilddokumenten dargestellt. Reinbek: Rowohlt, 1990. 156 pp., illus., facsims., bibl. (152–154). (Rowohlts Monographien, 472.)

27747. — BEN-CHORIN, SCHALOM: *Realismus und Innerlichkeit: Franz Werfel – Grenzgänger zwischen Judentum und Christentum.* [In]: Tribüne, Jg. 29, H. 115, Frankfurt am Main, 1990. pp. 180–184.

27748. — EICHMANN-LEUTENEGGER, BEATRICE: *Judentum und Christentum bei Franz Werfel (1890–1945).* [In]: Orientierung, Jg. 54, H. 15–16, Zürich, 1990. Pp. 168–171.

27749. — HUBER, LOTHAR, ed.: *Franz Werfel, an Austrian writer re-assessed*: Oxford: Berg, 1989. 237 pp., illus., ports.

27750. — JUNGK, PETER STEPHAN: *A life torn by history: Franz Werfel 1890–1945.* London: Weidenfeld & Nicolson, 1990. 318 pp., illus., ports., chronology, notes (239–302), bibl. of works by F. W. (303–304). [Book also discusses W.'s Jewish background.]

27751. WISTEN, FRITZ. *Drei Leben für das Theater: Stuttgart 1919–1933; Jüdischer Kulturbund; Berlin 1945–1962.* Hrsg. von der Akademie der Künste. Berlin: Edition Hentrich, 1990. 215 pp., illus., bibl.

27752. WITTGENSTEIN, LUDWIG. MONK, RAY: *Ludwig Wittgenstein: the duty of genius.* London: Jonathan Cape, 1990. XVIII, 646 pp., illus., ports., bibl. (640–646).

——   WOLF, FRIEDRICH. [See No. 27730.]

27753. WOLF, KONRAD. SILBERMAN, MARC: *Remembering history: the film maker Konrad Wolf.* [In]: new german critique, No. 49, Ithaca, N.Y., Winter 1990. Pp. 163–187, notes. [K.W., 1925–1982, son of Friedrich Wolf, emigrated to Soviet Union, returned to Berlin with the Red Army, became journalist, then film director for Defa.]

27754. WOLF, THEODOR: *Die Wilhelminische Epoche: Fürst Bülow am Fenster und andere Begegnungen.* Hrsg. von Bernd Sösemann. Frankfurt am Main: Athenäum, 1989. 435 pp.

27755. WRONKOW, LUDWIG. BOHRMANN, HANS, ed.: *Ludwig Wronkow, Berlin – New York: Journalist und Karikaturist bei Mosse und beim 'Aufbau'.* Eine illustrierte Lebensgeschichte. Bearb. von Michael Groth und Barbara Posthoff. München; New York: Saur, 1990. 231 pp., 126 illus. (Dortmunder Beiträge zur Zeitungsforschung, Bd. 46.) [L.W., Dec. 3, 1900 Berlin – July 12, 1982 Lisbon, journalist and cartoonist, emigrated to France in 1933 and in 1938 via Czechoslovakia to New York where he worked for 'Aufbau'.]

27756. ZADEK, WALTER. STERNER, GREGOR: *Ein Zeitzeuge besonderer Art: Walter Zadek, Journalist, Pressefotograf und Antiquar, wurde 90 Jahre alt.* [In]: Tribüne, Jg. 29, H. 114, Frankfurt am Main, 1990. Pp. 69–71, illus.

27757. ZWEIG, ARNOLD. SCHILLER, DIETER: *Arnold Zweigs 'Bilanz der deutschen Judenheit 1933'.* [In]: Weimarer Beiträge, Jg. 36, H. 5, Berlin, 1990. Pp. 805–814.

27758. — STERNBURG, WILHELM von: *Arnold Zweig.* Frankfurt am Main: Hain, 1990. 272 pp., illus., ports., facsims., bibl. (264–267).

27759. — THIELKING, SIGRID: *Auf dem Irrweg ins 'Neue Kanaan'? Palästina und der Zionismus im Werk Arnold Zweigs vor dem Exil.* Frankfurt am Main: Lang, 1990. XI, 374 pp. (Europäische Hochschulschriften: Reihe 1, Bd. 1178.]

VIII. AUTOBIOGRAPHY, MEMOIRS, LETTERS, GENEALOGY

27760. BENDIX, REINHARD: *Von Berlin nach Berkeley: deutsch-jüdische Identitäten.* Übers. von Holger Fliessbach. Frankfurt am Main: Suhrkamp, 1990. 491 pp., notes (467–[492]). (Suhrkamp-Taschenbuch, 1797.) [Paperback edn.; for American orig. and data of author's father, the lawyer Ludwig Bendix, see No. 22769/YB XXXI. See also: Ein Soziologenleben zwischen den Kulturen: zum Tode von Reinhard Bendix [Ruth & Hans-Jörg Schweizer-Meyer] [In]: Neue Zürcher Zeitung, Nr. 69, Zürich, 23./24. März 1991, p. 27.] [R.B., Feb. 25, 1916 Berlin – March 1991, California, professor of political science and sociology, emigrated to the USA in 1938.]

27761. BERMANN FISCHER, GOTTFRIED/BERMANN FISCHER, BRIGITTE: *Briefwechsel mit Autoren:* Hrsg. von Reiner Stach unter redaktioneller Mitarbeit von Karin Schlapp. Mit einer Einführung von Bernhard Zeller. Frankfurt am Main: S. Fischer, 1990. 846 pp., notes (699–802), list of names, bibl. [Incl. Ilse Aichinger, Hermann Broch, Paul Celan, Alfred Döblin, Erika Mann, Samuel Saenger, Friedrich Torberg, Franz Werfel, Kurt Wolff, Viktor Zuckerkandl,

Carl Zuckmayer, Stefan Zweig. [Cf.: Sehr geehrter Herr Verlag: die Familie Fischer und ihre Autoren (Walter Hinck) [in]: Frankfurter Allg. Zeitung, Nr. 10, 12. Jan. 1991 (Literaturbeilage). Ein Dokument der Zeitgeschichte (Paul E. Proskauer) [in]: Aufbau, 57, No. 4, New York, Feb. 15, 1991. P. 6.] [See also No. 27771.]

—— BETTELHEIM, BRUNO: *Freud's Vienna and other essays.* [See No. 27625.]

27762. BLOCH, ERNST. RÖMER, RUTH: *Erinnerungen an Ernst Bloch.* Berlin 1990 (privately printed). 50 pp. [Available in the LBI, London.]

27763. BLOCHMANN, ELISABETH. HEIDEGGER, MARTIN/BLOCHMANN, ELISABETH: *Briefwechsel 1918– 1969.* [See No. 27156.] [E.B., 1892–1972, professor at the Pädagogische Akademie Halle, dismissed in 1933, emigrated to England, returned to Univ. Marburg in 1952.]

—— BODENHEIMER, MAX. BODENHEIMER, HENRIETTE HANNAH: *Max Bodenheimer 1865–1940: political genius for Zionism.* [See No. 27565.]

27764. BONDY, FRANÇOIS: *Mein dreiviertel Jahrhundert: Erinnerungen, Gespräche, Porträts.* Hrsg. von Iso Camartin. Zürich: Ammann, 1990. 288 pp. [F.B., Jan. 1, 1915 Berlin, journalist, emigrated after 1933, living in Zürich from 1940.]

—— BRECHT, BERTOLT: *Letters 1913–1956.* [See No. 27885.]

27765. BUBER, MARTIN: *Briefwechsel Martin Buber – Ludwig Strauss.* Hrsg. von Tuvia Rübner und Dafna Mach. Frankfurt am Main: Luchterhand, 1990. 351 pp. (Veröffentlichungen der Deutschen Akademie für Sprache und Dichtung Darmstadt, Bd. 64.) [Incl. more than 600 letters and the essay 'Ludwig Strauss: sein Leben und Werk' by Dafna Mach.] [On Ludwig Strauss see also No. 27913.]

27766. BUBER-NEUMANN, MARGARETE. *Milena: the story of a remarkable friendship.* Transl. from the German by Ralph Manheim. New York: Schocken Books, 1989. VII, 213 pp. [Biography of Milena Jesenska, friend of Kafka; author befriended her when they were both prisoners in Ravensbrück concentration camp.]

27767. COHN, FREDERICK G.: *Signals: a young refugee's flight from Germany in the thirties.* Penzance, Cornwall: United Writers, 1990. 1 vol. [Autobiographical account of a the author's escape from Breslau to England via Czechoslovakia, Poland, Soviet Union, Sweden, Prague, Kattowice, Sweden.] [Cf.: 'A belated diary' (David Maier) [in]: AJR Information, Vol. 45, No. 11, London, Nov. 1990. P. 3.]

27768. DRACH, ALBERT: *'ZZ' das ist Zwischenzeit: ein Protokoll.* München: Hanser, 1990. 346 pp. [Autobiography, covers the years 1935–1938: from death of father to flight from Vienna; for sequel and author's data see No. 25794/YB XXXIV.]

27769. ELSAS, FRITZ: *Auf dem Stuttgarter Rathaus 1915–1922: Erinnerungen.* Hrsg.: Manfred Schmid. Stuttgart: Klett-Cotta, 1990. 240 pp., illus., ports., facsims., bibl. (Veröffentlichungen des Archives der Stadt Stuttgart, Bd. 47.) [Incl. Fritz Elsas: eine biographische Skizze (9–22), refers also to F.E.'s role in the German resistance.] [F.E., 1890 Stuttgart-Cannstadt – Jan. 1945 concentration camp Sachsenhausen, jurist, local politician, mayor of Berlin 1931– 1933, consultant for emigration from 1933, imprisoned for granting refuge to Carl Goerdeler in 1944 and subsequently shot.]

27770. FISCHER, RUTH/MASLOW, ARKADIJ: *Abtrünnig wider Willen:* aus den Briefen und Manuskripten des Exils. Hrsg. von Peter Lübbe. Mit einem Vorwort von Hermann Weber. München: Oldenbourg, 1990. XVI, 675 pp., illus., ports. [R.F., orig. Elfriede Eisler, Dec. 11, 1895 Leipzig – March 13, 1961 Paris, Communist politician, publicist, sister of the Communist functionary Gerhart Eisler and the composer Hanns Eisler, lived together with Arkadij Maslow, emigrated in 1933 to various countries, in 1941 to the USA where she became an anti-communist agitator. A.M., orig. Isaak Cemerinskij, March 9, 1891 Southern Russia – 1941 Havana, Cuba, Communist functionary, journalist, lived in Germany from 1899, emigrated in 1933, together with R.F. to various countries.]

27771. FISCHER, SAMUEL/FISCHER, HEDWIG: *Briefwechsel mit Autoren.* Hrsg. von Dierk Rodewald und Corinna Fiedler. Mit einer Einführung von Bernhard Zeller. Frankfurt am Main: Fischer, 1989. 1201 pp., notes (833–1110), list of names, bibl. [Incl. Peter Altenberg, Leopold Andrian, Richard Beer-Hofmann, Otto Brahm, Alfred Döblin, Moritz Heimann, Hugo von Hofmannsthal, Walther Rathanau, Felix Salten, Arthur Schnitzler, Jakob Wassermann, Carl Zuckmayer, Stefan Zweig. Cf.: Sehr geehrter Herr Verlag; Die Familie Fischer und ihre Autoren (Walter Hinck) [in]: Frankfurter Allg. Zeitung, Nr. 10, 12. Jan. 1991 (Literaturbeilage).] [See also No. 27761.]

27772. FLESCH, CARL F.: *'. . . und spielst du auch Geige?': der Sohn eines berühmten Musikers erzählt und blickt hinter die Kulissen..* Zürich: Atlantis Musikbuch-Verl., 1990. 1 vol. [On the author's father, the violinist and teacher Carl Flesch (1873–1944) and other musicians, among them many German and Austrian Jews. Author came to England as a refugee from Nazi Germany.] [Cf.: Monument to a famous father (Marianne Ehrenberg). [In]: AJR Information, Vol. XLV, No. 9, Sept. 1990, p. 3.]

—— FREUD, SIGMUND: *The letters of Sigmund Freud to Eduard Silberstein.* Ed. by Walter Boehlich. [See No. 27667.]

27773. GOLDSCHMIDT. PETER. GOLDSCHMIDT, MANUEL R.: *Mein Bruder Peter 1923–1987: eine biographische Skizze.* [In]: Castrum Peregrini 194–195, Amsterdam 1990. Pp. 9–40, illus. [P.G., April 11, 1923, Berlin – 1987, Netherlands, architect, graphic artist, of partly Jewish descent, emigrated to the Netherlands, survived during the German occupation in hiding, co-founder, with the author, of Castrum Peregrini.]

27774. GRANACH, ALEXANDER: *Da geht ein Mensch: Roman eines Lebens.* Erweitert um einen Bildteil, eine ausführliche Zeittafel und ein Glossar. München: Piper, 1990. 440 pp., illus., ports., facsims. (Serie Piper, Bd. 959.) [Augmented edn. of the actor's memoirs.] [A.G., data see No. 19617/YB XXVIII.]

27775. HEAVENRICH, MARIAN BLITZ: *Recollections.* [In]: Michigan Jewish History, Vol. 30, Southfield, Mich., Oct. 1989. Pp. 4–13, illus., ports. [Recollections of the Blitz family.] [M.B.H. 1879, Louisville, Ky. – 1970, Detroit, grandfather from Frankfurt am Main.]

27776. HERZL, THEODOR: *Briefe und Tagebücher.* Hrsg. von Alex Bein (s.A.), Hermann Greive (†), Moshe Scharf, Julius H. Schoeps, Johannes Wachten. Bd. 4: Briefe; Anfang Mai 1895 – Dezember 1898. Bearb. von Barbara Schäfer, in Zusammenarbeit mit Sofia Gelmann [et al.]. Frankfurt am Main: Propyläen, 1990. 833 pp., index of names, bibl. [Incl. Einführung: Theodor Herzls zionistische Briefe (Alex Bein, 9–209).]

27777. HEYM, STEFAN: *Nachruf.* Frankfurt am Main: Fischer-Taschenbuch-Verl., 1990. 847 pp. (Fischer-Taschenbücher 9549) [Paperback edn. of autobiography, orig. published in 1988, see No. 25803/YB XXXIV.] [St. H., data see No. 17741/YB XXVI.]

27778. HOFFER, GERDA: *Ererbt von meinen Vätern: 400 Jahre europäisches Judentum im Spiegel einer Familiengeschichte.* Köln: Verl. Wiss.u.Politik, 1990. 160 pp. [On the Utitz family of Bohemia and Prague.] [Gerda Hoffer, born 1921 in Vienna, writer, daughter of the author Stefan Pollatschek, emigrated to Czechoslovakia in 1938 and to London in 1939, lives in Jerusalem.]

27779. HOFMANNSTHAL, HUGO von: *Richard Strauss und Hugo von Hofmannsthal: Briefwechsel.* Hrsg. von Willi Schuh. München: Piper; Mainz: Schott, 1990. 751 pp., illus., music examples. (Serie Musik Piper Schott). [Augmented and revised paperback edn.]

27780. KAFKA, FRANZ: *Briefe an die Eltern aus den Jahren 1922–1924.* Hrsg. von Josef Cermák und Martin Svatos. Frankfurt am Main: Fischer, 1990. 141, [2] pp., notes (87–131), index of names.

27781. KERR, JUDITH: *Eine eingeweckte Kindheit.* Berlin: Argon, 1990. 56 pp., illus. [Reminiscences of Alfred Kerr's daughter on her childhood in Berlin before forced emigration.]

27782. KLEMPERER, VICTOR: *Ausgegrenzt von Anbeginn: aus dem Tagebuch 1933.* [In]: Neue Deutsche Literatur. 38. Jg., H. 453, Berlin, Sept. 1990. Pp. 108–120. [Excerpts from his diary.] [V.K., literary historian, Romanist, data see No. 26813 and 26814/YB XXXV.]

—— KRISS, SUSANNE [et al.]: *Wien – Belgien – Retour?* [See No. 27195.]

27783. KUCZYNSKI, JÜRGEN: *Schwierige Jahre – mit einem besseren Ende? Tagebuchblätter 1978 bis 1989.* Berlin: Tacheles-Verl., 1990. 219 pp. [Cf.: Ein orthodoxer Dissident. Wie Jürgen Kuczynski in seinem Tagebuch das Ende der DDR erlebte (Volker Ulrich) [in]: Die Zeit, Nr. 15, Hamburg, 5. Apr. 1991. P. 37, port.] [J.K., Sept. 17, 1904 Elberfeld, professor of economic history, emigrated to England in 1936, returned in 1945 to East Germany.]

27784. KUH, EMIL: *Gottfried Keller – Emil Kuh: Briefwechsel.* Hrsg. und erläutert von Irmgard Schmidt und Erwin Streitfeld. Stäfa, Schweiz: Verl., Theodor Gut, 1988. 1 vol., ports., facsims., notes. [E.K., Dec. 13, 1828 Vienna – Dec. 30, 1876 Meran, writer, friend and first biographer of Friedrich Hebbel.]

27785. LANGGÄSSER, ELISABETH: *Briefe 1924–1950.* Hrsg. von Elisabeth Hoffmann. Bd. 1–2. Düsseldorf: Claassen, 1990. 2 vols. 1296 pp. [Cf.: Mutter, geliebte, gehaßte Mutter. Elisabeth Langgässer in ihren Briefen (Walter Hinck) [in]: Frankfurter Allg. Zeitung, Nr. 114, 10. Mai 1991.] [E.L., Feb. 23, 1899 Alzey – July 25, 1950 Rheinzabern, writer, of partly Jewish descent; for memoirs of her daughter Cornelia Edvardson who survived Theresienstadt and Auschwitz, see No. 23251/YB XXXII; the editor E.H. is the daughter of C.E.]

27786. LANSBURGH, WERNER: *Feuer kann man nicht verbrennen: Erinnerungen eines Berliners.* Frankfurt am Main: Ullstein, 1990. 288 pp., illus. (by the author). [W.L., 1912 Berlin – Aug. 20, 1990 Uppsala, writer, studied law in Berlin and Basle, emigrated to Sweden via Spain, Italy, returned to Hamburg in 1980.]

27787. LUDWIG, RUTH: *Pistolen im Zucker: ein Leben zwischen zwei Welten*. Berlin: Ullstein, 1990. 240 pp. (Ullstein-Taschenbuch, Nr. 20678.) [R.L., born 1906 in Berlin, grew up in an assimilated German-Jewish family, studied in Heidelberg, emigrated to Palestine after 1933, pioneer life in a kibbutz, then settled in Jerusalem, where her house became one of the headquarters of the Haganah; her memoirs end with the founding of the State of Israel.]

27788. LUXEMBURG, ROSA: *Herzlichst Ihre Rosa: ausgewählte Briefe*. Hrsg. von Annelies Laschitza und Georg Adler. 2. Aufl. Berlin: Dietz-Verl., 1990. 557 pp., illus., ports. [Collection of 190 letters written between 1893 and 1919.]

27789. MENDELSSOHN FAMILY. KLESSMANN, ECKART: *Die Mendelssohns: Bilder aus einer deutschen Familie*. München: Artemis, 1990. 192 pp., 126 illus., ports., facsims. [On Moses Mendelssohn, his children, and his grandchildren, especially Felix Mendelssohn Bartholdy.]

27790. MEYER, EDUARD/EHRENBERG, VICTOR: *Ein Briefwechsel 1914–1930*. Hrsg. von Gert Audring [et al.]. Berlin: Akademie-Verlag; Stuttgart: B.G. Teubner, 1990. 162 pp., append., bibl., index of names.

27791. MEYER, LEONORE: *Velvet and steel: the life of Johanna Meyer*. Philadelphia, Pa. (1320 W. Somerville Av., Apt. 606): Leonore J. Meyer, 1989. 96 pp., illus., ports., facsims. [Priv. print., available in the LBI New York.] [Life-story of Johanna Meyer and her parental family Loevinson, Berlin and Rome, told by her daughter, the reciter and teacher Leonore Meyer, born 1911 in Berlin and emigrated to the USA in 1938.]

—— PAEPCKE, LOTTE: *Ein kleiner Händler der mein Vater war*. [See No. 27363.].

—— PAEPCKE, LOTTE: *Unter einem fremden Stern: ('Ich wurde vergessen')*. [See No. 27364.]

27792. POSENER, JULIUS: *Fast so alt wie das Jahrhundert*. Berlin: Siedler, 1990. 320 pp., illus. [Cf.: Rauhputzcharme des Menschlichen (Mathias Schreiber) [in]: Frankfurter Allg. Zeitung, Nr. 27, 1. Feb., 1990, p. 38.] [J.P., 1904 Berlin, architect, journalist, after 1933 emigrated to France, England, Palestine, Malaysia.]

27793. RICHTER, EVA & ILJA: *Der deutsche Jude*. Orig.-Ausg. München: Droemer Knaur, 1989. 110 pp. (Knaur, 2766: Satire.) [Reflections on the German Jew throughout the centuries, incl. personal reminiscences by E. R. on her family, on persecution during the Nazi period, and on German-Jewish relations today.]

27794. SAHL, HANS: *Memoiren eines Moralisten, [1]*. Frankfurt am Main: Luchterhand, 1990. 219 pp., index of names (223–229). [Paperback edn. of No. 20704/YB XXIX.] (Sammlung Luchterhand, 932.) [H.S., born May 20, 1902 in Dresden, writer, film and theatre critic, emigrated in 1941 via various countries to the USA.]

27795. SAHL, HANS: *Das Exil im Exil*. Frankfurt am Main: Luchterhand, 1990. 228 pp., ports. (Hans Sahl: Memoiren eines Moralisten, 2.) (Veröffentlichungen der Deutschen Akademie für Sprache und Dichtung Darmstadt, 63.) [Autobiography 1933–1945.]

—— SCHMITT, HANS A.: *Lucky victim: an ordinary life in extraordinary times, 1933–1946*. [See No. 27387.]

27796. SILBERMANN, ALPHONS: *Verwandlungen: eine Autobiographie*. Bergisch Gladbach: Lübbe, 1989 (3. Aufl. 1990). 574 pp., bibl. A. Silbermann (559–574). [A.S., born Cologne, Aug 11, 1909, sociologist, emigrated in 1933 to the Netherlands, France, Australia, returned to Europe about 1950, director of the Institut für Massenkommunikation at the University of Cologne until 1974, lives in Cologne.]

27797. SPIEL, HILDE: *Welche Welt ist meine Welt? Erinnerungen 1946–1969*. München: List, 1990. 331 pp., illus., ports. [Sequel to No. 26838/YB XXXV.] [Obituaries: Hilde Spiel Lauterkeit: Österreichs grösste Publizistin starb 79jährig in Wien (Joachim Kaiser) [in]: Süddeutsche Zeitung, Nr. 276, München, 1./2. Dez. 1990, p. 15, port. Leben zwischen zwei Welten: zum Tode von Hilde Spiel und zum zweiten Buch ihrer Erinnerungen (Hansres Jacobi) [in]: Neue Zürcher Zeitung, Nr. 281, 3. Dez. 1990, p. 21. See also No. 27736.] [H. Spiel, Vienna Oct. 19, 1911–Nov. 30, 1990.]

27798. STERN, HELLMUT: *Saitensprünge*. Berlin: Transit Buchverl., 1990. 256 pp., illus. [Autobiography.] [H. St., born May 21, 1928 in Berlin, violinist, emigrated to China in 1938, to Israel in 1949, to the USA in 1957, living in Berlin from 1961.]

27799. STERN, JOSEF: *Stark wie ein Spiegel*. Gießen: Wilhelm Schmitz, 1990. XXXIV, 282 pp. [Partly autobiographical, partly fictional story of the author's emigration from Gießen to Palestine.

Cf.: Geschichts- und Selbstbewußt (Niels Hansen) [in]: Tribüne, Jg. 29, H. 116, Frankfurt am Main, 1990, pp. 186–187.]

—— STRAUSS, LUDWIG: *Briefwechsel Martin Buber – Ludwig Strauss*. [See No. 27765.]

27800. TERJESEN, MARIANNE: *Riesen til byen som ikke finnes*. Oslo: Gyldendal Norsk Forlag, 1990. 189 pp., illus. [Norwegian journalist writing on her partly Jewish family and the Breslau Jewish community.]

27801. TOLLER, ERNST: *Spanisches Tagebuch*. Hrsg. und eingeleitet mit dem Essay: 'Traum und Wirklichkeit: Ernst Tollers spanische Hilfsaktion' von Richard Dove und Stephen Lamb. [In]: Exil, Jg. 10, Nr. 1, Maintal, 1990. Pp. 5–26, notes. [Publ. for the first time.]

27802. VIGEE, CLAUDE: *Leben in Jerusalem = Vivre à Jerusalem*. Hrsg. und aus dem Franz. übers. von Paul Assall. Bühl-Moos: Elster, 1990. 246 pp. [Autobiography 1960–1984.] [C.V., orig. Strauss, born 1921 in Bischweiler, Alsace, joined the resistance in France, emigrated to the USA in 1943, lecturer in French literature, settled in Israel in 1960.]

27803. WARBURG, LOTTE: *Eine volkommene Närrin durch meine ewigen Gefühle: aus den Tagebüchern der Lotte Warburg, 1925–1947*. Hgrsg., bearb. und kommentiert von Wulf Rüskamp. (Einleitung von Peter Meyer-Viol.) Bayreuth: Druckhaus Bayreuth, 1989. 456 pp., illus., ports., geneal. table. [L.W. 1884 Hamburg – 1948 Bayreuth, (daughter of the physicist Emil Warburg and sister of the Nobel Prize winning chemist Otto Warburg, Nobel Prize 1931) writer, journalist, married to Gottfried Meyer-Viol, emigrated via Switzerland to the Netherlands in 1937, returned to her estate Grunau near Bayreuth in 1945.]

27804. WARBURG-SPINELLI, INGRID: *Die Dringlichkeit des Mitleids und die Einsamkeit, nein zu sagen: Lebenserinnerungen 1910–1989*. Hamburg: Dölling und Galitz, 1990. 480 pp. [Cf.: Ein deutsches Schicksal: die Biographie der Ingrid Warburg-Spinelli (Volker Ullrich) [in]: Das Parlament, Nr. 5, Bonn, 25. Jan. 1991, p. 10.] [I. W.-S., 1910 Hamburg, daughter of the banker Fritz Warburg, emigrated in 1936 to the USA, co-founder of the 'Emergency Rescue Committee', lives in Rome.]

27805. WEILL, KURT. SCHEBERA, JÜRGEN: *Kurt Weill in Texten, Bildern und Dokumenten, 1900–1950: eine Biographie*. 1. Aufl. Mainz: Schott; Leipzig: Deutscher Verl. für Musik, 1990. 301 pp., illus., ports., facsims., bibl. (285–288), diskogr. (289–293). [Incl. some letters published for the first time in German, illuminating K.W.'s life and work in exile in the USA.]

27806. —— *Vom Kurfürstendamm zum Broadway: Kurt Weill (1900–1950)*. Hrsg. im Auftrag von Heinrich-Heine-Institut Düsseldorf [et al.] von Bernd Kortländer [et al.] Düsseldorf: Droste, 1990. 164 pp., illus., ports., facsims. (Veröffenlichungen des Heinrich-Heine-Instituts Düsseldorf.)

—— WEINBERG, HARRY: *Against the tide*. [See No. 27301.]

—— WEININGER, OTTO: *Eros und Psyche: Studien und Briefe 1899–1902*. Hrsg. von Hannelore Rodlauer [See No. 27745.]

27807. WITTGENSTEIN, LUDWIG. *Wittgenstein: Biographie, Philosophie, Praxis*. Eine Ausstellung der Wiener Secession (13. Sept.–29. Okt. 1989). Vorwort (Joseph Peter Stern, pp. 11–31) [Offprint].

27808. WOLF, FRIEDRICH. MÜLLER, HENNING: *Wer war Wolf? Friedrich Wolf (1888–1953) in Selbstzeugnissen, Bilddokumenten und Erinnerungen*. Köln: Röderberg, 1988. 263 pp. (Reihe Röderberg.) [See also No. 27415.]

27809. ZWEIG, ARNOLD: *'Soweit für heute . . . morgen mehr': Brief Arnold Zweigs an Solomon Liptzin aus dem Jahre 1945*. Eine Erstveröffenlichung. Kommentiert von Heidrun Loeper. [In]: Nachrichtenblatt des Verbandes der Jüdischen Gemeinden in der DDR, Dresden, Juni 1990. Pp. 7–11, facsim.

IX. GERMAN-JEWISH RELATIONS

A. General

27810. ARNIM, GABRIELE von: *Das grosse Schweigen: von der Schwierigkeit, mit den Schatten der Vergangenheit zu leben*. München: Kindler, 1989. 344 pp., bibl. (339–344). [On Germans' difficulties in mastering their historical past, particularly the Nazi period and the persecution of the Jews.]

27811. *Babylon*. Beiträge zur jüdischen Gegenwart. H. 7. Hrsg.: Micha Brumlik [et al.]. Frankfurt am Main: Verlag neue Kritik, Sept. 1990. [Incl.: Volk und Gesetz: über Erich Froms Dissertation (Hermann Kocyba, 116–124). Das jüdische Gesetz: zur Soziologie des

Diaspora-Judentums (Erich Fromm, 125–127). Further essays are listed according to subject.]

27812. DACHS, GISELA: *Der nationale Traum als Trauma: die deutschen Juden tun sich schwer mit der Einheit.* [In]: Die Zeit, Nr. 19, Hamburg, 4. Mai 1990. P. 2.

27813. DACHSELMÜLLER, CHRISTOPH: *Volkskultur und ihr nationales Bewusstsein: jüdische Volkskunde und ihr Einfluss auf die Gesellschaft der Jahrhundertwende.* [In]: Jahrbuch für Volkskunde, N.F. 12, Würzburg, 1989. Pp. 135 ff.

27814. *deutschland-berichte.* Hrsg.: Rolf Vogel. Jg. 26, Nr. 1–12. Bonn, 1990. 11 issues. [Final volume, publication suspended. Cf.: Dank an Rolf Vogel [in]: 'Allgemeine', Nr. 45/25, Bonn, 21. Juni 1990, p. 12.]

—— FREYERMUTH, GUNDOLF S.: *Reise in die Verlorengegangenheit: auf den Spuren deutscher Emigranten.* [See No. 27136.]

27815. FRIEDLANDER, ALBERT H.: *A thread of gold: journeys towards reconciliation.* Transl. by John Bowden. London: SCM Press; Philadelphia: Trinity Press International, 1990. 147 pp., ports. [For German edn. see No. 26858/YB XXXV.]

27816. FRIEDLANDER, EVELYN: *German-Jewish history: an interfaith exploration.* Report. [In]: Christian Jewish relations, Vol. 22, Nos. 3 & 4, Autumn/Winter 1989. Pp. 97–100.

27817. GIORDANO, RALPH: *Die zweite Schuld oder von der Last ein Deutscher zu sein.* München: Droemer Knaur, 1990. 367 pp. (Knaur, 3943: Sachbuch.) [Paperback edn. of No. 24757/YB XXXIII.]

27818. GIORDANO, RALPH: *Erfahrungen mit einem Buch (Die zweite Schuld oder von der Last ein Deutscher zu sein):* (ein Vortrag). Passau: Wiss. Verl. Rothe, 1989. 45 pp. (Kleine Rothe-Reihe, Bd. 1) [Lecture summarising the reception of R.G.'s book (first publ. in 1987; see No. 24757/YB XXXIII.).]

27819. GRASS, GÜNTER: *Schreiben nach Auschwitz.* Frankfurter Poetik-Vorlesung. Frankfurt am Main: Luchterhand, 1990. (Sammlung Luchterhand, 925.) [Discusses 'Vergangenheits-bewältigung' up to 1990.]

27820. HEIN, JÜRGEN: *Unfreiwillige Zwillinge? Christen und Juden im Wiener Volkstheater: Zusammenfassung.* [In]: Nestroyana, Jg. 8, H. 1/2, Wien, 1988. Pp. 21–28.

27821. The JEW IN LITERATURE. ANGRESS-KLUGER, RUTH: *Jewish characters in Thomas Mann's fiction.* [In]: Horizonte: Festschrift für Herbert Lehnert zum 65. Geburtstag. Tübingen: Niemeyer, 1990. Pp. 161–172.

27822. — NAUMANN, URSULA: *'Für einer Zeitung Gnadenlohn'?* Schillers Gedicht Die berühmte Frau und Sophie Ludwigs Buch Juda oder der erschlagene Redliche. [In]: Philologie, Bd. 109 (Sonderheft) H. 2, Pp. 16 ff.

27823. — WIECZOREK, JOHN P.: *Questioning philosemitism: the depiction of Jews in the prose work of Johannes Bobrowski.* [In]: German Life and letters, Vol. 44, No. 44, Oxford, 1990/1991. pp. 122–132.

27824. MAISLINGER, ANDREAS: *'Vergangenheitsbewältigung' in der BRD, der DDR und Österreich: Vergleich psychologisch-pädagogischer Massnahmen.* [In]: Zukunft, 6, Wien, Juni 1990. Pp. 48–54, notes (53–54).

27825. PAUCKER, ARNOLD: *Gedanken eines ehemaligen deutschen Juden.* Köln: Deutschlandfunk, 3. Okt. 1990. [Typescript of a broadcast on Oct. 3, 1990 on the occasion of the re-unification of Germany (available in the LBI London).]

27826. RINTELEN, KARL LUDWIG: *Der David-Kreis und die linke Minderheit.* Anmerkungen zum Problem des 'Handlungsspielraums' der mehrheitssozialdemokratischen Führung bis 1918/1919. [In]: Internationale wissenschaftliche Korrespondenz zu Geschichte der deutschen Arbeiterbewegung, Jg. 26, H.1, Berlin, März 1990. Pp. 14–34, notes. [Deals with factionalism and the split in the Social-Democratic movement of that period which was often expressed in antisemitism, often directed towards the Jewish members of the SPD, e.g. E. Bernstein, O. Cohn, H. Haase, J. Herzfeld, R. Hilferding.]

27827. SCHMITT, SAMUEL: *Am Rande notiert: Anmerkungen zum christlich-jüdischen Zusammenleben.* Schriesheim: Frank Albrecht Verl., 1990. 95 pp.

—— SCHOEPS, JULIUS H.: *Leiden an Deutschland: vom antisemitischen Wahn und der Last der Erinnerung.* [See No. 26960.]

27828. *Semit: die unabhängige jüdische Zeitschrift.* Hrsg.: Abraham Melzer. Dreieich (Buchschlager-Allee 28): Semit-Verl., Jan. 1989 ff. [A new periodical in the format Time Magazine, publ. 6 times a year.]

27829. STERN, FRANK: *Philosemitism – the whitewashing of the yellow badge in West Germany 1945–1952.* [In]: Holocaust and Genocide Studies, Vol. 4, No. 4, Oxford, 1989. Pp. 463–477.

27830. *Tribüne*. Zeitschrift zum Verständnis des Judentums. Jg. 29, H. 113–116. Hrsg. von Elisabeth Reisch. Frankfurt am Main: Tribüne-Verl., 1990. 4 issues. [All issues cont. various reports and articles on German-Jewish and German-Israeli relations. Further contributions are listed according to subject.]

27831. VOLKOV, SHULAMIT: *Deutsche und Juden im Zeitalter der Emanzipation: Überlegungen zu historischen Erfahrungen.* [In]: Neue Zürcher Zeitung, Nr. 208, 8./9. Sept. 1990. P. 66.

27832. WOLFFSOHN, MICHAEL: *Keine Angst vor Deutschland.* Erlangen: Straube-Verl., 1990. 240 pp.

B. German-Israeli Relations

27833. BEN-ARI, JITZHAK: *Israel und die Bundesrepublik: eine Bilanz besonderer Beziehungen.* [In]: Aus Politik und Zeitgeschichte: Beilage zur Wochenzeitung Das Parlament, Bonn, 6. Apr. 1990. Pp. 3–7.

27834. *Eindrücke von Jugendlichen bei ihrem Besuch in Israel.* [25. bis 27. Juni 1990]. [In]: Das Parlament, Nr. 30–31, Bonn, 20./27. July 1990. P. 15.

27835. *Der Einfluss der mitteleuropäischen Alijah auf Gesellschaft und Kultur in Israel.* Tagung, veranstaltet vom Irgun Olei Merkas Europa (IOME) in Zusammenarbeit mit dem Leo Baeck Institut und dem Goethe Institut, 11. Juni 1990. Report. [In]: MB, Jg. 58, Nr. 59, Tel-Aviv, Juni 1990. P. 2.

27836. HANSEN, NIELS: *Verbindungen in die Zukunft: 25 Jahre diplomatische Beziehungen zwischen Deutschland und Israel.* [In]: Aus Politik und Zeitgeschichte; Beilage zur Wochenzeitung Das Parlament, Bonn, 6. Apr. 1990. Pp. 8–18.

27837. KLOKE, MARTIN W.: *Israel und die deutsche Linke: zur Geschichte eines schwierigen Verhältnisses.* Frankfurt am Main: Haag & Herchen, 1990. 228 pp. (Schriftenreihe des Deutsch-Israelischen Arbeitskreises für Frieden im Nahen Osten e.V., Bd. 20.)

27838. MEROZ, YOCHANAN: *Israel, Jews and German unity.* [In Hebrew, with English summary]. [In]: Gesher, No. 122, Jerusalem, Winter 1990/1991. Pp. 7–16. [On the Jewish and Israeli perspectives of German reunification.]

27839. RENDTORFF, ROLF: *Freundschaft mit Israel: Erfahrungen – Einsichten – Konsequenzen: Rolf Rendtorff im Gespräch.* Frankfurt am Main: Haag & Herchen, 1990. 26 pp., (Israel & Palästina, Sonderheft, 23).

27840. VOGEL, ROLF, ed.: *Der deutsch-israelische Dialog: Dokumentation eines erregenden Kapitels deutscher Aussenpolitik.* Bd. 1–8. München; New York [et al.]: Saur, 1987–1990. 8 vols. [Cont.: *Teil 1: Politik.* 1987–1988. Bde. 1–3. *Teil 2: Wirtschaft, Landwirtschaft.* 1989. Bde. 4–5. *Teil 3: Kultur. 1989–1990.* Bde. 6–8.]

C. Church and Synagogue

27841. BATTENBERG, FRIEDRICH: *Reformation, Judentum und Landesherrliche Gesetzgebung: ein Beitrag zum Verhältnis des protestantischen Landeskirchentums zu den Juden.* [In]: Reformation et reformationes: Festschrift für Lothar Graf zu Dohna. Darmstadt: Technische Hochschule, 1989. Pp. 315–346.

27842. *Bilanz nach 40 Jahren Staat Israel: Christen und Juden im Gespräch.* Manfred Görg [et al.] Regensburg: Pustet, 1989. 108 pp., bibl. [Cont. (titles condensed): Jüdisches im Christentum – Christliches im Judentum. (M. Görg). Juden und Christen im Wandel der Zeit (Moshe Zimmermann). Der Dialog hat erst begonnen (Rolf Rendtorff). Hat sich der jüdisch-christliche Dialog nach 1945 gelohnt? (Nathan P. Levinson). Jüdisches Selbstverständnis und der Staat Israel (Michael Toch). Die Christen und der Staat Israel (H. Maier).]

27843. BONHOEFFER, DIETRICH. MÜLLER, CHRISTINE-RUTH: *Dietrich Bonhoeffers Kampf gegen die nationalsozialistische Verfolgung und Vernichtung der Juden: Bonhoeffers Haltung zur Judenfrage.* Ein Vergleich mit Stellungnahmen aus der evangelischen Kirche und Kreisen des deutschen Widerstandes. München: Kaiser, 1990. 352 pp. [Cf.: Dem Rad in die Speichen fallen (Beatrice Wolter) [in]: Das Parlament, No. 14–15, March 29/April 5, Bonn 1991.]

27844. DÖLLINGER, IGNAZ. *Geschichtlichkeit und Glaube: Gedenkschrift zum 100. Todestag Ignaz von Döllingers.* Hrsg. von Georg Denzler und Ernst Ludwig Grasmück. München: Wewel Verl., 1990. [Incl.: Döllingers Stellung zum Judentum (Manfred Görg, pp. 449–458).] [I.v.D., 1799–1890, Catholic theologian and historian.]

—— EHRLICH, ERNST LUDWIG: *Christen und Juden auf meinem Weg.* [See No. 27482.]

—— FRIEDRICH, NORBERT: *Der Beitrag evangelischer Theologen im Kampf gegen den Antisemitismus.* [See No. 27857.]

27845. HERMLE, SIEGFRIED: *Evangelische Kirche und Judentum: Stationen nach 1945.* Göttingen: Vandenhoeck & Ruprecht, 1990. 422 pp.

27846. JANSEN, REINER: *Christliche Kirche und Judentum von den Kirchenvätern bis zu den Reformatoren.* [In]: Judaica, Jg. 46, H. 3, Basel, Sept. 1990. Pp. 134–163, notes.

—— ROTHSCHILD, FRITZ A., ed.: *Jewish perspectives on Christianity: the views of Leo Baeck, Martin Buber, Franz Rosenzweig, Will Herberg, and Abraham J. Heschel.* [See No. 27514.]

27847. STEIN, EDITH. SCHANDL, FELIX M.: *'Ich sah aus meinem Volk die Kirche wachsen!':* jüdische Bezüge und Strukturen in Leben und Werk Edith Steins (1891–1942). Mit einer Einführung von Waltraud Herbstrith. Sinzi: Sankt-Meinrad-Verl. für Theologie Esser, 1990. XXII, 278 pp., illus., bibl. (262–278). (Sinziger theologische Texte und Studien, Bd. 9.)

27848. —— BÖCKEL, MATTHIAS: *Edith Stein und das Judentum.* Mit einem Vorwort von Maria Amata Neyer. Ramstein: Paque, 1989. 1 vol. (ca. 90 pp.) [Obtainable from M. Böckel, Am Bahnhof 3 a, D-6749 Klingenmünster.]

27849. —— SCHLICKEL, FERDINAND: *Edith Stein seliggesprochen: Jüdin und Ordensfrau.* 2., erweiterte Auf. München: Schnell & Steiner, 1988. 31 pp. [E. St., data see No. 22718/YB XXXI.]

—— ZAK, ADAM: *Aufgeschobene Begegnung – Franz Rosenzweigs Konzeption der Beziehung zwischen Judentum und Christentum.* [See No. 27513.]

D. Antisemitism

27850. ALMOG, SHMUEL: *Nationalism and antisemitism in modern Europe 1815–1945.* Oxford: Pergamon Press, 1990. 130 pp., illus. (Studies in antisemitism.) [Incl. the Austro-Hungarian Empire; Romania, Imperial Germany; the Weimar Republic; Antisemitism and the Holocaust.]

27851. ALLSWANG, BENZION: *The final resolution: combating anti-Jewish hostility.* New York, Jerusalem: Feldheim, 1989. IX, 293 pp. [Study of philosophical and psychological causes of antisemitism, incl. German antisemitism.]

—— AUSTRIA. [See also No. 27194.]

—— — MARIN, BERND: *Ein historisch neuartiger 'Antisemitismus' ohne Antisemiten?* [See No. 27115.]

—— — PAULEY, BRUCE F.: *Politischer Antisemitismus im Wien der Zwischenkriegszeit.* [See No. 27115.]

—— — PULZER, PETER: *Spezifische Momente und Spielarten des österreichischen und des Wiener Antisemitismus.* [See No. 27115.]

—— — SCHEICHL, SIGURD PAUL: *Nuancen in der Sprache der Judenfeinde.* [See No. 27115.]

—— — STAUDINGER, ANTON: *Katholischer Antisemitismus in der Ersten Republik.* [See No. 27115.]

—— — WISTRICH, ROBERT S.: *Sozialdemokratie, Antisemitismus und die Wiener Juden.* [See No. 27115.]

—— — WODAK, RUTH: *Opfer der Opfer? Der 'alltägliche Antisemitismus' in Österreich.* [See pp. 292–319 in No. 27855.]

—— BÄHTZ, DIETER: *Die jüdischen Salons in Berlin zu Beginn des 19. Jahrhunderts in der antisemitischen Historiographie der Faschisten.* [See No. 26994.]

27852. BÄRSCH, CLAUS-E.: *Das Katastrophenbewusstsein eines werdenden Nationalsozialismus: der Antisemitismus im Tagebuch des Joseph Goebbels vor dem Eintritt in die NSDAP.* [In]: Menora, Bd. 1, München, 1990. Pp. 125–151, notes.

27853. BECKER, PETER EMIL: *Wege ins Dritte Reich. Teil 2: Sozialdarwinismus, Rassismus und Völkischer Gedanke.* Stuttgart; New York: Thieme, 1990. X, 644 pp., illus. [Part 1 appeared under the title: Zur Geschichte der Rassenhygiene: Wege ins Dritte Reich. Stuttgart; New York: Thieme, 1988. X, 403 pp., illus., tabs.]

27854. BENZ, WOLFGANG, ed.: *Legenden – Lügen – Vorurteile: ein Lexikon zur Zeitgeschichte.* München-Gräfelfing: Moos & Partner, 1990. [See No. 27427.]

27855. BERGMANN, WERNER/ERB, RAINER, eds.: *Antisemitismus in der politischen Kultur nach 1945.* Opladen: Westdeutscher Verl., 1990. 348 pp. [Cont. the sections: I. Kontinuität und Diskontinuität des Antisemitismus (with the essays): Das Judentum als Antithese (Christhard Hoffmann, 20–37). Der Holocaust als Epochenscheide der Antisemitismusgeschichte (Herbert A. Strauss, 38–56). Nationale Identität und Antisemitismus in Deutschland (Bernd Estel, 57–78). Kollektive Erinnerungen und gesellschaftliche Lernprozesse (Max Miller, 79–107). II. Ergebnisse der Umfrageforschung zum Antisemitismus (with the essays): Sind die Deutschen antisemitisch? Meinungsumfragen von 1946–1987 in der BRD (Werner Bergmann, 108–130). Umfragen zum Antisemitismus: ein Vergleich zwischen vier Nationen

(Frederick D. Weil, 131–179). III: Antisemitismus in der politischen Kultur (with the essays): Entstehung, Bedeutung und Funktion des Philosemitismus in Westdeutschland nach 1945 (Frank Stern, 180–196). Die Evangelische Kirche und das Judentum nach 1945 (Siegfried Hermle, 197–217). Jugend als Symbol des politischen Neubeginns (Sybille Hübner-Funk, 218–237). Die Rückerstattung: ein Kristallisationspunkt für Antisemitismus (Rainer Erb, 238–252). Antisemitismus als politisches Ereignis: die antisemitische Schmierwelle im Winter 1959/1960 (Werner Bergmann, 253–277). Moralkommunikation und Kommunikationsmoral (Jürgen Bellers, 278–291). Opfer der Opfer? Der 'alltägliche Antisemitismus' in Österreich (Ruth Wodak, 292–319). IV. Zur gesellschaftlichen Rolle der Juden im Nachkriegsdeutschland (with the essays): Staat und Minorität: Antisemitismus und die gesellschaftliche Rolle der Juden in der Nachkriegszeit (Y. Michal Bodemann, 320–331). Die jüdische Gemeinde Ost-Berlins und ihre Integration in die DDR (Robin Ostow, 332–344).]

—— BIECHELE, WERNER: *Jüdische Intellektuelle im Spannungsfeld von bürgerlichem Demokratie-Verständnis und antisemitischem Rassenwahn.* [See No. 27730.]

27856. BRANDES, GEORG: *Die Bewegung gegen die Juden in Deutschland.* [In]: Brandes, Georg: Berlin als deutsche Reichshauptstadt: Erinnerungen aus den Jahren 1877–1883. Aus dem Dänischen übers. Hrsg. von Erik M. Christensen und Hans-Dieter Loock. Berlin: Colloquium, 1989. (Wissenschaft und Stadt, Bd. 12.) Pp. 390–398.

27857. FRIEDRICH, NORBERT: *Der Beitrag evangelischer Theologen im Kampf gegen den Antisemitismus, dargestellt am Verein zur Abwehr des Antisemitismus in der Weimarer Republik.* Bochum, Staatliches Prüfungsamt für Erste Staatsprüfungen für Lehrämter an Schulen in Dortmund – Aussenstelle Bochum, Mai 1990. III, 205 pp., bibl. (184–200). [Mimeog., available in the LBI London.] [Deals specifically with Otto Baumgarten, Emil Felden, Eduard Lamparter, Hans Tribukait; incl. chap. on the Verein zur Abwehr des Antisemitismus (18–53).]

27858. GERBER, BARBARA: *Jud Süß: Aufstieg und Fall im frühen 18. Jahrhundert.* Ein Beitrag zur Historischen Antisemitismus- und Rezeptionsforschung. Hamburg: Hans Christians Verl., 1990. 754 pp., notes, illus., bibl. (577–640), index (751–754). (Hamburger Beiträge zur Geschichte der deutschen Juden, Bd. 16; zugl.: Hamburg, Univ. Diss.)

27859. *Geteilter Feminismus: Rassismus, Antisemitismus, Fremdenhass.* (Hrsg.: Sozialwissenschaftliche Forschung und Praxis für Frauen e.V., Red.: Ute Annecke [et al.].) 1. Aufl. Köln: Verein Beiträge zur Feministischen Theorie und Praxis, 1990. 183 pp., illus., map, bibl. (Beiträge zur feministischen Theorie und Praxis, H. 27.]

27860. HITLER, ADOLF: *Hitler, speeches and proclamations 1932–1945: the chronicle of a dictatorship.* Vol. 1, 1932–1934. Ed. by Max Domarus. Transl. from the German by Mary Fran Gilbert. Wauconda, Ill.: Bolchazy-Carducci Publ., 1990. 611 pp., illus. [First of four-volume set, incl. Hitler's speech announcing the beginning of the boycott against the Jews. Editor's introd. discusses Hitler's antisemitism.]

27861. HUNGARY, BIBO, ISTVAN: *Zur Judenfrage: am Beispiel Ungarns nach 1944.* Aus dem Ungar. von Béla Rásky. Frankfurt am Main: Verlag Neue Kritik, 1990. 181 pp. [Orig. publ. in 1948; on the roots of Hungarian antisemitism and the reasons why Hungarian society did not oppose the persecution of Jews during the Nazi period, also on persisting antisemitic prejudice after 1945.]

—— — KORBULY, DEZSÖ: *Im Zeichen 'rassischer Notwehr'. Politischer Katholizismus und Antisemitismus in Ungarn (1890–1944).* [See No. 27124.]

27862. KLÖNNE, ARNO: *Völkisch-antisemitische Herkünfte des Nationalsozialismus.* [In]: Opfer und Täter: zum nationalsozialistischen und antijüdischen Alltag in Ostwestfalen-Lippe. Hrsg. von Hubert Frankemölle. (Im Auftrag der Gesellschaft für Christlich-Jüdische Zusammenarbeit, Paderborn. Bielefeld: Verlag für Regionalgeschichte 1990. Pp. 13–25. [See No. 27410.]

27863. LANGMUIR, GAVIN I.: *History, religion, and antisemitism.* Berkeley: Univ. of California Press, 1990. XI, 380 pp. [Incl. German medieval antisemitism.]

27864. LANGMUIR, GAVIN I.: *Toward a definition of antisemitism.* Berkeley: Univ. of California Press, 1990. 200 pp. [Incl. German antisemitism.]

27865. LINK, JERE H.: *Semitism in German literary politics: the special case of the Deutsche Schillerstiftung.* [In]: LBI Year Book XXXV, London, 1990. Pp. 371–383, notes.

27866. LUTHER, MARTIN. BERING, DIETZ: *Eine Tragödie der Nähe? Luther und die Juden.* [In]: Architectura poetica: Festschrift für Johannes Rathofer zum 65. Geburtstag. Köln: Böhlau, 1990. Pp. 327–344.

—— MAASS, HANS: *Verführung der Unschuldigen: Beispiele judenfeindlicher Kinderliteratur im 3. Reich.* [See No. 27326.]

27867. NIEWYK, DONALD L.: *Solving the 'Jewish Problem' Continuity and change in German antisemitism 1871–1945.* [In]: LBI Year Book XXXV, London, 1990. Pp. 335–370, notes.

—— OESTERREICHER, JOHANNES: *Zur Genealogie von Hitlers Judenhass.* [See No. 27277.]

27868. PATSCHOVSKY, ALEXANDER: *Judenverfolgung im Mittelalter.* [In]: Geschichte i. Wissenschaft u. Unterricht, H. 1, Stuttgart, 1990. Pp. 1–16, notes.

27869. PAUL, GERHARD: *Aufstand der Bilder: Die NS-Propaganda vor 1933.* Bonn: J.H.W. Dietz, 1990. 432 pp. [Incl. survey of effectiveness of racist and antisemitic propaganda.]

—— PETERS, PAUL: *Heinrich Heine 'Dichterjude': die Geschichte einer Schmähung.* [See No. 27694.]

27870. RAPHAEL, FREDERIC: *The necessity of antisemitism.* [In]: The Jewish Quarterly, Vol. 37, (137), London, Spring 1990. Pp. 26–34.

—— RÖLL, WALTER: *Ein antijüdisches Flugblatt von 1670 als sprachliche Quelle.* [See No. 26983.]

27871. ROHRBACHER, STEFAN: *Ritualmord-Beschuldigungen am Niederrhein: christlicher Aberglaube und antijüdische Agitation im 19. Jahrhundert.* [In]: Menora, Bd. 1, München, 1990. Pp. 299–326, notes.

27872. ROHRBACHER, STEFAN: *Volksfrömmigkeit und Judenfeindschaft: zur Vorgeschichte des politischen. Antisemitismus im katholischen Rheinland.* [In]: Annalen des Historischen Vereins für den Niederrhein 192/193, Pulheim 1990. Pp. 125–144, notes.

27873. ROSE, PAUL LAWRENCE: *Revolutionary antisemitism in Germany from Kant to Wagner.* Princeton, N.J.: Princeton Univ. Press, 1990. 395 pp. [Historical survey of antisemitism from Luther to Wagner.]

27874. SCHECHTER, RIVKA: *Paulus, Luther, Goethe, Hitler: from gnosticism to the Third Reich.* [In Hebrew, with English summary]. [In]: Nativ: a journal of politics and the arts, Vol. 3, No. 1, Tel-Aviv, Jan. 1990. Pp. 30–37. [Also on German antisemitism.]

—— SCHLOTZHAUER, INGE: *Ideologie und Organisation des politischen Antisemitismus in Frankfurt am Main, 1880–1914.* [See No. 27025.]

27875. SCHMIDT, MICHAEL: *Schacher und Wucher: ein antisemitischer Stereotyp im Spiegel christlicher und jüdischer Autobiographien der Goethezeit.* [In]: Menorah, Bd. 1, München, 1990. Pp. 235–277, notes.

—— SCHOEPS, JULIUS H.: *Leiden an Deutschland: vom antisemitischen Wahn und der Last der Erinnerung.* [See No. 26960.]

—— SCHREINER, KLAUS: *Von der Judentoleranz zur Judenemanzipation.* [See No. 26962.]

27876. SCHUBERT, KURT: *Antisemitische Verwertung jüdischer Traditionen und ihre Widerlegung.* Wien (Burggasse 35): Informationszentrum im Dienste der Christl. – Jüd. Verständigung, 1990. 27 pp. (IDCIV-Vorträge, 26.)

27877. SHEDLETZKY, ITTA: *Majestätsbeleidigung und Menschenwürde: die Fatalität des Antisemitismus in Heinrich Manns Roman 'Der Untertan'.* [In]: Bulletin des LBI, 86, Frankfurt am Main, 1990. Pp. 67–81, notes.

27878. STRAUSS, HERBERT A./BERGMANN, WERNER/HOFFMANN, CHRISTHARD, eds.: *Der Antisemitismus der Gegenwart.* Frankfurt am Main: Campus, 1990. 276 pp. [Incl.: Der Protest zwischen Neuanfang und Beharrung (Ekkehard W. Stegemann, 49–65, bibl.). Antisemitismus im internationalen Rechtsextremismus [incl. Germany] (Juliane Wetzel, 101–123, notes). Kathartische Zerreißproben: zur Israel-Diskussion in der Partei Die Grünen (Martin W. Kloke, 124–148, notes.).].

27879. SWITZERLAND. KAMIS-MÜLLER, AARON: *Antisemitismus in der Schweiz 1900–1930.* Zürich: Chronos, 1990. 547 pp. & [25 pp.] summaries in English, French and Hebrew, illus., bibl.

27880. VERBEECK, GEORGI: *Marxism, antisemitism and the Holocaust.* [In]: LBI Year Book XXXV, London, 1990. Pp. 385–396, notes.

27881. VOLKOV, SHULAMIT: *Jüdisches Leben und Antisemitismus im 19. und 20. Jahrhundert. Zehn Essays.* München: Beck 1990. 234 pp., notes. [Individual essays are listed under No. 26970.]

27882. WEINDLING, PAUL: *Health, race, and German politics between national unification and Nazism 1870–1945.* Cambridge: Cambridge Univ. Press, 1989. X, 641 pp., illus. [Cf.: To purify the tribe (Michael Burleigh) [in]: TLS, London, June 1–7, 1990, p. 592. Review (Ronald Smelser) [in]: German Studies Review, Vol. 13, No. 2, Tempe, Az., May 1990, pp. 354–355.]

27883. YARDENI, MYRIAM: *Anti-Jewish mentalities in early modern Europe.* Lanham, Md.: Univ. Press of America, 1990. 297 pp., notes. [Collection of essays on antisemitism, incl. Alsace, and a chap. on Huguenots and Jews in 17th-century Brandenburg and Prussia.]

27884. ZENTRUM FÜR ANTISEMITISMUSFORSCHUNG: *Bibliographie zum Antisemitismus: die Bestände der Bibliothek des Zentrums für Antisemitismusforschung der Technischen Universität Berlin* = A bibliography on antisemitism. Hrsg. von Herbert A. Strauss. Bearb. von Lydia Bressem

(Katalog) und Antje Gerlach (Sachregister). Bd. 1–4. München; New York: Saur, 1989 ff. Bd. 1: A–G. 1989. XX, 433 pp. Bd. 2–3: H–P; Q–Z. 1990. 435–938; 939–1374 pp. [Vol. 4: Subject index will follow.]

E. Noted Germans and Jews

27885. BRECHT, BERTOLT: *Letters 1913–1956*. Transl. by Ralph Manheim. Ed. with commentary by John Willett. London: Methuen, 1990. 720 pp., editor's notes (567–691). [Incl. many letters from B.B.'s German-Jew correspondents, e.g. Döblin, Feuchtwanger, Kisch, Kortner.]

27886. BUSCH, FRITZ. FUHRMANN, PETER: *Ein ganzer Mann und Künstler*: Erinnerung an den Dirigenten Fritz Busch, der vor 100 Jahren geboren wurde. [In]: Die Zeit, Nr. 15, Hamburg, 6. Apr. 1990. P. 31. [F.B., March 13, 1890 Siegen – Sept. 14, 1951 London, German conductor, general music director of Dresden State Opera from 1922, forced to leave Germany in 1933 due to public protest against the Nazi regime and its policies towards Jews, emigrated to Argentina and to England, performed in various countries.]

27887. ELLERIN, BRUCE ELKIN: *Nietzsche among the Zionists*. Ithaca, N.Y., Cornell Univ. Thesis, 1990. XLIV, 450 pp., illus. [How Nietzsche's philosophy influenced early Zionist thinking.]

27888. HEIDEGGER, MARTIN. HEIDEGGER, MARTIN/JASPERS, KARL: *Briefwechsel 1920–1963*. Hrsg. von Walter Biemel und Hans Saner. Frankfurt am Main: Klostermann; München: Piper, 1990. 299 pp. [Letters refer also to Heidegger's attitudes towards Nazism and Jews during the Nazi period.]

27889. — JURT, JOSEPH: *The philosopher and politics: new studies on Heidegger and National Socialism*. [In]: Journal of European Studies, Vol. 20, No. 78, Cambridge, June 1990. Pp. 167–177, notes. [Deals with Heidegger's antisemitism and his lack of insight after the war.]

27890. — LILLA, MARK: *What Heidegger wrought*. [In]: Commentary, Vol. 89, No. 1, New York, Jan. 1990. Pp. 41–51. [On the Heidegger controversy, particularly the book by Victor Farias, see No. 26914/YB XXXV.]

27891. — LYOTARD, JEAN-FRANÇOIS: *Vortrag in Wien und Freiburg Heidegger und 'die Juden'*. (Aus dem Französ. von Clemens Pornschlegel u. Werner Rappl.) Deutsche Erstausg. Wien: Passagen-Verl., 1990. 64 pp. [Also French edn. under the title: Conférence à Vienne et Freiburg Heidegger et 'les juifs'.]

27892. — RUBENSTEIN, RICHARD: *The philosopher and the Jews: the case of Martin Heidegger*. [In]: Modern Judaism, Vol. 9, No. 2, Baltimore, 1989. Pp. 179 ff.

27893. — VIETTA, SILVIO: *Heideggers Kritik am nationalsozialismus und an der Technik*. Tübingen: Niemeyer, 1989. 105 pp [Discusses also Heidegger and antisemitism.] [Cf.: Besprechung (Martin Bauer) [In]: Das Historisch-Politische Buch, Jg. 38, H. 7, Göttingen, 1990, pp. 209–210.]

27894. — ZIMMERMAN, MICHAEL E.: Heidegger's confrontation with modernity: technology, politics, art. Bloomington: Indiana Univ. Press, 1990. XXXVII, 306 pp., notes. [Incl. also H.'s antisemitism and his involvement with National Socialism.]

27895. HIRSCH, HELMUT: *Zur Dichotomie von Theorie und Praxis in Bettines [v. Arnim] Äußerungen über Judentum und Juden*. [In]: Internationales Jahrbuch der Bettina-von-Arnim-Gesellschaft, Bd. 1989, Berlin 1989. Pp. 153–172, notes.

27896. MANN, GOLO: *Reminiscences and reflections: growing up in Germany*. Transl. by Krishna Winston. London: Faber, 1991. XIII, 338 pp. [Incl. G.M.'s friendship with Leopold Schwarzschild and many other German Jews; also his views on antisemitism.]

27897. MANN, THOMAS: *The letters of Thomas Mann, 1895–1955*. Selected and transl. by Richard and Clara Winston. Berkeley, Ca.: Univ. of California Press, 1990. 550 pp. [Incl. letters to Adorno, Freud, Einstein, Schönberg, a.o. Orig. edn. 1975.]

27898. MELLEN, PHILIP: *Gerhart Hauptmann and Alfred Kerr: a further consideration*. [In]. The Germanic Review, Vol. 65, No. 4, Washington, D.C. Fall 1990. Pp. 159–170, notes. [Discusses their long and problematic relationship, especially K.'s criticism of H.'s silence about the fate of his Jewish friends during the Nazi period.]

27899. MORRIS, RODLER F.: *From Weimar philosemite to Nazi apologist: the case of Walter Bloem*. London: The Edwin Mellen Press, 1988. 256 pp., notes, bibl (229–239). (Studies in German Thought and History Vol. 7.) [Deals with Bloem's novel 'Brüderlichkeit']

27900. RATHER, L. J.: *Reading Wagner: a study in the history of ideas*. Baton Rouge: Louisiana State Univ. Press, 1990. XIII, 349 pp. [Also covers Wagner's antisemitism.]

X. FICTION, POETRY and HUMOUR

27901. ADLER, H. G.: *Neun Gedichte aus Theresienstadt*. [In]: europäische ideen, Heft 70, Berlin 1989. Pp. 14–17. [Incl. biographical postscript by Jeremy Adler. For H.G.A.'s data see No. 25665/ YB XXXIV.]

27902. APPELFELD, AHARON: *The healer*. Transl. by Jeffrey M. Green. London: Weidenfeld & Nicolson, 1990. 184 pp. [Cf.: The fictional world of Aharon Appelfeld (Lothar Kahn) [In]: Jewish Frontier, Vol. 47, No. 1, New York, Jan./Feb., pp. 16–18.]

27903. CANETTI, VEZA: *Die gelbe Strasse*. Roman. Mit einem Vorwort von Elias Canetti und einem Nachwort von Helmut Göbelö. München: Hanser, 1990. 180 pp. [Novel by Elias Canetti's first wife, orig. publ. in the Vienna 'Arbeiterzeitung', 1932/1933: describes scenes and characters from Vienna's Leopoldstadt.] [V.C., née Venetiana Taubner-Calderon, 1897 Vienna – 1963 London, author.]

27904. DALOS, GYÖRGY: *Die Beschneidung*. Aus dem Ungar. von György Dalos und Elsbeth Zylla. Frankfurt am Main: Insel, 1990. 199 pp. [Story of a 12-year-old Hungarian boy not circumcised as a baby because of the war, now wishing to be barmitzvah.] [Cf.: Problematik jüdischer Identität in Ungarn (E.H.) [In]:] Neue Zürcher Zeitung, Nr. 62, Zürich, 15. März 1990, p. 77.

27905. DESAI, ANITA: *Baumgartners Bombay*. Roman. Aus dem Engl. übers. von Peter Torberg. München: List 1989. 277 pp. [Cf.: Roman über einen nach Indien emigrierten Berliner Juden (Renate Schostack) [in]: Frankfurter Allgemeine Zeitung, Nr. 73, Frankfurt am Main, 27. März 1990, p. 34.]

27906. DISCHE, IRENE: *Der Doktor braucht ein Heim*. Erzählung. Aus dem Amerikan. von Reinhard Kaiser. Frankfurt am Main: Suhrkamp, 1990. 51 pp. [Cf.: Eine erotische Elegie: Irene Dische erzählt vom Wahnsinn, der sich Liebe nennt (Verena Auffermann) [in]: Süddeutsche Zeitung, Nr. 261, München, 13 Nov. 1990. p. VII.]

27907. FICHTE, HUBERT: *The orphanage*. Transl. by Martin Chalmers. London: Serpent's Tail, 1990. 161 pp. [Novel tells of the survival of a half-Jewish child in war-time Germany who grows up in a Catholic orphanage. First publ. in German in 1965.]

—— FLORSHEIM, STEWART J., ed.: *Ghosts of the Holocaust: an anthology of poetry by the second generation*. [See No. 27288.]

27908. FUKS, LADISLAV: *Reise ins gelobte Land*. Roman. Aus dem Tschech. von Eckhard Thiele. Mindelheim: Sachon-Werl., 1990. [On the failed attempt of a group of Jews from Vienna to escape to Palestine.] [Cf.: Die Illusion der Erlösung (Susanne Roth) [In]: Neue Zürcher Zeitung, Nr. 274, 24./25. Nov. 1990, p. 104.]

27909. HALEWY, BEN RAFAEL: *Newo. Zeitroman*. Frankfurt am Main: Haag & Herchen, 1990. 167 pp. [On the fate of German Jews under Nazism.]

27910. NUROWSKA, MARIA: *Postscriptum für Anna und Miriam*. Roman, aus dem Polnischen übersetzt von Albrecht Lempp. Frankfurt am Main: Fischer Taschenbuch, 1990. 155 pp. [On long-term consequences of Holocaust.] [Cf.: Minen in Annas Kopf (Klaus-Peter Walter). [In]: Frankfurter Allg. Zeitung, No. 97, April 26, 1991, p. 34.]

27911. SANDEN, HANS-HEINZ: *Der Makel: eine Jugend zwischen Rassen und Klassen*. München: Iniversitätsverl. in Fa. A. Herbig, 1990. 393 pp. [Based on the author's own autobiography, the novel describes childhood and youth of a "half-Jewish" child in Nazi-Germany, torn between his Jewish father and his non-Jewish mother and her second husband who have turned into fervent Nazis.] [Cf.: Besprechung (Ludger Heid) [In]: Das Historisch-Politische Buch, Jg. 39, H. 2, Göttingen 1991, p. 51.]

27912. STEWART, FRED MUSTARD: *The glitter and the gold*. New York: New American Library, 1989. 429 pp [A fictional account of a family fleeing from antisemitism in Germany and coming to America in 1849 to find a better life.]

27913. STRAUSS, LUDWIG: *Das verpaßte Verbrechen und andere Prosa*. Hrsg, und mit einem Nachwort versehen von Gregor Ackermann und Werner Jung. Aachen: Alono, 1990. 192 pp. [Cf.: Den Kleinbürger am Kragen gepackt (Horst Seferens) [In]: 'Allgemeine', Nr. 46/14, Bonn 4. April 1991, p. 11.] [L.S., born 1892 in Aachen, died 1953 in Jerusalem, prof. of German literature at the Univ. of Aachen, emigrated to Palestine in 1935, teacher at Ben Shemen, prof. at the Hebrew Univ. Jerusalem.

Index to Bibliography

List of Contributors

BORUT, Jacob, M.A., b. 1956 in Jerusalem. Doctoral candidate at the Hebrew University, Jerusalem. Author of i.a. 'Frankfurt am Main', in Israel Gutman (ed.), *Encyclopedia of the Holocaust*, vol. II (1990); 'Frankfurt am Main, 1824–1945' and other shorter articles for *Pinkas Hakehillot. Encyclopaedia of Jewish Communities from their Foundation till after the Holocaust. Germany. Part 3: Hessen* (1991, in Hebrew). Currently editing *Pinkas Hakehillot. Germany. Part 4: Rhine Province, Westphalia, Palatinate, Saarland* (in Hebrew).

CARON, Vicki, Ph.D., b. 1951 in Chicago. Assistant Professor, Judaic Studies Program, Brown University. Author of i.a. *Between France and Germany. The Jews of Alsace-Lorraine, 1871–1918* (1988); 'The Ambivalent Legacy. The Impact of Enlightenment and Emancipation on Zionism', in *Judaism* 4 (Fall 1989); 'Franco-Jewish Assimilation Reassessed. A Review of the Recent Literature', in *Jewish History* (Spring 1991). (Contributor, with Paula Hyman, to Year Book XXVI and contributor to Year Books XXVIII and XXX.)

COCKS, Geoffrey, Ph.D., b. 1948 in the USA. Professor of History, Albion College, Michigan. Author of *Psychotherapy in the Third Reich. The Göring Institute* (1985). Co-editor of *Psycho/History. Readings in the Method of Psychology, Psychoanalysis and History* (1987); *The Unfree Professions. German Lawyers, Teachers and Engineers, 1900–1950* (1990).

DALE JONES, Priscilla, Ph.D., b. 1953 in Newport, R.I. Historical researcher and writer. Author of several articles and reviews, i.a. 'The Finaly Affair. Issues and Implications', in *Religion* (July 1983); and 'Trials of "Minor" German War Criminals Conducted by British Military Courts in Germany and Elsewhere', in Israel Gutman (ed.), *Encyclopedia of the Holocaust* (1989).

ENGEL HOLLAND, Eva J., Ph.D., b. 1919 in Dortmund. Editor-General of *Moses Mendelssohn Jubiläumsausgabe* and Editor of vol. IV (1977), vol. VI.2 (1981) and vols. V.1c and V.2 (1991). Author of i.a. *Jean Paul's Schulmeisterlein Wuz* (1962) and of books and numerous articles on German literature and philosophy. (Contributor to Year Book XXIV.)

FRIESEL, Evyatar, Ph.D., b. 1930 in Germany. Professor of Modern Jewish History, Hebrew University, Jerusalem. Author of *Zionist Policy after the Balfour Declaration* (1977, in Hebrew); *Atlas of Modern Jewish History* (1983, in Hebrew). (Contributor to Year Books XXXI and XXXIII.)

GOSCHLER, Constantin, cand. Dr. phil., b. 1960 in Göppingen. Author of i.a. 'Controversy about a Pittance. The Compensation of Forced Laborers from

593

Concentration Camps by Germany's Post-War Industry', in *Dachau Review*, 1 (1988). Co-editor of *Wiedergutmachung in der Bundesrepublik Deutschland* (1989).

HALLO, William W., Ph.D., b. 1928 in Kassel. William M. Laffan Professor of Assyriology and Babylonian Literature and Curator of the Babylonian Collection, Yale University. Co-author of i.a. *Heritage, Civilization and the Jews*, 2 vols. (1984). Co-editor of *Scripture in Context*, vols. I–III (1980, 1983, 1990). Translator of Franz Rosenzweig, *The Star of Redemption* (1971).

HERZBERG, Arno, Dr. jur., b. 1907 in Poznań. Formerly jurist, Germany (to April 1933); manager, Jewish Telegraphic Agency Berlin (1934–1937) and contributor to Jewish newspapers; later Certified Public Accountant in the USA. Author of numerous articles on taxes and accounting.

HOFFMANN, Christhard, Dr. phil., b. 1952 in Lüneburg. Wissenschaftlicher Assistent at the Zentrum für Antisemitismusforschung, Technische Universität Berlin. Author of i.a. *Juden und Judentum im Werk deutscher Althistoriker des 19. and 20. Jahrhunderts* (1988); 'The Contribution of German-speaking Jewish Immigrants to British Historiography', in Werner E. Mosse *et al.* (eds.), *Second Chance. Two Centuries of German-speaking Jews in the United Kingdom* (1991); *Zerstörte Geschichte. Studien zur Emigration der Jüdischen Geschichtswissenschaft aus dem nationalsozialistischen Deutschland nach England und in die USA* (forthcoming).

JARAUSCH, Konrad H., Ph.D., b. 1941 in Magdeburg. Lurcy Professor of European Civilization, University of North Carolina. Author of i.a. *The Enigmatic Chancellor. Bethmann Hollweg and the Hubris of Imperial Germany* (1973); *Students, Society and Politics in Imperial Germany. The Rise of Academic Illiberalism* (1982). Co-editor of *The Unfree Professions. German Lawyers, Teachers and Engineers, 1900–1950* (1990).

KNIGHT, Robert G., Ph.D., b. 1952 in Stoke-on-Trent. Lecturer in European Studies, Loughborough University. Author of articles on Austrian antisemitism and de-Nazification. Editor of *"Ich bin dafür, die Sache in die Länge zu ziehen". Die Wortprotokolle der österreichischen Bundesregierung von 1945 bis 1952 über die Entschädigung der Juden* (1988).

KWIET, Konrad, Dr. phil., b. 1941 in Swinemünde. Associate Professor, School of German Studies, University of New South Wales. Author of i.a. *Van Jodenhoed tot Gele Ster* (1973). Co-author of *Selbstbehauptung und Widerstand. Deutsche Juden im Kampf um Existenz und Menschenwürde 1933–1945* (^{2}1986). Editor of *From the Emancipation to the Holocaust. Essays on Jewish Literature and History in Central Europe* (1987). Co-editor of *On being a German-Jewish Refugee in Australia. Experiences and Studies* (1985). (Contributor to Year Books XXI, XXIV and XXIX.)

LEVITT, Cyril, Dr. phil., b. 1946 in Toronto. Professor of Sociology at McMaster University, Ontario. Author of *Children of Privilege. Student Revolt in the Sixties*

(1984); editor of *The Social Compulsions of Ideas* (1985); co-author of *The Riot at Christie Pits* (1987).

LOWENSTEIN, Steven M., Ph.D., b. 1945 in New York. Isadore Levine Professor of Jewish History, University of Judaism, Los Angeles. Author of i.a. 'The Rural Community and the Urbanization of German Jewry', in *Central European History* (1980); 'The 1940s and the Creation of the German-Jewish Religious Reform Movement', in *Revolution and Evolution. 1848 in German-Jewish History* (1981); *Frankfurt on the Hudson. The German-Jewish Community of Washington Heights, 1933–1983. Its Structure and Culture* (1989); and numerous articles on German-Jewish social history, demography, religious change and Western Yiddish. (Contributor to Year Books XXI, XXIV, XXVIII and XXX.)

MEINEKE, Stefan, M.A., b. 1959 in Bonn. Research student and Co-editor of the *Walther-Rathenau-Gesamtausgabe*. Author of articles on twentieth-century German politics and historiography. Currently working on an intellectual biography of Friedrich Meinecke.

MEYER, Michael A., Ph.D., b. 1937 in Berlin. Professor of Jewish History, Hebrew Union College – Jewish Institute of Religion, Cincinnati. Author of i.a. *The Origins of the Modern Jew. Jewish Identity and European Culture in Germany, 1749–1824* (1967); *Ideas of Jewish History* (1974); *Response to Modernity. A History of the Reform Movement in Judaism* (1988); *Jewish Identity in the Modern World* (1990); and of numerous articles on Judaism and Jewish history. Fellow of the LBI, New York and Member of its Executive Committee. (Contributor to Year Books XI, XVI, XXIV, XXV and XXXV.)

MORGENTHALER, Sibylle, M.A., b. 1962 in Bern. Research assistant at the Hochschule für Jüdische Studien, Heidelberg.

NA'AMAN, Shlomo, Ph.D., b. 1912 in Essen. Professor emeritus of Mediaeval and Modern Social History. Author of i.a. *Lassalle* (1970); *Die Konstituierung der deutschen Arbeiterbewegung 1862/63* (1975); *Emanzipation und Messianismus. Leben und Werk des Moses Hess* (1982); *Der Deutsche Nationalverein, die politische Konstituierung des deutschen Bürgertums 1859–1867* (1987). (Contributor to Year Book XXXIV.)

NICOSIA, Francis R., Ph.D., b. 1944 in Philadelphia. Professor of History, St. Michael's College, Vermont. Author of i.a. *The Third Reich and the Palestine Question* (1985); and numerous articles on German Zionism and German Middle East Policy during the inter-war period. Editor of *Archives of the Holocaust. The Central Zionist Archives, Jerusalem*, 2 vols., in Sybil Milton and Henry Friedlander (eds.), *Archives of the Holocaust* (1990); co-editor of *Germans Against Nazism. Nonconformity, Opposition and Resistance in the Third Reich* (1990). (Contributor to Year Books XXIV, XXXI, XXXII and XXXIII.)

RINGER, Fritz, Ph.D., b. 1934 in Germany. Mellon Professor of History and Professor of the History and Philosophy of Science, University of Pittsburgh. Author of i.a. *Education and Society in Modern Europe* (1979); *The Decline of the German Mandarins. The German Academic Community, 1890–1933* (^{2}1990); *Fields of Knowledge. French Academic Culture, 1890–1920, in Comparative Perspective* (1990).

ROSE, Paul Lawrence, Dr. Hist., F.R.Hist.S., b. 1944 in Glasgow. Hecht Professor of History, University of Haifa. Author of i.a. *Revolutionary Antisemitism in Germany from Kant to Wagner* (1990); *Wagner. Race and Revolution* (1991); *Heisenberg's Lie. The Myth of the German Atomic Bomb 1939–1976* (1991). Editor of *Selected Writings of Jean Bodin on Religion, Philosophy and Politics* (1980); *Heine's History of Religion and Philosophy in Germany* (1982).

SCHWARTZ, Daniel R., Ph.D., b. 1952 in Syracuse, New York. Associate Professor of Jewish History, Hebrew University, Jerusalem. Author of *Agrippa I. The Last King of Judaea* (1990); various articles on ancient Jewish history and religion and on modern historiography.

STERN, Fritz, Ph.D., LL.D., b. 1926 in Breslau. Seth Low Professor of History, Columbia University, New York. Author of i.a. *The Politics of Cultural Despair* (^{2}1974); *Gold and Iron. Bismarck, Bleichröder and the Building of the German Empire* (^{5}1984); *Dreams and Delusions. The Drama of German History* (1989). Editor of i.a. *The Varieties of History* (1986). Author of numerous books and articles on general and European history and politics. Fellow of the LBI, New York. (Contributor to Year Books VIII, XX and XXV.)

TOURY, Jacob, Ph.D., b. 1915 in Beuthen. Professor emeritus of Jewish History, Tel-Aviv University. Author of i.a. *Die politischen Orientierungen der Juden in Deutschland. Von Jena bis Weimar* (1966); 'Der Eintritt der Juden ins deutsche Bürgertum', and 'Die Revolution von 1848 als innerjüdischer Wendepunkt', in *Das Judentum in der Deutschen Umwelt 1800–1850* (1977); *Soziale und politische Geschichte der Juden in Deutschland* (1977); *Die Jüdische Presse im Österreichischen Kaiserreich 1802–1918* (1982); *Jüdische Textilunternehmer in Baden-Württemberg 1683–1938* (1984). (Contributor to Year Books XI, XIII, XVI, XXII, XXVI, XXX and XXXIII.)

General Index to Year Book XXXVI
of the Leo Baeck Institute

597

The Latest Publication of the Leo Baeck Institute

Second Chance

Two Centuries of German-speaking Jews in the United Kingdom

Co-ordinating Editor
WERNER E. MOSSE

Editors
JULIUS CARLEBACH, GERHARD HIRSCHFELD,
AUBREY NEWMAN, ARNOLD PAUCKER,
PETER PULZER

This volume marks the first systematic attempt to evaluate the German-Jewish experience in Britain. It covers the process of migration, including the legal and administrative problems that needed to be overcome, the patterns of settlement, the difficulties of adaptation and the two-way process of integration. The essays in this collection show both what the newcomers received from British society and what they were able to contribute. In attempting to draw up a balance sheet the evidence suggests that for both parties the movement to Britain of German-speaking Jews was an advantageous bargain neither side had cause to regret.

J. C. B. MOHR (PAUL SIEBECK), TÜBINGEN

CONTENTS

Preface by CLAUS MOSER

PATHS TO ACCEPTANCE

1991 – XIV, 658 pages (Schriftenreihe wissenschaftlicher Abhandlungen des Leo Baeck Instituts 48). ISBN 3–16–145741–2 cloth.

PLACE YOUR ORDER WITH
YOUR BOOKSELLER OR
THE LEO BAECK INSTITUTES IN
LONDON : JERUSALEM : NEW YORK